UNDERSTANDING THE BIBLE

FOURTH EDITION

Stephen L. Harris

California State University, Sacramento

Mayfield Publishing Company

Mountain View, California

London • Toronto

Library of Congress Cataloging-in-Publication Data

Harris, Stephen L.
 Understanding the Bible / Stephen L. Harris.—4th ed.
  p.   cm.
 Includes bibliographical references and index.
 ISBN 1-55534-655-8
 1. Bible—Introduction. I. Title.
BS475.2H32   1996
220.6' 1—dc20   96-20085
                                                 CIP

Manufactured in the United States of America
10 9 8 7 6 5 4 3 2 1

Mayfield Publishing Company
1280 Villa Street
Mountain View, California 94041

Sponsoring editor, James Bull; production, Mary Douglas, Rogue
Valley Publications; manuscript editor: Robin Kelly; art director:
Jeanne M. Schreiber; cover designer: Susan M. Breitbard;
manufacturing manager: Randy Hurst. The text was set in 10/12
Bembo by Thompson Type and printed on 45# Restorecote Thin by
Malloy Lithographing, Inc.

Cover image: A page from Genesis. Bible written in Hebrew.
Provence, probably Avignon, c. 1422. The Pierpont Morgan Library/
Art Resource, NY.

Excerpts from *The New English Bible.* © The Delegates of the Oxford
University Press and The Syndics of the Cambridge University Press,
1961, 1970. Reprinted by permission. Excerpts from *The Jerusalem
Bible,* copyright © 1966 by Darton, Longman & Todd, Ltd. and
Doubleday, a division of Bantam Doubleday Dell Publishing Group,
Inc. Reprinted by permission. Excerpts from Genesis 1:1–2 translated
from *The Torah: The Five Books of Moses* © 1962, 1967 by the Jewish
Publication Society of America. Reprinted by permission.

 This book is printed on acid-free, recycled paper.

Contents

PART 5 The Prophets (Nevi'im) II: Collections Attributed to Individual Prophets   156

P A R T   6   *The Writings (Kethuvim): Books of Wisdom, Poetry, Short Fiction, and Sacred History   195*

P A R T   7   *Deuterocanonical, Apocalyptic, and*
Extracanonical Works   235

THE NEW TESTAMENT *The Christian-Greek Scriptures*   305

PART 10   A Christian History and the Pauline Letters   400

PART 12   *Beyond the Canon: The Judeo-Christian Bible and Subsequent History   479*

Maps, Illustrations, Boxes, and Tables

Maps

Illustrations

Boxes

Tables

Preface

To bring readers up to date on important advances in biblical scholarship, the fourth edition of *Understanding the Bible* features several major changes. In particular, discussions of the historical and cultural environments in which the Hebrew Bible (Old Testament) developed have been considerably expanded. Also, parallels between the religion of ancient Israel and that practiced in the older civilizations of ancient Mesopotamia, Egypt, and Canaan are more explicitly drawn. Therefore, students now undertaking a systematic study of the Bible can easily recognize the diverse multicultural forces that helped to create the world's first ethical monotheism, the inspiration of three global religions—Judaism, Christianity, and Islam.

To help clarify the link between historical events and the growth of religious ideas, much of the text has been reorganized. The fourth edition still generally follows the canonical order of books in the Hebrew Bible (Tanak) to emphasize its threefold division into the Law (Torah), the Prophets (Nevi'im), and the Writings (Kethuvim). The second division of the Tanak, however, is now covered in two separate parts. Part 4 (The Prophets) discusses the Deuteronomistic History, the historical narratives encompassing the books of Joshua through 2 Kings. Part 5 examines the second half of the Prophets, the fifteen books bearing the names of individual prophets, from Amos and Hosea to Malachi and Jonah.

Discussions of the Writings (Kethuvim) have also been rearranged to highlight connections between Israel's historical experience and the literature that the nation's writers produced.

The books by Israel's Wisdom authors are treated as a discrete unit, while the Psalms and a collection of poetry and short stories, known as the Festival Scrolls, form another. The books of Chronicles, Ezra, and Nehemiah, which trace Israel's history from the beginning of the monarchy to the period of Persian domination, constitute a third unit. These three historical works, among the last written in the Hebrew Bible canon, provide a review of Israel's former monarchical glories as well as an introduction to Israel's later diminished existence as a small province in a huge Gentile empire.

As presently revised, Part 7 offers a summary of political events that brought the biblical community under the sway of Alexander of Macedonia and an all-pervasive Hellenistic culture. Both the canonical book of Daniel and numerous deuterocanonical books—works belonging to a second, later biblical canon—were produced during the Hellenistic period. The books of 1 and 2 Maccabees are considered first because they provide historical continuity between the end of the Persian era and the conquests of Alexander and his Hellenistic successors. The Maccabean narratives also provide the political and cultural background for the rise of apocalyptic ideas, such as those embodied in Daniel and noncanonical documents such as I Enoch. Descriptions of the books of Enoch, along with other works of the Pseudepigrapha, complete this section.

Part 8 now contains a more comprehensive survey of political and cultural movements that took place between the time that the last book of the Hebrew Bible was written and the events that led to the composition of the New Testament. This section offers a more thorough discussion of Hellenistic philosophy and religion and of Jewish religious parties and denominations, including expanded coverage of the Essenes and the Dead Sea Scrolls.

Reflecting the enormous increase in public and scholarly interest in the historical Jesus and the origins of Christianity, Part 9 includes fuller, more detailed analyses of the four Gospels, and an entirely new section on the continuing quest to recover the historical facts of Jesus' life. Essays on the book of Acts and Paul's teaching (Part 10) have also been revised to acknowledge scholars' increasing awareness of the tension between Paul's own views, as expressed in his letters, and the portrait of him given in Acts.

Virtually every part of this book—from additional questions and essays in Part 1 to updated presentations of scholarly theories about the composition of the Torah (Pentateuch) in Part 3, to added discussions of the New Testament Apocrypha in Part 12—has been modified to incorporate the latest available biblical research. In addition to separating the informational "Questions for Review" from the more speculative issues raised in "Questions for Discussion and Reflection" and adding numerous new bibliographic references to the "Recommended Reading" lists, the fourth edition includes many new tables, sidebars, and charts that highlight or summarize important data.

The book's format has been rearranged to include new topic headings that call attention to major ideas, break up the text into more accessible units, and make reading and learning easier and more efficient. This edition also utilizes numerous other reader-friendly devices, including the placement of "Key Themes" at the beginning of every unit and lists of authoritative sources which may be consulted for further study. The list of "Terms and Concepts to Remember" featured at the end of each major section contains all terms that appear in **boldface** type in that section. All of these important terms are concisely defined in the Glossary at the back of the book. No other general introduction to the Bible includes so extensive a selection of indispensable terms for quick reference. The fourth edition of *Understanding the Bible* is a textbook that not only invites students to enjoy becoming acquainted with the world's most famous and influential book but helps to make the learning process as trouble-free as possible.

The field of biblical scholarship is vital and growing, each year adding valuable information from the labors of archaeologists, historians, textual critics, theologians, and literary analysts. The revised general bibliography reflects many of the current scholarly investigations that significantly increase our knowledge and appreciation of the biblical world. My debt to the experts represented in this list, as well as in the bibliographic references cited at the end of most sections, is vast and gratefully acknowledged.

Some comment needs to be made about an issue that troubles an increasing number of Bible readers: reference to the Judeo-Christian Deity as "he." Virtually all writers of both the Old and New Testaments employ the masculine pronoun when alluding to supernatural beings, whether gods, angels, or demons. (Significant exceptions include the prophetic denunciations of Ishtar, "Queen of Heaven"; Astarte, Baal's female consort; and other fertility goddesses worshipped by Israel's neighbors.) In discussing such passages, the author tries to avoid sexist language. When dealing with the idea of divinity, a moment's reflection reminds us that the Supreme Being cannot be limited by human gender. But the reader must distinguish between current beliefs about spiritual reality and the assumptions of a patriarchal society out of and for which the authors of Scripture wrote. Viewing the universal sovereign as male is indeed culture-bound, but it is the practice followed in the texts transmitted to us. To respect the historical integrity of the biblical text and minimize reader confusion, this book employs the same pronouns that appear in the passages being discussed. In the broader world of Church liturgy, theology, and philosophic speculation, the reader will recognize that the Being with whom the Bible writers seek to communicate is above and beyond merely human attributes, including gender.

Among those who have helped make the fourth edition a reality, I particularly wish to thank the reviewers who have used this textbook in class and were able to offer practical advice on improving its usefulness as a teaching tool. The reviewers are Paul Brians, Washington State University; H. David Brumble, University of Pittsburgh; James A. Freeman, University of Massachusetts, Amherst; Terry Giles, Gannon University; Valeria Gomez Harvell, Penn State University, Abington Campus; Pamela Monaco, La Salle University; Mar Peter Raoul, Marist College; Herbert Schneidau, University of Arizona; Ann K. Wetherilt, Emmanuel College; and Roy G. White, Sheldon State Community College.

Questions Readers Ask About the Bible: A Survey of Biblical Themes and Topics

Age, Authorship, and Original Languages

1. What Is the Bible?

Known as the Good Book, as if it were a single volume, the Bible is a collection or library of many small books written over a period of more than 1000 years. Christians divide this anthology of ancient Hebrew and Greek writings into the Old Testament and the New Testament. The Old Testament, however, is more accurately known as the Hebrew Bible, the holy Scriptures of Judaism. It is also called the **Tanak** (also spelled Tanakh), an acronym derived from the initial consonants of the Hebrew Bible's three main divisions: **Torah** (Law or Instruction); **Nevi'im** (the Prophets); and **Kethuvim** (the Writings).

To the original Hebrew Bible, Christians add the New Testament, consisting of four narratives of Jesus' life (Gospels), a theological account of the early Church (Acts), twenty-one letters, and the Apocalypse (revelation of future history). Most Protestant Bibles contain sixty-six books (thirty-nine from the Hebrew Bible and twenty-seven from the New Testament). Roman Catholics, most Eastern churches, and some Protestants, however, include several ad-ditional books from a Greek edition of the Hebrew Bible. These books, accepted as authoritative Scripture by Roman Catholic and Orthodox groups, are known to most Protestants as the Apocrypha.

2. What Does the Word Bible Mean?

The word *bible* means "little books." It is derived from the Greek term *biblion,* the diminutive form of *byblos,* which means "papyrus" or "book." That usage in turn comes from the ancient Phoenician city of Byblos, where papyrus plants were cut and dried in strips for use as writing paper. The manuscript material thus produced was called after the place of its manufacture, Byblos.

3. Why Should Anyone Study the Bible? How Is This Ancient Collection Relevant to Modern Life?

Until a few generations ago, virtually every educated person was familiar with biblical stories and expressions. Besides regularly hearing the Bible read aloud in church, people also attended chapel or other religious services in schools, where knowledge of biblical themes was an integral part of everyone's literary education. Almost every English poet, from Shakespeare and

Milton to T. S. Eliot and W. H. Auden, could count on readers recognizing their numerous allusions to biblical phrases or characters. Most people who were intimately familiar with the Authorized (King James) Version or some other English translation knew that the "apple of his eye" referred to Jacob's love for his son Joseph and that the fond father's gift of a "coat of many colors" incited murderous jealousy in Joseph's brothers.

Although many people in Judeo-Christian societies are no longer able to quote—or even recognize—biblical references, their cultures are permeated by ethical and religious principles originating in the Bible. For example, the Western legal and judicial system is deeply influenced by biblical law. Western law courts remain divided over issues raised by Israel's prophets and lawmakers, controversies ranging from capital punishment to the rights of women to society's moral responsibility for the poor and powerless. Biblical statements made thousands of years ago—from taboos on homosexuality to speculations about the end of the world—continue to be passionately debated. Approximately 2.0 billion people, more than a third of the world's population, embrace Judaism, Christianity, or Islam, religions based on the biblical tradition. For this reason, few can afford not to know what these writings say and how and why they came to express the particular views they do.

4. Who Wrote the Bible?

According to ancient Jewish tradition, **Moses** was considered to be the author of the Torah, the first five books of the Bible (also known as the **Pentateuch**). Similar traditions commonly ascribed authorship to the persons after whom individual books were named. Thus, such narrative books as Joshua, Samuel, Ezra, and Nehemiah were assumed to have been written by the Israelite leaders whose names they bore. However, two centuries of intense literary and historical analysis have left some doubts. Most modern scholars conclude that the evidence does not confirm traditional authorship. The Torah and the historical writings that follow appear to be products of a centuries-long and complex process that involved multiple authorship and repeated editing. (See parts 3 and 4 of this text.)

Although some conservative scholars and clerics continue to argue that Moses wrote the Torah, a large scholarly majority believes that these books did not reach their present form until about 700 to 800 years after Moses' death. The historical books that record Israel's rise and fall as a nation—Joshua, Judges, Samuel, Kings, and Chronicles—are the work of nameless priests, scribes, and archivists. None makes any direct statement about its origin, date, or compiler. Some Bible scholars, such as R. E. Friedman, suggest that the authors' distinctive theological interests give clues to the priestly or prophetic circles in which they originated. Final compilation of the long narrative, Joshua through Kings (called the **Deuteronomistic History***), may have been associated with the prophet Jeremiah and/or his secretary Baruch. (See the recommended reading, Friedman.)

It is essential to remember that only a tiny percentage of the ancient world's population knew how to read or write. In Israel, most of the literate few were associated with the royal court, wisdom schools, or Temple priesthood in Jerusalem. Most books of the Hebrew Bible generally reflect the views of a small group of educated scribes or priests who were associated with and actively promoted Jerusalem's central sanctuary, dedicated to the Yahweh, the Hebrew God.

According to the prophets, several of whom were connected with the Jerusalem court, many common people mixed their worship of Yah-

---

*In this text, the adjective *deuteronomic* refers exclusively to the Book of Deuteronomy and the philosophy of history it promotes. By contrast, the term *Deuteronomistic* refers to material pertaining to the historical narratives (Joshua through Kings). The Deuteronomistic History is abbreviated DH.

weh with elements drawn from Israel's foreign neighbors. This blending of religious practices into a new whole is known as **syncretism**. To the biblical writers who interpreted and passed moral judgment on their nation's history, attempts to combine Yahwism with other religious practices was unacceptable. The writers believed that the people's syncretistic practices violated Israel's vow to honor Yahweh alone. Biblical authors tended to impose a rigidly consistent pattern on their interpretation of Israel's historical experience. The military and political disasters that overtook Israel were seen as divine punishment for breaking Yahweh's law. Voicing the religious views of Israel's educated elite—urban sages, priests, and scribes—authors of the Hebrew Bible succeeded in promulgating the world's first and most enduring ethical **monotheism**, the worship of one god.

The same anonymity that characterizes Tanak authors prevails in the New Testament. Although Church traditions of the late second century attributed various Gospels and letters to prominent followers of Jesus or his disciples, most of the texts made no claims of authorship. The conspicuous exceptions are Paul's genuine letters—the oldest surviving Christian documents, written between about 50 and 62 C.E. (The common era, abbreviated as C.E., is a religiously neutral term for marking dates that can be used by Jews, Christians, Moslems, and others. As a chronological symbol, it corresponds to A.D., *anno Domini,* Latin for "in the year of the Lord." The term B.C.E., "before the common era," is synonymous with B.C., "before Christ.") Although the author of the two-volume Luke-Acts may have been a Gentile (non-Jew), all other Bible writers were Jewish, members of the Israelite nation.

RECOMMENDED READING

Friedman, Richard. *Who Wrote the Bible?* New York and San Francisco: Harper & Row, 1987. A clear

introduction to scholarly theories about the authorship and composition of the Bible.

5. *When Was the Bible Written?*

Most scholars date the first connected written account of biblical history—from the creation of *'adam* (humanity) in Genesis 2 to Israel's conquest of Palestine—at about the tenth century B.C.E. This document, which forms the oldest narrative strand in the Pentateuch, is characterized by its relatively consistent use of the personal name Yahweh for the Hebrew God and is usually called **J**, for *Jahveh,* the German form of the divine name.

Before J was written, Israel's history had been transmitted orally in the form of isolated songs, cultic recitations, and poetry. Stories concerning Israel's most famous ancestors—the patriarchs and matriarchs (tribal fathers and mothers) Abraham, Sarah, Isaac, Rebekah, Jacob, Leah, and Rachel—had been passed by word of mouth through many generations until they were incorporated into J. Early priests, prophets, and other national leaders also recited accounts of the central events in Israel's past—Yahweh's rescuing his people from slavery in Egypt and giving them his Torah (Law) on Mount **Sinai**—at public festivals and ceremonies. These creedlike recitals of the Moses–Sinai story, once isolated fragments of oral tradition, are now embedded in longer narratives. (See 1 Sam. 12:7–15; Deut. 26:6–10; Josh. 24:1–13.)

Some poems that celebrate decisive historical victories are thought to be older than the written context in which they now appear. A good example is Miriam's song of Yahweh's triumph at the Sea of Reeds (Exod. 15:21), which may have circulated independently of other oral material and was included in the J narrative around 950 B.C.E. The final editing of the long narrative sequence from Genesis through 2 Kings is believed to have taken place during and after Israel's exile in Babylon (the century following 587 B.C.E.). The last books of the Hebrew Bible were composed only a century or two before the birth of Jesus; some of the Apocrypha, such as the Wisdom of Solomon and 2 Esdras, were written even later.

Whereas the library of the Hebrew Scriptures took approximately a millennium to complete, the New Testament was composed during a much shorter period, probably between about 50 C.E. (for Paul's earliest letters) and 150 C.E. (for the final form of 2 Peter). In all, biblical literature represents a time span of approximately 1100 years.

6. Is the Bible the World's Oldest Book?

No. At one time, biblical scholars believed that the Bible was the only significant literary production of the ancient Near East. During the past century, however, archaeologists have found remains of other ancient libraries, such as that of the Assyrian Emperor Ashurbanipal IV (668–627 B.C.E.), in the ruins of whose palace at Nineveh, capital of the Assyrian Empire, were discovered hundreds of clay tablets inscribed with a wedge-shaped writing known as **cuneiform**. Ashurbanipal's tablets were in **Akkadian**, a Semitic language used by Assyrians and Babylonians, but they seem to have included translations from the much older literature of Sumer, the first known high civilization of the ancient Near East. The Sumerians, whose culture was later invaded by Akkadian-speaking peoples, were a non-Semitic group that built city-states along the southern Euphrates River near the head of the Persian Gulf in what is now Iraq.

For Bible scholars, perhaps the most important finds were eleven tablets recounting the adventures of **Gilgamesh**, a legendary king of Uruk, a leading Sumerian city. The "Epic of Gilgamesh" includes a vivid account of a great flood, which only a single man, Gilgamesh's ancestor Utnapishtim, survived. Directed by Ea, the god of wisdom, Utnapishtim built an ark (a box-shaped boat) on which he, his family, servants, and various animals were preserved. In numerous details, including the sending out of birds to find dry land and the offering of sacrifice after the flood waters receded, the Gilga-mesh flood story remarkably parallels that in Genesis. Scholar Alexander Heidel believes that both the Sumero-Babylonian and the biblical accounts go back to a single source, although the Gilgamesh version is clearly the older of the two.

Mesopotamia, as the Greeks called the Sumero-Babylonian area between the Tigris and Euphrates rivers, produced other counterparts to familiar Bible stories. The Mesopotamian creation account known as the ***Enuma Elish*** (meaning "when above") is sometimes called the Babylonian Genesis. Old Testament laws and legal practices are also paralleled in Sumerian and Akkadian inscriptions, the most famous of which occurs on a black stone monument called the Stele of Hammurabi. Ruler of the short-lived Old Babylonian Empire, **Hammurabi** revised and codified preexisting laws about 1690 B.C.E. Carved in stone for public view, Hammurabi's code is reflected in several Mosaic laws of the Pentateuch. Like Moses, Hammurabi claimed to have received his ordinances from a god, in his case the Babylonian sun deity Shamash.

Although Sumero-Babylonian literature is polytheistic (presenting a world with many gods), works like the *Enuma Elish* and *Epic of Gilgamesh* did have an impact on the authors who composed the Bible. The common Mesopotamian belief in the divine creation of life and the gods' control of earthly events influenced the development of Israel's religious thought. According to Genesis and Joshua, Israel's ancestors had worshiped Mesopotamian gods. At a later period, the Israelite captives in Babylon (587–538 B.C.E.) absorbed considerable Mesopotamian myth and folklore, some of which, refined by Hebrew monotheism, later appeared in Scripture. The priestly account of creation in Genesis 1 may have been a response to witnessing the splendid public performance of the *Enuma Elish* at the Babylonian New Year festival.

Besides Mesopotamian influences, which were particularly intense during the Assyrian and Neo-Babylonian hegemony of the eighth

Copies of the mosaic Torah are found in virtually every Jewish temple or synagogue. This elegant manuscript, although beautifully decorated, is approximately one-third of the size of the standard Torah scroll. (Courtesy of the Jewish Museum, London)

through sixth centuries B.C.E., Egyptian and Canaanite ideas also affected religious thought in Israel. Among other Egyptian borrowings, Proverbs 22:17–23:11 contains what is virtually a Hebrew translation of passages written or compiled by Amenemope, one of Egypt's leading wise men.

Some scholars believe that Egyptian ethical and religious motifs, such as the concept of **Maat**—which combined justice, truth, right thought, and conduct—helped shape ancient Israel's view of divine righteousness. One of Egypt's most controversial rulers, Amenhotep IV, who ruled from 1364 to 1347 B.C.E., introduced a radical new approach to religion—the worship of a single god, Aton, symbolized by the solar disc. Changing his name to **Akhenaton** ("It Is Well with Aton") and his capital from Thebes to Akhetaton (now known as Tell el-Amarna), this "heretic pharaoh" actively discouraged veneration of any deity except for that represented by the sun, giver of light and life.

Some historians believe that the Aton cult represents the world's first experiment in monotheism, although the powerful Egyptian priesthood restored traditional veneration of Egypt's many gods after Akhenaton's death. Others regard it as more likely to have been a **monolatry**, the worship of one god while conceding the existence of others. The Hebrew prophet Moses, who was reputedly educated at the Egyptian court, achieved a longer-lasting religious innovation than Akhenaton's.

Many similarities and affinities exist between ancient Egyptian and Israelite cultures. For example, Moses' name, like those of many subsequent Israelite priests, is Egyptian. His name is derived from the Egyptian verb *msw* ("to be born") or the noun *mesu* ("child, son"). The same root appears in such Egyptian names as Thutmose and Ahmose.

Another possible connection between the Egyptian and Israelite religions also appears in the way in which the two peoples housed their gods. In Egypt, statues of the gods—visible symbols of the divinity's invisible presence—were hidden away in windowless sanctuaries. Because the statues were protected from public gaze by massive stone walls, the god's holiness was enhanced by elements of secrecy and mystery. Only official priests and the pharaoh himself were allowed into the inner room that contained the deity's sacred image. In Israel, King Solomon built a similar kind of temple to house Yahweh's *kavod* (glory). In the Bible writers' judgment, however, Solomon allied himself too closely with Egypt, marrying the pharaoh's daughter and erecting shrines to the gods of his many foreign wives in the Temple precincts (1 Kings 9:16–18, 21; 11:1–8). Even after Solomon's time, the temple rituals continued to resemble those of Egypt: Only the hereditary high priest was permitted to enter the sanctuary's innermost chamber, the Holy of Holies that sheltered Yahweh's unseen presence.

Until relatively late in its history, the Israelite community did not adopt one of the Egyptian religion's central tenets: the expectation of a joyous afterlife. A firm conviction that the next world offered rewards for good behavior inspired the Egyptians' famous practice of embalming their beloved dead and placing them in richly decorated tombs. By the second century B.C.E., however, apocalyptic visionaries such as the authors of Daniel and Enoch began to express hope in a future resurrection similar to that of the Egyptian religion.

The apocalyptic concept of postmortem judgment, which Egyptian faith had honored for millennia, was eventually passed on from Judaism to Christianity. The Christian Apocalypse (Revelation) pictures cosmic judgment, in which names are read from a "book of life," in terms echoing ancient Egyptian belief (Rev. 20). Egyptian artworks depicting **Osiris**, god of the dead, weighing the deceased's heart on a scale balanced by the feather of truth, anticipate Judeo-Christian doctrines about the afterlife and final judgment.

When the Israelites left Egypt under Moses' leadership about 1250 B.C.E. and entered **Canaan** (the land that God promised their ancestors) a generation later, they encountered a wide variety of native religions. As they settled in Canaan, the Israelites gradually took over many older Canaanite shrines and sanctuaries, such as those at Bethel, Shechem, and Salem (Jerusalem). As a study of Canaanite literature reveals, the Israelites also adopted at least some Canaanite hymns, poems, and religious titles to apply to Yahweh's worship. Documents found at **Ugarit** (Ras Shamra) include prayers and epic poems celebrating **Baal**, the Canaanite fertility god, and **El**, father of all gods, in terms that later appear in biblical writings (cf. Pss. 82, 50:2–3; Gen. 21:33; Ezek. 16:3; Judg. 5:4–5). Genesis includes a brief narrative that shows how Abraham, ancestor of the Israelites, identified Yahweh with El Elyon ("God Most High") of the Canaanite city of Salem. (See the recommended readings Coogan and Cross.)

RECOMMENDED READING

Baines, J. and Malek, J. *Atlas of Ancient Egypt.* New York: Facts on File, 1980.

Coogan, Michael D. *Stories from Ancient Canaan.* Philadelphia: Westminster Press, 1978. A paperback collection of Canaanite myths and their biblical parallels.

Cross, Frank M., ed. *Canaanite Myth and Hebrew Epic, Essays in the History of the Religion of Israel.* Cambridge, Mass.: Harvard University Press, 1973.

Dalley, Stephanie. *Myths from Mesopotamia: Creation, the Flood, Gilgamesh, and Others.* New York: Oxford University Press, 1989.

Foster, Benjamin R. *From Distant Days: Myths, Tales, and Poetry of Ancient Mesopotamia.* Bethesda, Md.: CDL Press, 1995.

Gray, John. *Near Eastern Mythology.* New York: Peter Bedrick Books, 1982.

Heidel, Alexander. *The Gilgamesh Epic and Old Testament Parallels.* Chicago: University of Chicago Press, 1949.

———. *The Babylonian Genesis,* 2nd ed. Chicago: University of Chicago Press, 1951. A paperback translation of the *Enuma Elish* with commentary.

Ions, Veronica. *Egyptian Mythology.* New York: Peter Bedrick Books, 1982.

O'Connor, David. *A Short History of Ancient Egypt.* Pittsburgh, Penn.: Carnegie Museum of Natural History, 1990.

Pritchard, James B., ed. *The Ancient Near East in Pictures Relating to the Old Testament.* Princeton, N.J.: Princeton University Press, 1965. A companion volume to *Ancient Near Eastern Texts.*

———, ed. *The Ancient Near East: An Anthology of Texts and Pictures.* Princeton, N.J.: Princeton University Press, 1965. A less expensive work containing excerpts from the preceding book and *Ancient Near Eastern Texts.*

———, ed. *Ancient Near Eastern Texts Relating to the Old Testament.* 3rd ed., supp. Princeton, N.J.: Princeton University Press, 1969. Translations of relevant Egyptian, Babylonian, Canaanite, and other ancient literatures—the standard work.

Redford, Donald B. *Egypt, Canaan, and Israel in Ancient Times,* Princeton, N.J.: Princeton University Press, 1992. A new scholarly study of the first civilizations in north Africa and western Asia.

Sandars, N. K. *The Epic of Gilgamesh.* Baltimore, Md.: Penguin Books, 1972. A freely translated version of the *Epic of Gilgamesh* with a scholarly introduction.

Wolkstein, Diane and Kramer, S. N. *Inanna: Queen of Heaven and Earth, Her Stories and Hymns from Sumer.* New York: Harper & Row, 1983.

7. In What Languages Was the Bible Originally Written?

Most of the Old Testament was written in classical Hebrew, the Semitic tongue spoken by the Israelites. Certain later books were composed in **Aramaic**, an Aramean (Syrian) dialect closely related to Hebrew and probably also the language spoken by Jesus. The entire New Testament is in **koine** Greek, the international language of the first-century workaday world. Koine is derived from the fusion of classical Greek with the commercial vernacular of Near Eastern peoples conquered by the armies of **Alexander of Macedonia**. The blending of Oriental and Greek elements produced a cosmopolitan culture known as **Hellenism**. Arbitrarily dated as beginning with the death of Alexander in 323 B.C.E. Hellenistic culture exerted considerable influence on the thinking of late Old Testament authors and early Christian theologians. Merely phrasing age-old religious ideas in Greek, a language in which even the commonest terms were loaded with philosophical implications, subtly changed their religious meaning.

8. How Should We Study the Bible? Are There Differences Between the Way the Bible Is Read in Church and in the Classroom?

Bible reading in church is usually part of a worship service, devotional in nature. The short excerpts read aloud are commonly chosen to inculcate ethical principles: Stories of biblical heroes or villains serve to provide good or bad models of behavior for the congregation.

In a university setting, however, the Bible is typically studied as any other literary document from the ancient world would be. Using a methodology borrowed from the physical sciences, students consider such issues as the evidence for authorship, the original social setting, historical context, implied audience, and the author's philosophical outlook and religious assumptions. In analyzing a particular passage, such as the explanations given in 2 Kings for Yahweh's permitting his people to suffer at the hands of nonbelieving enemies, readers will wish to know why the writer promotes a particular view: What is the author's religious agenda? What lesson from history does the writer wish his readers to draw?

Some people read the Bible to learn more about the ideas and events that inspired three world religions. Others read it as an act of faith. Approaching the Bible as if every word were literally factual, many read as if tools for critical study do not exist. As New Testament scholar Marcus Borg observed, in the prescientific era people simply assumed that biblical writers objectively recorded irrefutable facts of history; they automatically adopted a naive or unconscious literalism. Since the rise of the fundamentalist movement early in the twentieth century, however, some believers now manifest a deliberate or conscious literalism. Reacting negatively to scholars who question the absolute historicity of some biblical narratives, such as the Genesis accounts of a six-day creation and a global flood, fundamentalists typically reject any historical-critical analysis of the biblical text. Generally refusing to reconcile an understanding of Judeo-Christian Scripture with the scientific discoveries of physics, astronomy, geology, or anthropology, fundamentalism tends to force its adherents to choose between faith and intellect.

Most Catholic, Protestant, and Jewish scholars do not accept fundamentalism's false dilemma. They do not think it necessary—or even defensible—to adopt the equivalent of Islamic fundamentalism's attitude toward the *Qur'an* (Koran), regarding it as infallible and inerrant. Aware that the discourse of religious thought is commonly metaphoric—that it uses images, parables, and figures of speech to convey its message—scholars of world religions suggest that we avoid undue literalism when reading the Bible. During the past century and a half, American and European scholars have analyzed the biblical text extensively, discovering that its authors freely used ancient **myth**, legends, and folktales to tell their story. The biblical writers' primary goal was not to record mere fact but to interpret a story's theological meaning. When narrating historical events, such as Babylon's demolition of Jerusalem in 587 B.C.E., biblical authors were not concerned with preserving a comprehensive and objective account of the disaster but were trying to understand God's purpose in allowing the triumph of a pagan empire over his chosen people. When they adopted traditions about creation inherited from the older civilizations of Mesopotamia, the writers exploited these origin myths to celebrate their God's creative majesty.

Some biblical writers apparently understood, as many modern readers do not, that myths are not deceptions or untruths but vehicles, in a prescientific age, for expressing universal insights into the nature of the world and human society. When used in this way, myths express values that transcend the accidents of history.

Modern scholars urge readers to view a given biblical book in its original cultural and historical context, ever mindful of the long historical process—sometimes involving centuries of composition, revision, and editing—by which individual books assumed their present form. Comparing biblical documents with other ancient literary texts heightens readers' awareness of both the similarities and differences between Israel's Scripture and the literature produced by other nations. Innumerable parallels to individual myths, beliefs, and traditions exist between the Bible and other texts of antiquity, but these are generally in the form of analogous ideas and motifs. No ancient Near Eastern nation besides Israel created documents that surpass the incomparable narrative—extending from the world's beginnings to the fall of Judah—encompassed in Genesis through 2 Kings. Other cultures produced many prophetic oracles and provocative wisdom literature but nothing to match the work of Israel's greatest prophets, such as Isaiah, Hosea, or Ezekiel, or the brilliant wisdom books of Job, Ecclesiastes, and Jesus Ben Sirach.

Avoiding the artificial dilemma that misleadingly distinguishes between "works of man" and "works of God," students of biblical literature can appreciate that the worth or significance of a religious text does not rest on its relation to concrete fact but on its continuing relevance to the human spirit. Whatever the mysterious force called inspiration may be, it operates independently of factual accuracy or error, transcending the limitations of an individual writer's inadequacies to reveal concepts of reality beyond the reach of ordinary experience.

RECOMMENDED READING

Several excellent one-volume reference books provide reliable scholarly discussions of biblical exegesis, especially

Achtemeier, Paul J., ed. *Harper's Bible Dictionary.* San Francisco: Harper & Row, 1985. A good place to start basic Bible research.

Brown, Raymond E.; Fitzmyer, Joseph A.; and Murphy, Roland E. *The New Jerome Biblical Commentary,* 2nd ed. Englewood Cliffs, N.J.: Prentice-Hall, 1990. A standard work of Roman Catholic scholarship.

Mays, James L., ed. *Harper's Bible Commentary.* San Francisco: Harper & Row, 1988. Offers accessible commentary on all canonical and deuterocanonical books.

Metzger, Bruce M.; and Coogan, Michael D., eds., *The Oxford Companion to the Bible.* New York: Oxford University Press, 1993. Offers carefully nuanced exposition of biblical topics mostly by British and American scholars.

Manuscripts and Translations

9. When Was the Bible First Translated?

The first translation of the Hebrew Bible was begun in Alexandria, Egypt, in the mid-third century before Christ, when leaders of the Jewish colony there found that the younger generation of Jews no longer understood classical Hebrew. According to legend, seventy scholars were appointed to translate the Scriptures into koine Greek, and after laboring for seventy days, they produced seventy identical versions. According to historical fact, however, this landmark translation, known as the **Septuagint**, abbreviated **LXX** (after the seventy or seventy-two elders who supposedly produced it), took more than two centuries to complete. The Pentateuch (Genesis through Deuteronomy) was translated first, followed gradually by the prophetic books and the Writings (poetic and wisdom literature), and eventually by works that later became known as the Apocrypha. A Hellenistic Jewish work, the *Letter of Aristeas,* gives a popular version of the Septuagint's origin. (See Part 7, "Pseudepigrapha.")

The Septuagint was extremely influential among Jews living outside Palestine and was the Bible adopted by the early Greek-speaking Christians. Most of the Old Testament passages cited in the New Testament are either direct quotations or paraphrases of the Septuagint Bible. Indeed, so completely did Christians take over this Jewish translation that the Jews were forced to produce another version for their own use.

The next great step in making the Bible available to a wider audience was St. Jerome's production of the Latin **Vulgate**. Commissioned by the bishop of Rome to render the Scriptures into the common tongue for the Latin-speaking Western church, Jerome, between 385 and 405 C.E., produced what became the official Bible of Roman Catholicism. Following the collapse of the western Roman Empire in the late fifth century, literacy rapidly declined. Accordingly, no other major translation of the Bible was published for nearly 1000 years. Pre-Reformation translators at first merely rendered Jerome's Latin into the languages of modern Europe. Not until the 1500s were translations again made from the Bible's original Hebrew, Aramaic, and Greek.

RECOMMENDED READING

Klein, Ralph W. *Textual Criticism of the Old Testament: The Septuagint After Qumran.* Philadelphia: Fortress Press, 1974.

10. In What Forms Has the Bible's Text Been Preserved?

No original copy of any biblical book has survived. The oldest extant forms of Scripture are manuscript (handwritten) copies on papyrus

This page from the Book of Leviticus belongs to one of the oldest copies of the Hebrew Torah, the Masoretic ("traditional") Text, dating from the mid-ninth century C.E. (Courtesy of the British Library)

(paperlike sheets made from the papyrus plant) and parchment (dried and treated animal skins). Countless ancient copies of the Hebrew Bible, or parts thereof, were undoubtedly lost during the repeated destruction of Jerusalem and its Temple, such as those by the Babylonians in 587 B.C.E. and by the Romans in 70 C.E. Wars, persecutions, and mob violence also account for the loss of many Hebrew manuscripts kept in synagogues (Jewish meeting places for instruction and worship) throughout the Greco-Roman world.

Before the Dead Sea Scrolls were discovered in 1947 (see question 17 and Part 8), the oldest complete copies of the Hebrew Bible available were those made in the ninth and tenth centuries. These manuscripts were largely the work of **masoretes** (from an Aramaic word meaning "tradition"), medieval Jewish scribes who added vowel symbols to the consonantal Hebrew script. The **Masoretic Text** (**MT**) is the standard form of the Hebrew Bible today. Although only the scroll of Isaiah was found complete, the discovery of the Dead Sea Scrolls produced at least fragments of every Hebrew canonical book, some of which date from as early as about 150 B.C.E. and represent the most ancient surviving texts.

Although there are no complete New Testament texts earlier than the fourth century C.E., the oldest manuscript fragments date from the second century and include versions preserved in Greek, Syriac, Latin, Ethiopic, and other languages. No two extant New Testament manuscripts are exactly alike. Surviving texts contain an estimated 400,000 variations, ranging from minor differences in phrasing to the presence or absence of entire passages.

Of the thousands of surviving Old and New Testament manuscripts or fragments, no two are precisely alike, which presents the textual critic or translator with a formidable challenge. He or she must compare variations among them and try to determine which one, or which combination of several, appears closest to the supposed original. Because all manuscripts differ from one another to some degree, a given text's exact relationship and fidelity to the (forever lost) original is virtually impossible to determine. The scholar's task of sorting out new manuscript finds and comparing them with previously known versions, thus to enhance the quality and reliability of the biblical text, is a continuously ongoing process known as lower (textual) criticism.

11. How Did Our Modern English Translations Come About?

Although none of his work has survived, the first man credited with translating the Bible into his native English was the Venerable Bede, a Benedictine monk and historian of Anglo-Saxon England. In the 730s, Bede rendered part of Jerome's Latin Vulgate into Old English. During the tenth and eleventh centuries, a few other Bible books, including the Psalms and Gospels, also appeared in English, but it was not until the fourteenth century that the entire Bible would be translated into that language. Except to Roman Catholic Church leaders and a few scholars, Latin had by then become a dead language, and the Vulgate Bible was incomprehensible to most Christians. To make the Scriptures accessible to the British, John Wycliffe, an English priest, translated both Old and New Testaments, completing the project around 1384. But the Roman Catholic Church, fearing the effect of Bibles in the popular tongue, in 1408 condemned Wycliffe's version and forbade any future translations.

Two historical events ensured that the Bible would find a large reading public in English. The first was Johann Gutenberg's invention of movable type in 1455, a revolutionary advance that made it possible to print books relatively quickly rather than copying them laboriously by hand. The second was a strong religious movement known as the Protestant Reformation, begun in Germany in 1517. In that year, a German priest named Martin Luther vigorously protested administrative corruption and other practices within the Roman Catholic Church. Luther's German translation of the Bible (1522–1534) was the first version in a modern European language based not on the Latin Vulgate but on the original Hebrew and Greek.

The first English translator to work directly from Hebrew and Greek manuscripts was William Tyndale; under the threat of church persecution, he fled to Germany, where his translation of the New Testament was published in 1525 (revised 1534). Official hostility to his work prevented him from completing his translation of the Old Testament, and in 1535 to 1536 he was betrayed, tried for **heresy**, and burned alive at the stake. Tyndale's superb English phrasing of the New Testament has influenced almost every other English translation since.

Although the church forbade the reading of Wycliffe's or Tyndale's translations, it nevertheless permitted free distribution of the first printed English Bible—the Coverdale Bible (1535), which relied heavily on Tyndale's work. Matthew's Bible (1537), containing additional sections of Tyndale's Old Testament, was revised by Coverdale, and the result was called the Great Bible (1539). The Bishop's Bible (1568) was a revision of the Great Bible, and the King James Version was commissioned as a scholarly revision of the Bishop's Bible. The Geneva Bible (1560), which the English Puritans had produced in Switzerland, also significantly influenced the King James Bible.

The King James Bible (Authorized Version)

By far the most popular English Bible of all time, the King James translation was authorized by James I, son of Mary, Queen of Scots, who appointed fifty-four scholars to make a new version of the Bishop's Bible for official use in the English (Anglican) church. After seven years' labor, during which the oldest manuscripts then available were diligently consulted, the king's scholars produced in 1611 the Authorized, or King James, Version. One of the masterpieces of English literature, it was created at a time when the language was at its richest and most vivid. In the beauty of its rhythmic prose and colorful imagery, the King James Version remains unsurpassed in literary excellence. Later translations may be more accurate and have the advantage of being based on older and more authoritative Hebrew and Greek manuscripts, but none has phrased the Scriptures in so memorable or quotable a fashion.

Despite its wonderful poetic qualities, however, the King James Version has grave disadvantages as a text for studying the Bible. The very attributes that contribute to its linguistic elegance—the archaic diction, poetic rhythms,

The oldest surviving manuscript of a New Testament book, these fragments of the Gospel of John date from about 125 C.E. Preserved for 1800 years in the dry sands of an Egyptian grave, these tiny scraps of papyrus contain four verses from John 18 (Rylands Greek Papyrus 457 [also known as P52]). (Courtesy of the Director and University Librarian, the John Rylands University Library of Manchester)

and Renaissance vocabulary—tend to obscure the explicit meaning of the text for many readers. Translated by scholars who grew up on the then-contemporary poetry of Edmund Spenser and William Shakespeare, the King James text presents real problems of comprehensibility to the average American student. Students who have difficulty undertaking *Hamlet* cannot expect to follow Paul's sometimes complex arguments when they are couched in terms that have been largely obsolete for centuries.

Modern English and American Translations of the Bible

Realizing that language changes over the years and that words lose their original meanings and take on new connotations, Bible scholars have repeatedly updated and reedited the King James text. The first Revised Version of the King James was published in England between 1881 and 1885; a slightly modified text of this edition, the American Standard Revised Version, was issued in 1901. Using the (then) latest studies in archaeology and linguistics, the Revised

Standard Version (RSV) appeared between 1946 and 1952. Because modern scholarship continues to advance in understanding of biblical languages and textual history, an updated edition, the New Revised Standard, with the Apocrypha, was published in 1991.

Readers can now choose from a wide selection of modern translations, most of which incorporate the benefits of expert scholarship that draws on interdisciplinary fields of linguistic, historical, and literary studies. These include the Jerusalem Bible (JB) (1966), which transliterates several Hebrew terms for God—notably the personal name Yahweh and the title El Shaddai—into the English text. A recently published text that captures the flavor of the original Hebrew is *The Five Books of Moses* (1995), translated by Everett Fox. Although the text contains only the first part of the Tanak, it is an extraordinarily vivid rendering of the Hebrew Bible. The New English Bible (NEB) (1970; 1976), the product of an international body of Roman Catholic, Jewish, and Protestant scholars, was further refined and reissued as The Revised English Bible (1989). Unless otherwise indicated, this textbook uses the Jerusalem Bible for all quotations from the Tanak and the NEB for citations from the New Testament.

The widely used New International Version (NIV), completed in the 1970s, reflects a generally conservative Protestant viewpoint. A popular Roman Catholic translation, the New American Bible (NAB) (1970), is also highly readable. Like the Jerusalem Bible and the New (and Revised) English Bible, it includes fresh renderings of the deuterocanonical books (the Apocrypha). Most of these new translations are available in paperback editions, which contain extensive annotations, maps, and scholarly commentary.

Some translations favored by many students need to be used with caution. Whereas the Good News Bible offers a fluent paraphrase of the original languages in informal English, many scholars think that the Living Bible strays so far from the original texts that it is unreliable and misleading. Some doctrinally oriented versions, such as the New World Translation, published by the Watchtower Society (Jehovah's Witnesses), consistently tend to render controversial passages in a way that supports their distinctive beliefs.

The multivolume Doubleday Anchor Bible is an excellent study aid. A cooperative effort by Protestant, Roman Catholic, and Jewish scholars, each volume in the series is the work of an individual translator, who provides extensive interpretative commentary. The Scholars Version (SV) is another in-progress multivolume translation with extensive annotation. Intended as an aid in discovering the historical Jesus, the Scholars Version of *The Five Gospels* (1993), including the Gospel of Thomas, uses a color code to indicate the relative authenticity of sayings ascribed to Jesus. Sayings considered most likely to be accurate memories of Jesus' actual words are printed in red or pink, doubtful sayings in gray, and those deemed not to represent his authentic voice in black. The SV translators have also issued *The Complete Gospels,* which compiles all known canonical and noncanonical

Gospel material from the first three centuries of Christianity.

RECOMMENDED READING

Bruce, F. F. *History of the Bible in English,* 3rd ed. New York: Oxford University Press, 1978. A concise history and critical evaluation of all major English translations from Anglo-Saxon times to the present.

Fox, Everett, ed. *The Five Books of Moses.* The Schocken Bible, Vol. 1. New York: Schocken Books, 1995. The first part of the Tanak in unusually vivid prose.

The Jerusalem Bible. Garden City, N.Y.: Doubleday, 1966. A vivid Roman Catholic translation in paperback that uses the name Yahweh throughout the Old Testament. The hardbound edition contains scholarly introductions and many informative notes.

Lewis, Jack P. *The English Bible from KJV to NIV: A History and Evaluation.* Grand Rapids, Mich.: Baker Book House, 1982. A scholarly review of major English translations from the King James Version to the New International Version.

Sandmel, Samuel, ed. *The New English Bible with the Apocrypha: Oxford Study Edition.* New York: Oxford University Press, 1976. A clear, readable paperback translation with helpful footnotes.

The Revised English Bible with the Apocrypha. Oxford University Press, Cambridge University Press, 1989. Brings some of the British idioms into line with American usage.

The Canon of the Hebrew Bible

12. What Is Meant by Canon?

The term **canon** refers to a list of books officially approved for use in a given community; it also refers to the standard of measurement by which books are included or excluded from the authoritative list. In Greek, canon means a "straight stick by which something is ruled or measured." The Hebrew word *qaneh* also refers to measurement or the norm by which something is judged.

13. How Did the Biblical Canon Come into Being, and Which Parts of the Bible Were First Accepted as Canonical?

Bible scholars emphasize that canonization occurs as a historical *process,* not by arbitrary decrees of a religious council or other authority. The Hebrew Bible grew by degrees, its contents expanding to incorporate new documents as Israel's writers over many generations recorded and interpreted their nation's political and spiritual experiences. The end result of a long period of development, canonization took place as the community of faith gradually accepted the religious authority of a book or books.

A Woman's Role in the Canonization Process
The first event in which a particular document is pronounced authoritative—a representation of Israel's faith—is commonly overlooked. About 621 B.C.E., a woman named Huldah, a Jerusalem prophetess, was asked to determine the authenticity of a manuscript that is generally presumed to be an early edition of Deuteronomy. Huldah's validation of the "book of the law" marks the first step in a canonization process that extended over several centuries.

As centuries passed, Israel's legal and prophetic writings grew ever more venerable and were quoted, debated, and read publicly in the synagogues until familiarity with their teaching and their recognized consistency with the Mosaic tradition made them by use and habit part of the Hebrew Bible.

By about 400 B.C.E., the Jews regarded the first five books of the Bible (the Pentateuch) as authoritative and binding. These five scrolls constituted the Torah, meaning the "law," "teaching," or "instruction" that Yahweh gave to Israel through Moses.

Next to be accepted were the prophetic books, which form the second major division of the Hebrew canon. By about 200 B.C.E., the Former Prophets (Joshua, Judges, Samuel, and Kings) and the Latter Prophets (the three Major Prophets, which occupy one scroll each, and the twelve Minor Prophets, which are encompassed on a single scroll) were regarded as sacred.

As early as the mid-second century B.C.E., a third category of Scripture was recognized. In the preface to his Greek translation of Ecclesiasticus (Wisdom of Jesus ben Sirach), the translator speaks of "the Law and the Prophets and the *other volumes of the fathers*" (italics added). These "other volumes" are the Writings (in Hebrew, the Kethuvim), whose contents were not clearly defined for many generations. Not until after the Romans had destroyed Jerusalem in 70 C.E. did the Jewish community attempt to set a precise limit on the number of books comprising the Writings. Then the problem was not so much what to include, considering the vast number of religious volumes available, as what to omit.

Following the Roman destruction of the Jewish state, a group of distinguished rabbis (teachers of the Law) founded the **Academy of Jamnia** on the Palestinian coast to define and consolidate the essential teachings of the Jewish religion, including a statement about which books of the Hebrew Bible were to be accepted as sacred and authoritative. The Jamnia assembly of about 90 C.E. was not the last such body to debate the issue, but it appears that the rabbis exercised their moral authority to favor use of the following books and no others: Psalms, Proverbs, Job, the five scrolls to be read on major holy days (Song of Songs, Ruth, Lamentations, Ecclesiastes, and Esther), Daniel (the only fully apocalyptic work to be included), and the work of the Chronicler (1 and 2 Chronicles, Ezra, and Nehemiah). Some historians have suggested that the rabbis also acted to exclude the writings of the heretical new Christian sect as well as a number of books found in the Greek Septuagint Bible. Many of the latter were extremely popular among Greek-speaking Christians, however, and today are included in the Roman Catholic and most Eastern canons as part of the Old Testament.

RECOMMENDED READING

Sanders, James A. "Canon: Hebrew Bible." In D. N. Freedman, ed., *The Anchor Bible Dictionary,* Vol. 1, pp. 837–852. New York: Doubleday, 1992.

———. *Torah and Canon.* Philadelphia: Fortress Press, 1972. A concise and helpful introduction to canon formation.

Sheppard, Gerald T. "Canon." In Mircea Eliade, ed. *The Encyclopedia of Religion,* Vol. 3, pp. 62–69. New York: Macmillan, 1987.

14. What Are the Apocrypha? Why Do Some Editions of the Old Testament Contain the Apocrypha but Others Do Not?

The word **apocrypha** is the plural form of a Greek adjective meaning "hidden," a designation that at one time may have applied to writings thought to contain some kind of "secret" doctrine. By the fourth century C.E., however, the influential Christian scholar Jerome (c. 342–420 C.E.) used the term *apocrypha* to denote books not accepted as part of the Hebrew Bible canon. Consequently, Jerome did not include most of them in his Latin translation of the Bible, the Vulgate.

The books or parts of books that Jerome deemed outside the canon had been included in early Christian manuscripts of the Greek Septuagint. These documents, most of which were composed in Semitic languages between about 300 B.C.E. and C.E. 100, represent the same literary categories found in the canonical Hebrew Bible. The Apocrypha include two outstanding examples of wisdom literature—Ecclesiasticus (Wisdom of Jesus ben Sirach) and the Wisdom of Solomon, a Greek work combining Hebraic and Hellenistic ideas. Two prose romances, Tobit and Judith, dramatize the lives of pious Jews

living in the **Diaspora**, the settling of Jews outside their Palestinian homeland. Historical works such as 1 and 2 Maccabees record Jewish resistance to Hellenistic oppression.

Added to later editions of the Vulgate, the Apocrypha were officially declared part of a **Deuterocanon** ("second canon") in 1546 at the Roman Catholic Council of Trent. Although the Council of Trent deleted three apocryphal books—1 and 2 Esdras and the Prayer of Mannaseh—from its official list, the rest of the Apocrypha, including the Additions to Esther and Daniel, are always published in Roman Catholic editions of the Old Testament. Whereas the Roman Catholic, Greek Orthodox, Armenian, and Ethiopian churches accord the Apocrypha deuterocanonical status, most Protestant churches do not. During the Protestant Reformation, many reformers argued that because the Old Testament represents the faith of pre-Christian Israel, its contents should include only those books found in the original Hebrew Bible as defined by the rabbis at Jamnia. (See "Tanak—The Three-Part Hebrew Bible" on page 16.)

RECOMMENDED READING

de Lange, Nicholas, *Apocrypha: Jewish Literature of the Hellenistic Age.* New York: Viking Press, 1978.

Charlesworth, James H. "Apocrypha and Pseudepigrapha." In Mircea Eliade, ed., *The Encyclopedia of Religion,* Vol. 2, pp. 173–183. New York: Macmillan, 1987.

15. Is Inclusion of the Apocrypha the Only Difference Among Jewish, Protestant, and Roman Catholic Bibles?

Unfortunately, no. To compound the confusion, both Protestants and Roman Catholics retained the Septuagint's general ordering of contents, which differs appreciably from the Hebrew (Table 1.1 on pp. 18–19). The threefold

---

Tanak—The Three-Part Hebrew Bible

A comparatively recent term for the Hebrew Bible, Tanak (also spelled Tanakh) is an acronym composed of consonants designating the first letters of the three major divisions of the Hebrew Scriptures. Vowel sounds are inserted between the consonants.

- **T** Torah (the five books of Moses)
  Genesis, Exodus, Leviticus, Numbers, Deuteronomy
- **N** Nevi'im (the Prophets)

  - The Former Prophets (Deuteronomistic it history): Joshua, Judges, 1 and 2 Samuel, 1 and 2 Kings

- The Latter Prophets (compiled in the prophets' names): Isaiah, Jeremiah, Ezekiel, and the Scroll of the Twelve (Amos, Hosea, Micah, Joel, etc.)
- **K** Kethuvim (the Writings)

  - Poetry: Psalms
  - Wisdom: Job, Proverbs, Ecclesiastes
  - Festival scrolls: Ruth, Song of Songs, Lamentations, Esther
  - Acpocalyptic literature: Daniel
  - Priestly history: Ezra, Nehemiah, 1 and 2 Chronicles

Hebrew division of Scripture into Law, Prophets, and Writings is in some respects a more logical (and chronological) arrangement than is the Septuagint's interspersing of prophets with historical writings and poetic books.

In Christian Bibles, then, the distinction between the Prophets and the Writings is seriously obscured. The traditional Christian catalog separates the Festival Scrolls, such as Ruth, Esther, and the Song of Songs, from one another, with the result that their devotional and cultic significance is no longer clear. The original arrangement is more meaningful, insofar as some of these short books were probably adopted into the canon because of their long association with particular holy days on which they were read aloud. Their long-term familiarity to the Jewish community of faith may largely have determined their canonization.

16. Are There Any Other Jewish Writings That Were Not Received into the Bible?

Yes, these noncanonical Jewish books are known collectively as the **Pseudepigrapha** because some of them were piously but inaccurately attributed to revered biblical figures of the distant past, such as Enoch and Moses. Dating from about 200 B.C.E. to 200 C.E., the Pseudepigrapha include a rich variety of legendary and apocalyptic material that significantly influenced Jewish and early Christian thought. Many pseudepigraphal works were found among the **Dead Sea Scrolls**, an ancient library of biblical and other religious documents found in caves near the **Dead Sea** settlement named **Qumran**. (Individual books of the Pseudepigrapha are discussed in Part 7.) Although most of the fifty-two books classified among the Pseudepigrapha—including 1 and 2 Enoch—are of Jewish origin, some manuscripts apparently were revised by Christian scribes, indicating that they circulated among and were read by members of the early church.

RECOMMENDED READING

Charles, R. H., ed. *The Apocrypha and Pseudepigrapha of the Old Testament in English,* vols. 1 and 2. New York: Oxford University Press, 1913, reprinted 1963.

Charlesworth, James H. "Biblical Literature: Apocrypha and Pseudepigrapha." In Mircea Eliade,

ed., *The Encyclopedia of Religion,* Vol. 2, pp. 173–
183. New York: Macmillan, 1987.
———, ed. *The Old Testament Pseudepigrapha.* Vol. 1,
Apocalyptic Literature and Testaments. Garden City,
N.Y.: Doubleday, 1983. A monumental scholarly
edition of the Pseudepigrapha, with new transla-
tions and notes.
———. *The Old Testament Pseudepigrapha.* Vol. 2,
*Expansion of the "Old Testament" and Legends, Wis-
dom and Philosophical Literature.* Garden City, N.Y.:
Doubleday, 1985.
Eissfeldt, Otto. *The Old Testament: An Introduction.*
New York: Harper & Row, 1965.
Nickelsburg, George W. E. *Jewish Literature Between
the Bible and the Mishnah: A Historical and Literary
Introduction.* Philadelphia: Fortress Press, 1981.
Rost, Leonard. *Judaism Outside the Hebrew Canon: An
Introduction to the Documents.* Nashville, Tenn.:
Abingdon Press, 1976.
Soggin, J. Alberto. *Introduction to the Old Testament,*
3rd ed. Louisville, Ky.: Westminster/John Knox
Press, 1989.

17. What Are the Dead Sea Scrolls?

Until about thirty years ago, the oldest known extant manuscript copies of the Hebrew Scriptures were the Masoretic Texts, which dated from about the ninth and tenth centuries C.E. In 1947, however, according to a popular version of the story, a Bedouin shepherd boy threw a stone into a cave at Qumran near the Dead Sea and heard pottery shattering inside. Investigating later, he found hidden in the cave clay jars containing leather scrolls. On examining the site, scholars found an entire library of religious books dating from about the second century B.C.E. to the first century C.E.

Many of these scrolls were copies of canonical works of the Hebrew Bible—such as Isaiah, the Psalms, Deuteronomy, and Daniel—as well as commentaries on them. There were also original writings, which most scholars believe were produced by a monastic group of **Essenes**, a Jewish sect that occupied the Qumran area over the three-century period during which the manuscripts were written. These original works included a Manual of Discipline for the Qum-

ran community and a set of military instructions for fighting the cosmic battle between Good and Evil, the imminent War of the Sons of Light against the Sons of Darkness. Many other tracts, sermons, and biblical explications were found in various caves.

This find was significant in several ways. First, it provided copies of at least fragments of all books of the Hebrew Bible that were almost 1000 years older than any other extant manuscripts. Second, it demonstrated that whereas many biblical texts contained numerous variations from the received copies, the Book of Isaiah, represented in a scroll twenty-four feet long, had been transmitted for nearly ten centuries with little appreciable change. Third, it confirmed the enormous diversity of Jewish thought during the period between the third century B.C.E. and 68 C.E., when Roman armies destroyed Qumran. The Dead Sea Scrolls not only contain a wide variety of religious texts, from purity laws to apocalyptic visions; some of them also include themes and practices that anticipate Christianity, including ceremonial immersion (baptism), a ritual meal open only to initiates, and a new covenant community that alone represents true Israel. (See Part 8.)

RECOMMENDED READING

Betz, O. "Dead Sea Scrolls." In G. A. Buttrick, ed.,
The Interpreter's Dictionary of the Bible, Vol. 1,
pp. 790–802. New York and Nashville, Tenn.:
Abingdon Press, 1962.
———. "Essenes." In G. A. Buttrick, ed., *The Inter-
preter's Dictionary of the Bible: Supplementary Vol-
ume,* pp. 277–279. Nashville, Tenn.: Abingdon
Press, 1976.
Cross, Frank M. *The Ancient Library of Qumran,* 2nd
ed. Grand Rapids, Mich.: Baker, 1980.
Gaster, Theodore H. *The Dead Sea Scriptures in En-
glish Translation.* Garden City, N.Y.: Doubleday,
1976.
Shanks, Hershel, ed. *Understanding the Dead Sea
Scrolls.* New York: Random House, 1992. A col-

Table 1.1 Order of Books in the Old Testament (Tanak)

Hebrew Bible (Masoretic Text)	Greek Septuagint Bible	Roman Catholic and Greek Orthodox Old Testament	Protestant Old Testament
Torah *Pentateuch*	*Pentateuch*	*Pentateuch*	*Pentateuch*
Bereshith (Genesis)	Genesis	Genesis	Genesis
Shemoth (Exodus)	Exodus	Exodus	Exodus
Wayiqra (Leviticus)	Leviticus	Leviticus	Leviticus
Bemidbar (Numbers)	Numbers	Numbers	Numbers
Debarim (Deuteronomy)	Deuteronomy	Deuteronomy	Deuteronomy
Nevi'im (Prophets)	*Historical Books*	*Historical Books*	*Historical Books*
Former Prophets	Joshua	Josue (Joshua)	Joshua
Yehoshua (Joshua)	Judges	Judges	Judges
Shofetim (Judges)	Ruth	Ruth	Ruth
	1–2 Regnorum (1–2 Samuel)	1 and 2 Kings (1–2 Samuel)	1–2 Samuel
Shemuel (1–2 Samuel)			1–2 Kings
Melakim (1–2 Kings)	3–4 Regnorum (1–2 Kings)	3–4 Kings (1–2 Kings)	
	1–2 Paralipomenon	1–2 Paralipomenon	1–2 Chronicles
	(1–2 Chronicles)	(1–2 Chronicles)	Ezra
	1 Esdras	1–2 Esdras (Ezra-Nehemiah)	Nehemiah
	2 Esdras (Ezra-Nehemiah)		Esther
	Esther	Tobias (Tobit)*	
	Judith	Judith*	
	Tobit	Esther (with additions)	
	1–4 Maccabees	1–2 Maccabees*	
	Poetry and Wisdom	*Poetry and Wisdom*	*Poetry and Wisdom*
	Psalms	Job	Job
	Odes	Psalms	Psalms
	Proverbs	Proverbs	Proverbs
	Ecclesiastes	Ecclesiastes	Ecclesiastes
	Song of Songs	Canticle of Canticles (Song of Solomon)	Song of Solomon
	Job		
	Wisdom of Solomon	Wisdom of Solomon*	
	Sirach (Ecclesiasticus)	Ecclesiasticus* (Wisdom of Jesus ben Sirach)	
	Psalms of Solomon		
Latter Prophets	*Prophetic Books*	*Prophetic Books*	*Prophetic Books*
Yeshayahu (Isaiah)		Isaias (Isaiah)	Isaiah
Yirmevahu (Jeremiah)		Jeremias (Jeremiah)	Jeremiah
		Lamentations	Lamentations
		Baruch (including the epistle of Jeremias)*	

Table 1.1 (*continued*)

Hebrew Bible (Masoretic Text)	Greek Septuagint Bible	Roman Catholic and Greek Orthodox Old Testament	Protestant Old Testament
Yehezqel (Ezekiel)		Ezechiel (Ezekiel)	Ezekiel
		Daniel (with additions; Prayer of Azariah and Song of the Three Young Men;* Susanna;* Bel and the Dragon*)	Daniel
Tere Asar (Book of the Twelve)			
	Hosea	Osee (Hosea)	Hosea
	Amos	Joel	Joel
	Micah	Amos	Amos
	Joel	Abidas (Obadiah)	Obadiah
	Obadiah	Jonas (Jonah)	Jonah
	Jonah	Micheas (Micah)	Micah
	Nahum	Nahum	Nahum
	Habukkuk	Habucuc (Habakkuk)	Habakkuk
	Zephaniah	Sophonias (Zephaniah)	Zephaniah
	Haggai	Aggeus (Haggai)	Haggai
	Zechariah	Zacharias (Zechariah)	Zechariah
	Malachi	Malachias (Malachi)	Malachi
Kethuvim (Writings)	Isaiah		
Tehillim (Psalms)	Jeremiah		
Iyyob (Job)	Baruch		
Mishle (Proverbs)	Lamentations		
Ruth	Epistle of Jeremiah		
Shir Hashirim (Song of Solomon)	Ezekiel		
	Susanna		
Qoheleth (Ecclesiastes)	Daniel		
Ekah (Lamentations)	Bel and the Dragon		
Ester (Esther)			
Daniel			
Ezra-Nehemyah (Ezra-Nehemiah)			
Dibre Hayamin (1–2 Chronicles)			

*Not in Jewish or most Protestant Bibles; considered deuterocanonical by Catholic scholars and relegated to the Apocrypha by Protestants.

lection of popular essays from the *Biblical Archaeology Review.*

Vermes, Geza. *The Dead Sea Scrolls, Qumran in Perspective.* Philadelphia: Fortress Press, 1977.

———. *The Dead Sea Scrolls in English,* 3rd ed. London: Penguin Books, 1987.

Yadin, Yigael. *The Temple Scroll: The Hidden Law of the Dead Sea Sect.* New York: Random House, 1985.

The New Testament Canon

18. What Does the Term Testament *Mean, and How Do the Old and New Testaments Differ in Respect to That Meaning?*

In biblical terms, **testament** is a synonym for **covenant**, which means an "agreement" or "promise." In the Hebrew Bible, Yahweh initiated a covenant with Israel that gave the Old Testament its name. At Mount Sinai, where Yahweh had brought the Israelites after rescuing them from Egyptian slavery, he promised to be their God, and they vowed to obey him. Because this agreement was mediated through Moses, it was called the Mosaic Covenant or Testament, and this legal bond between Israel and Israel's God is the central theme of the Torah. But several of Israel's prophets felt that the people had so grievously broken their covenant obligations that a new, more spiritual agreement was needed. Jeremiah, in particular, predicted that Yahweh would make a new covenant with his people (Jer. 31:31).

Christians believe that Jesus inaugurated that new covenant at the Last Supper: "And he took the cup, and gave thanks, and gave it to them, saying, Drink ye all of it: For this is my blood of the new testament . . ." (Matt. 26:27–28; King James Version). (The adjective *new,* not present in the earliest manuscripts, was added later to emphasize the change in God's relationship with humankind. Both the Revised Standard Version and the Jerusalem Bible omit *new* and use *covenant* instead of *testament* in this passage.)

To Christians, then, the Jewish Scriptures, dealing with the older Mosaic Covenant, came to be known as the Old Testament; the Greek writings about Jesus and his disciples were called the New Testament. The Christian community regarded both parts of the Bible as authoritative and suitable for religious instruction.

19. How and When Was the New Testament Canon Formed?

The process by which the twenty-seven books of the New Testament were canonized spanned a period of approximately four centuries. Although most of the early Christian writings that eventually became part of the New Testament were composed between about 50 and 120 C.E., it was not until 367 C.E. that a list of books appeared that corresponds exactly to the present canon. Even after Athanasius, then bishop of Alexandria, issued this list in his Easter Letter of 367, Christians in different parts of the Roman Empire continued to recognize a variety of official lists. By the late fourth century C.E., most—but not all—churches accepted the four Gospels and Paul's letters as authoritatively representing the Christian faith. At the same time, many churches rejected such books as Revelation, 2 Peter, Jude, and Hebrews, while accepting several others, such as the Epistle of Barnabas and the Apocalypse of Peter, that ultimately did not become part of the canon.

Each book in the New Testament originated as a separate document and at first circulated independently of the others. Paul's letters, the oldest extant Christian writings, were sent individually to different small congregations in Greece and Asia Minor. The four familiar Gospels—Matthew, Mark, Luke, and John— were similarly composed for particular Christian communities, such as **Antioch** or Ephesus, where they probably served as foundation documents for that distinct group.

Many scholars believe that the first step in bringing together these diverse documents occurred toward the end of the first century, when one or more of Paul's admirers collected his letters. By the mid-second century, when 2 Peter (believed to be the last-written canonical work) was published, Paul's letters had been recognized as Scripture—at least in some circles (2 Pet. 3:15–16). In the meantime, a large number of Gospels, all purporting to represent Jesus' life and teachings, had also been written. Until well into the second century, most churches apparently used only the one Gospel known to their local group; not until about 150 C.E. did a Christian leader, Justin Martyr, refer to the existence of several different Gospels. By the end of the second century, however, the international church reached a compromise between the single Gospel championed by individual churches and the many different Gospels then in circulation. In accepting the present four, the Christian communities rejected numerous others, such as the Gospel attributed to Peter and the **Gospel of Thomas**, consigning them to disuse and ultimate oblivion. In 1945, a complete copy of the Thomas Gospel, containing 114 sayings ascribed to Jesus, was found in an Egyptian cemetery. Except for this "Fifth Gospel," all of the others survive only in small fragments.

The notion that only a single, consistent Gospel—rather than four diverse and sometimes contradictory accounts—should be the church norm was expressed in the *Diatessaron* of Tatian (c. 170 C.E.). This version, which for centuries prevailed in the East, particularly Syria, ingeniously wove together the contents of Matthew, Mark, Luke, and John, as well as elements from oral tradition, into a unified narrative.

Whereas a collection of Paul's letters and four Gospels were widely accepted by the end of the second century, many other New Testament books—particularly Hebrews and the seven brief letters known as the **Catholic Epistles**—took an additional two or three centuries to find general recognition. The Muratorian Canon, which scholars once dated to the late second or early third century but now believe was com-

piled in the fourth century, is typical of the mixed bag of canonical and apocryphal books found in different church lists. Listing twenty-four books, the Muratorian Canon approves the four Gospels, Acts, thirteen letters ascribed to Paul (but excluding Hebrews), Jude, 1 and 2 (but not 3) John, the Wisdom of Solomon, Revelation, and the Apocalypse of Peter. The Muratorian list excludes five books that finally achieved canonical status, but it includes a Greek Wisdom book that was ultimately assigned to the Old Testament and an "apostolic" vision of hell that failed to be included in any canon.

The Codex Claromontanus is a sixth-century Greek-Latin manuscript that contains a list also thought to derive from the fourth century. Besides enumerating most of the (ultimately) canonical works, this codex includes the Epistle of Barnabas, the Shepherd of Hermas, the Acts of Paul, and the Apocalypse of Peter—all four of which were finally excluded from the canon. Even the Codex Sinaiticus, one of the oldest (fourth century) and most important manuscripts containing all twenty-seven New Testament books, also includes the Epistle of Barnabas and the Shepherd of Hermas. As late as the fifth century, a Greek manuscript known as the Codex Alexandrinus included both 1 and 2 Clement as part of the Christian testament. Whereas 1 Clement is a letter written around 96 C.E. by an historical bishop of Rome, 2 Clement is pseudonymous (composed by an unknown writer in the name of a famous person). **Pseudonymity** was common among many Greco-Roman, as well as Jewish and Christian, authors in the Hellenistic world.

Writing in the fourth century C.E., the church historian Eusebius divided sacred Christian literature into three categories. The "acknowledged" works include twenty-one canonical books; the "disputed" books include Revelation, James, Jude, 2 Peter, 2 and 3 John, the Acts of Paul, the Shepherd of Hermas, the Apocalypse of Peter, the Epistle of Barnabas, and the Didache (a compilation of early Christian teachings). Eusebius's "rejected" books are the Gospels attributed to Peter, Thomas, and Matthias and the Acts of Andrew, John, and other works judged spurious.

At no time did a single church authority or group of church leaders formally decide on the contents of the Christian Scriptures. The long, hotly debated process by which the present New Testament took its final form involved several historical events or movements. It was formerly thought that the canonization process began as a response to Marcion (c. 140 C.E.), a Roman Christian who advocated a Gnostic Christianity and who insisted that believers reject the entire Hebrew Bible, replacing it with an edited version of Luke's Gospel and Paul's letters. According to this older view, church leaders began to compile official lists of sacred writings—including a validation of the Greek Old Testament—to counteract Marcion's radically abbreviated canon. Noting that Paul's letters had already been collected together before Marcion, scholars now believe that the evolution of the New Testament canon resulted from circumstances broader than Marcion's provocative challenge. As in the case of the Hebrew Bible, some books, such as the Gospels, Acts, and Paul's letters, were widely used in worship services and in teaching converts. Read aloud in churches from Syria to Gaul, some books proved their long-term usefulness in maintaining a connection with Christianity's origins. Gospels that preserved the accepted words and deeds of Jesus served the dual purpose of keeping the church anchored to its roots and of standardizing its chief doctrines. Documents that enunciated the Christian community's essential beliefs and practices and that, over a period of centuries, came to represent orthodoxy (right teaching) earned canonical recognition. Books that were deemed to present heretical (officially incorrect) views, were discarded and condemned. A universally accepted canon of authoritative books provided a unifying force for churches scattered throughout the Roman Empire, imparting standards of belief and behavior.

RECOMMENDED READING

Gamble, Harry Y. "Canon, New Testament." In D. N. Freedman, ed., *The Anchor Bible Dictionary*, Vol. 1, pp. 852–861. New York: Doubleday, 1992.

Grant, Robert M. *The Formation of the New Testament.* New York: Harper & Row, 1965.

von Campenhausen, Hans F. *The Formation of the Christian Bible.* Translated by J. A. Baker. Philadelphia: Fortress Press, 1972.

20. What Are the Christian Apocrypha?

Books generally called the Christian Apocrypha are early writings that did not find a place in the New Testament but that were nonetheless popular reading in some parts of the church. These include the First Epistle of Clement, a sermon from the bishop of Rome to the Corinthian congregation. Dated about 95 C.E., 1 Clement is closer to genuine apostolic times than several later books, such as 2 Peter and the Pastorals, which were admitted to the canon. The Didache (Teaching of the Twelve Apostles), which contains moral instruction and regulations for the rites of baptism and communion, may be the first organized document on ecclesiastical policies produced by the Church. The Shepherd of Hermas (which was at times accepted as canonical) and the Epistle of Barnabas were influential as well. The New Testament Apocrypha also includes variant Gospels, such as the Gospel of Thomas, a Gnostic document dating as early as the late first century C.E. (See Part 10, "The New Testament Apocrypha.")

RECOMMENDED READING

Hennecke, Edgar. In W. Schneemelcher, ed., *New Testament Apocrypha.* Vol. 1, *Gospels and Related Writings*; Vol. 2, *Writings Related to the Apostles, Apocalypses, and Related Subjects.* Translated by R. McL. Wilson. Philadelphia: Westminster Press, 1963. This important work offers both a good translation of the New Testament apocryphal books and a discussion of their relation to the official canon.

Koester, Helmut. *Introduction to the New Testament.* Vol. 2, *History and Literature of Early Christianity.* Philadelphia: Fortress Press, 1982.

The Israelites and Their God

21. Who Were the Israelites?

In biblical terminology, the Israelites are descendants of the patriarch Jacob, whose name was changed to Israel. Chosen by their God to represent him among the nations, the Israelites formed a twelve- (later two-) tribe country that occupied Palestine from the thirteenth century before Jesus to the first century after, when they were dispersed by the Romans.

The anthropological origins of Israel, however, are much more complex and obscure. According to the national credo given in Deuteronomy 26:5, "a wandering [or 'perishing'] Aramean" was their "father" or progenitor. The Arameans (Syrians), with whom the Israelites were ethnically connected, were originally a nomadic people who migrated westward from the Arabian Desert. About 2000 B.C.E., a Semitic group known as Amorites or "Westerners" infiltrated Mesopotamia, the land between the Tigris and Euphrates rivers in what is now Iraq, and settled there. The Arameans may also be related to this group.

It was in **Mesopotamia**, home of the world's oldest known civilizations, that Israel's national traditions began. In Genesis, the Aramean family of **Abraham**, chief ancestor of the chosen people, is represented as moving northward from **Ur**, a major city in lower Mesopotamia, to **Haran**, 600 miles distant in what is now southern Turkey. (Some scholars place Abraham's original home in *northern* Mesopotamia, but most commentators identify it with the ancient Sumerian site.) From Haran, Abraham traveled southward with his flocks and herds to Canaan (Palestine). Recent archaeolog-

ical excavations in the Haran area have confirmed the existence of practices and customs during the first half of the second millennium B.C.E. that are depicted in Genesis. Although the Genesis stories were not written until centuries after the tribal movements they describe, some of their details were transmitted orally with impressive accuracy.

The Israelites belonged to and eventually developed from a larger group of Arameans known as the **'Apiru** (or **Habiru**)—apparently less a racial or ethnic group than a class of "outsiders" who lacked a definite or accepted place in ancient Near Eastern society. Racially mixed, they wandered from place to place serving as shepherds, caravan drivers, mercenary soldiers, slaves, and outlaws. Although the term *'Apiru* may be equivalent to the biblical word *'ibri,* meaning "**Hebrew**," not all the 'Apiru were biblical Hebrews. The Israelites were Hebrews, but they were only one small part of a much larger class of nomadic 'Apiru who moved rootlessly throughout the ancient Near East. After the biblical Hebrews settled in Canaan to found the nation of Israel, they were known as Israelites, traditional descendants of Abraham, Isaac, and Jacob.

In Scripture, the word *Israel* has several meanings. As used by many prophets, it denotes the collective descendants of Jacob, Yahweh's covenant people. In a political sense, it also refers to (1) the united twelve-tribe kingdom under David and Solomon and (2) the northern ten-tribe kingdom that split from Judah (the Davidic state) in 922 B.C.E.

RECOMMENDED READING

Albright, William F. *From the Stone Age to Christianity.* Garden City, N.Y.: Doubleday, 1957.

———. *The Biblical Period from Abraham to Ezra.* New York: Harper & Row, 1963.

Bright, John. *A History of Israel.* Philadelphia: Westminster Press, 1972.

de Vaux, Roland. *Ancient Israel, Its Life and Institutions.* Translated by D. Smith. New York: McGraw-Hill, 1961.

————. *The Early History of Israel.* Translated by D. Smith. Philadelphia: Westminster Press, 1978.

Hermann, Siegfried. *A History of Israel in Old Testament Times.* Philadelphia: Fortress Press, 1981.

Jagersma, Henk. *A History of Israel in the Old Testament Period.* Philadelphia: Fortress Press, 1983.

Mendenhall, George E. *The Tenth Generation: The Origins of the Biblical Tradition.* Baltimore: Johns Hopkins University Press, 1973.

Noth, Martin. *The History of Israel.* New York: Harper & Row, 1960.

Orlinsky, Harry M. *Ancient Israel.* Ithaca, N.Y.: Cornell University Press, 1960.

Wolff, Hans W. *Anthropology of the Old Testament.* Translated by M. Kohl. Philadelphia: Fortress Press, 1981.

22. By What Different Names Did the Israelites Know Their God, and What Is the Significance of These Differences?

Bible manuscripts contain a number of different names and titles for the Hebrew Deity. Genesis 1, for example, uses the generic name **Elohim**, a plural form denoting "gods" or "divine powers," although this does not necessarily imply that the Hebrews believed in many gods. Even the most monotheistic prophets continued to use the name Elohim.

In Genesis 2:4b occurs the first appearance of the **Tetragrammaton**, a Greek term designating the four sacred letters (YHWH) of the Hebrew God's personal name. Because the Hebrew language was originally written without vowels, we are not certain precisely how the divine name was pronounced, although most biblical scholars agree that **Yahweh** is a close approximation. (The familiar English name **Jehovah** derives from a Latin rendition of the Tetragrammaton, to which the vowels from Elohim and Adonai were added. This version of the divine name can be traced to Petrus Galatinus, confessor to Pope Leo X, 1518 C.E.)

According to one widely accepted theory, the name Yahweh is derived from the Hebrew verb meaning "to be" or "to cause to be," as God reveals to Moses when he states, "I Am who I Am" (Exod. 3). God is here speaking in the first person; in the third person singular, the phrase becomes *Yahweh* ("he is"). The divine name, occurring nearly 7000 times in the Old Testament, expresses both Yahweh's eternity (he always is) and his purposiveness, his causing all things to be or happen. The meaning of *Yahweh* is thus closely tied to the Hebrews' view of their God as the Lord of history.

To avoid profaning (taking in vain) the divine name, by the third century B.C.E. Jewish rabbis began to substitute the Semitic term **Adonai** (meaning "lord" or "master") when reading aloud passages containing the four sacred letters. Eventually, the name was pronounced but once a year, by the high priest on the Day of Atonement. For centuries Protestant and Roman Catholic Bibles followed the Jewish practice of substituting "Lord" or "God" whenever the Tetragrammaton occurred, but recent scholarly translations, such as the Doubleday Anchor Bible and the Jerusalem Bible, have restored *Yahweh* to its rightful place in the English text. (The King James translators indicated textual occurrences of the Tetragrammaton by printing GOD or LORD in small capitals where *Yahweh* had originally appeared. The Revised Standard Version and the New English Bible also follow this practice.)

Other names and titles of God, confined chiefly to the Pentateuch and Job, include *El Elyon,* "God Most High" (Gen. 14:19–22), *El Olam,* "God Everlasting" (Gen. 21:33), and such terms as "the Shield of Abraham" (Gen. 15:1) and "the Fear of Isaac" (Gen. 31:42, 53). Particularly interesting is the term **El Shaddai,** which is usually translated "God Almighty," although some experts think that it means "God of the Mountain." Certainly, it is on Mount Sinai that El Shaddai, who identifies himself as "the God of Abraham, the God of Isaac, and the God of Jacob," reveals that he is also Yahweh (Exod. 3 and 6) and commands Moses to bring Israel back to that mountain to worship him. Similarly, it is to Mount Sinai that El Shaddai descends when he reveals his law and makes his covenant with Israel.

Different names for the Deity, particularly Elohim and Yahweh, are associated with distinct literary styles and theological attitudes in the biblical text. This realization first led scholars to discover in the biblical narratives different strata or literary strands that seemed to derive from different sources, each of which tended to use a distinctive name or names for God. For a fuller explanation of the major sources that experts have found in the first five books of the Bible, see Part 3.

RECOMMENDED READING

Albright, William F. *Yahweh and the Gods of Canaan: A Historical Analysis of Two Contrasting Faiths.* Garden City, N.Y.: Doubleday/Anchor Books, 1969.

Cross, Frank M., ed. *Canaanite Myth and Hebrew Epic, Essays in the History of the Religion of Israel.* Cambridge, Mass.: Harvard University Press, 1973.

Good, Robert M. "Baal," and "El." In P. J. Achtemeier, ed., *Harper's Bible Dictionary,* pp. 84–85, 252–253. San Francisco: Harper & Row, 1985.

Rose, Martin. "Names of God in the OT." In D. N. Freedman, ed., *The Anchor Bible Dictionary,* Vol. 4, pp. 1001–1011. New York: Doubleday, 1992. An extremely important discussion of the different names of God in the Hebrew Bible.

Smith, Mark S. *The Early History of God: Yahweh and the Other Deities in Ancient Israel.* San Francisco: Harper & Row, 1990.

Thompson, Henry O. "Yahweh." In D. N. Freedman, ed., *The Anchor Bible Dictionary,* Vol. 6, pp. 1011–1012. New York: Doubleday, 1992. Discusses the significance of the personal name of Israel's God.

23. How Did the Concept of Israel's God Develop?

The Israelites' concept of God seems to have developed slowly over time, as a synthesis or composite of several earlier beliefs about divine beings. Bible writers are frank about admitting that the diverse tribes who eventually united to form the nation of Israel worshiped other deities. The Book of Joshua refers to "the gods your ancestors served beyond the River [Euphrates]" (Josh. 24:15), an allusion to the ancient divinities of Mesopotamia that presumably were recognized by the Genesis patriarchs.

Although the deep reverence that Egyptians and Mesopotamians expressed for their gods must have impressed the Israelites, they were apparently even more deeply influenced by the religions of Canaan. From the time they entered Canaan in the late thirteenth century B.C.E. until well after their return from the Babylonian exile in the sixth and fifth centuries B.C.E., the Israelites were repeatedly attracted to Canaanite gods such as Baal and his consort Asherah. Representing the natural forces of storm, rain, and fertility, these Canaanite deities were endlessly denounced by Israel's prophets, who saw them as rivals to their covenant God Yahweh.

Although Israel's distinctive faith developed in conscious opposition to Canaanite fertility cults, recent archaeological studies reveal that certain Canaanite descriptions of Baal and his attributes were commonly applied to Yahweh. The closest link between Canaanite religion and that of Israel—which evolved in a fully Canaanite environment—appears in the thematic affinities connecting Yahweh with Baal's father, El. (A general Semitic term for "god," El occurs more than 200 times in the Hebrew Bible.) Studies of Canaanite literature, such as the cuneiform texts from Ugarit, a Bronze Age site in Syria, reveal numerous parallels between El, the father-god of the Canaanite pantheon, and Yahweh. (See the discussion of the Ugaritic El, Part 2.)

Like El, who in Canaanite mythology presided over the celestial assembly of gods, Yahweh is depicted as the most prominent figure among "the holy ones in heaven":

> Yahweh, the assembly of holy ones in heaven
> applaud the marvel of your faithfulness.
> Who in the skies can compare with Yahweh?
> Which of the heaven-born can rival him?
> Psalms 89:5–6

Threatening the observer with a club in his raised right hand and brandishing a thunderbolt in his left, Baal appears as the Canaanite storm god. This limestone stele was found at Ugarit. Whereas most biblical prophets railed against any recognition of Baal, at specific periods of Israel's history Canaanite descriptions of his powers and functions were freely ascribed to Yahweh. (Courtesy of Musée du Louvre)

Yahweh is distinguished ethically from other powers in the heavenly council by his superior "faithfulness"—his justice and loyalty to his word:

> God, dreaded in the assembly of holy ones,
> great and terrible to all around him.
> Yahweh, God of Sabaoth, who is like you?—
> mighty Yahweh, clothed in your faithfulness!
> Psalms 89:7–8

A similar passage in Psalm 82 depicts Israel's God standing with other gods in heaven's "divine assembly." Unlike other "sons of the Most High [Elyon]," Elohim shows a passionate devotion to justice and a remarkable concern for people whom rival deities apparently despise. God declares himself the champion of the poor and powerless, determined to rescue "the weak and needy" from both divine and human oppressors. Although "[they] too are gods," he tells members of the heavenly council, he will see to it that they will perish like mere mortals, relegated to oblivion for their failure to enforce justice (Ps. 82:1–7).

An ancient poem appended to Deuteronomy recalls that when the guardianships of earth's nations were apportioned out among heavenly beings, Yahweh inherited Israel:

> When the Most High gave the nations their
>   inheritance,
> when he divided the sons of men,
> he fixed their bounds according to the number
>   of the sons of God
> but Yahweh's portion was his people,
> Jacob [Israel] his share of inheritance.
> Deuteronomy 32:8–9

The "Most High" referred to (in Hebrew, Elyon) is an epithet of El, who is called "God Most High" (El Elyon) at the Canaanite shrine of Salem, a deity whom Abraham identifies with his patron Yahweh (Gen. 14:18–22). As in the Ugaritic texts, in the deuteronomic passage (El) Elyon functions as administrative chief of the divine council, assigning other members their spheres of earthly influence.

Although Bible writers gradually attributed to Yahweh many of the qualities and functions of some older Canaanite gods, the Deity was not thought of as originating in Canaan. According to Deuteronomy,

> Yahweh came from Sinai.
> For them [Israel], after Seir, he rose on the
>   horizon,
> after Mount Paran he shone forth.
> For them he came, after the mustering at
>   Kadesh,
> from his zenith as far as the foothills.
>
> Deuteronomy 33:2

The geographical locations cited in this verse lie in desert regions south of Israel, including Edom (also called Seir). According to tradition, Edom was founded by Jacob's [Israel's] twin brother, Esau (Gen. 36:1). (See also Judg. 5:4–5.)

The historical origins of Israel's earliest concept of its God Yahweh are still far from resolved. Some older scholars traced the earliest cult of Yahweh to the Kenites, a people listed among the pre-Israelite inhabitants of Canaan (Gen. 15:19). Moses' father-in-law, **Jethro** (also called Reuel or Hobab), a priest of Midian (Exod. 2:15–18, 3:1, 18:1; Num. 10:29), is identified as a Kenite (Judg. 1:16, 4:11). Because Moses first encountered Yahweh on the slopes of Mount Sinai while working for Jethro and because his father-in-law is shown as a superior or teacher of Moses, blessing him, sacrificing to Yahweh, and instructing him (Exod. 18:17–27), some commentators speculated that Moses learned of Yahweh from the Kenites. Although suggestive, this "Kenite hypothesis" is not widely accepted. The historical source of the tribal deity who became the universal God of the world's three great monotheistic religions—Judaism, Christianity, and Islam—remains shrouded in mystery.

RECOMMENDED READING

Miles, Jack. *God: A Biography.* New York: Alfred A. Knopf, 1995. Examines the Israelite God as he appears as a literary character in the Hebrew Bible (Tanak).

Smith, Mark S. *The Early History of God: Yahweh and the Other Deities in Ancient Israel.* San Francisco: Harper & Row, 1990.

24. Is There a Single "Biblical View" of Israel's God? In What Ways Do Old and New Testament Authors Differ in Their Portraits of the Deity?

The reader will better appreciate the Bible's portrait of Israel's God by remembering that each individual writer of Scripture had a personal, and therefore necessarily limited, understanding of the Deity. Because the Bible authors also wrote from a variety of theological viewpoints and from an ever-changing cultural perspective during the approximately 1100 years that it took to complete the biblical canon, each gave a somewhat different emphasis to the divine nature. The scriptural portrait that emerges is thus extremely complex, even contradictory, a composite portrait to which many diverse authorial personalities contributed.

To some writers, Yahweh was primarily strength; to others, Israel's Deity was a military leader who gave victory to his people; to still others, he was an unknowable intelligence, the ineffable creator and sustainer of the universe. The highest concepts of the biblical God, in which the Creator appears as supreme wisdom, love, and mercy, are found in the Prophets of the Hebrew Bible and in the teachings of Jesus and the Johannine literature of the New Testament. Prophets like Isaiah, Hosea, and Micah saw God as an almighty power who could judge the world harshly but who was also kind, loving, and deeply concerned for humanity. Jesus typically presented God as a gracious parent ever near to those who would seek a relationship with the divine. The author of 1 John achieved an even more essential vision: To him, God is love.

In general, Bible writers pictured God as representing or embodying those qualities that they themselves most needed or valued in their given time and circumstances. Because they wrote from a patriarchal viewpoint, biblical authors tended to regard their Deity as a masculine force—a warrior, lawgiver, judge, or executioner. Thus, when the early Hebrews were a powerless, oppressed minority in Egypt, they looked to Yahweh to show his power—his ability to deliver them from their enemies. The ten plagues that Yahweh inflicted upon pharaoh and the Egyptians were a demonstration of his irresistible might, proof that he was stronger than other gods. In the Exodus narrative, the writers show little concern for Yahweh's objective justice or mercy, for such qualities would have been seen as irrelevant to those who needed a god with a strong arm.

Yahweh as Warrior   Although the biblical God first appears in Genesis as creator of the universe, historically it is likely that Israel first knew him as a warrior god fighting to bring them victory. Scholars believe that Israel's earliest writings, like those of all other ancient people, took the form of poetry. Some of the oldest prebiblical poetry, composed orally, included songs and hymns praising Yahweh's prowess on the battlefield, slaughtering Israel's enemies. In compiling their narratives in the Torah and the historical books that follow, some Bible authors drew on previously existing collections of Israelite war poetry, citing such sources as the Book of Jashar (or the Book of the Just), now lost. A verse quoted from that volume contains the famous command for sun and moon to "stand still over Gibeon," in evoking nature's cooperation so that Israelite troops can take full military "vengeance on their enemies" (Josh. 10:13).

A similar poetic anthology, the Book of the Wars of Yahweh, is quoted in Numbers 21, where Yahweh supplies Israel's invading armies with fresh well water, enabling them to sweep like a "fire" over Sihon, an Amorite king who refuses Israel's tribes passage through his territory (Num. 21:15, 18, 28–30). Other ancient war poetry, incorporated into the Bible's prose narratives, appears in the Song of Deborah, which extols the woman Jael for murdering **Sis-**

era, a Canaanite prince who took refuge in her tent. Deborah's war poem shows Yahweh advancing from the nation of Edom like a personification of natural chaos—earthquake and storm:

> Yahweh, when you set out from Seir,
> as you trod the land of Edom,
> earth shook, the heavens quaked,
> the clouds dissolved into water.
> The mountains melted before Yahweh,
> before Yahweh, the God of Israel.
>
> Judges 5:4–5

In this passage, Yahweh's violent advance is described in language similar to that applied to Baal when he attacks his opponents. Perhaps equally ancient is Moses' song praising Yahweh as a supernatural fighter who has drowned Egypt's army at the Sea of Reeds.

> Yahweh I sing: he has covered himself in glory,
>   horse and rider he has thrown into the sea.
> Yah is my strength, my song.
> he is my salvation. . . .
> Yahweh is a warrior;
> Yahweh is his name.
>
> Exodus 15:1–3

When the Israelites are about to invade Canaan, their leader Joshua sees a man who grasps a "naked sword" and who identifies himself as "captain of the army of Yahweh." The divine warrior may have been Yahweh himself: Joshua is told to remove his sandals because he stands on ground made holy by the presence of divinity, the same command given Moses when Yahweh appears at the burning bush (cf. Josh. 5:13–15 and Exod. 3:2–15). As he faces the giant Goliath, young David epitomizes his God's function: "Yahweh is the lord of the battle" (1 Sam. 17:47).

Whereas Israel's oldest conception of Yahweh may be as warrior, his supreme holiness is also an essential part of the composite biblical portrait. To the priestly writers of Leviticus, Chronicles, Ezekiel, and similar material, their God was absolutely holy, set apart from ordinary life and approached only through elaborate rituals and sacrifices. As presented in the New Testament, the Sadducees who officiated at the Jerusalem Temple services held a similar view. The deuteronomistic writers of Israel's historical books, such as Judges and Kings, saw Yahweh as the Lord of history, the manipulator of human events who causes the rise and fall of nations. In this role, Yahweh is also Judge of the earth, the impartial administrator of rewards and punishments according to the recipient's moral behavior. The authors of Genesis 1, Psalm 104, and Job 38–42 saw their God as an invisible power transcending nature, whose word alone is enough to create the world and whose incomparable wisdom eludes human understanding.

In contrast, some Bible writers pictured their God as all too human, attributing to him both the virtues and defects of a human personality. At times, their Deity is represented as a typical Near Eastern king—powerful and fundamentally just—but quick-tempered, prone to jealousy, and easily provoked to punish insubordination. This God is a destroyer as well as a creator, venting his wrath through flood, famine, plague, drought, earthquake, and fire from heaven. Because it was commonly believed that the biblical God controlled everything that happened (Amos 3:3–8), natural disasters were interpreted as his express will, though occasionally a Bible writer injected a note of doubt about this. For the author of Ecclesiastes, for example, the Deity is remote from and uninvolved in ordinary life, leaving the element of chance to control human affairs:

> I see this too under the sun: the race does not go to the swift, nor the battle to the strong; there is no bread for the wise, wealth for the intelligent, nor favor for the learned; all are subject to time and mischance.
>
> Ecclesiastes 9:11

Many of the prophets (see Part 5), who raised Israel's religion to its greatest heights, balanced the fear-inspiring aspects of their God's strength by also emphasizing his *hesed,* a term denoting steadfast love, loyal kindness, and a devotion beyond mere duty. Hosea presents Yahweh as punishing disobedience but also as recoiling from his intention to destroy Israel because of his great love for his people (Hos. 11:9). The Torah, with its demands that the Israelites are to love Yahweh with their whole being (Deut. 6:5–6) and to love their neighbors as themselves (Lev. 19:18), implies a similarly generous emotion in Yahweh.

Perhaps the single most sublime description of divinity in either Old or New Testament occurs in Isaiah 40–43, where the poet articulates a vision of Israel's God philosophically unmatched elsewhere in Scripture. All the basic tenets of ethical monotheism are made explicit: Yahweh is One—eternal, almighty, and omniscient. Unrivaled, he holds the universe under his absolute control.

Rejecting the existence of other gods, the poet of Isaiah 45 faces the implications of his monism—the belief that a single power rules the cosmos. Since he alone is God, Yahweh is the source of all things, including both good and evil.

> I am Yahweh, unrivaled,
> I form the light and create the dark.
> I make good fortune and create calamity,
> it is I, Yahweh, who do all this.
>
> Isaiah 45:7

As the single source of moral opposites, Yahweh's transcendent supremacy raises troubling questions. Authors of the Wisdom literature, such as Job and Ecclesiastes, pondered the mystery of a Deity who is at once all-good and all-powerful but who permits evil to exist and allows his righteous worshipers to suffer undeservedly. Basing their reflections on observed experience—in which the wicked commonly escape punishment and the innocent are cruelly exploited—the anonymous writers of Job and Ecclesiastes reject the notion that the universe operates according to recognizable laws of retributive justice, a principle that biblical historians rigorously apply to their interpretation of

Israel's sufferings. (See the discussions of Deuteronomy through 2 Kings parts 3 and 4.) Job accuses God of administering a world without ethical meaning, demanding that divine power come to empathize with the experience of human pain, to see and feel as intelligent creatures condemned to death must:

> Is it right for you [Yahweh] to injure me,
>   cheapening the work of your own hands
>   and abetting the schemes of the wicked?
> Have you got human eyes,
>   do you see as mankind sees?
> Is your life mortal like man's,
>   do your years pass as men's days pass?
>
> Job 10:3–5

When Yahweh, cloaked in darkness and storm cloud, answers Job from the whirlwind, he refuses to acknowledge his responsibility for humanity's excessive suffering, focusing instead on the vast disparity between his cosmic power and human insignificance (Job 38–42).

Although Job does not resolve the issue of divine justice and the problem of evil, a new understanding of the close relationship between humanity—imprinted with the divine image (Gen. 1:26–27, 5:2)—and its creator began to emerge among some later writers of the Bible. The deuterocanonical Wisdom of Solomon, written about 50 B.C.E., adopts the Greek belief that God and humans share the quality of immortality and a heavenly destiny. Although he does not mention Job's challenge that God must learn what it means to endure the human condition, the author of the fourth Gospel paints an unprecedented scenario in which the Deity—or his eternal attribute of creative Wisdom, the Logos (Word)—takes on flesh as Jesus of Nazareth. By becoming a man to suffer evil directly, God—as depicted in John's Gospel—bridges the gap between invincible Deity and vulnerable humanity, learning, as Job had prompted, to see with human eyes and know the agony of mortality (John 1:1, 14). A shocking departure from Judaism's vision of a Deity who never trespasses the boundary between spirit and flesh, John's picture of God incarnate as Jesus opened a breach between the Jewish and Christian faiths that has yet to be closed.

Despite the potential reconciliation between God and humanity portrayed in the Gospels, however, the power of Evil continued to distort and mar human life. By the beginning of the common era, both Jewish and Christian thinkers regarded the Deity as Absolute—immutable in truth, love, wisdom, and mercy; the harsher qualities once attributed to Yahweh were now seen as belonging to his cosmic enemy, the "devil."

25. Who Is the Devil? What Relationship Has This Figure to the Biblical Deity?

Although the **devil** looms large in the popular imagination, the term occurs relatively infrequently in the New Testament and not at all in the Hebrew Bible. From the Greek word *diabolos, devil* means "accuser" or "slanderer." Revelation 12:9–12 identifies the "devil" with the Genesis serpent and the Hebrew "satan," but this correlation took place very late in biblical history, appearing first in pseudepigraphal works like the books of Adam and Eve.

Despite this late identification of the two figures, the "satan" of the Old Testament is not the same entity as the "devil" of the New. The concepts rendered by these two different terms developed independently of each other. The word *satan* derives from a Hebrew root meaning "obstacle"; personified (given human qualities), it means "opposer" or "adversary."

Viewed from a purely historical perspective, the satan figure evolved from the psychic shadow of Yahweh himself. According to many historians, the satan emerges from negative elements in Yahweh's morally ambiguous character and eventually becomes an embodiment of all the violent and destructive attributes once considered part of the divine nature. This historical development is evident if one traces the satan concept chronologically from earliest to latest biblical references. At the outset, some Bible writers saw all things, good and evil alike, as emanating from a single source—Yahweh. Israel's strict monotheistic credo decreed that Yahweh alone caused both joys and sorrows, prosperity and punishment (Deut. 28). In the oldest literary source of Genesis, Yahweh first creates a world of sentient creatures, then "regrets" this creative work, annihilating virtually all living things, both animal and human (Gen. 6:6–8). At this stage in Israel's religious evolution, Yahweh not only is creator and destroyer, but also is represented as tormentor and deceiver. Thus, we read in 1 Samuel 16:14–23 that Yahweh personally sends an "evil spirit" to madden King Saul; in 1 Kings 22:18–28, he dispatches a "lying spirit" to mislead Ahab. Both these incidents show "evil" (defined from a human viewpoint and applied exclusively to disobedient people) as one of the means Yahweh employs to effect his will. As late as the sixth century B.C.E., the anonymous prophet called "Second Isaiah" presents Yahweh as the originator of both Light and Darkness, Good *and* Evil (Isa. 45:7).

Israel's writers reach a second stage of development when they place the source of human trouble not in Yahweh himself but in one of the *bene ha Elohim* (literally, "sons of the gods"). These mysterious beings are depicted as members of Yahweh's heavenly court; among them is the "satan," who plays the role of "accusing" Yahweh's people and testing the loyalty of Yahweh's subjects (Job 1–2; Zech. 3:1–9). Although the satan is by this time a henchman separate from Yahweh himself, he remains completely under the Deity's control and thus functions as a manifestation of the Deity's negative qualities, generating suspicion and demanding punishment for human frailty. In Job, Yahweh allows himself to be "tempted" by **Satan** (now a proper name) and permits the undeserved calamities that befall the faithful Job. By contrast, in Zechariah's vision of the celestial throne room, Yahweh resists the adversary's

contempt for sinful humanity and wills his compassion and mercy to prevail.

It should be noted that, in each of the few Old Testament passages in which the satan is a personage, he is always the adversary of *humanity,* not of God. The satan figure acts as Yahweh's spy and prosecuting attorney whose job is to bring human misconduct to the Deity's attention and, if possible, persuade Yahweh to punish it. Throughout the Old Testament, the satan remains among the divine "sons," serves as God's administrative agent, and thus reveals a facet of the divine personality.

The clearest example of Satan's assumption of the darker aspects of Yahweh's nature occurs in the two accounts of King David's census. In the first version, which dates from the tenth century B.C.E., Yahweh puts it into David's head to sin by taking a census of Israel—always hated by the people because it was done for purposes of taxation and military conscription —for which act God punishes not David but the people with a plague (2 Sam. 24:1–25). In the second version, written hundreds of years later, it is not Yahweh but the "satan" who inspires the census (1 Chron. 21:1–30); Yahweh only punishes. Evidently, with the passage of time and the development of an expanded sense of justice, it was no longer possible to see Yahweh as both the cause and enemy of sin and as the vindictive avenger of sin as well. The negative qualities that earlier writers had assumed to be in their God were eventually transferred to his opposite.

Following the Babylonian exile (after 538 B.C.E.), when Judah was dominated by the Persian Empire, Persian and other foreign religious ideas apparently infiltrated Jewish thinking. **Zoroastrianism**, the official Persian religion, was dualistic, holding that the universe was ruled by two opposing supernatural forces. The powers of Good (Light) were led by Ahura Mazda, while those of Evil were directed by Ahriman, the Zoroastrian devil. According to this belief, at the end of time a climactic battle between Good and Evil would result in Evil's destruction and the triumph of Light. Until then, the two powers struggled incessantly, resulting in alternating elements of happiness and misery in human existence.

With its hierarchies of angels and demons, systems of rewards and punishments in an afterlife, and concept of an all-good god waging war against a wicked opponent (the devil), Zoroastrianism strongly influenced later Hebrew ideas about the satan as not only humanity's but also Yahweh's enemy. Significantly, no Hebrew literature written before the Persian period pictures the satan as an individual. Only in postexilic books like Tobit and Daniel are individual angels, such as Michael, Gabriel, and Raphael, or demons, such as Asmodeus, given personal names. With the influx of Greek and other ideas following Alexander's conquest of the Near East in 330 B.C.E., views of an afterlife populated with angels and demons proliferated. (See the Pseudepigrapha, Part 7.) By New Testament times, Persian, Greek, Syrian, and other foreign notions had been thoroughly Hebraized and subordinated to the religion of Yahweh. After the first century C.E., however, Judaism rejected many of these Persian or Hellenistic concepts. The canonical Hebrew Bible grants the satan scant space and little power.

Whereas the Old Testament satan can do nothing without Yahweh's express permission, in the New Testament he behaves as an independent force who competes with the creator for human souls. According to the temptation scenes in the Synoptic Gospels (Matthew, Mark, and Luke, which adopt a "single view" of Jesus' life), he even attempts to win the allegiance of the Messiah. Interestingly, Jesus does not dispute Satan's claim to control the world or to offer it to whomever he wishes (Mark 1:12–13; Matt. 4:1–11; Luke 4:1–13; 2 Cor. 4:4). According to Mark's Gospel, one of Jesus' major goals is to break up Satan's kingdom and the hold that he and lesser evil spirits exercise on the people. Hence, Mark stresses Jesus' works of exorcising devils and dispossessing the victims of demonic control. The New Testament,

then—in sharp contrast to the Old—shows Satan and the "Devil" as one, a focus of cosmic Evil totally opposed to the Creator God. This "Evil One" is the origin of lies, sin, suffering, sickness, and death. But his power is limited only to the present age; he is doomed to annihilation in Revelation's symbolic "lake of fire" (Rev. 20:1–5).

Religious Divisions and "Satanic" Influences
In the centuries immediately before the birth of Christianity, beliefs about Satan's activities began to assume new forms. Whereas Hebrew Bible writers typically viewed Israel's enemies as external—Gentile nations that posed political or military threats—during the last two centuries B.C.E. some Jewish groups began to perceive an "intimate enemy" among their own people. Sectarian groups, such as the Essenes, saw themselves as the only Jews who were truly faithful to Yahweh's commands. Their Torah-keeping community was composed of "sons of light." By contrast, other Jews—especially those supporting a Temple priesthood that the Essenes regarded as illegitimate—were "sons of darkness." Walking blindly in spiritual night, Jews outside the Essene covenant community were actually under the power of Satan and served as his unsuspecting agents.

In *The Origin of Satan,* Elaine Pagels traces the development within Hellenistic Judaism of a sectarian worldview that branded one's religious opponents as "Satanic." This demonizing of members of one's own religious community who held opposing views was a significant development in Judeo-Christian history. Some New Testament authors adopted the Essenes' ethical dualism, declaring that not only non-believers but also some ostensible Christians were Satan's agents. Writing to the Corinthians, Paul explained that "unbelieving minds are so blinded by the god of this passing age [i.e., Satan]" that they cannot accept the Christian message (2 Cor. 4:4). Outraged that his fellow Jews did not share his conviction that Jesus was God's Word made flesh, the author of John's Gospel denounced all non-Christian Jews as children of the devil, who is the "father of lies" (John 8: 44–47). The New Testament writers' equating of all religious opponents with the Evil One had profoundly divisive consequences in later history, creating a strongly negative attitude toward both Jews and Christians who differed from mainstream church teachings. Reenacting the Essenes's earlier identification of people outside their group as God's enemies, official Christianity viewed both Jews and Christian dissenters as part of Satan's legions, fostering wars and persecutions that continue into this century.

RECOMMENDED READING

Pagels, Elaine. *The Origin of Satan.* New York: Random House, 1995. Pagels traces the "social history of Satan," showing how religious sects—particularly the Essenes—and some New Testament authors associated their opponents with demonic powers of darkness.

Russell, Jeffrey B. "Hebrew Personifications of Evil" and "The Devil in the New Testament." In *The Devil: Perceptions of Evil from Antiquity to Primitive Christianity,* pp. 174–220 and 221–249. Ithaca, N.Y.: Cornell University Press, 1978.

TERMS AND CONCEPTS TO REMEMBER

These and all other terms printed in boldface are defined in the glossary at the end of this book. Check listings in the index for additional information.

Abraham
Academy of Jamnia
Adonai
Akhenaton
Akkadian (Accadian)
Alexander of Macedonia
Antioch
'Apiru
Apocrypha
Aramaic
Baal
Canaan
canon
Catholic Epistles
covenant
cuneiform
Dead Sea
Dead Sea Scrolls
Deuterocanon
Deuteronomistic History (DH)
devil
Diaspora
El, Elohim (pl.)
El Shaddai
Enuma Elish
Ephesus
Essenes
Gilgamesh
Gospel of Thomas
Habiru
Hammurabi
Haran
Hebrew

heresy
Israel
J (Yahwist)
Jehovah
Jethro
Kethuvim
koine
Maat
masoretes
Masoretic Text (MT)
Mesopotamia
monolatry
monotheism
Moses
myth, mythology
Nevi'im
Pentateuch
Pseudepigrapha
pseudonymity
Qumran
Satan
Septuagint (LXX)
Sinai
Sisera
syncretism
Tanak
testament
Tetragrammaton (YHWH)
Torah (Law)
Ugarit
Ur
Vulgate
Yahweh
Zoroastrianism

THE HEBREW BIBLE

(Tanak, or Old Testament)

2

History and Geography of the Near East

Although human beings had inhabited numerous campsites, villages, and other small settlements throughout the Fertile Crescent for thousands of years, it was not until about 3200 B.C.E. that the first real cities were established. Originating in Mesopotamia (southern Iraq), the first urban civilization (Sumer) produced a written literature about the gods, creation of the world, and the afterlife that significantly influenced the biblical worldview. Whereas Sumerian and Babylonian city-states remained relatively small and autonomous, the Egyptians created the first unified national state in the mid-third millennium B.C.E. For most of its history, Israel, located geographically between powerful empires in Egypt and Mesopotamia, was dominated politically by a succession of Egyptian, Assyrian, Babylonian, Persian, and Greek invaders. For an outline of major historical events, see Table 2.1. For a chronology of the Hebrew Bible, see Table 2.2.

The Ancient Near East

A Prolog to Biblical History

For thousands of years before Israel came into existence, the **Fertile Crescent**—a strip of arable land curving from the head of the Persian Gulf northwestward to Syria and then southward through Canaan into Egypt—was studded with tiny villages and other settlements. At Jericho, famous for its walls that tumbled before the blast of Joshua's trumpets, archaeologists have discovered evidence of human habitation dating back to 9000 B.C.E. Lying six miles west of the Jordan River, north of the Dead Sea, Jericho is the world's oldest known walled town. Archaeological excavations have uncovered the ruins of a circular stone tower thirty feet high, as well as plastered, painted skulls with eyes made from seashells. Like other figurines from the Stone Age, these reconstructions of human faces probably had a religious meaning that is now impossible to know.

Repeatedly abandoned and then resettled, perhaps because of invasions or fluctuations in the climate, Jericho's ruins now form a high mound of rubble called a **tell**. Composed of numerous layers of debris, each representing a different period of settlement, tells mark the sites of ancient cities throughout the Near East, including **Ur**, the city of Abraham.

The Ancient Civilizations of Mesopotamia

The world's first great civilizations began to develop along river valleys in Mesopotamia and Egypt shortly before about 3000 B.C.E. Although some historians give Egypt chronological precedence, most scholars regard

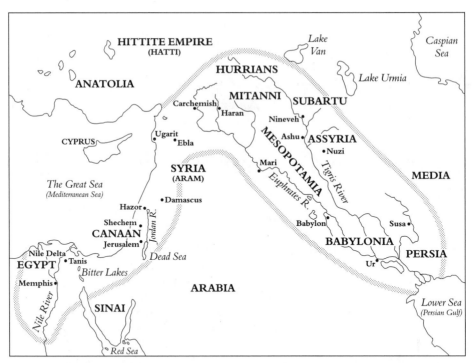

Ancient Middle East and Fertile Crescent

Mesopotamia, the low-lying region between the **Tigris** and **Euphrates** rivers, as the site of the world's oldest cities. Between about 3500 and 3300 B.C.E., the Sumerians occupied the Euphrates delta area at the head of the Persian Gulf, where they built urban centers such as Ur, Eridu, and Uruk (the city of Gilgamesh). Constructing elaborate irrigation systems and erecting monumental temples to their gods, the Sumerians fashioned a complex urban society. Besides devising laws to protect property and foster social order, they also invented the wheel (fourth millennium B.C.E.), thus facilitating travel, trade, and economic prosperity. At an early date, Sumerian merchants exported goods to Egypt, which was simultaneously evolving a highly sophisticated civilization in northeast Africa. To record inventories and other business transactions, Sumerian scribes invented writing as early as 3300 B.C.E. Imprinting wedge-shaped symbols, known as **cuneiform**, on soft clay tablets, the Sumerians produced tens of thousands of inscribed tablets that, when dried or baked, proved almost indestructible. As Samuel Noah Kramer observed, recorded history began at **Sumer**, where the literate upper classes left behind a wealth of information about their gods, kings, and heroes. Some Sumerian traditions provided models for the later Genesis accounts. These include myths that involve creation from a watery chaos and myths about a universal flood. The Sumerian view of the afterlife—that the dead exist only as powerless shadows in a dark, gloomy underworld—anticipates the biblical concept of **Sheol**, the term Bible writers use to denote their equally bleak notion of the netherworld.

Sumer's lasting contribution to subsequent cultures ranges from religion and literature to mathematics and architecture. Devising a numerical system based on sixty, symbol of the sky god Anu, head of their pantheon, the Sumeri-

Table 2.1 Some Major Events in the History of Biblical and Other World Religions

Approximate Date	Event	Biblical Reference
15,000 B.C.E.	Elaborate cave paintings are created at Lascaux, France; rituals of magic and religion evolve.	
10,000 B.C.E.	Pleistocene (Ice Age) glaciers retreat; Stone Age settlements are built in Canaan.	
9000 B.C.E.	The first permanent settlement occurs at Jericho.	
7000–5600 B.C.E.	Catal Huyuk, a town in south-central Turkey, is the apparent center of fertility cult, goddess worship.	
6000 B.C.E.	Neolithic pottery and figurines are crafted at Jericho.	
c. 3500 B.C.E.	The wheel is invented in Mesopotamia; trade, commerce, and the communication of ideas expand.	
I Early Bronze Age (c. 3400–2100 B.C.E.)		
3300 B.C.E.	Sumerian city-states form; cuneiform writing is invented; ancient Mesopotamian traditions about creation and divine-human relationships develop; temples are built to honor gods.	
c. 3000 B.C.E.	The first nation-state forms in Egypt; traditions of creation and divine justice evolve.	
c. 2500 B.C.E.	The Egyptian pyramids are built (First through Third dynasties); a powerful priestly class develops; rituals are encoded to ensure a happy afterlife.	
c. 2500 B.C.E.	Pre-Hindu civilization flourishes in Indus Valley.	
c. 2330 B.C.E.	Sargon I conquers Mesopotamian city-states and creates the first empire; Sargon supports the worship of Sin, Akkadian moon god, for whom Mount Sinai is named.	
II Middle Bronze Age (2100–1550 B.C.E.)		
c. 2000–1450 B.C.E.	Minoan civilization flourishes on Crete; worship of goddess figures develops.	
c. 1850–1700 B.C.E.	Age of Biblical Patriarchs: Nomadic Hebrews roam the Fertile Crescent.	Genesis 12–50
c. 1700 B.C.E.	Hammurabi of Babylon produces law code endorsed by sun god Shamash, protector of justice.	
III Late Bronze Age (1550–1200 B.C.E.)		
1500 B.C.E.	Compilation of Vedic literature begins in India; Stonehenge is built in England.	
c. 1350 B.C.E.	Akhenaton orders the worship of one god, the sun, which briefly establishes the world's first monolatry.	
c. 1250 B.C.E.	Moses leads Israelite slaves from Egypt and establishes the worship of Yahweh at Mount Sinai (formerly sacred to the moon god Sin).	Exodus 13–34
c. 1250–1200 B.C.E.	Mycenaean Greeks besiege Troy in northwestern Turkey, the source event of Homer's *Iliad* and *Odyssey* (written eighth century B.C.E.).	
IV Iron Age Begins (c. 1200 B.C.E.)		
c. 1200 B.C.E.	Israelite tribes settle in Canaan; Yahwism competes with the worship of Baal and Asherah.	Joshua 1–24; Judges 1–21

Table 2.1 (*continued*)

Approximate Date	Event	Biblical Reference
c. 1000 B.C.E.	David becomes king of united Israel.	2 Samuel 2–21
c. 950 B.C.E.	Solomon builds Yahweh's Temple in Jerusalem; A Yahwist writer composes the earliest account of Israel's history (J document).	1 Kings 3–11
922 B.C.E.	Israel splits into rival kingdoms of Judah (south) and Israel (north).	2 Kings 12–13
c. 860–840 B.C.E.	Prophets Elijah and Elisha denounce Canaanite influences and promote Yahwism alone.	1 Kings 17–22; 2 Kings 9
c. 850–750 B.C.E.	Greek poets Homer and Hesiod describe forms, qualities, and functions of Greek gods.	
750 B.C.E.	Prophets Amos and Hosea are active in Israel; a northern Israelite author compiles an account of Israelite history (E document).	Amos 1–9; Hosea 1–14
721 B.C.E.	Assyrian armies destroy northern ten-tribe nation of Israel; the prophet Isaiah is active in Judah.	2 Kings 17–20; Isaiah 36–37; 2 Chronicles 32–34
621 B.C.E.	Book of Deuteronomy is discovered in Solomon's Temple; King Josiah's reforms centralize Yahwism in Jerusalem.	2 Kings 22–23
c. 604 B.C.E.	Traditional birth date of Lao Tzu, founder of Taoism.	
c. 600 B.C.E.	Birth of the prophet Zoroaster, founder of dualistic religion Zoroastrianism, which becomes Persia's state religion; in Judah, the prophet Jeremiah advocates submission to Babylonian dominion.	Jeremiah 1–26
587 B.C.E.	Babylonians under Nebuchadnezzar destroy Jerusalem, ending the royal Davidic dynasty.	2 Kings 24; Psalms 74, 89
587–538 B.C.E.	Babylonian captivity begins the Jewish Diaspora; in Babylon, Jewish priests begin the final process of compiling the Torah and revising the Deuteronomistic History.	
563–483 B.C.E.	In India, Siddhartha Gautama, experiences mystical enlightenment, becoming the Buddha.	
551–479 B.C.E.	In China, Master Kung (Confucius) enunciates a religious philosophy that becomes the basis of the Chinese educational system.	
539 B.C.E. and after	After Cyrus the Great conquers Babylon in 539 B.C.E., the Jewish upper classes return to Jerusalem; the postexilic prophets Haggai and Zechariah urge the rebuilding of the Temple.	Ezra 1–6; Haggai 2
538–330 B.C.E.	Persia rules Judah; the influence of Zoroastrianism promotes a belief in cosmic dualism, angelology.	
515 B.C.E.	A new sanctuary is completed on the site of Solomon's Temple.	
500–400 B.C.E.	The great Hindu epics *Ramayana* and *Mahabharata* are composed.	
445 B.C.E.	Ezra brings an edition of the Torah from Babylon and promulgates reforms in Jerusalem.	Nehemiah 8
336–323 B.C.E.	Alexander of Macedonia conquers most of the known world, bringing Greek culture and ideas to the ancient Near East.	1 Maccabees 1
167–164 B.C.E.	Greek-Syrian king Antiochus IV attempts to eradicate Judaism; the Maccabean revolt begins; the Book of Daniel, adapting Zoroastrian dualism to Yahwism, predicts the final conflict between cosmic Good and Evil.	2 Maccabees 4; Daniel 1–12

Table 2.1 (*continued*)

Approximate Date	Event	Biblical Reference
142–63 B.C.E.	Hasmonean (Maccabean) kings rule Judah.	1 Maccabees
63 B.C.E.	Pompey makes Judea part of the Roman Empire.	
c. 4–30 C.E.	Jesus of Nazareth preaches Torah reforms and is executed by Roman governor Pontius Pilate.	
c. 30 C.E.	The first Christian community is formed in Jerusalem.	
35–62 C.E.	Paul, a Diaspora Jew who converted to Christianity, founds a series of non-Jewish Christian churches in Syria, Asia Minor, and Greece; he teaches that Gentile converts need not keep Torah ordinances, including circumcision and dietary restrictions.	
66–73 C.E.	The Jews revolt against Rome.	
c. 66–70 C.E.	The first narrative of Jesus' life, Gospel of Mark, is written.	
70 C.E.	Roman armies destroy Jerusalem and its Temple.	
80–90 C.E.	Gospels of Matthew and Luke are written.	
90 C.E.	Rabbinical Council at Jamnia leads the reconstruction of Judaism after the Roman destruction of the Jewish state.	
200 C.E.	The Mishnah, first part of the Talmud, is compiled.	
313 C.E.	Roman Emperor Constantine issues the Edict of Milan, making Christianity a legally recognized religion.	
c. 500 C.E.	Compilation of the Talmud is complete.	
570–632 C.E.	The Prophet Mohammed writes the *Qur'an* and founds the religion of Islam.	
632–750 C.E.	Islam spreads rapidly through the Near East, north Africa, and into Spain and France.	

ans invented the practice of dividing the hour into sixty minutes and the circle into 360 degrees. Because their flat, swampy territory lacked the granite and limestone used by Egyptian builders, the Sumerians mass produced clay bricks, typically baked and glazed, with which they constructed large temple complexes. Their most famous architectural form was the **ziggurat**, a massive multitiered, pyramidal structure with several terraced levels, each of which was recessed from the one below it. At the top level stood a chapel or shrine for the divinity it honored. Towering ziggurats erected at Ur and later at Babylon are thought to have inspired the Tower of Babel story in Genesis 11. Historians, however, do not think that the Sumero-Babylonian temples were intended to enable humans to invade the heavens, as Genesis would have it, but to serve as mountain-like pedestals by which the gods could descend to earth. The dream in which Jacob saw supernatural beings ascending and descending a celestial ladder seems to represent the ziggurat's function: It was a staircase connecting the divine and human realms (Gen. 28:10–13).

Invasion of Akkadians: The First Empire

About 2350 B.C.E., Sumer was invaded by a Semitic people known as the **Akkadians**. Assimilating the sophisticated Sumerian culture, including its cuneiform script, which they adapted to transcribe their own language, the Akkadians established the world's first empire.

Table 2.2 A Chronology of Tanak (Hebrew Bible) Writings

Approximate Date	Composition
c. 1200–900 B.C.E.	Oldest biblical poetry, such as the Song of Deborah (Judg. 5), Song of Miriam (Exod. 15:21), verses from the Book of Jashar (Josh. 10:13), and other poems hailing Yahweh as warrior (e.g., Num. 21) are orally composed.
c. 950–850 B.C.E.	First prose narrative of Israel's origins, the Yahwist (J) account, composed in Judah; J's narrative is preserved in parts of the present editions of Genesis, Exodus, and Numbers. Some J passages may also survive in parts of the Deuteronomistic History (DH).
c. 950–587 B.C.E.	Royal archives are compiled at the courts of Israel and Judah, sources for the Deuteronomistic account of the monarchy (Samuel through Kings).
c. 850–750 B.C.E.	The Elohist (E) account of Israel's origins is composed in the northern kingdom of Israel. E passages appear in parts of the Torah and (perhaps) DH.
c. 750 B.C.E.	The prophet Amos delivers his message orally; his disciples commit Amos's oracles to writing at an unknown later date.
c. 746–735? B.C.E.	Hosea delivers his oral message in Israel; disciples later compile his words in written form.
c. 740–701 B.C.E.	Isaiah of Jerusalem delivers his prophetic oracles warning of Assyria's threat to Judah; disciples later preserve Isaiah's words in parts of Isaiah 1–39.
c. 740–700 B.C.E.	Micah delivers prophetic oracles that are later recorded and preserved in the Jerusalem Temple (Jer. 26:16–18).
c. 700–621 B.C.E.	The central part of Deuteronomy (Chs. 12–29) is composed.
c. 630–609 B.C.E.	Prophetic oracles of Zephaniah are compiled.
621 B.C.E.	The prophetess Huldah begins the process of biblical canonization by affirming the authenticity of an early edition of Deuteronomy.
c. 621–609 B.C.E.	The first edition of the Deuteronomistic History (Joshua through 2 Kings), incorporating older poetic and prose documents, is written (perhaps by the scribe Baruch in Jerusalem).
c. 612 B.C.E.	Nahum delivers his oracles on Nineveh's fall.
c. 609–598 B.C.E.	Habukkuk delivers his oracles on the Babylonian threat.
c. 600–587 B.C.E.	Some prophetic oracles of Jeremiah are recorded by his secretary Baruch.

Sargon I of Agade, also rendered Akkad (c. 2334–2279 B.C.E.), rose from obscurity to become the earliest ruler to forge a union of previously independent Mesopotamian city-states. After conquering Ur, he appointed his daughter as high priestess of the moon god, Nanna, an important deity known to the Akkadians as **Sin**. For the next 1800 years, Mesopotamian rulers followed Sargon's practice of appointing their daughters to officiate at the moon god's temple.

Sargon's role as an innovative empire builder who successfully reigned for more than fifty years made him a legendary figure. According to one legend, Sargon, as a baby, had been placed in a reed basket that was sealed with bitumen and cast adrift on the Euphrates River. Rescued and raised as a gardener, the young Sargon was said to have won the affection of **Ishtar**, the Akkadian name of Inanna, Sumerian goddess of love, war, and fertility. This legend expresses a theme common to the stories of several biblical leaders: A male child destined for future greatness narrowly escapes death, grows up in humble circumstances, and as an adult suddenly manifests unparalleled abilities that

Table 2.2 (*continued*)

Approximate Date	Composition
c. 587 B.C.E.	Obadiah denounces Edom's part in Babylon's devastation of Judah and Jerusalem.
c. 580 B.C.E.	Ezekiel's visions in the Babylonian captivity are recorded. Baruch compiles more of Jeremiah's oracles, adding biographical material.
c. 550–500 B.C.E.	Collections of legal and ritual material by priestly writer(s) are inserted into JE narratives and preserved in parts of Exodus, Leviticus, and Numbers.
c. 540s B.C.E.	Second Isaiah delivers oracles of hope in Babylon, which are recorded later in Isaiah 40–55.
c. 520 B.C.E.	Post-exilic prophets Haggai and Zechariah encourage rebuilding of Jerusalem Temple.
c. 500 B.C.E.	Deuteronomistic and priestly reediting of older documents continues in postexilic Jerusalem.
c. 500–450 B.C.E.	Third Isaiah delivers oracles that are later incorporated into Isaiah 56–66.
c. 500–400 B.C.E.	Poetic dialogues in Job are composed and inserted into the framework of an old prose tale.
500–300 B.C.E.	Additional psalms are composed and used in worship at the Second Temple.
c. 490–400 B.C.E.	The prophetic books of Malachi, Joel, and Jonah are compiled. An old folk tale is rewritten, creating the Book of Ruth.
c. 450–400 B.C.E.	Priestly editor(s) complete the revision of legal material in Exodus, Leviticus, Numbers, and Deuteronomy; Ezra returns from Babylon to Jerusalem with a revised edition of the Torah.
c. 400 B.C.E.	The Book of Proverbs is compiled.
c. 400–300 B.C.E.	The process of canonization of the Torah is completed. The Book of Esther is composed. Disciples of a Jerusalem sage compile the Book of Ecclesiastes. The Books of Chronicles and Ezra-Nehemiah are written.
c. 250 B.C.E.	The Torah is translated into Greek, forming the first part of the Septuagint Bible.
c. 200–100 B.C.E.	Collections of the prophets are canonized.
c. 165 B.C.E.	The Book of Daniel is composed.
c. 90–100 C.E.	Jewish scholars at the Academy of Jamnia preside over the compilation of the Writings, completing the final part of the Hebrew Bible.

change the course of history. In both Greek and Hebrew tradition, national heroes or future gods such as Heracles, Perseus, Dionysus, Moses, and Jesus of Nazareth manifest this pattern of the endangered infant who is preserved unexpectedly and later is exalted by his divine patron.

Sargon's most celebrated successor, his grandson Naram-Sin, proclaimed himself "king of the four quarters of the earth," indicating that he may have extended his rule over most of Mesopotamia. Among Naram-Sin's many exploits was his destruction of **Ebla**, a major city in northern Syria. In 1975, archaeologists excavated Ebla's royal archives, uncovering an extensive library written in cuneiform. Dating to the twenty-third century B.C.E., Ebla's collections of hymns, proverbs, myths, and rituals offer a fascinating glimpse into a highly sophisticated northwest Mesopotamian culture that flourished several centuries before Abraham. Shortly after Ebla's discovery, a few scholars made sweeping claims about its supposed connection to the Bible. One proposed that Ebla's

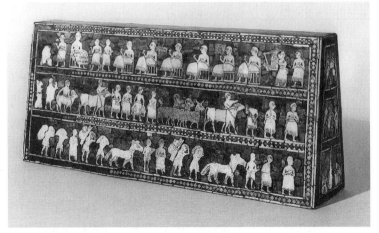

In the 1920s, archaeologists found remarkable works of art in the royal tombs of Ur's Third Dynasty (c. 2060–1950 B.C.E.), including this Standard of Ur, a decorative mosaic of inlaid shell and lapis lazuli. The bottom scene depicts men and animals carrying goods, perhaps from a military victory that the seated figures (top level) are celebrating. Note the musician entertaining the banqueteers (top right). (Courtesy of the Trustees of the British Museum)

The Sumerians built the world's first skyscrapers, towers of sunbaked bricks known as ziggurats. In this artist's reconstruction of the ancient ziggurat at Ur, the chapel to Nanna, god of the moon, crowns the temple structure. These artificial mountains served as pedestals to which heavenly beings could descend to earth, treading the sacred stairways linking the human and divine worlds. Jacob's dream at Bethel (Gen. 28:2–11) envisions a similar "gateway to heaven." (Courtesy of the Trustees of the British Museum)

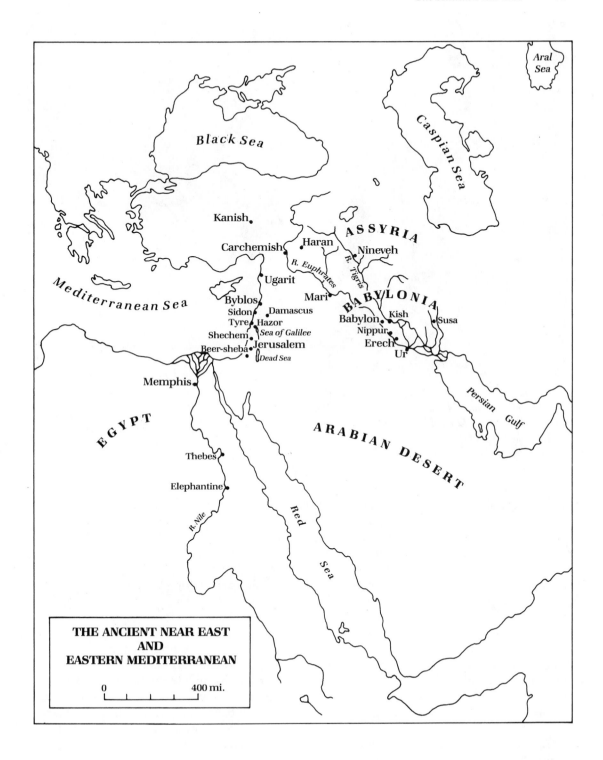

Aral Sea

Black Sea

Caspian Sea

Kanish

Carchemish Haran ASSYRIA
Nineveh

R. Euphrates *R. Tigris*

Ugarit

Mediterranean Sea

Byblos Mari BABYLONIA
Sidon Damascus Kish
Tyre Hazor Babylon Susa
Shechem *Sea of Galilee* Nippur
Beer-sheba Jerusalem Erech
Dead Sea Ur

Memphis Persian Gulf

EGYPT ARABIAN DESERT

Thebes

Elephantine

R. Nile Red Sea

**THE ANCIENT NEAR EAST
AND
EASTERN MEDITERRANEAN**

0   400 mi.

The wealth and elegance of Ur's Third Dynasty are reflected in this splendid gold headdress found in Lady Pu-Abi's tomb, which Sir Leonard Woolley excavated in the 1920s. (Courtesy of the University Museum, University of Pennsylvania [Neg. #S8-139343])

One of the oldest—and most durable—documents of world history, this clay prism records a cuneiform list of Sumerian kings "from the time that kingship was lowered [to human society] from heaven." Probably derived from a Sumerian original composed about 2100 B.C.E., the purpose of this compilation was to demonstrate that the gods selected one city—Uruk, Ur, or another—to rule successively over its Mesopotamian neighbors. These citations of the lengths of each king's reign anticipate the genealogies of Genesis and the Israelite dynastic records of Kings and Chronicles. (Courtesy of the Ashmolean Museum, Oxford)

pantheon included a god named Ya, an abbreviated form of Yahweh, and that a king called **Ebrum** may have been a forefather of Abraham. The majority of scholars have since rejected such assertions as premature and unverifiable, however, and much further study needs to be done before Ebla's relevance to prebiblical times is well understood. One personal name found among the documents—*Ishra-il*—seems too similar to *Israel* to be merely coincidental. Genesis states that Jacob, Abraham's grandson, had his named changed to *Israel* after a mysterious encounter with God at Peniel, but the Ebla reference suggests that the name existed long before it was bestowed on the progenitor of Israel's twelve tribes.

After dominating Mesopotamia for two centuries, Sargon's empire fell to a new invader,

the **Amorites** (or "Westerners"), who swept through many parts of the Fertile Crescent. Merely raiding and looting some areas, the Amorites settled in others, building new towns in northern and western Canaan and founding two important city-states in Mesopotamia—Mari on the middle Euphrates and Babylon on the river's south segment. Located near the modern border of Syria and Iraq, the **Mari** site has yielded more than 20,000 clay tablets approximately 4000 years old. Some of these cuneiform texts seem to contain information

Fashioned of limestone, this Sumerian figurine dates from about 2500 B.C.E. The shaved head and long flounced tunic were typically Sumerian styles of dress. (Courtesy of the University Museum, University of Pennsylvania [Neg. #S5-23215])

In this stele commemorating a victory of Naram-Sin, grandson of the Akkadian empire-builder Sargon I, the king ascends a mountain whose peak reaches into heaven, while his enemies are crushed beneath his feet. During Naram-Sin's thirty-seven-year reign in the twenty-third century B.C.E., the Akkadian Empire reached its height. (Courtesy of Musée du Louvre)

about Bronze Age social customs that would provide valuable background for the Genesis stories about Abraham, Isaac, and Jacob. A similar literary find at Nuzi on the upper Tigris River promised to illuminate legal and marital practices of the mid-second millennium B.C.E., a period shortly after the traditional dates for the patriarchal age. Despite alleged parallels to the domestic arrangements of Abraham and Sarah or Jacob and Laban, however, continued study of the Nuzi tablets inclines many scholars to doubt that the artifacts can provide valid background to the Genesis narratives. Although archaeologists can uncover material remains of vanished civilizations presumably contempora-neous with biblical events, they have not been able to verify the activities or even the historical existence of Israel's ancestors.

The Law Code of Hammurabi

The city of Babylon first achieved prominence when the Amorites founded a dynasty there, but it was not until the reign of **Hammurabi**, sixth king in the Amorite line, that the city

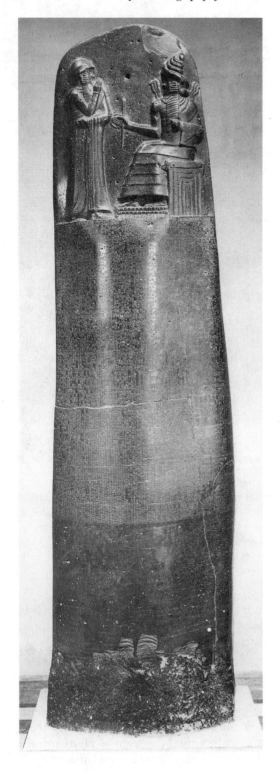

became the center of a new Mesopotamian empire. Uniting all Mesopotamian city-states under his rule, Hammurabi created a broad dominion that rivaled that of Sargon I. Because of the enormous difficulties in establishing a definitive chronology for events in the remote past, historians do not agree on Hammurabi's dates; many scholars place his forty-two-year reign between 1792 and 1750 B.C.E., whereas another widely accepted chronology gives his dates as 1728 to 1686 B.C.E. An effective general and capable administrator, Hammurabi is best remembered for a code of law published later in his reign. Divided into 282 separate units by modern scholars, the **Code of Hammurabi** is inscribed on a solid **stele** of black diorite nearly eight feet tall. Originally erected for public reading in the Babylonian city of Sippar, the block was later carried off by Elamites to Susa, where archaeologists found it more than 3000 years later. At the top of the diorite column, a sculptor carved a bas-relief portrait of Hammurabi receiving the laws from the sun god **Shamash**, exactly as Moses is later represented as receiving the Torah from Yahweh at Mount Sinai.

Hammurabi's laws are expressed in the same literary structure and, in some instances, have the same content as Mosaic decrees. Both the Hammurabic and Mosaic legal formats employ the casuistic form: If such and such happens, then such and such will be the punishment. Part of the Mosaic legislation is also codified in a manner resembling the older Babylonian model, as in the section of Exodus known as the Book

The legacy of Babylon's first important king, the Stele of Hammurabi—a basalt slab nearly eight feet tall—records an ancient Sumero-Babylonian legal code that contains statutes resembling laws found in the Mosaic Torah. Erected in the eighteenth century B.C.E., it reflects legal principles common to ancient Mesopotamia, the original home of the Israelite ancestors. (Courtesy of Musée du Louvre)

In the ancient Near East, law codes—which kings and other leaders imposed on their people—were commonly ascribed to the nation's gods. In this scene at the top of Hammurabi's Stele, Hammurabi (with hands clasped reverently) receives legal commands from the enthroned sun god, Shamash, just as Moses is represented as receiving Torah laws from Yahweh 500 years later. (Courtesy of Musée du Louvre)

of the Covenant (Exod. 20:22–23, 33; 24:7). Babylonian, Egyptian, and Israelite traditions commonly reflect similar concepts of justice, including protection of society's poor and powerless members. Both the Hammurabic and Mosaic laws refer specifically to "widows and orphans" as representing a class of people who need to be shielded from exploitation.

Hammurabi declares that his purpose is to "promote the welfare of the people, . . . to cause justice to prevail in the land, to destroy the wicked and the evil, that the strong might not oppress the weak." As in earlier Mesopota-

mian law codes, however, Hammurabi's system did not offer equal protection to people belonging to different classes. In general, the nobility fared far better than the social classes beneath them: Whereas an aristocrat was allowed to pay a fine for manslaughter, a slave was automatically condemned to death. Merely injuring a person who stood higher in the social hierarchy brought more severe penalties than would murdering a slave.

Both Mesopotamian and Mosaic laws levied the death penalty for numerous offenses, and both allowed physical mutilation of the condemned. Under Hammurabi, if a nobleman injured a social equal he was to suffer an equivalent maiming:

> If a seignior [nobleman] has destroyed the eye of a member of the aristocracy, they shall destroy his eye.
> If he has broken another seignior's bone, they shall break his bone. . . .
> If a seignior has knocked out the tooth of a seignior of his own rank, they shall knock out his own tooth.
> Code of Hammurabi, Sections 196, 197, 200

Using the same examples found in Hammurabi's code, the Mosaic Torah perpetuated the ancient Near Eastern demand for exact retaliation:

> If a man injures his neighbor, what he has done must be done to him: broken limb for broken limb, eye for eye, tooth for tooth. As the injury inflicted, so must the injury be suffered.
> Leviticus 24:19–20

Judges and executioners are to "show no pity" (Deut. 19:21) in enforcing the biblical **lex talionis**, the law of retaliation. This principle of inflicting precisely the same kind of injury that had been inflicted on a victim was central to the Israelite sense of justice. Bible writers considered the *lex talionis* so important that they proclaimed it in three of the five books of Torah (Exod. 21:23–25; Lev. 24:19–21; Deut. 19:21).

The Mosaic and Hammurabic codes also agree in permitting upper-class offenders to compensate social inferiors without suffering wounds corresponding to those they had caused. According to Babylonian law, a nobleman who blinds or knocks out the tooth of a commoner must pay a fine; if he seriously harms another nobleman's slave, he must pay one-half the slave's value (Hammurabi, Sections 199, 201, etc.). The Torah also permits someone to avoid the punishment accorded those who harm a social equal:

> When a man strikes the eye of his slave, male or female, and destroys the use of it, he must give him his freedom to compensate for the eye. If he knocks out the tooth of his slave, male or female, he must give him freedom to compensate for the tooth.
>
> (Exod. 21:26–27)

As the *lex talionis* permitted vengeance to go no further than inflicting injuries exactly equivalent to those one had received, so the biblical law restricted masters' physical abuses of their slaves. Beatings that resulted in specified injuries could cost an owner his human property.

Egypt: The First National State

The name **Egypt** derives from *Aiguptos,* the Greek version of *Hut-Ptah,* the "Temple of Ptah," the term by which the Egyptians identified their country. The "temple," or holy dwelling place of Ptah, the Egyptian creator god, was the strip of fertile land bordering the Nile River. Beyond this narrow cultivated zone, watered by annual inundations of the Nile, stretched vast, inhospitable deserts that effectively isolated Egypt from its neighbors. Whereas the broad plains of Mesopotamia were easily—and frequently—invaded by foreign armies, Egypt's unique geographical features allowed it to develop independently of most foreign influences. Surrounded by arid wastes on the east and west and on the south by a rugged terrain through which the Nile flowed in impassable cataracts, ancient Egypt enjoyed an uninterrupted period of stability and nation building.

From Kingdom to Empire   Beginning as a coalition of small political districts called nomes, Egypt first evolved into two distinct kingdoms, known as Upper Egypt and Lower Egypt. About 3100 B.C.E., the two kingdoms were merged under the rule of Narmer, king of Upper (southern) Egypt. From this point on, Egyptian pharaohs wore a headdress combining the white crown of Upper Egypt with the red crown of Lower Egypt.

Historians divide subsequent Egyptian history into three major periods: the Old Kingdom or Pyramid Age (Third to Sixth Pharaonic Dynasties, about 2686–2160 B.C.E.); the Middle Kingdom, or Feudal Age (the Eleventh and Twelfth Dynasties, about 2030–1720 B.C.E.); and the New Kingdom, or Empire (the Eighteenth to Twentieth Dynasties, about 1570–1075 B.C.E.). Under the Empire, New Kingdom pharaohs such as Thutmose I extended Egypt's dominion northeastward into Canaan. About 1490 B.C.E., Egyptian forces defeated a coalition of more than one hundred rulers of Syrian and Canaanite city-states at the Battle of **Megiddo**, a site that in later history marked several decisive Israelite defeats. (Apparently regarded as of crucial significance in biblical history, sixteen centuries later Megiddo lent its name—*Har-Megiddo* [Armageddon]—to identify the place where cosmic Good and Evil would fight their ultimate battle [Rev. 16:16].) Until near the end of the New Kingdom, Egypt maintained a line of military fortresses in Canaan, guarding against unwanted incursions from Mesopotamia or Asia Minor.

Egypt's Enduring Legacy   The Egyptian system of writing in pictorial characters—hieroglyphs—developed about the same time, or shortly after, the invention of cuneiform script in Mesopotamia. The Egyptians also made spectacular advances in mathematics and astronomy, devising a calendar based on the solar year of 365 days. This calendar featured twelve months of thirty days each, to which five festival days were added to round out the year.

The familiar practice of dividing the day into twenty-four hours and beginning a new day at midnight is also a legacy from ancient Egypt.

Egypt's numerous gifts to the modern world include the science of geometry. Devising methods to compute the areas and volumes of abstract geometric forms, Egyptian architects applied these skills to build the world's first large-scale structures in stone. An edifice of massive grandeur, the multitiered Step Pyramid was constructed for King Zoser (Djoser) about 2650 B.C.E. Erected shortly afterward, the enormous pyramids at Giza still tower hundreds of feet above the Nile valley, the sole survivors of the ancient world's Seven Wonders.

Egypt's great pyramids and colossal sphinx at al-Jizah were already many centuries old when Abraham's grandson Jacob and his eleven sons, driven by famine in Canaan, sought refuge in the Nile's prosperous land. Because the Nile supplied Egypt's extensive irrigation system even in many drought years when crops in neighboring areas failed, Ptah's land attracted many nomadic peoples hoping to secure Egyptian grain. According to Genesis, Israel's ancestors—the tribes of Jacob (Israel)—were among many who settled temporarily in the delta region.

One popular theory states that Semitic nomads were welcome in Egypt at the time Israelite tribes entered because Egypt was then ruled by foreigners known as the **Hyksos**. Although native Egyptian control of the country was rarely surrendered, in the seventeenth century B.C.E. the Semitic Hyksos infiltrated the population, eventually usurping pharaoh's throne. In 1560 B.C.E., an Egyptian revolt expelled the Hyksos rulers and established the Eighteenth Dynasty. This native royal line included some of Egypt's most famous rulers, including Queen Hatshepsut, the great military strategist Thutmose III, and Amenhotep IV.

Amenhotep IV, who changed his name to **Akhenaton**, scandalized the Egyptian priesthood by ordering that only a single deity, the sun god **Aton**, be universally acknowledged.

Whereas some historians believe that Akhenaton established the world's first monotheism, many think that his cult of Aton was really an example of **henotheism**—worship of a single god while conceding the existence of other deities. Although Akhenaton's religious experiment was brief—his youthful successor Tutankhamen revoked his reforms—it may have set a precedent that influenced Moses' concept of Yahweh's "jealousy." The revolutionary belief that a single god could require his devotees to honor no other gods is the cornerstone of the Mosaic religion.

Correspondence preserved in the ruined archives of Tell el-Amarna, the site to which Akhenaton moved his capital, gives a vivid picture of Egypt during the dominion of Aton. The **Amarna Age**, the period of Akhenaton's reign, and the exclusive cult of the sun were largely forgotten by 1306 B.C.E., when Rameses I founded a new royal dynasty, the nineteenth. Under Rameses II (1290–1224 B.C.E.), the Egyptian Empire reached its zenith in prosperity and prestige. Many historians believe that **Rameses II**, a vigorous—and vainglorious—leader was the pharaoh of the Exodus. Rameses made a habit of recording his military defeats, as well as his genuine victories, as complete triumphs. If a band of Hebrew slaves did escape from Egypt during his long reign, it is not surprising if court scribes did not think fit to mention it.

The earliest known reference to Israel as a distinct people appears on a victory inscription of **Merneptah**, Ramses II's son and successor. Merneptah boasts of his conquests in Canaan, claiming to have laid Israel waste, indicating that the Israelites were already established in Canaan shortly after 1220 B.C.E., the approximate time of Merneptah's campaign.

One of the most important finds of modern archaeology is the justly famous **Rosetta Stone**, a large flat slab of basalt inscribed with the same message in three different scripts—Greek, hieroglyphic, and demotic. In the 1820s, a French scholar, Jean-François Champollion,

This granite statue of Rameses II (1290–1224 B.C.E.) only suggests the Egyptian ruler's enormous power. Appearing deceptively mild, Rameses wears the distinctive royal headdress and holds the scepter symbolizing his absolute control of the state. Many historians believe that Rameses II was the unnamed pharoah of the Exodus. (Courtesy of Alinari/Art Resource)

The Stele of Merneptah (c. 1224–1211 B.C.E.), son and successor of Rameses II, contains the first extrabiblical reference to Israel's existence. Advertising his victories over various Canaanite states, Merneptah claims that he has so devastated Israel that its "seed [offspring] is not," a conventional military boast. A double figure of the god Amon appears at the top center, with Pharoah Merneptah (also in double representation) standing on either side of the deity. (Courtesy of Egyptian Museum/PhotoEdit)

deciphered the inscriptions and thereby discovered the key to reading Egyptian hieroglyphics. Champollion's breakthrough allowed scholars for the first time to understand previously inaccessible works of Egyptian literature. Scholars have since translated many Egyptian documents related to the biblical text, finding several parallels to the Book of Proverbs, Job, and other examples of wisdom writing. (See Part 6.) Some

Egyptian traditions appear to have served as models for Bible writers, such as the "Story of Two Brothers," a narrative in which an innocent young man working in his brother's household rejects his sister-in-law's sexual advances, only to have her falsely accuse him of attempted seduction. As in the Genesis story of Joseph and Potiphar's wife (Gen. 39:6–20), the Egyptian youth suffers undeserved disgrace before being elevated to a high position at Pharaoh's court.

Perhaps Egypt's most lasting contribution to biblical religion was the ritual practice of **circumcision**. The surgical removal of the foreskin (prepuce) from the penis, circumcision was a physically distinguishing mark on all Israelite males. According to the Greek historian Herodotus, this originally Egyptian practice spread to a few other nations, whereas the majority of men "leave their private parts as nature made them" (*The Histories,* Book 2, 37; cf. Josh. 5:2–6 and Jer. 9:25–26). In ancient Israel (and in modern Judaism), all male infants, when eight days old, routinely had the foreskin amputated (Gen. 17:12; Lev. 12:3; Luke 1:59; Phil. 3:5). This ancient Egyptian rite, in fact, is interpreted as the indelible "sign" of God's covenant with Abraham and all his descendants: "My Covenant shall be marked on your bodies as a Covenant in perpetuity" (Gen. 17:9–14). In New Testament times, the issue of circumcising non-Jewish converts to Christianity initiated the first great division in the early Church (cf. Acts 15 and Gal. 1–5).

Some Canaanite Contributions to Biblical Religion

In the stretch of the Fertile Crescent between Mesopotamia and Egypt—Syria, Phoenicia, and Canaan—other important urban centers also flourished, some of which were under sporadic Egyptian control. Various groups known as Canaanites, whose fertility religions proved so attractive to many Israelites, had settled not only in Canaan but also along Syria's southwestern coast, known in biblical times as Phoenicia and Lebanon. The seagoing Phoenicians, whose phonetic alphabet passed via the Greeks into modern languages of the West, built the trade-rich ports of Tyre, Sidon, and Byblos, with which Israel's kings made profitable commercial arrangements. To the north stood **Ugarit**, a Canaanite stronghold that seems to have had ties to the Mycenaean world (a proto-Greek civilization) farther west. The ruins of Ugarit, also known by its modern Arabic name **Ras Shamra**, preserved a cuneiform library of texts in a hitherto unknown Semitic language that, when deciphered, showed affinities with biblical Hebrew. The Ugaritic texts, dating from about 1600–1400 B.C.E., are a major source of information about the Canaanite religion, which Israel's later prophets denounced as the insidious rival of Yahwism. Containing myths of conflicts between gods and natural forces, such as the primordial sea and death-dealing drought, Ugaritic literature reveals that the chief god, **El**—the general Semitic term for deity—was thought of in much the same way as the earliest Israelite concepts of Yahweh. Called "Father of Years," "Eternal," "Compassionate," and "Father of Humankind," El is also referred to in epithets suggesting that he is the world creator and source of the Deep (the watery abyss of Gen. 1:1).

Although Israelite religion staunchly resisted any compromise with El's son **Baal**—the Canaanite god of storm, rain, and fecundity—many scholars believe that qualities and attributes of El were assimilated into the biblical portrait of Yahweh. According to the priestly account in Exodus 6, before Yahweh revealed his name to Moses he had been known to Abraham and the other patriarchs as **El Shaddai** (El associated with the cosmic mountain where divine beings held council). In Genesis, the patriarchal deity typically appears as El in the Canaanite environment. Abraham's concubine Hagar encounters *El Roi* (Heb., "God of Seeing") (Gen. 16:7–14); Abraham worships *El Olam* (Heb., "God Eternal") at Beersheba (Gen. 21:33); and at the Canaanite sanctuary of Salem he identifies *El Elyon* ("God Most High") with his personal god Yahweh (Gen. 14:18–20). *El Berith* ("God of the Covenant") is associated with **Shechem**, site of Israel's first covenant-renewal ceremony with Yahweh (cf. Josh. 24 and Judg. 9:46). According to many historians, when Israel settled in Canaan, it adopted some aspects of the older Canaanite veneration of El, whom it identified as a local manifestation of Yahweh.

Imperial Threats to Israel's Survival

Israel's settlement in Canaan coincided with a period during which the great Near Eastern empires were relatively weak. The struggle to wrest possession of the Promised Land described in Joshua, Judges, and 1 Samuel pitted the Israelites against only local tribes and small city-states. The **Philistines**, a maritime people who gave Palestine (Canaan) its name, arrived after the Israelite occupation had begun but proved the most serious military threat to Israel's survival. It was not until the reign of David (c. 1000 B.C.E.), the first effective Israelite king, that the Philistines were finally subdued and their territory incorporated into an Israelite state.

The Israelite empire that David and Solomon built, extending from the borders of Egypt northward to the Euphrates River, was militarily successful only in the near-absence of competition from more powerful neighbors. As soon as the long-quiescent Mesopotamian states revived, however, Israel—by then divided into the two smaller kingdoms of Israel and Judah—suffered repeated defeats and lost much of its former territory. In the ninth century B.C.E., the **Assyrians**, a people named for **Assur**, their god of war, began a series of conquests that created the most hated and feared of all Mesopotamian empires. Superbly organized and ruthlessly aggressive, Assyrian armies terrorized the Near East with their iron war chariots and seemingly invincible cavalry. Walled cities that refused to surrender were mercilessly sacked and burned, and the populations were enslaved and deported to distant parts of the empire. Prisoners were routinely tortured, flayed alive, and hideously mutilated—an effective means of discouraging resistance.

By the eighth century B.C.E, both Israel and Judah were practically vassals of the Assyrian emperor, who extorted vast sums of tribute, impoverishing both states. When Israel revolted against Assyrian oppression, **Sargon II** laid siege to the Israelite capital, Samaria, destroying it in 722–721 B.C.E. and deporting the upper classes. According to 2 Kings, the Assyrians settled foreigners in Israel's former territory who mixed with the remaining Israelites and adopted the Yahwist religion. Their descendants came to be known as **Samaritans** and were harshly condemned as perverters of the Mosaic faith by their compatriots in Judah.

Another Assyrian emperor, **Sennacherib**, invaded Judah and destroyed most of the area's fortified cities, although he failed to capture **Jerusalem**. This apparently miraculous deliverance of Judah's holy city appeared to confirm that Davidic kings who ruled there would be protected by Yahweh's presence. Jerusalem escaped the fate of Samaria, but its rulers had to pay crushingly heavy tribute to keep the Assyrians at bay (2 Kings 18:13–16).

As the seventh century B.C.E. drew to a close, Assyria's collapse brought both rapid change and a new set of masters for Judah. When **Nineveh**, the Assyrian capital, fell in 612 B.C.E. to a coalition of Medes and Babylonians, a general sense of relief must have swept through the Near East. The little Book of Nahum reflects Judah's rejoicing at the prospect of a world freed from Assyrian violence. Judah's respite from foreign domination was short-lived, however, because in 609 B.C.E. the Egyptian pharaoh Necho killed the popular Judean king **Josiah** at Megiddo, ending Josiah's important religious reforms. After defeating Egypt at the epochal Battle of **Carchemish** in 605 B.C.E., **Babylon** emerged as the Near East's supreme power.

The Fall of Jerusalem

Reduced to vassalage under the Neo-Babylonian Empire, Judah revolted in 597 B.C.E., resulting in the sacking of Jerusalem by King **Nebuchadnezzar** and the deportation of its ruling classes to Babylon. Among the exiles was the priest-prophet Ezekiel. More than a century earlier, the prophet Isaiah had assured King Hezekiah that Yahweh would not permit the Assyrians to desecrate the city where he had placed his name (2 Kings 19:32–34). By contrast, during Judah's Babylonian crisis the prophet **Jeremiah** preached a strikingly different message: Neither Yahweh's presence in the Temple nor his promise to maintain the Davidic dynasty would save Judah. Jeremiah urged Zedekiah, the last Davidic king to reign, to submit to Babylon as Yahweh's rod of correction. When Zedekiah's advisors, hoping for aid from Egypt, persuaded the king to revolt in 587 B.C.E., Nebuchadnezzar promptly marched on Jerusalem, leveling it along with Solomon's Temple. A large part of the population was removed to Babylon, leaving only the poor behind.

Scholars believe that much of the Bible, including the Torah and historical books (Joshua through 2 Kings) was rewritten and reedited during the **Babylonian exile** (587–538 B.C.E.). (See the overview to the structure of the Hebrew Bible on page 56.) Without a Davidic ruler, without a sanctuary, and even without a land, the Jewish exiles pondered deeply on the national disaster that had robbed them of all the divine promises made to Abraham and David.

The long historical account of Yahweh's covenant people, beginning in Genesis and extending through 2 Kings, ends abruptly with the Babylonian captivity. At that low point in their history, it may have seemed as if God had entirely abandoned Abraham's descendants. Israel's story, however, was far from over: After almost half a century had passed in exile, a new prophet, whom scholars call Second Isaiah, proclaimed to his fellow Judeans that Yahweh had forgiven them and would soon return them to the Promised Land in a new exodus (Isa. 40–55). In 539 B.C.E., **Cyrus the Great** of **Persia**

captured Babylon and a year later, as part of a general policy to enlist the loyalty of Babylon's former subjects, permitted the exiles to return to the ruins of Jerusalem and restore the worship of their God.

The drama of Judah's unexpected restoration is recorded in the third division of the Hebrew Bible, the Writings. (See Part 6.) The books of Ezra and Nehemiah depict the postexilic community undergoing a difficult and painful readjustment as it strives to keep its unique religious identity intact under Persian rule. Later writings, such as the books of Maccabees and Daniel, show the Jewish people responding to an even greater threat—a foreign king's attempt to eradicate their religion. (See Part 7.) The tests and challenges facing God's people as they are successively dominated by Babylonian, Persian, Greek, Syrian, and Roman empires are discussed in parts 6, 7, and 8.

RECOMMENDED READING

Cottrell, Arthur, ed. *The Penguin Encyclopedia of Ancient Civilizations.* New York and London: Penguin Books, 1980.

Gordon, Cyrus. *The Ancient Near East,* 3rd ed. New York: Norton, 1965.

Harris, Roberta L. *The World of the Bible.* London: Thames and Hudson, 1995. An illustrated survey of biblical history and archaeology.

Hobson, Christine. *The World of the Pharaohs: A Complete Guide to Ancient Egypt.* New York: Thames and Hudson, 1987.

Ions, Veronica. *Egyptian Mythology.* New York: Peter Bedrick Books, 1982.

Jacobson, Thorkild. *The Treasures of Darkness: A History of Mesopotamian Religion.* New Haven, Conn.: Yale University Press, 1976.

Kramer, Samuel N. *History Begins at Sumer.* New York: Doubleday/Anchor Books, 1959.

———. *The Sumerians.* Chicago: University of Chicago Press, 1963.

———. *Cradle of Civilization.* New York: Time-Life Books, 1967.

The Structure of the Hebrew Bible (Tanak): An Overview

The structure of the three-part Hebrew Bible (Tanak) reflects an important aspect of its meaning. Each major section of the Tanak, as arranged by the editors responsible for its final contents, opens and/or closes with a statement about God's repeated promises to give Israel a national homeland. After a brief survey of human origins, Genesis begins Israel's story with Yahweh's sudden appearance to Abraham, unconditionally promising that Abraham's descendants will possess the land of Canaan "forever." Deuteronomy, the fifth book of the Torah, ends with Abraham's multitudinous descendants poised to enter Canaan. Their leader, Moses, is permitted to glimpse the Promised Land from afar but is not allowed to share his people's inheritance. That Moses dies before he personally can experience the culmination of Israel's national hopes introduces a theme of divine promise and deferred fulfillment that helps to shape the Bible's structure as a whole.

The second part of the Hebrew Bible—the Prophets (Nevi'im)—opens with a long prose narrative—the Books of Joshua through 2 Kings—recounting more than six hundred years of Israel's history (c. 1200–562 B.C.E.). In the Book of Joshua, Moses' successor Joshua conducts a lightning-fast military conquest of Canaan, which gives Abraham's progeny (almost) full possession of that territory. The books of Samuel and 1 Kings describe the successful rise of Israel as a nation, culminating in the establishment of a powerful Israelite monarchy under King David. Although Yahweh voluntarily promises to make David's heirs rule over Israel "forever," 2 Kings reports that the Davidic monarchy comes to a disastrous end when Babylon destroys Jerusalem and its Temple in 587 B.C.E.

Whereas the first books of the Prophets (Deuteronomistic History) tell how Israel acquired Canaan and then lost it, the second part of this division of the Hebrew Bible is a collection of books named for individual prophets, most of whom were active during the period of the Davidic-monarchy. Observing Tanak order, this section begins with the Book of Isaiah, a prophet who advised Davidic kings when invading Assyrian armies seized most of Israel's northern territory. It closes with the short Book of Malachi, named for the messenger who warned that Yahweh threatens to afflict "the land" with yet another curse.

The third great division of the Hebrew Bible, the Writings (Kethuvim), opens with the Book of Psalms, devotional poetry sung during services at the Jerusalem Temple, the religious and geographical center of the Jewish state. The important end position of the Hebrew Bible—literally the final word of Israel's Scriptures—is given to the Book of 2 Chronicles. A late retelling of the history of Israel's monarchy—and its fall to Babylon—2 Chronicles ends on a note of hope. It concludes with a decree of Cyrus, Emperor of Persia, who defeated Babylon in 539 B.C.E. and allowed exiled Jews to return to their homeland. The historical event that concludes the Hebrew Bible is Cyrus's order to rebuild Jerusalem's Temple.

Although the Books of Chronicles are followed chronologically by the Books of Ezra and Nehemiah, which describe conditions under Persian rule in the restored Jerusalem community, the final editors of the Hebrew Bible chose to place Cyrus's edict—with its attendant call for faithful Jews to return to the Promised Land—as the climactic summation of Israel's historical experience. Cyrus's recreation of Israel—the climax of a narrative that began with Elohim's creation of the universe in Genesis 1—is not accomplished by military aggression, as was Joshua's original conquest of Canaan. Instead, Cyrus, who had pursued a policy of encouraging local religions throughout his vast empire and whom Second Isaiah boldly calls Yahweh's "Messiah" (Isa. 45:1–3), uses his imperial might to reassemble Israel peacefully. Human rulers, acting as Yahweh's instruments, become guarantors of Israel's future possession of its homeland.

Matthews, Victor H. and Benjamin, Don C. *Old Testament Parallels: Documents from the Ancient Near East.* Mahwah, N.J.: Paulist Press, 1991.

Pritchard, James B., ed. *Ancient Near Eastern Texts Relating to the Old Testament,* 3rd ed., supp. Princeton, N.J.: Princeton University Press, 1969.

———. *The Harper Atlas of the Bible.* New York: Harper & Row, 1987.

Roaf, Michael. *Cultural Atlas of Mesopotamia and the Ancient Near East.* New York and Oxford, Eng.: Facts on File, 1990.

Sandars, N. K. *Poems of Heaven and Hell from Ancient Mesopotamia.* New York and London: Penguin Books, 1971.

Wilson, John A. *The Culture of Ancient Egypt.* Chicago: University of Chicago Press, 1963.

The Promised Land

The land of Canaan (Palestine) probably has more religious associations for more people than any other part of the earth's surface, for it is the Holy Land to Catholic, Eastern Orthodox, Protestant, Jew, and Muslim alike. During the past 4000 years, more wars have been fought for its possession than for almost any other geographical area. From Egyptian, Amorite, and Israelite in the ancient world to Turk, Arab, Palestinian, and Israeli in modern times, millions have died attempting to gain or hold this small territory, which is roughly the size of Maryland. The generalized map of Palestine on page 58 shows the location of some major sites mentioned in the Hebrew Bible.

Much of the area's importance arises from its location. A relatively narrow strip (roughly 150 miles long and 70 miles wide) between the eastern end of the Mediterranean Sea and the inland deserts, Canaan was a land bridge between the three great civilized centers of the ancient world. Egypt lay to the southwest, Asia Minor to the northwest, and Mesopotamia to the northeast. Except for brief periods when these areas were militarily weak, armies repeatedly marched through the Palestinian corridor, generally devastating the regions they occupied. During peaceful times, however, Canaan flourished, as traders and caravans bearing grain, spices, gold, hides, and textiles traveled along the three main trade routes that crossed the country. Control of these international commercial highways provided considerable wealth for which many nations contended.

One thinks of modern Palestine as dry and rather barren, but in biblical times it was at least partly forested and relatively well watered. Then as now, however, the climate varied considerably in the country's four major regions. The western region is a low coastal plain, twenty to thirty miles wide at most. This narrow strip, which provided the chief highway to Egypt, was under Egyptian rule when the Israelites first invaded Canaan following 1250 B.C.E., although the Philistines occupied it during most of Israel's history. (Ironically, the whole country came to be known as **Palestine**, a name derived from Philistia, the hated scourge of the Israelites.)

Inland, running roughly north–south, is the second major region, a limestone ridge of low mountains and small valleys. This central hill country, much less fertile than the coastal plain, extends from the Valley of **Beersheba** in the south to the mountains of Lebanon in the north. The hilly range is broken in the north by the broad Plain of Megiddo, formed by the Kishon River, which flows northwestward to the Mediterranean Sea just north of Mount Carmel, a precipitous rocky massif that juts into the sea and forms the northern boundary of the coastal plain.

Megiddo's level fields join the Valley of **Jezreel** to the east, near Mount Gilboa, forming an east–west–trending greenbelt, the most fertile part of the country. The site of several bloody and decisive battles in Israel's history, the Megiddo area is cited in Revelation 16:16 as the location of **Armageddon**, the final cosmic war between God and the Devil. Not far to the north, where the limestone hills rise steeply to merge with the Lebanon Range, was the small

58

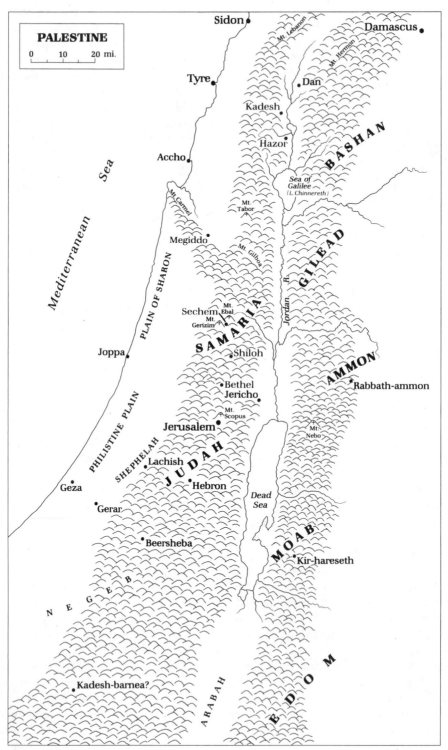

This map of Canaan, the land promised to Abraham's descendants, shows the areas occupied by Judah and Samaria after the fall of the northern kingdom of Israel in the late eighth century B.C.E.

Photographed from a U.S. spacecraft, this view of the southeastern corner of the Mediterranean shows southern Palestine (top left) and the Sinai desert (center). The Gulf of Suez lies below the Sinai peninsula and the Gulf of Aqabah above it. The long troughlike depression extending northward from Aqabah holds the Dead Sea, Jordan Valley, and the Sea of Galilee. (Courtesy of NASA)

village of Nazareth, where Jesus grew to manhood. A poor, rather bleak area, it afforded few attractions other than its southward view of Megiddo's gentle plains.

Between Palestine's mountainous backbone and the Transjordan hills to the east is the Great Rift Valley, which runs from north to south the full length of the country. This geological fault zone provides the channel for the **Jordan River**, which rises in the **Sea of Galilee** and flows sixty-five miles south to the **Dead Sea**, a great salt lake 1290 feet below sea level, the lowest point in the earth's land surface. Paralleling the Jordan on both sides is a lush band of vegetation; around the Dead Sea, however, nothing grows, making it a striking image of utter desolation. According to local folktales, the sea now covers the remains of Sodom and Gomor-

rah, which had lain near its shores before the area was decimated by a natural catastrophe.

Located east of the Jordan River, the fourth general region, **Transjordan**, is a rugged mountainous terrain cut by deep canyons that flood during heavy rains. Extending from the plains of southern Syria east of Galilee to the Brook Zered at the southern end of the Dead Sea, Transjordan averages about 1500 feet above sea level, although many of its peaks rise to twice that height. Legend has it that Jesus' family fled to Transjordan when the Romans temporarily lifted their siege of Jerusalem, and it is probable that some Palestinian Christians found refuge in this sparsely populated area during the Roman wars (66–70 C.E.).

But Palestine's division into four distinct regions is more meaningful than ordinary geographical sectioning might suggest. In terms of Israel's history, radically different areas meant that their inhabitants were relatively self-contained and somewhat culturally isolated from fellow citizens who inhabited topographically dissimilar areas. Farmers cultivated the fertile plains, small valleys, and terraced hillsides, growing wheat, barley, olives, and grapes. On nearby stony ridges, shepherds pastured sheep or goats that subsisted on occasional tufts of grass. By contrast, Israel's chief cities, located in the central hill country, were trade centers open to considerable cultural exchange with itinerant traders from Egypt, Mesopotamia, Syria, Phoenicia, and other affluent urban civilizations.

Palestine's regional and economic diversity sometimes led to suspicion and distrust among the three main occupational groups—farmers, shepherds, and commercial city dwellers. Shepherds, living a seminomadic outdoor life, regarded the cities as sources of financial exploitation and corruption, and eighth-century B.C.E. prophets, such as Amos and Hosea, typically sided with the country people in this regard. City people in turn regarded farmers and villagers as backward and given to compromising their faith by the worship of agricultural and fertility deities. To a degree then, Israel's class and religious conflicts emanated from the economic and cultural divergences caused by Palestine's unusually diverse geography.

Even more decisive than its diverse internal geography was Palestine's position between the great powers of the ancient world. Except for a few decades during the reigns of David and Solomon, this strategic land bridge joining Asia to Africa was continually trampled on by other nations. Israel's successive military domination by Assyria, Babylon, Medo-Persia, Macedonian Greece, and Rome gave its thinkers a distinctive philosophy of history and of their God's will. The Bible writers saw in their nation's relentless sufferings not an accident of geography but the inevitable consequences of their national sins, a belief that will be discussed further in the summaries of Deuteronomy and the Deuteronomistic History (Part 4).

The Bible's North-South Polarities

Many important events in biblical history reflect a sharp division between the northern and southern parts of Israel. Just as the United States was divided between the North and South during the American Civil War (1861–1865), so Israel was split into two rival states for much of its history. United briefly under their first three kings, Saul, David, and Solomon, the twelve tribes of Israel divided into two hostile camps following Solomon's death in 922 B.C.E. The ten northern tribes, which controlled most of the nation's territory, formed the kingdom of Israel, while the tribes of Judah and Benjamin formed the much smaller kingdom of Judah.

The tension between north and south—with each of the two kingdoms claiming to represent Yahweh's covenant people—strongly influenced their respective religious traditions. Whereas Israel's kings established Yahwist shrines at Bethel and Dan, Judah's leaders insisted that Yahweh accepted worship only at the Jerusalem sanctuary. In the Books of Kings, Judean writers consistently condemn all of Israel's rulers for their failure to recognize the Jerusalem Temple's supremacy. After Assyria destroyed the northern capital of Samaria and deported much of Israel's population (721 B.C.E.), refugees from the northern kingdom fled south to Judah, bringing with them traditions of their nation's past, some of which Judean editors later revised and incorporated into the biblical text. (See Part 3.)

Even after Jerusalem's destruction by Babylon and eventual restoration in 538 B.C.E., Judah's hostility toward Jews occupying Israel's former territories persisted. By New Testament times, inhabitants of this area were called Samaritans and regarded as violators of true Judaism. In the Gospel of Mark, which scholars believe was the first Gospel written, Jesus' life is arranged according to a geographical north-south division that is reminiscent of Israel's ancient polarities. In Mark (as well as Matthew and Luke), most of Jesus' ministry takes place in the northern region of Galilee, where he performs miracles, draws large crowds, and successfully proclaims the kingdom of God. In the second part of Mark's narrative, however, Jesus travels south to Judea and Jerusalem, where he is rejected, arrested, and executed. Although Mark reverses the compass directions—designating the north as the area in which Jesus flourishes and the south as the place of his suffering and death—his Gospel echoes the Hebrew Bible's emphasis on north-south geographical divisions and their significance in the working out of God's historical design.

RECOMMENDED READING

Cottrell, Arthur, ed. *The Penguin Encyclopedia of Ancient Civilizations.* New York and London: Penguin Books, 1980.

Gordon, Cyrus. *The Ancient Near East,* 3rd ed. New York: Norton, 1965.

Hobson, Christine. *The World of the Pharaohs: A Complete Guide to Ancient Egypt.* New York: Thames and Hudson, 1987.

Jacobson, Thorkild. *The Treasures of Darkness: A History of Mesopotamian Religion.* New Haven, Conn.: Yale University Press, 1976.

Kramer, Samuel N. *History Begins at Sumer.* New York: Doubleday/Anchor Books, 1959.

———. *The Sumerians.* Chicago: University of Chicago Press, 1963.

———. *Cradle of Civilization.* New York: Time-Life Books, 1967.

Matthews, Victor H. and Benjamin, Don C. *Old Testament Parallels: Documents from the Ancient Near East.* Mahwah, N.J.: Paulist Press, 1991.

Pritchard, James B., ed. *Ancient Near Eastern Texts Relating to the Old Testament,* 3rd ed., supp. Princeton, N.J.: Princeton University Press, 1969.

———. *The Harper Atlas of the Bible.* New York: Harper & Row, 1987.

Redford, Donald B. *Egypt, Canaan, and Israel in Ancient Times.* Princeton, N.J.: Princeton University Press, 1992. An up-to-date analysis of what we know about cultures surrounding ancient Israel.

Roaf, Michael. *Cultural Atlas of Mesopotamia and the Ancient Near East.* New York and Oxford: Facts on File, 1990.

Sandars, N. K. *Poems of Heaven and Hell from Ancient Mesopotamia.* New York and London: Penguin Books, 1971.

Wilson, John A. *The Culture of Ancient Egypt.* Chicago: University of Chicago Press, 1963.

Approaching the Bible

Before beginning a discussion of individual biblical books, it is helpful to review some of the major events of Bible history. In referring to Table 2.1, however, the reader is cautioned to remember that the dates are only roughly approximate and that scholars differ in their attempts to correlate events in Egypt, Mesopotamia, and Palestine with the biblical record. The ancient world had no common method of reckoning time; dating of events before the seventh or sixth centuries B.C.E. is especially conjectural.

It should further be noted that no attempt has been made in the following brief essays to discuss every aspect of the contents of the thirty-nine books of the Hebrew Bible. The summaries provide introductory material necessary or helpful to understanding individual books but do not substitute for reading the Bible itself. In general, only those themes or events that the author thought most significant are included, and these are signaled by headnotes with corresponding scriptural readings. Recommended readings at the end of each major section will direct the student to authoritative works that offer more thorough coverage of particular biblical topics.

TERMS AND CONCEPTS
TO REMEMBER

Akhenaton	Jordan River
(Amenhotep IV)	Josiah
Akkadian (Accadian)	*lex talionis*
Amarna Age	Mari
Amorites	Megiddo
Armageddon	Merneptah
Assur (Asshur)	Mesopotamia
Assyria	Nebuchadnezzar
Aton	Nineveh
Baal	Palestine (Canaan)
Babylon	Persia
Babylonian exile	Philistines
Beersheba	Rameses II
Carchemish	Ras Shamra
circumcision	Rosetta Stone
Code of Hammurabi	Samaritans
cuneiform	Sargon I
Cyrus the Great	Sargon II
Dead Sea	Sea of Galilee
Ebla	Sennacherib
Ebrum	Shamash
Egypt	Shechem
El	Sheol
El Shaddai	Sin
Euphrates River	stele
Fertile Crescent	Sumer
Hammurabi	tell
henotheism	Tigris River
Hyksos	Transjordan
Ishtar	Ugarit
Jeremiah	Ur
Jerusalem	ziggurat
Jezreel	

QUESTIONS FOR REVIEW

1. List some of the contribution that ancient Sumer made to world civilization. When were the first urban centers built in Mesopotamia? When was writing invented? What contribution did the Sumerians make to the measurement of time and space?

2. About when and how did the Akkadian Sargon I establish a political model that many later world leaders would follow?

3. Name some important archaeological findings at Ebla, Mari, and Ugarit. What are some of the possible connections between some of the artifacts unearthed at these ancient sites and the culture that produced the Bible?

4. Who was Hammurabi and why is his law code considered significant in understanding the Bible's legal material? Cite some parallels between Hammurabi's code and Mosaic laws.

5. What political innovations did the ancient Egyptians make when they merged Upper Egypt and Lower Egypt into a single kingdom? Describe some of the major contributions that Egypt made in mathematics, science, and technology. What kind of religious experimentation did Akhenaton initiate? Would you classify Akhenaton's cult of Aton as true monotheism or monolatry? Specify which of Egypt's traditions and practices may have influenced Israelite religious rites.

6. Why is the record of Merneptah's campaign important to our knowledge of Israel's earliest history? What is the Rosetta Stone? How did translating its inscriptions help scholars learn more about ancient Egypt?

7. How did Assyria's imperial expansion affect the northern kingdom of Israel? How did the Neo-Babylonian empire under Nebuchadnezzar affect the southern kingdom of Judah?

QUESTION FOR DISCUSSION
AND REFLECTION

Discuss some of the religious beliefs, practices, or concepts in ancient Egypt, Canaan, and Mesopotamia that parallel or anticipate later biblical themes or ideas. In what ways do you think that the Bible writers were influenced by the older civilizations around them?

3

The Torah (Divine Instruction)

Five Books of History and Sacred Teaching

An extended creation account, from the world's beginning to the formation of the Israelite community, the first division of the Hebrew Bible contains five books of narrative and legal material. Known as the **Torah**—sacred instruction—these books present human history as a progressive revelation of the divine will. In Genesis, God's revelation to Israel's ancestors are partial and incomplete, taking the form of covenant promises for land, nationhood, and blessing that will be fulfilled only in the distant future. Exodus records Yahweh's active intervention to create a people for his name, to whom he reveals his guidelines for human behavior at Mount Sinai (Horeb). These legal and ethical commands (Torah) include hundreds of directives enumerated in the latter parts of Exodus, Leviticus, and the first part of Numbers. The fifth book, Deuteronomy, reviews the vast body of Yahweh's legal requirements, emphasizing the necessity of obedience and invoking curses that will bring national ruin if Israel strays from loyalty to the covenant transmitted through Moses at Sinai. The Torah is the first unit of a long narrative section that traces Israel's history from the founding father and mother, Abraham and Sarah, through the crea-tion of a national empire under kings David and Solomon, to Israel's destruction by Babylon in the sixth century B.C.E. (Genesis through 2 Kings).

The Historical Growth of Torah Traditions

To a citizen of ancient Israel and to modern Jew alike, the Torah (the first five books of the Tanak) forms the core of Judaism. Also known as the **Pentateuch** (five scrolls), these books—Genesis, Exodus, Leviticus, Numbers, and Deuteronomy—comprise the law or divine teaching that Yahweh gave to Israel through Moses. The Torah contains not only the Ten Commandments (listed in Exod. 20 and Deut. 5) but also more than 600 other statutes, ordinances, and minute directions on diet, sacrifice, and worship, which regulated almost every phase of Israel's daily and religious life.

The heart of the Torah is Exodus, the second book of the Hebrew Bible. Exodus records the mighty acts by which Yahweh rescued his people from slavery in Egypt and led them to Mount Sinai (also called Horeb), where he bound Israel to himself in a sacred contract or covenant. In return for becoming Yahweh's chosen people, the Israelites promised to recognize him alone as God and to do all that he commands. The first of the Ten Commandments makes this covenant relationship clear:

> I am Yahweh your God who brought you out of
>   the land of Egypt, out of the house of slavery.
> You shall have no gods except me . . .
> For I Yahweh your God am a jealous God and I
>   punish the father's fault in the sons . . . but I
>   show kindness to thousands of those who love
>   me and keep my commandments.
>   Exodus 20:1–6

Although this solemn pact—the **Mosaic Covenant**—is named after Moses, its mediator, the real hero of Exodus and of the rest of the Torah is Yahweh himself. All that the human characters do, all that they achieve by war, conquest, or any other means, is explicitly ascribed to Yahweh's actions. Moses, his brother Aaron, and even the Egyptian rulers are merely instruments that Yahweh maneuvers to fashion his grand historical design. When pharaoh refuses to allow Israel's release, Yahweh announces that he will use the king's stubbornness to make a "name" or international reputation for himself. "Had I stretched out my hand to strike you and your subjects with pestilence," God declares, "you would have been swept from the earth. But I have let you live for this: to make you see my *power* and to have *my name* published throughout the world" (Exod. 9:15–16, italics added).

Besides directing historical events to publicize his "name" and power to the world at large, Yahweh also identifies himself as a God who demands total commitment from his people. When the Israelites fail to trust his ability to grant them victory over their Canaanite opponents, he angrily threatens to destroy them for their lack of faith. Although Moses persuades Yahweh not to wipe out the people he had delivered from Egypt (and thereby blemish his reputation among foreign nations), God nonetheless punishes Israel by delaying for forty years its entrance into the Promised Land. Except for Moses' loyal assistants Joshua and Caleb, none of the adult generation that left Egypt is permitted to enjoy possession of a national homeland (Num. 13:16–14:38).

The tension between Yahweh's promises and intentions for Israel and the people's repeated failure to live up to their God's expectations permeates the Torah's picture of Israel's national character. As the Torah writers present it, there exists a fundamental incompatibility between God's perfect holiness and humanity's imperfection. Yahweh's relationship with the people to whom he has chosen to reveal his instruction is therefore sharply conflicted: Beset by fears of Canaan's military strength and a natural desire for the food and security they had known in Egypt, the Israelites seem incapable of responding consistently or wholeheartedly to the invisible power that had led them from slavery to freedom.

The imperfect bond between Yahweh and his people is reflected in the Torah's strangely inconclusive ending. After forty years of leading Israel through the Sinai desert, Moses is allowed only a glimpse of the Promised Land beyond the Jordan River. Like the majority of Israelites who had left Egypt, Moses dies before experiencing fulfillment of Yahweh's promises. The Torah anticipates Israel's conquest and possession of Canaan, but it does not include a literal realization of Yahweh's vow that Abraham's descendants—the people of Israel—would inhabit the land "forever." Breaking off before the people's hopes are answered, the Torah points to the future, an unspecified time when God and his people will dwell together in peace.

Instead of granting a materialization of Yahweh's vow to Abraham's progeny, the Torah's last book challenges Israel to remember to keep the terms of the Mosaic Covenant. Represented as Moses' three farewell speeches to an Israel about to invade Canaan, the Book of Deuteronomy reminds the people that their future success depends on strict adherence to Yahweh's laws. Whereas obedience will result in national prosperity, disobedience will bring God's curses, resulting in economic, military, and political disaster (Deut. 28). Responsibility for future success or failure lies directly on the people's shoulders.

Authorship of the Torah

Tradition unanimously credits Moses with the composition of Genesis through Deuteronomy. Most of the ancient rabbis—teachers and interpreters of the Hebrew Scriptures—accepted Mosaic authorship, as did many New Testament writers (Matt. 8:4; 19:7–8; Mark 1:44; 7:10; 10:3–5; 12:19; Luke 5:14; 16:29; 24:27, 44; John 1:17; 5:45–47; 7:19; 8:5; Acts 3:22; 13:39; 15:5, 21; Rom. 10:19; 1 Cor. 9:9). New Testament references to the "law (*torah*) of Moses" or "Books of Moses," however, do not necessarily mean that Moses wrote the Pentateuch *as we have it now*. Statements about Mosaic authorship probably mean no more than that associating the Torah with Moses was a convenient means of alluding to it in ordinary speech, a kind of shorthand reference to the Bible's legal component. Most modern scholars regard the laws ascribed to Moses as a natural but later outgrowth of a nuclear Mosaic tradition.

Problems with Mosaic Authorship   Although there is no verification that Moses composed the Torah in its present form, there are real difficulties with traditional assumptions about his authorship. Even casual readers will note that Moses is always referred to in the third person, as an author writing *about* him would do. Moses, for example, is described as the "humblest man on earth" (Num. 12:3), an unlikely statement for a genuinely modest person to make about himself. Readers will also notice Deuteronomy's many repetitions of the phrase "until this day," a clear indication that the writer looks back from his time to that of a distant past (Deut. 3:14; 34:6, etc.). Deuteronomy's account of Moses' death might be seen as a postscript by a later hand, were it not in exactly the same style

as that of the rest of the book—*and* in language virtually identical to that in the historical books that follow. (See Part 4.) Some comments in Genesis, such as "At that time the Canaanites were in the land" (Gen. 12:6, 13:7), refer to an epoch centuries after Moses' time, when Canaan's original inhabitants had been expelled or assimilated by the Israelite population. References to territories east of the Jordan River as lying beyond "the other bank" presuppose a vantage point on the west side of the river, but the tribes did not occupy this western region until long after Moses' era (cf. Gen. 50:10; Num. 21:1). Other anachronisms, such as the Genesis list of Edom's rulers who reigned "before an Israelite king ruled" (Gen. 36:31), indicate that the author(s) lived at a period after the Israelite monarchy had been established, centuries after Moses' day.

The Documentary Hypothesis

In studying Genesis through Deuteronomy, readers will encounter numerous repetitions, contradictions, and abrupt shifts in tone, style, and theological viewpoint. (For more on biblical criticism, see the feature on pages 68–69.) The same incident, such as Yahweh's pledge of an eternal homeland for Abraham's heirs (Gen. 12, 17, 22) or the revelation of the divine name to Moses (cf. Exod. 3, 6) is commonly presented in two or even three different versions. The present form of the global Flood story (Gen. 6–8) combines two different narratives that can be separated to yield two distinct but complete accounts of the deluge. Moses' spectacular parting of the waters to save Israel from pursuing Egyptian armies also consists of two different stories about the same event that have been combined to produce a single narrative (Exod. 14).

Twice-told tales that parallel but often significantly differ from each other are particularly characteristic of the Torah's first four books,

Table 3.1 Four Principal Sources of the Pentateuch

Source	Characteristics	Approximate Date B.C.E.
J (Yahwist)	Uses the personal name *Yahweh* for God; vivid, concrete style; anthropomorphic view of Deity; begins with creation (Gen. 2:4b); uses term *Mount Sinai* for place where Mosaic Covenant was concluded; composed in the southern kingdom (Judah).	About 950
E (Elohist)	Uses *Elohim* (plural form of "divine powers") for God; style more abstract, less picturesque than J's; view of God less anthropomorphic than earlier source; uses term *Horeb* for covenant mountain; begins with story of Abraham; composed in northern Israel (Ephraim).	About 850
D (Deuteronomist)	Reflects literary style and religious attitudes of Josiah's reform (621 B.C.E.); insists that only one central sanctuary acceptable to Yahweh; best represented in Deuteronomy; composed in the north (?); (later D school also edits histories of Joshua through 2 Kings).	About 650–621
P (Priestly)	Emphasizes priestly concerns, legalistic and cultic aspects of religion; dry, precise style; lists censuses and genealogies; derived from priestly preservation of Mosaic traditions during and after Babylonian exile (following 587 B.C.E.).	About 550–400

Genesis through Numbers. Genesis opens with two strikingly different versions of creation: In Genesis 1, which has a lofty, majestic style, Elohim creates human beings, male and female, simultaneously, both in his own image. In Genesis 2, which has a more vivid, earthy style, it is Yahweh Elohim who fashions the first man and, at a later date, derives the first woman from his rib. Whereas Genesis states that Adam's grandson Enoch was "the first man to invoke the name Yahweh" (Gen. 4:26) and that Israel's ancestors freely used the divine name, Exodus states categorically that people did not know God's personal name before he confided it to Moses (Exod. 6:3–4).

During the past two centuries, an international community of Bible scholars has carefully analyzed the Torah's many discrepancies and has proposed several theories to account for them. Although some disagree, the theory that most scholars believe best accounts for the textual duplications and contradictions is the **documentary hypothesis**. Also called

the Graf-Wellhausen hypothesis, named for the nineteenth-century German scholars who most cogently presented evidence for it, this theory holds that redundancies and inconsistencies in the Pentateuch can be explained most simply by recognizing that it is a composite work. In most scholars' view, the Torah is a literary patchwork in which at least four originally separate documents—dating from four different periods of Israelite history—have been sewn together (Table 3.1). The interweaving of four once-independent sources explains both the repetitions and the discrepancies in the text.

The J (Yahwist) Source According to the documentary hypothesis, the earliest source is called **J** because its author typically uses the name *Yahweh* (in German, *Jahweh*) for God. Also known as the **Yahwist** writer, J—who some critics think may have been a woman—is the first to compose a continuous narrative of Israel's origins. J's work incorporates ancient oral traditions about human prehistory as well as tales of the ancestral fathers and mothers. Beginning his (or her) account with the creation of Adam and Eve (Gen. 2), J includes an old Hebrew version of the Mesopotamian Flood story, the saga of Abraham and Sarah and their descendants, the Israelite tribes' descent into and Exodus from Egypt, the Mosaic Covenant, and Israel's settlement in Canaan. Although it is difficult to determine exactly where J's narrative ends, some scholars believe that it originally included the establishment of the Davidic monarchy, regarded as the historical culmination of Yahweh's promises to Abraham. Whereas a minority of scholars discern fragments of J embedded in the later historical books of Joshua, Judges, and even Samuel, a majority believe that J's work survives primarily in Genesis, Exodus, and parts of Numbers.

Most scholars believe that the Yahwist narrative was produced in response to the great changes that affected Israelite life during the tenth century B.C.E., when Israel's tribes first united under a centralized government. This revolutionary transformation of the nation's social, political, and religious life—with both kings and priests now centered at the new capital of Jerusalem—elicited J's literary affirmation of the new order. In some respects, J's narrative may have been a foundation document validating the Davidic monarchy's innovations, connecting the striking achievements of David, Solomon, and their successors, with Yahweh's vow to make Abraham's progeny a "great nation" and a line of kings.

Certainly the J material woven into the Torah focuses on **Judah**, the name of both the tribe to which David belonged and the southern territory over which he and his heirs ruled. To emphasize the importance of Judah in Israel's past, J associates many of the **patriarchs** with geographical sites that are also significant to Judah's reigning dynasty. Thus, in J's account Abraham dwells in Hebron or Mamre (Gen. 13:18, 18:1), the location of Judah's first capital city, where David's reign was first acclaimed (2 Sam. 2–5), and the hometown of Zadok, who

The facial expression on this statuette of an ancient Egyptian scribe reveals the intelligence and consciousness of power characteristic of the literate professional class that controlled the preservation and interpretation of Egypt's history. In common with its Near Eastern neighbors, Israel developed a scribal class associated with the royal court that played a major role in creating the Bible. (Courtesy of Hirmer Fotoarchiv, München)

served as the nation's high priest under David and Solomon. J's description of the boundaries of the land that was promised to Abraham (Gen. 15:18) corresponds to the political frontiers of David's kingdom. By contrast, J gives a negative account of Shechem (Gen. 34), which in the late tenth century B.C.E. had become the capital of anti-Judean northern tribes that had seceded from the Davidic kingdom. Because J emphasizes Judah's central role in Israel's story, he (or she) is regarded as a native of Judah, perhaps a member of royal court at Jerusalem, giving J's literary symbol a double meaning.

E, the Elohist Source   After Israel's twelve tribes had split into the two rival kingdoms of

Some Representative Methods of Biblical Criticism

Although the word *criticism* may awaken negative feelings in some people—perhaps implying fault finding or an unfavorable judgment—in biblical study it is a positive means of understanding scriptural texts more accurately and objectively. Criticism derives from the Greek word *krino,* which means "to judge" or "to discern," to exercise rational analysis in evaluating something. In the fields of art and literature, it involves the ability to recognize artistic worth and to distinguish among the relative merits or defects of a given work. In biblical study, it refers to the scholarly methods used in analyzing the historical, theological, and compositional processes that brought individual books of the Bible into being.

Literary Criticism

Literary criticism is particularly helpful in studying the Bible and is a skill many careful readers have acquired. Every experienced student is a literary critic to some extent. The student reads not only to acquire information but also to recognize the author's main interest and themes and the elements of character, plot, setting, and style by which the writer's views are expressed. The reader automatically picks up clues—characteristic words, images, and phrases—that suggest the author's intent or purpose. In reading different parts of the Torah, Prophets, or Gospels, students will note that different writers emphasize differ-

ent ideas about God's actions through characters such as Moses, Isaiah, or Jesus and that each repeatedly employs distinctive terms to convey his interpretation of events.

Historical Criticism

Whereas literary criticism seeks to discover the meaning of a written text as we now have it, **historical criticism** attempts to understand the historical circumstances in which that text was first written. The historical critic investigates such matters as the time and place of a document's composition, its authorship, the author's sources, and the intended recipients, or audience, of the work. The historian also examines various social and cultural forces that may have influenced the writer's views of his subject.

In examining the long historical narrative from Joshua through 2 Kings, for example, the historical critic must ask, What really happened? After comparing the biblical version of events with extrabiblical sources—ancient inscriptions, records from other Near Eastern kingdoms, and archaeological excavations—the critic must inevitably realize that biblical authors write history not for the sake of preserving objective fact but to illustrate their views of history's theological significance. In addition, the historical investigator must compare the early edition of Kings—which triumphantly culminates in King Josiah's religious

Judah and Israel (following 921 B.C.E.), a writer in the northern kingdom of Israel produced a second narrative of his people's origins. Perhaps consciously designed as a corrective to J's Judah-oriented version, the northern account uses *Elohim* as the preferred term for God. Focusing on traditions associated with the northern part of Israel, the **E,** or **Elohist,** writer does not review early human history as J had done, beginning instead with the stories of Abraham, Isaac, and Jacob. While providing parallel versions

of some patriarchal and Mosaic traditions, E introduces some striking differences. Whereas J had specified Mount Sinai as the sacred mountain where Moses received the Torah, E names it **Horeb.** J calls the inhabitants of Palestine Canaanites, whereas E calls them Amorites; J refers to Moses' father-in-law as Ruel or Hobab, whereas E knows him as Jethro, priest of Midian.

According to J, people knew of and worshipped Yahweh long before Noah's flood (Gen.

reforms—with the final version that was revised after Josiah's promising reforms were swept away in the catastrophic fall to Babylon.

Form Criticism

Form criticism combines the tools of literary and historical criticism. It recognizes that the Torah and historical narratives are made up of many individual units—ancient folk memories, priestly regulations, genealogies, court archives, war hymns, traditional poetry, creeds formerly recited at cult festivals, and fragments from numerous other sources. Some elements in the narrative, such as battle accounts, victory poems, parables, or creedal recitals, are generally self-contained units that have clear-cut beginnings and endings and can stand alone. These individual units, called **pericopes**, had an independent existence before editors incorporated them into a continuous narrative. They are the building blocks out of which the present biblical text is constructed.

Form criticism looks behind the written form of a pericope to discover the older oral form in which it circulated before being written. The form critic tries to ascertain the circumstances, social and historical, in which an individual pericope originated. Oral traditions about the Moses–Sinai covenant were probably repeated annually at various covenant-renewal ceremonies, gathering new meanings and added interpretations as Israel's political and religious situations changed over the many generations that passed before they achieved written form in the Torah.

Redaction Criticism

Form criticism concentrates on the stages of development that orally transmitted traditions undergo before they are committed to writing. **Redaction criticism** (from the German *Redaktions-geschichte*) emphasizes the role of the individual Bible writer as he weaves these older units into a literary composition. Redaction refers to the authorial process of editing and shaping material. This discipline's emphasis on the author's part in assembling, rearranging, and reinterpreting older material applies equally to the formation of both the Old and New Testaments. Redaction analysis reveals that the Gospel writers, like the compilers of Torah, were not only mere recorders of fact or tradition but also conscious interpreters of their subject. As different writers contributed different traditions about Moses that eventually were blended together in the Torah, so each Gospel writer presented Jesus' life from a distinctive theological perspective consistent with his individual understanding of Jesus' nature and role. (See Part 9.)

During the past 200 years, scholars throughout the Western world have refined their techniques of analysis and interpretation to illuminate the forces and circumstances in which individual biblical books were composed and edited. A representative selection of the most recent and authoritative scholarly publications are listed at the end of each section of this book.

4:26), but E, who is responsible for the famous scene that describes Moses at the burning bush, states that Yahweh kept his personal name a secret until Moses' day (Exod. 3:15). Whereas J's portrait of God is strongly anthropomorphic (possessing human shape or qualities), E paints a more abstract and remote Deity. J pictures Yahweh strolling through Eden to enjoy a cooling breeze, dining with Abraham under the oaks of Mamre, personally wrestling with Jacob, and appearing directly to Moses. The Elohist tends to present God as transcendent, typically employing an angelic go-between when speaking to Abraham or Moses. Recounting Jacob's dream at Bethel, E depicts the invisible link between heaven and earth with the image of a celestial stairway trod by divine beings (Gen. 28:10–19). Whereas J sets many of the ancestral tales in Judah's territory, E prefers sites connected with the northern tribes, the most prominent of which was **Ephraim**, thus also giving the "E" symbol a twofold significance.

Of the four hypothetical documentary sources for the Torah, the E document is perhaps the least well preserved. Because it appears only at widely scattered intervals in the finished Torah narrative, some scholars doubt that the E document ever existed as an independent and continuous story. Some critics believe that the E document merely represents variations of Israel's oral tradition, which editors or **redactors** added to expand or enrich the story of Israel's formation.

The JE Epic   Elohist material, whether oral or written, may have been added to J's account after 721 B.C.E., when the northern kingdom of Israel fell to the Assyrians. Israelite refugees fleeing south into Judah may have brought Elohist traditions with them to Jerusalem, where they eventually were incorporated into J's story. If E was indeed a written source, it is not surprising that the unknown Judean scribe or editor who combined it with J rigorously subordinated material to J's narrative framework, breaking it up into short fragments that supplemented the Yahwist document. The resultant composite work, **JE**, inevitably contained innumerable conflicts and repetitions, such as the two versions of Abraham's wife being captured by a foreign ruler, a tale that occurs again in slightly altered form in the story of **Abimelech** and Isaac's wife, Rebekah (cf. Gen. 12:10–20, 20:1–18, 26:6–11). The JE editor skillfully dovetailed these redundant passages, retaining even contradictory accounts as equally venerable.

D, the Deuteronomist Source   The third principal source of the Pentateuch is known as **D**, the **Deuteronomist**. Whereas J and E strands are found throughout Genesis, Exodus, and Numbers, D's work is confined to the fifth book of Torah, Deuteronomy. Scholars believe that Deuteronomy, or at least its legal core (Chs. 12–28), was the "Book of the Law" discovered in 621 B.C.E. during repairs on the Jerusalem Temple. Discovery of this "Mosaic" document

helped validate an important religious reform conducted by King **Josiah**, who zealously followed Deuteronomy's injunction to centralize Judah's worship "at the place [Yahweh] will choose . . . to set his name there and give it a home" (Deut. 12:4–6). Acting on Deuteronomy's declaration that Yahweh would accept sacrifices only at the "place" designated—assumed to be Jerusalem—Josiah systematically destroyed all other altars and shrines, including those associated with the patriarchs (2 Kings 22:3–23:25; 2 Chron. 34–35). Josiah's other reforms, such as the celebration of a national Passover feast, also echo policies advocated in Deuteronomy.

A Woman's Role in Forming the Biblical Canon   Interestingly, the Temple officials who found this early edition of Deuteronomy took it to Huldah, a "prophetess" who decided that it represented Yahweh's authentic word. (Additional material was added to a later edition of Deuteronomy after the fall of Judah in 587 B.C.E.) Apparently regarded as an authority on the Mosaic tradition, **Huldah** was the first person known to pronounce on the canonicity of a biblical document. Huldah's ruling on Deuteronomy's religious authenticity placed her at the forefront of a long line of scribes, prophets, priests, and editors who eventually gave the Tanak its present form.

Deuteronomy's Theory of History   Although Deuteronomy probably includes much older material, scholars believe that the book's central section was composed in the mid-seventh century B.C.E., with the opening and closing chapters appended considerably later. With its crystal-clear theology of history, Deuteronomy exerted a profound influence on later Bible authors. (In the Torah, obedience brings military victory and economic abundance; disobedience to Yahweh's law triggers national disaster.) The deuteronomic theory of history expressed Israel's official view of its rise and subsequent fall: political domination by such foreign powers as

Assyria, Babylon, or Persia was the result of Israel's having violated its covenant vows to Yahweh.

A conviction that their nation's welfare was conditional upon the people's loyalty to Yahweh and their adherence to Torah requirements determined the way in which subsequent writers presented Israel's story. The prose narratives that follow Deuteronomy—the Books of Joshua through 2 Kings—relate Israel's historical experience almost entirely in terms of deuteronomic theory. Because it is so thoroughly permeated by Deuteronomy's equation of disobedience with national failure, these books are called the **Deuteronomistic History**. (See Part 4.)

Thematically, Deuteronomy belongs with the deuteronomistic narratives that follow it and that promote exactly the same philosophy of history. These are Joshua, Judges, Samuel, and Kings. Although these books form a cohesive literary unit, the Bible's editors ultimately placed Deuteronomy as the fifth book of Torah, concluding the Pentateuch with Moses' warnings about the painful consequences of covenant breaking.

P, the Priestly Source   The fourth and final contribution to the Torah was the work of priests who lived during and after the Babylonian exile (from 587 to the fourth century B.C.E.). Given the scholarly designation of **P**, the **priestly** writers(s) labored to collect, preserve, and edit Israel's religious traditions at a time when their continued existence was threatened by a hostile environment. Compilations of the priestly heritage, including the hundreds of laws and regulations governing Israel's worship, was crucial to ensure that Israel's sense of unique religious purpose survived intact.

According to the documentary hypothesis, it was the priestly writers and editors who were responsible for the final shape and structure of the Torah. The P author(s) extensively revised the JE epic of old Israel, inserting the vast body of legal material that extends from Exodus 35,

through all of Leviticus, to Numbers 10. Although the priestly component is largely concerned with ritual, purity laws, genealogies, and the minutiae of cult sacrifice, it also includes significant additions to the JE narrative. P interwove his tradition of the Flood story with that of J, producing a considerably expanded (and self-contradictory) version of a global deluge. (See "Two Versions of the Flood Story" on pages 72–73.)

P's explicitly priestly concerns appear throughout his expansions of J and E material: His version of creation (Gen. 1) culminates in Yahweh's observance of the first Sabbath, a cosmic validation of that priest-regulated institution. P gives exhaustively detailed directions for building Israel's portable shrine, the Tabernacle, a dwelling place for God that is rendered in terms similar to those that describe the creation (Exod. 25–31, 35–40). The elaborate machinery of the sacrificial cult, including offerings to expiate sin and guilt—also under priestly jurisdiction—occupies most of the Book of Leviticus. P rewrites J's account of Israel's deliverance at the Sea of Reeds, heightening the miraculous element and emphasizing Yahweh's parting of the sea so that Israel passes between two standing walls of water, an echo of Genesis 1 in which Elohim separates the primordial waters of chaos (Exod. 14). P also augments Aaron's role in the Exodus-Sinai story, making him Moses' spokesman before pharaoh and the founder of Israel's only legitimate line of high priests. Finally, P wrote the account of Moses' death that ends Deuteronomy, thus providing the structural framework for the entire Torah.

Ezra and the Torah   The P material may represent a long succession of priestly editors who, over a century or more, reshaped Israel's ancient and sometimes conflicting traditions into a semblance of literary unity. By binding an expanded and edited version of Deuteronomy to the JE narrative, P created the five-part Torah we know today. According to the Book of Nehe-

Two Versions of the Flood Story

The present text of Genesis relating the story of a universal deluge combines two Flood accounts, attributed, respectively, to the Yahwist writer (J) and the priestly writer (P). Each of the two accounts stands alone as a complete and independent narrative in this translation from the Jerusalem Bible.

The Yahwist Account of the Flood

Yahweh said to Noah, "Go aboard the ark, you and all your household, for you alone among this generation do I see as a good man in my judgment. Of all the clean animals you must take seven of each kind, both male and female; of the unclean animals you must take two, a male and its female (and of the birds of heaven also, seven of each kind, both male and female), to propagate their kind over the whole earth. For in seven days' time I mean to make it rain on the earth for forty days and nights, and I will rid the earth of every living thing that I made." Noah did all that Yahweh ordered. . . .

Noah with his sons, his wife, and his sons' wives boarded the ark to escape the waters of the flood. . . . Seven days later the waters of the flood appeared on the earth. . . . It rained on the earth for forty days and forty nights. . . . And Yahweh closed the door behind Noah.

The flood lasted forty days on the earth. The waters swelled, lifting the ark until it was raised above the earth. The waters rose and swelled greatly on the earth, and the ark sailed on the waters. The waters rose more and more on the earth so that all the highest mountains under the whole of heaven were submerged. The waters rose fifteen cubits higher, submerging the mountains. . . . Everything with the breath of life in its nostrils died, everything on dry land. Yahweh destroyed every living thing on the face of the earth, man and animals, reptiles, and the birds of heaven. He rid the earth of them, so that only Noah was left, and those with him in the ark. . . .

Rain ceased to fall from heaven; the waters gradually ebbed from the earth. . . . At the end of forty days Noah opened the porthole he had made in the ark. . . . Then he sent out the dove, to see whether the waters were receding from the surface of the earth. The dove, finding nowhere to perch, returned to him in the ark, for there was water over the whole surface of the earth; putting out his hand he took hold of it and brought it back into the ark with him. After waiting seven more days, again he sent out the dove from the ark. In the evening, the dove came back to him and there it was with a new olive branch in its beak. So Noah realized that the waters were receding from the earth. After waiting seven more days he sent out the dove, and now it returned to him no more. . . . Noah lifted back the hatch of the ark and looked out. The surface of the ground was dry! . . .

Noah built an altar for Yahweh, and choosing from all the clean animals and all the clean birds he offered burnt offerings on the altar. Yahweh smelled the appeasing fragrance and said to himself, "Never again will I curse the earth because of man, because his heart contrives evil from his infancy. Never again will I strike down every living thing as I have done.

"As long as earth lasts, sowing and reaping, cold and heat, summer and winter, day and night shall cease no more."

Genesis 7:1–8:22

The Priestly Account of the Flood

God [Elohim] said to Noah, ". . . Make an ark out of resinous wood. Make it with reeds and line it

---

miah, in the fifth century B.C.E. the priest-scribe **Ezra** brought back the "Book of the Law [Torah] of Moses which Yahweh had prescribed for Israel" from the Babylonian exile. Many scholars think that Ezra's edition of the Torah, which he promulgated to the assembled citizens of Jerusalem, represents essentially the Pentateuch in its final form, a priestly amalgamation of JE and D. Others believe that the editorial process that resulted in the finished Torah persisted well into the next century.

Once the Torah reached its ultimate form and had circulated throughout postexilic Israel, it is doubtful that any other major changes took

with pitch inside and out. This is how to make it: the length of the ark is to be three hundred cubits, its breadth fifty cubits, and its height thirty cubits. Make a roof for the ark . . . put the door of the ark high up in the side, and make a first, second and third deck.

"For my part I mean to bring a flood, and send the waters over the earth, to destroy all flesh on it, every living creature under heaven; everything on earth shall perish. But I will establish my Covenant with you, and you must go on board the ark yourself, your sons, your wife, and your sons' wives along with you. From all living creatures, from all flesh, you must take two of each kind aboard the ark, to save their lives with yours; they must be a male and a female. Of every kind of bird, of every kind of animal and of every kind of reptile on the ground, two must go with you so that their lives may be saved. For your part provide yourself with eatables of all kinds, and lay in a story of them, to serve as food for yourself and them." Noah did this; he did all that God [Elohim] had ordered him.

Noah was six hundred years old when the flood of waters appeared on the earth. . . . (Of the clean animals and the animals that are not clean, of the birds and all that crawls on the ground, two of each kind boarded the ark with Noah, a male and a female, according to the order God gave Noah.) . . .

In the six hundredth year of Noah's life, in the second month, and on the seventeenth day of that month, that very day all the springs of the great deep broke through, and the sluices of heaven opened. . . .

That very day Noah and his sons Shem, Ham and Japheth boarded the ark, with Noah's wife and the three wives of his sons, and with them wild beasts of every kind, cattle of every kind, reptiles of every kind that crawls on the earth, birds of every kind, all that flies, everything with wings. One pair of all that is flesh and has the breath of life boarded

the ark with Noah; and so there went in a male and a female of every creature that is flesh, just as God had ordered him. . . .

And so all things of flesh perished that moved on the earth—birds, cattle, wild beasts, everything that swarms on the earth, and every man. . . .

The waters rose on the earth for a hundred and fifty days. But God had Noah in mind, and all the wild beasts and all the cattle that were with him in the ark. God sent a wind across the earth and the waters subsided. The springs of the deep and the sluices of heaven were stopped. . . . After a hundred and fifty days the waters fell, and in the seventh month, on the seventeenth day of that month, the ark came to rest on the mountains of Ararat. The waters gradually fell until the tenth month when, on the first day of the tenth month, the mountain peaks appeared. . . .

At the end of forty days Noah opened the porthole he had made in the ark and he sent out the raven. This went off, and flew back and forth until the waters dried up from the earth. . . .

It was in the six hundred and first year of Noah's life, in the first month and on the first of the month, that the water dried up from the earth. . . . In the second month and on the twenty-seventh day of the month the earth was dry.

Then God said to Noah, "Come out of the ark, you yourself, your wife, your sons and your sons' wives with you. As for all the animals with you, all things of flesh, whether birds or animals or reptiles that crawl on the earth, bring them out with you. Let them swarm on the earth; let them be fruitful and multiply on the earth." So Noah went out with his sons, his wife, and his sons' wives. And all the wild beasts, all the cattle, all the birds and all the reptiles that crawl on the earth went out from the ark, one kind after another.

Genesis 6:13–8:19

---

place. Indeed, so careful were later scribes in copying the Torah that they counted every word and letter in a manuscript line, starting afresh if they discovered any errors in transcription. Accepted by the covenant community as sacred and complete, the Torah became the immovable foundation of Jewish faith.

Some Scholarly Modifications of the Documentary Hypothesis

Oral Sources for the Torah In reviewing scholarly theories about the four hypothetical sources underlying the Pentateuch, readers must not assume that biblical criticism is altogether clear-cut or simple. Although most contemporary scholars, Catholic, Protestant, and Jewish, accept some form of the documentary hypothesis, they do not necessarily agree about which particular passages belong to which source document. One modification of the Graf-Wellhausen proposal argues that the various strands of tradition woven into the Pentateuch derive largely from **oral traditions** about Israel's national cult, particularly oral recitations of allegiance to Yahweh, such as those preserved in Deuteronomy 5 and Joshua 24. The term that anthropologists and historians of religion commonly use to designate a people's formal rites and practice of worship is **cult**. This term applies to Israel's organized system of sacrifices and ceremonies. Throughout Israel's history, priestly leaders accorded enormous importance to maintaining the Temple cult in Jerusalem, which the deuteronomistic historians insisted was the only sanctuary on earth at which Yahweh would accept Torah-mandated offerings.

Before Josiah's reforms centralized worship late in the seventh century B.C.E., public recitations of the laws, rituals, and historical memories associated with Moses or tribal ancestors were performed at many different shrines and religious centers scattered throughout Israel. At seasonal festivals, Israel's various tribes would assemble at one of their local holy places, such as those at Shechem, Kadesh, Shiloh, or Jerusalem, where they would renew their covenant vows to Yahweh. Evolving differences between individual tribal stories recited at these various local sanctuaries may have contributed to the different strata of thought or theological viewpoints found in the Torah.

According to this theory, the Torah rituals and narratives were assembled from diverse blocks of previously independent oral (and some written) material at a relatively late date, perhaps the fifth century B.C.E. or even later. Some advocates of this view have recently proposed that the first four pentateuchal books, Genesis through Numbers, are largely the work of a single author-editor who first incorporated Israel's extremely diverse oral traditions into a continuous narrative during the late fifth or fourth century B.C.E. If this is true, then the Book of Deuteronomy, which was probably composed during the mid-seventh century B.C.E., is considerably older than the rest of the Torah. Because the scribal editor responsible for the Pentateuch's final form was most likely a post-exilic priest, it is not surprising that he validated a large body of legal and cultic traditions that had developed over several centuries by attributing all of them to Moses. Thus, laws promulgated during the monarchy and later, as well as liturgical practices of the Second Temple period (after 515 B.C.E.) were made part of the Mosaic revelation at Sinai. (For these and other recent scholarly theories about the making of the Pentateuch, see the recommended readings, Whybray, Rendtorff, and Quinn and Kikawada.)

To some scholars, the Torah's authorship and date remain an open question. Many conservative clergy, including some Orthodox rabbis and Evangelical Protestants, still endorse Mosaic authorship of the entire Pentateuch. A scholarly minority promotes a new thesis that a single priestly writer, working after the Babylonian exile, created all five books of the Torah. To most scholars, however, some version of the documentary hypothesis most efficiently accounts for otherwise inexplicable duplications, inconsistencies, contradictions, and stylistic and theological differences that characterize the first five books of the Bible. Students who wish to review a clear summary of the evidence for multiple sources in the Torah will find Richard E. Friedman's thoughtful work a great help. (See Recommended Readings.)

Equipped with an awareness of the Torah's multiple sources and long history of editorial revision, readers will appreciate the rich and varied texture of its vivid narratives. Stories retold in different forms, anachronisms, and even contradictions, such as conflicting traditions about the use of Yahweh's name and whether human beings could actually *see* God's form (cf. Exod. 24:9–11, 33:11, 19–23; Deut. 34:10–11), point to the diversity of religious experience that the Bible's authors thought fit to preserve.

RECOMMENDED READING

Anderson, Gary A. "Introduction to Israelite Religion." In *The New Interpreter's Bible,* Vol. 1, pp. 272–283.

Blenkinsopp, Joseph. "Introduction to the Pentateuch." In *The New Interpreter's Bible,* Vol. 1, pp. 305–318. Nashville, Tenn.: Abingdon Press, 1994.

———. *The Pentateuch: An Introduction to the First Five Books of the Bible.* New York: Doubleday, 1992.

Ellis, Peter. *The Yahwist: The Bible's First Theologian.* Notre Dame, Ind.: Fides, 1968.

Fohrer, Georg. *Introduction to the Old Testament.* Nashville, Tenn.: Abingdon Press, 1968.

Fox, Everett, ed. *The Five Books of Moses.* The Schocken Bible, Vol. 1. New York: Schocken Books, 1995. An extraordinary new translation of the Torah that captures the flavor of the original Hebrew text.

Friedman, Richard E. "Torah (Pentateuch)." In D. N. Freedman, ed., *Anchor Bible Dictionary,* Vol. 6, pp. 605–622. New York: Doubleday, 1992. Gives detailed but clear evidence that supports the documentary hypothesis.

———. *Who Wrote the Bible?* New York and San Francisco: Harper & Row, 1987. An excellent introduction to scholarly speculations about authorship of the Hebrew Bible.

Jenks, Alan W. "Elohist." In D. N. Freedman, ed., *The Anchor Bible Dictionary,* Vol. 2, pp. 478–482. New York: Doubleday, 1992. A description of the Elohist writer's characteristics.

Milgrom, Jacob. "Priestly ('P') Source." In D. N. Freedman, ed., *The Anchor Bible Dictionary,* Vol. 5, pp. 454–461. New York: Doubleday, 1992. Summarizes literary and theological characteristics of the priestly writer(s).

Pury, Albert de. "Yahwist ('J') Source." In D. N. Freedman, ed., *The Anchor Bible Dictionary,* Vol. 6, pp. 1013–1020. New York: Doubleday, 1992. Reviews literary style and theological viewpoint of the Yahwist (J) author.

Quinn, Arthur and Kikawada, Isaac. *Before Abraham Was: The Unity of Genesis 1–11.* Harrison, N.Y.: Ignatius Press, 1989. Argues for a single author of the primeval history.

Rendtorff, Rolf. *The Problem of the Process of Transmission of the Pentateuch.* Sheffield: JSOT Press, 1990. Argues that the deuteronomistic school compiled the Torah and denies the existence of earlier written sources, such as J or E.

Tigay, Jeffrey. "The Evolution of the Pentateuchal Narratives in the Light of the Evolution of the Gilgamesh Epic." In Jeffrey Tigay, ed., *Empirical Models for Biblical Criticism.* Philadelphia: University of Pennsylvania Press, 1985. Compares the development of the Sumero-Babylonian epic to the growth of the Pentateuch.

Whybray, R. N. *The Making of the Pentateuch: A Methodological Study.* Sheffield: JSOT Press, 1987.

TERMS AND CONCEPTS TO REMEMBER

Abimelech	J (Yahwist)
cult	JE (Yahwist/Elohist)
D (Deuteronomist)	Josiah
Deuteronomistic History	Judah
	literary criticism
documentary hypothesis	Mosaic Covenant
	oral tradition
E (Elohist)	P (priestly)
Ephraim	patriarch
Ezra	Pentateuch
form criticism	pericope
historical criticism	redaction criticism
Horeb, Mount	redactor
Huldah	Torah

Genesis

KEY THEMES

An account of human origins, Genesis introduces themes that will dominate most of the Bible's historical narratives. After establishing Yahweh-Elohim as creator of the universe and surveying the primeval history of humanity (Chs. 1–11), Genesis focuses on the Deity's relationships with Israel's ancestors, noting that divinely initiated covenants with chosen individuals will ultimately convey a blessing to all people. The theme of divine promise and its delayed fulfillment, first sounded in the two creation accounts, reappears in Yahweh's voluntary pledge (the Abrahamic Covenant) to grant land and multitudinous descendants to Abraham, whose story occupies the book's second section (Chs. 12–24). God's wrestling with recalcitrant humanity, marred from the beginning by disobedience and rebellion, is epitomized in the struggle at Peniel between the Deity and Jacob, whose new name, Israel, is said to mean "strong against God" (32:25–32). The morally ambiguous qualities of Jacob, prototype of strengths and weaknesses in Israel's national character, and his gradual ethical development are highlighted in his two contrasting prayers at Bethel and Peniel. After the long Jacob saga (Chs. 25–36), Genesis concludes with the story of Joseph and his brothers, whose quarrels and descent into Egypt further delay the promised blessings of homeland and nationhood (Chs. 37–50).

> God saw all he had made, and indeed it was very good.
>
> Genesis 1:31

The Primeval History

The Priestly Account   From Elohim's creation of heaven and earth in Chapter 1 to Joseph's confident prophecy about Israel's return to the Promised Land in the final chapter, Genesis presents world history as the inevitable outworking of the divine purpose. An exciting epic of human and national origins, Genesis opens with two discrete accounts of creation. In the first (1:1–2:4a), attributed to the priestly writer, Elohim fashions the cosmos out of a dark, watery chaos by the six-step process of separation and distinction. Although later theologians interpreted Genesis 1 as creation *ex nihilo*—out of

nothing—most scholars now believe that the Hebrew text should be translated as it is by the Jewish Publication Society of America: "When God [Elohim] began to create the heaven and the earth—the earth being unformed and void, with darkness over the deep [*tehom*] and a wind from God sweeping over the waters . . .*" "The deep," translated from the Hebrew *tehom,* refers to the primordial abyss, a boundless, formless waste of undifferentiated sea—the primeval substance that Elohim proceeds to illuminate, divide, and shape into an orderly system.

P's statement that the precreation world was an amorphous, storm-tossed body of water echoes a Mesopotamian tradition familiar to the Israelites. Genesis traces Abraham's origins back to Ur, an ancient city located in the water-saturated flatlands of Mesopotamia, an area near the Persian Gulf that was repeatedly inundated by flooding of the Euphrates and Tigris rivers. The Sumerians and Babylonians inhabiting this region could directly observe new land emerging from watery wastes as the rivers deposited large quantities of silt in their intermingled deltas. Noting the distinctly Mesopotamian ambience of Genesis 1, many scholars recommend that readers approach the biblical creation account—not as if it were a scientific report on astronomical and geologic events that formed our planet—but in the light of other ancient Near Eastern creation stories, such as the Babylonian **Enuma Elish**.

Dating from about the twelfth century B.C.E., the *Enuma Elish* celebrates the victory of Marduk, chief god of Babylon, over an older generation of Mesopotamian deities. After defeating their leader, the goddess Tiamat—who represents the primordial inertia of undifferentiated salt water—Marduk splits Tiamat's mollusklike carcass in two, using one-half to make

---

*The Torah: The Five Books of Moses. Philadelphia: The Jewish Publication Society of America, 1967. Note that the editors of this version translate Genesis 1:1 to show that creation does not begin from nothing but is a process of shaping chaotic matter into an orderly system.

earth and the other to form the vault (firmament) of heaven. Almost as an afterthought, Marduk then fashions humans out of the blood of Kingu, Tiamat's slain consort. In the Babylonian tale, humanity's function is to serve the gods as slaves, maintaining their temples and keeping their sacrificial fires burning.

Comparison of the *Enuma Elish* with Genesis reveals a number of parallels. Both accounts begin with a gloomy, windy chaos; both proceed in six distinct stages—the six generations of Babylonian gods corresponding to Genesis's six creative days—and in both, the creative process culminates in the appearance of humans.

The old Mesopotamian mythology of warring gods has been banished from Genesis, but allusions to it appear in other biblical passages about creation. Psalm 89 alludes to the ancient myth of Yahweh's long-ago battle with **Rahab**, who seems to be a Canaanite version of Tiamat, the primordial, raging sea:

> You [Yahweh] control the pride of the ocean,
> when its waves ride high, you calm them;
> you split Rahab in two like a carcass
> and scattered your enemies with your
>   mighty arm.

Yahweh's ancient battle with chaos to create the present world order also resounds through Psalm 74:

> By your power you split the sea in two,
> and smashed the head of monsters on the waters.
> You crushed Leviathan's heads,
> leaving him for wild animals to eat,
> you opened the spring, the torrent,
> and dried up inexhaustible rivers.
> You are master of day and night,
> you instituted light and sun,
> you fixed the boundaries of the world,
> you created summer and winter.

The order of Yahweh's actions in this poetic summary of creation is instructive: The sea is divided; sea monsters and the mysterious **Leviathan** (probably the Canaanite Lotan) are annihilated; floods are dried up, turned to dry land; sources of light are created; cosmic boundaries established; and the seasons instituted—a sequence roughly paralleling events in both Genesis and the *Enuma Elish*. (See also references to Yahweh's triumph over the "Wild Sea Beast" in Job 12:12 and 26:1–14.)

Despite some lingering echoes of Mesopotamian lore, however, the biblical texts present a qualitatively different picture of creation, one that defines important aspects of Israel's religious faith. Some scholars believe that Genesis 1 was composed during Israel's exile in Babylon (587–538 B.C.E.) as a conscious response to the annual public recitation of the *Enuma Elish* in Marduk's honor. Perhaps based on an earlier hymn of praise sung at the Jerusalem Temple, Genesis 1 proclaims the absolute supremacy of Israel's God. In striking contrast to Mesopotamian **polytheism**, P's liturgy exalts an eternal, omnipotent creator who exercises undisputed control of the universe, bringing order out of chaos and light out of darkness through the power of his word alone (1:3). As the priestly writer understood him, Elohim has no rivals.

The six days of P's creation week are arranged in two sets of three, the first set dealing with Elohim's creative acts of separation. On day one, Elohim separates light from darkness; on day two, he creates the "vault" (formerly translated "**firmament**"), an arch or dome that divides the primeval waters above the sky from those on the earth's surface. (Note that these atmospheric waters will be released to inundate the earth again when God returns the world to its original chaotic state during the Flood [Gen. 6:11–12].) On the third day, God separates dry land from the surrounding seas.

In the second three-day unit, Elohim creates life forms to inhabit the three regions he had previously separated and shaped from the primeval watery substance. As light came into being on the first day, so on day four Elohim creates the sources of light—sun, moon, and stars. Although many Near Eastern cultures worshiped these celestial objects, P does not even name them, stating that they exist only to regulate, or "govern," day and night—perhaps

The "Demythologizing" Tendency of Bible Authors

Virtually every known culture expresses its social values and religious views through myth—generally accepted traditions that tell how the world, its gods, its people, and its values and customs—came to be as they are. Torah writers and editors were probably aware of the numerous ancient tales—Canaanite, Mesopotamian, and Egyptian—that explained the origin of the universe, including divine and human beings. Some of the mythic elements that Yahweh apparently once shared with other ancient Near Eastern gods—largely absent from Torah narratives—are partly preserved in some biblical poetry. The Book of Job, Isaiah 27:1, and Psalm 89, for example, allude to the myth of Yahweh's primordial battle with Rahab or Leviathan, monsters that embody the chaos that preceded creation.

Poetic allusions to other myths include that of Yahweh's membership in a council of gods. In Psalm 82, God (Elohim) presides over a convocation of deities, whom he denounces for their failure to enforce justice. Although these gods are "sons of the Most High (the Canaanite *Elyon*)," they are condemned to die like men. In a similar picture of the celestial "divine assembly," a poem embedded in Deuteronomy shows the "Most High" (*Elyon*) allotting different nations to their particular patron deities and assigning Israel to Yahweh (Deut. 32:8–9). Whereas Psalm 89 shows Yahweh as one amid a heavenly assembly of many "holy ones," Job 1–2 portrays him reigning over a court composed of "*bene ha elohim*" (literally, "sons of the gods").

In describing God's (Elohim's) creative acts, the priestly author of Genesis 1 does not include the divine council in his account. This omission may confuse Bible readers, who will have no idea to whom God speaks when he suddenly addresses some unseen auditor: "let *us* make man in *our own image*, in the *likeness of ourselves*" (Gen. 1:26, italics added). Based on the tradition of the *bene ha elohim*, the Creator apparently is consulting members of his heavenly court, who serve as models for the earthly race. As a psalmist noted, God made his human image only "little less than a god" (Ps. 8:5), only slightly inferior to the "Sons of God(s) (*bene ha elohim*)" present at creation (cf. Job 38:7).

A similar tendency to demythologize appears in the Yahwist creation narrative, when Yahweh

---

because the Hebrew word for sun, *shamesh,* is virtually identical to that for Shamash, the Babylonian solar deity.

On day five, Elohim generates creatures to swim through the earthly seas and fly through the sky vault he had separated on day two. Days three and six also correspond in P's methodical account: The dry land and plants created on the third day provide a sustaining environment for the animals and humans formed on the sixth.

The creation of humanity, male and female together, both "in the image of God," is the climax of P's creation hymn. Readers will notice that this is the only project on which Elohim consults his heavenly court, the assembly of mysterious spirit beings who appear in some later biblical depictions of God's throne room (see Isa. 6 and Job 1–2; see also, "The 'Demythologizing' Tendency of Bible Authors" on pages 78–79). "Let us," Elohim invites his invisible courtiers, "make man in our own image, in the likeness of ourselves," to let "them" (notice the plural to include both sexes) become "masters" of earth and all its diverse creatures. This statement is remarkable not only for its unexplained reference to Elohim's heavenly companions but also for its astounding declaration about the godlike nature and role of humans. Although the context implies that humanity resembles the Deity primarily in its assigned role as ruler and beneficiary of creation's abundance, it also implies a link between the human and

observes that the first man had "become *like one of us,* with his knowledge of good and evil" (Gen. 3:22, italics added). Both the priestly and Yahwist writers decline to identify whom God consults during the creative process. Lacking a context for God's implied audience, readers are left wondering whom the Creator regards as "one of us," heavenly beings like himself.

God's unidentified companions reappear in the introduction to the Flood story when the *bene ha elohim* mate with mortal women to produce a generation of celebrated heroes (Gen. 6:1–4). The Book of Enoch, dating from the third to second centuries B.C.E., contains a more extensive account of these "sons of the gods" and their relationship to humanity. (See Part 7.) In their wish to emphasize God's solitary autonomy, however, the Genesis writers do not provide any explanation that would evoke the old mythology of El's cosmic assembly of divine beings.

The same principle holds true in the Genesis Flood account. In the original traditions inherited from Mesopotamia, two major gods are involved: Enlil (in Akkadian, Ellil), irascible god of storm and wind, brings on the deluge, but Ea, a wiser and more compassionate deity, warns Utnapishtim (the Babylonian Noah) to build an ark so he can preserve representative animals and at least one human family through the catastrophe. In Genesis, where only one God orders events, Yahweh takes on the roles of both Enlil and Ea: He is both destroyer and preserver, drowning most of the human race but saving Noah's family. This combining of two distinct divine personalities in one God has a paradoxical effect: the creator who pronounces everything "very good" in Genesis (1:31) comes to regret having created in the first place and resolves to annihilate his "own creation" (Gen. 6:6–8).

In thus revising and reinterpreting ancient religious traditions inherited from older Near Eastern civilizations, the Torah writers boldly separated their concept of God from his mythological trappings. Despite fragmentary references to earlier beliefs found in the Tanak, Bible writers ultimately succeeded in presenting an omnipotent, single Deity who creates and rules the universe almost entirely independent of mythic associations. In their radical insistence on "Yahweh alone," biblical authors posited a creator who tolerates no rival deities, eventually reducing the mysterious *bene ha elohim* to the rank of mere "messengers" (angels) and banishing all others from the universe.

divine that suggests an almost unlimited human potential. Psalm 8, a meditation on this concept, observes that God "made [humanity] little less than a god." Surveying "all that he had made," with humanity constituting the apex of creation, Elohim pronounces the entire arrangement "very good" (Gen. 1:31).

The Yahwist Version of Humanity's Creation

Whereas P presents a cosmic view of creation, ending with God's resting from his labors on the seventh day, the **Sabbath**, J's narrative (Gen. 2: 4b–25) brings creative events down to earth, portraying a Deity with decidedly human qualities and a humanity (in Hebrew, *'adam*) fashioned from dust of the ground (*adamah*). P's cosmos emerges out of an oceanic abyss, but J's precreation environment is a rainless, sterile desert that Yahweh irrigates with subterranean waters (2:5–6).

J also gives a different order to creation. In P, men and women are created at the same time, at the end of a long creative sequence; in J, Yahweh creates a human first, a composite being made of "soil" and animated by Yahweh's breath. After settling the human creature in a lush oasis, Yahweh then fashions "wild beasts and birds" (Gen. 2:18–19), apparently expect-

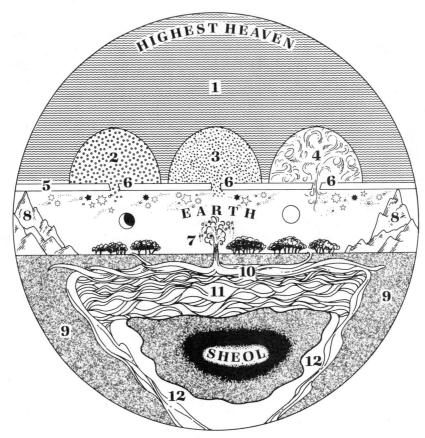

This artist's recreation of the ancient biblical view of the universe shows (1 and 11) the waters above and below the earth; (2, 3, and 4) chambers or storehouses of hail, rain, and snow; (5 and 6) the firmament with its openings or sluices; (7) fountains of the deep; (8) the mountain pillars on which the firmament rests; (9) the pillars of the earth; (10) the navel of the earth; and (12) the watery abyss. Sheol, abode of the dead, is the dark cavern at the center of the lower hemisphere.

ing 'adam to select a mate from this menagerie. When the creature finds no suitable counterpart among nonhuman species, Yahweh designs a woman, **Eve**, from a rib of the presumably androgynous 'adam. J emphasizes the bond and likeness between the two human creatures: The man (ish) and woman (ishshah) are of the same "bone" and "flesh," united metaphorically as "one body" (Gen. 2:21–24). Because 'adam is not a proper name but the Hebrew term for 'earth creature' or humanity, the J writer makes it clear that the human creation is complete only when both male and female are formed.

Adam, Eve, and the Serpent

Human enjoyment of **Eden**, the paradise garden that Yahweh provides for the first couple, is interrupted by one of the Deity's animal creations, the **serpent**. Described not as evil but as "shrewd" or "subtle," the serpent persuades Eve to taste the fruit of a tree that Yahweh had planted in Eden, but which he had forbidden humans to eat. Recognizing that the tree "was desirable for the knowledge that it could give" (Gen. 3:6), Eve shares the fruit with her husband. This joint act instantly destroys the couple's childlike innocence, forcing a painful awareness of their "nakedness," their vulnerability, and dread of Yahweh's reaction. Like naive children, they attempt to hide from Yahweh, who, not yet informed of their misbehavior, soon appears for his customary walk through the garden.

Yahweh's judgment is swift and severe. The crafty serpent who had pointed out that humans could "be like gods" (Gen. 3:5) is stripped of its legs and reduced to an object of human loathing (Gen. 3:14–15). (The notion that the serpent represents Satan, conventionally viewed as a fallen angel who corrupted the first human couple, does not appear in the Hebrew Bible but can be found in the noncanonical Life of Adam and Eve, written about the first century C.E. [See Part 7.]) Yahweh condemns the woman to intensified pain in childbirth and social domination by her husband—a reflection of woman's subordination to males in J's patriarchal society but not part of the original divine plan. For the man, Yahweh blights the soil, consigning males to the endlessly frustrating labor that peasant farmers experience in trying to wrest a living from arid Near Eastern fields. The cost of seizing knowledge without divine permission or guidance also includes a new consciousness of human mortality, and Yahweh reminds the pair that they must return to the soil from which they had been formed. The Deity later retracts his curse of the ground (Gen. 8:21), but not until the last-written book of the Hebrew Bible does he explicitly offer humanity a hope of transcending death (Dan. 12:1–3).

J's parable of humanity's alienation from God is never mentioned again in the Hebrew Bible. Not until about the first century B.C.E. do a few Hellenistic Jewish writers begin to attribute the origin of human death to the "devil's envy" (e.g., Wisdom of Solomon 2:24). Later Christian theologians, such as Augustine (early fifth century C.E.), read even more into J's story of Adam and Eve's expulsion from paradise, seeing it as a tragic "**Fall** from grace." According to Augustine's doctrine of "original sin," Adam's

eating the forbidden fruit corrupted human nature so that the entire human race, inheriting the original parents' sinfulness, is born depraved and under divine condemnation. Terms that later commentators use to interpret Genesis 3, however—*sin, evil, rebellion, disobedience, punishment, damnation*—are entirely absent from J's story. Modern theologians, both Protestant and Roman Catholic, have challenged Augustine's pessimistic view of humanity's innate defilement. Some recent commentators have transferred attention from human responsibility for the race's alienation from God to analyze the ethical ambivalence inherent in J's portrait of the Deity. Considerable tension exists between God's (Elohim's) creation of humanity in the divine image and Yahweh's strange refusal to grant the human pair wisdom, the ability to distinguish good from evil. J's picture of godlike knowledge as something to be acquired by magic—eating a forbidden fruit—is also troubling.

Equally problematic is J's explanation of Yahweh's motive for expelling humanity from Eden. "The man," Yahweh observes, "has become as one of us, with his knowledge of good and evil." Lest the man also eat from the "tree of life" and "live forever," Yahweh posts **cherubim**—winged creatures, part-animal, part-human, depicted in Mesopotamian art—to keep humanity from acquiring another attribute of divinity (Gen. 3:22–24). In the ancient world, the two chief qualities that distinguish gods from mortals were the former's superior knowledge and immortality. Alert to humanity's newborn assertiveness. Yahweh—apparently jealous of divine prerogatives—acts to prevent them from becoming fully like the quasi-divine beings in his heavenly court.

J's theme of competition between Yahweh and his intelligent creatures reappears in the Tower of Babel episode (Gen. 11:1–9) when Yahweh realizes that a humanity united in a common language and culture will find "nothing too hard for them to do." To weaken the human potential, he overthrows their united efforts—represented by their building a temple tower, or ziggurat—confuses their languages, and scatters them over "the whole face of the earth." J, concerned about humanity's misuse of freedom to work mischief, regards the **Babel** incident as an example of hubris, pride that defies the gods.

J's Portrait of God   The first writer to fashion the literary image of God that has dominated Judeo-Christian thought for 3000 years, J portrays Yahweh as if he were an embodiment of both the creative and destructive aspects of the universe. After creating humanity, Yahweh annihilates all but eight persons in a flood (Gen. 6–8) and later incinerates the entire populations of five cities (Gen. 19). At times, J pictures Yahweh as "a devouring fire," a mighty force so full of turbulent energy that he can scarcely restrain his own violent tendencies. In Exodus 4, Yahweh suddenly launches a murderous night attack on his loyal servant Moses, stopping only when Moses' wife appeases him by circumcising her child with a flint knife (Exod. 4:24–26). In Exodus 33, a passage in which the J and E strands are intricately blended, Yahweh twice warns Moses that he cannot bear to keep company with the Israelites because their conduct so enrages him that he cannot trust himself not to slaughter them all on sight (Exod. 33:3–5). After slaying the Egyptian first-born males, Yahweh also attacks his own people, exterminating countless thousands and threatening to wipe out the entire nation (Exod. 32–33; Num. 14, 16; etc.). J's Deity inspires terror not only because he is a righteous judge who does not hesitate to execute offenders but also because his wrath, of cosmic proportions, is perceived as arbitrary and unpredictable.

But J also reveals Yahweh as the one who cares for, rescues, and redeems his people, a God capable of surprising tenderness. Before evicting his human creation into the harsh world of adult experience, Yahweh makes clothes of animal skins to cover their nakedness. After the exile, he continues to supervise the human family: Eve bears her first son, **Cain**, "with the help of Yahweh" (Gen. 4:2). When Cain jealously murders his younger brother **Abel**, Yahweh marks the fugitive Cain to protect him from people (of unexplained origin) who would kill the man guilty of the first fratricide (Gen. 4: 13–16). Despite Yahweh's oversight, J pictures the human condition as rapidly deteriorating. The cost of knowledge is not only disruption of the divine–human and male–female relationships but also the introduction of fratricide and the proliferation of uncontrolled violence. J's list of Cain's descendants culminates in **Lamech**'s savage declaration that he avenges every wrong "seventy-sevenfold," a bloodthirsty egoism that defies Yahweh's plan for humanity (Gen. 4:17–24) and runs counter to the later Mosaic principle of strict retaliatory justice (Exod. 21:24).

Enoch   Chapter 5 is P's genealogy of the descendants of **Adam** (now used as a proper name), whose extraordinary longevity seems to echo the even longer life spans credited to antediluvian rulers in the Mesopotamian king lists. Especially remarkable are **Methuselah**, who lives to be 969 years old, and **Enoch**, who dies at the comparatively youthful age of 365 (perhaps representing a solar year). Enoch's fate— "he vanished because God took him" (Gen. 5:24)—has kindled considerable speculation. Like the prophet Elijah, swept heavenward centuries later in a fiery chariot (another symbol of the sun), Enoch became a figure of myth who, after touring heaven, returned to earth to reveal its mysteries. The three pseudepigraphal books of Enoch, one of which is quoted in the New Testament book of Jude, were supposedly written by the Genesis patriarch. (See the discussion of 1 and 2 Enoch in Part 7.)

The Composite J-P Flood Story

Noah and the Flood   J borrows from another ancient Near Eastern myth—the rebellion of divine beings who fall from heaven—for his introduction to the story of Noah's Flood. "Sons of God," the same term used for members of the celestial court in Job 1–2, violate Yahweh's boundaries between matter and spirit by mating with mortal women, producing a hybrid offspring, the Nephilim. As in classical Greek myths about the Titans' ejection from heaven and gods siring human children such as the strongman Heracles, the Nephilim produce a race of celebrated heroes (Gen. 6:1–4). Although J makes no explicit connection, he implies that these "famous men" are responsible for the general "wickedness" that corrupts earth's population, making the Deity "regret" having created humanity (Gen. 6:5–8). Even while planning to eliminate the vast majority of humanity as a failed experiment, however, Yahweh also intervenes to preserve Noah and his family—a saving act that expresses the Bible writers' belief that God redeems those who obey or "walk with [him]" as Noah does (Gen. 6:8).

The Genesis **Flood** narrative is a composite work, incorporating originally independent accounts by J and P. Although now intricately blended together, separating two complete versions of the story and placing them side-by-side is possible. Using the divine name *Yahweh*, J states that **Noah** took seven pairs of clean and two pairs of unclean animals into the **ark** (Gen. 7:2–3). P, who uses the generic term *Elohim* and believes that legal distinctions between clean and unclean were not revealed until the time of Moses, states that only one pair of each kind was taken aboard (6:19–20). J has the Flood last forty days and nights (7:4–12), as opposed to P's view that the Flood crested after 150 days (7: 24). The J and P duplications include two different divine commands to enter the ark (P in 6:18–20; J in 7:1–3), two separate entrances by Noah and his family (7:7 and 7:13), and two divine promises never again to drown the earth (8:21 and 9:11). Behind both accounts lie much older Mesopotamian traditions of a global deluge in which the wise god Ea instructs a favored

patriarch to build a ship that will carry pairs of all life forms. The most complete surviving texts occur in the Sumero-Babylonian *Epic of Gilgamesh* and the *Atrahasis Epic,* which offer exceptionally detailed parallels to the J and P story. (See "Excerpts from the Mesopotamian Flood Story in the Gilgamesh Epic" on pages 84–85.) Although geologists have found no evidence that a single catastrophic flood ever overwhelmed all of Mesopotamia, much less the entire planet, these ancient tales of divine retribution continue for many to function as prototypes of future world judgment (2 Pet. 3:3–7).

Emphasizing that in God's purpose even disaster involves a creative and saving element, Chapter 9 presents the postdiluvian world as a new beginning for humanity. After repeating his command to "be fruitful" and repopulate the earth (cf. Gen. 1:28 with 9:7), God unilaterally institutes the first of four important Old Testament covenants. The covenant with Noah and his descendants is universal, encompassing all of humanity. Described as "everlasting," it includes a declaration of the sacredness of life, both human and animal, and a divine promise never again to drown the earth (Gen. 9:1–11). Like the later Abrahamic and Mosaic covenants, the pact with Noah (referred to as the Noachan) has a "sign"—the rainbow as a visible symbol of God's reconciliation with humanity. (See "The Covenants with Noah and Abraham" on pages 86–87.) The Flood narrative thus concludes with another echo of the Gilgamesh epic. In the Sumero-Babylonian account, after the flood has abated, the goddess Ishtar expresses her relief by flinging her jeweled necklace into the sky. Ishtar's gems remain as a sparkling pledge that the gods will refrain from returning the world to its original state of watery chaos.

Chapters 10 and 11 trace the genealogies of Noah's three sons, **Shem, Ham,** and **Japheth,** who represent the three principal branches of the human family known to the ancient Hebrews. From Shem came the Semitic peoples, among them the Babylonians, Assyrians, Arabs, and Israelites. Ham was the eponymous

Excerpts from the Mesopotamian Flood Story in the Gilgamesh Epic

Living on a floodplain bordering the Euphrates and Tigris rivers, the ancient inhabitants of Mesopotamia repeatedly experienced severe floods, some of which destroyed early centers of civilization. Two Mesopotamian poems, the epics of Gilgamesh and Atrahasis, render ancient flood traditions in terms of a single catastrophic event that wipes out all of humanity, except for a single patriarch who survives by building an ark. In the Sumero-Babylonian epic of Gilgamesh, the title hero, seeking everlasting life, visits his ancestor Utnapishtim, the only man to survive the global deluge. Utnapishtim tells Gilgamesh that long ago when the gods, led by Enlil, deity of storm and wind, determined to drown all humanity, Ea, the kindly god of wisdom, warned Utnapishtim of the coming disaster. Like the biblical Noah, Utnapishtim is ordered to construct a wooden ark, stock it with supplies, and take aboard animals and birds.

> Utnapishtim spoke to him, to Gilgamesh,
> 'Let me reveal to you a closely guarded matter, Gilgamesh,
> And let me tell you the secret of the gods.
> Shuruppak is a city that you yourself know,
> Situated [on the bank of] the Euphrates.
> That city was already old when the gods within it
> Decided that the great gods should make a flood.
> There was Anu their father,
> Warrior Ellil their counsellor . . .
> Far-sighted Ea swore the oath (of secrecy) with them,
> So he repeated their speech to a reed hut,
> "Reed hut, reed hut, brick wall, brick wall,
> Listen, reed hut, and pay attention, brick wall.
> (This is the message:)
> Man of Shuruppak, son of Ubara-Tutu,

> Dismantle your house, build a boat.
> Leave possessions, search out living things.
> Reject chattels and save lives!
> Put aboard the seed of all living things, into the boat.
> The boat that you are to build
> Shall have her dimensions in proportion,
> Her width and length shall be in harmony,
> Roof her like the Apsu."
> I realized and spoke to my master Ea,
> "I have paid attention to the words that you spoke in this way,
> My master, and I shall act upon them.
> But how can I explain myself to the city, the men and the elders?"
> Ea made his voice heard and spoke,
> He said to me, his servant,
> "You shall speak to them thus:
> "I think that Ellil [Enlil] has rejected me,
> And so I cannot stay in your city,
> And I cannot set foot on Ellil's land again.
> I must go down to the Apsu and stay with my master Ea . . ."
> I put on board the boat all my kith and kin.
> Put on board cattle from open country, wild beasts from open country, all kinds of craftsmen.
> Shamash had fixed the hour:
> "In the morning cakes/"darkness",
> In the evening a rain of wheat/"heaviness"
> (I) shall shower down:
> Enter into the boat and shut your door!"
> That hour arrived;
> In the morning cakes/"darkness", in the evening a rain of wheat/"heaviness" showered down.
> I saw the shape of the storm,
> The storm was terrifying to see.
> I went aboard the boat and closed the door.
> To seal the boat I handed over the (floating) palace with her cargo to Puzur-Amurru the boatman. . . .

(name-giving) ancestor of the Egyptians and their (then) dependents, including the Canaanites, and Japheth was the supposed progenitor of the Aegean Sea peoples, including the Greeks and Philistines. This "table of nations" concludes Genesis' summary of primeval history.

The Story of Abraham and Sarah

After surveying the human race as a whole (Chs. 1–11), the Genesis account narrows in Chapter 12 to focus on the ancestors of a single

[Storm gods bring the Flood, returning the world
to a dark watery chaos.]
Everything light turned to darkness.
On the first day the tempest [rose up],
Blew swiftly and [brought (?) the flood-weapon],
Like a battle force [the destructive *kašūšu*-weapon]
passed over [the people]
No man could see his fellow,
Nor could people be distinguished from the sky.
Even the gods were afraid of the flood-weapon.
They withdrew; they went up to the heaven of
Anu.
The gods cowered, like dogs crouched by an out-
side wall.
Ishtar screamed like a woman giving birth;
The Mistress of the Gods, sweet of voice, was
wailing,
"Has that time really returned to clay,
Because I spoke evil in the gods' assembly?
How could I have spoken such evil in the gods'
assembly?
I should have (?) ordered a battle to destroy my
people;
I myself gave birth (to them), they are my own
people,
Yet they fill the sea like fish spawn!"
The gods of the Anunnaki were weeping with
her.
The gods, humbled, sat there weeping.
Their lips were closed and covered with scab.
For six days and [seven (?)] nights
The wind blew, flood and tempest overwhelmed
the land;
When the seventh day arrived the tempest, flood
and onslaught
Which had struggled like a woman in labour, blew
themselves out (?).
The sea became calm, the *imhullu*-wind grew
quiet, the flood held back.

I looked at the weather; silence reigned,
For all mankind had returned to clay.
The flood-plain was flat as a roof.
I opened a porthole and light fell on my cheeks.
I bent down, then sat. I wept.
My tears ran down my cheeks.
I looked for banks, for limits to the sea.
Areas of land were emerging everywhere (?).
The boat had come to rest on Mount Nimush.
The mountain Nimush held the boat fast and did
not let it budge. . . .
When the seventh day arrived,
I put out and released a dove.
The dove went; it came back,
For no perching place was visible to it, and it
turned round.
I put out and released a swallow.
The swallow went; it came back,
For no perching place was visible to it, and it
turned round.
I put out and released a raven.
The raven went, and saw the waters receding.
And it ate, preened (?), lifted its tail and did not
turn round.
Then I put (everything ?) out to the four winds,
and I made a sacrifice. . . .
The gods smelt the fragrance,
The gods smelt the pleasant fragrance,
The gods like flies gathered over the sacrifice.
As soon as the Mistress of the Gods arrived
She raised the great flies which Anu had made to
please her:
"Behold, O gods, I shall never forget (the signifi-
cance of) my lapis lazuli necklace,
I shall remember these times, and I shall never
forget.
[As in Genesis, the rainbow (Ishtar's jeweled neck-
lace) serves to remind the gods of the conse-
quences of their destructive impulses.]

nation, Israel. The remainder of Genesis (Chs. 12–50) is devoted to tracing the stories of Abraham, progenitor of the future Israel, and his colorful descendants through four turbulent generations. Opening with God's call to Abraham in **Haran**, northwestern Mesopotamia, the action then shifts all over the map of the Fertile Crescent, ending with Abraham's now-numerous descendants settled in Egypt. Despite the variety in their stories and their constant journeyings between the Euphrates and the Nile, however, a series of over-arching themes

The Covenants with Noah and Abraham

An extremely important biblical concept, a covenant (Hebrew, *berit*) is a vow, promise, contract, agreement, or pact. The Bible writers commonly use the term to express Yahweh's purposeful relationship with an individual or a nation. In the ancient Near Eastern culture out of which the Bible grew, there were two principal forms of covenant: (1) the *suzerainty covenant,* a political treaty between a superior party who dictated the terms of the arrangement and an inferior party who obeyed them, and (2) the *parity covenant,* an agreement between equals who were both obligated to observe its provisions.

In the Hebrew Bible, Yahweh, the great king or suzerain, initiates four major covenants—all an expression of divine graciousness in God's voluntarily binding himself to a person or a people. Genesis contains the texts of two formal covenants—the Noachan and Abrahamic—and some commentators believe that others are implied in the two creation accounts. Although *berit* is not mentioned in Genesis 1, some scholars believe that a covenant relationship is suggested when Elohim grants humanity dominion over the earth and a command to populate it (Gen. 1: 26–31). A comparable legal implication occurs in Yahweh's directive to cultivate Eden and his prohibition against tasting the tree of knowledge (Gen. 2:16–17). The first explicitly stated covenant, a recapitulation of God's order to procreate, is promulgated through Noah (Gen. 9:1–17). Universal in scope, encompassing all living creatures, both human and animal, it emphasizes the sacredness of life and the faithfulness of God, who promises never again to inundate the world. Its "sign" is the rainbow.

The second formal covenant that Yahweh initiates in Genesis is with Abraham for the benefit of his descendants. Because ancient compilers apparently used a variety of sources, Genesis contains several versions or aspects of the Abrahamic covenant. In Genesis 15, Yahweh, like a powerful king making a land grant to a favored subject, promises the land of Canaan (Palestine) to Abraham's progeny (the Israelites). The oath is ratified by an ancient ritual in which Yahweh passes between the two halves of a dismembered sacrificial animal. (A parallel covenant rite is described

unifies the diverse adventures of Israel's patriarchs and matriarchs. Genesis's unifying motifs include the varied human responses to a divine call: Abraham always reacts immediately and obediently when he hears God's voice, whereas his grandson, the wily **Jacob**, usually responds cautiously, even ambivalently. Abraham's wife, **Sarah**, laughs out loud in Yahweh's presence after he promises the long-infertile—and very elderly—woman a child. Others, such as Jacob's half-brother Esau, seem deaf to divine promptings.

Besides the call-response theme and the endless patriarchal wanderings they elicit, the Genesis stories are characterized by a series of obstacles that threaten to defeat God's promise to make Abraham's heirs a great and populous nation. The first obstacle takes the form of a difficulty common in folklore, the "barren wife." Even before relating Yahweh's sudden appearance to Abraham, the author notes that Sarah is infertile (Gen. 11:30), a condition that will also afflict the next two generations of Hebrew matriarchs, Rebekah and Rachel. With Sarah's inability to bear children already announced, the Yahwist's sense of ironic humor is evident when he has Yahweh proclaim that the aged and childless Abraham will produce enough descendants to populate an entire country (Gen. 12:1–3).

When Abraham dutifully travels to Canaan, Yahweh appears again, at **Shechem**, a Cain Jer. 34:18–21.) A later priestly account of the covenant (Gen. 17) repeats Yahweh's pledge about Canaan, states that Abraham will father a "multitude of nations," including a line of kings, and stresses circumcision of all Jewish males as a sign "in perpetuity" of the God's self-imposed bond with Israel. Yahweh also promises that "all the nations of the earth" will "bless themselves" because of Abraham (Gen. 12:3, 22:18).

The theme of kingly descendants anticipates the Davidic Covenant, in which Yahweh vows to keep King David's royal heirs on Judah's throne forever (2 Sam. 7:8–17; Ps. 89:19–37). The Deity's pacts with both Abraham and David are similarly unconditional, with the human beneficiaries required to do nothing in return, although circumcision functions as evidence that Abraham's progeny recognize their covenant status. Because the Genesis covenants assumed their literary form during and after the Davidic monarchy, many scholars believe that the Deity's oath to produce a royal line from Abraham is modeled on the pact with David. (See Part 4.)

The Noachan, Abrahamic, and Davidic covenants differ strikingly in degree, if not entirely in kind, from the Mosaic Covenant articulated in Exodus. (See "The Mosaic Covenant at Mount Sinai" on pages 102–103.) Although Noah, Abraham, and David display a trusting obedience to Yahweh's demands, which is presumably the reason for their being selected as covenant bearers, the Genesis and Davidic covenants place much less stress on reciprocal obligation from the human parties involved. According to the priestly rendition of the Abrahamic vow, the patriarch is to "bear himself blameless," implying a continuing moral relation between him and Yahweh (Gen. 17:1–2), but the Deity does not require an oath of obedience or a long list of legal stipulations comparable to that enunciated in the Mosaic pact. (The priestly reference to Abraham's keeping statutes and laws [Gen. 26:4–6] may be an effort to bring the Abrahamic tradition, at least partially, in line with the later Mosaic arrangement.) Throughout the historical narratives from Genesis to 2 Kings, and many of the prophetic books as well, a painful tension exists between the two different kinds of covenant: Yahweh's unconditional promises to Abraham (for land, progeny, and blessing) and to David (for an everlasting royal dynasty) seem to run counter to the conditional terms of the Mosaic covenant, in which God's help and protection depend almost entirely on Israel's loyal obedience to divine law.

naanite shrine and future holy place of Israel's northern tribes. The tantalizing promise to give Abraham's as yet nonexistent heirs the land of Canaan is reiterated, but new difficulties arise, keeping the tension alive between Yahweh's apparent intentions and their actual fulfillment. A famine strikes Canaan, sending Abraham away from the Promised Land to Egypt, where the pharaoh, overcome by Sarah's mature beauty, takes her into his harem. God maneuvers pharaoh to release Sarah unharmed and the couple returns to Canaan, but there is still no sign of an heir. After successfully fighting a coalition of Canaanite princes who had kidnapped his nephew **Lot**, Abraham offers a tribute from his spoils of war to the mysterious **Melchizedek**, king-priest of Salem (probably the future site of Jerusalem).

The Abrahamic Covenant

When Yahweh next appears to him, Abraham pointedly reminds his God that he remains childless, eliciting a renewed promise of an heir that will be his "own flesh and blood." Yahweh then conducts an elaborate animal sacrifice ratifying his compact—covenant—with Abraham (Gen. 15:1–18). The Abrahamic Covenant, four different versions of which are included in Genesis (Gen. 12:2–3; 15:1–21; 17:1–22; 22:15–18), is a solemn contractual agreement by which Yahweh pledges to make Abraham "the father of a multitude of nations" (particularly the future Israel); to give Abraham's "countless" descendants "the whole land of Canaan"; and to be their God in a special covenant relationship forever. The version given in Chapter 15 specifies the Promised Land's boundaries, which are to encompass all of the territory from the "wadi of Egypt to the Great River" Euphrates (Gen. 15:18). Not until the reigns of David and Solomon during the tenth century B.C.E. did Israel's frontiers extend to these limits, and then only for a brief period. In Genesis 17 (a priestly source), Yahweh stipulates that he requires **circumcision**—surgically removing the foreskin of the male organ—of Abraham and all of his male progeny. Ritually performed on infants eight days old, circumcision became the physical sign of the Israelite's covenant relationship with Yahweh. (In New Testament times, this practice became a source of intense controversy between Jewish Christians and their Gentile converts; see Paul's letter to the Galatians, Part 10.)

At age 86, eleven years after first receiving Yahweh's sworn oath to give him heirs, Abraham finally has a son—**Ishmael**—but by an Egyptian slave girl, **Hagar**, not by his wife, Sarah. Another thirteen years pass, and Abraham is ninety-nine, before Yahweh appears again to proclaim that within a year the patriarch and his wife will have a son. Sarah, who overhears the visitor's prophecy, reflects on the physical impossibility of fulfillment: She has long passed the time of menstruation and her husband is "an old man," sexually incapable, she presumes, and she laughs derisively (Gen. 18:1–15). In the Genesis tradition, however, it is precisely *because* the couple has reached an advanced age and cannot reproduce that the divinely planned moment has finally arrived. Within a year, Abraham and Sarah have an heir of their "own flesh and blood"—**Isaac**, whose name ("laughter") echoes his mother's mirth at hearing an "impossible" prediction.

Abraham's Debate with God

At the time of Yahweh's visit under the oak tree at Mamre, Isaac's birth still lies in the future and Abraham is presently concerned about the value his God places on human life. Yahweh states that he is on his way personally to inspect the cities of **Sodom** and Gomorrah, for he has heard rumors of their wickedness. Perceiving Yahweh's intention to annihilate the cities' entire populations, Abraham is appalled. "Will the Judge of the whole earth not administer justice?" he asks. Apparently cornered by Abraham's meek but persistent questioning, Yahweh finally declares that he will not destroy the cities for the sake of even ten righteous souls. In popular opinion, Yahweh's anger against Sodom is commonly alleged to have been kindled by its residents' homosexuality. Later Bible writers, however, cite quite different reasons for the city's destruction, including its failure to help the "poor and needy" and its inhospitable violence to strangers. (See Ezekiel's comparison of Sodom and Judah [Ezek. 16:48–58].)

Before fire from heaven consumes Sodom and its four sister cities, Yahweh, out of regard for Abraham, rescues Lot and his two daughters. Like Noah after an even greater cataclysm, Lot becomes intoxicated and—his wife having been changed into a pillar of salt—commits incest with his two daughters, whose sons subsequently become the eponymous ancestors of Moab and Ammon, two small nations that border Israel. The Genesis authors commonly present a single individual as the progenitor of an entire people or state. Jacob's brother **Esau** literally "is **Edom**" (Gen. 36:1); Jacob is identified as Israel (35:10), and the names of his twelve sons are identical with the later **twelve tribes of Israel** (Gen. 29:31; 30:24; 35:16–20; 49:16).

After all of the delays and misadventures that had prevented Sarah and Abraham from having an heir through whom a "great nation" would derive, it is a shock to find that Yahweh himself becomes the next obstacle toward fulfilling his

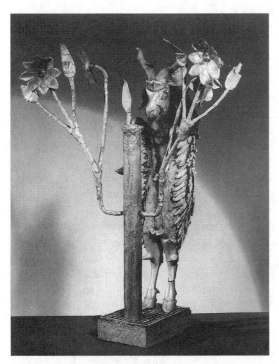

A treasure from the Royal Cemetery of Ur, this ornamental goat stands on its hind legs, leaning against a golden plant. Probably a fertility icon, the goat has horns and eyes of lapis lazuli, with face, horns, and legs of wood overlaid with gold. (Courtesy of the University Museum, University of Pennsylvania [Neg. S5-23190])

"all nations of the earth" (Gen. 22:15–18; italics added) will someday bless themselves because of him, an oath that expresses the universality of God's purpose for humanity.

"Overwhelmed . . . with blessings," Abraham dies at age 175 and is buried near Sarah's grave in Canaan (Gen. 25:7–11)—the only tiny piece of the Promised Land that Abraham ever owns. A model of the righteous person ever sensitive to the divine presence, Abraham stands at the head of a line of biblical heroes leading to Moses, Isaiah, King David, and, in the New Testament, Jesus of Nazareth. As "father of the Jews," he is covenant-bearer and forefather of the nation by which global blessings will come. The first person in the Hebrew Bible to argue with God on behalf of human rights and to persuade the Almighty to acknowledge his obligation to preserve life, Abraham establishes a pattern of divine-human interaction that later was pursued by Moses and Job. As some New Testament writers observed, Abraham is a person both of faith (Gal. 3:6–9; Heb. 11:8–10) and of active obedience (James 2:21–23). It is Abraham's self-surrender, his willingness to submit every part of his life to Yahweh's will, that sets him apart from other people. His devotion to Yahweh is surpassed only by Yahweh's wish to honor him as he had honored no other human being. Illustrating the biblical theme of divine election—God's practice of voluntarily initiating close relationships with favored persons—Yahweh vows to give Abraham the only form of immortality recognized in Torah, posthumous survival through progeny and a reputation "so famous it will be used as a blessing." In the Genesis tradition, a favorable response to Abraham is tantamount to standing right with God:

vow. After Isaac is nearly grown, God abruptly demands that Abraham offer the boy as a blood sacrifice. Abraham's willingness to comply, and his silence in the face of this horrific demand, are not altogether surprising in their historical context. As the tradition preserved in Exodus states, the firstborn son, as well as the firstborn of flocks and herds of cattle, belongs to Yahweh and is his to command (Exod. 22:30, 34:20). Abraham has already lifted the knife to cut his son's throat when an angel intervenes, substituting a ram in the lad's place. Yahweh then reaffirms his covenant promises and adds that as a reward for Abraham's supreme obedience,

> I will bless those who bless you.
> I will curse those who slight you.
> All the tribes of the earth
> shall bless themselves by you.
> Genesis 12:2–3

The Story of Jacob and His Family

After devoting a dozen chapters to Abraham, Genesis passes briefly over the career of Isaac, a relatively passive figure who is more notable for what is done to him—his youthful brush with sacrificial death and the deceptions perpetrated on him in his old age—than for anything he initiates himself. A much stronger and more vivid character is that of Isaac's wife, **Rebekah**, who behaves with telling decisiveness. Rebekah first appears in Genesis 24 when Abraham's servant returns to the patriarch's homeland in northwestern Mesopotamia to find Isaac a mate who has the same ethnic background. Rebekah at once manifests the hospitality that marks an admirable person and then, recognizing a divinely presented opportunity, courageously volunteers to accept an unknown bridegroom and cast her lot in a strange land. She later demonstrates a similar initiative in manipulating Isaac, child of the promise, to bless his (potentially) more worthy son, her favorite, Jacob. Depicted as having received Yahweh's prenatal revelation of intent concerning her younger child, Rebekah plays a major part in Israel's destiny, ensuring that the covenant promises are transmitted through Yahweh's chosen agent (Gen. 27:5–28:5). By placing a woman at the center of his account of the second-generation ancestors, the JE narrators achieve a meaningful balance between male and female participation in fulfilling the Deity's goals for humanity.

A spiritual cousin of the quick-witted Greek hero Odysseus (Ulysses), Jacob begins his career by persuading his older twin brother, Esau, to give him the birthright (inheritance) that traditionally belonged to the eldest son (Gen. 25:29–34). Under Rebekah's influence, Jacob tricks the blind and dying Isaac into bestowing the paternal blessing on him rather than on Esau, earning his brother's understandable enmity. Later, Jacob outwits his father-in-law, Laban (for whom he had labored fourteen years to earn his favorite wife, **Rachel**), escapes with Laban's status-conferring household idols (the teraphim), and eventually becomes a rich man (Gen. 25:19–34; 27:1–32:2).

Jacob's Vision at Bethel While traveling toward Haran, still inhabited by his Mesopotamian kinfolk, Jacob has his first significant experience of the divine. Sleeping outdoors with a stone for his pillow, he dreams of a "ladder" reaching from earth to heaven on which angels are ascending and descending (as Mesopotamian deities invisibly tread the ceremonial stairway of a Babylonian ziggurat). Yahweh appears in the dream and restates the Abrahamic Covenant, adding a promise to ensure Jacob's personal safety on his journey. On awakening, Jacob is awed by the sanctity of the place, which he renames **Bethel**, "house of God" (Gen. 28:10–22). Unwilling to commit himself to Yahweh on the basis of a mere dream, however, he vows to make Yahweh his god only on certain conditions: "*If* God goes with me and keeps me safe . . . *if* he gives me bread to eat and clothes to wear, and *if* I return home safely . . . *then* Yahweh shall be my God" (Gen. 28:20–22, italics added).

A more direct encounter occurs at **Peniel**, where Jacob literally wrestles with God, from whom he coerces a blessing and who consequently changes Jacob's name to Israel, interpreted here as "he who has been strong against God" (Gen. 32:23–32). This mysterious incident, in which he feels that he has "seen God face to face," indicates that even the wily Jacob has inherited some of his grandfather Abraham's spirituality. His two encounters with the supernatural, at Bethel and Peniel, suggest a progress in Jacob's maturation. In the first, he had bargained with God, consenting to acknowledge him only if the Deity guaranteed his safety and worldly ambitions; in the second, he intimately experienced his God's presence, undergoing a transformation signified by his change of name.

In a second version of the account in which Jacob's name is changed to Israel, the event takes place not at Peniel but at Bethel, where God—here called El Shaddai—renews his covenant vow and adds that Jacob's descendants will include kings (Gen. 35:1–14). Divine favor is further confirmed when Esau, the brother whom Jacob had repeatedly cheated and whose revenge he fears, welcomes him graciously (Gen. 32:32–33). Jacob's improved relationship with God also results in the blessing of another son, **Benjamin**, by his beloved wife, Rachel.

Joseph in Egypt

Joseph and His Brothers   With the exception of a brief interpolated tale involving Judah and Tamar (Gen. 38), the remainder of Genesis tells the success story of Jacob's favored son, **Joseph**. Although a self-contained literary unit, the Joseph saga significantly advances the general historical plan of Genesis, for here we see Yahweh's will operating in the lives of unsuspecting individuals for the accomplishment of his predestined purpose. Interestingly, it is only a petty family squabble among brothers that sets the elaborate story in motion and, in the Hebrew view, ultimately changes the course of world history.

As Yahweh had favored Abraham and Jacob above all others, so God favors Joseph, making him the chief representative of the fourth patriarchal generation. Singled out as the recipient of prophetic dreams—and given the sage's ability to interpret others' dreams as well—Joseph rashly antagonizes his ten older brothers by telling them two dreams that foreshadow his future greatness. In the first dream, the ten brothers bow low before Joseph, honoring his superiority; in the second, even the sun, moon, and stars do obeisance. When Joseph in effect presents himself as a figure of cosmic stature—a deity—his jealous brothers take the first opportunity to get rid of their offensively ambitious sibling.

The present text combines the originally independent J and E traditions, offering two con-

flicting versions of the plot against Joseph. In E's version, after Reuben (representing a northern tribe) persuades his brothers not to kill Joseph, they throw the youth into a well, where passing Midianites extricate him and take him to Egypt. In J's account, Judah (representing the southern tribe) intercedes for his seventeen-year-old brother, suggesting that Joseph not be harmed but be sold as a slave to a caravan of Ishmaelites, who then transport him to Egypt.

As a result of editors' bringing together two different literary strands, Joseph is twice sold into Egyptian slavery, first by E's Midianites (37:36) and then by J's Ishmaelites (39:1–2). In both cases, his buyer and new master is Potiphar, an important official at pharaoh's court. At this point, the author apparently makes creative use of an ancient Egyptian tale about a virtuous young man who resists the attempt of his master's wife to seduce him and who subsequently rises to become one of Egypt's top administrators. (See the recommended reading, Pritchard.) Although he rejects the advances of Potiphar's wife, Joseph (as in the Egyptian "Tale of Two Brothers") is falsely accused of betraying his master and is thrown in prison.

Even in jail, Yahweh is "kind" to Joseph, making him "popular with the chief jailer," who places the Hebrew in charge of the other prisoners. His ability correctly to interpret the dream of one of pharaoh's imprisoned courtiers eventually leads to his being released from jail and brought to pharaoh's court. Joseph's famous interpretation of pharaoh's dreams of seven years of prosperity followed by seven years of famine leads to his being appointed governor of all Egypt. The next stage of Yahweh's plan is now manifest: Joseph's spectacular rise from slavery to power, followed by a famine that afflicts the whole Near East, will bring the ten sons of Jacob (Israel) to Egypt seeking grain.

Although they do not recognize him, Joseph—after putting his brothers and aged father through years of anguish—eventually reveals his identity and, with impressive self-dramatization, forgives them. At pharaoh's invitation, the elderly Jacob also comes to Egypt along with his sons' families and livestock. Grateful to Joseph for making Egypt well-fed and secure during a period of international hunger and unrest, pharaoh grants land to the previously nomadic Hebrews who, according to one version of the story, settle in Goshen, an area of the Nile Delta. Genesis concludes with Abraham's descendants settled in a foreign country, far from the land God had promised them. Even so, Joseph's prophetic gifts are used to foretell Israel's future return to Canaan: The dying patriarch asks that when the Israelite tribes leave Egypt, his mummified remains be carried away with them (Gen. 50:24–26).

The Hyksos

Some historians have suggested that the pharaoh who welcomed Joseph's family into Egypt belonged to a foreign dynasty, the **Hyksos**, Asiatic invaders who had established their rule in the delta area during the late eighteenth century B.C.E. It was reasoned that, because many of the Hyksos invaders were Semitic, they favored other Semitic immigrants—thus accounting for Joseph's spectacular rise in pharaoh's service. After the native Egyptian Eighteenth Dynasty expelled the Hyksos, however, there arose a pharaoh who "knew nothing of Joseph" (Exod. 1:18) and began to oppress his people.

Although this view would help explain the drastic reversal of the Hebrews' fortunes, from honored administrators to slaves, most historians now find the Hyksos theory untenable. No evidence exists to support the notion that the Hyksos occupation coincided with the period that the Israelite tribes spent in Egypt. Neither Egyptian records nor archaeological investigations have been able to verify the Hebrews' presence in Egypt, much less to establish a date for it. According to Exodus 12:40, the tribes remained in Egypt for 430 years, which would place their arrival in the first half of the nineteenth century B.C.E., too early for the Hyksos. The chronology becomes more complex when another Torah reference, Exodus 6:16–20, states that only four generations—Jacob's son **Levi** to Moses—lived in Egypt.

Like the later compilers of Israel's history, the Genesis authors are less interested in recording literal fact than in conveying the religious meaning of humanity's historical experience. Viewing Yahweh-Elohim as Sovereign of the universe and Lord of history, they emphasize God's actions in directing historical events to fulfill his grand design, the reconciliation of humans with their creator, from whom their disobedience has estranged them. Exalting the Deity's saving acts, Genesis sets the stage for the next step in the Torah's long creation story—the formation of a people bearing Yahweh's name.

RECOMMENDED READING

Anderson, Bernhard W. *Creation Versus Chaos: The Reinterpretation of Mythical Symbolism in the Bible.* New York: Association Press, 1967.

———, ed. *Creation in the Old Testament.* Philadelphia: Fortress Press, 1984.

Bailey, Lloyd R. *Genesis, Creation, and Creationism.* Mahwah, N.J.: Paulist Press, 1991. A professor of Hebrew Bible examines the claims of fundamental creationists.

Coats, George W. *Genesis.* Grand Rapids, Mich.: Eerdmans, 1983.

Eissfeldt, Otto. "Genesis." In G. A. Buttrick, ed., *The Interpreter's Dictionary of the Bible,* Vol. 2, pp. 366–380. New York and Nashville, Tenn.: Abingdon Press, 1962.

Ellis, Peter. *The Yahwist: The Bible's First Theologian.* Notre Dame, Ind.: Fides, 1968.

Fox, Everett, ed. *The Five Books of Moses.* The Schocken Bible, Vol. 1. New York: Schocken Books, 1995. A superb new translation that captures the flavor of the original Hebrew.

Fretheim, Terence E. "The Book of Genesis." In *The New Interpreter's Bible*. Vol. 1, pp. 321–674. Nashville, Tenn.: Abingdon Press, 1994. Contains extensive scholarly commentary on the Genesis text.

Hendel, Ronald S. "Genesis, Book of." In D. N. Freedman, ed., *The Anchor Bible Dictionary*, Vol. 2, pp. 933–941. New York: Doubleday, 1992.

Jeansonne, Sharon P. *The Women of Genesis: From Sarah to Potiphar's Wife*. Minneapolis: Fortress Press, 1990.

Kikawada, Isaac M. "Primeval History." In D. N. Freedman, ed., *The Anchor Bible Dictionary*, Vol. 5, pp. 461–466. New York: Doubleday, 1992. Examines Genesis 1–11, placing biblical narrative in the context of Near Eastern creation and flood myths.

Levenson, Jon D. *Creation and the Persistence of Evil: The Jewish Drama of Divine Omnipotence*. San Francisco: Harper & Row, 1988.

Niditch, Susan. *Chaos to Cosmos: Studies in Biblical Patterns of Creation*. Chico, Calif.: Scholars Press, 1985.

Pritchard, James B., ed. *Ancient Near Eastern Texts Relating to the Old Testament*, 3rd ed. Princeton, N.J.: Princeton University Press, 1969. Contains "The Story of Two Brothers" that an Israelite author adapted for the Joseph story in Genesis.

Sarna, Nahum M. *Understanding Genesis*. New York: Schocken Books, 1970.

Scullion, John J. "Genesis, The Narrative of." In D. N. Freedman, ed., *The Anchor Bible Dictionary*, Vol. 2, pp. 941–962. New York: Doubleday, 1992.

Speiser, E. A., ed. *Genesis* (Anchor Bible). Garden City, N.Y.: Doubleday, 1964. Scholarly translation with extensive notes.

Trible, Phyllis. *God and the Rhetoric of Sexuality*. Philadelphia: Fortress Press, 1978. A close examination of Genesis 2–3 and other relevant biblical texts.

von Rad, Gerhard. *Genesis*. Philadelphia: Westminster Press, 1972. A standard work.

Westermann, Claus. *Genesis 1–11*. Minneapolis: Augsburg, 1984.

———. *Genesis 12–36*. Minneapolis: Augsburg, 1985.

———. *Genesis 37–50*. Minneapolis: Augsburg, 1986.

TERMS AND CONCEPTS TO REMEMBER

Abel	Edom
Adam	Enoch
ark	*Enuma Elish*
Babel	Esau
Benjamin	Eve
Bethel	Fall, the
Cain	firmament
cherub, cherubim (pl.)	Flood, the
	Hagar
circumcision	Ham
Eden	Haran
Isaac	Hyksos
Ishmael	polytheism
Jacob	Rachel
Japheth	Rahab
Joseph	Rebekah (Rebecca)
Lamech	Sabbath
Levi	Sarah
Leviathan	serpent
Lot	Shechem
Melchizedek	Shem
Methuselah	Sodom
Noah	twelve tribes of Israel
Peniel	

QUESTIONS FOR REVIEW

1. Give three possible definitions of *Torah* and explain its traditional connection to the figure of Moses.

2. List some characteristics of the Torah that cause many scholars to doubt traditional Mosaic authorship. Define the documentary hypothesis, including the significance of the letters J, E, D, and P in designating different writers who supposedly contributed to the composite text. What are the distinguishing characteristics of the Yahwist, the Elohist, the Deuteronomist, and the priestly writers?

3. Describe some of the differences between the two creation accounts in Genesis 1 and

2. What issues concern the priestly author? Why do you suppose that in the Yahwist's account Yahweh creates the animals *after* Adam (humanity) is already formed?

4. Reread the two separate versions of Noah's flood that are interwoven in Genesis 6–8. What differences do you find between the Yahwist and the priestly accounts?

5. Describe some of the personal qualities and attributes that typify the Yahwist's portrait of Yahweh. In what ways does the Yahwist combine both creative and destructive aspects of God's nature?

6. Who were Abraham and Sarah? Describe the terms of Yahweh's promises to Abraham (the Abrahamic Covenant). In what ways is God's vow to Abraham like the oath God made to Noah after the flood? What test of Abraham's loyalty does Yahweh make of his servant? Does Abraham live to see the divine promises fulfilled?

7. What roles do Sarah, Rebekah, and Rachel play in the Genesis story of Israel's origins?

8. Describe Jacob's character. In what specific ways does his career depend upon trickiness or deceit? Why does he fear the anger of his brother Esau? How do Jacob's prayers to God change over time?

9. Explain how the twelve sons of Jacob come to dwell in Egypt. How does Joseph attain a position that allows him to fulfill his dream of lording it over his older brothers? At the end of Genesis, are Abraham's descendants any closer to possessing the Promised Land?

QUESTIONS FOR DISCUSSION AND REFLECTION

1. If scholars are correct in believing that Genesis is a composite work in which the ancient Yahwist and Elohist narratives were later re-edited by a priestly redactor to produce the present biblical text, would this affect your view of the book's value? Do you think that biblical authors were more concerned about achieving factual objectivity or about presenting an ethical or religious interpretation of the remote past?

2. Is the modern theory of biological evolution incompatible with Genesis's claim that God created humanity in his own image? Given the geological and paleontological evidence, particularly the fossil record (which was unknown to ancient writers), do you think it was possible that God could have employed the gradual evolution of species over long eons of time as his *method* of creation?

3. Why does Genesis picture God as initiating special relationships with particular individuals, such as Noah, Abraham, Jacob, and Joseph? Do you find any distinctive qualities—ethical or psychological—that these figures have in common that would make them suitable recipients of divine selection? Do you suppose that God initiated similar relationships with persons living in other parts of the world, areas unknown to Bible writers?

Exodus

KEY THEMES

A continuation of the creation epic, Exodus opens with the birth of Moses and climaxes with the birth of Israel's covenant community at Mount Sinai. The themes of conflict, separation, and distinction that characterize the biblical creation tradition reappear in Yahweh's contest with pharaoh, the separation of Israel from Egypt, the dividing of the Reed Sea, and the establishment of Yahweh's cult, which distinguishes his worshipers from all others. The book's main sections include the story of Moses (Chs. 2–6), the ten plagues and Passover (Chs. 7–13), the miraculous sea crossing and desert wanderings (Chs. 14–18), the theophany at Sinai and inauguration of the law covenant

(Chs. 19–24; 32–34), and instructions for the cult (Chs. 25–31; 35–40).

> I am Yahweh your God. . . . You shall have no gods but me.
>
> Exodus 20:1–3

Israel in Egypt

Exodus expresses the core of Israel's faith more than any other book in the Old Testament. An elaborate expansion of ancient creeds orally recited at Israelite sanctuaries (Deut. 26:6–10; Josh. 24:2–13), Exodus celebrates the origins of Israel's special relationship to Yahweh. Rather than an objective history in the modern sense, this second volume of the Torah is a composite record concerned with theologically interpreting national memories of the great events that bind Israel to Yahweh forever. Dominating the narrative are Yahweh's two saving acts that brought the nation into existence: the escape from slavery in Egypt and the revelation of the Torah at Mount Sinai. Combining narrative, legal codes, poetry, and theology, the book presents a vivid characterization of Yahweh and his loyal servant **Moses**.

As in Genesis, the disparate strands of J, E, and P are intricately interwoven. According to most scholarly analyses of the text, the Yahwist writer (J) supplies the main narrative, supplemented by excerpts from the E (Elohist) document. The final priestly editors (P) apparently thoroughly reworked the JE story, adding considerable genealogical, legal, and ritual material (such as that describing the tabernacle in Chapters 35–40). They also seem to have added numerous details to J's account, heightening the miraculous quality of Israel's passage through chaotic waters—called the **Sea of Reeds** in the Jerusalem Bible—and providing a second version of Moses' reception of the divine name (Exod. 6:3–13).

To date, historians and archaeologists have been unable to verify any of the events described in Exodus. No known Egyptian records refer to the escape of Hebrew slaves or the drowning of pharaoh's army. Nor do Egypt's many surviving archives mention the biblical Moses or the devastating plagues that his god Yahweh reputedly inflicted on the country. The authors do not identify either the **pharaoh** of the oppression or the **Exodus**, making it extremely difficult for scholars to establish a reliable chronology. Although some historians believe that Pharaoh **Rameses II** (c. 1290–1224 B.C.E) was Moses' opponent, no hard evidence exists to support this view. The single reference to an extrabiblical datum, the Hebrews' building "store cities of Pithom and **Rameses**" (1:11), is inconclusive, for these particular names were not widely used until the seventh century B.C.E. Some scholars believe that this statement was interpolated by a later editor.

The Story of Moses

Moses   No figure looms larger in Israel's history than Moses, the man who simultaneously fills the roles of lawgiver, prophet, judge, military leader, and founder of the Yahwist religion. Described as initially reluctant to take on the tasks Yahweh assigns him (Exod. 4:10–17), Moses becomes not only God's chief instrument in creating Israel but also God's intimate friend, speaking with Yahweh "face to face" (Deut. 34:10–11). Whereas Yahweh may commune indirectly with others by vision or dream, with Moses he "speaks plainly and not in riddles," permitting him to "see the form of Yahweh" (Num. 12:8). The books of Exodus through Deuteronomy, in effect, are Moses' biography; the first begins with his birth and the last closes with his death. Even the detailed legal material that forms the Torah's core (Exod. 35 through Num. 10) is part of Moses' story, because Moses is the mediator through whom Yahweh communicates his law. As Yahweh himself describes

The temple of Amon at Karnak, Egypt, has 134 gigantic columns bearing hieroglyphic inscriptions, one of which records Pharaoh Shiskak's invasion of Palestine (c. 918 B.C.E.). The massive structure was probably completed during the reign of Rameses II (c. 1290–1224 B.C.E.). (Courtesy of Erich Lessing / Magnum Photos)

Moses' role, this exceedingly meek man (Num. 12:3) with a debilitating speech impediment (Exod. 4:10–11) acts as "a god for pharaoh" (Exod. 7:1), a human embodiment of divine power.

In any other Near Eastern tradition than that of Israel, Moses would undoubtedly be accorded superhuman status, made another Sargon or Gilgamesh—a glorious hero who defies Egypt's tyrant, releases chaotic waters to drown pursuing armies, and leads his people through a dangerous wilderness to freedom and nationhood. While affirming Moses' unique contri-

bution to Israel's history, however, the Torah writers are careful to subordinate him to the God he serves. Rather than a hero in his own right, Moses is always Yahweh's obedient spokesman. The priestly authors who prepared the final edition of the Torah took pains to explain why Yahweh did not allow his most loyal servant to enter the Promised Land. "Because you did not believe that I could proclaim my holiness in the eyes of the sons of Israel," Yahweh tells Moses and Aaron, "you shall not lead the assembly" into Canaan (Num. 20:12). Although the precise nature of Moses' offense is uncertain, many commentators assume that it is the lawgiver's failure to give Yahweh full credit when he brings water gushing from a rock (Num. 20:10). Considering Moses' self-sacrificing devotion to Yahweh and his people—including his refusal to accept Yahweh's offer to make the family of Moses, and not Israel, his chosen nation (Num. 14:12)—God's verdict may seem unduly harsh. For the Torah writers, however, Moses is both a model of humble service *and* a demonstration that even the greatest of human beings cannot measure up to Yahweh's standard of perfect righteousness.

Moses' Early Life Scholars recognize that the Torah narrative combines too many differing strands of tradition to permit an accurate recovery of the "historical Moses." Whatever the deeds of the real figure of history, the Torah portrait as we have it includes legend and folklore. According to Exodus 1–2, Moses is born under pharaoh's command that all boys of his race be drowned, a fate he escapes when his mother secretly sets him adrift on the Nile in a watertight cradle. A childless daughter of pharaoh finds the boy and raises him as her own. Moses, a Levite, thus becomes familiar with the royal court and, according to a later tradition, is educated in "all the wisdom of the Egyptians" (Acts 7:22). Tales involving an infant who narrowly escapes death and later becomes a national hero are common throughout the ancient world. According to Akkadian legend, when the mother of **Sargon I** cast him adrift on the Euphrates in a pitch-sealed basket, he was rescued not by a princess but by an ordinary laborer who subsequently raised the child as his own. From such humble origins, Sargon rose to displace the Sumerian monarch Ur-Zababa as the ruler of Kish and to found the first Mesopotamian empire. By adding this element of deliverance to J's story of Moses, a later editor emphasizes the specialness of Moses' role, a variation of another biblical theme, the "barren mother" who unexpectedly bears a son chosen to become a leader of his people, such as Isaac, Jacob, Joseph, or Samuel.

Yahweh Reveals His Name

After killing an Egyptian overseer who had abused two Hebrew slaves, Moses flees the country and settles in Midian, a desert area south of Edom, where he marries and lives as a shepherd for forty years. At this point, Moses undergoes an experience of the numinous, the holy, mysterious presence of divinity that can suddenly inspire the career of a great religious leader. Climbing Mount Horeb (or Mount Sinai in J's version) to investigate a bush that burns without being consumed, Moses hears a voice announce that he is in the divine presence, on holy ground: "I am the God [Elohim] of your father," the voice announces, "the God of Abraham, the God of Isaac, and the God of Jacob." Revealing that he intends to free his people from Egyptian bondage and settle them in Canaan, he commands Moses to return to Egypt and confront pharaoh with the demand to "let my people go."

When Moses, reluctant to undertake so formidable a task, demurs, suggesting that the Hebrews will not know which god is sending him, the voice replies: "I Am who I Am. . . . You are to say to the sons of Israel: **Yahweh**, the God of your fathers . . . has sent me to you. This is my name for all time; by this name I shall be invoked for all generations to come" (Exod. 3: 14–15). Whereas J has used Yahweh's name

from Genesis 2 onward, the Elohist writer of this extremely important passage believes that the divine name was not revealed until God communicated it to Moses. Although there is no scholarly consensus on the origin and exact meaning of the name, E indicates that it is derived from the Hebrew verb "to be" ("I am," first person singular). Yahweh—"he is"— is thus defined as a god of action, one who brings new things into being. In Exodus he is about to transform a group of slaves into a new nation and guide them to a new understanding of his nature and purpose. Note that although E identifies Yahweh with the God [Elohim] known to Israel's ancestors, the priestly author (P) states that the patriarchs knew Yahweh as El Shaddai (Exod. 6:2–13), an archaic term commonly translated as "God Almighty" but which may refer to a deity of the cosmic mountain where ancient gods, such as the Greek Olympians, were believed to dwell.

Yahweh's War Against Pharaoh

The Ten Plagues and the Passover The Hebrews in Egypt at first openly doubt Moses' authority to lead them, a response that foreshadows their future complaints and rebellions in the wilderness. Pharaoh also refuses to recognize the authority of either Moses or his God, declaring that he knows nothing of Yahweh. Angered, Yahweh displays his power through ten plagues calculated to break pharaoh's pride. Beginning with a bloody pollution of the Nile and other Egyptian waters, the plagues gradually increase in severity. Swarms of frogs, then mosquitoes, then gadflies afflict the Egyptians, showing Yahweh's control of nature. Pharaoh begs Moses to end the plagues but treacherously goes back on his word when the pests disappear.

The Exodus writers characteristically attribute pharaoh's stubbornness to Yahweh, who is depicted as deliberately hardening pharaoh's heart (Exod. 7:3; 10:1, 20, 27; 14:8), thus

NEUES REICH
Dyn.XVIII.

THEBEN
aus einem Grabe von Abd el Qurna.

This Egyptian tomb painting depicts slaves making bricks for the building enterprises of an Eighteenth Dynasty pharaoh. Although the work pictured is almost identical to that ascribed to Hebrew slaves in the Book of Exodus, archaeologists—despite Egypt's wealth of extant inscriptions, archival records, and other artifacts—have been unable to find any physical evidence corroborating the Hebrews' presence there. (Courtesy of the Oriental Division, the New York Public Library, Astor, Lenox and Tilden Foundations)

forcing him to "sin" in refusing to let Israel go. God's apparent interference with the Egyptian ruler's free will may distress modern readers, but in the Exodus tradition pharaoh's resistance was necessary to the Deity's purpose. He *had* to be uncooperative in order for Yahweh's power to be revealed (Exod. 9:15–16; 10:1–2). If Egypt had meekly submitted to Moses' demands, there would have been no awesome plagues, no "signs and wonders" demonstrating the supremacy of Israel's God.

As pharaoh's stubbornness persists, the plagues increase in horror. The fifth brings sickness and death to Egyptian livestock, although the Hebrew flocks remain untouched. In the sixth, boils and sores break out on human and beast, though the Hebrews are again unaffected. In the seventh, a tremendous storm of lightning and hail destroys Egyptian crops. The eighth brings an invasion of locusts that devour what is left of Egypt's vegetation. In the ninth, total

darkness covers the entire land except where the Hebrews live. Pharaoh then orders Moses out of his presence, refusing to see in these calamities the hand of the God of slaves.

The First Passover   Theologically, the tenth and last plague is the most important. In a final demonstration of divine power, Yahweh, or his Angel of Death, passes over Egypt at midnight and takes the life of every Egyptian first-born male, from pharaoh's crown prince to the son of the slave woman who grinds the corn. This time the Hebrews do not sit passively by; Moses orders each family to sacrifice a lamb, smear its blood on their doorposts, and stay in their homes to eat a ceremonial meal—the solemn feast of unleavened bread and bitter herbs. Thus, according to Exodus, the **Passover** ritual was established during Israel's last night of slavery while the divine executioner "passed over" their dwellings, made secure by the symbolic "blood of the lamb." This feast remains one of the most important of Jewish observances and is the forerunner of Jesus' Last Supper and the Christian Communion.

Deliverance at the Sea of Reeds

For the ultimate demonstration of Yahweh's might, pharaoh is maneuvered into leading his army in pursuit of the Israelites. Trapped between Egyptian charioteers and the Sea of Reeds, perhaps a lake or marshland along the Mediterranean coast, the Israelites are unexpectedly rescued by a phenomenon attributed to Yahweh's direct intervention. According to J's version of events,

> Yahweh drove back the sea with a strong easterly wind all night, and he made dry land of the sea. . . . [I]n the morning watch, Yahweh looked down on the army of the Egyptians. . . . He so clogged their chariot wheels that they could scarcely make headway. "Let us flee from the Israelites," the Egyptians cried. "Yahweh is fighting for them against the Egyptians!"
>
> Exodus 14:22, 25

In J's account, the Egyptian army is forced to retreat when its vehicles bog down in mud and is then "overwhelmed" when the "sea returned to its bed," perhaps in the form of a tsunami wave. To emphasize the divine presence in this event, P transforms it into a spectacular repeat of God's parting the waters of chaos during creation, so that the Israelites, marching between walls of water on either side, are symbolically re-created as God's special people (Exod. 14:23, 26, 29). By Yahweh's saving act, Israel literally becomes a community of faith, for the first time unanimously acknowledging Yahweh and his agent Moses (Exod. 14:30–31).

The Song of Miriam (Exod. 15:21), which may be one of the oldest passages in the Hebrew Bible, gives still another version of Israel's deliverance, stating that Yahweh somehow threw pharaoh's cavalry into the sea. The expanded victory hymn ascribed to Moses makes the same statement (Exod. 15:4–5), adding that by this act Yahweh had publicly established himself among the world's recognized powers:

> Who among the gods is your like, Yahweh?
> Who is your like, majestic in holiness,
> terrible in deeds of prowess, worker of wonders?
> Exodus 15:11

Throughout Old Testament history, Yahweh's saving act at the Reed Sea is referred to as the decisive moment in Israel's past, the moment at which Yahweh made Israel his own.

The Route of the Exodus More than 3000 years after the event, scholars remain divided on the question of Israel's route from Egypt to Canaan. The problem is compounded by the fact that few of the sites mentioned in the Exodus narrative have been positively identified. Even the point at which the Israelites crossed the Reed Sea is unknown. Various lakes and swampy areas north of the Gulf of Suez have been suggested, but neither Lake Sirbonis (Lake Bardawil) nor a southern extension of the present Lake Menzaleh have received general scholarly acceptance as the location of Israel's deliverance. Because the Egyptians then maintained a line of heavy fortifications along the Mediterranean coast, the most direct approach to Canaan (Exod. 13:17–19), the Israelites were forced to follow an inland route through an arid wilderness. A plausible reconstruction of Israel's path across the Sinai peninsula appears in the map on page 100.

The Theophany at Sinai

Mosaic Covenant The climactic act in the national epic is consummated at Mount **Sinai**, the holy mountain where Moses had experienced his **epiphany** (manifestation of God) and back to which Yahweh had commanded him to lead the Israelites. At Sinai (whose exact location has never been positively identified), Yah-

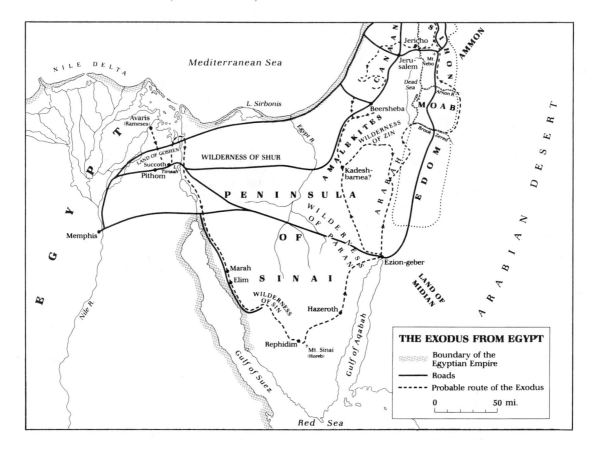

THE EXODUS FROM EGYPT

Boundary of the Egyptian Empire
Roads
Probable route of the Exodus

0   50 mi.

weh calls Moses and the symbolic seventy elders of Israel for special communion (Exod. 24). Out of the Mount Sinai **theophany** (revelation of God), Moses brings the **Ten Commandments** and the **Covenant Code**, the nucleus of Israel's Torah (Exod. 19–24). The Mosaic law in its entirety eventually included all of the hundreds of rules and regulations found in the Pentateuch, although many of these derive from a time later than that of Moses. (See "The Mosaic Covenant at Mount Sinai" on pages 102–103.)

Although the Hebrew people have heard the law read to them and have willingly accepted its terms, a reaction soon occurs. While Moses remains on Mount Sinai communing with Yahweh, the people become restive and rebellious. In order not to forfeit his leadership over them, Moses' brother **Aaron** makes them **golden calves** as physical objects of worship (Exod. 32). On returning from the mountain, however, such is Moses' fury at the Israelites' apostasy that he shatters the stone tablets on which the **Decalogue** had been inscribed (though Yahweh later makes new tablets, which are traditionally kept in the portable **Ark** [chest] **of the Covenant**, described in minute detail in Chapters 35–40 of Exodus).

The Israelites' thoughtless abandonment of Yahweh sparks a debate between Moses, the people's advocate, and Yahweh, whose anger at Israel is so great that he proposes to destroy them and make a nation derived from Moses instead. As Abraham had argued with God not to destroy Sodom, so Moses now pleads for his fellow Hebrews: Why give the Egyptians an opportunity to mock Yahweh, saying that he can-

This rugged peak in the Sinai desert is the traditional site at which Yahweh communicated the Torah to Moses. Known as Mount Sinai in J's account, it is called Horeb in E's tradition. Although much of the Torah's action takes place in Sinai's shadow, where the Israelites camp for almost two years (Exod. 19:2 to Num. 10:12), archaeologists have been unable to find any physical evidence of the tribes' sojourn there. (Courtesy of Alan Oddie/PhotoEdit)

not finish what he has begun, not preserve alive the people he has led out of Egypt? God, suggests Moses, must also remember his promise to Abraham.

"So Yahweh relented and did not bring on his people the disaster he had threatened" (Exod. 32:11–14). Elsewhere in the Pentateuch (notably Num. 14:10–19), we find Moses again reminding Yahweh that his reputation depends on Israel's continued existence and future success as a nation. In Numbers 14, he even quotes the Deity's own earlier recital of Yahweh's beneficent qualities (stated in Exod. 34:6–8) and appeals to his sense of fairness and consistency. Such passages illustrate Israel's slowly growing awareness of Yahweh as an ethical and responsible god.

Instructions for the Cult   Except for Chapters 32–34, which recount Israel's apostasy with the golden calf and the subsequent covenant-renewal ceremony, the last part of Exodus consists of instructions for building the **tabernacle**, a portable tent to house the Ark (Exod. 25–31)

and its construction (Exod. 35–40). Although these extensive blocks of ritual and other liturgical material that the P writer(s) inserted into the JE narrative may seem tiresome or irrelevant to many readers, they held great significance for Israel's priesthood. Many ancient Near Eastern creation accounts end with the construction of a shrine for the creator-god. The P author(s) describe the completion of the wilderness tabernacle in language similar to that employed at the end of Genesis 1, when God completed his creative work (cf. Gen. 1:31–2:3 with Exod. 39:32, 42–43; 40:33). God, who had walked in Eden with the first human couple (and with only a few others since), was now prepared to accompany his people on their long journey toward the Promised Land.

RECOMMENDED READING

Beegle, Dewey M. "Moses." In D. N. Freedman, ed., *The Anchor Bible Dictionary*, Vol. 4, pp. 909–918. New York: Doubleday, 1992. An examina-

The Mosaic Covenant at Mount Sinai

The central expression of Yahweh's unique relationship to Israel, the Mosaic Covenant is the standard by which most biblical historians and later prophets measure Israel's successes and failures. (Neither the early prophets, whose careers took place before the Mosaic traditions were widely disseminated, nor the Wisdom writers, whose moral reflections are based on thoughtful observation rather than divine revelation, commonly cite Mosaic authority.) Named for Moses because he acts as the mediator between God and his people, this solemn agreement commits the Israelites to recognize Yahweh alone as their God and to observe unquestioningly the vast collection of laws, statutes, rituals, and ordinances enumerated in Exodus through Deuteronomy. This body of law incorporates many legal traditions inherited from the older cultures of the Near East (see Part 2) but transforms them into a means by which the Israelites can—through dedication and obedience—demonstrate their appreciation for Yahweh's unseen presence in their midst. In the Exodus version of the covenant, Yahweh makes no promises to his worshipers assembled at Mount Sinai, except the implied assumption that he will act as Israel's divine patron and protector. By contrast, Deuteronomy's later restatement of the covenant depicts Yahweh as offering peace, prosperity, and other material blessings—all conditional on Israel's loyalty and obedience (Deut. 28).

Although scholars believe that the more than 600 commandments and stipulations found in the Pentateuch developed gradually over a long period of time, Israelite tradition attributes to Moses

all legal material in the Torah. More than 3000 years after the event, it is now probably impossible to determine precisely the terms of the original Mosaic pact between Yahweh and the Israelites. Numerous references scattered throughout Exodus, Leviticus, and Deuteronomy suggest that in legal form the covenant may have resembled a Hittite treaty. A study of ancient Near Eastern treaties shows that they commonly included the following provisions:

1. A preamble
2. An account of historical circumstances leading to the treaty
3. The stipulations and requirements
4. Arrangements for public reading of the text and its safekeeping at a shrine
5. A list of divine witnesses to the treaty
6. A vivid catalog of blessings for abiding by its terms and curses for violating them

All these elements occur in the Torah, although they are found in widely scattered fragments throughout the biblical text.

Exodus 19 describes the awe-inspiring presence of Yahweh on the sacred mountain, shrouded in clouds rent by lightning. In Exodus 20, the traditional preamble and historical recapitulation are reduced to a brief statement identifying the suzerain—"I am Yahweh"—and his subjects' reason for being grateful to the Deity, because Yahweh brought them "out of the land of Egypt, out of the house of slavery." Terms of the treaty between God and the people are then specified. The Israelites' public vow to obey does not im-

tion of the Torah's diverse strands of tradition regarding Moses' role.

Brueggmann, Walter. "The Book of Exodus." In *The New Interpreter's Bible.* Vol. 1, pp. 677–981. Contains extensive scholarly commentary on the Exodus text.

Childs, Brevard S. *The Book of Exodus.* Philadelphia: Westminster Press, 1974. A standard commentary.

Clifford, Richard J. "Exodus." In R. E. Brown, et al., eds., *The New Jerome Biblical Commentary,* pp. 44–60. Englewood Cliffs, N.J.: Prentice-Hall, 1990.

de Vaux, Roland. *The Early History of Israel.* Translated by D. Smith. Philadelphia: Westminster Press, 1978. Analyzes the Exodus and Sinai traditions.

mediately follow the Decalogue because P editors have inserted a large block of legal material between Chapters 20 and 24, where the ceremony of ratification now appears. The Israelites are pictured as unanimously accepting the covenant obligations, "with one voice" swearing to abide by all of Yahweh's demands (Exod. 24:3). Moses then performs a binding ritual, slaughtering sacrificial animals and casting part of the blood on an altar representing Yahweh, thus sealing the covenant bond. After Moses reads from the Book of the Covenant and the people again swear to uphold all its provisions, he sprinkles the Israelites with the rest of the sacrificial blood, thereby confirming the people's commitment to their divine suzerain.

No witnesses to Israel's solemn pledge to worship Yahweh exclusively are mentioned in Exodus. Deuteronomy, however, calls "heaven and earth" to witness against the Israelites if they break their vows, an invocation many scholars have seen as a possible reference to Near Eastern earth and sky deities (Deut. 30:19). Joshua 24, which describes a covenant-renewal ceremony at the old Canaanite sanctuary of Shechem, contains several parallels to ancient treaty conventions. In one passage, the people themselves testify to their legal obligation to serve Yahweh alone (Josh. 24:22). In another, a memorial stone "has heard all the words" of Yahweh and acts as witness against the people should they default. Consistent with Near Eastern custom, Joshua proclaims the covenant terms and then places the text in the shrine at Shechem. Promised benefits for keeping the covenant and curses for violating it are detailed in Leviticus 26 and Deuteronomy 28. Scholars believe that most of these passages are much later than the JE accounts preserved in Exodus, but the later texts accurately reflect ancient models in treaty making. They also echo the then-current mode of formal cursing typical of international pacts. Yahweh's threat to trap future covenant breakers in a harsh world, with the heavens like "brass" and the earth beneath it like "iron" (Deut. 28:23; Lev. 26:19), is almost identical to the metallic imagery of curses listed in a treaty that Esar-haddon, King of Assyria, concluded about 677 B.C.E.

The legal form in which Israelite covenant laws are expressed, as well as some of the content, is also paralleled in other Near Eastern legal codes. **Apodictic law**, such as the Ten Commandments, with their imperative absolutes ordering the people not to steal, kill, or bear false witness, is unusual in form, but the ethical principles expressed are commonly recognized in ancient cultures. **Case law**, with its typical formula "if such and such is the case, then . . . must be done," characterizes many Near Eastern laws. The *if-then* pattern appears throughout the famous Code of Hammurabi (about 1690 B.C.E.) and characterizes much legal material in the Torah (Exod. 20:22–23:5; Lev. 1–7, 12–15; etc.).

The Abrahamic and Davidic covenants contrast markedly with the Moses–Sinai agreement. Whereas the Mosaic Covenant demands total cooperation and obedience of the human parties, Yahweh's promises to Abraham and David—for land, descendants, and royal status—are unconditional. The tension between traditions in which Yahweh pledges unqualified benefits and those in which benefits are based entirely on the people's fidelity pervades much of biblical literature. (See the discussion of the Davidic Covenant in Part 4.)

Kitchen, K. A. "Exodus, The." In D. N. Freedman, ed., *The Anchor Bible Dictionary*, Vol. 2, pp. 700–708. New York: Doubleday, 1992.

Mendenhall, George E. *Law and Covenant in Israel and the Ancient Near East.* Pittsburgh: Biblical Colloquium, 1955. An influential study of correspondences between ancient treaty documents and the growth of Israel's covenant tradition.

———. "Covenant." In G. A. Buttrick, ed., *The Interpreter's Dictionary of the Bible,* Vol. 2, pp. 714–723. New York and Nashville, Tenn.: Abingdon Press, 1962. A concise, insightful summary of the biblical concept of covenant relationships.

Noth, Martin. *Exodus.* Philadelphia: Westminster Press, 1962.

Sarna, Nahum M. "Exodus, Book of." In D. N. Freedman, ed., *The Anchor Bible Dictionary,* Vol. 2, pp. 689–700. New York: Doubleday, 1992.

——. *Understanding Exodus.* New York: Schocken Books, 1987.

TERMS AND CONCEPTS TO REMEMBER

Aaron	pharaoh
apodictic law	Rameses
Ark of the Covenant	Rameses II
case law	Sargon I
Covenant Code	Sea of Reeds
Decalogue	Sinai
epiphany	tabernacle
Exodus, the	Ten Commandments
golden calf	(Decalogue)
Moses	theophany
Passover	Yahweh

QUESTIONS FOR REVIEW

1. Summarize the story of Moses. How does he become Yahweh's agent in humbling the Egyptian ruler and rescuing Israel from bondage? What series of events transforms Moses from an outlaw in Egypt to a lawgiver at Sinai?

2. What kinds of plagues does Yahweh bring against Egypt? What is the connection between the tenth plague, the Angel of Death, and the Passover meal? How does Yahweh rescue Israel at the Sea of Reeds?

3. Describe the nature of the Mosaic Covenant. How do its *conditional* terms differ from the absolute promises of the Abrahamic Covenant? What must the Israelites do to keep Yahweh's favor?

QUESTIONS FOR DISCUSSION AND REFLECTION

1. Discuss the theophany (revelation of God) at Mount Sinai and the nature of the laws de- livered in Exodus 20–23. After having res- cued his people from slavery in Egypt, why does Yahweh still permit the institution of human slavery (Exod. 21:1–11)?

2. Why does Exodus contain two distinct ver- sions of the revelation of the divine name to Moses (Exod. 3 and 6) and of the ratification of the Mosaic Covenant (Exod. 24 and 34: 10–28)? Why did the Torah editors include two apparently contradictory statements about Yahweh's appearing visibly to Moses and the elders (cf. Exod. 24:9–11 with Exod. 33:11 and 33:18–23)?

3. Why did the Torah writers depict Yahweh as "like a devouring fire" (Exod. 24:17–18), "jealous," and so wrathful that Moses must repeatedly dissuade him from annihilating his people (cf. Exod. 33:3–5; 34:6–9; and Num. 14:10–38)?

Leviticus

KEY THEMES

A vast collection of legal and liturgical material, Leviticus contains priestly instructions about maintaining the ritual and ethical purity of the Israelite community, an obligation necessitated by Yahweh's abiding presence in the tabernacle. Each individual Israelite must remain "holy," scrupulously observing priestly distinctions be- tween "clean" and "unclean" in diet, private life, and public behavior, thus avoiding a con- tamination that offends the Deity and brings punishment on the entire community. The first section deals with laws of sacrifice (Chs. 1–7); the second with the ordination of Aaron and his sons and the consecration of the tabernacle (Chs. 8–10); the third with various kinds of de- filement and cleansing (Chs. 11–15); the fourth with the ritual of Yom Kippur, the Day of Atonement (Ch. 16); the fifth with regulations concerning holiness in blood sacrifice, sexual activity, human relations, and priestly conduct

(Chs. 17–21); the sixth with the religious calendar and festivals, including the Jubilee Year (Chs. 22–25); the seventh with curses for disobedience (Ch. 26); and the eighth with miscellaneous holy things (Ch. 27).

> You therefore must be holy because I am holy.
> Leviticus 11:44

Now one of the least read parts of the Bible, Leviticus nevertheless represents an important stage in the development of Israel's religion. Scholars believe that Israelite priests assembled the book during and shortly after the Babylonian exile (587–538 B.C.E.), when the entire Jewish nation lay in ruins and its upper classes were held captive in Babylon. Responding to a threatened loss of national and religious identity, the priests attempted to preserve and standardize Israel's forms of worship. The result is the enormous body of cult material cataloged in the Torah.

Although most of Leviticus's laws and regulations presuppose a return to the homeland and Temple, it also contains rules on circumcision and diet that could be observed even in exile. These rituals and legal stipulations, which begin in Exodus 25–31 and 35–40 and carry over into Numbers 1–10, belong almost exclusively to the priestly document (P). Their purpose is to demonstrate that by conscientiously observing all the legal and liturgical requirements set forth by the priests, the Israelite people will remain distinct and different from the Gentile nations that endeavor to overwhelm or absorb them, thereby helping ensure continuance of Israel's unique legacy.

Israel's Purity Laws

Despite the Septuagint title, Leviticus has little to do with the **Levites** or their law; it concentrates almost exclusively on the descendants of Aaron and their priestly functions. The opening section (Chs. 1–7) regulates sacrificial offerings, both voluntary and required, to provide the means for Yahweh's worshipers to remove guilt and sin, perceived as a disruption of divinely instituted order that defiles not only the individual offender but also the entire community and the land it inhabited (see also Lev. 18:26–30). Providing guidelines for laypeople on how to make proper **sacrifices** of animals or grain, this section covers procedures appropriate for the high priest (Lev. 4:3–12), the community (Lev. 4:13–26), and the individual (Lev. 4:27–35, 5:1–13).

The second section (Chs. 8–10) describes the exacting ceremonies for installing the Aaronite priests. The third section (Chs. 11–15), outlining rules to distinguish "clean" from "unclean" foods and practices, also defines ritual defilements and their expurgation. Because Israel's priests viewed the world as consisting of mutually exclusive categories separated by boundaries that it was a sin to violate, they are deeply concerned about keeping different kinds of things from being mixed. Thus, Israel is forbidden to weave wool and linen into a single garment or boil a kid in its mother's milk, thus wrongly blending two distinct kinds of fabric or combining meat with a different animal product. The priestly belief that everything must be of a single kind or nature also appears in the rules concerning leprosy. When a priest finds a man with mottled skin, part flaky and white with leprosy and part of normal color and texture, he must pronounce him "unclean" (Lev. 13:9–11). But if the disease spreads over the entire body so that the skin is uniformly leprous, the priest may judge the man "clean": "Since it has all become white, he is clean" (Lev. 13:12–17). It is not the disfiguring diseases, or the possibility that it may infect others, that contaminates; it is the leper's simultaneously manifesting two different conditions that belong in separate categories.

The priestly concern with sexual taboos displays a similar abhorrence toward the mixing of kinds. A man may not have intercourse with a menstruating woman because life-giving semen should not mix with a flow of blood, which is associated with death. Any sexual contact also renders both partners "unclean" because the bodily fluids produced during intercourse have trespassed their natural boundaries within the body (Ch. 15:16–24).

Women's biological functions are regarded as essentially "unclean." Merely touching an object previously used by a menstruating woman contaminates a person (Lev. 15:19–32). Because birth produces a flow of blood, a woman who delivers a male child is considered unclean for seven days, and for another thirty-three days she cannot participate in the social or religious life of the community. If she delivers a female baby, the period of her ostracism is doubled, rendering her unclean for fourteen days and depriving her of normal activities for sixty-six days (Lev. 12:1–8).

Chapter 18 lists many other sexual prohibitions that forbid a variety of erotic combinations, ranging from taking both a woman and her sister into a man's harem (Lev. 18:18) to making love to a menstruating wife (18:19) to lying "with a man as with a woman" (18:22), all of which transgress the priestly notion of acceptable boundaries. Leviticus also forbids a liaison with the wife of a brother, although Deuteronomy unequivocally states that an Israelite—to remain in good standing—must marry his brother's widow, presumably to perpetuate the deceased's name and consolidate family property (Deut. 25:5–10).

Rituals of Atonement

Day of Atonement   Chapter 16 describes one of Israel's most significant ceremonies, the **scapegoat** offering. Annually, on the **Day of Atonement** (**Yom Kippur**), the high priest is instructed to prepare two goats for sacrifice. At the Tent of Meeting (another name for the tabernacle), the priest draws lots for the goats, slaughtering one as a blood sacrifice to Yahweh and keeping the other alive as a symbolic bearer of the people's collective sins. Ritually laying hands on the live goat, the priest transfers the nation's guilt to the animal, which, metaphorically laden with Israel's misdeeds, is then led out

into the desert "to **Azazel**." The scapegoat thus removes the punishable object of Yahweh's wrath from the community and transfers it to the uninhabited wilderness. (Scholars remain undecided whether Azazel is a place or a desert demon that destroys the "sinful" goat.)

The term *scapegoat* has come to mean any innocent person who suffers for the crimes of others; its fullest expression in the Hebrew Bible is found in Isaiah's Song of the Suffering Servant, a poem in which a guiltless man bears the sins of his people and by so doing wins forgiveness for them:

> On him lies a punishment that brings us
>   peace,
> and through his wounds we are healed.
> Isaiah 53:5

By taking away the people's collective offenses, the scapegoat ceremony lets them become "at one" with their God, effecting a reconciliation that restores harmony between Yahweh and the Israelites. Through such priestly rituals, the participants are cleansed or spiritually re-created and brought closer to the divine image in which humanity was originally formed.

Yahweh's Holy People

Holiness Code   Chapters 17–26, with their reiterated refrain "I am Yahweh," represent a distinctive body of material known as the **Holiness Code**. Covering a wide variety of human sins, sacrifices, seasonal festivals, and cleansing formulas, this portion of the book emphasizes Yahweh as the source of holiness and of the laws that Israel must observe to acquire a holiness appropriate for his special people. Despite the code's stress on ritual, it is important to remember that the P writers presuppose the worshiper's ethical integrity—sacrifice was no substitute for honorable behavior (cf. Micah 6:6–8).

Amid rather dry priestly regulations for making burnt offerings, the reader will find passages of great ethical and psychological insight. On the matter of social justice, for example, we are told: "You must neither be partial to the little man, nor overawed by the great; you must pass judgment on your neighbor according to justice. . . . You must not bear hatred for your brother in your heart. . . . You must love your neighbor as yourself. I am Yahweh" (Lev. 19: 15–18). Besides containing the only command in the Pentateuch to love one's neighbor as a religious duty, Leviticus also enjoins the Israelites to treat strangers and foreign residents with compassion, remembering that they themselves were once outsiders in a strange land (Lev. 19:34).

The Holiness Code concludes by placing Israel's laws and ceremonies in the general context of her covenant with Yahweh. In a passage reminiscent of the deuteronomic school of thought, Chapter 26 enumerates the respective blessings or curses that will follow obedience or disobedience to the laws contained in this book. Security, divine protection, military victory, and material prosperity are guaranteed if Israel keeps all her God's commandments; drought, famine, disease, poverty, military defeat, and total ruin are predicted if the nation fails to honor these edicts (Lev. 26:3–43). Promising to remember his covenant with Abraham, the Deity also promises to rescue his people from their enemies' power and restore them to Canaan. Although there was probably an ancient tradition that national disaster would befall a disobedient Israel, this description of the Babylonian exile and return indicates a relatively late date for this particular passage.

Noting similarities between the Holiness Code and legal material in the Book of Ezekiel, some critics believe that Leviticus dates from the time of Ezekiel or later, the sixth or fifth centuries B.C.E. Other scholars date the Levitical rituals governing sacrifices to the Second Temple period (roughly fifth through second centuries B.C.E.). A contemporary of Ezekiel, the prophet Jeremiah categorically denied that any of the sacrificial practices observed in his day actually originated during the Mosaic era. According to Jeremiah, Yahweh gave the Exodus generation "no orders about holocaust and sacrifice," implying that such elaborate ceremonies were a later priestly innovation (Jer. 7:22).

RECOMMENDED READING

Brueggemann, Walter. "The Kerygma of the Priestly Writer." In W. Brueggemann and H. W. Wolff, eds., *The Vitality of Old Testament Traditions,* pp. 101–113. Atlanta: John Knox Press, 1975.

Cross, Frank M., ed. "The Priestly Houses of Early Israel." In *Canaanite Myth and Hebrew Epic: Essays in the History and the Religion of Israel,* pp. 293–325. Cambridge, Mass.: Harvard University Press, 1973. Indispensable for understanding how the priests edited the Pentateuch.

de Vaux, Roland. *Studies in Old Testament Sacrifice.* Cardiff: University of Wales Press, 1964.

Eissfeldt, Otto. "The Holiness Code." In *The Old Testament: An Introduction,* pp. 233–239. New York: Harper & Row, 1965.

Kaiser, Walter C., Jr. "The Book of Leviticus." In *The New Interpreter's Bible,* Vol. 1, pp. 985–1191. A scholarly interpretation and reflection on Israel's liturgical codes. Nashville: Abingdon Press, 1994.

Levine, B. A. "Priestly Writers." In G. A. Buttrick, ed., *The Interpreter's Dictionary of the Bible: Supplementary Volume,* pp. 683–687. Nashville, Tenn.: Abingdon Press, 1976.

Noth, Martin. *Leviticus.* Philadelphia: Westminster Press, 1975. Provides information about the priestly tradition and Israel's cultic worship.

TERMS AND CONCEPTS
TO REMEMBER

Azazel	Levites
Day of Atonement (Yom Kippur)	sacrifice
	scapegoat
Holiness Code	

QUESTIONS FOR REVIEW

1. Describe the priestly writer's concern with purity laws—distinguishing ceremonially "clean" and "unclean" objects and per-

sons—and the religious concept of holiness. In what way does P envision Israel as a "holy nation of priests"?

2. What is the purpose of animal, grain, and other sacrifices prescribed in the Torah? What statement does the person offering sacrifice make to God?

3. Describe the scapegoat ritual on the annual Day of Atonement (Yom Kippur). How does this ceremony relate to later concepts of vicarious suffering and redemption, such as that presented in Isaiah 53?

QUESTIONS FOR DISCUSSION AND REFLECTION

1. Analyze the priestly tendency to separate and categorize all things according to their "kind," or intrinsic nature (a way of looking at the world that also was present in the first creation account [Gen. 1]). Why is a person whose skin is entirely leprous "clean," whereas a person only partly leprous is "unclean" (Lev. 13:9–17)?

2. Does the priestly attitude toward blood and women's menstrual cycles contribute toward a social devaluation of women? Is this ancient taboo behind some modern religious attempts to restrict women's roles in church or synagogue?

Numbers

KEY THEMES

A partial account of Israel's forty-year wandering in the Sinai wilderness, Numbers is a transitional work that links Yahweh's revelation of the Torah at Mount Sinai with Israel's subsequent long journey to Canaan. Beginning with a census of the twelve tribes, the first ten chapters also enumerate a variety of laws that are an intrinsic part of the Mosaic Covenant. The remaining chapters (10:11–36:13) record Israel's itinerary as the people march from camp to desert camp, at last reaching the plains of Moab, near the Jordan River. Intermixing narrative and legal material, Numbers focuses on issues of leadership and obedience as the people complain about their hardships and rebel against Moses. When the people fail to believe that Yahweh can drive out the Canaanites for them, God condemns the entire older generation—including Moses, Aaron, and Miriam—to die in the wilderness.

> It is you, Yahweh, . . . you go before them in a pillar of cloud by day and a pillar of fire by night.
>
> Numbers 14:14

Although Numbers—which mixes genealogies, laws, rituals, legends, poetry, and narrative—may appear disorganized and difficult to follow, the book does have thematic unity. Numbers takes its title from its Greek name, *arithmoi,* referring to the census or "numbering" of the people described in the first four chapters. The Hebrew title, *bemidbar,* means "in the wilderness," designating the location of Israel's forty-year journeying between Sinai and the borders of Canaan. The combined elements of numbering and wilderness travel suggest part of Numbers's meaning. Israel's male population is counted twice: at the beginning of the book while the people are still receiving the Sinai revelation and again years later after the older generation has perished for refusing to trust Yahweh (cf. Num. 1–4, 26). In between are narrative examples of the people's collective failure to appreciate the law Yahweh has given them or to cooperate with his appointed leader, Moses.

Whereas the early chapters are linked to the Sinai experience, Numbers's final section looks ahead to Israel's future military victories over the Canaanites and the allocation of different areas in the Promised Land to the twelve tribes (Num. 32–35). Besides connecting the Mosaic

Torah with Israel's ultimate possession of Canaan, Numbers achieves thematic unity by emphasizing the importance of submitting to Yahweh's governing arrangements and ethical directions.

Israel in the Desert

Israel's Rebellions and Yahweh's Anger The key event in Numbers is the Israelites' apparent inability to recognize or honor Yahweh's presence in their midst. From the moment they leave Sinai and head into the wilderness, Yahweh visibly guides them, appearing as a columnar cloud by day and a towering flame by night (Num. 10:33–34, 14:14). Despite these phenomena that confirm Yahweh's nurturing presence, however, the people incessantly complain, their discontent culminating in a series of outright rebellions against Moses—and against the God he represents. Although Yahweh earlier had tolerated the people's grumbling, after having made them the gift of divine instruction at Sinai, he no longer restrains his anger at their ingratitude or lack of trust. His patience apparently exhausted, Israel's savior now threatens to become its destroyer.

Whereas Yahweh presumably had intended to lead the Israelites directly to Canaan, their cowardly dread of the land's inhabitants causes him to delay fulfilling his promises for an additional forty years. According to Chapters 13: 25–14:38, ten of the twelve spies sent to reconnoiter Canaan return with discouraging reports of impregnably fortified cities and savage giants. Terrified, the people are ready to stone **Joshua** and **Caleb**, the only two spies who give a favorable view of their prospects. Provoked beyond endurance—do the people not remember his triumph as a warrior at the Sea of Reeds?—Yahweh is ready to annihilate the entire nation. Acting as intercessor between the faithless people and their wrathful God, Moses pleads with Yahweh to change his mind, reminding him

that the Gentile nations are watching his experiment with Israel and that he stands to lose face if he allows his people to perish in the desert. Yahweh must also recall his oath to Abraham as well as his words to Moses on Mount Sinai:

> Yahweh is slow to anger and rich in
>   graciousness,
> forgiving faults and transgressions . . .
> Numbers 14:18, 19

In the "abundance of his graciousness," then, Yahweh must not exterminate the people.

Yahweh's forgiveness is limited, however. He does not obliterate them but decrees that no Israelite over the age of twenty will live to enter Canaan; for every day that the spies reconnoiter the area, Israel must wander a year, until their "dead bodies . . . fall" in the desert. Practically speaking, the forty-year gap between leaving Egypt and settling in Canaan had its cultural and religious advantages. The older generation, imperfectly versed in the Yahwist faith and contaminated by their repeated lapses into idolatry, would be eliminated. Only those younger Israelites thoroughly indoctrinated in the Mosaic religion would be allowed to form the new nation. The two exceptions were Joshua and Caleb who, alone among the elder group, had faith in Yahweh's ability to defeat the Canaanite militia.

Israel Rebels Against Moses Although Moses has repeatedly deflected Yahweh's wrath from smiting Israel, his protective role is unappreciated by the people he defends. Early in the wilderness trek, the Israelites complain bitterly about their restricted diet. Yahweh supplements the daily supply of **manna**—a powdery food that falls from heaven each night—by sending them quail to eat but also sends a plague to punish them for wanting more than he had volunteered to provide. Moses' authority is more seriously undermined in his own household when his brother Aaron and sister **Miriam** declare that their communication with God is as good as his. For her presumptuousness, Miriam

This bronze statuette of a bull—seven inches long and five inches high—was found at a Palestinian cultic site dating from the period of Israel's judges (about 1200 B.C.E.). Representing masculine strength and virility, the bull was commonly associated with both Baal and Yahweh. (Courtesy of Zev Radovan/PhotoEdit)

(but not her equally presumptuous brother) is struck with leprosy (Num. 12). Moses, kind-hearted as always, intervenes with Yahweh, and after a seven-day excommunication from the camp, Miriam is cured.

The principal challenge to Moses' position, however, comes from a respectable group of Israel's leaders, including **Korah**, who is a Levite, and Dathan, Abiram, and On of the tribe of Reuben, along with 250 other "men of repute," who argue that because all Israel is consecrated to Yahweh's service, Moses and Aaron have no right to assume so much authority. During a confrontation between the rebels and Moses at the Tent of Meeting, the earth opens to swallow Korah and the others, including their wives, children, and possessions. The 250 men associated with the revolt are consumed when Yahweh sends fire from heaven (Num. 16:28–35).

Balaam's Blessing   Interpolated into the account of Israel's insurrections against Moses and Yahweh is an old folktale that illustrates how a Near Eastern fortune teller of the late Bronze Age performed his job (Chs. 22–24). This is the humorous story of **Balaam**, a Canaanite prophet hired by King Balak of Moab to curse Israel, whose presence in the area he regards as a military threat. Although Balaam conscientiously tries to earn his fee by invoking the customary curses, Yahweh turns the curses into blessings. Even Balaam's donkey, which miraculously finds a voice to reprimand her master, plays a part in thwarting Balak's designs. Neither pagan king nor hired prophet can resist Yahweh's plans for Israel.

The Balaam story, in which even an idolatrous soothsayer involuntarily serves Israel's welfare, functions as an ironic counterpoint to the chosen people's scandalous behavior at Peor, a site in Moab. Here Israelite men succumb to "the daughters of Moab," who persuade them to worship Baal, a Canaanite fertility god that becomes Yahweh's chief rival after his people settle in Canaan. This episode appears to blend disparate sources, adding the affair of Zimri, an Israelite who takes a **Midianite** wife. Outraged at this mixing with foreign women, the Aaronite priest Phinehas seizes a lance and stabs Zimri and his mate "right through the groin," an act that Yahweh interprets as zeal for his cause and that earns Phinehas's line the reward of an eternal priesthood. Although Moses himself had married a Midianite wife, Zipporah (Exod. 2:15–21), the editors of Numbers employ this incident to condemn intermarriage with Canaanite women, a practice they believe later corrupted Israelite worship of Yahweh. To demonstrate their God's displeasure at mixed marriages, the editors note that Yahweh sends a plague that kills 24,000 of his people, presumably the last contingent of the Exodus generation (Num. 25:1–18). The orgy at Peor is also used to justify slaughtering all Midianites (who are also descendants of Abraham [Gen. 25:1–2]), including women and children—except for Midianite virgins, who are seized to populate Israelite harems (Num. 31:1–24).

To most contemporary readers, the picture that Numbers paints of Yahweh is not altogether sympathetic. As pictured in the Midianite episode, the Deity seems little more than capricious, amoral, impatient, and destructive—a God who is easy to fear but difficult to love. Even after scribes and priests extensively revised the text, these ancient narratives represented Yahweh as essentially the national God of Israel, a supernatural being who shows little concern for other peoples except to slaughter them when they impede Israel's progress. As in Exodus, it is Yahweh's awe-inspiring strength and determination to fulfill his pledge to Abraham that wholly absorb the writers' attention. In the fifth volume of Torah, Deuteronomy, Yahweh pursues the same policy he had invoked against the Midianites—a holy war demanding the pitiless extermination of virtually every human being in Canaan.

RECOMMENDED READING

Milgrom, Jacob. "Numbers, Book of." In D. N. Freedman, ed., *The Anchor Bible Dictionary*, Vol. 4, pp. 1146–1155. New York: Doubleday, 1992.

Noth, Martin. *Numbers*. Philadelphia: Westminster Press, 1968.

TERMS AND CONCEPTS TO REMEMBER

Balaam	manna
Caleb	Midianites
Joshua	Miriam
Korah	

QUESTIONS FOR REVIEW

1. According to Numbers, why does Yahweh condemn the Israelites to wander for forty years in the Sinai wilderness? In what ways would the new Mosaic religion benefit from an enforced isolation from other nations until all the people familiar with the older Egyptian culture died off?

2. Why does Yahweh threaten to exterminate Israel? How does Moses persuade him to relent? What does this episode in Chapter 14 say about Yahweh's character and manner of dealing with his chosen people?

3. Summarize the episodes involving Balaam and the Israelites' orgy at Peor. Why does the latter incident begin with Moabites and suddenly change to an involvement with Midianites? Do you think that two different sources or traditions have been combined?

Deuteronomy

KEY THEMES

Cast in the form of Moses' three farewell speeches to a new generation of Israelites poised to enter the Promised Land, Deuteronomy presents an elaborate reworking of the Moses–Sinai traditions. Scholars believe the book's core (Chs. 12–26) originated during the eighth century B.C.E. in the northern kingdom of Israel, after which it was brought to Judah, thoroughly revised, and "discovered" at the Jerusalem Temple during King Josiah's religious reforms (c. 621 B.C.E.). Composed to meet Israel's political and religious crises, Deuteronomy provides a powerful standard by which to interpret Israel's national successes and failures: Obedience to the Mosaic Torah ensures prosperity and divine protection; disobedience brings national defeat and death. This philosophy of history inspired the school of writers who produced the deuteronomistic History (DH), the heavily edited narrative of Israel's history from the conquest of Canaan in the book of Joshua (c. 1200 B.C.E.) through the Babylonian destruction of Judah (587 B.C.E.) in 2 Kings. In Deuteronomy's opening section, Moses reviews Israel's historical experience from Mount Horeb (Sinai) through the wilderness (Chs. 1–4). In his second speech, Moses restates Yahweh's law, including the Ten Commandments (Chs. 5–26, 28). His third discourse emphasizes the "two ways" of life and destruction (Chs. 29–30). Chapter 27 describes a covenant-renewal ceremony at Shechem, and Chapters 32 and 33 contain ancient poetry about Yahweh and the twelve tribes. The book closes with a priestly appendix recounting Moses' death (Ch. 34).

> Listen, Israel: Yahweh our God is the one Yahweh.
>
> Deuteronomy 6:4

The Second Law of Moses

The Greek-speaking Jews from the second century B.C.E. onward called the Pentateuch's fifth book Deuteronomy (literally, "second law"). But the Hebrew title *Eleh Hádevarim* ("These are the words [of Moses]") is more accurate, because, unlike the other books of the Torah in which Yahweh directs his words to Moses who then transmits them to Israel, Deuteronomy shows Moses speaking directly to the people. The book takes the form of three farewell sermons that Moses delivers shortly before his death. The scene is the plains of Moab east of Jordan, along which the Israelites are massed just prior to their invasion of Canaan. Deuteronomy is thus the final recapitulation of Israel's covenant faith before Yahweh leads them into the land he had promised their ancestors.

Although canonized as the Torah's final book, Deuteronomy, in its literary history and origins, has little to do with the JE narratives that precede it. In style and theological outlook, Deu-

teronomy actually belongs to the historical books that follow it. The alert reader will notice, even in English translation, striking differences in style, phrasing, vocabulary, and theological assumptions between Deuteronomy and other parts of the Pentateuch. Because it purports to be a cycle of public addresses, the book is highly rhetorical, even artificial, in style, and the hortatory tone prevails throughout in such phrases as "with all your heart and soul," "in order that it may go well with you," "be thankful," "in a place he himself will choose," "a land where milk and honey flow," and "if only you obey the voice of Yahweh your God."

Compared with earlier sections of the Torah, too, Deuteronomy offers a more humane, sophisticated teaching, stressing both Yahweh's "steadfast love" for Israel and the people's moral obligation to "remember" his heroic acts on their behalf by loving him with their entire being. More than most other parts of the Pentateuch, Deuteronomy emphasizes social justice, personal ethics, and neighborly responsibilities, and it is therefore not surprising that later Jewish writers cite it frequently. In the New Testament, Jesus is shown employing Deuteronomy to refute the Devil himself (Matt. 4; Luke 4).

Josiah's Reforms   Most biblical historians agree that the Book of the Law that was found in 621 B.C.E. when King Josiah was conducting Temple repairs (2 Kings 22:3–10) was Deuteronomy, or at least its nucleus (Chs. 12–26). According to 2 Kings 22–23, this discovery reinforced Josiah's radical program to bring Judah's worship into strict conformity with the Mosaic tradition. Because Deuteronomy 12 demanded that Israel sacrifice only at a single (unnamed) sanctuary, which both king and priests took to be the Temple at Jerusalem, Josiah ordered the wholesale destruction of outlying altars, shrines, and cult sites at which the country people had worshiped for centuries.

Although it was officially published in Josiah's time, an early form of Deuteronomy was probably compiled about two centuries before.

Most scholars believe that the deuteronomic core originated in the northern kingdom of Israel when a writer or group of writers attempted to curtail religious and social abuses by composing an appeal to the Mosaic heritage. The author(s) may have incorporated traditions stemming from covenant-renewal ceremonies such as the one that Joshua conducted at Shechem (cf. Deut. 27 and Josh. 24). Later transferred to the old tribal sanctuary at Shiloh during the period of the judges (c. 1200–1020 B.C.E.), these rites were preserved among the northern Israelites. According to this theory, the protodeuteronomic material was probably brought south to Jerusalem by refugees from the Assyrian destruction of Samaria in 721 B.C.E. Extensively reedited from a Judaean perspective, the book was kept underground during King Manasseh's reign, a period of foreign religious influence when devoted Yahwists were not encouraged to insist on Israel's strict allegiance to the Mosaic Torah (see 2 Kings 21). With Josiah's ascension to the Davidic throne and a decline in Assyrian power, however, a revival of the national religion made welcome the reappearance of Deuteronomy. Ironically, a text intended to enhance a cult center in the northern kingdom was ultimately used to support the preeminence of Solomon's Temple.

It seems likely that Deuteronomy was added to and reedited even after Josiah's reign. The book has two introductions, one of which may have been appended after the seventh century B.C.E. The miscellaneous poetry at the end, such as the Song of Moses (Ch. 32) and the Blessing of Moses (Ch. 33), seems to represent ancient traditions about the great lawgiver that later editors wished to preserve as part of the Mosaic legacy. When Deuteronomy was placed with the JE narratives as the concluding volume of the Torah, priestly scribes also added a tradition about Moses' death (Ch. 34).

Moses' First Two Speeches In his first discourse, Moses reminds a new generation of Israelites (whose parents died in the wilderness) of all that has happened since the departure from Mount Horeb (Sinai), pointing out that Yahweh has faithfully kept his covenant promises and urging the younger generation to honor their obligations by obeying Yahweh's laws (Deut. 1:1–4:44). Moses' second speech comprises the bulk of Deuteronomy (Chs. 5–26, 28), including an expanded version of the Decalogue (Deut. 5:6–21), the **Shema**—a classic definition of Israel's essential faith (Deut. 6: 4–9)—and the deuteronomic code, a long list of ordinances covering such diverse matters as the central place of worship, dietary restrictions, divorce, the role of prophets, and various social regulations (Chs. 12–26). Much of this resembles material found in Exodus 20–23 and parts of Leviticus and Numbers.

In general, it appears that the Judean editors of Deuteronomy wished to update and revise Israel's ancient legal and sacrificial practices in the light of seventh-century B.C.E. understanding of the Mosaic heritage. The emphasis on a central sanctuary (Ch. 12), which Josiah's policies enforce, necessitates a revolution in national worship. The abolition of sacrifices at all rural shrines, which throws many Levites out of work, a reduction in the number of yearly festivals, and an insistence that all Israelites must travel to Jerusalem to observe institutionalized holy days such as Passover profoundly disrupt old customs. The effect is political as well as religious: Centralization of the national religion in Jerusalem serves to augment the prestige and influence of the Davidic dynasty reigning there.

Much of the second discourse is devoted to laws regulating civil organization, marriage and divorce (which can be initiated only by men), social welfare, and criminal justice. Because the Torah makes no provisions for building prisons, convicted criminals must either pay fines, submit to ritual mutilation, or be executed. For persons committing involuntary manslaughter, cities of refuge are established, but Deuteronomy also recognizes the ancient right of the deceased's relatives to avenge a kinsman's death. If the "blood avengers" catch and kill the accidental slayer before that person reaches a designated place of asylum, they may legally do so.

Deuteronomy imposes the death penalty on many kinds of behavior, ranging from premeditated murder to juvenile delinquency and religious nonconformity. Idolatry, blasphemy, heresy, and the practice of magic or attempted communion with the dead are also capital offenses, commonly punished by stoning or burning. Deuteronomy's compilers repeat the **lex talionis**—law of retaliation—given in Exodus: "Life for life, eye for eye, tooth for tooth, hand for hand, foot for foot" (Deut. 19:21). Although harsh to modern sensibilities, this principle of retributive justice controls the extent to which an injured party can demand vengeance. One may not take a life to satisfy the loss of an eye; one must inflict only the precise equivalent of one's own injury (cf. Exod. 21:23–24 and Lev. 24:19–20). (For the commentary of a Jewish teacher of the first century C.E. concerning retaliation, see Matt. 5:38–48.)

After describing a covenant-renewal ceremony to be held at Mount Ebal in northern Israel after the people cross the Jordan River (Deut. 27), the book provides a list of material rewards (blessings) if Israel keeps the law and a much longer list of punishments (curses) if it disobeys the law (Deut. 28). This passage expresses the essence of what is known as the deuteronomic hypothesis of history. Briefly, it states that Israel's future is totally conditional on her collective religious behavior. Obedience to the Torah will bring national prosperity; disobedience will result in national disaster, including military defeat and exile. This bleak vision closes Moses' second sermon.

Moses' Third Speech   The third and final speech (Deut. 29–30) seems more like a rhetorical conclusion to the second address than a separate discourse. Here Moses enumerates additional sufferings destined to befall Israel if she sins. "In anger, in fury, in fierce wrath," Yahweh will devastate their land and inflict so much misery that even survivors will wish they had died. In common with the prophets, however, there is a promise that when the people repent their sins and return to Yahweh, he will forgive them and restore a small remnant of them to their homeland. The people are repeatedly reminded that the responsibility for their future rests squarely on their own shoulders.

In truly "winged words," Yahweh emphasizes the people's freedom of choice. Setting before them "life and prosperity" or "death and disaster," he urges them to choose a life in which they and their descendants can live to enjoy the love of their God. The ancient song ascribed to Moses (Deut. 32) is actually a hymn glorifying Yahweh and denouncing the people's misuse of their free will:

> He [Yahweh] is the rock, his work is perfect,
> for all his ways are Equity.
> A God faithful, without unfairness,
> Uprightness itself and Justice.
> They [the people] have acted perversely,
> those he begot without blemish,
> a deceitful and underhand brood.
> Is this the return you make to Yahweh?
> O foolish, unwise people!
>
> Deuteronomy 32:4–6

Evil fortune, then, is directly the community's responsibility, for both Yahweh and his creation are perfect.

Moses' Last Days and Death   After the Blessing of Moses (Deut. 33), which strongly resembles Jacob's blessing (Gen. 49), Deuteronomy records Moses' death. Prohibited from entering the Promised Land for an unspecified reason (perhaps his taking credit for bringing water from the rocks at Meribah [Num. 20:2–13]), the 120-year-old Moses glimpses Canaan from a high mountain and dies alone, hidden from the people he has guided for forty years. His unfulfilled career provides an effective symbol for his nation's future experience. As an awed commentator penned in conclusion, "Never has there been such a prophet in Israel as Moses, the man Yahweh knew face to face" (Deut. 34:10). No stronger argument could be given for the absolute necessity of adhering to the Mosaic teachings—as presented in Deuteronomy.

In its literary excellence and generally humanitarian spirit, Deuteronomy is a fitting capstone to the Pentateuch, the five-part epic of Israel's creation. Because it provides the theoretical framework for the historical books that follow, Deuteronomy also functions as an introduction to the second major division of the Hebrew Bible, the long narrative section extending from Joshua through 2 Kings. Scholars believe that the same religious school or group that compiled and edited Deuteronomy also produced this sequence of historical books, which interpret Israel's later history in terms of deuteronomic principles. Although readers may find the deuteronomic formula, which attributes all of Israel's political and military defeats to covenant breaking, unconvincing when rigidly applied to the complexities of human experience, this view almost exclusively determines the deuteronomistic historians' judgment on their nation's history. In the books that follow, the DH writers are unswerving in their conviction that Israel was to be evaluated by one test alone—its collective obedience to Yahweh's covenant.

RECOMMENDED READING

Fretheim, Terence E. *Deuteronomic History.* Nashville, Tenn.: Abingdon Press, 1983. A brief introduction to the DH compositions.

Friedman, Richard E. *Who Wrote the Bible?* New York: Harper & Row, 1987. A brilliant analysis of the historical and theological forces at work behind the compilation and reediting of Deuteronomy and the deuteronomistic histories.

McKenzie, Steven L. "Deuteronomistic History." In D. N. Freedman, ed., *The Anchor Bible Dictionary,* Vol. 2, pp. 160–168. New York: Doubleday, 1992. Examines the influence of Deuteronomy's view of history on the books of Joshua through Kings.

Nicholson, E. W. *Deuteronomy and Tradition.* Philadelphia: Fortress Press, 1967.

von Rad, Gerhard. *Deuteronomy.* Philadelphia: Westminster Press, 1966.

———. *Studies in Deuteronomy.* Studies in Biblical Theology, No. 9. London: SCM Press, 1953. A form-critical approach.

Weinfield, Moshe. *Deuteronomy and the Deuteronomic School.* Oxford, Eng.: Clarendon Press, 1972.

———. "Deuteronomy, Book of." In D. N. Freedman, ed., *The Anchor Bible Dictionary,* Vol. 2, pp. 168–183. New York: Doubleday, 1992. Discusses the origin and content of the Torah's fifth book.

TERMS AND CONCEPTS TO REMEMBER

lex talionis   Shema

QUESTIONS FOR REVIEW

1. Why is Deuteronomy called "the second law"? What are the supposed circumstances of Moses' three speeches in this book?
2. According to most contemporary scholars, when was Deuteronomy actually written, and under what circumstances was it "discovered" and published?
3. Define the deuteronomic hypothesis. According to Deuteronomy 28–29, on what kinds of behavior does the Israelites' national future depend? Explain the philosophy of history promulgated in the deuteronomic view of covenant keeping or breaking.

QUESTION FOR DISCUSSION AND REFLECTION

Why do you suppose that Deuteronomy ends with Israel still outside the Promised Land and with Moses dying before he can experience the fulfillment of Yahweh's promises? Why do the biblical narratives repeatedly emphasize the theme of *deferred* realization of divine promises? According to Proverbs 13:12, "hope deferred makes the heart sick." Do Yahweh's delays have an adverse effect on the well-being of his people?

4

The Prophets (Nevi'im) I: The Deuteronomistic History

The second major section of the Hebrew Bible, the **Prophets** (Nevi'im), is divided into two distinct parts. The first part, traditionally known as the Former Prophets, is a long prose narrative that traces Israel's history from the conquest of Canaan in the late thirteenth century B.C.E. to the destruction of the Jewish state in the sixth century B.C.E. The second part, called the Latter Prophets, is a collection—mostly in poetry—of fifteen prophetic books that bear the names of individual prophets, such as Isaiah, Jeremiah, or Hosea. The historical accounts, Joshua through 2 Kings, provide necessary background for the teachings of Israel's prophets, who typically appear in times of political crisis to proclaim Yahweh's viewpoint in a particular historical situation. Isaiah, for example, serves as both prophet and political adviser to several Judean kings during the late eighth century B.C.E. When Assyrian armies overrun the northern kingdom of Israel and threaten to gobble up Judah as well, Isaiah counsels King Hezekiah not to fear because Yahweh has resolved to protect Jerusalem from capture (2 Kings 19).

The Deuteronomists' Theory of History

Scholars refer to the Former Prophets as the **Deuteronomistic History** because these theologically oriented narratives rigorously interpret Israel's historical experience according to rules laid down in the Book of Deuteronomy. As noted above, Deuteronomy's philosophy of history is inflexible: When Israel worships Yahweh alone and faithfully keeps all Torah regulations, the nation will win all its battles and prosper economically. But if the people—or their individual leaders—mix Yahweh's cult with Canaanite elements, the nation will suffer military defeat, financial ruin, and eventual enslavement to foreign masters (Deut. 28).

Scholars believe that there were two main editions of the Deuteronomistic History. The first version was composed during the reign of Josiah (640–609 B.C.E.), the Judean king who thoroughly purged Yahwism of Canaanite influences and led the people in a renewal of their covenant vows. Josiah's sweeping reforms were conducted according to "everything that was said in the book of the covenant found in the Temple of Yahweh" (2 Kings 23:1–3). As Part 3 explains, scholars think that the "book of the covenant" responsible for Josiah's revival of exclusive Yahwism was Deuteronomy, with its insistence on a single central sanctuary, directives for observing Passover, and list of curses for disobedience (cf. Deut. 12–28; 2 Kings 22–23).

Composed at the high tide of Josiah's triumphant religious and military campaigns, the first edition of the Deuteronomistic History praised Josiah in terms accorded no other Davidic king. Not only did he please Yahweh "in every respect" (2 Kings 22:2), Josiah "turned to Yahweh . . . with all his heart, all his soul, all his strength, in perfect loyalty to the law of Moses" (2 Kings 23:25). Josiah's total devotion to Yahweh, in fact, is rendered in terms that fulfill Deuteronomy's supreme command—to love Israel's God absolutely (Deut. 6:4–6).

In its original form, the Deuteronomistic History had a remarkable literary symmetry. The first edition began with an account of Joshua's stunning military and religious exploits and ended in 2 Kings with a summary of Josiah's Yahwist reforms and partial reconquest of the Promised Land. Backed by Yahweh's invisible armies, Joshua successfully led Israel in a holy war, capturing Canaanite strongholds, seizing large Canaanite territories, and overthrowing Canaanite shrines. At the conclusion of the narrative, Josiah performs similar feats, leading Jewish troops into northern territories that had been previously lost to Assyria, and systematically demolishing illicit places of worship throughout his kingdom (cf. Josh. 1–11; 2 Kings 23). Both men are pictured as national heroes who exemplify deuteronomistic piety in action. Joshua's gathering the tribes together for a solemn covenant-renewal ceremony—witnessed by a stone monument that Joshua sets up to commemorate the event (Josh. 24)—is paralleled by Josiah's conducting a comparable ritual "beside the [Temple] pillar." In both cases, the covenant terms are read aloud to the people, who then swear to uphold them (cf. Josh. 24:24–28; 2 Kings 23:3).

Probably written to help promote Josiah's crusade to honor Yahweh alone, this first version of the Deuteronomistic History could give Israel's story a happy outcome. Although the 600-year-long period from Joshua to Josiah had witnessed many reversals, attributed to the people's covenant-breaking, in the long run Yahweh and his people finally were united under a king "like his father David"—one through whom God could rule effectively. Promulgating Deuteronomy's laws as his country's constitution, Josiah presided over a Judean theocracy.

After Josiah's early death (609 B.C.E.) and Judah's subsequent fall to Babylon, however, the Deuteronomistic historian(s) had to revise their neatly symmetrical presentation of Israel's history. Josiah's reign could no longer be seen as the climactic fulfillment of the covenant people's relationship to Yahweh, for this glorious moment was soon followed by national calamity (2 Kings 25). Viewing Israel's history from the perspective of exile in Babylon, the Deuteronomistic editors found a way to explain their nation's collapse and the extinction of the Davidic dynasty, which Yahweh had promised would govern his people forever (2 Sam. 7). It was one of Josiah's predecessors, wicked King Manasseh, who was responsible for the catastrophe. Immediately following the passage in which they extolled Josiah's life-giving reforms, the editor(s) inserted this declaration:

> Yet Yahweh did not renounce the heat of his great anger which blazed out against Judah because of the provocation Manasseh had offered him. Yahweh decreed, "I will thrust Judah away from me too, as I have already thrust Israel. I will cast away Jerusalem, this city I had chosen, and the Temple of which I had said: There my name shall be."
>
> 2 Kings 23:26–27

The fathers' sins would be visited upon their great-grandchildren, because "Yahweh would not forgive" (2 Kings 24:4).

Revised during the Babylonian exile to reflect a devastating historical reality, the books of Joshua through Kings now present Israel's history according to a single principle—the fatal consequences of disobedience to Yahweh. As the Deuteronomistic historian(s) saw it, the nation's survival was *always conditional* on the people's strict adherence to their covenant obligations. Josiah's heroic efforts were ultimately futile, because too many other kings, predominantly Manasseh, had flagrantly violated Torah commands. In the Deuteronomistic view, these ancient failures perfectly account for every lost battle, foreign invasion, crop failure, drought, famine, plague, or political humiliation. All historical figures and events in the Former Prophets are subordinated to that view. By scattering brief references to the coming national defeat and exile throughout the narrative, the reviser(s) transformed the Deuteronomistic History, their foreshadowings making the ultimate disaster appear inevitable (cf. Deut. 4:26–27; Deut. 28: 36, 63–64; Josh. 23:16; 1 Kings 9:7; 11:35–36; 15:3–4; 2 Kings 8:18–19; 20:16–19, etc.).

Identity of the Deuteronomist(s)   According to R. E. Friedman, a careful study of the Deuteronomistic History indicates that the first edition was compiled during Josiah's reign by a single priestly writer associated with the royal court. Friedman suggests further that the same person revised the text during the exile, adding the account of Josiah's unsatisfactory successors and the passages foreshadowing Judah's destruction. For Friedman, the most likely candidate is the prophet Jeremiah, who repeatedly warned Judah's last kings of the dire results of covenant-breaking, although Jeremiah's secretary Baruch probably did the actual writing. (See Part 5.) Archaeologists recently found a clay stamp used to seal documents. The stamp contains the inscription, "Belonging to Baruch, son of Neriyah the scribe." Friedman speculates that this item may represent the author or editor of eight books of the Bible. Some other scholars, however, maintain that the Deuteronomistic History was composed by a school or circle of anonymous Judean scribes.

Sources   In compiling their account, the Deuteronomistic historian(s) drew upon both oral tradition, such as stories about the prophets Elijah and Elisha, and several written documents, including collections of archaic poetry, such as the Book of Jashar (Josh. 10:13; 2 Sam. 1:18). Royal archives that list the deeds of Israelite and Judean rulers were frequently cited, including the Book of the Acts of Solomon (1 Kings 11: 41), the Book of the Annals of the Kings of Judah (1 Kings 14:29), and the Book of the Annals of the Kings of Israel (1 Kings 14:19). These court records would doubtless have provided more extensive coverage of the various rulers' economic, political, and social accomplishments than the Deuteronomistic author(s) cared to preserve. Unfortunately, none has survived.

Major Events and Their Meaning

Although the six books of Joshua through 2 Kings provide a sweeping overview of Israel's history, they do not contain all the factual information that a modern historian would consider essential. The Deuteronomistic writer(s)' goals are not those of a scientific investigator who seeks to assemble a complete and objective picture of the social, economic, cultural, and religious forces that created ancient Israel. Writing from a deliberately limited viewpoint, the Deuteronomistic author(s) proposed only one factor to account for Israel's rise and fall—its loyalty or disloyalty to Yahweh. Events that a twentieth-century historian would view as the natural consequences of specific political or military conditions, the Deuteronomistic writers attributed solely to Israel's state of religious health. The rise of new, aggressive Mesopotamian empires that repeatedly invaded Canaan during the eighth and sixth centuries B.C.E. thus were not considered the inevitable result of imperialist expansionism but the means that Yahweh used to punish his people. Assyria and Babylon were merely the instruments of his wrath.

Emphasizing the theological meaning rather than the mere facts of historical change, the Deuteronomistic History covers seven crucial periods or events:

1. The **conquest of Canaan** under Joshua's leadership
2. The twelve-tribe confederacy and its battles with assorted Canaanite city-states (Judges)
3. The Philistine crisis leading to tribal unification and establishment of the monarchy, which reaches its apex under kings David and Solomon (1 and 2 Samuel; 1 Kings)
4. The secession of the northern ten tribes after Solomon's death and the development of two kingdoms of Judah and Israel (1 Kings)
5. The parallel dynastic histories of the divided kingdoms, culminating in Assyria's destruction of Israel and its capital, Samaria, in 721 B.C.E. (2 Kings)
6. King Josiah's religious reforms in Judah following 621 B.C.E.
7. Babylon's obliteration of Judah and the Jerusalem Temple in 587 B.C.E. (2 Kings)

Besides ascribing every military victory to Yahweh's pleasure at the people's loyalty and every defeat to his anger at their unfaithfulness, the Deuteronomistic History is characterized by the following traits:

1. Yahwist prophets such as Elijah and Elisha are pictured as heroic crusaders against the cult of Baal and other Canaanite impurities. (Behaving as warriors as well as prophets, Elijah and Elisha attack and massacre practitioners of Baalism.)
2. The text emphasizes the preeminence of Jerusalem, the only site at which Yahweh accepts the sacrifices mandated by the Mosaic Torah. Because the northern kingdom (after 922 B.C.E.) maintained several rival sanctuaries, *all* of its kings were uniformly blacklisted.
3. Besides condemning every ruler in the northern kingdom, the DH also adversely judges every king of Judah who was not a thoroughgoing Yahwist. Painting David as the ideal monarch, the prototype of the God-favored ruler with whom Yahweh makes an "everlasting covenant," the Deuteronomistic narrative presents only two Davidic successors—Hezekiah and Josiah—as measuring up to Mosaic standards.

Although the books of Samuel appear to have been edited only slightly, the other books—Joshua, Judges, and Kings—reflect a heavy hand by the Deuteronomistic author(s), who appear to have shaped the narrative to underscore the moral causes of historical effects.

Although its main thrust is to demonstrate that Israel had earned its tragic fall, the Deuteronomistic History ends with a glimmer of hope. After briefly describing the ruling class's exile to Babylon, the account concludes with a minor but possibly significant event: After the death of Nebuchadnezzar, Judah's King Jehoiachin is released from prison and allowed to dine at the new Babylonian ruler's table (2 Kings 25:27–30). Did the final editor, after all, dare hope that, true to his word, Yahweh would soon restore the Davidic royal line?

Observing the Order of the Hebrew Bible

In the Hebrew Bible, the Deuteronomistic History and the prophetic books form a coherent unit separate from the third great division of the Tanak—the Writings (Kethuvim). This separation makes sense chronologically because most of the prophets were active during the historical period covered by the books of Kings (tenth through sixth centuries B.C.E.). Rabbinical editors place narratives of Israel's later history—after the Babylonian exile—such as Ezra and Nehemiah, among the Writings. Following the order in the Tanak, this book will first discuss the preexilic histories and then the individual prophets (Part 5). In Part 6 we will resume tracing the course of Israel's history in the postexilic books of Chronicles, Ezra, and Nehemiah. Although the little Book of Ruth appears after Judges in most Protestant and Roman Catholic Bibles, we will observe the Jewish placement and discuss it among the Writings (Part 6).

RECOMMENDED READING

Fretheim, Terence E. *Deuteronomic History.* Nashville, Tenn.: Abingdon Press, 1983.

Friedman, Richard E. *Who Wrote the Bible?* New York: Harper & Row, 1987.

McKenzie, Steven L. "Deuteronomistic History." In D. N. Freedman, ed., *The Anchor Bible Dictionary,* Vol. 2, pp. 160–168. New York: Doubleday, 1992. An excellent introduction to the topic.

Joshua

KEY THEMES

Integrating a variety of older sources into a Deuteronomistic framework, Joshua presents Israel's conquest of Canaan as a direct result of its obedience to the Mosaic Covenant. After an introduction emphasizing the link between Torah observance and military victory (Ch. 1), the book describes a rapid series of successful attacks on Canaanite centers (Chs. 2–12). The second half of the book lists the apportioning of land among the twelve tribes (Chs. 13–22), concluding with Joshua's farewell speech and an intertribal covenant-renewal ceremony (Chs. 23 and 24).

> As for me and my house, we will serve
>   Yahweh.
>
>   Joshua 24:15

The first unit of the Deuteronomistic History, the Bible's sixth book—Joshua—dramatizes the deuteronomic thesis in action. Rather than give an objective account of the twelve Israelite tribes' settlement in Canaan near the

beginning of the Iron Age, Joshua presents history through the eyes of faith. Using a variety of battle scenes to demonstrate its point, the book shows that Yahweh—portrayed as an invincible Warrior-King—directs Israel's assault on the Canaanites, granting the tribes total victory when they are fully loyal to their covenant with him.

The conviction that God will defeat all enemies of an obedient Israel is expressed in Joshua's vision of the supernatural "captain" of Yahweh's army, who appears in human form, brandishing "a naked sword" (Josh. 5:13–15). Fighting invisibly alongside Israel's soldiers, the presence of this heavenly commander reveals that God has predetermined Israel's success. Whereas the older Israelite generation had failed to believe that Yahweh could annihilate the Canaanites or capture Canaan's seemingly impregnable walled towns, Joshua's troops show an exemplary faith. The first military operation, the siege of Jericho, is accomplished without material weapons: Its defensive walls crumble at the sound of priestly trumpets and a "mighty war cry" shouted by the "whole people" (Josh. 6:1–5, 14–16). By contrast, a temporary lapse into disobedience causes the Israelites to fail in their siege of the nearby town of 'Ai. Only after executing the guilty parties do they take the city (Josh. 7).

Sources   Like the Torah, this story of the conquest betrays a variety of sources, probably including fragments of the JE document. Even older are quotations from the now-lost **Book of Jashar,** which seems to have been a collection of early Israelite war hymns and other poems, some of which may have been contemporaneous with the victories they celebrate. Using oral traditions as well as these written texts, the Deuteronomistic author(s) compiled Joshua's main narrative, creating their highly idealized version of a faithful Israel's military invincibility. The priestly writer(s) who produced the final edition during the Babylonian exile added some genealogical and other mate-

Like many cities throughout Canaan, Lachish was attacked repeatedly by invading armies. This Assyrian bas-relief from the royal palace at Nineveh realistically portrays the armies of Sennacherib laying siege to Lachish (701 B.C.E.). Although Lachish, along with forty-six other Judean towns, was totally demolished (2 Kings 23:18), Jerusalem miraculously survived the Assyrian invasion. Note the assault ramp built against Lachish's gates and the civilian inhabitants fleeing by a side exit (right), while three naked captives are impaled on pointed wooden stakes (lower center). (Courtesy of the Trustees of the British Museum)

rial, primarily to the book's second half. A composite work, Joshua thus includes material that spans a lengthy period—poetry that was first composed orally during the conquest and priestly commentary from the postexilic age.

The Conquest of Canaan as a Continuation of the Exodus

Joshua as Another Moses   Despite repetitions and sometimes disjointed narratives that result from the authors' use of multiple sources, Joshua gives an exciting picture of the conquest of Canaan. The charismatic leader of twelve tribes united by Yahwistic faith, Joshua is presented as a second Moses. Like Moses, he leads the people through parted waters—this time those of the Jordan River, which is held back at floodtide to permit Israel's crossing. Instead of Moses' staff, however, it is the Ark of the Covenant, carried by priests, that effects the miracle (Josh. 3–4). Like Moses, too, Joshua experiences a theophany, a vision of Yahweh's divine

general whose participation guarantees victory over the Canaanites. He also resembles the great lawgiver in adding to the Book of the Covenant, in proclaiming Yahweh's commandments, and in presiding over a reenactment at **Shechem** of the pact that binds Israel to Yahweh (Josh. 4:1–9; 23–24).

The Fall of Jericho   After entering Canaan, the Israelites do not at once begin their military campaign. Instead, all males born during the forty-year wandering assemble at **Gilgal** to be circumcised, an operation that incapacitates them for several days, though the threatened residents of nearby **Jericho** make no attempt to take advantage of their vulnerability (Josh. 5:1–12). Now ritually acceptable, the warriors still do not immediately attack the Canaanite stronghold but follow Joshua's instructions to march silently around the city seven times until a signal is given, when they are to raise a loud shout, blow their trumpets, and charge Jericho's ramparts (Josh. 6). That is the earlier of two ac-

The world's "oldest walled town," Jericho was first occupied by prehistoric settlers about 9000 B.C.E. The round tower, twenty-five feet high, dates from the earliest Neolithic (New Stone Age) period (8000–7000 B.C.E.). Erosion has removed most of Jericho's remains from the late Bronze Age period, the time of Israel's invasion of Canaan described in the Book of Joshua (about 1200 B.C.E.). (Courtesy of PhotoEdit)

non-Hebrews in Canaan may shock modern sensibilities, but the concept of holy war plays an important part in the history of many Near Eastern religions.

After the spectacular victory at Jericho, the Israelites suffer a setback at **'Ai** (Josh. 7). Inquiring of Yahweh why his people have been ignominiously routed, Joshua is told that Yahweh was not with them because an Israelite soldier has violated the ban on Jericho by stealing and hiding some booty. Casting lots, Joshua eliminates all citizens except a man named Achan, who admits having taken some of Jericho's valuables for himself. Achan, his wife, children, and flocks are then stoned to death. After they have purged the sinner from their midst, the Israelites easily succeed in capturing 'Ai (Josh. 8).

The campaign is thereafter an uninterrupted series of Israelite triumphs. All enemies are defeated, including the giant race of Anakim who had intimidated the Israelite spies forty years earlier (Num. 13:33). Thirty-one kings and their armies are vanquished, although large areas, such as the Philistine territory to the southwest, remain unconquered. Joshua divides the conquered country among the twelve tribes (Josh. 13–22), thus bringing to a satisfactory conclusion the first part of Yahweh's plan for the region.

Farewell Speech and Covenant Renewal Joshua's final speech to the people (Josh. 23–24) is modeled on Moses' farewell address in Deuteronomy, which it resembles in diction, style, and sense of urgency. Like his predecessor, Joshua reminds Israel of her debt to Yahweh and of the people's obligation to obey the law faithfully. Asking them to choose today between Yahweh and the gods their fathers had worshiped beyond the Euphrates River in Mesopotamia, he sets the proper example: "As for me and my house, we will serve Yahweh" (Josh. 24:15).

After reciting the covenant laws before the assembled community at Shechem, Joshua erects a stone pillar to act as witness that the people

counts of Jericho's fall that have been woven imperfectly into a single narrative. The second version emphasizes the priests' role in carrying the Ark of the Covenant and sounding ram's-horn trumpets during some thirteen circuits of the town (Josh. 6:4, 8–9, 11–13).

On the final day, the city walls collapse except for that part supporting the house of **Rahab** the harlot (possibly the priestess of a Canaanite fertility cult), who had hidden Israelite spies when they had reconnoitered the city. The entire population is placed under the "sacred ban," which means that the people are massacred as an offering to Yahweh. The Israelites' belief that Yahweh required the deaths of all

Some archaeologists believe that this monolith may be the stone that Joshua erected at Shechem to hear and bear witness to Yahweh's covenant with Israel (Josh. 24:26–28). Located forty-one miles north of Jerusalem between Mount Ebal and Mount Gerizim, Shechem was an ancient Canaanite sanctuary that became the first religious center of Israel's tribal confederacy. (Courtesy of Erich Lessing/ Magnum Photos)

have heard Yahweh's commandments and have agreed to abide by them. This covenant ceremony (Josh. 24) is regarded as one of the most important passages in the Old Testament, because it embodies an authentic tradition of Israel's earliest reaffirmation in Canaan of the Sinai covenant. It has been suggested that the Israelites held the ceremony at Shechem, which they did not have to fight to possess, because the area—an ancient cult center of Baal Berith ("Lord of the Covenant")—was already occupied by related tribes or at least by a people friendly to the Israelites.

Did these people who worshiped the Canaanite El (to whom Jacob had built an altar

nearby) also embrace the Yahwist religion of the new arrivals? Did they agree to accept Yahweh, his mighty acts in Egypt, and the desert experience as part of their own heritage? Some prominent scholars see in the Shechem covenant ceremony an extension of the covenant provisions to kindred tribesmen who had not participated in the exodus experience. If true, this would explain why there is no record of the Israelites' having to struggle for control of the highly desirable Shechem region.

The Conquest and Archaeological Evidence

Although the first part of Joshua depicts Israel's invasion of Canaan as lightning fast and totally successful, a careful reading of specific passages gives a different impression. Most of the conquest stories deal only with the central hill country, while Joshua 13 records that much of Israel's future territory had yet to be captured (Josh. 13:1–6). Historians believe that the first chapter of Judges gives a more accurate picture, noting that even after Joshua's death most of the Promised Land remained under native Canaanite control. Archaeological excavations confirm that Israel's occupation of Canaan was a slow and gradual process, a piecemeal settlement rather than a swift conquest, as Joshua depicts it. Excavations at several sites, such as Lachish, Debir, and Hazor, show that a few towns were attacked and burned about 1200 B.C.E. At these places, a relatively advanced Canaanite civilization was replaced by a materially inferior culture, possibly that of invading Israelites. At other sites, such as Jericho and 'Ai, however, archaeology does not support the biblical record. Radiocarbon dating proves that Jericho had been destroyed centuries before Joshua's time and that if any settlement then existed at the site, it was insignificant, a far cry from the massively fortified city that the Bible depicts. In Joshua's day, the town of 'Ai had been abandoned for an even longer period; its very name means "ruin."

Although Joshua bears some relation to historical events—Israel did eventually settle in

Canaan—the book was not written to record raw fact but to teach the religious significance of events. As in other parts of the Deuteronomistic History, the drama of Israel's struggle to possess—and keep—its homeland is carefully crafted to express the writer(s)' insight that Yahweh shapes history to reveal his will. A sixth act to the Pentateuch, Joshua marks the beginning of Israel's historical transition from a nomadic, rootless way of life to a settled agrarian existence. The desert wanderings are over; now Israel must face the challenge of living up to its vow to recognize Yahweh alone—while surrounded by the temptations of Canaanite religion and culture. Like Moses' last speeches in Deuteronomy, Joshua's final warnings against compromising Yahwism with the cults of Baal and Asherah, gods who preside over both human and agricultural fecundity, resound with new force.

RECOMMENDED READING

Boling, Robert, G. *Joshua*. Garden City, N.Y.: Doubleday, 1982.

———. "Joshua, Book of." In D. N. Freedman, ed., *The Anchor Bible Dictionary*, Vol. 3, pp. 1002–1015. New York: Doubleday, 1992.

Dever, William G. "Israel, History of (Archaeology and the 'Conquest')." In D. N. Freedman, ed., *The Anchor Bible Dictionary*, Vol. 3, pp. 545–558. New York: Doubleday, 1992.

Gottwald, Norman K. *The Tribes of Yahweh: A Sociology of the Religion of Liberated Israel, 1250–1050 B.C.E.* Maryknoll, N.Y.: Orbis Books, 1979.

Kaufmann, Yehezkel. *The Biblical Account of the Conquest of Palestine*. Translated by M. Dagut. Jerusalem: Magnes, 1955.

Kenyon, Kathleen M. *Archaeology in the Holy Land*, 3rd ed. New York: Praeger, 1970. By an authority on the excavations at Jericho.

Soggin, J. Alberto. *Joshua*. Philadelphia: Westminster Press, 1972.

Wright, G. Ernest. *Biblical Archaeology*, 2nd ed. Philadelphia: Westminster Press, 1962. An expert introduction to archaeological discoveries in Palestine, including those relating to the conquest.

Judges

KEY THEMES

A transitional book surveying the period between Joshua's death and the formation of the monarchy (c. 1200–1020 B.C.E.), Judges describes an often brutal struggle between Yahwist leaders and Canaanite culture for the possession of Israel's soul. After a double introduction (Chs. 1 and 2) stressing the dire consequences of assimilation with Canaanites, Judges recounts the exploits of a series of charismatic military leaders, called judges, who fight Israel's many enemies. Major episodes include Deborah and Barak (Chs. 4 and 5), Gideon and Abimelech (Chs. 6–9), and Samson and Delilah (Chs. 13–16). Concluding with miscellaneous anecdotes not integrated into the main narrative, such as the war against Benjamin (Chs. 19–21), the book laments the savage state of affairs when no king ruled over Israel.

> In those days there was no king in Israel,
> and every man did as he pleased.
> Judges 21:25

Dramatizing the Deuteronomic Theory of History

Era of the Judges   Combining a wide variety of ancient poems, riddles, battle hymns, military annals, and legendary anecdotes, the Deuteronomistic editors create a picture of the hectic days before Israel's independent tribes united under a single ruler. The DH writers attempt to impart some coherence to those extraordinarily chaotic and primitive times, when Israel fought desperately to keep a toehold in the Palestinian hill country and to maintain its integrity as a covenant community. Applying the Deuteronomistic theology of history to extremely heterogeneous material, the editors organize Israel's history into a cyclical pattern. When a faithful judge presides and the people worship Yahweh exclusively, the whole nation prospers, winning battles against the Canaanites and reaping the benefits of their heritage. After the Yahwist judge dies, the people soon "prostitute themselves to **Baal**," causing Yahweh to desert them and deliver them into their enemies' power. In their anguish, the people cry out to Yahweh, who "feels pity" and raises up a new judge to overthrow the oppressors. After a generation of revived Yahwism, the people again backslide, and the whole cycle begins again. The DH theory of history is explicitly set forth in Judges 2: 11–23, which ends with the writers' theological explanation of Israel's inability to expel the Canaanites from the territory promised Abraham's descendants:

> Then Yahweh's anger flamed out against Israel, and he said, "Since this people has broken the covenant . . . I will not evict any of the nations that Joshua left in the land . . ."; this was to test them by means of these nations, to see whether Israel would or would not tread the paths of Yahweh as once their ancestors had trodden them.
>
> Judges 2:20–22

The dozen **judges** who rescue Israel from foreign domination are not judicial figures in the legal sense; they do not preside over a court or usually render verdicts among disputing parties. They are charismatic ("spirit-filled") military leaders who drive off local tribes that repeatedly raid Israel's territory in the Palestinian hill country. In general, the judges did not rule over all twelve Israelite tribes as Joshua, the first judge, is reported to have done. At most, an individual judge can muster support from two or three tribes, sometimes only a clan or two. Thus, the judges did not reign successively over a united Israel, and individual leaders were able to influence only a small portion of the Israelite confederacy, a term some scholars use to describe the extremely loose political structure of Israel in the days before monarchy (kingship) was established. Historically, the judges' administrations probably overlapped, but the Deuteronomistic History presents them as a chronological series in order to make each judge's career appear as another example of the sin-punishment-restoration cycle.

Deborah and Barak   The Bible writers did not regard this period of Israel's history, in retrospect, as an admirable era. Not only was Israel repeatedly devastated by enemy attacks and humiliated by the Philistines, but the whole tenor of life was both precarious and savage. Judges 4 records the activities of a celebrated female judge, the prophetess **Deborah**, and her associate Barak, who commanded 10,000 men against a Canaanite coalition. The completeness of their victory is epitomized by the act of a "mere" woman, **Jael**, who single-handedly strikes down the fleeing Canaanite general Sisera (Judg. 4:4–22).

Jael's patriotic murder of her foreign guest is commemorated in a long poem (Judg. 5:1–31), which scholars believe to be one of the oldest parts of the Bible. An individual death on behalf of the nation also climaxes the episode involving **Jephthah**, another military leader who, to repay Yahweh for his victory over the Ammonites, sacrifices his only child, an unnamed daughter (Judg. 11:29–40).

Gideon and Abimelech   Even a basically inspirational story like that of **Gideon**, who with his band of only 300 men routed the Midianites, is marred by episodes of cruelty (Judg. 6–8). Still worse, however, is the account of Gideon's son **Abimelech**, who after murdering his seventy brothers, manages to have himself crowned at Shechem, the old sanctuary of the tribal confederacy. Abimelech rules only a few northern clans living near Shechem and his reign lasts only three years, but before he is killed he tortures, maims, and slaughters thousands of his compatriots. The brief reign of Gideon's son vividly illustrates the evils of a despotic kingship and helps support the antimonarchical view encountered in subsequent books of the Former Prophets.

Samson and Delilah   One of the most vividly remembered of Israel's folk heroes, **Samson**—famous for his brawn and his riddles—is strangely unlike any of the other judges whose exploits have been recorded. An angel twice foretells his birth to a childless couple who, as divinely instructed, dedicate the child as a Nazirite. As visible signs of their consecration to Yahweh, **Nazirites** were to abstain from wine and other alcoholic drinks, eat only ritually "clean" foods, and leave their hair uncut. A man of strong passions as well as superhuman physical strength, Samson grows up far from the Nazirite ascetic ideal. His battles with the Philistines are less the result of a divine calling than the often accidental byproduct of his amatory adventures. A seafaring people who then occupied the southwest coast of Canaan, the **Philistines** had already mastered the techniques of manufacturing iron weapons and horse-drawn war chariots, skills the Israelites apparently lacked. In the books of Judges and Samuel, they are the primary threat to Yahweh's people.

Unlike Gideon or Jephthah, Samson does not lead an army against the enemy but fights the Philistines single-handedly, typically for personal reasons involving his relationships with women. Samson's sexual affairs, whether with wife or harlot, repeatedly involve him in dangerous confrontations with the enemy (Judg. 14:1–15:8; 16:1–3). The hero's most celebrated entanglement is with **Delilah**, whom the Philistines bribe to betray her hitherto invulnerable lover. Breaking his Nazirite vow by revealing the secret of his strength, Samson, shorn of his hair, is abandoned by Yahweh to be captured, blinded, and enslaved. Only when his hair begins to grow again does Yahweh's spirit empower Samson to exact a final revenge on his tormentors. In pulling down the temple of **Dagon** upon 3000 Philistine idolators, the blinded hero surpasses his previous achievements: "Those he killed at his death outnumbered those he had killed in his life" (Judg. 16:30).

Some critics regard Samson, whose name means "sun" or "solar," as a mythological figure whom a Hebrew writer transformed into an Israelite champion. Certainly if Samson is a historic character, his fellow Israelites do not perceive him as Yahweh's chosen instrument against the Philistines (Judg. 15:9–20). The Deuteronomistic historian, however, may have regarded him as an example of Yahweh's ability to use even the most unlikely human agents to accomplish his purpose. When Samson crushes thousands of Dagon worshipers, he proves himself an obedient officer of Yahweh the divine warrior.

The War Against Benjamin   The Deuteronomistic editors reserved the most barbarous narrative in Judges for the conclusion. Chapters 19–21 describe the rape-murder by the Benjaminites of a Levite priest's concubine, whose body the Levite cuts into eleven pieces and sends to eleven Israelite tribes, asking them to avenge the atrocity by declaring holy war on the Benjaminites. The tribe of **Benjamin** is thereafter almost totally exterminated. Having sworn never to marry their own daughters to any Benjaminite, the other tribes conspire to get around their vow by encouraging the few surviving men of Benjamin to kidnap the women of **Shiloh**. In this way, the nearly extinct Benjaminites can recruit mates from fellow Israelites without the other tribes' breaking their oaths. Like the sorry tale of Abimelech, this episode may at one time have served an antimonarchical purpose, because Israel's first king, Saul, was both a failure and a Benjaminite, the scion of a tainted group.

Apparently shocked at the social and moral disorders he transcribed, Judges' editor could not resist penning a final disapproving comment: "In those days there was no king in Israel, and every man did as he pleased." Compared with this anarchy, the monarchy with its centralized government seemed a decided improvement.

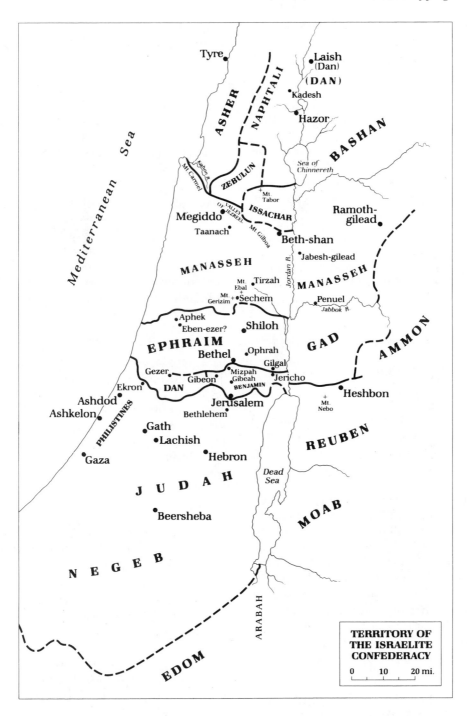

Tyre

Laish
(Dan)
(DAN)

Kadesh

Hazor

ASHER

NAPHTALI

BASHAN

Mediterranean Sea

Kishon R.

Mt. Carmel

ZEBULUN

Sea of
Chinnereth

+ Mt.
Tabor

ISSACHAR

*VALLEY
OF
JEZREEL*

Megiddo

Taanach

Mt. Gilboa

Beth-shan

Ramoth-
gilead

Jabesh-gilead

Jordan R.

MANASSEH

Mt.
Ebal

Tirzah

MANASSEH

Mt.
Gerizim +

+ Sechem

Penuel

Jabbok R.

Aphek

Eben-ezer?

Shiloh

EPHRAIM

Bethel

Ophrah

GAD

AMMON

Gilgal

Gezer

Mizpah

Gibeah

Jericho

Heshbon

Gibeon

DAN

BENJAMIN

Ekron

Ashdod

Jerusalem

+ Mt.
Nebo

Ashkelon

PHILISTINES

Bethlehem

Gath

Lachish

REUBEN

Gaza

Hebron

J U D A H

*Dead
Sea*

MOAB

Beersheba

N E G E B

ARABAH

EDOM

**TERRITORY OF
THE ISRAELITE
CONFEDERACY**

0   10   20 mi.

RECOMMENDED READING

Albright, William F. *Yahweh and the Gods of Canaan: A Historical Analysis of Two Contrasting Faiths.* Garden City, N.Y.: Doubleday/Anchor Books, 1969.

Boling, Robert G. *Judges.* Garden City, N.Y.: Doubleday, 1975.

Cross, Frank M. *Canaanite Myth and Hebrew Epic, Essays in the History of the Religion of Israel.* Cambridge, Mass.: Harvard University Press, 1973.

de Vaux, Roland. *The Early History of Israel.* Translated by D. Smith. Philadelphia: Westminster Press, 1978.

Fretheim, Terence E. *Deuteronomic History.* Nashville, Tenn.: Abingdon Press, 1983.

Webb, Barry G. *The Book of Judges: An Integrated Reading.* Sheffield, Eng.: JSOT Press, 1987.

1 Samuel

KEY THEMES

A remarkably vivid theologizing of history, 1 Samuel traces the origin and development of kingship in Israel. Incorporating several different sources, including one favorable to the new institution of monarchy and another strongly opposing it, the first section records the career of Samuel (Chs. 1–12) and the second narrates the rise and tragic fall of Saul, Israel's first king (Chs. 13–31). Priest, prophet, and judge, Samuel functions as Yahweh's kingmaker and kingbreaker, initially anointing Saul and, after this first choice proves unsatisfactory, later secretly anointing David, represented as the recipient of God's permanent favor. The book's second half relates Saul's psychological and political decline, to which the account of young David's ascent to power serves as an ironic counterpoint.

> It is not you [Samuel] they have rejected; they have rejected me [Yahweh] from ruling over them.
>
> 1 Samuel 8:8

In Hebrew, which was originally written without vowels, the Book of Samuel was contained on a single scroll. When the book was translated into Greek, however, it required two scrolls; the Septuagint translators therefore divided the work into 1 and 2 Samuel. A coherent narrative unit, the two volumes present one overarching theme—the rise of David from obscure shepherd boy to king of "all Israel." As the figure of Moses dominates four books of Torah, so that of David overshadows this account of Israel's political growth from a weak group of loosely confederated tribes to a powerful, united monarchy. David, in fact, is the pivotal character in the Deuteronomistic History: His appearance as Yahweh's divinely appointed ruler occupies the two central books. The first two, Joshua and Judges, act as a prolog to David's story, highlighting the chaotic conditions that prevailed "when there was no king in Israel," before David arrived to rescue the covenant people from their own disorganization. The last two books, 1 and 2 Kings, evaluate the reigns of David's successors, most of whom compare unfavorably to their forefather David, the one Yahweh favors. In vowing to maintain David's heirs on the royal throne forever (2 Sam. 7), Yahweh binds himself to David and his descendants as to no other Israelite constituency, guaranteeing that Davidic hopes are inextricably part of Israel's future history.

Historical Narrative of the Davidic Line

Historical Accuracy In recent years, a significant minority of historians have denied any reliability or historicity to the books of Joshua through Kings. Noting a number of inconsistencies and factual errors in the text, they dismiss the entire history as mere fiction, a work compiled late in the postexilic period to create an attractive past for the (then) politically impotent people of Judah. According to this "minimalist" view, David and his Israelite empire represent wishful thinking, a glamorous but mythical king and kingdom. While acknowledging that the Deuteronomistic author was more concerned about advancing a theological agenda than dispassionately recording history, the majority of scholars believe that David, Solomon, and their successors were historical personages. Two recent archaeological discoveries, the Tel Dan stela and a stela of the Moabite king Mesha (both ninth century B.C.E.), refer to the "House [Dynasty] of David," providing extrabiblical confirmation that the Davidic line existed.

The Narrative as Literature   Long before the Greek historian Herodotus compiled his account of the Persian War (c. 450 B.C.E.), as Baruch Halpern has observed, Israelite scribes created masterpieces of historical narrative, albeit highly theologized. (See the recommended reading, Halpern.) In parts of Judges, Samuel, and Kings, one finds passages that feature superb characterization, psychological insight, and a sure grasp of historical cause and effect—particularly the interconnection between human ambition and social and military consequences—unmatched elsewhere in ancient Near Eastern literature.

Scholars have long recognized that the present books of Samuel represent several discrete stages of development, at different times incorporating sources that were originally separate documents. These sources include a narrative about the Ark of the Covenant, including its capture by the Philistines (1 Sam. 4:1–7:1); an account of Saul's abortive kingship (9:1–11:15); the story of David's spectacular early achievements (16–31); and a long narrative about the various struggles of David's heirs to take over the throne, a document variously called the Court History or Succession Narrative (2 Sam. 9–20 and 1 Kings 1–2). Some critics have argued that much of Samuel was derived from the group that produced the J document, which forms the main narrative framework of the Pentateuch. Certainly, the final version contains poems of great antiquity, such as the Song of Hannah (1 Sam. 2:1–10), David's beautiful eu-

logy for Saul and Jonathan (2 Sam. 1:19–27), David's lament over Abner (2 Sam. 3:33 ff.), and the Hymn of David (2 Sam. 22). Apparently less thoroughly revised to conform to Deuteronomy's principles than Joshua, Judges, or Kings, the books of Samuel nonetheless include some passages interpolated by the Deuteronomistic editors (e.g., 1 Sam. 8 and 12).

Conflicting Views of the Monarchy   Alert readers will notice that 1 Samuel features two strikingly different attitudes toward the monarchy, one positive and the other decidedly negative. In Chapter 8, the antimonarchical source represents Samuel as declaring that installing a king to reign over Israel is tantamount to rejecting Yahweh's theocratic rule. According to this passage, the establishment of a monarchy stems from the people's failure to trust in Israel's God to govern them directly, or through temporarily appointed deliverers, such as the judges. Samuel then warns the people of all the hardships—taxation, military conscription, tyranny—that await them if they insist on imitating other nations by having a king. Although cast in the form of prophecy, Samuel's warning actually represents Deuteronomistic hindsight, a looking back at the oppressive burden that the expensive splendors of David's royal dynasty imposed on Israel. A second version of Samuel's antimonarchical warning (1 Sam. 10:17–27) and a longer Deuteronomistic judgment (1 Sam. 12:1–25) make it clear that Yahweh only reluctantly consents to the people's demand for a king. As if coerced by popular pressure, Yahweh grudgingly permits Samuel to anoint Saul (Chs. 9 and 10), virtually assuring Saul's eventual failure. Only when Yahweh chooses freely, does he select a king whom he will consistently support (1 Sam. 16:1–13).

In contrast to these negative views of the monarchy, some passages favorably portray Saul and his early accomplishments, such as the accounts of his anointing and his military victory over the Ammonites (1 Sam. 9:1–10:16; 11:1–15). When Saul has been eliminated and replaced by David, a generally promonarchical view prevails, implying that Yahweh is generally well served by the Davidic rulers (2 Sam. 7). After the negative verdict in 1 Samuel 12, no further criticism of the monarchy *as an institution* occurs in the Deuteronomistic History. Individual kings are condemned, but the legitimacy of the Davidic line itself is henceforth never questioned.

Observing Yahweh's Rule   Besides the theme of divine election, the books of Samuel emphasize the absolute necessity of Israel's leaders adhering faithfully to Yahweh's commands. As commentators have pointed out, this theme is introduced at the opening of 1 Samuel, when Hannah offers her prayer of thanksgiving for Samuel's birth. Declaring that Yahweh exercises total control over human lives, awarding success to the humbly obedient and a catastrophic downfall to the arrogant, Hannah articulates the standard that will determine the fate of Israelite rulers:

> For Yahweh is an all-knowing God
> and his is the weighing of deeds.
> The bow of the mighty is broken
> but the feeble have girded themselves with
>   strength.

* * *

> Yahweh makes poor and rich,
> he humbles and also exalts.
> 1 Samuel 2:3–4, 7

Supporting the weak and overthrowing the strong who grow proud or oppressive, Yahweh initiates unexpected reversals of fortune among Israel's leadership. In addition to exalting Samuel while removing Eli and his sons from priestly office at Shiloh, Yahweh brings about Saul's ruin even as he raises David from obscurity to unprecedented wealth and power. When David, in turn, grows overconfident and abuses his kingly prerogatives by murdering Uriah, Yahweh punishes his favorite by creating for David the same kind of trouble that the king had inflicted on others. Mirror images of their father's ambition, lust, or opportunism, David's sons Ammon and Absalom wreak havoc within the royal household. As if reenacting his father's undermining of Saul, Absalom captures the people's affections and temporarily drives David from power, causing him to experience what Saul must have felt when displaced by a younger rival. As Hannah had correctly observed, when dealing with Israel's God even kings must expect their political ups and downs to correlate precisely with their degree of loyalty to Yahwistic principles.

Samuel, Saul, and the Philistine Crisis

Although named for **Samuel**, the first major character to appear in the book, 1 Samuel is really David's story and that of the monarchy he founded. But there is no servile flattery such as is found in other Eastern dynastic histories. The court history is justly admired for its clear-sighted candor in recording the human weaknesses and flaws of one who was already a national hero. On comparing Samuel's portrait of **David**, with his admixture of courage, ambition, calculation, and religious fervor, with the idealized version in 1 Chronicles, Samuel's relative objectivity is immediately obvious.

Despite the diversity of materials it uses, 1 Samuel is a skillfully constructed work of literature, tying together disparate sources with the same theme of divine election that motivates the action in Genesis and Exodus. As Yahweh suddenly, with no reasons given, calls selected individuals like Abraham, Jacob, Joseph, or Moses to perform special tasks, so he chooses Samuel from before birth to serve him. The stories of the principal characters, each of whom is divinely elected in turn, are intricately interwoven. When **Eli**, the well-meaning but ineffectual high priest who acts as Samuel's mentor, declines into impotence, God elevates Samuel to a position of moral leadership, ensuring the continuity of the covenant and Ark traditions.

As Samuel replaces Eli, so he prepares **Saul**, who first appears in Chapter 8, to take over Israel's rulership. Saul no sooner ascends the throne (Ch. 13) than Samuel breaks with his protégé, becoming his chief critic (Ch. 15). David's appearance on the political stage (Chs. 16–17) introduces a new conflict, the jealous competition between King Saul and his predestined successor—a rivalry that ends with Saul's death (Ch. 31).

The Philistine Crisis The first seven chapters, describing Samuel's career, also paint a bleak picture of Israel's political and religious situation, which is now even more desperate than that portrayed in Judges. Eli is feeble, and his sons are corrupt; the Philistines inflict a humiliating defeat on the Israelite armies and capture the Ark of the Covenant, the portable shrine on which Yahweh is invisibly enthroned. Israel's loss of its most sacred possession is a terrible blow to national prestige, but its captors receive no benefits. The Philistines are afflicted with a strange plague of tumors, which they superstitiously attribute to the Ark's malignant presence. Although a twenty-year peace ensues following the Ark's return to Israel, continued Philistine hostility denies the Hebrews any real security.

Samuel and Saul With the Philistines and other aggressors pressing upon them, many Israelites may have doubted their nation's continued existence. Some may have recognized that the old tribal confederacy, with no central leadership and riven by uncooperative individualism, was no match against a tightly organized enemy headed by a warrior-king. With Israel's future uncertain, realistic tribal leaders seem to have decided that national survival required the political unity that only an able king could give. When the elders petition Samuel to appoint a king, however, no higher motive is assigned their request than a conformist desire to "be like the other nations" (1 Sam. 8:19).

Although the Deuteronomistic author(s) ed-

ited the books of Samuel more lightly than Joshua or Judges, their ambivalence toward the monarchy is evident here. Samuel warns the people that a monarchy will exploit the people economically, including outright confiscation of their best property (1 Sam. 8:10–22). But when the people insist, Samuel privately anoints Saul (c. 1020 B.C.E.), an obscure member of the tribe of Benjamin (1 Sam. 9:14–10:8; cf. the second account of Saul's being chosen king in 1 Sam. 10:17–27).

Scholars believe that the portrait of Saul that we now find in 1 Samuel is a distortion of an older account of his reign that his supporters composed. Regarding David's heirs as the nation's rightful rulers, pro-Davidic editors later retouched Saul's portrait, transforming him into the neurotic, paranoid failure he had to be in order for David to supplant him. Samuel's original choice of Saul to lead the nation out of its social confusion and military weakness is logical. Tall, handsome, and a brave soldier, Saul belonged to a tribe so small and insignificant that his election does not arouse tribal jealousies. The incidents over which Samuel withdraws his support (in David's favor) illustrate, even after editing, how impossible was Saul's historical role. When the prophet-priest fails to appear, to offer the sacrifices necessary before going into battle, and when the army is deserting in droves, Saul performs the ritual—only to be denounced as usurping priestly prerogatives (1 Sam. 13:8–15). (Both David and Solomon later routinely assume priestly duties.) The decisive break occurs when Saul, perhaps feeling pity for a fellow ruler, spares the life of Agag, an **Amalekite** king who has been "put under the ban," designated as a sacrifice to Yahweh. Furious, Samuel proceeds to butcher Agag as an offering to God (1 Sam. 15:10–33). Withdrawing the support of Israel's religious institutions, Samuel not only excommunicates Saul but also ensures his political demise. Depicted as suffering from epilepsy and extreme depression, Saul rapidly loses control of events, particularly when the Philistines launch a new attack.

The Rise of David

Saul and David   At this critical moment, the narrative's real hero appears, a charismatic youth destined to replace Saul as king and to establish a dynasty that will endure for more than four centuries. The writers' use of multiple sources is apparent in the two different versions of David's introduction to Saul's court. In the first, David is presented as a "brave man and a fighter" who is also a musician, a harpist whom Saul employs to drive out the "evil spirits" with which Yahweh afflicts the king (1 Sam. 16:14–23). In the second, David is introduced as a stranger to Saul (1 Sam. 17:55–56), a mere "lad" who volunteers to fight single-handedly the Philistine champion **Goliath**. Otherwise unarmed, he fells Goliath with a stone from his slingshot (1 Sam. 17:4–54). As a leader who would transform Israel from a faltering confederacy into a powerful, if short-lived, Near Eastern empire, David is credited with legendary feats, some of which may have been accomplished by his associates. An appendix to 2 Samuel states that Goliath was slain by one of David's soldiers: "Elhanan son of Jair from Bethlehem killed Goliath of Gath" (2 Sam. 21:19).

The biblical narrators are concerned less with historical accuracy than theological significance. As Yahweh's chosen one—Samuel secretly anoints him king even before he joins Saul's retinue (1 Sam. 16:1–13)—David acts as God's representative. When the writers portray him as an inexperienced shepherd boy who overcomes a heavily armed giant, the purpose is to demonstrate that Yahweh can use weak human vessels to accomplish great deeds. David's speech to Goliath makes clear that defeating an enemy is Yahweh's work, for which no human being can take credit:

> You come against me with sword and spear and javelin, but I come to you in the name of Yahweh. . . . Today Yahweh will deliver you into my hand and I shall kill you . . . so that all the earth may know that there is a God in Israel, and . . . that it is not by sword or by spear that Yahweh gives the victory . . .
>
> 1 Samuel 17:45–47

That David basks in divine favor is also illustrated by the declaration of love that Saul's son **Jonathan** lavishes on the victorious youth. As the king's presumed heir, Jonathan should be David's chief rival, but instead he works to promote David's advancement, stripping off his armor and giving it to his friend—an act that foreshadows David's taking his place as Saul's successor (1 Sam. 18:1–5). Jonathan's sister **Michal** also becomes devoted to David, who, by marrying the king's daughter, further cements his ties to the royal family. If David's conquest of his children does not arouse Saul's suspicions, the song of Israelite women indiscreetly praising David's superiority to the king makes him consider the potential danger to his reign inherent in David's ambitions: "Saul has killed his thousands, and David his tens of thousands." The king determines to eliminate his rival by having him lead assaults on the Philistines (1 Sam. 18).

Blessed with an ability to command personal loyalty, David uses the partisanship of Jonathan and Michal, both of whom prefer to help him rather than their father, to circumvent Saul's attempts to murder him. When forced to flee Israel and take refuge among the Philistines, David even wins the friendship of their ruler, on whom he also practices his abundant powers of deception (1 Sam. 19–23). An outlaw and guerrilla fighter, David survives by his wits, eluding capture and twice refusing to kill Saul when he has the opportunity to do so. His restraint is well paid, for when the Philistines eliminate Saul and Jonathan at the Battle of **Gilboa**, the way is open for David to ascend the throne (1 Sam. 24–31).

2 Samuel

KEY THEMES

2 Samuel describes the long reign of King David, beginning with accounts of his brilliant

military victories (Chs. 2–5), centralization of the national religion in his new capital (Ch. 6), and the inauguration of a royal covenant in which Yahweh swears to create a Davidic dynasty that will last forever. An abrupt reversal of his fortunes takes place, however, when David oversteps the ethical limits of kingly power by committing adultery with Bathsheba and murdering her husband, Uriah (Chs. 11 and 12). Although Yahweh does not abandon him, David's abuse of his position results in dire consequences—treachery and violence in his household (Chs. 13 and 14), and Absalom's rebellion that temporarily drives him from his throne (Chs. 15–20). An appendix of miscellaneous narratives and poetry closes the book (Chs. 21–24).

> Your House [the Davidic dynasty] and your
> sovereignty will be established forever.
> 2 Samuel 7:16

Because 1 and 2 Samuel were originally a single volume, there is no true break in the narrative between the two books. 2 Samuel opens with David's receiving news of Saul's death, a scene that sets the tone of David's rise to power and reflects the hero's sometimes ambiguous character. When Saul and his sons—human obstacles to David's career—are eliminated without his having to lift a hand against them, David typically punishes the men responsible for advancing his cause, acquiring a public reputation for piously mourning fallen enemies. By executing the Amalekite who claims to have slain the former king, David not only absolves himself of any responsibility for Saul's death but also proclaims the life of Yahweh's anointed ruler to be sacrosanct—a policy indispensable for protecting his own anointed status (2 Sam. 1:1–16). Acknowledged king of **Judah**, his own tribe, David has yet to become ruler of the northern ten tribes, who accept Saul's son Ishbaal as their rightful monarch. After two Benjaminite chieftains assassinate Ishbaal, bringing his head to David, the Judaean king explicitly refers to his treatment of the Amalekite messenger, sentencing his would-be benefactors to death (2 Sam.

4:1–12). Although he owes much of his success to **Joab**, commander of the army, David repeatedly condemns his general for dispatching the king's opponents (2 Sam. 3:22–39), particularly for Joab's removal of David's traitorous son **Absalom** (2 Sam. 18:9–19:9). David's exquisite laments over rivals that others have swept from his path are justly famous, especially that for Saul and Jonathan, whose love for him had been "more wonderful than the love of a woman" (2 Sam. 1:26).

After Ishbaal's murder, David, who had reigned over Judah at **Hebron** for seven years, is acclaimed king of all twelve tribes (2 Sam. 5:1–5). Freed from pursuing intertribal warfare with the House of Saul, David undertakes military campaigns that eventually expand Israel's borders to the limits promised in the Abrahamic Covenant. One of his first exploits is to capture the Jebusite city of **Jerusalem**, which Joshua and his successors had been unable to conquer (Judg. 1:21). On the border between the territories of Judah and Benjamin, this ancient Canaanite sanctuary (Gen. 14:18–24) was an ideal administrative site. By bringing the Ark of the Covenant to Jerusalem, David makes his well-fortified capital the religious as well as the political center of the newly united nation (2 Sam. 6).

A shrewd exploiter of the military and executive abilities of loyal followers like Joab, Abishai, and Elhanan (2 Sam. 21:15–22), David quickly routs the Philistines, drives back the Ammonites and Aramaeans, and reduces neighboring states like Edom, Moab, and Damascus to vassal dependents. At its greatest extent, David's empire stretches from the Euphrates River in the northeast to the frontiers of Egypt in the south. Seldom does a single person so rapidly transform the fortunes of a country, triggering a cultural revolution that affects almost every aspect of Israelite life. Commercial treaties with **Hiram** of **Tyre** and other trading peoples stimulate a flow of wealth and cosmopolitan influences into Israel such as it had never known before (Chs. 5 and 8). It is not surprising that in ages to come, when Israel had fallen far short of

Davidic splendor, popular memories concerning this "lion of Judah" would shape the people's hopes for a new deliverer like David. Yahweh's Anointed (Messiah)—a term applied to all Davidic rulers—was to resemble David, beloved of God, a conquering hero, a political savior of his people. (See Part 8, "The Messiah: First-Century Expectations.")

Yahweh's Promise to David and His Heirs

Davidic Covenant   Dwelling in a palace of cedar, David resolves to build a comparable house for Yahweh, at once honoring the God who had raised him to the pinnacle of earthly success and establishing the national cult under imperial jurisdiction. At first, the court prophet **Nathan** agrees because Yahweh has so obviously favored David in his many enterprises, but—perhaps after consulting Israel's conservative elders—Nathan replies that the Deity, accustomed to dwelling in a tent (the wilderness tabernacle) will not be confined to a material shrine. Instead, Yahweh will build David a "house," an "everlasting" dynasty ensuring that heirs of David will remain on Israel's throne in perpetuity.

Yahweh's oath to establish David's royal line forever is *unconditional,* a striking contrast to the terms of the Mosaic Covenant, whose continued validity depends on the people's obedience. (See "The Davidic Covenant" on pages 136–137.) Yahweh vows that although he may chastise Davidic heirs, he will never remove them from power as he had Saul (2 Sam. 7). The Deity's absolute promise to preserve the royal house, and by implication its capital city as well, eventually led to a popular belief in the impregnability of Jerusalem, an assumption later championed by Isaiah (Isa. 28:16; 29:5–8; 30:15;36–37) and still later violently denounced by Jeremiah (Jer. 7 and 26). After the Babylonians deposed Zedekiah, the last Davidic king, in 587 B.C.E., the David–Zion Covenant was commonly interpreted as applying to a future "son of David," the **Messiah**, who would restore his predecessor's kingdom. (See Part 8.)

David and Bathsheba   The refrain "Wherever David went, Yahweh gave him victory" (8:7, 14, etc.) accompanies the recital of David's conquests like a leitmotiv. The theme changes abruptly, however, after Chapter 11, when David abuses his kingly authority by having an adulterous affair with the wife of **Uriah,** one of his Hittite mercenaries. This episode, which forms part of a court chronicle known as the Succession Narrative (2 Sam. 9–20 and 1 Kings 1 and 2), reveals the fatal flaw that compromises David's relationship with Yahweh. Notable for its candor in depicting the moral errors and psychological weaknesses of a popular leader, the narrative shows David caught in the trap of his own schemes, for once unable to assign blame to others. After learning that **Bathsheba** is carrying his child, David, to cover his paternity, first tries to cajole Uriah into breaking his soldier's vow of celibacy. When Uriah, perhaps aware of the king's intentions, refuses to sleep with his wife, David contrives to send Uriah into the front lines of battle, where, according to the king's orders, he is betrayed and killed (2 Sam. 11:2–27). In any kingdom other than theocratic Israel, the matter would have ended there; the monarch would have satisfied his lust, and no one would have dared to protest. To the prophet Nathan, however, not even the king is above Yahweh's law. Appearing one day in court, he tells David of a rich man with many flocks who took the one lamb of a poor man and killed it. Indignant, David denounces the rich villain for his greed and lack of compassion. "You," Nathan answers, "are the man" (2 Sam. 12:1–15).

Perhaps in no other Near Eastern country would Nathan's head have remained on his shoulders after such an accusation. David, however, proves a model of submissive repentance, accepting Yahweh's verdict that the child born of his illicit union with Bathsheba must die. Yahweh's judgment extends far beyond the infant's death, precipitating a series of betrayals and rebellions that reduce David's royal household to a state of moral anarchy.

Having set the example of wrongdoing, David must now endure the consequences, which include incest and murder among his own children. After his son Ammon rapes his half-sister, **Tamar**, her full-brother Absalom avenges (his) honor by killing the rapist. The assault of brother against brother echoes that of Cain and Abel, as well as the recent fratricidal civil wars that divided the Houses of Saul and David (2 Sam. 2–4). When Absalom, whose physical good looks and gift for attracting followers are a mocking image of the young David, rebels against his father, the aging king is forced to abandon his capital and seek refuge east of the Jordan River. Then Joab, once again coming to his master's rescue, eliminates Absalom. The ostentatious grief that David shows over his traitorous offspring disgusts the army commander (Ch. 19). These disorders in the kingdom provide an opportunity for some Israelites, unhappy with the rule of a Judean king, to rebel. Although the revolt led by Sheba, a Benjaminite, is short-lived, it foreshadows the deep political discontent that will eventually strip the ten northern tribes from the Davidic monarchy (Ch. 20; see also 1 Kings 12–13).

Appendices An anthology of supplementary documents that have not been chronologically integrated into the main narrative forms the conclusion of 2 Samuel. The appendices preserve six incidents, of which the most interesting for their theological views are the first and last additions. In the first (2 Sam. 21), a three-year famine, conveniently interpreted as a sign of divine anger against Saul's family, gives David an excuse to eliminate Saul's seven surviving sons, obvious rallying points for future rebellions, whom he delivers to their old enemies the Gibeonites for impalement.

The last supplement (2 Sam. 24) presents Yahweh inciting David to take a census of the people; the Deity then punishes this act by sending a pestilence that kills 70,000 Israelites. (Later biblical historians, apparently noting the moral illogic of such divine capriciousness, revise the story to make "Satan" the instigator of the census, a highly unpopular move because numbering the population was primarily for purposes of taxation and military conscription [see 1 Chron. 21].) On the advice of the prophet **Gad**, David buys a Jebusite threshing floor and erects upon it an altar to Yahweh. Perhaps because it is offered on the site of the future Jerusalem Temple, David's sacrifice halts the Angel of Death in his tracks, thus ending the epidemic. This final narration of David's actions is consistent with 2 Samuel's depiction of his paradoxical character: David is both the cause of his people's troubles and the instrument of its cure.

RECOMMENDED READING

Clements, Roland. *Abraham and David, Studies in Biblical Theology*, 2nd ser., no. 5. Naperville, Ill.: Allenson, 1967.

Cross, Frank M., ed. "The Ideologies of Kingship in the Era of the Empire: Conditional Covenant and Eternal Decree." In *Canaanite Myth and Hebrew Epic: Essays in the History of the Religion of Israel.* Cambridge, Mass.: Harvard University Press, 1973.

Gordon, R. P. *1 and 2 Samuel.* Old Testament Guides. Sheffield, Eng.: JSOT Press, 1984.

Halpern, Baruch. *The First Historians: The Hebrew Bible and History.* San Francisco: Harper & Row, 1988.

Hertzberg, H. W. *The Books of Samuel.* Translated by J. S. Bowden. Philadelphia: Westminster Press, 1964.

Hillers, Delbert R. *Covenant: The History of a Biblical Idea.* Baltimore: Johns Hopkins University Press, 1969.

McCarter, P. Kyle. *I Samuel.* Garden City, N.Y.: Doubleday, 1980.

———. *II Samuel.* Garden City, N.Y.: Doubleday, 1984.

Miscall, Peter D. *I Samuel: A Literary Reading.* Bloomington: Indiana University Press, 1986.

The Davidic Covenant

The main thrust of the Davidic covenant (2 Sam. 7:8–17)—Yahweh's sworn guarantee that David's heirs will possess his throne forever—resembles the Abrahamic Covenant (Gen. 12:1–3, 17:3–8) in both content and language. In both cases, Yahweh voluntarily—and without stipulating any conditions—promises a favored individual that his descendants will enjoy special blessings including land, fame, and royal progeny. In David's case, God additionally vows to ensure that the Israelites will enjoy undisturbed peace, permanently free of the oppression they suffered during the days of the judges (2 Sam. 7:10–11).

Reserving the right to punish disobedient kings, Yahweh nonetheless swears that he will never withdraw his protection from David's line, as he had from Saul, David's predecessor. Through the prophet Nathan, David is told unequivocally, "Your house [royal dynasty] and your sovereignty will always stand secure before me [Yahweh] and your throne be established forever."

Confidence that Israel's God would honor his pledge to maintain the Davidic line in perpetuity helps explain the uninterrupted succession of Davidic kings who reigned in Jerusalem for more than four centuries. Whereas the northern kingdom of Israel, formed about 922 B.C.E., was repeatedly wracked by violent changes of ruling dynasties, the southern kingdom of Judah remained loyal to David's house. This remarkable political stability resulted largely from public acceptance of the royal covenant theology expressed in 2 Samuel 7.

As Yahweh revealed his faithfulness by blessing Abraham's line, so he maintained a special relationship with David's heirs, regarding them as his "sons" (Ps. 2). Each Davidic king was Yahweh's Messiah (Hebrew, *mashiach,* or "Anointed One"), consecrated with holy oil at his coronation to designate his chosen status (Pss. 2; 18; 20; 110; 132). When historical events, such as the secession of Israel's ten northern tribes in 922 B.C.E. and the fall of Judah to Babylon in 587 B.C.E., appeared to violate Yahweh's oath to David, some later Bible writers significantly revised the covenant terms. Deuteronomistic editors reinterpreted the original promises to conform with the terms of the Mosaic agreement, which made divine favor dependent on strict obedience to the

1 Kings

KEY THEMES

Opening with the death of David and the succession of Solomon, remembered for his wisdom, wealth, and enormous building projects (Chs. 1–10), 1 Kings presents a mixed judgment of Solomon's reign. The narrator attributes the breakup of the kingdom early in the reign of his heir Rehoboam to Solomon's cosmopolitan tolerance of foreign cults (Ch. 11). When Rehoboam foolishly refuses to change Solomon's oppressive policies, the northern ten tribes revolt against the Davidic monarchy. Led by Jeroboam I, the northern tribes establish an independent kingdom of Israel, with its first capital at Shechem (Chs. 12–14). Because the northern kings set up sanctuaries to rival the Jerusalem Temple, the Deuteronomistic account denounces them all for continuing the "sins of Jeroboam" (Chs. 15 and 16). The bitter contest between King Ahab and Elijah, archetypal prophet of the northern kingdom, concludes the book (Chs. 17–22).

> I [Yahweh] consecrate this house you [Solomon] have built; I place my name there forever.
>
> 1 Kings 9:3

Like the books of Samuel, 1 and 2 Kings were originally a single work that the Septuagint translators later divided into two parts. Together

Torah (1 Kings 2:4, 3:14–15, 6:12–14, 11:30–39, etc.). Thus, the abolition of David's ruling dynasty by Babylon's King Nebuchadnezzar was seen as the justifiable consequence of disobedient Davidic kings like Manasseh (2 Kings 23:26–27).

Other Bible writers rejected the simplistic Deuteronomistic view expressed in Kings and insisted that the promise to David's house was absolutely unconditional, as stated in 2 Samuel (7:13–16 and 23:1–5). The author of Psalm 89 states that the Davidic Covenant had been abrogated not by disloyal kings but by Yahweh's incomprehensible actions in allowing Israel's humiliating defeat (Ps. 89:19–51). By contrast, the prophet Jeremiah used the form of a covenant lawsuit to illustrate his belief that Israel deserved her fate for having broken the Moses–Sinai agreement (Jer. 2:2–37, 5:1–25, 11:1–17, etc.).

Although a remnant of Judah's deported population eventually returned from the Babylonian captivity (after 538 B.C.E.), the Davidic dynasty was never restored. The leadership of priests officiating at the rebuilt Jerusalem Temple replaced the rule of kings in the postexilic community. Remembering the former close association of the priestly Temple cult and Davidic royal family (2 Sam. 6–7; 1 Kings 5–9; Ps. 132), some later Bible writers rewrote the history of the Davidic monarchy, reinterpreting David's role as founder of priestly rituals, particularly the establishment of the Ark of the Covenant in Jerusalem. Although the postexilic Temple was no longer a royal shrine as it had been in Solomon's day, it remained the center of the national religion and provided a link with the monarchical past (Hag. 1–2; Zech. 3–4; 1 Chron. 13:15–17, 21–29; 2 Chron. 1–8, 24–28, 34–38; 36:22–23).

The authors of Chronicles and other postexilic books, accepting Yahweh's will in ending the Davidic kingship, were consoled with the rule of a priestly theocracy. Some later interpreters began to apply the old prophetic promises made to David and his house (Isa. 7, 9, 11; Pss. 2, 110; etc.) to a future royal prince who would restore the Davidic sovereignty as a political reality. Conceived as a conquering warrior like David before him, this future hero would be Yahweh's ultimate Anointed One. Hope for the restoration of David's royal line in Judah eventually led to keen expectations of a messiah figure who would revitalize Yahweh's people and lead them to triumph over their enemies. Such expectations flourished during the period in which the New Testament Gospels were written. (See Part 9.)

these volumes carry the history of Israel from the death of King David to the fall of Jerusalem and the Babylonian captivity (587 B.C.E.). As might be expected, the books are based on a number of older sources, including court archives and traditional material concerning the prophets Elijah and Elisha. The authors frequently refer to several dynastic histories that have since been lost: the Book of the Acts of Solomon (1 Kings 11:41), the Book of the Annals of the Kings of Israel (1 Kings 14:19), and the Book of the Annals of the Kings of Judah (1 Kings 14:29). These sources were rigorously edited and reshaped to conform to the theological viewpoint of the Deuteronomistic historians, who produced the first version of Kings after Josiah's religious reforms late in the seventh century B.C.E. The first edition of the DH account may have been issued to help justify and support Josiah's policies, which the authors regard as the climactic fulfillment of the Mosaic Torah prescribed in the Book of Deuteronomy. After Babylon's dismantling of the Jewish state, a second edition was prepared for the exiled community in order to explain why Yahweh had permitted Jerusalem's fall and the end of the Davidic royal house.

Drawing material selectively from older court records to illustrate their historical theory, the writer-editors rigidly apply Deuteronomy's standard of obedience to all rulers of Judah and Israel. Authorial judgment focuses almost exclusively on the issue of centralizing Yahweh's worship "only in the place he himself will choose from among all your tribes, to set his name there and give it a home" (Deut. 12:5). Although the place is not specified in Deuteronomy's text, the author(s) assume it to be Jerusalem and consequently condemn any ruler who tolerates sacrifices at the "high places," traditionally hilltop sites where Yahweh's rituals had been performed since the days of Abraham and Jacob. Because rulers of the northern kingdom set up rival shrines at Bethel and **Dan**, the Deuteronomistic writers denigrate them all, reserving their approval for a few of Judah's kings, primarily Hezekiah and Josiah, who consistently enforce centralization of the national cult at the Davidic capital.

The Reign of Solomon

Solomon's Succession and Reign (c. 961–922 B.C.E.)   1 Kings opens with an account of King David's last days, and Bathsheba's behind-the-scenes plotting to have her son **Solomon**, rather than David's older son **Adonijah**, succeed to the throne. (The story of Solomon's succession is probably based on the same court history that underlies 2 Sam. 9–20.) On his deathbed, David reminds Solomon that although he has promised to spare those of his enemies who are still alive, his successor is bound by no such vow. Solomon accordingly consolidates his power by murdering Adonijah and numerous others who might threaten the security of his crown. In a special blessing, Yahweh then grants him "a discerning judgment" and a heart "wise and shrewd" (1 Kings 3:4–15), so that he soon earns international fame for the astuteness of his policies (1 Kings 3–11).

Solomon's extensive building program includes erecting a magnificent royal palace with a special mansion for his most important wife, the daughter of pharaoh, with whom he has concluded a political alliance. In erecting the Temple in Jerusalem to house the Ark of the Covenant, thus further centralizing the national

religion in his capital city (1 Kings 5–7), he also allies Israel with **Phoenicia** by importing numerous planners, architects, and craftspeople capable of executing his ambitious designs. Public dedication ceremonies at the new **Temple**, which is built on the model of a Phoenician sanctuary, are the highlight of Solomon's reign (1 Kings 8).

In a cloud reminiscent of that which led Israel through the Sinai desert, Yahweh accepts the Temple as his earthly dwelling place, although Solomon acknowledges that heaven itself cannot contain God's true majesty, much less the house he has built. Solomon's prominent role in the dedication sacrifices reveals how much royal power has grown since the time of Saul, when the king was strongly condemned for assuming priestly functions (1 Sam. 13:8–15). Although the Temple consecration is seen as the culminating achievement in Israel's religious history, the DH writers inject an ominous note that shadows the occasion. Yahweh is shown warning Solomon that his oath to preserve the Davidic dynasty depends on wholehearted obedience to his "commandments and laws"—a striking contrast to the unconditional promise made to David in 2 Samuel 7. Composing this passage shortly after 562 B.C.E., the latest dated event in the books of Kings, the DH editors revise the Davidic Covenant to bring it in line with historical developments. At the time Kings received its final editing, Solomon's Temple lay in ruins (see the explicit reference to this fact in 1 Kings 9:8–9), and Babylonian conquerors had deposed the last Davidic ruler (2 Kings 25).

After an admiring survey of Solomon's unparalleled wealth, fame, military strength, and diplomatic prowess (1 Kings 10), the DH editor(s) conclude their evaluation of the reign by criticizing Solomon's numerous marriages to foreign women, whom he blames for seducing the king into idolatry. Out of respect for David, Solomon is allowed to die peacefully (922 B.C.E.), but his heirs will lose the largest part of the kingdom. Judah, however, the nucleus of

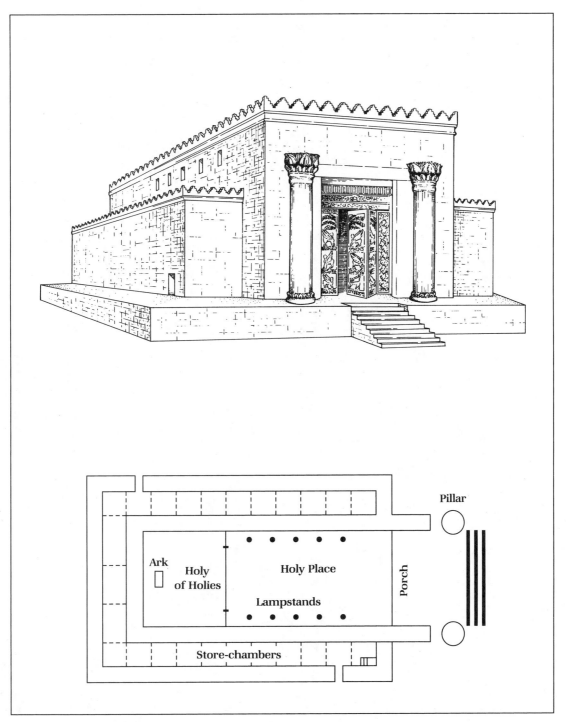

An artist's reconstruction of Solomon's Temple.

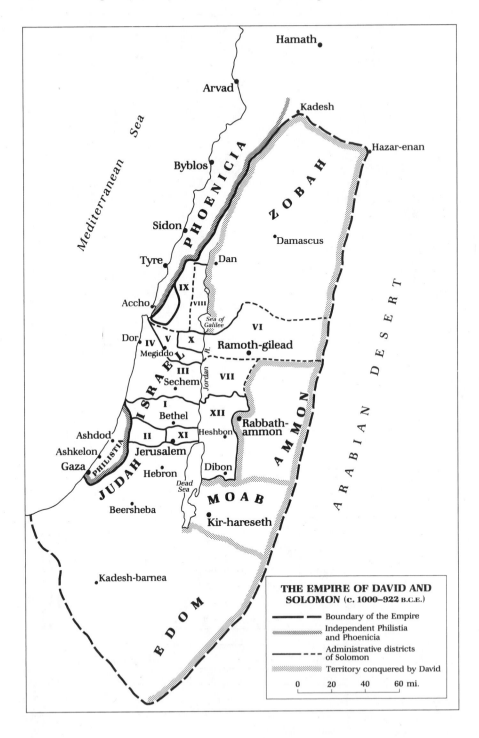

Hamath

Arvad

Kadesh

Hazar-enan

Mediterranean Sea

PHOENICIA

Byblos

ZOBAH

Sidon

Damascus

Tyre

Dan

Accho

IX

VIII

Sea of Galilee

VI

Dor

IV

V

X

Ramoth-gilead

Megiddo

III

Sechem

VII

Jordan R.

ISRAEL

I

Bethel

XII

Ashdod

II

XI

Heshbon

Rabbath-ammon

Ashkelon

Jerusalem

Gaza

PHILISTIA

Hebron

Dibon

JUDAH

Dead Sea

MOAB

Beersheba

Kir-hareseth

A R A B I A N   D E S E R T

AMMON

E D O M

Kadesh-barnea

THE EMPIRE OF DAVID AND SOLOMON (c. 1000–922 B.C.E.)

— — — Boundary of the Empire

Independent Philistia and Phoenicia

- - - - Administrative districts of Solomon

Territory conquered by David

0   20   40   60 mi.

the Davidic realm, is to remain under the rule of his successors "so that David may always have a [land] in [Yahweh's] presence" (1 Kings 11:12–13, 35–36), an assurance repeated when later Judean kings misbehave (1 Kings 15:3–4; 2 Kings 8:18–19). Scribes who produced the second edition of Kings during the Babylonian exile apparently agreed that Judah's Davidic kings, despite their faults, enjoyed an eternal commitment from Yahweh. When they added the tragic history of Josiah's heirs (2 Kings 23:26–25:30), the final editors did not delete the original writer's references to Yahweh's abiding by his promise to David (2 Sam. 7), perhaps because they regarded a restoration of the Davidic line as inevitable.

The Divided Kingdoms

The Great Schism   **Rehoboam** (922–915 B.C.E.), Solomon's successor, foolishly refuses to lighten the heavy burden of taxes and forced labor that Solomon's building projects have placed on the people (1 Kings 12), and his rejection of the northern tribes' plea for a more humane administration sparks a widespread revolt against the House of David. The ten northern tribes withdraw from the monarchy and form their own kingdom, to be called **Israel**:

> What share have we in David?
> We have no inheritance in the son of Jesse!
> 1 Kings 12:16

Remaining faithful to the Davidic rulers, the southern tribes of Judah and Benjamin form the smaller and poorer kingdom of Judah with its capital at Jerusalem.

Hereafter, Kings will record the history of a divided kingdom, alternately describing reigns in the northern kingdom and then events in Judah (Table 4.1). This jumping back-and-forth, coupled with a monotonous emphasis on obedience to the law, makes some of Kings rather turgid reading, although royal conflicts with certain prophets considerably enliven parts of the narrative.

The rebel leader **Jeroboam I**, the first king of northern Israel (c. 922–901 B.C.E.), sets up rival sanctuaries at Bethel and Dan, where he erects two golden calves, probably as pedestals for the invisibly enthroned Yahweh (1 Kings 12–13); indeed, most of the northern monarchs make some effort to follow the Mosaic faith. Whereas the southern nation of Judah, ruled by an unbroken succession of Davidic kings, maintains relative stability, the northern kingdom suffers repeated overthrows of its kings, none of whom is able to establish a dynasty as enduring as David's. Because the history is told from a disapproving southern (Judean) viewpoint, even **Omri** (876–869 B.C.E.), one of Israel's most effective rulers, is accorded only a few lines (1 Kings 16:23–24), although long after his dynasty had fallen the emperors of Assyria still referred to Israel as the "land of Omri."

Elijah and King Ahab (869–850 B.C.E.) Considerably more space is allotted to the misdeeds of Omri's successor, King **Ahab** (1 Kings 17–22), who is married to the notorious **Jezebel**, daughter of the king of Tyre. Ahab's endorsement of Baal worship brings him into confrontation with the most formidable prophet that Israel has yet produced, **Elijah** the Tishbite, who stages a contest between Yahweh and Baal on Mount **Carmel** near the Mediterranean coast (1 Kings 18). Despite their ritual antics, the Canaanite priests fail to arouse Baal to action, but Elijah's God sends fire from heaven, consuming the offered sacrifice. Triumphant, Elijah slaughters the priests of Baal and announces that Yahweh is ending the long drought that has afflicted Israel.

Driven from his homeland under Jezebel's threat of execution, the solitary prophet—who believes himself to be the only one alive still faithful to Yahweh—retreats to the desert origin of his faith, Horeb (Mount Sinai). Hidden in the same rocky cleft that had once sheltered Moses, Elijah, too, encounters Yahweh—not in wind, earthquake, fire, or other spectacular phenomena but in a "gentle breeze"—or, in

Table 4.1 Events and Rulers in the Divided Kingdom

Approximate Date B.C.E.	Mesopotamia and Egypt	Israel	Judah	Hebrew Prophets
	Twenty-second Dynasty of Egypt (935–725) Pharaoh Shishak invades Palestine (c. 918)	Jeroboam I (922–901)	Rehoboam (922–915) Abijah (915–913) Asa (913–873)	
900		Nadab (901–900) Baasha (900–877) Elah (877–876) Zimri (876) Omri (876–869) Ahab (869–850)	Jehoshaphat (873–849)	Elijah (Israel)
850	Shalmaneser III (859–825) of Assyria Battle of Qarqar (853) Hazael of Syria (842–806)	Ahaziah (850–849) Jehoram (849–842) Jehu's Revolt (842)	Jehoram (849–842) Ahaziah (842) Athaliah (842–837)	Elisha (Israel)
800		Jehu (842–815) Jehoahaz (815–801) Jehoash (801–786) Jeroboam II (786–746)	Joash (837–800) Amaziah (800–783) Uzziah (Azariah) (783–742)	Amos (Israel) Hosea (Israel)
750	Tiglath-pileser of Assyria (745–727) Shalmaneser V (726–722) Twenty-fourth Egyptian Dynasty (725–709)	Zechariah (746–745) Shallum (745) Menahem (745–738) Pekahiah (738–737) Pekah (737–732) Hoshea 732–724)	Jotham (742–735) Ahaz (735–715)	Isaiah (Judah) Micah (Judah)
725	Sargon II of Assyria (721–705) Twenty-fifth Egyptian Dynasty (716–663)	Fall of Israel (722/721)	Hezekiah (715–667)	
700	Sennacherib (704–681) Assyrian invasion of Judah (701) Esarhaddon of Assyria (681–669) Ashurbanipal (668–627)		Manasseh (687–642)	

Table 4.1 Events and Rulers in the Divided Kingdom (*continued*)

Approxi-mate Date B.C.E.	Mesopotamia and Egypt	Israel	Judah	Hebrew Prophets
650	Twenty-sixth Egyptian Dynasty (664–525)		Amon (642–640)	
			Josiah (640–609) Deuteronomic reforms (621 and following)	Jeremiah Zephaniah Nahum
	Fall of Nineveh (612)		Jehoahaz (609)	
	Pharaoh Necho (610–594)		Jehoiakim (609–598/597)	
600	Battle of Carchemish (605)		Jehoiachin (598/597)	
	Growth of Neo-Babylonian Empire under Nebuchadnezzar (605–562)		First Babylonian sack of Jerusalem (598/597)	Habakkuk
			Zedekiah (597–587)	Ezekiel
			Fall of Jerusalem (587)	Jeremiah taken to Egypt
			Babylonian captivity (587–538)	

SOURCE: In general, this table follows the dates derived from W. F. Albright, *Bulletin of the American School of Oriental Research,* no. 100 (December 1945), and adopted by John Bright, *A History of Israel* (Philadelphia: Westminster Press, 1972), pp. 480–481.

more familiar translation, a "still small voice" (1 Kings 19:9–18).

The narrative then shifts to Ahab's unlawful coveting of Naboth's vineyard, which Jezebel obtains for him by falsely accusing **Naboth** of blasphemy (1 Kings 21).

After the unfortunate Naboth has been stoned in accordance with Mosaic law, Elijah appears and pronounces doom upon Ahab and his descendants, who are to be exterminated. Like King David before him, Ahab admits his sin and repents, thus causing Yahweh to delay his punishment, though shortly afterward he is killed at the Battle of Ramoth-gilead (1 Kings 22). The book closes with brief summaries of the reigns of Ahab's ally **Jehoshaphat**, king of Judah (873–849 B.C.E.), and Ahab's son Ahaziah of Israel, who rules for only two years (850–849 B.C.E.).

2 Kings

KEY THEMES

Although 2 Kings originally ended with a celebration of King Josiah's religious reforms, the book was revised to its present form to explain not only why Yahweh permitted the northern kingdom of Israel to suffer annihilation (721 B.C.E.) but also why he consigned Judah to the same fate (587 B.C.E.). By amassing detailed examples of Israelite and Judean rulers' covenant-breaking, the Deuteronomistic authors prepare readers for the final catastrophe. The opening narratives review events in the northern kingdom following Ahab's death, which plunges the nation into turmoil and weakness, conditions abetted by Elisha's prophetic backing of Jehu's

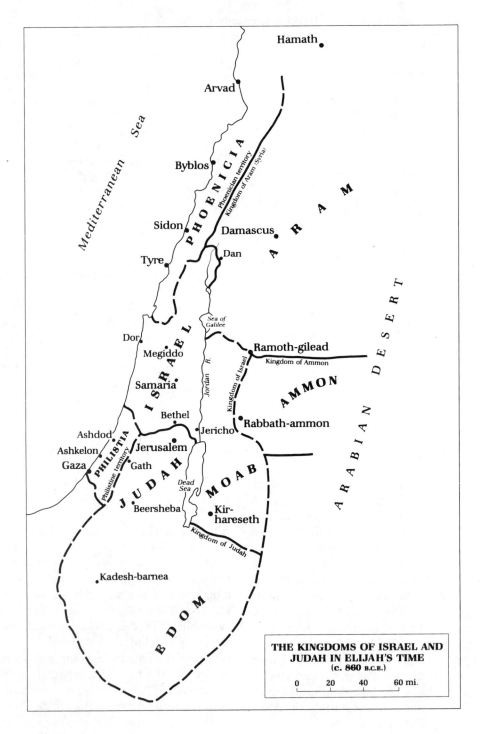

**THE KINGDOMS OF ISRAEL AND
JUDAH IN ELIJAH'S TIME**
(c. 860 B.C.E.)

0   20   40   60 mi.

fanatical Yahwism and slaughter of all Ahab's descendants (Chs. 1–10). The second part interweaves the reigns of Israelite and Judean monarchs with the rule of Queen Athaliah in Judah (c. 842–837 B.C.E.) briefly interrupting the Davidic line (Chs. 11–16). After succinctly describing the Assyrian conquest of Israel and the origin of the hated Samaritans (Ch. 17), the account focuses on the last days of Judah, giving qualified approval to the policies of Hezekiah (Chs. 18–20) and denouncing those of Manasseh, whose religious practices and detente with Assyria are blamed for Judah's collapse (Ch. 21). Josiah's hopeful reforms (Chs. 22–23) merely delay Yahweh's punishment of the nation for Manasseh's disloyalty. After Babylon has reduced Judah to the status of a vassal, Zedekiah, the last Davidic king, rashly rebels, inciting Nebuchadnezzar to destroy Jerusalem and raze Solomon's Temple (Chs. 24–25).

> No king before [Josiah] had turned to Yahweh as he did, with all his heart. . . . In perfect loyalty to the Law of Moses; nor was any king like him seen again. Yet Yahweh did not renounce the heat of his great anger which blazed out against Judah.
>
> 2 Kings 23:25–26

The Fall of Israel

Elisha and Jehu The history of Israelite and Judean rulers continues uninterrupted in 2 Kings. After reporting Ahaziah's death in Chapter 1, the historian returns in Chapters 2–8 to the Elijah–Elisha prophetic cycle. When Elijah, the archetypal man of God, is carried to heaven in a fiery chariot and whirlwind, he leaves his prophetic cloak behind for his disciple **Elisha**,

Hadad, Syrian god of storm, strides atop a bull in this basaltic stele. Grasping lightning bolts in each hand, Hadad invisibly rides an animal symbolizing power and terror. Because Canaanite artists commonly show El, father of the gods, also standing on a bull, many scholars believe that the notorious "golden calf" that Moses'

brother Aaron manufactured and the two calf sculptures that Jeroboam set up in Israel were not intended as rivals to Yahweh, but only as pedestals on which the Deity could be viewlessly enthroned (Exod. 32:1–35; 2 Kings 12: 26–33). (Courtesy of Musée du Louvre)

whose reported miracles are even more numerous and spectacular than those of his predecessor. In the course of his career, Elisha causes an iron axhead to float on water, a child to rise from the dead, jars of oil to fill magically, poisoned soup to become edible, twenty barley loaves to feed 100 men, and lepers to be cleansed, foretelling droughts, famines, victories, and deaths.

The prophet's political influence is equally impressive. Through a messenger, Elisha secretly anoints **Jehu**, a former captain of Ahab's guard, king of Israel. Jehu, supported by the army, plunges the nation into a bloodbath (2 Kings 9–10). Citing Elijah's curse on Ahab's house, Jehu massacres all of Ahab's surviving sons, grandsons, friends, priests, administrators, and political supporters, totally annihilating his dynasty. With **Jehonadab**, a Yahwist fanatic, Jehu then assembles all Baal worshipers in the great temple that Ahab had built in Samaria, the capital city, and after offering sacrifice to Baal, orders eighty trusted executioners to butcher everyone inside. The temple is demolished and its site turned into a public latrine.

For all his savage zeal, however, even Jehu does not entirely win the Deuteronomists' approval. In neglecting to remove Jeroboam's **golden calves** from Bethel and Dan, he did not serve Yahweh wholeheartedly. Nor was Jehu an effective king: His purges and massacres may have pleased some Yahwists, but he so depleted the nation's supply of trained and competent leaders that Israel rapidly lost territory on every side. When Jehu (842–815 B.C.E.) died after a

A witness to the Assyrian Empire's once irresistible might, the Black Obelisk of Shalmaneser III (859–825 B.C.E.) pictures representatives from five different regions—including King Jehu of Israel—bringing tribute to the Assyrian king. After Assyria destroyed the northern kingdom of Israel (721 B.C.E.), Judah maintained a precarious existence by stripping the Temple of its treasures to keep Assyrian armies at bay (2 Kings 18:13–16). (Courtesy of the Trustees of the British Museum)

reign of twenty-eight years (of which only the violent first year is described in Kings), he left Israel politically weak, without allies, and considerably smaller in size than it had been under Omri and Ahab (2 Kings 10:32–35).

Jehu's ultimate status is indicated on the Black Obelisk, a stone monument that pictures him—or his representative—groveling before his Assyrian overlord. A roughly contemporary inscription on the Moabite Stone records that after having been conquered by Omri, Moab broke free of Israel's "oppression," a national liberation achieved by the power of Chemosh, the Moabite god. (See "The Moabite Stone" on page 148.)

A Queen Rules Judah An indirect result of Jehu's massacre of Israelite and Judean royalty was the establishment of a queen on the Judean throne, her reign the only interruption of the Davidic line in its entire history. A daughter of Omri (or perhaps of Ahab and Jezebel), **Athaliah** (842–837 B.C.E.) was the wife of Jehoram, king of Judah. Their son was King Ahaziah. When Jehu murdered this king in 842 B.C.E., Athaliah seized control of Judah. Following Jehu's example, Queen Athaliah ordered the execution of all of Ahaziah's sons, rival heirs to the crown. Only one prince escaped when the chief priest Jehoiada secretly hid Ahaziah's infant son, Jehoash (Joash), in the Jerusalem Temple.

After Athaliah had reigned successfully for six years, the priest Jehoiada masterminded a palace revolt, having Athaliah murdered and placing the seven-year-old Jehoash on the throne. According to the DH, Jehoash's long reign (837–800 B.C.E.) was "pleasing" to Yahweh. Instructed by Jehoiada, Jehoash lavished Judah's resources on the Temple's care and upkeep (2 Kings 11–12).

Assyria and Judah Although the northern kingdom enjoyed renewed prosperity under such kings as **Jeroboam II** (786–746 B.C.E.), revolution and violent changes of rulership continued to undermine Israelite strength. At the same time, a new threat appeared: After centuries of relative stasis, **Assyria** was once again on the march, swallowing up kingdoms and peoples as it expanded. Assyria's territorial encroachments and increasing demands for tribute culminated in the siege of Samaria, which fell to **Sargon II** in 721 B.C.E. Because it was Assyria's policy to deport defeated populations to discourage future rebellions, the ten northern tribes were forcibly relocated elsewhere in the Assyrian Empire, and new people were moved into Israelite territory.

Chapter 17 describes a plague of lions that afflicted the resettled foreigners until a priest of Yahweh was brought back from exile to teach them the proper ritual to pacify the god of the land. This passage is intended to explain how the northern Israelites came to be "lost tribes"; its biased account of the origin of the **Samaritans**, an ethnically mixed group that practiced a form of the Jewish religion, is of doubtful historical value. Despised by the "true" Jews of Judah, the Samaritans were uncharitably regarded as foreign corrupters of the faith—a hostility still current in New Testament times, when Jesus probably shocked his Jewish audience by making a Samaritan the moral hero of a famous parable.

"Good" and "Evil" Kings: Hezekiah and Manasseh

Hezekiah's Reign Chapters 18 through 21 provide contrasting portraits of two very different Judean kings, **Hezekiah**, who receives praise for his adherence to the Mosaic Covenant, and his son **Manasseh**, whose fascination with foreign religions irrevocably angers Yahweh, dooming the nation. Hezekiah (715–686 B.C.E.) receives unstinted praise for abolishing the "high places," hilltop shrines where Yahweh was worshiped (possibly along with the Canaanite goddess Asherah), strongly enforcing the centralization of Yahweh's cult in Jerusalem. Besides smashing the poles and sacred pillars—symbols of the tree of life associated with

The Moabite Stone

Discovered in 1868, this flat basaltic slab is important because the message with which it is inscribed demonstrates that Israel's neighbors had developed a theology of history virtually identical to that promulgated in the books of Joshua through 2 Kings. The Deuteronomistic historians interpreted Israel's political and military fortunes according to their degree of obedience to the Mosaic Torah (Deut. 28). Ascribing all national defeats to Yahweh's anger, the Deuteronomists believed that Yahweh used pagan armies to punish Israel's religious disloyalties. As the Moabite Stone reveals, the same theological view of events prevailed in **Moab**, Israel's close neighbor and traditional enemy. According to the inscription, Mesha, king of Moab (middle to late ninth century B.C.E.) attributed his country's invasion and occupation by Israelite troops to the wrath of **Chemosh**, the Moabite national god. Moab's successful rebellion and liberation from Israelite domination is regarded as the result of Chemosh's blessing of his people. Ironically, Moab's ability to break away from Israel was the result of a Yahwist revival led by Jehu, who usurped the Israelite throne, slaughtered all male members of the previous royal family, and conducted a bloody purge of Baal's adherents (cf. 2 Kings 3:4–27; 9:1–10: 32). Jehu's fanatical policies irreparably weakened Israel, permitting formerly subject nations like Moab to regain their independence. Israel's decline under Jehu is also reflected on an Assyrian monument, the Black Obelisk, which shows the Yahwist king groveling before the emperor **Shalmaneser** III, to whom he was forced to pay tribute.

The enormously important Moabite Stone, found in 1868, records the victories of Mesha, king of Moab, over the northern state of Israel (ninth century B.C.E.). Grateful to Chemosh, the Moabite national god, for liberating him from the Israelite domination imposed by Omri and Ahab, Mesha articulates a Canaanite mirror image of the Deuteronomistic philosophy of history: "As for Omri, king of Israel, he humbled Moab many years, for Chemosh was angry at his land. And his son followed him and he also said, 'I will humble Moab.' In my time he spoke (thus), but I have triumphed over him and over his house, while Israel hath perished for ever!" (Courtesy of Musée du Louvre)

This panel of the Black Obelisk shows Jehu, king of Israel, groveling before the Assyrian emperor Shalmaneser III, to whom he pays tribute. The Deuteronomistic writers describe Jehu's revolt against Ahab's dynasty (842 B.C.E.) as a Yahwist-inspired movement (2 Kings 9:1–10:36), but as a result of Jehu's butchery of Israel's former ruling class, the nation was fatally weakened and eventually destroyed. Ironically, the Black Obelisk identifies Jehu as "son of Omri," founder of the royal line that the Yahwist usurper exterminated. (Courtesy of the Trustees of the British Museum)

Asherah—Hezekiah also destroyed the bronze serpent (called Nehushtan) that Moses had fashioned in the desert to cure people bitten by poisonous snakes (Num. 21:9). As a symbol of healing, the bronze image had become an object of veneration and hence a threat to Yahwist purity. No icon or relic, even one associated with God's spokesman Moses, could be permitted to deflect worship from Yahweh alone.

Although the Deuteronomistic author compares Hezekiah to David in adhering strictly to Yahwism and keeping Torah commands (2 Kings 18:3–8), the writer's attitude toward his reign as a whole is somewhat ambivalent. The text states that Yahweh made the king "successful in all he undertook" and notes with apparent approval Hezekiah's rebellion against Judah's Assyrian oppressors. At the same time it is clear that Hezekiah's "success" is perilously close to failure: His refusal to pay Assyria tribute causes **Sennacherib** (704–681 B.C.E.) to invade Judah, capture most of its important cities, and levy a ruinously heavy fine on the nation. Hezekiah is forced to strip Yahweh's Temple of its decorations and treasure, paying Sennacherib enormous sums of silver and gold, and then to submit again to the Assyrian yoke. Although Isaiah's confidence that Jerusalem will not be conquered is vindicated by the event, Hezekiah ends his long reign impoverished and ruling over only a tiny scrap of his former domain.

Jerusalem's Deliverance Assyrian and biblical records concerning Sennacherib's invasion of Judah in 701 B.C.E. differ strikingly. According to Sennacherib's boast, his troops sealed Hezekiah within Jerusalem "like a bird in a cage," but he says nothing about why he failed to take the city. In 2 Kings and a parallel account in Isaiah 36–37, Jerusalem's survival is attributed to divine intervention: In a single night, Yahweh's Angel of Death strikes down 185,000 Assyrian soldiers, forcing Sennacherib to lift his siege and return to Nineveh. The biblical version has some confirmation from nonbiblical sources, including the Greek historian Herodotus, but the exact cause of the Assyrian retreat and Jerusalem's deliverance is not clear. The holy city's unexpected escape from the Assyrian threat contributed to a popular idea that Jerusalem, site of Yahweh's Temple, would never fall into enemy hands—a view that the prophet Jeremiah would later vigorously attack (Jer. 7, 26).

Chapter 20 records an incident that evidently took place before Sennacherib's invasion, when Hezekiah still possessed great wealth. Apparently trying to recruit Babylon as an ally against Assyria, Hezekiah foolishly takes the Babylonian ambassador on a tour of his richly furnished palace and overflowing treasury, displaying all of Judah's resources to the foreigner's gaze. Appalled at the king's action, Isaiah then prophesies that the country's entire treasure will be swept away to Babylon—a direct reference to Nebuchadnezzar's sacking of Jerusalem more than a century later. Probably added to the text during the exile, this passage depicts a morally ambivalent Hezekiah. When Isaiah informs him that the disaster still lies in the future, the king finds the news "reassuring" because he will enjoy "peace and security" during his own lifetime (2 Kings 20:12–19).

Manasseh's Reign   The Deuteronomistic writer credits Hezekiah's son Manasseh with every Torah violation ever practiced by any king of Israel or Judah, including rampant Baalism, black magic, and human sacrifice. Promoting a syncretism abhorrent to Judah's prophets, Manasseh (687–642 B.C.E.) erects a "carved image of Asherah," perhaps conceived as a female consort to Yahweh, in the Jerusalem Temple. Accused of worse crimes than those perpetrated by the Canaanites whom Israel had driven from the land, Manasseh nonetheless reigned for approximately a half century, longer than any other Davidic ruler.

Manasseh's Conversion   The Book of Chronicles, written more than two centuries after the Deuteronomistic History, adds a surprising conclusion to Manasseh's story, one not even hinted at in 2 Kings. According to 2 Chronicles, Manasseh was taken captive to Babylon, where he underwent a sudden conversion to Yahwism, repenting of his former misdeeds. Moved by his prayer, Yahweh permitted Manasseh's restoration to Judah's throne, after which the humbled and penitent king conducted a thoroughgoing religious reform anticipating that of **Josiah**. (The Chronicler cites the "Annals of Hozai" as the source of this remarkable tale [2 Chron. 33:11–20].) If the Deuteronomistic editor knew about a tradition in which Manasseh had been transformed into an ardent Yahwist reformer, he did not use it. In the Deuteronomistic scheme, there is no place for a repentant Manasseh: The sorcerer-king is singled out as the primary cause of Judah's demise, and his character is allowed no redeeming qualities (2 Kings 21:10–17, 23:26–27).

Mosaic Yahwism Triumphant: The Reforms of Josiah

King Josiah   With the ascension of Josiah, Manasseh's grandson, Judah entered a new era in the development of Yahwistic faith. Reviving the policies of his ancestor Hezekiah, Josiah (640–609 B.C.E.) fulfills both the letter and the spirit of Deuteronomy's commands—to honor one God and sacrifice to him at one sanctuary only. Although its legal core was probably composed in the northern kingdom several generations earlier, the Book of Deuteronomy became Josiah's chief instrument in revitalizing Judah's national religion. Found during Temple repairs—renovations that probably involved removing Manasseh's Baalistic shrines and images—Deuteronomy brought the Mosaic tradition to general public notice, perhaps for the first time in Israel's history. The writer indicates that both king and people were unfamiliar with the laws and curses of the Mosaic legacy and notes that holding Passover ceremonies, so important in the Exodus account, were regarded as an innovation. No Passover celebration like Josiah's enactment of Deuteronomy's command had ever been observed "throughout the entire period of the kings of Israel and the kings of Judah" (2 Kings 23:21–23).

Taking advantage of Assyria's rapid decline in the late seventh century B.C.E., Josiah extends his reforms and political influence into the former northern kingdom, demolishing altars and desecrating tombs throughout the countryside. His renewal campaign is cut short, however, when Egypt's pharaoh **Necho** invades the area on his way to aid the last remnant of Assyrian power in northern Syria. Whereas Necho wanted a weakened Assyria to survive as a buffer state between Egypt and the newly revived empire of Babylon, Josiah may have hoped to rid Judah of all foreign occupation or, failing that, to support Babylon against Assyria. Attempting to intercept Necho's army, Josiah is killed at the battle of Megiddo, thus bringing his deuteronomic reforms to a premature end and leaving Judah in the hands of weak or incompetent successors.

Theology and History The Deuteronomistic theory of history equates Torah obedience with success and disloyalty with destruction. Yet, Manasseh, Judah's least faithful king, reigned longer than any other Davidic monarch and died peacefully in his palace bed. Conversely, Josiah, hailed as a ruler unprecedented in Yahwistic devotion, was cut down as a relatively young man while trying to defend his country—even though Yahweh's prophet Huldah had foretold that he would go to his grave "in peace" (cf. 2 Kings 22:20, 23:29–30). Despite the awkwardness of historical facts that would not fit into the deuteronomic framework, even the final edition of Israel's history adhered firmly to Deuteronomy's simple formula of retributive justice.

The Last Days of Judah

Babylonian Conquest In 612 B.C.E., Nineveh, Assyria's hated capital, had fallen to the combined forces of the Medes and Babylonians. Although Pharaoh Necho had rushed into the power vacuum that Assyria's collapse had created in the Near East, the Egyptians were soon defeated by Nebuchadnezzar, king of Babylon, at the Battle of **Carchemish** (605 B.C.E.). The tiny state of Judah must next submit to the Babylonian yoke; its last kings are merely tribute-paying vassals of **Nebuchadnezzar**, who is now master of the Near East.

Josiah's son **Jehoiakim** (609–598 B.C.E.), whom Nebuchadnezzar had placed on Judah's throne, unwisely rebels but dies before the Babylonians can capture Jerusalem, leaving his son and successor, **Jehoiachin**, to suffer the consequences of the revolt. In 598/597 B.C.E., Jehoiachin and his family are taken as prisoners to Babylon, the Temple is stripped of its treasures, and 10,000 members of Judah's upper classes are deported to Mesopotamia (2 Kings 24). Nebuchadnezzar then appoints Jehoiachin's uncle **Zedekiah** (597–587 B.C.E.) king in his place.

When Zedekiah, too, rebels against Babylon, Nebuchadnezzar captures and destroys the holy city and its Temple. The Babylonians demolish the city walls, loot and burn surrounding villages, and carry off most of the remaining population, leaving only the poorest citizens behind. Nebuchadnezzar appoints Gedaliah governor of the ruined city, but even this token of survival is lost when Gedaliah is assassinated by fanatical Jewish nationalists. Fearing Babylonian retaliation, many of the peasant survivors flee to Egypt.

Questioning the Deuteronomic Assumptions

The Aftermath The flight of Jerusalem's inhabitants to Egypt brings the story of Israel full cycle, back to conditions under which their pre-Mosaic ancestors had lived, strangers in a foreign land. Seeking to find moral sense in the national catastrophe, the Deuteronomistic historians blamed the victims: The covenant community deserved its sufferings because it had broken faith with Yahweh. Apostate rulers like Manasseh had led the way, but the people themselves were so deeply ingrained with guilt that a righteous Deity could not refrain from punishing them. Prophetic witnesses to the disaster who were also influenced by the deuteronomic view of history, such as Jeremiah, similarly attributed Judah's demise to its failure to keep the Mosaic Torah.

Not all Bible writers agreed with this view, however, and some were tormented by what seemed to be Yahweh's failure to keep his word. The author of Psalm 44 contrasts ancestral traditions about God's saving acts in the remote past with the Deity's present abandonment of his people:

> You let us go to the slaughterhouse like sheep,
> you scatter us among the nations;
> you sell your people for next to nothing,
> and make no profit from the bargain.

Contrary to the deuteronomic thesis, the writer declares that his community had not violated its Torah obligations:

> All this happened to us though we had not forgotten you,
> though we had not been disloyal to your covenant;
> though our hearts had not turned away,
> though our steps had not left your path;
> yet you crushed us in the place where the jackals live,
> and threw the shadow of death over us.
> Psalms 44:17–19

It is, the psalmist reminds God, "for *his* sake we are being massacred daily," suffering precisely because they have put their trust in Yahweh as savior (Ps. 44:11–22).

Another psalmist directly charges Yahweh with violating his oath to David, in which he swore "I will not break my covenant, . . . I have sworn on my holiness, once for all, and cannot turn liar to David":

> And yet you have rejected, disowned
> and raged at your anointed;
> you have repudiated the covenant with your servant
> and flung his crown dishonored to the ground.
> Psalm 89:38–39

Although the annihilation of the Davidic dynasty, never again restored to Judah's throne, brought into question the trustworthiness of the Deity's promises, the Jewish community in exile did not abandon Yahweh. Without land, kings, sacrifices, or temple, anonymous editors in Babylon—striving to understand their God's intentions—reworked ancient legal and prophetic traditions to produce the epic of Israel's creation and fall, Genesis through 2 Kings. Deuteronomistic writers found one single tangible hope: King Jehoiachin's release from prison (2 Kings 25:27–30), although this apparent harbinger of Davidic restoration was doomed to disappointment.

As presented in Genesis through 2 Kings, the totality of Israel's history is profoundly ironic. Israel's story begins with Abraham, a native of Ur in Mesopotamia, who receives Yahweh's promise that his descendants will possess land, multitudinous progeny, nationhood, and royal leaders. The long historical narrative ends with Abraham's last anointed descendant, King Jehoiachin, a deposed monarch without a country, the prisoner of a Mesopotamian ruler (cf. Gen. 11:28–12:3 and 2 Kings 25:27–30). (For a list of Babylonian kings and the Persian emperors who reigned over Yahweh's people after the exile, see Table 4.2.)

Despite this tragic loss, Israel's political failure was to become a new beginning. A few prophets in exile, such as the great poet known as Second Isaiah, proclaimed that Yahweh would lead a new Exodus back to the Promised Land. More than a millennium after Abraham's jour-

Table 4.2 Neo-Babylonian and Persian Empires

Date B.C.E.	Events in Babylon or Persia	Events in Judah
625	Nabopolassar of Babylon (626–605)	
600	Nebuchadnezzar creates New Babylonian Empire (605–562)	First captivity of Jerusalem (598/597)
		Ezekiel prophesies in Babylon
	Nebuchadnezzar conquers Judah (587)	Fall of Jerusalem and deportation of Jews (587)
	Amel-Marduk (562–560)	
	Neriglissar (560–556)	Exile
550	Nabonidus (556–539)	
	Cyrus (550–530) captures Babylon (539); founding of Persian Empire	Second Isaiah in Babylon
		Cyrus' edict freeing Jews (538)
		Jewish remnant returns to Judah
		Zerubbabel, governor of Judah
	Cambyses (530–522) extends Persian Empire to include Egypt	Haggai and Zechariah
	Darius I (522–486)	Temple rebuilt (520–515)
500		
	Persia invades Greece; defeated at Marathon (490)	Joel
	Xerxes I (486–465); second Persian invasion of Greece (480–479)	Malachi
	Artaxerxes I (465–424)	
450		
425	Xerxes II (423)	Nehemiah comes to Jerusalem (445)
	Darius II (423–404)	
400	Artaxerxes II (404–358)	Ezra's reforms; final (?) edition of Torah promulgated
350	Artaxerxes III (358–338)	
	Arses (338–336)	
	Darius III (336–331)	
	Alexander the Great of Macedonia (336–323); conquers Persia, Egypt, Mesopotamia, western India, etc.; begins Hellenistic period	

ney from Mesopotamia to Canaan, a small group of his chastened descendants would retrace his steps to Jerusalem, bringing with them copies of their nation's history and the words of the prophets, which comprise the next section of the Hebrew Bible.

RECOMMENDED READING

Cross, Frank M., ed. "The Themes of the Book of Kings and the Structure of the Deuteronomic History." In *Canaanite Myth and Hebrew Epic: Essays in the History and the Religion of Israel,* Chap.

10. Cambridge, Mass.: Harvard University Press, 1973.

Gray, John. *1 and 2 Kings,* 2nd ed. Old Testament Library. Philadelphia: Westminster Press, 1970.

Long, Burke O. *1 Kings.* Grand Rapids, Mich.: Eerdmans, 1984.

Montgomery, James A., and Gehman, Henry S. *The Books of Kings.* International Critical Commentary. New York: Scribner, 1951. A thorough critical examination of the texts.

TERMS AND CONCEPTS TO REMEMBER

Abimelech
Absalom
Adonijah
Ahab
'Ai
Amalekites
Assyria
Baal
Bathsheba
Benjamin
Book of Jashar
Carchemish
Carmel
Chemosh
conquest of Canaan
Dagon
Dan
David
Deborah
Delilah
Deuteronomistic History
Eli
Elijah
Elisha
Gad
Gideon
Gilboa
Gilgal
golden calf
Goliath

Hebron
Hezekiah
Hiram
Israel
Jael
Jehoiachin
Jehoiakim
Jehonadab
Jehoshaphat
Jehu
Jephthah
Jericho
Jeroboam I
Jeroboam II
Jerusalem
Jezebel
Joab
Jonathan
Josiah
Judah
judge
Manasseh
Messiah
Michal
Moab
Naboth
Nathan
Nazirites
Nebuchadnezzar
Necho
Omri

Philistines
Phoenicia
Prophets (Nevi'im)
Rahab (of Jericho)
Rehoboam
Samaritans
Samson
Samuel
Sargon II
Saul

Sennacherib
Shalmaneser
Shechem
Shiloh
Solomon
Tamar
Temple
Tyre
Uriah
Zedekiah

QUESTIONS FOR REVIEW

1. Define the theory of history given in the Book of Deuteronomy. How is this theory used to explain the rise and fall of Israel as presented in the books of Joshua through Kings? Why do scholars call this long narrative from the conquest of Canaan to the fall of Judah the Deuteronomistic History?

2. How does the Book of Joshua describe the Israelite invasion and takeover of Canaan? In what specific events—such as the capture of Jericho or the failed assault on 'Ai—does the author teach that Israel's military successes or defeats are tied to its loyalty to Yahweh?

3. Explain the concept of "holy war," including the "sacred ban" in which all people and animals in a defeated city are slaughtered. To support your explanation, use passages from Deuteronomy and Joshua in which Yahweh is shown demanding that Israel eradicate all Canaanites.

4. Describe the covenant-renewal ceremony in Joshua 24; how does this scene illustrate the deuteronomic requirement of total obedience to covenant laws? What choices are the Israelites—and readers—asked to make?

5. What incidents does the Book of Judges use to illustrate the principle that obedience to Yahweh leads to national success and disobedience to national disaster? How do the careers of the various judges illus-

trate this hypothesis? Is Samson a typical "judge" or military leader?

6. In 1 Samuel, what was the national crisis that brought about the formation of the Israelite monarchy? How does the story of the stolen Ark of the Covenant illustrate Israel's dire circumstances? Define the two opposing views of kingship—positive and negative—contained in 1 Samuel's account of the monarchy's establishment. What themes involving a reversal of fortune are emphasized in the story of King Saul's rise and decline?

7. Describe David's character and political career. Why do virtually all his ardent supporters end up dead, including his former king, his beloved companion Jonathan, and his most competent general, Joab? What qualities in David motivate him to commit the acts that bring about the domestic betrayals, political revolts, and personal losses that characterize his later reign?

8. Does Yahweh's pact with David (2 Sam. 7) more closely resemble the vow to Abraham or the *conditional* terms of the Mosaic Covenant? In what ways did the Davidic Covenant theology influence the narrative in 1 and 2 Kings about David's royal descendants, such as Solomon, Hezekiah, Manasseh, and Josiah?

9. From the Deuteronomistic History's standpoint, what were the major events and achievements of Solomon's reign? Why did the Davidic empire split into two separate kingdoms after Solomon's death?

10. Why does the Deuteronomistic author approve of *no* ruler in the northern kingdom of Israel? When and how did the northern ten-tribe state come to an end?

11. In the story of Israel's developing religion, why is Josiah's reign considered so important? What were the nature of Josiah's religious reforms? What book, found during Temple repairs, influenced the direction of Josiah's policies?

QUESTIONS FOR DISCUSSION AND REFLECTION

1. Does the Deuteronomistic hypothesis adequately explain the course of events in Israel's history between the conquest and the exile to Babylon? After Nebuchadnezzar destroyed Jerusalem and deported the upper classes, what questions were raised about Yahweh's justice and his sworn oath to David? If you were to compile a synopsis of Israel's history, would you link the nation's fate to Torah loyalty—as the Deuteronomistic author does—or would you evaluate it in more socio-political terms involving the military aggressiveness of Israel's imperialistic neighbors? Do you prefer the Deuteronomistic theory of retributive justice or the psalmists' questioning of that simple explanation?

2. Judging by the Deuteronomistic historian's numerous references to the Israelite people's habits of worshiping Yahweh alongside Baal and Asherah, do you think that Judah was a monotheistic community at the time Babylon conquered it? What do you think allowed Yahwism to survive the destruction of royal family, state, Temple, and priesthood that had fostered it? Of all the gods worshiped throughout the ancient Near East, why did Yahweh alone eventually become the paradigm of a single, universal Deity?

5

The Prophets (Nevi'im) II: Collections Attributed to Individual Prophets

Spokesmen for God

Whereas some Bible writers perceived Yahweh as absent, "hidden" (Ps. 89:46), or "asleep" (Ps. 44:23) during critical periods of Israel's history, the prophets (*nevi'im*) intensely felt his presence, which they communicated through oracles, pronouncements revealing the divine will or purpose. Israelite prophets, such as Nathan, Gad, Ahijah, Micaiah, Elijah, and Elisha, appeared prominently in the historical books of Samuel and Kings, but it was not until about 750 B.C.E. that a prophet's disciples began the practice of collecting and writing down their master's oracles under the individual prophet's name. Although emphasizing ethical and religious issues, the prophets also played leading roles in Israel's political affairs, intervening in dynastic disputes (1 Kings 1:11–53) or helping elevate or overthrow kings (1 Sam. 8:10–10:27; 13:8–15; 15:10–35; 16:1–13; 1 Kings 11:26–39; 2 Kings 9:1–13). Some prophets were associated with religious shrines like Shiloh or Bethel, but most clustered at royal courts, where they offered counsel or criticism to kings like David, Solomon, Jehu, or Ahab. As a national influence, prophecy's rise and decline corresponded almost exactly to that of the Davidic monarchy. Flourishing from the tenth to

the sixth centuries B.C.E., Hebrew prophecy almost disappeared shortly after the end of the Babylonian exile (about the fifth century B.C.E.). Its function of providing guidance during national emergencies was eventually taken over by priests, scribal interpreters of the Torah, and sages, the professional teachers of wisdom.

The Hebrew word for prophet, **navi** (singular), means "one who is called" or "one who announces." (The plural form is *nevi'im*.) Its Greek equivalent, *prophetes,* from which our English word is derived, means "a person speaking for God," one chosen to proclaim Yahweh's message, and includes both men and women.

To understand the nature and purpose of Israel's prophets, it is helpful to review what little is known about their historical development. In Deuteronomy 18 (which scholars believe was compiled in the seventh century B.C.E. when the *nevi'im* had already arisen in Israel), Moses is shown describing the prophetic office. The prophet is to function as a link between the people and Yahweh, who employs the prophet to convey Yahweh's "words" (oracles). The *navi* is specifically said to be Israel's means of ascertaining the divine will—in direct contrast to the Canaanite practices of seeking supernatural help by consulting sorcerers, soothsayers, or spirit mediums who "call up the dead," religious figures to whom some Israelites apparently were attracted (Deut. 18:9–12). Yahweh sends Israel the *nevi'im,* whose messages have the force of divine commands. Anyone ignoring the prophetic word and attempting to communicate directly with the unseen world—a practice the Torah labels a Canaanite "abomination"—risked death by stoning or fire (Lev. 20:27; Exod. 22:18).

Among the earliest Hebrew prophets were those called "ecstatic"—people who, seemingly possessed by Yahweh's spirit, worked themselves into a religious frenzy, throwing themselves writhing upon the ground and uttering unintelligible sounds. As with the later Orphic and Dionysic cults in ancient Greece, such emotional seizures were induced through orgiastic music or dance (1 Sam. 10:5–6; 2 Kings 3:15). According to 1 Samuel 10, Saul was seized by Yahweh's spirit shortly after the prophet Samuel had anointed him king. Joining a prophetic band that played "harp, tambourine, flute, and lyre," Saul is thrown "into an ecstasy" and "changed into another man," temporarily losing his individual identity. A later account of the incident adds details associated with the primitive ecstatic experience: Saul stripped off his clothes, fell into a trance, and "lay there naked all that day and night" (1 Sam. 19:18–24).

Even in later Israel, prophets were noted for their bizarre, even grotesque, behavior. Isaiah, naked except for a loincloth, paraded through Jerusalem's streets to illustrate the city's imminent humiliation and ruin. Jeremiah wore a yoke first of wood then of iron, symbolic of bearing the Babylonian oppression (Jer. 27). Ezekiel carried the prophets' symbolic acts to an even greater extreme, cooking his food over a fire of human excrement (Ezek. 4:12–15), refusing to mourn for his dead wife (Ezek. 24:15–27), and lying bound like a prisoner for 190 days on one side, then 40 days on the other (Ezek. 4:4–8). In these and other ways, the great prophets dramatized their messages through strangely expressive conduct.

According to 1 Samuel 9, Israel's early prophets were called **seers.** The old term is appropriate, for Yahweh was believed to grant seers special insight into a given situation, permitting them to apprehend spiritual realities not accessible to others. Seers and prophets (the terms are *almost* interchangeable) traditionally received Yahweh's oracles through dreams and visions (Num. 12:6). Some of the early prophets belonged to schools or brotherhoods called "sons of the prophets." Elijah and Elisha were apparently leaders of such guilds at Bethel, Jericho, and Gilgal (2 Kings 2:3–4; 4:38), though they were not permanently attached to a particular cultic center.

A careful reading of prophetic literature distinguishes Israel's classical prophets from certain modern concepts of the role. The *nevi'im* were not primarily fortune-tellers or prognosticators of future history. Their function was to perceive and then announce Yahweh's will in an immediate circumstance—in terms comprehensible or at least relevant to their original audience. Rather than predicting events in a far-distant future, the *nevi'im* endeavored to illuminate Yahweh's intentions in the present. They strove to bring Yahweh's people back into harmony with the Mosaic Torah or, failing that, to specify the punishments for disobedience.

The prophetic calling included women, the first of whom was Moses' sister Miriam (Exod. 15:20–21; Num. 12:2). In the period of the judges, Deborah was both a tribal leader and a prophet (Judg. 4:4). When priests discovered the lost manuscript of Deuteronomy during Josiah's reign, they brought the matter to Huldah, "a prophetess," for interpretation and advice (2 Kings 22:14). The prophetess Noadiah was one of Nehemiah's noted opponents in postexilic Jerusalem (Neh. 6:14; see also Isa. 8:2). Women participated in the prophetic dispensation well into New Testament times (Luke 2:36; Rev. 2:20).

The Hebrew Bible places the three Major Prophets—Isaiah, Jeremiah, and Ezekiel—first among the Latter ("writing") Prophets, a ranking that probably derives as much from their great length as from their enormous theological influence. The books of the twelve **Minor Prophets**—Hosea through Malachi—are minor only in length, not in religious significance. From the earliest, Amos, who prophesied during the eighth century B.C.E., to Jonah, a book written in the late sixth or early fifth century B.C.E., the twelve present a 300-year continuum of Yahweh's oracles to Israel. These Minor Prophets are arranged in roughly chronological order, although other factors, such as a book's size, also figured in their positioning. The following is an introductory survey of the Latter Prophets and a statement of the order in which the individual prophets appeared, if not that in which the books bearing their names were written.

The Three Great Crises

The Latter Prophets of Israel and Judah, like other contributors to biblical literature, appeared largely in response to urgent political or ethnical crises that troubled their people. Most of the Latter Prophets belong to one of three critical periods: (1) the Assyrian era, (2) the Babylonian crisis, or (3) the postexilic adjustment.

The Assyrian Crisis   The earliest of the "writing" prophets (those whose works were recorded in their names) were active during the second half of the eighth century B.C.E. A time of swift change and political upheaval, a revitalized Assyrian Empire then threatened the very existence of the two kingdoms of Israel and Judah. Amos and Hosea preached in the northern kingdom, warning of a terrible retribution for the people's faithlessness to the Mosaic Covenant ideals of social justice and loyalty to Yahweh. Within two decades after northern Israel's collapse before the Assyrian military juggernaut (722–721 B.C.E.), Judah seemed doomed to a

similar fate. Like their two predecessors in the north, the Judeans Isaiah and Micah interpreted the historical situation as Yahweh's punishment for Judah's religious and social sins. (The two prophets, however, manifest strikingly different attitudes toward the Davidic monarchy and royal sanctuary in Jerusalem.)

The Babylonian Threat   Another cluster of late seventh- and sixth-century prophets responded to a second period of international turmoil. In rapid succession Assyria fell (612 B.C.E.), inspiring Nahum's rejoicing, and Egypt's Pharaoh Necho attempted to fill the Near Eastern power vacuum (defeating and killing Judah's "good" King Josiah along the way), only to be defeated by Babylon's Nebuchadnezzar at the decisive Battle of Carchemish (605 B.C.E.). Judah, which had begun a profound religious reform and political expansion under Josiah (c. 621 B.C.E.)—developments made possible by Assyria's growing weakness—quickly found itself subject to a new imperial master, the Neo-Babylonian Empire. Reduced again to a tribute-paying vassal state, as it had been under Assyria, Judah plotted revolts against Nebuchadnezzar and looked to Egypt (a "frail reed") for military help.

During the Babylonian crisis the prophets Habakkuk and Jeremiah interpreted political events as signs of Yahweh's will working through human activity. Using the form of a legal prosecution or "covenant lawsuit" against lawbreaking Judah, Jeremiah urged political submission to Babylon, which unwittingly acted as Yahweh's punishing agent.

Deported to Babylonia (597 B.C.E.), Ezekiel similarly proclaimed that Yahweh had abandoned his dwelling place in Jerusalem's Temple because of the people's promoting injustice and religious corruption. Ezekiel also produced visions of a new Jerusalem and splendidly rebuilt Temple where a restored "remnant" would one day properly worship their God. These glowing visions of a happier future helped encourage the Judean captives and provided a rallying point of hope that Yahweh had not utterly forgotten the covenant community. Toward the close of the Babylonian period, the unknown prophet called Second Isaiah announced not only that the captives' return to the Judean homeland was near but also that Yahweh planned a glorious triumph for his "servant," Israel.

The Postexilic Readjustment   Second Isaiah's promises were not matched by the grim and impoverished realities of life in postexilic Jerusalem; the returned exiles nonetheless experienced prophetic encouragement. About 520 B.C.E., the prophets Haggai and Zechariah renewed promises of a brighter future and incited the apathetic Judeans to finish rebuilding Yahweh's Temple. Still later, Joel, Malachi, and the anonymous poet known as Third Isaiah added their **eschatological** (referring to a doctrine of "last things") hopes to the prophetic writings. After the time of Ezra—priest, scribe, and transmitter of the Mosaic law (c. 400 B.C.E.)— it was believed that traditional prophecy ceased. Late "prophetic" books like Daniel, for example, were not included among the canonical Prophets but were assigned to a later collection, the Writings.

Hosea (c. 746–735? B.C.E.)   Comparing Israel's disloyalty to Yahweh in its worship of Baal to the breaking of a marriage bond, **Hosea** renews Amos's theme of economic and social corruption and deserved national disaster but also stresses Yahweh's *hesed* (loving devotion) and likens Yahweh's concern for Israel to a spouse's distress over a beloved but faithless mate.

Isaiah of Jerusalem (c. 742–701 B.C.E.)   A prophet intimately associated with the Jerusalem sanctuary and Davidic royal family, **Isaiah** resembles the northern prophets in denouncing the ruling classes' acquisitive greed and callous disregard for the poor. Active during the Assyrian invasion of Judah, he counsels "isolationism," a total reliance on Yahweh's power to save, and predicts that a Davidic heir will establish universal peace and justice.

Micah   Unlike his contemporary Isaiah, **Micah** is a country villager who unequivocally condemns the rich urban landowners who "skin" and "devour" the peasant farmer. Criticizing the Jerusalem kings who permit such practices, Micah declares that the city and Temple will be destroyed (Mic. 3:9–12).

Order of the Prophets' Appearances

Eighth Century

Amos (c. 750 B.C.E.)   A Judean called to prophesy in the northern kingdom, **Amos** reverses popular assumptions about the "Day of Yahweh," when Yahweh appears to judge the world, he will punish Israel along with other nations that foster social and economic injustice. Amos vigorously denounces the upper classes' luxurious living based on an unjust exploitation of the poor. Claiming that Israel had perverted religion into an empty ritual, Amos predicts political disaster and exile.

Seventh Century

Zephaniah   Compiled during Josiah's reign (640–609 B.C.E.), the Book of **Zephaniah** opens with Yahweh's declared intention to sweep all life from the earth, continues with denunciations of Israel's neighbors, Moab and Ammon, and the oppressor, Assyria, but abruptly switches course and asserts that Yahweh has changed his mind and "repealed his sentence" against Judah (Zeph. 3:14–18). The prophet's abrupt change in attitude may have been a reaction to Josiah's religious reforms.

Nahum   Shortly before Nineveh's fall (612 B.C.E.), **Nahum** gloats over Assyria's destruction.

Habakkuk   Faced with Babylon's imminent conquest of Judah, **Habakkuk** ponders Yahweh's fairness, concluding that the righteous person must live having faith in God's ultimate justice.

Sixth Century

Jeremiah   During the reigns of Judah's last kings (Josiah to Zedekiah, about 626 until after 587 B.C.E.), **Jeremiah** stresses that Yahweh employs Babylon as the divinely appointed instrument of punishment against covenant-breaking Judah. Declaring that only those submitting to Babylon (and Yahweh) can escape destruction, Jeremiah envisions the future enactment of a covenant that will not be broken (Jer. 31:31). Unlike his predecessor Isaiah, who also advised Jerusalem's kings during foreign invasions, Jeremiah sees little merit in the Temple cult or the Davidic ruling family.

Obadiah   **Obadiah** condemns Edom for helping the Babylonians sack Jerusalem (587 B.C.E.).

Ezekiel   A priest and mystic exiled in Babylonia during Judah's last years (after 597 B.C.E.), **Ezekiel** declares that Yahweh is too holy to continue dwelling among an unjust and violent people. Envisioning Yahweh's "glory" abandoning Jerusalem to Babylon's power, Ezekiel also foresees a glorious rebuilt sanctuary and divinely protected new Jerusalem.

Second Isaiah   Living in Babylonia during Cyrus the Persian's rise to power (c. 550–539 B.C.E.), this anonymous poet, referred to as **Second Isaiah**, views Yahweh as the *only* God, the eternal foreordainer of human history who was then acting to restore Judah's faithful remnant to its homeland in Palestine. The four Servant Songs depict the redemptive role of Yahweh's chosen agent, Israel.

Haggai   Under Zerubbabel, a Davidic descendant whom the Persians appointed governor of the tiny restored community of Judah, **Haggai** argues that Yahweh will cause the wealth of nations to flow into Jerusalem if the Judeans will obediently rebuild the Temple.

Zechariah   A contemporary of Haggai (c. 520 B.C.E.), **Zechariah** produces a series of mystic visions involving the rebuilt Temple, the high priest Joshua, the Davidic governor Zerubbabel, and Yahweh's messianic intentions for Israel. A later hand added Chapters 9–12.

Late Sixth or Fifth Century

Third Isaiah   The third section of Isaiah (Chs. 55–66) includes oracles from almost the whole period of Israelite prophecy, including the work of a postexilic prophet, referred to as **Third Isaiah**, who is sharply critical of the restored community's religious failures.

Joel   Of uncertain date, Joel's book contains a series of apocalyptic visions that picture plagues and judgments signaling the Day of Yahweh. Calling for repentance, **Joel** foresees a climactic outpouring of the divine spirit upon all humanity.

Malachi   This anonymous prophet also predicts a coming judgment on the frightening day of Yahweh's visitation. Promising a "messenger" to purify the Temple cult, **Malachi** ends by announcing the future reappearance of Elijah.

Jonah   A moral fable contrasting **Jonah**'s narrow view of divine justice with Yahweh's universality and compassion, this humorous tale provides insight into the ethical value of an unfulfilled prophecy.

RECOMMENDED READING

Barton, John. "Prophecy (Postexilic Hebrew)." In D. N. Freedman, ed., *The Anchor Bible Dictionary,*

Vol. 5, pp. 489–495. New York: Doubleday, 1992.

Bright, John. *Covenant and Promise: The Prophetic Understanding of the Future in Pre-Exilic Israel.* Philadelphia: Westminster Press, 1976.

Buber, Martin. *The Prophetic Faith.* Translated by C. Witton-Davies. New York: Macmillan, 1949; Harper Torchbooks, 1960.

Heschel, Abraham J. *The Prophets.* New York: Harper & Row, 1963. A major work by a great Jewish scholar.

Huffmon, H. B. "Prophecy (Ancient Near Eastern)." In D. N. Freedman, ed., *The Anchor Bible Dictionary,* Vol. 5, pp. 477–482. New York: Doubleday, 1992.

Koch, Klaus. *The Prophets.* Vol. 1, *The Assyrian Age.* Translated by M. Kohl. Philadelphia: Fortress Press, 1982.

———. *The Prophets.* Vol. 2, *The Babylonian and Persian Period.* Philadelphia: Fortress Press, 1984.

Lindblom, Johannes. *Prophecy in Ancient Israel.* Philadelphia: Fortress Press, 1963. A major study by a Swedish scholar.

Schmitt, John J. "Prophecy (Preexilic Hebrew)." In D. N. Freedman, ed., *The Anchor Bible Dictionary,* Vol. 5, pp. 482–489. New York: Doubleday, 1992.

Scott, R. B. Y. *The Relevance of the Prophets,* rev. ed. New York: Macmillan, 1968.

Vawter, Bruce. *The Conscience of Israel.* New York: Sheed & Ward, 1961. Discusses preexilic prophecy.

von Rad, Gerhard. *Old Testament Theology.* Vol. 2, *The Theology of Israel's Prophetic Traditions.* Translated by M. G. Stalker. New York: Harper & Row, 1965.

Ward, James. *The Prophets.* Nashville, Tenn.: Abingdon Press, 1982.

Westermann, Claus. *Basic Forms of Prophetic Speech.* Translated by H. K. White. Philadelphia: Westminster Press, 1967.

Amos

KEY THEMES

Beginning with a series of oracles condemning Israel's neighbors (1:3–2:3), Amos also threatens the northern kingdom with destruction (2:4–16), delivering three warnings of judgment (Chs. 3–6) followed by five visions of disaster (Chs. 7–9). An epilog, promising restoration and peace, was added by a Judean editor (9:9–15).

> The Lord Yahweh do[es nothing] without revealing his plans to his servants the prophets.
>
> Amos 3:7

Although placed third among the Minor Prophets, Amos was the first biblical prophet to have his words recorded in book form and to introduce major themes that would thereafter become the staple of prophecy. Active about 750 B.C.E. during the reign of Jeroboam II, Amos was an older contemporary of Hosea and Isaiah of Jerusalem. A native of Judah from the small town of Tekoa, located about twelve miles south of Jerusalem, a shepherd and pruner of sycamore (fig) trees, Amos—as he insists—was not a professional prophet (Amos 7:14). Nonetheless, he answered Yahweh's call to proclaim a stern message of doom in the northern kingdom. His book shows considerable familiarity with northern customs, economic conditions, and religious practices, many of which he condemns astringently.

Yahweh Demands Economic Justice

Oracles of Doom　The first cluster of oracles, delineated in an abrupt, austere style, consists of denunciations against Israel's various neighbors—Syria, Philistia, Tyre, Edom, and Moab—that the prophet excoriates for their inhumane treatment of conquered peoples. Then, unexpectedly switching his target, Amos suddenly attacks his Israelite audience, castigating its leaders for behaving no better than greedy foreign princes. His point is that Yahweh not only refuses to tolerate cruelty among the people whom he had rescued from Egypt but also requires higher standards of ethical conduct from Israel than from those who do not enjoy Yahweh's special guidance.

Foremost among Israel's crimes was its exploitation of the poor. Although under Jeroboam the nation had grown rich and comfortable, the wealth had accumulated into too few hands, leaving many landless and in want. This unequal distribution of the nation's goods Amos condemned as abhorrent to Yahweh, who will punish them

> Because they have sold the virtuous man for
>   silver
> and the poor man for a pair of sandals,
> because they trample on the heads of ordinary
>   people
> and push the poor out of their path.
>
> Amos 2:6–7

Amos saw that behind the national prosperity and private luxury was a callous indifference to human rights, which was no less a sin than sacrificing to idols. He was the first prophet to argue that social justice is as vital to religion as worshiping one God alone (Amos 8:4–8).

Three Sermons   In the three sermons that follow (Amos 3–6), the prophet reminds Israel that Yahweh causes everything that happens, whether it be the fall of a city or the message of his prophets (Amos 3:3–8). He then predicts the destruction of Bethel's popular sanctuary and the ruin of the magnificent palaces and "houses of ivory" that the wealthy had built (Amos 3:13–15). Similarly, in Chapter 5 he foretells that the houses, fields, and vineyards that rich landowners have accumulated will never yield their benefits to those who cheat the poor and defenseless (Amos 5:7–12).

Nor is the ceremonial religion practiced by "respectable" citizens acceptable:

> I hate and despise your feasts,
> I take no pleasure in your solemn festivals.
> When you offer me holocausts,
> I reject your oblations. . . .
> Let me have no more of the din of your
>   chanting,
> no more of your strumming on harps.

> But let justice flow like water,
> and integrity like an unfailing stream.
>
> Amos 5:21–24

Amos's insistence that ethical behavior is more important than ritual observances is typical of Israel's prophets, but he was the first to emphasize this important concept.

The Day of Yahweh: A New Vision

Visions of Judgment   Amos fostered another significant reversal in Israel's religious outlook. Until his time, the Day of Yahweh was thought to be a time of rejoicing, a future era when Yahweh would vanquish all Israel's enemies and cover his people with glory. Blasting such complacent assumptions, Amos reversed popular expectations by proclaiming the Day of Yahweh to be a Day of Judgment, a period of darkness and grief for sinful Israel (Amos 5:18–20). This so distressed his hearers that Amaziah, the priest of Bethel, forbade the prophet to speak and expelled him from the sanctuary (Amos 7:10–17), which did not, however, prevent Amos from continuing his pronouncements of doom.

Israel, he said, was like a basket of summer fruit, ripe for destruction (Amos 8:1–4), and none will escape the day of wrath:

> Should they burrow their way down to Sheol,
> my hand will haul them out;
> should they scale the heavens,
> I will drag them down.
>
> Amos 9:2

Amos saw Yahweh as directing the fate of all nations, not of Israel alone. He had brought the Philistines from Crete just as he had brought Israel from Egypt; they and the Ethiopians were all the same to him (Amos 9:7–8). Assyria, then just beginning its imperial expansion, was also under Yahweh's jurisdiction and would be the chosen instrument to punish Israel. Amos thus foresaw the northern kingdom's fall to Assyria in 721 B.C.E., though he expressed this insight in terms of hyperbole and metaphor rather than by foretelling specific events and dates.

Epilog So unrelieved was Amos's pessimism that a later hand added a brief epilog predicting Israel's future restoration and prosperity (Amos 9:11–15). But his dire warnings and harsh judgments nevertheless set the tone for many later prophets, among them Jeremiah, who resembles the shepherd from Tekoa in delivering an unrelievedly gloomy message.

RECOMMENDED READING

Auld, A. Graeme. *Amos.* Sheffield, Eng.: JSOT Press, 1986.

Cathcart, K. J. "Day of Yahweh." In D. N. Freedman, ed., *The Anchor Bible Dictionary,* Vol. 2, pp. 84–85. New York: Doubleday, 1992.

Coote, Robert B. *Amos Among the Prophets: Composition and Theology.* Philadelphia: Fortress Press, 1981.

King, Philip J. *Amos, Hosea, Micah—An Archaeological Commentary.* Philadelphia: Westminster Press, 1988.

Koch, Klaus. *The Prophets.* Vol. 1, *The Assyrian Age.* Translated by M. Kohl. Philadelphia: Fortress Press, 1982.

Willoughby, Bruce E. "Amos, Book of." In D. N. Freedman, ed., *The Anchor Bible Dictionary,* Vol. 1, pp. 203–212. New York: Doubleday, 1992.

Wolff, Hans W. *Confrontations with Prophets.* Philadelphia: Fortress Press, 1983.

Hosea

KEY THEMES

Active during the last turbulent years of the northern kingdom, Hosea is the only native prophet of Israel whose oracles have been preserved in book form. Providing a unique view of late Israelite society and religion, Hosea uses the metaphor of an unhappy marriage to illustrate Yahweh's relationship with Israel. Comparing his people to an unfaithful mate, the prophet urges a national return to Yahweh's loving embrace, a reaffirmation of the bond that alone can save Israel from disaster. The first part (Chs. 1–3) describes Hosea's marriage, the second (Chs. 4–13) Israel's crimes and punishments, and the third (Ch. 14) a brief epilog promising future repentance and reconciliation.

> My people perish for want of knowledge.
> Hosea 4:6

Unlike Amos, the Judean shepherd who preceded him as a prophet in the northern kingdom, Hosea was a native son of Israel, the only Israelite prophet whose words have survived in a canonical book. Hosea also differs from his predecessor in tempering his announcements of Yahweh's punishments with expressions of grief at Israel's imminent sufferings and hope for his nation's future. Presenting a God who experiences mixed emotions—anger and wounded love—at his people's **apostasy**, Hosea began his career during the reign of **Jeroboam II** (c. 747 B.C.E.) and continued prophesying into the reign of Israel's last king, Hosea (732–724 B.C.E.). After the fall of the northern kingdom, his oracles were probably carried south to Judah, where Judean scribes wrote them down, adding references to the Davidic monarchy (Hos. 1:7; 3:5). A copyist appended a postscript urging readers to take the prophet's message to heart (Hos. 14:10).

Yahweh's Disloyal Mate

Hosea's Marriage The social, religious, and moral decay that marked the last days of the northern kingdom is reflected not only in the prophet's message but also in his private life. The book's first section (Hos. 1–3) is intended to show that Hosea's domestic situation exactly paralleled his prophetic view of Yahweh's relationship to Israel: Both he and his God were loving husbands who had suffered betrayal by their wives. Israel, Yahweh's bride (whom he had redeemed from slavery in Egypt), had betrayed her divine protector by worshiping Baal, the Canaanite fertility god. To illustrate the nation's faithlessness, Hosea had been commanded: "Go, and marry a whore, and get children with a whore, for the country has become nothing but a whore by abandoning Yahweh" (Hos. 1:2).

Hosea obediently married Gomer, who may have been a priestess of fertility in a Baalistic cult. The prophet fathered children by her, naming each one symbolically to reflect Yahweh's anger with Israel's religious infidelity. Hosea saw in Gomer's repeated adulteries a mirror image of Israel's "whoring" after Canaan's agricultural deities. It was to Baal the people looked to provide rain, bless their crops, and ensure general prosperity, having forgotten Yahweh's "marriage" covenant with them in the Sinai wilderness. Although for its sins Israel stands condemned to national death, the Deity will not permanently abandon his disloyal consort (Hos. 2). Yahweh's steadfast love will eventually reconcile him to his errant people, as Hosea is reunited with his faithless wife (Hos. 3).

Crimes and Punishments   Part 2 (Hos. 4–14) forms a somewhat random collection of poetic declarations against Israel's idolatries, foreign alliances, and exploitation of the poor. Hosea charges the corrupt priesthood with rejecting proper knowledge of their God (Hos. 4:4–11). Priests, nobles, and kings are the nation's ruin (Hos. 5:1–7); even the people's repentance is insincere and short-lived (Hos. 6:1–6).

Hosea particularly laments the popularity of cultic rituals and sacrifices, which keep the people from recognizing how empty their religion is (Hos. 8:11–13). What Yahweh desires is "love, not sacrifice; knowledge of God, not holocausts" (Hos. 6:6). The prophet foresees that the Israelites will be scattered, some returning to Egypt, others carried to Assyria, where they will "eat food that is unclean" (Hos. 9:3–6). Although he does not refer to these events, Hosea may have lived to experience the fulfillment of his oracles when Assyria devastated Samaria in 721 B.C.E. and deported many of the survivors.

Future Reconciliation   Despite their certain punishment, Hosea argues, Yahweh will remember his people. Chapter 11 contains one of the Bible's most moving expressions of divine love, which Hosea perceives as stronger than divine vengeance. Although the remaining chapters remind Israel of the reasons for its God's present wrath, they also assert that Yahweh waits to effect a reconciliation (Hos. 12:9–11). Indeed, Israel's exile may lead to a "second honeymoon" with Yahweh, like the Mosaic sojourn in the Sinai desert (Hos. 2:3, 16–17). The book concludes with a final call for Israel's return and a promise of future happiness (Hos. 14).

RECOMMENDED READING

Anderson, Francis I., and Freedman, David N. *Hosea.* Anchor Bible, Vol. 24. Garden City, N.Y.: Doubleday, 1980.

Mays, James L. *Hosea.* Philadelphia: Westminster Press, 1969.

Seow, C. L. "Hosea, Book of." In David N. Freedman, ed., *The Anchor Bible Dictionary,* Vol. 3, pp. 291–297. New York: Doubleday, 1992.

Ward, James M. *Hosea: A Theological Commentary.* New York: Harper & Row, 1966.

Wolff, Hans W. *Confrontations with Prophets.* Philadelphia: Fortress Press, 1983.

Isaiah

KEY THEMES

A diverse collection of Hebrew prophecy dating from the mid-seventh to the fifth centuries B.C.E., the Book of Isaiah is the work of at least three prophets responding to three different crises in Israel's history. In the first section (Chs. 1–39), the Assyrian Empire threatens to engulf tiny Judah, eliciting a series of poetic oracles from the historical Isaiah of Jerusalem (c. 742–

701 B.C.E.), who advises Davidic kings to rely exclusively on Yahweh for deliverance. A prosaic narrative recounting the Assyrian failure to capture Jerusalem ends this section (Chs. 36–39). In the second main division (Chs. 40–55), from which both the Assyrian threat and the figure of Isaiah are absent, an anonymous prophet speaks to Judean captives in Babylon, hailing Cyrus of Persia as Yahweh's Messiah, the divine agent of Israel's liberation from the Babylonian exile. The third part (Chs. 56–66) is a miscellaneous assemblage of prophetic oracles to an impoverished colony of exiles resettled in Judah, now under Persian rule.

> They shall beat their swords into plowshares,
> and their spears into pruning hooks;
> nation shall not lift up sword against nation,
> neither shall they learn war any more.
> Isaiah 2:4; King James Version

Preeminent among the prophetic books is that of Isaiah, which preserves some of the loftiest thoughts and most memorable poetry in world literature. Although traditionally regarded as a single, unified work, the Book of Isaiah is actually an anthology of many prophetic oracles produced over many years. Scholars who have analyzed Isaiah's sixty-six chapters have generally agreed that the book can be divided into at least three distinct parts, each portion representing a different time period and a different author.

The first thirty-nine chapters (except for 24–27, 33–35, and 36–39) are thought to be largely the work of Isaiah of Jerusalem, who prophesied between 742 and 701 B.C.E., when the Assyrian Empire engulfed Israel and threatened Judah as well. Chapters 40–55 present a historical situation in which Babylon, not Assyria, dominates. The differences in style, vocabulary, and theological perspective also indicate a new author at work. Chapters 56–66 seem to represent oracles from the eighth to the early fifth centuries B.C.E.—almost the whole age of prophecy. Scholars customarily treat each of Isaiah's three main divisions as a separate lit-

erary unit. Based on scholarly analyses of their style, literary form, theological content, and allusions to historical themes or events, the first and third sections are in turn divided into numerous smaller units. Isaiah 24–27 (the "little apocalypse") appears to belong to a period later than that of the historical Isaiah. Because of its elaborately developed eschatological concerns, this passage is generally assigned a postexilic date. Chapters 36–39 have been lifted almost verbatim from 2 Kings 18:13 through 2 Kings 20:19, which summarize events from late in Isaiah's ministry. The book's last ten chapters (Isa. 56–66) stem partly from the late sixth century and are addressed to members of the restored Jerusalem community, though they also include fragments from earlier centuries. As noted below, some of the book's most powerful utterances are directed to an audience eagerly awaiting release from captivity. This section (Isa. 40–55) speaks cogently to the needs of Judean exiles living in Babylon between about 550 and 539 B.C.E.

Isaiah of Jerusalem

According to Isaiah 1:1, the prophet was active during the reigns of four Judean kings: **Uzziah** (Azariah), Jotham, Ahaz, and Hezekiah. If Isaiah received his call to prophesy around 742–740 B.C.E. as Chapter 6 suggests, he could have devoted more than forty years to his ministry. Although the individual oracles represented in the Isaiah scroll are arranged neither chronologically nor topically, scholars have tentatively assigned various portions of the book to three principal crises of Isaiah's lifetime: the Syro-Ephraimite War (735–734 B.C.E.), Hezekiah's temptation to ally Judah with Egypt (c. 711 B.C.E.), and the Assyrian invasion of 701 B.C.E.

Oracles from the first phase of his career are contained in Chapters 2–11 (the first chapter is a general preface to the whole of Isaiah 1–39 and includes oracles from the prophet's entire career). Chapter 6 records what is generally regarded as Isaiah's call to prophesy. While worshiping at the Temple, Isaiah experiences a vision of Yahweh enthroned in heaven and encompassed by his angelic court. Overcome by a consciousness of his human imperfections, he feels his lips symbolically cleansed when touched by a burning coal, and he volunteers to carry Yahweh's word to Judah (Isa. 6:1–9). Having dedicated his life to the Deity, he demands comparable allegiance from his people.

Many of Isaiah's early messages are concerned with social justice. Like his contemporaries Amos and Hosea, who prophesied in the northern kingdom of Israel, Isaiah argues that Yahweh places greater importance on dealing mercifully and generously with widows, orphans, and strangers than he does on cultic observances. The nation will be judged harshly for its economic exploitation of the poor (Isa. 1:10–20; 3:13–15; 5:8–20; 10:1–4). For their sins, Israel and Judah will go into exile, though Yahweh will eventually restore a remnant (Isa. 11:10–16).

It is important to note that Isaiah never attributes the coming punishment to a breaking of the Mosaic Covenant. Scholars believe that Mosaic traditions now found in the Pentateuch were not widely known or influential during Isaiah's day and would not become truly authoritative until after the publication of Deuteronomy during Josiah's reign a century later. Instead of appealing to Mosaic legal obligations, Isaiah emphasizes Yahweh's special relationship to the Davidic dynasty in Jerusalem, a concept with which his audience seems more familiar (cf. 2 Sam. 7). This reliance on the Davidic royal line and the sanctity of the Davidic capital may explain why Isaiah regards every threat to Jerusalem and its anointed kings as an opportunity for the nation to demonstrate its absolute trust in Yahweh's sworn oath to preserve David's heirs. The prophet consistently urges Judah's rulers to rely exclusively on Yahweh's faithfulness to his promise rather than on diplomatic or military assistance.

Isaiah and the Syro-Ephraimite Crisis   Isaiah's policy is well illustrated by his prophetic advice during the Syro-Ephraimite War of the mid-730s B.C.E. As scholars reconstruct events, it appears that various Palestinian states, led by Syria and Israel (Ephraim), formed a coalition to resist Assyrian expansion into the area. When the kings of Damascus and Samaria besieged Jerusalem to force King **Ahaz** of Judah to join their alliance, Isaiah counseled a passive reliance on Yahweh to keep his vow to David and deliver the holy city (Isa. 7).

Ignoring Isaiah's counsel, Ahaz negotiated with Assyria, and thanks to Assyrian influence, the Syro-Ephraimite siege of Jerusalem was lifted. In saving his capital from the kings of Damascus and Syria, however, Ahaz made it subservient to Assyria, so that Judah was reduced to the level of a vassal state in the Assyrian Empire. Inevitably, Isaiah regarded Ahaz's compromise as a betrayal of Yahweh. He predicts that Assyria will soon become the "rod" of Yahweh's anger to punish those who have failed to show faith in their God (Isa. 7:18–25; 10:5–6, 28–32). Should Assyria exceed its mandate to chastise his people, however, Yahweh will in turn destroy it (Isa. 10:7–19).

As a sign that Yahweh would rescue his people from the Syro-Ephraimite crisis, Isaiah had prophesied that a young woman would conceive and bear a son whose name, **Immanuel** ("God [El] is with us"), signified that Yahweh would protect those who trusted in him (Isa. 7:13–17). Although the author of Matthew's Gospel, relying on the Greek translation of Isaiah's "young woman" as "virgin," interpreted this as a messianic prophecy (Matt. 1:22–24), it contains no direct reference to the Messiah but seems to imply the birth of a child in the prophet's own day.

Judging Ahaz as having failed to meet Yahweh's challenge of faith, Isaiah nonetheless foresees a future Judean king who by fully depending on Yahweh will reap the promised blessings, a king whose sovereignty will be worldwide and under whose glorious reign the earth will be transformed into another Eden (Isa. 9:2–7; 11:1–6). Because the term *messiah* simply means "anointed one," as Judah's kings were anointed with holy oil at their coronations, it is difficult to tell whether Isaiah envisions **Hezekiah**, Ahaz's son and heir, or another more distant descendant of David fulfilling this role. Whereas those passages associate a Davidic king with a renewed creation (Isa. 9:2–7; 11:6–9), other oracles present a new world order of universal peace, in which Jerusalem is the center, without mentioning a messianic ruler (Isa. 2:2–4; 29:17–21; 19:19–25).

Assyrian Crisis   The prophet's attention was brought back to more immediate problems when around 711 B.C.E. the Assyrians attacked the city of **Ashdod**, which bordered on Judah's southwest frontier. This time Egypt attempted to form a Palestinian coalition to protect its own boundaries. To dissuade King Hezekiah from involving Judah in this alliance, Isaiah paraded naked through the streets of Jerusalem, vividly illustrating the certainty of exile and slavery that would result from relying on Egypt instead of on Yahweh for deliverance (Isa. 20). Although Hezekiah did not then commit himself to Egypt, a decade later he did join Egypt in an anti-Assyrian alliance, and Isaiah castigated king, courtiers, and other national leaders for abandoning Yahweh to join forces with an unreliable ally (Isa. 28–31).

In 701 B.C.E., the Assyrians retaliated: King **Sennacherib** swept down from the north, cut off communication with Egypt, and laid siege to Jerusalem as Isaiah had predicted (Isa. 29:1–4). In a celebrated inscription, Sennacherib describes sealing up Hezekiah in Jerusalem "like a bird in a cage" and extorting enormous sums of gold and silver, as well as skilled artisans and royal children, as payment for ending the siege. Although Hezekiah thus succeeded in buying off Sennacherib and Jerusalem escaped destruction, the surrounding countryside was devastated, and Judah, humbled and impoverished, was relegated to a political dependence from which it would only briefly revive.

Chapters 36 and 37, however, present a strikingly different account (repeated almost verbatim in 2 Kings 18:13–19:37, but with the conspicuous addition that Hezekiah stripped the Temple and royal palace of their treasures to buy off Sennacherib, a pragmatic factor on which Isaiah is entirely silent). In the Isaiah–Kings version, Hezekiah is pictured as showing absolute faith in Yahweh's power to rescue Judah from the pagan hordes, a confidence that is rewarded by a miracle—total Assyrian withdrawal.

Whether the Isaiah–Kings version represents a second Assyrian siege (later than that described in Sennacherib's inscription) or whether both the Assyrian and biblical accounts are exaggerated versions of the same event is not known. In any case, Jerusalem did not suffer the same destruction visited on other rebellious Palestinian states, and its unexpected escape contributed dramatically to the belief that David's holy city was specially protected by the hand of Israel's God (see Jer. 7 and 26).

Some of the material in Chapters 1–39 is thought to have been added later by Isaiah's disciples, who apparently formed a prophetic school that preserved, edited, and eventually compiled their master's words. The apocalyptic passages (Isa. 24–27), various references to Babylon's fall, and the prose appendix that closes this section of the book (Isa. 36–39) are probably the work of followers or lesser prophets writing under Isaiah's influence. (The parts of Isaiah [Chs. 40–66] that scholars attribute to postexilic prophets are discussed in the sections "Second Isaiah" and "Third Isaiah.")

RECOMMENDED READING

Childs, Brevard S. *Isaiah and the Assyrian Crisis.* Studies in Biblical Theology, no. 3. London: SCM Press, 1967.

Daves, Eryl W. *Prophecy and Ethics: Isaiah and the Ethical Tradition of Israel.* Sheffield, Eng.: JSOT Press, 1981.

Hayes, John H., and Irvine, Stuart A. *Isaiah the Eighth-Century Prophet.* Nashville, Tenn.: Abingdon Press, 1987.

Kaiser, Otto. *Isaiah 1–12.* Philadelphia: Westminster Press, 1972.

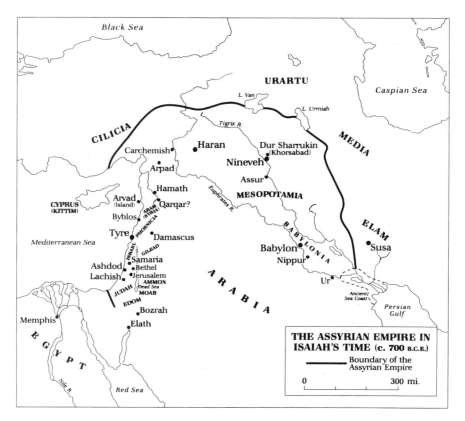

THE ASSYRIAN EMPIRE IN
ISAIAH'S TIME (c. 700 B.C.E.)

———— Boundary of the
Assyrian Empire

0   300 mi.

————. *Isaiah 13–39*. Philadelphia: Westminster Press, 1974.

Millar, William R. "Isaiah, Book of (Chaps. 24–27)." In D. N. Freedman, ed., *The Anchor Bible Dictionary*, Vol. 3, pp. 488–490. New York: Doubleday, 1992. Discusses the apocalyptic passages incorporated into the Isaiah collection.

Seitz, Christopher R. "Isaiah, Book of (First Isaiah)." In D. N. Freedman, ed., *The Anchor Bible Dictionary*, Vol. 3, pp. 472–488. New York: Doubleday, 1992.

Micah

KEY THEMES

Sharply critical of Jerusalem's ruling classes, including Davidic monarchs and priests, the rural prophet Micah prophesies doom upon Israel and Judah (Chs. 1–3). Expanded by later interpolations, Micah's oracles are edited to include predictions of Yahweh's future universal reign (Chs. 4 and 5), additional denunciations of social abuses, and hopes for restoration (Chs. 6 and 7).

> This is what Yahweh asks of you:
> only this, to act justly,
> to love tenderly,
> and to walk humbly with your God.
>
> Micah 6:8

Micah, fourth and last of the eighth-century B.C.E. prophets, was a younger contemporary of Isaiah of Jerusalem. Active between 740 and 700 B.C.E., he directed his earliest prophecies against Israel's idolatries, predicting the fall of the northern kingdom (Mic. 1:2–7). A native of Moresheth, a small town west of Jerusalem,

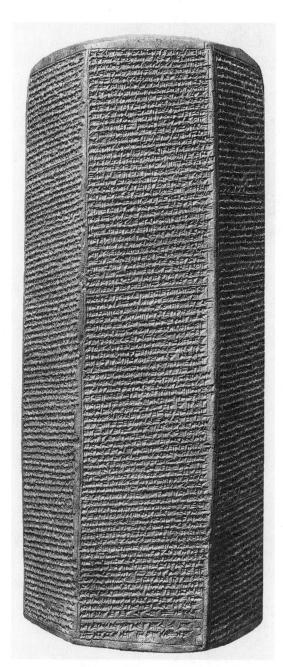

The cuneiform inscription on this hexagonal prism proclaims Sennacherib's military triumphs over Palestinian states and their Egyptian allies. Sennacherib, emperor of Assyria (704–681 B.C.E.), boasts that his armies overwhelmed Judah, his siege of Jerusalem trapping King Hezekiah (715–667 B.C.E.) "like a bird in a cage."

Micah took a country dweller's dim view of urban life and what he regarded as its inevitable corruption. He perceives the city as a source of sin that doomed both Samaria and Jerusalem (Mic. 1:5). He denounces the tyranny of dishonest merchants and greedy landowners (Mic. 2:1–5, 6–11; 3:1–4; 6:9–14), equating their guilt with that of Judah's corrupt princes, judges, priests, and false prophets (Mic. 3:9–12; 7:1–4).

Unlike Isaiah, Micah espouses the cause of the village peasant and is sharply critical of the Davidic dynasty and Temple cult. He scornfully denies that the sanctuary's presence in Jerusalem will protect the holy city from harm and predicts that both city and Temple will be reduced to rubble (Mic. 3:1–3, 9–12). Condemning the Jerusalem aristocracy and priesthood (Mic. 6:1–2, 9–16), he also rebukes hired seers who speak false comfort and fear to tell the people unwelcome truths (Mic. 3:5–8). Micah even rejects the belief that animal or any other sacrifice is required by Israel's Deity. In the book's most famous passage, he argues that Yahweh asks only for acts of justice and love and for humble communion with one's God (Mic. 6:6–8). Here the insight of the rural prophet wars with the prerogative of the city priest, for if Micah's words were to be taken literally, would Judah need either Levite or sanctuary?

Interpolations—Zion's Future Glory   Some scholars believe that Micah may have been one of Isaiah's disciples, which would account for a prediction of universal peace in almost exactly the same words as a passage in Isaiah (cf. Mic. 4:1–4 and Isa. 2:2–4). Other scholars suggest that the optimistic promises and visions of Judah's future glory (Mic. 4:1–5:15; 7:8–20) were

Accounts of Sennacherib's invasion and Jerusalem's deliverance appear in 2 Kings 18:13–19:37 and Isaiah 36:1–37:38. (Courtesy of the Oriental Institute Museum, University of Chicago)

The Cyrus Cylinder, describing Cyrus the Great's capture of Babylon (539 B.C.E.), illustrates the radically different ways in which non-Israelites and Bible writers interpreted the same historical events. Second Isaiah views Cyrus, liberator of Jewish captives, as Yahweh's national deliverer, his "messiah" (Isa. 45:1–3). Whereas the author of 2 Chronicles shows Cyrus attributing his victories to Yahweh (2 Chron. 36:23), the Cylinder presents Cyrus ascribing them to the chief Babylonian god Marduk, who inspires the Persian conqueror to restore the Near Eastern gods' neglected altars. The editors who arranged the Hebrew Bible's contents regarded Cyrus's actions as so important that they made his order to rebuild the Jerusalem Temple the climactic final act in the Bible canon, completing the creation sequence begun in Genesis 1:1. (Courtesy of the Trustees of the British Museum)

added by a later hand. According to the latter view, Micah originally condemned Judah for its violation of the Mosaic Covenant, and an editor subsequently inserted references to Yahweh's unconditional promise to preserve the Davidic kingdom. The references to a faithful remnant returning to Judah after exile, after which every citizen will sit under his or her vine and fig tree in peace and prosperity (Mic. 2:12; 4:4–8), may have been interpolated into the text after Micah's time. The famous prophecy that Bethlehem one day would become the birthplace of a ruler whose "origin goes back to the distant past, to the days of old" (Mic. 5:2) is viewed similarly as a later addition. Despite scholars' suspicion that Micah's original message underwent editorial modification, in its present form the book represents the typical prophetic paradox in which Yahweh is presented simultaneously as the stern judge and merciful savior of his people.

Although his words must have been unpopular with the authorities, Micah's oracles were preserved on a scroll housed in the Temple, an institution whose destruction he had foretold (Jer. 26:16–18).

RECOMMENDED READING

Hillers, Delbert R. *Micah.* Philadelphia: Fortress Press, 1984.

Laberge, Léo. "Micah." In R. E. Brown et al., eds., The New Jerome Bible Commentary, pp. 249–254. Englewood Cliffs, N.J.: Prentice-Hall, 1990.

Mays, James L. *Micah.* Philadelphia: Westminster Press, 1976.

Wolff, Hans W. *Micah the Prophet.* Translated by R. D. Gehrke. Philadelphia: Fortress Press, 1981.

Zephaniah

KEY THEMES

Expanding on Amos's theme, the fearful day of Yahweh's coming judgment, Zephaniah predicts universal catastrophe, cursing Gentiles as well as unfaithful Jerusalemites (Chs. 1–3). The assurances of forgiveness and restoration (3:11–20) probably belong to a later compiler.

> Seek Yahweh, all you, the humble of the
>   earth, . . .
> seek integrity, seek humility.
> Zephaniah 2:3

Day of Yahweh   With Zephaniah we return to the typical concerns of Israel's prophets: the condemnation of sin and declaration of Yahweh's impending wrath. Indeed, Zephaniah foresees a universal destruction in which all life forms—humans, beasts, birds, and fish—are to be exterminated (Zeph. 1:2–3). Yahweh will slaughter foreign kings, Judean royalty, greedy merchants, and skeptics alike who believe that "Yahweh has no power for good or for evil" (Zeph. 1:4–13). Like Amos, the prophet regards the Day of Yahweh as frighteningly near:

> A day of wrath, that day,
> a day of distress and agony,
> a day of ruin and devastation,
> a day of darkness and gloom,
> a day of clouds and blackness,
> a day of trumpet blast and battle cry. . . .
> I am going to bring such distress on men
> that they will grope like the blind . . .
> their blood will be scattered like dust,
> their corpses like dung.
> Zephaniah 1:15–17

On the day of Yahweh's "jealousy," the earth will be consumed, and all its inhabitants will be destroyed (Zeph. 1:18).

Although we do not know what specific conditions fostered the prophet's pessimism, he wrote during the reign of King Josiah (640–609 B.C.E.) but before the discovery of the Book of Deuteronomy (621 B.C.E.) had stimulated Josiah's sweeping religious reforms. The Jerusalem whose sins Zephaniah denounces was thus a prereform city that may have been contaminated by the pro-Assyrian idolatries of Manasseh's administration. It seems, then, that Zephaniah was the first prophet to speak out after the long silence that Manasseh and his immediate successor, Amon, had imposed on the Yahwist religion.

After categorically asserting that Yahweh will spare no living thing, Zephaniah concedes that a few humble people who keep the commandments "may perhaps find shelter" on the day of wrath (Zeph. 2:3). In fact, Chapter 2 implies the survival of a faithful remnant, for after Philistia, Moab, and Ammon have been destroyed, Jewish survivors will confiscate their land (Zeph. 2:6–7; 9–10).

Curses and Promises   Chapter 3 attacks the "rebellious," "defiled," and "tyrannical" leaders of Jerusalem who have failed to learn justice from the object lessons to be found in the destruction of other cities. As a result, Yahweh will gather the nations to pour out his fury on Judah (Zeph. 3:8). After painting a bleak future for humanity, however, Zephaniah concludes by offering some rays of hope. In a series of terse oracles, he asserts that the Gentile states will come to worship Yahweh (Zeph. 3:9–10), that a humble remnant of Israel will seek refuge in Yahweh (Zeph. 3:11–13), and that Jewish exiles will be delivered from their oppressors (Zeph. 3:19–20).

It is tempting to suppose that the following uncharacteristically joyous passage was Zephaniah's response to King Josiah's reform movement:

> Shout for joy, daughter of Zion. . . .
> Yahweh has repealed your sentence;
> he has driven your enemies away.
> Yahweh, the king of Israel, is in your midst;
> you have no more evil to fear.
> Zephaniah 3:14–15

If this surmise is true, perhaps Zephaniah believed that Josiah's cleansing of the Temple and his reinstituting the Passover and other Mosaic observances had restored Yahweh's presence to the Judean community. Josiah's military successes may also have indicated to the prophet that Yahweh had changed his mind about obliterating a nation stained with Manasseh's sins. In any case, the prophet's image of Yahweh dancing invisibly at Judah's festivals (Zeph. 3:18) represents a striking shift in his vision.

RECOMMENDED READING

Achtemeier, Elizabeth. "Zephaniah." In J. L. Mays, ed., *Harper's Bible Commentary*, pp. 742–744. San Francisco: Harper & Row, 1988.

Nahum

KEY THEME

The prophet rejoices over Nineveh's deserved fall.

> Yahweh is a jealous and vengeful God,
> Yahweh avenges, he is full of wrath.
> Nahum 1:2

Of Nahum's personal life or theological beliefs we know nothing except that his message was unlike that of any other known Hebrew prophet. He neither decried his people's sins nor prophesied their retribution; instead, his entire book is composed of three poems rejoicing over the ruin of Nineveh, capital of the Assyrian Empire. His gloating, unmitigated by compassion, contrasts markedly with the merciful attitude found in Jonah.

Fall of Nineveh   Nahum probably wrote about 612 B.C.E., either while the combined Medes and Babylonians were besieging Nineveh or shortly after the city's capture. In any case, the Medo-Babylonian coalition brought an end to Assyrian hegemony in the Near East, and the Jews were undoubtedly not alone in celebrating their enemy's downfall. A notoriously cruel taskmaster, Assyria had not only deported whole populations from their homelands but also had routinely performed atrocities that included physically mutilating and disfiguring captured persons, butchering women and children, and leading away chained prisoners with metal hooks in their jaws.

Nahum sees Nineveh's collapse as evidence of Yahweh's vengeance on Assyrian inhumanity (Nah. 1:2–3), for Yahweh is here perceived as the universal Sovereign. Although he had used Assyria as his "rod of correction" to punish Israel and Judah for their sins, Assyrian savagery had determined that it, too, must be humbled. Chapters 2 and 3 provide excellent examples of Hebrew poetry at its most vivid. Nahum's description of armed legions marching against Nineveh and plundering its treasures is harrowingly realistic (Nah. 2); his enumeration of Assyria's crimes is equally eloquent (Nah. 3).

Nahum interprets Nineveh's fate as part of Yahweh's long-range plan to improve the condition of his people. Released from Assyrian bondage, perhaps Israel but certainly Judah will enjoy a happy era of freedom (Nah. 1:15; 2:2), "for never again shall the wicked come against you" (Nah. 2:15; Revised Standard Version). This optimism is unjustified, however, for only three years later King Josiah is killed by Pharaoh Necho as Egyptian troops pass through the Plain of Megiddo on their way to support remnants of the Assyrian army (2 Kings 23:29–35). Egypt then controlled Judah's affairs until about 605 B.C.E., when the Babylonians defeated Egyptian forces at the Battle of Carchemish and assumed jurisdiction over Palestine, reducing Judah once again to a vassal state.

Dominating the ancient Near East for two and a half centuries, the Assyrians effectively discouraged revolt by a policy of terror. This Assyrian bas-relief depicts the torturing and flaying alive of captives—defeated soldiers and civilian prisoners alike. When Nineveh, Assyria's capital, was about to fall to a coalition of Medes and Babylonians in 612 B.C.E., the prophet Nahum saw the event as Yahweh's punishment of a bloodthirsty nation (Nah. 3). (Copyright British Museum)

RECOMMENDED READING

Christensen, Duane L. "Nahum." In J. L. Mays, ed., *Harper's Bible Commentary*, pp. 736–738. San Francisco: Harper & Row, 1988.

Leslie, E. A. "Book of Nahum." In G. A. Buttrick, ed., *The Interpreter's Dictionary of the Bible*, Vol. 3, pp. 498–499. New York and Nashville, Tenn.: Abingdon Press, 1962.

Habakkuk

KEY THEMES

Composed when Babylon was about to devastate Judah, Habakkuk contains a miniature theodicy, reflecting the prophet's effort to find a worthy purpose in Yahweh's permitting the destruction of his people by unbelieving foreigners.

> The upright man will live by his faithfulness.
> Habakkuk 2:4

The Babylonian Threat

Yahweh's Justice   Habakkuk is less a book of prophecy than a collection of philosophical meditations and a psalm describing Yahweh as a world conqueror. The first section (Hab. 1–2) is cast as a poetic dialog between Yahweh and Habakkuk, who bitterly complains of his God's inaction in world affairs. Apparently written between about 600 and 587 B.C.E., when the Babylonian (Chaldean) armies threatened Judah, the first chapter asks why Yahweh remains silent while this "fierce and fiery" nation plunders and murders innocent people, including people much better than they.

The answer is that such Gentile oppressors are Yahweh's "instruments of justice" (Hab. 1:12), chosen to carry out his will even though they do not recognize him as God. The implication is that Babylon's task is to punish Judah. Unlike Jeremiah or Ezekiel, however, Habakkuk does not argue that Judah's sins deserve so catastrophic a punishment. Indeed, he differs strikingly from the Deuteronomistic historians of the period in *not* asserting that the people's suffering is a result of their collective guilt.

In Chapter 2, Habakkuk declares that he will "stand on [his] watchtower" and await Yahweh's response, which is simply this: "The upright man will live by his faithfulness." That is, people must have faith that their God will eventually see justice done; this confidence in divine control of the outcome will sustain the righteous soul in its trials.

The balance of Habakkuk 2:5–20 is a veiled threat of vengeance on Babylon (or some other oppressor of the chosen people), whose punishment for abusing Yahweh's heritage is certain though it may not be swift. This section closes with a satire against idolatry, juxtaposed with the statement that "Yahweh is in his Holy Temple" and the nations should keep silent before him. Although this passage indicates that the Temple was still standing at the time of writing, it may come from a later hand than Habakkuk's and thus refer to the postexilic sanctuary.

Judge of the Earth   The third chapter pictures Yahweh as angrily striding from the east amid storm clouds and lightning—a mighty warrior flashing his arrows, hurling his spear, and riding in horse-drawn chariots. This manifestation of divine strength is probably a response by a later writer to Habakkuk's original skepticism that Yahweh would bring justice to world affairs. In Chapter 3, the Deity is clearly willing and able to execute immediate vengeance on Israel's oppressors. This vision decisively answers Habakkuk's plaintive cry about "how long" Yahweh will tolerate wrongdoing (Hab. 1:2). The militant psalm, which was probably sung in the sec-

ond Temple, concludes with a quiet affirmation of trust in the Deity.

RECOMMENDED READING

Sweeney, Marvin A. "Habakkuk." In J. L. Mays, ed., Harper's Bible Commentary, pp. 739–741. San Francisco: Harper & Row, 1988.

Jeremiah

KEY THEMES

Proclaiming a message of submission to the Babylonian Empire, which he viewed as Yahweh's punitive instrument against Judah for its covenant breaking, Jeremiah suffered rejection and condemnation as a traitor. The book containing his oracles of warning and doom, considerably revised and expanded by later disciples and postexilic editors, can be divided into four parts: (1) poetic oracles uttered during the reigns of Judah's last kings, particularly Jehoiakim and Zedekiah (Chs. 1–25); (2) biographical narratives interspersed with prophetic material, such as the promise of a "new covenant" (Chs. 26–45); (3) a collection of diatribes against pagan nations (Chs. 46–51); and (4) a brief historical appendix closely resembling 2 Kings 24–25 (Ch. 52).

> See the days are coming—it is Yahweh who speaks—
> when I will make a new covenant
> with the House of Israel (and the House of Judah).
>
> Jeremiah 31:31

In its present form, the Book of Jeremiah is a bewildering collection of poetic prophecies and prose narratives, intermixed with introspective monologs, lamentations, messianic oracles, declarations of imminent disaster, and intimations of future hope. According to the opening verses, Jeremiah began his career during the reign of Josiah (c. 626 B.C.E.), perhaps inspired by the king's sweeping reforms and his attempt to bring national policy in line with the deuteronomic concept of the Mosaic Covenant. With Josiah's death in 609 and the rapid growth of Neo-Babylonian power that threatened to crush the tiny state of Judah, Jeremiah apparently became increasingly disillusioned with the policies of Josiah's Davidic successors. Although some dispute the claim, many scholars argue that Jeremiah perceived the deuteronomist reforms as superficial, a zealous cultivation of ritual masking deep social ills, especially a lack of social justice and economic equity. While supporting the Temple cult, the ruling classes did little to improve social conditions. "Wicked men among my people," Yahweh announces, "spread their nets" to catch the poor and powerless:

> Like a cage full of birds
> so are their houses full of loot;
> they have grown rich and powerful because of it,
> fat and sleek. . . .
> [T]hey have no respect for rights,
> for orphans' rights, to support them;
> they do not uphold the cause of the poor.
> And must I not punish them for such things
> —it is Yahweh who speaks—
> or from such a nation exact my vengeance?
>
> Jeremiah 5:26–29

In Jeremiah's view, Judah's failure to enforce Mosaic principles that protected impoverished laborers and their families, coupled with the government's implied mandate for the rich to use any means, including fraud and violence, to increase their wealth compelled Yahweh to bring the entire system to an end. Rejecting a state that does not recognize the ethical implications of his worship, Yahweh feels no obligation to preserve a corrupt Davidic monarchy or Aaronic priesthood.

Chapter 36 gives a valuable insight into how at least part of the book took form. During the winter of 605–604 B.C.E., Jeremiah dictated to his secretary, **Baruch**, a scroll summarizing all the prophecies about Judah and Jerusalem that he had delivered during the previous twenty years. After Baruch read the scroll to an assembly in the Temple, word of it reached King **Jehoiakim**, who ordered it read in his presence.

As a royal scribe intoned excerpts from the scroll, Jehoiakim cut them from the manuscript, contemptuously burned them in an open brazier, and then ordered the arrest of Jeremiah and Baruch, who had already gone into hiding. Undeterred by the king's response, Jeremiah dictated a whole new scroll to Baruch, adding many similar prophecies. This second scroll may form the nucleus of our present Book of Jeremiah, for it probably contained large portions of Chapters 1–6 and 10–23, which are written mostly in the first person.

Jeremiah's Unpopular Message

Oracles Against Judah   Acting under the conviction that Yahweh intended to crush Judah for abandoning his covenant, Jeremiah viewed Babylon as the Deity's chosen means of implementing his decision. Convinced that Judah's moral failures necessitated its punishment, Jeremiah issued pronouncements brimming with negative judgments and images of loss and suffering. Although he agonized over Judah's fate, Jeremiah believed that the punishment was deserved, because king and people alike abused the poor and powerless. Literally as well as metaphorically, exploitative nobles "filled the streets of Jerusalem with innocent blood."

If the introductory chronology is correct, Jeremiah delivered his unpopular message of doom for approximately forty years, causing him to be hated, shunned, and persecuted. Many of his fellow Judeans regarded his call to surrender to Babylonian domination as a shameful betrayal of his country (Jer. 26:7–11; 32:1–5; 37:11–15; 38:14–28). Using the classic form of a covenant lawsuit—indictment and punishment—Jeremiah proclaimed Yahweh's verdict on the nation's collective guilt. In failing to up-

The splendor of Nebuchadnezzar's Neo-Babylonian Empire is reflected in this museum reconstruction of the ceremonial Gate of Ishtar, Babylonian goddess of love, fertility, and war. While upper-class Jews were held captive in Babylon (587–538 B.C.E.), they probably witnessed the annual New Year's festival in honor of Marduk, creator of heaven and earth, which featured an elaborate parade that passed through these portals. Note that the figures decorating the enameled brick include a serpent with legs (a dragon), reminiscent of the Genesis serpent. (Courtesy of Vorderasiatisches Museum, Berlin)

ize that the newly reborn Babylonian Empire was Yahweh's judgment on his people for their faithlessness, idolatry, and social injustice (Jer. 21; 22:1–9; 36; 37:16–21; 38:14–28). After Nebuchadnezzar had had thousands of Judah's religious and political leaders deported to Babylon in 598–597 B.C.E., Jeremiah wrote to the exiles telling them not to expect an early return but to build houses, plant gardens, and settle down as comfortably as possible for a long captivity (Jer. 29).

Jeremiah seems to have regretted the nature of his prophetic calling and to have suffered greatly at having to proclaim such a harsh view of Yahweh's intentions:

> Woe is me, my mother, for you have borne me to be
> a man of strife and of dissension for all the land.
> I neither lend nor borrow,
> yet all of them curse me.

* * *

> Yahweh, remember me, take care of me,
> and avenge me on my persecutors.
> Your anger is very slow; do not let me be snatched away.
> Realize that I suffer insult for your sake.
>
> Jeremiah 15:10, 15

Weary of rejection, he even tried to stop preaching to those who had no wish to hear it but found that the undelivered word burned "like a fire in [his] bones" and that he had to continue his work.

Biographical Narratives   We know Jeremiah's inner life, his love for his people, and his unhappiness at being ostracized from them not only from several "confessions" (Jer. 11:18–23; 12: 1–5; 15:10–11, 15–20; 17:14–18; 18:18–23; 20:7–11) but also from the memoirs of Baruch, which are contained in Chapters 26–45. From these biographical sections, we learn that the prophet was born of a priestly family of Anathoth, a village three to four miles north of Jerusalem, that he was called to prophesy while still

hold the Mosaic Covenant, Judah's ruling classes had committed a capital offense; unless they repented instantly, they would pay the penalty of death (Jer. 7–8; 11:21–22; 26–28).

The prophet urged Judah's kings, particularly Jehoiakim and Zedekiah, to see that Babylon's supremacy was not merely a political reality against which it would be disastrous to struggle. Burdened with a sense of the ruling class's guilt, Jeremiah struggled to make Judah's leaders real-

An artist's reconstruction of Babylon at the time of King Nebuchadnezzar (605–562 B.C.E.), founder of the Neo-Babylonian Empire and conqueror of Judah (587 B.C.E.), illustrates the city's massive fortifications. During their captivity in Babylon, Judah's former ruling classes re-edited and/or produced much of the literature that now forms the Hebrew Bible. The towering ziggurat at the left, an artificial mountain crowned with a chapel to the Babylonian gods, is characteristic of Mesopotamian religious architecture; its predecessors at Ur and elsewhere may have inspired the "Tower of Babel" legend (Gen. 11). (Courtesy of the Oriental Institute Museum, University of Chicago)

a boy, and that he witnessed rapid historical changes during his youth. Assyria's power was broken with Nineveh's fall in 612 B.C.E.; King Josiah's religious reforms and the accompanying territorial expansion were halted by the king's untimely death in 609 B.C.E. At the Battle of Carchemish in 605 B.C.E., the Babylonians, who there defeated Pharaoh Necho, became the dominant world power.

An "Unpatriotic" Prophet   Although at one time Jeremiah probably supported Josiah's reforms, he seems to have become disillusioned when the people observed the correct sacrificial forms prescribed by Deuteronomy but did not otherwise change their behavior (Jer. 3:6–10). Under King Jehoiakim, who tried to escape Babylon's control by allying Judah with Egypt, Jeremiah's bitter denunciation of such resistance as contrary to Yahweh's will was greeted with ridicule and charges of treason. After Nebuchadnezzar captured Jerusalem and deported many of its leading citizens, Jeremiah intensified his warnings. When the prophet Hananiah falsely promised deliverance from Babylon, Jeremiah contradicted him by going about Jerusalem wearing a wooden yoke, the symbol of coming slavery. When Hananiah angrily smashed the wooden yoke, Jeremiah returned wearing one of iron (Jer. 27–28).

During the Babylonians' final siege of Jerusalem, the prophet was accused of attempting desertion (Jer. 37) and was thrown into a muddy well to die (Jer. 38). This persecution was the Judean government's response to Jeremiah's "treason." The prophet advocated a radical—and "unpatriotic"—solution to the Babylonian threat: Jerusalem was to open its gates and surrender to the enemy. If the city capitulated, Jeremiah argued, it would not be burned, and its citizens would escape with their lives. In a secret interview with King **Zedekiah**, last of the Davidic monarchs, Jeremiah urged the king to act boldly, ignore his counselors' mistaken will to resist, and submit to Nebuchadnezzar, thereby sparing his people the horrors of slaughter and destruction when Jerusalem inevitably fell. The prophet's recommendations were not based on political expedience, a policy of survival at all costs. Instead, he offered Zedekiah and the nation a religious challenge—to place their *trust* entirely in Yahweh's power to save. But Zedekiah, who was as weak and vacillating as his father, Josiah, had been zealous and resolute, failed to accept Yahweh's offer of safety (Jer. 38: 14–28). As a result of the king's timid decision to heed his official advisers and not the prophet, Zedekiah saw his sons killed before his eyes and the holy city in flames. He was then blinded, chained, and led into captivity (Jer. 39:1–8).

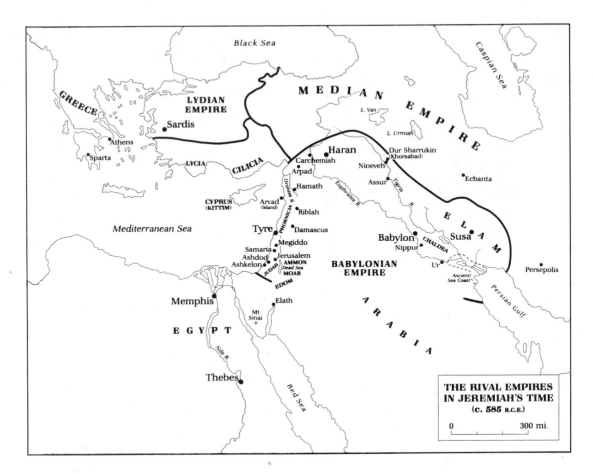

THE RIVAL EMPIRES
IN JEREMIAH'S TIME
(c. 585 B.C.E.)

0   300 mi.

To the Jerusalem leadership, Jeremiah's attitude toward Solomon's Temple was as offensive as his "defeatist" pacifism. Throughout the siege, he declared that those who believed that the sanctuary, center of sacrificial worship, could protect them were relying on an illusion (Jer. 7 and 26). Rather than depending on a mere building, which the corrupt had profaned, Judah must cleanse itself of crime and idolatry to regain Yahweh's favor and protection.

Shortly before Jerusalem fell, Jeremiah made a rare gesture of faith in the future. As his world was disintegrating around him, he bought a field in Anathoth to demonstrate his belief that land ownership in Judah would someday again be profitable (Jer. 32). In 587 B.C.E., however,

after a harrowing siege, Nebuchadnezzar took Jerusalem, demolishing its walls, palaces, and Temple.

Jeremiah in Egypt   Having learned of Jeremiah's policy of submission, the Babylonians offered to take him to Babylon along with other prominent Jews, but the prophet preferred to remain among the poor in the ruined city. After Gedaliah, Nebuchadnezzar's governor, was murdered, Jeremiah was forcibly carried into Egypt, where we last see him, aged but unmellowed, violently attacking the refugees in Egypt for worshiping the **Queen of Heaven** (perhaps envisioned as Yahweh's feminine consort) (Jer. 43–45). Though he was paid no more attention in exile than during his forty-year preaching in

Jerusalem, legend suggests that the prophet was silenced only by martyrdom.

Promised New Covenant   Perhaps Jeremiah's greatest contribution to the survival of the Jewish religion was his perception that Judah's faith did not depend on outward signs of Yahweh's presence or protection. David's throne, the holy city, Solomon's Temple, even the nation itself could vanish. When all the national religious symbols were destroyed, Yahweh would nonetheless maintain his relationship with those who believed in him. As the prophet's own communication with his God was not broken in the idolatrous land of Egypt, neither would the faithful in Babylon lose contact with Yahweh, who could be worshiped without a temple anywhere in the world.

Jeremiah's most famous prophecy foretold a time when the old covenant that Yahweh had made through Moses would be replaced by a new and better covenant.

> See, the days are coming—it is Yahweh who speaks—when I will make a new covenant with the House of Israel (and the House of Judah), but not a covenant like the one I made with their ancestors on the day I took them by the hand to bring them out of the land of Egypt. . . . No, this is the covenant I will make. . . . Deep within them I will plant my Law, writing it on their hearts. Then I will be their God and they shall be my people.
>
> Jeremiah 31:31–33

This new covenant inscribed on human hearts would not be a superficial or short-lived reform but an everlasting bond between Yahweh and his people because it would spring from the worshiper's deepest emotion, an inborn love for the covenant God.

RECOMMENDED READING

Blank, Sheldon H. *Jeremiah: Man and Prophet.* Cincinnati: Hebrew Union College Press, 1961.

Bright, John. *Jeremiah.* Anchor Bible, Vol. 21. Garden City, N.Y.: Doubleday, 1965. A fine commentary.

Carroll, Robert P. *Jeremiah.* Philadelphia: Westminster Press, 1986.

Ludrom, Jack R. "Jeremiah (Prophet)." In D. N. Freedman, ed., *The Anchor Bible Dictionary,* Vol. 3, pp. 684–698. New York: Doubleday, 1992. Discusses the life and times of the prophet.

———. "Jeremiah, Book of." In D. N. Freedman, ed., *The Anchor Bible Dictionary,* Vol. 3, pp. 706–721. New York: Doubleday, 1992. Discusses the content and composition of the biblical book.

McKane, William. *A Critical and Exegetical Commentary on Jeremiah.* Edinburgh: Clark, 1986.

Obadiah

KEY THEME

The prophet blasts Edom for benefiting from Judah's destruction.

> As you have done, so will it be done to you.
> Obadiah 15

Oracles Against Edom   Shortest of the Old Testament prophetic books, Obadiah is a single chapter of oracles against Israel's near neighbor **Edom**, probably delivered shortly after the Babylonians had destroyed Jerusalem in 587 B.C.E. Apparently, Edom had joined in the plundering of Judah, for which the writer bitterly condemns Edom and predicts its imminent desolation. The **Edomites'** gloating over fallen Judah is seen as particularly heinous because, according to ancient traditions, they were descended from Esau, Jacob's (Israel's) twin brother. (See Gen. 25:19–27:45; 36:1–19.) Their unbrotherly conduct will be repaid in kind (Obad. 15), but Judah's exiles will return to occupy Mount Zion (Obad. 19–21). Other Bible writers also cite Edom's ungenerous actions (Jer. 29:7–22; Ezek. 25:12–14; Ps. 137:7).

RECOMMENDED READING

Floyd, Michael H. "Obadiah." In J. L. Mays, ed., *Harper's Bible Commentary,* pp. 726–727. San Francisco: Harper & Row, 1988.

Ezekiel

KEY THEMES

A younger contemporary of Jeremiah, the priest-prophet Ezekiel was taken to Babylon during the first deportation of Judah's ruling classes in 597 B.C.E. Although tightly structured, with the oracles arranged in generally chronological order, Ezekiel's prophecies and mystical visions are filled with strange and grotesque images puzzling to modern readers. The first set of oracles (Chs. 1–24) describes the prophet's call (Chs. 1–3) and conveys messages of judgment and doom on Judah and the Jerusalem Temple, from which Ezekiel sees Yahweh's "glory" (*kavod*) depart, abandoning the holy city to Babylonian invaders (Chs. 8–11). Breaking with Mosaic principles that punished younger generations for their elders' misdeeds, Ezekiel emphasizes individual responsibility (Ch. 18). The second part records oracles of judgment against foreign nations such as Tyre (Ch. 28) and ends with news of Jerusalem's fall (Chs. 25–33), providing a transition to the third section, oracles and visions of Israel's rebirth (Chs. 34–39) and a future restoration of the Temple cult (Chs. 40–48).

> When I bring them [Israel] back from the countries of their enemies, when I reveal my holiness in them for many nations to see, they will know that I am Yahweh their God. . . . I shall never hide my face from them again.
>
> Ezekiel 39:27–29

The symbols that Ezekiel evokes to describe his visions are at once so bizarre and so compelling that in medieval times Jewish teachers commonly forbade anyone under thirty years of age to read the book. Whereas the prophet's strange images of Yahweh's celestial throne were once thought too likely to seduce young minds unready for venturing into serious mysticism, today they often inspire wild speculation among untrained readers. One popular author, for example, maintains that in his picture of Yahweh's blazing chariot (Ezek. 1:4–28; 11:22–23) the prophet is describing alien spaceships and visitors from outer space. Even without this peculiarly twentieth-century slant, however, readers are sure to find Ezekiel's metaphors bewildering. No other prophetic book in the Hebrew Bible, with the possible exception of Zechariah, features such hallucinatory material. Even Daniel's animal symbolism is less perplexing.

Ezekiel's Prophetic Warnings

Visions and Symbols   The narrative begins in 593 B.C.E., during the fifth year of deposed King Jehoiachin's exile, when Ezekiel is living in a Jewish community on the "River Chebar," a large irrigation canal near the Euphrates River in Babylonia. In a trance, Ezekiel sees four winged animals "of human form" that closely resemble the colossal stone cherubs that guarded the gates of many Mesopotamian cities and would have been familiar sights to the prophet and other exiles.

The accompanying image of wheels within wheels having eyes along their rims probably represents Ezekiel's attempt to picture Yahweh among his heavenly servants in other than strictly anthropomorphic terms. The prophet characteristically speaks of Yahweh's "glory" in the Jerusalem Temple rather than of the God himself. Certainly, images of fiery beings, a sapphire throne, and spiritual voices vividly express the awe and sense of mystery that Ezekiel feels during his communion with the divine (Ezek. 1–2).

After eating a scroll (representing Yahweh's message to Judah) that tastes like honey, Ezekiel is appointed watchman over the House of Israel, earning his own salvation by warning others

This stone cherub, over ten feet tall, once guarded the entrance to an Assyrian palace at Calah (Nimrud). A hybrid creature associated with Mesopotamian religion, the cherub (plural, cherubim) commonly has a human face (symbolizing intelligence), the body of a bull or lion (representing strength), and the wings of an eagle (indicating its supernatural swiftness as the gods' emissary). Yahweh's cherub guards the tree of life (Gen. 3:24), and a pair of cherubim extend their wings over the Ark of the Covenant, figuratively sheltering God's throne (Exod. 37:6–9; Ps. 99:1). In Ezekiel's vision, cherubim with four faces draw Yahweh's heavenly chariot (Ezek. 1; 10), grotesque beasts far removed from the chubby infants of popular tradition. (Courtesy of the Trustees of the British Museum)

of the impending judgment (Ezek. 2:8–3:21). Those who heed the warning will be spared the holocaust; those who ignore it will suffer destruction. Ezekiel here sounds the note of free

will and individual responsibility that recurs throughout the book.

In the first of many strange actions that Ezekiel performs to dramatize parts of his message, the prophet begins his ministry by being struck dumb and hence unable to communicate his warning (Ezek. 3:22–27). He cooks his food over human excrement to foreshadow how people trapped during Nebuchadnezzar's siege will be forced to eat "unclean food." When his wife dies, he neither weeps nor mourns; his actions are intended to illustrate that Yahweh will not mourn the loss of his polluted Temple (Ezek. 4:9–17; 24:15–27).

Ezekiel's public displays sometimes border on the abnormal. Tightly bound in ropes, he lies down on one side for 190 days to symbolize the duration—each day for a year—of the northern kingdom's exile, then lies on his other side for another 40 days to designate the length of Judah's captivity (Ezek. 4:1–8). Finally, he shaves off his beard and the hair on his head, burning a third of the hair, striking another third with a sword, and scattering the last third to the winds, retaining only a few stray hairs that he binds up in his robe. This demonstration is to inform the people that a third of them will die of pestilence and famine, a third by violence, and the remaining third will become captives in Babylon. The few hairs that he keeps represent those whom God will allow to escape (Ezek. 5).

Yahweh's Abandonment of Jerusalem

Departure of Yahweh's Glory   Chapters 8–11 form a unit concerning the profanation of the Temple and the departure of Yahweh's "glory" from Jerusalem. Stationed in Babylon, Ezekiel feels himself lifted by the hair and carried to Jerusalem where he envisions the idolatry that pollutes the sanctuary. Women there weep for **Tammuz**, a young fertility deity similar to the Greek Adonis, while Judah's corrupt elders secretly burn incense to hideous reptilian deities. Yahweh sends an angelic scribe who strides through the city marking the foreheads of those who deplore the religious abominations committed in the Temple. Those unmarked, who have compromised their Yahwist faith with pagan rites, are to be slain by six divine executioners.

Ezekiel then sees the "glory of Yahweh" rise from its traditional seat between the gold cherubim in the temple's innermost sanctuary and pass through the city gates to the east. This strange event is probably meant to show that Yahweh's *kavod* (a Hebrew term that can be translated as "glory" or "influence") has permanently abandoned the Temple and now roams the world, operating in new and unpredictable ways. Like Jeremiah, Ezekiel realized that Yahweh did not need a material shrine in which to house his presence, nor would he protect a sanctuary that had been contaminated. With Yahweh's departure from the Temple, he could be with his people anywhere, including idolatrous Babylon.

Revision of a Torah Principle

Individual Responsibility   Chapters 12–17 deal with a variety of themes, most of which depict the sins that have alienated God from Judah. Chapter 18, however, minutely examines the moral consequences of the national disaster for the individual Jews who have survived it. Here Ezekiel declares that God will no longer judge and punish the people collectively; now that the nation is gone, each individual has responsibility for his or her own fate. The sinner will still be punished but not for the wrongdoing of others.

Ezekiel thus assumes the authority of a lawgiver, a latter-day Moses who corrects the old misconception of the second commandment in which Yahweh is represented as vowing to punish the father's sins in the sons even to the fourth generation (Exod. 20:5). Why, Ezekiel asks, cling mindlessly to the inherent injustice of the old system or persist in repeating the old proverb that when fathers eat sour grapes the sons' teeth are set on edge? "As I live—this is the Lord Yahweh who speaks—there will no longer be

any reason to repeat this proverb in Israel. See now: all life belongs to me; the father's life and the son's life, both alike belong to me. The man who has sinned, he is the one who shall die" (Ezek. 18:3–4).

Like Joshua, Ezekiel emphasizes the individual's freedom of choice—Yahweh and life or disobedience and death: "House of Israel, in future I mean to judge each of you by what he does—it is the Lord Yahweh who speaks. Repent, renounce all your sins . . . and make yourselves a new heart and a new spirit! Why are you so anxious to die, House of Israel? I take no pleasure in the death of any one. . . . Repent and live!" (Ezek. 18:31–32).

Oracle Against the King of Tyre   Chapters 25–32 are devoted to denunciations and judgments against various foreign nations. Of particular interest is the oracle attacking the king of Tyre, a powerful Phoenician port city (Ezek. 28). This passage, like Isaiah 14, uses brilliant imagery to describe the downfall of a pagan king who opposes Yahweh's rule:

> You were once an exemplar of perfection,
> full of wisdom,
> perfect in beauty;
> you were in Eden, in the garden of God.
>
> * * *
>
> Your heart has grown swollen with pride
> on account of your beauty.
> You have corrupted your wisdom
> owing to your splendor.
> I have thrown you to the ground.
>   Ezekiel 28:13, 17

It is possible that the prophet, a political prisoner who knew the value of symbolism, discreetly aimed his barbs at the Tyrian monarch rather than at Nebuchadnezzar, the real object of his attack.

Ezekiel's Visions of the Future

Promises of Restoration and Defense   Chapter 33, which is pivotal, briefly describes Jerusalem's fall and the miserable fate of those remaining amid the ruins. After this event, the prophet abandons his visions of judgment and concentrates on Israel's future restoration (Ezek. 33–39), foreseeing that Yahweh will send a shepherd, a descendant of David, to guide Israel, with whom God will conclude a covenant of peace so that they will live in perfect security (Ezek. 34). The prophet, however, does not foresee a restoration of the Davidic monarchy. Yahweh declares that he will take vengeance on the nations who desolated Israel and Judah, not because he pities his people but to vindicate his name, to convince them that he is supreme among gods. The phrase "then they will know that I am Yahweh" resounds throughout this section (Ezek. 36).

Perhaps the most influential of Ezekiel's visions occurs in Chapter 37. Beholding a long valley littered with human bones, he hears a voice ask, "Son of man, can those bones live?" Miraculously, the fragmented skeletons reassemble themselves and are again clothed in flesh. Yahweh directs the winds to breathe life into them, and their **resurrection** is complete. Here Ezekiel predicts the rebirth of Israel, which was symbolically dead; this image of rebirth was eventually to become part of Israel's religious hope. It is not until the Book of Daniel was written four centuries later that a belief in the individual's resurrection is explicitly promulgated (Dan. 12:1–3).

Once the nation was restored to its homeland, however, what was to prevent its being devastated again by Gentile armies? To assure the people that Yahweh would protect Israel's future security, the prophet introduces the strange allegory of **Gog** and **Magog** (Ezek. 38–39). In an eschatological vision, Ezekiel sees Jerusalem's would-be attackers destroyed by Yahweh's direct intervention, and Israel's slain enemies are so numerous that it takes seven months to bury their corpses.

This spectacular rescue is performed not only for the nation's sake but also for the additional vindication of Yahweh, whose stature in the eyes of other nations had been seriously reduced by the humiliating defeat of his people and destruction of his Temple. To restore his international prestige and reputation, Yahweh resolves to act resolutely in the future. Chapter 39 closes with his reaffirmation to return to Jerusalem all who are currently scattered among foreign countries so that the heathen will be forced to "know that I am Yahweh their God."

Future Israel   The final section (Ezek. 40–48), a kind of blueprint for the future Israelite theocracy, offers a concrete hope to the Jewish exiles in Babylon. Room-by-room and court-by-court, giving exact measurements and dimensions, Ezekiel describes the rebuilt Temple, then envisions Yahweh's return to his restored sanctuary:

> I saw the glory of the God of Israel approaching from the east. A sound came with it, like the sound of the ocean, and the earth shone with his glory. . . . The glory of Yahweh arrived at the Temple by the east gate. . . . I saw the glory of Yahweh fill the Temple.
>
> Ezekiel 43:1–6

The prophet's visions have thus come full cycle, from beholding Yahweh deserting the doomed sanctuary to beholding Yahweh's "glory" returning to a greater Temple.

The idealized new Temple was to be administered not by the Levites but by descendants of the priest **Zadok**, whose name means "righteous." Levites may serve as attendants, but only Zadokites are to enjoy full priestly authority. After listing regulations and liturgical details of Temple worship, Ezekiel (or the disciples who compiled and edited his work) paints a final vision of a life-giving stream of water issuing from beneath the sanctuary, a fitting symbol of the spiritual cleansing that Yahweh will provide at his restored shrine.

In several ways, Ezekiel's message resembles that of Jeremiah. Both attribute the nation's political troubles to its many sins, especially social injustice and idolatry. Both predict that Yahweh will assuage his anger with a national catastrophe culminating in the destruction of Jerusalem and exile in Babylon. Both emphasize individual responsibility for one's life and foretell a return from the Babylonian captivity. A priest as well as a prophet, however, Ezekiel emphasizes the necessity of practicing Jewish rites, customs, holidays, dietary observances, and communal worship even in exile, realizing that the exiles' moral behavior *and* strict adherence to ceremonial requirements would ensure their national and religious survival. With this emphasis, Ezekiel became the spiritual progenitor of later **Judaism**.

RECOMMENDED READING

Ackroyd, Peter R. *Exile and Restoration: A Study of Hebrew Thought in the Sixth Century B.C.E.* Philadelphia: Westminster Press, 1968.

Boadt, Lawrence. "Ezekiel, Book of." In D. N. Freedman, ed., *The Anchor Bible Dictionary*, Vol. 2, pp. 711–722. New York: Doubleday, 1992.

Eichrodt, Walther. *Ezekiel*. Philadelphia: Westminster Press, 1970.

Greenberg, Moshe. *Ezekiel, 1–20*. Garden City, N.Y.: Doubleday, 1983.

Klein, Ralph W. *Ezekiel: The Prophet and His Message*. Columbia: University of South Carolina Press, 1988.

Raitt, Thomas M. *A Theology of Exile*. Philadelphia: Fortress Press, 1977.

Zimmerli, Walther. *Ezekiel 1–2*. Hermenica. Philadelphia: Fortress Press, 1983.

"Second Isaiah"

KEY THEMES

In Isaiah 40–55, an anonymous prophet comforts Judean exiles in Babylon, declaring that Yahweh has forgiven Judah's collective sins. The prophet hails Cyrus of Persia as Yahweh's agent of liberation from the Babylonian captivity.

New Exodus   In perusing the Book of Isaiah, even the casual reader is likely to notice the sudden shift in tone, style, and theological viewpoint between Chapters 39 and 40. Whereas Isaiah of Jerusalem had proclaimed that Assyria was God's instrument of future punishment, the author of Chapters 40–55 declares that the time of punishment is past. The social and geographical background is no longer Jerusalem under the Assyrian threat of the eighth century B.C.E. but a group of exiles in Babylon almost two centuries later. An anonymous poet, known as **Deutero-Isaiah** (Second Isaiah), addresses a Judean audience already chastened for its sins and about to be redeemed from imprisonment and despair.

Active in the 540s B.C.E., Second Isaiah sees world events as about to culminate in the salvation of a faithful remnant of Judean exiles, who will participate in a "new exodus" to the Promised Land. The prophet regards **Cyrus**, the Persian commander who was then conquering country after country in the Near East, as Yahweh's "Messiah" (Isa. 45:1), a Gentile anointed for the task of liberating Jewish captives and restoring them to their homeland (Isa. 44:28–45; 45:1–6; 48:12–16, 20–22). Second Isaiah confidently predicts Cyrus's conquest of Babylon, which takes place in 539 B.C.E., as evidence of Yahweh's absolute control of history (Isa. 47; 48:12–15). Consoling and encouraging those who may have doubted Yahweh's concern or ability to re-create his people, he reminds the covenant community that Yahweh is both all-powerful and all-loving, celebrating his God in joyous poetry unsurpassed in world literature.

As a theologian, Second Isaiah is an uncompromising monotheist who makes explicit what had been only implied by Israel's earlier prophets. Yahweh alone exists, creates life, and directs human events, shepherding foreign nations as well as Israel. His God declares,

> I am the first and the last;
> there is no God besides me.
> Isaiah 44:6

Isaiah 40:12–31 contains monotheism's greatest hymn—a sweeping denial that other gods have any reality and an incomparable description of Yahweh's magnificence.

To the poet, Yahweh is both *transcendant*—above and beyond the world he creates—and *immanent*—personally involved in human affairs, for he not only manipulates history for his purpose but announces through the prophets what he intends to occur:

> Who from the very beginning foretold the
> future?
> Let them tell us what is yet to come.
> Have no fear, do not be afraid;
> have I not told you and revealed it long ago?
> Isaiah 44:7–8

In Second Isaiah's emphasis on Yahweh's wisdom, foreknowledge, and redeeming love, we reach the high point of Old Testament prophecy.

The Servant Songs   One of the most intriguing components of Second Isaiah's message is the series of poems, which scholars call the Servant Songs (Isa. 42:1–4; 49:1–6; 50:4–9; 52: 13–53:12). These beautiful passages describe the ministry of a righteous servant of Yahweh who even before birth realizes that he is chosen to receive God's spirit and bring justice to the world. Despite his noble work, however, he is misunderstood, classified with sinners, and condemned to an agonizing, humiliating defeat.

The most celebrated of these poems, the Suffering Servant, paints him as "despised and rejected of men: a man of sorrows, and acquainted with grief" (Isa. 53:3; King James Version); yet, the servant transforms Israel's awareness of what suffering means. Traditionally, as in the Deuteronomistic Histories of Joshua through Kings, misery was regarded as God's punishment for sin. In Second Isaiah, however, the afflicted person is guiltless and willingly takes the punishment for others' wrongdoing, suffering on their behalf:

> Surely he hath borne our griefs,
> and carried our sorrows: . . .
> But he was wounded for our transgressions,

> he was bruised for our iniquities:
> the chastisement of our peace was upon him;
> and with his stripes we are healed.
> Isaiah 53:4–5; King James Version

The identity of the servant has provoked considerable scholarly debate. In some passages, Second Isaiah clearly equates this unnamed agent with Israel as a whole (Isa. 43:10); in others, he seems to be an individual (Isa. 52:13–53:12). Some commentators suggest that the prophet regards him as both a person and a people, an individual who represents the community of Israel and God's chosen group as a collective entity, suffering by and for its persecutors. In the New Testament, the suffering servant is occasionally interpreted as prophetic of Jesus' crucifixion, a voluntary act by which the Messiah (Christ) vicariously takes upon himself the punishment that justly belongs to all humanity. (See Acts 8:29–35.)

Respecting the integrity of the Hebrew Bible, some scholars have recently pointed out that the rejected servant is probably Second Isaiah himself, a prophet whose bold declaration that Cyrus would soon crush Babylon would certainly arouse the ire of Babylonian authorities. Jeremiah had urged submission to Babylon, a policy many Jewish exiles undoubtedly followed. According to traditions preserved in the Book of Daniel, some Jewish leaders served honorably in the Babylonian government (Dan. 1–5) and may have regarded Second Isaiah's frankly political oracles as a dangerous threat to the security of the Jewish community. The persecution, imprisonment, and possible death of the anonymous sufferer—followed by public vindication—described in Isaiah 52: 13–53:12 may reflect the prophet's checkered career as understood by the disciples who collected, edited, and poetically interpreted his prophecies.

RECOMMENDED READING

Clifford, Richard J. "Isaiah, Book of (Second Isaiah)." In D. N. Freedman, ed., *The Anchor Bible*

Dictionary, Vol. 3, pp. 490–501. New York: Doubleday, 1992.

Gottwald, Norman K. *The Hebrew Bible: A Socio-Literary Introduction.* Philadelphia: Fortress Press, 1985. Includes an insightful analysis of Second Isaiah.

McKenzie, John L. *Second Isaiah.* Garden City, N.Y.: Doubleday, 1968.

Muilenburg, James. "Introduction and Exegesis to Isaiah 40–66." In G. A. Buttrick, ed., *The Interpreter's Bible,* Vol. 5, pp. 151–773. New York and Nashville, Tenn.: Abingdon Press, 1956. An excellent commentary.

North, Christopher R. *Isaiah 40–55.* New York: Macmillan, 1964.

———. *The Suffering Servant in Deutero-Isaiah,* 2nd ed. New York: Oxford University Press, 1956. A helpful review of different interpretations of the "servant" passages.

Smart, James D. *History and Theology in Second Isaiah: A Commentary on Isaiah 35, 40–66.* Philadelphia: Westminster Press, 1965.

Westermann, Claus. *Isaiah 40–66.* Philadelphia: Westminster Press, 1969.

Haggai

KEY THEME

Anticipating renewed prosperity and a restoration of the Davidic kings, Haggai urges the apathetic community of returned exiles to rebuild Jerusalem's Temple.

> I will shake all the nations and the treasures of
> all the nations shall flow in,
> and I will fill this Temple with glory. . . .
> Haggai 2:7–8

Yahweh's Temple   Although a remnant of devout Jews had returned from Babylon around 538 B.C.E. and laid the foundations of a new sanctuary on the site of Solomon's Temple, they had since become discouraged and allowed the work to lapse. Economic conditions were bad, and the tiny postexilic community struggled merely to survive. Interpreting the repeated crop failures and subsequent famine as signs that Yahweh is angry because his shrine has not been completed (Hag. 1:4–11), Haggai, who prophesied in the year 520 B.C.E., urges the governor and the high priest to persuade the people to return to the project, which they do enthusiastically. Older Jews who remember the glories of Solomon's Temple are disappointed in the modest dimensions of the new sanctuary, but Haggai promises that it will soon be filled with treasures flowing into Jerusalem from all nations (Hag. 2:7).

Zerubbabel   The prophet also conveys Yahweh's plan to "shake the heavens and the earth," to "overturn the thrones of kingdoms" (Hag. 2:22), and to establish **Zerubbabel**, Jerusalem's governor and a descendant of one of the last Davidic kings, as "a signet ring." The implication seems to be that the Persian Empire, of which Judah was then a small part, would be overthrown and Judah's independence restored with Zerubbabel as its reigning monarch. Haggai thus seems to regard the governor as a political "messiah" or anointed king (Hag. 2:23). Zechariah, an exact contemporary of Haggai, apparently had the same hope (Zech. 4:6–10); but Zerubbabel soon afterward disappears from history, and we hear no more of him.

RECOMMENDED READING

Ackroyd, Peter R. *Exile and Restoration: A Study of Hebrew Thought in the Sixth Century B.C.E.* Philadelphia: Westminster Press, 1968.

Meyers, Carol L., and Meyers, Eric M. *Haggai, Zechariah 1–8.* Garden City, N.Y.: Doubleday, 1987.

Peterson, David L. *Haggai and Zechariah 1–8.* Philadelphia: Westminster Press, 1984.

Wolff, Hans W. *Haggai.* Minneapolis: Augsburg, 1988.

Zechariah

KEY THEMES

A contemporary of Haggai, Zechariah employs a series of eight visions to encourage his fellow returned exiles to rely on Yahweh, restore Jerusalem and the Temple, and expect the reestablishment of the Davidic line (Chs. 1–8). The second half of the book contains increasingly obscure oracles from a later prophet, known as Second Zechariah (Chs. 9–14).

> Many peoples and great nations will come
> to seek Yahweh . . . in Jerusalem
> and to entreat the favor of Yahweh.
> Zechariah 8:22

Whereas Haggai's message was direct and straightforward, that of Zechariah, his fellow prophet of the postexilic period, is often ambiguous and obscure. The Book of Zechariah makes clear that Yahweh wishes to have the Temple rebuilt and that Zerubbabel is a likely candidate to restore Judah's political fortunes, but beyond that all certainty vanishes. Scholars divide the book into two parts. The first eight chapters are mostly by the "Historical Zechariah," who began prophesying in 520 B.C.E. Chapters 9–14, called the "Second Zechariah," seem to have been written by other seers, perhaps a Zecharian school of prophets, at various later dates.

Historical Zechariah   Zechariah, who appears to have come from a priestly family, lived in a restored community in which want and insecurity had taken the place of the glorious future predicted by Second Isaiah. Although Zechariah stressed the necessity of rebuilding the Temple to attain Yahweh's favor and material blessings, he also addressed himself to the community's underlying disillusionment in eight visions (Zech. 1–6), which, interpreted by an angelic figure, are generally aimed at calming the people's apprehensions about what Yahweh intends to do with them. Hopes that Zerubba-

bel would mount the throne of David are dashed when Darius, emperor of Persia, quells an incipient revolt and consolidates his power. After Zerubbabel disappears from history, Zechariah concentrates on the prospects of Joshua, the high priest, to whom he refers as the "branch" or shoot from David's stock (Zech. 3: 8–10).

Particularly interesting is Zechariah's vision in Chapter 3 of Joshua standing before Yahweh's celestial throne. When Satan (the Adversary) appears to accuse the high priest (who represents the Judean remnant), Yahweh's angel removes Joshua's dirty garments—symbolic of the community's sins—and reclothes him in splendid robes. This change of attire shows that Yahweh has forgiven his people's sins and that the period of national mourning is over; if the community henceforth keeps Yahweh's commandments, it will prosper. Zechariah's mystical experience thus provides hope that Yahweh is at last acting to improve the condition of his restored nation.

A Restoration of Davidic Kings?

Similarly, the vision in 6:9–15 emphasizes Joshua's messianic role as "the branch," the person destined to rebuild the sanctuary, wear the royal insignia, and "sit on his throne as ruler" (Zech. 6:13). Because this passage also refers to cooperation between a restored king and priest, scholars have suggested that the prophecy originally applied to the Davidic Zerubbabel who, with Joshua, was joint leader of the community. After Zerubbabel's aspirations came to nothing, however, scribes substituted Joshua's name for that of the former governor. Although plans for a renewed Davidic monarchy had become both futile and dangerous, it was still possible to envisage the high priest as Yahweh's anointed and spiritual leader of the Jewish state.

Chapters 7 and 8, respectively, survey the moral meaning of Israel's rise and fall as a nation and promise the people ultimate redemption through a Messiah who will create a new dispensation in which the whole earth will become a paradise. This section concludes with the prediction that not only will powerful nations come to Jerusalem to worship Yahweh but also that ten foreigners will cling to a single Jew, begging him to teach them Yahweh's law. With its emphasis on Zion (or Jerusalem) as the religious center of the universe, this section echoes ideas first expressed in Isaiah 2, 9, and 11.

"Second Zechariah"

The second half of Zechariah contains diverse oracles, some from as late as the Greek period in the fourth century B.C.E. These strange visions and predictions appear to be the work of several apocalyptic writers whose intended meanings are now nearly impossible to grasp, although the section (which resembles the apocalyptic passages in Isaiah 24–27) was a favorite with early Christians, who found numerous messianic references in it.

Messianic Visions   Zechariah 9:9 declares that Jerusalem's king will come to the city "humble and riding on a donkey, on a colt, the foal of a donkey." The author of Matthew's Gospel, perhaps misunderstanding the poet's use of parallelism here, depicts Jesus as riding on two different animals at once (Matt. 21:1–7). Zechariah also mentions "thirty shekels of silver" (Zech. 11:13–14), the sum for which Judas betrays his Master. A particularly obscure oracle pictures Jerusalem as mourning "one whom they have pierced" (Zech. 12:10), in a passage where Yahweh also promises to make "the House of David like God" leading victorious armies. Equally cryptic is the allusion to striking a shepherd and scattering his sheep (Zech. 13:7), which follows an apparent declaration that the gift of prophecy has been removed from Israel (Zech. 13:2–6).

Chapter 14 is a full-fledged eschatological vision describing the end of history. In a climactic battle, Yahweh will gather all nations to Jerusalem. The enemy will plunder the city and slaughter nearly all its inhabitants; but at the last desperate moment, Yahweh will intervene, striding from the Mount of Olives—which will be sundered by titanic earthquakes—to fight for Israel.

After annihilating his enemies, Yahweh will transform the earth and its climate. Cold and frost will cease, streams will issue from Jerusalem, mountains will disappear, and all Palestine will become a plain (a highly desirable change for farmers and shepherds). Meanwhile, non-Jewish nations will suffer a plague that rots their eyes in the sockets and causes them to attack one another irrationally. The nations that survive this catastrophe will henceforth make pilgrimages to Jerusalem, then elevated above all other cities, to worship at Yahweh's Temple, and Yahweh "will be king of the whole world."

RECOMMENDED READING

Ackroyd, Peter R. *Exile and Restoration: A Study of Hebrew Thought in the Sixth Century B.C.E.* Philadelphia: Westminster Press, 1968.

Petersen, David L. "Zechariah." In J. L. Mays, ed., *Harper's Bible Commentary,* pp. 747–752. San Francisco: Harper & Row, 1988.

"Third Isaiah"

KEY THEMES

Isaiah 56–66 preserves a miscellaneous assemblage of prophetic oracles drawn from the entire era of Israelite prophecy. An anonymous prophet ("Third Isaiah") directs his message to an impoverished colony of exiles resettled in Judah, now under Persian rule.

Disappointments in the Restored Community Parts of the third section of the Book of Isaiah appear to depict conditions in postexilic Judah when the returned exiles confronted an unsatisfying reality of poverty and political helplessness that was painfully different from the brilliant prospects that Second Isaiah had envisioned. At this juncture, a new member of the prophetic school descended from Isaiah of Jerusalem—known for want of a better title as "Third Isaiah"—added new messages to the prophetic collection, denouncing the restored community's lapses into idolatry, social injustice, religious apathy, and failure to keep the Sabbath properly.

The opening and closing parts of this section (Isa. 56:1–8; 66:18–23) reveal a new dimension to Yahweh's worshiping community—the inclusion of foreigners who the prophet declares are to be integrated completely into Judah's religious life. These Gentile converts may have included the Jews' fellow victims of Babylonian oppression, as well as other former citizens of Mesopotamia.

Third Isaiah also injects an apocalyptic element, looking beyond the bleak present to "new heavens and a new earth" in which Judah's sins are forgotten and the land becomes an earthly paradise, enjoying peace, plenty, and longevity for all (Isa. 65:17–25). This promise of a renewed creation, repeated in Isaiah 66: 22–23 to include "all mankind," would become an important eschatological hope of early Christianity (2 Pet. 3:13; Rev. 21:1). The penultimate chapter of the last book of the Christian Bible describes the still-future fulfillment of Third Isaiah's vision (Rev. 21:1–4).

RECOMMENDED READING

Blank, Sheldon H. *Prophetic Faith in Isaiah.* New York: Harper & Row, 1958.

Stuhlmueller, Carroll. "Deutero-Isaiah and Trito-Isaiah." In R. E. Brown et al., eds., *The New Jerome Biblical Commentary,* pp. 329–348. Englewood Cliffs, N.J.: Prentice-Hall, 1990. Discusses the work of Second and Third Isaiah in the prophets' historical context.

Joel

KEY THEMES

After comparing a plague of locusts then devastating Judah (Ch. 1) to Yahweh's imminent day of wrath, Joel predicts an outpouring of the divine spirit on all humanity and proclaims judgment on foreign nations (Ch. 4).

> I will pour out my spirit on all [humanity].
> Your sons and daughters shall prophesy.
> your old men shall dream dreams,
> and your young men see visions.
>
> Joel 2:28

The Book of Joel presents some of the most striking imagery found in the Old Testament. Although it gives no conclusive evidence of the time it was written, the conditions it describes—locust invasions, drought, and crop failure—suggest that the prophet was active during the fifth century B.C.E., a period of severe economic hardship for the restored community of Judah.

Plague of Locusts   The book consists of two parts. The first (Joel 1:1–2:27) vividly relates the devastation wrought by a plague of locusts, which Joel, following the prophetic-deuteronomic tradition, interprets as a sign that Yahweh is angry with his people. He urges the Judeans to repent (Joel 2:12–17), promising that Yahweh will then graciously end the plague (Joel 2:18–27). Chapter 2 either describes an invading army or likens the locusts to a foreign invasion. Which of the two is meant is unknown, but the crisis inspires Joel to declare that the Day of Yahweh, a gloomy time of judgment that Amos had previously announced (Amos 5: 18–20), is at hand.

Day of Yahweh   The second part of Joel (Joel 2:28–3:21) presents some difficulties because the manuscript text appears to have many passages out of order. For this reason, some modern editors, such as those of the Jerusalem Bible, have reconstructed the sequence of several verses to make better sense of Joel's message. The main theme, however, is clear enough: The locust or military invasion heralds Yahweh's imminent visitation of both Judah and the nations, an event of cosmic terror: "The sun will be turned to darkness, and the moon to blood, before the great and terrible day of the Lord comes" (Joel 2:31; Revised Standard Version).

Although the Day of Yahweh will involve "portents in the heavens and on earth, blood and fire and columns of smoke" (Joel 2:30), it will also provide an opportunity to obtain individual salvation, for at that time "all who call on the name of Yahweh will be saved" (Joel 2: 32). After repentance, Joel foresees the dawn of a new age. Not only will the land recover from its present desolation and prosper, but Yahweh will pour out his spirit upon all humanity so that dreams, visions, and prophecies will reopen channels of communication between the Deity and his creation (Joel 2:28–29).

Glorious Future   In his climactic vision of the "End Time," Joel predicts that godless nations will be summoned to the Valley of Decision (Joel 3:14), where the ultimate war between Good and Evil (called Armageddon in Rev. 16: 12–16) will take place. In a reversal of Isaiah's prophecy (Isa. 2:4), Joel sardonically urges the pagan warriors to

> Hammer your plowshares into swords,
> your sickles into spears.
>
> Joel 4:10

After the Gentile hosts suffer final defeat, Yahweh will send his people unprecedented blessings:

> When that day comes,
> the mountains will run with new wine,

and the hills flow with milk,
and all the river beds of Judah run with water.

Joel 3:18

Joel specifically promises that Yahweh will never again make Judah a public shame, as he had done when it was conquered by Babylon (Joel 2:20), and foresees that Yahweh will always protect his holy city:

> But Judah will be inhabited for ever,
> Jerusalem from age to age . . .
> and Yahweh will make his home in Zion.
>
> Joel 3:19–21

Joel contains in miniature the pattern for Judgment Day and the New Age on which later Bible writers elaborated in such books as Daniel, 2 Esdras, and Revelation. The eschatologic features that Joel foresees as occurring at the End of history include (1) a series of natural, political, and supernatural disasters—"signs" in heaven and earth—that portend the wrath to come; (2) a cosmic battle fought in both the material and spiritual realms, in which Yahweh and his people triumph over their enemies; (3) an outpouring of Holy Spirit on Yahweh's people; and (4) the divine presence among the faithful.

Understandably, Joel is frequently quoted by later Jewish and Christian writers. The pseudepigraphal Book of Enoch reflects Joel's ideas and imagery, as does the New Testament Book of Acts, which interprets the Pentecostal miracle as the fulfillment of Joel 2:28–29 (see Acts 2:1–4, 7–21). The Synoptic Gospels cite Joel's references to astronomical phenomena as events heralding Jesus' Second Coming (see Mark 13: 24–25; Luke 21:11, 25; Matt. 24:29).

RECOMMENDED READING

Kapelrud, Arvid S. *Joel Studies.* Uppsala, Sweden: Almquist & Wiksells, 1948.

Wolff, Hans W. *Joel and Amos.* Philadelphia: Fortress Press, 1977.

Malachi

KEY THEMES

Contrasting foreign nations that honor Yahweh with Judah's apathetic sacrificial cult, the prophet instructs a dispirited, disorganized audience of Judeans on how to please their God (Chs. 1 and 2) and predicts the future day of Yahweh, evoking the reappearance of Elijah and the coming of Yahweh's irresistible messenger of the covenant (Ch. 3).

> Look, I am going to send my messenger
> to prepare a way before me. . . .
> Who will be able to resist the day of his
>   coming?
>
> Malachi 3:1–2

In Protestant and Catholic Bibles, Malachi appears as the last Old Testament book, an appropriate placement because the book concludes with a prediction that Yahweh will send a "messenger" who will prepare his people for the climactic event of history, the Day of Yahweh. The title of the book, *Malachi,* means "my messenger"; it may have been taken from the reference at 3:1 and may not be the name of a historical prophet. Although the text gives no information about the writer or time of composition, the book is customarily dated in the fifth century B.C.E., shortly before the time when traditional prophecy in Israel is thought to have ceased.

Pleasing Yahweh   The first two chapters contribute little to Israel's prophetic legacy. Casting his message in question-and-answer form, the writer presents Yahweh's complaints that the people offend him by sacrificing defective animals at the Temple. The author's concern is exclusively with the physical aspects of worship; he has nothing to say about the moral implications. Even so, one can assume that he views the offering of an unblemished animal, as Mosaic law required, as the outward symbol of a worshiper's wholehearted attempt to please his God; to do less betrayed an imperfect commitment to Yahweh. Chapter 2 ends with a vigorous attack on divorce, which the prophet also regards as breaking faith with Yahweh. Some commentators see this passage as a reaction against the policies of Ezra and Nehemiah, who compelled Jewish men to divorce their non-Jewish wives (Ezra 10:3, 44; see also Neh. 13:23–29).

The Coming Messenger   Malachi's prediction that the Temple will be inspected and cleansed by Yahweh's messenger, "the angel of the Covenant" (Mal. 3:1), is thematically connected with the earlier denunciations of inferior sacrifices, but in Chapter 3 the prophet broadens his charge to include responsibilities to widows, orphans, strangers, and the poor. The author briefly returns to mundane functions, like tithing (Mal. 3:6–12), but then asserts that Yahweh's justice will prevail only when the God himself intervenes to champion the righteous and punish the wicked. Although in this life the arrogant and ruthless often exploit the humble and faithful, justice will triumph when the Day of Yahweh arrives. It consequently behooves one to keep the commandments, even though one may temporarily suffer for it.

Finally, Malachi promises that before "that great and terrible day" arrives Yahweh will send Elijah the prophet—who in 2 Kings 2:11–12 had been carried off alive to heaven—to reconcile the generations, fathers and children, lest Yahweh "strike the land with a curse" (Mal. 3:24). The belief that Elijah would return to prepare the way for the Messiah or the kingdom of God and Day of Judgment played a significant part in later Jewish expectations. Even today a place is set for Elijah, the long-awaited guest, at Passover observances. In the first century C.E., the Synoptic Gospels identify John the Baptist with Elijah's eschatological role (Mark 9:11–12; Matt. 17:9–13).

RECOMMENDED READING

Hanson, Paul D. "Malachai." In J. L. Mays, ed., *Harper's Bible Commentary,* pp. 753–756. San Francisco: Harper & Row, 1988.

Jonah

KEY THEMES

In this parable describing Jonah's painful learning experiences when he tries to avoid prophesying to the Assyrians at Nineveh, an unknown author illustrates the relationship between a prophet and his God, who turns out to be both more powerful and more merciful than the reluctant prophet had supposed.

> Am I [Yahweh] not to feel sorry for Nineveh,
>   the great city . . . ?
>
> Jonah 4:11

Unique among the prophetic writings, the Book of Jonah is not a collection of oracles but a brief prose tale about a narrow-minded man whose God is much greater than he had anticipated. The style of the book is terse, its intent broadly humorous, and the joke is on those who think that Yahweh condemns all people except those belonging to a particular religious or racial group. Although the time of writing is unknown, it is probably postexilic, its theme of toleration perhaps a reaction to Ezra's severe and rigid view of Judaism (Part 6).

Yahweh's Mercy: A Lesson for Judah

A Reluctant Prophet   Jonah's story occupies but four brief chapters. In the first, Yahweh calls Jonah to preach at Nineveh, capital of the hated Assyrian Empire, but the reluctant prophet decides instead to leave Palestine and take ship for Spain at the opposite end of the Mediterranean. Yahweh stops the ship with a great storm that terrifies the Gentile sailors. Casting lots, they learn that Jonah is the cause of their danger but are too humane to cast the Hebrew jinx overboard. Only after begging Yahweh's forgiveness do they hurl Jonah into the sea, where God has arranged for a large fish to swallow him.

The second chapter consists largely of Jonah's prayer from the belly of the sea creature. It is the only poetic passage in the book and may have been inserted by a later writer. Although Jonah's lament reveals little religious insight—he still seems to think that Yahweh hears prayers only at the Jerusalem Temple—Yahweh has the fish spew Jonah out near shore.

The humor of the totally improbable dominates Chapter 3. After his "resurrection" from the fishy grave, Jonah finally goes to Nineveh. Tersely announcing that the city will be destroyed in forty days, he is unpleasantly surprised when the entire Assyrian population, from the king downward, immediately repents; even the animals wear sackcloth in the hope that Yahweh will relent and spare their city. Noting their improved behavior, Yahweh changes his mind and does not obliterate the Assyrians, which infuriates Jonah. Though in Chapter 4 he pretends to have known all along that Yahweh is compassionate, he is privately indignant that Yahweh did not act on his original plan. Feeling betrayed, he asks to die.

While the prophet sulks outside Nineveh's gates, Yahweh causes a leafy plant to grow and shade him from the sun. When a worm kills the plant, Jonah again complains and wishes for death. The book ends with Yahweh questioning Jonah about his (Yahweh's) right to pardon whom he pleases, especially religiously blind people like the Ninevites "who cannot tell their right hand from their left." There is no record that Jonah ever understands the meaning of Yahweh's catechism.

It is difficult to assess the purpose of this curious tale because the author does not spell out his message. The work seems to be an amusing parable teaching that Yahweh is universal and considers the lives of pagan nations to be as valuable as those of his chosen people. If so, is the book a tract against the Jewish exclusiveness that prevailed after the time of Ezra? Certainly its details were not meant to be taken seriously. For who would believe that Nineveh was so gigantic that it took a man three days to walk across it? Or that Jonah literally stayed three days in the stomach of a fish? Or that the Ninevites' domestic animals walked about in mourning garb? Such touches are surely aspects of the author's slyly humorous design.

RECOMMENDED READING

Ceresko, Anthony R. "Jonah." In R. E. Brown et al., eds., *The New Jerome Biblical Commentary,* pp. 580–584. Englewood Cliffs, N.J.: Prentice-Hall, 1990.

Fretheim, Terence E. *The Message of Jonah.* Minneapolis: Augsburg, 1977.

TERMS AND CONCEPTS
TO REMEMBER

Ahaz	Jeremiah
Amos	Jeroboam II
apostasy	Joel
Ashdod	Jonah
Baruch	Judaism
Cyrus	Magog
Deutero-Isaiah	Malachi
(Second Isaiah)	Micah
Edom, Edomites	Minor Prophets
eschatology	Nahum
Ezekiel	*navi*
Gog	Obadiah
Habakkuk	Queen of Heaven
Haggai	resurrection
Hezekiah	Second Isaiah
Hosea	seer
Immanuel	Sennacherib
Isaiah (of Jerusalem)	Tammuz
Jehoiakim	Third Isaiah
Uzziah (Azariah)	Zedekiah
Zadok	Zephaniah
Zechariah	Zerubbabel

QUESTIONS FOR REVIEW

1. Define the nature and function of Israel's prophets. During what three crucial periods of Israel's ancient history did most of the prophets appear? Were they typically more concerned about foretelling the far distant future or about declaring Yahweh's views on pressing ethical and social issues of their own day?

2. During the eighth century B.C.E., when the threat of Assyrian invasion loomed on the horizon, which prophets were active in the northern kingdom of Israel? What were the messages about economic and social justice? Which two prophets were active in Judah? Did Isaiah and Micah have the same opinion of the Davidic royal dynasty?

3. What was Judah's political situation during the decades that Isaiah counseled Jerusalem's kings? What "miraculous" event occurred during Hezekiah's reign in 701 B.C.E.?

4. Why do scholars believe that the Book of Isaiah represents the work of at least three different prophets from three different historical periods? Why does the Assyrian threat dominate the first part of Isaiah, whereas after Chapter 40 Babylon becomes the chief foreign power? Which passages in Isaiah 40–55 do you find most significant in establishing Judaism as a universal, monotheistic religion?

5. Habakkuk, Jeremiah, and Ezekiel prophesied during the Babylonian crisis. To what social abuses and failures of leadership does Jeremiah attribute the fall of Jerusalem? How does Ezekiel attempt to prepare his people for the future? Do you see any connection between Jeremiah's promise of a "new covenant" (Jer. 31:31) and Ezekiel's visions of a restored holy city and Temple?

6. Haggai and Zechariah were active after a Judean "remnant" had returned to Jerusalem from Babylon. What were their hopes about Zerubbabel's restoring Davidic rule in Judah? What role did the two prophets play in rebuilding Yahweh's Temple?

QUESTIONS FOR DISCUSSION AND REFLECTION

1. Historically, prophecy rose with the establishment of the Davidic monarchy and rapidly declined after its destruction in 587 B.C.E. How do you explain this phenomenon? Do you think that the rise of priestly leadership and political control in the post-exilic community may have contributed to the disappearance of officially recognized or "genuine" prophets? Do you think that contemporary "spokesmen for God" who are the equivalent of Amos or Jeremiah would be encouraged to prophesy in churches or synagogues today?

2. According to Deuteronomy 18, how could one distinguish between a true prophet and an imposter? Was clairvoyance, an ability to foresee future political events, essential to Israelite prophecy? In what ways can people today learn to detect the will of God in a difficult or even ethically ambiguous situation? Should prophetic ideas be legally adopted as part of modern government policies?

6

The Writings (Kethuvim): Books of Wisdom, Poetry, Short Fiction, and Sacred History

An Anthology of Sacred Literature

The third major division of the Hebrew Bible, the Writings (*Kethuvim*), was the last to be accepted as canonical. In theme and literary form, it is also the least unified part of the Bible. The diverse material in the Torah is bound together by Yahweh's series of promises or covenants with the patriarchs and with Israel at Sinai. The historical narratives of Joshua through Kings (the Former Prophets) are unified by the writer's controlling intent to show Yahweh as Lord of history, expressing his will through Israel's political rise and fall. Even the fifteen books of the Latter Prophets, for all their diverse responses to changing political and religious circumstances over a period of four centuries, form a coherent tradition. By contrast, the Writings present a wide variety of viewpoints expressing the multifaceted religious experiences of postexilic Israel.

Whereas the long line of prophets began during the early monarchy and ended soon after Judah's return from exile, the Writings belong primarily to the postexilic period (approximately the fifth to the second centuries B.C.E.). This miscellaneous collection includes poetry (Psalms, Song of Solomon, Lamentations), wise sayings (Proverbs), short stories (Ruth and Esther), priestly history (Ezra, Nehemiah, and Chronicles), magnificent wisdom literature (Job and Ecclesiastes), and apocalyptic visions of the end of time (Daniel). See "The Writings: A Tribute to Israel's Religious Vitality" on page 196 for more about this division of the Hebrew Bible.

Wisdom Literature

In ancient Israel, people belonging to three callings or professions could speak with authority—the priest, the prophet, and the sage. According to Jeremiah (18:18), the priest's business was to instruct in covenant law (the Torah), the prophet's function was to convey Yahweh's "word," and the sage's office was to provide wise advice. (See also Ezek. 7:26.) The "wise," including both men and women, held positions of public respect and commonly served as counselors to kings (2 Sam. 14:21, 16:23, 20:14–22). Prophets were sometimes critical of the professional class of sages—as they were of priests—but the wisdom movement ultimately outlasted

195

The Writings: A Tribute to Israel's Religious Vitality

"Can these bones live?" When Yahweh asked this question of Ezekiel, who was then a captive in Babylon, the covenant people resembled dessicated skeletons scattered in a boneyard. The nation of Judah had perished in the flames rising from Jerusalem and Solomon's Temple and, as had happened to many other small states crushed by the Babylonian juggernaut, it looked as if Judah would vanish forever, buried in history's graveyard. Yahweh, however, regarded Judah's political death and interment—punishment for its faithlessness—as only a temporary state: "these bones [that were] the whole House of Israel" would live again. In Ezekiel's vision of his nation's future resurrection, the prophet witnesses Yahweh's miraculous reenactment of Adam's creation. Infusing Judah's apparently lifeless corpse with his spirit, Yahweh recreates a people for his name (Ezek. 37:1–14).

The third major division of the Hebrew Bible, the Writings (Kethuvim), expresses the enormous vitality of Judah's postexilic religious community. Composed between the sixth and second centuries B.C.E., the Writings contain a rich diversity of responses to Judah's rebirth and radically changed circumstances. Poets and sages explored the possible meanings of Israel's sufferings and partial restoration, creating such Wisdom books as Job and Ecclesiastes. Rejecting the simplistic deuteronomic thesis that equated prosperity with religious obedience, and misery with sin, the authors of Job and Ecclesiastes boldly questioned older biblical teachings, including the traditional concept of God.

The unknown author of Ruth similarly contributed to a new skepticism about conventional religious attitudes, portraying a Moabite woman—and presumably a worshiper of the Moabite god Chemosh—as entirely sympathetic. The Torah had pictured foreign women, whether Moabite or Midianite, as wanton temptresses who caused Israelite men to sin, and hence to deserve death (cf. Num. 31:1–20; Deut. 7:1–16, 16; 20:17–18). Whereas Ruth celebrates marriage between a foreign widow and her Yahwist husband, the conventional bias against intermarriage with non-Israelite women resurfaced in postexilic times and is a major theme of Ezra and Nehemiah. Representing a broad range of literary categories, from lyric poetry and short fiction to long historical narratives, the Writings bear eloquent testimony to the diversity and speculative freedom of Judah's postexilic thinkers.

Books of the Writings

- Proverbs (a compilation of wise sayings, largely practical and conventional wisdom)
- Job (a philosophical exploration of Yahweh's ethical character and relation to humanity)
- Ecclesiastes (a sage's quest for meaning and delight in paradox)
- Psalms (an anthology of deeply felt religious poetry)
- Ruth (a short story about a Moabite woman's new life in Israel during the time of the Judges)
- Song of Songs (a collection of erotic love poems)
- Lamentations (an anguished complaint over Yahweh's destruction of his people)
- Esther (a short story about Jewish survival in a foreign empire)
- 1 and 2 Chronicles (a priestly revision of the Deuteronomistic History, emphasizing the Temple cult)
- Ezra (a composite account of Ezra, the priest-scribe who brought the Torah from Babylon to recreate the covenant community in postexilic Jerusalem)
- Nehemiah (a narrative about rebuilding Jerusalem's fortifications under Persia's sponsorship)
- Daniel (an apocalypse, or revelation, that includes mystical visions of events leading to the end of time)

The last-written book in the Hebrew Bible canon, Daniel is discussed in its historical context in Part 7.

the prophetic line and produced some of the greatest books in the Bible.

The origins of Israel's wisdom tradition are unknown, but archaeological discoveries have revealed that long before Israel came into existence, thinkers in Egypt, Mesopotamia, Edom, and Phoenicia had produced astute guides to the "good life." Among Hebrew writers, however, wisdom material acquired a new tone and emphasis: "The fear of Yahweh is the beginning of knowledge" (Prov. 1:7). Although the writers of many proverbs—short, memorable sayings summarizing insights about life—stressed observation and experience as a source of knowledge, they regarded wisdom as much a divine gift as the prophetic word (Prov. 2:6). Wisdom, rather than the Torah, was envisioned as Yahweh's first creation and, personified as a gracious divine woman, acted as a liaison between the Deity and humanity (Prov. 8). This theme of Wisdom as a creative spirit linking humanity with a primary attribute of the Creator is most fully developed in a late apocryphal work, the Wisdom of Solomon (7:22–9:18).

Renowned for his shrewd judgments, King Solomon—the reputed author of 3000 proverbs—stood at the head of Israel's wisdom tradition (1 Kings 3:1–28, 4:29–34). Later ages, honoring Solomon's role in establishing a national institution of wise government counselors and other sages, attributed a large body of wisdom writings to him. These include the canonical books of Proverbs, Ecclesiastes, and Song of Solomon, the apocryphal Wisdom, and the pseudepigraphal poetry collections known as the Psalms and Odes of Solomon.

In Hebrew literature, wisdom was expressed in many different literary forms. Early types include riddles, fables, and proverbs (Judg. 9: 18–15, 14:14; 1 Kings 4:32). In later times, anonymous sages produced far more complex and sophisticated works, such as the Book of Job, where subtle theological arguments are sustained through lengthy debates about divine justice and the meaning of human suffering. Works like Ecclesiastes contain an amalgam of the sage's personal reflections on life's futility and meditations on death, as well as paradoxic maxims, proverbs, and expressions of skeptical pessimism.

The author of only one wisdom book is known—Jesus ben Sirach, who compiled the observations, teachings, and experiences of a lifetime in Ecclesiasticus. This weighty volume, the longest of its kind in the Bible, reveals the existence of "wisdom schools" at which young people were educated by a recognized wisdom authority. One of the last-written books of the Apocrypha, the work entitled Wisdom of Solomon (written around the first century B.C.E.) is the only work in the Hebrew Bible that specifically links the righteousness born of wisdom to hopes of personal immortality (Wisdom 1: 12–3:9; 5:4–24, etc.).

Besides these works, various psalms also contain wisdom motifs (Pss. 1, 8, 16, 17, 19, 34, 37, 49, 73, 92, 104, 112, 119, and 139) as do the prose tales of Joseph and Daniel, wise men loyal to their Jewish heritage, who rose to power in foreign nations (Gen. 39–41; Dan. 1–6). Both of these figures are depicted as recipients of a divine gift, the wisdom to interpret dreams that foreshadow the future. The greatest **wisdom literature**, however, is based on the authors' profound reflections on the significance of ordinary life, with its unequal distribution of good and evil fortune, unexpected calamities, and the ambiguity of its ethical "message."

Because of its diversity in outlook, thought, and form, wisdom material defies easy classification. Its characteristic themes are strikingly different from those in the Torah and the Prophets. Wisdom books typically make no references to the covenant relationship that bound Israel to Yahweh. Neither Job nor Ecclesiastes even mentions the Mosaic Torah; but both agree that many religious assumptions, such as a divinely favored "right side's" winning in life's battles, are unjustified by human experience. The deuteronomic thesis that Yahweh directs human history, of which individual lives are a part, is also conspicuously absent.

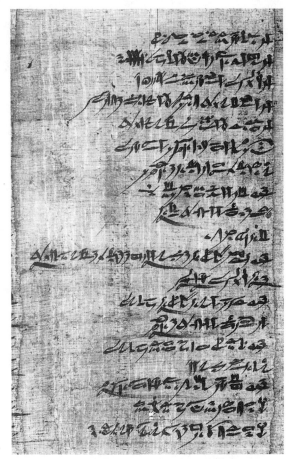

An ancient Egyptian papyrus recording the Wisdom of Amenemope (c. 1200 B.C.E.) contains sage advice that was later incorporated into the Book of Proverbs (Prov. 22:17 to 24:22). The wisdom movement permeated virtually the entire ancient Near East, creating an international legacy shared by Egypt, Mesopotamia, and Israel. (Copyright British Museum)

shared by the Deuteronomistic historians, who interpreted Israel's growth and destruction as the consequence of keeping or breaking covenant laws. Among the Hebrews thinkers who vigorously disputed this simplistic view of life was the anonymous poet who wrote Job.

RECOMMENDED READING

Brueggemann, Walter A. *In Man We Trust: The Neglected Side of Biblical Faith*. Richmond, Va.: John Knox Press, 1972.

Bryce, Glendon E. *Israel and the Wisdom of Egypt*. Lewisburg, Pa.: Bucknell University Press, 1975. Analyzes the influence of Egyptian wisdom on the book of Proverbs.

Crenshaw, James L. *Studies in Ancient Israelite Wisdom*. New York: KTAV Publishing House, 1976.

———. *A Whirlpool of Torment: Israelite Traditions of God as an Oppressive Presence*. Philadelphia: Fortress Press, 1984.

Grabbe, Lester L. *Priests, Prophets, Sages: A Socio-Historical Study of Religious Specialists in Ancient Israel*. Valley Forge, Penn.: Trinity Press International, 1995. Provides cross-cultural parallels to Israel's religious office in the ancient Near East.

Humphreys, W. Lee. *The Tragic Vision and the Hebrew Tradition*. Philadelphia: Fortress Press, 1985.

Lambert, W. G. *Babylonian Wisdom Literature*. Oxford, Eng.: Clarendon Press, 1960.

Murphy, Roland E. *Seven Books of Wisdom*. Milwaukee: Bruce, 1960.

———. *Wisdom Literature and Psalms*. Nashville, Tenn.: Abingdon Press, 1983.

Scott, R. B. Y. *The Way of Wisdom in the Old Testament*. New York: Macmillan, 1971.

Evaluating the ethical quality of human life from a variety of perspectives, the wisdom authors typically come to rather seditious conclusions. Their observations and analyses of experience tend to subvert some other Bible writers' interpretation of Israel's history. The prophetic tradition held that Yahweh observed all people's actions, inevitably punishing the bad and rewarding the good, an assumption

Proverbs

KEY THEMES

Although ascribed to Solomon, traditional founder of Israel's wisdom schools, the Book of Proverbs contains practical advice drawn from diverse sources, ranging from ancient Egypt through many generations of Israelite thought. Besides "Solomonic" maxims (Chs. 10–22), the book's highlights include reflections on the value of wisdom (Chs. 1–6), personifications of Wisdom and Folly (Chs. 7–9), and a portrait of the "perfect wife" (Ch. 31).

> Yahweh created me [Wisdom] when his purpose first unfolded,
>   before the oldest of his works.
> From everlasting I was firmly set,
>   from the beginning, before earth came into being.
>
> Proverbs 8:22–23

Whereas examples of speculative wisdom, such as Job and Ecclesiastes, deal with theological inquiries about the nature of God and the purpose of human life, the Book of Proverbs is devoted to advocating practical wisdom and with guiding readers to find their proper place in the social and religious order. *Proverb* translates from the Hebrew term *mashal,* which means a "statement of truth" or "standard of appropriate behavior." The biblical proverbs are typically based on observation and experience rather than on divine revelation and are commonly nonreligious in tone. Thus,

> The rich man's wealth is his stronghold,
> poverty is the poor man's undoing.
>
> Proverbs 10:15

is simply an observed fact of life: Riches give security and poverty the opposite.

Like much wisdom literature, Proverbs is not peculiarly Jewish; most of its admonitions could apply equally well in a pagan society totally different from Israel's theocracy:

> The generous man is his own benefactor,
> a cruel man injures his own flesh.
>
> Proverbs 11:17

It is not surprising, then, that archaeologists have found almost word-for-word parallels of biblical proverbs in Mesopotamia and Egypt; indeed, a whole passage from the wisdom book of the Egyptian sage Amenemope has been taken over almost verbatim in Proverbs 22: 17–23:11. Scholars now realize that proverbs and other wisdom writings were produced in many New Eastern cultures and that Israel's sages in some cases borrowed from older literary collections.

Proverbs Attributed to Solomon　Because King Solomon, who was credited with more than 3000 proverbs (1 Kings 4:29–33), has been traditionally associated with the production of adages or wise sayings, the superscription ascribing Proverbs to Solomon (Prov. 1:1) may mean no more than that these proverbs are written in the "manner" of Solomon. Other writers, in fact, are specifically cited. Agur, son of Jakeb, is the author of Chapter 30; Lemuel, king of Massa, of Chapter 31; and various unnamed sages of 24:23–24. Like the Psalms, Proverbs grew from many different sources over a span of centuries.

The Role of Wisdom

Value of Wisdom　What principally distinguishes some of Israel's proverbs from those of Edom, Babylonia, or Egypt is the theme that true wisdom promotes loyalty to Yahweh and sensitivity to the divine will. The wise person makes his or her behavior accord with divine law (Prov. 3; 19:16); the wise person is the righteous person who harmonizes his or her conduct with Yahweh's will (Prov. 16:1, 9; 19:21, 23). Proverbs also affirms the orthodox theme that in this world the righteous are rewarded and the wicked punished (Prov. 11: 17–21; 21:21). Fearing Yahweh, observing the commandments, and behaving discreetly will ensure a long and prosperous life. Only the fool rejects admonition and suffers accordingly.

Proverb's emphasis on the pragmatic "getting ahead" in life endeared it to Israel's middle and upper classes. The directive to "study the ant, thou sluggard" (Prov. 6:6–11) is one of several that attribute poverty to laziness. (See also Prov.

24:30–34.) Considerable proverbial wisdom is aimed at young people who wish to establish themselves at court and become the counselors of kings. Others offer advice on table manners and how to behave in the company of rich and powerful persons whom one wishes to impress favorably. The sages point out that achieving these ambitious goals requires self-discipline, reverence for Yahweh, and the special combination of humility and penetrating insight that enables the wise to perceive the cosmic order and attain one's place in it.

Wisdom as Yahweh's Companion   The writer of Proverbs characteristically assumes the role of a father advising his son against bad company in general and seductive women in particular (Prov. 1–2). Folly (lack of wisdom) is likened to a harlot who corrupts youth, whereas Wisdom is personified as a noble woman who seeks to save young men from their own inexperience and bad judgment. In Chapter 1, Wisdom is pictured as calling from the streets and housetops, promising rich treasure to those not too ignorant to appreciate her. The theme of "Lady Wisdom's" supreme value climaxes in Chapter 8, in which she is presented as nothing less than Yahweh's associate in creation:

> Yahweh created me when his purpose first
>   unfolded,
>   before the oldest of his works.
> From everlasting I was firmly set,
>   from the beginning, before earth came
>   into being.

* * *

> I was by his side, a master craftsman
>   [alternatively, "darling child"],
>   delighting him day after day,
>   ever at play in his presence,
> at play everywhere in his world,
>   delighting to be with the sons of men.
>   Proverbs 8:22, 23, 30, 31

This passage, which shows Yahweh creating the world with Wisdom, a joyous feminine

companion at his side, seems to have influenced such later Jewish thinkers as **Philo Judaeus**, who lived in Alexandria, Egypt, during the first century C.E. Philo's attempt to reconcile Greek philosophy with Hebrew revelation included his doctrine of the **Logos** ("**Word**") by which God created the universe. (*Logos,* a masculine term in Greek, became more acceptable to Hebrew patriarchal thinking than *Sophia,* "Wisdom," which is feminine.) The Hymn to Logos with which John opens his Gospel is derived from Philo's (and ultimately Proverbs's) assumption that a divine mediator stands between God and the world.

The Perfect Way   The book closes with a famous alphabetic poem on the perfect wife. Although promiscuous women and domineering wives receive considerable censure throughout Proverbs, the wife who works hard and selflessly to manage her husband's estate and increase his wealth is praised as beyond price (Prov. 31).

RECOMMENDED READING

Bryce, Glendon E. *Israel and the Wisdom of Egypt.* Lewisburg, Pa.: Bucknell University Press, 1975.

Camp, Claudia. *Wisdom and the Feminine in the Book of Proverbs.* Sheffield, Eng.: Almond Press, 1985.

McKane, William. *Proverbs.* Philadelphia: Westminster Press, 1970.

Scott, R. B. Y. *Proverbs. Ecclesiastes.* Anchor Bible, Vol. 18. Garden City, N.Y.: Doubleday, 1965.

Whybray, R. N. *Wisdom in Proverbs: The Concept of Wisdom in Proverbs 1–9.* Studies in Biblical Theology, No. 45. London: SCM Press, 1965.

Job

KEY THEMES

A supreme masterpiece of religious thought, the Book of Job dramatizes the plight of a rep-

court in which the Deity and humanity's Adversary agree to test Job's loyalty. In the long poetic central section (Chs. 3–31), the author exposes the inadequacy of conventional religious explanations about divine–human relationships, expressly discrediting the deuteronomic thesis that God is pledged to protect and reward the righteous, a position taken by Job's three friends who argue that suffering is an inevitable result of sin. After Elihu's interpolated discourse (Chs. 32–37), Yahweh delivers two speeches emphasizing cosmic wonders beyond human comprehension (Chs. 38–41). The prose epilog recounts Job's restored fortunes (42:7–17).

> It is all one, and this I dare to say:
>   innocent and guilty, he [Yahweh] destroys all
>   alike.
> When a sudden deadly scourge descends,
>   he laughs at the plight of the innocent.
> When a country falls into a tyrant's hand,
>   it is he who blindfolds the judges.
>   Or if not he, who else?
>
> Job 9:22–24

The Bible's prime example of *speculative wisdom*—the kind of intellectual activity that questions the principles and assumptions commonly accepted by society—the Book of Job is a profound exploration of the issue of God's responsibility for evil and the extent to which he is morally bound, by the intrinsic goodness of his own nature, to protect sentient creatures from unmerited pain. It is also concerned with the psychological relationship between humanity and God, as well as with the intellectual honesty of a righteous person whose integrity does not allow him to evade the dilemma by falsely confessing to sin in order to justify his god's harsh treatment of him. The author's rejection of conventional explanations and his unorthodox demand that Yahweh meet Job on equal terms to explain his (Yahweh's) questionable morality undoubtedly shocked pious readers when the book was new, as it may still shock some readers today. Because the questions it raises have

The cuneiform script on this clay tablet narrates a Sumerian variation of the Job story. Like the Book of Job, this text records the humiliating ordeals of a righteous man who nonetheless clings to his faith and is at last delivered from his undeserved sufferings. The problem of Evil, with its conflict between the concept of a good God and the fact of unmerited human pain, was a perplexing theme explored in Egyptian, Babylonian, and Israelite literature. (Courtesy of the University Museum, University of Pennsylvania [Neg. #S8-68052b])

resentative human whose tragic sufferings inspire him to question the ethical nature of a god who permits evil and the unmerited pain of sentient creatures. The prose prolog (Chs. 1 and 2) features two scenes in Yahweh's heavenly

never been satisfactorily resolved, the book is as provocative now as it was 2500 years ago. Commentators have proposed innumerable interpretations of this perplexing masterpiece; the discussion here encompasses a variety of possible viewpoints.

Scholars do not agree on when Job was written. Although Hebrew tradition ascribed the book to Moses, both its language and theological outlook are later than the Mosaic period. The book seems to be the product of a troubled age when the moral assumption of the deuteronomic thesis had lost much of its former authority. The Book of Deuteronomy had argued that the good person, obedient to Yahweh's regulations, would automatically enjoy security, prosperity, and long life, but the history of Israel did not support this comfortable belief. After the Babylonians under Nebuchadnezzar had demolished both Yahweh's sanctuary and the Israelite state—acts involving the suffering and deaths of hundreds of thousands of people—it was necessary to rethink Israel's traditional philosophy of history.

During the Babylonian exile, then, Israel's wisdom writers had to grapple with troubling questions. How could Yahweh allow such a disaster to afflict his chosen people? How could he permit his holy Temple to fall into pagan hands? The prophets had answered that Israel suffered defeat because the Israelites had, by sinful disobedience to the Mosaic Covenant, forfeited their privilege of divine protection. Because it is unthinkable that Yahweh does wrong, individuals must deserve whatever evils befall them.

The anonymous author of Job, writing sometime after the exile, probably in the fifth century B.C.E., could not agree that Israel's oppression was justified either by Deuteronomy's simplistic system of rewards and punishments or by the prophets' insistence that the people had earned their miseries. Combining the traditional reverence for Yahweh with an acutely critical intelligence and demand for moral logic, he uses an old folktale of the legendary patriarch Job to illustrate his conviction that neither the God-

fearing person nor the blasphemer receives what he or she deserves in this life. But if God is in control of the universe, why is this so? The writer's attempt to probe this mystery leads him to reexamine the basic concept of divinity.

While most of Job is in poetry, the prolog and epilog are in prose, and most scholars believe that the prose sections represent an old fable that the author used as a framework for his central poetic drama.

Yahweh's Heavenly Court

Prolog The prolog presents Job as a thoroughly upright and godly man who in no way deserves the evils inflicted on him. Described as "sound and honest," one "who feared God and shunned evil" (Job 1:1 and 2:3), he is meant to represent a universal type, the person of good will found everywhere throughout history. For this reason the writer does not make him a Jew but a native of Uz (perhaps south of Edom) who lived long before Israel's birth. So scrupulous is Job about not offending God, however, that he offers sacrifices for his children in case they, even in thought, have sinned. No wonder Yahweh declares that "there is no one like [Job] on the earth" (Job 1:8).

Ironically, Job's outstanding righteousness attracts the interest of "the satan," a heavenly being who acts as Yahweh's prosecuting attorney. Appearing among "the Sons of God" before Yahweh's throne, he suggests that Job will not remain loyal if deprived of family, property, and reputation. For reasons known only to himself, Yahweh accepts this challenge, withdrawing the protective "wall" with which he had previously shielded Job from misfortune. Job now experiences the power of chaos—the sudden injection of violent change into his formerly stable environment. Predatory nomads sweep away his flocks and herds; "the fire of God" consumes his sheep and shepherds; a fierce wind demolishes the house where Job's children are feasting, killing them all. Stripped of everything he holds dear by chaotic forces of earth, air, and sky, Job still blesses Yahweh's name (1:1–2:21). As if tempting God to doubt further the integrity of his human creation, "the satan" next persuades Yahweh to infect his faithful worshiper with a painful and disfiguring disease, although Yahweh protests that such persecution is unjustified, "without cause" (2:1–10). In contrast to Yahweh, who yields to his prosecutor's suggestions, Job rejects his wife's despairing plea to "curse God and die."

The Central Poetic Drama

Sufferings and Complaints   In Chapter 3, the action shifts from the heavenly court to Job's dungheap, where, in a long monolog, he prays to have the process of creation reversed, asking for a return to the primeval darkness that shrouded all before God illuminated the cosmos. (See Gen. 1:1–2.) If light and life are mere vehicles for pain, it is better not to exist or, once born, to sink quickly into the oblivion of **Sheol**, the dark subterranean realm where the human dead remain in eternal nothingness. (See also Eccl. 9:5, 10.) The lack of moral meaning in Job's fate is such that he evokes **Leviathan**, the mythical dragon of chaos, the "fleeing serpent," embodiment of the darkness and disorder that Yahweh subdued—but apparently did not annihilate—when creating the world (cf. Job 3:8; 26:10–14; 40:20–41:25; Pss. 74:12–13; 89:9–10; Isa. 27:1; etc.). Leviathan's significance is crucial to the problem of evil explored in the Book of Job, for Yahweh's reply to Job's accusations about divine injustice climaxes in a final evocation of Leviathan's chaotic role in the universe (Ch. 41).

The Central Debate   The hero is joined by three friends, **Eliphaz**, **Bildad**, and **Zophar**, who, following the comfortable assumptions of conventional wisdom, insist that Job's present misery must be the result of some vile but unknown sin. Each friend gives a speech, and Job in turn replies, refuting his contention. As the debates become more heated, Job's early patience gives way to a realization of two unorthodox truths: (1) that his humanity entitles him to certain moral rights, which Yahweh seems to ignore in permitting him to suffer undeservedly; (2) that if he is guiltless and God is truly all-powerful, then the Deity himself must be responsible for the evil that he and all other people endure.

In Chapters 9 and 10, Job challenges Yahweh to appear before him as a human being so that their conflict may be settled in terms of human justice. Anticipating Yahweh's appearance in the whirlwind, however, he realizes that he has no chance to present the justice of his cause before so formidable an opponent. A human is no match for the strength of God. Furthermore, the power that afflicts him is the same power that will judge him.

> Suppose I am in the right, what use is my
>   defense?
>   For he whom I must sue is judge as well.
> If he deigned to answer my citation,
>   could I be sure that he would listen to my
>   voice?
> He, who for one hair crushes me,
>   who, for no reason, wounds and wounds
>   again,
> leaving me not a moment to draw breath,
>   with so much bitterness he fills me.
> Shall I try force? Look how strong he is!
>   Or go to court? But who will summon *him*?
>   Job 9:15–19 (italics added)

With courage born of his honest recognition that good people can be more compassionate and moral than their gods seem to be, Job suggests that Yahweh must learn what it is like to be human, to bear the sorrows of mortality.

> I shall say to God, "Do not condemn me.
>   but tell me the reason for your assault.
> *Is it right* for you to injure me,
>   cheapening the work of your own hands
>   and abetting the schemes of the wicked?
> Have *you* got *human eyes*,
>   do *you* see as *mankind sees*?
> Is *your* life *mortal* like man's,
>   do your years pass as men's days pass?

You, who inquire into my faults
    and investigate my sins,
you know very well that I am innocent,
    and that no one can rescue me from your
    hand."
                Job 10:2–7 (italics added)

Reversing the traditional wisdom that asks us to look at things from the Deity's perspective, Job boldly demands that God try to see the world from the vantage point of pain-ridden, mortal humanity.

In his famous essay *Answer to Job,* the psychologist Carl Jung suggests that Job's challenging Yahweh to abandon his icy distance from human suffering had an enormous impact on the development of religious thought. Many centuries later, as a branch of first-century Judaism evolved into early Christianity, the concept of a remote, omnipotent Deity was radically transformed into the notion that Israel's God assumed human shape to suffer as the man Jesus. No longer conceived as utterly distinct from humanity, God—through the Incarnation—placed himself amid the human predicament, subject to the pain and evil that had afflicted Job. (See the discussion of John's Gospel, Part 9.)

Elihu's Speeches   Most scholars believe that the lengthy words of **Elihu**, a young man who suddenly appears in Chapter 32, are a later addition to the Book of Job. Except to sharpen the accusations against Job—of self-righteousness, pride, or secret sin—Elihu's speeches add little to the discussion, although he claims to resolve the entire theological problem that Job's case presents. Verbose and overconfident, Elihu betrays his absurd pretentiousness in speaking "on God's behalf":

I will range far afield for my arguments
    to prove my Maker just.
What I say to you contains no fallacies,
    I assure you,
        you see before you an enlightened man.
                    Job 36:2–4

After six chapters of Elihu's rehashing the friends' arguments, readers may well feel that the opening question in Yahweh's first speech applies to him rather than to Job: "Who is this obscuring my designs with his empty-headed words?" (38:2).

Yahweh Reveals His Universe

Yahweh Speaks   As Job foresaw in Chapter 9, when Yahweh appears, it is not in human form to debate the cause of injured innocence but in a superhuman display of power that ignores the mental anguish and disillusionment in divine goodness that are the principal source of Job's suffering. Speaking from the whirlwind as if to underscore the untractable, amoral energy of the natural world he has created, Yahweh emphasizes the enormous distance between divinity and humanity. His first speech (38:1–39:30) parades images of cosmic grandeur before Job's dazzled eyes, sardonically demanding that Job inform God about the miracle of creation, astronomical phenomena, and the curious habits of wildlife. Note that Yahweh invites Job to share his creative pride in the world of animal violence, such as the fearless warhorse that delights in battle (39:19–25). In his final horrific example, Yahweh describes the eagle or vulture that "feeds her young on blood," feasting on the bodies of dying humans, oblivious to their pain (39:27–30).

Job did not need to be told about Yahweh's cosmic might, of which he was already thoroughly aware (9:1–10), but he had hoped for reassurance about God's intrinsic goodness, compassion, and paternal concern for suffering humanity. Instead, Yahweh recites a catalog of impersonal natural wonders and a pitiless survey of predatory nature, "red in tooth and claw."

When Yahweh asks if Job, now deluged with examples of the savage and inexplicable, is ready to give up, Job merely replies that he will speak no more. Yahweh has refused to answer any of humanity's questions about the ethical principles by which he rules the universe and has arbitrarily limited the debate to a display of omnipotence that avoids addressing the real issue—his questionable moral character. As many readers have observed, Job's silence before God's self-disclosure is not reverent submission but the numbness of moral shock.

Apparently unsatisfied with Job's half-hearted acquiescence, Yahweh then launches into a second long speech in which he strikes at Job's deepest fear: that in the absence of a recognizable divine ethic, humans will have to create—out of emptiness—their own meaning of life. When Yahweh asks "Do you really want to reverse my judgment, and put me in the wrong to put yourself in the right?" (Job 40:8), Job's response must be no, for it is the necessary function of an omniscient God, not fallible man, to enforce a recognizable moral order. Faced with the total failure of the prophetic or deuteronomic attempts to explain human loss and pain in terms of an ethical Creator, Job is next compelled to stare even more deeply into the magnificence—and horror—of the universe Yahweh has fashioned.

Yahweh begins by inducing Job to examine the sphere of human activity, asking him if he can duplicate the divine thunder that (when it chooses) can obliterate the wicked. But Yahweh does not linger over his strangely inconsistent enforcement of justice in human society; instead, he demands that Job consider the untamable **Behemoth**, "the masterpiece of all God's work," a monster so powerful, so grotesque, and so removed from any possible relation to human experience that God's admiration of the creature forces Job to realize that the world is not a place designed for human welfare. The universe Yahweh unveils is God-centered, frightening in its vast indifference to human needs. (Compare the Genesis tradition of humanity's position as the pinnacle of creation [Gen. 1:26–31].)

Scholars used to think that Behemoth and Leviathan were, respectively, the hippopotamus and the crocodile, but since the discovery of Ugaritic texts referring to Baal's defeat of Lothan, the primeval sea monster, it is known that Leviathan is a mythological beast representing the chaos that existed before creation. The Canaanite Lothan and Hebrew Leviathan are variant forms of **Rahab**, the chaotic beast that Yahweh subdued when bringing order to the cosmos (Ps. 89:9–10). Note that Yahweh describes Leviathan in mythological terms, as a dragon belching fire and smoke (41:10–12) from whom the ocean waves flee (41:14, 17).

Whereas Yahweh's might has tamed Leviathan, the monster still has power to disrupt the world order, spasmodically returning the world, at least in part, to the primordial watery chaos described in Genesis 1.

> When he stands up, the waves themselves take fright,
> the billows of the sea retreat.

> * * *

> He churns the depths into a seething caldron,
> he makes the sea fume like a scent burner.
> Behind him he leaves a glittering wake—
> a white fleece seems to float on the deeps.
> He has no equal on earth,
> being created without fear.
> He looks the haughtiest in the eye;
> of all the sons of pride he is the king.
> Job 41:16–17, 22–26

God and Chaos

Yahweh's climactic reference to Leviathan's supreme "pride" recalls the beginning of his speech in which the Deity described his ability to overthrow "the haughty" and the "proud" (41:6–14). Although Yahweh crushes human pride, he does not annihilate Leviathan, the embodiment of chaos that lies coiled like a serpent around the visible cosmos, primal energy unassimilated into the stable order, that periodically rears its head to shatter the peace of both nature and humanity.

In Job, Yahweh seems to tolerate the chaotic forces that still permeate creation, but in Isaiah he is represented as vowing to destroy Leviathan—on the last day when he fully imposes his universal sovereignty.

> That [final] day, Yahweh will punish,
> with his hard sword, massive and strong,
> Leviathan, the fleeing serpent,
> Leviathan, the twisting serpent:
> he will kill the sea dragon.
>
> Isaiah 27:1

The final overthrow of the chaotic principle inherent in creation, as in human experience, began with Yahweh's initial ordering of the cosmos but will not be complete until Yahweh's Day of Judgment, when his righteousness ultimately defeats the dragon of chaos. (Compare Yahweh's promised overthrow of Leviathan with the mythic image of the Dragon, "the serpent of old that led the whole world astray, whose name is Satan, or the Devil" in Revelation 12:3–9.)

Job's total submission after Yahweh's Leviathan speech is commonly understood as a recognition of humanity's puny insignificance when confronted with Yahweh's irresistible power or a simple case of Job's moral right trampled under God's implacable might:

> I know that you are all-powerful;
> what you conceive, you can perform.
> I am the man who obscured your designs
> with my empty-headed words.
> I have been holding forth on matters I cannot
> understand,
> on marvels beyond me and my knowledge.
>
> Job 42:2–3

God and Human Pain

When Job hears Yahweh's acknowledgment of Leviathan's continuing power, he recognizes that his earlier questions about God's ethical character are irrelevant. The universe is as it is, an unfolding process in which Light and Dark, Gentle and Violent, and Good and Evil are intrinsic components. "The satan," who (unknown to Job) attends Yahweh's heavenly court as one of the "Sons of God," and the primordial sea beast Leviathan, whom Yahweh has reduced to a plaything, are perhaps manifestations of the same mysterious, seditious force that Yahweh tolerates as part of the cosmic whole.

Job's reconciliation to the God who had permitted his unspeakable misery arises from a new understanding of divinity:

> I knew you then only by hearsay;
> but now, having seen you with my own eyes,
> I retract all I have said,
> and in dust and ashes I repent.
>
> Job 42:5–6

Job's concept of God and of the divine–human relationship is radically altered by Yahweh's self-revelation, particularly the Deity's climactic invocation of Leviathan. The chaotic monster's very presence suggests God's ongoing struggle to shape and maintain the created order—a struggle in which Job places himself on Yahweh's side. Although Job's unqualified submission suggests that he has attained a more profound understanding of his God, questions about the insights that motivate him abound.

Because Yahweh is eternal, having neither beginning nor end, the origin of chaos remains problematic. If cosmic violence did not precede Yahweh's emergence as Creator, it must bear some relationship to the Deity himself, an expression of the divine nature—a concept suggested by Second Isaiah:

> I am Yahweh, unrivaled,
> I form the light and create the dark.
> I make good fortune and calamity,
> It is I, Yahweh, who do all this.
>
> Isaiah 45:7

As strict monotheists, do Second Isaiah and the author of Job imply that a single universal Being encompasses all opposites, including what humans call Good and Evil, Order and Chaos?

Does Job "see" Yahweh embodying all things, including a counterforce inimical to the order he has created, a chaotic element represented by his "shadow," "the satan"? Or does Job perceive that Yahweh's power is somehow limited by the persistence of chaotic forces—from violent mass extinctions of species on earth to exploding suns in distant galaxies—the erratic outbursts of "Leviathan" that randomly disrupt an evolving universe? Perhaps, as Carl Jung suggests, Job's challenge has caused Yahweh to become aware of hitherto unconscious aspects of his character, to acknowledge the link between the vast, inhuman complexities of the cosmos and the suffering of intelligent beings whom he had fashioned in his image. God's frightening self-absorption in his cosmic glory must give way to a compassionate identification with human mortality. For the author of John's Gospel, this identification occurs when divine Wisdom becomes embodied in human flesh. (See the discussion of John's Gospel, Part 9.)

At the least, the author of Job demonstrates the intellectual and ethical inadequacy of the deuteronomistic theory of history. Eliphaz, Bildad, and Zophar argue passionately that God is just and that everyone gets exactly what he deserves. By contrast, the God-centered world Yahweh describes is *not* based on retributive justice, and human misery is *not* consistently the result of wrongdoing. Conventional moral logic is contradicted by Job's experience.

To some commentators, the prose epilog in which Job becomes wealthier than before and begets more sons and daughters to replace those Yahweh had allowed to be killed seems a tacked-on fairy-tale ending that undercuts the main thrust of the poetic dialogs. Note, however, that in this prosaic conclusion Yahweh condemns the three friends who had so ardently defended God's justice, declaring that they had not spoken "truthfully about me as my servant Job has done" (42:7). Yahweh prefers Job's honest doubts about the divine character to the friends' doubtful orthodoxy. God's restoration and double blessing of Job do not resolve the perplexing issue of evil and undeserved suffering. To Job, however, this divine goodness may foreshadow the time when Yahweh will permanently expel Leviathan, the "fleeing serpent," from our universe.

RECOMMENDED READING

Crenshaw, James L., ed. *Theodicy in the Old Testament*. Philadelphia: Fortress Press, 1983.

Dhorme, Edouard P. *A Commentary on the Book of Job*. Translated by H. Knight. London: Thomas Nelson, 1967. Reprint of a major study of Job, first published in 1926.

Gordis, Robert. *The Book of God and Man: A Study of Job*. Chicago: University of Chicago Press, 1965.

Hone, Ralph E., ed. *The Voice Out of the Whirlwind: The Book of Job*. San Francisco: Chandler, 1960. Includes the King James Version of the text of Job and a collection of interpretive essays.

Kallen, H. M. *The Book of Job as a Greek Tragedy*. New York: Moffat, Yard, 1918. A stimulating comparison of Job to the tragedies of Aeschylus and Euripides.

Levenson, Jon D. *Creation and the Persistence of Evil*. San Francisco: Harper & Row, 1988. A lucid study of divine omnipotence and the problem of evil.

MacKenzie, R. A. F., and Murphy, R. E. "Job." In R. E. Brown et al., eds., *The New Jerome Biblical Commentary*, pp. 466–488. Englewood Cliffs, N.J.: Prentice-Hall, 1990. Offers a more conventional reading of the poem.

Pope, Marvin H. *Job*. Anchor Bible, 5th ed. Garden City, N.Y.: Doubleday, 1978. An up-to-date translation with many useful notes.

Sanders, Paul S., ed. *Twentieth-Century Interpretations of the Book of Job: A Collection of Critical Essays*. Englewood Cliffs, N.J.: Prentice-Hall, 1968. Offers a variety of viewpoints.

von Rad, Gerhard. *Wisdom in Israel*. Translated by J. D. Martin. Nashville, Tenn.: Abingdon Press, 1973. An excellent theological study.

Ecclesiastes

KEY THEMES

The Bible's finest example of skeptical wisdom, the book of Ecclesiastes is ascribed to King Solomon but is actually the work of an anonymous Israelite sage who calls himself Koheleth (Qoheleth), one who presides over a circle of learners. Delighting in paradox, Koheleth denies the possibility of knowing anything for sure, except the inescapable facts of death and the ultimate futility of all human effort.

> The race [of life] does not go to the swift, nor battle to the strong; . . . all are subject to time and mischance.
>
> Ecclesiastes 9:11–12

If life is a tragedy to those who feel, as Horace Walpole once remarked in a letter of 1776, it is a comedy to those who think. Although both are works of speculative wisdom that unflinchingly acknowledge the world's moral anarchy, the books of Job and Ecclesiastes present radically different responses to cosmic injustice. Deeply committed to exploring the mystery of undeserved suffering, the author of Job challenges readers to share Job's pain and to question God's purpose in permitting good to go unrewarded and evil to flourish. Whereas Job demands our emotional involvement in contemplating Yahweh's ultimate responsibility for cosmic violence and spiritual evil, the author of Ecclesiastes adopts an emotionally neutral position of coolly ironic detachment. An aloof observer of human folly, he derives a certain dry amusement from his ivory-tower perspective on the human predicament. He is puzzled by Yahweh's apparent unwillingness to enforce ethical principles, but he simply concludes that God chooses to operate with no coherent moral plan—at least not one that human beings can perceive (Eccl. 8:10–14, 16–17).

An element of Proverbs's practical wisdom also permeates the work. Having experienced much, the writer has found that there is "nothing new under the sun" that has not been seen, said, or felt a thousand times before. He therefore advises his readers not to be taken in by the world's sham innovations. True wisdom lies in observing everything, knowing how little has genuine value, and refusing to become committed to the hopeless pursuits to which most people blindly devote their lives.

Although the superscription to the book attributes its authorship to Qoheleth or **Koheleth**, "son of David, king in Jerusalem"—presumably Solomon—most scholars regard this as merely a literary device that offers the writer an elevated position from which imaginatively to experience everything enjoyed by Israel's wealthiest and wisest monarch (Eccles. 1:12–2:12). The Solomon persona is soon dropped and is not referred to after the second chapter.

Koheleth means "one who presides over a congregation," a term the Septuagint translators rendered as "Ecclesiastes," from the Greek *ekklesia* ("assembly"). But Koheleth was not a preacher as some English translations call him; he was a professional sage living in Jerusalem who may have assembled a circle of student-disciples about him. Because the author seems familiar with various strands of Greek philosophy, including that of Heraclitus, Zeno the Stoic, and Epicurus, experts tend to place the book's composition sometime during the Hellenistic era, after the campaigns of Alexander of Macedonia had brought Greek culture to Palestine. In its present form, the book resembles a somewhat rambling essay studded with aphorisms, short poems, and meditations on the futility of existence. An epilog (Eccles. 12:9–14) preserves some later editorial reactions to Koheleth's unorthodox teaching.

The Impossibility of Finding Meaning in Life

Futility of Human Aspiration Most of Ecclesiastes' principal ideas are stated in the first two chapters. The remaining ten mainly illustrate and elaborate the basic perception that the rewards of humanity's customary activities are either short-lived or nonexistent. The book opens with a description of the eternal cycle of nature, in which all things—sun, rivers, seas—are seen as moving in endless circles and eventually returning to their place of origin to begin the same cycle again. It is merely society's bad memory that causes people to imagine that anything new ever occurs. Individual observers simply are not around long enough to recognize that, in the long view, all that is repeats itself without essential change.

Aware that knowledge is a burden because wisdom makes the illusion of happiness impossible, Koheleth nonetheless determines to sample the various pursuits that are commonly believed to provide fulfillment in life. He first tries pleasure, a deliberate savoring of "folly." Although he enjoys being able to "deny his eyes nothing they desired" and "refuse his heart no pleasure" (Eccles. 2:10), he finds the experiment in hedonism empty. He next tries "great" enterprises, such as elaborate building programs, but finds these endeavors equally unsatisfying. He then concentrates on amassing wealth but concludes that this, too, is meaningless. Koheleth acknowledges some valid pleasure in hard work but cautions that all effort is ultimately "vanity" and a "chasing of the wind" (Eccles. 2:1–11).

The author offers several reasons for his negative view of human activity:

1. No matter what he achieves in life, he must ultimately die and leave everything to someone else, perhaps an unworthy heir who will waste it all.
2. Regardless of his successor's conduct, time itself will destroy whatever he builds or creates.
3. No matter how hard he labors or how wisely he plans, life can never compensate him for the toil and sacrifice expended to achieve his goals.
4. Death will inevitably frustrate all his intentions and hopes.

Sheol Lurking behind the author's pessimism is a conviction that death is the absolute end to life, that there is no conscious existence beyond the grave (Sheol) to which all will descend without reaping either rewards or punishments that the present world does not offer. He has no hope that the Deity will distinguish between human and animal lives, let alone between virtue and sin.

> Indeed, the fate of man and beast is identical; one dies, the other too, and both have the self-same breath; man has no advantage over the beast, for all is vanity. Both go to the same place [Sheol]; both originate from the dust; and to the dust both return. Who knows if the spirit of man mounts upward or if the spirit of the beast goes down to the earth?
>
> Ecclesiastes 3:19–21

In view of the traditional Old Testament belief that *all* the dead are indiscriminately housed in the grim underworld of Sheol, the author's question here should be understood as purely rhetorical, emphasizing the inequitable fact that the righteous worshiper fares no better after death than an animal. Indeed, it is better, the writer ironically continues, to be a "live dog" (living Gentile) than a "dead lion" (deceased king of Judah), for "the living know at least that they will die, the dead know nothing; no more reward for them, their memory has passed out of mind. Their loves, their hates, their jealousies, these all have perished, nor will they ever again take part in whatever is done under the sun" (Eccles. 9:5–6).

The dead in Sheol are eternally oblivious, without hope of future resurrection. Hence, Koheleth advises the living to live fully now (Eccles. 9:7–9), for "there is neither achievement, nor planning, nor knowledge, nor wisdom in Sheol where you are going" (Eccles. 9:10). Such counsel resembles that of the Epicurean philosophy, which held that humans are a chance collection of atoms that disintegrates at death. The consciousness or "soul" is as physical as the body and, like the body, perishes utterly.

Like the Roman poet Horace, Koheleth advises the wise person to seize the day and wring from it whatever pleasures are possible.

The writer also entertains some typically Stoic ideas. Chapter 3, which begins with "there is a season for everything, a time for every occupation under heaven," seems to imply that a providence directs all things. Because the author is a Hebrew, he probably regarded Israel's God as the enforcer of the cosmic timetable. But Koheleth's God is apparently interested only in enforcing natural laws, not in giving meaning or order to human lives. Even the Stoic idea of a providentially managed universe is modified by Epicurean warnings that chance typically determines one's fate: "The race [of life] does not go to the swift, nor the battle to the strong; there is no bread for the wise, wealth for the intelligent, nor favor for the learned; all are subject to time and mischance" (Eccles. 9:11). It would be almost impossible to make a declaration more at variance with Israel's Prophets or the Deuteronomistic historians.

Paradoxes   The author's love of paradox is a characteristic of the book that troubles some readers; he seldom makes a statement that he does not somewhere else contradict. Advising one to savor life and to drink wine with a joyful heart (Eccles. 9:7), he also states that it is better to frequent the house of mourning than the house of feasting (Eccles. 7:3). The day of death is better than the day of birth (Eccles. 7:1), but he would rather be a "living dog" than a "dead lion" (Eccles. 9:4). All people are "in the hand of God" (Eccles. 9:1) and should live righteously (Eccles. 8:10–13); but it is as much a mistake to behave too virtuously (Eccles. 7:16) as it is to be excessively wicked (Eccles. 7:17).

These paradoxic views are among the book's chief strengths, however, for the writer is not contradicting himself but asserting that life is too complex for absolute certainties. Just as there is a time to live and a time to die, there are occasions when radically different attitudes and behaviors are appropriate. Koheleth refuses

to be confined to any single philosophical position. Whereas many Greek thinkers made logical consistency the test of truth, Ecclesiastes' author perceives the irrational elements in life and refuses to omit observable variety in the interests of theoretical coherence. In a world where the Deity does not seem to act (and it is significant that Yahweh, the Lord of history, is mentioned by name nowhere in the work), illogic and absurdity must be acknowledged. Koheleth's admonition is to be aware and take no chances.

Postscripts   The book closes with a poignant allegory of old age and death (Eccles. 12:1–8), but later writers added a series of brief postscripts. In the first, a disciple praises Koheleth for his wisdom and "attractive style" and adds a proverb extolling the value of wise teachers (Eccles. 12:9–11). A later editor, perhaps scandalized by the author's human-centered philosophy, warns the reader that writing and studying books is exhausting (Eccles. 12:12). It was perhaps a still later redactor who appended the final admonition to "fear God" and keep the commandments (Eccles. 12:14). The presence of this orthodox advice—inserted elsewhere into Koheleth's text as well (e.g., Eccles. 5:6b)—could have been partly responsible for the eventual admission into the biblical canon of this deeply skeptical, religiously uncommitted book.

RECOMMENDED READINGS

Crenshaw, James L. *Ecclesiastes*. Philadelphia: Westminster Press, 1987.

Gordis, Robert. *Koheleth: The Man and His World.* New York: Jewish Theological Seminary of America Press, 1951. A translation with interpretative notes.

Scott, R. B. Y. *Proverbs and Ecclesiastes.* Anchor Bible, Vol. 18. Garden City, N.Y.: Doubleday, 1965.

Wright, Addison G. "Ecclesiastes (Qoheleth)." In R. E. Brown et al., eds., *The New Jerome Biblical*

Commentary, pp. 489–495. Englewood Cliffs, N.J.: Prentice-Hall, 1990.

———. "The Riddle of the Sphinx: The Structure of the Book of Qoheleth." In L. Crenshaw, ed., *Studies in Ancient Israelite Wisdom*, pp. 245–266. New York: KTAV Publishing House, 1976.

TERMS AND CONCEPTS TO REMEMBER

Behemoth	Philo Judaeus
Bildad	Rahab
Elihu	Sheol
Eliphaz	wisdom literature
Koheleth	Zophar
Leviathan	the Word
Logos	

QUESTIONS FOR REVIEW

1. What diverse categories of literature appear in the third major division of the Hebrew Bible, the Writings? In what ways—subject matter, themes, and theological concerns—do these books commonly differ from the Torah, Deuteronomistic History, or Prophets?

2. Describe some of the principal concerns of "practical" wisdom, such as the pragmatic advice and memorable aphorisms contained in the Book of Proverbs. How does conventional proverbial wisdom differ from the speculative or philosophic wisdom of Job and Ecclesiastes? In what ways do Wisdom writers challenge such assumptions as the belief that God reveals his nature and future plans through the prophets or that he directly manipulates historical events to reward the righteous and to punish wrongdoers?

3. Who puts the idea in Yahweh's mind to test his servant Job? Who are the *bene ha elohim* (sons of God) gathered in the celestial court, and why does Yahweh permit one of them to initiate his affliction of Job? Who are Eli-phaz, Bildad, and Zophar, and of what do they accuse Job? Do these three "friends" interpret Job's misfortunes according to Deuteronomistic principles? In Chapters 9–10 and 14, what does Job say about God's justice? What does Yahweh say to Job from the whirlwind?

4. Koheleth delights in collecting conventional sayings or proverbs that contradict each other. What examples of contradictory statements can you find in Ecclesiastes? Why does Koheleth state that humans cannot recognize any clear moral pattern or unmistakable sign of God's activity in the world? Why does he regard Death as the supreme evil? What were Koheleth's beliefs about humans' posthumous state in Sheol?

QUESTIONS FOR DISCUSSION AND REFLECTION

1. A profound questioning of the conventional view of God, the Book of Job dramatizes the problem of Evil, particularly God's responsibility for undeserved suffering. The author uses none of the traditional explanations—sin inherited from Adam, a demonic rebellion against the Deity, or a future immortality to compensate for earthly pain—to excuse Yahweh's permitting humanity's torment. In keeping his integrity, why must Job refuse to put himself in the wrong? What revelation about his universe does Yahweh make from the whirlwind?

2. Do you think that the Wisdom books can help people cope with the violence and injustice that millions of people endure every day? Are the questions that Job poses about the character of God intensified by historical events like the Holocaust, in which six million Jews—in addition to millions of political dissenters, homosexuals, and gypsies—were deliberately annihilated? Do natural catastrophes over which we have no control and the terminal illnesses of children keep

the Jobian issues alive? What advice would you give to victims of chaotic Evil?

Hebrew Poetry

Like most ancient poetry, that of the Hebrews grew out of dance and song, pleasing the ear not through rhyme but through its musical rhythms. Israel's poets balanced ideas so that the first line of a poem was typically paralleled in the second line by a similar thought expressed in slightly different words. This structure and balance of two poetic lines is called **parallelism**, of which there are three basic types.

In *synonymous parallelism,* the idea in the first part of a line is duplicated in the second part but with a few changes in phrasing:

> Who else is God but Yahweh,
> who else a rock save our God?
> Psalm 18:31

> The heavens declare the glory of God,
> the vault of heaven proclaims his handiwork.
> Psalm 19:1

In *antithetical parallelism,* the first part of a line expresses one thought and the second part its opposite. Proverbs includes many examples of this:

> A wise son is his father's joy,
> a foolish son his mother's grief.
> Proverbs 10:1

> The slack hand brings poverty,
> but the diligent hand brings wealth.
> Proverbs 10:4

Synthetic or *formal parallelism* is not, strictly speaking, parallelism at all. In this poetic form, the first line states a thought, the second adds a new idea, and the third completes the statement. David's lament over the fallen Saul and Jonathan illustrates this pattern:

> O Jonathan, in your death I am stricken,
> I am desolate for you, Jonathan my brother.

> Very dear to me you were,
> your love to me more wonderful
> than the love of a woman.
> 2 Samuel 1:26

This repetition, variation, and expansion of a central theme or idea is characteristic of Hebrew poetry from its earliest war chants to its most sophisticated lyrics. Even in English translation, Hebrew poetry's repetitiveness, concreteness, and imagistic vividness stir the feelings as do few other works of world literature.

Psalms

KEY THEMES

A superb anthology of Hebrew religious poetry, the Book of Psalms covers a wide variety of subjects, including hymns of praise, trust, or thanksgiving (Pss. 8, 19, 23, 24, 46, 93, 96–99, 103, 104, 114, 115, 118, 131, 136, 139, 150); enthronement, royal, or messianic psalms (Pss. 2, 21, 45, 72, 110); psalms of lament, petition, and indebtedness (Pss. 22, 33, 55, 74, 78–80, 89, 105, 106); psalms of blessing or cursing (Pss. 1, 109, 137); and psalms of wisdom, meditation, and instruction (Pss. 33, 37, 49, 52, 73, 90, 112, 119, 128).

> Let everything that breathes praise Yahweh.
> Psalm 150:6

The Book of Psalms is a collection of 150 sacred poems that in their totality express virtually the full range of the Israelites' religious faith. The title derives from the Greek *psalmoi,* which denotes religious songs performed to musical accompaniment. The Septuagint uses *psalmoi* to translate the Hebrew title *Tĕhillim,* "Praises," an appropriate name for an anthology in which many psalms are hymns praising Yahweh.

Although the Psalms as a group have been described as the hymnal of the second Temple, this designation is only partially accurate. Although the psalms were not collected into a book for use in worship until the postexilic period, some of them belong to a much earlier age. Several seem to have been composed specifically for performance at royal coronations, which means that they were written when Davidic kings still reigned in Jerusalem. One, Psalm 45, was used to celebrate the marriage of an Israelite monarch with a foreign bride.

The tradition that David wrote the Psalms is probably owing to David's popular reputation as a musician and poet. In fact, however, the Psalms are Davidic mainly in the sense that they belong to a literary development that may have stemmed from a royal patronage of poetry. The biblical text, while attributing many psalms to David, also ascribes number 72 to Solomon, number 90 to Moses, and various others to Asaph and the sons of Korah. Most scholars believe that few, if any, can be ascribed to David himself. Number 137 unmistakably dates from the Babylonian captivity, as does number 74, which laments the destruction of Solomon's Temple. Few others can be precisely dated. In its final form, the Book of Psalms represents many generations of devotional poetry.

Structurally, Psalms is divided into five different books representing collections of varying ages: (1) Psalms 1–41, which may be the oldest edition of the work; (2) Psalms 42–72; (3) Psalms 73–89; (4) Psalms 90–106; and (5) Psalms 107–150. Psalm 1 acts as a general introduction to the collection; Psalm 150 is a concluding doxology (expression of praise) to the whole. In an effort to organize the poems thematically, scholars have created various categories and classifications, grouping them according to their principal topics or functions. No matter how one classifies them, however, it should be remembered that nearly all psalms were composed for public performance at the Temple as communal expressions of Israel's faith.

In ancient Israel, there seems to have been little distinction between private prayer and public worship. The Israelite attending Temple services communed with God as a member of the covenant community, not as an isolated individual. The Psalms, then, can be said to be cultic songs, performed at the nation's religious festivals, which centered at the Temple. Psalm 24, for example, appears to have been sung at a holy procession during which the Ark of the Covenant was brought to **Zion**, "the mountain of Yahweh," on which the Temple stood.

Israel's Songs of Faith and Sorrow

Hymns of Praise The hymn, or song of praise, typically celebrates God's majesty, creative power, or faithfulness in directing Israel's history. Some, such as Psalm 8, express confidence that God has fashioned an orderly universe, placing man, who is "little less than a god," at the apex of his earthly hierarchy. Declaring that the visible heavens and earth manifest divine glory, Psalm 19 extols the two "books" that together reveal God's perfection: physical nature and Israel's Torah. Psalm 104, which seems to be dependent on an Egyptian hymn to the sun god credited to Pharaoh Akhenaton, similarly pays tribute to the Deity's creative wisdom. Whereas many hymns echo Genesis 1 in presenting God's effortless creativity, others recall his battle with the primordial dragon of chaos—Leviathan, Rahab, or the Sea (Pss. 74:13–14; 89:7–14; 104:7–8, 25–26).

God's intervention in history to rescue Israel offers another occasion for praise: Psalm 78 recounts Yahweh's mighty acts during the Exodus, while Psalm 114 recalls the saving grace of the first Passover. Still others focus on Zion or Jerusalem, the city made holy by God's dwelling in the Temple there (Pss. 46, 48, 84, 87, 122). Another group of "divine enthronement" hymns proclaims Yahweh as Israel's reigning king, lord of history, and universal sovereign (Pss. 47, 93, 95–99).

Psalms of Thanksgiving Psalms of thanksgiving are typically prayers offered in gratitude for God's having saved or delivered the psalmist from danger. Depicting their plight as a torrent of chaotic waters or the abyss of death, the poets rejoice in Yahweh's graciousness for having rescued them (Pss. 18, 30, 40, 66, 116, 118). Probably the best known poem in the collection, Psalm 23 offers thanks for God's comforting presence. Asserting that "Yahweh is my shepherd," the psalmist so beautifully expresses the believer's trust in divine care that in the Judeo-Christian world it has become an inspirational companion at life's major crises.

Royal or Messianic Psalms   As Psalms 95 through 97 honor God's rulership of the world, so "royal" psalms pay tribute to his anointed Davidic kings. Psalm 45 celebrates a royal marriage, while number 101 paints the portrait of an ideal ruler. Celebrating the coronation or installation of Davidic (or perhaps later Maccabean) rulers, Psalms 2, 18, 20, and 110 present Judean monarchs as Yahweh's representatives on earth. Alluding to foreign rulers' chaotic resistance to Yahweh's royal agent, Psalm 2 urges immediate submission to the Judean king because he is also God's adopted son. Similarly, Psalm 110 associates the king with Yahweh's heavenly power, ensuring that royal armies will crush enemy opposition. Connecting the monarch with the priestly tradition of Melchizedek—the king-priest of Salem whom Abraham honored (Gen. 14:17–20)—may indicate that this psalm was composed for a Maccabean (Hasmonean) ruler. This line of non-Davidic kings ruled Judah from about 142 to 63 B.C.E. and typically assumed the high priesthood as well. Because the Maccabees were not descended from the Aaronic line, they may have claimed descent from the mysterious Melchizedek to justify their dual office.

Psalms of Lament, Petition, or Indebtedness "Lament" or "petition" psalms include both individual and communal supplications. In the individual prayers, the petitioner commonly praises God, then asks for rescue from his enemies and vengeance upon them (Ps. 55). Although many laments are concerned with forgiveness of personal sins (Pss. 38, 51), some imply that God himself has been slow to rectify injustice (Pss. 10, 58, 59). Communal laments

such as Psalm 74 stress Israel's misfortunes and beg Yahweh to retaliate against the nation's oppressors. Psalm 44 is particularly interesting in rejecting the traditional deuteronomic view and stating flatly that the people had done nothing wrong but had suffered simply because Yahweh was their God (Ps. 44:17–22). In contrast to psalms of lament or complaint are those that recapitulate Yahweh's past historical acts on Israel's behalf—the exodus and conquest of Canaan, providing reviews of the people's indebtedness to the national Deity (Pss. 78, 105, 106).

Psalms of Blessing and Cursing   Another category—psalms of blessing and cursing—may appear somewhat shocking to modern sensibilities attuned to the concept that religion teaches the return of Good for Evil. Psalm 1, for example, arbitrarily divides all people into two classes—the righteous and the wicked—and promises doom for the latter; no shades of gray are acknowledged. In Psalm 109, the poet enthusiastically lists disasters with which the writer asks God to afflict persons who have offended him or her. These include the wish that one's enemies be condemned by a corrupt judge, punished for the sins of their ancestors, and tormented by the certainty that their orphaned children will be driven in poverty from their homes. Psalm 137, which begins in lyrical beauty ("By the streams of Babylon"), concludes in vindictive fury, promising a blessing on the person who will seize Babylonian infants and dash out their brains against a rock. From these and other examples, it is obvious that the orthodox worshiper regarded retaliatory justice as more religiously fitting than mercy.

Psalms of Wisdom, Meditation, and Instruction There are, to be sure, other possible ways of classifying the various psalms, many of which are mixed types, combining praises with petitions for mercy and curses with requests for divine aid. Psalm 22, for example, begins as a lament ("My God, my God, why have you deserted me?"), changes in verse 22 to a hymn of praise ("Then I shall proclaim your name to my brothers, praise you in full assembly"), and ends on a note of confident triumph ("The whole earth, from end to end, will remember and come back to Yahweh"). Other psalms are mixtures of thanksgiving and instruction, royal and lament, or praise and supplication. In general, however, Psalms constitutes a microcosm of Israel's deepest religious insights and convictions. Although some were composed nearly 3000 years ago, the emotions they inspire are as relevant to the contemporary reader as they were to the "sweet singers of Israel" who brought them into being.

RECOMMENDED READING

Anderson, Bernard W. *Out of the Depths: The Psalms Speak for Us Today.* Philadelphia: Westminster Press, 1974.

Barth, Christoph. *Introduction to the Psalms.* Translated by R. A. Wilson. New York: Scribner, 1966. An illuminating introduction.

Gunkel, Hermann. *The Psalms: A Form-Critical Introduction.* Translated by T. M. Horner. Introduction by James Muilenburg. Philadelphia: Fortress Press, 1967. By a pioneer of the form-critical method.

Kselman, John S., and Barré, Michael L. "Psalms." In R. E. Brown et al., eds., *The New Jerome Biblical Commentary,* pp. 523–552. Includes a brief discussion of each psalm.

Mowinckel, Sigmund. *The Psalms in Israel's Worship,* Vols. 1 and 2. Translated by D. R. Ap-Thomas. Nashville, Tenn.: Abingdon Press, 1962.

Terrien, Samuel L. *The Psalms and Their Meaning for Today.* Indianapolis: Bobbs-Merrill, 1952. A nontechnical study.

Weister, Artur. *The Psalms.* Old Testament Library. Translated by H. Hatwell. Philadelphia: Westminster Press, 1962.

TERMS AND CONCEPTS TO REMEMBER

parallelism   Zion

QUESTIONS FOR REVIEW

1. After reading some of the "royal psalms," such as 2 and 110, explain how you would distinguish between their original application to the coronation of Davidic kings in ancient Israel and their later reinterpretation as messianic prophecies of Christ.

2. Some of the subversive elements permeating wisdom literature can also be found in the Psalms. How do poems like Psalms 89 and 44 challenge the Deuteronomistic theory of history promulgated in the books of Kings?

3. The Psalms constitute some of the world's most beloved poetry, partly because they invite readers to share in the writers' personal relationship to God. How do you account for the emotional power of psalms 23 and 91?

Festival Scrolls

The five books of the Festival Scrolls, or **Megillot**—Ruth, Song of Songs, Ecclesiastes, Lamentations, and Esther—were used, respectively, at the five principal festivals of the Jewish liturgical year (Table 6.1). Placed together as a unit in the Hebrew Bible, they are scattered among the Prophets and Writings in most English translations, a practice that derives from the Septuagint but obscures the books' original relationship. (Because it forms an integral part of Israel's wisdom tradition, Ecclesiastes is discussed along with Job and Proverbs, pp. 208–211.)

Although they differ greatly in style, tone, and theological content, the five scrolls collectively present a multifaceted view of human nature, ranging from the elegant cynicism of Ecclesiastes to the tender love story of Ruth. The Deity is seldom mentioned in these books; except in Lamentations; in Esther he is not referred to at all. There are no legalistic absolutes here such as we find in the Law, or certainties about Yahweh's will such as we hear in the

Table 6.1 The Megillot and Associated Festivals

Book	Festival
Ruth	**Pentecost** The harvest festival
Song of Songs	**Passover** Annual holiday that commemorates the end of slavery for the Israelites in Egypt
Ecclesiastes	**Feast of Tabernacles** or **Feast of Booths** Autumn agricultural feast of thanksgiving
Lamentations	**Fast of the Ninth of Ab** (July–August) Mourning for the destruction of the Jerusalem Temple by the Babylonians in 587 B.C.E. and the Romans in 70 C.E.
Esther	**Purim** or **Festival of Lots** (February–March) Celebration of Jewish deliverance from Persian attack

Prophets. Each book offers a different suggestion for handling life's problems; and each, despite the various crises and sorrows it depicts, affirms that life is good.

Ruth

KEY THEME

A short story set in the time of Israel's judges, Ruth is the tale of a Moabite woman who became one of Yahweh's people and the great-grandmother of King David.

> You left your own father and mother . . .
> to come among a people whom you knew
>   nothing about. . . .
> May Yahweh reward you for what you have
>   done!
>
> Ruth 2:11–12

Ruth's Uniqueness A masterpiece of the storyteller's art, the Book of **Ruth** occupies a distinctive place in the Hebrew Bible. Unlike the books of Esther and Judith, which bear the names of Jewish national heroines, the titular character in Ruth is a foreigner, a person born and bred outside the covenant community. The Book of Ruth is one of only two canonical works named for a central character who is a

non-Israelite; the other work is the Book of Job. Ruth, a childless Moabite widow, and Job, an Edomite sage, also share the distinction of being Gentiles in whom Israel's God takes a special interest. Both Job and Ruth experience a fully realized divine-human relationship, albeit in strikingly different ways. Whereas Job relates to God by challenging him to reveal moral logic in human suffering, Ruth, who also suffers painful losses—her husband, family, and social identity—quietly builds a relationship with Yahweh through the people and events he brings into her life. In Job, God ultimately discloses himself through terrifying images of wild nature and cosmic violence; in Ruth, Yahweh manifests the tender, caring aspects of the divine nature. Although Yahweh does not speak or intervene directly in Ruth, the characters' frequent references to him suggest his invisible presence, gently shaping human destinies.

Like the poet-sage who created Job, Ruth's unknown author takes the radical step of portraying Gentiles as sympathetic figures, worthy of both Yahweh's and the reader's respectful attention. In Deuteronomy and the Deuteronomistic History, Canaanites and other foreigners are categorically denied human value and condemned to mass extermination because their continued existence would tempt Israel to imitate their "abominable" religious practices. As a gentle protest against Israel's xenophobia, the writer depicts a Moabite heroine whose behavior is exemplary and whom Yahweh selects to fulfill his purpose in creating David's royal dynasty.

Moab as Israel's Ancient Enemy   To appreciate the impact of a marriage between an Israelite male in good standing, **Boaz**, and a Moabite, it is illuminating to remember how harshly other Bible writers condemned intermarriage with foreigners. Viewing the practice as "treachery" to God and the Jewish state, Ezra, leader of the postexilic Judeans, forced all of his fellow countrymen to divorce their foreign wives, whether Egyptian, Canaanite, Ammonite, or Moabite (Ezra 9–10). Had Boaz lived in Ezra's Jerusalem, he would have been compelled to send Ruth away, along with any children they might have had.

Ruth's native land, Moab, along with its close ally, Ammon, were traditionally regarded as Israel's enemies. According to Genesis, the Moabites and Ammonites were descended from Lot's incestuous union with his two daughters (Gen. 19:30–38). This tale of Moabite origins was intended to denegrate the entire nation. During the period of the Judges, the purported time of Ruth's story, a Moabite king named Eglon reportedly conquered and "enslaved" Israel (at least part of Benjamin's territory), tyrannizing over them for eighteen years (Judg. 3:12–30). For some time Moab was incorporated into David's empire. Later, it successfully revolted against Israelite domination and regained its national independence (cf. 2 Sam. 8: 2; 2 Kings 3; see also Part 4, the Moabite Stone). The Book of Ruth, however, offers no hint of hostile relations between citizens of Moab and Israel—or between their respective gods, **Chemosh** and Yahweh; the author's purpose is to represent a Moabite woman as the peer of biblical heroines such as "Rachel and Leah who together built up the House of Israel" (Ruth 4:11).

Date and Placement in the Canon   In the Hebrew Bible, the Book of Ruth stands first in the Megillot, probably because it is set "in the days of the Judges" (1:1), chronologically the earliest period attributed to any of the five scrolls. In Jewish liturgy, Ruth was read at Pentecost, a harvest festival also called the Feast of Weeks, or Shabuoth. Following the Septuagint order, most English Bibles insert Ruth between Judges and 1 Samuel, a placement that puts the gentle figure of Ruth between the barbarous account of the Levite's murdered concubine (Judg. 19–20) and the story of Hannah's answered prayers to conceive a son, Samuel (1 Sam. 1–2). Although Ruth's story supposedly took place when warlike Judges led Israel (see Part 4), the setting at Bethlehem is remarkably peaceful, a serene landscape of farm laborers harvesting rich fields of grain. Unlike the Torah narratives, the Deuteronomistic History, or the Books of Esther and Judith, Ruth is marked by the absence of great historical events, wars, or other violence. Focusing exclusively on the private lives of three ordinary people, Ruth shows God unobtrusively operating even in the most intimate of human relationships—friendship, love, and marriage.

Although the action takes place in the premonarchical period, Ruth is a difficult book for which to establish a date of origin; there is no scholarly agreement about when it was composed. Some critics think that it was written while Judean kings still reigned, as part of a literature celebrating Davidic ancestry. Others assign it to the postexilic period, seeing in Ruth's story a counterargument to the prohibition against foreign wives enunciated in Ezra and Nehemiah. (The prophet Malachi's protest against divorce—separating from the bride of one's youth—is thought to reflect similar opposition to the Ezra-Nehemiah policies (Mal. 2).)

Structure and Content of the Book   Literary critics have noted that Ruth is artfully crafted, with a symmetrical structure in which the three sections of the book's first half (Chs. 1–2) parallel, in reverse order, three sections of the second half (Chs. 3–4). (See the recommended reading, Trible.) Most scholars believe that the narrative featuring Naomi, Ruth, and Boaz was orally composed and transmitted for many generations before being written down. Advanced largely through dialogue, the simple plot is skillfully developed. Because of a famine that afflicts Israel, the Judean Elimelech, his wife **Naomi**, and their two sons settle in Moab, which is located on Israel's southeastern border. After Elimelech dies, his two sons marry Moabite women, Orpah and Ruth, for whom Naomi develops a strong affection. Ten years later, the sons also die, leaving Naomi alone in a country typically regarded as enemy territory.

Ruth and Naomi   When she hears that Israel's famine has ended and grain has become plentiful in Judah, Naomi determines to return to her home city of Bethlehem, advising her two widowed daughters-in-law to go back to their families and find new husbands. After expressing warm feelings for Naomi, Orpah returns to her people, but Ruth refuses to part from the Israelite woman she has come to love. In words that the King James translation has made a classic expression of devotion, Ruth declares, "Entreat me not to leave thee, or to return from following after thee: for whither thou goest, I will go: and where thou lodgest, I will lodge: thy people shall be my people, and thy God my God" (Ruth 1:16). The intensity of Ruth's wish to identify herself completely with Naomi is matched in the Bible only by Jonathan's passionate attachment to young David. Jonathan "made a pact . . . to love him [David] as his own soul" (1 Sam. 18:1–5; cf. 2 Sam. 1:26).

Ruth and Boaz   Naomi and Ruth travel together to Bethlehem—future birthplace of King David—where, according to the Mosaic provision for the poor, Ruth gleans the fields of Boaz, a relation of Elimelech. Following Naomi's shrewd advice, Ruth makes a nocturnal visit to Boaz, who falls in love with her. In one

of the fine psychological touches of this brief story, the middle-aged Boaz praises the young Moabite woman for having the perception to prefer him to a younger man. The kindly and wealthy landowner then makes sure that one of Elimelech's nearer kinsmen does not care to exercise his legal right to redeem—that is, to buy from Naomi—her dead husband's property, and with it Ruth's hand in marriage. Then Boaz is free to do so. By acquiring the dead man's estate and marrying Ruth, Boaz acts to perpetuate Elimelech's memory in Israel. Although Ruth is actually Elimelech's son's widow, in this legal arrangement she ranks as Elimelech's widow so that a son later born to Ruth and Boaz will in effect belong to Naomi and Elimelech, ensuring the dead man an heir. Rejoicing that "a son has been born for Naomi," the women of Bethlehem name the child Obed. This child grows up to become the father of Jesse, the father of David, king of Israel.

Although Yahweh neither speaks nor appears in the narrative, the Book of Ruth illustrates that Yahweh actively assists both the living and the dead. His is the invisible presence that guides the lives of Naomi, Ruth, and Boaz. He is the life force that ensures that a man long dead will have a grandson to perpetuate his name and that an aged widow, Naomi, will again nurse her "own son" (Ruth 4:13–16). That son, in turn, will become the grandfather of David, founder of Israel's God-appointed royal family. Yahweh's selection of a Moabite woman—one of the people of Chemosh—to carry out his purpose suggests that Gentiles, as well as Israelites, are part of the divine plan for humanity. Those who insist on ethnic exclusivity, such as Ezra, Nehemiah, or the Deuteronomistic historian, do not necessarily express the attitude of Israel's universal God.

RECOMMENDED READING

Campbell, Edward F. *Ruth*. Garden City, N.Y.: Doubleday, 1975.

Trible, Phyllis. "Ruth, Book of." In D. N. Freedman, ed., *The Anchor Bible Dictionary,* Vol. 5, pp. 842–847. New York: Doubleday, 1992. A clear summary of current scholarship.

Sasson, Jack M. *Ruth.* Baltimore: Johns Hopkins University Press, 1979.

Song of Songs

KEY THEME

A cycle of erotic poems celebrating sensual love, the Song of Songs presents a lyric drama of human passion.

> I am sick with love.
>   Song of Songs 5:8

The only erotic poetry in the Bible, the Song of Songs defies easy classification or interpretation. Its frank celebration of sexual passion challenges interpreters to explain the book's presence in sacred scripture. Puzzled or embarrassed by the poet's joyous reveling in physical sensuality, many commentators have labeled the work an **allegory**—a fictional narrative in which characters, objects, and actions symbolize some higher truth. To Jews, the Song became an allegory of Yahweh's love for Israel; to Christians, it became an expression of Christ's love for his "bride," the Church. To most modern scholars, this collection of love lyrics is precisely what it appears to be, an affirmation of the human capacity for sexual pleasure.

That ancient commentators, both Jewish and Christian, regarded the book as functioning allegorically, however, suggests that the poem's eroticism may have a spiritual dimension. Perhaps suggesting the psychological affinity between sexual and spiritual ecstasy, in the final section the poet evokes cosmic images of death, the afterworld, and a "flame" (divine love) emanating from Yahweh. Equating the power of love with that of death, and sexual jealousy with the inexorability of Sheol, the subterranean

abode of the dead, the author also invokes Yahweh, the "jealous God who acts as Israel's lover" (cf. Exod. 20:1–5; Hos. 2–3). Israel's God is a passionate Deity whose yearning for human reciprocity resembles "a flash of fire, a flame of Yahweh himself" (Song 8:6–7).

Authorship and Purpose   Like the books of Proverbs and Ecclesiastes, the Song of Songs is traditionally ascribed to Solomon (3:1), paradoxically famous for both his wisdom and his 1,000 wives and concubines. Although presumably an expert in the art of love, Solomon, nonetheless, is not thought to be the author. Some scholars believe that these erotic poems originated as hymns associated with a Near Eastern fertility goddess, such as Asherah, who was married to the god El (in Ugaritic lore) or Baal (in Canaanite tradition). If so, the Asherah-El-Baal cultic elements have entirely disappeared from the extant texts. Other scholars propose that these verses were intended to be sung at country weddings in ancient Israel.

Assuming that the Song of Songs echoes rustic marriage rites, editors of the Jerusalem Bible have edited the various lyrics to form a poetic drama in which individual lyrics are alternately sung by the bride and bridegroom. With choral responses interspersed throughout the work, it is easy to imagine the Jerusalem Bible version as a music drama or chorale of the kind performed at bucolic weddings. More recent scholarship, however, tends to reject this view of the collection. Noting that references to marriage are almost entirely absent from the poems—the notable exception is an idealized description of Solomon's wedding procession (3:6–11)—most scholars now look for other ways to understand or classify them.

Of surviving ancient Near Eastern literature, the Song of Songs has the closest affinity with Egyptian love poetry, in which the female beloved is typically addressed as "sister" (4:8–10). Regardless of their literary precedents or original function, however, this cycle of love songs enthusiastically validates the universality of human desire, its tantalizing frustrations and joyous fulfillments. Whereas some poems lament the lover's absence, others rejoice in physical proximity with an extravagance of language unmatched elsewhere in the Bible. Intoxicated by emotion, the poet pours forth torrents of images that compare the human body—both male and female—to fruits, flowers, animals (both domestic and wild), and even topographical features. Containing numerous terms, including geographical place-names, that appear nowhere else in Scripture, the lyrics place the lovers in lush, scented environments where passion can flourish unrestrained. All of nature, rich in nourishment and sensation, provides metaphors for the lovers' intensely focused enjoyment of each others' bodies. As the pair create a private Eden in their passionate absorption in one another, love overwhelms all thoughts of the outside world of mundane life. Only at the poem's conclusion is human love placed in a larger context that recognizes the existence of joy's limits: Death, the Underworld, and Yahweh. Even then, however, love is asserted to be as "strong as Death," and Yahweh, "a flash of fire," is himself both the source and paradigm of human love (8:6–7).

Writing in prose, a later commentator validated the poet's vision of love's surpassing value: If a rich man were to offer all of his wealth in exchange for love, "contempt is all he would purchase" (8:7). Both elusive and irresistible, human love is paradoxical: Desired by all, it cannot be commanded.

RECOMMENDED READING

Murphy, Roland E. "Song of Songs, Book of." In Freedman, D. N. *The Anchor Bible Dictionary,* Vol. 6, pp. 150–155. New York: Doubleday, 1992. Surveys the Song's history of interpretation.

Pope, Marvin H. *The Song of Songs.* Anchor Bible. Garden City, N.Y.: Doubleday, 1977.

Lamentations

KEY THEMES

Ascribed to Jeremiah, Lamentations is a collection of five poetic dirges over the Babylonian destruction of Jerusalem. The lyrics explore the causes of evil, suffering, and Yahweh's reasons for permitting the triumph of unbelieving nations.

> For the Lord does not reject mankind
>   forever and ever.
> If he has punished, he has compassion
>   so great is his kindness;
> since he takes no pleasure in abasing
>   and afflicting the human race.
>   Lamentations 3:31–33

Dirges and Laments   Lamentations is the work that is chanted in sorrow when Jews gather each year to mourn the destruction of Jerusalem. According to tradition, the city fell to the Babylonians on August 9, 587 B.C.E., and again on the same day and month to the Romans in 70 C.E. The five poetic dirges and laments composing this brief book express the people's collective grief for the loss of their holy city. While the prophetic books record public pronouncements of doom against the Judean capital, Lamentations embodies the private anguish of individuals who witnessed the fulfillment of Yahweh's harsh judgment.

Although a relatively late tradition assigns Lamentations to the prophet Jeremiah, its authorship is unknown. The book itself does not mention the writer, and many scholars believe that it is the work of two or three different poets. The oldest parts are thought to be Chapters 2 and 4, which were written shortly after Jerusalem's capture by Nebuchadnezzar. Chapters 1 and 3 appeared somewhat later in the sixth century B.C.E., and Chapter 5 at some point between 540 and 325 B.C.E. The first four poems are **acrostics**: Each has twenty-two verses in which the first word of each verse begins with a different letter of the alphabet in sequential order. The last chapter also has twenty-two verses, but these are not arranged alphabetically.

From such artifice, it is apparent that Lamentations is not a spontaneous outpouring of emotion, although the poets' feelings run deep and many passages are extremely moving. Chapters 2 and 4 seem to be the work of an eyewitness to the horror of the holy city's devastation:

> My eyes wasted away with weeping,
> my entrails shuddered,
> my liver spilled on the ground
> at the ruin of the daughters of my people,
> as children, mere infants, fainted
> in the squares of the citadel.
>
> They kept saying to their mothers,
> "Where is the bread?"
> as they fainted like wounded men
> in the squares of the city,
> as they poured out their souls
> on their mothers' breasts.
>
> Lamentations 2:11–12

The poet reports that some mothers ate the flesh of their infants during the famine caused by Nebuchadnezzar's siege. Formerly vigorous young men, wasted "thin as a stick," collapsed from hunger and died in the streets (Lam. 4: 7–10). Corpses became too numerous to bury.

The writers of Chapters 1, 2, and 4 agree that Jerusalem's fall was the direct result of its sins, particularly those of the priests and prophets who had falsely promised deliverance (Lam. 4:13). The question now is, Has Yahweh forsaken his people permanently? Because they have suffered so greatly for their mistakes, will Yahweh at last show pity? Perhaps because he lived to see Jerusalem's restoration, the poet of Chapter 3 is confident that Yahweh takes no pleasure in continuing to abuse his human creation (Lam. 3:31–33). But the writer of Chapter 5, to whom Yahweh's future intentions remain a mystery, simply asks,

> You cannot mean to forget us for ever?
> You cannot mean to abandon us for good?
>
> Lamentations 5:20

RECOMMENDED READING

Gordis, Robert. *The Song of Songs and Lamentations,* rev. ed. New York: KTAV Publishing House, 1974.

Gottwald, Norman K. "Book of Lamentations." In G. A. Buttrick, ed., *The Interpreter's Dictionary of the Bible,* Vol. 3, pp. 61–62. New York and Nashville, Tenn.: Abingdon Press, 1962.

Hillers, Delbert R. *Lamentations.* Garden City, N.Y.: Doubleday, 1972.

Esther

KEY THEME

Depicting the plight of Jews scattered throughout the Persian Empire, Esther is a strongly nationalistic story in which a beautiful Jewish queen risks her life to help save her people from Haman's plot to annihilate them. This secular tale of heroic resistance to Gentile persecution celebrates the origin of the festival of Purim.

> The king granted the Jews, in whatever city they lived, the right to . . . slaughter and annihilate any armed force of any people . . . that might attack them.
>
> Esther 8:11

Although the apocryphal Greek version of the tale of Esther reverts to the traditional view that Israel's God controls history and manipulates events to save his people, the Hebrew version of the story offers virtually no religious teaching. Though the Jews are here threatened with genocide, the writer does not mention the Deity but implies that if Jews are to survive in a hostile world, it will not be through divine intervention but by their own efforts. Set in the days when **Ahasuerus (Xerxes I)** ruled the Persian Empire (486–465 B.C.E.), the tale purposes to explain how the joyous nationalistic feast of Purim came to be established. A long short story or novella, the Book of Esther lacks the

This bas-relief at Persepolis, the Greek-designed capital of the Persian Empire, shows an enthroned Darius I (522–486 B.C.E.), with his son and successor Xerxes I (486–465 B.C.E.) standing directly behind him. Both emperors launched ill-fated invasions of Greece, only to be routed by the Athenians and their allies at Marathon (490 B.C.E.) and Salamis (480 B.C.E.). (Courtesy of The Oriental Institute of The University of Chicago)

sensitive characterization of the Book of Ruth but offers instead an exciting melodrama.

King Ahasuerus's Edict   When Ahasuerus divorces Queen **Vashti** for her refusal to exhibit herself before his male courtiers, **Mordecai**, who is both a supremely devout Jew and a loyal subject of the Persian emperor, maneuvers events so that his beautiful cousin **Esther**, whom he has adopted (Esther 2:7), becomes queen. In the meantime, Mordecai has discovered a conspiracy against the emperor's life but is able to send a warning in time so that the conspirators are discovered and executed. Although Mordecai's deed is recorded in the Persian court annals, Ahasuerus does not know that he owes his life to a Jewish subject.

Haman, whom the emperor has promoted to chief administrator at the court, becomes furious when Mordecai refuses to bow down before him and resolves not only to murder the Jew but also to liquidate his entire race. Telling Ahasuerus that an "unassimilated" people who obey their own customs rather than the emperor's laws are settled throughout the empire, Haman persuades Ahasuerus to issue an edict permitting their mass execution and confiscation of their property. Haman casts lots (*purim*,

hence the name of the festival) to determine the date of the massacre, which is to be the thirteenth day of the month of Adar (February-March).

Haman Outwitted   Having previously been commanded by Mordecai to keep her Jewishness a secret, Esther is now persuaded to appear unbidden before the emperor—even though to intrude on the royal presence uninvited carries a penalty of death—and beg him to rescind his decree. As Haman erects a lofty gallows on which to hang Mordecai for disobeying the chief vizier, Ahasuerus learns from the court annals that Mordecai has saved his life, and Haman is duped into suggesting high honors for the emperor's rescuer. Esther then reveals Haman's evil machinations, which were intended to destroy her, a Jew, and Mordecai, to whom Ahasuerus owes his life. Dramatic justice is served when Haman is hanged on the gallows he had built for Mordecai.

Feast of Purim   Unfortunately, the Jews living in the Persian Empire are still in danger, for the law of the Medes and Persians does not permit the theoretically infallible monarch to retract his orders. Ahasuerus does, however, issue a second edict instructing all Jews to fortify and defend themselves, which they do with spectacular success (Esther 8). Chapter 9 recounts how the Jews slew all who would have murdered them, after which they hold a victory celebration, the feast of **Purim**. The irony is that their triumph falls on the very day that Haman had selected for their extermination.

Most scholars, Jewish as well as Christian, regard the Book of Esther as patriotic fiction rather than historical fact: despite its authentic picture of Persian court life and political intrigue during the fifth century B.C.E., the book contains several historical errors. Although we know much of Xerxes I, for example, there is no record that he was married to Vashti or that he had a Jewish queen named Esther. The Persian Empire was never (as the book insists) divided into 127 different provinces, nor did Xerxes order Jews in his territories to attack his Persian subjects. Mordecai, moreover, is said to have been deported to Persia from Babylon, which would make him at least 100 years old during Xerxes' reign, and the alluring Esther could not have been much younger.

There are, then, decidedly more fictional than historical elements in the story. The name Esther itself is a variation of "Ishtar," the Babylonian goddess of love and fertility. The name Mordecai derives from "Marduk," the leading Babylonian deity. Indeed, some interpreters have suggested that the book's Jewish author deliberately fictionalized an old Babylonian myth in which Marduk defeats his demonic enemies (Haman and his cohorts in this narrative). Certainly, the present book is a clear-cut example of the forces of Good triumphing over Evil as they did in the ancient myth.

At all events, Esther has found a vital place in the Jewish consciousness; to many pious Jews, it is the most significant book in the Megillot. The annual reading of the book at Purim does not merely commemorate the Jews' turning the tables on their enemies in ancient Persia; it is also a profound statement about the heroic resistance necessary, in the face of overwhelming anti-Semitic aggression, to ensure Jewish survival at any place and any time in the modern world.

RECOMMENDED READING

Berg, Sandra B. *The Book of Esther.* Chico, Calif.: Scholars Press, 1979.

Dumm, Demetrius. "Esther." In R. E. Brown et al., eds., *The New Jerome Biblical Commentary,* pp. 576–579. Englewood Cliffs, N.J.: Prentice-Hall, 1990.

Humphreys, W. Lee. "Book of Esther." In G. A. Buttrick, ed., *The Interpreter's Dictionary of the Bible: Supplementary Volume,* pp. 279–281. Nashville, Tenn.: Abingdon Press, 1976.

LaCocgne, André. *The Feminine Unconventional: Four Subversive Figures in Israel's Tradition.* Minneapolis, Minn.: Fortress Press, 1990.

Moore, Carey A. *Esther.* Garden City, N.Y.: Doubleday, 1971.

TERMS AND CONCEPTS TO REMEMBER

acrostic	Mordecai
Ahasuerus (Xerxes I)	Naomi
allegory	Passover
Boaz	Pentecost
Chemosh	Purim (Festival
Esther	of Lots)
Fast of the Ninth	Ruth
of Ab	Feast of Tabernacles
Haman	(Feast of Booths)
Megillot	Vashti

QUESTIONS FOR REVIEW

1. Why were the five books of the Megillot placed together as a discrete unit of the Hebrew Bible? What common interests or themes connect such diverse works as Lam-

entations and the Song of Solomon? What place does a work of erotic poetry have in the Bible?

2. Why does the author of Ruth make his heroine a Moabite? Do you think that the writer is reacting against the ethnic exclusivism advocated by the Deuteronomistic historians and the books of Ezra and Nehemiah (discussed later in this section)? Compare and contrast the respective characters and situations of Ruth, Naomi, and Esther. How does Esther act to save her people?

Chronicles, Ezra, and Nehemiah: Reinterpreting Israel's History for the Postexilic World

During their exile in Babylon, many Judean leaders had followed Jeremiah's advice, buying property and putting down roots in Mesopotamian soil (Jer. 29). When Cyrus, emperor of the new Persian Empire, captured Babylon (539 B.C.E.) and issued his famous decree permitting the exiles to return to their homeland, many displaced Judeans opted to remain in their adopted country. Those remaining included an intellectual leadership that, over many generations, produced extensive commentaries on the Torah, adapting Mosaic laws to new circumstances of Jewish life in the **Diaspora** ("scattering" of Jews abroad). Approximately 1100 years after the exile had begun, Mesopotamian Jewish scholars compiled the Babylonian **Talmud**, a vast compendium of oral tradition that eventually became the supreme guidebook of rabbinical Judaism. (See Part 8.)

Another group of Judeans had fled Jerusalem's ruins and taken refuge in Egypt, where they established permanent settlements. After Alexander of Macedonia conquered Egypt (c. 330 B.C.E.) and founded the great port city of Alexandria, a large colony of Jews flourished there. From the thriving Alexandrian commu-

nity came the first translation of the Hebrew Bible into Greek, the Septuagint. Alexandrian Jews also produced a significant body of original literature, including the Wisdom of Solomon, which became part of Roman Catholic and Greek Orthodox Bibles.

The group most responsible for the creation of the Hebrew Bible, however, was a relatively small contingent of priests, scribes, and other influential leaders who returned from Babylon to Judah after 538 B.C.E. Perhaps inspired by the optimistic rhetoric of Second Isaiah, the first exiles to make the arduous trek back to Judah found conditions very different from those the prophet had envisioned. Instead of recovering paradise, they had to eke out a bare subsistence in an impoverished land that Nebuchadnezzar's troops had thoroughly ravaged. Disappointed and dispirited, the former refugees were motivated to rebuild Yahweh's Temple only when the prophets Haggai and Zechariah promised that the "treasures of all the nations" would flow in to finance the project (Hag. 2:7).

Adjusting to New Political Realities

Haggai and Zechariah also had fed the people's hopes that their new masters, the Persians, might allow a restoration of the Davidic monarchy. Because the Persian emperor had appointed **Zerubbabel**, a grandson of the deposed King Jehoiachin, as governor of Judah, the next step might be to recognize him as a legitimate king (1 Chron. 3:17–19). The Persians apparently refused to take that step, however, and Zerubbabel's unexplained disappearance from the scene left David's throne—in spite of Yahweh's sworn oath (2 Sam. 7; Ps. 44)—permanently vacant. The postexilic Judean community, forced to grapple with irreversible change, entered a new phase of history. Instead of being ruled by Yahweh's anointed kings, Judah, stripped of political or economic importance, would henceforth be led by anointed priests. As the covenant community had survived the transition from charismatic Judges to divinely ordained monarchs almost five centuries earlier, the covenant people of Judah now would prosper without Davidic leadership or even national autonomy. Reaffirming the Mosaic law as their eternal heritage, Judean priests resolved to maintain their people's identity as a Torah-keeping group. Taking the lead from a new Joshua—the Aaronic High Priest who, with Zerubbabel, helped lead postexilic Judeans—the covenant people could, in effect, become a theocratic "nation of priests."

The Work of the Chronicler

Recognizing that Yahweh, Lord of history, had radically changed the direction of Israel's historical development, postexilic scribes undertook the necessary task of reinterpreting the nation's past. Whereas the first edition of the Deuteronomistic History had seen Israel's story culminating in Josiah's splendid reforms, the second edition, revised during the Babylonian exile, had presented it as culminating in Yahweh's destruction of the nation. Writing more than a century after the exiles' return, an anonymous priestly author known as the Chronicler again surveyed Israel's past, this time discovering national fulfillment in the restoration of Yahweh's worship at the rebuilt Jerusalem Temple. In the Chronicler's view, Israel's destiny was not necessarily to exercise political power on the world stage, but to promote Yahweh's cult with ethical and ritual purity—a view that historical events seemed to vindicate.

Authorship Because of their generally consistent priestly orientation, the four books of 1 and 2 Chronicles, Ezra, and Nehemiah are commonly assigned to the same redactor or editor. Many scholars, however, dispute the claim that the same person—the Chronicler—compiled all four, pointing to differences in attitude and theology that distinguish Ezra or Nehemiah from the two books of Chronicles. Although

some commentators argue that the same priestly scribe provided the final editing of the four volumes, preserving older material that differed from his viewpoint and adding commentary to impart thematic unity, the majority of scholars now believe that the books of Ezra and Nehemiah, which underwent a series of complex revisions before reaching their present state, represent the work of an author different from the writer responsible for 1 and 2 Chronicles.

Sources and Themes The books of 1 and 2 Chronicles are largely rewrites of Samuel and Kings, but with a significant change in emphasis. Instead of portraying David and Solomon as creators of a powerful—though short-lived—Israelite empire, the Chronicler depicts them as priest-kings whose main concern was always the building, furnishing, and maintenance of the Jerusalem Temple. The stream of Israelite history thus flows not toward the goal of imperial success but toward the "proper liturgical service of Yahweh" at Jerusalem's rebuilt sanctuary—a religious mission that could be carried out regardless of Judah's political fortunes (2 Chron. 35:16, 36:22–23; Ezra 1:1–11; 5–7).

Samuel and Kings are the Chronicler's primary sources. He also borrows genealogical lists from the Pentateuch and passages from various psalms, as well as otherwise unknown documents, such as the "Annals of Samuel the seer, the Annals of Nathan the prophet, and the Annals of Gad the seer" (1 Chron. 29:29–30; see also references to Solomonic archives [2 Chron. 9:29] and those of Hezekiah [2 Chron. 32:32]). As for the historical reliability of the Chronicles material that did not appear in the Deuteronomistic History, scholars disagree about whether added—and extensive—passages about Hezekiah's reforms (2 Chron. 29–31) and Manasseh's repentance (2 Chron. 33) represent the author's use of authentic sources or his own creative imagination. As scholars have observed, the account of Manasseh's sins, deportation to Babylon, and promotion of religious reforms following his return to Jerusalem exactly parallel what happened to Judah. In the Chronicler's revisions, Manasseh comes to embody the covenant people's collective experience, that of a sinner redeemed by suffering and repentance.

The two parts of Chronicles were originally one volume, until the Septuagint editors divided the work into two scrolls entitled *Paralipomenon,* meaning "what was omitted" (that is, information not included in the books of Samuel and Kings). When translating the Latin Vulgate, Jerome called the work *Chronicon,* the Latin name from which the English title is derived. This closely approximates the Hebrew title, *Dibre Hayamim,* which means "annals" (literally, "the book of the acts of days"). As with Ezra and Nehemiah, the books of Chronicles show an overriding interest in genealogies (especially of priestly families), dates, Temple liturgy, and sacerdotal functions.

1 Chronicles

KEY THEMES

First Chronicles retells the story of King David's career from a priestly viewpoint, emphasizing his association with the Ark of the Covenant, the Jerusalem cult, and the elaborate preparations for building the Temple. Portraying David as a monarch-priest, the account omits unflattering material from the older histories, such as David's adultery with Bathsheba and murder of Uriah (Chs. 10–29).

> David grew greater and greater, and
> Yahweh Sabaoth [of armies] was with him.
> 1 Chronicles 11:9

First Chronicles opens with a genealogical survey of world history, beginning with Adam and culminating in lists of Judeans (particularly Levites) who returned from the Babylonian captivity (1 Chron. 1:1–9:34). After a brief and

negative judgment on the reign of King Saul—whose failure is set as a foil to his successor (9:35–10:14)—the remaining twenty chapters focus on King David's splendid accomplishments. In idealizing David, the Chronicler reminds his audience that past faithfulness to Yahweh's covenant brought Israel unprecedented blessings, thus recalling them to their present religious obligations.

In Chapters 11–29 David is depicted not as a military and administrative genius but as a devout religionist who establishes the elaborate Temple cult, contributes heavily to its support, and recruits whole retinues of artisans and musicians for its services. In the Chronicler's story, preparation for building the sanctuary becomes the main goal of David's kingship, as constructing, dedicating, and maintaining the sanctuary became the chief objective of Solomon's administration.

David as King-Priest

Times of David   With regard to the times of King David, the author's major alterations of his source material include the following:

1. Making Saul's death a judgment caused by his visit to the witch of Endor (1 Chron. 10:13–14), an obvious betrayal of the Yahwist cult

2. Having David proclaimed king of all Israel at Hebron (1 Chron. 12:23–40), when historically only Judah first acknowledged him there

3. Interpolating a long prayer by David when he brings the Ark of the Covenant to Jerusalem (1 Chron. 16:7–36), thus clothing the monarch in priestly garb

4. Insisting that David contributed enormous sums of gold toward building the Temple as a good example to later Israelites (1 Chron. 22:14–16; 28:14–19)

5. Stating that David was responsible for assigning the Levites—cantors, gate keepers, and bakers—their Temple duties (1 Chron. 23:2–27:34)

6. Asserting that David determined the plans, furnishings, and functions of the Temple

and that Solomon merely carried them out (1 Chron. 28:1–31)

7. Deleting all references to David's misdeeds, including his adultery with Bathsheba and murder of Uriah

8. Attributing to David a final speech in which he urges generous financial support for the construction and upkeep of the Temple (1 Chron. 29:1–20)

9. Implying that David transferred the reins of power to Solomon while he was still alive and that Solomon ascended the throne without opposition (1 Chron. 29:22–28)

The Chronicler's primary intent here is not to provide fresh insights into David and Solomon (whose faults, recorded in 2 Samuel and 1 Kings, he omits) but to insist that the nation's principal mission is to worship Yahweh wholeheartedly and to demonstrate that the failure of later kings to honor the Jerusalem sanctuary led to the monarchy's collapse. By showing how royal apostasy and lack of zeal for Temple worship caused the nation's downfall, he hopes to rouse his audience from its apathy and revive participation in the Levitical services. And although his distortions of historical fact to make this point may be debatable, his thesis is nevertheless consistent with the rest of Israel's sacred history.

2 Chronicles

KEY THEMES

Continuing the priestly saga of preparation for and building of the Jerusalem Temple, 2 Chronicles depicts Solomon's reign as almost exclusively focused on the national cult and then recapitulates the narrative of Judah's Davidic rulers (derived largely from 1 and 2 Kings) through the reign of Josiah (Chs. 1–35). Adding a claim that Mannasseh allegedly repented of his apostasy (Ch. 33), the book ends with Cyrus's

decree restoring the exiled Jews to their homeland (Ch. 36).

> I [Yahweh] chose Jerusalem for my name to make its home there, and I chose David to rule over Israel my people.
> 2 Chronicles 6:6–7

Second Chronicles opens with the glories of Solomon's reign and then surveys Judah's history from the time of his successor, Rehoboam, to the issuing of Cyrus's edict permitting the return of the Jews to Jerusalem. Unlike the author of Kings, the Chronicler does not attempt to give a parallel history of the divided kingdom but concentrates almost entirely on Judah, referring to the northern kingdom only when it concerns Judah's affairs. As in the first book, the writer's interest revolves around the Temple.

The Royal Temple Cult

Solomon to Josiah   The first nine chapters recount the splendors of Solomon's legendary wealth and his building program, emphasizing the construction, dedication, and divine consecration of the Temple; nothing is said about Solomon's weaknesses or eventual corruption by his many foreign wives. He repeats the dramatic confrontation between Rehoboam and the rebellious northern tribes who withdraw from the monarch when the new king refuses to modify his harsh policies (2 Chron. 10–11).

Thereafter, the Chronicler rapidly scans the line of Judean rulers, pausing to elaborate on the reigns of four "good" kings—Asa, Jehoshaphat, Hezekiah, and Josiah—and to expand passages dealing with the prophets. He devotes much more space than the author of Kings to enumerating the reforms of Hezekiah, who is miraculously delivered from the Assyrian menace, and Josiah, whose reinstitution of the Passover feast became a standard for later observances (2 Chron. 28–32 and 34–35).

Manasseh's Sins and Repentance   Between these two approved monarchs came **Manasseh**, whose forty-five-year reign exceeded that of any other Judean king (2 Chron. 33). 2 Kings lists Manasseh's crimes, which include burning his son as a pagan sacrifice, but the text is silent on his alleged repentance. The Chronicler, however, states that while a captive of the Assyrians in Babylon, Manasseh sought Yahweh, who relented and restored him to his throne (though the Chronicler does not explain how this astonishing reversal occurred). Manasseh then personally conducted a religious reform, cleansing the Temple of the pagan cults he had established there and rebuilding Yahweh's altar. The writer notes that the prayer that moved Yahweh to rescue the former "black magician" was preserved in the Annals of Hozai (2 Chron. 33:20), which is not the same as the Prayer of Manasseh included in the Apocrypha.

Unexpectedly, portions of 2 Chronicles make somewhat more interesting reading than does the rather dry version of David's reign in the first book, where the author's ecclesiastical apparatus overwhelms the narrative. Although 2 Chronicles repeats much of 2 Kings, it adds some colorful details and ends with a hopeful promise of the people's liberation. As the last book in the Hebrew Bible canon, it apparently anticipates a future for Judaism in which the priest rather than the king will play the dominant role.

Although the events it narrates take place before those recorded in Ezra and Nehemiah, the rabbinical editors who arranged the order of canonical books placed 2 Chronicles last, according it the climactic end position in the Hebrew Bible. Cyrus's decree promises restoration of Yahweh's religion in the Promised Land and thus forms a counterpoise to the final scene at the end of the Torah, a poignant moment in which Moses looks across Jordan to the land he will not enter. Whereas the Torah closes with the pledges made through Abraham and Moses about to be fulfilled, the second division of the Hebrew Bible (Joshua through 2 Kings) recounts the tragic story of Israel's gain—and loss—of the promised homeland. To balance

the Deuteronomistic vision, the Chronicler ends with another account promising Israel's repossession of its land. It is significant that the last words spoken in the Hebrew Scriptures are those of a Gentile conqueror who espouses the Jewish cause—the same **Cyrus** whom Second Isaiah called Yahweh's "Messiah" (Isa. 45:1). The Persian king, to whom Yahweh "has given . . . all the kingdoms of the earth," calls to Jews scattered throughout the world to return to worship at the holy city: "Whoever there is among you of all his people, may his God be with him! Let him go up" (2 Chron. 36:23).

RECOMMENDED READING

Klein, Ralph W. "Chronicles, Book of 1–2." In D. N. Freedman, ed., *The Anchor Bible Dictionary*, Vol. 1, pp. 992–1002. New York: Doubleday, 1992.

Meyers, Jacob M. *1 Chronicles.* Garden City, N.Y.: Doubleday, 1965.

———. *2 Chronicles.* Garden City, N.Y.: Doubleday, 1965.

Noth, Martin. *The Chronicler's History.* Sheffield, Eng.: JSOT Press, 1987.

Ezra

KEY THEMES

The Book of Ezra pictures the difficult conditions that prevailed in the postexilic community of Judah, then a small part of the vast Persian Empire (Chs. 1–6). The Persian emperor authorizes Ezra, a priestly scribe returned from Babylon, to reorganize the restored Jewish community according to principles of the Mosaic Torah (Ch. 7). To prevent assimilation with the Gentile population, Ezra forbids intermarriage between Jews and foreign women (Chs. 9 and 10).

> Artaxerxes, king of kings, to the priest Ezra, scribe of the Law . . . you are to appoint scribes and judges to administer justice for . . . all who know the law of your God. You must teach those who do not know it.
>
> Ezra 7:12, 25

Although Ezra and Nehemiah probably formed a single book originally, the two histories present conflicting information about the sequence of events they record. Part of the confusion arises because we do not know who first returned to help rebuild Jerusalem—the priest-scribe **Ezra** or the Persian-appointed governor of Judah, **Nehemiah**. The Chronicler precisely dates his history by citing particular years of the Persian emperor **Artaxerxes**; but because two monarchs of this name ruled during the fifth century B.C.E., scholars are uncertain which one the writer meant. Although even experts do not agree on the basic order of events, it seems likely that Nehemiah came to Jerusalem first (around 445 B.C.E.) and that Ezra appeared during the governor's second twelve-year term.

Return from Exile   Ezra opens with Cyrus's proclamation endorsing the return of the Jews from Babylon to Jerusalem to rebuild Yahweh's Temple (around 538 B.C.E.), an edict consistent with the Persian ruler's policy of tolerating and even encouraging local religious cults throughout his empire. A long list of repatriated exiles follows in Chapter 2, whereas Chapter 3 describes the first sacrifices on a rebuilt altar "set up on its old site" and the laying of foundations for a second Temple. Poignantly, the tears of those old enough to remember the much larger dimensions of Solomon's Temple mingle with the joyous shouts of the younger generation as the priests lead the people in singing praises.

Chapters 4–6 record the Jewish leader **Zerubbabel**'s rejection of Samaritan aid in reconstructing the sanctuary. Consequently, Judah's slighted neighbors conspire to persuade the Persian emperor (then Xerxes I) that Jerusalem is a potentially rebellious city whose rebuilding should be stopped. The emperor agrees, and the

Temple remains unfinished until two postexilic prophets, Haggai and Zechariah, convince Zerubbabel and **Joshua**, the high priest, to start work again. (For a discussion of these prophets, Haggai and Zechariah, see Part 5.)

When a Persian official questions the legality of this project, the Jewish elders appeal to the

This silver figurine from the court of Artaxerxes I (465–424 B.C.E.) shows the kind of tunic, trousers, and hood that biblical figures such as Ezra, Nehemiah, and Haman may have worn, as officials associated with the Persian emperor's court. After Cyrus the Great defeated Babylon in 539 B.C.E. and encouraged former captives to restore the cults of their respective national gods, the Jews returned to Palestine, rebuilt Yahweh's Temple, and enjoyed two centuries of Persia's remarkably tolerant rule. (Courtesy of Vorderasiatisches Museum, Berlin)

new Persian emperor, **Darius**, to investigate the court records for Cyrus's original authorization to erect a new Temple. Cyrus's edict not only is found and enforced, but it obligates the Persians to supply money for rebuilding and procuring sacrifices. The second Temple is completed and dedicated in about 515 B.C.E., permitting a Passover celebration at Yahweh's sanctuary for the first time in more than seventy years.

Ezra's Mission   Chapter 7 introduces Ezra, a Babylonian Jew who had devoted himself to intense study and teaching of the Mosaic law and who is represented as the first in a long line of distinguished rabbis who were decisive in forming and preserving Judaism. Emperor Artaxerxes commissions Ezra to travel to Jerusalem to supervise the Temple, to evaluate conditions in the Judean province according to Mosaic standards, and to appoint scribes and judges to administer civil and moral order for the whole Jewish population (Ezra 7:11–26). Chapter 8 lists the new returnees and the treasures of silver and gold that Ezra had been appointed to bring to the Temple.

Foreign Wives   Chapters 9 and 10 record Ezra's distress at the returned exiles' intermarrying with foreign women. He was raised in exclusively Jewish circles in Babylon, where strict adherence to legal and ethnic exclusiveness were observed, so he determines to enforce his concept of the nation's duty. After begging his God to forgive the people for marrying those who follow pagan religions, Ezra calls on the people to reject these mixed alliances at a great assembly before the Temple. Weeping, the men agree to divorce their non-Jewish wives, and Ezra arranges to see that the resolution is enforced. The book ends with a list of those guilty of unsanctified marriages.

The Book of Ezra gives a positive view of the Persian government's remarkable cooperation with and consideration for Jews in its empire, a view that accords with the picture of Jews dispersed amid the Persian state presented in the

books of Esther and Tobit. Ezra himself, the priest and learned scribe who brings a copy of the Mosaic law with him from Babylon to regulate and unify Jewish life in the restored community, is a key figure in the further development of Judaism. Both the Pharisees and later rabbis could trace their roots to this zealous promoter of Mosaic traditions, as could the writers of several apocryphal books, such as 1 and 2 Esdras (the Greek form of Ezra).

Nehemiah

KEY THEMES

Appointed governor of postexilic Judah by Emperor Artaxerxes, Nehemiah oversees the rebuilding and reorganization of Judah (Chs. 1–7). After promulgating a version of the Mosaic Torah compiled and edited during the Babylonian exile (perhaps the final form of today's Pentateuch), the priest Ezra institutes an atonement ceremony (Chs. 8–10). A report of Nehemiah's reforming zeal, enforcing Sabbath keeping and the ban on foreign marriages, concludes the book (Ch. 13).

> And Ezra read from the Law of God, translating and giving the sense, so that the people understood what was read.
> Nehemiah 8:8

Return to Jerusalem   Originally combined with Ezra, the Book of Nehemiah enlarges our picture of conditions in postexilic Judah and Jerusalem. The book opens with an account of Nehemiah's grief when, as an official cupbearer to the emperor at Susa, the Persian capital, Nehemiah learns of the miserable conditions in Jerusalem. Weeping over reports of the city's poverty and ruin, he persuades Emperor Artaxerxes to commission his return to Jerusalem to rebuild the city.

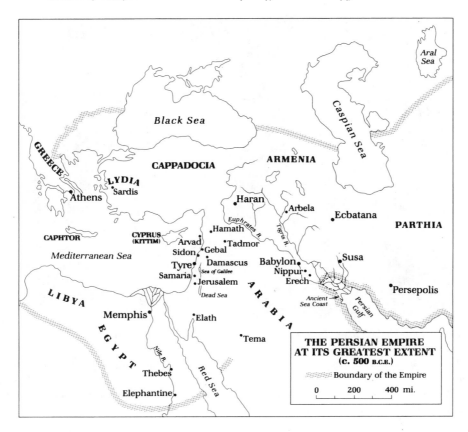

THE PERSIAN EMPIRE
AT ITS GREATEST EXTENT
(c. 500 B.C.E.)

Nehemiah travels with an armed guard to Jerusalem, where he encounters local opposition to the refortification of the city. (Reconstructing the city's defensive walls would naturally increase its apparent independence, which the Jews' enemies could interpret as subversive to Persian rule.) When Sanballat (the governor in Samaria), Tobiah the Ammonite, and Geshem the Arab first deride and then threaten to attack Nehemiah's workmen, Nehemiah arms his builders, who thereafter complete the city walls in record time. After Artaxerxes officially appoints Nehemiah governor, Nehemiah is able to maintain order and to institute significant economic and social reforms, such as canceling debts and freeing slaves.

Ezra Proclaims the Torah

Promulgation of the Mosaic Law Perhaps the most significant incident recorded in the Book of Nehemiah is Ezra's extended public reading of the Mosaic law (Neh. 8). Apparently the resettled Judeans no longer understood the classical Hebrew in which the Torah was written, because Ezra, after declaiming aloud from the sacred scrolls, translated and "gave the sense"— that is, interpreted the law's meaning—"so that the people understood what was read" (Neh. 8:8). Scholars have debated exactly which form of the Torah Ezra presented to the people, but it may well have been the Pentateuch that we have now, for during the Babylonian captivity, schools of priests and scribes labored to com-

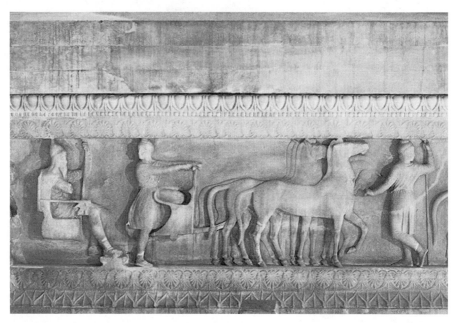

This bas-relief depicts a Persian satrap, or governor. The Persians divided their enormous empire into twenty administrative units called satrapies, each locally autonomous but ruled by the emperor's appointed governor. As the books of Ezra, Nehemiah, and Esther reveal, some upper-class Jews, including those from priestly families, rose to influential positions within the Persian administration. Because the Persians did not permit the restoration of the Davidic royal line, many priests assumed leadership roles in postexilic Judah. (Courtesy of Erich Lessing/Magnum Photos)

pile, preserve, and interpret Israel's Mosaic legacy for their own day.

Whether the Torah that Ezra brought back to Jerusalem was the entire Pentateuch or merely a collection of legal material later integrated into it, his work thereafter became the basis and standard for the Jewish community. The religious reforms that Ezra and Nehemiah inculcated in the national consciousness included revivals of such age-old festivals as the Feast of Tabernacles and a covenant-renewal ceremony (Neh. 9), the latter featuring additional public teaching of the law and a long poetic recital of Israel's history, emphasizing its covenant obligations to Yahweh.

Nehemiah's Zeal   Chapters 10–13 record the people's vow to abide by the covenant to support the Temple service, which involved nu-

merous financial and other responsibilities. Marriages to foreign women are again forbidden, and strict observance of the **Sabbath** is enjoined. Chapters 11 and 12 report the repopulating of Jerusalem, Levitical genealogies, and the formal dedication of the new city wall. The final chapter concludes Nehemiah's memoir, recounting how he bustled about the city personally enforcing Sabbath keeping, persuading individuals to give up their foreign wives, and asking God to remember his good works "for [his] happiness."

Like Ezra, Nehemiah was a conscientious proponent of Jewish exclusivism, tolerating neither Gentile customs nor non-Jewish women in the holy city. While his rigid insistence on ceremonial and racial particularism may strike the modern reader as unsympathetic, these requirements were deemed necessary at a time when

The Hebrew inscription on this pottery fragment, which dates from the eighth or seventh century B.C.E., refers to the "gold of Ophir." According to the books of Kings and Chronicles, King Solomon imported vast quantities of this precious metal from Ophir, famous for the high quality of its gold. Although Egyptian documents also refer to Ophir, its location, perhaps somewhere in eastern Africa, is now unknown. (Courtesy of the Israel Antiquities Authority)

the Jews were few in number and surrounded by enemies. Without such separatism, both national and religious identity might have been lost.

RECOMMENDED READING

Blenkinsopp, Joseph. *Ezra, Nehemiah.* Philadelphia: Westminster Press, 1988.

Eskenazi, Tamara C. *In an Age of Prose.* Atlanta: Scholars Press, 1988.

Fensham, F. Charles. *The Books of Ezra and Nehemiah.* Grand Rapids, Mich.: Eerdmans, 1982.

Meyers, Jacob M. *Ezra, Nehemiah.* Garden City, N.Y.: Doubleday, 1965.

North, Robert. "The Chronicler: 1–2 Chronicles, Ezra, Nehemiah." In R. E. Brown et al., eds., *The New Jerome Biblical Commentary,* pp. 362–398. Englewood Cliffs, N.J.: Prentice-Hall, 1990.

Williamson, H. G. M. *Ezra and Nehemiah.* Sheffield, Eng.: JSOT Press, 1987.

TERMS AND CONCEPTS TO REMEMBER

Artaxerxes	Manasseh
Cyrus	Nehemiah
Darius	Sabbath
Diaspora	Talmud
Ezra	Zerubbabel
Joshua	

QUESTIONS FOR REVIEW

1. Following the return from the Babylonian exile, what group replaced Davidic kings as leaders of the restored Judean community? Given Judah's changed circumstances and leadership, why do you think that the Chronicler prepared a revised edition of Israelite history?

2. How does the Chronicler's account of King David differ from that in the Deuteronomistic History? What episodes in David's personal life does he omit? In his revisionist account, what does the Chronicler depict as the main objective of David's reign?

3. In the Chronicler's view, what is the most important function of the postexilic Judean community?

4. What historical figure made Judah's restoration possible? Under what political control did the covenant people live, between 538 and about 330 B.C.E.?

5. Describe Ezra's contribution to the development of Judaism. What role did he play in perpetuating the Mosaic tradition?

6. In what ways did Ezra and Nehemiah try to preserve the religious and ethnic identity of the postexilic community? Why were Israelite men forced to divorce their foreign

wives? Would the author of Ruth have regarded all foreign women as inherently subversive of Yahwism?

QUESTIONS FOR DISCUSSION AND REFLECTION

1. After Ezra reintroduced the Torah to the postexilic Judean community, why did the institution of prophecy cease? Did publication of the Torah inhibit and replace the living prophetic voice? What role did the increase of priestly control and influence have on this process?

2. Most Judeo-Christian groups emphasize the teachings in the Torah and the Prophets and devote much less attention to the Writings. Although selected psalms are commonly read in most churches, the challenge of Israel's sages is often largely ignored. Why is this the case? Do you think most people find that obeying a set of legal decrees—such as the Ten Commandments—and seeing history as the Deuteronomistic historian interpreted it offers a more clear-cut and easily acceptable view of religion?

3. Do you think that such books as Job, Ecclesiastes, and Ruth present an acceptable version of religious experience? Can people relate to God by criticizing—and perhaps rejecting—conventional religious ideas? Can people sufficiently experience God through the quiet events of private relationships, as pictured in Ruth? Why do the Wisdom authors prefer rational observation and critical thought to the revelations and visions found in the Torah and Prophets? In compiling the final edition of the Hebrew Bible, why did Jewish scribes include *both* divine revelations and writings that were skeptical of such revelations?

7

Deuterocanonical, Apocalyptic, and Extracanonical Works

The Covenant People in the Hellenistic World

Books of the "Second Canon"

As validated by Jewish scholars meeting at Jamnia about 90 C.E., the Hebrew Bible (Tanak) closes with the books of Chronicles. The rabbis at Jamnia apparently decided not to recognize as authoritative Scripture about fourteen books—including several additions to canonical Daniel and Esther—that had been included in the Septuagint or other Greek translations of the Tanak. The early Christian community, however, which used Greek editions of the Hebrew Bible, regarded these fourteen books as **deuterocanonical**—belonging to a later "second canon." In Roman Catholic and Greek Orthodox Bibles, deuterocanonical works are interspersed among the Prophets and the Writings. Following the Protestant Reformation in the sixteenth and seventeenth centuries C.E., however, most Protestant editions of the Bible either omitted deuterocanonical books altogether or relegated them to a separate unit between the Old and New Testaments (see Table 7.1). Taking the name assigned them by Jerome in the fourth century C.E., these "supplementary" books were called the **Apocrypha**. (See Part 1.)

Whether considered deuterocanonical or apocryphal, this group of books represents an indispensable record of evolving Jewish thought between the Old and New Testament periods. Like the canonical Writings, deuterocanonical works encompass a variety of literary categories, including Wisdom books, short stories, poetry, and historical narratives. As the canonical Writings reflect differing theological responses to the postexilic world when Judah was part of the Persian Empire, so the deuterocanonical books reflect responses to yet another challenge—the Hellenistic world.

Alexander's Conquests and the Hellenistic World

In the Writings, books such as Esther, Ezra, and Nehemiah give a generally favorable picture of Persian rule. Except when influenced by anti-Jewish advisers, such as Haman, Persian emperors tended to support Jewish causes, particularly Yahweh's worship in the Judean homeland. While the Persian Empire lasted (539–330 B.C.E.), the Jewish people enjoyed two centuries of relative peace and stability. Conditions changed rapidly in the late fourth century B.C.E., however, when a new world conqueror

235

Table 7.1 Deuterocanonical (Apocryphal) Books

The Hebrew Bible (Tanak) omits fourteen books or parts of books that some Christian churches regard as part of the Old Testament. This table presents the canonical status—the acceptance or rejection—of the deuterocanonical (apocryphal) writings by various representative groups. A dash (—) indicates that the writing is not accepted. An empty circle (○) indicates that the book is not part of the canon but is given some religious value. A dark circle (●) indicates that the writing is included in the Bible but is not equal in authority to the Old and New Testaments. A dark square (■) means that the book is accepted as part of the Old Testament.

Book	Jewish	Protestant	Roman Catholic	Eastern Orthodox	
				Greek	Russian
1 Maccabees	—	○	■	■	●
2 Maccabees	—	○	■	■	●
Additions to Daniel	—	○	■	■	●
Tobit	—	○	■	■	●
Judith	—	○	■	■	●
Additions to Esther	—	○	■	■	●
Baruch	—	○	■	■	●
Letter of Jeremiah	—	○	■	■	●
Ecclesiasticus (ben Sirach)	—	○	■	■	●
Wisdom of Solomon	—	○	■	■	●
2 Esdras (4 Ezra)	—	○	○	■	●

For additional information on deuterocanonical and extracanonical works, see James H. Charlesworth, "Biblical Literature: Apocrypha and Pseudepigrapha." In Mircea Eliade, ed., *The Encyclopedia of Religion*, Vol. 2, pp. 173–183. New York: Macmillan, 1987.

burst onto the international scene. Blazing across the eastern Mediterranean region like a brilliant comet, Alexander of Macedonia (356–323 B.C.E.) rapidly conquered the entire Persian Empire. Extending his dominion over parts of three continents—from Greece to Egypt to Afghanistan and western India—Alexander created the largest empire the world had yet known. (See the map on page 237.) Changing forever the way people lived, Alexander brought Greek language, art, literature, philosophy, and social customs to the millions of subjects inhabiting his vast domain. For the first time in history, a European power dominated—militarily, politically, and culturally—the older Near Eastern and Indian centers of civilization.

Before he could carry out his presumed goal of forging a single world government unified by Greek culture, however, Alexander died—at age thirty-two—of a sudden fever at Babylon. After Alexander's death, his empire slowly disintegrated, but large sections remained under the control of his successors, known collectively as the *diadochoi*. For biblical history, the two most important successors were **Ptolemy I**, who founded a dynasty that ruled Egypt for three centuries, and **Seleucus**, whose descendants ruled Syria, then a large territory stretching from Asia Minor (modern Turkey) to Mesopotamia (modern Iraq). The Ptolemaic dynasty, with its capital at **Alexandria**, controlled **Judea** until 199 B.C.E., when it was taken over by the Seleucid dynasty of Syria.

This mosaic, in which Alexander of Macedonia (left) defeats the Persian Emperor Darius III (right center) at the Battle of Issus (333 B.C.E.), pictures a decisive moment in later biblical history. Alexander's conquest of the older Near Eastern centers of power, including Egypt, Palestine, Mesopotamia, and Iran, introduced a new era in which Greek language, art, literature, science, and philosophy transformed the biblical world. By the time of Jesus, Judaism had been largely Hellenized—even in Palestine—and the New Testament was composed for a Greek-speaking audience molded by Greek ideas and culture. (Courtesy of Alinari/Art Resource, NY)

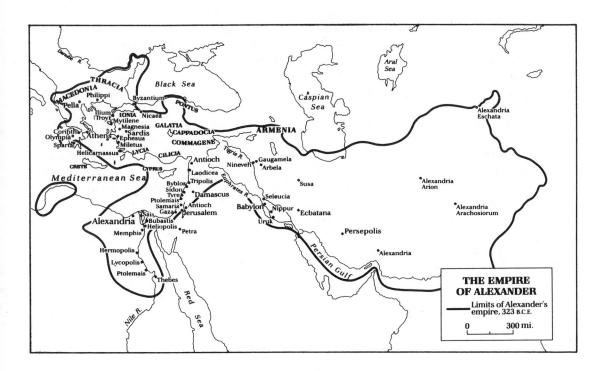

Although Alexander's successors did not achieve his vision of a permanently united world, they did preside over a new international culture known as **Hellenistic**. A mixture of the classical Greek (Hellenic) civilization with the older cultures of the Near East, the Hellenistic synthesis produced a creative flowering of Greek and Oriental motifs in religion, philosophy, and the creative arts. Arbitrarily dated as beginning with Alexander's death in 323 B.C.E., the Hellenistic epoch chronologically overlaps the period of Roman expansion and the early Christian centuries. (See Part 8.)

Judaism and Hellenistic Assimilation

Israel's religion had originally developed in the geographically limited area of Canaan. After Alexander's conquests, however, Judeans were suddenly forced to cope with life in a much larger, more culturally complex environment. Throughout the Hellenistic kingdoms of Alexander's successors, people began to regard themselves not as citizens of a particular city-state (*polis*) but of the world (*cosmos*) as a whole. This *cosmopolitan* outlook helped break down barriers between different national traditions, allowing an integration of Greek with other ethnic customs, a process by which even many Jews became partly Hellenized.

The deuterocanonical books present several strikingly different reactions to the covenant people's encounter with Hellenism. For some authors, Hellenistic culture and the practice of an authentic Jewish religion peacefully coexisted. This view prevails in the book of Tobit, which purports to be set in the days of Assyria and actually represents Jewish life during the Hellenistic **Diaspora**. The Book of Wisdom, attributed to King Solomon, similarly manifests an easy integration of Israelite tradition and Hellenistic philosophy. In sharp contrast, the books of **Maccabees** show faithful Jews heroically resisting a government-imposed policy of enforced Hellenization. Written in Greek, these

two accounts vividly illustrate the life-and-death struggle between Torah loyalists and a Hellenistic king who tried to eradicate their religion. This extreme crisis—in which Jewish assimilation into the larger Hellenistic culture is seen as a threat to the covenant people's religious identity and purpose—is given a cosmic dimension in the canonical Book of Daniel. The only fully apocalyptic work in the Hebrew Bible, Daniel pictures human history as a series of Gentile empires that repeatedly attempt to compromise the faith of pious Jews. Because it concerns the same historical crisis that inspired the Maccabean revolt, Daniel is included here among discussions of the deuterocanonical works.

Traditionally, the deuterocanonical books are arranged with those attributed to Ezra (Esdras) first and the Maccabean histories last. In order not to interrupt the chronological flow of biblical history from the Persian into the Hellenistic periods, however, we will consider 1 and 2 Maccabees first. Depicting Antiochus's frontal attack on Judaism, these two narratives record a major shift in Israel's religious experience. For the first time, Judeans find themselves battling a foreign power, not to defend their state militarily but to defend their religion. Unlike previous Assyrian, Babylonian, and Persian conquerors, who permitted Judeans to worship Yahweh and keep the Torah, Antiochus deliberately set out to destroy Judaism. Determined to crush opposition to state-enforced assimilation, Antiochus made loyalist Jews suffer *for their faith*. Many Jews who refused to abandon their ancestral laws were imprisoned, tortured, and killed. This "great tribulation," as the author of Daniel saw it, produced the first saints and martyrs, initial victims in what would become a long line of Jewish and Christian religious heroes who kept their integrity unto death. Antiochus's persecutions form the historical context of Daniel's eschatological visions, images of an ordeal so painful that it was thought to mark the climactic consummation of history.

This text surveys the Maccabean conflict, the rise of apocalyptic literature, and the deuterocanonical works that depict the trials and temptations of Jewish life in the Hellenistic world. Although deleted from the Roman Catholic canon by the Council of Trent (in the sixteenth century C.E.), the apocalypse of 2 Esdras is included here because it combined Wisdom and eschatological themes current in both Hellenistic Judaism and early Christianity. Deuterocanonical books—and canonical Daniel—are discussed in the following order:

• 1 Maccabees (an historical account of the Jewish revolt against the oppression of the Syrian king Antiochus IV)

• 2 Maccabees (a vivid elaboration of the persecutions and tortures that Antiochus IV inflicted on Jewish martyrs)

• Daniel (a canonical work—written during the persecutions of Antiochus IV—that combines quasi-historical narrative and apocalyptic visions of end time)

• Additions to Daniel (prayers and anecdotes about Daniel added to the Septuagint edition)

• Tobit (a short story about faithful Jews in the Diaspora)

• Judith (an historical romance that highlights dangers threatening Diaspora Jews)

• Additions to Esther (pious sentiments added to a book that does not mention God)

• Baruch (a quasi-prophetic narrative about Jews living in foreign realms)

• Ecclesiasticus or Wisdom of Jesus ben Sirah (a compendium of proverbial wisdom and ethical advice to Jewish students, written by a Jerusalem sage about 180 B.C.E.)

• Wisdom of Solomon (a Wisdom book, written during the first century B.C.E., combining Jewish and Hellenistic ideas)

• 2 Esdras (a speculative apocalyptic work written after the Roman destruction of Jerusalem and the Second Temple, about 100 C.E.)

1 Maccabees

KEY THEMES

A remarkably accurate history of the Jewish revolt against Greek-Syrian oppression in the mid-second century B.C.E., 1 Maccabees recounts the persecution of Jews by Antiochus IV (Ch. 1); the uprising led by Mattathias and his sons (Ch. 2); the guerrilla war led by Judas Maccabeus (Chs. 3–9), which after his death is carried on by his brothers Jonathan (Chs. 9–12) and Simon (Chs. 13–16) and Simon's son, John Hyrcanus I, the first priest-king of a new Maccabean (Hasmonean) dynasty.

> A terrible oppression began in Israel; there was nothing like it since the disappearance of prophecy among them.
> 1 Maccabees 9:27

The most accurate and valuable historical work in the Apocrypha, 1 Maccabees covers the tumultuous period from about 168 to 134 B.C.E., during which the Jews overthrew their Greek-Syrian overlords and established an independent state. Without this and the less trustworthy account in 2 Maccabees, we would have virtually nothing of Israel's history between Ezra's reforms (about 400 B.C.E.) and the New Testament period.

Probably written about 100 B.C.E., 1 Maccabees gives an apparent eyewitness description and remarkably unprejudiced account of the fight for religious freedom by **Judas Maccabeus** (for whom the book is named) and his brothers during the persecutions of the Syrian tyrant **Antiochus IV**. Besides its objectivity, 1 Maccabees is notable for its plain, swiftly moving style and for the complete absence of miracles, supernatural elements, and divine interventions from the narrative. Like the canonical Book of Esther, it presents historical events as the result of purely human activity.

While his protagonists offer prayers and strictly observe the Mosaic law, the author never attributes their military or political victories to God's direct help, though he does seem to indicate that faithful Jews who are willing to sacrifice their lives to oppose the heathen will achieve success. Because he never refers to divine providence or to the hope of immortality for the faithful dead, many scholars believe the unknown writer belonged to the Sadducee party, a religiously conservative group that developed during this period.

Antiochus's Persecution and the Maccabean Revolt

The Great Persecution   A brief preface recounts Alexander's conquest of Persia and his successor's division of the Macedonian Greek Empire. (Palestine was first awarded to the Ptolemies of Egypt and then conquered by the Syrian Antiochus III; see Table 7.2.) The book then focuses on Antiochus IV's misguided effort to impose religious unity on all his subjects by outlawing the Jewish religion. Antiochus burns copies of the Mosaic law and forbids the offering of sacrifices to any but Hellenistic gods, the circumcision of infants, and the keeping of Sabbath or other holy days. To enforce his prohibitions, he erects a fortress citadel in Jerusalem and fills it with Syrian soldiers. Finally, he builds an altar to Zeus in Yahweh's Temple and sacrifices pigs and other ceremonially unclean animals at the sanctuary.

Revolt of the Maccabees   Fearful of the Syrians' power, many Jews reluctantly compromise their faith and sacrifice to the state-imposed gods. Others, attracted by Greek culture and philosophy, more willingly support Antiochus's policies. A large number, however, refuse to abandon their ancestral faith; among these is the priest **Mattathias**, who with his five sons— John, Simon, Judas, Eleazar, and Jonathan— moves from Jerusalem to their native village of Modein. When one of Antiochus's commissioners tries to bribe Mattathias into publicly

obeying the royal edict, the old man kills both the commissioner and a fellow Jew who had sacrificed, then flees to the hill country with his sons (1 Macc. 2).

After Syrian soldiers massacre 1000 Jews who piously refuse to defend themselves on the Sabbath, Mattathias and his followers prudently decide that self-defense does not violate Sabbath rules. Fighting a guerrilla war against the occupation troops, Mattathias's group destroys many pagan altars and forcibly circumcises many Jewish boys. Near death, Mattathias appoints the most capable of his sons, Judas Maccabeus (in Greek, the "hammer") as his successor.

Judas Maccabeus   Chapters 3–9 recount the incomparable service of Judas Maccabeus to the Hebrew nation. Against tremendous odds, he defeats the Syrian armies in several decisive battles, then marches into Jerusalem where he cleanses the ransacked Temple and rebuilds its altar. He then institutes the joyous festival of rededication (**Hanukkah**)—according to tradition, three years after the day on which Antiochus had polluted the sanctuary. When Antiochus unexpectedly dies in 163 B.C.E., Judas concludes an armistice with the Syrians, assuring his people religious freedom. After war is resumed three years later, Judas defeats the Syrian general Nicanor, who had rashly threatened to burn the Temple.

Among the most significant of Judas's deeds is his treaty of friendship with Rome, the mighty new empire then rising in the West. The author of 1 Maccabees (who must have written before Rome took over Palestine in 63 B.C.E.) ironically regards Rome as the champion of peace and political integrity, the protector of smaller states who willingly place themselves within its sphere of influence.

Jonathan   After Judas falls in battle, his brother Jonathan becomes leader of the Jews (160–142 B.C.E.). Sharing his predecessor's charismatic gifts, Jonathan rallies the people against further Syrian aggression, which is repelled. Alexander, the new claimant to the Syrian throne,

Table 7.2 Hellenistic Successors of Alexander the Great (336–323 B.C.E.)

| Date B.C.E. | Rulers over Palestine | | Events in Judah |
	Egypt (Ptolemys)	Syria (Seleucids)	
323	Ptolemy I Lagi (323–285)		
		Seleucus I (312–280)	
300			
	Ptolemy II Philadelphus (285–246); Alexandrine Jews begin translation of Torah and Prophets (Septuagint Bible)		
		Antiochus I (280–261)	
		Antiochus II (261–246)	Judah under Ptolemaic control
250			
	Ptolemy III Euergetes (246–221)	Seleucus II (246–226)	
		Seleucus III (226–223)	
		Antiochus III (223–187)	
	Ptolemy IV Philopator (221–203)		
200	Ptolemy V Epiphanes (203–181)	Seleucids capture Palestine (200–198/197)	Judah under Seleucid control
	Ptolemy VI Philometer (181–146)	Seleucus IV (187–175)	Persecution of Jews; desecration of the Temple (168 or 167)
		Antiochus IV Epiphanes (175–163)	
		Antiochus V (163–162)	Maccabean revolt under Mattathias (d. 166) and Judas Maccabeus (d. 160); rededication of the Temple (165 or 164)
150		Demetrius I (162–150)	
			Judah independent under Hasmoneans (142–163)

shrewdly concludes a peace settlement with Jonathan and in 152 B.C.E. appoints him high priest, by this time a political as well as religious office. This act establishes a line of **Hasmonean** (an ancestral name of the Maccabees) priest-kings that lasts until 40 B.C.E., when the Romans appoint Herod king of the Jews. During later political turmoil, however, Jonathan is led into the Syrian camp and treacherously slain (1 Macc. 9:23–12:53).

Simon   The last of the Maccabean brothers, Simon now assumes military leadership and eventually the high priesthood as well. Although he marshals an army, he fights fewer battles than did his brothers; his forte seems to have been diplomacy, because he bribes Syrian troops to withdraw and thus ensures peace for about seven years. Taking advantage of this lull and of Syria's internal strife, Simon builds numerous fortresses around the country and forms an alliance with the Syrian ruler, who confirms his appointment as high priest and simultaneously releases the Israelites from taxation and tribute. This act effectively ensures Jewish autonomy (142 B.C.E.) and marks a new independence for the Jewish state.

John Hyrcanus   In 134 B.C.E., however, the Syrians again attack, and many Jews are impris-

The coin on the right was struck during the time of John Hyrcanus II (67–40 B.C.E.), the Hasmonean ruler who invited the Roman occupation of Judea in 63 B.C.E. The bronze coin on the left features a menorah, the seven-branched lampstand kept in the Temple, and was issued during the brief reign of Antigonus (40–37 B.C.E.), last of the Hasmonean dynasty. Herod I, the Roman-appointed king of Judea, had Antigonus beheaded and ruthlessly eliminated all other Hasmonean claimants to the throne. (Courtesy of Erich Lessing/Magnum Photos)

oned or killed. The aged Simon commissions two of his sons, Judas and John, who lead the Jewish army victoriously against the invaders. After Simon and his other sons, Mattathias and Judas, are murdered by Simon's traitorous son-in-law, John (surnamed "Hyrcanus") becomes Judah's priest-king (1 Macc. 16). This event is the last recorded in Old Testament history. (For a summary of Judean history in Roman times, see Part 8.)

Although the author of 1 Maccabees ignores the possibility of supernatural aid in the Jewish struggle for independence from Syria, his theme that faithfulness and courage under persecution can result in freedom is undeniably inspirational. The hectic period he describes, with its excesses on both sides, also provides the historical background for such canonical books as Esther, which similarly depicts the Jews fighting for their lives against pagan oppressors, and Daniel, which recounts the struggles between the Seleucids and Jews in eschatological terms (Dan. 11:21–12:13).

RECOMMENDED READING

Bickerman, Elias. *From Ezra to the Last of the Maccabees.* New York: Schocken Books, 1962. A brief introduction to the period.

de Lange, Nicholas. *Apocrypha: Jewish Literature of the Hellenistic Age.* New York: Viking Press, 1978.

Goldstein, Jonathan A. *1 Maccabees.* Garden City, N.Y.: Doubleday, 1976. Covers the Maccabean period thoroughly and includes a translation and interpretation of 1 Maccabees.

Hengel, Martin. *Judaism and Hellenism,* vols. 1 and 2. London: SCM Press, 1974.

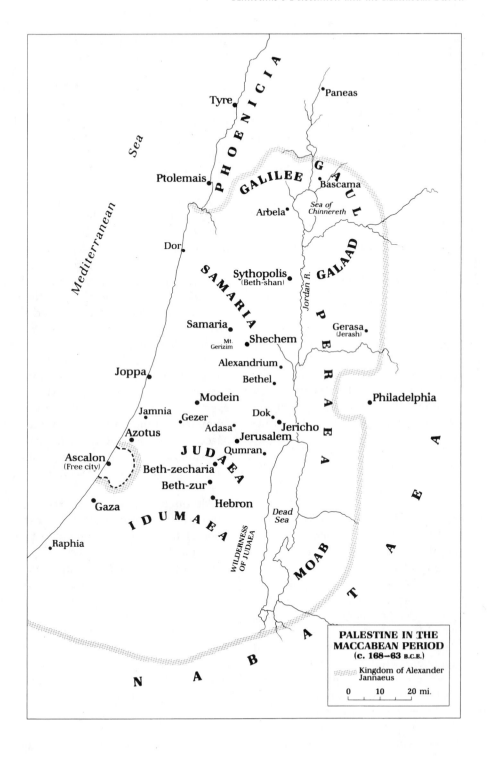

**PALESTINE IN THE
MACCABEAN PERIOD**
(c. **168–63** B.C.E.)

Kingdom of Alexander
Jannaeus

0   10   20 mi.

———. *Jews, Greeks, and Barbarians: Aspects of the Hellenization of Judaism in the Pre-Christian Period*. Philadelphia: Fortress Press, 1980.

Nickelsburg, George W. E. *Jewish Literature Between the Bible and the Mishnah*. Philadelphia: Fortress Press, 1981. A survey of both apocryphal and pseudepigraphal works in their historical context.

Stone, Michael. *Scriptures, Sects and Visions: A Profile of Judaism from Ezra to the Jewish Revolts*. Philadelphia: Fortress Press, 1980. A concise, clearly written discussion of ideas during the pre-Christian period.

2 Maccabees

KEY THEMES

An expanded revision of the first seven chapters of 1 Maccabees, 2 Maccabees is a theologically oriented interpretation of events, emphasizing tales of official corruption, persecution, and the integrity of martyred Torah loyalists (Chs. 1–15). The unknown author interpolates numerous innovative religious beliefs into the narrative (Chs. 6, 7, 10, 12, 15).

> The Hebrews were invincible because the mighty God fought for them.
>
> 2 Maccabees 11:13

A Greek work, probably written in Alexandria, Egypt, after 124 B.C.E., 2 Maccabees is not a continuation of the history of 1 Maccabees but a revised version of events related in the first seven chapters of the earlier book. According to the compiler's preface (2 Macc. 2:19–32), the book is an edited abridgement of a five-volume historical work (since lost) by "Jason of Cyrene," who is otherwise unknown. The period covered is approximately 176–161 B.C.E.

While 1 Maccabees is a relatively straightforward, reliable, and human (perhaps Sadducean) account of the Jewish revolt against Antiochus IV's enforced Hellenization of Judah, the second book's credibility is undermined by its emphasis on exaggerated numbers, miracles, and supernatural apparitions. The writer of 2 Maccabees, who seems to have been a Pharisee, not only presents the successful rebellion as an act of God (2 Macc. 11:13; 15:27) but injects considerable religious commentary into his narrative (2 Macc. 5:17–20; 6:12–17; 8:36; 12:40), along with such typical Pharisaic doctrines as belief in a bodily resurrection (2 Macc. 7:9; 14:46).

Corruption, Persecution, and Integrity   The book opens with two letters from Palestinian Jews to their fellow Jews in Egypt, urging them to observe Hanukkah, the festival of the Temple's rededication (2 Macc. 1:1–2:18). After outlining his sources in a preface (2 Macc. 2:19–32), the "abbreviator" traces the increasing corruption of the high priesthood in the persons of Jason and Menelaus (2 Macc. 3–4); Antiochus IV's campaign to unify his ethnically diverse subjects by imposing Hellenistic culture and religion on them; the Jews' consequent sufferings (2 Macc. 5–7); Judas Maccabeus's unexpectedly effective guerrilla resistance, which culminates in the purification of the Temple (2 Macc. 8–10); and Judas's further battles against such foes as Nicanor, chief general of Demetrius I, one of Antiochus's successors (2 Macc. 10–15).

Although some of its material is of doubtful authenticity, 2 Maccabees offers vivid descriptions of the greed, intrigue, and treachery of Jason and Menelaus (2 Macc. 4–5), who betray their people for personal gain. Equally memorable are the author's depictions of the tortures endured by Jews who refuse to compromise their faith. The nobility of the ninety-year-old Eleazar, a distinguished teacher who is bludgeoned to death, and the courage of seven brothers and their mother, all of whom are mutilated and burned alive by Antiochus, are classic examples of Jewish integrity (2 Macc. 6–7).

Religious Beliefs   Also noteworthy is the author's theological philosophy of history, which attributes the Jewish people's martyrdom under Antiochus to their God's wish to discipline them. Intense suffering is here seen, paradoxically, as a sign of divine benevolence; whereas the Deity allows the pagan nations to multiply their crimes and guilt—with the implication that the coming retribution will be all the more severe—Israel is punished *before* its "sins come to a head." That numerous disasters befall the Jews, in short, is evidence that their God has *not* deserted them (2 Macc. 6:12–17).

The writer's other religious beliefs apparently include a future resurrection of the dead (2 Macc. 7:9; 14:46), a belief in the efficacy of a prayer to release the dead from sin (2 Macc. 12: 43–45), the doctrine that the righteous dead can intervene on behalf of the living (2 Macc. 15:12–16), and the concept that God created the world out of nothing (2 Macc. 7:28). Such Pharisaic beliefs appear to have been increasingly prevalent in the time of Hellenistic Judaism. Certainly, such notions as prayers for souls in Purgatory and the intercessory prayers of saints later became important in Roman Catholicism. Perhaps because it supported these doctrines, 2 Maccabees was condemned in Protestant circles.

RECOMMENDED READING

Goldstein, Jonathan A. *2 Maccabees.* Garden City, N.Y.: Doubleday, 1979.

TERMS AND CONCEPTS TO REMEMBER

Alexandria	Judas Maccabeus
Antiochus IV	Judea
Apocrypha	Maccabees
deuterocanonical	Mattathias
Diaspora	Ptolemy I
Hanukkah	Seleucus
Hasmonean	

Apocalyptic Literature and the Book of Daniel

No form of biblical literature is more bewildering to the average reader than the apocalyptic, a term derived from the Greek *apokalypsis,* which means "an unveiling, an uncovering, a stripping naked of what is normally hidden." As a literary category, an **apocalypse** is a revelation of dimensions or events ordinarily closed to human view, such as the invisible realm of heaven or the future course of history. In the Hebrew Bible, only Daniel is a fully apocalyptic work, although there are apocalyptic elements in the visions of Yahweh's heavenly court, described by Isaiah (6:1–12), Zechariah (3:1–10), and a few other prophets. The "little apocalypse" of Isaiah 24–27 and the obscure predictions about Israel's future redemption and the final defeat of its enemies in Ezekiel (Chs. 30, 37–39) and Zechariah (9–14) also illustrate apocalyptic concerns about the ultimate fate of God's people. From the time the earliest parts of 1 Enoch were written in the third century B.C.E. through the end of the first century C.E. when 2 Esdras (4 Ezra) and the New Testament Book of Revelation were composed, Jewish and Jewish-Christian authors produced a flood of **apocalyptic literature**. With the exception of Daniel, most of these visionary works were not included in the Hebrew Bible canon and are now classed among the Apocrypha or Pseudepigrapha, including 2 Esdras, 1 and 2 Enoch, 2 and 3 Baruch, and the Sibylline Oracles. (Pseudepigraphal books are discussed later in this part.) Much of the New Testament is permeated with apocalyptic thought, particularly the forecasts of Jesus' return (Mark 13, Matt. 24, and Luke 21), Paul's early letters (1 and 2 Thess. and 1 Cor.), and the epistles of Peter and Jude, the last of which quotes 1 Enoch as if it were Scripture.

Apocalyptic literature is typically concerned with **eschatology**—speculations about "last things," such as the final consummation of history, the prophetic "Day of Yahweh" in which Israel's God judges the nations, rewards the righteous, and annihilates the wicked. Besides its "end of the world" aspects, eschatology also concerns the ultimate fate of individual persons: death, posthumous judgment, heaven, hell, and resurrection. Belief that people will experience an afterlife, typically through **resurrection** of the body, is a byproduct of the apocalyptic movement (Dan. 12:1–3).

The authors of the first two divisions of the Hebrew Bible, the Torah and the (Former) Prophets, showed little or no interest in eschatological matters, but the situation changed near the close of the Old Testament period when apocalyptic speculation reached its height. During the Hellenistic era, a general belief arose that Israelite prophecy had ceased after the time of Ezra (about 400 B.C.E.). When Israel accepted the notion that prophets no longer spoke "in the name of Yahweh," writers who desired to communicate their understanding of the divine will commonly published their works under the name of some famous leader of the distant past. From about 250 B.C.E. to 100 C.E., numerous Jewish authors practiced the art of **pseudonymity**, attributing their writings to such revered figures as Enoch, Abraham, Moses, Daniel, or Ezra. Pseudonymity was a device that allowed apocalyptic writers, such as the author of Daniel, to review past history as if it were prophecy and then to predict the imminent outcome of the issue or crisis that had inspired his work. While such practices today might be regarded as dishonest or fraudulent, in the Hellenistic world both Jewish and Greco-Roman authors commonly wrote pseudonymously to honor an ancient luminary, presenting what they believed would be his views were he still alive. Some New Testament writers, with no thought of forgery, penned sermons or epistles in the name of apostles such as Peter or Paul. (See the discussions of 2 Peter, Timothy, and Titus, Part 10.)

Recent studies of the sociological background of apocalyptic writings indicate that they commonly originate during times of crisis and tension, responding either to severe persecutions of the writer's religious community or to other forces that threaten the group's welfare, such as a widespread decline in religious enthusiasm or a growing consciousness of the disparity between the group's apocalyptic expectations and the social or political realities they were actually experiencing. Thus, both Daniel and Revelation were composed to encourage their respective audiences to remain faithful before the threat of state persecution, foretelling their persecutors' certain doom and rekindling hopes of future blessedness following the present tribulation.

While differing significantly from both, apocalyptic literature seems to draw from a twofold source: Israel's prophetic and wisdom traditions. Like the prophets, apocalyptists exhort their audience to remain faithful to the ancestral religion; like the wisdom writers, they explore the mysterious principles by which God rules the universe, seeking to learn the divine will as communicated through natural phenomena, human experience, and the arcane learning preserved in religious books. Thus, Jesus ben Sirach, the head of a wisdom school in Jerusalem, observes that the professional sage

> . . . researches into the wisdom of all the
>   Ancients,
>   he occupies his time with the prophecies.
> He preserves the discourse of famous men,
>   he is at home with the niceties of parables.
> He researches into the hidden sense of proverbs,
>   he ponders the obscurities of parables.
> He enters the service of princes,
>   he is seen in the presence of rulers.
> He travels in foreign countries,
>   he has experienced human good and human
>   evil. . . .
> He will grow upright in purpose and learning,
>   he will ponder the Lord's hidden mysteries.
> Ecclesiasticus 39:1–5, 10

Jesus ben Sirach's description of an educated **scribe** pondering on cosmic secrets, ancient wisdom, and the cryptic language of sages may well apply to the class of persons who composed apocalyptic literature. The hero of the Book of

Daniel, who combines Torah loyalty with arcane wisdom and divination, may also represent an idealized self-portrait of the apocalyptist. A devout Jew serving a foreign government, Daniel becomes one of several Jewish trainees whom King Nebuchadnezzar selects to be educated in a Babylonian wisdom school. Daniel is "trained in every kind of wisdom," taught "the language and literature of the Chaldaeans," and, most important for apocalyptic purposes, granted the divine "gift of interpreting every kind of vision and dream" (Dan. 1:3–4, 17–18). Although earlier Bible writers had warned against practicing the mantic arts—interpreting omens, portents, and dreams, and forecasting future events (Deut. 18:10–11; Jer. 14:14; etc.)—the author of Daniel implicitly identifies his central character with the professional class of Babylonian wise men, including the court "magicians and enchanters, sorcerers, and Chaldaeans [persons skilled in the art of divination]" (Dan. 2:1–4, 14–19). After successfully explaining Nebuchadnezzar's dream as a preview of future history, Daniel is made "head of all the sages of Babylon" (Dan. 2:24–49). A clue to the author's own identification as a sage versed in studying signs and portents in order to discern God's will is given at the end of the book: "The learned [the wise] will shine as brightly as the vault of heaven, and those who have instructed many in virtue, as bright as stars for all eternity" (Dan. 12:3). This linking of sages with the stars recalls the astronomical section of 1 Enoch (Chs. 72–82), which combines observation of sun, moon, planets, and stars with eschatological predictions. And as Daniel notes, only "the learned will understand" the significance of eschatologic developments (Dan. 12:10).

Characteristics of Apocalyptic Writing

Although apocalyptists drew on Israel's prophetic and wisdom traditions, the literature they produced is distinguished from these older schools by several characteristics. Besides the practice of pseudonymity discussed above, apocalypses are typified by the following:

1. *Universality.* In contrast to prophetic oracles, which focus almost exclusively on Israel and its immediate neighbors, apocalyptic visions are universal in scope. Although the writers' religious communities (Israel or the Church) stand at the center of their concern, their work encompasses the whole of human history and surveys events in both heaven and earth. Apocalyptists view all spirit beings, as well as all nations and peoples, as swept together in a conflict of cosmic proportions.

2. *Cosmic dualism.* The apocalyptic worldview borrows much of its cosmology from Greek philosophical ideas about parallel worlds of matter and spirit. Postulating a dualistic "two-story universe" composed of visible earth and invisible heaven, apocalyptists see human society profoundly influenced by unseen forces, angels and demons, operating in a celestial realm. Events on earth, such as persecution of the righteous, reflect the machinations of these heavenly beings.

3. *Chronologic dualism.* Besides dividing the universe into two opposing domains of physical matter and viewless spirit, apocalyptists regard all history as separated into two mutually exclusive periods of time, a current wicked era and a future age of perfection. Seeing the present world situation as too thoroughly evil to reform, apocalyptists expect a sudden and violent change in which God or his Messiah imposes divine rule by force. In the apocalyptic vision, there is no normal historical progression from one age to the next and no real continuity between them. Thus, the Book of Daniel depicts God's kingdom as abruptly interrupting the ordinary flow of time, shattering all worldly governments with the impact of a colossal meteorite (Dan. 2:31–45).

4. *Ethical dualism.* In the apocalyptic view, there are only two kinds of human beings, just as there are only two epochs of world history and two levels of existence—material and spiritual. Apocalyptists see humanity divided into two opposing camps of intrinsically different ethical quality. The vast majority of people walk in spiritual darkness and are doomed victims of

God's wrath. Only a tiny minority—the religious group to which the writers belong and direct their message—remains faithful and receives salvation. Deeply conscious of human imperfection and despairing of humanity's ability to meet God's standards, apocalyptists take a consistently pessimistic view of society's future.

5. *Predestination.* Whereas most biblical writers emphasize that historical events are the consequences of our moral choices (e.g., Deut. 28–29; Josh. 24; Ezek. 18), apocalyptists view history as running in a straight line toward a predetermined end. Just as the rise and fall of worldly empires occurs according to God's plan (Dan. 2, 7–8), so will the end take place at a time God has already set. Human efforts, no matter how well intended, cannot avert the coming disaster or influence God to change his mind. The vast complexity of human experience means nothing when confronted with the divinely prearranged schedule.

6. *Exclusivism.* Many apocalypses, including Daniel and Revelation, were composed to encourage the faithful to maintain integrity and resist temptations to compromise with "worldly" values or customs. Apocalyptists typically equate religious fidelity with a total rejection of the ordinary goals, ambitions, social attachments, and other pursuits of unbelieving society. Regarding most people as condemned, apocalyptists commonly urge their audience to adopt a rigidly sectarian attitude, avoiding all association with unbelievers.

7. *Limited theology.* Consistent with this strict division of history and people into divinely approved or disapproved units, apocalyptists usually show little sympathy for differing viewpoints or compassion for nonbelievers. All modes of life are either black or white, with no psychological or spiritual shades of gray in between. As a result of the author's mental set, the apocalyptic picture of God is ethically limited. The Deity is almost invariably portrayed as an enthroned monarch, an omnipotent authority who brings history to a violent conclusion in order to demonstrate his sovereignty, confound

his enemies, and preserve his few worshipers. The notion that God might regard all people as his children or that he might establish his kingdom by less catastrophic means does not appeal to the apocalyptic temperament or satisfy the apocalyptic yearning.

8. *Belief in a violent God.* Assuming that the Deity achieves control over heaven and earth through a cataclysmic battle with a formidable opponent (the dragon of chaos, or, in the New Testament, Satan), apocalyptists imagine this transference of power by picturing God as a destroyer who exterminates much of his sentient creation. Using the Exodus story of the ten plagues that Yahweh inflicted on Egypt as their model, apocalyptists typically show God angrily punishing disobedient humanity with a devastating series of natural disasters, famines, and loathsome diseases. That the use of evil to defeat evil is ethically questionable does not seem to trouble the apocalyptic mentality.

9. *Eschatological preoccupations.* Along with uncovering the mysteries of the invisible world, apocalyptists reveal the posthumous fate of people during God's terrifying judgment. Because they were commonly written at a time when fidelity brought no earthly rewards but only the danger of imprisonment, torture, and death, apocalyptic works pioneered the way in popularizing new beliefs about compensatory blessings in the New Age. Apocalyptists were the first Bible writers to speculate about the nature of the afterlife, which they commonly pictured as resurrection of the body rather than as the survival of an immortal soul (Dan. 12:1–3). The apocalyptists' rejection of the old Hebrew belief that human souls were consigned to eternal oblivion in **Sheol** (the Underworld) and their insistence that God makes moral distinctions between virtuous and wicked lives marked a theological innovation that was adopted by several later Jewish groups, including the Pharisees, Essenes, and early Christians.

10. *The use of symbols and code words.* Perhaps because they are the work of sages immersed in arcane learning, almost all apocalypses contain

deliberately obscure language that veils as well as expresses the author's meaning. In addition, most were written during periods of crisis and persecution, a situation that encouraged apocalyptists to use terms and images that their original audiences could understand but that will bewilder outsiders. In Enoch, Daniel, Revelation, and other apocalypses, the authors employ symbols from a wide variety of sources, both pagan and biblical.

In its broadest sense, a **symbol** is a sign that represents something other than itself, typically an abstract quality or religious concept. Symbols take the form of persons, places, objects, or actions that suggest an association or connection with another dimension of meaning. Both Daniel and Revelation depict **Gentile** nations as animals because, to the authors, they resemble wild beasts in their savage and irrational behavior. Kings who demand worship are symbolized as idols, and paying homage to them is labeled idolatry. Using code words for a pagan opponent, such as the "little horn" to denote the persecutor Antiochus IV (Dan. 7:8, 24–27; 8:23–26; 11:21–39), a contemporary of Daniel's author, also shields the apocalyptist's seditious message.

Daniel

KEY THEMES

Written to encourage Jewish Torah loyalties during the persecutions of Antiochus IV (mid-second century B.C.E.), the Book of Daniel reviews past history as though it were prophecy, assuring readers that even when Israel is scattered and oppressed by Gentile powers, its God still controls all nations. A two-part drama of supernatural deliverance, the book portrays Daniel, one of Nebuchadnezzar's court magicians, and his three young friends as scrupulous Torah observers whom the Deity miraculously

rescues from unjust punishments (Chs. 1–6). The second part (Chs. 7–12) consists of a series of apocalyptic visions surveying the rise and fall of Near Eastern empires, from Babylon to the Hellenistic states of Syria and Egypt, that dominated Palestine in the author's day, and ending with the public vindication and physical resurrection of the wise, who remained faithful under persecution.

> In the time of these kings the God of heaven will set up a kingdom which shall never be destroyed, and this kingdom will not pass into the hands of another race; it will shatter and absorb all the previous kingdoms, and itself last forever.
>
> Daniel 2:44

Although the Book of Daniel purports to have been written during the Babylonian captivity in the sixth century B.C.E. when its author was successively a member of the Babylonian, Median, and Persian courts, scrupulous examination of the text reveals that it was composed between about 167 and 164 B.C.E. when the Jews were suffering intense persecution by the Macedonian-Syrian ruler **Antiochus IV** Epiphanes. It is chronologically the latest written book in the canonical Hebrew Bible. This fact, together with its striking differences in form and style from the prophetic books, may explain why it was not included among the Prophets but instead placed among the Writings; Daniel is not a typically prophetic work but seems a deliberately literary creation whose main character embodies and reflects the long tradition of Israel's sacred literature.

Daniel himself is, like Joseph (see Gen. 39–41), a devout Jew transported to a foreign nation of idol worshipers. Like Joseph, he remains faithful to his God under severe testing and is elevated by pagan rulers to positions of high honor. Like Joseph, too, he is basically a solitary figure, although an unusually shrewd one. Educated in the "wisdom of the **Chaldeans** [Babylonian practitioners of the mantic arts]," empowered to reveal the meaning of divinely inspired dreams and thereby predict the future, supernaturally aided in his escapes from danger, Daniel is not an ordinary person, and it is difficult to regard him as merely a role model for Jews struggling to maintain their religious integrity under adverse circumstances.

If, however, Daniel were as outstanding a figure during the sixth century B.C.E. as the present book represents him, it is strange that he is never mentioned by his contemporaries or by later historians. Ezekiel, a prophet who lived in Babylon during the exile, thrice refers to an ancient sage named "**Danel**" who is associated with the patriarchs Noah and Job as a prototype of righteousness (Ezek. 14:4, 20; 20:3), but the Old Testament nowhere speaks of a "Daniel" who lived with Ezekiel in captivity. Because archaeological discoveries at Ugarit have also revealed the existence of a legendary King Danel who was a model of wisdom and rectitude, it is possible that over the centuries the Israelites adopted this originally foreign character and reclothed him in typically Jewish virtues until he eventually became the exemplar cited by Ezekiel. Later, a writer of the second century B.C.E., wishing to create a representative figure whose name and reputation for godliness would be well known but whose life and career were shrouded in mystery, chose "Daniel" as his hero.

Daniel divides naturally into two main sections. The first six chapters—which may have been written well before Antiochus's persecutions—recount Daniel's adventures under the successive reigns of Nebuchadnezzar, Belshazzar, "Darius the Mede," and Cyrus the Persian. The apocalyptic elements are subdued in this part, which concentrates on Daniel's strict allegiance to his God and the conflict into which it brings him with various Gentile authorities.

Like Esther and Mordecai, Daniel is a victim of court intrigue. Unlike the Jews in the Book of Esther, however, he scrupulously observes Hebrew dietary laws (which makes him stronger than those who dine on the "king's food") and publicly manifests his Jewishness by refusing to participate in the religious ceremonies of his Babylonian or Persian overlords. A thematically important event in the biographical portion of the book is Daniel's interpretation of Nebuchadnezzar's dreams, the contents of which prepare the reader for the apocalyptic visions in Chapters 7–12, which compose the second main section of the book.

Interpreting Dreams and Resisting Assimilation

Nebuchadnezzar's Dreams   According to Chapter 2, Nebuchadnezzar has dreamed of a huge statue with a head of gold, chest and arms of silver, belly and thighs of bronze, legs of iron, and feet of mixed iron and clay. Suddenly a great stone uncut by human hands hurtles from heaven to smash the idol's clay feet; the colossus disintegrates, and the stone grows into a mountain that fills the entire earth. Daniel interprets the various metals composing this statue as symbolizing a series of kingdoms that rule his part of the world.

Nebuchadnezzar (Babylon) is the head of gold; and the nations that follow him—though Daniel does not specify them—are probably Media (silver), Persia (bronze), Macedonian Greece (iron), and the lesser Hellenistic kingdoms of Egypt and Syria (iron combined with clay to signify the weaker successors of Alexander's ironlike empire). The gigantic meteorite represents the kingdom of God that is destined to obliterate and replace all pagan governments and last forever (Dan. 2:44).

Chapter 3 tells of three faithful Hebrew youths—known by their Babylonian names as **Shadrach**, **Meshach**, and **Abednego**—who are thrown into a hot furnace for declining to worship Nebuchadnezzar's golden image. After they emerge unsinged, the Babylonian king is represented as enthusiastically praising the Jews' "Most High God" who so miraculously delivers his servants (Dan. 3:24–30). Despite this reputed lip service, however, Nebuchadnezzar is given another lesson in that Deity's omnipotence.

In another dream, the king beholds an enormous tree sheltering all forms of bird and animal life but hears a heavenly authority order the tree cut down and given a "beast's heart" until all around acknowledge the sovereignty of the "Most High" (Dan. 4:11–14). Called to explain the dream, Daniel, the "chief of magicians" (Dan. 4:6), says that Nebuchadnezzar is the tree and that he is to be struck down—to lose his reason and kingship—"seven times" until he fully realizes that all power, political as well as celestial, comes from Daniel's God.

A short time later, while Nebuchadnezzar is touring his capital and boasting that he had built it by his own power, he is afflicted with a form of insanity that drives him to flee society and live like a beast. When he finally extols the "Most High" as the universal king, his sanity is restored (Dan. 4:25–34). This first-person narrative concludes with Nebuchadnezzar's prayerful recognition that Daniel's God humbles "those who walk in pride" (Dan. 4:34).

There is no record, however, that Nebuchadnezzar, a successful conqueror and able administrator, ever suffered a seven-year fit of insanity or that he temporarily adopted the monotheistic beliefs of the Jews he held as prisoners and slaves. The modern reader's credulity may be strained by the notion that a polytheistic ruler in Babylon repeatedly and publicly praised the God whose Temple he had destroyed and whose nation he had defeated; but at the time these tales were first circulated, they may have provided a hope that whatever ungodly monarch then oppressed the Jews might still be taught humility before Yahweh.

Fall of Babylon   In Chapter 5, **Belshazzar** is ostensibly Babylon's ruler, though historically he was merely acting governor or prince regent for his father, King Nabonidus. At the height of a riotous celebration—possibly the Babylonian New Year festival—handwriting mysteriously appears on the palace walls. Summoned to interpret the cryptic signs, Daniel declares that Belshazzar is doomed to have his kingdom stripped from him and given to "the Medes and the Persians" (Dan. 5:25–31). That night, one "Darius the Mede" (unknown to history) takes the city. The author's blunder is puzzling because other biblical works, including Second Isaiah, Ezra, and Chronicles, make it clear that Cyrus of Persia captured Babylon (539 B.C.E.).

Chapter 6 states that Daniel underwent yet another test of his faith under the new "Median" administration. Like Ahasuerus in the Book of Esther, Darius is tricked by Daniel's rival courtiers into issuing an edict that for thirty days forbids anyone to pray except to the monarch. Loyal to his Jewish rites, Daniel is caught disobeying and is confined in a den of lions. When he leaves the den unharmed, the "Median ruler's" reaction to the miracle exceeds even that of Nebuchadnezzar. Darius not only confesses the supremacy of Daniel's God but orders that everyone in his far-flung empire learn to fear the Jewish Deity (Dan. 6:26–28).

Daniel's Visions of End Time

Eschatological Visions   The strange visions and predictions of the second portion of Daniel, which is fully apocalyptic, make it the most controversial part of the Old Testament, particularly among some fundamentalist groups. During the past few centuries, hundreds of sects have been founded on differing interpretations of Daniel's eschatology. Most experts agree, however, that Daniel's visions were intended primarily for the author's fellow Jews during the terrible days of Antiochus IV's attempt to eradicate the Jewish religion, perhaps just before the Maccabean revolt (c 168–164 B.C.E.).

Chapters 7–12 contain four main visions that survey Near Eastern history from the sixth to the second centuries B.C.E. from the perspective of a Babylonian or Persian captive. Chapter 7 disguises the Babylonian, Median, Persian, and Macedonian empires as beasts: a lion with eagle's wings (Babylon); a bear with ribs in its mouth (Media); a winged leopard with four heads (Persia); and a ferocious ogre with iron

These decorative bull heads were originally designed as the capitals of columns that supported massive wooden rafters in the imperial palace at Susa (Shushan), summer capital of the Persian Empire. Several biblical characters are associated with this city, including Daniel (Dan. 8:2), Nehemiah (Neh. 1:1), Esther, and Haman (Esther 1:2, 4). (Courtesy of Musée du Louvre)

kingdom to replace the bestial Gentile nations that rule in his own day. This section closes with more veiled remarks about the "little horn" (Antiochus IV) who makes war on the "saints" (devout Jews), tries to change the "law" (Temple observances), and attempts to abolish the Mosaic religion altogether. Again, it is certain that the persecutor will be overwhelmed by the coming kingdom.

The vision of Chapter 8—supposedly given when Daniel was living at Susa, the Persian capital—depicts a ram with two horns (the dual power of Medes and Persians) being gored by a he-goat sporting a great horn (Alexander of Macedonia), which in turn is broken and replaced by four smaller horns (the four divisions of Alexander's empire made after his death). From one of these lesser horns (the Seleucid dynasty of Syria) springs a prodigious horn (again Antiochus), which tramples the "Land of Splendor" (Judea), challenges the "armies of heaven," takes away the "perpetual sacrifice" (Antiochus forbade offerings at the Jerusalem Temple), and institutes an "abomination of desolation" (the Syrian king slaughtered a pig on the Temple altar and erected a statue of Zeus in the inner court as part of his policy to force the Jews into accepting a Hellenistic way of life). The angel **Gabriel** makes most of this vision explicit to Daniel, except for the part concerning Antiochus, which for reasons of safety had to be kept vague. Following this angelic exegesis, Daniel collapses and is ill for several days.

Chapter 9 features Daniel's most moving prayer, in which he confesses his people's sins and asks his God to deliver them from their enemies, for the first time in the book using the personal name Yahweh, God of the covenant and Lord of history (Dan. 9:5–19). This prayer leads to the angel Gabriel's revisionist explanation of Jeremiah's prophecy that Jerusalem would lie desolate for "seventy years" after the Babylonian conquest and then be restored. Why has the city been so consistently enslaved by foreign powers since then? Jeremiah, explains Gabriel, meant that "seventy weeks of years" (490

teeth and ten horns (the Macedonian Greeks and their successors, the Ptolemies of Egypt and the Seleucids of Syria). The boastful "little horn" that also turns up is probably Antiochus, who intended to coerce the Jews into abandoning their traditional worship.

Daniel's parade of monsters is interrupted by a more traditional prophetic vision of the "Ancient of Days," who confers "glory and kingship" on "one like a Son of Man," presumably a Messiah figure, although Daniel nowhere mentions the Messiah by title (Dan. 7:10–14). The passage implies, however, that the writer expects a supernaturally appointed, everlasting

years?) were to pass before the consummation of all things. In the second century B.C.E., when this interpretation was written, the expected fulfillment was imminent.

Chapters 10–11 are a tangled thicket of prophecies about battles between "the King of the South" (Ptolemies) and "the King of the North" (Seleucids) and the further machinations and fall of Antiochus. There seem to be allusions to the Maccabean wars here; although at the time these passages were written it appears that the Maccabees had not yet recaptured the Temple and rededicated its altar, the author correctly foresees that the Temple will be cleansed and priestly services resumed in the near future. He is less accurate in predicting Antiochus's punishment, however, because that fanatical king dies a natural death abroad, not in Palestine (Dan. 11:21–45).

Resurrection   Undoubtedly regarding Antiochus's depredations as inaugurating the "end time," the author of Daniel postulated a resurrection to compensate contemporary Jews who had died defending their faith against the Syrian persecutor, and this explicit affirmation of a life after death (Dan. 12:2–3) was to be the most enduring part of his message.

In Chapter 12, Gabriel tells Daniel that when history draws to its *predetermined* climax in the pagan nations' assault on the righteous, Michael (described as the prince or guardian spirit of Israel) will "stand up" for his people and decisively defeat their enemies. At that point, a resurrection of "many" just and unjust persons who had been "sleeping in the dust" will occur. Daniel—who as a literary character is placed during the Persian era—is told to sleep among his ancestors until he is raised for his "share" at the end of time (Dan. 12:1–13).

Although a familiarity with the apocalyptic mode makes it evident that Daniel was not composed for people living the last quarter of the twentieth century, the book's fundamental themes remain universally relevant. Its picture of the Deity firmly in control of earthly his-

tory, aiding the devout to survive adversity, and promising the ultimate triumph of life and faith over death and evil make Daniel an integral part of the biblical heritage.

RECOMMENDED READING

Charles, R. H. *Eschatology: The Doctrine of a Future Life in Israel.* New York: Schocken Books, 1963 (reprint).

Collins, John C. "Daniel, Book of." In D. N. Freedman, ed., *The Anchor Bible Dictionary,* Vol. 2, pp. 29–37. New York: Doubleday, 1992.

Hanson, Paul D. *The Dawn of Apocalyptic.* Philadelphia: Fortress Press, 1975.

Hartman, Louis F., and De Lella, Alexander A. *The Book of Daniel.* Garden City, N.Y.: Doubleday, 1978.

Koch, K. *The Rediscovery of Apocalyptic.* London: SCM Press, 1972.

Lacocque, André. *The Book of Daniel.* Atlanta: John Knox Press, 1978.

Mowinckel, Sigmund. *He That Cometh.* Nashville, Tenn.: Abingdon Press, 1956.

Nickelsburg, George W. E. *Jewish Literature Between the Bible and the Mishnah.* Philadelphia: Fortress Press, 1981.

Porteous, Norman W. *Daniel.* Philadelphia: Westminster Press, 1965.

Russell, D. S. *Apocalyptic, Ancient and Modern.* Philadelphia: Fortress Press, 1978.

———. *The Method and Message of Jewish Apocalyptic: 200 B.C.–A.D. 100.* Philadelphia: Westminster Press, 1964.

Stone, Michael, *Scriptures, Sects and Visions: A Profile of Judaism from Ezra to the Jewish Revolts.* Philadelphia: Fortress Press, 1980.

Additions to Daniel

KEY THEMES

A poetic prayer and two prosaic narratives were added to the Greek translation of Daniel: The Song of the Three Holy Children (Ch. 3); the

The difficulties that some early Christians experienced in Greco-Roman society are perhaps echoed in this third-century C.E. painting of an episode from the Additions to Daniel. Two elders, representing accepted religious authority, point accusingly at Susanna, whom they falsely charge with immorality. Daniel (left) observes the scene, about to pronounce on Susanna's innocence. (Courtesy of Alinari/Art Resource, NY)

tale of Susanna and the Elders (Ch. 13); and a primitive detective story, Bel and the Dragon (Ch. 14).

> "You are great, O Lord, God of Daniel,"
> Cyrus exclaimed, "there is no god but you."
> Bel and the Dragon 14:42

The Song of the Three Holy Children The Greek version of Daniel includes, among many briefer additions, three relatively long poetic and narrative units not found in the Hebrew canon. The first of these consists of psalms or hymns reputedly sung by Shadrach, Meshach, and Abednego while confined in a Babylonian furnace. Their songs are inserted into the Hebrew-Aramaic text of Daniel between verses 23 and 24 of Chapter 3 (forming verses 3:24–90 in Catholic Bible editions).

The opening poem, the Prayer of Azariah (the Hebrew name of Abednego), is a lament confessing Israel's collective sins and beseeching its God for mercy, though the psalm strangely never alludes to Azariah's fiery ordeal. The references to Jewish suffering under "an unjust king, the worst in the whole world" (Song of Three Children 3:32) and to the suppression of Temple services (Song of Three Children 3:38–40) indicate that the poem may have been composed during the persecutions of Antiochus IV, perhaps about the same time the apocalyptic portions of Daniel 7–12 were written.

The choral psalm that the three young men sing in unison (Song of Three Children 3:52–90) is a vigorous hymn of praise extolling the "God of [their] ancestors" and inciting the natural elements—earth, air, sea, and sentient life—to praise the Deity. Some critics have suggested that this poem, which resembles the canonical Psalm 148 in thought and Psalm 136 in form, may be a popular hymn of thanksgiving for Maccabean victories. Experts are not agreed, however, on either the exact time of composition or the original language of these poems. Like other additions to Daniel, they may have been written in Hebrew, Aramaic, or Greek during the late second or early first century B.C.E.

Susanna   Because Daniel is still a "young boy" (Sus. 13:46) when the story's action takes place, this cleverly plotted short story is sometimes placed at the beginning of the book, although some modern Catholic translations such as the Jerusalem Bible include it as Chapter 13.

In Babylon during the captivity (587–539 B.C.E.), Susanna, a beautiful and virtuous young wife, rejects the lustful advances of two Jewish elders who are also judges. When they spitefully accuse her of adultery and she is condemned to death by their testimony, the "holy spirit" inspires Daniel to demand a more thorough investigation. Separating the elders, who then give contradictory evidence, he convicts them of bearing false witness, so that they suffer the fate they had planned for Susanna. Although commonly regarded as a suspenseful "detective story," Susanna's experience was probably recorded to criticize corrupt judges of the Jewish **Diaspora** who abused their legal authority.

Bel and the Dragon   This third apocryphal addition, usually appended to Daniel as Chapter 14, is a prose account of three incidents in which Daniel demonstrates either his superior powers of deduction or the deceitful machinations of heathen priests who attempt to ruin him. In the first incident, Daniel proves to "King Astyages" (Cyrus of Persia, who now rules at Babylon) that the great statue of **Bel** (the Babylonian god Marduk) does not eat the food left before it but that the offerings are consumed by lying priests and their families (Bel and Dragon 14:1–22). Disabused of his superstition, Cyrus orders the priests and their relatives slain and commissions Daniel to destroy Bel's idol and temple.

In the next episode, Daniel poisons a dragon, or large serpent, to show his credulous ruler that it is not a god but a mortal reptile (Bel and Dragon 14:23–27). When Babylonians who had revered the serpent learn that Daniel has killed it, they accuse the king of "turning Jewish" and persuade him to throw the iconoclastic foreigner into a lions' pit, where he remains for six days. During this period, an angel carries the prophet Habakkuk from Judah to Babylon so that he can feed Daniel, then immediately returns the prophet to Judah. When the king discovers on the seventh day that Daniel is still uneaten, he releases him, praises his God, and hurls his rivals into the pit, where they are promptly devoured (Bel and Dragon 14:28–42).

As in the story of Susanna, the author here emphasizes that the Hebrew God will "not desert those who love him" (Bel and Dragon 14:39). Indeed, like the canonical Daniel, the Additions consistently dramatize that the Jewish Deity watches over those who faithfully keep his commandments and reject the snares of idol-worshiping pagans.

RECOMMENDED READING

Moore, Carey A. *Daniel, Esther, and Jeremiah: The Additions.* Garden City, N.Y.: Doubleday, 1977.

Tobit

KEY THEMES

A fictional narrative depicting the life of an exiled Israelite family (Tobit, Tobias, and Sarah) living in Nineveh, capital of the Assyrian Empire, during the seventh century B.C.E., Tobit demonstrates that God hears and answers the prayers of his landless and dispossessed faithful. Perhaps influenced by Zoroastrian mythology, the book contains the Bible's first account of an exorcism (Chs. 5–8).

> The prayer of each of them [Tobit and Sarah] found favor before the glory of God, and

The notorious "little horn" of Daniel's vision (Dan. 7:8, 20–22, 24–26; 11:21–45), Antiochus IV Epiphanes (175–163 B.C.E.) was the Seleucid ruler of Hellenistic Syria who profaned the Jerusalem Temple by erecting a statue of Olympian Zeus there, an "abomination" that resounds through the books of Daniel and 1 Maccabees and resurfaces as a sign of End time in the Gospels of Mark and Matthew (Mark 13:14; Matt. 24:15–16). Shown in profile on this Greek coin, Antiochus IV tended to identify his rule with that of Zeus, king of the gods. (Courtesy of Hirmer Fotoarchiv, München)

Raphael was sent to bring remedy to them both.

Tobit 3:16

Life in the Diaspora

Although the Septuagint editors placed Tobit among the historical books, it is really a work of imaginative fiction. The action is set during the seventh century B.C.E. when many Jews from the northern kingdom were scattered throughout the Assyrian Empire. The central figure, Tobit, an aged and pious Jew of the Naphtali tribe, is an exile living in Nineveh, the

Assyrian capital. Though remarkably true in its psychology of character and artistic handling of plot and theme, the book contains several historical and geographical errors. Although the customs, attitudes, and theological beliefs presented in the story suggest that it was written during the Hellenistic period, perhaps about 185–175 B.C.E., the author is unknown.

Tobit, Tobias, and Sarah   The book's purpose is to encourage Jewish exiles to maintain their religious integrity; the author insists that Israel's God hears their prayers and will eventually reward the faithful. This message is dramatized in a well-constructed plot consisting of three closely related narrative strands. The main plot concerns Tobit, an exemplary Jew who strictly observes all aspects of the law but who suffers the illnesses and privations of a latter-day Job. A subplot involves his kinswoman Sarah, a beautiful virgin whose seven husbands have all been killed on their wedding night by the jealous demon Asmodeus. A second subplot concerning Tobit's son Tobias, who travels to Media, exorcises the demon and marries Sarah, effectively ties all the narratives together.

Tobit's story is joined to Sarah's when the Deity hears their simultaneous prayers for death (Tob. 3:16–17). Tobit prays to die because, for piously burying slaughtered Israelites, he has not only been stripped of all his possessions but also has been blinded by bird droppings (Tob. 2:9–3:6). Sarah, unhappy that a maid has accused her of murdering her seven husbands, similarly longs to end her life (Tob. 3:7–15). The earthly connection is provided when Tobias journeys to Ecbatana in Media to claim money that Tobit had entrusted to his kinsman Raguel, who is also Sarah's father.

The archangel Raphael, disguised as a man named Azariah, guides young Tobias to Ecbatana, provides the necessary instructions to exorcise Asmodeus (who flees to Egypt, where an angel binds him), and permits the union of Tobias and Sarah. Raguel, who had spent the wedding night digging a grave for his new son-in-law, is astounded by Tobias's survival. Upon Tobias's triumphant return to Nineveh with the money and a new wife, Raphael also cures Tobit's blindness with fish gall (Tob. 11:10–15).

A treasure house of second-century Jewish social customs and beliefs, this delightful tale deals with such matters as guardian angels (Tob. 5:21; 12:12–13), priestly distinctions (Tob. 1:6–7), dietary restrictions (Tob. 1:10–12), personal prayers (Tob. 3:2–15; 8:5–8), the importance of a decent burial (Tob. 1:17–19; 2:3–8; 14:12), the power of demons and the use of fish entrails in exorcising them (Tob. 3:8; 6:6–8; 8:1–3), seven angels of the heavenly court (Tob. 12:15), and the value of wise parental advice (Tob. 4:3–19). Tobit's popular view of angels, guardian spirits who act as intercessors (Tob. 12:12), and demons seems to reflect the influence of Persian dualism (Zoroastrianism) with its doctrine of warring spirits of Good and Evil.

The last chapters—Tobit's thanksgiving psalm (Tob. 13) and an epilog recounting his advice that Tobias and Sarah leave Nineveh to escape the city's impending destruction (Tob. 14)—may be later additions. The final section, in which Tobias prophesies Nineveh's fall and Jerusalem's restoration, contains the remarkable prediction that "all the nations of the world will be converted to the true worship of God" (Tob. 14:6).

RECOMMENDED READING

Nowell, Irene. "Tobit." In R. E. Brown et al., eds., *The New Jerome Biblical Commentary,* pp. 568–571. Englewood Cliffs, N.J.: Prentice-Hall, 1990.

Judith

KEY THEME

An anonymous historical romance, Judith resembles Esther in depicting the dangers and difficulties of Jews living in the Diaspora (scattering abroad). Set during the Assyrian threat to Israel (Chs. 1–7), the book presents Judith's killing of Holofernes as an act of national heroism (Chs. 8–16).

> The Lord our God is with us still, displaying his strength in Israel and his might against our enemies.
>
> Judith 13:11

Like Tobit, Judith is a historical romance written by an unknown author during the Hellenistic period and set in the distant past. The book begins with a glaring historical error—that Nebuchadnezzar (605–562 B.C.E.) reigned in Nineveh over the Assyrians, when in reality his father, the king of Babylon, had destroyed Nineveh in 612. This error may have been intentional, to show at the outset that the narrative was not meant to be factual history. The true political situation is probably that of the Syrian oppression of the Jews under Antiochus IV (175–164/163 B.C.E.). Nebuchadnezzar, then, represents Antiochus, the despot who tried to eradicate Israel's religion (1 Macc. 1:14–50; Dan. 3:3–15), and the writer advises armed revolt, asserting that Israel's God will defend his people if they remain faithful to him (Jth. 13:11; 16:17).

A National Heroine

Judith was probably written around 150 B.C.E., about a decade after the Maccabees had successfully repulsed the Syrians. The heroine's name, the feminine form of "Judah," literally means "Jewess" and may be intended to symbolize the nation or to remind the reader of Judas, its Maccabean leader. Judith embodies the traditional biblical heroism of the solitary Israelite struggling against a pagan superpower, as David fought Goliath or as Jael felled Sisera (1 Sam. 17:20–54; Judg. 4:17–24; 5:25–30). Judith's triumph over Holofernes, the Assyrian commander, is her nation's victory over their collective enemies.

Assyrians Threaten Judah   The book is divided into two parts. The first (Jth. 1–7) states that after conquering Media, Nebuchadnezzar sent Holofernes to punish countries that had not supported his campaign. After overrunning various other nations, the Assyrians laid siege to Bethulia, a fortified city that may represent Jerusalem, which Antiochus had sacked. When Bethulia is ready to submit, the ruler Uzziah decrees that Israel's Deity be given another five days to rescue the people.

Judith Slays Holofernes   In the second part (Jth. 8–15), Judith, a beautiful widow, berates the leaders who put their God to the test and volunteers to save the city herself. After offering a prayer, she perfumes herself, dresses in her gayest clothes and jewelry, and enters the Assyrian camp, pretending to defect because of her admiration of Holofernes. Flattered, the Assyrian commander invites the seductive woman into his tent, where, after plying him with wine, she takes his sword and decapitates him.

Stowing the head in her travel bag, Judith and her maid convey it to Jerusalem, where it is displayed on the city wall. Dispirited by their leader's death, the Assyrians withdraw, allowing the Jews to loot their camp. Judith dedicates her share of the booty to the Jerusalem Temple. In an epilog, Judith hails her God for protecting his people (Jth. 16:17). After her death at an advanced age, she is honored by her compatriots as a national heroine.

Although Judith was written at a time when slaughtering an enemy could be regarded as an act of religious piety, it is more than a nationalistic war story. Its emphasis on the power of Israel's God to rescue an obedient people echoes a theme recurrent in biblical history: It is not "by sword or spear" that Israel carries the day but only through the will of its God, who can save by the frail hand of a lone woman. (See also 1 Sam. 17:46–47.)

RECOMMENDED READING

Craven, Toni. "Judith." In R. E. Brown et al., eds., *The New Jerome Biblical Commentary*, pp. 572–575. Englewood Cliffs, N.J.: Prentice-Hall, 1990.

de Lange, Nicholas. *Apocrypha: Jewish Literature of the Hellenistic Age.* New York: Viking Press, 1978, pp. 114–128.

Moore, Carey A. *Judith.* Garden City, N.Y.: Doubleday, 1985.

Additions to Esther

KEY THEME

An unknown editor interpolated prayers and pious sentiments into the essentially secular Book of Esther, which originally did not even mention God (Chs. 10–16).

> And Mordecai said, "All this is God's doing."
> Additions to Esther 10:3a

The Septuagint version of the Book of Esther contains six parts not found in the Hebrew original. Although a few scholars hold that the Additions existed first in Hebrew, most believe they were not composed and interpolated into the biblical text until 114 B.C.E. when Esther was translated into Greek. The Septuagint editors interspersed the Additions at various points in the story, weaving the Hebrew original and Greek expansions into a single whole; but when Jerome prepared the Latin Vulgate, he removed the Additions from the main body of the work and placed them at the end (Add. to Esther 10: 3a–16:24).*

Modern translations that include the apocryphal excerpts handle the textual problem in various ways. The Jerusalem Bible restores the Additions to the canonical Hebrew narrative

*Chapter and verse numbers in the Additions follow Jerome's ordering of the Vulgate text.

but prints them in italics to distinguish them from the Hebrew text. The New English Bible places them among the Apocrypha and, for coherence, translates the entire Greek version of Esther with the supplements fitted into their proper sequence.

Making Esther a Torah Loyalist

Religious Interpolations The Additions were apparently intended to heighten the religious implications of Esther's story. Although the Hebrew version contains neither prayers nor references to Israel's God, the Additions emphasize the efficacy of prayer and the Deity's saving power (Add. to Esther 13:8–18, 14:3–19, 15:8); they even preface the account with an apocalyptic dream of Mardochaeus (Mordecai) that places the Jews' deliverance from Persian attack in the context of Yahweh's ultimate victory over all worldly powers (Add. to Esther 11:2–12).

A devout practitioner of Torah Judaism and Kosher dietary laws, the Esther of the Greek version refuses to eat Gentile food (Add. to Esther 14:17) and finds her marriage to a non-Jewish husband, Emperor Ahasuerus (Xerxes I), repellent (Add. to Esther 14:15). These added touches stress the strict observance of Jewish law and abhorrence of having to comply with the requirements of a pagan environment by a heroine who implores the Deity:

> As for ourselves, save us by your hand,
> and come to my help, for I am alone
> and have no one but you, Lord.
> You have knowledge of all things,
> and you know that I hate honors from the
>   godless,
> that I loathe the bed of the uncircumcised,
> of any foreigner whatever.
> You know I am under constraint,
> that I loathe the symbol of my high position
> bound round my brow when I appear at court;
> I loathe it as if it were a filthy rag
> and do not wear it on my days of leisure.
> Your handmaid has not eaten at Haman's table,

> nor taken pleasure in the royal banquets,
> nor drunk the wine of libations.
> > Additions to Esther 14:14–17

The Additions increase the suspense of Esther's unsolicited interview with the emperor by dramatizing the emotions it arouses (Add. to Esther 15:6–19). They also attempt to lend authenticity by reproducing the text of Artaxerxes' letter condemning Haman (who turns out to be a Macedonian spy), praising the king's Jewish subjects and commanding them to defend themselves when attacked (Add. to Esther 16:1–24). Like the Hebrew original, the Additions present the Jewish characters operating in an atmosphere of intrigue and competition instigated by jealous pagans. But unlike the canonical tale, the Additions transform the violent episode of Jewish self-defense into a declaration of their God's omnipotence; for here, even Artaxerxes testifies to this Deity's control of events (Add. to Esther 16:4, 21).

RECOMMENDED READING

Moore, Carey A. *Daniel, Esther, and Jeremiah: The Additions.* Garden City, N.Y.: Doubleday, 1977.

Baruch

KEY THEMES

A composite work by at least three different writers, Baruch purports to be a prophetic document written by Jeremiah's secretary early in the Babylonian captivity. The book includes a prayer of the Jewish exiles (Chs. 1–3), a hymn to Wisdom and religious poems (Chs. 3–5), and a letter of Jeremiah (Ch. 6).

> [Wisdom is revealed in] the book of the
>   commandments of God,
> the Law that stands for ever;

those who keep her live,
those who desert her die.

Baruch 4:1

Baruch is the only book of the Apocrypha whose mode resembles the prophetic. Although it purports to have been written about 582 B.C.E. (Bar. 1:2) by the secretary and companion of the prophet Jeremiah (Jer. 36:4–10), scholars agree that it is a composite work to which at least three different writers anonymously contributed. The book's four parts have been dated from about 200 B.C.E. for the earliest additions to after 70 C.E. for the latest additions. Although set during the Babylonian exile, it more accurately reflects the problems of non-Palestinian Jews dispersed throughout the Hellenistic world.

Counsel for Jewish Exiles

Exiles' Prayer   The first part (Bar. 1:1–3:8) contains several confusing contradictions. It states, for example, that the "book of Baruch" was written in Babylon five years after the Babylonians had burned Solomon's Temple (Bar. 1:2), yet it pictures the exiles asking the high priest and his assistants in Jerusalem to offer prayers in "the house of the Lord" (Bar. 1:14). Equally confusing is the statement that Baruch read "this book" to an assembly of Jewish exiles living in Babylon (Bar. 1:1–4), when it is clear that the book relates events that occurred long after the public reading.

The rest of this prose section (Bar. 1:15–3:8), which resembles parts of Daniel (see Dan. 9:4–19), depicts the exiled Jews confessing the sins that caused their nation's downfall (Bar. 1:15–2:10; 2:20–26) and beseeching divine mercy (Bar. 2:11–19; 3:1–8). It also contains a prophecy that the scattered people will be restored to their homeland (Bar. 2:27–35).

Hymn and Poems   The second part (Bar. 3:9–4:4), apparently by a different author, is a didactic hymn praising Israel's God for revealing his wisdom in the Mosaic law. The third section (Bar. 4:5–5:9), echoing motifs in Second Isaiah and Lamentations, contains poems of hope and comfort as well as of sorrow for Jerusalem's fall. The poet realizes that Israel's exile is a punishment for its violations of the law but foresees a joyous return to Palestine (Bar. 5:1–9).

Letter of Jeremiah   Although the ancient manuscripts place this document after Lamentations, the Latin Vulgate and most English Bibles that include the Apocrypha attach it to Baruch, where it appears as Chapter 6. (The New English Bible prints it as a separate book following Baruch.) Purporting to be a letter from Jeremiah to Jews about to be deported to Babylon, the document is in fact a much later work, apparently modeled on the prophet's authentic sixth-century letter to Babylonian exiles. (See Jeremiah 29.) Estimates on the date of composition vary from 317 to about 100 B.C.E.

The writer's theme is the evil of idolatry, to which he devotes the most virulent and extensive attack in the Bible. Although the only heathen god specifically mentioned is Bel (Marduk) (Bar. 6:4), scholars believe that he is really denouncing Hellenistic deities that Jews scattered abroad might for social and political reasons be tempted to worship. "Babylon" would then be a symbol for areas outside Palestine where Jews had been dispersed.

The author extends Jeremiah's prediction that the exile would last seventy years (Jer. 25:12) to "seven generations" (Bar. 6:3), which, taking a biblical generation as forty years (Num. 32:13), would mean that the Jews would remain exiled until the end of the fourth century B.C.E. The letter thus updates earlier biblical themes and applies them to contemporary situations in the Hellenistic Diaspora.

RECOMMENDED READING

Moore, Carey A. *Daniel, Esther, and Jeremiah: The Additions.* Garden City, N.Y.: Doubleday, 1977.

Ecclesiasticus
(Wisdom of Jesus ben Sirach)

KEY THEMES

A poetic compilation of proverbs, sage advice, and philosophical reflections, Ecclesiasticus was written early in the second century B.C.E. by Jesus (Joshua), son of Sirach, the head of a professional wisdom school in Jerusalem. Translated into Greek and published in 132 B.C.E. by Jesus' grandson, it contains a lengthy collection of wise sayings and practical counsel (Chs. 1–42), including a famous speech by Wisdom herself (Ch. 24). The second part consists of hymns and a eulogy of famous Israelites (Chs. 42–51), ending with a biographical postscript.

> Thoughts are rooted in the heart,
> and this sends out four branches,
> good and evil, life and death.
> Ecclesiasticus 37:17–18

The longest Wisdom book in the Bible, Ecclesiasticus is also the only apocryphal writing whose author, original translator, and date are known. The writer identifies himself as Jesus ben (son of) Sirach (Ecclus. 50:27), a professional teacher of wisdom who conducted a school or house of learning in Jerusalem (Ecclus. 51:24). In a preface to the main work, ben Sirach's grandson reveals that he brought the book to Egypt, where he translated it from Hebrew into Greek at a date equivalent to 132 B.C.E.; his grandfather had composed it in Jerusalem about 180 B.C.E. The title, which means "church book," may reflect either its extensive use in church worship or the fact that though the Jews eventually denied it a place in the Hebrew Bible, the Christian Church received it into the canon.

Sayings and Reflections　Written in the tradition of Proverbs, Ecclesiasticus is largely a collection of wise sayings, moral essays, hymns to wisdom, practical advice to the young and inexperienced, instructions in proper social and religious conduct, private meditations, and extended reflections on the human condition. Like other postexilic sages, ben Sirach perceives an ordered design in the universe and counsels others to conform their lives to it. A learned, respected, influential representative of upper-class Judaism, his tone is genial, pragmatic, and urbane. Writing more than a decade before the persecutions of Antiochus IV, he believes that life can be a positive experience if one only learns to conduct oneself with prudence, insight, and the right degree of shrewdness.

Wisdom and the Good Life

Completely a man of the present, ben Sirach rejects any belief in angels, demons, or life after death. Apocalyptic enthusiasms are not for him. "The son of man," he asserts, "is not immortal" (Ecclus. 17:30). With his emphasis on the law, Temple service, good works, and denial of a resurrection or afterlife, ben Sirach seems to be a forerunner of the Sadducees. Like that intensely conservative, aristocratic party that largely controlled the priesthood and Temple in the first century C.E., he appears to regard the law as final and unchanging, an essentially static guidebook to both the moral and material good life.

Ecclesiasticus also resembles Proverbs and the Wisdom of Solomon in consisting mostly of poetry, chiefly couplets of parallel lines. The first forty-two chapters, containing many brief aphorisms interspersed with longer discourses, offer advice and admonition on many diverse topics: the fear of God as the basis of wisdom (Ecclus. 1:20; 32:14–33:3), humility (Ecclus. 3:17–26), generosity to the poor (Ecclus. 4:1–11; 7:32–40), choosing prudent friendships (Ecclus. 6:5–17; 12:8–19; 22:19–32), trusting in God (Ecclus. 2:1–23; 11:12–30), humanity's moral responsibilities (Ecclus. 16:24–17:13), female spite (Ecclus. 25:13–36), a good wife (Ecclus. 26:1–23), proper manners and control of drinking at banquets (Ecclus. 31:12–32:17),

Discovered at Masada, the hilltop fortress where the last important band of Jewish rebels held out against Roman armies (73 C.E.), this fragment of the Book of Ecclesiasticus (Wisdom of Jesus ben Sirach) is approximately 2000 years old. (Courtesy of PhotoEdit)

honoring doctors and respecting scholars (Ecclus. 38:1–15; 31:1–15), and the human predicament and fate of the wicked (Ecclus. 40:1–11; 41:5–16).

Chapter 24:1–30 contains a splendid oration by Lady Wisdom, whom ben Sirach explicitly identifies with the Mosaic law (Ecclus. 19:20, 24:23):

> I came forth from the mouth of the Most High,
>   and I covered the earth like a mist . . .
> From eternity, in the beginning, he created me,
>   and for eternity I shall remain.
> I ministered before him in the holy tabernacle,
>   and thus was I established on Zion.
> In the beloved city he has given me rest,
>   and in Jerusalem I wield my authority.
>   Ecclesiasticus 24:3, 9–11

Hymns and a Eulogy Chapters 42:15–43:33 comprise a hymn praising the Deity's glory as revealed in physical nature, a poem that rivals Psalm 19 in beauty. This is followed by the best-known passage in the book—"let us now praise famous men"—a eulogy of twenty-nine Old Testament heroes, from Enoch to Nehemiah, including Abraham, Joseph, Aaron (Israel's first high priest, who is given more space than the lawgiver Moses), David, Hezekiah, and Elijah. Ezra's name is conspicuously absent, presumably because this great interpreter of the law was regarded as the progenitor of a religious movement that culminated in Pharisaism, a development of which ben Sirach strongly disapproved.

The tribute to Israel's ancestors climaxes in the praise of Simon the high priest (about 225–200 B.C.E.), whom ben Sirach lauds as personifying the best of his nation's traditions (Ecclus. 50:1–24). As intercessor between the people and their God, Simon was privileged to enter the Temple's **Holy of Holies** annually on the Day of Atonement (see Lev. 16) and there pronounce the divine name Yahweh, which by Hellenistic times was considered too sacred to utter publicly. The book concludes with an epilog containing ben Sirach's hymn of personal thanksgiving (Ecclus. 51:1–12) and an autobiographical résumé of the rewards of pursuing wisdom (Ecclus. 51:13–30).

The emphasis that ben Sirach places on the practical advantages of strict moral conduct, wealth, and worldly success and his view that Temple services are the most important part of Israel's worship well represent attitudes characteristic of latter Sadduceeism. His assumption that his God's intentions for humanity were completely and unchangingly revealed in the Mosaic code and Temple liturgy helps explain why the Sadducees as a party did not long survive the Roman destruction of Jerusalem and its sanctuary in 70 C.E. Ironically, a fragment of ben Sirach's work was found recently at Masada, site of the final zealot hold-out against the Romans.

RECOMMENDED READING

Hengel, Martin. *Judaism and Hellenism.* London and Philadelphia: SCM Press, 1979.

Skehan, Patrick W., and Di Lella, Alexander A. *The Wisdom of Ben Sira.* Garden City, N.Y.: Doubleday, 1987.

Snaith, John G. *Ecclesiasticus: or The Wisdom of Jesus Son of Sirach.* Cambridge Bible Commentary on the New English Bible. London: Cambridge University Press, 1974.

The Wisdom of Solomon (Wisdom)

KEY THEMES

Although attributed to Solomon, this brilliant collection of poems, proverbs, and sage meditations was composed by an anonymous Hellenized Jew living in Alexandria, Egypt, during the last century B.C.E. A creative synthesis of Hebrew wisdom traditions with speculative Greek philosophy, the book surveys the nature of divine Wisdom and the rewards of virtue and immortality it imparts (Chs. 1–5) and describes the origin, character, and value of Wisdom (Chs. 6–9). The more prosaic second half surveys the role of Wisdom in Israel's sacred history (Chs. 10–19).

> Wisdom is a spirit, a friend to man.
> Wisdom of Solomon 1:6

Although the Wisdom of Solomon presents itself as King Solomon's address to the world's rulers (Wisd. of Sol. 1:1), it is really the work of an anonymous writer aimed at Jews living in exile, some of whom were apparently tempted to compromise or relinquish their religion under the allurements of Greek culture and philosophy or the pressure of Gentile discrimination. The author's familiarity with Greek terms and philosophic ideas (Wisd. of Sol. 8:7, 19–20; 12:1) indicates that he lived during the Hellenistic period, perhaps about 100 B.C.E. He appears to have been a well-educated member of the Jewish community in **Alexandria**, Egypt, a populous cosmopolitan city that then rivaled Athens as the world's leading intellectual center.

By demonstrating that Judaism's ethical and religious wisdom is superior to that of the Gentiles, the author hopes to encourage Jews to maintain their traditional allegiances. He endeavors also to show that his religion offers a view of world history and divine justice that will appeal to the moral and rational Gentile as well. A creative synthesis of Hebrew and Greek thought, the Wisdom of Solomon is theologically one of the most important books in the Apocrypha and a major contribution to biblical wisdom literature. The book may be divided into three parts: (1) the rewards of Wisdom (personified as God's Spirit) and the promise of immortality (Wisd. of Sol. 1–5); (2) the origin, character, and value of Wisdom (Wisd. of Sol.

6–9); and (3) the Wisdom of Israel's Deity operating in human history (Wisd. of Sol. 10–19).

Rewards of Wisdom   The first section contrasts the fate of the wicked—whose twisted reasoning is vividly rendered in 2:1–20—with that of the righteous. Although the ungodly may prosper on earth and oppress the good, the soul's survival after death (different from the bodily resurrection depicted in Dan. 12:2) guarantees that the Deity's justice will ultimately prevail. Asserting that "God created man for immortality" and "made him the image of his own eternal self" (Wisd. of Sol. 2:23), the author assures his readers that "the souls of the just are in God's hand and torment shall not touch them" (Wisd. of Sol. 3:1).

Foolish skeptics might believe that the just perish utterly but that their sufferings are merely a test to refine their worth and their deaths are a disguised blessing; they are destined to judge nations and rule over the world (Wisd. of Sol. 3: 2–8; see also Rev. 2:26–27; 20:4). The ungodly, meanwhile, are punished not arbitrarily but according to their own evil designs (Wisd. of Sol. 3:10). This concept of an afterlife in which immortal souls are rewarded for their good deeds on earth is the author's response to the problem of undeserved suffering that had troubled writers of such other Wisdom books as Job. Here the Deity's justice toward his human creation is vindicated because he provides an eternity of bliss to compensate for temporary earthly pain.

Origin, Character, and Value of Wisdom
Comparable Greek ideas appear in the second section, which features "Solomon's" praise of Lady Wisdom, the bringer of immortality (Wisd. of Sol. 6:1; 8:13). The speaker, who takes Wisdom as his "bride," implies that the soul exists in heaven prior to its incarnation or imprisonment in a physical body (Wisd. of Sol. 8:19–20; 9:15). This belief in an immaterial, preexistent soul that escapes to the spirit realm

at the body's dissolution is typical of Platonic and neo-Platonic thought.

Similarly representative of Greek ethical philosophy is the author's exposition of the four classical virtues, which became the four cardinal virtues of Christian morality:

> Or if it be virtue you love,
> why, virtues are the fruit of her labors,
> since it is she who teaches temperance
>   and prudence,
> justice and fortitude;
> nothing in life is more serviceable to men
>   than these.
>
> Wisdom of Solomon 8:7

Wisdom in Sacred History   In the lengthy third part, the author presents an idealized survey of early humanity (Wisd. of Sol. 10) and of Israel's history, contrasting the Deity's judgments on the heathen with his saving care of the chosen people, to whom Wisdom lent strength and understanding. The moralistic discussion of Israel and Egypt (Wisd. of Sol. 11–19) is interrupted by a diatribe against idolatry (Wisd. of Sol. 13:1–15:17) that is reminiscent of Second Isaiah's castigation of the Babylonian gods (Isa. 40, 46). The imaginative reinterpretation of Israel's past in the final chapters may have been intended to inspire hope among the exiled Jews that their God still intervened in human affairs on their behalf (Wisd. of Sol. 16:7–8; 19:22).

The author attributes the presence of evil and death to the "Devil's spite" (Wisd. of Sol. 2:23–24), an interpretation of the serpent's role in Genesis 3 that would culminate in the doctrine of inherited sin expounded by Paul (Rom. 5) and the writer of 2 Esdras 3:7. (For other passages that influenced New Testament writers, compare Wisd. of Sol. 1:7 with Col. 1:17; Wisd. of Sol. 3:7 and Matt. 13:42; Wisd. of Sol. 3:14 and Matt. 19:12; Wisd. of Sol. 5:16 and Rev. 2:10; Wisd. of Sol. 5:16–19 and Eph. 6: 11–17; Wisd. of Sol. 6:3–4 and Rom. 13:1–12; Wisd. of Sol. 14:22–31 and Rom. 1:18–32.)

Finally, the reference to divine Wisdom manifesting itself as God's "all-powerful Word" leaping "down from the heavens, from the royal throne" into the "heart of a doomed land" where "he touched the sky, yet trod the earth" (Wisd. of Sol. 18:15, 16) anticipates the doctrine of the Word (Logos) developed by **Philo Judaeus**, a later Alexandrine Jewish scholar. Philo's Logos concept was then adopted and modified by the author of John's Gospel to explain the incarnation of the prehuman Jesus (John 1:1, 14). Such foreshadowing of ideas popular in Christianity may explain why the Wisdom of Solomon was recommended reading in many early churches and was included with New Testament writings in the Muratorian Canon.

RECOMMENDED READING

Reese, James M. *Hellenistic Influence on the Book of Wisdom and Its Consequences.* Rome: Biblical Institute Press, 1970.

Winston, David. *The Wisdom of Solomon.* Garden City, N.Y.: Doubleday, 1979.

Wright, Addison G. "Wisdom." In R. E. Brown, et al., eds., *The New Jerome Biblical Commentary,* pp. 510–522. Englewood Cliffs, N.J.: Prentice-Hall, 1990.

2 Esdras (4 Ezra)

KEY THEMES

Attributed to the historical Ezra, a priestly scribe credited with assembling the final edition of the Mosaic Torah, 2 Esdras was actually written about 100 C.E., thirty years after the Roman destruction of Jerusalem. Combining themes from wisdom and apocalyptic literature, the book includes a theodicy, a perceptive examination of the conflict between religious faith and the reality of Evil (Chs. 3–8); apocalyptic visions of future history and Israel's redemption (Chs. 9–13); and an account of Ezra's author-

ship of the Hebrew Bible and Apocrypha (Ch. 14). Composed about the same time as the New Testament Book of Revelation, 2 Esdras was later framed by Christian additions (Chs. 1, 2, and 15).

> To what end has the capacity for understanding been given me? For I did not mean to ask about ways above, but about those things which pass by us every day; why Israel . . . whom you loved [is] given up to godless tribes.
>
> 2 Esdras 4:22–23

2 Esdras is a composite work of Jewish and Christian origin and one of the latest books to find its way into the Apocrypha. Although Chapters 3–14, the central portion of the book, purport to have been written by the historical priest Ezra while he was a captive in Babylon about 557 B.C.E., scholarly analysis of the text indicates that this section was probably composed in either Hebrew or Aramaic late in the first century C.E., after the Romans had destroyed Jerusalem and the Temple. Like the New Testament Book of Revelation, which it greatly resembles in theme and outlook, 2 Esdras reflects the tension existing between loyal Jews and Greco-Roman society.

After 2 Esdras had been translated into Greek, an anonymous Christian writer added Chapters 1 and 2 around 150 C.E. Perhaps a century later, another Christian, also writing in Greek, appended Chapters 15 and 16. But 2 Esdras did not appear in the Septuagint; it entered Christian Scripture via Old Latin translations and Jerome's Vulgate, although conflicting Ethiopic, Syriac, Greek, Arabic, Armenian, and other versions exist as well.

The Problem of Evil in Human History

Ezra's Theodicy The first two chapters are mainly Christian apologetics implying that God has repudiated "natural" Israel as his chosen people and adopted instead a "spiritual" Israel, the Christian Church, as his own. Chapters 3–

14 consist of seven apocalyptic visions, of which the first three are cast in the form of philosophical dialogs between Ezra and various angels. These angelic mentors counter Ezra's repeated questioning of his God's justice with attempts to defend the Deity's ways to humans. In general, Ezra's questions are more penetrating than the answers he receives.

If Babylon (read "Rome") was God's chosen instrument to punish Israel, Ezra asks, why are Babylon's citizens so much worse behaved than the Jewish people Babylon oppresses? Why has God allowed an enemy nation that mocks him to destroy those who have at least tried to worship him (2 Esd. 3:25–32)? Would not God's lesson to both Jewish and pagan nations be less equivocal if he punished directly, "with his own hands," rather than through an ungodly intermediary like Babylon (Rome) (2 Esd. 5:28–30)? Is it not better to remain unborn than to live and suffer without knowing why (2 Esd. 4:12)? The angels' reply is that God will act to dispense justice in good time. The flourishing of wickedness is only temporary; it will be terminated according to a foreordained timetable (2 Esd. 4: 27–32), and it is not humanity's business to worry about the divine schedule.

Ezra is concerned about not only the earthly plight of his people but also the fate of their souls after death. Reluctantly agreeing that many act wrongly while only a few are righteous, he nonetheless disputes the justice of condemning sinners to everlasting torment without any further chance of repentance. Chapter 7, vividly picturing the blessings of salvation and the agonies of the damned, is the most complete picture of afterlife and judgment in the Old Testament Apocrypha.

2 Esdras gives us, in addition, the Old Testament's first statements of *original sin*—the belief that all humanity has inherited Adam's sin and is therefore born deserving death (2 Esd. 5: 21–26; 7:46–48, 70–72). This doctrine of humanity's inherent propensity toward vice is also expounded by the Apostle Paul in Romans 5 and has since become dogma in many Christian denominations. Finally, the author also seems to express a belief in the existence of the human soul before birth (2 Esd. 4:42).

Apocalyptic Visions   In Chapter 9, the book changes from a Jobian theodicy to a more purely apocalyptic preview of the "last days." The fourth vision depicts a woman who mourns her dead son and who is suddenly transformed into a thriving city. Uriel explains that the woman is Jerusalem, her lost son the destroyed Temple, and the splendid city a future glorified Zion (2 Esd. 9–10). Chapters 11 and 12, with their portrait of a mighty eagle, are reminiscent of John's visions in Revelation. This proud eagle (Rome) that now dominates the earth is destined to disappear when a lion (the Messiah) appears to judge it for its persecution of the righteous (2 Esd. 11:38–12:34). The sixth vision emphasizes the certainty of the Messiah's imminent appearance and his just destruction of the pagans who oppress Jerusalem (2 Esd. 13).

Ezra's Production of the Deuterocanonical Books Ezra's pre-eminent importance to Jewish religion is emphasized in Chapter 14, where the "Most High" inspires him to write ninety-four sacred books. Twenty-four of these books are canonical Scripture—the published Hebrew Bible—and the remaining seventy are reserved for the "wise" who alone can understand them. This passage indicates that the author credited Ezra with replacing the Hebrew Bible that the Babylonians had allegedly destroyed. The extrabiblical books are presumably the deuterocanonical books (Apocrypha) and other apocalyptic works, such as 2 Esdras itself.

Following his literary efforts, Ezra is transported to heaven to dwell with other holy men. In light of the Jewish traditions on which the author draws, Ezra is clearly seen as a heroic figure who embodies the virtues of priest, prophet, and lawgiver. A second Moses, he also incorporates the honors of Elijah and the antediluvian patriarch Enoch, both of whom had been similarly caught up to heaven.

The two final chapters, a Christian addition of the second century C.E., emphasize the Deity's coming vengeance on the wicked. Predicting a series of terrors and calamities (again reminiscent of Revelation), the book assures the reader that the ungodly nation (Rome), as well as all other empires that afflict the righteous, will fall and that the guilty will be consumed by fire (2 Esd. 15–16).

RECOMMENDED READING

de Lange, Nicholas. *Apocrypha: Jewish Literature of the Hellenistic Age.* New York: Viking Press, 1978.

Dentan, Robert C. *The Apocrypha: Bridge of the Testaments.* Greenwich, Conn.: Seabury Press, 1954.

Goodspeed, Edgar J., ed. and trans. "The Second Book of Esdras." In *The Apocrypha: An American Translation,* pp. 39–106. New York: Random House, 1959.

Meyers, Jacob M. *1 and 2 Esdras.* Anchor Bible. Garden City, N.Y.: Doubleday, 1974.

Nickelsburg, George W. E. *Jewish Literature Between the Bible and the Mishnah.* Philadelphia: Fortress Press, 1981.

TERMS AND CONCEPTS TO REMEMBER

Abednego	Gabriel
Alexandria	Gentile
Antiochus IV	Holy of Holies
apocalypse	Meshach
apocalyptic literature	Philo Judaeus
Bel	pseudonymity
Belshazzar	resurrection
Chaldean	scribe
Danel	Shadrach
Diaspora	Sheol
eschatology	symbol

QUESTIONS FOR REVIEW

1. Define the term *deuterocanonical.* After reviewing Questions 12 through 16 in Part 1, explain why Roman Catholic and Greek Orthodox persons regard some books that appeared only in the Septuagint as deuterocanonical, whereas most Protestant groups classify them as Apocryphal.

2. What effect did the campaigns of Alexander of Macedonia have on the biblical world? Which two kingdoms ruled by Alexander's successors sequentially controlled Judea?

3. Identify Antiochus IV and describe his policies concerning the Jewish religion. What actions did he take against the Jerusalem Temple and the practice of the Jewish religion?

4. Summarize the main events in the books of Maccabees. Who were the Maccabees and why did they lead a revolt against Antiochus? What political changes did they bring to the land of Judah by 142 B.C.E.?

5. How did the "great tribulation" of Antiochus's persecutions and the creating of martyrs for the Jewish faith stimulate apocalyptic ideas? What is an apocalypse? Define *eschatology* and its relation to apocalyptic writings.

6. Enumerate ten major characteristics of apocalyptic literature. What part does ethical and cosmic *dualism* play in apocalyptic thought? In what ways is the Book of Daniel apocalyptic? What new eschatological idea about a future life does it introduce?

7. When and under what circumstances do scholars believe that the Book of Daniel was composed? Describe the author's view of Gentile empires and Israel's suffering. What lessons for Jews living outside Judah do the stories of Daniel and the three Hebrew youths try to teach? Should Jews of the Diaspora retain their traditional customs, or should they follow the traditions of their host countries? Why is this issue important in Daniel?

8. What message do the books of Tobit and Judith have for Jews living under foreign ruler? Identify Raphael and Holofernes.

9. To what general category do the books of Ecclesiasticus and Wisdom of Solomon be-

long? List some of their principal themes. When and where were they written, and for what presumed audience? What specific information do we have about the author, translator, and editor of Ecclesiasticus?

QUESTIONS FOR DISCUSSION AND REFLECTION

1. Why did apocalyptic ideas become so popular among many Jews between about 200 B.C.E. and 200 C.E.? Compare and contrast the apocalypses of Daniel and 2 Esdras. Why are each of these books written in the name of a long-dead sage? Describe the differing political circumstances at the time of their respective compositions. What great national disaster does 2 Esdras lament? Which book—Daniel or 2 Esdras—deals more profoundly with the problem of Evil and the purpose of human suffering? Which shows the more highly developed eschatology?

2. Discuss the nature and function of divine Wisdom in Ecclesiasticus and the Wisdom of Solomon. What role does God's Wisdom play in human history? In what ways do these two books contribute to Israel's wisdom tradition? How does the concept of immortality promised in the Wisdom of Solomon add an important new dimension to the problem of undeserved suffering dramatized in older Wisdom books like Job?

Pseudepigrapha

In addition to the deuterocanonical works, Hellenistic Jewish writers also produced a body of religious literature known collectively as the **Pseudepigrapha**, books that were not admitted to the canons of either the Hebrew or Greek editions of the Bible. Although designated as pseudonymous—ascribed by anonymous writers to luminaries of the past, such as Enoch,

Noah, Moses, or Isaiah—some books of the Pseudepigrapha, such as 3 and 4 Maccabees, make no claims of illustrious authorship.

Dating from about 200 B.C.E. to 200 C.E., these documents include a variety of literary types, ranging from apocalypses and sacred legends to interpretative retellings of canonical narratives, such as the Book of Jubilees. Like the Apocrypha, pseudepigraphal books appeared in Hebrew, Aramaic, and Greek. Because of limited space, only brief summaries of some representative works that may have influenced later Judeo-Christian thought are given here.

RECOMMENDED READING

Charles, R. H. *Apocrypha and Pseudepigrapha of the Old Testament,* Vol. 2. Oxford, Eng.: Clarendon Press, 1913. Charles provides translations, with critical introductions and numerous annotations of the texts, of most of the pseudepigraphal books. Because this volume appeared long before discovery of the Dead Sea Scrolls, however, the reader must approach some of the author's conclusions with caution.

Charlesworth, James H., ed. *The Old Testament Pseudepigrapha.* Vol. 1, *Apocalyptic Literature and Testaments.* Garden City, N.Y.: Doubleday, 1983. A scholarly new edition of the Pseudepigrapha (including several documents not in Charles's collection), with new translations and historical-critical annotations on the text. A major work of scholarship.

———. *The Old Testament Pseudepigrapha.* Vol. 2, *Expansions of the "Old Testament" and Legends, Wisdom and Philosophical Literature, Prayers, Psalms and Odes, Fragments of Lost Judeo-Hellenistic Works.* Garden City, N.Y.: Doubleday, 1985. Includes annotated editions of Jubilees, Letter of Aristeas, and 3 and 4 Maccabees.

de Lange, Nicholas. *Apocrypha: Jewish Literature of the Hellenistic Age.* New York: Viking Press, 1978. Discusses several pseudepigraphal works.

Eissfeldt, Otto. *The Old Testament: An Introduction.* New York: Harper & Row, 1965. In this English version of a standard German work, the author includes précis of the background and content of fourteen pseudepigraphal books.

Nickelsburg, George W. E. *Jewish Literature Between the Bible and the Mishnah*. Philadelphia: Fortress Press, 1981.

Rost, Leonhard. *Judaism Outside the Hebrew Canon: An Introduction to the Documents*. Nashville, Tenn.: Abingdon Press, 1976.

1 Enoch (Ethiopic Book of Enoch)

KEY THEMES

Perhaps the oldest surviving example of Jewish apocalyptic literature, 1 Enoch combines imaginative visions of the spirit world with images of End time (eschatology). Using a rich mythology involving cosmic conflict, fallen angels, and a tour of heaven, the apocalypse is editorially divided into five books: (1) the Watchers (Chs. 1–36), (2) the Similitudes (Parables) (Chs. 37–71), (3) the Astronomical Writings (Chs. 72–82), (4) the Dream Visions (Chs. 83–90), and (5) the Epistle of Enoch (Chs. 91–107).

> And the first heaven shall depart and pass
> away,
> And a new heaven shall appear . . .
> And all shall be in goodness and
> righteousness,
> And sin shall no more be mentioned forever.
> 1 Enoch 91:16, 17

Ascribed to **Enoch**, the antediluvian patriarch who was reputedly transported alive to heaven (Gen. 5:24), the Book of Enoch is a heterogeneous collection of the work of many unknown authors. Composed and compiled during the Hellenistic period, it is designated as Ethiopic because its text has been transmitted in that language.

The oldest materials in the compilation (found in 1 En. 6–11; 54–55:2; 60; 65–69; and 106–107) are believed to be fragments of a Book of Noah or Book of Lamech (mentioned in Bk. Jub. 10:13 and 21:10), which may date from the first half of the second century B.C.E. The Ten

Weeks Apocalypse (1 En. 93 and 91:12–17), which apparently antedates the Book of Daniel, may have appeared about 170 B.C.E. Most of Enoch's other components may be assigned to the late second and first centuries B.C.E., with the "Similitudes" (1 En. 37–71)—with their messianic references to the "Son of man"—probably dating from the first century C.E. or slightly earlier.

Emulating the Pentateuch, Psalms, Proverbs, and Ecclesiasticus, an editor-compiler arranged the Enoch collection into five distinct parts. Its division into 108 chapters did not become standard until the nineteenth century. After a prefatory speech in which Enoch is depicted proclaiming the ultimate destinies of the wicked and righteous (1 En. 1–5), section 1 describes the fall of the Watchers (angels who mated with the daughters of humans to produce the giants; see Gen. 6:1–4), their punishment, and Enoch's metaphysical journeys though the earth and Underworld (1 En. 6–36).

Section 2 contains a series of parables concerning a variety of topics, including the Messiah, the rewards of the righteous, judgment by the **Son of Man**, the torments of the fallen angels, and similar eschatological matters (1 En. 37–71). Section 3 includes a primitive scientific treatise on astronomy, a discussion of the sun, moon, and planets and of human calendars based on them (1 En. 72–82). Section 4 presents a sequence of dream visions, notably of the (then) coming Flood, and an allegoric panorama of world history that designates Jews as tame animals and pagans as wild beasts. It begins with Adam as a white bull and culminates in the appearance of the Messiah as a lamb who becomes a "great animal" with black horns (1 En. 83–90).

Section 5 is a book of exhortation that includes Enoch's admonition for his children, an apocalypse in which world history is divided into periods of ten weeks of varying length, and pictures of blessings for the righteous and woes for the godless (1 En. 91–105). The book concludes with a fragment from the Book of Noah describing miracles occurring at the patriarch's birth and Enoch's last words of encouragement for the pious who await their God's day of reckoning (1 En. 106–198).

From even this cursory survey of its contents, it is apparent that the Book of Enoch—an anthology of history, astronomy, law, poetry, eschatological doctrines, and apocalyptic visions—provided a wealth of theological ideas, some of which were extremely influential on Hellenistic Judaism. After the disastrous wars with Rome (66–73 and 132–135 C.E.), however, which were apparently inspired in part by apocalypse-fed expectations, the Jews largely repudiated this kind of writing. By then, Christians had taken up many of these speculations and eschatological hopes and adapted them to their own doctrinal needs.

Among the early Christians, then, Enoch was understandably popular, although after the fourth century C.E. its influence declined. In time, all complete manuscripts of this Hebrew-Aramaic work vanished. It was not until the end of the eighteenth century that an Ethiopic translation was found in Abyssinia. The first English version of the entire book appeared in 1821. In 1952, a number of Aramaic fragments of Enoch were found among the Dead Sea Scrolls, and some scholars believe that the book probably originated in the Qumran community.

RECOMMENDED READING

Charles, R. H. "Book of Enoch, with an Introduction." In *Apocrypha and Pseudepigrapha of the Old Testament,* Vol. 2, pp. 163–281. Oxford, Eng.: Clarendon Press, 1913.

Charlesworth, James H., ed. *The Old Testament Pseudepigrapha.* Vol. 1, *Apocalyptic Literature and Testaments.* Garden City, N.Y.: Doubleday, 1983, pp. 5–100.

Knibb, Michael A., trans. *The Ethiopic Book of Enoch: A New Edition in the Light of the Aramaic Dead Sea Fragments.* Oxford, Eng.: Clarendon Press, 1978.

Milik, Jozef T. *The Books of Enoch: Aramaic Fragments of Qumran Cave 4.* Oxford, Eng.: Clarendon Press, 1976.

Nickelsburg, George W. E. *Jewish Literature Between the Bible and the Mishnah.* Philadelphia: Fortress Press, 1981, pp. 43–55, 145–160.

2 Enoch (Slavonic Book of Enoch)

KEY THEMES

An apocalyptic interpretation of the Enoch traditions, 2 Enoch describes a mystical journey through the ten levels of heaven (Chs. 1–21), a purview of human history (Chs. 22–38), an admonition based on Enoch's intimacy with the divine realm (Chs. 39–66), and a conclusion summarizing his supernatural experiences (Chs. 67 and 68).

> [Enoch's] books are many, and in them you will learn all the Lord's works, all that has been from the beginning of creation, and will be till the end of time.
>
> 2 Enoch 47:2

The Slavonic Book of Enoch (so called because it has survived only in a Slavonic translation) was originally written in Greek. Although the book's present form may represent a Christian edition from as late as the seventh century C.E., it undoubtedly arose from a Jewish original dating from perhaps the first century C.E. Injunctions to visit the Jerusalem Temple three times a year (2 En. 51:4) and references to ongoing sacrificial procedures (2 En. 59:1–2; 61:4; 62:1) indicate that at least these portions were written before 70 C.E. R. H. Charles suggests Alexandria, Egypt, as the likely place of composition. A first-person narrative of sixty-eight chapters, it describes Enoch's ascension to the tenth heaven, where he beholds the face of God and is taught all knowledge; his thirty-day return to earth to transmit this wisdom to his sons; and his permanent return to heaven.

The first section of the book (2 En. 1–21)

offers a fascinating survey of the ten levels of the spirit world through which Enoch ascends. Although the concept may seem strange to modern theology, the author makes several of the levels places of darkness and torment. The "second heaven," for example, is a gloomy prison for rebellious angels (2 En. 7); the "third heaven" is divided into a sensuous Eden for the righteous and a flaming darkness for sinners (2 En. 8–10); the fifth level contains the giant angel who had provoked a revolt against God and whom Enoch persuades to beseech the Deity's pity (2 En. 18). Enthroned in the "tenth heaven" is God himself, a formidable image with a face burning "like iron made to glow in fire" (2 En. 22:1). This section is an outstanding example of Hebrew mysticism and occult beliefs of the late Hellenistic period.

In the second part of the book (2 En. 22–38), the Deity instructs Enoch in the mysteries of creation and interprets human history from the time of Adam to the Flood. The third section (2 En. 39–66) shows Enoch imparting to his sons what he has learned and admonishing them to study his 366 books containing the divine wisdom. Typical of apocalyptic mentality is the author's insistence that all history, including that of individual lives, is predetermined (2 En. 53:2–3). The last two chapters record Enoch's final ascension and a summary of his extraordinary accomplishments (2 En. 67–68).

2 Enoch may have appeared too late to influence Christian thought directly, but its views of heaven and of the rewards and punishments of the afterlife remarkably parallel some New Testament beliefs. Certainly, its picture of the ten celestial stages strongly affected Dante's presentation of heaven in the *Divine Comedy*.

RECOMMENDED READING

Charles, R. H. "The Book of the Secrets of Enoch, with an Introduction." In *Apocrypha and Pseudepigrapha of the Old Testament,* Vol. 2, pp. 425–469. Oxford, Eng.: Clarendon Press, 1913.

Charlesworth, James H., ed. *The Old Testament Pseudepigrapha.* Vol. 1, *Apocalyptic Literature and Testaments.* Garden City, N.Y.: Doubleday, 1983, pp. 91–221.

Letter of Aristeas

KEY THEME

A fictionally embroidered account of the origin of the Septuagint, the first Greek translation of the Hebrew Bible, this document illustrates the increasing Hellenization of Judaism.

> The good life consists in the keeping of the enactments of the law.
> Letter of Aristeas, verse 127

This document is ostensibly a letter from Aristeas—a courtier of the Egyptian monarch Ptolemy II (285–246 B.C.E.)—to his brother Philocrates, containing an eyewitness account of the origin of the **Septuagint** Bible. A treatise rather than a letter, it relates how Ptolemy, when informed by the head of the Alexandria library that his collection lacks a copy of the Jewish Torah, sends Aristeas and Andreas to Jerusalem to obtain the original text.

The book describes negotiations with the high priest Eleazar, the selection of six leading scholars from each tribe of Israel, the reception of the seventy-two Jewish experts at the Ptolemaic court, their labors in translating the Hebrew text into Greek, and their production in seventy-two days of seventy-two identical translations, the reliability of which is affirmed by leaders of Alexandria's constituency. In popular usage, however, the number of translators was rounded off to seventy, a figure that gave the Septuagint its name.

Despite its wealth of concrete detail, scholars regard this story as more legend than historical fact. It is possible that in the mid-third century B.C.E. a librarian added a Greek transcription or translation of the Pentateuch to his official collection and that the reigning king may have sponsored the acquisition; but the royal honors that the author claims were showered on the Jewish translators are surely fictional.

Moreover, the Letter of Aristeas was not written by a contemporary of Ptolemy II but about 150 years later. The author was probably an Alexandrine Jew familiar with the Egyptian court, who wrote to demonstrate the authority of the Septuagint and the superiority of Hebrew wisdom (manifested in the law) to Greek learning. Hence, the writer features extended dialogs between Torah-trained Jews and Greek philosophers, with the former triumphing in every dispute.

In this regard, the book well illustrates the tension between the Hebraic and Hellenic cultures that prevailed in the cosmopolitan setting of Hellenistic Alexandria. The fact that well-educated Jews found Greek ideas attractive made a Greek version of the Torah all the more necessary. Although an eventual fusion of Greek and Hebrew thought fertilized the growth of Hellenistic Judaism, later Palestinian rabbis rejected most of the synthesis.

RECOMMENDED READING

Charles, R. H. "The Letter of Aristeas, with an Introduction." In *Apocryphya and Pseudepigrapha of the Old Testament,* Vol. 2, pp. 83–122. Oxford, Eng.: Clarendon Press, 1913.

Charlesworth, James H., ed. *The Old Testament Pseudepigrapha.* Vol. 2, *Expansions of the Old Testament and Other Legends, Wisdom, and Philosophical Literature.* Garden City, N.Y.: Doubleday, 1984.

Book of Jubilees

KEY THEME

A Pharisaic expansion of Genesis and part of Exodus, Jubilees postulates the eternity of the Mosaic Torah, which predates the world's creation.

> And the Jubilees shall pass by, until Israel is cleansed
> from all guilt . . . and error,
> and dwells with confidence in all the land,
> and there shall be no more a Satan or evil one,
> and the land shall be clean from that time forevermore.
>
> Book of Jubilees 50:5

The Book of Jubilees takes its name from the fact that the author divides world history into "Jubilees," or periods of forty-nine years, based on the **Jubilee** concept given in Leviticus 25. He further partitions each forty-nine-year epoch into seven weeks of years, all of which contain seven solar years of 364 days. This rigid compartmentalizing of the world's chronology is typical of the writer's priestly and legalistic approach.

Jubilees is also known as "Little Genesis" because it reproduces almost the entire narrative of the first Bible book, adding interpretative commentary and details from Jewish oral tradition along the way. In this expansion and elaboration of the canonical text, the author provides a virtual **Midrash** characteristic of the late second century B.C.E. when Jubilees was written. (*Midrash* is a Hebrew term meaning an "explanation or scholarly interpretation of Scripture," typically produced by scribes and rabbinical Pharisees.)

As the Chronicler imbued Israel's monarchical history with a priestly slant, so the author of Jubilees retells the story of Genesis (and the first twelve chapters of Exodus) from a Pharisaic viewpoint, emphasizing the absolute supremacy of the law, both canonical as preserved in the written Torah and oral as retained in the Pharisees' traditions. He thus makes the patriarchs Abraham, Isaac, and Jacob fervent practitioners not only of the Mosaic legal system but also of the Pharisaic additions to that law. His purpose is to show that the law existed from the beginning, that it is thus the supreme moral value in the universe, and that its delivery to Moses on Mount Sinai was a complete and final manifestation of divine wisdom.

Jubilees presents an angel relating the whole story (Gen. 1 through Exod. 12) so that Moses can preserve it in the Pentateuch. As noted, however, Jubilees' version of Israel's prehistory includes many anachronistic elements. At age fourteen, Abraham is said to have rejected his father's idols and embraced a perfect monotheism (Bk. Jub. 11:16–18). After describing Abraham's death (Bk. Jub. 23:1–8), the author interjects a long apocalyptic prophecy in which the angel tells Moses of the disasters to follow humanity's disobedience and Israel's future forsaking of the covenant; but after the chastened Israelites return to studying the law and heeding its commands, their God will again restore them to long life and prosperity (Bk. Jub. 23: 13–32).

Such eschatological predictions give the author's theology a more flexible quality than his rather pedantic legalism might indicate. (See also Book of Jubilees 1:4–29 for a parallel eschatological prophecy.) At the same time, however, Jubilees strictly enjoins the reader to observe all distinctions between things clean and unclean, to avoid idolatry and other heathen contaminations, and to honor the Sabbath fully. The author insists, in addition, upon circumcision (Bk. Jub. 15); upon keeping all the ritual feast days; upon obligatory fruit, grain, and animal offerings; and upon regulations concerning women's sexual impurities (Bk. Jub. 3:8; 15:31–32; 21; 22:16–20; 30:7–17; 50:6–13).

Some scholars have detected a resemblance between Jubilees' theology and that expressed in several documents recovered from the Qumran community; the presence of fragments from nine manuscripts of the original Hebrew version of the book found among the Dead Sea Scrolls confirms the link. Although written first in Hebrew, Jubilees survives most completely in an Ethiopic translation. Both it and Latin translations are taken from a Greek edition of the Hebrew original, which may be dated at about 100 B.C.E.

RECOMMENDED READING

Charles, R. H. "The Book of Jubilees, with an Introduction." In *Apocrypha and Pseudepigrapha of the Old Testament,* Vol. 2, pp. 1–82. Oxford, Eng.: Clarendon Press, 1913. Complete text in English with critical introduction and copious notes.

Charlesworth, James H., ed. *The Old Testament Pseudepigrapha.* Vol. 2, *Expansions of the Old Testament.* Garden City, N.Y.: Doubleday, 1984.

Davenport, Gene L. *The Eschatology of the Book of Jubilees.* Leiden, Netherlands: Brill, 1971.

Eissfeldt, Otto. *The Old Testament: An Introduction.* New York: Harper & Row, 1965.

Sibylline Oracles

KEY THEMES

An adaptation of classical traditions about the Sibyl, this composite work is a miscellaneous collection of Hellenistic Jewish, Christian, and pagan oracles covering several centuries of Greco-Roman history.

> But when Rome shall rule over Egypt as
> well, which she still hesitates to do,
> then the mightiest kingdom of the Immortal
> king over men shall appear.
> Sibylline Oracles 3:46–48

The Sibyl, after whom this collection of prophecies is named, was a prophetess or series of prophetesses famous in classical Greece and Rome. Inspired by Apollo, the Sibyl foretold the fate of individuals and nations, although most such predictions were written down long after the events foretold had already occurred. During the second century B.C.E., this time-honored method of ascribing prophecies of more recent historical events to a figure of the remote past was taken up by Jewish writers who by this means could review past occurrences as if foretelling them and then go on to predict the immediate future. Such was the mode of apocalyptic writing that replaced Israel's classical prophecy, which was thought to have ended after Ezra's day.

Adopted by Jewish apocalyptists, the Sibyl became a daughter-in-law of Noah and thus associated with the very beginning of the present world system (Sib. Or. 3:826). In this new guise, she was moved to prophesy Israelite as well as Greek history and to denounce both idolatry and the Jews' political enemies. In all, fifteen books of oracles were collected in which pagan, Jewish, and Christian elements are combined, edited, and revised. Of the twelve books that survive (Books 1–8 and 11–14), the largest block of mainly Jewish writings occurs in Books 3, 4, and 5; Books 6, 7, 8, and 13 are of Christian origin. These diverse materials were collected by a Christian editor in the sixth century C.E.

Especially noteworthy in Book 3, which contains a Jewish revision and expansion of earlier pagan material, is an eschatological passage foretelling the coming of a messiah at a time "when Rome shall rule over Egypt" (Sib. Or. 3: 46–61) and predictions of disaster for heathen nations when the messianic kingdom arrives (Sib. Or. 3:573–812). Throughout Book 3, the author somewhat incongruously blends Gentile history with exhortations to unbelieving pagans and descriptions of eschatologic catastrophes. References to the Egyptian monarch Ptolemy VII lead scholars to believe that the book was mostly written during his reign (145–116 B.C.E.). Allusions to later events—such as the second triumvirate (43 B.C.E.) and Cleopatra (about 30 B.C.E.)—were probably added by a later editor.

Book 4, a series of cryptic utterances in which some historical events are cited as signs of imminent calamity, was written after the great eruption of Vesuvius in 79 C.E. (Sib. Or. 4: 130–136). The veiled reference to Nero's return from the dead at the head of an invading army (Sib. Or. 4:137–139; 8:140–155) ex-pressed a belief popular in the late first century C.E. (See also the use of this legend in Revelation 17:8–9.)

Book 3 was written in Egypt; Book 4's place of origin is not known. Book 5, which includes a lament over the fall of Jerusalem (Sib. Or. 5: 397–413), probably appeared in Egypt toward the close of the second century C.E. Some of the Christian books were probably written even later.

RECOMMENDED READING

Charles, R. H. "The Sibylline Books [3, 4, and 5 only], with an Introduction." In *Apocrypha and Pseudepigrapha of the Old Testament,* Vol. 2, pp. 377–406. Oxford, Eng.: Clarendon Press, 1913.

Collins, J. J. *Sibylline Oracles.* In J. H. Charlesworth, ed., *The Old Testament Pseudepigrapha,* Vol. 1. Garden City, N.Y.: Doubleday, 1983. Includes the entire corpus, plus an introduction and notes.

Testaments of the Twelve Patriarchs

KEY THEMES

Each of Jacob's twelve sons, reputed founders of Israel's twelve tribes, gives ethical advice based on his life experiences.

> As the heaven is higher than the earth,
> so is the priesthood of God higher than the earthly kingdom.
> Testaments of the Twelve Patriarchs 21:4

This apocalyptic work purports to be the last words or testaments of the twelve sons of Jacob to their descendants. Although modeled on the Blessing of Jacob to his twelve sons (Gen. 49), the Testaments of the Twelve Patriarchs does not for the most part contain prophecies about the individual tribes' future destiny; it consists mainly of exhortations by each patriarch, using his own particular character and moral behavior as a model either to shun or to emulate. With its many ethical precepts and wise sayings, the Testaments would seem a part of Israel's wisdom literature were it not that many passages embody visions or revelations of divine secrets, such as the nature of angels and the heavenly world.

The deathbed advice given by Jacob's twelve sons is summarized below:

1. Reuben, citing his own case (see Gen. 35:22, 49:4), warns against "the seven spirits of deceit," which inspire lust and foster immorality.

2. Simon, referring to his murderous jealousy of Joseph, cautions against envy.

3. Levi, who has been privileged to visit the seventh heaven and receive direct divine appointment to the priesthood, urges respect for the Torah and for wisdom and states that he learned from the Book of Enoch that his progeny would corrupt the office until a messianic high priest appeared to establish the New Age.

4. Judah instructs his sons to avoid wine, women, and greed and to subordinate themselves to Levi's descendants. (The exaltation of the Levitical priesthood suggests that the Testaments have a priestly source.) He also notes that his tribe will produce a messianic king but that he will be secondary to the priestly Anointed One.

5. Isaachar promotes the values of a pious country-dweller.

6. Zebulun asks his sons to behave charitably.

7. Dan exhorts against wrath and lying.

8. Naphtali advises his progeny to conduct themselves with piety, purity, and kindliness, thus reflecting the harmony of the cosmos, though he also prophesies that Israel will rival Sodom in wickedness until, through Levi and Judah, their God ushers in the New Age.

9. Gad warns against hatred and urges brotherly love.

10. Asher exhorts his heirs to candor and honest dealings with their fellows.

11. Joseph delivers an elaborate oration on chastity.

12. Benjamin, who refuses any longer to be called "ravenous wolf" (Gen. 49:27), recommends uprightness in all things and cites Joseph as a model of godly conduct.

There is much scholarly debate about the origin of this work. Some experts believe that it is fundamentally a Jewish work with Christian interpolations; others believe that it is a Christian work incorporating an older Jewish text; still others maintain that it was composed by the Essenes or the Essene-like community of Qumran, which had many doctrinal similarities to Christianity. Estimated dates for its various parts range from the second century B.C.E. to the second century C.E.

Biblical critics agree, however, that pseudepigraphal works like the Testaments contain many *haggadic* elements, a term that refers to the Hebrew **Haggadah**—stories, legends, or explanatory narrations of the first centuries C.E. that supplement or expand the nonlegal sections of the Pentateuch. Typically, haggadic narratives are imaginative developments of a thought suggested by the Pentateuch, as are the sometimes fanciful additions to Genesis found in the Book of Jubilees and the Testaments. Such commentaries preserve a rich tradition of oral legends that have otherwise been lost.

RECOMMENDED READING

Charles, R. H. "The Testaments of the Twelve Patriarchs, with an Introduction." In *Apocrypha and Pseudepigrapha of the Old Testament,* Vol. 2, pp. 296–367. Oxford, Eng.: Clarendon Press, 1913.

Charlesworth, James H., ed. *The Old Testament Pseudepigrapha.* Vol. 1, *Apocalyptic Literature and Testaments.* Garden City, N.Y.: Doubleday, 1983, pp. 775–828.

Eissfeldt, Otto. *The Old Testament: An Introduction.* New York: Harper & Row, 1965. Pages 631–636 provide a good review of problems in determining the Jewish or Christian origin and date of the Testaments of the Twelve Patriarchs.

Nickelsburg, George W. E. *Jewish Literature Between the Bible and the Mishnah.* Philadelphia: Fortress Press, 1981, pp. 231–241.

Books of Adam and Eve

KEY THEMES

Imaginative interpretations of postbiblical traditions about the first human beings' Fall from grace, these two works present ideas later incorporated into basic Christian theology, identifying the Edenic serpent with the Devil, a rebel angel.

> The Devil spake: "O Adam! all my hostility,
> envy, and sorrow is for thee,
> since it is for thee that I have been
> expelled from my glory, which I
> possessed in the heavens. . . ."
>
> Life of Adam and Eve 12:1

Jewish and early Christian writers delighted in producing fictional accounts of the first human pair. The haggadic narratives under consideration here, which derive from Hebrew sources but are in their present form Christian works, consist of two supplementary and sometimes contradictory tales: (1) the Life of Adam and Eve (*Vita Adae et Evae*), which survives in a Latin version translated from the Greek, and (2) a parallel Greek narrative that is misnamed the Apocalypse of Moses.

As the following summary will indicate, some elements of the Adam and Eve story are found only in the Life, others only in the Apocalypse, and still others in both. In R. H. Charles's standard edition of the Pseudepigrapha, however, passages from the Life and Apocalypse are interspersed to present a coherent narration. Analogous selections from a Slavonic translation of the Life are also included.

The Life opens with Adam and Eve already expelled from paradise. Unable to find nourish-ment, they attempt to assuage the Deity's wrath through prayer and penitence. But Eve, who punishes herself by standing immersed in the icy Tigris River, is again deceived by Satan into relinquishing her ascetic task, for which lapse Adam reproaches her (Life 1–11).

When Adam complains that Satan persecutes them without reason, the latter replies that Adam was the cause of his expulsion from heaven. For after man was created "in God's image," the Deity commanded all the heavenly host to worship this human replica of the divine. Refusing to adore a younger and inferior creature, the Devil and those who sided with him were permanently cast out of the celestial abode. By thus observing the Old Testament prohibition against idolatry and further pursuing the Mosaic law of retaliation, the Devil instigated Adam's deprivation of "joy and luxury" as he himself had been deprived for the man's sake (Life 12–17). Unmoved, Adam endures forty days' penance in the Jordan River.

The Life continues with the birth of Cain and **Abel**, Abel's murder, and the birth of **Seth** and of sixty additional children (Life 18–24). Adam then tells Seth of an earlier vision in which the Deity had described Adam's coming death (Life 25–29). When Adam is dying, Seth and Eve try to obtain the healing oil from the "tree of mercy," but the archangel Michael orders them back from the gates of paradise and affirms the finality of Adam's death (Life 30–44; Apoc. M. 5–14). Eve then gives her version of the Fall (Apoc. M. 15–34), and Adam dies at age 930 (Life 45–48).

After Adam's soul is conveyed to paradise in the third heaven, angels accompany the Deity to earth, where he entombs Adam's body and the hitherto unburied corpse of Abel. Adam and all his progeny are promised a resurrection (Apoc. M. 35–42). Six days later, Eve also dies, praying to be buried in her husband's unknown tomb, after which Michael instructs Seth never to mourn on the Sabbath, which is a holy day symbolic of future life and the New Age (Life 49–51; Apoc. M. 52–53).

Although fanciful, the narrative is a sensitive re-creation by unknown Hellenistic Jews of what the original human couple's life was conceived to be like after the Fall. The Hebrew versions on which the later Christian edition is based may have been composed during the first century C.E., before the Roman destruction of Jerusalem.

RECOMMENDED READING

Charles, R. H. "The Books of Adam and Eve, with an Introduction." In *Apocrypha and Pseudepigrapha of the Old Testament,* Vol. 2, pp. 123–154. Oxford, Eng.: Clarendon Press, 1913.

Charlesworth, James H., ed. *The Old Testament Pseudepigrapha.* Vol. 2, *Expansions of the "Old Testament" and Other Legends, Wisdom and Philosophical Literature, Prayers, Psalms, and Odes, Fragments of Lost Judeo-Hellenistic Works,* pp. 249–295. Garden City, N.Y.: Doubleday, 1984.

TERMS AND CONCEPTS TO REMEMBER

Abel

Enoch

Haggadah

Jubilee

Midrash

Pseudepigrapha

Septuagint

Seth

Son of Man

QUESTIONS FOR REVIEW

1. What are the Pseudepigrapha, and what kinds of literature do they contain? During what period of history were they composed?
2. What tradition about the translation of the Septuagint Bible is found in the Letter of Aristeas? How much of this account do you think is reliable?
3. To what category of Jewish literature do the Book of Jubilees and the books of Adam and Eve belong? In what ways do they supplement the canonical accounts in Genesis and Exodus?

QUESTION FOR DISCUSSION AND REFLECTION

As examples of apocalyptic literature, what worldview do the books of 1 and 2 Enoch present? Why do you suppose that these works were composed in the name of Enoch, who was said to have been "taken" by God (presumably into heaven)? Is the Enochan view of history similar to that in Daniel and 2 Esdras? Note that both Daniel and 1 Enoch refer to heavenly beings as the "Watchers," a practice that indicates the two books' use of a common eschatological tradition. Why do you suppose that Daniel was accepted into the canon whereas Enoch was not?

Between the Old and New Testaments:
Hellenistic Culture and the Growth
of Multiple Judaisms

Political Events

The Maccabean revolt (beginning about 168 B.C.E.), supported by many of the **hasidim** ("pious ones," loyal to the Mosaic Torah), eventually resulted in expelling the Syrian occupation forces. In 142 B.C.E., an independent Jewish state was established, ruled by a Maccabean dynasty known as the **Hasmoneans**. The sufferings of the hasidim, many of whom were commonly tortured and executed by Antiochus's decree, had significant consequences for some later writers of the Hebrew Bible, as well as for the early Christian community. Antiochus's desecration of the Jerusalem Temple, its rededication by Judas Maccabeus three years later, and the atrocities perpetrated on Torah loyalists, who became models of the faithful martyr, helped ignite the fires of apocalyptic speculation among Hellenistic Jews. The authors of the Book of Daniel and several New Testament documents, including the Synoptic Gospels and Revelation, are deeply preoccupied with the imminent consummation of human history. (For a discussion of the Maccabean period, with its "great tribulation" for the people of God, review the sections cover-

ing the Books of Daniel and 1 and 2 Maccabees in Part 7.)

The Roman Occupation of Judea Weakened by endless wars with neighboring Hellenistic kingdoms, Syria and Palestine were absorbed into the Roman Empire in 63 B.C.E. Led by Pompey, the great military rival of Julius Caesar, Roman legions arrived in Palestine as ostensible peacekeepers, invited there to settle a dynastic dispute between two brothers contending for the Hasmonean throne. John Hyrcanus II appealed to Rome for help in ousting his younger sibling, Aristobulus II, who had made himself both high priest and king. After overthrowing Aristobulus, Pompey installed John Hyrcanus (63–40 B.C.E.) as high priest and ethnarch (provincial governor) over a Jewish state much reduced in size and prestige. The change in title from "king" to "ethnarch" is significant, because after 63 B.C.E. Jewish rulers were mere puppets of Rome, and the Holy Land merely another province in the empire.

Herod "the Great"

After the death of John Hyrcanus, the Roman Senate appointed **Herod**, son of a powerful Id-

278

King Herod I's extensive renovations of the Jerusalem Temple, begun about 20 B.C.E., had been completed only a few years before the Romans destroyed it in 70 C.E. According to Josephus, the bejeweled curtain veiling the Sanctuary's innermost room, the Holy of Holies, depicted a panorama of heaven. Visible through the main entrance (shown here in a modern scale model), the curtain is said to have been "torn in two from top to bottom" at the moment of Jesus' death (Mark 15:38). In Mark's Gospel, this event corresponds to the heavens being "torn open" at the time of Jesus' baptism (Mark 1:10). (Courtesy of Erich Lessing/Magnum Photos)

umean (Edomite) governor, king of Judea, a territory he eventually extended to include much of Palestine. Although politically successful, Herod's long reign (40–4 B.C.E.) was unpopular with the Jews. Only half-Jewish himself, Herod tried to win his subjects' favor with an elaborate building program that transformed Jerusalem into one of the showplaces of the eastern Roman Empire. His most famous project, an extensive reconstruction of the Jerusalem Temple, was completed only a few years before the Roman armies destroyed it in 70 C.E. An unstable mixture of shrewdness, suspicion, and savagery, King Herod ended his reign in paranoid homicide, executing three sons and his favorite wife, the Hasmonean Mariamne. His tyrannic behavior and violent reaction toward any person who might threaten his

power forms the historical backdrop to Matthew's story of Herod's slaughtering the children of Bethlehem (Matt. 2:16–17).

On Herod's death, his kingdom was divided among his three surviving sons. **Herod Archelaus**, who received Judea, Idumea, and Samaria (4 B.C.E.–6 C.E.), was a despot whom the Emperor **Augustus** banished to Gaul, following which Archelaus's territory was administered by a Roman prefect or procurator who was directly responsible to the emperor. **Herod Antipas**, the second son, ruled Galilee and Perea (4 B.C.E.–39 C.E.), an area east of the Jordan River. An inept and unpopular leader, Antipas—whom Jesus styled "that fox"—ordered John the Baptist beheaded and, according to Luke's Gospel, gave Jesus a private hearing after his arrest (Luke 23:6–12). Whereas Antipas is the

In this scale model of Jerusalem (first century C.E.), the simple flat-roofed tenements housing the general population contrast with the monumental public buildings that Herod I (40–4 B.C.E.) erected. The heavily fortified Temple area appears in the top left. (Courtesy of Erich Lessing/PhotoEdit)

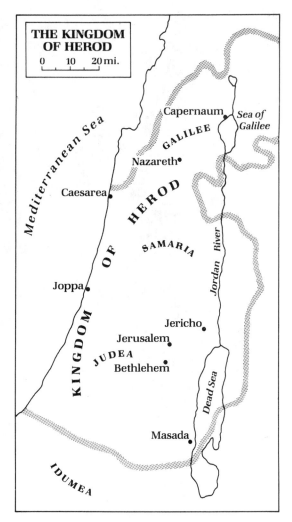

Herod mentioned most often in the New Testament, Herod's third son, **Herod Philip II**, was apparently the most able, reigning over the region northeast of Galilee (4 B.C.E.–34 C.E.) without notoriety.

The Jewish War Against Rome (66–73 C.E.)

A grandson of Herod the Great and a favorite of the Emperor Claudius, **Herod Agrippa I** (reigned 41–44 C.E.) briefly reunited Palestine, but after his premature death his kingdom reverted to direct Roman control. Between the Jews and their Roman overlords, suspicion and hatred mounted until in 66 C.E. open revolt broke out, the Judean countryside was devas-

tated, and in 70 C.E. Jerusalem was besieged, captured, and demolished. At the command of General **Titus**, son of the Emperor **Vespasian**, the Temple was razed, ending forever the daily sacrifices prescribed by the Mosaic Torah. As Jesus had forewarned, correctly assessing the political trends of his day, not a stone remained upon a stone of the sanctuary where Yahweh had placed his name (Mark 13). A last attempt to recover Jewish freedom in 132–135 C.E. was ruthlessly crushed by the Emperor Hadrian, who built a shrine to Jupiter at the site where

A shrewd and experienced soldier, Vespasian was dispatched by Nero to quell the Jewish revolt. After Nero's assassination (68 C.E.) and the year of political chaos that followed, the Roman legions declared Vespasian emperor (69–79 C.E.). (Copyright British Museum)

The son of Vespasian who captured Jerusalem and ordered its Temple destroyed (70 C.E.), Titus ruled as emperor for only two years (79–81 C.E.). The best-known event of his brief reign was the eruption of Mount Vesuvius that buried Pompeii and Herculaneum (79 C.E.). (Copyright British Museum)

Herod's magnificent Temple had once stood. As a result of the two failed uprisings against the Roman occupation of Palestine, the Jewish people were dispersed throughout the empire. Almost 1900 years would pass before they again established an autonomous state on the land promised to Abraham's descendants.

The difficult relations caused by overlapping political jurisdictions in first-century Palestine are well illustrated in the Gospel accounts of Jesus' trials, in which Jewish, Roman, and Herodian authorities compete in handling a delicate religiopolitical situation. The measure of religious liberty that the Romans accorded Jews was concentrated in the **Sanhedrin**, or Great Council, which was headed by the **Sadducees**.

The council, a religious body, allegedly condemned Jesus for blasphemy, but it apparently lacked the legal right to execute him. **Pontius Pilate**, a representative of Rome, quizzed Jesus on his claim to be king of the Jews—a treasonous act against the Emperor **Tiberius**—but finding the accused to be a Galilean, Pilate sent him to Herod Antipas, the ruler of Galilee, who happened to be in Jerusalem at the time. It was Pilate, however, who gave the order to crucify Jesus on the grounds of sedition against Rome (Luke 22:66–23:25).

The historical period during which the canon of the Hebrew Bible was completed and the first books of the New Testament were com-

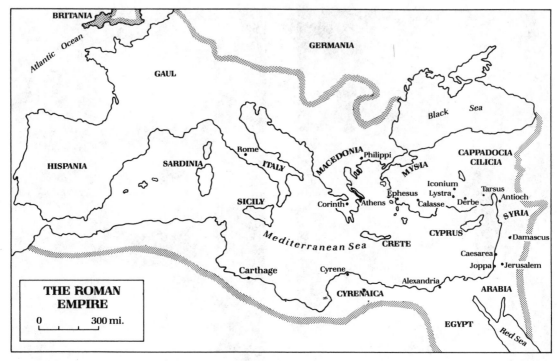

By the reign of Augustus (30 B.C.E.–14 C.E.), the Roman Empire controlled most of the known world.

posed is bracketed by two Jewish wars of independence. The first, in which the Maccabee patriots and other Torah loyalists rebelled against Greek-Syrian oppression (168–142 B.C.E.), was successful, resulting in the formation of a free Jewish state. The second, in which Palestinian Jews revolted against Rome—which had almost infinitely larger armies and other resources to draw on than had the Seleucid kings—ended in catastrophe, with the total annihilation of the Jewish political community (66–73 C.E.). The life of Jesus, as well as the writing of the oldest surviving Christian literature—the letters of Paul and the Gospel of Mark—are thus framed by two "great tribulations" for the biblical communities, cataclysmic historical events that shaped the outlook of several Bible writers.

RECOMMENDED READING

Boardman, John; Griffin, Jasper; and Murray, Oswyn. *The Oxford History of the Classical World.* New York: Oxford University Press, 1986. A collection of informative essays by leading historians and other scholars.

Boren, H. C. *The Ancient World: An Historical Perspective,* 2nd ed. Englewood Cliffs, N.J.: Prentice-Hall, 1986. A readable history surveying the world from ancient Sumer to the fall of Rome.

Cohen, Shaye J. D. *From the Maccabees to the Mishnah.* Philadelphia: Westminster Press, 1987. Surveys the period of Jewish history that gave rise to Judaism and Christianity.

Green, Peter. *Alexander to Actium: The Historical Evolution of the Hellenistic Age.* Berkeley: University of California Press, 1990. A scholarly examination of classical history from the time of Alexander's conquests to the establishment of the Roman Empire under Augustus.

This silver shekel was coined about 67 C.E. during the Jewish revolt against Rome. Faith in the city that contains Yahweh's Temple is voiced in the inscription, "Jerusalem the holy." (Courtesy of the American Numismatic Society, New York)

Josephus, Flavius. *The Jewish War*, rev. ed. Translated by G. A. Williamson. Edited by E. M. Smallwood. New York: Penguin Books, 1981. The most important contemporary source for conditions in Palestine during the first century C.E.

Hellenistic Thought, Culture, and Religion

Hellenistic culture dominated the world, including that of Jews and Christians, from the time of Alexander through the reign of Marcus Aurelius in the late second century C.E., a span of 500 years. This period, during which the last books of the Hebrew Bible and the entire contents of the New Testament were written, also saw the production of a large body of noncanonical Jewish and Christian literature, most of which was significantly influenced by Greek thought. (See discussions of Jewish and Christian Apocrypha and Pseudepigrapha, Parts 7 and 12.) The Greek passion for learning, intense intellectual curiosity, and confidence in the power of reason and logic to discover truth shaped educational standards throughout the Greco-Roman world. The Greek heritage not only offered a language with a huge vocabulary of scientific, religious, and philosophical terms but also transmitted an incomparably rich legacy of art, architecture, literature, and speculative thought.

The Greek Love of Wisdom

A Greek book that reflects the Hellenistic environment in which it originated, the New Testament also reveals its dual inheritance of Jewish biblical traditions and Greek philosophical concepts. A term meaning "love of wisdom," *philosophy* is an attempt to understand and interpret the nature of reality, including the purpose of human life. At first indistinguishable from primitive science, philosophy began at Miletus in the late seventh century B.C.E. when creative thinkers such as Thales began applying rational analysis to a body of observable facts. By the fifth century B.C.E., Athens emerged as the intellectual center of the Greek world, home to numerous schools of thought that used the tools of logic to discredit old superstitions and to construct new theories about the universe. Some philosophers ("lovers of wisdom"), such as the Athenian Socrates (c. 469–399 B.C.E.), focused on ethical questions, particularly the mental disciplines by which one could discover and lead the "good life," that worthy of responsible and intelligent human beings.

Greek Philosophy   Combining brilliant originality with a delightful sense of humor, Socrates regarded human life as an ongoing quest for truth, a pilgrimage toward the unseen world of spirit and eternal ideals, the ultimate goal of the human soul trapped in an earthly body. Questioning every belief that his fellow Athenians cherished as "obviously" true, Socrates good-naturedly cross-examined tradesmen, teachers, and politicians alike—demanding to learn how people could be so sure that their beliefs were valid.

While attracting a small circle of devoted followers, Socrates also irritated many of Athens's most influential citizens, some of whom viewed this "gadfly" with his stinging questions as dangerous to conventional morality. As a result, Socrates was eventually tried and executed for criticizing the ethical inadequacy of his opponents' policies and practices, the only thinker in Athens's long history to be put to death for expressing unpopular ideas.

Many readers find suggestive parallels between the respective careers of Socrates and Jesus, both of whom followed a divine calling, advocated cultivating spiritual values and eschewing the usual goals of a materialistic culture, and paid the supreme penalty for voicing ideas that leaders of their respective communities deemed subversive. Although both men were sages who taught that the ultimate realities were divine powers before whom all people's conduct would be judged posthumously, their cultural differences were perhaps greater than the roughly analogous patterns of their public ministries and martyrs' deaths.

Plato   The historical situations for Jesus and Socrates are alike in one important respect, however: Neither Socrates nor Jesus left anything in writing. In both cases, their teachings were reconstructed by later writers whose accounts of their subjects' lives may owe as much to editorial interpretation as they do to biographical fact. Socrates' youthful disciple **Plato** (c. 427–347 B.C.E.) made his teacher the hero of a series of philosophical dialogs in which a saintly and impish Socrates always outargues and outwits his opponents. Because virtually all of Plato's compositions, which he continued to produce until his death at eighty years of age, feature Socrates as the chief speaker, separating Plato's ideas from those of his master is difficult. New Testament scholars face a similar problem in trying to distinguish Jesus' authentic sayings from the added commentary of the Gospel writers, who wrote between forty and sixty-five years after Jesus' death.

Although he was a philosopher and logician, Plato profoundly influenced the history of Western religion, particularly later beliefs about the immortality of the soul and the effects that decisions made in this life can have on posthumous rewards and punishments. Plato's dualistic view of reality also deeply affected subsequent religious thought. He posited the coexistence of two distinct worlds: one the familiar physical environment of matter and sense impressions and the other an invisible realm of perfect, eternal ideas. In this worldview, our bodies belong to the material sphere and are chained to the physical process of change, decay, and death. Our souls, however, originate in the unseen spirit world and after death return to it for posthumous judgment. Education involves recognizing the superiority of the soul to the body and cultivating those virtues that prepare the soul for its immortal destiny. Hence, the person

Perhaps the most creative and influential thinker of all time, Plato (c. 427–347 B.C.E.) wrote a series of philosophical dialogues in which his mentor, Socrates, debates major ethical and cosmological questions. Plato's celebrated Theory of Ideas, which postulates the existence of a dualistic universe composed of parallel worlds of perishable matter and eternal spirit, underlies the New Testament worldview. (Courtesy of the Bettmann Archive)

Condemned to death for challenging the religious assumptions of his fellow Athenians, Socrates' (c. 469–399 B.C.E.) life in some ways anticipated that of Jesus. (Copyright British Museum)

who truly loves wisdom, the genuine philosopher, will seek the knowledge of eternal truths that make real goodness possible, helping others along the way to realize that ambitions for worldly power or riches are false idols. The wise seek the perfect justice of the unseen world and, with the pure spirits of divinity, find eternal life.

Over the centuries, Plato's ideas were modified and widely disseminated until, in one form or another, they became common knowledge during the Hellenistic era. Some New Testament writers, such as the author of Hebrews, used Platonic concepts to illustrate parallels and correspondences between the spiritual and physical worlds (Heb. 1:1–4, 9:1–14). This book's famous definition of faith is primarily a confession of belief in the reality of the invisible realm (Heb. 11:1–2).

Stoicism   Another Greek philosophy that became extremely popular among the educated classes during Roman times was **Stoicism**. Founded in Athens by Zeno (c. 336–263 B.C.E.), the Stoic school emphasizes the order and moral purpose of the universe. In the Stoic view, reason is the divine principle that gives coherence and meaning to our complex world. Identified as **Logos** (a Greek term for "word," or rational utterance that directs and shapes the universe), this cosmic intelligence unifies the world and makes it intelligible to the human intellect. Human souls are sparks of the divine Logos, which is symbolized by cosmic fire and sometimes associated with a supreme god. In the prolog of John's Gospel, the prehuman Jesus is identified with the Logos, the creative Word of God (John 1:1, 14).

Stoic teaching urges the individual to listen to the divine element within, to discipline both body and mind to attain a state of harmony with nature and the universe. Stoics must practice self-control, learning self-sufficiency and noble indifference to both pleasure and pain. The Stoic ideal is to endure either personal gain or loss with equal serenity, without any show of emotion. When the Apostle Paul discusses self-discipline or the ability to endure want or plenty, he echoes Stoic values that were commonplace in Greco-Roman society (Phil. 4: 11–14).

A strikingly different philosophical outlook appears in the teachings of Epicurus (c. 342–270 B.C.E.). Whereas the Stoics believed in the soul's immortality and a future world of rewards or penalties, Epicurus asserts that everything is completely physical, including the soul, which after death dissolves into nothingness along with the body. The gods may exist, but they have no contact with or interest in humanity. Without a cosmic intelligence to guide them, people must create their own individual purposes in life. A major goal is the avoidance of pain, which means that the shrewd person will avoid public service or politics, where rivalry may destroy one's contentment. Cultivating a private life,

the wise forgo merely sensual indulgences that weaken physically and mentally. Using reason not to discover ultimate truth—which is unattainable—but to live well, the enlightened mind seeks intellectual pleasure because such enjoyments outlast those of the body.

Epicurus's emphasis on the material, perishable nature of both body and soul found support in the philosopher Democritus's atomic theory. Democritus (born about 460 B.C.E.) taught that all things are formed of tiny invisible particles called atoms. It is the nature of atoms to move and collide, temporarily forming objects, including sentient ones like animals and human beings, and then to disintegrate and re-form in other objects elsewhere. Wise or foolish, all persons are mere chance collections of atoms destined to dissolve without a trace. According to the Book of Acts, Paul debated both Epicurean and Stoic philosophers when he introduced Christianity to the Athenians about 50 C.E. (Acts 17).

Pre-Christian Cults of Savior Gods and Goddesses

The Mystery Religions   Besides the principal schools of philosophy, with their ethical stress on one's duties to the gods and state, the Hellenistic world also fostered a number of "underground religions," which countless thousands of people found intellectually and emotionally satisfying. In their common emphasis on universal brotherhood, spiritual rebirth, and the life to come, some of these cults anticipated important elements in Christianity. Known as the **mysteries** (Greek, *mysteria*) because their adherents took oaths never to reveal their secret rites, several mystery cults honored young male gods born of a divine father and human mother, heroes who underwent death, a descent into the **Hades** (the Underworld), and a resurrection to immortality. In some of these secret religions, celebrants shared a communal meal in which they symbolically ate the flesh and drank the blood of their god. By thus absorbing the god's presence into themselves, worshipers hoped to attain a similar deathlessness.

Dionysus The most famous of the dying and resurrected gods was **Dionysus**, son of **Zeus** (king of the Olympian gods, known to the Romans as Jupiter) and Semele, a human princess of ancient Thebes. According to some versions of the myth, the young Dionysus was murdered by the Titans, rebellious gods whom Zeus had cast from heaven and imprisoned in Tartarus, the bottomless pit below Hades. Zeus raised his son from the dead, granting him everlasting divinity. As god of "the vine"—representing wine, the most universally popular beverage in the ancient world—Dionysus was an embodiment of fertility and growth, symbolized by the cycle of vegetation, which ostensibly dies in the winter only to be reborn in the spring.

In the Orphic Mysteries, people were initiated into the secrets of Dionysus's mystic resurrection and shown visions of the future life. This cult is commonly called Orphism because Orpheus, the first poet and musician, is said to have composed poems revealing doctrines about the afterlife. Those who strictly kept the Orphic code of moral and ritual purity were granted joy in the next world, while wrongdoers faced a painful ordeal to purge them of their sins. Orphism also taught the transmigration of souls, a belief that individual souls are eventually reborn in new bodies to work out their final destinies.

Mithras Practiced the length and breadth of the Roman Empire, Mithraism became one of Christianity's main competitors during the first centuries C.E. According to Persian myth, Mithras was the youthful god of light who killed a sacred bull, from whose blood and semen new life was generated. A cult in which absolute secrecy was rigorously enforced, Mithraism was extremely popular among the Roman common people, soldiers, and tradesmen. Only men were admitted into the religion, after which

ceremony initiates were said to have been "born again" and henceforth lived under the god's special protection.

By the end of the third century C.E., Mithraism had become the official cult of the Roman Empire, supported by emperors who needed a strong deity to defend Rome against the never-ending waves of barbarian invaders. Associated with the sun, Mithras was said to have been born on December 25, about the time of the winter solstice, the moment when the divine sun is reborn and hours of daylight begin to lengthen. Because the solstice appropriately symbolizes the birth of God's Son, the "Light of the world" (as well as the rebirth of the Mithraic solar deity), the Roman church eventually chose Mithras's birthday to celebrate as that of Jesus.

Whereas Mithraism excluded women, other mystery religions emphasized the importance of a female deity, a mother goddess who can offer her worshipers help in this life and also intervene for them in the next world. Demeter ("earth mother"), goddess of the grain harvest, and her daughter Persephone were honored at Eleusis and elsewhere in the eastern Mediterranean. Originally concerned with agricultural fertility and the cycle of the seasons, the Eleusinian Mysteries developed into a mystical celebration of death and rebirth.

Isis and Osiris Even more popular in Roman time was **Isis**, an Egyptian mother goddess whom artists typically depicted as a madonna holding her infant son Horus. Representing motherly compassion allied with divine power, Isis was the center of a mystery cult that promised initiates personal aid in resolving life's problems as well as the assurance of a happy existence after death. As an embodiment of creative intelligence and cosmic wisdom, Isis was known as the goddess of "a thousand names," a maternal deity whom the whole world recognized in one form or another. Offering the individual worshiper far more comfort than the official state religions of Greece or Rome, the

In this Roman bas-relief, the youthful Mithras slays a sacred bull. Extremely popular with soldiers, merchants, and traders throughout the Roman Empire, the Mysteries of Mithras involved a cleansing baptism with the blood of a sacrificial animal and a ritual fraternal meal. As with the cults of Isis and Dionysus, initiation ceremonies offered glimpses of the spirit world and assurances of the soul's immortality. (Courtesy of Giraudon/Art Resource, NY)

Isis cult found dedicated adherents throughout the Roman Empire.

The myth of **Isis** involved her male consort **Osiris**, originally a mortal ruler of ancient Egypt. Like Dionysus, Osiris suffered death by being torn in pieces but was resurrected to new life as a god. Through arcane rituals uniting the worshiper with Osiris, king and judge of the dead, the initiate theoretically lost the fear of death and looked forward to a posthumous union with the divine.

Christianity's Appeal to Mystery Cult Followers   The Hellenistic world offered people a wide variety of religious options. This multiplicity of philosophies and religions, both public and secret, suggests that many persons in Greco-Roman society felt a need to find spiritual direction and purpose in their lives. Offer-

ing practical help in this world and immortality in the next, many mystery cults focused on the promise inherent in myths dramatizing the death of a young male figure who is raised to eternal life. Others stressed the wisdom and compassion of a mother goddess, such as the beloved Isis. Virtually all such cults involved a devoted community that met privately to share a ritual or sacred meal in which the devotees experienced the exhilaration of spiritual regeneration.

During the century following Jesus' death, Christianity developed and spread in competition with these older philosophies and cults. Addressing persons familiar with the symbols, rites, and concepts of the Hellenistic world, New Testament writers commonly phrased their message about Jesus in terms their Greek readers would understand. In a cosmopolitan environ-

The *"goddess of a thousand names,"* Isis was an Egyptian deity worshiped throughout the Roman Empire. Her devotees believed that Isis, the eternal Mother and Protector of her human children, manifested herself in different cultures as Ishtar, Gaia, Demeter, Ceres, or Venus. Promiser of immortality to those initiated into her cult, she is commonly pictured holding the infant Horus. Together, they are a prototype of the Christian Madonna and child. *(Courtesy of Alinari/Art Resource, NY)*

This Greco-Roman mural depicts an African priest of Isis directing a sacrifice to the goddess at her temple in Herculaneum. (Courtesy of the Ancient Art and Architecture Collection)

ment that provided so many different answers to important religious questions, Paul, the Gospel authors, and others strove to articulate Christianity's distinctive vision of life's purpose.

RECOMMENDED READING

Burkert, Walter. *Ancient Mystery Cults.* Cambridge, Mass.: Harvard University Press, 1987.

Fox, R. L. *Pagans and Christians.* New York: Knopf, 1987. A comprehensive and insightful investigation of Greco-Roman religious life from the second to the fourth century C.E.

Grant, F. C., ed. *Hellenistic Religions: The Age of Syncretism.* Indianapolis: Bobbs-Merrill, 1953. A collection of Greco-Roman religious writings.

Hengel, Martin. *Jews, Greeks, and Barbarians: Aspects of the Hellenism of Judaism in the Pre-Christian Period.* Philadelphia: Fortress Press, 1980.

———. *Judaism and Hellenism,* vols. 1 and 2. Philadelphia: Fortress Press, 1974. A thorough and detailed analysis of Hellenistic influences on Jewish thought during the period between the Old and New Testaments.

Detail from the Arch of Titus, which the Roman Senate erected in the Forum of Rome about 100 C.E. Created in honor of Titus's victories in the Jewish War, this frieze depicts Roman soldiers carrying off loot from the Jerusalem Temple, including the menorah—the seven-branched candelabrum formerly housed in the sanctuary. (Courtesy of Alinari/Art Resource, NY)

Kee, H. C. *The New Testament in Context: Sources and Documents.* Englewood Cliffs, N.J.: Prentice-Hall, 1984. An important collection of Greco-Roman documents containing parallels to New Testament ideas and teachings.

Koester, Helmut. *Introduction to the New Testament.* Vol. 1, *History, Culture, and Religion of the Hellenistic Age.* Philadelphia: Fortress Press, 1982. A scholarly study.

Kramer, Ross S., ed. *Maenads, Martyrs, Matrons, Monastics: A Sourcebook on Women's Religion in the Greco-Roman World.* Minneapolis, Minn.: Fortress Press, 1988.

Lohse, Eduard. *The New Testament Environment.* Translated by J. E. Steely. Nashville, Tenn.: Abingdon Press, 1976.

Seltzer, Robert M., ed. *Religions of Antiquity,* 2nd ed. New York: Macmillan, 1989.

The Diverse World of First-Century Judaisms

Probably during the Maccabean period, Judaism fragmented into a variety of religious parties or denominations. In *Wars of the Jews* 2.8, an account of the revolt against Rome, **Flavius Josephus**, the first-century Jewish historian, describes the four major groups, two of which—the Pharisees and the Sadducees—the Gospel writers present as Jesus' leading opponents. In reviewing these four principal groups, however, it should be emphasized that most Jews of Jesus' day did not belong to such parties. Many of them probably admired the Pharisees' erudition and piety but followed no strict party line themselves. Classed as unteachable "sinners" by the orthodox, the people of the land worshiped as best they might (Mark 2:15), and it was to these generally poor and uneducated masses that Jesus directed his message.

The Pharisees

Although scholars have estimated that the **Pharisees** (from a word that apparently means "separatists") never had more than about 6000 members, their influence was nevertheless tremendous. According to Josephus (*Antiquities of the Jews* 13.10), so great was their authority that they were able to dictate public opinion on kings, priests, and nearly all religious matters. In New Testament times, they were Judaism's chief interpreters of Scripture, particularly of the Torah.

The Pharisees accepted as binding not only the Pentateuch, the Prophets, and the Writings (the three major divisions of the Hebrew Bible) but also the "oral law." This "tradition of the elders" (Mark 7:3), an extensive and growing body of legalistic interpretation that the rabbis had compiled over many generations, was later codified in the **Mishnah** ("that which is learned by repetition"). This record, compiled about 200 C.E. by Rabbi Judah ha-Nasi, is the first document of rabbinic Judaism. An informal term meaning "master" or "teacher" in Jesus' day, after the two Jewish wars against Rome, *rabbi* became a title designating scholars ordained or officially recognized as authoritative in their practice and exposition of Jewish law. In time, the Mishnah became the basis of further commentary, resulting in the **Gemara** ("completion"), which was added to the Mishnah to form the **Talmud** ("teaching"), an immense compendium of rabbinic scholarship containing about 2.5 million words. Two Talmuds developed, one in Palestine (also known as the Jerusalem Talmud) about 400 C.E. and one in Babylon about 550 C.E. The Babylonian Talmud, in thirty-six tractates or books, became the chief regulator of Jewish religious life.

Although many scholars believe that Pharisaism evolved into the rabbinic Judaism that eventually produced the Talmud—and hence modern Judaism—the rabbinic compilers never refer to themselves as Pharisees and seem to avoid the term. After the Temple's destruction, however, it was Pharasaic emphasis on reapplication of the Torah to the Jewish people's radically changed circumstances that helped make possible the survival of their religion and distinctive way of life.

Hillel and Shammai Two influential Pharisaic leaders whose teachings are remembered in the rabbinic commentaries were Hillel and Shammai, who lived into the first decades of the first century C.E. A famous anecdote illustrates the striking differences in temperament of these two eminent Pharisees. It was said that a **Gentile** persistently besought Shammai, known for his aloof personality and strict interpretation of the Law, to explain the essential meaning of the Law while the Gentile stood on one foot. Appalled that anyone could be simple enough to imagine that the profundities of the Mosaic revelation could be articulated in a single phrase, Shammai sent the Gentile packing. Undaunted, the Gentile then went to Hillel with the same question. Taking the man's inquiry as sincere, Hillel is said to have replied: "Do not do to your neighbor what is hateful to yourself. That is the entire Torah. All the rest is commentary." Although expressed negatively, Hillel's concise summary of the Law's human significance anticipates Jesus's expression of the golden rule (Matt. 7:12).

Despite his remembered disagreements with Pharisees on how the Law should be practiced, Jesus is known to have been on good terms with some of their number, dining at their homes, and even benefiting from a friendly warning about a plot on his life (Luke 7:36–50; 13:31–32). Matthew's Gospel depicts Jesus as sharing the Pharisees' view that the Law is eternally binding (Matt. 5:17–19) and that it be interpreted correctly (Matt. 23:2–3). On numerous matters of belief, Jesus and the Pharisees see eye-to-eye (Mark 11:18–26). Unlike the Sadducees, they believe in a coming judgment day, resurrection of the dead, a future life of rewards and penalties based on deeds in this life, and the existence of angels, demons, and other inhabitants of the invisible world. By devotedly studying the Hebrew Bible and flexibly adapting its principles to the constantly changing situation in which Jews found themselves, the Pharisees depended on neither the possession of the Temple nor the Promised Land to perpetuate the Jewish faith. Some may have been rigid or overly ingenious in their application of the Torah's requirements, perhaps making the Law impossible for the poor or ignorant to keep (Matt. 23:6–23). As a group, however, they pursued a standard of religious commitment and personal righteousness that was virtually unique in the ancient world.

Gamaliel   According to the Book of Acts, it was Rabbi **Gamaliel**, a leading first-century Pharisee, who protected the early Jesus movement from excessive repression by the Jerusalem authorities (Acts 5:34–42). Depicted in Acts as the apostle Paul's teacher and an advocate of religious tolerance, Gamaliel is rarely mentioned in the Mishnah, although the document observes that "when he died the glory of the Torah ended." Acts portrays Paul, even after his conversion to Christianity, as remaining proud of his Pharisaic background and appealing for support from his fellow Pharisees when he stood trial before the Jerusalem religious council (Acts 23:6–9; Phil. 3:4–7).

The Academy of Jamnia (Yavneh)

After Rome's destruction of the Jewish state in 70 C.E., Roman authorities apparently wished to show their goodwill toward prominent Jews who had not advocated violent revolt against the empire. The leading force behind this Roman-endorsed movement to reorganize the postwar Jewish faith was Yohanan ben Zakkai

(c. 1–80 C.E.), an eminent Pharisee. According to one tradition, during the Roman siege of Jerusalem, ben Zakkai—who favored a peaceful settlement with Rome—escaped from the city by feigning death and being carried in a coffin outside Jerusalem's walls for burial. Like the historian Josephus, who also went over to the Romans, ben Zakkai won the favor of Vespasian, the general (and later emperor) whom Nero had dispatched to quell the insurrection. Ben Zakkai received Vespasian's permission to travel to Jamnia (also called Javneh, Jabneh, or Yavneh), a city west of Jerusalem on the Mediterranean coast that had not participated in the Jewish Revolt.

At Jamnia, ben Zakkai gathered other Pharisaic teachers together and presided over an already-existing Jewish council there, the *Bet Din* (House of Judgment). During the years following 70 C.E., the pronouncements and interpretations of ben Zakkai and other sages of the **Academy of Jamnia** exercised tremendous influence over Judaism, which thus entered into a new stage of development known as formative Judaism. The Jamnia rabbis successfully confronted the challenge of enabling Judaism to survive without the Temple, an officiating priesthood, or even a homeland. It is said that when ben Zakkai visited the ruins of Jerusalem with another rabbi, his companion lamented the fact that, with the Temple gone, their religion had no means of making the atonement sacrifices necessary to cleanse the people from sin. Ben Zakkai reportedly answered that from henceforth "deeds of love"—humanitarian service—would replace the old system of animal sacrifice. He then quoted the Scripture in which God declares, "I require mercy, not sacrifice" (Hosea 6:6), a passage that Jesus is also said to have emphasized (Matt. 9:13).

After his retirement or death, ben Zakkai was succeeded by Gamaliel's grandson, Gamaliel the Younger (c. 30–100 C.E.). Along with debating the official contents of the Hebrew Bible, the Jamnia scholars also sought to define the essential requirements—and limits—of Judaism.

According to a Talmudic tradition, the benediction against the *Minim* (heretics) was formulated during this period (about 90 C.E.). Many scholars believe that this interdiction was aimed at the Christians, whose beliefs about Jesus' superiority to Moses, transmitter of God's Torah, increasingly separated them from Jamnia's views of acceptable Judaism. It seems probable that after 85 or 90 C.E. Jewish Christians were sporadically expelled from the **synagogues**, Jewish meeting places for study, prayer, and explication of the Scriptures. This expulsion caused a bitter division between the Christian and Jewish communities. The Gospel of John appears to reflect this exclusion of Jesus' followers (John 9:22, 34), as does the Gospel of Matthew, which vehemently denounces Pharisaic policies while simultaneously commending their general teachings (Matt. 23).

The Sadducees

Since none of their writings survive, we know the Sadducees only through brief references in the New Testament and in other secondary sources, such as Josephus. Represented as among Jesus' chief opponents, the Sadducees were typically members of the Jewish upper class, wealthy landowning aristocrats who largely controlled the priesthood and the Temple. Their name (Greek *Saddoukaioi,* from the Hebrew *Zaddukim* or *tsaddiqim*) means "righteous ones" and may be descriptive, or it may reflect their claim to be the spiritual heirs of Zadok, the High Priest under David and Solomon (1 Kings 1:26). Because the prophet Ezekiel had stated that only the "sons of Zadok" could "approach Yahweh" in the Temple service (Ezek. 40:46), the Sadducees, the officiating priests at the Jerusalem sanctuary, emphasized their inherited right to this role. High Priests like **Caiaphas** (who condemned Jesus) were apparently always of their number. Along with their opponents the Pharisees, the Sadducees dominated the Great Council (Sanhedrin), Judaism's highest court of religious law.

The Sadducees and the Romans   Although the New Testament and Josephus give us an incomplete picture of the group, the Sadducees seem to have acted as the chief mediators between the Jewish people and the occupying Roman forces. As beneficiaries of the Roman-maintained political order, the Sadducees had the most to lose from civil disorder and typically opposed a Jewish nationalism that might attempt to overthrow the status quo. Their adoption of Hellenistic customs and their friendship with Rome made it possible for them to manipulate some Palestinian political affairs. The Sadducees' determination to preserve the uneasy accommodation with Rome is revealed in their eagerness to get rid of Jesus, whom they apparently regarded as a potential revolutionary and a threat to Judea's political security. Their view that rebellion against Rome would lead to total annihilation of the Jewish nation was vindicated during the Jewish revolt (66–73 C.E.), when Roman troops decimated Jerusalem and Judea.

As conservative religiously as they were politically, the Sadducees practiced a literal reading of the Torah, rejecting the Pharisees' "oral law" and other interpretations of the biblical text. It is uncertain how much of the Prophets or Writings they accepted, but they did not share Pharisaic beliefs about a coming judgment, resurrection, angels, or demons (Mark 12:18; Acts 23:8). As a group, the Sadducees did not survive the first Christian century. Their close association with Rome; their refusal to accept developing ideas based on the Prophets, the Writings, and the Apocrypha; and their narrow concentration on Temple ritual—all spelled their doom. After the Temple's destruction (70 C.E.), the Sadducees disappeared from history. The Pharisees, emphasizing education and progressive reinterpretation of Scripture, became the leaders in formulating post-70s Judaism.

The Essenes and the Dead Sea Scrolls

In 1947 began a series of sensational discoveries that have revolutionized scholars' understand-

An apocalyptic sect that awaited Yahweh's call to battle the Romans, the Essenes maintained a monastic colony at Qumran near the northwest shores of the Dead Sea. After the Essenes had hidden their library—the Dead Sea Scrolls—in nearby caves, the Roman army destroyed Qumran (68 C.E.), the ruins of which have since been excavated. (Courtesy of Jacques Benbassat / Leo de Wys)

ing of Judaism's complexities during the early New Testament period. According to one version of the story, in that year a Bedouin shepherd boy, who had been idly throwing stones into the mouth of a cave near the Dead Sea, heard a sound like shattering pottery. When he climbed into the cave to investigate, he found pottery jars full of ancient manuscripts, now world famous as the **Dead Sea Scrolls**.

Before the young shepherd made his astonishing find, scholars had almost no Jewish literature dating from the centuries immediately before or during the formative period of Christianity. Books of the Hebrew Bible are considerably older than the time of Jesus, and the Mishnah was compiled almost two centuries after Jesus' death. With the unexpected discovery of the Dead Sea Scrolls, however, scholars now have an entire religious library that was composed or transcribed between the mid-second century B.C.E. and late first century C.E., not only encompassing the chronological period

when Christianity first developed but also originating in a place near the Judean wilderness where John the Baptist held his revival campaign—the locale in which Jesus began his ministry.

Some scholars recently have proposed that the Dead Sea library represents not one but a variety of Jewish groups, a collective witness to the religious diversity and eschatological interests of first-century Judaisms. A large majority of scholars are convinced, however, that the scrolls were produced by the **Essenes**, an ascetic Jewish sect that flourished in Palestine from about 140 B.C.E. until 68 C.E., when it was destroyed or dispersed by Roman armies. First-century Jewish authors, such as **Philo Judaeus** of Alexandria and Josephus, had described some of the Essene beliefs and practices, but only after 1947 did their own extensive writings—found in eleven different caves—gradually become available. When some of the Dead Sea Scrolls were first published in English, a few scholars

This Dead Sea Isaiah Scroll represents the oldest surviving example of a complete book of the Hebrew Bible. Found in a cave near the Essene monastery of Qumran, it is almost 1000 years older than the Masoretic Text. (Courtesy of PhotoEdit)

theorized that the Essene group was an early form of Christianity. More recently, some commentators have speculated that the "Teacher of Righteousness"—the sect's founder and early leader—was none other than Jesus of Nazareth or perhaps his brother (kinsman) **James**, who was known as "James the Righteous." Other critics have claimed that Paul, who rejected Torah-keeping in favor of divine grace, was the

"wicked priest" whom the scrolls condemn. One commentator has even assigned the "wicked priest" role to Jesus!

Despite a few extreme—and almost universally repudiated—claims, the scholarly consensus holds that the primary value of the scrolls in studying Christian origins is the evidence they provide for the Palestinian roots of earliest Christianity. Many ideas, terms, and phrases previously thought to have arisen in a non-Palestinian Hellenistic environment were actually present in Jesus' homeland during his lifetime. Documents outlining the Essenes' mode of worship, communal meals, purification rites involving immersion in water, and conviction that they alone formed a "New Covenant" community representing true Israel demonstrate abundant parallels to Christian teachings. Rather than prove that the Jesus movement developed out of Essene beliefs, however, the scrolls generally show that a marginal Jewish religious group anticipated a number of Christian practices. Some rituals, such as a shared meal of bread and wine or water baptism of initiates, are not unique to Christianity but are paralleled in earlier Essene rituals, just as Greco-Roman myths about a dying and rising savior deity foreshadow theological interpretations of Jesus' life and death.

Qumran Although many Essenes lived in cities, one particularly rigorous group settled in **Qumran**, located near the northwest corner of the Dead Sea. The Qumran group apparently pursued a monastic existence, renouncing marriage, holding all possessions in common, and unquestioningly obeying their priestly superiors. The Qumran community may have been founded shortly after the Maccabean revolt when Hasmonean rulers assumed the office of High Priest, a practice the Essenes abhorred as an illegal usurpation that polluted the Temple. Withdrawn from the world in their isolated desert community, the Essenes patiently awaited the arrival of two **Messiahs**—a priestly Messiah descended from **Aaron**, Moses' brother and Israel's first High Priest, and a second "Messiah of Israel," a leader descended from King David. The only Jewish sect known to expect two such leaders, the Essenes may have influenced the author of the New Testament Book of Hebrews, which is unique in presenting the risen Christ as both a Davidic and a high priestly Messiah. Essene interest in **Melchizedek**, a mysterious king-priest mentioned briefly in the books of

Genesis and Psalms, is similarly reflected in the Book of Hebrews's comparison of Christ to Melchizedek, the only canonical writing to do so. (See Part 11, "Hebrews").

Contents of the Qumran Library The Dead Sea documents, which the Essenes may have hidden in caves shortly before the Roman armies razed Qumran, are enormously important for biblical research. First, the manuscripts contain the oldest surviving copies of the Hebrew Bible, some fragments of which date back to the second century B.C.E. The complete **scroll** of Isaiah, which is perhaps 900 years older than any other previously known Isaiah manuscript, shows few variations from the Hebrew **Masoretic Text** (MT), the medieval edition of the Hebrew Bible from which most translations are made. Other Qumran copies of Scripture differ significantly from the "standard" Masoretic edition. Extensive variations between some of the Qumran biblical texts and later copies of the Hebrew Bible suggest that by the first century C.E. Jewish scholars had not yet adopted a universally recognized version of their sacred writings.

Second, the Qumran scrolls include copies and fragments of apocryphal and pseudepigraphal works, such as Tobit, 1 Enoch, and the Book of Jubilees. Generally written later than the canonical books of the Hebrew Bible, Pseudepigrapha are typically ascribed to eminent figures of the distant past such as Enoch (mentioned in Genesis 5:21–24), who reputedly was carried up to heaven where he witnessed sacred mysteries and then returned to disclose esoteric knowledge to a select few. The presence of 1 Enoch (fragments were also found at the nearby fortress of Masada) interspersed among canonical books indicates that the Essenes may have accepted a larger canon than that eventually promulgated at Jamnia (Yavneh). Whether the Essenes regarded works like Enoch or the Book of Jubilees (a retelling of Genesis and part of Exodus) as part of the Bible is open to question, but numerous fragments of these and similar compositions among the Dead Sea Scrolls reveal that they were carefully preserved and studied. Like the Essenes, some New Testament writers apparently accepted the authority of Enoch, which is quoted repeatedly in the Book of Jude. (See Part 11.)

Third, some of the most notable documents are Essene commentaries on canonical books, such as those on the prophets Habakkuk, Isaiah, Hosea, and Micah. The Habakkuk commentary is particularly illuminating because it shows that the Essenes used the same methods of interpreting biblical texts later employed by many New Testament writers. Gospel authors such as Matthew regard the Hebrew Bible as a repository of prophetic texts foretelling events fulfilled in his own day among his own community, an approach also adopted by the Habakkuk commentator, who interprets Habakkuk's words as predictions about recent Essene leaders and experiences. Both Essene and New Testament writers characteristically view their own group as God's only loyal worshipers and hence the culmination of the divine plan for humanity.

Finally, besides preserving the earliest extant copies of canonical and noncanonical biblical texts and commentaries typical of Christian **exegesis**, the scrolls include numerous compositions produced entirely by and for the Essene community. Although a minority of scholars argue that the Dead Sea collection represents a cross-section of Hellenistic Jewish beliefs, most still attribute its rule books and eschatological literature to Essene composition. Containing numerous works whose existence had not been previously suspected, this fourth group of scrolls includes the following:

1. A "Manual of Discipline" giving requirements and regulations for life in the Qumran monastery. Also called "The Community Rule," this document features a declaration that all humanity is divided into two mutually exclusive categories: (a) The "children of light" are guided by a "spirit of truth" and are ruled by the "Prince of Light"; (b) by contrast, the "children of falsehood" walk in darkness under an "Angel of Darkness." This truth–error and light–dark dichotomy also typifies the language of John's Gospel.

2. A compendium of messianic rules designating qualities of age, physical condition, ritual purity, and doctrinal orthodoxy for members of the community—especially relevant to Christians for its description of a solemn meal of bread and wine that strikingly resembles Gospel accounts of Jesus' Last Supper.

3. An extensive collection of Essene hymns that were probably sung during Qumran worship services. Because the Essenes rejected the Jerusalem Temple as contaminated by its (to them) illegitimate Sadducean priests, they attempted to duplicate certain rituals and ceremonies in their own settlement.

4. Liturgical fragments containing blessings for the obedient and cursings for the wicked.

5. The "Zadokite Document" (a version of which had been discovered in a Cairo synagogue in the 1890s), which outlines the "New Covenant" made in the "land of Damascus" (presumably a code word for the Qumran establishment) under which the Essene group lived.

6. Passages of biblical interpretation on such topics as the Blessing of Jacob, the Admonition of Moses, a prayer attributed to the Babylonian king Nabonidus, an exposition of signs marking the last days, and an anthology of messianic predictions.

7. A scroll entitled the "War of the Sons of Light Against the Sons of Darkness," a surprisingly mundane battle plan for the cosmic war that would culminate in the defeat of the ungodly and the establishment of God's kingdom.

The New Testament is silent on the Essenes, their desert monastery, and their austere lives of pious scholarship. The absence of references to the Essenes may reflect the fact that by the time the Gospels were written the sect had ceased to exist as an identifiable group. Some historians, however, suggest that the Gospels' silence may reflect their authors' consciousness that Jesus and his first disciples may have been influenced by Essene teachings.

Although a few scholars argue that Jesus spent the "lost years" between ages twelve and thirty as a member of the Essene community, the suggestion has not been widely accepted. By contrast, **John the Baptist**—whom the Gospels paint as a desert ascetic condemning Jewish religious and political leadership and preaching a doctrine of repentance before an impending holocaust—seems to echo some of the Essenes' characteristic views. What relationship John might have had to the Essene movement, however, remains conjectural.

The Zealots

Known for their passionate commitment to Jewish religious and political freedom, the **Zealots** formed a party dedicated to evicting the Romans from Palestine. Opposition to the Roman occupation that began in 63 B.C.E. flared repeatedly during the first century C.E., climaxing in the Jewish War against Rome (66–73 C.E.). In 6 C.E. a Jewish patriot known as **Judas the Galilean** led an armed rebellion that fueled nationalistic hopes but which the Romans crushed easily. **Simon**, one of Jesus' disciples, is called a "zealot" (Luke 6:15; Acts 1:13), and in Acts a parallel is drawn between Jesus' activity and that of Judas (Acts 5:37–39), causing some historians to suspect that Jesus may also have been involved in some form of rebellion against Rome. Most scholars, however, believe that Simon's designation as a "zealot" probably refers to his zeal or enthusiasm for the Law and that Jesus firmly refused to become involved in any political schemes (Mark 8:33, 10:38–39; Luke 24:21; Acts 1:6).

Although many Jews had fought against foreign oppression since the time of the Maccabees, the Zealots did not constitute an identifiable political party until shortly after the revolt against Rome began in 66 C.E. According to

Josephus, the Zealots' blind nationalism forced the Palestinian Jews on a suicidal course. In his history of the Jewish War, Josephus argues that it was the Zealots' refusal to surrender, even after Jerusalem had been captured, and their occupation of the Temple precincts that compelled the Romans to destroy the sanctuary. According to Josephus, General Titus, and Roman commander-in-chief, had not originally intended to commit this desecration. This catastrophe and the later bar Kochba rebellion of 132–135 C.E. discredited both the Zealot party and its apocalyptic hope of divine intervention in achieving national liberation. Thanks to the Zealot failures, both armed revolution and end-of-the-world predictions were henceforth repudiated by mainstream Judaism.

The Messiah: First-Century Expectations

Given the vast diversity of first-century Judaisms, we should not expect to find general agreement among different Jewish groups about the nature and function of the Messiah. It seems that many Jews did not make expectation of a coming Messiah a major part of their religious hope. The Sadducees apparently denied that there would be one, while the Essenes anticipated two separate figures who would, respectively, fill either a priestly or a political role. The Christian view that Jesus of Nazareth was the Messiah was not accepted by mainstream Judaism for a variety of reasons that will become clearer as we study the Gospels. (See Part 9.) Among other things, it appears that many Jews questioned the biblical correctness of Jesus' teaching and the "shameful" manner of his death. The Hebrew prophets did not foresee that Israel's deliverer would be executed as a criminal by Gentiles (John 7:12, 27, 31, 40–44), making the crucifixion "a stumbling block" to scripturally literate Jews (1 Cor. 1:23). Mark's Gospel reflects these objections and emphasizes the unexpected or "hidden" quality of Jesus' messiahship.

The Royal Covenant of King David

Despite the heated debates between Jewish and Christian viewpoints preserved in the Gospels, it is possible to draw a general picture of Israel's concept of the Messiah by tracing its development in the Hebrew Bible. Derived from the Hebrew word *mashiah,* Messiah means "anointed one" and refers to the ceremony in which priests anointed (poured oil) on the heads of persons singled out or commissioned by God for some special undertaking. In the Hebrew Bible, *mashiah* is most frequently applied to the kings of ancient Israel, particularly those descended from King David (Pss. 18:50; 89:20, 38, 51; 132:10, 17). Because of his outstanding success in establishing a powerful Israelite state, David was regarded as the prototype of the divinely favored ruler and his kingdom a foreshadowing of the reign of God on earth. According to 2 Samuel 7, Yahweh concluded an "everlasting covenant" or treaty with David's "house" (dynasty). The covenant terms specified Yahweh's unconditional promise to maintain an unending line of Davidic kings on the throne of Israel. If some of David's royal descendants misbehaved, Yahweh would punish them, but he vowed never to remove them from the throne (2 Sam. 7:8–17; 23:1–5). Perhaps as a result of this "royal covenant theology," David's heirs ruled uninterrupted over the land of Judah for nearly 400 years (961–587 B.C.E.). (By contrast, the northern kingdom of Israel, separated from Judah in 922 B.C.E., saw many changes of ruling families before its destruction by the Assyrians in 721 B.C.E.)

Historical End of the Davidic Dynasty   As described in Part 4, David's line of reigning kings came to an abrupt end in 587 B.C.E., when Nebuchadnezzar of Babylon destroyed Jerusalem and removed the last Davidic monarch, Zedekiah, from the throne. When a remnant of Judah's former leadership returned to Jerusalem from Babylon in 538 B.C.E., the Davidic monarchy was not restored. During the centuries that followed, the land of Judah was ruled by a succession of foreign powers—the empires of Persia, Macedonian Greece, Syria, and Rome.

Under Persia's administration of Judah, the first appointed governor was Zerubbabel, a descendant of the Davidic line. Zerubbabel apparently became the focus of national hopes for a restoration of the Davidic kingdom and was hailed in messianic terms by the prophets Haggai and Zechariah (Hag. 2:20–23; Zech. 2:10, 6:12). Hopes for a renewed Davidic state failed to materialize, however, and the figure of Zerubbabel disappeared from history. Israel was never again to have a Davidic king, the "anointed of God."

During the long years of Persian rule, the Jewish people looked mainly to the spiritual leadership of their High Priest (who was also anointed with holy oil when installed in office [Lev. 4:3, 5]). The High Priest and his many priestly assistants administered the rebuilt Temple and provided a focus of communal religious identity. Without a king or political autonomy, Judah became increasingly a theocratic (God-ruled) community, guided by a priestly class that supervised the Temple sacrifices and interpreted the Mosaic Torah.

Israel's Hopes for a New Davidic King

Israel's collective memory of the Davidic Covenant, however, did not fade. Yahweh's sworn oath that his people would have a Davidic heir to rule them forever (2 Sam. 7; 23:1–5; Ps. 89: 19–31) was reinforced by Israel's prophets who envisioned a future golden age when a man like David, "anointed of God," would rise to liberate Israel, defeat its enemies, and help bring God's kingdom to earth.

The prophet Isaiah of Jerusalem, a staunch supporter of the Davidic monarchy, had delivered unforgettable oracles (prophetic words) from Yahweh:

For a boy has been born for us, a son given to us
  to bear the symbol of dominion on his
  shoulder;
and he shall be called
in purpose wonderful, in battle
God-like,
Father for all time, Prince of peace.

Great shall the dominion be and boundless the
  peace
  bestowed on David's throne and on his
  kingdom,
  to establish it and sustain it with justice and
  righteousness from now and for evermore.

The zeal of the LORD [Yahweh] of Hosts shall
  do this.

Isaiah 9:6–7

Isaiah's further allusions to a righteous king "from the stock of Jess (David's father)" (Isa. 11: 1–9) and visions of a Davidic Jerusalem to which the Gentile nations would flock (Isa. 2: 1–4) not only enhanced the prestige of the Davidic royal family but also associated it irrefutably with the coming earthwide reign of Yahweh.

The Messiah as a Political Leader   All of Israel's Davidic kings were literally messiahs, "anointed ones." They ruled as Yahweh's "sons," adopted as such at the time of their consecration or coronation (Ps. 2:7). Because the prophets had conceived of the Messiah as a warrior-king like David, a hero whom Yahweh chose to act as his agent in establishing a dominion of universal peace, the messianic leader was typically regarded as primarily a political figure. His function was to demonstrate the omnipotence of Israel's God by setting up an earthly kingdom whose righteous government would compel the nations' respect for both Yahweh and his chosen people (Isa. 11; Dan. 2:44).

Messianic Claimants Before and After Jesus

Judea's troubled relationship with Rome inspired a series of prophets, revolutionaries, and other leaders who typically promised the Jewish people relief from Roman economic and social oppression. Some rebel leaders reputedly claimed the title of Jewish king, the crime for which Pontius Pilate executed Jesus. Most of those aspiring to royal status did not claim to be a "*son* [descendant] of David" but merely to be "*like* David," a previously obscure youth who was raised from among the common people to become Israel's champion against a foreign military threat. It could be said of these popular national leaders what the psalmist's God said of David: "I have conferred the crown on a hero, and promoted one chosen from my people" (Ps. 89:19).

In his accounts of peasant uprisings against the Romans or their **Herodian** puppets, Josephus reported that several prominent rebels were also messianic pretenders (i.e., they assumed the function of Israel's *anointed* kings). Most of these popular kings appeared either during the turmoil following the death of Herod the Great (4 B.C.E.) or during the greater upheaval of the Jewish War against Rome (66–73 C.E.). After Herod's death, a rebel named Judas, son of a brigand or terrorist named Hezekiah, led Galilee in a revolt against Roman occupational forces. According to Josephus, this Judas was motivated by an ambition to achieve "royal rank" (*Antiquities of the Jews,* 17.271–272).

Another messianic pretender, Simon bar (son of) Giora, led the largest and most powerful force resisting the Roman reconquest of Jerusalem. Josephus states that after Titus's soldiers had captured and demolished the Temple, Simon, arrayed in royal robes, suddenly appeared among the ruins. If he hoped for a last-minute divine intervention to vindicate his kingly aspirations, he was disappointed: The Romans took him as a prisoner to Rome, where he was executed.

The most famous messianic claimant was Simon bar Kochba, who led the second Jewish Revolt against Rome in 132–135 C.E. Akiba, a prominent rabbi, proclaimed that bar Kochba fulfilled the promise in Numbers 24:17 that "a star shall go forth from Jacob." Although Rabbi Akiba and other supporters called Simon "bar Kochba," which means "son of the star," his detractors derisively labeled the revolutionary "bar Koziba"—"son of the lie." His attempt to liberate Judea and restore a theocratic state was doomed by Roman might, which again annihilated Jewish armies and brought a terrible end to Jewish political messianic hopes.

A Christian View of the Messiah

As presented in the Gospels, Jesus of Nazareth takes a view of the Messiah's role and the kingdom of God that was disappointing or perplexing to many. Despite some modern commentators' attempts to associate him with the Zealot or revolutionary party, Jesus (as portrayed by the Evangelists) does not present himself as a military or political savior of Israel. As John's Gospel concludes, Jesus' "kingdom does not belong to this world" (John 18:36).

Jesus' Multiple Role   Despite Jesus' reluctance to assert his right to rule Israel, the Gospel writers nonetheless were convinced that he was the same Messiah whose life Isaiah and the other Hebrew prophets foresaw. In identifying Jesus as Israel's Messiah, however, the New Testament authors broadened his role beyond that of the largely political nature of the prophesied Davidic ruler. To defend Jesus against charges that he "failed" to reestablish David's kingdom, early Christians pointed to specific passages in the Hebrew Bible that seemed to them to illustrate the nature of Jesus' unexpected messiahship. In Christian interpretations of the Messiah, Jesus became the "prophet like Moses" described in Deuteronomy (18:15–20) and the mysterious "suffering servant" in Isaiah (52:13–53:12). In the original texts, neither the Mosaic prophet nor the anonymous servant is associated with the Messiah, and we do not know whether these two unidentified figures were given a messianic emphasis before the Christian period. Isaiah's "Song of the Suffering Servant," dramatizing the unjust punishment of a righteous man who suffers for the sins of others and thereby somehow redeems them, became a crucial text for explaining the theological significance of Jesus' death (Mark 10:45). Psalm 22, which records the lament of a man tormented by Gentile enemies, was also used to reinforce the Christian view that the true Messiah was destined to suffer. The Christian concept of the Messiah is a paradox: a God-anointed king who is rejected and dies, but whose voluntary death is a triumph over forces of darkness and evil and a source of hope for mortal humanity.

TERMS AND CONCEPTS TO REMEMBER

Aaron	Masoretic Text (MT)
Academy of Jamnia	Melchizedek
Augustus	Messiah
Caiaphas	Mishnah
Dead Sea Scrolls	mysteries
Dionysus	Osiris
Essenes	Pharisees
exegesis	Philo Judaeus
Flavius Josephus	Pontius Pilate
Gamaliel	Plato
Gemara	Qumran
Gentile	rabbi
Hades	Sadducees
hasidim	Sanhedrin
Hasmoneans	scroll
Hellenistic	Simon
Herod	Stoicism
Herod Agrippa I	synagogue
Herod Antipas	Talmud
Herod Archelaus	Tiberius
Herod Philip II	Titus (Flavius
Herodian	Sabinius
Isis	Vespasianus Titus)
James	Vespasian
John the Baptist	Zealots
Judas the Galilean	Zeus
Logos	

RECOMMENDED READING

Charlesworth, James H., ed., *Jesus and the Dead Sea Scrolls.* New York: Doubleday, 1995. A collection of highly readable essays by expert scholars.

Cohen, Shaye J. D. *From the Maccabees to the Mishnah.* Philadelphia: Westminster Press, 1987. A readable survey of evolving Jewish religious ideas that gave birth to both rabbinic Judaism and Christianity.

Cross, Frank M. *Qumran and the History of the Biblical Text.* Cambridge, Mass.: Harvard University Press, 1975.

———. *The Ancient Library of Qumran,* 2nd ed. Grand Rapids, Mich.: Baker, 1980.

Finkelstein, Louis. *The Pharisees,* vols. 1 and 2. Philadelphia: Jewish Publication Society of America, 1962. Provides reliable information.

Gaster, Theodor H. *The Dead Sea Scriptures in English Translation.* Garden City, N.Y.: Doubleday, 1976.

Hengel, Martin. *Judaism and Hellenism,* vols. 1 and 2. Philadelphia: Fortress Press, 1974. A thorough and detailed analysis of Hellenistic influences on Jewish thought during the centuries preceding the birth of Christianity.

———. *Jews, Greeks, and Barbarians: Aspects of the Hellenism of Judaism in the Pre-Christian Period.* Philadelphia: Fortress Press, 1980.

Horsley, Richard A. "Messianic Movements in Judaism." In D. N. Freedman, ed., *Anchor Bible Dictionary,* Vol. 4, pp. 791–797. New York: Doubleday, 1992. An excellent introduction to political messianic claimants at the time of Jesus.

Horsley, Richard A., and Hanson, John S. *Bandits, Prophets, and Messiahs: Popular Movements at the Time of Jesus.* Minneapolis/Chicago/New York: Winston Press, 1985.

Josephus, Flavius. *Josephus: Complete Works.* Translated by W. Whiston. Grand Rapids, Mich.: Kregel Publications, 1960. A dated translation but one that contains the complete texts of *The Antiquities of the Jews* and *The Jewish War,* as well as the "Discourse on Hades."

———. *The Jewish War,* rev. ed. Translated by G. A. Williamson. Edited by E. M. Smallwood. New York: Penguin Books, 1981. The most important contemporary source for conditions in Palestine during the first century C.E.

Murphy, Frederick J. *The Religious World of Jesus: An Introduction to Second Temple Palestinian Judaism.* Nashville, Tenn.: Abingdon Press, 1991. A survey of pertinent cultural and religious groups at the time of Jesus.

Neusner, Jacob. *From Politics to Piety: The Emergence of Pharisaic Judaism.* Englewood Cliffs, N.J.: Prentice Hall, 1973.

Newsome, James D. *Greeks, Romans, Jews: Currents of Culture and Belief in the New Testament World.* Philadelphia: Trinity Press International, 1992. A superbly researched compendium of historical documents relevant to Jewish religious thought and practice during the era of Christianity's inception.

Sandmel, Samuel. *Judaism and Christian Beginnings.* New York: Oxford University Press, 1978.

Shanks, Hershel, ed. *Christianity and Rabbinic Judaism.* Washington, D.C.: Biblical Archaeological Society, 1992. A collection of scholarly essays profiling the parallel development of Christianity and formative Judaism.

———. *Understanding the Dead Sea Scrolls.* New York: Random House, 1992. A collection of popular essays from the *Biblical Archaeology Review.*

Stone, M. E. *Scriptures, Sects, and Visions: A Profile of Judaism from Ezra to the Jewish Revolts.* Philadelphia: Fortress Press, 1980. A readable introduction to the period.

Talmon, Shemaryahu, ed. *Jewish Civilization in the Hellenistic Period.* Philadelphia: Trinity Press International, 1991. A collection of scholarly essays about the fusion of Hebraic and Hellenistic culture that gave birth to rabbinic Judaism and Christianity.

Ulrich, Eugene and VanderKam, James, eds. *The Community of the Renewed Covenant.* Chicago: University of Notre Dame Press, 1995. A collection of up-to-date scholarly essays on the Dead Sea Scrolls.

Vermes, Geza. *The Dead Sea Scrolls: Qumran in Perspective.* London: Collins, 1977.

QUESTIONS FOR REVIEW

1. What rapidly expanding empire gobbled up the Hellenistic kingdoms of Syria and Egypt during the last centuries B.C.E.? How and when did Judea come under the rule of this new empire?

2. Who was King Herod, and for what great building project is he famous? Identify Herod Antipas and Herod Agrippa I.

3. Describe the two Jewish revolts against Rome (66–73 C.E. and 132–135 C.E.). What were the political consequences to the Jewish people?

4. Define *Hellenistic,* and describe some of the main characteristics of Hellenistic culture. Identify Socrates and Plato and explain some of their influential ideas. Define Stoicism.

5. What were the "mystery religions"? What benefits did initiation into the cults of Dionysus, Mithras, Isis, or Osiris confer upon the worshiper?

6. Why do historians refer to "multiple Judaisms" when speaking of the period before 70 C.E., when the Romans destroyed the Jewish state? Describe the major groups and their distinctive beliefs, including Pharisees, Sadducees, Essenes, and Zealots.

7. Describe the importance of the Academy at Jamnia (Yavneh) for the development of modern rabbinical Judaism. What was the religious purpose of the Jamnia group?

8. Define the Dead Sea Scrolls. What kinds of documents do they include? When were they written, and when were they found? What is their probable connection to the Essenes?

9. Summarize the concept of the Messiah found in the Hebrew Bible. To what degree is the biblical Messiah a political figure related to the restoration of King David's royal dynasty? In what ways do New Testament writers modify the concept of the Davidic Messiah?

QUESTIONS FOR DISCUSSION AND REFLECTION

1. Discuss some of the beliefs that Pharisees, Essenes, and early Christians held in common. In what ways did their beliefs differ?

2. After the conquests of Alexander, Hellenistic art, philosophy, literature, and customs permeated the entire Mediterranean world, causing many assimilated peoples to adopt the Greek way of life. Which aspects of Hellenistic culture seem to conflict with the biblical traditions? Why did the hasidim view many Greek ideas as threats to the purity of their ancestral religion?

3. Greek philosophy, particularly Plato's spiritual dualism and concept of the immortal soul, exercised great influence on later religious thought. Do you think that philosophy, with its emphasis on rational method and logical deduction, is inherently incompatible with the concept of a divinely revealed religion such as Judaism or Christianity? Can scientific reason (our Hellenic inheritance) and religious faith (the Hebraic legacy) complement each other? Does the current debate over evolution and creationism represent a continuing split between reason and revelation in the Western psyche?

4. Historians have discerned many parallels between some Hellenistic mystery cults of savior gods and later Christian beliefs about Jesus of Nazareth. Do you think that the apparent similarities result from the older cults' influence on the Christian movement's deification of Jesus or from common psychological needs shared by adherents of both old and newer religions?

THE NEW TESTAMENT

The Christian-Greek Scriptures

9

The Books of the New Testament: The Gospels

Literary Categories in the New Testament

A collection of twenty-seven early Christian documents that the Church added to the Greek version of the Hebrew Scriptures, the New Testament roughly parallels the three-part organization of the Hebrew Bible. The four Gospels, which form the first unit of the New Testament, relate the actions and teachings of Jesus, just as the first section of the Hebrew Bible—the Torah—contains material traditionally ascribed to Moses. The second unit, the Book of Acts, is a narrative about the birth and growth of the Christian community, corresponding to the Deuteronomistic History (the Former Prophets) found in Joshua through 2 Kings. The thirteen letters commonly attributed to Paul are analogous to the fifteen prophetic books (the Latter Prophets) of the Tanak. The third section of the New Testament includes a miscellaneous assortment of books—Hebrews, the Catholic (general) epistles, and Revelation—and roughly corresponds to the third main division of the Hebrew Bible, the Writings. (Refer to "Organization of the Hebrew and Christian Greek Scriptures" on page 308.)

A literary category invented by the early Christian community, the Gospels—a term de-

rived from the Greek *evangelion,* meaning "good news"—are vehicles for transforming previously oral preaching about Jesus into the form of his biography. As scholars have learned, however, the **Gospel** authors—the **Evangelists**—do not pursue the same historical goals as modern biographers, who, ideally, attempt to compile an objective, complete, and factually accurate picture of their subject. The Gospel writers are primarily Christian believers presenting their confessions of faith in Jesus through biographical narratives. The author of John's Gospel speaks for all Evangelists when he states that his purpose in writing is explicitly theological: He writes "in order that you [the reader] may hold the faith that Jesus is the Christ, the Son of God, and that through this faith you may possess life by his name" (John 20:31). The Evangelist also notes that he is aware of many traditions about Jesus that he does not include in his Gospel, which contains only those elements that will illustrate his theological objective (John 20:30). Thus, the Evangelists focus on Jesus' adult ministry and **Passion**—his suffering and death—excluding almost all information that today's biographer would regard as essential to help us understand Jesus as a historical personage, such as his relationship with his parents and family, his education, the kind of

Organization of the Hebrew and Christian Greek Scriptures

The contents of the New Testament are arranged in a way that approximates the order of the Hebrew Bible, which is also called the Tanak, a term whose consonants represent the three principal divisions of the Hebrew Scriptures: the **T**orah *(Law), the* **N**evi'im *(Prophets), and the* **K**ethuvim *(Writings).*

OLD COVENANT (TESTAMENT)	NEW COVENANT (TESTAMENT)
T Torah (five books of Moses) **A**	Four Gospels (story of Jesus)
N Nevi'im (Prophets) Deuteronomistic History of Joshua through 2 Kings Books of the Prophets **A**	Book of Acts (church history) Letters of Paul and other church leaders
K Kethuvim (Writings) Books of poetry, wisdom, and an apocalypse (Daniel)	Book of Hebrews, catholic epistles, and an apocalypse (Revelation)

religious instruction he received, and the cultural and intellectual forces that shaped his mind and character. Except for the infancy narratives in Matthew and Luke and the brief episode about the twelve-year-old Jesus in the Temple (Luke 2:41–51), the Gospel authors concern themselves entirely with Jesus' brief public career, emphasizing his miraculous deeds and teachings about the kingdom of God. Like the historians of the Hebrew Bible, the Evangelists are less interested in recording factual events than in proclaiming the hand of God operating through the life of their hero, which they view as the crucial turning point in the divine plan to redeem humanity (Luke 16:16). (See Table 9.1 for an outline of major historic events.)

The Evangelists were convinced that Jesus of Nazareth was both the long-awaited Jewish **Messiah** and the universal Savior, the divine agent through whom Israel's God had chosen to make the ultimate revelation of his will. Composed about forty to sixty-five years after Jesus' death, the canonical Gospels represent four different attempts to crystallize in final, written form what four different Christian communi-

ties believed was important about the Christ figure. Although scholars believe that they incorporate many authentic traditions about Jesus, the Gospels function largely to promote their authors' understanding of Jesus' theological significance. This theological orientation, along with the supernatural events associated with Jesus' death and resurrection, provides scholars with a formidable challenge as they attempt to evaluate the Gospels in terms of ordinary historical analysis.

The fifth book of the New Testament, Acts was composed by the same author as the Gospel of Luke and shows the same religious preoccupations. Rather than a scientific inquiry into the origin and social dynamics of the early Christian movement, Acts—written at least half a century after the events it describes—is an idealized interpretation of the sometimes chaotic struggles of the primitive Church to define itself.

Written almost two decades before the first Gospel, Paul's letters to newly founded churches in Asia Minor, Greece, and Italy are the oldest surviving Christian documents. Paul's use of the letter form proved so effective and popular that most of the later New Testament writers adopted this literary device. Even the Book of Revelation, a visionary work responding to a perceived threat of Roman oppression, uses letters, showing the glorified Jesus dictating seven missives to churches in Asia Minor.

Except for Paul's genuine letters, written between 50 and 62 C.E., most New Testament books—including at least three of the Gospels, the Book of Acts, and Revelation—appeared during the last three decades of the first century, following the Roman destruction of Jerusalem in 70 C.E. The last books accepted into the canon, ascribed to leaders of the early Jerusalem church, are several of the general (catholic) epistles, such as Jude and 2 Peter, which were probably not composed until the mid-second century C.E.

Table 9.1 Major Events in New Testament History

Approximate Date	Event	Biblical Source
332 B.C.E.	Alexander the Great of Macedonia includes Palestine in his empire.	1 Macc. 1:1–5
323–197 B.C.E.	The Ptolemys of Egypt rule Palestine (Hellenistic period).	1 Macc. 1:6–10
197–142 B.C.E.	Seleucid dynasty of Syria rules Palestine.	2 Macc. 4
167–164 B.C.E.	Antiochus IV attempts to force Hellenistic religion on the Jews and pollutes the Temple.	1 Macc. 1:10–67
164 B.C.E.	The Maccabean revolt is successful; the Temple is cleansed and rededicated.	1 Macc. 2–6; 2 Macc. 8–10; Dan. 7:25, 8:14, 9:27, 12:7
142–63 B.C.E.	The Jews expel the Seleucids; Judea becomes an independent kingdom under the Hasmonean dynasty.	1 Macc.
63 B.C.E.	General Pompey makes Palestine part of the Roman Empire and partitions Judea.	
40–4 B.C.E.	Herod the Great rules as Roman-appointed king of Judea; he rebuilds the Temple.	
30 B.C.E.–14 C.E.	Augustus Caesar rules as emperor of Rome.	
6–4 B.C.E.	Birth of Jesus.	Matt. 2; Luke 2
4 B.C.E.–39 C.E.	Herod Antipas rules as tetrarch of Galilee.	Luke 13:31–32; Mark 6:14–29
5–10 C.E.	Birth of Saul at Tarsus (the Apostle Paul).	
14–37 C.E.	Tiberius Caesar rules as emperor of Rome.	Luke 3:1
26–36 C.E.	Pontius Pilate serves as procurator of Judea.	
27–29 C.E. (?)	Ministry of John the Baptist.	Mark 1:2–11, 6:17–29; John 1:19–36, 3:22–36
27–30 or 29–33 C.E. (?)	Ministry of Jesus.	Matt., Mark, Luke, John
30–33 C.E. (?)	Crucifixion and resurrection of Jesus.	Matt., Mark, Luke, John
33–35 C.E. (?)	Conversion of the Apostle Paul.	Acts 9:1–19, 22:1–21, 26:1–23; Gal. 1:11–16
41–54 C.E.	Claudius serves as emperor of Rome; he banishes the Jews from Rome (49 C.E.?).	Acts 18:2
41–44 C.E. (?)	Herod Agrippa I is king of Judea; he imprisons Peter; he beheads James and possibly John as well (44 C.E.?)	Acts 12

Table 9.1 (continued)

Approximate Date	Event	Biblical Source
47–56 C.E.	Paul conducts missionary tours among the Gentiles.	
49 C.E.	Paul attends the first Church council held in Jerusalem.	Acts 15; Gal. 2
50 C.E.	Paul writes 1 and 2 Thessalonians; the "Sayings" of Jesus are compiled (?).	
54–68 C.E.	Nero serves as emperor of Rome.	
54–62 C.E.	Paul writes a series of letters to various churches he had founded or visited.	1 Cor. (54–55 C.E.); 2 Cor. (55–56 C.E.); Gal. (56 C.E.); Rom. (56–57 C.E.); Col. (61 C.E.?) Philem. (61 C.E.); Phil. (62 C.E.)
60–62 or 63 C.E. (?)	Paul under house arrest in Rome.	
62 C.E.	James, brother of Jesus, is martyred.	
64 C.E.	Rome is burned, and Christians are persecuted.	
66–70 C.E. (?)	Gospel of Mark is written.	
66–73	Jewish Revolt against Rome, destruction of Jerusalem	
69–79 C.E.	Vespasian serves as emperor of Rome.	
79–81 C.E.	Titus, conqueror of Jerusalem, is emperor.	
80–85 C.E.	Gospel of Matthew is written.	
80–90 C.E.	Gospel of Luke and Acts are written.	
80–100 C.E.	Letter of James is written.	
81–96 C.E.	Domitian is emperor; Christians in Asia Minor experience general hostility.	
85–90 C.E.	Book of Hebrews is written.	
90 C.E. (?)	Letter to the Ephesians is written; Paul's letters are collected (?).	
90–100 C.E.	1 Clement is written; Gospel of John is composed.	
90–91 C.E. (?)	Rabbis hold council at Jamnia; third part of the Hebrew Bible—the Writings—is defined.	
95–100 C.E.	Various Jewish and Christian apocalypses are composed: 2 Esdras, Revelation, and 3 Baruch.	
98–117 C.E.	Trajan serves as emperor and persecutes the Christians.	
100–110 C.E.	Letters of 1, 2, and 3 John are written.	
100–140 C.E.	The Didache, Shepherd of Hermas, and Epistle of Ignatius are written; canonical New Testament books of 1 and 2 Timothy, Titus, 1 Peter, and Jude also appear.	
117–138 C.E.	Hadrian is emperor.	
132–135 C.E.	Jews revolt against Rome for the last time.	
150 C.E. (?)	2 Peter is written.	

The line above marks the end of both the Jewish state and the original apostolic church.

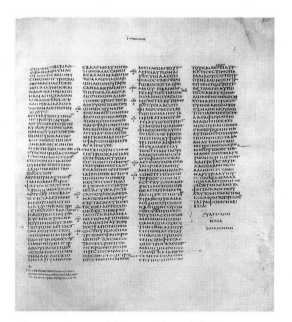

Christians pioneered the use of the **codex,** *manuscript pages bound together like a modern book. This Greek text from the Gospel of John contrasts with older copies of New Testament books, which typically survive in only fragmentary form. After Constantine recognized Christianity as a legal religion in the early fourth century, New Testament manuscripts increased in number and quality. (Courtesy of the British Library, no. 4445 f 85r)*

As literature, the Christian Greek Scriptures lack the poetic richness and diversity that characterize the Hebrew Bible. Despite some memorable passages, such as Matthew's Sermon on the Mount and Paul's discourses on love and resurrection (1 Corinthians 13 and 15), the New Testament offers little comparable to the poetry of Second Isaiah or Hebrew wisdom literature, particularly the innovative speculations found in Job and Ecclesiastes. It should be remembered, however, that whereas the Hebrew Bible was created over approximately 1100 years, the compositional time span of the New Testament was much briefer, perhaps only 100 years (from about 50 to 150 C.E.). Moreover, instead of dramatizing the history of an entire nation as the Hebrew Bible does, the New Tes-

tament focuses on the lives and thoughts of a relatively few people—Jesus, his disciples, and a handful of other early Christians. Although the New Testament adds only one story to world literature, that story—the ministry and Passion of Jesus—has been described by some as the greatest story ever told.

The following discussion of the twenty-seven canonical New Testament books is intended to familiarize the reader with some of the basic events and themes contained in the Christian Greek Scriptures. (See "New Testament Books: Approximate Order of Composition," on page 312 for a listing of these twenty-seven books.) This text makes no attempt to cover every aspect of Christian teaching. For additional information on specific topics, consult the list of "Recommended Readings" at the end of individual essays. Unless otherwise noted, all quotations are from the New English Bible (NEB).

The Synoptic Gospels

Of the four Gospels, the first three—Matthew, Mark, and Luke—are so alike that they are known as the **Synoptics,** sharing a common viewpoint in the order in which they present Jesus' story. In general, scholars can place their three accounts of the same event side-by-side and find remarkably parallel versions of similar sayings or narrative episodes. Whereas Matthew, Mark, and Luke generally follow the same sequence of events and show Jesus teaching in the same style—creating earthy parables and issuing succinct pronouncements—the fourth Gospel, attributed to John, presents a strikingly different chronology (order of events) and manner of teaching.

The Synoptic Problem Because the Synoptic Gospels resemble each other so closely, scholars recognize a close literary kinship; their attempts to analyze the nature of this apparent relation-

New Testament Books: Approximate Order of Composition

APPROXIMATE DATE (C.E.)	TITLE OF BOOK	AUTHOR
50	1 Thessalonians	Paul
	2 Thessalonians (if by Paul)	
54–55	1 and 2 Corinthians	Paul
56	Galatians	Paul
56–57	Romans	Paul
61	Colossians (if by Paul)	Paul
61	Philippians	Paul
62	Philemon	Paul
66–70	Gospel of Mark	Anonymous
66–73	*Jewish War Against Rome: Destruction of Jerusalem and Temple*	
80–85	Gospel of Matthew	Anonymous
85–90	Gospel of Luke and Acts	Anonymous
85–95	Hebrews, 1 Peter, Ephesians, James	Anonymous
90–95	Gospel of John	Anonymous
95	Revelation (the Apocalypse)	John of Patmos
95–100	Letters of John (1, 2, and 3 John)	The Elder
110–30	1 and 2 Timothy, Titus	Anonymous
130–50	Jude, 2 Peter	Anonymous

ship, to discover which Gospel was a source for the others, along with related questions of authorship, chronologic priority, dates of composition, and other aspects of possible interdependence, are known as the **Synoptic Problem**.

For many years, it was assumed that Mark, the shortest Gospel, was a conflation and abridgement of Matthew and Luke. This belief is known as the Griesbach theory, named for Johann Griesbach (1745–1812), who first published this solution to the Synoptic Problem. The belief that Mark is an abbreviated version of the two longer Gospels is still held by a minority of conservative scholars. Approximately 90 percent of today's scholars, however, are convinced that Mark was the first Gospel written and that it is the major source of both Matthew and Luke.

The Two-Document Hypothesis   The most widely accepted explanation of the Synoptic's literary relationship, the two-document hypothesis argues that Matthew and Luke used Mark as their basic narrative source, to which they added teaching material drawn from a now-lost document known as Q. **Q** (usually defined as *Quelle,* the German for "source") is a hypothetical collection of Jesus' sayings; its former existence is presumed because many sayings not found in Mark occur in both Matthew and Luke. Because many of Jesus' statements appear in Matthew and Luke in almost identical form, or in very similar phrasing, scholars believe that they come from a written document rather than an orally transmitted memory of Jesus' words. The shared sayings, absent from Mark, include such famous passages as the "beatitudes" (blessings) (cf. Matt. 5:1–1 with Luke 6:9–13) and the "Lord's Prayer" (Matt. 6:9–13; Luke 11:1–4). The disappearance of this hypothetical source can be attributed to the fact that once Q's contents had been incorporated into Matthew and Luke, there was no reason to preserve it as a separate document. Even so, the lack of proof that Q ever existed is a weakness in the theory.

Whatever the origin of their shared sayings, Matthew and Luke also use material peculiar to their individual gospels. The writers of both documents add genealogies and birth stories, but each does so according to his distinctive themes. Whereas Matthew's genealogy emphasizes Jesus' ancestral link (through Joseph) to the major figures of Israel's past, particularly Abraham and David, Luke's genealogy traces Jesus' lineage all the way back to Adam, "the son of God." Matthew's initial emphasis on Jesus as the fulfillment of God's promises to Israel and Luke's stress on Jesus' universality are not accidental but reflect the characteristic special interests of each Gospel writer. Thus, the great parables found only in Luke, such as those involving the good Samaritan, the prodigal son, and Lazarus and the rich man, all embody a typically Lukan emphasis on sudden reversals of ordinary expectations. With his special interest in principles governing the Christian community, we are not surprised to find that only Matthew uses the term for **Church** (*ekklesia*) and only he provides guidelines for its governance (Matt. 10 and 18).

Six Stages in the Gospels' Development

Oral Preaching About Jesus   Scholars have inferred six hypothetical developments behind the writing of the Gospels. First, for probably twenty years or more after Jesus' death, the Christian testimony about him was entirely oral. Eyewitness memories about Jesus' deeds and words were transmitted by word of mouth without any consistent reference to the time, place, or circumstances of their origin. As preserved in the Christian *kerygma* (proclamation),

individual sayings circulated independently of one another, so free-floating that when later incorporated into the Gospels each Evangelist placed them in a different narrative setting. Compare the four strikingly different contexts given to the story of the woman who anointed Jesus with oil: Matthew 26:6–13; Mark 14:3–9; Luke 7:36–50; John 12:1–8. Clusters of sayings may have accumulated in major Christian centers—Jerusalem, Antioch, Caesarea, Ephesus—where they were interpreted and reapplied to the rapidly changing social environment of the early Christian congregations.

The Q Document   A second development took place about 50–60 C.E., when an anonymous Christian scribe made the first significant collection of Jesus' sayings, the hypothetical Q document. Using this source independently, Matthew and Luke later composed about 250 verses based on Q. Whether these sayings were compiled primarily for teaching purposes or to keep Jesus' words from being forgotten as the first generation of Christians began to die off is not known.

When Jesus' expected early return did not materialize, it became necessary to preserve authoritative accounts of his actions and teachings that could set standards of belief and behavior for the increasingly diverse Christian communities. Arguments about the nature of Christ, the extent to which a Gentile Christian must observe the Mosaic Torah, and many other theological issues hastened the process of creating foundation documents that preserved community leaders' understanding of the "correct" view of Jesus. After the apostolic witness disappeared and particularly after the mother church at Jerusalem was destroyed in 70 C.E., the center of Church governance shifted from Palestine and Syria to Greco-Roman centers such as Ephesus and Rome. As Gentile converts flooded the originally Jewish churches, definitive written accounts of Jesus' message became increasingly vital in reeducating former pagans.

Mark's Gospel   A third development was the Gospel of Mark, composed, perhaps in Rome, on the eve of the Roman destruction of Jerusalem. According to Eusebius, the author of a fourth-century history of the Church, Mark was not an eyewitness of Jesus' ministry but had become a disciple of Peter in Rome and had based his Gospel on Peter's testimony. Eusebius quotes Papias, an earlier churchman (c. 140 C.E.), who noted that Mark had not known Jesus personally but had merely recorded Peter's recollections, which were "not in [proper chronologic] order" (*Ecclesiastical History* 3.39). Despite Eusebius's plausible claims, however, most scholars now conclude that the author of Mark drew on numerous oral traditions about Jesus, rather than the memoirs of a single disciple. If Mark's secondhand account of Jesus' life does not observe the proper historical chronology, it was nonetheless followed closely by the authors of Matthew and Luke, who reproduce his sequence of events.

Matthew's Gospel   A fourth development was the Gospel of Matthew, composed to answer Jewish criticism of Christian claims about Jesus and to emphasize Jesus' adherence to the Jewish Torah. The Gospel of Matthew, probably written in Antioch about 85 C.E., incorporated 90 percent of Mark's account but greatly expanded the teaching content, for which he drew on the Q document as well as a source unique to his Gospel, designated *M*. Matthew framed Mark's narrative with accounts of Jesus' infancy and postresurrection appearances; most distinctively, he presented Jesus' birth and ministry as fulfilling prophecies from the Hebrew Bible. He cites about 130 scriptural passages to refute Jewish claims that Jesus had not lived up to Old Testament predictions about the Messiah.

Whereas Mark introduces Jesus as "Son of God," Matthew initially identifies him as "son of David, son of Abraham," implying that his subject is the culmination of Jewish messianic hopes, embodying all the promises made to Israel's progenitor. Reflecting his community's concern for Jewish law, Matthew portrays Jesus as a greater Moses who inaugurates a higher level of Torah observance and a new covenant. The Evangelist arranges Jesus' teachings in the form of five separate sermons corresponding to the five books of the Mosaic Torah. So successful was his integration of Jesus' ethical teachings with Mark's older narrative that Matthew's Gospel—with its strong orientation toward the Church—soon became the most popular, ranking first among the four.

Luke and Acts   During the 90s C.E., perhaps only five to ten years after the appearance of Matthew, the most literate and formally correct of the Synoptics was composed. The writing of Luke and Acts marked the fifth stage in the development of the Gospels. Perhaps the work of the only Gentile author in the Bible, Luke's Gospel reproduces about half of Mark along with generous portions of Q and the author's own source, known as L, which comprises about a third of his account. The first part of a two-volume narrative about Christian origins, Luke and its sequel, Acts, form the largest contribution of any single author to the New Testament.

John's Gospel   The last stage is marked by the composition of the Gospel of John—the fourth Gospel and apparently the last written. This document is so different from the Synoptics that scholars regard it as a special case. John covers the same period of Jesus' life as do the Synoptics, beginning with his baptism and ministry in Galilee and concluding with his trial and execution near Jerusalem. But this Gospel presents so different a picture of Jesus' character and teaching that most scholars are at a loss to determine its historical value. In the fourth Gospel, Jesus' manner of teaching is radically transformed. Instead of speaking in earthy images and parables drawn from the experience of his peasant audience, John's Jesus delivers long philosophical monologs about his relationship to the Father and reascension to heaven. The

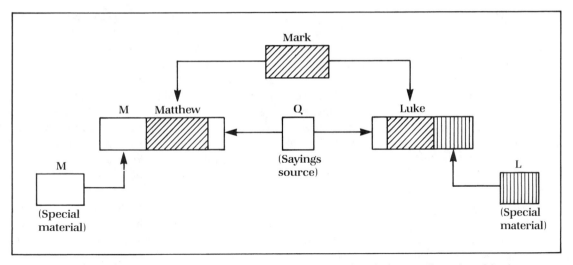

This drawing illustrates the two-document theory, an attempt to explain the literary relationship of the three Synoptic Gospels. Note that this theory takes Mark's Gospel as a major source for Matthew and Luke. In addition, both Matthew and Luke incorporate teaching material from Q (Quelle, a hypothetical collection of Jesus' sayings). Matthew also uses special material unique to his Gospel, here designated M; Luke similarly includes material found only in his account, here labeled L.

thrust of Jesus' instruction is also different. Rather than focusing on the inbreaking kingdom of God and a reinterpretation of the Jewish law, Jesus dwells primarily on the nature of his own being and his significance to the believer. Whereas Mark, Matthew, and Luke show Jesus promulgating a modified form of traditional Judaism, John is less interested in preserving Jesus' own religion than he is promoting a religion *about* Jesus, an approach in which the teacher, rather than his historical message, becomes the object of veneration. John's insistence upon Jesus as a divinity walking the earth in human form renders his biography of the Galilean highly problematic to scholars who attempt to retrieve the actual facts of Jesus' life.

Four Distinctive Portraits of Jesus

The reader who lets each Gospel speak for itself will find that each creates a distinctive portrait of Jesus that reflects the individual author's concept of Jesus' theological meaning. Some readers may wonder why the early Church produced four such diverse accounts of its Master's career or why a single harmonious version, free of the contradictions, discrepancies, and repetitions that characterize the four, was not substituted for the present quartet. The answer may lie in the historical processes that gave birth to the Gospels. Mark seems to have been written in response to the double crisis of the Jewish revolt against Rome, which ended in the destruction of the original apostolic church in Jerusalem, and the first state persecution of Christians, which Nero conducted to penalize an unpopular group for the fire that ravaged much of Rome in 64 C.E. Shaping the *kerygma* into biographical form, Mark emphasizes Jesus' sufferings and humiliating death as a model that his followers can expect to emulate. Whether composed in Rome or Syria, Mark's Gospel provided his persecuted community with a beleaguered Jesus with whom they could identify.

After the Jewish revolt had failed and the Jerusalem Temple at which both Jews and Christians had worshiped was no more, relations between synagogue and Church quickly deteriorated. Long-standing controversies between Matthew's church in Antioch, home to the second-oldest Christian community as well as a large Jewish population, and his Pharisaic opponents inspired the Evangelist to create a new edition of Mark. Portraying Jesus as the fulfillment of Israel's religious traditions, Matthew gleaned as many "proof texts" from the Hebrew Bible as possible to demonstrate that Jesus was indeed the expected Jewish Messiah.

Whereas Matthew's Gospel addressed the concerns of Jewish Christians in Syria confronting Jewish hostilities, the needs of a Hellenistic Gentile group were met with Luke's edition of Mark. Designed as a two-volume demonstration proving that both Jesus and his international body of followers were innocent of any sedition against Rome, Luke and Acts show that from its inception Christianity is a religion with a world savior and is compatible with and suitable for all people dwelling throughout the Roman Empire.

While the Synoptics were being composed for apologetic purposes, a small community of Christian mystics who envisioned Jesus as the Incarnation of God's creative Word developed a version of Jesus' life that roughly paralleled but significantly diverged from the first three Gospels. Based on the meditations of an unnamed disciple whom Jesus loved, the fourth Gospel presented a "high Christology," an exalted interpretation of Jesus' divinity that far exceeded the Synoptic's claims for their hero but that eventually became the standard of belief for the international Church. By the close of the second century C.E., the Church had adopted all four Gospels, works that had originated anonymously and circulated independently of each other in four geographically separated areas, had been written for specific audiences to meet particular social and religious needs, and had created significantly distinct theological views of

the meaning of Jesus' life and death. By 200 C.E., each of the four Gospels, disseminated throughout the Christian world, had been commonly used in teaching and worship, had achieved an authoritative status, and had enjoyed support in one or more branches of the international community of faith. Read and studied among large segments of the Christian population, the four separate versions were too widely known and had too many partisans to be reduced to a single homogenous account. Accepting all four, the Church acknowledged a quartet of portraits (Table 9.2) that hint at the mysterious power of the historical figure on whom they are based and whom they intermittently reveal.

RECOMMENDED READING

Bultmann, Rudolf. *The History of the Synoptic Tradition.* Translated by J. Marsh. New York: Harper & Row, 1963. A masterful, if somewhat technical, study by the great German scholar.

Farmer, W. R. *The Synoptic Problem.* New York: Macmillan, 1964. Argues for the priority of Matthew.

Funk, Robert W., ed. *New Gospel Parallels.* Vol. 1, *The Synoptic Gospels;* Vol. 2, *John and the Other Gospels.* Philadelphia: Fortress Press, 1985. The most valuable scholarly tool for comparing the Gospel texts.

Funk, Robert W.; Hoover, Roy W.; and the Jesus Seminar. *The Five Gospels: The Search for the Authentic Words of Jesus.* New York: Macmillan, 1993. The New Scholars Version of the Gospels, with Jesus' sayings printed in red, pink, gray, or black, depending on the scholars' view of their probable authenticity.

Jacobson, Arland D. *The First Gospel, An Introduction to Q.* Sonoma, Calif.: Polebridge Press, 1992. A study of Q's development and theology.

Kloppenborg, John S. *The Formation of Q: Trajectories in Ancient Wisdom Collections.* Studies in Antiquity and Christianity. Philadelphia: Fortress Press, 1987. A scholarly study of the presumed Q text that finds two layers of traditions—the first presenting Jesus as a wisdom teacher and the second, later addition picturing Jesus as an apocalyptic judge.

Kloppenborg, John S.; Meyer, Marvin W.; Patterson, Stephen J.; and Steinhauser, Michael G. *Q Thomas Reader.* Sonoma, Calif.: Polebridge Press, 1990. Includes an annotated reconstruction of the presumed sayings source.

Koester, Helmut. *Introduction to the New Testament.* Vol. 2, *History and Literature of Early Christianity.* Philadelphia: Fortress Press, 1982. Translated from the original German, this is a major and incisive study of New Testament origins.

Neirynck, Frans. "Synoptic Problem." In R. E. Brown et al., eds., *The New Jerome Biblical Commentary,* pp. 587–595. Englewood Cliffs, N.J.: Prentice Hall, 1990. A detailed examination of the literary kinship of the Synoptics.

Streeter, B. H. *The Four Gospels.* London: Macmillan, 1924. A landmark scholarly study arguing that Mark is the earliest Gospel.

Tannehill, Robert C. "The Gospels and Narrative Literature." In L. E. Keck, ed., *The New Interpreter's Bible,* Vol. 8, pp. 56–70. Nashville, Tenn.: Abingdon Press, 1995.

Tuckett, Christopher M. "Jesus and the Gospel." In L. E. Keck, ed., *The New Interpreter's Bible,* Vol. 8, pp. 71–86. Nashville, Tenn.: Abingdon Press, 1995.

———. "Synoptic Problem." In D. N. Freedman, ed., *The Anchor Bible Dictionary,* Vol. 6, pp. 263–270. New York: Doubleday, 1992. A lucid introduction to theories about the interdependence of Matthew, Mark, and Luke.

Mark's Gospel

KEY THEMES

Considered the first Gospel written, Mark reflects the crisis affecting the Christian community between about 66 and 70 C.E. The Church at Rome had just suffered Nero's devastating persecution, and Jerusalem, home of the first Church, was about to be destroyed by Roman armies. Portraying Jesus as a "hidden Messiah" whose true identity is revealed only through his suffering and death, Mark presents his hero as universally misunderstood, rejected by his own people and condemned by the Romans, thus reminding his audience that Jesus' story anticipated their own harrowing experiences. Mark's Jesus is an apocalyptic preacher, healer, and exorcist whose Galilean campaign heralds the arrival of God's rule and imminent world judgment. The Gospel's five main divisions include a prelude to Jesus' public ministry (1:1–13), the Galilean campaign inaugurating God's kingdom (1:14–8:26), the journey from Caesarea Philippi to Jerusalem (8:27–10:52), the Jerusalem ministry (11:1–15:47), and a postlude in which women disciples discover the empty tomb (16:1–8).

> For even the Son of Man did not come to be served but to serve and to give up his life as a ransom for many.
>
> Mark 10:45

Although he seems to have been the first author to transform oral traditions about Jesus into a biographical narrative, Mark was not the first Christian writer. About twenty years before Mark created his Gospel, Paul, Christianity's most successful missionary to the Gentiles, began composing a series of letters (c. 50–62 C.E.) in which he makes the risen Jesus his central focus. Except for the essential facts of Jesus' crucifixion and resurrection, however, Paul shows little interest in Jesus' earthly life or teachings. Paul's only extended quotation from Jesus is taken from a **tradition** passed on to him about Jesus' final meal with his disciples, the Last Supper (1 Cor. 11:23–26). One or two written collections of Jesus' sayings—Q and perhaps an early edition of the Gospel of Thomas—were probably also circulating among some Christian communities when Mark wrote, but if he was aware of their existence he chose not to use them. The Gospel of Mark, in fact, cites relatively few of Jesus' teachings, instead emphasizing Jesus' actions, particularly his miraculous healings and willingness to sacrifice himself for others.

Table 9.2 Some Parallels Among the Four Gospels

Mark (c. 66–70 C.E.)	Matthew (c. 80–85 C.E.)
· · ·	· · ·
· · ·	· · ·
· · ·	1. Introduction to the Messiah: genealogy and infancy narrative (1:1–2:23)
1. Prelude to Jesus' public ministry (1:1–13)	2. The beginning of Jesus' proclamation: baptism, temptation, inauguration of Galilean ministry (3:1–4:25)
· · ·	3. First major discourse: the Sermon on the Mount (5:1–7:29)
2. The Galilean ministry: inaugurating the kingdom (1:14–8:26)	4. First narrative section: ten miracles (8:1–9:28)
· · ·	5. Second major discourse: instructions to the Twelve Apostles (10:1–42)
· · ·	6. Second narrative section: questions and controversies (11:1–12:50)
· · ·	7. Third major discourse: parables on the kingdom (13:1–52)
3. The journey to Jerusalem (8:26–10:52)	8. Third narrative section: from the rejection in Nazareth to the Transfiguration (13:53–17:27)
· · ·	9. Fourth major discourse: instructions to the church (18:1–35)
	· · ·
4. The Jerusalem ministry and Passion story (11:1–15:47)	10. Fourth narrative section: the Jerusalem ministry (19:1–22:46)
5. Postlude: the empty tomb (16:1–8)	11. Fifth major discourse: warning of Final Judgment (23:1–25:46)
· · ·	12. Fifth and final narrative section: the Passion story and postresurrection appearances (26:1–28:20)
	· · ·

· · ·   Indicates that the Gospel in question does not have material found in another Gospel. Note that John's Gospel contains much material not present in the Synoptics.

Mark's Historical Setting

The earliest reference to Mark's Gospel comes from Papias, an early Christian writer who was bishop of Hierapolis in Asia Minor about 130–140 C.E. As quoted by Eusebius, Papias states that Mark had been the apostle **Peter's** disciple in Rome and based his account on Peter's reminiscences of Jesus. Papias notes that Mark "had not heard the Lord or been one of his followers" so that his Gospel lacked "a systematic arrangement of the Lord's sayings" (Eusebius, *History,* 3.39).

Table 9.2 (continued)

Luke (c. 85–90 C.E.)	John (c. 90–100 C.E.)
	1. Prolog: Hymn to the Logos (Word); testimony of the Baptist (1:1–51)
1. Formal preface	
2. Infancy narratives of the Baptist and Jesus (1:5–2:52)	

3. Prelude to Jesus' ministry: baptism, genealogy, and temptation (3:1–4:13)	2. The Book of Signs (2:1–11:57)
	  a. The miracle at Cana
	  b. The assault on the Temple (compare Mark 11)
	  c. Dialog with Nicodemus
	  d. Conversations with a Samaritan woman and a woman taken in adultery

4. Jesus' Galilean ministry and Luke's "lesser interpolation" (4:14–9:50)	e. Five more miraculous signs in Jerusalem and Galilee; Jesus' discourses witnessing to his divine nature
5. Jesus' teachings on the journey to Jerusalem; Luke's "greater interpolation" (9:51–18:14)	f. The resurrection of Lazarus (the seventh sign)

6. The Jerusalem ministry: Jesus' challenge to the holy city (18:31–21:38)	3. The book of Glory (12:1–20:31)
	  a. The plot against Jesus
	  b. The Last Supper and farewell discourses

7. The final conflict and Passion story (22:1–23:56)	c. The Passion story
8. Epilog: postresurrection appearances in the vicinity of Jerusalem (24:1–53)	d. The empty tomb and postresurrection appearances in Jerusalem
	4. Epilog: postresurrection appearances in Galilee; parting words to Peter and the Beloved Disciple (21:1–25)

Mark's author offers few hints about where or for whom he wrote, except for his insistence that following Jesus demands a willingness to suffer for one's faith. Mark's near-equation of discipleship with suffering suggests that he directed his work to a group that was then undergoing severe testing and needed encouragement to remain steadfast. (See Mark 8:34–38, 10:38–40.) This theme of "carrying one's cross" may derive from the effects of Nero's persecution (c. 64–65), when numerous Roman Christians were crucified or burned alive. Papias and Iranaeus, another early Church leader, agree that Mark wrote shortly after Peter's martyrdom, which, according to tradition, occurred during Nero's attack on Rome's Christian community.

Although Rome is the traditional place of composition, a growing number of scholars think it more likely that Mark wrote for an audience in Syria or Palestine. Critics favoring a Palestinian origin point to Mark's emphasis on the Jewish revolt (66–73 C.E.) and concurrent warnings to believers who were affected by the uprising (Mark 13). In Mark's view, the "tribulation" that climaxes in Jerusalem's destruction is the sign heralding Jesus' **Parousia**, his return in heavenly glory. The association of wars and national revolts with persecution of believers and Jesus' Second Coming gives an eschatological urgency to Mark's account.

Even though Papias and other second-century writers ascribe the Gospel to John Mark, a companion of Peter and Paul (Philem. 24; Col. 4:10; Acts 12:12–25, 14:36–40), the author does not identify himself in the text. The superscription—"The Gospel According to Mark"—is a later church embellishment, for second-century churchmen tried to connect extant writings about Jesus with Apostles or their immediate disciples. The Gospel is anonymous; for convenience, we refer to the author as **Mark**.

Mark's Puzzling Attitude Toward Jesus' Close Associates

Historical Sources   Strangely, Mark does not seem to have regarded Jesus' relatives—or any other ordinary source a modern biographer would consult—as worthy informants. One of the author's prevailing themes is his negative presentation of virtually everyone associated with the historical Jesus. (See "Mark's Leading Characters" on page 321.) From "his [Jesus'] mother and brothers" (3:31) to his most intimate followers, Mark portrays all of Jesus' companions as oblivious to his real nature and/or as obstacles to his work. Mark's Gospel consistently renders all Jesus' Palestinian associates as incredibly obtuse, unable to grasp his teachings, and blind to his value.

The Markan picture of Jesus' family implies that they, too, failed to appreciate or support him. "When his relatives heard of this [his drawing large crowds around him], they set out to take charge of him, convinced he was out of his mind" (3:21, Jerusalem Bible). When "his mother and his brothers" send a message asking for him, apparently demanding that he cease making a public spectacle of himself, Mark has Jesus declare that "whoever does the will of

God is my brother, my sister, my mother"—a startling repudiation of his blood ties—and an implication that, in the Markan Jesus' view, his relatives were not doing the divine will (3:31–35). The force of this antifamily episode is intensified because Mark uses it to frame a controversy in which Jesus' opponents accuse him of expelling demons by the power of Beelzebub, another name for the devil. Jesus countercharges that those who oppose his work are defying the **Holy Spirit**, an "unforgivable sin" (3:22–30). At this point in the narrative, Mark shows Jesus' family attempting to interrupt his ministry, thus subtly associating them with his adversaries. (See also John 7:1–9.)

Mark also depicts Jesus' acquaintances in **Nazareth** as hostile to a local carpenter's unexpected career as prophet and healer, questioning his credentials as sage and teacher. " 'Where does he get it from?' " his neighbors ask. " 'What wisdom is this that has been given him?' and 'how does he work such miracles? Is not this the carpenter, the son of Mary, the brother of James and Joseph and Judas and Simon? And are not his sisters here with us?' So they [turned against] him" (6:2–3). In this incident of Jesus' revisiting his home turf, Mark argues that those who thought they knew Jesus best not only doubted his right to be a religious leader but also his legitimacy—note Mark's reference to "the son of Mary," a contrast to the biblical custom of identifying a son through his male parentage even if his father were dead. The Nazarenes' refusal to see any merit in him results in a troubling diminution of Jesus' power: "He *could work no miracle there* . . . " except for some routine healings (6:6; italics added). Mark thus seems to dismiss both family and hometown citizens as acceptable channels of biographical tradition: They all fail to trust, comprehend, or cooperate with his hero.

Mark's allusion to Jesus' "brothers" and "sisters" (see also Matt. 13:54–56) may disturb some readers. Because his Gospel does not include a tradition of Jesus' virginal conception or birth, the existence of siblings may not have been an

---

Mark's Leading Characters*

<table>
<tr>
<td>

♦ John the Baptist (1:4–9); executed (6:17–29)

♦ Jesus introduced (1:9) final words (15:34)

♦ Simon Peter and his brother Andrew (1:16–18); Peter's imperfect discipleship (8:27–33; 9:2–6; 14:26–31, 66–72)

♦ James and John, the fishermen sons of Zebedee (1:19–20); wish to be first in the kingdom (10:35–45)

♦ Levi (Matthew), a tax collector (2:13–17)

♦ The Twelve (3:13–19).

♦ Judas Iscariot, Jesus' betrayer (3:19; 14:17–21, 43–46)

♦ Mary, Jesus' mother, and other family members (3:20–21, 31–35; 6:3)

♦ The Gerasene demoniac (5:1–20)

♦ Herod Antipas, ruler of Galilee (4 B.C.E.–39 C.E.) (6:17–29; 8:15)

</td>
<td>

♦ The Syrophoenician (Canaanite) woman (7:14–30)

♦ A rich young man (10:17–22)

♦ The woman who anoints Jesus at Bethany (14:3–9)

♦ The High Priest Caiaphas (14:53–64)

♦ Pontius Pilate, procurator of Judea (26–36 C.E.) (15:1–15, 43–44)

♦ Barabbas, the terrorist released in place of Jesus (15:6–15)

♦ Simon of Cyrene, the man impressed to carry Jesus' cross (15:21)

♦ Joseph of Arimathaea, the Sanhedrin member who buries Jesus (15:42–46)

♦ Mary of Magdala (in Galilee) (15:40–41, 47; 16:1)

♦ Mary, mother of James and Joseph (15:40, 47; 16:1)

</td>
</tr>
</table>

*Characters are listed in general order of appearance, along with the chief quality or event that distinguishes them in Mark's narrative.

---

issue with the Markan community (as it apparently was not for the Pauline churches; none of Paul's letters allude to a virgin birth). Matthew, however, explicitly affirms that Jesus was virginally conceived (Matt. 1:18–25), and Luke strongly implies it (Luke 1:26–38). Some Protestant Christians believe that following Jesus' delivery, his mother may have borne other children in the ordinary way. According to Roman Catholic doctrine, however, Mary remains perpetually virgin. Jesus' "brothers" (translating the Greek *adelphoi*) are to be understood as close male relatives, perhaps cousins or stepbrothers (sons of Mary's husband Joseph by a previous marriage).

The Disciples Mark's opinion of the Galilean **disciples** whom Jesus calls to follow him (3:13–19) is distinctly unsympathetic, although these are the Twelve Apostles on whose testimony the Christian faith is traditionally founded.

Almost without exception, Mark paints **the Twelve** as dull-witted, inept, unreliable, cowardly, and, in at least one case, treacherous. When Jesus stills a storm, the disciples are impressed but unaware of the act's significance (4:35–41). After his feeding of the multitudes, the disciples "had not understood the intent of the loaves" because "their minds were closed" (6:52). The harshness of Mark's judgment is better rendered in the phrase "their hearts were hardened" (as given in the Revised Standard Version). This is the same phrase used to describe the Egyptian pharaoh when he arrogantly "hardened his heart" and refused to obey Yahweh's commands (Exod. 7:1–14, 10:1–27). After listening for months to Jesus' teaching, the disciples are such slow learners that they are still ignorant of "what [Jesus' reference to] 'rising from the dead' could mean" (9:9–10). They not only fail to grasp the concept of sharing in Jesus' glory (10:35–41), but even the simplest, most obvious **parables** also escape their comprehension (4:10–13). As Jesus asks, "You do not understand this parable? How then will you understand any parable?" (4:13).

Although he has "explained everything" (4:33–34; see also 8:31–32) and the disciples have presumably recognized him as the Messiah (8:27–32), they desert him after his arrest (14:30). Peter, who had earlier confessed Jesus to be the Messiah, three times denies knowing him (14:66–72). Almost the only character in Mark shown as recognizing the significance of Jesus' death is an unnamed Roman soldier who perceives that "truly this man was a son of God!" (15:39).

Mark's antipathy toward the historical Jesus' closest associates and the original Jerusalem church is puzzling. Does this apparent hostility mean that the group for which Mark wrote wished to distance itself from the Jerusalem community, whose founders included Jesus' closest family members, Mary and James (Acts 1:14; 12:17, etc.)? Does Mark's negative attitude represent a power struggle between his branch of Gentile Christianity and the Jewish-Christians who (until 70 C.E.) headed the original church? Most scholars caution that one should not necessarily postulate an historical tension between the Markan community and Palestinian Jewish Christians. Ancient historians and biographers commonly portray their heroes as enormously superior to their peers, depicting a subject's followers or disciples as constitutionally incapable of rising to his level of thought or achievement. Writing in this literary tradition, Mark may have emphasized the deficiencies of Jesus' contemporaries to underscore his hero's unique status: By magnifying Jesus' image, Mark demonstrates that Jesus alone does God's work and declares God's will.

Mark's Narrative Structure

Organizational and Bipolar Structure Whatever the historicity of Mark's version of Jesus' career, it eventually exerted a tremendous influence on the greater Christian community, primarily through the enlarged and revised editions of Mark produced by Matthew and Luke. Because the two other Synoptic Gospels generally follow Mark's order of events in Jesus' life, it is important to understand the significance of Mark's bipolar organization. Mark arranges his narrative around a geographical north–south polarity: The first half of his narrative takes place in **Galilee** and adjacent areas of northern Palestine, a largely rural area of peasant farmers where Jesus recruits his followers, performs numerous miracles, and—despite some opposition—enjoys considerable success. The second half (after Chapter 8) relates Jesus' fatal journey southward to Judea and Jerusalem, where he is rejected and killed. Besides dividing Jesus' career into two distinct geographical areas, Mark's Gospel presents two contrasting aspects of Jesus' story. In Galilee, Jesus is a figure of power, using his supernatural gifts to expel demons, heal the sick, control natural forces, and raise the dead. Representing the Hellenistic concept of an awe-inspiring divine man (*theios aner*), the Galilean Jesus speaks and acts with tremendous authority, effortlessly refutes his detractors, and affirms or invalidates the Mosaic Torah at will. Before leaving **Caesarea Philippi**, however, Jesus makes the first of three Passion predictions, warning his uncomprehending disciples that he will go to Jerusalem only to suffer humiliation and death (8:30–38, 9:31–32, 10:33–34).

By using the Passion predictions as a device to link the indomitable miracle worker in Galilee with the helpless figure on the cross in Judea, Mark reconciles the two seemingly irreconcilable components in his portrait of Jesus. The powerful Son of God who astonishes vast crowds with his mighty works is also the vulnerable **Son of Man** who, in weakness and apparent defeat, sacrifices his life "as a ransom for many" (10:45). Thus, the author balances older Christian traditions of his hero's phenomenal deeds with a bleak picture of Jesus' sufferings, devoting the last six chapters to a detailed account of the Passion. (See "Mark's Order of Events in

Jesus' Life" on pages 324–325; see also the map of Palestine on page 364.)

Mark's Gospel can be divided into five parts:

1. Prelude to Jesus' public ministry (1:1–13).
2. The Galilean ministry; inaugurating the kingdom (1:14–8:26)
3. The journey to Jerusalem (8:27–10:52)
4. The Jerusalem ministry (11:1–15:47)
5. Postlude: the empty tomb (16:1–8)

Prelude to Jesus' Public Ministry

Like the writer of a classical epic, Mark plunges into the middle of the action, providing no background about his hero but introducing him with apocalyptic suddenness. The opening line, "here begins the gospel [good news] of Jesus Christ" (1:1), simultaneously announces his epic theme and echoes Genesis 1, alerting the reader to see that in Jesus God has begun a new creative activity. Jesus is the **Christ** (Greek translation of the Hebrew *mashiah*) and the "Son of God," titles that Mark seldom uses in his narrative, because one of his purposes is to demonstrate that in his lifetime the majority of people did not recognize Jesus' divine sonship. No person calls Jesus a "son of God" until almost the very end of Mark's Gospel. Significantly, at that point Jesus is already dead and the speaker is neither a Jew nor a disciple but a Roman centurion (15:39).

By citing a blend of passages from Isaiah (40:3) and Malachi (3:1)—that a divinely appointed "herald" and a "voice crying aloud in the wilderness" are preparing a path for the Lord—Mark immediately places Jesus' story in the context of the Hebrew Bible. Mark identifies the "herald" with **John the Baptist**, a desert ascetic then conducting a religious campaign in the Jordan River, where John baptizes converts "in token of repentance, for the forgiveness of sins" (1:4). Jesus, implicitly included among the repentant, appears for **baptism**, perhaps as John's disciple. Mark has John predict a "mightier" successor, although he does not show the Baptist as explicitly identifying Jesus as that successor.

Empowered by the Holy Spirit at his baptism, Jesus resists **Satan**'s temptations in the desert (1:12–13). In Mark's view, God's Son has arrived. Jesus' **exorcisms**—the casting out of demons who have possessed human beings—are an important Markan theme and are given proportionately greater space in Mark than in any other Gospel. (By contrast, John's Gospel does not contain a single reference to Jesus performing exorcisms.)

The Galilean Ministry: Inaugurating the Kingdom

Mark's Eschatological Urgency　Mark launches Jesus' career with a startlingly eschatological message: "The time has come, the kingdom of God is upon you; repent and believe the Gospel" (1:15). Mark's sense of eschatological urgency permeates his entire Gospel, profoundly affecting his portrayal of Jesus' life and teaching. With the tradition that Jesus had prophesied the Temple's fall about to be fulfilled, Mark, writing about 70 C.E., sees the *eschaton*—the end of history as we know it—about to take place (13:1–4, 7–8, 14–20, 24–27, 30, 35–37). He therefore paints Jesus as an eschatological figure whose words are reinterpreted as specific warnings to Mark's generation. In the thought world Mark creates, the apocalyptic Son of Man who is about to appear in glory (13:24–31) is the same as the Son of Man who came forty years earlier to die on the cross (8:31, 38; 9:9–13, 31). The splendor of the One to come casts its radiance over Mark's portrait of the human Jesus (9:1–9).

Mark's style conveys his urgency: He uses the present tense throughout his Gospel and repeatedly connects the brief episodes, or **pericopes**, of his narrative with the transition word *immediately*. Jesus scarcely finishes conducting a healing or exorcism in one Galilean village before he "immediately" rushes off to the next town to perform another miracle. In Mark's breathless

---

Mark's Order of Events in Jesus' Life

Beginning of Jesus' Ministry
(Approximately 27 or 29 C.E.)

Jesus is baptized by John at the Jordan River (1:9–11).

Jesus withdraws alone into the Judean desert (1:12–13).

Jesus begins preaching in Galilee (1:14–15).

Jesus recruits Peter, Andrew, James, and John to be his first disciples (1:16–20).

Jesus performs miraculous cures and exorcisms in Capernaum and throughout Galilee (1:21–3:12).

Jesus appoints twelve chief disciples from among his many followers; he explains the meaning of parables to this inner circle (3:13–34).

Jesus repeatedly crosses the Lake of Galilee, healing Jews on the western side and non-Jews on the eastern side (4:35–5:43).

Jesus returns to Nazareth, where his neighbors reject him (6:1–6).

Jesus sends the Twelve out on a mission to heal the sick and exorcise demons (6:7–13).

Herod Antipas beheads John the Baptist (6:14–29).

Jesus miraculously feeds a Jewish crowd of 5000 (6:30–44).

End of Jesus' Ministry
(Approximately 30 or 33 C.E.)

Jesus debates Torah rules with the Pharisees, who increasingly oppose his teaching (7:1–23).

Jesus leaves Galilee and travels through non-Jewish territories in Phoenicia and the Decapolis (7:24–37).

Jesus miraculously feeds a second crowd, this time a group of Gentiles (8:1–10, 14–21).

Jesus cures a blind man, and, near the town of Caesarea Philippi, Peter's eyes are opened to Jesus' true identity as the Messiah; Jesus rebukes Peter for failing to understand that the Messiah must suffer and die (8:22–9:1).

Jesus is gloriously transfigured before Peter, James, and John (9:1–13).

Jesus travels with the Twelve through Galilee to Capernaum, instructing them privately (9:30–50).

Jesus travels south to Judea, teaching the crowds and debating with Pharisees (10:1–33).

---

presentation, the world faces an unprecedented crisis. Jesus' activity proclaims that history has reached its climactic moment.

Mark represents Jesus as promising his original hearers that they will experience the *eschaton*—"the present generation will live to see it all" (13:30). The kingdom, God's active rule, is so close that some of Jesus' contemporaries "will not taste death before they have seen the kingdom of God already come to power" (9:1). The long-awaited figure of Elijah, the ancient prophet whose reappearance is to be an infallible sign of the last days (Mal. 4:5), has already materialized in the person of John the Baptist

(9:12–13). Such passages indicate that Mark's community anticipated the imminent consummation of all things.

Mark as Apocalypse So pervasive is Mark's eschatology that some scholars regard the entire Gospel as a modified apocalypse, a revelation of unseen realities and a disclosure of events destined soon to climax in God's final intervention in human affairs. Mark's use of apocalyptic devices is particularly evident at the beginning and ending of his Gospel. God speaks directly as a disembodied voice (a phenomenon Hellenistic Jews called the *bath gol*) at Jesus' baptism and

On the road to Jerusalem, Jesus for the third time predicts his imminent suffering and death (the Passion predictions) (8:31–33, 9:30–32, 10:32–34).

Approaching Jerusalem via Jericho, Jesus performs his last public miracle, curing a blind man (10:46–52).

Events of the Last Week of Jesus' Life

Palm Sunday: Jesus arranges his public entry into Jerusalem; his followers hail him in terms of the Davidic kingdom (11:1–11).

After a night at the Jerusalem suburb of Bethany, Jesus returns to Jerusalem and drives the money-changers out of the Temple (11:15–19).

Jesus debates the "chief priests," Sadducees, Pharisees, and other Jewish religious leaders in the Temple (11:27–12:40).

Seated on the Mount of Olives opposite Jerusalem, Jesus predicts the imminent destruction of the Temple (13:1–37).

Jesus' enemies conspire to kill him; Judas betrays Jesus (14:1–11).

Jesus holds a final Passover meal with the Twelve (14:12–31).

After the Last Supper, Jesus is arrested at Gethsemane on the Mount of Olives outside Jerusalem (14:32–52).

Jesus is tried on charges of blasphemy before the High Priest Caiaphas and the Sanhedrin (14:53–65).

After all of Jesus' followers have abandoned him, Peter denies ever having known him (14:66–72).

Good Friday: Jewish leaders accuse Jesus before Pontius Pilate; Jesus is declared guilty of treason, flogged, and condemned to crucifixion (15:1–20).

A passerby, Simon of Cyrene, is impressed to carry Jesus' cross to Golgotha, where Jesus is crucified (15:21–39).

A group of Galilean women witness the Crucifixion; Joseph of Arimathaea provides a tomb for Jesus (15:40–47).

Easter Sunday: Mary of Magdala and other women discover that Jesus' tomb is empty; a young man instructs them to look for Jesus in Galilee, but the women are too frightened to tell anyone of their experience (16:1–8).

---

again at the **Transfiguration**, an **epiphany** (manifestation of divine presence) in which the disciples see Jesus transformed into a luminous being seated beside the ancient figures of Moses and Elijah (1:11; 9:2–9). In this apocalyptic scene, Jesus appears with Moses and Elijah (who represent, respectively, the Torah and the prophets) to demonstrate his continuity with Israel's biblical tradition and his role as the one who embodies God's ultimate revelation to humanity.

Jesus as Son of Man   The author presents virtually all events during Jesus' final hours as revelatory of God's unfolding purpose. At the Last Supper, Jesus emphasizes the eschatological "Son of Man is going the way appointed for him" and that he will "never again" drink wine with his disciples until he will "drink it new in the kingdom of God" (14:21, 25). At his trial before the **Sanhedrin**, the Jewish leaders' highest judicial council, Jesus reveals his true identity for the first time: He confesses that he *is* the Messiah and that the officiating High Priest "will see the Son of Man seated at the right hand of God and coming with the clouds of heaven" (14:62–63).

This disclosure—found only in Mark—associates Jesus' suffering and death with his ulti-

The Synoptic Gospels' Use of the Term Son of Man

The authors of the Synoptic Gospels use the expression Son of Man *in three distinct ways, all of which they place on the lips of Jesus to denote three important aspects of his ministry. The three categories identify Jesus as the Son of Man who serves on earth, the Son of Man who must suffer and die, and the Son of Man who will be revealed in eschatological judgment. Representative examples of these three categories appear below.*

The Earthly Son of Man

Mark 2:10 (Matt. 9:6; Luke 5:24): Has authority to forgive sins.

Mark 2:27 (Matt. 12:8; Luke 6:5): Is Lord of the Sabbath.

Matthew 11:19 (Luke 7:34): Son of Man comes eating and drinking.

Matthew 8:20 (Luke 9:58): Son of Man has no-where to lie his head.

Luke 19:20: Son of Man came to seek and save the lost.

The Suffering Son of Man

Mark 8:31 (Luke 9:22): Son of Man must suffer.

Mark 9:12 (Matt. 17:12): Son of Man will suffer.

Mark 9:31 (Matt. 17:22; Luke 9:44): Son of Man is delivered into hands of men.

Mark 10:33 (Matt. 20:18; Luke 18:31): Son of Man is delivered to chief priests, condemned to death.

Mark 10:45 (Matt. 20:28): Son of Man came to serve and give his life.

Mark 14:41 (Matt. 26:45): Son of Man is betrayed to sinners.

Matthew 12:40 (Luke 11:30): Son of Man will be three days in the earth.

The Eschatological Son of Man

Mark 8:38 (Matt. 16:27; Luke 9:26): Comes in glory of the Father and holy angels.

Mark 14:26 (Matt. 24:30; Luke 21:27): They will see Son of Man coming with clouds and glory.

Mark 14:62 (Matt. 26:64; Luke 22:69): You will see Son of Man sitting at the right hand of power.

Luke 12:40 (Matt. 24:44): Son of Man is coming at an hour you do not expect.

Luke 17:26 (Matt. 24:27): As it was in days of Noah, so in days of Son of Man.

Matthew 24:30: Then will appear the sign of the Son of Man.

Luke 17:30: So it will be on the day when the Son of Man is revealed.

For a fuller discussion of the Son of Man concept and its use by the Synoptic authors, see George Eldon Ladd, A Theology of the New Testament *(Grand Rapids, Mich.: Eerdmans, 1974), pp. 145–158.*

mate revelation as the eschatological Son of Man. A designation that appears almost exclusively in the Gospels and then always on the lips of Jesus, Son of Man is Mark's favored expression to denote Jesus' three essential roles: an earthly figure who teaches with authority, a servant who embraces suffering, and a future eschatological judge. (See the feature on this page regarding the term *Son of Man*.) Although

many scholars question whether the historical Jesus ever used this title, many others regard it as Jesus' preferred means of self-identification. Still other scholars postulate that Jesus may have used the title *Son of Man* to designate another, future-coming figure who would vindicate Jesus' own ministry and that the later church, because of its faith in Jesus' resurrection, retrojected that title back into the account of Jesus' life where it originally did not appear. In Mark's view, however, Jesus himself is clearly the eschatological Son of Man.

In Mark's modification of the Son of Man concept, he is both an apocalyptic ruler and a servant who must suffer and die before attaining the kind of heavenly glory that Daniel 7 and 1 Enoch attribute to him (cf. Mark 8:30–31; 10:45; 13:26–27; 14:62). It is as the Son of Man in his earthly role that Mark's Jesus claims the authority to exercise immense religious authority. As Son of Man, the Markan Jesus assumes the right to prescribe revolutionary changes in Jewish law and custom (2:10). Behaving as if he already reigns as world judge, Jesus forgives a paralytic's sins (2:1–12) and permits certain kinds of work on the Sabbath (3:1–5). The Torah-keeping Pharisees are outraged that the Galilean presumes to revoke Moses' inspired command to forbid all labor on God's day of rest (Exod. 20:8–10; Deut. 5:12–15). As Mark presents the case, it is Jesus' flexible attitude toward Sabbath observance that incites some Pharisees and supporters of Herod Antipas to hatch a murder plot against the Nazarene healer (3:5–6).

Conflict Stories   Mark devotes considerable space to recounting Jesus' controversies with four hostile groups:

1. Pharisees, who object to his apparently cavalier attitude toward the Mosaic Torah
2. Scribes, the preservers and copyists of the Torah, who resent what they see as unjustified claims to reinterpret the Mosaic tradition
3. Sadducees, the priestly aristocracy, who view him as disrupting their tenuous armistice with Rome
4. Herodians, who believe that he, like John the Baptist, threatens the rulership of Herod Antipas

Although these groups normally oppose one another, Mark pictures them as uniting to attack Jesus as subverting the security of the Jewish nation.

Throughout his Galilean campaign, Jesus is shown debating the Pharisees and scribes, who variously accuse him of blasphemy in daring to forgive sins (2:5), associating with "tax collectors and sinners" (2:15–17), violating Sabbath laws (2:23–28), using Satan's help in performing exorcisms (3:22–27), and profaning tradition by neglecting to wash ritually before a meal (7:1–8). Most of Mark's conflict stories end with Jesus issuing a pronouncement on some aspect of Torah observance: declaring all foods "clean" (7:14–23), making the Sabbath relevant to human needs (2:23–3:6), and revoking Moses' permission for men to divorce their wives (10:2–12). In each case, Jesus demonstrates authority to approve or invalidate both written and oral Torah.

Jesus and the Demons   Following his exorcisms at **Capernaum**, Jesus performs similar feats in Gentile territory, "the country of the Gerasenes." Driving a whole army of devils from a Gerasene madman, Jesus casts them into a herd of pigs—the religiously unclean animals becoming a fit home for spirits who drive people to commit unclean acts (5:1–20). The demons' name—"legion"—is an unflattering reference to the Roman legions (large military units) then occupying Palestine (and in Mark's day assaulting Jerusalem).

Mark arranges his material to show that Jesus does not choose to battle Evil in isolation. At the outset of his campaign through Galilee, Jesus gathers followers who will form the nucleus of a new society, one presumably free from demonic influence. Recruiting a band of Galilean fishermen and peasants, Jesus selects two sets of brothers, Simon Peter—also called **Cephas**—and **Andrew**, and **James** and **John**—sons of **Zebedee** also known as "**sons of thunder**" or *Boanerges*—to form his inner circle (1:16–20). Later he adds another eight disciples to complete the Twelve, a number probably representing the twelve tribes of Israel: **Philip**; **Bartholomew**; **Matthew**; **Thomas**; **James**, son of Alphaeus;

Thaddeus; **Simon** the Canaanite; and **Judas** Iscariot (3:16–19; cf. the different list in Acts 1).

Jesus Accused of Sorcery   In another incident involving demonic possession (3:22–30), Mark dramatizes a head-on collision between Jesus and opponents who see him as a tool of the devil. The clash occurs when "doctors of the law" (teachers and interpreters of the Torah) from Jerusalem accuse Jesus of using black magic to perform exorcisms. Denying that Evil can produce good, Jesus countercharges that persons who attribute good works to Satan "slander the Holy Spirit," the divine force manifested in Jesus' actions.

Matthew's version of the incident explicitly links Jesus' defeat of evil spirits with the arrival of the kingdom of God. The Matthean Jesus declares, "If it is by the Spirit of God that I drive out the devils, then be sure the kingdom of God has already come upon you" (Matt. 22–28). To both Evangelists, Jesus' successful attack on demonic control is a revelation that through his presence God now rules. Willful refusal to accept Jesus' healings as evidence of divine power is to resist the Spirit, an obstinacy that prevents spiritual insight.

The Existence of Demons   Mark, like other New Testament authors, reflects a common Hellenistic belief in the existence of unseen entities that influence human lives for Good or Evil. Numerous Hellenistic documents record charms to ward off demons or free one from their control. In Judaism, works like the deuterocanonical Book of Tobit reveal a belief that demons could be driven out by the correct use of magical formulas (Tob. 6:1–8, 8:1–3). Josephus, who was Mark's contemporary, relates a story about Eleazar, who allegedly exorcised a demon in the presence of the emperor Vespasian (69–79 C.E.), drawing the malign spirit out through its victim's nose (*Antiquities*, 8.46–49).

Jesus the Healer   Physical cures, as well as exorcisms, characterize Jesus' assault on Evil. In Mark's portrayal, one of Jesus' most important functions is to bring relief to the afflicted. He drives a fever from Simon Peter's mother-in-law (1:29–31), cleanses a leper (1:40–42), enables a paralyzed man to walk (2:1–12), restores a man's withered hand (3:1–6), stops a woman's chronic hemorrhaging (5:25–34), and resuscitates the comatose daughter of **Jairus**, a synagogue official (5:21–24, 35–43).

Presenting Jesus' healing campaign as a triumphant procession through Galilee, Mark summarizes the effect Jesus' actions had on the Galilean public: "Wherever he went, to farms . . . villages, or towns, they laid out the sick in the market-places and begged to let them simply touch the edge of his cloak; and all who touched him were cured" (6:56). To Mark, Jesus' restoration of physical health to suffering humanity is an indispensable component of divine rule, tangible confirmation that God's kingdom is about to dawn.

The Journey to Jerusalem: Jesus' Predestined Suffering

Mark's Central Irony   In Chapter 8, which forms the central pivot on which the entire Gospel turns, Mark ties together several themes that convey his essential vision of Jesus' ministry and what Jesus requires of those who would follow him. Beginning on a joyous note with his account of Jesus feeding a large crowd (8:1–10), this section continues through a crisis of misunderstanding between Jesus, Peter, and the other disciples (8:11–21, 27–33) and ends with Jesus' warning (to Mark's community) that he will disown unfaithful followers (8:38). The narrative movement from elation to gloom involves the disciples' failure to comprehend either the significance of Jesus' miracles or the purpose of his life and death.

Besides repeating the theme of the disciples' obtuseness, Chapter 8 also sounds Mark's concurrent themes of the hidden or unexpected quality of Jesus' messiahship—especially the necessity of his suffering—and the requirement that all believers must be prepared to embrace a comparably painful fate. In contrast to John's Gospel, in which Jesus' identity is publicly affirmed at the outset of his career, no one in Mark's Gospel even hints that Jesus is the Messiah until almost the close of the Galilean campaign when Peter—in a flash of insight—recognizes him as such (8:29). The Markan Jesus then swears the disciples to secrecy, as he had earlier ordered other witnesses of his deeds to keep silent (1:23–24, 34; 3:11–12; 5:7; 7:36; 8:30; see also 9:9). Jesus' reluctance to have news of his miracles spread abroad is known as the messianic secret, a term coined by the German scholar William Wrede (1901).

Most scholars believe that Mark's theme of the messianic secret represents the author's theological purpose. For Mark, people could not know Jesus' identity until *after* he had completed his mission. Jesus had to be unappreciated in order to be rejected and killed—to fulfill God's will that he "give up his life as a ransom for many" (10:45).

A conviction that Jesus must suffer an unjust death—an atonement offering for others—to confirm and complete his messiahship is the heart of Mark's **Christology** (concepts about the nature and function of Christ). Hence, Peter's confession at Caesarea Philippi that Jesus is the Christ (Messiah) is immediately followed by Jesus' first prediction that he will go to Jerusalem only to die (8:29–32). When Peter objects to this notion of a rejected and defeated Messiah, Jesus calls his chief disciple a "Satan." Derived from a Hebrew term meaning "obstacle," the epithet *Satan* labels Peter's attitude an obstacle or roadblock on Jesus' predestined path to the cross. Peter understands Jesus no better than outsiders, regarding the Messiah as a God-empowered hero who conquers his enemies, not as a submissive victim of their brutality.

At the end of Chapter 8, Mark introduces a third idea: True disciples must expect to suffer as Jesus does. In two of the three Passion predictions, Jesus emphasizes that "Anyone who wishes to be a follower of mine must leave self behind; he must take up his cross, and come with me" (8:27–34, 10:32–45). Irony permeates the third instance when James and John, sons of Zebedee, presumptuously ask to rule with Jesus, occupying places of honor on his right and left. As Jesus explains that reigning with him means imitating his sacrifice, Mark's readers are intended to remember that when Jesus reaches Jerusalem, the positions on his right and left will be taken by the two brigands crucified next to him (15:27).

The Jerusalem Ministry

Jesus in the Temple If Mark had been aware of Jesus' other visits to Jerusalem (narrated in John's Gospel), he dismisses them as unimportant compared with that made during Jesus' last week on earth. In Chapter 11, a crowd, probably of Galilean supporters, enthusiastically welcomes Jesus to Jerusalem, hailing him as restorer of "the coming kingdom of our father David" (11:9–10). For the first time, Jesus publicly accepts a messianic role, one that Roman guards at the city gate could interpret as a political claim to Jewish kingship and an act of treason to Rome (11:1–10). During his few days in the holy city, Jesus behaves in a manner that alienates both the Roman and Jewish administrations, arousing the hostility of almost every religious party and institution in official Judaism. His assault on the Temple (11:15–19)—overturning the moneychangers' tables and disrupting the sale of sacrificial animals—is seen as a dangerous attack on the Sadducean priesthood in charge of maintaining the Sanctuary, an act that probably seals his fate with the chief priests and Temple police.

As Jesus moves through the Temple courts, thronged with Passover pilgrims, Mark depicts him scoring success after success in a series of hostile confrontations. The Pharisees and Herod's party attempt to trap Jesus on the controversial issue of paying taxes to Rome, a snare he eludes by suggesting that Caesar's coins may

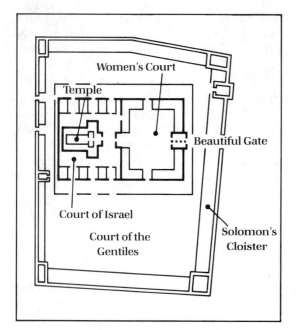

Outline of Herod's Temple, Jerusalem. With its great courtyards and porticoes, the Temple covered many acres. The main sanctuary, however, was a simple rectangular building with an outer porch, a long inner room, and an innermost chamber known as the Holy of Holies. A heavily bejeweled curtain separated the two inner chambers.

be returned to their source, while God claims the rest.

The Sadducees also suffer defeat when they try to force Jesus into an untenable position they hope will illustrate the illogic of a belief in resurrection to future life. When asked to which husband a woman who has been widowed six times would be married when all the former spouses are raised, Jesus states that there will be no ethical problem because those resurrected are no longer confined to human sexual identities but are "like angels in heaven" (12:18–25). Citing the Torah, the only part of the Hebrew Bible that the Sadducees accept, he quotes Yahweh's words to Moses at the burning bush— that Yahweh is the God of Abraham, Isaac, and Jacob (Exod. 3:6)—arguing that because Yahweh is "not God of the dead but of the living," the ancient patriarchs must still be alive from the Deity's perspective (12:26–27).

Attracted by this clever refutation of the Sadducees, a Torah expert asks Jesus to name the most important commandment. Agreeing that love of God (Deut. 6:4) and love of neighbor (Lev. 19:18) are paramount, the lawyer and Jesus exchange compliments. Although not a follower, the Jerusalem leader sees that love is the essence of religion, a perception that Jesus says makes him "not far from the kingdom of God" (12:14)—a more favorable verdict than Jesus ever passes on the Twelve.

Jesus' Prophecy of the Temple's Fall

In Chapter 13, Mark highlights the crisis that then deeply concerned his community—Rome's imminent destruction of the holy city and its Sanctuary, with all its implications for the original center of Christianity. The long speech predicting the Temple's doom appears to combine material from a variety of sources, particularly Jewish apocalyptic material. How much of the discourse on Jerusalem's destruction and the reappearance of the Son of Man originated with Jesus and how much represents interpretations by visionaries and prophets in Mark's church is unknown. Readers will notice that Mark incorporates two somewhat contradictory views of the eschaton. He states that a swarm of disasters and frightening astronomical phenomena will provide unmistakable "signs" that the End is near, just as the budding fig tree heralds the arrival of spring (13:8, 14–20, 24–31). Conversely, neither the Son nor his followers can know the time of Judgment, so one must keep constant watch because the End will occur without previous warning (13:32–37).

Mark's strong emphasis on political and social upheavals as portents of the End can be explained by the turbulent era in which he composed his Gospel. If, as historians believe, Mark wrote during the Jewish revolt when battles and insurrections were daily occurrences, along with intense suffering of the Palestinian Jews and Roman Christians, these events seemed to be a turning point in history, a crisis in which the Messiah's appearance was widely antici-

A typical example of early Christian art in the catacombs of Rome, this wall painting shows communicants celebrating the Eucharist, or communal meal. The fish and the baskets recall Jesus' twin miracles of feeding 4000 and 5000 in Mark's Gospel. (Courtesy of Alinari/Art Resource, NY)

pated. In the 60s C.E., great earthquakes (13:8) shook the eastern Mediterranean, as well as central Italy, where Pompeii, Herculaneum, and Naples suffered heavy damage—precursors of Vesuvius's eruption in 79 C.E. Notice that Mark is concerned that Christians are not misled by rumors of new messiahs or impostors claiming to be Jesus returned. Mark's anxiety about false prophets indicates that his community was familiar with predictions about Jesus' reappearance that were disproved when they failed to materialize (13:5–6, 21–23).

This painful tribulation, which threatens the people of God, will be ended by the Son of Man returning with his angels to gather the faithful. Mark shows Jesus warning the disciples that all these horrors and wonders will occur in the lifetime of his hearers, although no one knows the precise day or hour (13:24–32). Mark's eschatological urgency, which Matthew and Luke later mute in their respective versions of the apocalypse (cf. Matt. 24–25 and Luke 21), vividly conveys both the fears and hopes of Mark's Christian generation.

Last Supper   Withdrawing with his disciples to an "upper room" in Jerusalem, Jesus presides over a **Passover** feast of unleavened bread, an observance that solemnly recalls the Jews' last night in Egypt where the Angel of Death "passed over" their homes to slay the Egyptian firstborn (Exod. 11:1–13:16). In a ritual at the close of their meal, Jesus gives the Passover a new significance, stating that the bread is his "body" and the wine his "blood of the [New] Covenant, shed for many" (14:22–25), a foreshadowing of his crucifixion. Mark's account of this Last Supper, the origin of the Christian celebration of the **Eucharist**, or Holy Communion, closely resembles Paul's earlier description of the ceremony (1 Cor. 11:23–26).

Jesus' Passion   In describing Jesus' Passion—his final suffering and death—Mark's narrative irony reaches its height. Although the author emphasizes many grim details of Jesus' excruciatingly painful execution, he means his readers to see the enormous disparity between the *appearance* of Jesus' vulnerability to the world's evil and the actual reality of his spiritual triumph. Jesus' enemies, who believe they are ridding Judea of a dangerous radical, are in fact making possible his saving death—all according to God's design.

Even so, Mark's hero is tested fully—treated with savage cruelty (14:65; 15:15–20), deserted by all his friends (14:50), and even (in human eyes) abandoned by God (15:34). The agony begins in **Gethsemane**, a grove or vineyard on the **Mount of Olives** opposite Jerusalem to which Jesus and the disciples retreat after the Last Supper. In the Gethsemane episode (14:28–52), Mark places a dual emphasis on Jesus' fulfilling predictions in the Hebrew Bible (14:26–31, 39) and on his personal anguish. By juxtaposing these two elements, Mark demonstrates that while the Crucifixion will take place as God long ago planned (and revealed in Scripture), Jesus' part in the drama of salvation demands heroic effort. While the disciples mindlessly sleep, Jesus faces the hard reality of his impending torture, experiencing "grief" and "horror and dismay." To Mark, his hero—emotionally ravaged and physically defenseless—provides the model for all believers whose loyalty is tested. Although Jesus prays that God will spare him the humiliation and pain he dreads, he forces his own will into harmony with God's. Mark reports that even during this cruel testing of the heavenly Father/Son of Man relationship, Jesus addresses the Deity as "*Abba,*" an Aramaic term expressing a child's trusting intimacy with the parent (14:32–41).

Mark's skill as a storyteller—and interpreter of the events he narrates—is demonstrated in the artful way he organizes his account of Jesus' Passion. Peter's testing (14:37–38) and denial that he even knows Jesus (15:65–72) provide the frame for and ironic parallel to Jesus' trial before the Sanhedrin, the Jewish council headed by **Caiaphas**, the high priest. When Peter fulfills Jesus' prediction about denying him, the disciple's failure serves a double purpose: confirming Jesus' prophetic gifts and strengthening readers' confidence in Jesus' ability to fulfill other prophecies, including those of his resurrection (14:28) and reappearance as the glorified Son of Man (14:62).

Mark contrasts Peter's fearful denial with Jesus' courageous declaration to the Sanhedrin that he is indeed the Messiah and the appointed agent of God's future judgment (14:62). The only Gospel writer to show Jesus explicitly accepting a messianic identity at his trial, Mark may do so to highlight his theme that Jesus' messiahship is revealed primarily through humility and service, a denial of self that also effects humanity's salvation (10:45). Like the author of Hebrews, Mark sees Jesus' divine sonship earned and perfected through suffering and death (Heb. 2:9–11; 5:7–10).

At daybreak on Friday, the "whole council held a consultation" (15:1)—perhaps implying that the night meeting had been illegal and therefore lacked authority to condemn Jesus—and sends the accused to **Pontius Pilate**, the Roman prefect or procurator who was in Jerusalem to maintain order during Passover week. Uninterested in the Sanhedrin's charge that Jesus is a blasphemer, Pilate focuses on Jesus' reputed political crime, seditiously claiming to be the Jewish king. After remarking that it is Pilate himself who has stated the claim, Jesus refuses to answer further questions. Because Mark recreates almost the entire Passion story in the context of prophecies from the Hebrew Bible, it is difficult to know if Jesus' silence represents his actual behavior or the author's reliance on Isaiah 53, where Israel's suffering servant does not respond to his accusers (Isa. 53:7).

As Mark describes the proceedings, Pilate is extremely reluctant to condemn Jesus and does so only after the priestly hierarchy pressures him to do so. Whereas the Markan Pilate maneuvers to spare Jesus' life, the historical Pilate (procurator of Judea from 26–36 C.E.), whom Josephus describes, rarely hesitated to slaughter troublesome Jews (cf. *Antiquities*, 18.3.1–2; *The Jewish War*, 2.9.4). When a mob demands that not Jesus but a convicted terrorist named **Barabbas** be freed, Pilate is pictured as having no choice but to release Barabbas (the first person to benefit from Jesus' sacrifice) and order the Galilean's crucifixion.

Stripped, flogged, mocked, and crowned with thorns, Jesus is apparently unable to carry the crossbeam of his cross, so Roman soldiers impress a bystander, **Simon** of Cyrene, to carry it for him (15:16–21). Taken to Golgotha ("Place of the Skull") outside Jerusalem, Jesus is crucified between two criminals (traditionally called "thieves" but probably brigands similar to those who formed the Zealot party in Mark's day). According to Pilate's order, his cross bears a statement of the political offense for which he is executed: aspiring to be the Jewish king— a cruelly ironic revelation of his true identity (15:22–32).

Although Mark's description of Jesus' undergoing a criminal's shameful death is almost unendurably harsh, his Passion story effectively conveys his dual purpose: creating a paradigm for Christians facing a similar fate and showing that out of human malice and blindness the divine goal is accomplished. The disparity between what witnesses to the Crucifixion think is happening and the saving work that God actually achieves through Jesus' death is expressed in Mark's report of Jesus' last words. Just before dying, Jesus cries out in Aramaic, *"Eli, Eli, lema sabachthani?":* "My God, My God, why hast thou forsaken me?" (15:33). In placing this question—a direct quotation of Psalm 22:1— on Jesus' lips, the author invites readers to remember the psalm in its totality. The psalmist opens his poem with a cry of despair, describing the savage attacks of enemies who try to destroy him. Midway through his song, however, the poet abruptly changes to a positive tone, ending in a joyous affirmation of God's reign over all nations of the earth (Ps. 22:19–31). In Mark's eschatological vision, the horror of Jesus' agony is similarly transformed by God's intervention to raise his Son in glory.

Jesus' Burial   As in all four Gospels, **Mary of Magdala** provides the key human link connecting Jesus' death, burial, and the subsequent discovery that his grave is empty (15:40–41, 47;

16:1). **Joseph of Arimathaea**, a mysterious figure introduced suddenly into the narrative, serves a single function: to transfer Jesus' body from Roman control to that of the dead man's disciples. Acquainted with Pilate, a member of the Sanhedrin and yet a covert supporter of Jesus' ministry, he bridges the two opposing worlds of Jesus' enemies and friends. Not only does Joseph obtain official permission to remove Jesus' body from the cross—otherwise it would routinely be consigned to an anonymous mass grave—but he also provides a secure place of entombment, a rock-hewn sepulcher that he seals by rolling a large flat stone across the entrance (15:42–47).

Postlude: The Empty Tomb

Because the Jewish Sabbath begins at sundown Friday, the day of Jesus' execution, the female disciples cannot prepare the corpse for interment until Sunday morning. Arriving at dawn, the women find the entrance stone already rolled back and the crypt empty except for the presence of a young man dressed in white.

Mark's scene at the vacant tomb recalls themes recurring throughout his Gospel. Like the male disciples who could not understand Jesus' allusion to resurrection (9:9–10), the women are bewildered, unable to accept the youth's revelation that Jesus is "risen." Fleeing in terror, the women say "nothing to anybody" about what they have heard (16:8), leaving readers in suspense, wondering how the "good news" of Jesus' resurrection ever got started. The Gospel thus concludes with a frightened silence, eschewing any account of Jesus' postresurrection appearances (16:8).

Resurrection or Parousia?   Mark's belief in the nearness of Jesus' Parousia may explain why the risen Jesus does not manifest himself in the earliest Gospel. Some scholars think that Mark, convinced that the political and social chaos of the Jewish revolt will soon climax in Jesus' return, refers not to a resurrection phenomenon but to the Parousia. Forty years after the Crucifixion, Mark's community may believe that their wandering through the wilderness is almost over: They are about to follow Jesus across Jordan into "Galilee," his promised kingdom (16:6).

Conversely, Mark's climactic image of the empty tomb may express his wish to emphasize Jesus' *absence:* Jesus is present neither in the grave (that is, in death), nor yet as triumphal Son of Man. Mark's Jesus lives both in memories evoked by the Gospel story and in his enduring power over the lives of his followers.

Added Conclusions   Mark's inconclusiveness, his insistence on leaving his story open-ended, must have seemed as unsatisfactory to later Christian scribes as it does to many readers today. For perhaps that reason, Mark's Gospel has been heavily edited, with two different conclusions added at different times. All the oldest manuscripts of Mark end with the line stressing the women's terrified refusal to obey the young man's instruction to carry the resurrection message to Peter. In time, however, some editors appended postresurrection accounts to their copies of Mark, making his Gospel more consistent with Matthew and Luke (Mark 16:9–2 and 16:20b).

RECOMMENDED READING

Achtemeier, Paul J. "Gospel of Mark." In D. N. Freedman, ed., *The Anchor Bible Dictionary,* Vol. 4, pp. 541–557. New York: Doubleday, 1992. Applies the two-source hypothesis to Mark.

Funk, Robert W., and Hoover, Roy W. *The Five Gospels: The Search for the Authentic Words of Jesus.* A Polebridge Press Book. New York: Macmillan, 1993. A fresh, colloquial translation, with clear, scholarly annotations comparing Markan passages with parallels in Matthew, Luke, and Thomas.

Harrington, Daniel J. "The Gospel According to Mark." In R. E. Brown, et al., eds. *The New Jerome Biblical Commentary.* Englewood Cliffs, N.J.: Prentice Hall, 1990, pp. 596–629.

Kee, Howard C. *Community of the New Age: Studies in Mark's Gospel.* Philadelphia: Westminster Press, 1977. Reprint, Macon, Ga.: Mercer University Press, 1983. Examines the probable historical circumstances of Mark's community.

Kelber, W. H. *Mark's Story of Jesus.* Philadelphia: Fortress Press, 1979. A penetrating but succinct analysis of Mark's rendition of Jesus' life.

———. *The Oral and the Written Gospel: The Hermeneutics of Speaking and Writing in the Synoptic Tradition, Mark, Paul, and Q.* Philadelphia: Fortress Press, 1983. A major scholarly study of Mark's place in the Jesus tradition.

Ladd, George Eldon. *A Theology of the New Testament.* Grand Rapids, Mich.: Eerdmans, 1974.

Mann, C. S. *Mark: A New Translation, Interpretation, and Commentary.* Anchor Bible, Vol. 27. Garden City, N.Y.: Doubleday, 1986. Argues the Griesbach hypothesis that Mark is a conflation of Matthew and Luke.

Perkins, Pheme. "The Gospel of Mark." In *The New Interpreter's Bible,* Vol. 8, pp. 509–733. Nashville, Tenn.: Abingdon Press, 1995.

Schmidt, Daryl D. *The Gospel of Mark: The Scholars Bible I.* Sonoma, Calif.: Polebridge Press, 1991. A vivid new translation with scholarly annotations.

Streeter, B. H. *The Four Gospels: A Study in Origins.* New York: Macmillan, 1924. A classic statement of the relationship of the Synoptic Gospels, arguing Mark's priority.

Matthew's Gospel

KEY THEMES

Most scholars believe that Matthew's Gospel is an expanded edition of Mark, which the author frames with accounts of Jesus' birth (Chs. 1 and 2) and postresurrection appearances (Ch. 28). Although retraining Mark's general sequence of events, Matthew adds five blocks of teaching material, emphasizing Jesus as the inaugurator of a new covenant (26:26–29) who definitively interprets the Mosaic Torah and, through fulfilling specific prophecies in the Hebrew Bible, proves his identity as Israel's Messiah. Writing a

Representative Examples of Material Found Only in Matthew

- A "Table of Descent [genealogy]" listing Jesus' ancestors (1:1–17)
- Matthew's distinctive version of Jesus' miraculous conception and birth at Bethlehem (1:18–2:23)
- Some parables, sayings, and miracles unique to Matthew:

1. The dumb demoniac (9:32–34)
2. Wheat and darnel [weeds] (13:24–30)
3. Buried treasure (13:44)
4. The pearl of "special value" (13:45)
5. Catching fish in a net (13:47–50)
6. A learner with treasures old and new (13:51–52)
7. Earthly rulers collecting tax (17:25–26)
8. Finding a coin in a fish's mouth to pay Temple tax (17:27)
9. The unforgiving debtor (18:23–35)
10. Paying equal wages to all vineyard laborers (20:1–16)
11. The two sons and obedience (21:28–32)
12. The improperly dressed wedding guest (22:11–14)
13. The wise and foolish virgins (25:1–13)
14. The judgment separating sheep from goats (25:31–46)
15. Judas and the chief priests (27:3–10)
16. The dream of Pilate's wife (27:19)
17. The resurrection of saints (27:52–53)
18. The Easter morning earthquake (28:2)
19. The chief priests' conspiracy to deny Jesus' resurrection (28:11–15)

decade or two after the Roman destruction of Jerusalem, Matthew somewhat softens Mark's portrait of an apocalyptic Jesus, adding parables that imply a delay in the Parousia (Second Coming) (Chs. 24 and 25), an interval of indefinite length devoted to the missionary work of the Church (*ekklesia*). Matthew's principal discourses include the Sermon on the Mount (Chs. 5–7). Instructions to the Twelve (Ch. 10), Parables of the Kingdom (Ch. 13), Instructions to the Church (Ch. 18), and Warnings of Final Judgment (Chs. 23–25).

> Do not suppose that I have come to abolish the Law and the prophets; I did not come to abolish, but to complete.
>
> Matthew 5:17

New Characters Introduced in Matthew

- Joseph, husband of Mary (1:16, 18–25; 2:13–14, 19–23)
- Herod the Great, Roman-appointed king of Judea, 40–4 B.C.E. (2:1–8, 16–19)
- The Magi, astrologers or "wise men" from the east (2:1–12)
- Satan, the devil (as a speaking character) (4:1–11)
- Two blind men (9:27–31)
- A dumb demoniac (9:32–34)
- Revised list of the Twelve (10:1–4)
- The mother of James and John, sons of Zebedee (20:20–21)

Christ with the Sick Around Him, Receiving Little Children *by Rembrandt (1606–1669). In this painting, healing light radiates from the central figure of Jesus and creates a protective circle of illumination around those whom he cures. (Courtesy of Metropolitan Museum of Art. Bequest of Mrs. H. O. Havemeyer, 1929. The H. O. Havemeyer Collection. 29.107.35)*

Matthew's Gospel: A Link Between Old and New Testaments

If the Gospel of Mark was the first Gospel written, as most scholars believe, why does Matthew's account stand first in the New Testament canon? The original compilers of the Christian Scriptures probably assigned Matthew its premier position for several reasons. Besides offering a more extensive coverage of Jesus' teaching than any other Gospel, it was important to early churchmen because of the author's concern with the nature and function of the Church, a term (*ekklesia*) that appears only in Matthew's Gospel (Chs. 10 and 18). As both an instructional tool and a rudimentary guidebook to administering the Christian community, Matthew was supremely useful.

Placing Matthew at the opening of the New Testament is also thematically appropriate because it forms a strong connecting link with the Hebrew Bible. Matthew starts his account with a genealogy to associate Jesus with the most prominent heroes of ancient Israel, particularly Abraham and David (1:1). More than any other Evangelist, he presents Jesus' entire life, from conception to death, in terms of fulfilling biblical law and prophecy. Besides quoting or paraphrasing the Hebrew Bible at least 60 times (some scholars have found as many as 140 scriptural allusions), Matthew commonly employs a literary formula that drives home the link between ancient prophecy and events in Jesus' life; "All this happened in order to fulfill what the Lord declared through the prophet . . . ," Matthew writes, and then cites a biblical passage to support his contention (1:22–23; 2:15; 2:23; etc.; see Table 9.3).

Matthew takes great pains to show that Jesus both taught and observed the principles of the Mosaic Torah (5:17–20), which he presents as still binding on his church. Regarded as the "most Jewish" of the Evangelists, the author is well versed in the methods of interpreting a biblical text practiced in the Judaism of his day. Like the Essenes of Qumran, Matthew interprets the Hebrew Bible as applying exclusively to his group of believers, whom he regards as the true Israel. He also typically presents Jesus' teaching as a kind of Midrash on the Torah. A detailed exposition of the underlying meaning of a scriptural passage, a **Midrash** includes an interpretation of the Scripture's legal rules for daily life (called **Halakah**) and explanation of nonlegal material (called **Haggadah**). At various points in his Gospel, Matthew shows Jesus providing halakic interpretations of the Torah (see 5:17–48), particularly on such legal matters as Sabbath keeping and divorce (12:1–21; 19:3–12).

Authorship and Date   Although an early tradition assigns the Gospel of Matthew to Jesus' apostle of that name, the book itself makes no such claim. The assumption that the author is the "publican" or tax collector mentioned in Matthew 9:9–13 (and called "Levi" in Mark 2:14) dates from the second century C.E. and cannot be verified. According to Papias (c. 140 C.E.), whom Eusebius quotes in his *History of the Church,* "Matthew compiled the Sayings [*logia*] in the Aramaic language, and everyone translated them as well as he could" (*History* 3.39.16).

As many commentators have observed, the Sayings, or *logia,* are not the same as the "words" [*logoi*] of Jesus, nor are they the same as the Gospel of Matthew we have today. Papias may refer simply to an early Christian, perhaps named Matthew, who assembled a list of Old Testament messianic prophecies, a collection that the creator of our present Gospel may have used. The main difficulty in accepting Matthew's authorship is that the writer relies heavily on Mark as a source. Scholars believe it extremely unlikely that one of the original Twelve would depend on the work of Mark, who was not an eyewitness of the events he describes. Like all the Gospels, Matthew was originally composed in Greek and circulated anonymously.

A Greek-speaking Jewish Christian, Matthew (we use the traditional author's name to avoid confusion) may refer to himself or a "school" of early Christian interpreters of the Hebrew Scriptures when he states, "When, therefore, a teacher of the law [a scribe] has become a learner [disciple] in the kingdom of Heaven, he is like a householder who can produce from his store both the new and the old" (Matt. 13:52–53). The author effectively combines "the new" (Christian teaching) with "the old" (Torah Judaism), providing a continuity between the two testaments.

The oldest reference to Matthew's Gospel appears in the letters of Ignatius, who was bishop of Antioch in Syria about 110–115 C.E. The Gospel text itself implies that it was written after the destruction of Jerusalem, which is apparently referred to in 22:7, and after the split between Church and synagogue, which occurred about 85–90 C.E. (9:35; 10:17; 12:9; 13:54). Hence, most scholars believe that it was composed in Antioch, a major Jewish-Christian center, in the late 80s or early 90s C.E.

Table 9.3 Representative Examples of Matthew's Use of the Hebrew Bible to Identify Jesus as the Promised Messiah

Matthew: "All this happened in order to fulfil what the Lord declared through the prophet. . . ." (Matt. 1:22)	Hebrew Bible Source
1. "The Virgin will conceive and bear a son, and he shall be called Emmanuel." (Matt. 1:22)	1. A young woman is with child, and she will bear a son and will call him Immanuel. (Isa. 7:14)
2. "Bethlehem in the land of Judah, you are far from least in the eyes of the rulers of Judah; for out of you shall come a leader to be the shepherd of my people Israel." (Matt. 2:5–6)	2. But you, Bethlehem in Ephrathah, small as you are to be among Judah's clans, out of you shall come forth a governor for Israel, one whose roots are far back in the past, in days gone by. (Mic. 5:2)
3. So Joseph . . . went away . . . to Egypt, and there he stayed till Herod's death. This was to fulfill what the Lord had declared through the prophet: "I called my son out of Egypt." (Matt. 2:15)	3. When Israel was a boy, I loved him; I called my son out of Egypt. (Hos. 11:1)
4. Herod . . . gave orders for the massacre of all children in Bethlehem and its neighborhood, of the age of two years or less. . . . So the words spoken through Jeremiah the prophet were fulfilled: "A voice was heard in Rama, wailing and loud laments; it was Rachael weeping for her children, and refusing all consolation, because they were no more." (Matt. 2:16–18)	4. Hark, lamentation is heard in Ramah, and bitter weeping, Rachel weeping for her sons. She refuses to be comforted: they are no more. (Jer. 31:15)
5. "He shall be called a Nazarene." (Matt. 2:23)	5. Then a shoot shall grow from the stock of Jesse, and a branch [Hebrew, *nezer*] shall spring from his roots. (Isa. 11:1)
6. When he heard that John has been arrested, Jesus withdrew to Galilee; and leaving Nazareth he went and settled at Capernaum on the Sea of Galilee, in the district of Zebulun and Naphtali. This was to fulfil the passage in the prophet Isaiah which tells of "the land of Zebulun, the land of Naphtali, the Way of the Sea, the land beyond Jordan, heathen Galilee," and says: The people that lived in darkness saw a great light: light dawned on the dwellers in the land of death's dark shadow (Matt. 4:12–16)	6. For, while the first invader has dealt lightly with the land of Zebulun and the land of Naphtali, the second has dealt heavily with Galilee of the Nations on the road beyond Jordan to the sea. The people who walked in darkness have seen a great light: light has dawned upon them. dwellers in a land as dark as death. (Isa. 9:1–2)

Table 9.3 (continued)

Matthew: "All this happened in order to fulfil what the Lord declared through the prophet. . . ." (Matt. 1:22)	Hebrew Bible Source
7. And he drove the spirits out with a word and healed all who were sick, to fulfill the prophecy of Isaiah: "He took away our ill-nesses and lifted our diseases from us." (Matt. 8:16–17)	7. Yet on himself he bore our sufferings, our torments he endured, while we counted him smitten by God, struck down by disease and misery. (Isa. 53:4)
8. Jesus . . . gave strict injunctions that they were not to make him known. This was to fulfil Isaiah's prophecy: Here is my servant, whom I have chosen, my beloved on whom my favour rests; I will put my spirit upon him, and he will proclaim judgment among the nations. He will not strive, he will not shout, nor will his voice be heard in the streets. He will not snap off the broken reed, nor snuff out the smouldering wick, until he leads justice on to victory. In him the nations shall place their hope. (Matt. 12:16–21)	8. Here is my servant, whom I uphold, my chosen one in whom I delight, I have bestowed my spirit upon him, and he will make justice shine on the nations. He will not call out or lift his voice high, Or make himself heard in the open street. He will not break a bruised reed, or snuff out a smouldering wick; he will make justice shine on every race, never faltering, never breaking down, he will plant justice on earth, while coasts and islands wait for his teaching. (Isa. 42:1–4)
9. In all his teaching to the crowds Jesus spoke in parables; in fact he never spoke to them without a parable. This was to fulfil the prophecy of Isaiah: I will open my mouth in parables; I will utter things kept secret since the world was made. (Matt. 13:34–35)	9. Mark my teaching, O my people, listen to the words I am to speak. I will tell you a story with a meaning, I will expound the riddle of things past, things that we have heard and know, and our fathers have repeated to us. (Ps. 78:2—*not* in Isaiah)
10. [Jesus instructs his disciples to bring him a donkey and her foal.*] "If any speaks to you, say 'Our Master needs them'; and he will let you take them at once." This was to fulfil the prophecy which says, "Tell the daughter of Zion, 'Here is your king, who comes to you riding on an ass, riding on the foal of a beast of burden.'" (Matt. 21:2–5)	10. Rejoice, rejoice, daughter of Zion, shout aloud, daughter of Jerusalem; for see, your king is coming to you, his cause won, his victory gained, humble and mounted on an ass, on a foal, the young of a she-ass. (Zech. 9:9)

*Matthew shows Jesus mounted on two beasts—the donkey *and* her foal. See Luke 19:29–36, in which a single mount is mentioned.

Matthew's Structure and Themes

Sources Analysis of Matthew's text suggests that he used at least four different sources. Besides incorporating about 90 percent of Mark into his account, Matthew apparently used the Q document as well. A hypothetical collection of Jesus' sayings compiled between about 50 and 60 C.E., Q contained numerous kingdom parables, instructions to the disciples, and prophecies of the Second Coming (Parousia) that are present in both Matthew and Luke but absent from Mark.

Besides Mark and Q, Matthew had a source peculiar to his Gospel, known as M (Matthean). M includes sayings and parables, such as the stories about the vineyard laborers (20:1–16) and many of the kingdom pronouncements in Chapter 13 (13:24–30, 44–45, 47–52). Finally, Matthew used his special versions of Jesus' ancestral background and infancy, as well as his distinctive account of the postresurrection appearances (28:8–20).

Organization Matthew adheres to Mark's north-south polarity, presenting Jesus as making only one journey southward from Galilee to Jerusalem. Closely reproducing Mark's order of events, which forms the narrative framework of his Gospel, he inserts five large sections of teaching material into the Markan sequence and brackets it with his unique accounts of Jesus' birth and resurrection. This discussion focuses on Matthew's distinctive contribution to Jesus' story, particularly the five speeches the author ascribes to his hero (Chs. 5–7, 10, 13, 18, and 23–25).

Matthew's Editing of Mark While preserving most of his Markan source, Matthew edits it to convey his theological views. He thus modifies or omits Markan elements that do not reflect the Torah-respecting practices of the Matthean church, deleting Mark's assertion that Jesus declared all foods "clean" (cf. Mark 7:18–23 with Matt. 15:15–20) and changing the absolute prohibition against divorce to permit it in cases of "unchastity" (cf. Mark 10:11–12 and Matt.

5:31–32). (For more examples of Matthew's editing of Markan material, see the feature on pages 342–343.)

Matthew also edits Mark to emphasize the miraculous and supernatural character of Jesus' mission. In recounting Jesus' unfriendly reception in Nazareth, Matthew changes Mark's observation that Jesus "could work no miracle there" (Mark 6:5) to the declaration that "he did not work many miracles there," eliminating the implication that the human Jesus had any limit to his powers (13:58). He similarly omits Mark's definition of John's baptism as a rite performed "for the forgiveness of sins" (3:2, 6, 11; Mark 1:4), transferring the exact phrase to his account of the Last Supper (26: 26–28). Matthew may have effected this change to ensure that readers understood that "forgiveness of sin" comes not from John's baptism but from Jesus' expiatory death.

Matthew's edition of the Passion narrative also intensifies the supernatural element. In Gethsemane, the Matthean Jesus reminds his persecutors that he has the power to call up thousands of angels to help him (26:53), a claim absent from Mark. Matthew's Christ allows himself to be arrested only to fulfill Scripture (26:54).

Matthew also revises Mark's crucifixion account, inserting several miracles to stress the event's cosmic significance. To Mark's plague of darkness and the rending of the Temple curtain, Matthew adds that a violent earthquake occurred, severe enough to open graves and permit suddenly resurrected "saints" (holy persons) to rise and walk the streets of Jerusalem (27: 50–53). (This mysterious raising of saints is not mentioned elsewhere in the New Testament but probably appears here to express Matthew's conviction that Jesus' death makes possible the resurrection of the faithful.) Matthew introduces yet another earthquake into his description of the first Easter morning, stating that the women disciples arrive at Jesus' tomb in time to see a divine being descend and roll away the stone blocking the tomb entrance. Mark's linen-clad youth becomes an angel before whom the

Roman guards quake in terror (28:1–4). What Mark's account implies, Matthew's typically makes explicit, ensuring that the reader will not miss the hand of God in these happenings. Nor does Matthew leave the Galilean women wondering and frightened at the empty sepulcher. Instead of being too terrified to report what they have seen, in Matthew's version the women joyously rush away to inform the disciples (28:8; Mark 16:8). In this retelling, the women set the right example by immediately proclaiming the good news of Jesus' triumph over death (28:19).

The Infancy Narrative

Except for Matthew and Luke, no New Testament writers refer even briefly to the circumstances surrounding Jesus' birth. Nor do Matthew and Luke allude to Jesus' virginal conception in the main body of their Gospels. In both cases, the infancy narratives are self-contained units that act as detachable prefaces to the central account of Jesus' public ministry.

Matthew constructs his narrative (1:18–2:23) with phrases and incidents taken from the Hebrew Bible. Jesus is born in Bethlehem to fulfill Micah 5:2 and to a virgin (Greek, *parthenos*) to fulfill the Greek version of Isaiah 7:14. Foreshadowing that the child will be worshipped by many non-Jews, Matthew describes the nativity visit of foreign astrologers, "wise men" from Persia or Babylonia who apparently had concluded from a horoscope of Judah that its king was then due to appear. Roused by the news, King Herod—the Roman-appointed ruler of Judea—attempts to eliminate a potential rival by ordering the slaughter of all Bethlehem children under the age of two (2:1–18). Herod's "massacre of the innocents" is intended to parallel a similar tradition about Moses' infancy, when the child was threatened by pharaoh's murderous schemes (Exod. 1:8–2:25). It is also cited as fulfillment of a prophecy in Jeremiah.

The holy family's flight into Egypt to escape Herod's wrath is similarly explained as a fulfillment of Hosea 11:1 ("out of Egypt I called my son"). Because Hosea refers not to the Messiah's infancy but to Israel's Exodus under Moses and is clearly cited out of context, many scholars doubt the historicity of the entire Herod episode. Some critics have questioned whether Matthew, in his eagerness to find or create analogies between Moses and Jesus, the dominant figures of the old and new covenants, has not invented some aspects of the infancy story. The only other New Testament account of Jesus' birth (Luke 2) does not mention either Herod's plot or the Egyptian journey, nor does Josephus or any other contemporary source refer to Herod's alleged murder of Jewish infants.

In fairness to Matthew's use of Old Testament proof texts to validate Jesus as the expected Messiah, it should be noted that biblical **exegesis**—analysis and interpretation of the text—was in first-century Palestine a very different discipline from what it is today. Modern scholars respect the integrity of a text, endeavoring to discover its primary meaning by placing it in its original social and historical setting. In Matthew's time, however, every word, sometimes even every letter, of Scripture was regarded as having an inspired meaning. In this view, a passage's original context did not matter if a single word or phrase seemed applicable to the interpreter's theological purpose.

The Beginning of Jesus' Proclamation

Matthew starts his account of Jesus' adult life (3:1–4:25) at exactly the same point as Mark (1:1–13), giving no information about Jesus' life during the thirty years (Luke 3:1, 23) that separate his birth from his baptism. Note that Matthew revises Mark's baptism narrative to emphasize Jesus' superiority to John by omitting the reference to baptismal "forgiveness" and adding a brief dialog in which the Baptist admits Jesus' greater authority (3:13–17).

Mark (1:12–13) alludes to Satan's tempting Jesus in the desert, uninhabited wastes where demons were popularly believed to roam, but Matthew expands the scene to include a dramatic dialog between the Messiah and his Ad-

Examples of Matthew's Editing of Markan Material

MARK	MATTHEW

Jesus' Baptism

It happened at this time that Jesus came from Nazareth in Galilee	Then Jesus arrived at the Jordan from Galilee, and came to John to be baptized by him. **John tried to dissuade him, "Do you come to me?" he said. "I need rather to be baptized by you." Jesus replied, "Let it be so for the present; we do well to conform in this way with all that God requires." John then allowed him to come.** After baptism Jesus came up out of the
and was baptized in the Jordan by John. At the moment when he came up out of the water, he saw the heavens torn open and the Spirit, like a dove, descending upon him. And a voice spoke from heaven: "Thou art my Son, my Beloved; on thee my favour rests."	water at once, and at that moment heaven opened; he saw the Spirit of God descending like a dove to alight upon him; and a voice from heaven was heard saying, "**This is my Son,** my Beloved, on whom my favour rests."
(Mark 1:9–11)	(Matt. 3:13–17)

In comparing the two accounts of Jesus' baptism, the reader will note that Matthew inserts a speech by John into the Markan narrative. Recognizing Jesus as "mightier" than himself, John is reluctant to baptize him. By giving John this speech, Matthew is able to stress Jesus' superiority to the Baptist. Matthew also changes the nature of Jesus' experience of the "Spirit" after his baptism. In Mark, the heavenly voice is addressed directly to Jesus and apparently represents Jesus' own private mystical experience of divine sonship at the event. Matthew changes "thou art," intended for Jesus' ears, to "this is," making the divine voice a public declaration heard by the crowds.

Jesus' Healings

That evening after sunset they brought to him all who were ill or possessed by devils; and the whole town was there, gathered at the door. He healed many who suffered from various diseases, and drove out many devils.	When evening fell, they brought to him many who were possessed by devils;
	and **he drove the spirits out with a word and healed all who were sick. This was**
He would not let the devils speak, because they knew who he was.	to fulfill the prophecy of Isaiah: "He took
(Mark 1:32–34)	**away our illnesses and lifted our diseases from us.**"
	(Matt. 8:16–17)

versary (4:1–11). As Matthew and Luke present the incident, apparently drawn from Q, it functions to clarify the nature of Jesus' messiahship. Notice that Satan prefaces his first two temptations with the phrase "if you are the Son of God," an attempt to capitalize on any doubts that the human Jesus may have entertained

about his origins or his future legitimacy as God's agent. In the second temptation, Satan quotes from Psalm 91, a poem in which the Deity vows unconditionally to shield from harm his Chosen One. By placing this passage in the Devil's mouth, Matthew may wish to refute Jews who quoted this passage as evidence

MARK	MATTHEW

In reproducing Mark's story, Matthew edits it in several ways that are characteristic of his particular concerns as an author: (1) He condenses Mark's narrative, omitting various details to focus on a single aspect of Jesus' miraculous power, in this case the exorcising of "devils." (2) He emphasizes the totality or comprehensiveness of Jesus' power, changing Mark's "he healed many" to "healed all." (3) Most characteristically, he adds to the account a quotation from the Hebrew Bible, citing Isaiah's poem about the suffering servant (Isa. 53:4), to demonstrate that Jesus' activities fulfilled ancient prophecy. (Matthew's chief editorial changes are printed in boldface type.)

Jesus' Reception by His Neighbors in His Hometown of Nazareth

He left that place and went to his home town accompanied by his disciples. When the Sabbath came he began to teach in the synagogue; and the large congregation who heard him were amazed and said, "Where does he get it from?", and, "What wisdom is this that has been given him?", and, "How does he work such miracles? Is not this the carpenter, the son of Mary, the brother of James and Joseph and Judas and Simon? And are not his sisters here with us?"
So they [turned against] him. Jesus said to them, "A prophet will always be held in honour except in his home town, and among his kinsmen and family." He could work no miracle there, except that he put his hands on a few sick people and healed them; and he was taken aback by their want of faith.

(Mark 6:1–6)

Jesus left that place, and came to his home town, where he taught the people in their synagogue.

In amazement they asked,

"Where does he get this wisdom from, and these miraculous powers? **Is he not the carpenter's son? Is not his mother called Mary,** his brothers James, Joseph, Simon, and Judas? And are not all his sisters here with us? Where then has he got all this from?" So they [turned against] him, and this led him to say, "A prophet will always be held in honour, except in his home town, and in his own family." And **he did not work many miracles there: such was their want of faith.**

(Matt. 13:54–58)

In editing Mark's account of Jesus' unsatisfactory reunion with his former neighbors in Nazareth, Matthew reproduces most of his source but makes some significant changes and deletions. He omits Mark's reference to the Sabbath, as well as Mark's brief list of Jesus' "few" deeds there and Jesus' apparent surprise at his fellow townsmen's refusal to respond to his healing efforts. Matthew also substitutes the phrase "the carpenter's son" for Mark's "the son of Mary," with its implication of Jesus' illegitimacy. In both accounts, the Nazareans' familiarity with Jesus' background and family (naming four "brothers" and referring to two or more "sisters") is enough to make them skeptical of Jesus' claims to special wisdom or authority.

that God's true Messiah would not have died a shameful criminal's death as did the Baptist's disciple. The third attempt to subvert Jesus' understanding of his role is Satan's offer to make Jesus master of all the world's kingdoms—if he would but "do homage" to the Evil One. The lure of political power—perhaps the popular concept of a Davidic Messiah as conquering hero—Jesus also rejects. To rule as Alexander and Augustus —or King David—had ruled would inevitably

entail bloodshed, a use of the Devil's methods that honors not God but Satan.

First Major Discourse: The Sermon on the Mount

After showing his hero rejecting some of the functions then commonly associated with the Messiah, Matthew demonstrates how radically different Jesus' concept of his messiahship is

Virgin and Child. *In this conception of Mary and the infant Jesus, the artist pictures the Madonna as an archetypal image of abundance and fertility, giving her a crown to depict her queenly status and surrounding her with flowers to suggest her association with natural fecundity. This twentieth-century rendition of the Virgin by F. Botero of Uruguay effectively demonstrates her thematic connection with nurturing goddesses of pre-Christian antiquity. (Courtesy of Lee Boltin)*

from the popular expectation of a warrior-king who delivers Israel from its pagan oppressors. The celebrated Sermon on the Mount, which Matthew constructs from widely scattered sayings and the Q material (cf. Luke's version, the Sermon on the Plain, Luke 6:17–7:1), represents Jesus' view of the kingdom as the arts of peace, service, and endurance in doing good. Delivering his catalog of ethical instructions like a greater Moses, Jesus introduces a radical con-

cept of "higher righteousness" that must surpass and transcend the older values of the Mosaic Torah.

The sermon opens with the **Beatitudes** ("blessings" or "happinesses"), assertions that some kinds of people—the sorrowful, the peacemakers, the hungry, the persecuted—uniquely enjoy divine favor. Jesus' statements significantly challenge assumptions typical of some biblical thought. Deuteronomy and Proverbs had ar-

other churches—primarily those established by Paul, who declared Christianity's independence of the law covenant (see Part 10)—do not share this conviction. Conceding that such nonobservant believers are still part of "the kingdom of Heaven" (a term Matthew sometimes applies to the Church), the author nonetheless regards them as ranking below Torah loyalists:

> If any man therefore sets aside even the least of the Law's demands, and teaches others to do the same, he will have the lowest place in the kingdom of Heaven, whereas anyone who keeps the Law, and teaches others so, will stand high in the kingdom of Heaven.
>
> Matthew 5:19

The Antitheses   To Matthew, Jesus gives the Torah renewed vitality by asking followers to go beyond mere obedience and to cultivate an inner grace that excels the old Mosaic requirements. The author shows Jesus illustrating the Torah's eternal validity in the six antitheses, a series of rhetorical statements in which Jesus formally contrasts opposing ideas in similar or parallel verbal structures. Matthew typically begins a statement with the declaration "you have learned that our forefathers were told" and balances it with Jesus' contrasting "but what I tell you is this: . . . ." In this part of the sermon, Jesus contrasts Torah commandments with new interpretations based exclusively on his own personal authority: "You have learned that they [the biblical Israelites] were told 'Eye for eye, tooth for tooth.' But what I tell you is this: Do not set yourself against the man who wrongs you. If someone slaps you on the right cheek, turn and offer him your left" (5:38–39).

The *lex talionis*, or law of retaliation, that Jesus quotes is central to the Mosaic concept of justice and appears in three different Torah books (Exod. 21:23–25; Lev. 24:19–20; Deut. 19:21). Notice that Matthew's Jesus explicitly repudiates the concept, insisting that his people give up the power to avenge personal wrongs. Instead, the victim of wrongdoing is asked to surrender whatever an enemy wants to take. Al-

Virgin and Child. *This wooden sculpture from Africa shows the infant Jesus being nursed by Mary, a rendition illustrating the archetypal image of mother and child, nurturer and bearer of new life, as well as an image of black holiness. (Wood polychromed. Melanesia. Courtesy of Lee Boltin.)*

gued that material prosperity and earthly success were signs of God's approval, whereas poverty and suffering were evidence of divine punishment. In the Beatitudes, Jesus reverses these traditional views, affirming that Israel's God takes the part of those suffering grief or loss. The poor and powerless persons lauded here are exactly those to whom Jesus will direct his ministry.

Matthew's Torah-Abiding Community.   Although Matthew presents Jesus as a staunch upholder of the Mosaic Torah, he is aware that

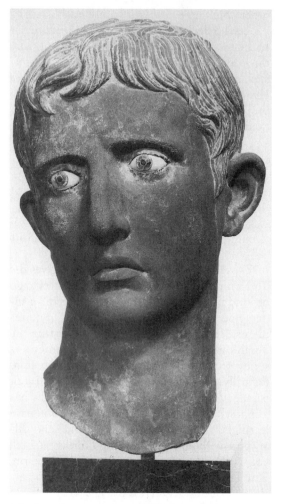

This bust shows Octavius, grandnephew of Julius Caesar, as a thoughtful youth. After defeating his chief rival, Marc Antony, at the Battle of Actium (31 B.C.E.), Octavius became the sole ruler of the Roman Empire (30 B.C.E.–14 C.E.), accepting the title Augustus. Absolute monarch of the largest empire the world had yet known, Augustus established the pax romana—*the Roman peace that brought lasting order and stability to the entire Mediterranean world. (Copyright British Museum)*

cycle of retaliatory justice that can blight individual lives and entire nations alike.

In the final antithesis and its accompanying commentary (5:43–48), Jesus contrasts the command to love one's neighbor (Lev. 19:18) with the assumption that it is permissible to hate an enemy. Again, he demands a "higher righteousness" that surpasses mere legal compliance in order to encompass both friend and stranger in God-like love (5:43–45). Jesus urges his audience to put no limit, legal or doctrinal, on their goodwill or affection because "there must be no limit to your goodness, as your heavenly Father's goodness knows no bounds" (5:48). Believers must imitate the heavenly Parent, who sends rain and sun to all, regardless of their merit. Seeking first the kingdom (6:33) requires submission to these divine principles of beneficence.

The sermon ends with Jesus' parable about the advantages of building one's life firmly on the rock of his teachings (7:24–27), after which, Matthew reports, the crowds "were astounded" because "unlike their own teachers he taught with a note of [his personal] authority" (7:28). Note that Matthew's phrase "when Jesus had finished this discourse," or a variation thereof, marks the conclusion of the four other blocks of teaching material in his Gospel (11:1, 13:53, 19:1, 26:1).

Second Major Discourse: Instructions to the Twelve

In his second major collection of ethical teaching, Matthew presents Jesus' instructions to the twelve chief disciples (listed by name in 10:2–4). Notice that the Twelve are sent exclusively to the "lost sheep of the house of Israel" and forbidden to preach to Gentiles or Samaritans (10:5–6), an injunction found only in Matthew. (By contrast, both Luke and John show Jesus leading his disciples on a brief Samaritan campaign [Luke 9:52–56; John 4:3–42]. Matthew himself ends the Gospel with a command to convert people of all nations [28:19–20].) The Twelve are to preach the kingdom's imminent

though critics have accused Jesus of instituting a "slave morality" in which the strong exploit the weak, his intention may have been to end the

appearance, the same apocalyptic message that the author attributes to both the Baptist (3:2) and Jesus at the outset of his career (4:17). While healing the sick, cleansing lepers, and raising the dead—thus replicating Jesus' spectacular miracles—the disciples are to expect hostility and persecution. This extended warning (10:16–26) seems to apply to conditions that existed in the author's generation, rather than to the time of Jesus' Galilean ministry. Matthew's apparent practice of combining Jesus' remembered words with commentary relating them to later experiences of the Christian community is typical of all the Gospel writers.

A strong eschatological tone pervades the entire discourse. Followers are to be loyal at the time of testing because destruction in Gehenna awaits the unfaithful. The New Testament name for a geographical location, the "Valley of the Son of Hinnom," **Gehenna** is commonly rendered as "hell" in English translations, although it is uncertain that the later Christian notion of a metaphysical place of punishment accurately expresses the original meaning of Gehenna. A site of human sacrifice in Old Testament times (Jer. 7:32; 1 Kings 11:7; etc.), the Valley of Hinnom later housed a garbage dump that was kept permanently burning, a literal place of annihilation for "both soul and body" (Matt. 10:28; 18:8; 25: 30, 46; etc.).

Equally arresting is the statement that before the Twelve have completed their circuit of Palestine "the Son of Man will have come" (10:23). Writing more than half a century after the events he describes, Matthew surprisingly retains a prophecy that was not fulfilled, at least in historical fact. The author's inclusion of this apocalyptic prediction indicates that he may not have understood it literally. Matthew may have regarded the "Son of Man" as already spiritually present in the missionary activity of the Church. If so, this suggests that many of Matthew's other references to "the end of the age" and Jesus' Parousia (Chs. 24 and 25) are also to be understood metaphorically.

Third Major Discourse: Parables of the Kingdom

Matthew brackets Jesus' third discourse with his version of Jesus' alienation from his family (12:46–50; cf. Mark 3:31–35) and Jesus' rejection by the citizens of Nazareth (13:54–58; Mark 6:1–6). The author divides Jesus' parable teachings into two distinct episodes: the first public, the second private (13:10–23). Although only the Twelve are initiated into the secrets of God's rule, Matthew softens Mark's explanation of Jesus' reasons for speaking in parables. Instead of using figures of speech to *prevent* understanding (Mark 4:11–12), Matthew says that Jesus speaks metaphorically because most people have the wrong attitude and unconsciously shut their mental eyes and ears (13:11–15; Isa. 6:9–10). Notice that Matthew's version of the parable lesson explicitly states that the Twelve *do* understand and appreciate Jesus' teaching (13:16–17, 51–52), thus banishing Mark's picture of the disciples' chronic stupidity.

Fourth Major Discourse: Instructions to the Church

In Chapter 18, Matthew assembles disparate sayings of Jesus and applies them to the Christian community of the writer's generation. Taken together, Chapters 10 and 18 form a rudimentary instruction manual for the early Church. The author skillfully combines numerous small literary units to achieve his intended effect. A brief glimpse of the disciples' squabbling for power (18:1–2) introduces opposing images of a powerless child and a drowning man (18:2–7), which are quickly followed by pictures of self-blinding and the flames of Gehenna 18:8–9). The variety of literary forms gathered together here makes the author's prescription for an ideal Christian community intensely vivid. The writer's devices include hyperbole, exaggeration for rhetorical effect; parable (the lost sheep and the unforgiving debtor [18:12–14, 23–35]); advice on supervising troublesome people (18:15–17); prophetic promises (18:10, 18–20); and direct commands (18:22). In Matthew's view of the Church, service, humility, and endless forgiveness are the measure of leadership. Practicing the spirit of Torah mercy, the Church is the earthly expression of divine rule (18:23–35), a visible manifestation of the kingdom.

Note that Matthew gives the individual "congregation" the right to exclude or ostracize disobedient members (18:15–17). During later centuries, this power of *excommunication* was to become a formidable weapon in controlling both belief and behavior. Notice also that the same authority accorded Peter in Jesus' famous "keys of the kingdom" speech (16:16–20) is also given to individual congregation leaders (18:18).

Fifth Major Discourse: Warnings of Final Judgment

This fifth and final block of teaching material summarizes the Matthean Jesus' adverse judgment on Jerusalem, particularly its Temple and religious hierarchy (Chs. 23–25). It opens with a blistering denunciation of the scribes and Pharisees—professional transmitters and interpreters of the law—upon whom Jesus is pictured as heaping "seven woes," perhaps corresponding to the curses on a disobedient Israel listed in Deuteronomy 28. According to Matthew, Jesus blames the Pharisees and their associates for every guilty act—every drop of innocent blood poured out—in Israel's entire history. He condemns the religious leadership to suffer for their generation's collective wrongdoing as well as that of their distant ancestors.

Matthew implies that the Roman devastation of Jerusalem in 70 C.E., an event that occurred during the author's lifetime, is tangible proof of God's wrath on Israel (23:35–36). Matthew intensifies this theme in his version of Jesus' trial before Pilate (Ch. 27); note that Matthew represents a Jerusalem crowd demanding the Messiah's crucifixion, hysterically inviting the Deity to avenge Jesus' blood upon them and their children (27:25). Matthew edits Mark's Passion narrative by adding that Pilate, symbol of imperial Rome, washed his hands of responsibility for Jesus' death—even while ordering Jesus' execution (27:24). All four Gospel writers shift the blame from the Roman government to the Jewish leadership, but only Matthew extends responsibility to the Jews' as-yet-unborn descendants.

Many commentators find an ethical paradox in Matthew's vindictive attitude toward his fellow Jews who did not accept Jesus as the national Messiah. Earlier in his Gospel, Matthew presents Jesus as repudiating the *lex talionis* (5:38–40), stressing instead the necessity of practicing infinite forgiveness (6:12, 14–16; 18:21–35) and exercising mercy (5:7). In dealing with his church's opponents, however, Matthew judges without compassion, apparently regarding Jewish rejection of his Messiah as falling beyond the tolerable limits of charity. The author, in effect, reintroduces the old law of retaliation that Jesus himself rejected. Historically, the consequences of New Testament writers attributing collective guilt to the Jewish people helped fuel the waves of anti-Semitism that repeatedly swept through the Western world for centuries afterward. Throughout Europe, Jews were indiscriminately persecuted as "Christ-killers," often with the blessing of ecclesiastical authorities. Only in 1974 did the Roman Catholic church absolve modern Jews from responsibility for Jesus' crucifixion.

To place Matthew's negative verdict on the first-century Jewish establishment in historical perspective, we must remember that he condemns only the Jerusalem leadership, not Judaism itself. Despite his dislike of Pharisaic customs, the author agrees with Pharisaic teaching. He reminds his readers to "pay attention to their words" and "do what they tell you," for they occupy "the seat of Moses" and their teachings are authoritative (23:1–3).

The Fall of Jerusalem and the Parousia

Signs of the Times   The second part of Jesus' fifth discourse is based largely on Mark 13, the prediction of Jerusalem's impending destruction. Whereas Mark states that the disciples asked only about when the Temple would fall (Mark 13:1–4). Matthew expands the disciples' question to include an apocalyptic inquiry into Jesus' Second Coming (the Parousia) and the "end of the age," the End of human history as we know it (24:1–3). Jesus' reply is a good illustration of how first-century Jewish eschatology was incorporated into the Christian tradition.

Matthew's presentation of the "signal" or "signs" leading to Jesus' return are a complex mixture of first-century historical events, such as the Jewish wars, and prophetic images from the Hebrew Bible, particularly Daniel, Joel, Zechariah, and the pseudepigraphical 1 Enoch. All three Synoptic writers link the Jewish revolt against Rome (66–73 C.E.) with supernatural portents of End time and Jesus' reappearance. Mark, the first to make this association of events, seems to have written at a period when the revolt had already begun (note the "battles" and "wars" in 13:7–8) and Jerusalem was about to fall. These cataclysmic events he called "the birth pangs of the new age." Both Matthew and Luke follow Mark's lead and connect these political upheavals with persecution of believers, perhaps allusions to Nero's cruel assault on Roman Christians (about 64–65 C.E.). The Synoptic authors concur that attacks on the Church, then a tiny minority of the Greco-Roman population, are of critical importance. The sufferings of the Christian community will bring God's vengeance on all humanity.

Jesus' cryptic reference to an "abomination of desolation" (24:15), echoing Daniel 9:27, 11:31, and 12:11, may refer to the Zealot party's violent occupation of the Temple in 67–68 C.E. and their polluting its sacred precincts with the blood of their victims, which may have included some Christians. Matthew's caution— "let the reader understand" (24:16)—suggests that the passage is not from Jesus' oral teaching but from a written source. In his version of the Parousia prediction, Luke omits the mysterious "abomination" reference and substitutes an allusion to Roman armies besieging Jerusalem instead (Luke 21:20–24). To Matthew, the Temple's pollution is a warning for believers to flee Judea because it introduces a time of distress so severe that if not "cut short, no living thing could survive" (24:21–22)—unmistakable allusions to the Roman troops' destructive assault on Jerusalem, home of the apostolic Church. Matthew may refer to ancient traditions about a group of Judean Christians who fled the besieged holy city to seek refuge in Pella, east of Jordan.

Both Mark and Matthew are aware that in the white heat of apocalyptic expectation there were many false reports of the Messiah's return (Mark 13:21–23; Matt. 24:23–27). Some Christians must have experienced crushing disappointment when their prophets' "inspired" predictions of Jesus' reappearance failed to materialize. Thus, both Evangelists caution that even "the Son" does not know the exact date of the Parousia (Mark 13:32; Matt. 24:36). Matthew adds that when the Son does return, his coming will be unmistakable in its universality, "like lightning from the east, flashing as far as the west" (24:27).

Matthew preserves the "double-vision" nature of the Parousia found in Mark. Jesus' supernatural coming will be preceded by unmistakable "signs" that it is near (24:21–22, 29–35); at the same time, he will come without warning and when least expected (24:42–44). Although contradictory, both concepts apparently existed concurrently in the early Church, which was deeply influenced by eschatological thinking.

Although the author of Revelation connects End time with cosmic catastrophe, other New Testament writers (perhaps aware of the repeated failure of attempts to calculate the date of the Parousia) stress that the Son's return is essentially unheralded (1 Thess. 5:1–5; 2 Peter 3:10).

Matthew probably wrote about two decades after Mark's Gospel was composed, but he retains the Markan tradition that persons who knew Jesus would live to see his predictions come true (24:34; Mark 13:30). To Matthew, the Roman annihilation of the Jewish state, which coincided with the emergence of the Christian Church as an entity distinct from Judaism, may essentially have fulfilled Jesus' words, or at least an important part of his prophecy. From the writer's perspective, the "New Age" had already dawned with God's overthrow of Israel and the Church's new and decisive role in future human history (28:19–20).

Parables of Jesus' Return   Chapters 24 and 25 contain three parables and a prophetic vision of Jesus' unannounced Parousia. Whatever their original meaning to Jesus, in Matthew they serve to illustrate believers' obligation to await faithfully and patiently their absent Lord's return. The first parable contrasts two servants, one of whom abuses his fellow employees until the master suddenly reappears to execute him (24:45–51)—a clear warning to Church members to treat others honorably. The parable about a delayed bridegroom similarly contrasts two kinds of believers, those who are alert and prepared for the wedding event and those who are not. Note that the "bridegroom" is "late in coming," a hint that Christians must reconcile themselves to a delay in the Parousia (25:1–13).

The parable of the talents, in which a master's servants invest huge sums of money for him, emphasizes the necessary growth and productivity of the Church during its Lord's prolonged absence (25:14–30). Once again, the servants—the master's Church—are unexpectedly called to account, in this case to demonstrate that they have significantly increased the value of the treasure entrusted to them.

The fourth and final judgment parable concerns not only the Church but also "the nations." The term *nations* refers primarily to Gentiles living outside of the Mosaic law, but it may be intended to include all humanity—Jewish, Christian, and those belonging to other world religions as well. In the parable about separating worthy "sheep" and unworthy "goats," all are judged exclusively on their behavior to-

ward Jesus' "little ones," Matthew's favored term for Christian disciples (25:31–46).

Matthew's eschatological vision makes charitable acts, rather than "correct" religious doctrines, the standard of distinguishing good people from bad. In such passages, Matthew reflects the ancient Israelite prophets who regarded service to the poor and unfortunate as acts of worship to God. The Book of James, which defines true religion as essentially humanitarian service to others (James 1:27), espouses a similar view.

The Passion Story and Resurrection

Although Matthew's account of Jesus' last two days (Thursday and Friday of Holy Week) generally follows Mark's narrative sequence, he adds details from his own distinctive source. Perhaps drawing from oral traditions in his community, he states that the chief priests paid Judas Iscariot thirty pieces of silver for betraying Jesus (26:14–16). He also links Judas's treachery to the fulfillment of a passage in Jeremiah, although the relevant text actually appears in Zechariah (26:14–15, 20–25, 47–50; 27:3–10; Jer. 32:6–13; Zech. 11:12–13). The theme of a warning dream, used frequently in the infancy narrative, reappears when Pilate's wife, frightened by a dream about Jesus, urges her husband to "have nothing to do with that innocent man" (27:19).

Besides adding his mysterious reference to the sudden resurrection of "God's saints," a phenomenon associated with the Final Judgment (27:50–53), Matthew also states that not only Mark's centurion but also his men confess Jesus' divinity (27:54). This editorial change may express Matthew's view that the Roman soldiers' belief foreshadows that of the future Gentile Church.

Roman Guards at the Tomb   Matthew's principal addition to Mark's account of Jesus' burial is the posting of Roman soldiers to guard the tomb, an effort to prevent Jesus' disciples from stealing the body and then claiming that he had been raised from the dead (27:62–66). Matthew also reports a Jewish conspiracy to undermine belief in Jesus' resurrection; Jerusalem priests bribe the guards to say that the disciples had removed and hidden Jesus' corpse (28:11–15).

Matthew implies that Jews of his day used the soldiers' false testimony to refute Christian preaching about the resurrection. However, his counterargument that Roman soldiers had admitted falling asleep while on duty is not convincing. Severe punishment, including torture and execution, awaited any Roman soldier found thus derelict. A rumor about the possible theft of Jesus' body undoubtedly circulated but probably not for the reasons that Matthew gives.

Postresurrection Appearances In Mark's Gospel, Jesus promises that after his crucifixion he will reappear in Galilee (14:28; 16:7), a tradition that Matthew also follows in his extremely brief account of the resurrection. When the eleven disciples encounter the risen Jesus at a prearranged mountain site, Matthew observes that some disciples had doubts about seeing him, as if mistrusting the evidence of their own senses. The author seems to imply that absolute proof of an event so contrary to ordinary human experience is impossible (28:16–17).

The concluding command to recruit followers from "all nations" further emphasizes Matthew's theme that the Church has much work to do before Jesus returns. It suggests that the author's tiny community has only begun what was to become a vast undertaking—a labor extending into the far-distant future.

In composing a new version of Jesus' life, Matthew accomplishes several purposes. Citing Old Testament prophecies, he argues that Jesus of Nazareth is the expected Messiah foretold in the Hebrew Bible. Into Mark's narrative about Jesus' mighty deeds, he incorporates five large blocks of teaching material, emphasizing Jesus' authority to reinterpret the Torah for the Christian community (Chs. 5–7) and to direct its future behavior (Chs. 10 and 18). While retaining Mark's apocalyptic themes, he significantly modifies them to stress the Church's global task during the interval between Jesus' resurrection and Parousia. A guidebook providing instruction and discipline for the community of faith, Matthew's Gospel became the Church's major source of *parenesis*—advice and didactic encouragement to all believers.

RECOMMENDED READING

Beare, F. W. *The Gospel According to Matthew.* New York: Harper & Row, 1982. A standard introduction.

Boring, M. Eugene. "The Gospel of Matthew." In *The New Interpreter's Bible,* Vol. 8, pp. 89–505. Nashville, Tenn.: Abingdon Press, 1995. Extensive scholarly commentary on origin, purpose, and text of Matthew.

Brown, R. E. *The Birth of the Messiah: A Commentary on the Infancy Narratives in Matthew and Luke.* New York: Doubleday, 1977. A thorough analysis of traditions surrounding Jesus' birth.

———. *The Death of the Messiah,* Vols. 1 and 2. New York: Anchor-Doubleday, 1994. An exhaustive analysis of the Gospel accounts of Jesus' arrest, trial, and execution by a leading Roman Catholic scholar.

Edwards, R. A. *Matthew's Story of Jesus.* Philadelphia: Fortress Press, 1985. An introductory study.

Farmer, W. B. *Jesus and the Gospel: Tradition, Scripture, and Canon.* Philadelphia: Fortress Press, 1982. An argument for the primacy of Matthew's Gospel.

Gundry, R. H. *Matthew: A Commentary on His Literary and Theological Art.* Grand Rapids, Mich.: Eerdmans, 1982. A thorough scholarly analysis and exposition.

Kee, H. C. *Jesus in History: An Approach to the Study of the Gospels,* 2nd ed. New York: Harcourt Brace Jovanovich, 1977. A respected exploration of the Gospel texts.

Kingsbury, J. D. *Matthew: Structure, Christology, Kingdom.* Philadelphia: Fortress Press, 1975.

———. *Matthew as Story.* Philadelphia: Fortress Press, 1986. A more advanced analysis of the Gospel.

Meier, John P. *The Vision of Matthew: Christ, Church and Morality in the First Gospel.* Theological Inquiries. New York: Paulist Press, 1979.

———. "Matthew, Gospel of." In D. N. Freedman. ed., *The Anchor Bible Dictionary,* Vol. 4, pp. 622–641. New York: Doubleday, 1992. A lucid survey of current scholarship on the origin and purpose of Matthew's Gospel.

Stendahl, Drister. *The School of St. Matthew and Its Use of the Old Testament.* Philadelphia: Fortress Press, 1968.

Luke's Gospel

KEY THEMES

The first part of a two-volume work (Luke-Acts), Luke's Gospel presents Jesus' career not only as history's most crucial event but also as the opening stage of an indefinitely extended historical process that continues in the life of the Church (Acts 1–28). Writing for a Greco-Roman audience, Luke emphasizes that Jesus and his disciples, working under the Holy Spirit, are innocent of any crime against Rome and that their religion is a universal faith intended for all people. The parables unique to Luke's Gospel depict the unexpected ways in which God's inbreaking kingdom overturns the normal social order and reverses conventional beliefs. After a formal preface and extended nativity account (Chs. 1 and 2), Luke generally follows Mark's order narrating the Galilean ministry (Chs. 3–9); he then inserts a large body of teaching material, the "greater interpolation" (9:51–18:14), supposedly given on the journey to Jerusalem, returning to Mark for his narration of the Jerusalem ministry and Passion story (18:31–23: 56). Luke's final chapter reports postresurrection appearances in or near Jerusalem (Ch. 24).

> But [Jesus] said, "In the world kings lord it over their subjects; and those in authority are called 'Benefactors.' Not so with you: on the contrary, the highest among you

must bear himself like the youngest, the chief of you like a servant. . . . Here I am among you like a servant."

Luke 22:25–27

Luke's Historical Vision

The author of Luke-Acts is unique among New Testament writers, manifesting a breadth of historical vision comparable to that shown in the sweeping narrative of Israel's history from the conquest of Palestine to the first destruction of the Jewish state (the Hebrew Bible books of Joshua through 2 Kings). Consciously working within the tradition of Hellenistic historians, who labored not only to preserve facts but also to interpret their moral significance, Luke ambitiously seeks to trace the course of a new world religion from its inception in a Bethlehem stable to its (hoped-for) status as a legitimate faith of the Roman Empire. Thus, Luke's two-volume work places Jesus' career precisely at the center of time, his life forming the connecting link between Israel's biblical past and the future age of a multinational Gentile Church. Luke views John the Baptist, whose birth story he interweaves with that of Jesus, as both the last of Israel's prophets and the forerunner of the Messiah: "Until John, it was the Law and the prophets; since then there is the good news of the kingdom of God, and everyone forces his way in" (16:16).

By making Jesus' life the central act of a three-part drama that begins with Israel and continues with the Christian Church, Luke offers a philosophy of history that is important to Christianity's later understanding of its mission. Instead of an apocalyptic End, Jesus' ministry is a new beginning that establishes a heightened awareness of God's intentions for humanity. Note that Luke ties Jesus' resurrection to the disciples' job of evangelizing the world (24:44–53; Acts 1: 1–8). He creatively modifies early Christianity's initial emphasis on eschatological expectations to focus on the future work of the Church. Acts thus portrays the disciples entering a new historical epoch, the age of the Church, and thereby extends the new faith's operations indefinitely into the future. Acts concludes not by drawing attention to the Parousia but with Paul's resolve to concentrate on ministering to the Gentiles (28:27–28).

The Author and His Sources

The most important early reference to the author of Luke-Acts confirms that, like Mark, he was not an eyewitness to the events he describes. In the Muratorian list of New Testament books (compiled about the fourth century C.E.), a note identifies the author as **Luke**, "the beloved" physician who accompanied Paul on some of the Apostle's missionary tours. It also states that he did not know Jesus. A few years earlier, Irenaeus, a bishop of Lyons in Gaul (France), also referred to the author as a companion of Paul, presumably the same Luke named in several Pauline letters (Col. 4:14; Philem. 24; 2 Tim. 4:11).

Although some scholars accept the author's traditional identification as Paul's travel companion, a great many do not, pointing out that the writer seems unaware of Paul's letters and never refers to his writing. Although Paul dominates the second half of Acts, Luke only twice refers to him as an Apostle, a title for which the historical Paul vigorously fought. Even though the author's identity is not conclusively settled, for convenience we refer to him as Luke. Because of his interest in the Gentile mission and his fluency in the Greek language (he has the largest vocabulary and most polished style of any Evangelist), the writer may have been a Gentile, the only non-Jewish writer of the Bible.

According to most scholars, Luke-Acts was written after 70 C.E., when Titus demolished Jerusalem. Luke reveals detailed knowledge of the Roman siege (21:20–24), referring specifically to the Roman method of encircling a town, a military technique used in the assault on Jerusalem: "Your enemies will set up siege-works against you; they will encircle you and hem you in at every point; they will bring you to the ground, you and your children within your walls, and not leave you one stone standing on another" (19:43–44). It appears that Luke-Acts was composed at some point after the Jewish wars of 66–73 C.E. and before about 90–95 C.E., when Paul's letters were first collected and published. Many scholars place the Gospel and its sequel in the mid-to-late 80s and favor Ephesus, a Hellenistic city in Asia Minor with a relatively large Christian population, as the place of composition.

Preface   Luke is the only Gospel author to introduce his work with a formal statement of purpose. In this preface (1:1–4), he briefly refers to the methods used in compiling his Gospel and addresses it to Theophilus, the same person to whom he dedicates the Book of Acts (1:1; Acts 1:1). Mentioned nowhere else in the New Testament, **Theophilus**, whose name means "lover of God," may have been a Greek or Roman official, perhaps a well-to-do patron who underwrote the expenses of publishing Luke's work.

Luke states that he wishes to write "a connected narrative," supplying readers with "accurate knowledge." Luke's use of the term translated as "connected narrative" or "coherent account" may not refer to attempting a chronologically accurate biography, for Luke generally follows Mark's order of events. Luke's use of the phrase probably voices his intention of arranging his subject's life in a proper literary form acceptable to an educated Gentile audience.

Use of Sources   As a Christian living two or three generations after Jesus' time, Luke must rely on other persons' information, including orally transmitted recollections about Jesus and traditional Christian preaching. Besides using memories of "eyewitnesses" and later missionary accounts, the author depends on his own research skills—the labor he expends going

A victory monument commemorating Rome's success in crushing the Jewish Revolt (66–73 C.E.), the Arch of Titus still stands in the Roman Forum. After his father, Vespasian, became emperor (69 C.E.), Titus laid siege to Jerusalem, capturing and destroying the city and its Temple in August 70 C.E. Titus's campaign ended not only 1000 years of Jewish Temple sacrifices but also the hegemony of the apostolic church centered there. (Courtesy of Alinari/Art Resource, NY)

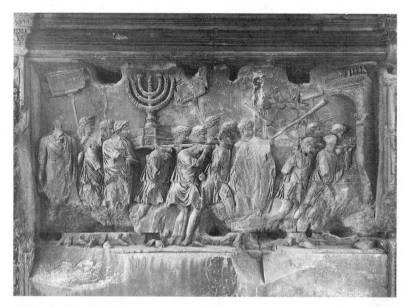

This bas-relief inside the Arch of Titus shows Roman soldiers and captives transporting treasures looted from Herod's Temple in 70 C.E., including the menorah, a seven-branched lampstand that formerly illuminated the sanctuary. (Courtesy of Alinari/Art Resource, NY)

"over the whole course of these events in detail" (1:1–4).

Luke is aware that "many" others before him produced Gospels (1:1). His resolve to create yet another suggests that he was not satisfied with his predecessors' efforts. As Matthew did, he chooses Mark as his primary source, incorporating about 45 to 50 percent of the older work into his narrative. Editing Mark more extensively than did Matthew, he omits several large units of Markan material (such as Mark 6:45–8: 26 and 9:41–10:12), perhaps to make room for his own special additions. Adapting Mark to his creative purpose, Luke often rearranges the sequence of individual incidents to emphasize his particular themes. Whereas Mark placed Jesus' rejection at Nazareth midway through the Galilean campaign, Luke sets it at the beginning (4:16–30). Adding to Mark's account, a claim that the Nazarenes attempted to kill Jesus, he uses the incident to foreshadow his hero's later death in Jerusalem.

In addition, Luke frames Mark's central account of Jesus' adult career with his own unique stories of Jesus' infancy (Chs. 1 and 2) and resurrection (Ch. 24). Luke further modifies the earlier Gospel by adding two large sequences of teaching material. The first section—called the "lesser interpolation" (6:20–8:3)—includes Luke's version of the Sermon on the Mount, which the author transfers to level ground. Known as the Sermon on the Plain (6:20–49), this collection of Jesus' sayings is apparently drawn from the same source that Matthew used, the hypothetical Q document. Instead of assembling Q material into long speeches as Matthew does, however, Luke scatters these sayings throughout his Gospel.

Luke's second major insertion into the Markan narrative, called the "greater interpolation," is nearly ten chapters long (9:51–18:14). A miscellaneous compilation of Jesus' parables and pronouncements, this collection supposedly represents Jesus' teaching on the road from Galilee to Jerusalem. It is composed almost exclusively of Q material and Luke's special source, which scholars call L (Lukan). After this interpolation section, during which all narrative action stops, Luke returns to Mark's account at 18:15 and then reproduces an edited version of the Passion story.

Like the other Synoptic writers, Luke presents Jesus' life in terms of images and themes from the Hebrew Bible, which thus constitutes another of the author's sources. In Luke's presentation, some of Jesus' miracles, such as his resuscitating a widow's dead son, are told in such a way that they closely resemble similar miracles in the Old Testament. Jesus' deeds clearly echo those of the prophets Elijah and Elisha (1 Kings 17–19; 2 Kings 1–6). Luke introduces the Elijah–Elisha theme early in the Gospel (4: 23–28), indicating that for him these ancient men of God were prototypes of the Messiah.

Special Lukan Material   Although he shares material from Mark, Q, and the Hebrew Bible with Matthew, Luke gives his "connected narrative" a special quality by including many of Jesus' words that occur only in his Gospel (the L source). Only in Luke do we find such celebrated parables as those of the prodigal son (15: 11–32), the lost coin (15:8–10), the persistent widow, the good Samaritan (10:29–32), and Lazarus and the rich man (16:19–31). These and other parables embody consistent themes, typically stressing life's unexpected reversals and/ or God's gracious forgiveness of wrongdoers.

Despite the inclusion of some of Jesus' "hard sayings" about the rigors of discipleship, Luke's special material tends to picture a gentle and loving Jesus, a concerned shepherd who tenderly cares for his flock (the community of believers). Luke has been accused of "sentimentalizing" Jesus' message; however, the author's concern for oppressed people—the poor, the socially outcast, and women—is genuine and lends his Gospel a distinctively humane and gracious ambience. (See "Representative Examples of Material Found Only in Luke" on page 356 and "New Characters Introduced in Luke" on page 357.)

Representative Examples of Material Found Only in Luke

* A formal preface and statement of purpose (1:1–4)
* A narrative about the parents of John the Baptist (1:5–25, 57–80)
* Luke's distinctive story of Jesus' conception and birth (1:26–56; 2:1–40)
* Jesus' childhood visit to the Jerusalem Temple (2:41–52)
* A distinctive Lukan genealogy (3:23–38)
* The Scripture reading in the Nazareth synagogue and subsequent attempt to kill Jesus (4:16–30)
* Details on the Roman siege of Jerusalem (19:43–44; 21:21–24)
* Jesus' hearing before Herod Antipas (23:6–12)
* The sympathetic criminal (23:39–43)
* Jesus' postresurrection appearances on the road to Emmaus (24:13–35)

Some parables, sayings, and miracles unique to Luke:

1. A miraculous catch of fish (5:1–11)
2. Raising the son of a Nain widow (7:11–17)
3. Two forgiven debtors (7:41–43)
4. Satan falling like lightning from heaven (10:18)
5. The good Samaritan (10:29–37)
6. The friend asking help at night (11:5–10)
7. The rich and foolish materialist (12:13–21)
8. Remaining alert for the Master's return (12:36–38)
9. The unproductive fig tree (13:6–9)
10. Healing a crippled woman on the Sabbath (13:10–17)
11. Curing a man with dropsy (14:1–6)
12. A distinctive version of the kingdom banquet (14:12–24)
13. Counting the costs of going to war (14:31–33)
14. Parable of the lost coin (15:8–10)
15. The prodigal (spendthrift) son (15:11–32)
16. The dishonest manager (16:1–13)
17. Lazarus and the rich man (16:19–31)
18. Healing ten lepers (17:11–19)
19. The unjust judge (18:1–8)
20. The Pharisee and the tax collector (18:9–14)
21. Restoring the ear of a slave (22:47–53)

Some Typical Lukan Themes

A number of Luke's themes appear in both the Gospel and the Book of Acts, such as his emphasis on prayer, forgiveness, compassion, interest in the poor, concern for women, the active role of the Holy Spirit, God's direction of human history, the universality of Jesus' messiahship, and the new religion's positive relationship with the Greco-Roman world. Both of Luke's books argue that Jesus' career and the growth of Christianity are not historical accidents but the direct result of God's will, which is expressed through the Holy Spirit. Luke uses the term *Holy Spirit* a total of fourteen times, more than Mark and Matthew together. It is by the Spirit that Jesus is conceived and by which he is anointed after baptism. The Holy Spirit leads him into the wilderness (4:1) and empowers his ministry in Galilee (4:14). The spirit is conferred through prayer (11:13), and at death the Lukan Jesus commits his "spirit" to God (23:46).

The Holy Spirit reappears with overwhelming power in Acts 2 when, like a "strong driving wind," it rushes upon the 120 disciples gathered in Jerusalem to observe Pentecost. Possession by the Holy Spirit confirms God's acceptance of Gentiles into the Church (Acts 11:15–18). To Luke it is the Spirit that is responsible for the rapid expansion of believers throughout the Roman Empire. Like Paul, Luke sees the Christian community as charismatic, Spirit-led and Spirit-blessed.

New Characters Introduced in Luke

Elizabeth and the priest Zechariah, parents of the Baptist (1:5–25, 39–79)

Gabriel, the angel who announces Jesus' Virginal conception (1:26–38)

Augustus, emperor of Rome (2:1–2)

Simeon, who foretells Jesus' messiahship (2:25–35)

Anna, an aged prophetess (2:36–38)

The widow of Nain (7:11–16)

The unidentified sinful woman whom Jesus forgives (7:36–50)

The sisters Mary and Martha (10:38–39)

Zacchaeus, the wealthy tax collector (19:1–10)

Herod Antipas, as one of Jesus' judges (22:7–12; also 9:7–9)

Cleopas and another unidentified disciple (24:13–35)

Additional minor characters include a crippled woman (13:10–17), a man with dropsy (14:1–4), and ten lepers (17:11–19).

Early Christian artists commonly pictured Jesus in the guise of earlier Greco-Roman gods or heroes, particularly Apollo, Dionysus, or Orpheus, all of whom were associated with music, inspiration, and flocks and shepherds. In this mosaic at Ravenna, Christ appears as the Good Shepherd. (Courtesy of Erich Lessing/ PhotoEdit)

In Luke's view, from its inception Christianity is a saving faith that God offers to people of "all nations." As Simeon prophesies over the infant Jesus, the child is destined to become "a revelation to the heathen [Gentiles]" (2:32). In Acts, the risen Christ's final words commission his followers to bear witness about him from Jerusalem "to the ends of the earth" (1:8).

Besides presenting Christianity as a universal religion, Luke asserts that it is a peaceful and lawful faith, posing no threat to the Roman government. Hence, he emphasizes that Jesus is guilty of no sedition against Rome (23:22) and that his followers, when hailed before Roman courts, are equally innocent of political subversion.

Finally, Luke portrays Jesus in a guise that his Greek and Roman readers will understand. Matthew had labored to prove from the Hebrew Bible that Jesus was the Davidic Messiah. In his account of Jesus' infancy, Luke also sounds the theme of prophetic fulfillment. But he is also aware that his Gentile audience is not primarily interested in a Jewish Messiah, a figure traditionally associated with Jewish nationalism. Although Mark and Matthew had declared their hero "Son of God," Luke further universalizes Jesus' appeal by declaring him "Savior" (1:69; 2:11; Acts 3:13–15). He is the only Synoptic writer to do so. Luke's term (the Greek *soter*) was used widely in the Greco-Roman world and was applied to gods, demigods, and human rulers alike. Hellenistic people commonly worshiped savior deities in numerous mystery cults and hailed emperors by the title "god and savior" for the material benefits that they conferred upon the public. For Luke, Jesus is the "Savior" of repentant humanity, one who delivers believers from the consequences of wrongdoing, as the judges of ancient Israel "saved" or delivered their people from military oppressors. (The NEB translators therefore use the English term *deliverer* for *soter* in Luke [1:24, 69; 2:11].)

Infancy Narratives in Luke

Only the Gospel of Luke tells of the aged priest **Zechariah** and his barren wife **Elisabeth**, who become the parents of John the Baptist, precursor of Jesus (1:5–25, 39–45, 57–80). To Luke, John the Baptist is the culmination of Israel's purpose—to prepare the way for the Christ: "Until John, it was the Law and the prophets, since then there is the good news of the kingdom" (16:16). Jesus' birth begins a new stage in God's plan for human salvation.

Luke opens his Christmas story with the angel **Gabriel's** announcement to **Mary** that she will bear a son conceived by the Holy Spirit (1:26–28). In Latin translation, Gabriel's salutation to Mary becomes the *Ave Maria*, one of Christendom's most celebrated prayers. Mary's praise of the Deity's graciousness—the *Magnificat* (1:46–53)—is typical of the formal set pieces, apparently drawn from liturgies in Luke's worshiping community, that the author incorporates into his Gospel. This prayer is modeled on **Hannah's** song in 2 Samuel (2:1–10), in which a previously childless wife rejoices in conceiving a son.

Luke's depiction of Jesus' birth in a stable in the Davidic city of **Bethlehem** (2:1–40) differs from Matthew's account (Matt. 2:13–23) in several respects. Luke tells of humble Judean shepherds visiting the infant, rather than of foreign astrologers, as in Matthew; he also omits any reference to Herod's attempt to kill the child or a flight to Egypt. Jesus' presentation at the Jerusalem Temple a month after his circumcision is the occasion for Simeon's prophecy that the babe will be a "light" and "revelation" benefiting "all the nations"—the Nunc Dimittis hymn (2:29–32)—which expresses Luke's theme that Christianity is intended as "good news" to "all people" (2:10, Revised Standard Version), non-Jews as well as Israelites.

Jesus' Boyhood   Luke includes the only tradition about Jesus' boyhood contained in the New Testament, an anecdote about the twelve-year-old boy's visit to the Temple in which he impresses some learned scribes with the acuteness of his questions and understanding (2:41–52). The statement that Jesus "advanced in wisdom and in favor with God and men" (2:52) almost exactly reproduces the Old Testament description of young Samuel (1 Sam. 2:26) and is probably a conventional observation rather than a historically precise evaluation of Jesus' youthful character.

The Galilean Ministry

While reproducing much of Mark's account, Luke modifies it to articulate his distinctive themes. By placing Jesus' rejection in Nazareth at the outset of the Galilean campaign (rather than after Jesus' ministry is well underway, as Matt. 13:54–58 and Mark 6:1–6 do), Luke anticipates the final rejection in Jerusalem. He also introduces specifically Lukan motifs by having Jesus read from Isaiah (61:1–2 and 58:6), announcing the kind of Messiah the author takes him to be—a Spirit-empowered bringer of health and joy to society's "broken victims," particularly the poor, the imprisoned, and the physically afflicted. Luke's references to Elijah and Elisha performing miracles among non-Jewish peoples also foreshadow Christianity's later mission to the Gentiles.

Luke's Sermon on the Plain   Luke also changes Mark's sequence of events by placing Jesus' call of the Twelve after the Nazareth episode (6:12–19). This transposition serves to introduce Jesus' first public discourse, the Sermon on the Plain (6:20–49). The Sermon opens a long section, the "lesser interpolation," in which Luke interweaves material shared with Matthew (presumably from Q) with material that appears only in his own Gospel (6:20–8:3).

In comparing Matthew's Sermon on the Mount with Luke's version, notice that the Lukan Beatitudes are shorter, simpler, and directed at the hearer-reader—"you!" Note, too, that whereas Matthew spiritualizes their meaning, blessing "those who hunger and thirst to see right prevail," Luke gives a bluntly material version: "how blest are you who now go hungry, your hunger shall be satisfied" (6:21). Luke's "poor" are the financially destitute, the powerless to whom God gives his kingdom. Finally, notice

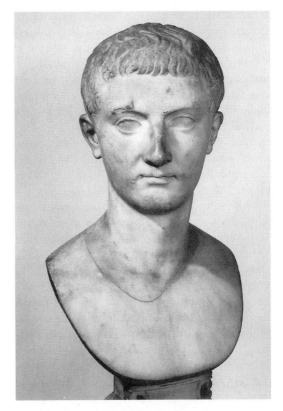

Bust of the Emperor Tiberius (14–37 C.E.). According to Luke, Jesus was "about thirty years old" when he began his Galilean campaign during the fifteenth year of Tiberius's reign (c. 27–29 C.E.) (Luke 3:1, 23). (Copyright British Museum)

that Luke concludes the Beatitudes with "woes" ("alas for you") in which the "rich" and "well-fed" are cursed with future loss and hunger. Persons who benefit unduly from the present world order will see a total reversal of their fortunes (6:24–26).

To Luke, Jesus is the model of compassionate service whom Christians are to imitate. When Jesus raises a widow's son from the dead (7:11–17), the miracle (found only in this Gospel) expresses the twin Lukan themes of God's special love for the poor and deprived and Christ's role as Lord of the resurrection.

The Importance of Women in Luke   Luke commonly uses Jesus' interaction with women to reveal his concept of Jesus' character, stressing his hero's combination of authoritative strength and tenderness. After restoring the widow of Nain's son, Jesus reveals compassion for a different kind of vulnerable woman, a prostitute. All four Gospels contain some version of this incident, in which a woman anoints Jesus' feet, but Luke uses it in a special way to show Jesus accepting an act of devoted love from an anonymous woman whom others consider unfit because of her "immoral life" (7:36–50; cf. Mark 14:3–9; Matt. 26:6–13; John 12:1–8).

Luke's sympathetic interest in women appears throughout his Gospel. He alone relates the parables of the persistent widow and the woman's lost coin, the conversations between Mary and her cousin Elizabeth (1:29–56), the words of the old prophetess Anna (2:36–38), the grieving widow of Nain, and the female disciples who help support Jesus and his male followers "out of their own resources" (8:1–3). Mary Magdalene (from the Galilean suburb of Magdala), from whom Jesus drove seven devils, and Joanna, whose husband is a steward to Herod Antipas, are present at the crucifixion and are also among the women who find Jesus' tomb empty (23:55–24:12). The sisters Mary and Martha, whose differing personalities allow Jesus to teach a lesson in spiritual values (10:38–42), number among his closest friends.

Jesus' Teaching on the Journey to Jerusalem

The "Greater Interpolation"   Luke begins this long section (9:51–18:14), known as the "greater interpolation," with the declaration that Jesus "set his face resolutely towards Jerusalem," signaling Jesus' resolve to confront the Jerusalem authorities who will reject and condemn him. Although ostensibly the record of a journey from Galilee to Judea, this part of the Gospel is largely a miscellaneous collection of brief anecdotes, sayings, and parables. Here the author intermixes Q material with his individual source (L), including most of the parables unique to his Gospel.

Jesus' brief tour through **Samaria** and his sending forth seventy-two disciples to evangelize the countryside (10:1–16) anticipate the later Christian mission to Samaria described in Acts 8. In Jewish terminology, the number seventy or seventy-two represents the sum total of non-Jewish nations. As the Twelve sent to proselytize Israel symbolize the traditional twelve Israelite tribes (9:1–6), so the activity of the seventy-two foreshadows Christian expansion among Gentiles in the Roman Empire.

The Parable of the Good Samaritan   Notice the context in which Luke sets the parable of the good **Samaritan**. In 10:25–28, a Torah expert defines the essence of the Mosaic law in the twin commandments to love God (Deut. 6:5) and neighbor (Lev. 19:18). Jesus confirms that in loving thus a person "will live." This episode provides a good example of the way in which Luke adapts Markan material to his theological purpose. Whereas Mark places this dialog with the Torah instructor in the Jerusalem Temple, Luke transfers it to an unidentified site on the road to Jerusalem and uses it to introduce his parable of the kindly Samaritan. The author creates a transition to the parable by having the instructor ask Jesus to explain what the Torah means by "neighbor."

In typical rabbinic fashion, Jesus does not define the concept but instead tells a story in which the questioner must find his own meaning in a specific human situation. Analyzing the tale (10:29–35), most students will find that it not only follows Luke's customary theme of the unexpected but also contains some distinctively subversive themes.

In making a Samaritan the moral hero of this tale, Jesus asks his hearers to find nobility in a class of people whom observant Jews must despise as apostates and pariahs. Note that the priest and Levite who fail to help the robbers' victim do so in order to obey Torah rules. If the victim were dead and they touched his corpse, they would automatically become ritually unclean and disqualified from performing their

Temple duties. Jesus' directive to behave as the Samaritan does stresses a typical Lukan reversal: The person his audience regarded as an unclean foreigner and heretic becomes the model to emulate. Ignoring both religious and racial barriers, the Samaritan recognizes the injured Jew as his neighbor, thereby fulfilling the Torah commands that the legal expert had cited.

Parables About Wealth and Poverty   The parables of the rich fool (12:13–21) and Lazarus and the rich man (16:19–31) illustrate Luke's dim view of a life spent acquiring great wealth. The Lukan Jesus urges his disciples to sell their possessions, give to the poor, and thus earn "heavenly treasures" (12:22–34; 14:12–14). Luke consistently emphasizes that helping the deformed and unattractive, society's rejects and have-nots, must be the Christian's primary concern in attaining Jesus' ultimate approval (14: 15–24). One version of the author's ideal social order is the commune that the disciples establish following Pentecost, an economic arrangement in which the well-to-do sell their goods, share the proceeds, and hold "everything in common" (Acts 2:42–47).

Jesus' Association with Outcasts   The Synoptic authors agree that Jesus sought the company of "tax-gatherers and sinners," a catch-all term referring to the great mass of people in ancient Palestine who were socially and religiously unacceptable because they did not or could not keep the Torah's requirements. This "unrespectable" group stood in contrast to the Sadducees, the Pharisees, the scribes, and others who conscientiously observed all Torah regulations in their daily lives. In the Synoptic tradition, Jesus ignores the principle of contamination by association. He eats, drinks, and otherwise intimately mixes with a wide variety of persons commonly viewed as both morally and ritually "unclean." At one moment, we find him dining at the homes of socially honored Pharisees (7:36–50) and the next enjoying the hospitality of social outcasts like Simon the leper (Matt.

26:6–13) and Zacchaeus the tax collector (19: 1–10). Jesus' habitual associations lead some of his contemporaries to regard him as a pleasure-loving drunkard (7:34). According to Luke, Jesus answers such criticism by creating parables that express God's unfailing concern for people whom the "righteous" dismiss as worthless.

The Prodigal Son   The parable of the prodigal son might better be called the story of the forgiving father, because the climax of the narrative focuses on the parent's attitude to his two very different sons (15:11–32). The younger son violates the most basic standards of Judaism, squandering his inheritance and reducing himself to the level of an animal groveling in a Gentile's pigpen. Vivid exaggerations characterize Jesus' authentic parables, and he here paints a youth who is totally insensitive to his religious heritage and as "undeserving" as a human being can be. Even his decision to return to his father's estate springs from an unworthy desire to eat better food.

Yet, the parable's focus is not on the ungrateful son but on the father's love for both his children, the obedient older brother as well as the prodigal. Notice that the father acknowledges his elder son's superior claim to his favor and attempts to explain the unlimited quality of his affection. The father's nature is to love unconditionally, making no distinction between the deserving and undeserving. The parable illustrates the character of the divine Parent, who "is kind to the ungrateful and wicked," whom Luke describes in his Sermon on the Plain (6: 35–36).

The Jerusalem Ministry: Jesus' Conflict with Rome

Although returning to Mark's narrative in 18:15 for his account of the Jerusalem ministry, Luke significantly modifies his source to soften the older Gospel's intense apocalypticism and to emphasize his major theme that Jesus is innocent of plotting treason against Rome. Luke's account retains elements of primitive Christian apocalypticism, including admonitions to be constantly alert and prepared for the eschaton, but he also distances the End, placing it at some unknown time in the remote future.

In Luke's Gospel, we find Jesus' sayings about the imminence of the kingdom intermixed with exclusively Lukan material about the kingdom already being a reality present in Jesus' miraculous deeds and teaching. When the Pharisees accuse Jesus of exorcising demons by the power of "Beelzebub [Satan]," he answers, "If it is by the finger of God that I drive out the devils, then be sure the kingdom of God has already come upon you" (11:20). Jesus thus challenges onlookers to see in his successful fight against Evil the in-breaking reign of God. A similar concept of the kingdom appears in Jesus' answer to some Pharisees who ask when God's dominion will begin: "You cannot tell by observation when the kingdom of God comes. There will be no saying, 'Look, here it is!' or 'there it is!'; for in fact the kingdom of God is among you [or in your midst]" (17:20–21).

Predictions of Jerusalem's Fall   Luke retains Mark's eschatological prediction of Jerusalem's destruction (Mark 13) but edits it extensively to show that a period of indefinite length intervenes between the city's fall and the actual Parousia (Ch. 21). The author is aware that many of Jesus' followers expected his ministry to culminate in God's government being established visibly on earth. He reports that "because [Jesus] was so close to Jerusalem . . . they thought the reign [or kingdom] of God might dawn at any moment" (19:11), an expectation that persisted in the early Church (Acts 1:6–7). Luke counters this belief with a parable explaining that their Master must go away "on a long journey" before he returns as "king" (19:12–27). (Matthew uses this parable of the talents [Matt. 25:14–30] for the same purpose of explaining the delayed Parousia.)

Luke separates historical events preceding Jerusalem's destruction from cosmic events that signal Jesus' return. After the Romans decimate the city and raze the Temple, an indefinitely extended period of secular history will intervene. Luke's Jesus states that "Jerusalem will be trampled down by foreigners until their day has run its course" (21:24). This reference to an epoch of Gentile domination occurs only in Luke and replaces the apocalyptic "sign" of the "abomination of desolation" that appears at this point in Mark's apocalyptic prophecy (Mark 13: 14; Matt. 24:15). The fact that Luke follows his Gospel with an account of the Church—the Book of Acts—indicates that he foresees a long earthly history for his religion. Luke's emphasis on the Church's long-range commission to witness about Jesus "to the ends of the earth" (Acts 1:8) expresses his belief that Christians have much unfinished business to accomplish before the End.

It is also important to note that Luke may regard the astronomical phenomena—"portents . . . in sun, moon, and stars"—that immediately precedes Jesus' reappearance (21: 25–28) as essentially metaphoric. In Acts, Peter is shown declaring that such celestial wonders, prophesied in the Hebrew Bible's Book of Joel, were historically fulfilled in the spiritual activities of the early Church (Acts 2:16–24). In presenting the Holy Spirit's visitation in images associated with Jesus' Parousia, Luke anticipates the doctrine of realized eschatology in John's Gospel.

Jesus As Servant   Although Luke's account of Jesus' last days roughly parallels that of Mark (14:1–16:8), Luke introduces several variations to express his particular theological views and to demonstrate that Jesus is innocent of any sedition against Rome (22:1–23:56). Mark had stated that Jesus' death was sacrificial: His life is given "as a ransom for many" (Mark 10:45). In the Lukan equivalent of this passage (placed in the setting of the Last Supper), Jesus merely says that he comes to serve (cf. Mark 10:42–45 and Luke 22:24–27). Luke's theology of the cross does not interpret Jesus' crucifixion as a mystical atonement for human sin. Instead, Jesus appears "like a servant," providing an example for others to imitate, the first in a line of Christian models that includes Peter, Stephen, Paul, and their companions in the Book of Acts.

Luke's version of the Last Supper also expresses his theological intent. In the Lukan ceremony, the wine cup is passed first and then the unleavened bread. The author may present this different order in the ritual because he wants to avoid giving Jesus' statement about drinking wine again in the kingdom the apocalyptic meaning that Mark gives it. Luke also omits the words interpreting the wine as Jesus' blood, avoiding any suggestion that Jesus sheds his blood to ransom humanity from sin or that he gives his blood to establish a new covenant. In Luke, Jesus' only interpretative comment relates the bread (Eucharist) to his "body" (22:17–20). The author also inverts Mark's order by having Jesus announce Judas's betrayal after the ritual meal, implying that the traitor was present and participated in the communion ceremony.

Luke's Passion Story

Luke's Passion story emphasizes a theme that will also dominate Acts: Jesus, like his followers after him, does nothing illegal or threatening to the peace and stability of Roman rule. In Luke the Sanhedrin can produce no witnesses and no conviction of charges of blasphemy. Its members bring Jesus to Pilate strictly on political terms: The accused "subverts" the Jewish nation, opposes paying taxes to Rome, and claims to be the Messiah, a "king," and therefore a traitor to Caesar. In his account of the trial before Pilate, Luke repeatedly has the Roman governor pronounce Jesus innocent. The episode in which Pilate sends Jesus to **Herod Antipas** (23:6–12), a tradition found only in Luke, serves to reinforce the author's picture of an innocent Jesus. Pilate twice declares that the prisoner "has done nothing to deserve death" (23:15) and is legally "guilty of [no] capital offense" (23:22). The Roman procurator, whom other contemporary historians depict as a ruthless tyrant contemptuous of Jewish public opinion, is here only a weak pawn manipulated by a group of his Jewish subjects.

The same theme reappears in the crucifixion scene, where one of Jesus' fellow victims remarks that "this man [Jesus] has done nothing wrong" (23:41). Whereas in Mark and Matthew the Roman soldier confesses that Jesus is divine, in Luke it is his political innocence that the centurion affirms: "Beyond all doubt, . . . this man was innocent" (23:47).

Other typically Lukan themes are sounded in Jesus' "last words" on the cross. Only in Luke do we find Jesus' prayer to forgive his executioners because they do not understand the meaning of their actions (23:24). Because the author regards both Jews and Romans as acting in "ignorance" (see Acts 2:17), Jesus' request illustrates the principle of all-encompassing love that freely pardons enemies (6:27–38) and ends the cycle of retaliation that perpetuates evil in this world. Jesus' final words are to the Father whose Spirit he had received following baptism (3:21; 4:1, 14) and to whom in death he commits his own spirit (23:46–47). Rather than being a sacrifice for sin, the Lukan Jesus is an example of compassion and forgiveness for all who receive the Spirit to emulate.

Postresurrection Appearances

Because early editions of Mark contain no resurrection accounts, it is not surprising that Matthew and Luke, who follow Mark through the discovery of the empty sepulcher, differ widely in their reports of Jesus' postresurrection appearances. Consistent with his emphasis on Jerusalem, Luke omits the Markan tradition that Jesus would reappear in Galilee (Mark 16:7; Matt. 28:7, 16–20) and places all experiences of the risen Jesus in or near Jerusalem. The first posthumous appearance, on the road to Emmaus, suggests Luke's understanding of the risen Jesus' relationship to followers left behind on earth. The two disciples, Cleopas and an unnamed companion, who encounter Jesus do not recognize him until they share a meal together. Only in breaking bread—symbolic of the Chris-

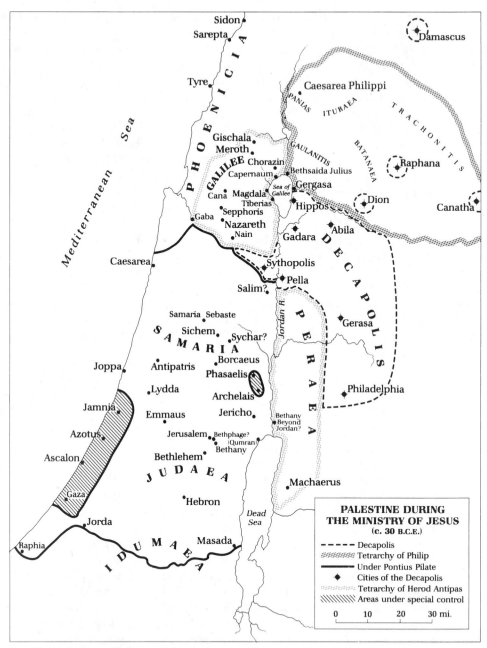

Sidon
Sarepta
Damascus

Tyre
Caesarea Philippi
PHOENICIA
PANIAS
ITURAEA
TRACHONITIS

Gischala
Meroth
GALILEE Chorazin
Capernaum
Bethsaida Julius
GAULANITIS
BATANAEA
Raphana

Cana Magdala
Sea of Galilee
Gergasa
Dion
Canatha

Tiberias
Sepphoris
Hippos

Gaba
Nazareth
Nain
Gadara
Abila
DECAPOLIS

Mediterranean Sea

Caesarea
Sythopolis

Salim?
Pella

Samaria Sebaste
SAMARIA
Sichem
Sychar?
Jordan R.
PERAEA
Gerasa

Joppa
Antipatris
Borcaeus
Phasaelis

Lydda
Archelais
Philadelphia

Jamnia
Emmaus
Jericho
Bethany Beyond Jordan?

Azotus
Jerusalem Bethphage?
(Qumran)
Bethany

Ascalon
Bethlehem
JUDAEA

Gaza
Hebron
Machaerus

Dead Sea

Jorda
Masada

Raphia
IDUMAEA

PALESTINE DURING THE MINISTRY OF JESUS
(c. 30 B.C.E.)

- - - Decapolis
Tetrarchy of Philip
—— Under Pontius Pilate
◆ Cities of the Decapolis
Tetrarchy of Herod Antipas
Areas under special control

0   10   20   30 mi.

The political divisions of Palestine during the ministry of Jesus (c. 30 C.E.). Note that Rome directly administered Judea and Samaria through its procurator Pontius Pilate; Herod Antipas ruled Galilee (Jesus' home district) and Peraea; another son of Herod the Great, Philip, ruled an area to the northeast. The Decapolis was a league of ten Greek-speaking cities on the east side of the Jordan River.

tian communion ritual—is Jesus' living presence discerned.

Luke's second postresurrection appearance takes place inside Jerusalem, reinforcing themes expressed in the Emmaus incident. After having appeared to Peter—an event that Luke does not describe but that was an early Church tradition (see 1 Cor. 15:1–5)—Jesus materializes in the midst of a large group, including the Eleven. Reporting that this apparition was sudden and stunning, Luke states that the resurrected figure displayed familiar physical qualities, perhaps to demonstrate the continuity between the human Jesus and the risen Christ. Thus, the Lukan Jesus bears the marks of crucifixion and shares ordinary food (communion) with his disciples (24:33–43).

Linking the Emmaus and Jerusalem events, Luke emphasizes that the resurrected Jesus offers teaching that connects his ministry and death with the Hebrew Bible. By showing the risen Christ interpreting biblical texts (24:13–32), the author expresses his belief that Jesus continues to guide the Christian community, inspiring fresh insights into the meaning of the Jewish Scriptures. To Luke, neither the Bible nor Jesus' life can be clearly understood except in the light radiated through Christ's resurrection.

Luke ends his Gospel with Jesus' promise to send the disciples his "Father's gift," the Holy Spirit that enables the Church to appreciate Jesus' significance and hear his continuing voice. That living voice instructs them to remain in Jerusalem, awaiting "power from above" (24:44–53; fulfilled in Acts 2).

Emphasizing God's compassion and willingness to forgive all, the Lukan Jesus provides a powerful example for his followers to imitate in service, charity, and good works. An ethical model for Jews and Gentiles alike, Jesus establishes a Spirit-led movement that provides a religion of salvation for all people. The primitive belief that the Son of Man would return "soon" after his resurrection from the dead is replaced with Luke's concept of the disciples' role in carrying on Jesus' work "to the ends of the earth": a commission that extends the time of the End indefinitely into the future. In the meantime, a law-abiding and peaceful Church will convey its message as a Savior for all nations throughout the Roman Empire—and beyond.

RECOMMENDED READING

Conzelmann, Hans. *Theology of St. Luke*. Translated by G. Buswell. New York: Harper & Row, 1960. An influential and incisive analysis of Luke's theological purposes.

Danker, F. W. *Luke*. Philadelphia: Fortress Press, 1976. A good general introduction.

Edwards, O. C., Jr. *Luke's Story of Jesus*. Philadelphia: Fortress Press, 1981.

Fitzmyer, J. A., ed. *The Gospel According to Luke*, vols. 1 and 2 of the Anchor Bible. Garden City, N.Y.: Doubleday, 1981, 1985.

Johnson, Luke Timothy. "Luke-Acts, Book of." In D. N. Freedman, ed., *The Anchor Bible Dictionary*, Vol. 4, pp. 403–420. New York: Doubleday, 1992. A lucid summary of current scholarly studies of Luke's two-volume work.

Karris, Robert J. "The Gospel According to Luke." In R. E. Brown et al., eds., *The New Jerome Biblical Commentary*, pp. 675–721. Provides detailed commentary on Lukan account.

Leaney, A. R. C. *A Commentary on the Gospel According to St. Luke*, 2nd ed. Harper's New Testament Commentary. London: Black, 1966.

Talbert, C. H. *Reading Luke: A Literary and Theological Commentary on the Third Gospel*. Los Angeles: Crossroads, 1982.

———. *Luke-Acts: New Perspectives from the Society of Biblical Literature Seminar*. New York: Crossroads, 1984.

John's Gospel

KEY THEMES

In John's Gospel, the order of events and the portrayal of Jesus and his teaching are strikingly different from those in the Synoptic accounts.

Whereas the Synoptics depict Jesus as an eschatological healer-exorcist whose teachings deal primarily with Torah reinterpretation, John describes Jesus as an embodiment of heavenly Wisdom who performs no exorcisms and whose message centers on his own divine nature. In John, Jesus is the human form of God's celestial Word, the primeval expression of divine intelligence by which God created the universe. As the Word incarnate (made flesh), Jesus reveals otherwise unknowable truths about God's being and purpose. To John, Jesus' crucifixion is not a humiliating defeat (as Mark characterizes it) but a glorification that frees Jesus to return to heaven. John's Gospel preserves no tradition of a Second Coming (the Parousia). Instead it argues that the risen Christ is eternally present in the invisible form of a surrogate—the Paraclete, or Holy Spirit, that continues to inspire and direct the believing community. The Gospel is commonly divided into a prolog (1:1–51); a Book of Signs recounting seven miraculous deeds (2:1–11:57); the Book of Glory, a reinterpretation of the Passion (12:1–20:31); and an epilog (21:1–25).

> He who has faith in me will do what I
>   am doing; and he will do greater things
>   still. . . . Your Advocate [Paraclete], the Holy
>   spirit . . . will teach you everything, and
>   will call to mind all that I have told you.
>   John 14:12, 26

A Different Gospel

The Gospel of John is so different from the Synoptics that most scholars conclude that it is fundamentally not a portrait of the historical Jesus but a profound meditation on his theological significance. The community that produced this Gospel held a uniquely high view of Jesus' divinity, ascribing to him a heavenly preexistence before his coming to earth and equating him with an eternal attribute of God, the divine Wisdom used to create the universe. A mystical reflection upon Jesus' cosmic meaning and a tribute to his divinity, the fourth Gospel presents Jesus' earthly life almost exclusively in terms of his postresurrection glory. According to the unnamed author, it represents an understanding of Jesus' career that the **Paraclete** (Holy Spirit) later bestowed on a small "brotherhood" originally founded by a "disciple whom Jesus loved."

The author clearly states his purpose: to inspire faith in Jesus' divinity. He describes Jesus' miracles—which he calls "signs"—"in order that you may hold faith that Jesus is the Christ, the Son of God, and that through this faith you may possess life by his name" (20:31). This declaration follows the Gospel's climactic scene—a postresurrection appearance in which the reality of Jesus' living presence conquers the doubts of his most skeptical disciple, Thomas. Confronted with a sudden materialization of the risen Jesus, Thomas recognizes him as "My Lord and my God!"—a confession of faith, which the reader is intended to echo.

The Authorship of John

Since the late second century C.E., the Gospel has been attributed to the Apostle John, son of Zebedee and brother of James. According to one tradition, John eventually settled in Ephesus, where he lived to an exceptionally great age, writing his Gospel, three letters, and the Book of Revelation. These five works are known collectively as the "Johannine literature."

The tradition ascribing authorship to the son of Zebedee is relatively late. Before about 180 C.E., Church writers do not mention the Gospel's existence. After that date, opinion on its origin is divided, with some leading churchmen accepting it as John's composition and others doubting its authenticity. Some even suggested that it is the work of Cerinthus, a Gnostic teacher.

Most contemporary scholars doubt that the Apostle John wrote the document that bears his name. The Gospel itself does not mention the author's identity, stating instead that it is based on the testimony of an anonymous disciple "whom Jesus loved" (21:20–24). Some traditions identify this "**beloved disciple**" with John (whose name does not appear in the text), but scholars can find no evidence to substantiate this claim. Jesus predicted that John would suffer a death similar to his (Mark 10:39), whereas the Gospel implies that its author, unlike Peter, James, and John, did not die a martyr's death (21:20–22). Many historians suggest that Herod Agrippa may have executed the Apostle John along with his brother James, about 41–43 C.E. (Acts 12:1–3).

A few critics propose that another John, prominent in the church at Ephesus about 100 C.E., is the author. Except that he was called "John the Elder" *(presbyter),* we know nothing that would connect him with the Johannine writings. Lacking definite confirmation of traditional authorship, scholars regard the work as anonymous. For convenience we refer to the author as John.

The Beloved Disciple   Although the Gospel text does not identify its author, editorial notes added to the final chapter associate him with the unnamed beloved disciple, suggesting that at the very least this disciple's teachings are the Gospel's primary source (21:23–24). Whether or not this anonymous personage was a historical character, he is certainly an idealized figure, achieving an intimacy and emotional rapport with Jesus unmatched by Peter or the other disciples. In the Gospel, he does not appear (at least not as the one "Jesus loved") until the final night of Jesus' life, when we find him at the Last Supper, lying against his friend's chest (13:23). (The Twelve dined in the Greco-Roman fashion, reclining two-by-two on benches set around the table.)

Designed to represent the Johannine community's special knowledge of Christ, the beloved disciple is invariably presented in competition with Peter, who may represent the larger apostolic church from which the disciple's exclusive group is somewhat distanced. At the Last Supper, the beloved disciple is Peter's intermediary, transmitting to Jesus Peter's question about Judas's betrayal (13:21–29). Acquainted with the high priest, he has access to Pilate's court, thus gaining Peter's admittance to the hearing, where Peter denies knowing Jesus (18:15–18). The only male disciple at the cross, he receives Jesus' charge to care for Mary, becoming her "son" and hence Jesus' "brother" as well (19:26–27).

Outrunning Peter to the empty tomb on Easter morning, he arrives there first and is the first to believe that Jesus is risen (20:2–10). In a boat fishing with Peter on the Sea of Galilee, the disciple is the first to recognize the resurrected Jesus standing on the shore, identifying him to Peter (21:4–7). Peter, future "pillar" of the Jerusalem church, is commissioned to "feed" (spiritually nourish) Jesus' "sheep" (future followers), but Jesus has a special prophecy for the beloved disciple's future: He may live until the Master returns (21:20–22). (This reference to the Second Coming is virtually unique in John's Gospel.)

Editorial comments appended to the Gospel, apparently after the favored disciple's death, indicate how the Johannine church interpreted Jesus' prophecy. The editor notes that, although Jesus' remark had circulated among "the brotherhood" (the community in which the Gospel originated), the saying did not mean that the "disciple would not die." It meant only that Jesus' intentions for his favorite did not involve Peter (21:21–23). The editor's comments hint at the differences between the Johannine and most apostolic Christian communities, which, during the first century C.E., were generally independent of one another. The disciple's "brotherhood" would produce a Gospel promoting Jesus' theological meaning in ways that paralleled the Petrine churches' teachings but revealing, they believed, Jesus' "glory" (1:14) more fully than other Gospel accounts.

Place of Composition and Date   Despite the use of Hellenistic terms and ideas in John's Gospel, recent studies indicate that this book is deeply rooted in Palestinian tradition. It shows a greater familiarity with Palestinian geography than the Synoptics and reveals close connections with first-century Palestinian Judaisms, particularly concepts prevailing in the Essene community at Qumran. Study of the Dead Sea Scrolls from Qumran reveals many parallels between Essene ideas and those in John's Gospel and letters. Like the Essene authors, John typically contrasts pairs of abstract terms, such as light (symbolizing Truth and Goodness) and darkness (symbolizing Deceit and Evil), to distinguish between his group and the rest of the world. He sees the universe as a duality, an arena of polar opposites in which the Devil (synonymous with "liar") and his "spirit of error" oppose Jesus' "spirit of truth" (8:44; 14:17; 15:26; 1 John 4:6). As the "light of the world," Jesus comes to illuminate humanity's mental and spiritual darkness. The Gospel's use of such terminology does not necessarily imply borrowing from Essene sources but suggests that the author's thought developed in a Palestinian religious environment.

Many scholars favor a Palestinian or Syrian location for the Gospel's place of composition, but others accept the traditional site of Ephesus. A wealthy, populous seaport and capital of the Roman province of Asia (the western part of modern Turkey), Ephesus was a crossroads for Greek and Near Eastern religious ideas and home to many Jews and early Christians. A center for Paul's missionary work, it was also the base of a John-the-Baptist sect (Acts 19:1–7). If the Gospel originated in a territory where the Baptist was viewed as Jesus' superior, it would explain the writer's severe limitation of John's role in the messianic drama, denying that he represents Elijah and reducing his function to a mere "voice" bearing witness to Jesus (1:6–9, 19–28).

Some critics once believed that John's Gospel was composed late in the second century (when Christian authors first mention it), but tiny manuscript fragments of John discovered in the Egyptian desert have been dated at about 125 and 150 C.E., making them the oldest surviving copy of a New Testament book. Allowing time for the Gospel to have circulated abroad as far as Egypt, the work could not have originated much later than about 100 C.E. The Gospel's references to believers being expelled from Jewish synagogues (9:22, 34–35)—a process that began about 85 or 90 C.E.—suggest that the decisive break between Church and synagogue was already in effect when the Gospel was written. Hence, the Gospel is usually dated between about 90 and 100 C.E.

Differences in John's Portrait of Jesus

Although John's Gospel contains a few close verbal parallels to Mark's (e.g., John 6:7 and Mark 6:37; John 12:3, 5 and Mark 14:3, 5), indicating that the author was familiar with the Synoptic tradition, he takes such a fresh and novel approach that most scholars conclude that the fourth Gospel does not depend on the earlier accounts. Concentrating on Jesus as a heavenly revealer of ultimate truth, John presents his hero not as a vulnerable man of sorrows but as a divine being who projects his heavenly radiance even while walking the earth.

The following passage lists a dozen of the principal differences between John and the Synoptic accounts, along with brief suggestions about the author's possible reasons for omitting so many characteristic Synoptic themes. (See also "Representative Examples of Material Found Only in John" on page 369.)

1. John has no birth story or reference to Jesus' virginal conception, perhaps because he sees Christ as the eternal Word (**Logos**) who "became flesh" (1:1, 14) as the man Jesus of Nazareth. John's doctrine of the **Incarnation** (the spiritual Logos becoming physically human) makes the manner of Jesus' human conception irrelevant.

2. John includes no record of Jesus' baptism by John, emphasizing Jesus' independence of and superiority to the Baptist.

3. John reports no period of contemplation in the Judean wilderness or temptation by Satan. His Jesus possesses a vital unity with the Father that makes worldly temptation impossible.

Representative Examples of Material Found Only in John

1. Doctrine of the Logos: Before coming to earth, Jesus preexisted in heaven, where he was God's mediator in creating the universe (1:1–18).

2. Miracle at Cana: Jesus changes water into wine (the first "sign") (2:1–12).

3. Doctrine of spiritual rebirth: conversation with Nicodemus (3:1–21; see also 7:50–52; 19:39).

4. Jesus is the water of eternal life: conversation with the Samaritan woman (4:1–42).

5. Jesus heals the invalid at Jerusalem's Sheep Pool (5:1–47).

6. The "I am" sayings: Jesus speaks as divine Wisdom revealed from above, equating himself with objects or concepts of great symbolic value, such as "the bread of life" (6:22–66), "the good shepherd" (10:1–21), "the resurrection and the life" (11:25), "the way," "the truth" (14:6), and "the true vine" (15:1–17).

7. Jesus, light of the world, existed before Abraham (8:12–59).

8. Cure of the man born blind: debate between church and synagogue (9:1–41).

9. The resurrection of Lazarus (the seventh "sign") (11:1–12:11).

10. A different tradition of the Last Supper: washing the disciples' feet (13:1–20) and delivering the farewell discourses; promise of the Paraclete, the Spirit that will empower the disciples and interpret the meaning of Jesus' life (13:31–17:26).

11. Resurrection appearances in or near Jerusalem to Mary Magdalene and the disciples, including Thomas (20:1–29).

12. Resurrection appearances in Galilee to Peter and to the Beloved Disciple (21:1–23).

---

4. John never mentions Jesus' exorcisms, preferring to show Jesus overcoming Evil through his personal revelation of divine truth rather than through the casting out of demons (which plays so large a role in Mark's and Matthew's report of his ministry).

5. Although he reports some friction between Jesus and his brothers (7:1–6), John does not reproduce the Markan tradition that Jesus' family thought he was mentally unbalanced or that his neighbors at Nazareth viewed him as nothing extraordinary (Mark 3:20–21, 31–35; 6:1–6). In John, Jesus meets considerable opposition, but he is always too commanding and powerful a figure to be ignored or devalued.

6. John presents Jesus' teaching in a form radically different from that of the Synoptics. Both Mark and Matthew state that Jesus "never" taught without using parables (Mark 4:34; Matt. 13:34), but John does not record a single parable of the Synoptic type (involving homely images of agricultural or domestic life). Instead of brief anecdotes and vivid comparisons, the Johannine Jesus delivers long philosophical speeches in which Jesus' own nature is typically the subject of discussion. In John, he speaks both publicly and privately in this manner, in Galilee as well as in Jerusalem.

7. John includes none of Jesus' reinterpretations of the Mosaic law, the main topic of Jesus' Synoptic discourses. Instead of the many ethical directives about divorce, Sabbath keeping, ending the law of retaliation, and forgiving enemies that we find in Mark, Matthew, and Luke, John records only one "new commandment"—to love. In both the Gospel and the letters, this is Jesus' single explicit directive; in the Johannine community, mutual love among "friends" is the sole distinguishing mark of true discipleship (13:34–35, 15:9–17).

8. Conspicuously absent from John's Gospel is any prediction of Jerusalem's fall, a concern that dominated the Synopticists' imagination (Mark 13; Matt. 24–25; Luke 21).

Characters Introduced in John or Given New Emphasis

- Andrew, Peter's brother, as a speaking character (1:40–42, 44; 6:8–9; 12:20–22)
- Philip, one of the Twelve (1:43–49; 6:5–7; 12:20–22; 14:8–11)
- Nathanael, one of the Twelve (1:45–51)
- Mary, as a participator in Jesus' ministry (2:1–5); at the cross (19:25–27)
- Nicodemus, a leading Pharisee (3:1–12; 7:50–52; 19:39)
- A Samaritan woman (4:7–42)
- A paralyzed man cured in Jerusalem (5:1–15)
- Jesus' unbelieving "brothers" (7:2–10)
- The woman taken in adultery (8:3–11; an appendix to John in NEB)
- A man born blind (9:1–38)
- Lazarus, brother of Mary and Martha (11:1–44; 12:1–11)
- An unidentified disciple whom "Jesus loved" (13:23–26; 18:15–16; 19:26–27; 20:2–10; 21:7, 20–24)
- Annas, father-in-law of Caiaphas, the High Priest (18:12–14, 19–24)

9. Nor does John contain a prophecy of Jesus' Second Coming, substituting a view that Jesus is already present among believers in the form of the Paraclete, the Holy Spirit that serves as Christians' Helper, Comforter, or Advocate (14:25–26; 16:7–15). To John, Jesus' first coming means that believers have life now (5:21–26, 11:25–27). Presenting a **realized eschatology**, a belief that events usually associated with the eschaton (world's End) are even now realized or fulfilled by Jesus' spiritual presence among believers, John does not stress a future apocalyptic return.

10. Although he represents the sacramental bread and wine as life-giving symbols, John does not preserve a communion ritual or the institution of a new covenant between Jesus and his followers at the Last Supper. Stating that the meal took place a day before Passover, John substitutes Jesus' act of humble service—washing the disciples' feet—for the Eucharist (13:1–16).

11. As his Jesus cannot be tempted, so John's Christ undergoes no agony before his arrest in the Garden of Gethsemane. Unfailingly poised and confident, Jesus experiences his painful death as a glorification, his raising on the cross symbolizing his imminent ascension to heaven. Instead of uttering a cry of despair, as portrayed in Mark, in John, Jesus dies with a declaration that he has "accomplished" his life's purpose (19:30).

12. Finally, it must be emphasized that John's many differences from the Synoptics do not simply result from the author's attempting to "fill in" the gaps in his predecessors' Gospels. By carefully examining John's account, readers discover that he does not write to supplement earlier narratives about Jesus but that both his omissions and inclusions are determined almost exclusively by the writer's special theological convictions (20:30–31; 21:25). From his opening hymn praising the eternal Word to Jesus' promised reascension to heaven, every part of the Gospel is calculated to illustrate Jesus' splendor as God's fullest revelation of his own ineffable Being.

Differences in Chronology and Order of Events

Although John's essential story resembles the Synoptic version of Jesus' life—a public ministry featuring healing and other miracles followed by official rejection, arrest, crucifixion, and resurrection—the fourth Gospel presents important differences in the chronology and order of events. (See "Characters Introduced in John or Given New Emphasis" on this page.)

Significant ways in which John's narrative sequence differs from the Synoptic order include the following:

1. The Synoptics show Jesus working mainly in Galilee and coming south to Judea only during his last days. By contrast, John has Jesus traveling back-and-forth between Galilee and Jerusalem throughout the duration of his ministry.

2. The Synoptics place Jesus' assault on the Temple at the end of his career, making it the incident that consolidates official hostility toward him; John sets it at the beginning (2: 13–21).

3. The Synoptics agree that Jesus began his mission after John the Baptist's imprisonment, but John states that their missions overlapped (3:23–4:3).

4. The earlier Gospels mention only one Passover and imply that Jesus' career lasted only about a year; John refers to three Passovers (2: 13, 6:4, 11:55), thus giving the ministry a duration of three to nearly four years.

5. Unlike the Synoptics, which present the Last Supper as a Passover celebration, John states that Jesus' final meal with the disciples occurred the evening before Passover and that the crucifixion took place on Nisan 14, the day of preparation when paschal lambs were being sacrificed (13:1, 29; 18:28; 19:14). Many historians believe that John's chronology is the more accurate; it is improbable that Jesus' arrest, trial, and execution took place on Nisan 15, the most sacred time of the Passover observance.

John's Purpose and Method

Relation to Gnostic Ideas   John's stated intent is to elicit belief in his community's distinctively high Christology (17:3–5; 20:30–31), but other purposes can also be inferred from studying the text. Although he emphasizes Jesus' supernatural character, John also refutes Gnostic Christians who view Christ as pure spirit. A widespread and extremely diverse movement in early Christianity, **Gnosticism** argues that believers gain salvation through a special knowledge (*gnosis*) revealed through a spiritual Savior, presumably Jesus. Gnostic thinkers are dualists, viewing the world as composed of two mutually exclusive realms. The invisible world of spirit is pure and good, whereas the physical world is inherently evil, the inferior creation of a lesser god, whom some Gnostics identify with Yahweh. The divine redeemer who descends from heaven to bring saving knowledge to a spiritual elite belongs entirely to the spirit realm. Hence, some Christian Gnostics argued that Jesus only *seemed* to be human. Docetists (a name taken from the Greek verb "to seem") concluded that Christ was wholly spiritual, uncontaminated by a material body. At the crucifixion, he ascended to heaven, leaving behind another's corpse on the cross.

Although he uses typically Gnostic terms, John avoids Gnosticism's extremism by insisting on Jesus' physical humanity (1:14). Even after resurrection, Jesus displays fleshly wounds and consumes ordinary food (Chs. 20–21). To show that Jesus was a mortal person who truly died, John eliminates from his Passion story the tradition that Simon of Cyrene carried Jesus' cross (lest the reader think that Simon might have been substituted for Jesus at the crucifixion). John also introduces an incident in which a Roman soldier pierces Jesus' side, confirming physical death (19:34–35).

Despite including details to refute Gnostic beliefs, John also contains statements expressing classic Gnostic ideas. Knowing the divine Beings—Father and Son—is equated with "eternal life" (17:3). The assertion that the "spirit alone gives life; the flesh is of no avail" (6:63) and the unique emphasis on spiritual rebirth (Ch. 3) strikingly parallel Gnostic concepts.

Role of the Paraclete   Another of the author's implied goals is to picture Jesus as revealed through the Paraclete. A term found only in John's Gospel, the Paraclete is the Holy Spirit that Jesus bestows on his followers after his death. Variously translated as "Advocate," "Helper," "Comforter" or "Spirit of Truth," the Paraclete functions as a substitute for Jesus' own presence, his surrogate among the disciples. In John's view, the Paraclete inspires his community to continue Jesus' miraculous works of healing; it answers their prayers for power and knowledge; it provides defenses against their opponents' hostile criticism; and—most important for the presentation of Jesus' life and teachings—it enables the "brotherhood" to explain and interpret Jesus' full theological significance (14:12–26).

One of the Paraclete's main purposes is to unveil Jesus' true likeness, to portray the spiritual reality hidden during his human incarnation. Thus, John represents Jesus as saying that "he [the Paraclete] will glorify me," revealing Jesus' cosmic splendor to the author's privileged group (16:12–15). John's community thus creates a portrait of Jesus that not only preserves traditions about his historical ministry but also uses the insights into his character and nature that the Paraclete discloses to them. In John's Gospel, the author's task is not to record external facts about his subject's earthly biography but to fashion a picture of Jesus that duplicates what the Paraclete reveals. Because the Paraclete's function is to define Jesus' glory—both its heavenly origin and its continuing presence on earth—John's account must meet the formidable challenge of portraying the "true" Jesus, allowing his celestial radiance to shine through the man of flesh and history. (Compare John's method with Luke's similar implication that Jesus' real story can be told only in terms of his post-resurrection divinity [Luke 24:25–27, 44–53].)

John's portrait of Jesus is thus painted with supernal colors chosen by the Paraclete. His subject's self-revealing speeches, long metaphysical discourses—so different from the short, vivid pronouncements in Mark and Luke—appear to have a similar origin. Most scholars find it virtually impossible to detect the voice of the historical Jesus in the Johannine speeches; rather than being attempts to reconstruct Jesus' re-

membered words, they are confessions of faith in his divine nature and cosmic stature. As they stand in the Gospel, they are largely the author's creation—sublime tributes to Jesus' unique role in human redemption.

Jesus As Divine Wisdom

In the prolog (1:1–18), John identifies the human Jesus with the Logos (Word). A philosophical term since the time of Heraclitus (born before 500 B.C.E.), in John's day Logos was a concept that Stoic philosophers used to denote the principle of cosmic reason, the intelligent force that orders and sustains the universe, making it accessible and intelligible to the human mind. Greek philosophy also saw the Logos as a creative power that had formed the cosmos (world order) out of the original chaos (dark void). In the Hebrew biblical tradition, a similar concept developed. According to Proverbs (8: 22–31), Yahweh had **Wisdom**, personified as a gracious young woman, as his companion when he created the world. She not only was Yahweh's intimate helper in the creative process but also served as God's channel of communication with humanity. In later manifestations of this biblical idea, Wisdom became both the agent or means of creation and the revealer of the divine mind (Ecclus. 24; Wisd. of Sol. 6:12–9:18).

These parallel Greek and Hebrew ideas converge in the writings of **Philo Judaeus**, a Jewish scholar who lived in Alexandria during the first century C.E. A pious Jew profoundly influenced by Greek thought, Philo attempted to reconcile Hellenic logic with the revelation contained in the Hebrew Bible. Philo used the Hebrew concept of Wisdom as the creative intermediary between the transcendent Creator and the material creation, but he employed the Greek term *Logos* to designate its role and function (Philo may have preferred *Logos* because it is masculine in Greek, whereas *Wisdom* [*Sophia*] is feminine.) Philo's interpretation can be illustrated by an allegoric reading of Genesis 1, in which God's first act is to speak—create the

Word (Logos)—by which power heaven and earth come into being.

Echoing the Genesis creation account, John adapts Philo's doctrine to identify Jesus, in his prehuman existence, with the divine Logos that formed the universe (1:1–5, 9–14). The heavenly Logos then "became flesh" (1:14) to walk the earth as Jesus of Nazareth, the embodiment of God's creative Wisdom. With this statement of the **Incarnation** (the spiritual Logos becoming the man Jesus), John asserts his hero's innate superiority to all other divine messengers, whether angels or prophets, including John the Baptist. Jesus not only speaks the Word of God; he *is* that Word and reveals the divine nature fully.

The Book of Signs: Miracles Revealing Divinity

John organizes his account of Jesus' public ministry around seven miracles or "signs," among which he inserts long discourses and dialogs, including several "I am" sayings (2:1–11:57). (For a summary of the signs, see "The Book of Signs" on page 374.) The first sign occurs at the Galilean town of Cana, where Jesus contributes to the merriment of a wedding party by changing water into wine (2:1–11). This miracle, found only in John, is followed by the cleansing of the Temple in Jerusalem (2:13–22). John's reversal of the Synoptic order, placing the Temple incident at the beginning of his narrative, probably serves to express his conviction that Jesus is now the true Sanctuary, the living abode of God's spirit.

Jesus' conversation with **Nicodemus**, a Pharisee and member of the Sanhedrin, typifies John's method of presenting Jesus' teaching (3:1–21). In most of the Johannine dialogs, Jesus uses a figure of speech that someone misinterprets, causing Jesus to explain his metaphoric language in a long monolog that typically culminates in a meditation on his nature and unique relationship with the Father. Nicodemus takes Jesus' reference to spiritual rebirth literally, triggering a metaphysical discourse on Jesus' heavenly origin and role as "Light of the world."

John shares with Luke a tradition about Jesus' special concern for women and outsiders. These interests coincide in Chapter 4, in which Jesus scandalizes his male disciples by holding a public conversation with a Samaritan woman of questionable reputation. Note that Jesus selects this person—foreign, "immoral," a heretic, and a woman—to serve as his first non-Jewish prophet. Through her, "many Samaritans" become believers. Similar themes appear in the anecdote that concerns a woman about to be stoned for adultery. Although absent from many New Testament manuscripts and relegated to an appendix in the New English Bible, this episode (7:1–11) well illustrates Jesus' compassion for the powerless and oppressed.

The second miraculous sign takes place when Jesus, again in Cana, cures the dying son of a Roman centurion (4:46–54), the second non-Jew to whom he brings comfort. The third sign takes place when Jesus heals a chronic invalid (5:2–9) at the sheep-gate pool in Jerusalem, the significance of which appears in the discourse that follows (5:19–47). Here Jesus describes the Son's intimacy with the Father, who has committed powers of judgment and forgiveness to him.

The fourth sign is Jesus' feeding of the 5000, the only miracle that appears in all four Gospels (6:1–12; Mark 6:30–44; Matt. 14:13–21; Luke 9:10–17). In John, this event symbolizes Jesus' providing the world with spiritual nourishment (6:25–59), although, as usual in this Gospel, Jesus' hearers misunderstand his intent. This time they forcibly attempt to make him king (6:15), not realizing that his kingdom "does not belong to this world" (18:36). A fifth sign, Jesus' walking on water, quickly follows, demonstrating the Son's power over nature (6:16–21).

Jesus and Yahweh: The "I Am" Sayings This section contains the first of Jesus' "I am" pronouncements. Scholars believe that these discourses are modeled not on recollections of his actual words but on Wisdom's speeches in the

---

The Book of Signs

Many scholars believe that the author of John's Gospel used an earlier narrative of Jesus' miraculous deeds known as the Signs Gospel. The author's hypothetical source contained accounts of the following miracles (listed here in the Johannine order):

1. Turning water into wine at Cana (in Galilee, 2:1–11)
2. Healing an official's son (in Galilee, 2:12a; 4:46b–54)
3. Healing a crippled man (in Jerusalem, 5:2–9)

4. Feeding 5000 people (in Galilee, 6:1–15)
5. Walking on water (in Galilee, 6:16–25)
6. Restoring sight to a blind man (in Jerusalem, 9:1–8)
7. Raising Lazarus from the dead (near Jerusalem, 11:1–45)

Some scholars also think that the disciples' huge catch of fish (21:1–14) was originally a Galilean miracle that the Gospel's final editor incorporated into his appended account of Jesus' postresurrection appearances.

Hebrew Bible. Hebrew writers typically picture Wisdom speaking in the first person, using the phrase "I am" and then defining her activities as God's agent. John casts many of Jesus' discourses in exactly the same form, beginning with a declaration "I am" and then equating himself with a term of great religious significance. Compare some of Wisdom's utterances with those of the Johannine Jesus:

> The Lord created me the beginning of his works,
> before all else that he made, long ago.
> Alone I was fashioned in times long past,
> at the beginning, long before earth itself.
> *Proverbs 8:22–23*

Identifying Wisdom with God's verbal command to create light (Gen. 1:3), the author of Ecclesiasticus represents her as saying,

> I am the word which was spoken by the
>   Most High; . . .
> Before time began he created me,
> and I shall remain for ever. . . .
> *Ecclesiasticus 24:3, 9*

Sent by God to live among his people, Israel, Wisdom invites all to seek her favor:

> Come to me, you who desire me,
> and eat your fill of my fruit; . . .

> Whoever feeds on me will be hungry for more,
> and whoever drinks from me will thirst for more.
> *Ecclesiasticus 24:19, 21–22*

The Johannine Jesus echoes Wisdom's promise even while fulfilling it:

> Everyone who drinks this water [of Jacob's well] will be thirsty again, but whoever drinks the water that I shall give him will never suffer thirst any more. The water that I shall give him will be an inner spring always welling up for eternal life.
> *John 4:13–15*

Besides associating Jesus with the principle of eternal Wisdom, John's "I am" speeches also express an important aspect of his Christology. They echo Yahweh's declaration of being to Moses (Exod. 3:14), in which God reveals his sacred personal name. In the Hebrew Bible, only Yahweh speaks of himself (the "I Am") in this manner. Hence, Jesus' reiterated "I am . . . the bread of life" (6:35), "the good shepherd" (10:11), "the resurrection and the life" (11:25), or "the way," "the truth," and "the life" (14:6) stress his unity with god, the eternal "I am."

John attributes much of "the Jews'" hostility to his hero to their reaction against Jesus' apparent claim to divinity. When Jesus refers publicly to his prehuman existence, declaring that "be-

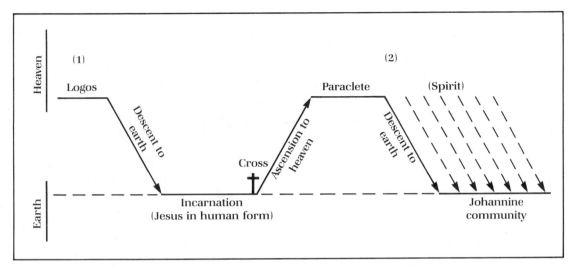

John's concept of the Incarnation (the Word made flesh). Note that Jesus' ascension to heaven (return to his place of spiritual origin) is followed by a descent of the Paraclete, Jesus' Spirit—an invisible surrogate that inspires the Johannine brotherhood. Whereas Jesus' human presence on earth was brief, John implies that the Paraclete abides permanently with the believing community.

This Ravenna mosaic shows Jesus conversing with a Samaritan woman drawing water from Jacob's well (John 2). Both Luke and John emphasize Jesus' characteristic concern for women. (Courtesy of Alinari/Art Resource, NY)

fore Abraham was born, I am," his outraged audience in the Temple attempts to stone him for blasphemy (8:56–59). Many scholars doubt that Jesus really made such assertions. According to this view, the attempted stoning represents Jewish leaders' response to the preaching of John's community, which made extraordinarily high claims about Jesus' divine status.

John's Double Vision   John's presentation of the sixth sign—restoring sight to a man born blind (9:1–41)—illustrates what some scholars refer to as the author's double vision or two-level drama. Careful analysis of this long passage suggests that the Evangelist is combining traditions about the miracles of the historical Jesus with healing activities of his own time and community. The two elements—Jesus and his later disciples—can be equated because the same Paraclete operates through both parties. Because Jesus had promised that his followers would accomplish "greater things" than the human Jesus had (14:12), the author's group could perceive their Master's continuing presence in their own ministry. In John's imaginative conflation of history, the human Jesus of the past and the believers of the present perform the same Spirit-empowered work.

In the episode of the man born blind, John skillfully combines historical past and present to tell his story. Notice that Jesus' miracle is followed by a series of debates and confrontations between the cured man, his parents, and officials of the synagogue. The Jewish officials' interrogation of the man reproduces circumstances prevailing not in Jesus' day but in the writer's own time, when Torah authorities cross-examined Jews suspected of regarding Jesus as the Jewish Messiah. Note, also, the references to the expulsion of Jesus' followers from the synagogue (9:23, 34), a situation that did not develop until well after Jerusalem's fall in 70 C.E.

The conversation with Nicodemus (Ch. 3) offers a similar blending of Jesus' past actions with the Johannine community's ongoing ministry. Jesus' pretended astonishment that one of Israel's most eminent teachers does not understand the Spirit that motivates Jesus' followers reflects the late first-century debate between the Jewish authorities and the author's group. Using the first-person plural "we" to signify the whole believing community, John affirms that his community experiences the Spirit's power, while "you" (the disbelieving opponents) refuse to credit the Johannine testimony (3:9–11). The reader will also observe that in this dialog Jesus speaks as if he has already returned to heaven (3:13), again expressing a belief held by the author's community.

Resurrection of Lazarus   The seventh and most spectacular sign—raising **Lazarus** from the dead (11:1–44)—demonstrates another Johannine conviction, that Jesus is the source of everlasting life. Concluding the Book of Signs, this episode connects the story of Jesus' ministry with his imminent Passion and resurrection. As John presents it, Jesus' ability to raise a man who has been dead for four days is the act that consolidates priestly opposition to him and leads directly to his death (11:45–53).

Although no other canonical Gospel mentions the climactic Lazarus event, John may draw on a primitive resurrection story that appears in an Egyptian edition of Mark. Discovered in 1958, this fragment called "Secret Mark" is quoted in a letter by Clement of Alexandria (about 200 C.E.). Secret Mark describes Jesus' resurrecting a rich youth whom he then initiates into the "mystery of the kingdom of God." According to Clement, the excerpt would appear in canonical Mark between verses 10:34 and 35. Although present editions of the Synoptics are silent about the episode, Secret Mark indicates that a version of John's resurrection story was once part of the Synoptic tradition.

Whatever the historical foundation of the Lazarus incident, John uses it to illustrate his theme of realized eschatology—that in Jesus' activity and presence events normally relegated to the End of time are now taking place. In a climactic "I am" speech, Jesus declares, "I am the resurrection and I am life. If a man has faith in me, even though he die, he shall come to life; and no one who is alive and has faith shall ever die" (11:25).

Faced with overwhelming evidence of Jesus' eschatological powers, the Jerusalem opposition resolves to eliminate him. The priests fear that if the Jewish people accept his messiahship (making him "king of the Jews"), their response will incite the Romans to destroy their state. (This passage refers to the Roman destruction of Jerusalem in 70 C.E.) The remark attributed to Caiaphas, the high priest—that "it is more to your interest that one man should die for the people, than that the whole nation should be destroyed" (11:50)—is deeply ironic in unwittingly expressing the Christian belief that Jesus redeems the world through his death.

The Book of Glory

In the second part of his Gospel, John pictures Jesus' final days in a way that transforms the Messiah's betrayal and suffering into a glorious triumph. After a joyous entry into Jerusalem, Jesus foretells his death in terms resembling Mark's description of the agony in Gethsemane but reinterpreted to stress the crucifixion's saving purpose: "Now my soul is in turmoil, and what am I to say? Father, save me from this hour [cf. Mark 14:32–36]. No, it was for this that I came to this hour. Father, glorify thy name" (12:27–28). When a celestial voice affirms that God is glorified in Christ's actions, Jesus interprets his "lifting up" (crucifixion) as God's predestined means of drawing all people to him, a process of human salvation that cannot occur without his death (12:28–33).

Jesus' Farewell Speeches   Chapters 13–17 contain Jesus' farewell discourses delivered at the Last Supper. John's account differs significantly from the Synoptic tradition, omitting all references to the communal bread and wine or a new covenant and presenting instead Jesus'

washing his disciples' feet (13:3–17). Note that John links this act of humble service to Jesus' foreknowledge of his imminent return to the Father and his "new commandment"—to love others in the way he has loved his own (13:1, 3, 34–35). In contrast to the many ethical directives found in the Synoptics, the Johannine tradition preserves only this single command (see also 15:11–14).

A Johannine composition, the farewell speeches (13:31–17:26) emphasize Jesus' unity with the Father and the work of the Paraclete, or "Spirit of Truth" (14:16–17). An invisible counterpart of Jesus, the Paraclete enables his disciples to understand the true significance of Jesus' teaching (16:1–15). By implication, the Paraclete also empowers the author to create a Gospel that fully portrays Jesus' glory.

In John's view, Jesus imparts the promised Paraclete (Advocate, or Spirit) at his resurrection, merely by breathing on the disciples and saying, "Receive the Holy Spirit" (20:21–23). The risen Lord's action recalls the creation scene in Genesis 2 when Yahweh breathes into Adam's nostrils "the breath of life," making him an animate being. As his Gospel begins with the Word creating the universe (1:1–5), so it closes with the Word breathing the pure spirit of life into his renewed human creation.

As he fixes the date of the Last Supper on the day before Passover (the slaying of the Passover lambs at that time suggests the symbolization of Jesus as God's sacrificial lamb), so John presents a version of Jesus' Passion that differs significantly from that in the Synoptics. Instead of appearing before the entire Sanhedrin (Mark 14), Jesus is examined secretly at the residence of **Annas**, father-in-law of the high priest Caiaphas. Many historians believe that John's account of an impromptu session in Annas' private quarters is more plausible than the Synoptic version of a full-scale (but probably illegal) Sanhedrin trial.

Although John parallels the Synoptics in citing prophetic fulfillments in the crucifixion scene (18:9, 32; 19:24, 29), he is the only Evan-

The Crucifixion *by Matthias Grunewald (c. 1470–1528). Painted on wood, this small version of Jesus' tortured death heightens the sense of the sufferer's physical pain and grief. Although his emphasis on Jesus' agony reflects Mark's account, Grunewald follows John's Gospel in showing Jesus' mother and the beloved disciple (as well as another Mary) present at the cross. (Courtesy of the National Gallery of Art, Washington, D.C. Samuel H. Kress Collection.)*

gelist to include the incident of the Roman soldier's spear thrust into Jesus' side. The blood and water pouring from Jesus express the typical Johannine themes that Christ is the source of salvation, his blood the sacramental wine, and the water a symbol of baptism and truth.

Postresurrection Appearances John's resurrection account also reveals his distinctive concerns.

Only John includes the race between Peter and the beloved disciple (the only male follower present at the crucifixion) to confirm Mary Magdalene's report of the empty sepulcher (Ch. 20). Only he reports Thomas's skepticism and subsequent confession of Jesus' divinity. To John, Jesus' resurrection is the final victorious "sign" toward which all his earlier miracles pointed.

Most scholars believe that Chapter 21, which

presents traditions about Jesus' posthumous appearances in Galilee, is the work of an editor, who may have prepared the Gospel manuscript for publication. This epilog reiterates the theme of differences between Peter, who represents the apostolic Church, and the beloved disciple, who represents the author's community, noting Jesus' distinctive messages to each. The Gospel ends with the editor's musing over the vast oral tradition surrounding Jesus. If his entire career were to be recorded in detail, the "whole world" could not contain "the vast number of books that would be produced" (21:25).

More than any other single book in the New Testament, John's Gospel lays the foundations for later theological interpretations of Christ's nature and function. In post–New Testament times, theologians came to interpret such Johannine statements as "the Father and I are one" as equating Christ and God. This high Christology viewed Jesus as the Second Person in the **Trinity** (a term that does not appear in canonical Scripture), coequal, cosubstantial, and coeternal with the Father. Although the Johannine writings do not articulate so formal a dogma, historically John's portrait of Jesus' divinity influenced Christendom's eventual understanding of its Master.

RECOMMENDED READING

Brodie, Thomas L. *The Quest for the Origin of John's Gospel: A Source-Oriented Approach.* New York: Oxford University Press, 1993. Argues that John composed his Gospel by theologically transforming the Synoptic accounts.

Brown, R. E. *The Gospel According to John,* vols. 29 and 29a of the Anchor Bible. Garden City, N.Y.: Doubleday, 1966 and 1970. Provides the most complete historical and theological background and the most thorough commentary on John's Gospel.

———. *The Community of the Beloved Disciple.* New York: Paulist Press, 1979. A readable and insightful study of the Christian group that produced the Gospel and the Letters of John.

———. *The Epistles of John,* Vol 30 of the Anchor Bible. Garden City, N.Y.: Doubleday, 1982. A thoroughly annotated edition.

Bultmann, Rudolf. *The Gospel of John.* Translated by G. R. Beasley-Murray. Philadelphia: Westminster Press, 1971. A somewhat dated but seminal interpretation.

Dodd, C. H. *Historical Tradition in the Fourth Gospel.* Cambridge: Cambridge University Press, 1963.

———. *The Interpretation of the Fourth Gospel.* Cambridge: University Press, 1965.

Fortna, R. T. *The Fourth Gospel and Its Predecessor: From Narrative Source to Present Gospel.* Philadelphia: Fortress Press, 1988. The definitive analysis of the hypothetical Signs source underlying John's Gospel.

Kysar, Robert. *John, the Maverick Gospel.* Atlanta: John Knox Press, 1976. An influential study of the Fourth Gospel.

———. "John, Epistles of." In D. N. Freedman, ed., *The Anchor Bible Dictionary,* Vol. 3, pp. 900–912. New York: Doubleday, 1992. Relates circumstances of the Gospel's composition to later epistles.

———. "John, the Gospel of." In D. N. Freedman, ed., *The Anchor Bible Dictionary,* Vol. 3, pp. 912–931. New York: Doubleday, 1992. A thoughtful review of Johannine literature and scholarship.

Martyn, J. L. *History and Theology in the Fourth Gospel,* 2nd ed. Nashville, Tenn.: Abingdon Press, 1979. A brilliant interpretation of John's method of composition that focuses on John 9.

Miller, Robert J., ed. *The Complete Gospels.* Sonoma, Calif.: Polebridge Press, 1992.

Olson, A. M., ed. *Myth, Symbol and Reality.* Notre Dame, Ind.: University of Notre Dame Press, 1981. Includes essays on the Logos.

Perkins, Pheme. "The Gospel According to John." In R. E. Brown et al., eds., *The New Jerome Biblical Commentary.* Englewood Cliffs, N.J.: Prentice Hall, 1990, pp. 942–985. An insightful commentary on the Gospel.

———. "The Johannine Epistles." In R. E. Brown et al., eds., *The New Jerome Biblical Commentary.* Englewood Cliffs, N.J.: Prentice Hall, 1990, pp. 986–995.

Schnackenburg, Rudolf. *The Gospel According to John,* vols. 1–3. Various translators. New York: Seabury Press, 1980, and Crossroads, 1982. Challenging but insightful analysis.

TERMS AND CONCEPTS
TO REMEMBER

Transfiguration
Trinity
Twelve, the

Wisdom
Zebedee
Zechariah

Andrew
Annas
apocalypse
baptism
Barabbas
Bartholomew
Beatitudes
beloved disciple
Bethlehem
Caesarea Philippi
Caiaphas
Capernaum
Cephas
Christ
Christology
codex
disciple
Elisabeth
epiphany
Eucharist
Evangelist
exegesis
exorcism
Gabriel
Galilee
Gehenna
Gethsemane
Gnosticism
Gospel
Haggadah
Halakah
Hannah
Herod Antipas
Holy Spirit
Incarnation
Jairus
James (Apostle)
James (Jesus' kinsman)
James (son of
    Alphaeus)
John (Apostle)
John the Baptist

Joseph of Arimathaea
Judas (Iscariot)
Lazarus
Logos
Luke
Mark (John Mark)
Mary
Mary of Magdala
    (Mary Magdalene)
Matthew
Messiah
Midrash
Mount of Olives
Nazareth
Nicodemus
parable
Paraclete
Parousia
Passion
Passover
pericope
Peter
Philip
Philo Judaeus
Pontius Pilate
Q (*Quelle*)
Samaria
Samaritan
Sanhedrin
Satan
Simon (the
    Canaanite)
Simon (of Cyrene)
Son of Man
sons of thunder
    (*Boanerges*)
Synoptic Problem
Synoptics
Thaddeus
Theophilus
Thomas
tradition

The Continuing Quest for the Historical Jesus

Because the Evangelists present Jesus' life almost exclusively in theological terms and non-Christian first-century writers refer only briefly to his existence, scholars face a formidable challenge in trying to distinguish the Jesus of history from the Christ of faith. In their ongoing quest to recover the historical Jesus, scholars have developed criteria by which they hope to evaluate the authenticity of words and actions that the early church ascribed to Jesus. Although most scholars generally agree on a methodology for screening traditions to find Jesus' authentic voice, they have reached strikingly different conclusions about his essential teachings and self-identity, particularly on the issue of his eschatology.

After reading four different accounts of Jesus' ministry—all of which are believers' tributes to his supernatural identity—students may wonder who the "real" Jesus of Nazareth may have been. Comparing Mark's Gospel with that of John, attentive readers see a great disparity in the way the two Evangelists present their subject: In Mark, Jesus is primarily an exorcist and healer who teaches, in brief parables and vivid figures of speech, about God's dawning rule. Framing Jesus' message in terms of an imminent eschatological judgment, Mark emphasizes a gradually revealed messiahship of human weakness and suffering.

In John, neither Jesus' innate divinity nor ultimate triumph are ever in doubt: He is proclaimed God's sacrificial "lamb" from the outset of his public career. The Johannine Jesus performs no exorcisms and creates no parables. Instead of earthy similes based on peasant life, he speaks in extended monologs about the mystery of his divine nature and his journeys from and back to heaven. To many, John's picture of an omniscient incarnation of celestial Wisdom is irresistible. His vision of Christ, a paradigm of cosmic power and absolute certainty, is probably the one that most attracts believers.

For all its spiritual appeal, however, John's depiction of Jesus' character and teaching seems too focused on the glory of the risen Christ to offer a realistic assessment of the historical person. Even Mark, with its emphasis on demonic possession, the impending *eschaton,* and Jesus' foreknowledge of the precise circumstances of his death, appears far removed from the normal standards of historicity.

New Testament scholars recognize that the Gospel authors do not attempt to record an objective, purely factual biography of Jesus but in their individual ways *interpret him theologically*. Aware of this fact, students often ask if it is possible to find the authentic man amid the sometimes conflicting sayings and deeds that the Evangelists attribute to their hero. Are there any "unbiased" historical sources that give us reliable information about the human Jesus?

Early Historical References to Jesus

Unfortunately, non-Christian writers tell us almost nothing about the Nazarene except that he existed, was crucified under Pilate, and inspired a new religious movement in the Roman Empire. The earliest writer to mention Jesus is Tacitus, a Roman senator and historian of the first century C.E., who seems to have based his report largely on secondhand evidence. His single allusion to Jesus is tantalizingly brief, stating merely that Jesus "had been executed in Tiberius's reign by the governor of Judea, Pontius Pilate" (*Annals* 15.44). Tacitus's statements about Jesus and his followers are incidental to the historian's main purpose—illustrating the cruelty and corruption of Nero, who tried to blame the Christians for a great fire that consumed much of Rome about 64 C.E.:

Nero had self-acknowledged Christians arrested. Then, on their information, large numbers of others were condemned—not so much for incendiarism as for their anti-social tendencies. Their deaths were made farcical. Dressed in wild animals' skins, they were torn to pieces by dogs, or crucified, or made into torches to be ignited after dark as substitutes for daylight. . . . Despite their guilt as Christians, and the ruthless punishment it deserved, the victims were pitied. For it was felt that they were being sacrificed to one man's brutality rather than to the national interest. (*Annals* 15.44)

Nero's persecution, which was apparently confined to the imperial capital, represents the Roman government's first official recognition of the new faith. That even an enlightened author such as Tacitus could regard Christians as so "notoriously depraved" that they deserved the death penalty indicates the extent to which Rome's ruling classes misunderstood the Jesus movement. Given first-century officialdom's ignorance of early Christian beliefs, it is likely that few educated non-Christians were in a position to know the facts of Jesus' life and teachings.

Suetonius, another Roman historian, records that, even before Nero, the emperor **Claudius** (reigned 41–54 C.E.) had expelled the Jews from Rome because of trouble arising from "Chrestus" (probably a variant spelling of Tacitus's "Christus" [the Greek *Christos,* or Christ]) (*Twelve Caesars* 25). The alleged "constant rioting" that Claudius punished about 49 C.E. may have resulted from conflicts between Roman Jews and Jewish-Christian missionaries who brought their innovative religion from Palestine. (The author of Acts refers to Claudius's expulsion of Jews, including Priscilla and Aquila, who met Paul in Corinth about 50 C.E. [Acts 18:2].)

Flavius Josephus, the first-century Jewish historian who interpreted his people's customs to a Greco-Roman audience, twice mentions Jesus. With its later Christian interpolations deleted, Josephus's comments originally may have run as follows:

> Now there was about this time [the administration of Pontius Pilate (26–36 C.E.)], Jesus, a wise man, . . . a doer of wonderful works, a teacher of such men as receive the truth with pleasure. He drew over to him . . . many of the Jews, . . . and when Pilate . . . had condemned him to the cross, those that loved him at the first . . . [believed] that he appeared to them alive again the third day. . . . [A]nd the tribe of Christians, so named from him, are not extinct at this day. (*Antiquities* 18.3.3) •

Josephus's second reference deplores the illegal execution of James, "the brother of Jesus, who was called Christ" (*Antiquities* 20.9.1). Although from a later date, allusions to Jesus in the Talmud, which condemns him for sorcery and "for leading Israel astray," similarly attests to Jesus' historicity.

Pliny the Younger, who governed the Roman province of **Bithynia** (north-central Turkey) from about 111 to 115 C.E., wrote to the emperor **Trajan** for advice about dealing with Christians who refused to participate in "emperor worship," a public ritual then popularly regarded as much an expression of patriotism as of religious commitment. Pliny's letter notes that Christians gathered to "partake of a meal [the Eucharist or Holy Communion]" and to sing "a hymn to Christ, as if to a god" (*Letters,* 97), adding that cities, villages, and even the rural districts had been "thoroughly infected" by the "seditious" cult.

Whereas the Greco-Roman authors' cursory allusions to Jesus tend to confirm his martyrdom under Pilate and posthumous influence, they offer almost no information with which to construct a biography. Virtually everything we can learn about Jesus derives from the New Testament and a few other Christian documents, such as the apocryphal Gospel of Thomas. The writers of these works are not objective historians but believers who regarded Jesus as qualitatively different from every other human being. To them, Jesus is the "image of the invisible God" in whom "the complete being of the Godhead dwells embodied" (Col. 1:15–20; 2: 9–10). He is the Incarnation of the Logos, the preexistent Word, who so fully reveals the Creator that he is represented as saying that "anyone who has seen me has seen the Father" (John 14:9).

These devotional affirmations of Jesus' metaphysical nature are not capable of scientific verification but must remain an expression of faith. Supernatural events that by definition occur outside life's normal historical process, such as Jesus' miraculous ability to control a storm, walk on water, or rise from the dead, cannot be studied in themselves but only in their conceptual development within the primitive Christian community. Scientific analysis cannot deal with Jesus conceived as divinity but must approach the living man as the only legitimate object of historical inquiry, leaving to theologians the task of interpreting the paradox of Jesus as both completely human and fully divine.

The Scholarly Search for the "Real" Jesus

Systematic analysis of the Gospels to separate theological interpretation of Jesus from the real figure of history began only after the rise of modern science gave scholars a model for the rational evaluation of evidence. In the eighteenth century, Hermann Samuel Reimarus (1694–1768) became the first major critic to subject traditional ideas about Christian origins to historical investigation. Reimarus, whose work was not published until after his death, argued that the "real" Jesus was a Jewish revolutionary who failed to overthrow the Romans and was instead executed by them. During the next century a growing number of scholars employed **source criticism** and other methodologies to discover the historical and social circumstances that eventually produced the written Gospels. H. J. Holtzmann (1832–1910) concluded that Mark was the earliest Gospel, while Johannes Weiss (1863–1914) pursued the historical Jesus by placing his teachings about the kingdom of God firmly in a first-century Judean context.

Weiss's thesis that Jesus was an eschatological prophet was adopted and extensively developed by Albert Schweitzer (1875–1965), whose monumental *Quest of the Historical Jesus* (1906/1961) both defined the movement and, for nearly a half-century, immobilized it. Schweitzer's book had a revolutionary impact, shattering many people's traditional image of Jesus. In Schweitzer's exhaustive study, Jesus is dominated by a conviction that he is God's chosen instrument to announce the impending consummation of history. Burning with eschatological zeal, he demands that followers abandon all earthly ties and work with him to hasten the arrival of God's kingdom, which will overturn the present satanic world order and usher in the New Age. Jesus' driving goal is to fulfill the prophetic conditions that will bring about a supernaturally inspired chain of events culminating in his cosmic reign as the Son of Man. When Jesus' early expectations do not materialize (Matt. 10:22–23), he marches to Jerusalem, confident that he can compel the kingdom's appearance through his voluntary death, the final "tribulation" leading to God's direct imposition of his sovereignty. The anticipated divine intervention does not occur, however, and Jesus is crushed by the system he defies.

Schweitzer's reading of Jesus as a devoted but misguided apocalyptist made Christianity's core figure seem irrelevant to the modern worldview. No matter how sincere, a prophet whose eschatological predictions had been disproved by the world's stubborn failure to end had little to say to twentieth-century thinkers accustomed to scientific rationalism. As a result of this uncongenial historical Jesus, scholars for the next several decades concentrated almost exclusively on the Gospels, employing **form criticism** and similar techniques to disentangle Palestinian traditions of the Jesus movement from later Hellenistic strands. The Jesus

of history, apparently tied to an outmoded and unacceptable eschatology, was ignored while theologians focused on the postresurrection Christ of faith.

Rudolf Bultmann (1884–1976) is perhaps the single most influential New Testament scholar since Schweitzer. In his *Jesus and the Word* (1934) and *Jesus Christ and Mythology* (1958), Bultmann provided an exhaustive analysis of the different literary forms contained in the Synoptic Gospels, arguing that in most cases the material indicates an origin, not in the life of Jesus but in the life of the early church. Bultmann also argued that the Gospels largely present Jesus in terms of Hellenistic **mythology**, portraying him as a supernatural figure who descends from heaven to reveal divine Wisdom. According to Bultmann, one can make Jesus' essentially timeless message relevant to modern believers only by translating the Gospels' mythic language into the principles of twentieth-century existentialism. Although it is both impossible and undesirable to recover the finite historical personality of Jesus himself, the universal concept for which Jesus stands can still summon people to make an existentialist decision of ethical commitment. For Bultmann, the human Jesus espoused a form of Judaism, while Christianity is essentially a Hellenistic creation, thus rendering the historical Jesus of only marginal significance to faith in the risen Christ.

The Continuing Scholarly Debate

The international scholarly community remains deeply divided on the issue of the historical Jesus' actions and teachings. A large number of distinguished scholars, including E. P. Sanders and Paula Fredriksen (see Recommended Reading), are convinced that Jesus' message emphasized an imminent eschatological judgment. According to this view, Jesus assaulted the Temple moneychangers because he believed (as the Hebrew prophets Micah and Jeremiah had earlier proclaimed) that God planned to destroy the

Jerusalem sanctuary and raise a new one in the dawning New Age—an eschatological event that would occur in the immediate future! Similarly, Jesus' intensification of Torah ethics—insisting on purity of motive as well as deed (Matt. 5–7)—served to prepare a faithful remnant of Israel for the coming kingdom. Like the Essenes, Jesus and his followers—symbolizing the renewed twelve tribes of Israel—saw themselves as a divinely supported group ethically purifying itself for the final consummation of history. If the historical Jesus in fact preached that God was about to bring an adverse judgment against both Jewish and Roman authorities—and replace them with direct divine rule—this pronouncement could plausibly account for his arrest and execution. Although Jesus apparently did not advocate armed rebellion against the Roman–Sadduceean alliance, his message of the established order's impending doom and the crowds that enthusiastically responded to the promise of their exploiters' overthrow would be enough to make Pilate eliminate this potential threat to the present system.

The Work of the Jesus Seminar

Whereas many scholars view the historical Jesus as having anticipated an imminent *eschaton,* others insist that his teaching had little to do with popular eschatology. Prominent among the exponents of a noneschatological Jesus is the **Jesus Seminar**, a group of about 100 leading North American New Testament scholars. Like other participants in the scholarly quest for the historical Jesus, members of the Jesus Seminar employed a set of criteria by which to evaluate the probable authenticity of sayings (and deeds) attributed to Jesus. (In its attempt to reconstruct Jesus' actual teachings, the Seminar examined both canonical and noncanonical sources of the first three centuries C.E., including the apocryphal Gospel of Thomas.) The methodology for distinguishing Jesus' words from those of later followers who preached about him and whose declarations of faith were ultimately incorpo-

rated into Jesus' Gospel speeches includes several important standards of evidence.

Because Jesus directed his teaching—in Aramaic—to a rural and largely illiterate peasant audience in first-century Galilee, the first criterion is that of *orality*. Jesus' authentic words, which were not written down for two or three decades after he spoke them, would have had to be vivid and striking enough to be remembered and repeated by unlettered hearers. Genuinely historical sayings, then, will be attention-getting and memorable, such as Jesus' advising people to get a beam out of their own eye before looking for a speck in someone else's. Jesus appears to have favored the **aphorism**—brief, pithy sayings that challenged or overturned conventional wisdom, forcing people to think about the world in new ways. "It is not what goes into a person that defiles," he said, "but what comes out" (Mark 7:15, Scholars Version)—an almost scatological criticism of biblical dietary laws. Although they resemble **proverbs** in form, Jesus' aphorisms are typically nonproverbial in rejecting commonsensical assumptions or customs, such as his declaration: "It's easier for a camel to squeeze through a needle's eye than for a wealthy person to get into God's domain" (Mark 10:25, SV). Such statements not only provoke a double-take among typical listeners, but they also reverse traditional assurances that wealth is a divine blessing (Prov. 6:6–11; 10:15; 24:30–34; Job 42:12; Deut. 28:1–14).

Besides speaking in aphorisms that typically shock with their audacity or provoke with their rejection of familiar, everyday expectations, Jesus also used parables to convey his message. Scholars of the Jesus Seminar found that Jesus characteristically used exaggeration—huge sums of money in the parable of the unforgiving steward (Matt. 18:23–35)—or surprise reversals of accepted values—a despised Samaritan turns out to be the moral hero of another famous parable (Luke 10:30–35). To distinguish Jesus' true voice from those of Christian preachers who modified his words in oral transmission or Gospel authors who fitted them into their theological preconceptions, Seminar members concluded that it was necessary to look for sayings that were peculiar to Jesus' distinctive style. This criterion resembles that of *dissimilarity*—sayings that differ from both typically Jewish *and* Christian teachings of the first century C.E. are more likely to prove authentic. In addition, sayings that are found in two or more different sources that are independent of each other, such as Mark, the Q document, *and* the Gospel of Thomas (or some other early noncanonical writing not derived from the Synoptics), have some chance of being genuine. This standard of *multiple attestation* suggests that if different groups (presumably with different Christologies) have preserved the same saying, it may go back to Jesus. As a result of this methodological screening, only about 20 percent of the words attributed to Jesus by Gospel writers were judged to have originated with him.

Results of the Seminar's work were published in *The Five Gospels* (1993), which features colloquial translations of the Greek texts and adds Thomas to the canonical four as a source of some reliable material. Subtitled *The Search for the Authentic Words of Jesus,* the book prints Jesus' words in red, pink, gray, or black, depending on the scholars' verdicts about their respective genuineness. Using only the sayings printed in red or pink to create a portrait of the historical Jesus, one will find him presented as a compassionate sage, a wisdom teacher deeply concerned with social justice—particularly for the poor and powerless—and with each person's intimate relationship with God.

Members of the Jesus Seminar believe that they have stripped away the Synoptic Gospels' eschatological overlay and the Johannine Gospel's high Christology to reveal a more unified and focused character portrait than is possible if one uncritically accepts *all* the claims the Evangelists make about their subject. In the view of some readers, the Seminar's red-letter Jesus seems more human and historically credible than John's omniscient figure who descends from heaven and serenely embraces his cross as

the necessary means of reclaiming his preexistent divinity. For some critics, discovering Jesus as a wisdom teacher, even a kind of Hellenistic-Jewish-Cynic philosopher, removes the embarrassment of regarding him as an apocalyptist whose promise to return (within his disciples' lifetimes) as the eschatological Son of Man was not kept.

Other scholars doubt that rescuing an historical figure from his eschatological misconceptions is a reputable criterion for scholarship. Many scholars point out that if Jesus did not advocate an eschatological viewpoint, it is extremely difficult, if not impossible, to fit him into his historical environment. There is general scholarly agreement that Jesus' immediate predecessor, John the Baptist, warned Judah of an impending divine visitation and that Jesus' most influential interpreter, the apostle Paul, eagerly anticipated Jesus' imminent return as eschatological judge. (See Part 10.) With Jesus' career closely bracketed by two such proponents of the approaching *eschaton*, advocates of a noneschatological Jesus face a formidable challenge in explaining the continuity (or lack of it) in the sequence from John to Jesus to Paul.

The work of the Jesus Seminar has helped rekindle public interest in recovering the "real" Jesus, but the scholarly community is still far from consensus on who Jesus believed he was or exactly what he taught. Students wishing to explore the issue further can find excellent recent studies by Marcus Borg, E. P. Sanders, Paula Fredriksen, John P. Meier, and J. Dominic Crossan, all of whom present cogent evidence for their respective—and highly divergent—interpretations of Jesus' self-identity and purpose. (See the recommended readings.)

Conflicting Theories   As many commentators have noted, the picture of Jesus that one attempts to paint typically says more about the painter than it does about the subject. Almost all attempts to reconstruct Jesus' personal character and motivation tend to be projections of qualities that the individual researcher consciously or unconsciously accepts as valuable. Students and scholars alike generally assume that Jesus, when found, will be relevant to contemporary needs and expectations. Most persons still reject the possibility that Jesus was too limited by his exclusively religious preoccupations to say anything truly meaningful to a largely secular and technological society.

The theory that presents Jesus as a fanatic, deluded and doomed by eschatological obsessions, however, does not satisfy most New Testament readers. Among many other considerations, the man embodied in the Gospels seems far too profound and insightful to attempt forcing an egocentric and literalist eschatology into historical fulfillment. The Jesus-as-apocalyptist view sees him as entirely the product of his own time, but the opposing theory on a noneschatological Jesus, a benign wisdom teacher who championed the rights of the oppressed, creates a Jesus who is highly congenial to the modern temperament.

To scholars who see Jesus as having promoted a realized eschatology, Jesus' challenge to discern that God's kingdom reigns now—if people can get over their spiritual blindness and recognize its transcendent power—is intellectually attractive. Perpetuating the Johannine doctrine of cultivating eternal life in the present, this view has the advantage of presenting a Jesus who transcends his ancient Palestinian milieu to speak directly to contemporary experience. Most scholars, however, advise us to beware discovering a Jesus who appears too acceptable by today's standards. No matter how much Jesus may have differed from his peers, the historical person was a first-century rural Jew and, in many ways, would undoubtedly seem disturbingly alien to late twentieth-century sensibilities.

Some General Agreements About the Historical Jesus

Although scholars have not achieved a consensus about Jesus' primary teachings, many do agree on the general outline of his life. The Gospel traditions contain numerous data about Jesus that are relatively "theology-free," particularly biographical information that is not cited as a fulfillment of biblical prophecy or to promulgate christological doctrine. We may accept the tradition, then, that Jesus was born late in the reign of Herod the Great (between 6 and 4 B.C.E.); that he was raised in Nazareth (which is not mentioned in the Hebrew Bible); that he was the presumed son of Joseph, a carpenter, and his wife, Mary; and that he had brothers (or close relatives) named James (a future leader of the Jerusalem church), Joseph, Simon, and Judas (Jude), and an unknown number of sisters (or step-sisters) (Mark 6; Matt. 13:55). If Jesus and his putative father were carpenters, it probably means that the family had lost its hereditary land, which reduced them to a social status below that of Galilee's land-owning peasants.

When "about thirty years old" (Luke 3:1), Jesus came to John the Baptist for baptism in the River Jordan (about 27 or 29 C.E., depending on how one calculates Luke's "fifteenth year of the emperor Tiberius"). Mark's report that John baptized Jesus "in token of repentance for the forgiveness of sins" (Mark 1:4) is not an event that the early church would have invented. Because official doctrine held that Jesus was "sinless" and superior to the Baptist, Mark's baptismal story could not have emerged unless there was a firm tradition that Jesus had indeed submitted to John's ministrations. Some scholars think it likely that Jesus was, for an indefinite period, a disciple of the Baptist and did not begin his own ministry until after Herod Antipas had arrested and beheaded the prophet. Although it is impossible to confirm this theory, it appears that Jesus held the Baptist in the highest regard, perhaps regarding him as a mentor.

Following his baptism and perhaps an interlude of solitary meditation, Jesus began proclaiming a distinctive variation of the Baptist's message—the kingdom of God is near (or perhaps already present). In Jesus' proclamation, God's burgeoning rule reversed ordinary social values and encompassed people who were typically devalued by respectable society. The Syn-

The Holy Family. *The unknown years of Jesus' boyhood are given a Japanese setting in this twentieth-century painting on silk. Shouldering his share of the family's work, the young Jesus carries wood to help Joseph, his carpenter father, while Mary, his mother, is busy at her spinning wheel. The themes of productive labor, mutual assistance, and familial harmony dominate the domestic scene in Nazareth, providing a contrast to the adult Jesus' later rejection of family ties and obligations (Mark 3). (Courtesy of Lee Boltin)*

optic tradition consistently shows Jesus as an active friend of the poor and outcast, going out of his way to share meals with known "sinners" and other disreputable people. Jesus' penchant for unsavory associations—along with his reputation as "a glutton and a drinker"—passes the credibility test because no believer would invent such tales (Matt. 10:18–19; Luke 15:1–3; 7:33–8:3). Some commentators have even suggested that Jesus' parable of the prodigal son—which features a young man who squanders his inheritance in riotous living, much to the dismay of his disapproving brother—may hint at a

situation in Jesus' own life before he underwent John's cleansing baptism. Although anything said about Jesus before his association with the Baptist is necessarily conjectural, the twin traditions of his public repentance and his unfailing sympathy for social pariahs suggest that he knew this class of people well (and may once have been counted among them). His family's objections to Jesus' suddenly embarking upon a controversial ministry and his neighbors' doubts about his new-found prophetic claims (Mark 3: 20–21, 31–35; 6:1–6) also suggest that Jesus' early life was qualitatively different from his later

The Holy Family. *In depicting Jesus, Mary, and Joseph as indigenous Americans, the twentieth-century painter Fr. John B. Giuliani emphasizes both the archetypal sacredness of the family and the tradition of spirituality attained by pre-Columbian peoples of North America. (Courtesy of Bridge Building Images, Burlington, VT.)*

career. The antifamily sentiments Jesus repeatedly expressed—including the "hard sayings" about hating father and mother and leaving "the dead to bury their dead"—emphasizes a sharp break with his former connections and way of life.

Whereas Jesus' Nazarene acquaintances had defined (and thereby limited) him in terms of his occupation and blood ties—he was merely "Mary's son," "the carpenter"—Jesus seems to have attained a radically new identity: He called God *Abba* (father). This divine-parent/human-child relationship appears to underlie some of his most distinctive pronouncements, such as his injunction to be as giving and gracious to other mortals as God is to all his children, regardless of their merits (Matt. 5:44–48). The paradoxical command to "Love your enemies!" is practicable because God perceives human "enemies" as potential allies and friends.

Jesus' invitation to share in the divine relationship seems to have been remarkably inclusive: He breaks bread with Pharisees, lepers, tax collectors, slaves, women, and children (who, in the Greco-Roman world, were at the bottom of the social hierarchy). While raising their spirits, he also shows concern for their bodies: *All the traditions agree that Jesus was a healer.* How Jesus accomplished his healings and exorcisms is not known, but people he helped were convinced that he had changed them for the better, not least by validating their intrinsic worth and accepting some of them among his disciples. Issuing witty, provocative statements that challenged widely accepted values and attitudes, baiting religious authorities, and imparting a sense of physical and spiritual health to persons desperately in need of curative attention, Jesus, whether he wished to or not, could not help attracting followers.

Pursuing an itinerant life of deliberately chosen poverty and wandering randomly through Galilee from village to village, Jesus inevitably drew around him a mixed group of Galilean fishermen, farmers, women, and other ordinary working people. In parables and other figures of speech, he illustrated the desirability of living under God's kingdom—or perceiving the real-

Ravenna Mosaic of Christ Separating Sheep from Goats. *This early sixth-century mosaic illustrates Matthew's parable of eschatological judgment (Matt. 25:31–46). At his Parousia (Second Coming), an enthroned Jesus, flanked by two angels, divides all humanity into two mutually exclusive groups: the sheep are gathered in the favored position at Jesus' right hand, whereas the goats, at Jesus' left, are condemned to outer darkness for their failure to help others. (S. Apollinare Nuovo, Ravenna. Courtesy of Hirmer Verlag, München.)*

ity of divine rule, despite the oppression of secular authority, in the worlds of nature and human society. Although the Synoptic writers imply that the Galilean campaign lasted about a year, John's Gospel may be right in stating that it extended over at least three years and included several visits to Jerusalem.

While attracting throngs of mostly powerless admirers, Jesus also aroused powerful opposition. Jesus' apparent habit of relying on his own authority to pronounce on religious observances, such as Sabbath keeping—so different from the rabbinic tradition of citing the honored view of one's predecessors—irritated some and outraged others. Whereas many disciples were probably delighted with Jesus' authoritative dismissal of some purity laws and criticism of the Temple's priestly administration, some influential Sadducean officials in Jerusalem were undoubtedly suspicious of his motives. The priestly leadership may have regarded him as blasphemous and a potential threat to the delicate balance between Roman rule and Jewish welfare.

Jesus' healings, preaching about God's kingdom, and his drawing of large, unruly crowds

This "Good Shepherd" is an early Christian painting of Christ on the ceiling of a crypt in the catacombs of St. Priscilla in Rome. Note that the artist pictures Jesus in a pose that would be familiar to a Greco-Roman audience: like earlier renditions of Apollo, the Greek god of prophecy, intellect, music, and shepherds, the youthful Jesus carries a lamb on his shoulders to demonstrate his concern for his human flock. Compare John 10:1–18, Matthew 18:12–14, and Luke 15:4–7. (Courtesy of Benedettine Di Priscilla)

may have inspired some persons who particularly hated Roman occupation of the Holy Land to speculate that he was Israel's Messiah—the promised deliverer who would rid them of Gentile domination. John's report that a crowd wanted to proclaim him "[a Davidic] king" (John 6:15) and Luke's observation that as Jesus approached Jerusalem to celebrate Passover there, his disciples "thought the reign of God might dawn at any moment" (Luke 19:11) may echo actual historical conditions. Although most scholars do not think that Jesus presented himself as Israel's Messiah, some of his followers may have viewed him as the one prophesied to restore David's monarchy. If such claims were being circulated on Jesus' behalf, it would explain Pilate's action in executing Jesus on the

charge of treason, pretending to be "king of the Jews." To the Roman procurator, Jesus was merely another messianic (royal) claimant, such as those who led popular uprisings after Herod the Great's death.

Jesus' crucifixion under Pilate, which Tacitus and other non-Christian historians confirm, was not the kind of death—public, shameful, and associated with slaves and criminals—believers would fabricate for their leader. In the considered opinion of many Jews, the fact that Jesus was crucified meant that he *could not* have been the Messiah: No passage in the Hebrew Bible even hinted that the Messiah would die, let alone be executed as a felon by Gentile agents. (Proof texts that Christians later cited, such as the suffering servant poem in Isaiah 53 or Psalm 22, to explain Jesus' death are not specifically messianic prophecies.) Paul candidly describes the awkward fact of Jesus "nailed to the cross" as a "scandal"—a "stumbling block to Jews" and "sheer folly" to the Greeks (1 Cor. 1:23, 18). The humiliating fact of Jesus' crucifixion—so contrary to scriptural expectations—was probably the chief obstacle that kept most Jews from taking Christian preaching about him seriously. Some scholars believe that an early narrative about Jesus' miracles (and perhaps including his Passion)—the hypothetical Signs Gospel presumably later incorporated into John's Gospel—was composed to demonstrate that Jesus *was* Israel's Anointed One and that he was killed only because people refused to believe in his wondrous deeds. (See Chapter 10.)

Jesus' Teaching About the Kingdom

God as Universal King Jesus' attempts to convey his vision of God's kingdom inspired some of his most celebrated parables and figures of speech. The English phrase "kingdom of God" translates the Greek expression *basileia tou theou*. *Basileia* refers primarily to the act or process of ruling, a quality or privilege that distinguishes a king or other ruler. To have *basileia* is to possess control, power, freedom, and independence. The biblical God, whose infinite kingship Israel's thinkers take for granted, has these attributes in abundance. Psalm 145 proclaims Yahweh's universal sovereignty:

> All thy creatures praise thee, Lord [Yahweh],
> and thy servants bless thee.
> They talk of the glory of thy kingdom
> and tell of thy might,
> they proclaim to their fellows how mighty are
> thy deeds,
> how glorious the majesty of thy kingdom.
> Thy kingdom is an everlasting kingdom, and thy
> dominion stands for all generations.
> Psalm 145:11–12

Israel's God is thus the supreme possessor of *basileia,* a concept that must be kept in mind when considering Jesus' possible intentions as he combines his kingdom teaching with assertions of his own autonomy and dominion.

Although he is never shown defining what he means by the term, in the Gospels Jesus is pictured using *basileia tou theou* in four major ways: (1) to express the kingdom's preeminence; (2) to defend his personal authority to represent the kingdom and interpret the divine will; (3) to imply the nature of his self-awareness—the views he holds about his relationship with God and the meaning of kingship; and (4) to proclaim the kingdom's radical demand for total commitment. Because it dominates his message throughout the Synoptic Gospels, we will concentrate on the first category, emphasizing those sayings that scholars believe are most likely to stem from the historical Jesus.

In the Sermon on the Mount, Matthew presents Jesus as giving top priority to seeking the kingdom. The disciple who puts God's kingdom and his "justice [righteousness]" "before everything else" will also receive all that ordinary life requires (Matt. 6:33). Matthew and the other Synoptic writers then present such a variety of conflicting, even contradictory references to the kingdom that it is difficult to harmonize these disparate statements into a coherent view of what is meant. In different pericopes, the Synoptic Jesus speaks as if the kingdom were (1) a prophesied future event, (2) an unexpected occurrence, (3) a hidden power that grows slowly, (4) a present reality, and (5) physically present but unnoticed.

The Kingdom as Future Event The Synoptic writers typically emphasize the eschatological nature of the kingdom, presenting Jesus' message as a continuation of John the Baptist's warning of imminent divine judgment (cf. Matt. 3:3 and 4:17). In the Synoptic view, the kingdom is so close that people who first hear it proclaimed will live to see "the kingdom of God already come in power" (Mark 9:1; Matt. 16:28; Luke 9:27). All three Synoptic authors link Jesus' death with the kingdom's nearness. At the Last Supper, Jesus tells the disciples that he will never again drink "from the fruit of the vine until the day when I drink it new in the kingdom of God" (Mark 14:25; Matt. 26:19; Luke 22:16, 18).

The Kingdom as an Unexpected Event   In their apocalyptic predictions that link Jerusalem's fall and Jesus' return in glory, the Synoptic Gospels also implicitly associate the Parousia with the kingdom's arrival (cf. Mark 13, Matt. 24, and Luke 21). These passages anticipating the *eschaton* are inherently paradoxical: While asserting that spectacular portents will herald the End, they also emphasize the suddenness and unexpectedness of divine intervention. Thus, the kingdom appears stealthily, "like a thief in the night," its abrupt materialization a striking contrast to the parables that stress its quiet growth (Mark 13:33; Matt. 24:42; 25:13; Luke 12:40, 21:36). These and other texts that relate the kingdom to the Second Coming incorporate traditional themes of Hellenistic-Jewish eschatology, including world judgment and resurrection. In this context, the kingdom's appearance signifies the End of history as we know it and the inception of a radical "New Age." As noted above, scholars continue to debate the extent to which the Synoptic writers' eschatological expectations accurately mirror Jesus' historical views of the kingdom.

The Kingdom as a Hidden Power That Grows Slowly   Many of the best-known parables depict the kingdom as a hidden power that grows slowly until it achieves greatness. In contrast to the apocalyptic tradition—in which God's kingdom bursts suddenly and catastrophically into human affairs (Dan. 2:44)—Jesus' kingdom parables typically reject destruction imagery in favor of similes depicting serene germination. Jesus compares the kingdom to a tiny mustard seed that develops "underground," gradually maturing into a "tree" that shelters wildlife (Mark 4:30–32; Matt. 13:31–32; Luke 13:18–19; Gosp. Thom. 20). That the mustard plant is a weed farmers do not want taking over their fields per-

haps adds an ironic dimension to Jesus' simple analogy.

The parable of "leaven" that causes bread dough to rise and expand also suggests the kingdom's slow and quiet maturation (Matt. 13:33; Luke 13:20–21; Gosp. Thom. 96). The parables comparing the kingdom to seeking what is lost or unexpectedly finding an invaluable object— a pearl, a buried treasure, or a lost coin—highlight a gradual and *private* process on the part of individuals. In parables of this kind, a solitary figure—a widow, a lone merchant, a shepherd— takes time to focus on the process of discovery, a quiet personal search that ends in rejoicing (Matt. 13:44; 18:12–13; Luke 15:4–6; Gosp. Thom. 107). Employing images of life as it is daily lived, Jesus' parables of planting, growing, and recognizing unforeseen treasures have little affinity with apocalyptic violence.

The Kingdom as a Present Reality   Jesus' metaphors of seeking and finding harmonize with pronouncements in which he declares the kingdom a present reality. In Luke 11:20, he tells opponents, "But if it is by the finger of God that I drive out the devils, then be sure that the kingdom has already come upon you" (see also Matt. 12:28). Expelling demons, traditionally an eschatological act, is here equated with psychological healing and spiritual power, an expression of God's invisible dominion. Jesus' response to the Baptist's disciples, who inquire if he is really the Messiah, similarly implies that Jesus' present activity is a realization of the kingdom. When John's disciples behold the blind restored to sight, the deaf restored to hearing, and the dead raised to life, we know that God now reigns (Matt. 11:2–6; Luke 7:22–23). When the seventy-two disciples return from a successful campaign of exorcisms, Luke has Jesus declare that he now sees Satan fall "like lightning" from heaven (Luke 10:18). The spiritual healings performed by Jesus and his followers are a defeat of Evil and a manifestation of divine sovereignty.

*The Kingdom as Physically Present Yet Un-
noticed* Luke preserves Jesus' most explicit statement about the kingdom's already being present:
"You can not tell by observation when the
kingdom of God comes. There will be no saying, 'Look, here it is!' or 'there it is!'; for in fact
the kingdom of God is among you" (or "right
there in your presence") (Luke 17:20). With
this startling declaration, Jesus informs the Pharisees that in his person and healing activity, they
can witness the kingdom in operation. Divine
rule, Jesus adds, is as immediately obvious and
universal as sheet lightning that flashes over the
entire sky (Luke 17:22–24). The same perception of the kingdom's paradoxically elusive yet
pervasive presence is also found in the Gospel of
Thomas: "It will not come by watching for it. It
will not be said, 'Look, here!' or 'Look, there!'
Rather, [the Father's] imperial rule is spread out
upon the earth, and people don't see it" (Gosp.
Thom. 113). As Jesus implies in his calling the
disciples' attention to the beauty of the flowers
growing in a field or the fall of a sparrow, God
rules the world unnoticed by unperceptive or
unappreciative humans.

Luke's assertion that the kingdom rules everywhere, even among Jesus' opponents, has
another parallel in the Thomas Gospel. Here
Jesus is represented as saying that

> the Kingdom is inside you, and it is outside of
> you. When you come to know yourselves, then
> you will become known, and you will realize
> that it is you who are the sons of the living Fa-
> ther. But if you do not know yourselves, you
> dwell in poverty and it is you who are that
> poverty.
>
> (Gosp. Thom. 3:1–2)

Whereas the Lukan saying depicts the kingdom appearing through Jesus' presence, that in
Thomas seems to equate it with a state of heightened spiritual awareness. Knowing the true
"self" (the divine "image" within each person)
means awakening to one's kinship with God.
Remaining ignorant of the "god within" is
"poverty." Despite alleged Gnostic elements in

the Thomas saying, this concept of an indwelling divine spirit—perhaps similar to what Paul
called the "mystery" of "Christ in [the be-
liever]" (Col. 1:27)—may represent an integral
part of Jesus' kingdom concept.

Scholars who champion a noneschatological
Jesus believe that the historical Galilean did not
preach about a future eschatological kingdom
of God, violently imposed by divine intervention. Instead, he taught that God's rule is presently active in creation but difficult for most
people to perceive. According to this view, Jesus
had a highly subtle sense of time, a vision of
divine immanence in which God's eternal presence operates unseen, drawing and guiding into
his dominion those who respond to his will.
Entering God's domain means discerning and
embracing the simultaneity of present and future, which conflate into a profound sense of
the unbroken continuity of divine rule.

Many other scholars object that if Jesus' concept of seeking the kingdom meant a persistent
quest for recognizing God's "finger" at work in
the overfamiliar world, how can one account
for an apocalyptically oriented John the Baptist,
an eschatologically driven Paul, and an early
Church that expected Christ's Second Coming
to occur at any moment? (See 1 Thess. 4:15–
17; Mark 13.) Would it not be more reasonable
to assume that Jesus was an eschatological
prophet similar to his predecessors, many Jewish
contemporaries, and successors? One possible
defense of a noneschatological view of Jesus is
that the Gospel traditions make it clear that even
his closest followers did not understand him.
Misconstruing his complex and subtle vision of
divine sovereignty, more pedestrian followers
simply applied their inherited eschatological
ideas to the one they accepted as Lord. Indeed,
if Jesus had *not* taught that the kingdom reigns
now in those doing the divine will, how did his
apocalyptist followers conceive of such sayings
as those expressed in Luke 11:20 and 17:20–21
and Gospel of Thomas 3 and 113? Because
these sayings run against the trend of later eschatologically oriented Christianity, they pass

the test of distinctiveness and may well represent Jesus' actual views. Still other scholars observe that, like many first-century Jews, Jesus may have promoted a double vision of the kingdom: God rules now through the work of his servants, but full implementation of *divine* sovereignty lies ahead in the future.

Wisdom and the Kingdom of God

In contrast to Mark and Matthew, who were apparently inspired by the apocalyptic disaster that befell Judea in 70 C.E., the authors of John and Thomas show that it was possible to follow a Jesus who was fundamentally an exponent of divine Wisdom rather than a purveyor of eschatological judgment. The Johannine writer rarely mentions the kingdom as an integral part of Jesus' teaching, but he may convey a significant historical truth when he makes the nature of Jesus' personal kingship the crucial issue on which Pilate's execution of Jesus hinges (John 18:33–19:22). During the confrontation with Pilate, the Johannine Jesus states that his kingdom is not of this world—that it is not political—but he fails to define either his government or his own kingly role (John 18:36).

John nonetheless gives his readers a relatively clear idea of what Jesus' kingdom involves. From the outset of his Gospel, the author identifies Jesus with the eternal Word, the expression of immortal Wisdom by and through which God created the universe (John 1:1–18; Prov. 8:22–36). In his person, Jesus reveals and shares with others the vital Wisdom by which God rules and communicates his will. As noted above, John firmly links Jesus with Israel's **wisdom literature**, the teachings of which associate the wise person with God's *basileia*—heavenly kingship.

The deuterocanonical Wisdom of Solomon expresses the affinity between Wisdom and divine kingship that may have influenced John's view of Jesus:

> For she [Wisdom] ranges [the earth] in search of those who are worthy of her. . . . The true beginning of wisdom is the desire to learn, and a concern for learning means the keeping of her laws; to keep her laws is a warrant of immortality; and immortality brings a man near to God. Thus the desire of wisdom leads to kingly stature [a *basileia*].
>
> Wisdom of Solomon 6:16–20

Notice that learning and keeping God's wise laws, the principles by which he orders the Cosmos, lead to eternal life and make the obedient possessor of Wisdom a king.

Wisdom also reveals the kingdom of God:

> She [Wisdom] guided him [Jacob, the embodiment of Israel] on straight paths; she showed him the *basileia tou theou* [literally, the kingdom or sovereignty of God].
>
> Wisdom of Solomon 10:10

In Israel's wisdom writings, Wisdom (Sophia, a personification of God's primary attribute) imparts knowledge, divine favor, and immortal life (Prov. 2:1–10; Job 28:12–23; Ecclus. 24; Wisd. 8:4, 13). She discloses secrets of the unseen world to those who seek her, satisfying their intellectual and spiritual thirst (Wisd. 7:17–29). The references to Jesus' unveiling the "secret" or "mystery of the kingdom of God" in Mark (4:11) and Secret Mark (2:10) may preserve a parallel to the Johannine tradition that Jesus' teaching focuses not on the eschatological but on Wisdom's revelation of previously hidden cosmic truths.

According to this view of Jesus' kingdom message, Jesus teaches that followers must come under God's rule by imitating and participating in the divine *basileia*. As noted above, *basileia* implies kingly autonomy, freedom, and self-determination—living one's life as the master of one's situation. The Johannine Jesus tells his followers that he had already "conquered the world" (John 16:33). The self-confidence or "authority" with which Jesus habitually teaches may derive from his profound sense of possessing the celestial Wisdom that sets people free (Matt. 7:28–29; Mark 1:22; John 8:22). At liberty to proclaim his personal views on the Torah, he inevitably antagonizes many rival teachers of the **Law**. As a sage through whom Wisdom speaks, he is also free to recognize his own kingship—the *basileia* that Wisdom imparts (Wisd. 6:17–20; 10:10). If Jesus publicly equated his wisdom teaching with kingship, the connection may have inspired Pilate's suspicion. As governor for Rome, Pilate could tolerate no Jew claiming to be a king of any kind.

The Johannine Jesus informs his disciples that he fully reveals the Father, the supreme reality with whom he—and they—enjoy a life-giving unity (John 17:1–8, 20–23). Spiritual union with the Deity confers a power upon Jesus' disciples that will enable them to accomplish greater deeds than he (John 14:10–14). The arrival of the Paraclete, or Spirit of Truth, endows believers with additional heaven-sent Wisdom and allows them to continue imitating Jesus' example of kingly rulership. Indeed, the Paraclete manifests the same power of *basileia* that characterizes Jesus (John 16:7–15). Initiated into the mystery of divinity and empowered by the Spirit, the Johannine disciple possesses a kingdom authority resembling that of Jesus himself (John 14:12–21).

Scholars in large part agree that the historical Jesus taught about God's kingdom (whatever his precise meaning by the phrase), but most question the belief that he taught about himself. Although he seems to have perceived the world and his mission from the vantage point of one who holds a peculiarly close relationship to God, he is not believed to have called himself Christ, Son of God, or the Holy One of Israel. All these honorific titles, scholars believe, were bestowed upon him posthumously by a community that—in retrospect—recognized him as Israel's Messiah and God's chief agent, the means by which the Deity reconciles humanity to himself. In telling Jesus' story so that readers could understand his true significance, it was natural for the Gospel writers to apply titles such as *Christ* and *Son of God* to the historical figure. In the Evangelists' view, they could not write the truth about who Jesus was unless they

presented him in the light of his resurrection and glorification. The Galilean prophet and teacher who had challenged the world's norms in the name of a radical egalitarianism for all God's children was—by his continuing life in the believing community—vindicated as divine, the Wisdom and love of God made flesh.

QUESTIONS FOR REVIEW

1. What is the literal meaning of the word *gospel,* and what New Testament Greek word does it translate? Define *Gospel* as a literary category. By definition, who and what must always be the subject of a Gospel?

2. Define *Synoptic* and describe the issue that scholars call "the Synoptic Problem." What is the hypothetical Q document? According to scholarly theory, approximately when was it written and what did it contain? In what two Gospels do its contents now appear?

3. Define the Griesbach hypothesis. According to the "two-source" hypothesis, which Gospel was written first? What relationship does this original Gospel have to the other two Synoptic Gospels? How does Q figure into the equation?

4. Describe six theoretical stages in the development of the four canonical Gospels. Begin with oral traditions—Christian oral preaching—about Jesus, and conclude with the composition of the fourth Gospel.

5. In compiling his account of Jesus' public career, what sources would you expect the author of Mark's Gospel to consult? What attitude does Mark express toward Jesus' family, former neighbors, disciples, and opponents? In Mark's view, did Jesus' contemporaries understand him or his purpose?

6. List the reasons that scholars often refer to Mark as a "wartime Gospel." Relate Mark's eschatological urgency—the author's expectation of an imminent End to history—

to the Jewish war against Rome and its catastrophic consequences (see Mark 13). Describe what happened to Jerusalem, Yahweh's Temple, the Jewish state, and the apostolic Christian Church in 70 C.E. What influence did Roman persecution of Christians have on Mark's equation of discipleship with suffering?

7. Summarize the order of events in Mark's Gospel, beginning with Jesus' baptism and ending with his arrest and execution. Describe Mark's division of Jesus' career into two distinct parts, the Galilean and Jerusalem ministries. Define the concept of the messianic secret, and explain how Mark uses the three Passion predictions to connect the two disparate segments of Jesus' life.

8. Describe the kinds of healings, exorcisms, and other miracles that Jesus performs. At what point in the narrative does Mark's Jesus cease performing powerful works? How does Mark explain the apparent failure of Jesus' mission in Jerusalem? Who is the first *human being* to recognize Jesus' divine sonship? Under what circumstances?

9. According to the two-source theory, in what ways is Matthew's Gospel a revised and expanded edition of Mark? What five blocks of Jesus' teaching does Matthew add to Mark's narrative? Summarize nativity and resurrection accounts with which the author frames his story. How does Matthew use the Hebrew Bible to demonstrate Jesus' messiahship? List some of Matthew's major themes, including his attitude toward keeping the Mosaic Torah.

10. Define *parable,* and give several examples from Mark 4 or Matthew 13. To what images or natural processes does Jesus compare the kingdom of God? What specific commands or principles in Matthew's Sermon on the Mount (Matt. 5–7) illustrate the nature of God's reign?

11. What does Matthew add to Mark's story of Jesus that tends to deemphasize early Christians' eschatological expectations? Compare Mark 13 with Matthew 24–25.

12. Describe some of the major themes in the two-volume Gospel and history known as Luke-Acts. According to Luke's preface, how did the author gather information for his Gospel? Do you think that the "many" previously existing Gospels the author consulted (Luke 1:1–4) included Mark?

13. After reading Luke's famous parables of the good samaritan, the prodigal son, the Pharisee and the tax collector, Lazarus and the rich man, and others, what impression of Jesus' teaching do you think Luke wants you to receive? Summarize Luke's major themes and special interests. Compare Luke's account of Jesus' crucifixion with that of Mark, particularly Jesus' words on the cross and the Roman centurion's remarks about Jesus. How does Luke use this scene to emphasize his themes of forgiveness and Christians' political innocence of any sedition toward Rome?

14. List some of the principal differences between the Gospel of John and the three Synoptic Gospels. Compare the order of events in Mark with those in John, specifying differences in chronology.

15. What role does the beloved disciple play in John's account? How does he compete with Peter?

16. Contrast the nature of Jesus' teaching in the Synoptics—his use of parables, aphorisms, and reinterpretations of Torah—with the teachings of the Johannine Jesus, which emphasize Jesus' divine preexistence and unique relationship to the Father. List as many differences as you can between John's portrait and the Synoptic picture of Jesus.

17. Define John's concept of realized eschatology and his view that Jesus' death is glorious, a *return* to his previous heavenly abode. How does the Paraclete substitute for the earthly Jesus?

18. Describe some of the criteria that modern scholars use to screen Jesus' authentic words

and deeds from those that may have been attributed to him by later Christians. Does use of these criteria help to distinguish the Jesus of history from the Christ of faith?

QUESTIONS FOR DISCUSSION AND REFLECTION

1. Why do you think that the early Christian community produced four distinct—and sometimes contradictory—accounts of Jesus' life rather than one completely consistent version? What present value, in matters of flexibility and tolerance, does the existence of four diverse portraits of Jesus have for today's many different Christian groups?
2. After reading the Sermon on the Mount (Matt. 5–7), do you think that its principles of nonviolence, selflessness, and antimaterialism can be practiced closely today, either by individuals, communities, or nations? Why is Jesus so concerned that none of his followers oppress or economically exploit other people?
3. The Synoptic Gospels consistently show Jesus gravitating toward economically and politically powerless persons, including women, social outcasts, and children. Do you believe that Jesus' example of concern for socially marginal and "unrespectable" people—such as prostitutes, notorious sinners, and tax collectors who collaborated with the "evil empire" of Rome—is recognized or honored by today's political leaders and policymakers? Can someone be a Christian and *not* follow Jesus' example of siding with the poor and oppressed? Explain.
4. Did the historical Jesus believe that the End of history would occur during his lifetime or as a result of his ministry? In emphasizing the imminence of the kingdom, did Mark accurately represent Jesus' authentic teachings? Did early Christianity's eschatological expectations derive from Jesus or some other source? If Christian leaders such as Paul and

the Synoptic writers were wrong about the *eschaton,* does that fact undermine the importance or truth of their teaching?
5. Why do you think that the author of John's Gospel emphasizes Jesus' divine nature—and his continuing presence in the Paraclete (Holy Spirit)—rather than the Synoptic traditions of exorcisms and predictions of the Second Coming? Is John's identification of the human Jesus with the divine Wisdom that created the universe—presented along with his concept of realized eschatology—an attempt to transcend competing beliefs about the impending Parousia and End of the world? Did John's picture of a Cosmic Christ who abides spiritually and permanently with a community of beloved friends enhance Christianity's appeal in the Greco-Roman world? If so, how? Suppose the three Synoptic Gospels were the only portraits we had of Jesus. Would Christianity be the same global religion that it is today?

TERMS AND CONCEPTS TO REMEMBER

aphorism	mythology
Bithynia	proverb
Claudius	realized eschatology
form criticism	source criticism
Jesus Seminar	Trajan
Law	wisdom literature

RECOMMENDED READING

Borg, Marcus J. *Jesus: A New Vision.* San Francisco: Harper & Row, 1988. Scholarly and perceptive, this study of the historical Jesus shows that his message was not primarily eschatological.
———. "Jesus, Teaching of." In D. N. Freedman, ed., *The Anchor Bible Dictionary,* Vol. 3, pp. 804–812. New York: Doubleday, 1992. A concise survey of Jesus' major teachings.

Bultmann, Rudolf. *History of the Synoptic Tradition,* rev. ed. Translated by John Marsh. San Francisco: Harper & Row, 1961. Representing a major achievement in New Testament scholarship, Bultmann's work shows how the Evangelists reinterpreted Jesus mythically.

Carlston, Charles E. "Jesus Christ." In P. J. Actemeier, ed., *Harper's Bible Dictionary,* pp. 475–487. San Francisco: Harper & Row, 1985. A good introduction to the subject; offers a clear survey of Jesus' principal teachings.

Crossan, John Dominic. *The Historical Jesus: The Life of a Mediterranean Peasant.* San Francisco: HarperSanFrancisco, 1991. A distinctive scholarly interpretation of Jesus as a sage advocating radical social egalitarianism.

———. *Jesus: A Revolutionary Biography.* San Francisco: HarperSanFrancisco, 1994. A distillation of Crossan's earlier book for the general reader.

Falk, Harvey. *Jesus the Pharisee: A New Look at the Jewishness of Jesus.* New York: Paulist Press, 1985. Shows the many similarities between the teachings of Jesus and those of the Pharisees, including parallels in both form and content.

Fredriksen, Paula. *From Jesus to Christ: The Origins of the New Testament Images of Jesus.* New Haven: Yale University Press, 1988. Traces the historical process by which the human Jesus became the divine Christ.

Funk, Robert W.; Hoover, Roy W.; and the Jesus Seminar. *The Five Gospels: The Search for the Authentic Words of Jesus.* A Polebridge Press Book. New York: Macmillan, 1993. Features a highly colloquial translation of the canonical Gospels and Thomas, with Jesus' authentic words printed in red or pink, doubtful sayings in gray, and speeches ascribed to him by tradition or Gospel authors in black.

Jacobson, Arland D. *The First Gospel: An Introduction to Q.* Sonoma, Calif.: Polebridge Press, 1992. A study and tentative reconstruction of material in the hypothetical sayings source.

Josephus, Flavius. *Josephus: Complete Works.* Translated by W. Whiston. Grand Rapids, Mich.: Kregel, 1960. A dated translation but one that contains the complete texts of *The Antiquities of the Jews* and *The Jewish War* as well as brief references to Jesus, John the Baptist, and Jesus' brother James.

———. *The Jewish War,* rev. ed. Translated by G. A. Williamson. Edited by E. M. Smallwood. New York: Penguin Books, 1981. Modern translation of Josephus's eyewitness account of the Jewish revolt and its consequences.

Kee, Howard C. *Jesus in History,* 2nd ed. New York: Harcourt Brace Jovanovich, 1977.

Kloppenborg, John S. *The Formation of Q.* Philadelphia: Fortress Press, 1987. Analyzes the stages or levels of oral tradition contained in the hypothetical sayings source.

Kloppenborg, John S.; Meyer, Marvin W.; Patterson, Stephen J.; and Steinhauser, Michael G. *Q Thomas Reader.* Sonoma, Calif.: Polebridge Press, 1990.

Koester, Helmut. *Ancient Christian Gospels: Their History and Development.* Philadelphia: Trinity Press International, 1990. A thorough and detailed study of the Gospels' literary evolution; for more advanced students.

Mack, Burton I. "The Kingdom Sayings in Mark." *Forum* 3, no. 1 (1987): 3–47. Argues that Jesus' kingdom teachings were not eschatological.

Meier, John P. "Jesus." In R. E. Brown et al., eds., *The New Jerome Biblical Commentary,* pp. 1316–1328. Englewood Cliffs, N.J.: Prentice Hall, 1990. A concise introductory essay.

———. *A Marginal Jew: Rethinking the Historical Jesus.* New York: Doubleday, 1991. The first volume of a projected two-part biography by an eminent Roman Catholic scholar, this work presents the Hellenistic-Jewish environment in which Jesus was nurtured.

Meyer, Ben. "Jesus Christ." In D. N. Freedman, ed., *The Anchor Bible Dictionary,* pp. 773–796. New York: Doubleday, 1992. Provides a good introductory review of contemporary scholarship on Jesus' life and teachings.

Miller, Robert J. *The Complete Gospels: Annotated Scholars Version,* rev. ed., 1994. HarperSanFrancisco. Includes all known Gospels, including fragments, produced during the first three Christian centuries.

Patterson, Stephen J. *The Gospel of Thomas and Jesus.* Sonoma, Calif.: Polebridge Press, 1993. Argues that the first edition of Thomas dates to the middle of the first century C.E. and contains authentic sayings of Jesus.

Rivkin, Ellis. *What Crucified Jesus? The Political Exe-*

cution of a Charismatic. Nashville, Tenn.: Abingdon Press, 1984. A Jewish scholar's investigation into the social and political forces that led to Jesus' execution by Rome.

Robinson, James M., ed. *The Nag Hammadi Library*, 3rd ed. San Francisco: Harper & Row, 1988. Contains English translations of Christian documents found at Nag Hammadi.

Robinson, John A. T. *Jesus and His Coming*. Philadelphia: Westminster Press, 1979. Argues that Jesus was not an apocalyptist and that beliefs about his Second Coming developed from a misunderstanding of his teachings.

Sanders, E. P. *Jesus and Judaism*. Philadelphia: Fortress Press, 1985. A scholarly and highly readable evaluation of the Gospel traditions about Jesus and his message, particularly about the kingdom and its original meaning in the context of Palestinian Judaisms.

———. *The Historical Figure of Jesus*. New York: Viking, 1994. A readable work of solid scholarship.

———. "The Life of Jesus." In Hershel Shanks, ed., *Christianity and Rabbinic Judaism,* pp. 41–83. Washington, D.C.: Biblical Archaeology, 1992. A lucid and commonsensical study of what we may know about the historical Jesus by a major New Testament scholar.

Sanders, E. P., and Davies, Margaret. *Studying the Synoptic Gospels*. Philadelphia: Trinity Press International, 1989.

Schweitzer, Albert. *The Quest of the Historical Jesus: A Critical Study of Its Progress from Reimarus to Wrede.* New York: Macmillan, 1961. The German original was published in 1906, but the issues Schweitzer raises in this monumental project still influence scholars' search for the real figure of history.

Sheehan, Thomas. *The First Coming: How the Kingdom of God Became Christianity*. New York: Random House, 1986. A Roman Catholic scholar's careful account of historical and theological developments that transformed the Jesus of history into the Christ of faith.

Tatum, W. Barnes. *In Quest of Jesus: A Guidebook*. Atlanta: John Knox Press, 1982. A helpful guide for beginners.

Wright, N. T. "Jesus, Quest for the Historical." In D. N. Freedman, ed., *The Anchor Bible Dictionary,* pp. 796–802. New York: Doubleday, 1992. A survey of scholars' efforts to discover the Jesus of history, including the work of the Jesus Seminar.

A Christian History and the Pauline Letters

The Book of Acts

KEY THEMES

In the Book of Acts, Luke continues his two-part narrative of Christian origins, depicting characters who, like Jesus, are models of Christian behavior and service. An idealized account of the Church's beginnings, Acts focuses on only two Christian leaders—Peter and Paul—whom the author uses to symbolize two consecutive phases of the religion's development. Dominating the first half of the book (Chs. 1–12), Peter represents the original Jewish Christianity centered in Jerusalem. After converting thousands of his fellow Jews to "the new Way," Peter completes his role by bringing the first Gentile—a Roman centurion named Cornelius—into the Church (Chs. 10–11).

Acts' second part (Chs. 13–28) narrates Christianity's historical transition from a Jewish to a Gentile religion, a movement represented by Paul's three missionary tours through the Greco-Roman world. Because Luke wishes to show the early Church as a paradigm of harmony and cooperation, he creates a picture of Paul significantly different from that revealed in Paul's own letters. Instead of the fiercely independent missionary defending his "gospel's" total freedom from the Jerusalem leadership (Gal. 1–2; 2 Cor. 10–13), the Lukan Paul is a team player who meekly accommodates himself to churchly authority. Emphasizing the same themes found in his Gospel, Luke paints Christianity as a Spirit-directed faith, innocent of sedition against Rome and divinely predestined to spread "to the ends of the earth" (Acts 1:8), a process that will continue indefinitely into the future.

The Purpose and Structure of the Book of Acts

In composing this sequel to his Gospel, Luke adopts the ancient historian's customary moral goals—to portray historical persons and events in a way that will clearly illustrate their ethical quality and meaning. Rather than write a comprehensive analysis of the complex social, economic, and theological forces that shaped the earliest Christian movement, Luke chooses to provide a smoothly flowing narrative that will demonstrate Christianity's divinely inspired birth and growth. The only first-century account of Christian origins, Acts preserves important traditions about the first Christians, even while revising them to minimize theological controversies and present Church leaders as exemplary models for his readers to imitate.

As history, Acts is a highly selective account, listing the original eleven apostles (1:13) but reporting almost nothing about anyone except Peter, who is depicted leading the original Christian community in Jerusalem in the period immediately following Jesus' ascension to heaven, an event mentioned only in Luke-Acts. Luke also reports that the eleven elect a replacement for Judas Iscariot (who has committed suicide)— a disciple named Matthias—but this new "twelfth apostle" is never heard from again. Even James and John, the two sons of Zebedee who were members of Jesus' inner circle, are mentioned only in passing, James merely to record his beheading by Herod Agrippa I (Acts 12:2). A more influential James, whom Paul calls the "Lord's brother" (Gal. 1:19; cf. Mark 6:3), eventually supplants Peter as head of the Mother Church in Jerusalem, but Luke does not explain where Peter goes or how James succeeds him (Acts 15:13–21, 21:18–26). Nor does the author record who introduced Christianity to Rome or when, merely remarking that there were already believers living there when Paul arrived at the capital (Acts 28:14–15). Acts traces the spread of Christianity from Jerusalem to Rome but concentrates exclusively on the northeastern corner of the Mediterranean, completely ignoring the faith's contemporaneous expansion into north African cities such as Alexandria and Cyrene.

A Universal Faith Addressed to the same Theophilus as Luke's Gospel, Acts is similarly directed to a Greek-speaking audience, one keenly interested in the process by which an obscure Jewish sect becomes a universal religion known throughout the Roman Empire. Part of the author's goal is to show that God kept his biblical promises to Israel (see Part 3) before opening the "new Way" (Acts 9:2) to non-Jews. In tracing Christianity's movement away from its Palestinian roots to Gentile soil, Luke reassures Theophilus and other Gentiles that God faithfully fulfilled his covenant vows in the work of Jesus and his Jewish followers. At the end of his Gospel and the beginning of Acts, Luke reminds the reader of Israel's hopes for a Davidic king. Approaching Jerusalem, the disciples wonder if the kingdom is at last about to materialize (Luke 19:11), a question they reformulate to Jesus immediately before his ascension to heaven. "Lord," they ask, "is this the time when you are to establish once again the sovereignty of Israel?" (Acts 1:6). Jesus' answer—that they must remain in Jerusalem to "receive power" from above and then evangelize the earth— implies a positive response to their question. In Luke's view, in creating a Spirit-empowered Jewish community in Jerusalem—the original Jewish-Christian Church—God reestablishes his rule over Israel's true citizens.

At Pentecost, when the Lukan Peter asserts that God's eschatological promise of Israel's Spirit-anointing is fulfilled (2:14–36), 3000 Jews join the Galilean disciples (2:37–41). Peter's second Jerusalem speech emphasizes the Lukan theme that Jews remain the "heirs of the prophets" and "within the covenant" that Yahweh made with Abraham. Hence, God sent his "servant" and offered his "blessing" to them first, keeping the oath he had sworn to Israel's patriarchs and prophets (3:25–26). As Luke presents his history of salvation, Jerusalem and its Temple—where Pharisees and Jewish Christians worship side-by-side—are the nucleus of God's redemptive acts for all humanity.

Organization Luke arranges his narrative in ten major sections:

1. Prolog and account of Jesus' **ascension** (1:1–11)
2. Founding of the Jerusalem church (1:12–2:47)
3. Work of Peter and the apostles (3:1–5:42)
4. Persecutions of the "Hellenist" Jewish Christians and the first missions (6:1–8:40)
5. Preparation for the Gentile mission: the conversions of Paul and Cornelius (9:1–12:25)
6. First missionary journey of Barnabas and Paul: the Jerusalem conference (13:1–15:35)

7. Paul's second missionary journey: evangelizing Greece (16:1–18:21)

8. Paul's third missionary journey: revisiting Asia Minor and Greece (18:22–20:38)

9. Paul's arrest in Jerusalem and imprisonment in Caesarea (21:1–26:32)

10. Paul's journey to Rome and his preaching to Roman Jews (27:1–28:31)

Prolog and Ascension

Luke is the only New Testament writer to state that Jesus' postresurrection appearances spanned a period of forty days and that he ascended visibly to heaven, indicating that he would return in a similarly quiet manner (1:9–11). He is also the only author to report that **Matthias** was chosen to replace **Judas Iscariot** (1:12–26), apparently to maintain an apostolic membership of twelve, symbolizing the complete tribes of Israel. This passage also defines Luke's understanding of an **apostle**, a person who had physically accompanied Jesus during his entire ministry and witnessed his resurrection (1:21–22). Because Paul had not personally known Jesus, Luke almost never calls him an apostle, although in his letters Paul passionately fights to make others acknowledge his right to that title (see Gal. 1).

Founding the Jerusalem Church: Role of the Holy Spirit

The first two chapters emphasize the divine power that transforms the **Jerusalem church** from a group of about 120 persons (1:15) to several thousand worshipers, including some priests (2:41; 4:4; 5:14–16; 6:1, 7). Symbolically rendered as wind and flame, the Holy Spirit inspires the disciples to speak in foreign tongues—representing the multinational nature of Christianity. Peter interprets this ecstatic phenomenon, known as **glossolalia**, as the fulfillment of Joel's prediction that in the last days "everyone" would prophesy (2:1–24; see Joel 2:28–32).

Peter's long speech, interpreting the theological meaning of **Pentecost**, is typical of other discourses that follow. Whether ascribed to Peter, Stephen, James, or Paul, the Acts speeches tend to sound alike, expressing the author's themes as much as remembered words of the historical characters to whom they are assigned. Like other historians of his day, Luke follows the standard Greco-Roman practice of advancing his narrative through speeches of his own composition, mingling historical traditions with what he deems appropriate to the occasion. Although we cannot know the extent to which Luke's speeches express ideas characteristic of the apostolic period—two or three generations earlier than his own time—some may preserve important aspects of early Christian teaching. Peter's declaration that by resurrecting Jesus, God has made him "both Lord and Messiah" does not reflect Luke's view that Jesus was Messiah during his lifetime, but it may transmit a primitive Jewish-Christian belief that Jesus—the "man singled out by God"—became confirmed as Messiah only upon his ascent to heaven (2:22).

Luke's picture of the original Jerusalem community repeats a theme prominent in his Gospel. He reports that believers sold their possessions, distributing the money to establish a community without rich or poor. Holding "everything" "in common" (2:43–45; 4:32–35), the Jerusalem church meets Jesus' challenge to sacrifice material goods to attain true discipleship (Luke 18:18–30).

The Work of Peter and the Apostles

In the next section (3:1–5:42), Luke presents a series of dramatic confrontations between the apostles and the Jerusalem authorities. He attributes much of the Church's trouble to the Sadducee party, whose priests control the Temple (4:1–6; 5:17–18). By contrast, many Pharisees tend to tolerate or even champion some Christian activities (5:34–40; 23:6–9). During Peter's second hearing before the Sanhedrin, the Pharisee **Gamaliel**, a famous first-century rabbinical scholar, is represented as protecting the infant Church.

Persecution of the Hellenists

In the following section (6:1–8:40), Sadducean hostility focuses on **Stephen**, a leading **Hellenist**, or Greek-speaking Jew of the Diaspora. The episode culminates in Stephen's impassioned "witness" to the Jews who stone him for blasphemy (6:8–7:60). The execution of this first Christian **martyr** and the persecution that follows have the unintended effect of promoting the Church's growth. Scattered throughout Judea and Samaria, Hellenist Christians carry the "new Way" to new populations, making such diverse converts as **Simon** the magician (8:9–13) and an Ethiopian eunuch, treasurer of Queen Kandake (Candace) (8:26–40).

Conversions of Paul and Cornelius

Luke represents the progress of Christianity from its origin as a Palestinian Jewish sect to its (hoped-for) status as a world religion in two additional conversion stories of monumental importance. In the first, **Saul of Tarsus**—a Pharisaic persecutor of the Church—is converted by a dazzling revelation of the risen Jesus (9:1–19). Henceforth known by his Roman name, **Paul** is seen as God's principal instrument of transforming Christianity into a largely Gentile religion (9:15). More than any other single individual, Paul is responsible for the future universality of the Church.

Luke devotes the next two chapters (10–11) to the second landmark conversion, that of **Cornelius**, the Roman **centurion**, and his household. Although Peter generally represents the conservative Jewish position in the Jerusalem community, the author here shows him as the agent who first opens the Church's door to Gentiles. Peter first receives a vision implying that all foods, as well as the non-Jewish people who eat them, are now "clean" and acceptable to God (10:9–16). Following the vision, a delegation brings Peter to Cornelius's house, where Peter, directed by the **Holy Spirit**, baptizes the entire family (10:1–8, 17–48). Stressing his view that the Spirit's presence validates a

The Descent of the Holy Spirit at Pentecost *by El Greco. (Courtesy of the Prado Museum, Madrid)*

religious decision, Luke shows Cornelius and his entire household speaking in tongues exactly as the Jewish Christians had at Pentecost. Peter then interprets the incident's religious meaning: "God has no favorites, but . . . in every nation . . . the God-fearing [person who] does what is right is acceptable to him" (10:34). Luke also represents Peter as persuading the "circumcision party" (Jewish Christians who strictly observe the Mosaic Torah) in Judea that "God has granted life-giving repentance to the Gentiles also" (11:18). When Gentiles flock to the church at **Antioch**, the Jerusalem Apostles dispatch **Barnabas**, a Greek-speaking Jewish Christian from Cyprus, to report on the situation. Impressed by the converts' zeal, Barnabas imports Paul, who had returned to Tarsus, to help instruct them (11:19–30).

Having demonstrated the fulfillment of Jesus' command to preach "all over Judea and Samaria" (1:8), Acts concludes its first half with an account of Herod Agrippa's persecution of the Jerusalem community. After executing James, "the brother of John," he imprisons Peter, who is promptly delivered by "an angel" (12:1–19). Decisive evidence of divine displeasure at Herod's arrogance is manifested when the king, after accepting divine honors, suddenly dies of a hideous disease, thus ending his reign (41–44 C.E.) over a briefly reunited Jewish kingdom (12:20–23).

First Missionary Journey of Barnabas and Paul

Acts' remaining sixteen chapters are largely devoted to the international missionary travels of Paul and his fellow workers. The first part of this section shows Barnabas and Paul successfully evangelizing among the "God-fearing" Gentiles who attend synagogues in various Hellenistic cities of Asia Minor (modern Turkey), although local Jewish leaders are typically depicted as violently opposing their efforts (13:1–14:28). Their tour is interrupted, however, when dissension breaks out between Gentile and Jewish Christians over adherence to the Mosaic Torah. Among other requirements, the Judaizing element insists that Gentile converts be circumcised and observe Jewish dietary laws.

The Jerusalem Conference   According to Acts 15, the first recorded Church council takes place at Jerusalem, where the apostles and "elders" gather to consider whether a believer must first become a Jew in order to be a Christian. Christian Pharisees demand that the entire Torah be kept, but Peter reportedly opposes this (15:10) and, citing his own key role in bringing uncircumcised Gentiles into the Church (15:7–11), thereby silences the Judaizers.

This dispute between Torah-keeping Christians who advocated **circumcision** and their opponents who denied its necessity bitterly divided the early Church. As a believing historian writing many years after the issue had been settled in favor of uncircumcised Gentiles, Luke does not attempt to reproduce the hostilities that then prevailed. His purpose is to create a model, or paradigm, for dealing peacefully with such internal controversies.

In describing the Jerusalem conference, held about 49 C.E., Luke presents an ideal of orderly procedure in which delegates from Antioch and Christian Pharisees agree unanimously on a compromise solution. After Peter advises against laying the Torah "yoke" upon converts, Barnabas and Paul plead their case for the Gentiles' freedom from Torah rules.

According to Luke, the deciding voice is that of **James** (Jesus' "brother" or kinsman), the person who later succeeds Peter as head of the Jerusalem church. Although Paul's letters paint James as a strongly conservative advocate of circumcision (see Gal. 2), the Lukan James is a "moderate" who imposes only limited Torah mandates. James' dietary restrictions are based on rules from Leviticus, in which both Jews and foreign residents are forbidden to eat blood or meat that has not been drained of blood (15:13–21; Lev. 17–18).

The author completes his example of model church procedures by illustrating the manner in which James' recommendation is carried out. Themes of unity and cooperation dominate Luke's account: the "whole church" agrees to send "unanimously" elected delegates back to Antioch with a letter containing the Jerusalem church's directive. Characteristically, Luke notes that the decision of this precedent-setting conference is also "the decision of the Holy Spirit" (15:22–29). To the author, the church's deliberations reflect the divine will.

Paul's Independence of the Apostolic Church
Luke's picture of Paul's cooperative relationship with the apostolic leadership in Jerusalem differs significantly from the account in Paul's letters. According to Luke, shortly after his conversion Paul went to Jerusalem, where he "tried to join the body of disciples there" but was rebuffed. After Barnabas took this zealous convert under his wing, however, Luke implies that Paul became an accepted member of Jerusalem's Christian community (9:26–30). In his own version of events, Paul categorically denies that he had early contact with the Jerusalem Church or that his teaching about Jesus owed anything to his apostolic predecessors. After describing his private "revelation" of the risen Jesus, Paul states: "without consulting any human being, without going up to Jerusalem to see those who were apostles before me, I went off at once to Arabia, and afterwards returned to Damascus" (Gal. 1:17). Three years later, Paul notes, he did make a trip to Jerusalem "to get to know Cephas [Peter]," but he did not confer "with any other of the apostles, except James, the Lord's brother" (Gal. 1:18–19). When Paul immediately adds: "What I write is plain truth; before God I am not lying" (Gal. 1:20), it is clear that he rejects any suggestion that he was ever under the influence or jurisdiction of the Jerusalem leadership.

Given Luke's policy of depicting Paul as an obedient churchman, willingly subject to apostolic decrees, it is not surprising that Acts' picture of the Jerusalem conference contrasts markedly with Paul's eyewitness report (Gal. 2:1–10). Whereas Acts shows the Gentile-Torah issue peacefully and unanimously settled, Paul declared that "not for one moment" did he compromise his position that Gentile Christians should live absolutely free of Torah "bondage." According to Galatians, Paul accepted no restrictions, whereas Acts states that he unhesitatingly agreed to James's four Torah prohibitions.

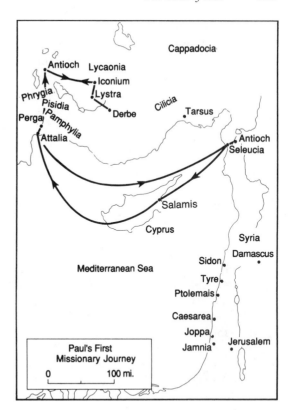

According to Acts, Paul made three major tours through the northeastern Mediterranean region. Although the account in Acts may oversimplify Paul's complex travel itineraries, it correctly shows him focusing his efforts on major urban centers in Asia Minor (modern Turkey).

In addition, Paul reveals an attitude toward eating meat sacrificed to Greco-Roman gods that differs from that ascribed to him in Acts (1 Cor. 8:8; 10:27).

Some historians believe that the apostolic decree involving dietary matters may have been issued at a later Jerusalem conference, one that Paul did not attend. In this view, Luke has combined the results of two separate meetings and reported them as a single event. Later in Acts, the author seems aware that Paul did not know about the Jerusalem church's decision regarding Torah-prohibited meats. During Paul's final Jerusalem visit, James is shown speaking about the dietary restrictions as if they were news to Paul (21:25).

Paul's Second Missionary Journey: Evangelizing Greece

Shortly after the Jerusalem conference, Paul and Barnabas separate. Acts attributes the parting to a quarrel over John Mark's alleged unreliability, but in Galatians Paul states that he and Barnabas differed over the question of Torah observance, Barnabas having been "carried away" by the "circumcision party" (Gal. 2:13). As a result, Paul and Silas alone visit the newly founded churches of **Syria** and Asia Minor until a vision directs Paul into **Macedonia** (15:40–16:10), where Luke shows him following his usual pattern of preaching in local synagogues and then being abused by Jewish leaders (16:11–17:15).

Driven from the Macedonian cities of **Philippi, Thessalonica**, and Beroea, Paul finds unusual tolerance in **Athens**, the brilliant center of Greek philosophy, where he is invited to speak before an intellectually curious group at the **Areopagus** (highest council) (17:16–34). After making few converts among the sophisticated Athenians, Paul enjoys greater success in **Corinth**, a prosperous Greek seaport, where he founds a thriving church. Paul's letters to the Corinthians (discussed later in this part) contain some of his most vivid writing.

Paul's Third Missionary Journey: Revisiting Asia Minor and Greece

A third missionary tour, in which Paul revisits the churches of Greece and Asia (Chs. 18–21), culminates in **Ephesus**, a cosmopolitan port in what is now western Turkey. Luke frames Paul's adventures in Ephesus with intimations of the apostle's final journey—to Rome. As Luke had pictured Jesus turning his face resolutely toward Jerusalem and the servant's death that awaited him there (Luke 9:51), so the author shows Paul determined to complete his last tour and head for the imperial capital (19:21–22). After summoning Ephesian church leaders to Miletus, an ancient Greek city on the Aegean, Paul delivers a farewell speech, predicting his imminent imprisonment and possible martyrdom (20:17–38).

The remainder of Acts is largely concerned with Paul's legal difficulties with the Roman government. Reinforcing his theme that Christianity offers no threat to Roman security, the author takes pains to demonstrate that Paul is charged with sedition only because "envious" Jews stir up trouble against him. Roman officials repeatedly testify that he is guilty of no punishable action. When some Corinthian Jews charge him with defaming God, the Roman proconsul **Gallio** throws the case out of court (18:12–17). Similarly, when the Greek silversmiths of Ephesus, who fashion images of the goddess Artemis (**Diana**) for sale to tourists, try to force Paul to stop his anti-idolatry campaign, local authorities argue that they have no legal cause to do so (19:21–40).

Paul's Arrest in Jerusalem and Imprisonment in Caesarea

On Paul's return to Jerusalem, Jewish resistance reaches a climax as certain "Jews from the province of Asia" (21:27) accuse him of blasphemy and of profaning the Temple. When a mob attacks him, Roman soldiers intervene and conduct him to the Sanhedrin. Disclosing that he is a Pharisee, Paul succeeds in dividing the Council so that scribes of his party call for his release while the Sadducees and others denounce him (21:27–23:10). The divine plan operating through Paul's suffering is now revealed: He must proclaim the Christian witness in Rome as he has in Jerusalem (23:11).

The Political Innocence of Christians   After being taken into protective custody by Lysias, a Roman army commander, Paul is imprisoned for two years at **Caesarea** under Governor **Antonius Felix**, who apparently has no plans to release his troublesome prisoner without receiving the customary bribe. Under Felix's successor, **Porcius Festus**, Paul exercises his birthright as a Roman citizen and "appeals to

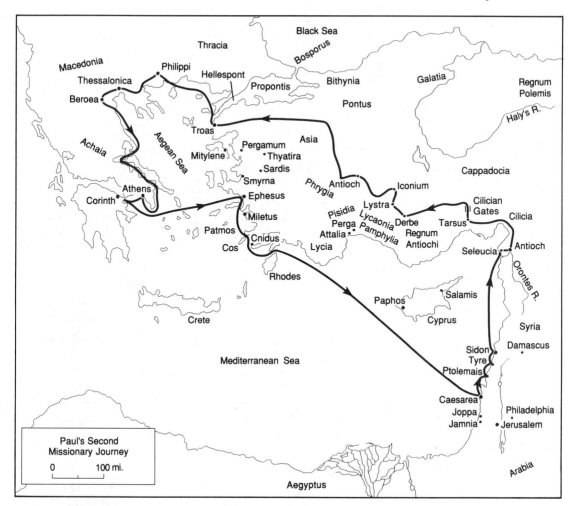

As Acts depicts it, Paul's second missionary journey brought Christianity to Europe, with new cells of Christians established in Philippi, Thessalonica, and Corinth. Note that Antioch in Syria is Paul's missionary headquarters.

Caesar," demanding to be tried in the emperor's own court (25:1–21). The detailed narration of Paul's defense before Festus, King **Herod Agrippa II**, and his sister Bernice (25:8–26:32) is intended to demonstrate his innocence of any religious or political crimes. Paul's long defense (26:1–29) is a vivid summary of his career as depicted in Acts, including a third account of his "heavenly" vision of the risen Jesus. Luke's main purpose in this courtroom scene is to establish Christianity's potentially friendly rela-

tionship to the **Roman Empire**. Echoing Pilate's opinion of Jesus, Governor Festus admits that Paul is guilty of "nothing that deserves death or imprisonment." Agrippa drives home the point: Paul could have been set free if "he had not appealed to the Emperor" (26:30–32). In Luke's introduction of the Christian church to his Greco-Roman audience, the author makes clear that missionaries like Paul are prosecuted in Roman courts only through officials' misunderstanding or the malice of false accusers.

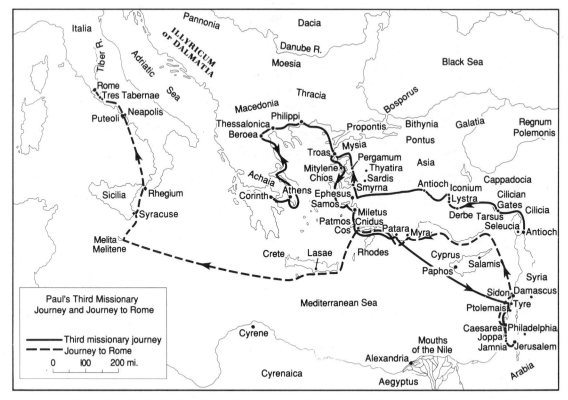

According to Acts, Paul's third missionary journey ended with his arrest in Jerusalem and two-year imprison-ment in Caesarea. The broken line shows the route of Paul's sea voyage to Rome, where he was taken to be tried in the imperial courts.

Paul's Journey to Rome and His Preaching to Roman Jews

Luke begins his final section—Paul's sea jour-ney to Rome—with an exciting description of a shipwreck (27:1–28:31). This segment of the narrative is told in the first person, one of several "we" passages appearing in the latter part of Acts. Scholars are unsure whether this represents an eyewitness report or is merely a literary device to heighten the immediacy of the account.

The author concludes his survey of the early Church with Paul's arrival in Rome, where, al-though under house arrest, he is free to preach "quite openly and without hindrance" (28:31). This final statement is probably a reminder to Roman authorities that Paul established a kind of legal precedent. Awaiting trial, and with full

knowledge of his captors, Christianity's greatest missionary continued to evangelize the Roman population.

Although Acts ends abruptly without telling us of Paul's subsequent fate, Luke has accom-plished his stated purpose of tracing Christiani-ty's expansion from Jerusalem to "the ends of the earth" (1:8), a goal metaphorically achieved by Paul's witness in Rome, heart of the pagan empire. His hero's last words emphasize another major Lukan theme: Paul (and his successors) will henceforth direct the gospel primarily to non-Jews, for "the Gentiles will listen" (28:28). Notice that Luke shows Paul quoting from Isa-iah 6, the same passage about Jewish refusal to heed the prophet's oracles that Mark had cited to explain why Jesus' people failed to accept his

Perhaps the world's most famous ruins, the Parthenon originally housed an ivory and gold statue of Athene Parthenos (Athene the Virgin). This gleaming marble temple to the goddess of wisdom and victory dominated the skyline of Athens when Paul visited the city in the late 40s C.E. and still does today, twenty-five centuries after it was built. (Courtesy of Erich Lessing/PhotoEdit)

teaching (see Mark 4:10–13). Luke does not use this Markan interpretation in his Gospel account of Jesus' parables but instead places it at the end of his Church history to express his view that Christianity's future belongs to the Gentiles.

TERMS AND CONCEPTS TO REMEMBER

Antioch	Corinth
Antonius Felix	Cornelius
apostle	Diana (of the
Areopagus	Ephesians)
ascension	Ephesus
Athens	Gallio
Barnabas	Gamaliel
Caesarea	glossolalia
centurion	Hellenists
circumcision	Herod Agrippa II

Holy Spirit	Philippi
James	Porcius Festus
Jerusalem church	Roman Empire
Judas Iscariot	Saul of Tarsus
Macedonia	Simon
martyr	Stephen
Matthias	Syria
Paul	Thessalonica
Pentecost	

RECOMMENDED READING

Bruce, F. F. *Commentary on the Book of Acts.* Grand Rapids, Mich.: Eerdmans, 1956.

Dillon, Richard J. "Acts of the Apostles." In R. E. Brown et al., *The New Jerome Biblical Commentary,* pp. 722–767. Englewood Cliffs, N.J.: Prentice-Hall, 1990. A thorough introductory study.

Haenchen, Ernst. *The Acts of the Apostles: A Commentary.* Philadelphia: Westminster Press, 1971. An excellent study.

The ruins of a magnificent city open to the sky mark the site of Ephesus, a Greco-Roman seaport in Asia Minor (western Turkey). This view looks across an amphitheater toward the Arcadian Way. A major base of Paul's missionary activity (Acts 19), Ephesus later became an important Christian center, as reflected in later traditions that the Apostle John took Jesus' mother there, whence she ascended bodily to heaven. (Courtesy of Sonia Halliday Photographs, photo by F. H. C. Birch)

Hanson, R. P. C. *The Acts.* New York: Oxford University Press, 1967.

Hengel, Martin. *Acts and the History of Earliest Christianity.* Philadelphia: Fortress Press, 1980.

Johnson, Luke Timothy. "Luke-Acts, Books of." In D. N. Freedman, ed., *The Anchor Bible Dictionary,* Vol. 4, pp. 403–420. New York: Doubleday, 1992.

Juel, Donald. *Luke-Acts: The Promise of History.* Atlanta: John Knox Press, 1984.

Talbert, C. H. *Acts.* Atlanta: John Knox Press, 1984.

QUESTIONS FOR REVIEW

1. A sequel to Luke's Gospel, the Book of Acts continues the story of Christian origins. Which of the same themes that appear in the Gospel are also found in Acts? Compare the account of Jesus' trial before Pilate with that of Paul before Pilate's successors, Felix and Festus.

2. How does Luke organize his account of Christianity's birth and growth to demonstrate fulfillment of Jesus' commission in Acts 1:8? Describe the major milestones in Luke's history of the "new Way" from Pentecost through the conversion of Cornelius, the first Church council in Jerusalem, Paul's missionary journeys, and Paul's arrival in Rome.

3. In what ways does the Jerusalem community described in Acts 2 put into operation the social and economic principles enunciated in Luke's Gospel? How does the early Church "equalize" wealth and poverty?

4. By adding a history of primitive Christianity to his Gospel narrative, how does Luke de-emphasize apocalyptic hopes of Jesus' early return? What does Paul's preaching in Rome forecast for the Church's future relationship with the Roman Empire?

Paul and the Gentile Mission

Paul, former Pharisee and persecutor of the Church who later spearheaded Christianity's mission to the Gentiles, dominates the second half of Acts. To an incalculable extent, he also dominates the later history of Christian thought. His letters, which form the third unit of the New Testament, represent the new religion's first—and in important ways the most lasting—attempt to interpret the meaning of Jesus' sacrificial death and its significance to human salvation. Paul's startling view is that Jesus' crucifixion introduced a radically different relationship between God and all humanity—Gentiles as well as Jews. Paul's declaration that faith in Christ superseded Torah obedience as the means of reconciliation to God transformed Christianity from a Jewish sect into a new world religion. In his letters to the Romans and Galatians, Paul outlined a theology of redemption through faith that has become central to Christianity's self-understanding. Later theologians as diverse as the Roman church father Augustine (354–430 C.E.) and Martin Luther (1483–1546), the German priest who sparked the Protestant Reformation, derived many of their doctrines from Paul's letters.

Many historians have remarked that there is perhaps more of Paul than Jesus in official Christianity. Even Mark, the earliest story of Jesus' life, bears the imprint of Pauline ideas in its bias toward Gentile believers, its account of the Last Supper, and its theology of the cross. Some

This cult statue of Diana of Ephesus, where the world's largest temple was erected in the goddess' honor, emphasizes her function as giver of fertility. Although the Romans identified Diana with Artemis, the Greek virgin goddess of wild creatures and the hunt, the Ephesian Diana bears a greater resemblance to older Near Eastern fertility deities such as Ishtar or Astarte. Acts records a confrontation between Paul and the silversmiths of Ephesus, whose livelihood making silver figurines of Diana was threatened by the apostle's monotheistic gospel (Acts 19: 23–41). (Courtesy of Alinari / Art Resource, NY)

This map shows the locations of the major churches at the end of Paul's ministry (about 62 C.E.). Note that most of the tiny cells of Christians are at the eastern end of the Mediterranean (Palestine and Syria) or in Asia Minor (present-day Turkey). Paul established most of the churches in western Asia Minor as well as the first churches in Greece (Philippi to Corinth). We do not know who founded the Italian churches, including the one in Rome. How or when Christianity was introduced to Egypt (Alexandria and Cyrene) is also unknown.

commentators accuse Paul, who did not know the historical Jesus, of largely ignoring Christ's original proclamation—God's active rule in individual human lives—in favor of promulgating a mystery cult *about* Jesus. Certainly, Paul almost never cites Jesus' kingdom teaching and instead emphasizes his own personal experience of the risen Christ, which he interprets in cosmic and mystical terms.

In contrast to Jesus, who apparently wrote nothing, Paul speaks directly to us through his letters, permitting us to compare what he says about himself with what later writers, such as Luke, say about him. Paul's position in the canon is unique: He is the only historical personage who is both a major character in a New Testament book and the author of New Testament books himself. Church tradition ascribes no fewer than thirteen canonical letters to Paul, in total length nearly one-third of the New Testament. Most scholars regard only seven as genuinely Pauline, but the presence of other works attributed to him shows in what high esteem he was held. His ideas and personality so captured the imagination of later Christian authors that they paid tribute to the great apostle by writing in his name and perpetuating his teachings.

Seeking the Historical Paul

As a Christian thinker, Paul never forgets his Jewishness. Although he fights to free Christi-

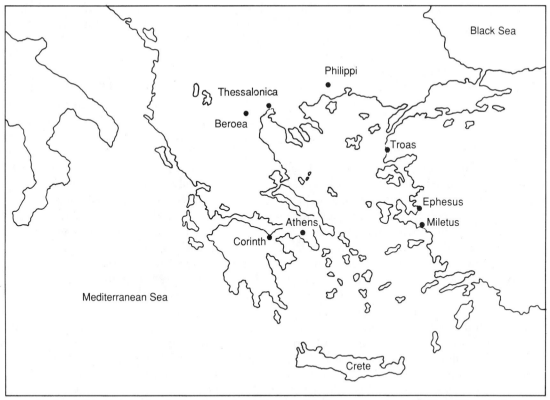

Paul established largely Gentile churches in the northeastern Mediterranean region at Philippi, Thessalonica, Beroea, and Corinth. Paul's teaching was also influential in the Asia Minor City of Ephesus, where he lived for at least two years.

anity from the "bondage" of Torah observance, Paul consistently stresses the unbroken continuity between **Judaism** and the new religion. For him, as for Matthew, Christianity is revealed through Jesus' ministry but shaped and largely defined by the Hebrew Bible. Throughout his letters, Paul quotes selected parts of the Hebrew Scriptures to support the validity of his particular gospel. Despite Paul's ambivalent attitude toward the Mosaic Torah, much of the Hebrew biblical tradition retains its teaching authority for him.

Our most reliable source of Paul's biography is his letters, where he repeatedly stresses his Jewish heritage. Describing himself as a circumcised "Hebrew born and bred" from the Israelite tribe of Benjamin (Phil. 3:5–6), Paul states

that as a "practicing Jew" he outstripped his Jewish contemporaries in strict observance of "the traditions of [his] ancestors" (Gal. 1:13–14). A member of the **Pharisee** sect, he obeyed the Torah completely. "In legal rectitude"—keeping the Torah commandments—Paul judges himself "faultless" (Phil. 3:6).

Before his call to follow Jesus, Paul demonstrated his loyalty to Pharisaic Judaism by persecuting those who believed that Jesus was the Jewish Messiah. Whatever the nature of Paul's supernatural encounter with the risen Christ (Acts 9:1–9, 22:3–11, 16:12–19), it radically changed his attitude toward Christianity without modifying his essential personality. According to Acts and his own testimony, he displayed the same quality of religious zeal before Jesus appeared to him as he does afterward. Paul's experience seems less a conversion from one religion to another (he always stresses the connection between Judaism and the new faith) than a redirection of his abundant energies. (See "A Tentative Sequence of Events in Paul's Life" on page 415.)

The Historical Reliability of Acts

Acts supplies much information about Paul not contained in his letters, but most scholars urge great caution about accepting Acts' data at face value. A great deal of the material in the letters is difficult to reconcile with Acts' narrative sequence. Where discrepancies occur, scholars prefer Paul's firsthand version of events. The author of Acts investigated various sources to compile his account of Christianity's beginnings (Luke 1:1–4), but he appears to have worked with inadequate documentation in recording Paul's career. As noted above, the author is either unaware of, or deliberately ignores, Paul's voluminous correspondence, his insistence claims to apostleship, and his distinctive teaching. Acts says virtually nothing about Paul's essential gospel—that people are saved not by obedience to Torah commands but by faith in Christ. A growing number of scholars believe that the writer of Acts set out to tame or domesticate Paul, minimizing his fierce independence and picturing him as a dutiful son of the institutional church. In his letters, Paul passionately defends his autonomy and recognizes no superior churchly authority.

Acts provides biographical details that Paul never mentions, such as his birth in **Tarsus**, capital city of Cilicia (now included in southeastern Turkey) and the belief that Paul's family possessed Roman citizenship. These and similar traditions—such as Paul's originally being named Saul, his studying at the feet of Rabbi Gamaliel (the leading Pharisee scholar of his day), and his supporting himself by tent making—are never referred to in the Pauline letters, so we have no way of verifying their

historical accuracy. (See the feature, "Some Differences Between Acts and Paul's Letters" on page 416.)

Paul's Experience of the Risen Jesus

In both Acts and Paul's letters, Paul's life can be divided into two contrasting parts. During his early career he was a devout Pharisee who "savagely" persecuted the first Christians. During his later years he was a Christian missionary who successfully implanted the new religion in non-Jewish territories and established the first churches of Europe. The event that changed Paul from a persecutor of Christians into an indomitable Christian evangelist was, in his words, "a revelation [*apokalypsis*] of Jesus Christ" (Gal. 1:12). Acts depicts the "revelation" as a blinding vision of the risen Messiah on the road to **Damascus**. The author stresses the importance of the event by narrating it fully three times (Acts 9:1–9, 22:3–11, 26:12–19). Paul's briefer allusions to the experience speak simply of being called by God's "grace" (Gal. 1: 15) to an "abnormal birth" and of witnessing a postresurrection appearance of Jesus (1 Cor. 15: 8–9). Paul does not state what form the apparition took, but he does imply that he maintained an ongoing communication with divine beings, experiencing a number of mystical visions (2 Cor. 12:1–10).

Paul's physical stamina—even today duplicating his travel itinerary would exhaust most people—is matched by the strength of his feelings. Paul's letters reveal their author's emotional intensity, ranging from paternal tenderness to biting sarcasm. In one letter, he insults his readers' intelligence and suggests that some of their advisers castrate themselves (Gal. 3:1; 5:12). In other letters, he reacts to criticism with threats, wild boasting, and wounding anger (2 Cor. 10–13). In still others, he expresses profound affection and gentle tact (1 Cor. 13; Phil. 1:3–9; 2:1–4; 4:2–3).

Paul's conviction that Jesus had privately revealed to him the one true gospel (Gal. 1–2)

A Tentative Sequence of Events in Paul's Life

Except for a few incidents, such as Paul's visit to Corinth when Gallio was proconsul in Achaea (Greece) (c. 51–53), scholars do not agree on the dates of major events in Paul's life. From references in Paul's letters and a cautious use of material in Acts, however, it is possible to reconstruct a general outline of Paul's biography.

* Paul is born a Hellenistic Jew (in Tarsus, first decade C.E.?). He is educated as a Pharisee (Phil. 3:5–6; 2 Cor. 11:22).
* [Jesus is crucified (c. 30 C.E.?).]
* Paul harasses members of the early Jesus movement (1 Cor. 15:9; Gal. 1:13–14).
* Paul encounters the risen Jesus (c. 32–34 C.E.) (1 Cor. 15:9–10; Gal. 1:11–12, 16).
* After his *revelation,* Paul travels to "Arabia" and then returns to Damascus (without visiting Jerusalem) (Gal. 1:16–17).
* "After three years," he visits Jerusalem to meet Peter (Cephas) and James "the Lord's brother" (Gal. 1:18–19).
* He then travels to "Syria and Cilicia [southeast Turkey]," presumably as a missionary to Gentiles (and steering clear of Jewish churches) (Gal. 1:22).
* "Fourteen years later," with Titus and Barnabas, Paul makes a second visit to Jerusalem (c. 49 C.E.), presumably to confer with Peter, John, James, and representatives from Antioch about admitting Gentiles as equal members of the church (Gal. 2:1–10; cf. Acts 15).

* After the Jerusalem consultation, Paul returns to Antioch, where he opposes Peter over the issue of dining with Gentiles (Gal. 2:11–14).
* Traveling from Antioch to Greece, Paul establishes the first Christian congregations of Europe (Philippi, Thessalonica, and Corinth); remains in Corinth for eighteen months (c. 49–51); writes letter to the Thessalonians (c. 50 C.E.). (See Acts 18:11–12.)
* Paul visits Ephesus (c. 52–55); writes 1 Corinthians (c. 54–55).
* Paul makes (second?) tour of Macedonia and Greece (Acts 19:1, 10, 22); writes various parts of 2 Corinthians (and Galatians?).
* He makes a third and final visit to Corinth; writes Romans; plans to revisit Jerusalem and then to stop by Rome en route to Spain (Rom. 15:23–29).
* Paul makes third visit to Jerusalem, where he is arrested and then imprisoned at Caesarea under Antonius Felix (procurator of Judea, c. 52–59 C.E.) and Felix's successor, Porcius Festus.
* Under armed guard, Paul is transported to Rome, where he remains under house arrest for two years (c. 60–62) (Acts 27–28).
* Paul is executed in Rome under Nero (c. 62–64).

isolated the apostle from many fellow believers. Acts and the letters agree that Paul quarreled with many of his intimate companions (Acts 15:37–39; Gal. 2:11–14) as well as with entire groups (Gal.; 2 Cor. 10–13). This sense of a unique vision, one not shared by most other Christians, may have shaped Paul's admitted preference for preaching in territories where no Christian had preceded him. The more distant his missionary field from competing evangelizers, the better it suited him. Paul's desire to impress his individual gospel upon new converts may have influenced his ambition to work in areas as far removed from established churches as possible (Rom. 15:20–23).

Paul's Letters

The Genuine Letters   New Testament historians generally agree that Paul became a Christian in the mid-30s C.E. and that he traveled extensively as a missionary during the 40s and 50s C.E., arriving in Rome about the year 60. Scholarly agreement disappears, however, in at-

Some Differences Between Acts and Paul's Letters

ACTS	PAUL'S LETTERS
Named Saul and raised in Tarsus.	Original name not mentioned (but born to tribe of Benjamin, whose first king was Saul [Phil. 3:5]).
Studied under Rabbi Gamaliel.	Studies under Gamaliel not mentioned.
Belonged to the Pharisee party.	Membership in Pharisee party confirmed in Philippians 3:6.
Persecuted Christians.	Persecution of Christians mentioned several times.
Experienced a vision of Jesus on the road to Damascus.	Received a "revelation" of Jesus (Gal. 1:12, 16).
Following his call, went immediately to Damascus, where he preached in synagogues.	Went to "Arabia" for an unspecified period (Gal. 1:17).
At first is shunned by Jerusalem disciples, is later introduced to apostles (9:26–30).	Did not go to Jerusalem until three years after return from "Arabia" and met only Peter and James (Gal. 1:17–20).
Receives Holy Spirit after Ananias baptizes and lays hands upon him.	Asserts he owes his apostolic gospel and commission to no one; never refers to baptism (Gal. 1:11–12, 16–17).
Attendance at apostolic conference is his third Jerusalem visit.	Conference marks Paul's second Jerusalem visit (Gal. 2:1–10).
Agrees to impose Torah dietary restrictions on Gentile converts.	Refuses to accept any legal restrictions (Gal. 2:5).
Agrees to forbid eating meat sacrificed to idols.	Regards eating such meat as undefiling (1 Cor. 8; 10:27; Rom. 14:13–15:6).

tempting to date Paul's letters or even establish the exact order in which he wrote them.

The majority of scholars accept seven letters as authentically Pauline. Virtually all scholars regard Romans, 1 and 2 Corinthians, Galatians, Philippians, 1 Thessalonians, and Philemon as Paul's own writing. Some also accept 2 Thessalonians and Colossians. By contrast, the majority doubt that Ephesians is genuine and are certain that three—Titus and 1 and 2 Timothy—were composed by a Pauline disciple after the apostle's death. Almost no reputable scholar believes that Hebrews, which is a sermon rather than a letter, is a Pauline composition. (Refer to "Paul's Letters: Authentic, Disputed, and Pseudonymous" on page 417.)

Order of Composition   Although scholars debate the exact order in which Paul composed his letters, they generally agree that 1 Thessalonians was written first (about 50 C.E.) and is thus the oldest Christian writing in existence. If Paul also wrote 2 Thessalonians, it also dates from about 50 C.E. 1 and 2 Corinthians are usually placed in the mid-50s, and the more theologically mature letters, such as Romans and Philippians, are dated later. Four letters—Colossians, Philemon, Philippians, and possibly Ephesians—were reputedly composed while Paul was imprisoned and are known as the "captivity letters." Unfortunately, Paul does not reveal in the letters where he was jailed, so we do not know whether he wrote them from

Paul's Letters: Authentic, Disputed, and Pseudonymous

Paul's genuine letters, composed between about 50 and 62 C.E., form the oldest surviving Christian literature. In the decades after Paul's death, his influence became so great that different Christian groups apparently competed for the role of authoritative interpreter of his teaching. Following the Hellenistic-Jewish practice of **pseudonymity** (writing in the name of an honored religious authority of the past, such as Moses or one of the apostles), some Christian authors composed letters in Paul's name, using their understanding of the Pauline heritage to address problems of their own day. Whereas Paul's genuine letters invariably deal with specific problems besetting individual congregations (and presume a relatively informal church structure), pseudonymous letters such as 1 and 2 Timothy and Titus (the **pastoral Epistles**) typically deal with such issues as maintaining the doctrinal purity of apostolic traditions and presume a much more structured church administration.

LETTERS BY PAUL	*LETTERS PROBABLY NOT BY PAUL*	*LETTERS DEFINITELY NOT BY PAUL*
1 Thessalonians (c. 50 C.E.)	2 Thessalonians	Ephesians
1 and 2 Corinthians	Colossians	1 and 2 Timothy
Galatians		Titus
Romans		Hebrews (Even in early Christianity, most churchmen did not believe that Hebrews was by Paul.)
Philemon		
Philippians		

Ephesus, Caesarea, or Rome, all cities in which he presumably suffered imprisonment. The canonical letters (others have been lost) were probably all written during a relatively brief span of time, the decade between about 50 and 60 C.E.

Paul's Use of the Letter Form   Paul is aware that his letters are persuasive documents. He consciously uses letters as substitutes for his own presence, making them an effective means of influencing people and events from a distance. Although he gives directions on a wide variety of matters, his primary object is to correct his recipients' beliefs and to discipline their behavior. His letters are also potent weapons for shooting down opposition to his teaching.

Writing to the Corinthians, Paul states that his critics contrast his "weighty and powerful" letters with his unimpressive physical appearance and ineffectiveness as a speaker (2 Cor. 10: 9–11). The apostle may exaggerate his defects for rhetorical effect, but he is right about his letters. From the time they were first written until now, they have exerted enormous influence on Christian thought and conduct.

Paul writes letters so effectively that he makes this literary category the standard medium of communication for many later Christian writers. The large majority of New Testament authors imitate Paul by conveying their ideas in letter form. Twenty-one of the twenty-seven canonical books are (at least theoretically) letters. Even the writer of Revelation uses this form to transmit Jesus' message to the seven churches of Asia Minor (Rev. 2–3).

Hellenistic Letters   In general, Paul follows the accepted Hellenistic literary form in his correspondence, modifying it somewhat to express his peculiarly Christian interests. Much Greco-Roman correspondence, both personal and

St. Paul in Prison by Rembrandt (1606–1669). In his murky cell, Paul composes letters to inspire faith and hope in the membership of his tiny, scattered churches. Notice that the light from the cell's barred window seems to emanate from Paul himself, surrounding his head like a halo and glowing from the pages of the manuscripts he holds. (Courtesy Staatsgalerie, Stuttgart)

business, has survived from early Christian times, allowing us to compare Paul's letters with those of other Hellenistic writers.

The Hellenistic letter writer typically begins with a prescript, identifying the writer and the reader, and a greeting, wishing good fortune to the reader and commonly invoking the blessing of a god. Paul varies this formula by mentioning the Christian allegiance of the writer and recipients, substituting "grace" and "peace" for the customary greetings, and frequently including an associate's name in the salutation. He also elaborates on the Hellenistic custom by giving praise, thanks, or prayers for the welfare of his recipients.

Paul also modifies his letters' prescripts according to his attitude toward the church he is addressing. Paul's letter to his trusted friends at Philippi opens with an effusive outpouring of affection and praise for the Philippians (Phil. 1: 1–11). By contrast, when he writes to the churches in Galatia, he is furious with the recipients and includes no warm or approving salutation (Gal. 1:1–5).

After stating the letter's principal message, the Hellenistic writer closes with additional greetings, typically including greetings from other people and sometimes adding a request that the recipient(s) convey the sender's greetings to mutual acquaintances. Paul often expands this custom to include a summary statement of faith and a benediction as well as a list of fellow Christians to be greeted (Rom. 16; 1 Cor. 16:10–21; Col. 4:7–18).

Role of Dictation   As was customary in Greco-Roman correspondence, Paul apparently dictated all his letters to a secretary or scribe, occasionally adding a signature or a few other words in his own hand. In antiquity, secretaries ordinarily did not record the precise words of those dictating but paraphrased the gist of what was said (Rom. 16:21–22; Gal. 6:11; Col. 4:18; Philem. 19; 2 Thess. 3:17), a practice that helps explain the spontaneous quality of Pauline letters.

Circumstances of Writing   Most of Paul's letters were composed under the pressure of meeting an emergency in a given church. With the exception of Romans, which is addressed to a congregation that he had not yet visited, every Pauline letter is directed to a particular group, and most of the groups are personally known by the writer. In virtually every case, the recipients are experiencing some form of crisis, either of belief or behavior, which the author tries to resolve.

Paul's main concern is always pastoral; he deals with individual problems caused by church members' teaching or conduct. In counseling these small groups of infant Christians, Paul typically invokes theological arguments or examples to reinforce his advice. Because Paul's presentation of theological issues is secondary to his counseling, the letters do not represent a complete or systematic statement of Pauline belief. In addition, the reader will find Paul's

thought changing and developing from one letter to another.

Paul's Major Topics and Themes

Pauline thought is commonly subtle and complex, so much so that even scholars are not able to achieve a consensus about the apostle's views on many important topics. Among the major Pauline topics and concepts are the following:

1. *Eschatology and mysticism.* Paul bases his authority as a Christian leader and the validity of his distinctive gospel on an *apokalypsis,* a private revelation of the postresurrection Jesus (Gal. 1:11–12, 15–17). This encounter with Christ, which he insists he received as a direct heavenly communication and not from any apostolic predecessor, informs Paul that the glorified Jesus now exists in two separate but related dimensions: the macrocosm (great world) of God's spiritual domain and the microcosm (little world) of human consciousness. This **dualism,** characteristic of apocalyptic thought, expresses Paul's conviction that Christ possesses both an objective and a subjective reality. Christ is at once a cosmic figure who will soon return to judge the world and a being who also mysteriously dwells within the individual believer. The tension between the transcendent and the imminent Christ, one who is simultaneously universal and yet intimately experienced by the faithful, appears in almost every letter Paul wrote.

Paul's mysticism—his powerful sense of union with an unseen spiritual reality—is an important component of his worldview. In 2 Corinthians, he writes of being "caught up as far as the third heaven," "into paradise," where he "heard words so secret that human lips may not repeat them" (2 Cor. 12:1–4). These "visions and revelations granted by the Lord," which undoubtedly played their part in sustaining Paul through the many dangers and hardships he endured, may not have occurred as often as he would have liked. He adds that to prevent him "from being unduly elated by the

The Apostle Paul by Rembrandt (1606–1669). Rembrandt's somber portrait shows Paul in a deeply reflective mood and stresses the apostle's consciousness of the enormous burden he bears—the task of communicating his unique vision of Christ to the Gentiles. In his letters, Paul expresses a wide variety of emotions —joy, anger, bitter sarcasm—but Rembrandt captures here the sense of melancholy and isolation that typically characterize this great missionary. (Courtesy of National Gallery of Art, Washington, D.C., Widener Collection)

magnificence of such revelations," he was given "a sharp physical pain," perhaps to remind him that even sporadic experiences of the infinite could not allow him to escape his finite humanity (2 Cor. 12:7–8).

Paul may have been familiar with the Book of 1 Enoch, which describes **Enoch**'s visionary tour of seven (or ten) heavens—or at least the tradition surrounding it—because he clearly shares its aspiration for mystical oneness with the divine. Paul also shares Enoch's apocalyptic viewpoint. His conviction that the Messiah's appearance has inaugurated the End of time permeates his thought and underlies much of his ethical teaching. Paul's advice on marriage, divorce, slavery, celibacy, and human behavior in general is largely shaped by his expectation of an imminent Final Judgment. In his oldest surviving letter, he states that he expects to witness the **Parousia**: "We who are left alive until the Lord comes . . . [will be] caught up in the clouds to meet the Lord in the air" (1 Thess. 4: 15–17).

In 1 Corinthians, his expectation to live until the End is equally certain; hence, he advises his correspondents that "the time we live in will not last long. While it lasts, married men should be as if they had no wives; . . . buyers must not count on keeping what they buy, nor those who use the world's wealth. . . . For the whole frame of this world is passing away" (1 Cor. 7:29–31). Eagerly anticipating the *eschaton,* he also tells the Corinthians, "Listen! I will unfold a **mystery** [emphasis added]: we shall not all die, but we shall all be changed in a flash, in the twinkling of an eye, at the last trumpet-call. For the trumpet will sound, and the dead will rise immortal, and we shall be changed" (1 Cor. 15:51–52).

Like many Jewish apocalyptists of the first century, Paul sees human history as divided into two qualitatively different ages, or periods of time. The present evil age will soon be replaced by a New Age, a new creation, in which God will reign completely (Gal. 6:14; 1 Cor. 15; 20–28; 2 Cor. 5:17). Because the Messiah's arrival denotes the final consummation of history, Paul regards his generation as the last. His letters thus burn with special urgency because he believes that his day marks the crucial transition period between the two ages. Those about to be judged, especially members of his infant churches, must therefore prepare for the impending visitation, pursuing lives of unblemished virtue.

2. *The centrality and preeminence of Jesus.* Absolutely central to Paul's thought is his conviction that in Jesus God accomplishes the world's salvation. Although Paul shows almost no interest in Jesus' earthly ministry or teachings (if he knew them in any detail), he sees the heavenly Christ in three roles: (1) as God's revealed Wis-

dom (1 Cor. 1–4), (2) as the divine Lord through whom God rules (Phil. 2:11; Rom. 10: 9; 1 Cor. 15:24–28), and (3) as the means by whom God's Spirit dwells in believers (Rom. 8; 14:17). The operation of the Spirit, God's active force denoting his presence and effecting his will in the world, characterizes all of Paul's churches.

3. *Christ and humanity.* In contrasting Christ with the symbol of earthly humanity, Adam (in Genesis, God's first human creation), Paul emphasizes the vast change Jesus' activity has effected for the human race. Prior to Jesus' coming, human beings existed in Adam's perishable image, victims of sin and death (Rom. 5:12–21). By contrast, believers now "in Christ" (living under his power) will also share in the glorified Christ's life-giving nature (1 Cor. 15:21–24, 45–49). "As in Adam all men die, so in Christ all will be brought to life. . . ."

4. *Christ as liberator from sin, Torah, and death.* In Paul's view, all human beings are negatively influenced by sin's power and hence alienated from the perfect God (Rom. 7). Sin's invariable consequence is death, a condition of the defective humanity we share with Adam (Rom. 5: 12–21). By defining the nature as well as the punishment of sin, the Torah increased its power, revealing the universality of sin and condemning all sinners—the entire human race (Rom. 1–3).

Christ's total obedience to the Father and his selfless death on the cross, taking unto himself the Torah's penalty for sin, liberates those persons accepting him (living fully under his power) from sin, death, and the Torah's curses (Gal. 3–5; Rom. 3–7). For Paul, "freedom in Christ" means deliverance from the old order of sin and punishment, including the Torah's power to condemn.

5. *Justification by faith.* Because union with Christ, coming under his rule and influence, is the only way provided to share in Christ's eternal life, good deeds or works of the Torah cannot save. To Paul, one is justified or "made right" before God only through placing **faith**

or complete trust in Jesus' power to save persons with whom he is spiritually united.

RECOMMENDED READING

Baird, W. R. "Paul." In *Harper's Bible Dictionary,* rev. ed., pp. 757–765. San Francisco: Harper & Row, 1985. Basic introduction to Paul's life and thought.

Beker, J. C. *Paul the Apostle: The Triumph of God in Life and Thought.* Philadelphia: Fortress Press, 1980.

Betz, Hans D. "Paul." In D. N. Freedman, ed., *The Anchor Bible Dictionary,* Vol. 5, pp. 186–201. New York: Doubleday, 1992. Surveys Paul's life and theological views.

Bornkamm, Gunther. *Paul.* New York: Harper & Row, 1971. An analysis of Paul's life and thought in the context of his Jewish and Hellenistic environments.

Dunn, James D. G. *Unity and Diversity Within the New Testament,* 2nd ed. Philadelphia: Trinity Press International, 1990. A careful study of the many different ways in which Jesus' significance was understood within the various groups that composed the first-century Christian community.

Fitzmyer, Joseph. *Paul and His Theology,* 2nd ed. Englewood Cliffs, N.J.: Prentice-Hall, 1989. A brief but careful introduction to Paul's central teachings.

———. "Paul." In Raymond E. Brown, Joseph A. Fitzmyer, and Roland E. Murphy, eds., *The New Jerome Biblical Commentary,* pp. 1329–1337. Englewood Cliffs, N.J.: Prentice-Hall, 1990. A helpful survey of Paul's contribution to Christian thought by an eminent Roman Catholic scholar.

Holmberg, B. *Paul and Power.* Philadelphia: Fortress Press, 1980. An incisive study of the social forces at work in the Pauline communities and of Paul's difficult relationships with other apostolic leaders.

Jewett, Robert. *A Chronology of Paul's Life.* Philadelphia: Fortress Press, 1979. Evaluates earlier systems of dating events in Paul's career and provides a new chronology.

Neyrey, Jerome H. *Paul, in Other Words: A Cultural Reading of His Letters.* Louisville, Ky.: Westminster Press/John Knox Press, 1990. The author analyzes Paul's writings to discover the underlying cultural and social assumptions on which Paul bases his worldview and theology.

Sanders, E. P. *Paul, the Law, and the Jewish People.* Philadelphia: Fortress Press, 1983. An excellent exploration of Paul's Jewish heritage.

Segal, Alan F. *Paul the Convert: The Apostolate and Apostasy of Saul the Pharisee.* New Haven, Conn., and London: Yale University Press, 1990. Examines Paul's views of the Christ event in the light of his Jewish heritage.

Soards, Marion L. *The Apostle Paul: An Introduction to His Writings and Teaching.* Mahwah, N.J.: Paulist Press, 1987. A clearly written introduction to Paul's thought, emphasizing his eschatology.

Theissen, Gerd. *The Social Setting of Pauline Christianity.* Philadelphia: Fortress Press, 1982. This study of the social dynamics operating in the church at Corinth is one of the most illuminating studies of primitive Christianity yet published.

1 Thessalonians

KEY THEMES

1 Thessalonians is Paul's earliest surviving letter and thus the oldest Christian document in existence. Written from Corinth about 50 C.E. to a church that Paul, with his companions **Timothy** and **Silas** (Silvanus), had recently founded, it is remarkable chiefly for its eschatology, particularly the urgent expectation of Christ's Parousia (5:1–11) and the resurrection of the dead (4:13–18).

> You [in Thessaloniki] have become a model for all believers . . . you turned from idols . . . to wait expectantly for the appearance from heaven of [God's] Son, Jesus, . . . our deliverer from the terrors of judgment to come.
>
> 1 Thessalonians 1:7, 9, 10

Thessalonica (now called Thessaloniki) was the capital city of the Roman province of **Macedonia**, homeland of Alexander the Great. The church that Paul and his companions had founded there only a short time before writing this letter was still so new that its members, most of whom were Greek converts from polytheistic religions, needed instruction in basic Christian beliefs. After the long introductory section (1: 1–4:12), Paul explains his principal reason for sending the letter—a clarification of his teaching about End time (4:13–5:11). Christians must cling firmly to their newfound faith and live ethically correct lives because Jesus will soon return to judge them. Apparently, some Thessalonians believed that the Parousia would occur so swiftly that all persons converted to Christ would live to see his Second Coming. That belief was shaken when some believers died before Jesus had reappeared. What would become of them? Had the dead missed their opportunity to join Christ in ruling over the world?

The Parousia and the Resurrection

Paul states that the recently dead are not lost but will share in the glory of Christ's return. Paul assumes that he will personally witness the Parousia, declaring that "we who are left alive until the Lord comes" will have no advantage over the faithful dead. Using the traditional language of Jewish apocalyptic works, Paul writes that when the trumpet call of Final Judgment sounds, the Christian dead will rise first. Simultaneously, Christians who are still alive—Paul and his associates among them—will be lifted from earth into the air to join the resurrected saints on their journey to heaven. In both life and death, then, the believer remains with Jesus (4: 13–18). (Compare 1 Thessalonians with Paul's more elaborate discussion of the resurrection in 1 Corinthians 15.)

Discouraging Speculation Although he eagerly expects Jesus' reappearance "soon," Paul has no patience with those who try to predict the exact date of the Parousia. He discourages speculation and notes that calculating "dates and times" is futile because the *eschaton* will arrive as quietly as a thief at midnight. Stressing the unexpectedness of the Parousia, Paul declares that it will occur while leaders proclaim "peace and security" (a common political theme in Roman times as well as the present).

Disaster will strike the nations suddenly, as labor pains seize a woman without warning.

In the Hebrew Bible, the Day of the Lord was the time of Yahweh's intervention into human history, his visitation of earth to judge all nations and to impose his universal rule (Amos 5:18; Joel 2:14–15). In Paul's apocalyptic vision, Jesus serves as the divinely appointed agent of the *eschaton*. As the eschatological Judge, Jesus serves a double function: He brings punishment to the disobedient ("the terrors of judgment") but vindication and deliverance to the faithful. Paul's cosmic Jesus is paradoxic: He dies to save believers from the negative judgment that his return imposes on unregenerate humanity. Returning to his main theme, Paul concludes that "we, awake [living] or asleep [dead]" live in permanent association with Christ (5:4–11).

Role of the Spirit With anticipation of Jesus' speedy return a living reality, Paul reminds the Thessalonians that the Holy Spirit's visible activity among them is also evidence of the world's impending transformation. As noted in Acts, the Spirit motivating believers to prophesy, heal, or speak in tongues was taken as evidence of the Deity's approval. Paul admonishes his readers not to "stifle inspiration" or otherwise discourage believers from prophesying. Christian prophets, inspired by the Spirit, play a major role in Pauline churches, but Paul is aware that enthusiastic visionaries can cause trouble. Believers are to distinguish between "good" and "bad" inspirations, avoiding the latter, but they are not to inhibit charismatic behavior. Besides providing evidence that the End is near, the Spirit's presence also validates the Christian message (see Joel 2:28–32; Acts 2: 1–21; 1 Cor. 2:9–16).

RECOMMENDED READING

Beker, J. C. *Paul's Apocalyptic Gospel: The Coming Triumph of God.* Philadelphia: Fortress Press, 1982.
Collins, R. F. "The First Letter to Thessalonians." In

The New Jerome Biblical Commentary, pp. 772–779. Englewood Cliffs, N.J.: Prentice-Hall, 1990.

Keck, L. E., and Furnish, V. P. *The Pauline Letters*. Nashville, Tenn.: Abingdon Press, 1984.

Krentz, Edgar M. "Thessalonians, First and Second Epistles to the." In D. N. Freedman, ed., *The Anchor Bible Dictionary*, Vol. 6, pp. 515–523, New York: Doubleday, 1992.

Marshall, I. H. *1 and 2 Thessalonians*. Grand Rapids, Mich.: Eerdmans, 1983.

Orr, W. F., and Walther, J. A., eds. *1 and 2 Corinthians and 1 and 2 Thessalonians*. Vol. 32 of the Anchor Bible. Garden City, N.Y.: Doubleday, 1976.

Reese, J. M. *1 and 2 Thessalonians*. Wilmington, Del.: Michael Glazier, 1979.

1 Corinthians

KEY THEMES

Paul's letters to Corinth urge the recipients to overcome their serious divisions, abandon competitive behavior, and strive for unity of belief and purpose. The most important topics include differences between human and divinely revealed wisdom (1:10–3:23), Christian ethics and responsibilities (5:1–11:1), proper conduct at Communion (11:17–34), appreciating gifts of the Spirit (Chs. 12–14), and resurrection of the dead (Ch. 15).

> When I came to you, I declared the attested truth of God without display of fine words or wisdom . . . And yet I do speak words of wisdom to those who are ripe for it, not a wisdom belonging to this passing age. . . . I speak God's hidden wisdom, his secret purpose framed from the very beginning to bring us to our full glory.
>
> 1 Corinthians 2:1, 6, 7

Paul's letters to the congregation in **Corinth**, a wealthy port city noted for its licentiousness and cult of the love goddess Aphrodite (Venus), mirror the problems of an infant church divided by doctrinal disputes, rival leaderships, and sexual immorality. His most extensive correspondence to any one group, the Corinthian letters are particularly valuable for their references to Paul's personal life, their portrait of a first-century Christian community, their theological content, and their memorable passages on love (1 Cor. 13) and a future life (1 Cor. 15; 2 Cor. 4: 7–5:10).

Promoting Christian Unity

Paul's first objective is to halt the rivalries that divide the Corinthians. Without imposing a dogmatic conformity, he asks his readers to work together cooperatively for their mutual benefit (1:8–10). Like all early Christian congregations, that at Corinth met in a private house large enough to accommodate the entire group. Although membership was small, numbering perhaps 50 or 100 persons, it was broken into several opposing cliques. Some members placed undue importance on the particular leader who had converted or baptized them— Paul, **Cephas** (Peter), or **Apollos**, an Alexandrine Jew whose eloquence had impressed many—and competed with each other over the prestige of their respective mentors.

A more serious cause of division may have sprung from the members' unequal social and educational backgrounds, particularly because the Corinthians included both slaves and slaveowners. Even among free citizens, some individuals apparently believed that they were demonstrably superior to their neighbors. Examining Chapter 1 carefully, the reader will see that Paul's attack on false "wisdom" is really an attempt to discourage human competitiveness. In Paul's view, all believers are fundamentally equal: "For through faith you are all [children] of God in union with Christ Jesus. . . . There is no such thing as Jew and Greek, slave and freeman, male and female; for you are all one person in Christ Jesus" (Gal. 3:26, 28). When Paul reminds the Corinthians that he taught his message as simply as possible, he does so to show that the new faith is essentially incompatible with individual pride or competitiveness. (Paul's relative lack of success debating Athenian philosophers just before coming to Corinth [Acts 17] may have influenced his decision to preach henceforth without any intellectual pretensions [1:23; 2:1].)

Wisdom: Human and Divine Paul's argument (1:17–2:5) is sometimes misused to justify an anti-intellectual approach to religion, in which reason and faith are treated as if they were mutually exclusive. The apostle's attack on "wisdom" is not directed against human reason or logic, however. It is aimed at individual Corinthians who boast of special insights that supposedly give them a deeper understanding than that granted their fellow Christians. This elitism led some persons to cultivate a false sense of superiority that devalued less educated believers, fragmenting the congregation into groups of the "wise" and "foolish."

Paul reminds the Corinthians that human reason by itself did not come to know God but that God revealed his saving purpose through Christ as a free gift (1:21). Because all are equally undeserving recipients of the divine benefits, no believer has the right to boast (1:21–31).

The apostle, however, does teach a previously hidden wisdom to persons mature enough to appreciate it. This wisdom is God's revelation through the Spirit that now dwells in the Christian community. The hitherto unknown "mind" of God—the ultimate reality that philosophers make the object of their search—is unveiled through Christ (2:6–16). The divine mystery, although inaccessible to rational inquiry, is finally made clear in the weakness and obedient suffering of Christ, the means by which God reconciles humanity to himself.

Having dealt with factionalism, Paul turns to the problem of sexual misconduct, another source of disunity among the Corinthians, urging the excommunication of a man who had scandalized the community by living openly

In this portrait uncovered at Pompeii (buried by the eruption of Mount Vesuvius in 79 C.E.), Terentius Neo and his wife proudly display the pen and wax tablets that advertise their literary skills. Similar young Roman couples of the professional classes undoubtedly were among the members of Paul's newly founded churches in Corinth and other Greco-Roman cities. (Courtesy of Erich Lessing PhotoEdit)

with his stepmother (5:1–8). This consigning to the outside world ("Satan") any Christian who is a slanderer, drunkard, idolator, or otherwise conspicuous sinner (5:9–13) was later to prove a formidable weapon, for the excommunicated person, deprived of both religious and social rights, became a pariah. Paul's theological justification for this practice is that the Christian's body is "a shrine of the indwelling Holy Spirit" (6:19) that must not be profaned by sinful acts such as intercourse with prostitutes. Finally, in Chapter 6, Paul orders the Corinthians to stop bringing lawsuits against fellow believers, stating that it is better to suffer a wrong than to expose other Christians to public criticism by airing their disputes in pagan courts (6:1–8).

Questions of Ethics and Behavior

Beginning in Chapter 7, Paul answers additional ethical and theological questions about which the Corinthians had written him. His dim view of marriage and unequivocal preference for a single life of sexual abstinence can be understood in the light of his eschatology. Expecting momentarily the return of Christ and the End of the world (7:26, 29–31), he believes that it is best to devote oneself wholeheartedly to the Lord's work (7:1–40). To a second problem—concerning whether a believer may lawfully eat food sold after it had been sacrificed on a pagan altar—Paul's solution is that the Christian, although technically free to act as he or she judges best, should do nothing that will trouble another believer's conscience (8:1–11:1).

Proper Behavior in Worship   To support his position on a third issue—the participation of women in worship services—Paul invokes what he assumes to be a divinely ordained hierarchy: As God is the head of Christ and as Christ is the head of humanity, so man is the head of woman (11:3). A woman who prophesies must veil her head, either as a sign of her holy office or as a concession to patriarchal prejudices.

Paul's argument for male superiority strikes many readers as labored and illogical. (Some scholars think that this passage [11:2–16] is the interpolation of a later editor, added to make Corinthians agree with the non-Pauline instruction in 1 Tim. 2:8–15.) Paul grants women an active role, praying and prophesying during worship, but at the same time he argues that the female is a secondary creation, made from man, who was created directly by God. The apostle uses the second version of human origins (Gen. 2) to support the sexual hierarchy, but he could as easily have cited the first creation account in which male and female are created simultaneously, *both* in the "image of God"

(Gen. 1:27). Given Paul's revelation that Christian equality transcends all distinctions among believers, including those of sex, class, and nationality (Gal. 3:28), many commentators see the writer's choice in a Genesis precedent as decidedly arbitrary.

The Eucharist (Lord's Supper)   A fourth problem involves the Corinthians' behavior during the **Lord's Supper** (known variously as Communion, Mass, or the Eucharist). First-generation Christians apparently celebrated the sacrament as part of a "love feast," a foretaste of the messianic banquet in which all participants shared a complete meal. In Corinth, however, the ritual had become another source of division. Wealthy members came early and consumed all the delicacies before the working poor arrived, thus relegating their social inferiors to hunger and public embarrassment (11:17–22).

Paul contrasts this inconsiderate behavior with the tradition coming directly from Jesus himself, quoting our oldest tradition of Christ's final meal with his friends. Repeating the sacramental distribution of bread and wine, he emphasizes that the ceremony is to be decorously repeated in memory of Jesus' death until he returns. This allusion to the nearness of the Parousia reminds the Corinthians of the seriousness with which they must observe the Last Supper ritual (11:23–34).

Spiritual Gifts   Yet another source of disruption was the phenomenon of **speaking in tongues** (12:1–31; 14:1–33), which Paul values least of all "spiritual gifts," such as prophesying, interpreting, and teaching. Reminding the Corinthians that he is more skilled than they at ecstatic speech, he nonetheless declares that he would rather "speak five intelligible words" than thousands in "the language of ecstasy" (14:18–19), for it is comprehensible instruction and prophecy that strengthen the Church (14:4–12).

Paul's emphasis on rational communication

among believers is consistent with his theme of Christian unity. At the outset of his letter, he urges the Corinthians to "be firmly joined in unity of mind and thought" (1:10). Although blessed with diverse spiritual gifts, they are all members of a single body, which he metaphorically compares to the human body with its many specialized parts. As the physical organs function cooperatively to achieve maximum benefits, so individual Church members must work together harmoniously (12:4–31), each person's ability contributing toward the success of the whole.

In his most celebrated burst of inspiration, Paul interrupts his advice on the use of spiritual gifts to show the Corinthians "the best way of all" (13:1–13). Only love, he declares, gives spiritual gifts their meaning. Using the Greek term *agapē*—meaning "selfless giving"—Paul emphasizes its human application: Love is infinitely patient, kind, forgiving. "There is no limit to its faith, its hope, and its endurance"; love once given is never withdrawn. Whereas other spiritual qualities are only partial reflections of the divine reality and will be rendered obsolete in the perfect world to come, the supreme trio of Christian virtues—faith, hope, and love—endures forever.

The Eschatological Hope: Resurrection of the Dead

The most important theological concept with which Paul struggles in this letter is his view of the afterlife. Apparently, some Corinthians had rejected the Jewish-Christian doctrine of **resurrection** or held that they were already spiritually "risen" through baptism and reception of the Holy Spirit. Some Greek Christians probably denied the necessity of a physical body rising from the dead. Following the teaching of Egyptian wisdom and Greek philosophers such as Pythagoras, Plato, and the neo-Platonists, Greek Christians may have concluded that the body is unimportant and that the **soul**—an invisible, immaterial, immortal consciousness—

survives the body's death and immediately ascends to the heavenly realm as pure spirit.

Although Paul agrees that the physical self cannot inherit the kingdom (15:50), he seems to argue for the Hebraic view that the soul and body form a unity, a mortal state requiring complete transformation to achieve eternal life. The bodily resurrection of Christ, he insists, is absolutely central to Christian belief; without it, Christian faith is vain, and the dead "are utterly lost" (15:16–19). In what form, then, are the dead raised? Although Paul does not answer directly, he implies that the resurrected being will be clothed in a "spiritual body" appropriate to a future life with Christ; what is perishable will receive imperishability, and what is mortal will acquire immortality. This triumph of life defeats the hostile power of death (15:3–57).

Returning abruptly from his cosmic vision of human destiny to take up earthly affairs again, Paul reminds the Corinthians of their previous agreement to help the Jerusalem church. They are to contribute money every Sunday, an obligation Paul had assumed when visiting the Jerusalem leadership (Gal. 2). The letter ends with Paul's invocation of Jesus' speedy return—*Marana tha* ("Come, O Lord")—an Aramaic prayer dating from the first generation of Palestinian Christians.

2 Corinthians

KEY THEMES

A composite work consisting of several letters or letter fragments, 2 Corinthians shows Paul defending his apostolic authority (Chs. 10–13); the first nine chapters, apparently written after Chapters 10–13, describe Paul's reconciliation with the church at Corinth.

Our eyes are fixed, not on the things that are seen, but on the things that are unseen: for what is seen passes away; what is unseen is eternal.

2 Corinthians 4:18

Whereas 1 Corinthians is a unified document, 2 Corinthians seems to be a compendium of several letters or letter fragments written at different times and reflecting radically different situations in the Corinthian church. Even casual readers will note the contrast between the harsh, sarcastic tone of Chapters 10–13 and the generally friendlier, more conciliatory tone of the earlier chapters. Many scholars believe that Chapters 10–13 represent the "painful letter" alluded to in 2 Corinthians 2:3–4, making this part necessarily older than Chapters 1–9. Some authorities find as many as six or more remnants of different letters in 2 Corinthians, but for this discussion we concentrate on the work's two main divisions (Chs. 10–13 and 1–9), taking them in the order in which scholars believe they were composed.

Apostolic Attacks on Paul's Authority

Troubles in Corinth   Behind the writing of 2 Corinthians lies a dramatic conflict between Paul and the church he had founded. After he had dispatched 1 Corinthians, several events took place that strained his relationship with the church almost to the breaking point:

1. New opponents, whom Paul satirizes as "superlative apostles" (11:5), infiltrated the congregation and rapidly gained positions of influence. Paul then made a brief, "painful" visit to Corinth, only to suffer public humiliation (2: 1–5; 7:12).
2. His visit a failure, he returned to Ephesus, where he wrote the Corinthians a severe reprimand, part of which is preserved in Chapters 10–13.
3. Having carried the severe letter to Corinth, his associate **Titus** then rejoins Paul in Macedonia, bringing the good news that the Corinthians are sorry for their behavior and now support the apostle (7:5–7).

4. Paul subsequently writes a joyful letter of reconciliation, included in Chapters 1–9.

Although this reconstruction of events is conjectural, it accounts for the sequence of alienation, hostility, and reconciliation found in this composite document.

The Severe Letter: Paul's Defense of His Apostolic Authority

In the last three chapters of 2 Corinthians, Paul writes a passionate, almost brutal defense of his apostolic authority. A masterpiece of savage irony, Chapters 10–13 show Paul boasting "as a fool," using every device of rhetoric to demolish his opponents' pretensions to superiority. We do not know the identity of these opponents, except that they were Jewish Christians whom Paul accuses of proclaiming "another Jesus" and imparting a "spirit" different from that introduced by *his* "gospel." The label "superlative apostles" suggests that these critics enjoyed considerable prestige, perhaps as representatives from the Jerusalem church. They may have been emissaries from James, "the Lord's brother," similar to those who drove a wedge between Peter and Paul in Antioch. In both cases, Paul describes their "gospel" as differing from his (Gal. 2: 11–15).

Paul's Authority   Although Paul's bitter sarcasm may offend some readers, we must realize that this unattractive quality is the reverse side of his intense emotional commitment to the Corinthians' welfare. Behind the writer's "bragging" and threats (10:2–6; 11:16–21; 13:3, 10) lies the sting of unrequited affection. The nature of love that Paul had so confidently defined in his earlier letter (1 Cor. 13) is now profoundly tested.

It is not certain that the "superlative apostles" (11:5) who question his teaching are the same as the "sham apostles" (11:13) whom Paul accuses of being Satan's agents (11:12–15). Whoever they were, these opponents apparently base their authority at least partly on supernatural visions and revelations. Paul responds by telling of his own mystical experience in "the third heaven" (in some extrabiblical beliefs, the spiritual Eden), where he learned secrets too holy to reveal to the uninitiated (12:1–13).

The Letter of Reconciliation

After Titus left to carry the disciplinary letter from Ephesus to Corinth, Paul began a journey to Macedonia. When Titus caught up with Paul, he brought the welcome news that the Corinthians had disavowed their divisive leaders and now gave Paul their full support, acknowledging him a genuine Apostle who had treated them honorably.

Despite the reconciliation, the Corinthian church is still troubled by Paul's rivals, whom he denounces as mere "hawkers" (salespersons) of God's word (2:17). Although he is more controlled than in Chapters 10–13, his exasperation is evident when he asks if he must begin all over again proving his apostolic credentials (3:1). Placing the responsibility for recognizing true apostolic leadership squarely on the Corinthians, the writer reminds them that *they* are his living letters of recommendation. Echoing Jeremiah 31:31, Paul contrasts the Mosaic Covenant—inscribed on stone tablets—with the new covenant written on human hearts. Inhabited by the Holy Spirit, the Christian reflects God's image more splendidly than Moses (3:2–28).

Nurturing a Spiritual Body In this section (4:16–5:10), Paul further develops his concept of a "spiritual body" that he had outlined in 1 Corinthians 15. In his earlier letter, Paul wrote that the believer will become instantly transformed—receive an incorruptible "spiritual body"—at Christ's return. He said nothing about the Christian's state of being or consciousness during the interim period between death and the future resurrection. In 2 Corinthians, Paul seems to imply that believers are already developing a spiritual body that will clothe them at the moment of death.

Paul appears to state that God has prepared for each Christian an eternal form, a "heavenly habitation," that endows the bearer with immortality. Yearning to avoid human death, he envisions receiving that heavenly form now, putting it on like a garment over the physical body, "so that our mortal part may be absorbed into life immortal." The presence of the Spirit, he concludes, is visible evidence that God intends this process of spiritual metamorphosis to take place during the present lifetime (5:1–5). United with Christ, the believer thus becomes a new creation (5:11–17).

The spiritual renewal is God's plan for reconciling humanity to himself. As Christ's ambassador, Paul advances the work of reconciliation; his sufferings are an act of love for them (5:18–6:13). Imploring the Corinthians to return his affection, Paul ends his defense of the apostolic purpose with a not-altogether-convincing expression of confidence in their loyalty (7:2–16).

Chapters 8 and 9, which concern Paul's collection for the Jerusalem poor, seem redundant and may have originated as separate missives before an editor combined them. Citing the generosity of Macedonia's churches, Paul reminds the Corinthians that "God loves a cheerful giver" (2 Cor. 9:7).

RECOMMENDED READING

Betz, H. D. "Corinthians, Second Epistle to the." In D. N. Freedman, ed., *The Anchor Bible Dictionary,* Vol. 1, pp. 1148–1154, New York: Doubleday, 1992.

Betz, H. D., and Mitchel, M. M. "Corinthians, First Epistle to the." In D. N. Freedman, ed., *The Anchor Bible Dictionary,* Vol. 1, pp. 1139–1148, New York: Doubleday, 1992.

Bruce, F. F. *1 and 2 Corinthians.* Grand Rapids, Mich.: Eerdmans, 1978.

Furnish, V. P. *Second Corinthians.* Anchor Bible Commentary, Vol. 32A. Garden City, N.Y.: Doubleday, 1984.

Georgi, Dieter. *The Opponents of Paul in Second Corinthians.* Philadelphia: Fortress Press, 1986.

Hooker, M. D. "Authority on Her Head: An Examination of 1 Cor. 11:10." *New Testament Studies* 10 (1963): 410–416.

Hurd, J. C. *The Origin of 1 Corinthians*. Macon, Ga.: Mercer University Press, 1983.

Meeks, Wayne. *The First Urban Christians: The Social World of the Apostle Paul*. New Haven, Conn.: Yale University Press, 1983. An insightful investigation into the cultural environment and socioeconomic background of the earliest Christians.

Murphy-O'Connor, Jerome. *St. Paul's Corinth: Text and Archaeology*. Wilmington, Del.: Michael Glazier, 1983. An archaeologist's illumination of the Corinthian life and customs in Paul's day.

Schmithals, Walter. *Gnosticism in Corinth: An Investigation of the Letters to the Corinthians*. Translated by J. Steely. Nashville, Tenn.: Abingdon Press, 1971.

Schütz, J. H., ed. *The Social Setting of Pauline Christianity*. Philadelphia: Fortress Press, 1982.

Scroggs, Robin. "Paul and the Eschatological Woman." *Journal of the American Academy of Religion* 40 (1972): 283–303; 42 (1974): 532–537.

Soards, Marian L. *The Apostle Paul: An Introduction to His Writing and Teaching*. New York: Paulist Press, 1987.

Talbert, C. H. *Reading Corinthians: A Literary and Theological Commentary on 1 and 2 Corinthians*. New York: Crossroad, 1987.

Theissen, Gerd. *The Social Setting of Pauline Christianity: Essays on Corinth*. Edited, translated, and with an introduction by J. H. Schütz. Philadelphia: Fortress Press, 1982.

Galatians

KEY THEMES

Like the letters to Corinth, this letter to the Galatian churches reflects Paul's ongoing struggle with opponents who challenged his apostolic authority and his "gospel" that believers must live free of the Mosaic law. An angry declaration of Christianity's independence of Judaism, Galatians vigorously defends Paul's doctrine of salvation through faith. The letter also proclaims Paul's independence of Jerusalem's Christian leadership.

> There is no such thing as Jew and Greek,
>   slave and free, male and female; for you are
> all one person in Christ Jesus.
>
> Galatians 3:28

An Angry Letter to the Galatians

A brief but extremely important letter, Galatians outlines Paul's most distinctive and innovative doctrine: Obedience to Torah commandments cannot justify a person before God. Only trust (faith) in God's gracious willingness to redeem humanity through Christ can now win divine approval and obtain a believer's salvation.

This uniquely Pauline gospel revolutionized the development of Christianity. By sweeping away all Torah requirements, including circumcision and dietary restrictions, Paul opened the church wide to Gentile converts. Uncircumcised former adherents of Greco-Roman religions were now granted full equality with Jewish Christians. Although the process was only beginning in Paul's day, the influx of Gentiles would soon overwhelm the originally Jewish church, making it an international community with members belonging to every known ethnic group. This swift transformation could not have been possible without Paul's radical insistence on the abandonment of all Mosaic observances, which for centuries had separated Jew from Gentile.

The Recipients   The identity of the Galatian churches Paul addresses is uncertain. In Paul's time, two different geographical areas could be designated "**Galatia**." The first was a territory in north-central Asia Minor (now Turkey) inhabited by descendants of Celtic tribes that had invaded the region during the third to first centuries B.C.E. Brief references to Galatia in Acts (16:6, 18:23) suggest that Paul traveled there, but this is not certain.

Black Sea

Galatia

Iconium

Lystra

Derbe

Antioch

Rhodes

Crete

Cyprus

Mediterranean Sea

The identity of Paul's Galatians is uncertain. The letter may have been directed to churches in the north-central plateau region of Asia Minor (near present-day Ankara, Turkey) or to churches in the southern coastal area of east-central Asia Minor (also in modern Turkey). Many scholars believe that the Galatians were Christians living in Iconium, Lystra, Derbe, and other nearby cities that Paul had visited on his first missionary journey.

The other possibility, which many historians support, is that Paul was writing to Christians in the Roman province of Galatia. The southern portion of this province included the cities of Iconium, **Lystra**, and Derbe, places where the apostle had established churches (Acts 14). If the "southern Galatia" theory is correct, it helps explain the presence of Judaizers (persons advocating circumcision for all converts), because the Roman province was much closer to Jewish-Christian centers at Antioch and Jerusalem than was the northern, Celtic territory.

The Identity of Paul's Opponents Some commentators identify Paul's opponents as emissaries of the Jerusalem church, such as those sent by James to inspect the congregation at Antioch (2:12). It is unlikely, however, that Jewish Christians from Jerusalem would be unaware that requiring circumcision also means keeping the entire Torah (5:2–3). Paul's opponents appear to combine aspects of a Greco-Roman cult that involved honoring cosmic spirits and observing religious festival days (4:9–10), with selected Torah requirements (6:12–14). This **syncretism** (mixing together elements of two or more different religions to create a new belief) suggests that the opponents are Galatian Gentiles. In Paul's view, their attempt to infuse Jewish and pagan components into Christianity misses the point of the Christ event.

Purpose and Contents   Writing from Corinth or Ephesus about 56 C.E., Paul has a twofold purpose: (1) to prove that he is a true apostle, possessing rights equal to those of the Jerusalem "pillars" (Chs. 1 and 2), and (2) to demonstrate the validity of his gospel that Christian faith replaces works of law, including circumcision. The letter can be divided into five parts:

1. A biographical defense of Paul's autonomy and his relationship with the Jerusalem leadership (1:1–2:14)
2. Paul's unique gospel: justification through faith (2:15–3:29)
3. The adoption of Christians as heirs of Abraham and children of God (4:1–31)
4. The consequences and the obligations of Christian freedom from the Mosaic law (5:1–6:10)
5. The final summary of Paul's argument (6:11–18)

Largely dispensing with his usual greetings and thanksgiving, Paul opens the letter with a vigorous defense of his personal autonomy. His apostolic rank derives not from ordination or "human appointment" but directly from the Deity (1:1–5). Similarly, his message does not depend on information learned from earlier Christians but is a direct "revelation [*apokalypsis*] of Jesus Christ" (1:12). Because he regards his gospel of faith as a divine communication, Paul sees no need to consult other church leaders about the correctness of his policies (1:15–17).

Paul's Freedom from Institutional Authority

In contrast to Acts, in Galatians Paul presents himself as essentially independent of the mother church at Jerusalem. Nonetheless, he apparently recognizes the desirability of having his work among the Gentiles endorsed by the Palestinian Christian leadership. His visit with the Jerusalem "pillars"—Peter (Cephas), John, and James—is probably the same conference described in Acts 15. According to Paul, the pillars agree to recognize the legitimacy of his Gentile mission. Imposing no Torah restrictions on Gentile converts, the Jerusalem trio ask only that Paul's churches contribute financially to the mother church, a charitable project Paul gladly undertakes (2:10; see 2 Cor. 8–9; Rom. 15).

After the Jerusalem conference, Paul meets Peter again at Antioch, a meeting that shows how far the Jewish-Gentile issue is from being resolved. Paul charges that Jesus' premier disciple is still ambivalent about associating with uncircumcised believers. When James sends emissaries to see if Antiochean Christians are properly observing Mosaic dietary laws, Peter stops sharing in communal meals with Gentiles, perhaps because he fears James's disapproval. Although Paul publicly denounces Peter's action as hypocrisy, claiming that Peter privately does not keep Torah regulations, we cannot be sure of Peter's motives. He may have wished not to offend more conservative Jewish believers and behaved as he did out of respect for others' consciences, a policy Paul himself advocates (1 Cor. 8:1–13).

Paul's Gospel of Justification by Faith

Paul's strangely negative attitude toward the Mosaic law puzzles many Jewish scholars. Why does a Pharisee trained to regard the Torah as God's revelation of ultimate Wisdom so vehemently reject this divine guide to righteous living? Is it because of a personal consciousness that (for him) the law no longer has power to

Because early church traditions assert that both Peter and Paul were executed in Rome during Nero's reign, their images are commonly paired, as in this fourth-century Roman lime relief depicting the two apostles. Paul's letter to the Galatians indicates that their historical relationship was not so close (Gal. 2:11–13). (Courtesy of Erich Lessing / PhotoEdit)

justify his existence before God? In both Galatians and Romans, Paul closely examines his own psychological state, attempting to show how the experience of Christ achieves for him what the law failed to do—assure him of God's love and acceptance.

In Paul's understanding of the crucifixion, Jesus' voluntary death pays the Torah's penalty for all lawbreakers (3:13–14). Thus, Paul can say that "through the law I died to law." He escaped the punishments of the Torah through a mystical identification with the sacrificial Messiah. Vicariously experiencing Jesus' crucifixion, Paul now shares in Christ's new life, which enables him to receive God's grace as never before (2:17–21).

Paul also appeals to the Galatians' experience of Christ, reminding them that they received the Spirit only when they accepted his gospel,

not when they obeyed the law (3:1–5). In addition, he provides what people versed in the rabbinic tradition expect in an argument over doctrine—a precedent from the Hebrew Bible. Paul argues that his formula—"faith equals righteousness"—is explicitly present in the Genesis story of Abraham. It is Abraham's "faith" in God's call, Paul notes, that "was counted to him as righteousness" (citing Gen. 15:6). Therefore, he reasons, people who exercise faith today are Abraham's spiritual children, heirs to the promise that God will "bless," or justify, pagan nations through faith (3:6–10). Faith, not obedience to law, is the key to divine approval.

In support of his appeal to biblical authority, Paul finds only one additional relevant text, Habakkuk 2:4: "He shall gain life who is justified through faith." Paul interprets the Habakkuk text as prophetic of the messianic era and contrasts its emphasis on faith with the law's stress on actions (3:11–12). The faith Habakkuk promised comes to the lawless Gentiles because Christ, suffering a criminal's execution, accepted the law's "curse" on unlawful people and allowed them to become reconciled to God (3:13–14).

Paul concludes his argument by citing the Genesis account of Abraham's two sons, which he interprets as an **allegory**. **Ishmael**, son of the slave girl **Hagar**, represents the Judaism of Paul's day, in bondage to both the law and Rome. Conversely, Isaac, son of the free woman Sarah, symbolizes the sons of Abraham by faith, the Christian community. They are citizens of the "heavenly Jerusalem," a free mother. Attempting to keep even one part of the law, such as circumcision, is futile, for those under law must observe it all. Paul emphasizes that "the only thing that counts is faith active in love" (5:6).

Paul's exasperation with the Galatians' failure to comprehend the distinction between law and grace inspires his most brutal insult. With savage irony, he suggests that those who insist on circumcision finish the job by emasculating themselves (5:7–12). Seizing the pen from his scribe, Paul adds a postscript in which he accuses his opponents of practicing circumcision only to escape persecution, presumably from Torah-abiding Jews. He summarizes his position with crystal clarity: Torah obedience is meaningless because it implies that God's revelation through Jesus is not sufficient; in truth, Jesus alone can reconcile or unite humanity with its Creator. Paul's closing words are as abrupt and self-directed as his opening complaint (1:6): "In future let no one make trouble for me" (6:11–17).

RECOMMENDED READING

Betz, H. D. *Galatians.* Hermeneia. Philadelphia: Fortress Press, 1979. A scholarly analysis.

Cousar, C. B. *Galatians, Interpretation.* Atlanta: John Knox Press, 1982.

Ebeling, Gerhard. *The Truth of the Gospel: An Exposition of Galatians.* Philadelphia: Fortress Press, 1985.

Romans

KEY THEMES

In Romans, Paul offers the most comprehensive statement of his views on God's plan for humanity's salvation. Probably written from Corinth about 56–57 C.E., this letter surveys the predicament of humanity, alienated from God and enslaved to imperfection, and argues that Jews and Gentiles suffer equally from the results of Adam's original disobedience and its punishment, death (Chs. 1–3). The Torah, although "holy" and "just," serves merely to increase our awareness of human inadequacy by condemning the universal failure to keep its standards. Only God's undeserved love expressed through Christ and accepted in faith can ethically justify humanity and reconcile people to their Creator (Chs. 4–8). The Jewish lack of faith in Jesus as the divinely appointed agent of redemption is only temporary, a historical necessity that allows believing Gentiles also to become God's people (Chs. 9–11).

> As the issue of [Adam's] misdeed was condemnation for all [people], so the issue of [Christ's] just act is acquittal and life for all [people].
>
> Romans 5:8

Paul's Gospel of Freedom from Torah and Justification by Faith

Whereas Galatians was dictated in the white heat of exasperation, Romans is a more calmly reasoned presentation of Paul's doctrine of salvation through faith. In this letter, written about 56–57 C.E. when he had not yet visited Rome but hoped to make the imperial capital his departure point for a pioneering mission to Spain, Paul offers the most comprehensive and systematic expression of his theology. Here the author thoughtfully explores an issue central to all world religions: how to bridge the gap between God and humankind, to reconcile imperfect, sinful humanity to a pure and righteous Deity. As a Jew, Paul is painfully aware of the immense disparity between mortals and the immaculate holiness of the Supreme Being, whose justice cannot tolerate human wrongdoing. Paul's gospel, or "good news," is that these seemingly irreconcilable differences between God and humanity are overcome in Christ, the Son who closes the gulf between perfect Father and imperfect children. In Paul's view, God himself takes the initiative by re-creating a deeply flawed humanity in his own transcendent image.

In form, Romans resembles a theological essay or sermon rather than an ordinary letter, lacking the kind of specific problem-solving advice that characterizes most Pauline correspondence. Some commentators regard Romans as a circular letter, a document intended to explain Paul's teachings to various Christian groups who may at that time have held distorted views of the apostle's position on controversial subjects. Most scholars view Chapter 16, which contains greetings to twenty-six different persons—more than the writer is likely to have known personally in a city he had never visited—as a separate missive. This section originally may have been a letter of recommendation for **Phoebe**, who was a deacon of the church at Cenchreae, the port of Corinth.

Organization The longest and most complex of Paul's letters, Romans can be divided into nine thematically related parts:

1. Introduction (1:1–15)
2. Statement of theme (1:16–17) and exploration of the human predicament: God's wrath directed at all humanity because all people are guilty of deliberate error (1:18–3:31)

3. Abraham is the model of faith (4:1–25)
4. Faith in Christ ensures deliverance from sin and death (5:1–7:25)
5. Renewed life in the Spirit (8:1–39)
6. The causes and results of Israel's disbelief (9:1–11:36)
7. Behavior in the church and the world (12:1–15:13)
8. Paul's future plans and greetings (15:14–33)
9. Appendix: letter recommending Phoebe (16:1–27)

Humanity's Need for Redemption

Human Error After an introductory greeting that affirms his apostolic authority (1:1–15), Paul boldly surveys the human predicament (1:18–3:20), a sorry condition in which all people, Jews as well as Gentiles, are incapable of justifying their existence before God. He announces his main theme by citing Habakkuk 2:4, the same verse proclaiming salvation "through faith" that he had earlier quoted to the Galatians (1:17; Gal. 3:11).

Echoing passages from the Wisdom of Solomon (see Part 7), Paul argues that the Gentiles' error is based on worshiping created objects—images of the Greco-Roman gods—rather than the Creator. His comments on male and female homosexuality, common in Hellenistic society, assume a deliberate turning from "natural" to "unnatural" behavior (1:26–28). Although this passage has been used frequently to condemn same-sex relationships, many medical researchers now believe that homosexual orientation is either genetically determined or formed at such an early stage of development that it is not a matter of moral choice. (Note that Paul's views of human sexuality in general are largely shaped by his eschatological assumptions [1 Cor. 7].)

Paul adds that Jews, despite possessing the law and covenant promises, fare no better than idolatrous Gentiles in achieving justification before God. The Torah, Paul asserts, cannot effect a right relationship between God and the lawkeeper; it serves only to make one conscious of sin (2:17–3:31).

Justification by Faith   In the next section (4:1–25), Paul argues that since Jesus' death and resurrection no one can gain God's approval solely by trying to keep the Mosaic law. Jesus has introduced a New Age in the history of salvation in which God can "justify" or declare a believer righteous through trust in Christ's saving power. This revelation was foreshadowed in Genesis when Abraham, "father of the Jews," received God's favor before he was circumcised and before the Torah came into being. True children of Abraham are therefore not necessarily those descended from him "in the flesh" but those who show faith in God's Son, believing Gentiles as well as Jews.

Christ and Adam   In Chapter 5, Paul combines theology and anthropology to create a theory of human history that has had a tremendous impact on Western civilization. Adapting a Hellenistic Jewish reading of Genesis 3, Paul interprets the disobedience of **Adam** (whose name means "humankind") as an act that introduced sin and death into the world. He then contrasts Adam and Christ as two opposing models of humanity: Persons existing in Adam's earthly likeness suffer corruption; those living "in Christ" experience his heavenly nature. As all Adam's offspring share his mortal fate, so all will share the reward of Christ's resurrection to life. It is the believer's faith in the saving power of Christ that makes him or her "righteous," enabling the just Deity to accept persons who trustingly respond to his call (5:12–21).

Some later theologians used Romans 5 to formulate a doctrine of original sin, a teaching that all human beings inherit an unavoidable tendency to do wrong and are innately corrupt. From Augustine, a father of the early Church, to John Calvin, a Protestant reformer, such theologians took a deeply pessimistic view of human nature, in some cases regarding the ma-

jority of humanity as inherently depraved and justly damned.

It is important to remember, however, that Paul's word for "sin"—*hamartia*—is a Greek archery term, meaning "to miss the mark," to fall short of a desired goal or standard of conduct. Instead of implying depravity or corruption, *hamartia* commonly refers to an error of judgment, as it does in Aristotle's *Poetics* when he uses it to denote the character flaw of the tragic hero. In Paul's moral scheme, it is not a biologically inherited condemnation that inflicts mortality on the human race. It is flawed humanity's failure to hit the target of reunion with God that brings death—permanent separation from the Source of life.

Paul's scheme of salvation history emphasizes the joyful aspects of God's reconciliation to humanity. It is the Creator who initiates the process, making God's "grace"—his gracious will to love and give life—far exceed the measure of human failings. So universally powerful is God's determination to redeem humanity that Paul implies he will ultimately succeed in saving all people, a concept the writer also alludes to in 1 Corinthians (cf. Rom. 5:18–19; 1 Cor. 15:21–23).

Although divine grace, received in faith, liberates believers from God's wrath and the consequences of sin, this freedom must be used wisely. Living free of Torah constraints does not permit unlawful behavior but offers opportunities to practice Christ-like virtues. There remains, however, the problem of human fallibility, which Paul explores in one of his most introspective passages (7:7–25). Mixing analysis with intuition, Paul plunges into the murky realm of psychological conflict, which he views as a battle between opposing forces of Good and Evil that apparently take over his psyche and function independently of his conscious will. "The good which I want to do, I fail to do," he laments, "but what I do is the wrong which is against my will" (7:9). With his reason delighting in the Torah but his lower nature fighting against it, he finds that he incurs the law's punishment—death. He bursts with desire to attain God's approval but always "misses the mark." In agony over his dilemma, he seeks some power to rescue him from an unsatisfying existence that ends only in death (7:21–25). Paul may be accused of attributing his personal sense of moral imperfection to everyone else, but his despairing self-analysis illustrates why he feels that the law cannot deliver one from the lethal consequences of fallible human nature (8:3).

Renewal in the Spirit   God rescues humanity through Christ. By sharing our imperfect nature and dying "as a sacrifice for sin," Christ transfers the Torah's penalties to himself, condemning it and not the human nature in which sin exists (8:3–4). Because Christ's Spirit now dwells within the believer, sin no longer exerts its former control, and new life can flourish in the Christian's body. Thus, Christians escape their imperfection, having put it to death with Christ on the cross (8:5–17).

Paul uses mystical language to describe not only human nature but also the physical cosmos itself struggling to be set free from the chains of mortality. During this period of cosmic renewal, the whole universe wails as if in childbirth. Believers now hope for a saving rebirth, but the reality is still ahead. Then they will be fully reshaped in the Son's image, the pattern of a new humanity reconciled to God (8:18–30):

> For I am convinced that there is nothing in death or life, in the realm of spirits or superhuman powers, in the world as it is or the world as it shall be, in the forces of the universe, in heights or depths—nothing in all creation that can separate us from the love of God in Christ Jesus our Lord.
>
> Romans 8:38–39

Israel's Disbelief   In Chapters 9–11, Paul discusses Israel's continuing role as God's chosen people, even though most have not accepted Jesus as the national Messiah. Paul suggests that his fellow Jews misunderstand God's purpose in Christ because they seek salvation through To-

rah obedience, allegedly depending on their own efforts to earn divine approval. True "children of Abraham," however, recognize the necessity of placing faith in Christ. Jews withhold their faith, but the Gentiles benefit from this refusal. In a famous analogy, Paul compares Gentile believers to branches from a wild olive tree that have been grafted onto the cultivated olive trunk, which is Israel. Paul also assumes that Israel's unbelief is only temporary. After the Gentiles have been attached to the main trunk, then the natural branches will be regrafted onto God's olive tree and "the whole of Israel will be saved" (11:16–27).

Behavior in the Church and the World   Paul's ethical instruction (Chs. 12–15) is closely tied to his sense of apocalyptic urgency. Because the New Age is about to dawn (13:11), believers must behave prudently in both public and private life. The apostle's policy toward the Roman government, composed before his imprisonment and prosecution, is strongly positive, advocating civil obedience and cooperation. Echoing the Stoic view that the state exists to maintain public order and punish wrongdoing, Paul argues that the Roman Empire is a "divine institution"— an opinion that contrasts with his earlier view that the present world is ruled by demonic forces (2 Cor. 4:4).

Although he emphasizes the Christian's duty to pay taxes and submit to legally constituted authority, Paul does not consider the ethical problem of a citizen's duty to resist illegal or unethical acts by the state. As Luke does in Acts, Paul advises accommodation with the empire, probably because he believes that the existing system would not endure long. (Compare Paul's similar acceptance of the state-supported institution of human slavery in Philemon, discussed later in this part.)

When Paul implied that voluntary cooperation with Rome might benefit Christians, he could not know that he soon would be among the first victims of a government persecution. Following the emperor **Nero**'s legal murder of many Roman believers (about 64–65 C.E.), some New Testament authors came to regard the state as Satan's earthly instrument to destroy God's people. After Rome destroyed Jerusalem (along with the original church there) in 70 C.E., the empire became the new Babylon in the eyes of many Christians. The author of Revelation pictures Rome as a beast and predicts its fall as a cause for universal rejoicing (Rev. 17–19). At the time Paul wrote, however, the adversarial relationship between Church and state was still in the future.

RECOMMENDED READING

Achtemeier, P. J. *Romans.* Interpretation. Commentary. Atlanta: John Knox Press, 1985.

Cranfield, C. E. B. *A Critical and Exegetical Commentary on the Epistle to the Romans.* International Critical Commentary. 2 Vols. Edinburgh: T. & T. Clark, 1975, 1979. A standard work incorporating the history of Pauline interpretation.

Fitzmyer, Joseph A. *Romans.* The Anchor Bible, Vol. 33. New York: Doubleday, 1993. A new translation with extensive commentary.

Kasemann, Ernst. *Commentary on Romans.* Grand Rapids, Mich.: Eerdmans, 1980. An intensely scholarly study for more serious readers.

Sanders, E. P. *Paul and Palestinian Judaism.* Philadelphia: Fortress Press, 1978. An important scholarly study of Paul's relationship to rabbinic Judaism.

———. *Paul, the Law and the Jewish People.* Philadelphia: Fortress Press, 1983.

Philippians

KEY THEMES

Paul's letter to the church at Philippi, the first church established in Europe, contains important biographical information about the author (3:4–8) and his imprisonment (either at Rome or Ephesus) (1:12–26). An unusually warm and friendly missive, it includes Paul's quotation of an early Christian hymn that depicts Jesus as the opposite of Adam—a humbly obedient son whose self-emptying leads to his heavenly exaltation (2:5–11).

> He [Jesus] did not think to snatch at equality with God, but made himself nothing, assuming the nature of a slave.
>
> Philippians 2:6–7

A Letter from Prison

This letter expresses Paul's special affection for the church at **Philippi**, the first in Europe, which he and his associate Timothy had founded (Acts 16:11–40). Paul's unusual intimacy with the Philippians is reflected in the warmth of his greetings (1:1–11) and by the fact that they were the only group from whom he would accept financial support (4:15–16).

According to an early Church tradition, Philippians is one of four canonical letters—including Philemon, Colossians, and Ephesians—that Paul wrote while imprisoned at Rome. Rigorous scholarly analysis of the four works, however, has raised serious questions about the time and place of their composition as well as the authorship of two of them. Whereas scholars accept Philippians and Philemon as genuine Pauline documents, a majority challenge Paul's authorship of Colossians, and nearly all doubt that he wrote Ephesians (discussed later in this part).

If Philippians was not written during Paul's house arrest in Rome (Acts 28), it may have originated in a prison at Ephesus. The letter implies that Paul's friends made four journeys between Philippi and Paul's place of imprisonment and that a fifth trip was planned (2:25–26). Because the distance between Philippi and Rome seems too great for such frequent trips, some historians propose that he wrote the letter in Ephesus, which is only about ten days' travel time from Philippi. Still other scholars suggest that Caesarea, where Paul spent two years in prison, was the place of origin (Acts 23–25).

Little remains of the Greco-Roman city of Philippi, where Paul established the first Christian church in Europe. This crumbling wall gives scant indication of the massive Roman structures that once occupied the site. (Courtesy of Erich Lessing / Magnum Photos)

Whereas numerous scholars retain the traditional view that Paul wrote Philippians at Rome, an increasing number believe the canonical work is a composite document, made up of several letter fragments written at different times. According to this theory, the note thanking the Philippians for their financial help (4:10–20 or 23) was composed first, followed by a letter warning the Church about potential troublemakers (partially preserved in 1:1–3:1a and 4: 2–9). A third letter bitterly attacks advocates of circumcisions (3:1b–4:1). The letter may be a unity, however, for Paul's letters typically leap from topic to topic, reflecting the author's quick changes of mood as he addresses different issues.

The Significance of Paul's Imprisonment

Paul gives a surprisingly mellow response to his prison experience, courageously stressing its positive results. His case, he believes, allows other believers the opportunity to witness publicly for Christ. Interestingly, not all of Paul's fellow Christians support him; some use his incarceration as a means of stirring up new troubles for the prisoner. The writer does not identify those Christians whose personal jealousies complicate his already difficult situation, but some commentators suggest they are the "advocates of circumcision" denounced in Chapter 3. In Acts' narration of Paul's arrest and imprisonment in Caesarea, the Jerusalem church leadership is conspicuously absent from his defense. Perhaps those who shared James's adherence to Torah obligations were in some degree relieved to see Paul and his heretical views under legal restraint.

The Hymn to Christ

Chapter 2 contains the letter's most important theological concept. Urging the Philippians to

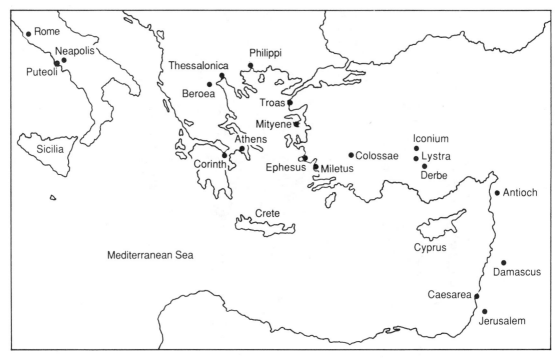

Paul may have written his "letters from prison" from Rome (in the far west on this map), from Ephesus (on the coast of present-day Turkey), or from Caesarea (in the far eastern Mediterranean). Note that Ephesus is much closer to Philippi than either of the other two cities.

avoid rivalry and cultivate humility, Paul cites Jesus' behavior as the model to emulate and quotes or paraphrases a liturgical hymn about Christ's self-emptying. The rhythmic and poetic qualities of this passage, as well as the absence of typically Pauline ideas and vocabulary, indicate that it is a pre-Pauline composition. The first stanza reads:

> Who though he was in the form of God,
> Did not count equality with God
> A thing to be grasped.
> But emptied himself,
> Taking the form of a servant,
> Being born in the likeness of men.
> And being found in human form
> He humbled himself
> And became obedient unto death.
> > Philippians 2:6–8
> > (Revised Standard Version)

The hymn's second stanza (2:9–11) describes how God rewards Jesus' selfless obedience by granting him universal lordship, which elevation glorifies "God, the Father."

Although this famous passage is commonly believed to demonstrate Jesus' heavenly preexistence and Incarnation, its depiction of Jesus' relation to the Father is ambiguously rendered. In view of Paul's explicit subordination of Jesus to God in 1 Corinthians 15:24–28, modern commentators are cautious about interpreting the hymn as a statement of Jesus' preexistent divine nature.

A growing number of scholars believe that Paul employs the hymn in order to contrast implicitly two "sons" of God—Adam (Luke 3:38) and Jesus. (The Adam–Christ contrast figures prominently in 1 Corinthians 15:21–23, 45–49, and Romans 5:12–19.) Paul's use of the term *form* (Greek, *morphe*) may refer to the divine image that both Adam and Jesus reflect (Gen. 1:27–28). But, whereas Adam tried to seize God-like status (Gen. 3:5), Jesus takes the form of a slave. Instead of rebelling against the Creator, he is submissively obedient unto death.

Finally, Adam's disobedience brings shame and death, but Jesus' total obedience brings glory and exaltation. Jesus' self-emptying earns him the fullness of God's reward, the bestowal of the "name above all names," before whom all creation bows. Consistent with his usual method of using theology to drive home behavioral advice, Paul implicitly compares the reward given Jesus' humility with that in store for humbly obedient Christians. Now shining like "stars in a dark world," they will inherit a future life similar to that which Jesus now enjoys (2:14–18).

The references to Timothy and **Epaphroditus**, two of his favorite companions, suggest Paul's capacity for friendship. Timothy, whose name appears as courtesy coauthor of this letter (1:1), is half-Jewish and half-Greek, a dependable supporter of Paul's radical policy toward recruiting Gentiles. In the apostle's absence, Paul trusts him to act as he would (2:19–24).

Epaphroditus, who had brought Paul the Philippians' monetary gifts, apparently touched Paul by the depth of his personal devotion. Epaphroditus's dangerous illness, which delayed his return to Philippi, may have resulted from having risked his life to help the prisoner. Paul implies his gratitude when urging the Philippians to give his friend an appreciative welcome home (2:25–3:1a).

Chapter 3, which may belong to a separate letter, contains flashes of Paul's old fire as he attacks Judaizers who insist on circumcising Gentile converts. Denouncing the practice as "mutilation," he contemptuously dismisses his opponents as "dogs"—the common Jewish tag for the uncircumcised. Paul provides valuable autobiographical information when he cites his ethnic qualifications—superior to those of his enemies—to evaluate the advantages of being a Jew. Despite his exemplary credentials—and his former perfection in keeping Torah regulations—he discounts his Jewish heritage as "garbage." All human advantages are worthless when compared to the new life God gives in Christ (3:1–11).

RECOMMENDED READING

Byrne, Brendan. "The Letter to the Philippians." In R. E. Brown et al., *The New Jerome Biblical Commentary,* 2nd ed., pp. 791–797. Englewood Cliffs, N.J.: Prentice-Hall, 1990.

Martin, R. P. *Carmen Christi: Philippians 2:5–11 in Recent Interpretation and in the Setting of Early Christian Worship,* rev. ed. Grand Rapids, Mich.: Eerdmans, 1983.

———. *Philippians.* New Century Bible Commentary. Grand Rapids, Mich.: Eerdmans, 1983.

Stendahl, K., ed. and trans. *Romans, Galatians, and Philippians.* Anchor Bible, Vol. 33. Garden City, N.Y.: Doubleday, 1978. A recent translation with editorial commentary.

Philemon

KEY THEME

In his only surviving private letter, Paul urges his recipients to treat the runaway slave Onesimus as a brother in Christ.

> I am sending [Onesimus] back to you, and in doing so I am sending a part of myself.
> Philemon 11

Although Paul's shortest letter, Philemon deals with a big subject—the problem of human slavery among Christians. From prison, Paul writes to **Philemon**, a citizen of Colossae, to plead for the runaway slave **Onesimus**, who had apparently stolen money from his master's household. Onesimus's flight brought him from Colossae to Rome (or Ephesus, if that is where Paul's captivity letters originated), where the slave was converted to Christianity, perhaps by Paul himself.

Compelled by Roman law, Paul has no choice but to send the slave back to his owner. Maintaining a fine balance between exercising his apostolic authority and appealing to the voluntary equality cultivated among all Christians, Paul asks Philemon to receive Onesimus kindly, treating him "no longer as a slave, but . . . as a dear brother" (v. 15). Paul also gives his guarantee that he will reimburse Philemon for any debt he may have incurred (or, perhaps, money he may have stolen) (vv. 18–20). Besides appealing to Philemon's compassion, Paul hints broadly that returning Onesimus deprives him of a major comfort: "I should have liked to keep him with me to look after me as you would wish, here in prison for the Gospel. But I would rather do nothing without your consent, so that your kindness may be a matter not of compulsion, but of your own free will" (vv. 13–14).

The Question of Slavery

Readers may be disappointed that Paul does not denounce human slavery as incompatible with Christian belief in God's equal love for all humanity. Instead, he merely accepts its existence as a social fact, nowhere ordering believers to free the human beings they owned as chattel. Paul's attitude is consistent with both the biblical tradition and the practices of Greco-Roman society.

The Hebrew Bible regulates slavery, distinguishing between Gentile slaves captured in battle and Hebrew slaves who sold themselves or their children to pay off debts. In Exodus, the law decrees that after six years' servitude a male Hebrew slave is to be set free. Any children born to him and one of his master's female slaves, however, are to remain the master's property. If at the end of six years' time, the freed man wishes to remain with his wife and family, he must submit to a mutilation of the ear (the organ of obedience) and remain a slave for life (Exod. 21:2–6; see Part 3).

Following the Torah and the institutions of society at large, the New Testament writers neither condemn slavery nor predict its abolition. At the same time, the persistence of slavery was strangely inconsistent with the principles of freedom and a human being's innate worth advocated in Paul's letters and the Gospels. In United States history, both proslavery and antislavery parties used the New Testament to support their conflicting views. Slavery's proponents argued that Bible writers, including Paul, implicitly accepted the institution as a "natural" condition. Those against slavery extrapolated from Paul's doctrine of freedom and Christian equality (Gal. 3:28) a corresponding social and legal freedom for all people.

RECOMMENDED READING

Barth, M., ed. and trans. *Colossians and Philemon.* Vol. 34a of the Anchor Bible. Garden City, N.Y.: Doubleday, 1974. A scholarly translation and analysis.

Knox, John. *Philemon Among the Letters of Paul,* rev. ed. New York: Abingdon Press, 1959. Develops Edgar Goodspeed's theory that about 90 C.E. a Paulinist—perhaps the former slave Onesimus, who may then have been bishop of Ephesus—collected Paul's letters and circulated them among the entire church.

TERMS AND CONCEPTS TO REMEMBER

Adam	Galatia
allegory	Hagar
apokalypsis	Ishmael
Apollos	Judaism
Cephas (Peter)	Lord's Supper
Corinth	Lystra
Damascus	Macedonia
dualism	mystery
Enoch	Nero
Epaphroditus	Onesimus
faith	Parousia

pastoral Epistles
Pharisee
Philemon
Philippi
Phoebe
pseudonymity
resurrection
Silas

soul
speaking in tongues
syncretism
Tarsus
Thessalonica
Timothy
Titus

QUESTIONS FOR REVIEW

1. Find the passages in 1 Thessalonians and 1 Corinthians indicating that Paul believed the End to be very near. If Paul was wrong about the occurrence of the Parousia during his lifetime, to what extent does his mistaken view affect a reader's confidence in Paul's teachings?

2. Paul regards the Messiah's death and resurrection as immediately inaugurating a new era of divine judgment and eschatological hope. In what ways do Paul's beliefs about the imminent resurrection of the dead (1 Thess. 4–5 and 1 Cor. 15) relate to his view of Christ as the "last Adam" (Rom. 5:12–19; 1 Cor. 15:45–49)?

3. What are the sources of Paul's difficulties with the church at Corinth? Why does Paul boast "as a fool" in 2 Corinthians 10–13 and cite his mystical vision of heaven as part of his apostolic credentials?

4. Both Galatians and Romans deal with Christianity's relationship to Torah Judaism. Define and explain Paul's gospel of justification by faith.

QUESTIONS FOR DISCUSSION AND REFLECTION

1. In both Galatians and Romans, Paul cites excerpts from Genesis 15 and Habakkuk 2 to prove that God always intended faith to be

the means by which humanity was to be "justified" or "made righteous." Compare Paul's interpretation of Abraham's example with that given by James (James 2:14–26). How do these two writers differ on the issue of faith versus "works"?

2. Although the hymn Paul quotes in Philippians 2 is commonly interpreted as describing Jesus' prehuman existence, many commentators believe that it contains instead an implied contrast between the disobedience of Adam (who was God's human image) and the obedience of Christ (who reflects the divine image perfectly). Discuss the arguments for and against these differing interpretations.

3. Identify Philemon and Onesimus and their connection to Paul. Why do you think that Paul does not condemn human slavery as an evil institution?

The Disputed Pauline Letters

Paul's continuing influence on the Church was so great that for years after his death various Pauline disciples composed letters honoring his name and spirit. Some documents written in his name, such as those purportedly addressed to Timothy and Titus, are universally rejected by modern scholars. The authorship of others, such as 2 Thessalonians and Colossians, is still vigorously disputed, with sizable minorities defending the documents' authenticity. Perhaps 90 percent of scholars, however, doubt that Paul wrote Ephesians.

2 Thessalonians

KEY THEMES

Although repeating themes from 1 Thessalonians, 2 Thessalonians reinterprets Paul's original eschatology, asserting that a number of traditional apocalyptic "signs" must precede the eschaton.

> Stand firm . . . and hold fast to the traditions which you have learned from us by word or letter.
>
> 2 Thessalonians 2:15

Authorship and Purpose

Many scholars question Paul's authorship of 2 Thessalonians. If Paul composed it, why does he repeat—almost verbatim—so much of what he had already just written to the same recipients? More seriously, why does the author present an eschatology so different from that given in the first letter? In 1 Thessalonians, the Parousia will occur stealthily, "like a thief in the night." In 2 Thessalonians, a number of apocalyptic "signs" will first advertise its arrival. The interposing of these mysterious events between the writer's time and that of the Parousia has the effect of projecting the eschaton further into the future—a contrast to 1 Thessalonians, in which the End is extremely close.

Scholars defending Pauline authorship advance several theories to explain the writer's apparent change of attitude toward the Parousia. In the first letter, Paul emphasizes the tension between the shortness of time the world has left and the necessity of believers' vigilance and ethical purity as they await Christ's return. In the second missive, Paul writes to correct the Thessalonians' misconceptions or abuses of his earlier emphasis on the nearness of End time.

If Paul in fact wrote this document, his purpose is twofold: to stop his recipients from assuming that the "Day of the Lord" had already arrived (2:2) and to insist that believers who lazily awaited the End must work to support themselves (3:11–12). The false notion that the Parousia had already occurred may have arisen partly from a misunderstanding of 1 Thessalonians, with its several references to the imminence of Christ's return (1 Thess. 1:10; 2:19; 4:

15–5:11). Now counseling his readers not to "lose their heads," the author outlines specific events or "signs" that must occur before the day arrives (2:3–12). Although still maintaining that the Parousia is near (1:6–10), he insists that it cannot come "before the final rebellion against God, when wickedness will be revealed in human form, the [person] doomed to perdition" (2:3). This unidentified "enemy" will attack all religion, claim to be a god himself, and even take "his seat in the Temple of God" (2:4).

Traditional (Non-Pauline?) Signs of the End

Paul rarely predicts specific events in the course of future history, particularly in the vague and cryptic language of 2 Thessalonians. Whoever the author, his statement that the mysterious enemy's identity will not be disclosed until the appointed time expresses a typically apocalyptic belief. All future history is predestined, and nothing can happen before its divinely prearranged hour. The present is linked to the coming revelation, however, because evil forces are already at work, secretly gathering strength until the unnamed "Restrainer" disappears, allowing the wicked personage to emerge in power.

In this passage, the writer paints a characteristically apocalyptic worldview, a moral dualism in which the opposing powers of Good and Evil have their respective agents at work on earth. The enemy figure is Satan's agent; his opposite is Christ. As Jesus is God's representative working in human history, so the wicked rebel is the Devil's tool. Operating on a cosmic scale, the conflict will culminate in Christ's victory over the demonic enemy, who has deceived the mass of humanity into believing the "Lie." An evil parody of the Messiah, the anonymous Satanic dupe functions as an **antiChrist** (2:3–12).

The author's language is specific enough to arouse speculation about the identities of the enigmatic "wicked man" and the "Restrainer" who at the time of writing kept the anti-Christ in check. It is also vague enough to preclude connecting any known historical figures—in the first century C.E. or any period since—with these apocalyptic roles. In typical apocalyptic fashion, the figures are mythic archetypes that belong to a realm beyond the reach of historical inquiry.

Return to Practical Advice   After his bedazzling preview of future history, the writer makes sure that the Thessalonians do not neglect the practical affairs of their present lives. Notice that this section (3:6–16) firmly reanchors the Church to its earthly obligations. The author cites Paul's example of hard work and directs his readers to avoid persons who sponge off others. When he asserts that people who do not work will not eat, the writer suggests that at least some Thessalonians lived in a Christian commune similar to that in Jerusalem (Acts 2), where leaders could control the food supply.

2 Thessalonians contains a warning that forged letters were already circulating in Paul's name (2:1–3) and ends by insisting that Paul verified his genuine letters with his own signature (3:17–18). Scholars doubting Pauline authorship view the pseudonymous writer as protesting overmuch, but the apostle appends similar comments to undisputed letters (1 Cor. 16:21–24; Gal. 6:11).

Colossians

KEY THEMES

In Colossians, which may be the work of a Pauline disciple, the author emphasizes Jesus' identity with the cosmic power and wisdom by and for which the universe was created. The divine secret is revealed as Christ's Spirit dwelling in the believer.

The secret is this: Christ in you, the hope of a glory to come.

Colossians 1:27

If Paul is the author of Colossians, as a large minority of scholars believe, he had not yet visited the town of Colossae when he wrote this theologically significant letter. A small town in the Roman province of Asia, **Colossae** was located about 100 miles southeast of Ephesus, the provincial capital. **Epaphras**, one of Paul's missionary associates, had apparently founded the church a short time prior to Paul's writing (1:7).

If genuine, Colossians was probably composed at about the same time as Philemon, to which it is closely related. In both letters, Paul (or a disciple) writes from prison, including his friend Timothy in the salutation (1:1) and adding greetings from many of the same persons cited in the earlier missive (4:9–18), including Onesimus, Epaphras, Mark, and Luke.

Purpose   The author, whom we call Paul for convenience, writes to reaffirm the validity of what Epaphras had preached and to refute a false "philosophy" that threatened to distort the proper understanding of Christ's uniqueness. Some members of the Colossian church were apparently involved in a cult that blended pagan and marginal Jewish speculations about angels and "elemental spirits of the universe," to which they accorded some form of worship (2:8, 18). The writer denounces these "hollow and delusive" notions that failed to recognize Christ's preeminence. Christ is not only supreme but also the only channel to spiritual reality; lesser spirit beings are merely his "captives," reduced to servants by his triumphant death and heavenly ascension.

The letter advances two important Christological concepts: (1) Christ is supreme because God's power now manifested in him is the same power that created the entire universe, including those invisible entities that the false teachers mistakenly worship; and (2) when they realize

Christ's supremacy and experience his indwelling Spirit, the Colossians are initiated into his mystery cult, voluntarily harmonizing their lives with the cosmic unity he embodies.

Christ: The Source of Cosmic Unity

In the opinion of some analysts, both the complex nature of the false teachings, which may represent a form of Gnosticism, and the **Christology** of Colossians seem too "advanced" for the letter to have originated in Paul's day. Other critics point out that if the letter was written late in Paul's career to meet a situation significantly different from others he had earlier encountered, it could well have stimulated the apostle to produce a more fully developed expression of his views about Christ's nature and function.

As in Philippians 2, the author appears to quote an older Christian hymn to illustrate his vision of the exalted Jesus' cosmic role:

> He is the image of the invisible God, the first-born of all creation;
> for in him all things were created, in heaven and on earth, visible and invisible, whether thrones or dominions or principalities or authorities
> all things were created through him and for him.

> * * *

> For in him all the fullness of God was pleased to dwell,
> and through him to reconcile to himself all things, whether on earth or in heaven,
> making peace by the blood of his cross.
> Colossians 1:15–16, 19–20
> (Revised Standard Version)

Like the prolog to John's Gospel, this beautiful poem is modeled on biblical and Hellenistic Jewish concepts of divine Wisdom (Prov. 8: 22–31; Ecclus. 24:1–22; see also the discussion of John's use of the Logos [Word], Part 9). Hellenistic Jews had created a rich lore of speculative thought in which God's chief attribute, his

infinite Wisdom, is the source of all creation and the means by which he communicates his purpose to humanity. Many historians believe that early Christian thinkers adopted these ready-made wisdom traditions and applied them to Jesus.

Recognizing the Colossian hymn's use of wisdom language, many scholars view it as a declaration that the same divine presence and power that created the universe now operates in the glorified Christ. The personified Wisdom whom God employed as his agent in fashioning the cosmos is now fully revealed in Christ, the agent through whom God redeems his human creation.

The phrase "image [*eikon*] of the invisible God" (1:15) may correspond to the phrase "form [*morphes*] of God" used in Philippians 2: 6. In both cases, the term echoes the words of Genesis, in which God creates the first human beings in his own "image" and "likeness" (Gen. 1:26–27; 5:1). The author believes that Christians reconciled to God also come to bear the divine "image" (3:10). Rather than asserting the Johannine view that the prehuman Jesus was literally present at creation, the hymn may affirm that he is the ultimate goal toward which God's world trends.

Whatever Christological origins he promotes, the writer's main purpose is to demonstrate Christ's present superiority to all rival cosmic beings. The "thrones, sovereignties, authorities and powers" mentioned (1:6) probably represent the Jewish hierarchy of angels. Christ's perfect obedience, vindicating God's image in humanity, and his ascension to heaven have rendered these lesser beings irrelevant and powerless. By his triumph, Christ leads them captive as a Roman emperor leads a public procession of conquered enemies (2:9–15).

Union with the Divine Image   Moving from Christ's supremacy to his own role in the divine plan, Paul states that his task is to deliver God's message of reconciliation. He is the agent chosen to reveal the divine "secret hidden for long ages"—the glorified Christ dwelling in the believer, spiritually reuniting the Christian with God. Christians thus form Christ's visible body, here identified with the Church (1:21–2:8).

The Mystical Initiation into Christ Employing the rather obscure language of Greek mystery religions (see Part 8), Paul compares the Christian's baptism to a vicarious experience of Christ's death and resurrection (2:12, 20; 3:1). It is also the Christian equivalent of circumcision, the ritual sign that identifies one as belonging to God's people, and the rite of initiation into Christ's "body" (2:12–14). Raised to new life, initiated believers are liberated from religious obligations sponsored by those lesser spirits who transmitted the Torah revelation to Moses.

Paul reminds the Colossians that they need not be intimidated by self-styled authorities who mortify the body and piously forbid partaking of certain food and drink, for Christ's death put an end to such legal discriminations. No longer is there "Greek and Jew, circumcised and uncircumcised, barbarian, Scythians, slave and freeman; but Christ is all, and is in all" (2:20–3:11). Like persons initiated into Greco-Roman mystery cults, Christians now enjoy a union of social and religious equality.

Characteristically, Paul moves from doctrinal matters to ethical exhortations: Christians are to live godly lives and to meet all domestic and social obligations. The list of vices (3:5–9) and virtues (3:12–25) is typical of other Hellenistic teachers of ethics, but the writer adds a distinctively Christian note: Believers conduct themselves well because they are being re-created in Christ's nature and "image" (3:10).

RECOMMENDED READING

Barth, Markus, ed. and trans. *Colossians and Philemon.* Anchor Bible, Vol. 34A. Garden City, N.Y.: Doubleday, 1974. A scholarly translation and analysis.

Giblin, Charles H. "The Second Letter to the Thessalonians." In R. E. Brown et al., eds., *The New Jerome Biblical Commentary,* 2nd ed., pp. 871–875. Englewood Cliffs, N.J.: Prentice-Hall, 1990. A Catholic scholar concludes that the letter is by a later Pauline disciple.

Lohse, Eduard. *Colossians and Philemon.* Hermeneia. Philadelphia: Fortress Press, 1971. A scholarly analysis, concluding that Colossians is by a Pauline disciple.

O'Brien, P. T. *Colossians, Philemon.* Word Biblical Commentary, 44. Waco, Tex.: Word Books, 1982. Defends Pauline authorship of Colossians; includes the author's translation.

Schweizer, Eduard. *The Letter to the Colossians: A Commentary.* Minneapolis: Augsburg, 1982. Less technical than works by Lohse and O'Brien, this study suggests that Timothy played a role in writing Colossians.

Ephesians

KEY THEMES

Scholars believe that Ephesians is a tribute to Pauline thought penned by a later disciple who modifies and updates Paul's ideas to address concerns of his own day. The writer argues that the unity of Christ and the cosmos must be reflected in the unity of the Church, whose members engage in spiritual warfare with supernatural Evil.

> For our fight is not against human foes, but against the authorities and potentates of this dark world, against the superhuman forces of evil in the heavens. Therefore, take up God's armour.
>
> Ephesians 6:12

Arguments for Non-Pauline Authorship

Many scholars question Paul's authorship of Colossians, but an overwhelming majority doubt that he composed the document we call Ephesians. Although it closely resembles Colossians (the style and theology of which also seem un-

The Book of Ephesians's famous description of a Christian's spiritual defenses against Evil is based on the armor and other military equipment used by Roman soldiers, depicted in this bas-relief (Eph. 6:13–17). (Courtesy of the Mansell Collection)

typical of Paul), Ephesians differs from the undisputed Pauline letters in (1) vocabulary (containing over ninety words not found elsewhere in Paul's writings); (2) literary style (written in extremely long, convoluted sentences, in contrast to Paul's usually direct, forceful statements; its quietly devotional tone and smoothly organized sequence of thoughts also differ from the apostle's usual hectic welter of ideas and impassioned language); and (3) theology (the absence of such typically Pauline doctrines as justification by faith and the nearness of Christ's return).

Despite its similarity to Colossians (75 of Ephesians's 155 verses parallel phrases in Colossians), it presents a different view of the sacred "secret" or "mystery" revealed in Christ. In Colossians, God's long-kept secret is Christ's mystical union with his followers (Col. 1:27),

but in Ephesians it is the union of Jew and Gentile in one Church (Eph. 3:6).

More than any other disputed letter (except those to Timothy and Titus), Ephesians seems to reflect a time in Church history significantly later than Paul's day. References to "Apostles and prophets" as the Church's foundation imply that these figures belong to the past, not the author's generation (2:20; 3:5). The Gentiles' equality in Christian fellowship is no longer a controversial issue but an accomplished fact; this strongly suggests that the letter originated after the Church membership had become non-Jewish (2:11–22). Judaizing interlopers no longer question Paul's stand on circumcision, again indicating that the work was composed after Jerusalem's destruction had largely eliminated the Jewish influence of the mother church.

When Paul uses the term *church* (*ekklesia*), he always refers to an individual congregation (Gal. 1:2; 1 Cor. 11:16; 16:19; etc.) By contrast, Ephesians's author speaks of the Church collectively, a universal institution encompassing all communities of faith. This view of the Church as a worldwide entity also points to a time after the apostolic period.

The accumulated evidence convinces most scholars that Ephesians is a **deutero-Pauline** document, a secondary work composed in Paul's name by an admirer thoroughly steeped in the apostle's thought and general theology. The close parallels to Colossians, as well as phrases taken from Romans, Philemon, and other letters, indicate that unlike the author of Acts this unknown writer was familiar with the Pauline correspondence. Some scholars propose that Ephesians was written as a kind of "cover letter," or essay, to accompany an early collection of Paul's letters.

The phrase "in Ephesus" (1:1), identifying the recipients, does not appear in any of the oldest manuscript copies. That fact, plus the lack of any specific issue or problem being addressed, reinforces the theory that Ephesians was intended to circulate among several churches in Asia Minor. It probably functioned to provide an updated summary of Paul's ideas, tailored to fit the changing needs of a largely Gentile and cosmopolitan church.

God's Plan of Salvation Through the United Body of Christ

Probably written between 90 and 100 C.E., Ephesians is more a sophisticated theological meditation than a real letter. Its principal theme is that the unity of the universe through Christ (Chs. 1–3) must be reflected in the unity of the Church, which is the earthly manifestation of the divine oneness (Chs. 4–6). God has now revealed his "hidden purpose": to bring "all in heaven and earth . . . into a unity with Christ" (1:10). Although the human race had become alienated from God, God's redemptive act in Jesus' death and resurrection has reconciled the believing world to him. The Deity's age-old secret plan is now clear: "The Gentiles are joint heirs with the Jews, part of the same body, sharers in the promise made in Christ Jesus" (3:6).

In the second part of his letter (Chs. 4–6), the author explores four areas in which the Spirit imparts unity. The first area is the Church, where all believers "at last attain to the unity inherent in our faith" (4:4–16), for there is "one body and one Spirit . . . one Lord, one faith, one baptism, one God" (4:5–6). The second area is the pagan world (4:17–5:20), whose ignorance and "foul desires" the Christian abandons to be "made new in mind and spirit," thus acquiring a "new nature of God's creating" (4:21–24). In the third area, the Spirit permeates family life so that husbands, wives, children, and slaves show mutual love and forbearance (5:21–6:9).

Finally, the Spirit offers protection against "cosmic powers" and "superhuman forces of evil in the heavens" (6:10–20). Using the analogy of a well-equipped Roman soldier, the writer urges the Christian to arm himself against the dark powers with such spiritual defenses as "the belt of truth" and the "shield of faith," with which one can quench the Devil's "flaming arrows" (6:13–17). Interestingly, the Devil's attack is not seen as part of a final apocalyptic conflict but as a present ongoing fight against invisible evil forces that inspire the vice and corruption of contemporary pagan society.

RECOMMENDED READING

Barth, Markus, ed. and trans. *Ephesians.* Vols. 34 and 34a of the Anchor Bible. Garden City, N.Y.: Doubleday, 1974. This extensive commentary defends Pauline authorship.

Bruce, F. F. *The Epistles to the Colossians, to Philemon, and the Ephesians.* New International Commentary on the New Testament. Grand Rapids, Mich.: Eerdmans, 1984.

Furnish, V. P. "Ephesians, Epistle to the." In D. N. Freedman, ed., *The Anchor Bible Dictionary,* Vol. 2, pp. 535–542. New York: Doubleday, 1992.

Goodspeed, E. J. *The Meaning of Ephesians.* Chicago: University of Chicago Press, 1933. An older but perceptive study arguing that Ephesians was written as a cover letter for the first collected edition of Paul's correspondence.

Mitton, C. L. *Ephesians.* New Century Bible. Grand Rapids, Mich.: Eerdmans, 1981. A brief study of Ephesians as a work produced by one of Paul's disciples.

Taylor, W. F., and Reumann, J. H. P. *Ephesians, Colossians.* Augsburg Commentary on the New Testament. Minneapolis: Augsburg, 1985.

TERMS AND CONCEPTS TO REMEMBER

anti–Christ

Christology

Colossae

deutero–Pauline

Epaphras

QUESTIONS FOR REVIEW

1. Why do scholars believe that 2 Thessalonians, Colossians, and Ephesians represent the work of later Pauline disciples rather than

that of the apostle himself? What subtle differences in style, theology, and outlook do you find in these disputed letters?

2. Summarize Paul's major contributions to Christian thought, including his beliefs about the eschaton, his teachings about the nature and function of Christ (Christology), and his doctrine of justification by faith.

QUESTION FOR DISCUSSION AND REFLECTION

Identify and interpret Ephesians's metaphor of Christian armor. How does the attitude in Ephesians toward Christians' continuing battle against supernatural evil differ from Paul's view of the imminent End of the present evil age?

The Pastoral Letters

The three letters addressed to Paul's young missionary companions, Timothy and Titus, are known as the **Pastoral Epistles** (from *pastor,* the "shepherd" of a flock). The Pauline authorship of 1 and 2 Timothy and Titus, however, has been under critical attack since the eighteenth century. Besides the fact that they do not appear in early lists of Paul's letters, the Pastoral Epistles (or Pastorals) seem to reflect conditions that prevailed long after Paul's day. Their views of ecclesiastical offices, "bishops," "elders," and "deacons" mirror the more tightly organized Church of the second century C.E. in which such offices had far more specialized functions than in Paul's time.

Lacking Paul's characteristic ideas about faith and the Spirit, the Pastorals are also un-Pauline in their flat style and different vocabulary (containing 306 words not found in Paul's undisputed letters). Scholars believe that a single Pauline disciple—who possessed little of his

mentor's fire or originality—wrote all three, between about 100 and 140 C.E.

1 Timothy

KEY THEME

Writing to Timothy as representing a new generation of Christians, an anonymous disciple (known as the pastor) warns his readers against false teachings and recommends the standards necessary for ensuring proper order and discipline within the church.

> I am writing these instructions to you so that
> . . . you may know how one ought to behave in the household of God, which is the church of the living God, the pillar and bulwark of the truth.
>
> 1 Timothy 3:14–15

The first two pastorals are addressed to **Timothy**, the son of a Jewish mother and Greek father (Acts 16:1). However, if scholars are correct in concluding that the pastorals are not by Paul but by an early to mid-second century Christian writer deeply influenced by Pauline thought, it becomes clear that "Timothy" is not the historical evangelist but a literary character intended to symbolize orthodox (correct) leadership in the postapostolic Church. Such pastors struggled to keep alive Paul's "wholesome doctrine" at a time when "subversive teachings [heresies] inspired by devils" threatened to disrupt Christian unity (4:2).

Establishing Orthodoxy and Institutional Order

Erroneous Doctrines   The writer's primary purpose is to combat "erroneous doctrines" (1:3) then circulating among the Church membership. As Christianity spread among diverse Gentile groups, some converts apparently brought ideas from older Greco-Roman religions and philosophies, which they applied to Christian traditions. Because the pastor does not offer a rational criticism of his opponents' errors, we do not know the exact nature of the beliefs attacked. Some commentators suggest that the false teachers practiced an early form of **Gnosticism**, a cult of secret "knowledge" mentioned in 6:20, but the letter reveals too little about the **heresies** taught to identify them as Gnostic.

The author describes such deviation from the true faith as involving "interminable myths," "genealogies," and fruitless "speculations" (1:3–4). Its practitioners may have included Jewish legalists, self-appointed "teachers of the moral Law" (1:7–11), and ascetics or "puritans" who forbade marriage and abstained from certain foods that, in the pastor's opinion, God intended everyone to eat (4:1–3). Timothy (and the pastorship he represents) must correct this misguided austerity by transmitting the correct Pauline teachings (4:11), thereby saving himself as well as those who obey him (4:16).

Qualifications for Church Offices   The pastor's second concern is to outline the qualifications for aspirants to Church offices (3:1–13). Church officers must demonstrate all the virtues typical of Hellenistic ethical philosophy: They are to be "above reproach" in public reputation, sober, courteous, hospitable, in control of their families, and good teachers (3:2–23). It is remarkable that the pastor's list of qualifications does not include either intellectual ability or possession of the Spirit. Instead of the spiritual gifts that prevailed in Paul's churches, the pastor's congregation seems content with typically middle-class respectability.

The pastor regards the institution of the Church—rather than the Spirit of Christ dwelling in the believer—as "the pillar and bulwark of the truth" (3:15). By the time this letter was composed, a tightly organized structure administered by a thoroughly conventional male leadership had replaced the dynamic and charismatic fellowship of the genuinely Pauline congregations.

Ranking the Church Membership   In 1 Timothy, the Church membership mirrors the social order of the larger Greco-Roman society out of which its members came. Bishops (overseers), deacons (assistants), and elders (seasoned congregants) govern a mixed group composed of different social classes, including heads of households, masters, slaves, wives, widows, and children—all of whom are ordered to submit to their respective superiors. Rather than the spontaneous equality Paul had advocated, in which slaves and masters, men and women, were urged to escape social categorization and stratification in Christian fellowship, the pastoral church adopted the rigid class system of the outside world.

Women's Roles   Whereas Paul recognizes women as prophets and speakers (1 Cor. 11:5), the pastor does not permit a woman to teach because the first woman, Eve, was weak-minded and tempted her husband to sin (2:8–15). The detailed instruction on women's dress and conduct probably applies to public worship and parallels the restricted position assigned women in some Hellenistic circles. Because it reflects thencurrent social customs, many commentators observe that the pastor's advice is not a timeless prescription for women's roles in the Christian community.

As Christians are to pray for government rulers (2:1–3), so slaves are to obey their masters (6:1–2). Yet, the rich and powerful are reminded to share their wealth (6:17–19). Those ambitious to acquire riches are told that a passion for money is the cause of much evil, a source of grief and lost faith (6:9–10).

In closing, the pastor instructs Timothy, the prototype of the wise Church supervisor, to safeguard the apostolic heritage and to avoid "so-called knowledge" disseminated by (Gnostic?) heretics (6:20–21). Anyone who disagrees with the pastor's interpretation of the Pauline legacy is "a pompous ignoramus" (6:3).

2 Timothy

KEY THEME

In a style more closely resembling that of Paul than the other pastoral Epistles, 2 Timothy counsels against various false teachings.

> Keep before you an outline of the sound
> teaching which you heard from me. . . .
> Guard the treasure put into your charge.
> 2 Timothy 1:13–14

2 Timothy more closely resembles Paul's genuine letters than either 1 Timothy or Titus. Although similarly concerned with refuting false teachings, its tone is more intimate and personal. Several passages in which the author depicts himself as abandoned by former associates and languishing alone in prison except for the companionship of "Luke" (1:15; 4:9–11, 16) are especially poignant. Although these and other flashes of Paul's characteristic vigor and emotional fluctuations (4:6–8, 17–18) have led some critics to speculate that the work contains fragments of otherwise lost Pauline letters, such proposals have not won general acceptance.

The part of 2 Timothy with the best claim to Pauline authorship is the section that ends the letter (4:6–22), in which the writer emulates the fluctuations between lofty thoughts and mundane practicalities so typical of the apostle. In the first part, he compares himself to a runner winning the athlete's coveted prize—not the Greek competitor's laurel crown but a "garland of righteousness" justifying him on Judgment Day (6:6–8). Switching abruptly to practical matters, the author then asks the recipient to remember to bring his books when he visits. In another quick change of subject, he complains that during his court hearing nobody appeared

in his defense and that the testimony of one "Alexander the coppersmith" seriously damaged his case. Then, in a seemingly contradictory about-face, the writer states that he has (metaphorically) escaped the "lion's jaws" and expects to be kept safe until the Parousia (6: 13–18).

Although such rapid shifts from gloom to optimism characterize Paul's authentic letters, most scholars believe that the entire document is the pastor's work. The more vivid passages are simply the writer's most successful homage to the apostle's memory.

In describing the false teaching within the Church that he identifies as signs of the last days, the pastor reveals that he is using Paul to predict conditions that characterize the writer's own time. During the world's final days (3:1), hypocrites insinuate their way into Christians' homes, corrupting the occupants. These predators typically prey upon women because, in the pastor's insulting opinion, even when eager to learn, women lack the ability to understand true doctrine (3:6–8). Instead of the false teachers' being punished at the Second Coming, the pastor implies that the mere passage of time will expose their errors (3:9).

As in 1 Timothy, the pastor does not refute the heretics with logical argument but merely calls them names and lists their vices (3:1–6, 13; 4:3–4), duplicating the catalogs of misbehavior common in Hellenistic philosophical schools. Whereas the Church is the stronghold of faith in 1 Timothy, in 2 Timothy the Hebrew Bible is the standard of religious orthodoxy (correct teaching) confounding error and directing the believer to salvation. Scripture also provides the mental discipline necessary to equip the believer for right action (3:15–17).

Concluding with his memorable picture of the apostle courageously facing martyrdom, the pastor graciously includes all of the faithful in Christ's promised deliverance. Not only Paul but all who trust in Jesus' imminent return will win victory's crown at the Parousia (6:6–8).

Titus

KEY THEME

The letter to Titus, who represents the post-apostolic Church leadership, urges him to preserve the Pauline traditions and sets forth the requirements and duties of elders and bishops.

> There are all too many . . . who talk wildly and lead men's minds astray. Such men must be curbed.
>
> Titus 1:10, 11

Although it is the shortest of the pastorals, Titus has the longest salutation, a fulsome recapitulation of Paul's credentials and the recipient's significance (1:1–4). This highly formal introduction would be inappropriate in a personal letter from Paul to his younger friend but is understandable as the pastor's way of officially transmitting Paul's authoritative instruction to a postapostolic successor.

The historical **Titus**, a Greek youth whom Paul refused to have circumcised (Gal. 2), accompanied the apostle on his missionary tours of Greece, acting as Paul's emissary to reconcile the rebellious Corinthians (Gal. 2:1, 3, 10; 2 Cor. 8:6, 16–23). Like the "Timothy" of the other pastorals, however, "Titus" is a symbolic figure, representing a late postapostolic generation interested in preserving Pauline traditions. Hence, "Titus" functions as a mediator to a later age who can establish the requirements and some of the duties of Church leaders who will adhere to Pauline orthodoxy.

Revising the Pauline Legacy

Qualifications for Church Officers   The writer states that he left "Titus" in Crete, an island center of Greek civilization, to install Church assistants (elders) in every town (1:5). Such persons must be socially respectable married men who keep their children under strict parental control (1:6). Whereas Paul had preferred Christians to remain single (1 Cor. 7), the pastor insists that Church leaders be married! Besides possessing these domestic credentials, bishops (Church supervisors) must also have a reputation for devotion, self-control, and hospitality (1:7–8). Again, the writer says nothing about the leaders' mental or charismatic gifts so highly valued in the Pauline churches (2 Cor. 11–14).

One of the bishop's main functions is to guard the received religion, adhering to established beliefs and correcting dissenters (1:7–9). Titus is the only book in the New Testament that uses the term *heretic* (3:10), which at the time of writing (early to mid-second century) probably meant a person who held opinions of which the elders disapproved. Such dissenters are to be warned twice and then ignored (excluded from the Church?) if they fail to change their ways (3:10–11).

The author reminds his audience that because they are Christians in a nonbelieving world, they must live exemplary lives of obedience and submission to government authorities (3:1). Men and women, old and young, slaves and masters are all to behave in a way that publicly reflects well on their religion (2:1–10). Christians must maintain an ethically pure community while awaiting Christ's return (2:13–14).

In a moving passage, the author contrasts the negative personality traits that many believers had before their conversion with the grace and hope for eternal life that they now enjoy (3:3–8). In counsel similar to that in the letter of James, he urges believers to show their faith in admirable and useful deeds and to refrain from "foolish speculations, genealogies, quarrels, and controversies over the Law" (3:9–10).

The Pastor's Contribution   Although the pastor's style is generally weak and colorless compared to Paul's (except for some passages in 2 Timothy), he successfully promotes Paul's continuing authority in the Church. His insistence that Paul's teaching (as he understood it) be followed and that Church leaders actively employ apostolic ideas to refute false teachers helped ensure that the international Christian community would build its future on a (modified) Pauline foundation.

Although the pastor values continuity and tradition, he does not seem to show an equal regard for encouraging the individual revelations and ecstatic experiences that characterized the Pauline churches. (Regarding the "laying on of hands" as the correct means of conferring authority [2 Tim. 1:16], he would probably not welcome another like Paul who insisted that his private experience of Jesus—not ordination by his predecessors—validated his calling.) Using Scripture, inherited doctrines, and the institutional Church as guarantors of orthodoxy, the pastor sees the Christian revelation as already complete, a static legacy from the past. He ignores Paul's injunction not to "stifle inspiration" or prophetic speech (1 Thess. 5:19–20); his intense conservatism allows little room for future enlightenment.

RECOMMENDED READING

Dibelius, Martin, and Conzelmann, Hans. *The Pastoral Epistles.* Hermeneia Commentary. Philadelphia: Fortress Press, 1972. Conzelmann's updating of Dibelius's famous commentary, first published in German in 1913.

Hanson, A. T. *The Pastoral Epistles.* New Century Bible. Grand Rapids, Mich.: Eerdmans, 1982. A brief but helpful treatment.

MacDonald, D. R. *The Legend and the Apostle.* Philadelphia: Westminster Press, 1983.

Quinn, J. D., ed. and trans. *1 and 2 Timothy and Titus.* Vol. 35 of the Anchor Bible. Garden City, N.Y.: Doubleday, 1976. A recent translation with commentary.

———. "Timothy and Titus, Epistles to." In D. N. Freedman, ed., *The Anchor Bible Dictionary,* Vol. 6, pp. 560–571. New York: Doubleday, 1992.

TERMS AND CONCEPTS TO REMEMBER

Gnosticism	Timothy
heresy	Titus
pastoral Epistles	

QUESTIONS FOR REVIEW

1. List the reasons that the large majority of New Testament scholars think that the pastoral Epistles were composed after Paul's time by later Christian writers deeply influenced by Pauline thought. What ideas are missing from the Pastorals that characterize Paul's genuine letters?

2. After reviewing the works addressed to Timothy and Titus, explain what you think motivated the author to write them. What ideas or principles is he writing to advocate?

QUESTIONS FOR DISCUSSION AND REFLECTION

1. All three pastorals have a similar purpose—to combat heresy and affirm the author's orthodox understanding of apostolic teachings. In what specific ways do the Pastorals reflect church conditions that are different from those obtaining in Paul's day?

2. Discuss the pastor's views about women, children, and slaves. How does his prescription for internal church order reflect the hierarchical organization of the contemporary Greco-Roman society? What similarities and differences do you see between the character and behavior of Jesus and the pastor's list of qualifications for church leaders? Would the historical Jesus, an unmarried itinerant prophet, have met the pastor's standards to qualify for church leadership?

General Epistles and a Vision of End Time

Hebrews and the Catholic ("General") Epistles

Paul's extensive use of the letter form influenced many later New Testament writers. Besides authors like the pastor, who wrote in Paul's name, other early Christians imitated the apostle by composing "letters" to instruct and encourage the faithful. Unlike Paul's genuine correspondence, these later documents commonly are not addressed to individual congregations but are directed to the Christian community as a whole. This group of eight disparate writings, headed by the Book of Hebrews, forms a discrete unit between the collection of letters traditionally ascribed to Paul and the Book of Revelation.

Because of their general nature, seven of these writings are known collectively as the **Catholic Epistles** (referring to the fact that they were intended for the Church at large). The seven—James; 1 and 2 Peter; 1, 2, and 3 John; and Jude—are called **epistles** because most of them are formal communications intended for public reading in many different churches. In this respect, they differ from genuine letters like those of Paul, which were composed for specific recipients known to the author and which are much less formal.

Even the term *epistle* does not adequately describe the diverse literary forms encompassed in these works. Of the three missives ascribed to John, for example, the first is actually a sermon or tract, the second is a warning letter to a specific group, and the third is a private note.

Pseudonymous Authorship Besides their dubious categorization as epistles, another significant factor links these seven writings. All are attributed to prominent leaders of the original Jerusalem church. Six are ascribed to the three Jerusalem "pillars"—Peter, James, and John (Gal. 2). The seventh, Jude, is purportedly by James's brother.

The practice of creating new works under the identity of a well-known but deceased person is called **pseudonymity**. In our discussion of the Pseudepigrapha (see Part 7), we noted that from about 200 B.C.E. to 200 C.E. many Jewish writers composed books attributed to famous leaders of the past, including Moses, Enoch, Isaiah, Solomon, Ezra, and Daniel. These pseudepigraphal works should *not* be thought of as forgeries but as attempts to perpetuate the teachings of great sages and prophets, updating them to address problems faced by later generations.

Early Christians followed the Jewish lead, producing numerous documents attributed to the apostles and their associates, including Peter,

John, James, Barnabas, and Paul (see Part 12). As mentioned in our discussion of the pastorals (Part 10), some of these pseudonymous writings were eventually included in the New Testament.

Hebrews

KEY THEMES

The work of an accomplished stylist who combines allegorical interpretation of the Hebrew Bible with elements of Greek philosophy, Hebrews argues that Jesus was both a kingly and priestly Messiah. The final and complete revelation of God's purpose, Christ now serves in heaven as an eternal High Priest and mediator for humanity.

> In this final age God has spoken to us in the Son whom he has made heir to the whole universe, and through whom he created all orders of existence: the Son who is . . . the stamp of God's very being.
>
> Hebrews 1:2

Authorship and Date of Hebrews

An old tradition that Paul wrote Hebrews, which was disputed even in the early Church, is now generally discredited. Besides differing in vocabulary and style, the book does not reflect Paul's characteristic thought on faith, justification, reconciliation, or union with Christ. Although various attempts have been made to show that Barnabas, **Priscilla** (mentioned in Rom. 16:3; 1 Cor. 16:19; 2 Tim. 4:19), or the eloquent Apollos of Alexandria was the author, most scholars now conclude that the work is anonymous.

The last section of Hebrews (13:18–25), with its salutations and first-person references to Timothy, may originally have been part of another document, which a later editor added to make Hebrews seem more like a letter. Despite this epistolary ending, however, Hebrews reads more like an oratorical treatise or sermon than a letter. Mixing theological analysis with exhortation, the work does not follow the rules prescribed by any particular literary form.

Because the text itself does not contain the phrase "to the Hebrews" or otherwise identify its recipients, scholars are also unsure of its intended destination. The final "greetings to you from our Italian friends" (13:24) suggests that it originated in Italy, perhaps in Rome, but some scholars have argued persuasively that it was written in Alexandria or Palestine. The date of composition is equally problematic, estimates ranging from about 65 to 100 C.E.

A Dualistic View and Methods of Interpretation

The Book of Hebrews was written by an anonymous Christian scholar who was equally well acquainted with the Hebrew Bible and with Greek philosophical concepts. The work challenges the reader as does no other New Testament book except Revelation. With the warning that he offers "much that is difficult to explain" (5:11), the writer presents a dualistic view of the universe in which earthly events and human institutions are seen as reflections of invisible heavenly realities. Employing a popular form of Platonic thought, the writer assumes the existence of two parallel worlds: the eternal and perfect realm of spirit above, and the inferior constantly changing world below. Alone among New Testament authors, he attempts to show how Christ's sacrificial death links the two opposing realms of perishable matter and eternal spirit. He is the only Bible writer to present Jesus as a heavenly priest who serves as an everlasting mediator between God and humanity.

Like **Philo Judaeus**, the Hellenistic Jewish scholar of Alexandria, the author of Hebrews uses a highly sophisticated method of biblical interpretation. In both Hebrews and Philo's work, the Hebrew Bible is not merely a record of Israel's history; it is an allegory in which earthly events symbolize heavenly realities.

Like all New Testament writers, however, Hebrews's author does not make subtle theological interpretation an end in itself but only a means of reinforcing his attempt to influence readers' ethical behavior. The theological argument—that Christ is the final and complete revelation of God's will—serves to remind believers that they must hold fast to their faith or risk destruction. Thus, the recipients are exhorted to remember their former loyalty during persecution and avoid the common pitfalls of apathy or indifference (10:32–34).

After an introduction (1:1–4), Hebrews is arranged in three main sections:

1. Christ, the image of God, is superior to all other human or heavenly beings (1:5–4:16).

2. The Torah's priestly regulations—including sanctuary, covenant, and sacrifice—foreshadowed Jesus' role as a priest like Melchizedek (5:1–10:39).

3. Believers must act on faith in unseen realities, emulating biblical figures of old (11:1–13:16).

Christ's Superiority to All Other Beings

Hebrews' principal theme is the supremacy and absolute finality of the divine revelation through **Jesus Christ**. As the perfect "image of God," Christ is superior to all biblical sages, prophets, angels, and the priesthood of the Mosaic Torah (4:44–7:28). Hebrews is the only canonical book to argue that Jesus was not only a Davidic Messiah-King but an eternal High Priest as well.

Christ as a King-Priest

To demonstrate that Jesus is greater than the Levitical priests who administered the Mosaic tabernacle (and by implication the Jerusalem Temple), the author cites the Torah story of Abraham and Melchizedek (Gen. 14:17–20)

and a reference to Israel's kings as "like Melchizedek" (Ps. 110:4). According to Genesis, Abraham, returning from a successful war, paid **Melchizedek**, the mysterious king of Salem and priest of "God Most High" (El Elyon), a tenth of his victor's spoils. Because the account mentions neither Melchizedek's ancestors nor descendants, the author concludes that his priesthood is without beginning or end. As king of righteousness and peace and an "eternal priest," Melchizedek is the prototype of Christ. Superior to Abraham, who paid him tithes, he is also superior to Abraham's Levitical descendants, the Jewish priests. Sinless, deathless, and confirmed by divine oath, Christ's priesthood endures forever (7:3, 21–28).

In the author's view, Christ's high priesthood supersedes that of the Levites, as do his Temple sanctuary, covenant, and sacrifice (8:1–10:39). Employing a form of Platonic **dualism**—an eternal world of spirit paralleling our perishable world of matter—Hebrews envisions Israel's earthly ceremonies of sacrifice and worship as reflections, or copies, of invisible heavenly realities (8:5). The author then provides an allegorical interpretation of priestly rituals on the **Day of Atonement** (Yom Kippur).

In the visible Israelite tabernacle (or Temple), the high priest enters the innermost Holy of Holies once a year on the Day of Atonement to make a sin offering for the people (Lev. 16)—an imperfect offering that must be renewed annually. Christ, however, has entered the spiritual reality—the heavenly Temple—once and for all time with the sacrifice of his life, thus canceling the need for any further sacrifices in the earthly sanctuary.

Christianity is thus the only true religion, the fulfillment of Judaism, which was but a shadow of the final revelation. Christ's sacrifice is superior to Israel's atonement offerings not only because it is sinless, perfect, and nonrepeatable but also because it inaugurates a new covenant (9:15). Like the Mosaic law, Christ's covenant is ratified by blood—that poured out at his crucifixion, for the author subscribes to the old priestly view that without blood no forgiveness of sin takes place (9:22). Whereas the old law demands endlessly repeated animal sacrifices, the new law has but one—Christ's—which is permanently effective.

Those benefiting by Christ's everlasting sacrifice can hope, like him, to enter the heavenly sanctuary, their sins forgiven and their salvation ensured (10:5–19). Meanwhile, Christians should loyally adhere to the true religion because the **Day of Judgment** is near. If they willfully sin after having known the truth, they are condemned because Christ cannot die for them a second time (10:20–31). Although this rigorous view was apparently common in early Christianity, no other New Testament author so categorically denies erring believers a second chance at salvation. (See also Heb. 6:4–9.)

Faith in Unseen Realities

In Chapter 11, one of the most famous passages in the Bible, the writer reaches the climax of his presentation—a soaring discourse on **faith**. The writer proposes that believers accept God's ultimate revelation in the Son through faith, which "gives substance to our hopes and makes us certain of realities we do not see" (11:1). Unlike Paul, who always associates faith with trust in Christ, the author of Hebrews defines the concept in classically Platonic terms—perception of an unseen universe transcending the material world (11:1–3). It is the invisible cosmos—the celestial realm where Christ sits at God's right hand—upon which the eyes of faith are fixed. After presenting a brilliant survey of Old Testament figures who lived by faith—from Abel, the first martyr, to the countless men and women who suffered death to attain the spiritual kingdom above—the author urges his readers to run a similar race for eternal life (11:2–12:2). Like the biblical characters who had only a glimpse of what was to come, the Christian, who has the reality, must stand firm, enduring suffering as a necessary discipline (12:3–13).

In a memorable image, the author reminds his readers that the ancient Israelites saw the To-

rah introduced with awesome phenomena: fire, thunder, and earthquake. Christians now witness an even more holy covenant, which is promulgated not on earthly Mount Sinai but "before Mount Zion and the city of the living God, heavenly Jerusalem." The Exodus imagery inspires a last warning: If the Israelites who disobeyed that law were punished by death, how much more severe will be the punishment of those who fail to keep the faith in the new dispensation (12:1–29).

RECOMMENDED READING

Attridge, Harold W. *The Epistle to the Hebrews.* Philadelphia: Fortress Press, 1989. An authoritative analysis of the book's origin and theology.

Bourke, Myles M. "The Epistle to the Hebrews." In R. E. Brown et al., eds. *The New Jerome Biblical Commentary,* pp. 920–941. Englewood Cliffs, N.J.: Prentice-Hall, 1990. A helpful introduction.

Buchanan, G. W., ed. and trans. *Hebrews.* Vol. 36 of the Anchor Bible. Garden City, N.Y.: Doubleday, 1972. Provides the editor's translation and commentary.

Fuller, R. H. "The Letter to the Hebrews, James, Jude, Revelation, 1 and 2 Peter." In G. Krodel, ed., *Proclamation Commentaries.* Philadelphia: Fortress Press, 1977.

Kasemann, E. *The Wandering People of God: An Investigation of the Letter to the Hebrews.* Minneapolis: Augsburg Publishing House, 1984.

James

KEY THEMES

A Jewish-Christian anthology of ethical instruction, James defines both religion and faith in terms of humanitarian action.

> The kind of religion that is without stain or fault . . . is this: to go to the help of orphans and widows in their distress. . . .
>
> James 1:27

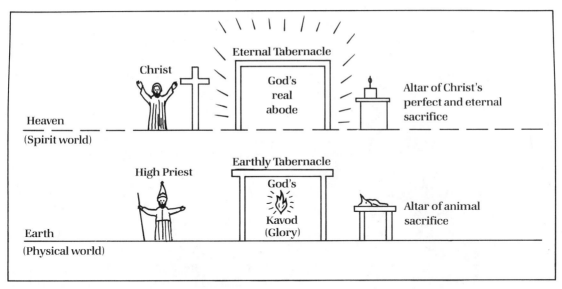

The Book of Hebrews expounds a theory of correspondences, the belief that reality exists in two separate but parallel dimensions—the spirit world (heaven) and the physical world (earth). Material objects and customs on earth are temporary replicas, or shadows, of eternal realities in heaven. The author's notion that Jesus' "perfect" sacrifice has rendered Jewish worship obsolete is clearly partisan and a claim that many scholars find highly unacceptable.

Although relatively late Church traditions ascribe this epistle to **James**, whom Paul called "the Lord's brother" (Gal. 1:19), most scholars question this claim. The work reveals no personal knowledge of either Nazareth or Jesus, to whose life or gospel the author never refers. According to Flavius Josephus, James was martyred by command of the high priest **Ananias II** (*Antiquities* 20.9.1) about 60–62 C.E. Scholars regard it as an anonymous compilation of early Christian ethical advice made between about 80 and 100 C.E. Accepted only reluctantly by the Western and Syrian churches—perhaps because of the writer's attack on the Pauline doctrine of faith—it was one of the last New Testament books to attain canonical status.

James is addressed to the "Twelve Tribes dispersed throughout the world" (1:1), which probably refers not to the Israelites of the Diaspora but to Christians scattered throughout the eastern Mediterranean region. Lacking salutations, greetings, or a complementary close, the work resembles a sermon more than a letter. A collection of ethical precepts and proverbial counsel, it strongly resembles Hebrew wisdom books. Its tone is impersonal and didactic; its advice is extremely general. Without a discernible controlling theme, it presents practical exhortation on a series of miscellaneous topics ranging from gossip to the misuse of wealth.

A Religion of Practical Effort

Although this book lacks a unifying theme, one principle that lends some coherence to the work is James's conception of religion, which he defines as typically Jewish good works (1:26–27), charitable practices that will save the soul and cancel a multitude of sins (5:19–20). The religion God approves is eminently practical: helping "orphans and widows" and keeping "oneself untarnished by the world" (1:27). In James's two-part definition, the "orphans and widows" are Judaism's classic examples of the poor and defenseless who need God's special care, and "the world" represents a society that repudiates

Mother of the Streets. *In painting this (homeless) black Madonna and Christ child, the artist Robert Lentz invites viewers to remember that the Judeo-Christian tradition emphasizes God's unceasing concern for the poor and powerless of society. In the Epistle of James, "true religion" is defined as displaying generosity toward persons who lack adequate food, clothing, shelter, or medical care. (Courtesy of Bridge Building Images, Burlington, VT)*

help others—is also its most controversial (2: 14–26). Many interpreters see James as attacking Paul's doctrine of salvation through faith (the apostle's rejection of "works" of Torah obedience in favor of trust in God's saving purpose in Christ). Like Paul, James cites the Genesis example of Abraham to prove his point, but he gives it a strikingly different interpretation. James asserts that it was Abraham's action—his willingness to sacrifice his son Isaac—that justified him in God's eyes. The writer's conclusion is distinctly un-Pauline: "A man is justified by deeds and not by faith in itself" (2:24). With its implication that one earns divine approval through hard effort and service to others, this conclusion apparently contradicts Paul's assertion that people are saved through a trusting acceptance of God's grace. (See Gal. and Rom. 1–8.)

James's conclusion that faith without actions is as dead as a corpse without breath (2:26) seems to repudiate Paul's distinctive teaching. Some commentators point out, however, that James may have intended only to correct a common misuse of Pauline doctrine. Paul himself was a model of "good works," laboring mightily for others' welfare, and condemning selfish indolence. Nonetheless, Martin Luther rejected James's argument, describing the work as "strawlike" for its failure to recognize the primacy of divine grace.

God. Thoroughly Jewish in its emphasis on merciful deeds, James's "true religion" cannot be formulated into doctrines, creeds, or rituals (cf. Matt. 25:31–46).

Addressing a problem that plagues virtually every human institution, whether religious or secular, James denounces all social snobbery, especially intimidation of the poor, whose cause God himself defends. Interestingly, the author does not quote from Jesus' sayings about care for the destitute but from the Torah (Lev. 19:18).

Criticizing Paul's Doctrine of Faith   The book's most celebrated passage—a denunciation of those who claim to have faith but do nothing to

Attack on the Rich   In another memorable passage (4:13–5:4), James provides the New Testament's most severe criticism of the rich. He denounces Christian merchants and landowners who use their wealth and power to exploit their economic inferiors. Without conscience or compassion, employers have defrauded their workers, delaying payment of wages on which the laboring poor depend to live. Such injustice outrages the Creator, who views the luxury-loving exploiters as overfed animals ripe for slaughter.

Reminding his audience that the Lord will return (5:7), presumably to judge those who economically murder the defenseless (5:6), James ends his sermon on a positive note for any who have strayed from the right path. Sinners and others who are "sick," perhaps spiritually as well as physically, can hope for recovery. God's healing grace operates through congregational prayer for the afflicted. A good person's prayer has power to rescue a sinner from death and to erase countless sins (5:13–20).

RECOMMENDED READING

Dibelius, Martin, and Greeven, Heinrich. *A Commentary on the Epistle of James.* Hermeneia Commentary. Translated by M. A. Williams. Philadelphia: Fortress Press, 1976. An excellent study.

Laws, Sophie. *A Commentary on the Epistle of James.* Harper's New Testament Commentary. San Francisco: Harper & Row, 1980.

Leahy, Thomas W. "The Epistle of James." In R. E. Brown et al., eds. *The New Jerome Biblical Commentary,* pp. 909–916. Englewood Cliffs, N.J.: Prentice-Hall, 1990.

1 Peter

KEY THEMES

Often compared to a baptismal sermon, 1 Peter reminds Christians of their unique privileges and ethical responsibilities.

> The end of all things is upon us, so you must lead an ordered and sober life. . . . Above all, keep your love for one another at full strength, because love cancels innumerable sins.
>
> 1 Peter 4:7, 8

Authorship, Date, and Structure

Scholars are divided on the authorship of 1 Peter. Traditionalists maintain that it is the work of the Apostle **Peter**, who reputedly composed it in Rome during Nero's persecution of Chris-

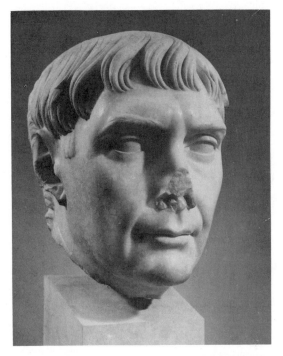

Under Trajan (98–117 C.E.) the Roman Empire reached its greatest geographical extent, stretching from Britain in the northwest to Mesopotamia (Iraq) in the east. Pliny the Younger's letters to Trajan about the proper method of handling Christians reveal that the emperor opposed anonymous accusations and ordered that accused persons who demonstrated their loyalty to the state by making traditional sacrifices should not be prosecuted. (Courtesy of Museo Archeologico di Ostia Antica [Lastra A 1066])

tians (64–65 C.E.). If true, it is surprising that the epistle is addressed to churches in Asia Minor (1:1), because official persecution was then confined to the imperial capital. The epistle's closing remarks note that it was written "through Sylvanus [Silas]" (5:12), which, among those who champion Petrine authorship, supposedly accounts for the work's excellent Greek.

Most scholars believe that 1 Peter is pseudonymous and was produced during postapostolic times. Its references to "fiery ordeals" (4:12–13) lead most experts to date it either during the time of **Domitian** (about 95 C.E.) or **Trajan** (about 112 C.E.). Because the situation it reflects closely parallels that described in the correspondence between Trajan and Pliny the Younger, governor of **Bithynia**, the latter date is commonly preferred (Pliny, *Letters* 97).

The greetings from "her who dwells in Babylon" (5:13) provide the key to the work's place of origin, for "her" refers to the Church, and "Babylon" (the Hebrew prophets' archetypal example of the ungodly nation) was a Christian code word for Rome. (See Rev. 14:8; 18:2.) The author's purpose is to encourage believers to retain their integrity (as Christians like Peter did in Nero's time) and to promote Christian ethics. He urges the faithful to live so blamelessly that outsiders can never accuse them of anything illegal or immoral. If one suffers persecution, it should be only "as a Christian" (4: 14–16).

Organization   The first letter of Peter is commonly described as a baptismal sermon, because it presents readers with a vivid survey of both the privileges and dangers involved in adopting the Christian way of life. The letter can be divided into three sections:

1. The privileges and values of the Christian called (1:3–20:10)
2. The obligations and responsibilities of Christian life (2:11–4:11)
3. The ethical meaning of suffering as a Christian (4:12–5:11)

The Rewards and Dangers of Christian Life

Addressing an audience who had not known Jesus, Peter emphasizes the rarity and inestimable value of the faith transmitted to them. They must regard their present trials and difficulties as opportunities to display the depth of their commitment and the quality of their love (1:3–7). Christians, including Gentiles, are the new "chosen race"—"a royal priesthood, a dedicated nation, and a people claimed by God for his own" (2:9–10).

Obligations and Responsibilities of Christian Life

The second section of 1 Peter focuses on the responsibilities and moral conduct of God's people (2:11–4:11). Many commentators have noted that these passages contain numerous Pauline ideas, particularly on matters of Christian behavior and obedience to the Roman state. Echoing Romans 13, the author advises peaceful submission to government authorities (3:13–15), just as servants should submit to their masters (2:18) and wives to their husbands (3: 1–2). Those who suffer unjustly from the burdens of this hierarchy must bear it as Jesus bore his sufferings (1:19–25; 3:13–18; 4:1–5).

This section includes two brief but fascinating allusions to Jesus' descent into the Underworld (Hades), presumably during the interval between his death and resurrection (3:18–20; 4:6), which inspired the medieval tradition that Jesus entered hell and rescued the souls of those who died before the way to heaven was open.

Ethical Meaning of Christians' Suffering

The third part of 1 Peter (4:12–5:11) examines the ethical meaning of suffering "as a Christian." Persons embracing the new faith should not be surprised by their "fiery ordeal" because as followers of Christ they must expect to share his sufferings (4:12–16). Judgment has come, and it begins "with God's own household"— the Church. If the righteous are but narrowly saved, what will happen to the wicked? (4:17–19). Elders must shepherd the flock with loving care; younger people must submit humbly to their rule (5:1–7); and all must remain alert because the Devil prowls the earth "like a roaring lion" seeking to devour the unwary. The faithful who resist him will share in Christ's reward.

RECOMMENDED READING

Best, Ernest. *I Peter.* London: Oliphants, 1971.

Brown, R. E.; Donfried, K.; and Reumann, J.; eds. *Peter in the New Testament: A Collaborative Assess-*

ment by Protestant and Roman Catholic Scholars. Minneapolis: Augsburg, 1973. A recommended study of Peter's role in the New Testament tradition and literature.

Dalton, William J. "The First Epistle of Peter." In R. E. Brown et al., eds., *The New Jerome Biblical Commentary,* 2nd ed., pp. 903–908. Englewood Cliffs, N.J.: Prentice-Hall, 1990.

Elliott, J. H. *A Home for the Homeless: A Sociological Exegesis of I Peter, Its Situation and Strategy.* Philadelphia: Fortress Press, 1981. A sociological analysis of historical conditions underlying the message and meaning of 1 Peter.

Kelly, J. N. D. *A Commentary on the Epistles of Peter and Jude.* New York: Harper & Row, 1969. A good introductory study.

Reicke, Bo. *The Epistles of James, Peter, and Jude.* Anchor Bible, Vol. 37. Garden City, N.Y.: Doubleday, 1964.

Jude

KEY THEME

Defending orthodoxy, Jude warns of impending judgment on false teachers.

> I appeal to you to join the struggle in defense of the faith which God entrusted to his people once and for all.
>
> Jude 3

Although the author identifies himself as **Jude** (Judas), "servant of Jesus Christ and brother of James"—and presumably also a kinsman of Jesus (see Mark 6:3; Matt. 13:55)—the text implies that the time of the apostles is long past and that their predictions are now coming true (v. 17). Scholars generally agree that the Letter of Jude is a pseudonymous work composed about 125 C.E., perhaps in Rome.

Warning Against False Teachers   Placed last among the general epistles, Jude is less a letter than a tract castigating an unidentified group of heretics. Its primary intent is to persuade the (also unidentified) recipients to join the writer in defending orthodox Christian traditions (v. 3). In literary style, Jude represents a kind of rhetoric known as invective—an argument characterized by verbal abuse and insult. Rather than specify his opponents' doctrinal errors or logically refute their arguments, the author merely calls them names, denouncing them as "brute beasts" (v. 10), "enemies of religion" who have wormed their way into the Church to pervert it with their "licentiousness" (v. 4). A "blot on [Christian] love feasts" (v. 12), they are doomed to suffer divine wrath as did Cain, Balaam, Korah, and other villains of the Hebrew Bible. Because the author does not try to correct their errors rationally but merely fires off bitter accusations along with threats of doom, Jude has been called the least creative book in the New Testament.

Use of Noncanonical Writings   Besides its vituperation, Jude is notable for citing several nonbiblical sources along with well-known passages from the Old Testament. In verses 14–15, the author directly quotes the pseudepigraphal books of Enoch and alludes to or paraphrases it elsewhere as well (cf. 1 En. 18:12; 1:1–9; 5:4; 27:2; 60:8; 93:2). From copies of Enoch preserved among the Dead Sea Scrolls, we know that the Essenes studied the work. Jude's use of the text to support his contentions proves that some early Christian groups also regarded Enoch as authoritative.

In addition, Jude's reference to a postbiblical legend about the archangel **Michael**'s contending with the Devil for Moses' body (v. 9) may be taken from the incompletely preserved Assumption of Moses, another pseudepigraphal work. To balance its largely vindictive tone, the epistle closes with a remarkably lyric **doxology** (vv. 24–25).

RECOMMENDED READING

Bauckham, R. J. *Jude, 2 Peter.* Word Biblical Commentary, 50. Waco, Tex.: Word, 1983.

2 Peter

KEY THEMES

Incorporating most of Jude into his second chapter, a second-century Christian writing in Peter's name attacks false teachers and urges a return to the apocalyptic hope of apostolic times. Explaining the delayed Parousia as God's means of allowing more people to repent, the author outlines the "three worlds" of apocalyptic history.

> Our Lord's patience with us is our salvation.
> 2 Peter 3:15

Meeting the Challenge of the Delayed Parousia

Only a few reputable New Testament scholars defend the Petrine authorship of 2 Peter, which is believed to have been written by an anonymous churchman in Rome about 140–150 C.E. The book's late date is confirmed by (1) the fact that it incorporates most of Jude (2:2–17), itself a second-century work; (2) its references to Paul's letters as "Scripture" (3:16), a status they did not attain until the mid-second century; and (3) its concern with the delayed Parousia (Ch. 3), which would not have been a problem for believers until after the apostolic generation. In addition, many leaders of the early Church doubted 2 Peter's authorship, resulting in the epistle's absence from most lists of "approved" books well into the fourth century. Not only was 2 Peter one of the last works to gain entrance into the New Testament, but scholars believe that it was also the last (eventually canonized) book written.

The author assumes Peter's identity for the purpose of representing the epistle's contents as embodying true apostolic doctrine. He takes pains to present himself in apostolic terms, mentioning his presence at the Transfiguration (1:17–18), Jesus' prediction of his death (1:14), his authorship of 1 Peter (3:1), and his association with Paul (3:15). Having thus established his credentials, he rails against the "false teachers" who pervert the apostolic traditions, upon whom judgment will fall as it did upon rebellious angels whom God chained in Tartarus (2:4), upon the corrupt world of Noah's day, and upon Sodom and Gomorrah (2:5–6).

The Delayed Parousia   In Chapter 3, the author reveals that his primary goal is to reinstate the early Christian apocalyptic hope of the **Parousia** (Second Coming). Skeptics may point out that the "fathers" (apostles) who promised Christ's early return have all died and yet the world continues on exactly as before, but they forget that the world has already been destroyed once in Noah's Flood (3:3–6). Similarly, the present world will be consumed by fire (3:7). In predicting a cosmic holocaust, the author apparently borrows the Stoic philosophers' theory that the cosmos undergoes cycles of destruction and renewal. Employing Stoic images and vocabulary, 2 Peter foretells a universal conflagration in which heaven will be swept away in a roaring fire and the earth will disintegrate, exposing all its secrets (3:10).

Citing either Revelation's vision (21:1–3) or the Isaiah passages upon which it is based (Isa. 65:17; 66:22), the author states that a third world will replace the previous two destroyed, respectively, by water and fire. "New heavens and a new earth" will host true justice (3:13), the apocalyptic kingdom of God.

2 Peter's Theodicy   The author is aware that some Christians who doubt the Parousia may do so because God, despite the arrival, death, and ascension to heaven of the Messiah, has not acted to conquer Evil and deliver the faithful. God's seeming delay, however, has a saving purpose. Holding back judgment, the Deity allows time for more people to repent and be spared the final catastrophe (3:9, 15). Although exercising his kindly patience in the realm of human time, God himself dwells in eternity where "a thousand years is like one day." From his vantage point, the Parousia is not delayed; his apparent slowness to act is only a manifestation of his will to save all people (3:8–9).

Because the universe is destined to perish in flames (an extreme view that even Revelation does not advocate), the author urges believers to shield themselves with good works, which will serve to "hasten" the End (3:11–12). While awaiting the fulfillment of the Lord's design, they must study the Scriptures (including Paul's letters), which the ignorant ruinously misinterpret (3:14–16). Some critics suggest that if 2 Peter originated in Rome, this reference to Paul's work as possessing scriptural authority may reflect a mid-second-century controversy in which Marcion and other Roman Gnostics claimed Paul's writings to support their doctrines.

RECOMMENDED READING

Bauckham, Richard J. "Peter, Letters of 2 Peter." In Metzger, Bruce M. and Coogan, Michael D., eds., *The Oxford Companion to the Bible,* pp. 586–588. New York: Oxford University Press, 1993.

Neyrey, Jerome H. "The Second Epistle of Peter." In R. E. Brown et al., eds., *The New Jerome Biblical Commentary,* 2nd ed., pp. 1017–1022. Englewood Cliffs, N.J.: Prentice-Hall, 1990.

1 John

KEY THEMES

An important tract directed against secessionists from the Johannine community, 1 John establishes a set of criteria by which to distinguish true belief from error.

> The message you have heard from the beginning is this: that we should love one another.
>
> 1 John 3:11

Letters from the Johannine Community

The three letters traditionally ascribed to the Apostle John give us some important insights into the Johannine community that produced and used the fourth Gospel as its standard of belief. The author of 2 and 3 John identifies himself as "the Elder" (*presbyteros*) (2 John v. 1; 3 John v. 1); the writer of 1 John does not mention his office or function in the Church.

Most scholars believe that the same person wrote all three documents but that he is not to be identified with either the Apostle John or the author of the Gospel. Although some critics link him with the editor who added Chapter 21 to the Gospel, most commentators view the letter writer as a separate party, albeit an influential member of the Johannine "brotherhood" (John 21:23). The majority of scholars date the letters at about 100–110 C.E., a decade or two after the Gospel's composition.

Rather than a letter, 1 John is a sermon or tract against former members who have recently withdrawn from the Johannine community. The author calls them "**anti-Christs**" who have deserted his church to rejoin the outside world (2:18–19), where they spread false ideas about the nature of Christ and Christian behavior.

Revealing a more conventional view about End time than the Gospel writer, the Elder opines that the "anti-Christ's" activity proves that the "last hour" has arrived (2:18; see also John 21:22–23). (In the Johannine church, the Gospel's "realized eschatology" may have existed side-by-side with more traditional ideas about the Parousia.) Like most early Christian churches, the Elder's community relied on prophetic inspiration, an ongoing communication with the Holy Spirit that continued the process of interpreting Jesus' message and meaning (John 15:26–27; 16:12–14). Problems arose when Christian prophets contradicted each other, as the anti-Christ secessionists were then doing. How was the believer to determine which among many opposing "inspirations" was truly from God?

Writing to a charismatic group long before a central Church authority existed to enforce orthodoxy, the Elder is the first Christian writer to propose standards by which believers can distinguish "the spirit of error" from "the spirit of truth" (4:1–6). He echoes the Apostle Paul, who experienced similar difficulties (1 Thess. 5: 19–21), when he asks Christians to "test the spirits" critically (4:1) to evaluate the reliability of their message.

Standards for Belief and Behavior

Because the Elder sets up his particular tests to refute the secessionists' errors, we can infer something about their teaching from the nature of his proposals. Basically, he offers two areas of testing—doctrinal and behavioral. His document is accordingly divided into two parts, the first beginning with his affirmation of the community's pristine teaching: "Here is the message we heard from him and pass on to you: that God is light" (1:5). The light from God illuminates the doctrinal truth about Jesus. In his prolog (1:1–7), which strikingly resembles the Gospel's Hymn to the Logos, the Elder claims that his group possesses a direct, sensory experience of Jesus' humanity. The Word was visible and physical; he could be seen and touched. Yet, those who abandoned the community apparently deny Christ's full humanity, causing the Elder to impose a christological test of the true faith: Jesus (the man) and Christ (the heavenly being) were one person, "in the flesh." Those who deny this "light" now walk in "darkness."

Many scholars suggest that the Elder's opponents were Gnostics or Docetists, who insisted that "the Christ" was a divine Revealer from heaven who temporarily occupied the body of Jesus, separating from the Galilean at death and reascending to the spirit realm. The Johannine community insists that Jesus and the Christ are the same being and that he truly suffered and died.

Next to the **Incarnation** test, the Elder places a requirement expressing his community's cardinal rule. He begins the second part of his discourse with a declaration that parallels his first criterion: "For the message you have heard from the beginning is this: that we should love

one another" (3:11). Like Cain, who murdered his brother, the secessionists fail to show love for the former associates whom they have abandoned. In his most quoted statement, the author declares that people who do not love cannot know God because "God is love" (4:8–9). Emphasizing the unity between divine and human love, the Elder reminds us that to love God is also to cherish God's human creation (4: 19–21).

Implying that the secessionists not only fail to love but also neglect Christian ethics, the author insists that loving God necessitates keeping his commandments (5:5). This means living as Jesus did, serving others' welfare (2:6). The author refers to "the old command" that his group has always possessed, apparently the single commandment that John's Gospel ascribes to Jesus—the instruction to love (John 13:34–35; 15:12, 17). The Elder can cite no other ethical injunction from his group's tradition.

2 John

KEY THEME

This letter is a warning against false teachings of the secessionists.

> Love means following the commands of God.
> 2 John 6

A letter of only thirteen verses, 2 John is from the Elder to another church in the Johannine community. As in 1 John, the writer's purpose is to warn of the "anti-Christ," the deceiver who falsely teaches that Jesus Christ did not live as a material human being (v. 7). He urges his recipients not to welcome such renegade Christians into the believers' homes or otherwise encourage them (vv. 10–11). As before, the author can counter the secessionists' attacks by citing only one cardinal rule, the love that is their community's sole guide (vv. 5–6).

3 John

KEY THEME

This letter is an appeal to show hospitality to an itinerant Johannine teacher.

> The well-doer is a child of God.
> 3 John 11

In 3 John, a private note to his friend Gaius, the Elder asks his recipient to extend hospitality to some Johannine missionaries led by Demetrius (otherwise unknown). The writer asks Gaius to receive these travelers kindly, honoring their church's tradition of supporting those who labor to spread their version of "the truth" (v. 8).

By contrast, one Diotrephes, a rival leader, offends the Elder by not only refusing his emissaries' hospitality but also expelling from the congregation any persons who attempt to aid them. We do not know if the spiteful charges Diotrephes brings against the Elder relate to the secessionists' false teaching denounced in 1 John. Although Diotrephes may not be one of the "anti-Christ" faction, his malice and lack of charity suggests that he does not practice the Johannine community's essential commandment.

RECOMMENDED READING

Brown, R. E. *The Community of the Beloved Disciple.* New York: Paulist Press, 1979. An extraordinarily insightful analysis of the Johannine group that produced the Gospel and letters of John.

——. *The Epistles of John.* Anchor Bible, Vol. 30. Garden City, N.Y.: Doubleday, 1982. A scholarly translation and commentary on the letters of John.

——. *The Churches the Apostles Left Behind.* New York: Paulist Press, 1984. A wonderfully concise study of several different Christian communities at the end of the first century C.E.

Culpepper, R. A. *1 John, 2 John, 3 John.* Knox Preaching Guides. Atlanta: John Knox Press, 1985.

Perkins, Pheme. "The Johannine Epistles." In R. E. Brown et al., eds., *The New Jerome Biblical Com-*

mentary, 2nd ed., pp. 986–995. Englewood Cliffs, N.J.: Prentice-Hall, 1990.

von Wahlde, Urban C. *The Johannine Commandments: 1 John and the Struggle for the Johannine Tradition.* New York: Paulist Press, 1990. For advanced study.

TERMS AND CONCEPTS TO REMEMBER

Ananias II	James
anti-Christ	Jesus Christ
Bithynia	Jude
Catholic Epistles	Melchizedek
Day of Atonement	Michael
Day of Judgment	Parousia
Domitian	Peter
doxology	Philo Judaeus
dualism	Priscilla
epistle	pseudonymity
faith	Trajan
Incarnation	

QUESTIONS FOR REVIEW

1. Describe the practice of pseudonymity among Jewish and early Christian circles. Why are pseudonymous works to be regarded not as deceptions or forgeries but as tributes to the persons in whose name and memory they are written?

2. Define the term *Catholic Epistle* and describe the general nature of these seven documents. According to tradition, to what specific group of authors are these works attributed? Why do most scholars conclude that all seven are pseudonymous?

3. Identify and explain the major themes in Hebrews. How does the author's belief in a dualistic universe—an unseen spirit world that parallels the visible cosmos—affect his teaching about Jesus as an eternal High Priest officiating in heaven?

4. Almost every book in this unit of the New Testament—Hebrews and the Catholic Epis-

tles—contains a theme or concept not found in any other canonical document. For example, only Hebrews presents Jesus as a celestial priest foreshadowed by Melchizedek; it is also unique in being the only New Testament work to define faith (Heb. 11:1).

Indicate which of the Catholic Epistles contains the following definitions or statements:

a. A definition of religion

b. A belief that Jesus descended into Hades (the Underworld) and preached to spirits imprisoned there

c. A definition of God's essential nature

d. A set of standards by which to determine the truth of a religious teaching

e. An argument that actions are more important than faith

f. A concept that human history is divided into three separate eras, or "worlds"

g. A defense of the primitive apocalyptic hope involving Jesus' Second Coming (the Parousia)

h. Citations from the noncanonical books of the Pseudepigrapha, including the Book of Enoch

i. The New Testament's most severe denunciation of the rich

A Vision of End Time

Revelation

KEY THEMES

Revelation affirms Christianity's original hope for an immediate transformation of the world and assures the faithful that God's prearranged plan, including the destruction of Evil and the advent of Christ's universal reign, is about to be accomplished. The book presents an *apokalypsis* ("unveiling") of unseen realities, both in heaven as it is now and on earth as it will be in the future. Placing government oppression and Christian suffering in a cosmic perspective, Revelation conveys its message of hope for believers in the cryptic language of metaphor and symbol.

> I saw a new heaven and a new earth, . . .
> Now at last God has his dwelling among men!
>
> Revelation 21:1, 3

Continuing the Eschatological Hope

Although Revelation was not the last New Testament book written, its position at the end of the canon is thematically appropriate. The first Christians believed that their generation would witness the end of the present wicked age and the beginning of God's direct rule over the earth. Revelation expresses that apocalyptic hope more powerfully than any other Christian writing. Looking forward to a "new heaven and a new earth" (21:1), it envisions the glorious completion of God's creative work begun in the first book of the Bible. In this sense, it provides the **omega** (the final letter of the Greek alphabet) to the **alpha** (the first letter) of Genesis.

Revelation's climactic placement is also fitting because it reintroduces Jesus as a major character. Its picture of an all-powerful heavenly Jesus provides a counterweight to the Gospels' portrait of the human Jesus' earthly career. In Revelation, Jesus is no longer Mark's suffering servant or John's embodiment of divine Wisdom. Revelation's Jesus is the Messiah of popular expectation, a conquering warrior-king who slays his enemies and proves beyond all doubt his right to universal rule. In striking contrast to the Gospel portraits, the Jesus of Revelation comes not to forgive sinners and instruct them in a higher righteousness but to inflict a wrathful punishment upon his opponents (19:11–21).

Revelation's depiction of Jesus' character and function, qualitatively different from that presented in the Gospels, derives partly from the author's rigorously apocalyptic view of human history. Like the authors of Jude and 2 Peter, the writer of Revelation perceives a sharp contrast between the present world, which he regards as hopelessly corrupt, and God's planned future world, a realm of ideal purity. In the author's opinion, the righteous new order can be realized only through God's direct intervention in human affairs, an event that requires Jesus to act as God's Judge and Destroyer of the world as we know it. Revelation's emphasis on violence and destruction, with its correspondingly harsher picture of Jesus' cosmic role, has led many commentators to question the book's theological or ethical validity. Many churches did not accept it as part of the biblical canon until after the fourth century C.E., and Martin Luther frankly doubted the authenticity of its Christology.

The Apocalyptic Tradition

Although the Gospels and Paul's letters contain strongly apocalyptic passages, Revelation is the only New Testament document composed entirely in the form of a literary **apocalypse**. Combining visions of the unseen world with previews of future history—all rendered in highly symbolic language—it belongs to a tradition that began with Enoch and Daniel in the early second century B.C.E. and continued well into the second century C.E. The apocryphal book of 2 Esdras, which was probably composed at almost the same time, is cast in the same visionary form and uses some of the same cryptic images. Revelation is unique in the New Testament, but it can best be understood by studying it in the context of the literary tradition to which it belongs. (See Part 7.) Although deliberately mystifying, the powerful **symbols** it employs—the **dragon, serpent,** beast, and Celestial Woman—represent the conventional vocabulary of apocalpytic discourse.

Origins and Structure of Revelation

Authorship and Date Although one tradition states that Revelation is the work of John the Apostle, son of Zebedee, and that he is the same person who wrote John's Gospel, this assertion was questioned even in the early Church. The author identifies himself only as "John," God's "servant" (1:1, 4, 9; 22:8), does not claim apostolic authority, never mentions having known the historical Jesus, and portrays Jesus' character as radically different from that shown in the Gospels. To him, the apostles belong to an earlier generation and have already become the twelve "cornerstones" of the heavenly Temple (21:14).

Eusebius suggests that another John, known as "the Elder" who lived at Ephesus about 100 C.E., may have been the author. A few critics accept this view, although the majority believe that we can know little about the writer except for his name and his assertion that he had been exiled to **Patmos,** a tiny Aegean island off the western coast of Asia Minor (western Turkey). From the contents of his work, scholars can infer something of John's background. He is intimately familiar with internal conditions in the seven churches addressed (Chs. 2 and 3), even though he seems to belong to none of them. To some commentators, this indicates that **John of Patmos** was an itinerant Christian prophet who traveled among widely scattered churches. Although he held no congregational office, his recognized stature as a mystic and visionary gave him considerable influence in the communities to which he directed his apocalypse.

Because he writes Greek as if it were a second language, phrasing idiosyncratically in a Semitic style, most scholars believe that John was a native of Palestine, or at least had spent much time there. A few critics suggest that he had some connection with the Johannine community, because, like the author of John's Gospel, he refers to Christ as Logos (Word), Lamb, Witness, Shepherd, Judge, and Temple. Both Revelation and the Gospel express a duality of spirit and matter, Good and Evil, God and the Devil. Both regard Christ as present in the Church's liturgy and view his death as a saving victory. Important differences range from the quality of the Greek—excellent in the Gospel and awkward in the apocalypse—to the writers' respective theologies. Whereas the Gospel presents

Christ over New York City. *In this painting on a steel door, an unknown Ukrainian-American artist projects the image of a cosmic Christ above the skyscrapers of Manhattan. Depicting two dimensions of reality, the painter contrasts New York's towers of cold steel and concrete—monuments to modern commerce and banking—with his vision of Jesus' unseen presence. Encompassing the largely unaware inhabitants of American secular society in his spiritual embrace, Christ extends his arms in a gesture that is both protective and beseeching. In his apocalyptic visions, John of Patmos exhibited a similar, if somewhat less compassionate, view of Christ's relation to the Roman Empire. (Ukrainian-American, twentieth century. Courtesy of Lee Boltin.)*

God's love as his primary motive in dealing with humanity (John 3:15–16), Revelation mentions divine love only once. The Johannine Jesus' preeminent command to love is pervasively absent from Revelation.

Writing about 180 C.E., the churchman Irenaeus stated that Revelation was composed late in the reign of **Domitian**, who was emperor from 81 to 96 C.E. Internal references to government hostilities toward Christians (1:9; 2:10, 13; 6:9–11; 14:12; 16:6; 21:4), policies then associated with Domitian's administration, support Irenaeus's assessment. Most scholars date the work about 95 or 96 C.E.

The Emperor Cult   Domitian was the son of Vespasian and the younger brother of Titus, the general who had successfully crushed the Jewish revolt against Rome and destroyed the Jerusalem Temple. After Titus's brief reign (79–81 C.E.), Domitian inherited the imperial throne, accepting divine honors offered him and allow-

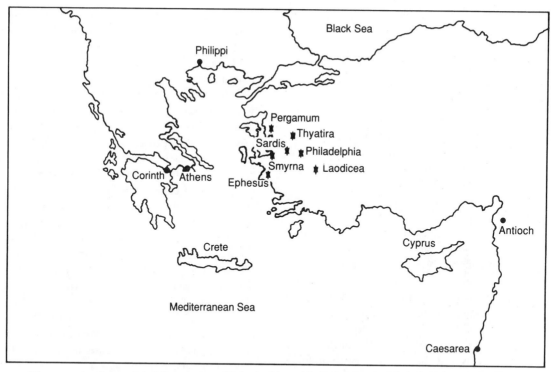

The seven churches in Asia Minor (western Turkey) addressed in Revelation 1–3 include Ephesus, one of the major seaports of the Roman Empire, and Sardis, once capital of the older Lydian Empire (sixth century B.C.E.). John pictures the heavenly Christ dictating letters to seven angels who act as invisible guardians of the individual churches. With this image, John reminds his audience that the tiny groups of Christians scattered throughout the Roman Empire do not stand alone. Although seemingly weak and insignificant, they are part of God's mighty empire of the spirit and are destined to triumph over their earthly oppressors.

ing himself to be worshiped as a god in various parts of the empire. We have no real evidence that Domitian personally enforced a universal observance of the emperor cult, but in some areas—especially in Asia Minor—governors and other local officials demanded public participation in the cult as evidence of citizens' loyalty and patriotism. During this period, persecution for Christians' refusal to honor the national leader seems to have been local and sporadic. Despite the lack of a concentrated official assault on the faith, however, John clearly feels a growing tension between Church and state, a sense of impending conflict that makes him regard Rome as a new Babylon, destroyer of God's people.

Purpose and Organization   Viewing the outside world as an increasingly hostile threat to his community, John writes to encourage believers to maintain a strict separation between themselves and Greco-Roman society. He defines his group in a rigidly sectarian way: a tiny point of light almost swallowed up by a dark world dominated by idolatry, oppression, and the soulless pursuit of wealth. Whether facing active persecution or the threat of social assimilation, the faithful must resist all compromise. To make the Christians' fight for integrity as graphic as possible, John describes the situation from a cosmic perspective—a conflict between invisible spirit forces of Good and Evil that contend for human allegiance.

Despite its vast complexities, Revelation can be outlined as follows:

1. Prolog: the author's self-identification and authority (1:1–20)

2. Jesus' letters to the seven churches of Asia Minor (2:1–3:22)

3. Visions from heaven: breaking seven seals on a scroll; seven trumpets (4:1–11:19)

4. Signs in heaven: visions of the woman, the dragon, the beast, the lamb, and the seven plagues (12:1–16:21)

5. Visions of the "great whore" and the fall of Babylon (Rome) (17:1–18:24)

6. Visions of the eschaton: the warrior Messiah, the imprisonment of the beast and Satan, judgment of the dead, and the final defeat of Evil (19:1–20:15)

7. Visions of the "new heaven and a new earth"; descent of the heavenly Jerusalem to earth (21:1–22:5)

8. Epilog: authenticity of the author's prophetic visions and the nearness of their fulfillment (22:6–21)

From this outline, we observe that John begins his work in the real world of exile and suffering (1:1–10), then takes his readers on a graphic tour of the spirit world—including a vivid dramatization of the imminent fall of Satanic governments and the triumph of Christ. He returns at the end to earth and gives final instructions to his contemporary audience (22:6–21). The book's structure thus resembles an immense circle starting and ending in physical reality but encompassing a panorama of the unseen regions of heaven and the future.

The Author's Use of Images from the Hebrew Bible

A consciously literary artist, John borrows many of his characteristic symbols and themes from the Hebrew Bible, particularly from apocalyptic sections in Daniel, Ezekiel, Joel, and Zechariah. Although he almost never directly quotes a biblical text, he paraphrases the Old Testament in almost every line. Scholars have counted approximately 500 such allusions. (The Jerusalem Bible helps the reader recognize John's biblical paraphrases by printing them in italics.)

John employs striking images largely to convey his vision of the unseen forces affecting his churches' experience in the world. The more powerful, even grotesque, his symbols are, the more they serve to alert readers to the spiritual realities operating behind the familiar modes of everyday existence. In describing persons whose teaching he opposes, for example, John gives them larger-than-life stature by identifying them with notorious figures from Old Testament times. Thus, a Christian prophetess in **Thyatira** is "Jezebel" (2:20–21) because she regards meat sacrificed at pagan rituals as acceptable food. (Note that Paul shares "Jezebel's" attitude in 1 Corinthians 8:1–13; 10:25–33.) A proponent of this policy in **Pergamum** is "Balaam," a latter-day Canaanite tempter (2:14–16). In his first portrait of a heavenly being (1:12–16), John paints a male deity with snow-white hair, flaming eyes, incandescent brass feet, and a sharp sword protruding from his mouth. These images derive chiefly from Daniel (Chs. 7 and 10). To universalize this figure more completely, John adds astronomical symbols. Like a Greek mythological hero transformed into a stellar constellation, the divinity is pictured as holding seven stars in his hand and shining with the radiance of the sun.

The next verses (1:17–19) reveal the figure's identity. As the "first and the last" who has died but attained immortality, he is the crucified and risen Christ. The author's purpose in combining biblical with nonbiblical imagery is now clear: In strength and splendor, the glorified Christ surpasses rival Greco-Roman gods like Mithras, Apollo, Helios, Amon Ra, or other solar deities worshiped throughout the Roman Empire.

John further explains his symbols in 1:20. There, Christ identifies the stars as angels and the lampstands nearby as the seven churches of

Son of Vespasian and younger brother of Titus, Domitian (81–96 C.E.) was a generally unpopular emperor whose reign ended with his assassination. According to some sources, he enjoyed being addressed as "Lord and God" and may have encouraged the cult of emperor worship, particularly in the province of Asia, which may have triggered sporadic persecution of Christians there for their "unpatriotic" refusal to honor the emperor. (Courtesy of Alinari / Art Resource, NY)

John's home territory. The identification reassures the author that his earthly congregations do not exist solely on a material plane but are part of a larger visible-invisible duality in which angelic spirits protect Christian gatherings. In his unveiling of spiritual realities, John implies that the seven churches are as precious as the golden candelabrum that once stood in the Je-rusalem sanctuary. Like the eternal stars above, they shed Christ's light on a benighted world.

Jesus' Letters to Seven Churches

Having validated his prophetic authority through the divine source of his prophecy, John now surveys conditions in the seven light-bearing churches of Asia Minor. Like his contemporary fellow apocalyptist, the author of 2 Esdras (14: 22–38), John presents himself as a secretary recording the dictation of a divine voice. (Mohammed later employed this device when dictating the Qur'an [Koran], the Scriptures of Islam.)

After reading Jesus' messages to Ephesus (2: 1–7), **Smyrna** (2:8–11), Pergamum (2:12–17), Thyatira (2:18–29), **Sardis** (3:1–6), **Philadelphia** (3:7–13), and **Laodicea** (3:14–22), students will have a good idea of John's method. The situation in each city is rendered in images that suggest the religious issues prevailing there. Thus, Pergamum is labeled the site of Satan's throne (2:13), probably because it was the first center of the emperor cult. The author regards any worldly ruler who claims divine honors as Satan's agent and hence an anti-Christ.

Visions from Heaven

John's visions of heaven resemble those in the books of Enoch, Daniel, and 2 Esdras. Entering the spirit realm through an open "door," John is caught up to God's throne, where—in cinematic style—he views pictures of events about to occur (4:1–2). In this long section (4:1–11: 19), John's purpose is not merely to predict future happenings but to remove the material veil that shrouds heavenly truths and to allow his readers to see that God retains full control of the entire universe.

The two series of visions that involve seven seals and seven trumpets serve to reassure Christians that their deliverance is near and that their enemies are predestined to suffer God's wrath. (The number *seven* corresponds to the seven days of the creative week [Gen. 1] and probably represents the completeness of divine action.) In the ancient world, paper documents were wrapped around a stick, forming a scroll, which was then sealed with hot wax. After the soft wax was imprinted with the writer's personal signet, the scroll could not be opened without breaking the seal, ensuring the privacy of its contents

until it reached the intended recipient. In John's vision, the lamb (Christ) opens each of the seven seals in sequence, disclosing either a predetermined future event or a further revelation of God's will. Opening the first four seals unleashes four horses and riders—the famous Four Horsemen of the Apocalypse—representing earthly disasters, including military conquest, war, famine, and death (6:1–8). Breaking the fifth seal discloses Christian martyrs who cry out for vengeance (6:9–11). Opening the sixth brings seismic and astronomical phenomena (6: 12–17), painting the End in livid colors of cosmic dissolution. During a quiet interval, a symbolic 144,000 Israelites and a "vast throng" (probably of Gentiles) are designated to worship at the celestial throne (7:1–17). The breaking of the seventh seal introduces the vision of seven trumpets, in which additional plagues afflict the earth (8:7–11:19).

Signs in Heaven

Chapter 12 opens a series of unnumbered visions dramatizing the cosmic battle between the lamb and the dragon. In this section (12:1–16: 21), John parallels unseen events in heaven with their experienced consequences on earth. The spiritual conflict (12:1–12) finds its earthly counterpart in the climactic battle of **Armageddon** (16:12–16).

The Woman   This section's first astronomical sign is rendered as a woman dressed in the sun, moon, and stars, a figure resembling Hellenistic portraits of the Egyptian goddess Isis. Despite its nonbiblical features, however, John probably means the figure to symbolize Israel, historically the parent of Christ. Arrayed in "twelve stars" suggesting the traditional twelve tribes, the woman gives birth to the Messiah. The author of 2 Esdras similarly represents Jerusalem, the mother of all believers, as a persecuted woman (2 Esd. 9:38–10:54). Like most of John's symbols, this figure is capable of multiple interpretations, including the Roman Catholic view that it denotes the Virgin.

The Dragon The seven-headed dragon—a composite of apocalyptic beasts—is identified as **Satan**, the "serpent of old" (12:9; Gen. 3:1, 14–15). Revelation's dragon image harkens back to ancient prebiblical Mesopotamian myths of creation. In the *Enuma Elish,* Marduk—the Mesopotamian creator-god, vanquishes Tiamat, the primordial dragon of chaos, and fashions the cosmos out of her dismembered body. In John's vision, the archangel **Michael**—the traditional spirit prince of Israel (Dan. 11:1)—defeats the chaotic reptile, permitting the birth of a new cosmic order. Expelled from heaven, as were the opponents of Marduk, the dragon then wars against representatives of God's earthly kingdom—the Church (12:5–9). By thus updating one of the world's oldest conflict myths, John simultaneously explains Roman society's sudden hostility toward his community and reassures the faithful that the One who overthrew the dragon will soon rescue them.

The Roman Beast Most scholars believe that the beast with "ten horns and seven heads" symbolizes Rome, the earthly focus of the dragon's power (13:8). The two-horned beast may represent the Roman priesthood that helps promote emperor worship (13:11–17). The occult "number of the beast" (666)—signifying a man's name—is a mystery that no commentator has been able to solve. Among apocalyptic groups, the trend has been to identify the beast with a contemporary figure whom the group fears or distrusts, commonly some prominent leader of the period. In John's day, all numbers, whether in Hebrew, Aramaic, or Greek, were represented by letters of the alphabet. Because each letter in a person's name was also a number, it was possible to assign individual names a numerical value. Noting that in Aramaic "Nero Caesar" corresponds to 666, some scholars think that John intended **Nero**, the first emperor to persecute Christians, as the archetypal beast or

This ancient coin shows a portrait bust of Nero (54–68 C.E.). According to the Roman historian Tacitus, Nero was the first emperor to persecute Christians. Nero's violence toward believers made him seem to some the image of bestial attacks on God's people. In depicting the "beast" who demands his subjects' worship, John of Patmos may have had Nero—and other worldly rulers who imitated the emperor's methods—in mind. (Courtesy of American Numismatic Society Photographic Services, NY)

anti-Christ. Although a popular first-century rumor speculated that Nero (54–68 C.E.) had not really committed suicide but would reappear at the head of a foreign army, most scholars do not accept the Neronian hypothesis. Even if we do not possess the key to unlock John's riddle, we must remember that the purpose of apocalyptic writing is not necessarily to predict specific persons and events but to create images of Good and Evil so powerful that they compel the reader to view human history on the author's cosmic terms.

Visions of the Great Whore

In asking us to perceive the universe as God sees it, John challenges his readers to respond emotionally and intuitively as well as intellectually

This bust of Julia, daughter of the Emperor Titus, shows the elaborate hair styles popular among aristocratic women of the late first century. Julia's contemporary, the author of Revelation, denounces Rome in the symbol of a vain and luxurious woman (Rev. 17). (Courtesy of Erich Lessing / PhotoEdit)

to his symbols. Thus, he pictures Rome not as a mighty empire ruling almost the entire known world but as a corrupt whore bedecked with jewels and gold (17:1–18:24). (Note that the wealth and precious stones, soon to be stripped from the harlot, will reappear to adorn the lamb's virgin bride, the heavenly Jerusalem [21:10–21].) The whore is the dragon's city—Rome—a new "Babylon" doomed to fall before God's sovereignty (18:1–24).

Visions of the Eschaton

John's last series of conflict visions (19:11–21:8) features the lamb's ultimate triumph over the dragon. An angel hurls the dragon into the abyss, the primordial void—the great "deep" of Genesis—that existed before God shaped the cosmos into its present order (20:1–3). With the dragon imprisoned, Christ's reign begins. Known as the **millennium** because it lasts 1000 years, it ends paradoxically with the dragon's release to wage yet another war on the faithful. The only New Testament writer to present a 1000-year prelude to God's kingdom, John states that during the millennium the **martyrs** who resisted the beast's influence are resurrected to rule with Christ (20:4–6).

The dragon's attack on God's people (based on Ezekiel's prophetic drama involving the mythical Gog of Magog [Ezek. 38–39]), climaxes with fire from heaven destroying the attackers. A **resurrection** of the dead ensues. Released from the control of death and Hades (the Underworld), they are judged according to their deeds (20:7–13).

John's eschatology includes a place of punishment represented by a lake of fire, an image drawn from popular Jewish belief. (See Flavius Josephus' "Discourse on Hades," in Whiston's edition.) Defined as "the second death" (20:15), it receives a number of symbolic figures, including death, Hades, the beast, the false prophet, and persons or human qualities not listed in God's book of life (19:20, 20:14–15). Although John uses his picture of eternal torment to encourage loyalty to Christ, his concept of hell incites many commentators to question the author's understanding of divine love, a quality almost entirely absent from Revelation's portrait of the Deity.

Unlike myths of some world religions, John's cosmic vision does not transcend the polar opposites of Good and Evil to achieve a universal harmony. In his vision, Evil—the subversive force of disorder troubling God's universe—is not transformed but simply annihilated. Whereas Yahweh astonished Job with his tolerance of Leviathan (another aspect of the chaotic dragon [Job 41–42; see also Part 6]), Revelation's God violently eliminates his opposition. John's solution ultimately compounds the problem of Evil, for his God not only fails to redirect chaotic energy to a higher Good but also eternally perpetuates the pain of sentient creatures (14: 9–11, 19:20, 20:14–15; cf. 2 Esd. 7:36–38). In some respects, it is difficult to distinguish between the natures of Revelation's Deity and his Adversary, the Devil. As John presents them, God and Satan use similar methods— violence, destructiveness, and the wholesale infliction of pain and suffering. Although John's God represents the Good, it is not recognizable as such until after the final conflict when the Deity at last expresses his beneficence (Rev. 21:1–4).

Visions of the New Heaven and the New Earth

Borrowing again from ancient myth in which epics of conflict are commonly ended in a union of supernatural entities, John pictures a sacred marriage (*hieros gamos*) of the lamb with the holy city that descends from heaven to earth. (Notice that human beings do not rise to heaven but that God's presence dwells with humanity, at last fulfilling the promise of Yahweh's sporadic visits to Eden [Gen. 3].) The "new heaven and a new earth" from which all pain and sorrow are excluded (21:1) includes a glorified capital, constructed of gems and precious metals like those stripped from imperial Rome. The new Eden provides **trees of life** that restore humanity to full health, completing the renewal of God's creation.

Whereas the prophet Daniel had been instructed to seal his vision until End time (Dan. 12:4), John is told not to do so because "the hour of fulfillment is near" (22:10). The writer apparently expected an immediate vindication of his eschatological hopes. Cursing anyone who tampers with his manuscript, the author ends his cosmic vision by passionately invoking Jesus' speedy return.

RECOMMENDED READING

Aune, David. *Prophecy in Early Christianity and the Ancient Mediterranean World*. Grand Rapids, Mich.: Eerdmans, 1983. Places Christian apocalypticism in historical perspective.

Batto, Bernard F. *Slaying the Dragon: Mythmaking in the Biblical Tradition*. Louisville: Westminster Press/John Knox Press, 1992. Although devoted mainly to the Hebrew Bible, this study also shows how New Testament writers used archetypal myths to express their understanding of Christ and the cosmic battle between God and the primordial dragon of chaos.

Collins, A. Y. *The Apocalypse*. Wilmington, Del.: Glazier, 1979.

———. *Crisis & Catharsis: The Power of the Apocalypse*. Philadelphia: Westminster Press, 1984. A carefully researched, clearly written, and rational analysis of the sociopolitical and theological forces affecting the composition of John's visions.

———. *Early Christian Apocalypticism: Genre and Social Setting*. Semeia 36. Decatur, Ga.: Scholars Press, 1986.

———. "The Apocalypse (Revelation)." In R. E. Brown et al., eds., *The New Jerome Biblical Commentary*, pp. 996–1016. Englewood Cliffs, N.J.: Prentice-Hall, 1990. A close reading of the text that places John's visions in their original Greco-Roman social and historical context.

Collins, J. J., ed. *Apocalypse: The Morphology of a Genre*. Semeia 14. Chico, Calif.: Scholars Press, 1979.

———, ed. *The Apocalyptic Imagination: An Introduction to the Jewish Matrix of Christianity*. Los Angeles: Crossroads, 1984.

Efird, J. M. *Daniel and Revelation: A Study of Two Extraordinary Visions*. Valley Forge, Pa.: Judson Press, 1978.

Hanson, P. D. *The Dawn of Apocalyptic: The Historical and Sociological Roots of Jewish Apocalyptic Eschatology*. Philadelphia: Fortress Press, 1979.

Josephus, Flavius. "Josephus' Discourse to the Greeks Concerning Hades." In *Josephus: Complete Works*. Translated by William Whiston. Grand Rapids, Mich.: Kregel Publications, 1960. Presents first-century Jewish views of the afterlife similar to those postulated in the Synoptic Gospels and Revelation.

Perkins, Pheme. *The Book of Revelation*. Collegeville, Minn.: Liturgical Press, 1983. A brief and readable introduction for Roman Catholic and other students.

Russell, D. S. *The Method and Message of Jewish Apocalyptic: 200 B.C.–A.D. 100*. Philadelphia: Westminster Press, 1964. A useful review of apocalyptic literature of the Greco-Roman period.

Stone, M. E. *Scriptures, Sects, and Visions: A Profile of Judaism from Ezra to the Jewish Revolts*. Philadelphia: Fortress Press, 1980.

TERMS AND CONCEPTS TO REMEMBER

alpha	omega
apocalypse	Patmos
apokalypsis	Pergamum
Armageddon	Philadelphia
Domitian	resurrection
dragon	Sardis
John of Patmos	Satan
Laodicea	serpent
martyr	Smyrna
Michael	symbol
millennium	Thyatira
Nero	tree of life

QUESTIONS FOR REVIEW

1. Define the term *apocalypse* and explain how the Book of Revelation unveils realities of the unseen spirit world and previews future events.

2. Connect John's apocalyptic visions with conditions prevailing in his own time. What events taking place during the late first century C.E. would cause Christians to despair of the present evil world and hope for divine intervention in the near future?

3. Describe some of the main symbols John uses to convey his understanding of the spiritual reality behind earthly appearances. Define the general meanings represented by the lamb, the dragon, the heavenly woman, the whore, and the marriage of the lamb and the heavenly city.

QUESTIONS FOR DISCUSSION AND REFLECTION

1. Revelation repeatedly shows God's kingdom triumphing only to be engaged again in further cosmic battles with Evil, until the symbol and source of Evil—the chaotic dragon—is finally exterminated by fire. Do you think that Revelation's frequently restaged conflicts between Good and Evil indicate a continuing cycle in which divine rule (the kingdom) alternates with wicked influences on humanity—a cycle in which each nation and individual participates until the final judgment? Cite specific passages to support your answer.

2. Martin Luther thought that Revelation did not truly reveal the nature of God or Christ. Discuss the ethical strengths and religious limitations of John's view of the Deity and the divine purpose.

12

Beyond the Canon: The Judeo-Christian Bible and Subsequent History

Noncanonical Christian Writings

*If [all that Jews did] were to be recorded in de-
tail, I suppose the whole world could not hold
the books that would be written.*

John 21:25

Besides the twenty-seven books officially accepted into the New Testament canon, early
Christianity produced a large number of other
writings, including Gospels, letters, apocalypses, and "memoirs" of the apostles. Some of
these works appear in early lists of New Testament books but were later denied canonical
status and consigned to oblivion. Although many
noncanonical writings are highly fanciful, some,
such as the Gospel of Thomas and Secret Mark,
may preserve authentic traditions about Jesus.

The early Christian community produced a
large number of writings besides the twenty-
seven books comprising the New Testament,
and many of them significantly influenced later
Christian thought. Some of these documents,
once included in church lists of "recognized
books" along with familiar New Testament titles, are as old as or older than many works
eventually accepted into the canon. No one
knows why particular works were accepted and
others were not. Paul wrote letters besides those

accorded canonical status (1 Cor. 5:9–11); we
cannot be sure that their exclusion was the result
of their being destroyed or otherwise lost. Specific works may have been accepted or rejected
primarily because of their relative usefulness in
supporting the traditional church teachings.

As noted in Part 1, as late as the fourth century and even later, many individual churches
rejected books like Hebrews, James, Jude, 2 Peter, and Revelation; others regarded them as
possessing only "doubtful" authority. By contrast, 1 Clement (a letter from the Roman
bishop to the Corinthian church, composed
about 95–96 C.E.) was commonly included
among the "recognized books" (Eusebius, *History* 3.16.24–26; 3.16.37; 6.13; etc.).

Works Included in Some Early Editions of the New Testament

The **Codex Sinaiticus,** an ancient Greek edition of the New Testament, contains several
books that supplemented the central canon.
These extracanonical works include the **Shepherd of Hermas,** a mystical apocalypse incorporating documents that may have been written
in the late first century C.E.; the **Didache** (also
called the Teaching of the Twelve Apostles), a
two-part volume that preserves a manual of

479

Selected List of Early Christian Noncanonical Gospels, Apocalypses, and Other Writings

Works Formerly Appearing in Some New Testament Lists

+ The Epistle of Barnabas (attributed to Paul's Jewish-Christian mentor)
+ The Didache (supposedly a summary of the Twelve Apostles' teachings on the opposing ways leading to life or death)
+ 1 Clement (letter by the third bishop of Rome to the Corinthians)
+ Apocalypse of Peter (visions of heaven and hell ascribed to Peter)
+ The Shepherd of Hermas (a mystical apocalyptic work)

Gospels Possibly Preserving Some of Jesus' Teachings or Other Historical Information About Him

+ The Gospel of Thomas (a compilation of 114 sayings of Jesus found in the Nag Hammadi Library)
+ The Gospel of Peter (a primitive account, ascribed to Peter, of Jesus' crucifixion, burial, and resurrection)
+ The Secret Gospel of Mark (two excerpts from an early edition of Mark preserved in a letter from Clement of Alexandria)
+ The Egerton Papyrus 2 (fragment of an unknown Gospel that may have provided a source for some of the Johannine discourses)
+ The Apocryphon of James (a private dialog between Jesus and two disciples, Peter and James)

Other Gospels, Most Surviving Only in Fragmentary Form

+ The Protoevangelium of James
+ The Dialogue of the Savior
+ The Gospel of the Egyptians
+ The Gospel of the Hebrews
+ The Gospel of the Nazoreans
+ The Gospel of the Ebionites
+ The Infancy Gospel of Thomas
+ Papyrus Oxyrhynchus 840

Miscellaneous Other Works

+ The Acts of Pilate
+ The Acts of John
+ The Epistula Apostolorum
+ 2 Clement
+ The Epistle to Diognetus

Other Important Early Christian Writings

+ The Epistles of Ignatius:
  + To the Ephesians
  + To the Magnesians
  + To the Trallians
  + To the Romans
  + To the Philadelphians
  + To the Smyrnaeans
  + To Polycarp
+ The Epistle of Polycarp to the Philippians
+ The Martyrdom of Polycarp

primitive church discipline perhaps dating back to apostolic times; and the **Epistle of Barnabas**, a moralistic commentary on the Hebrew Bible supposedly written by Paul's mentor and traveling companion.

Although these books are contained in an appendix to the codex, they apparently achieved a quasiauthoritative position in the church's list of approved books; several prominent early churchmen attributed considerable importance to them. Clement of Alexandria, who also cites the Secret Gospel of Mark, refers to the Didache as "Scripture," and Bishop Athanasius recommends its use for teaching Christian students. The Epistle of Barnabas (about 130 C.E.) and 1 Clement were also held in high esteem in numerous churches. All these works are probably older, and therefore closer to the apostolic era, than most of the canonical Catholic Epistles.

Another early list of New Testament books, the Muratorian Canon (which may be as late as the fourth century C.E.) accepts the **Apocalypse of Peter,** a visionary tour of hell based largely on the eschatological terrors described in Mark 13 and Matthew 24. Existing now only in an Ethiopic translation, this apocalypse—unlike the eventually canonical Revelation—paints no eschatological picture of future history or Jesus' Second Coming.

Among other writings that remained influential for centuries are the seven epistles of Ignatius, including letters to the congregations at Ephesus, Rome, Philadelphia, and Smyrna, all cities associated with Paul or the author of Revelation. The letters date from about the year 107 C.E., when Ignatius, the bishop of Antioch, was traveling under armed escort to Rome, where he was martyred. A few decades later in the second century, **Polycarp,** a bishop of Smyrna, wrote to Philippi, another important Pauline church. Polycarp, who was martyred about 155 C.E., possessed unusual authority because he was reputed to have been a disciple of the apostle John.

Works like the Didache, the Shepherd of Hermas, and the epistles of Clement, Ignatius, and Polycarp, as well as a few others, hovered for centuries on the fringe of the New Testament canon. Although they did not win final acceptance, they became known collectively as the "Apostolic Fathers" and continued to play a role in shaping church belief and practice.

The New Testament Apocrypha

In addition to works that for a time enjoyed near-canonical status, early Christian writers composed a large body of writings known as the New Testament **Apocrypha**. (Refer to the selected list of writings on page 480.) Many, but not all, of the Christian Apocrypha derived from Gnostic circles, which helps to account for their ultimate exclusion from church usage.

The Gospel of Thomas   Writers of the apocryphal books imitated the literary forms of canonical works—Gospels, apostolic histories, letters, and apocalypses. Many of the noncanonical Gospels are pseudonymous, ascribed to apostles like Thomas, Peter, and James, as well as to members of Jesus' family. Only fragments of these Gospels now exist—with one salient exception, the **Gospel of Thomas**. Found in 1945 among the documents buried in a Christian grave near Nag Hammadi, Egypt, the Gospel of Thomas survives complete in a Coptic translation. Originally composed in Greek and attributed to "Didymos [the twin] Judas Thomas" (according to some traditions, Jesus' twin brother), the Gospel is a compilation of 114 sayings, proverbs, parables, and prophecies that Jesus allegedly taught an inner circle of disciples. Containing almost no narrative material, it represents the kind of sayings collection that scholars imagine the hypothetical Q (source) document to have been.

Although some of the teachings ascribed to Jesus reflect Gnostic thought, many of the Thomas sayings parallel those in the canonical writings. According to many scholars, in some cases the Gospel of Thomas preserves an older (and perhaps closer to the original) form of Jesus' words, as well as genuine sayings not found in the canonical texts. Some historians believe that the Gospel of Thomas was compiled during the second half of the first century C.E., making it roughly contemporaneous with the Synoptic accounts.

The Gospel of Thomas promises that whoever finds the right "interpretation" of Jesus' "secret sayings" (i.e., understands the spiritual meaning of his metaphors) "will not experience death" (will not know what it is to die spiritually). This statement strikingly resembles the Johannine Jesus' declaration that people who believe in him will never die (John 11:25–26). Along with the "mysteries" and "secrets of the kingdom" in Mark and the concept of divine Wisdom in John, the Gospel of Thomas represents a distinctly metaphysical and otherworldly component of early Christianity, a tradition perhaps similar to but not necessarily identical to some Gnostic ideas. Future analysis of the text may reveal that Thomas contains essential aspects of Jesus' worldview that have long been ignored or neglected, particularly his views on the nature of reality, including the interpenetration of physical matter and spirit.

The Gospel of Peter   Although only a fragment remains, an early Gospel incorrectly ascribed to Peter narrates a version of Jesus' trial, crucifixion, and resurrection that some scholars believe is independent of the canonical tradition. The only Gospel to depict Jesus' actual rising from the tomb, Peter's account has even more supernatural elements than Matthew's: Late Saturday night, as Roman soldiers guarding the tomb watch, the heavens open and two celestial figures descend, rolling away the stone sealing the entrance and entering the burial chamber. Three towering figures then emerge from the sepulcher, two whose heads reach the sky and a third even taller, followed by a cross that speaks. The text breaks off with Peter fishing the Sea of Galilee, apparently about to witness a postresurrection appearance.

Whereas some critics regard this Gospel as a somewhat fantastic elaboration of Matthew, others believe that it contains a substratum preserving a more "primitive" (and thus older) "witness" to the Resurrection. A few scholars date it as early as the last third of the first century C.E. and suggest that, in its earliest form, the **Gospel of Peter** was a major source for the Passion stories in Mark and Matthew.

Secret Mark   A fragment of this Gospel was discovered in 1958, preserved in a letter by Clement of Alexandria (about 200 C.E.). The section of **Secret Mark** that Clement quotes narrates the resurrection of a rich young man whom Jesus then initiates into "the mystery of the kingdom of God." According to Clement, the excerpt would appear in canonical Mark between verses 10:34 and 35.

A second and briefer excerpt refers to the resuscitated young man as "the youth whom Jesus loved." Secret Mark is important because it provides a link between the Synoptic Gospels and the fourth Gospel's account of Lazarus' resurrection, as well as the Johannine tradition that Jesus had a particularly Beloved Disciple. Whereas the canonical editions of the Synoptic Gospels are silent about the episode, Secret Mark reveals that a primitive version of John's resurrection story was once part of the Synoptic tradition.

The Infancy Gospel of Thomas   Early Christian curiosity about Jesus' boyhood inspired several narratives that attempted to fill in the "missing years" of his youth. (Except for Luke's brief reference to Jesus' Temple visit at age twelve, the canonical Gospels offer no information about what happened between his infancy and his appearance at the Baptist's revival campaign thirty years later.) The **Infancy Gospel of Thomas**, dating from the mid–second century C.E., is ascribed to the apostle Thomas. Unrelated to the Coptic Gospel of Thomas, which was written much earlier, this infancy account uncritically incorporates popular legends and speculations about Jesus' youthful character and activities.

The Protoevangelium of James   Also called the Book of James, this work supplies background information on Jesus' parents and family, covering events that occurred up to and including his birth. Based partly on the infancy accounts in Matthew and Luke and partly on oral tradition, this prolog to Jesus' life story may contain a few historical facts among its legendary elements. The work implies that its author is James, Jesus' stepbrother, Joseph's son by a former marriage. The narrative focuses on the personal history of Mary, Jesus' future mother, who is born to a previously childless couple, Joachim and Anna. At age three, Mary is taken to the Jerusalem Temple, where she is raised by priests who later engage her to Joseph, a widower with children, who functions strictly as her guardian and respects her virginity.

The genealogies in Matthew and Luke both trace Jesus' Davidic ancestry through his presumed father, Joseph. By contrast, James states that Mary, too, descends from David. Thus, her virgin-born son inherits his messianic heritage directly from her. The Book of James provides the names of Mary's parents, the manner of her birth and upbringing, and a doctrine of her perpetual virginity. These traditions greatly contributed to the later veneration of Mary in the Greek Orthodox and Roman Catholic churches. The fact of its immense popularity in the church is reflected by the protogospel's survival in over 130 Greek manuscripts. Although never officially listed in the New Testament canon, in some Christian groups the book has exerted as much influence as the canonical Gospels.

Other Writings   Other pseudonymous works include the Apocryphon (meaning "secret book") of James, a Coptic-language edition of an originally Greek document that presents Jesus' teaching in the form of a conversation between the apostles Peter and James. The Dialogue of the Savior, found in the Nag Hammadi Coptic library, employs a similar device, rendering Jesus' message as a four-way discussion among Christ and the disciples Judas, Matthew, and Mariam, a woman follower. Similarly, the Gnostic Gospel of the Egyptians presents a brief dialog between Jesus and a female disciple named Salome.

Although the Apocryphon may well preserve some of Jesus' authentic sayings, most apocryphal gospels appear to contain editions of Christ's message that have been tailored to fit Gnostic preconceptions. These include the Gospel of the Hebrews, the Gospel of the Nazoreans, the Gospel of the Ebionites, and the Acts of Pilate, a dramatization of Jesus' confrontation with the Roman **procurator**. Except for the last named,

most of these gospels survive only in small fragments. Others are known by their titles alone.

The proliferation of new gospels continued for centuries, resulting in increasingly fanciful versions of Jesus' life and teachings. Exhausting the supply of "apostolic" writers, pseudonymous authors created gospels attributed to the Virgin, Nicodemus, Gamaliel, and even Eve!

Spurious apostolic histories modeled on the Book of Acts also abounded. Besides "Acts" purportedly describing the adventures of Peter and Paul, there were fictional narratives about Andrew (Peter's brother), Thomas, and John. Apocryphal letters also circulated under the apostles' names, and Christian mystics and prophets added to a collection of futuristic visions called the **Sibylline Oracles**. This was originally a Jewish compilation written in imitation of Greco-Roman prophecies attributed to Apollo's inspired **oracle**, the Sibyl.

RECOMMENDED READING

Cameron, Ron, ed. *The Other Gospels: Non-Canonical Gospel Texts*. Philadelphia: Westminster Press, 1982. Scholarly translations of several early Christian Gospels, including those attributed to Peter, James, and Mark.

Crossan, John D. *The Cross That Spoke: The Origins of the Passion Narrative*. San Francisco: Harper & Row, 1988. Analyzes the Gospel of Peter as source for the canonical Gospels.

Eusebius. *The History of the Church from Christ to Constantine*. Translated with an introduction by G. A. Williamson, Baltimore: Penguin Books, 1965. If the reader takes Eusebius' statements with caution, this history provides excellent atmospheric background for the early church and fascinating traditions about the apostles and second-century church leaders.

Josephus, Flavius. *The Jewish War*. Translated by G. A. Williamson. Revised by E. M. Smallwood. Baltimore: Penguin Books, 1981. An eyewitness account of political events in Palestine that provided the background for the birth and growth of Christianity, including the Jewish revolt against Rome

(66–73 C.E.), its causes and aftermath, and a few references to Jesus and the martyrdom of his "brother" James.

Koestler, Helmut. *Ancient Christian Gospels: Their History and Development.* Philadelphia: Trinity Press International, 1990. Provides technical analysis of all extant gospels and fragments.

Miller, Robert J., ed. *The Complete Gospels.* Annotated Scholars Version. Sonoma, Calif.: Polebridge Press, 1992. Includes complete texts of the Gospel of Thomas, Infancy Gospel of Thomas, Protoevangelium of James, Gospel of Peter, Secret Gospel of Mark, and numerous fragmentary works.

Musurillo, Herbert A. *The Fathers of the Primitive Church.* New York: New American Library, 1966. A useful paperback collection of early Christian writings through the fourth century.

Pagels, Elaine. *The Gnostic Gospels.* New York: Random House, 1979. Argues that the church suppressed Gnostic Christianity on political grounds.

Robinson, James M., ed. *The Nag Hammadi Library,* rev. ed. San Francisco: Harper & Row, 1988.

Schneemelcher, Wilhelm, ed. *New Testament Apocrypha,* rev. ed. Vol. 1, *Gospels and Related Writings,* Philadelphia: Westminster Press, 1990; Vol. 2, *Writings Relating to the Apostles.* Philadelphia: Westminster, 1992.

Staniforth, Maxwell. *Early Christian Writings: The Apostolic Fathers,* rev. ed. New York: Penguin Books, 1987. A paperback anthology of the more important Christian Apocrypha, with helpful prefaces and notes.

The Judeo-Christian Bible in Later History

The "great tribulation" that marked Rome's destruction of the Jewish state (70 C.E.)—along with the original center of Palestinian Christianity—offers a chaotic background to the formation of the Judeo-Christian Bible. The loss of homeland, Temple, sacrifice, and priesthood was a terrible blow to Palestinian Jews and also a shock to infant Christianity, which lost its mother church and center of apostolic teaching. Jerusalem's devastation evoked a series of religious responses that influenced not only modern Judaism and Gentile Christianity but also the form and content of their Scriptures.

Of the twenty-seven New Testament documents, only Paul's letters, Q (a collection of Jesus' sayings) and the Gospel of Mark existed at that time. Most of the Christian Greek Scriptures were yet to be written, and it would take centuries before the Church agreed upon their exact contents. Although the Hebrew Bible was complete, the precise number of books to be included had not yet been agreed upon.

Throughout the wars, trials, and persecutions of the calamitous late first century C.E., the Hebrew Bible remained the primary authority for both Judaism and the fledgling church. Led by Rabbi Yohanan ben Zakkai, a small group of rabbinical scholars assembled at Jamnia (Yavneh) on the Palestinian coast to provide essential leadership in coping with the post-70 C.E. crisis, particularly in shaping the final contours of the Old Testament canon. The rabbis at Jamnia did not formally close the biblical canon, but they seem to have applied several criteria that excluded numerous books used by Jewish congregations outside Palestine. Accepting the thesis that inspired prophecy had ceased shortly after the time of Ezra (about 400 B.C.E.), the Jamnia scholars apparently rejected books clearly composed after that period, such as Ecclesiasticus or 1 Maccabees. Only Daniel, of all the apocalypses, was accepted, because its author plausibly claimed to write during the sixth century B.C.E. Books that contradicted the Torah or that were not originally written in Hebrew, such as the Wisdom of Solomon, were also excluded. Whether or not some books that eventually achieved canonical status were appropriate, such as Ezekiel (which radically modified some Torah principles), Esther (which did not mention God), Ecclesiastes (which encouraged skepticism), and the Song of Songs (which celebrated erotic love), was hotly debated. In the end, the official Palestinian edition of the Hebrew Bible included these controversial documents but rejected many more that had found a place in Greek editions of the Scriptures. The Christian community, however, which adopted the Septuagint as its preferred version of the Bible, generally recognized the deuterocanonical status of these disputed books—commonly known as the Apocrypha—and later included them in its official Latin Bible, the Vulgate.

Order of Books in the Tanak   Jewish and Christian Bibles differ not only in the number of accepted books but also in the order that they arrange their contents. Rabbinical scholars place the books of Chronicles at the end of the canon, thus giving a climactic position to Cyrus the Great's order to repatriate Jewish exiles and rebuild the Jerusalem Temple (2 Chron. 36:22–23). This promise of national and cultic restoration, presented as Yahweh's intervention in Judah's history, may have voiced Jewish hopes that their God would again restore his people as he had done after the Babylonian captivity (587–538 B.C.E.). Interestingly, Cyrus's recreation of Israel—the culmination of a narrative that begins with Elohim's creation of the world in Genesis 1—is accomplished, not by an apocalyptic catastrophe, but through a Gentile ruler who favors the Jewish cause. Cyrus, the Persian empire-builder whom Second Isaiah calls Yahweh's Messiah (Isa. 45:1–3), is not only God's tool for achieving the divine plan but is also a symbol of any future Gentile power that might befriend the covenant people.

Order of Books in the Christian Bible   By contrast, Christian editions of the Hebrew Bible follow the Septuagint order and place Chronicles, despite its late date, among the Former Prophets and conclude the Old Testament with the twelve Minor Prophets (see Part 1, Table 1.1). The Christian Old Testament thus makes Malachi's prediction that "Elijah the prophet" will return to earth just before Yahweh's eschatological Day of Judgment (Mal. 3:22–24), the ultimate Old Testament message. (The Synoptic Gospel writers relate Malachi's prophecy to Christian origins, identifying John the Baptist,

seen as Jesus' forerunner, as the predestined Elijah [Mark 6:14–15; Matt. 11:10–14; Luke 7:27–28]). The Church's rearrangement of the Hebrew Bible expressed its christological interests, an assumption that the Jewish Scriptures serve largely to foretell and elucidate the Christ event.

When added to Greek translations of the Hebrew Bible canon, the twenty-seven New Testament books—all of which extensively quote from or allude to Israel's Scriptures—promulgate a christological fulfillment of Old Testament covenant promises. In the Christian reinterpretation, virtually the entire Hebrew Bible becomes prophetic of Christ, giving startlingly innovative meanings to familiar scriptural passages. Jesus of Nazareth becomes Eve's "seed" (Gen. 3:15), his death and resurrection are foreshadowed in the Abraham-Isaac drama (Gen. 22), and his universal rulership is anticipated by the reigns of Davidic kings (2 Sam. 7; Pss. 2, 110; Isa. 7, 11, etc.).

Jesus is also the commanding figure who binds together the diverse collection of narratives, letters, sermons, and apocalyptic visions that form the New Testament. The order in which the canonical books are arranged reinforces his dominance: The New Testament opens with Matthew's genealogy, proclaiming "Jesus Christ, son of David, son of Abraham," at the outset as the embodiment of Israel's prophetic hopes. Matthew and the other Gospels provide theological interpretations of Jesus' Jewish messiahship, and Acts and Paul's letters offer profound meditations on Jesus' meaning to the world at large. The pseudo-Pauline letters, Hebrews, and the general epistles further explore Jesus' continuing significance to the community developing in his name, typically distinguishing between correct and incorrect views about his being and nature.

The New Testament closes with John's dazzling revelation of the postresurrection Jesus as a cosmic divinity, empowered at last to establish the longed-for universal kingdom. As the first Gospel's opening verse roots Jesus in Israel's historical past, the "son" or heir of David and Abraham, so the last New Testament book concludes with a Christian mystic's passionate evocation of Jesus' return to finish the task he had begun on earth, echoing Malachi's fervent call for the reappearance of God's agent. Because Christianity emerged historically as an apocalyptic movement within first-century Judaism, it is fitting that its canonical text closes with the apocalyptic conviction that Christ is "coming soon," preserving as a final word the assurance of Jesus' imminent Parousia (Second Coming) (Rev. 22:17–21).

Before the end of the first century C.E., some Christians were keenly aware that expectations for a speedy Parousia had failed to materialize. Neither Christ nor the kingdom had rescued the Church from Rome's intermittent persecutions. In 1 Clement, an epistle included in some editions of the New Testament, Clement, Bishop of Rome, states:

> Let that Scripture be far from us which says: "Wretched are the double-minded, those who doubt in their soul and say, 'We have heard these things [predictions of the End] even in our fathers' times, and see, we have grown old and none of this has happened.'"
>
> 1 Clem. 23:3–5 (about 96 C.E.)

Two generations after Clement, in a work attributed to the apostle Peter, the problem of the "delayed Parousia" was again raised. Skeptics complained that Jesus' promised coming had proved to be a nonevent; everything "continues exactly as it has always been since the world began" (2 Pet. 3:1–10). The writer responded to this criticism of an unconfirmed doctrine by asserting that a delayed world judgment allowed time and opportunity for sinners to repent and was thus an act of divine mercy.

Nonetheless, Jesus' failure to return undoubtedly provoked a crisis of belief among many second-century Christians. Yet, the Church not only survived its initial disappointments, but prospered. Despite dashed hopes that the Parousia would follow any number of seemingly

"final" events—the Jewish revolt, the destruction of Jerusalem, the deaths of the last apostles, or the first- and second-century Roman persecutions, the believing community continued to grow in stature, wealth, and influence. By the fourth century it had become the state religion of the Roman Empire.

Constantine the Great

Following his victory at the Milvian Bridge over Maxentius, his rival for the imperial throne (312 C.E.), the Emperor Constantine effected one of the most unexpected reversals in human history. Having experienced a vision in which Jesus was revealed as the divine power that enabled him to defeat his enemies, Constantine began a slow process of conversion to the Christian faith. The emperor's ultimate championing of Christ as his chief god had immense repercussions throughout the empire, altering forever the relationship of Church and state.

Shortly before Constantine began his long reign (306–337 C.E.), his predecessor, Diocletian (284–305 C.E.) had initiated the most thorough and devastating persecution that Christians had yet endured, which ended only with Diocletian's abdication and death. When Constantine issued his celebrated decree of religious toleration, the Edict of Milan (313 C.E.), and subsequently began restoring confiscated Church property, consulting Christian leaders about official affairs, and appointing bishops to high public office, it was as if a miraculous deliverance of the faithful had occurred—as if a new Cyrus had arrived to rescue God's chosen ones. To many who benefited from Constantine's policy it seemed that Revelation's seventh angel had sounded his trumpet: "the sovereignty of the world has passed to our Lord and his Christ" (Rev. 11:15).

In a more modest metaphor, the churchman Eusebius, who later became Constantine's biographer, compared the emperor's enthusiastic support of the Church to the dawn of a brilliant new day, opening up glorious possibilities for

The Arch of Constantine, standing near the Roman Forum and Flavian Amphitheater (Colosseum), commemorates the political and military achievements of Rome's first Christian emperor. After defeating his rival Maxentius at the Battle of Milvian Bridge (312 C.E.), Constantine (306–337 C.E.) issued the famous Edict of Milan, legitimizing the Christian Church and ending centuries of intermittent persecution. (Courtesy of Archiv für Kunst und Geschichte, Berlin)

the Christian religion. With the exception of Julian (361–363 C.E.), who was known as the Apostate for trying to revive pagan cults, all of Constantine's successors were nominally Christians. For the last century and a half of its existence, the empire that had crucified Jesus was ruled by emperors who professed to be his servants.

The Church and the Secular World

Rome's belated emergence as a putatively Christian empire that supported and protected the Church was sometimes viewed as a historical fulfillment of apocalyptic expectations, with Christ now ruling through his imperial representatives on earth. In fact, historical developments during the fourth and fifth centuries C.E. bore out Luke's nonapocalyptic vision of a Church expanding in cooperation with the imperial power more than Revelation's picture of violent conflict between Church and state resolved only when God intervened to destroy the latter. Officially

muting sporadic revivals of apocalyptic fervor, the Church espoused the Gospel of John's doctrine of realized eschatology—with Jesus invisibly present among the believing community— as theologically desirable.

In part, the Church preserved eschatological principles by adapting and applying them to individual lives. Christianity originally borrowed most of its eschatological beliefs from Jewish sources, which emphasized the external and material triumph of Yahweh's sovereignty over Gentile nations. This general eschatology—the terrifying Day of Yahweh, cosmic battles between Good and Evil, divine judgment and the supernatural imposition of God's kingdom— was replaced by personal eschatology. Jewish eschatological literature, such as 2 Baruch, the Testament of Abraham, the books of Enoch, and 2 Esdras, had stressed Yahweh's (or the coming Messiah's) universal rule, violently imposed, but they had also provided graphic images of the consequences of apocalyptic events on individual human beings.

Only the head and other fragments of a colossal statue of Constantine (306–337 C.E.) remain, but they reflect the enormous power wielded by this remarkable general and administrator. Seeking the support of a unified church, Constantine summoned and presided over the Council of Nicaea (325 C.E.), which, amid intense theological controversy, formulated the Trinitarian creed affirming that the Son is coequal, cosubstantial, and coeternal with the Father. (Courtesy of Archiv für Kunst und Geschichte, Berlin)

After the two disastrous Jewish wars against Rome (66–73 C.E. and 132–135 C.E.) that may have been partly fueled by apocalyptic hopes, rabbinic Judaism rejected such visionary speculations as typically misleading. However, the Church embraced their eschatological revelations of heaven, hell, and the afterlife. In later Roman Christianity, eschatological ideas retained their emotional impact on a personal, individual level. All believers were faced with inevitable death and the attendant dangers and terrors of the next world. Jewish and Christian apocalyptic writers had painted memorable scenes of the fates await-

ing the righteous and the wicked. Anticipation of the world's End might fade, but to the believer, postmortem judgment involving permanent assignment to celestial joy or eternal torment seemed certain. The Church defined and regulated these eschatological concerns. While normative Judaism abandoned virtually all its eschatological literature, with its ethically problematic views of divine justice, the Christian community effectively transferred its inherited doctrines of "last things" to the human microcosm, postponing its hopes for the Parousia to an unknowable time in the indefinite future.

Whereas John of Patmos had eagerly anticipated Rome's fall, many Christian leaders who lived through the Roman Empire's disintegration regarded it as an unmitigated catastrophe for society, including the Church. Writing of Alaric the Goth's invasion of Rome in 410 C.E., **Jerome**—the scholar who created the Vulgate Bible—lamented the "great city's" humiliation.

Judaism and Christianity, originator and inheritor of the world's first ethical monotheism, endured the Roman Empire's slow collapse as they had survived the earlier destruction of Jerusalem, the crisis under Domitian that inspired the writing of Revelation, and far more intense attacks on the Judeo-Christian communities under later emperors. The Church replaced the state's crumbling authority with its own spiritual leadership. Along with descendants of the people who had created them, the Hebrew and Christian Scriptures survived the empire's demise, providing a continuity with Israel's ancient prophets and early Christian visionaries as well as a fixed standard of belief in a rapidly changing world.

During the sixteenth and seventeenth centuries, fierce religious conflicts divided Western Christendom. Debates between Roman Catholic and Protestant leaders over matters of belief and ritual brought the Bible—particularly the letters of Paul—into renewed prominence. Martin Luther claimed that "only Scripture"—not custom or tradition—was the correct basis of Christian teaching. As a result, many European believers studied the biblical documents with great fervor. In most Protestant circles, scriptural texts were thought to provide the sole means of defining Christian doctrine and practice.

The Bible's complex message retains its vitality in the modern world. Today, three main divisions of Judaism and literally thousands of Christian groups, each claiming the Bible as its doctrinal authority, compete for believers' allegiance. Some people regret the Judeo-Christian world's lack of unity, but those who carefully study the Bible's historical development possess an important clue to Christendom's present diversity. Both Old and New Testaments display a wide range of theological viewpoints. The Tanak encompasses works that testify to God's redemptive acts in history (such as the Torah) and works that question his justice (for example, the Book of Job) or his refusal to reveal his will (such as Ecclesiastes). Remembering the vastly diverse goals of different Bible writers, readers will recognize the comparably vast diversity of biblical thought. As 2 Peter observes, Paul's letters contain passages that are difficult to understand and open to more than one interpretation—a view that applies equally well to the rest of the biblical canon. The multiplicity of contemporary Christian denominations results less from the breaking up of an original monolithic biblical religion than from the rich variety of ideas embodied in both Jewish and Christian canonical literature.

The Bible's collection of documents—spanning 1100 years of human religious experience—does not conform to a single doctrinaire vision. Each biblical book reflects its individual writers' intensely personal response to God's impact on human life and history. Creating a multifaceted review of humanity's troubled and sometimes tenuous relationship with its Creator, the Bible validates the continuing power of the divine–human bond.

RECOMMENDED READING

Brown, R. E. *The Churches the Apostles Left Behind.* New York: Paulist Press, 1984. A concise but extremely important analysis of the theological diversity present in early Christian communities.

Dunn, J. D. G. *Unity and Diversity in the New Testament.* Philadelphia: Westminster Press, 1977. A thoughtful study of the variety of belief found among different canonical authors. Highly recommended.

Eusebius. *The History of the Church.* Translated by G. A. Williamson. Baltimore: Penguin Books, 1965. Eusebius is our principal source for the study of the growth and development of early Christianity.

Fox, R. L. *Pagans and Christians.* New York: Knopf, 1986. A comprehensive study of the historical processes that resulted in Constantine's conversion and the religious transformation of the Roman Empire.

Gonzalez, J. L. *The Story of Christianity.* Vol. 1, *The Early Church to the Dawn of the Reformation.* San Francisco: Harper & Row, 1984.

MacMullen, Ramsay. *Christianizing the Roman Empire, A.D. 100–400.* New Haven, Conn.: Yale University Press, 1984. A historical investigation of the social, political, and religious conditions under which the Roman people were converted.

Meeks, W. A. *The Moral World of the First Christians.* Philadelphia: Westminster Press, 1986. Explores the pagan and Jewish ethical context in which Christianity developed.

Robinson, J. M., and Koester, Helmut. *Trajectories Through Early Christianity.* Philadelphia: Fortress Press, 1971.

Wilken, R. L. *The Christians as the Romans Saw Them.* New Haven, Conn.: Yale University Press, 1984. A careful analysis of the social, educational, religious, and political conflicts between early Christians and their Roman critics.

QUESTIONS FOR REVIEW

1. Describe some early Christian Gospels, such as the Gospel of Thomas, Secret Mark, and the Gospel of Peter, that were not included in the New Testament canon. In what ways are they similar to or different from the canonical accounts of Jesus' life?

2. Describe some early Christian documents, such as the Shepherd of Hermas, the Epistle of Barnabas, and 1 Clement, that were once apparently on the margins of the New Tes-

tament canon but that were eventually deleted from the church's list of authoritative works. Define the term *New Testament Apocrypha*. What resemblances do you see between such accepted works as Revelation and the noncanonical Apocalypse of Peter?

3. After the ascension of Constantine to the imperial throne, Christianity's position in the Roman Empire changed dramatically. Describe and explain the church's role during the later empire. How did many leading Christians react to the barbarian invasions that eventually destroyed the Roman world? How did Jerome's reaction to Rome's fall differ from that of John of Patmos (see Rev. 17)?

QUESTIONS FOR DISCUSSION AND REFLECTION

1. Discuss the differences in attitude toward Rome expressed in Romans 13 (and 1 Peter) on the one hand and in Revelation on the other. What changing historical conditions can help account for the shift from the positive attitude of Paul to the negative judgment of John of Patmos?

2. Do you think that the New Testament canon is now irrevocably closed? What are the possibilities that existing noncanonical writings—or even books not yet written—will eventually be added to the Church's approved list? Describe the effect on Christian doctrine if such works as the Gospel of Thomas, Secret Mark, or the Book of Mormon were officially approved to be read in church as examples of legitimate Christian thought and experience.

TERMS AND CONCEPTS TO REMEMBER

Apocalypse of Peter	Jerome
Apocrypha	oracle
Codex Sinaiticus	Polycarp
Didache	procurator
Epistle of Barnabas	Secret Mark
Gospel of Peter	Shepherd of Hermas
Gospel of Thomas	Sibylline Oracles

Glossary of Major Biblical Characters, Terms, and Concepts

The following Glossary identifies or defines a representative selection of major characters, concepts, places, and terms found in the canonical Old and New Testaments. For a more comprehensive treatment of individual terms, the reader is directed to David Noel Freedman, ed. *The Anchor Bible Dictionary,* vols. 1–6 (New York: Doubleday, 1992), an indispensable and up-to-date resource. For useful one-volume references, consult Paul Achtemeir, ed., *Harper's Bible Dictionary* (San Francisco: Harper & Row, 1985); Raymond Brown, Joseph Fitzmyer, and Roland Murphy, *The New Jerome Biblical Commentary,* 2nd ed. (Englewood Cliffs, N.J.: Prentice-Hall, 1990); and B. M. Metzger and M. D. Coogan, eds., *The Oxford Companion to the Bible.* New York: Oxford University Press, 1993.

Aaron　The older brother of Moses and first head of the Israelite priesthood, Aaron was the son of Amram the Levite and his aunt Jochebed (Exod. 6:20). Because Moses reputedly had a speech defect, Aaron served as his spokesman before the pharaoh (Exod. 4:14). According to the Priestly source in the Pentateuch, which stresses Aaron's special role, Moses anointed him and his four sons as founders of Israel's priesthood (Num. 3:1–3), consecrating them to administer the tabernacle (see Lev. 8 and Exod. 29). Although he led in the worship of the golden calf (Exod. 32:1–6), Aaron remained in divine favor. His son Eleazar succeeded him as high priest of Israel.

Aaronites　Priestly descendants of Aaron's line (1 Chron. 12:27; Ps. 115:10). In the New Testament, Zechariah and Elisabeth, the parents of John the Baptist, were both Aaronites (Luke 1).

Abel　The second son of Adam and Eve (Gen. 4:2) and brother of Cain, who murdered Abel when his animal sacrifice was accepted by Yahweh whereas Cain's grain offering was rejected. This story of the first murder (Gen. 4:3–10) occurs in the J portion of the Pentateuch and is referred to in the New Testament by Jesus (Matt. 23:35) and the author of Hebrews (Heb. 11:4). In Hebrew, the name *Abel* means "breath" or "vanity."

Abigail　Wife of Nabal the fool, a wealthy shepherd who denied young David a share of his property. By wisely making a peace offering to David's guerrilla band, Abigail saved her husband's life. After Nabal's death, she married David (1 Sam. 25) and bore him a son, Chileab (2 Sam. 3:3).

Abimelech　(1) In Genesis, a king of Gerar at whose court Abraham presented his wife Sarah as his sister (Gen. 20:1–18). The ruler and patriarch later made a covenant with each other (Gen. 21:22–34). (2) A Philistine king at Gerar to whom Isaac passed off his wife Rebekah as his sister and with whom he, too, later established a covenant (Gen. 26:1–33). (3) In Judges, the son of Gideon who slew his seventy brothers and made himself king at Shechem until he was killed during a siege (Judg. 9).

Abraham　In Genesis 12–24, Abraham (at first called Abram, meaning "exalted father") is the supreme example of obedience to Yahweh and the founder of the Hebrew nation. By divine order, he leaves his adopted home in Haran, northern Mesopotamia, and travels to Canaan (Palestine), which land is promised to his descendants who are to become a mighty nation (Israel). Yahweh later demands that he sacrifice his only son by his wife Sarah. Because of Abraham's willingness to surrender Isaac, Yahweh reaffirms the Abrahamic covenant, by which the patriarch's descendants are to become as numerous as "the sands of the sea" and a source of blessing to all nations. According to Genesis, the twelve tribes of Israel are descended from Abraham's grandson Jacob. The Age of Abraham, a period of mass nomadic movement in the ancient Near East, occurred during the nineteenth or eighteenth century B.C.E.

Absalom　In 2 Samuel, the son of David and Maacah (2 Sam. 3:3). Noted for his physical beauty and fiery temperament, Absalom killed his half-brother Amnon to avenge the rape of his sister Tamar, fled to Geshur in

Aram, but was reconciled with his father three years later. He later rebelled against David and drove him from Jerusalem but was defeated and killed by the loyalist Joab (2 Sam. 13–14).

acrostic   In Hebrew poetry, a series of lines or verses of which the first word begins with consecutive letters of the alphabet. Examples of this alphabetic sequence are found in Lamentations 1–4 and Psalm 199.

Adam   In Genesis, the name *Adam* literally means "ruddy," from the Hebrew for "red"; it possibly derives from the Akkadian word meaning "creature." In the older creation account (Gen. 2:4–4:26) Adam is simply "the man [earthling]," which is not rendered as a proper name until the Septuagint version (about 250 B.C.E.). New Testament writers typically use Adam as a symbol of all humanity (as in 1 Cor. 15:21–49; Rom. 5:12–21). *See* Fall, the.

Adonai   The Hebrew word for "Lord," a title of honor and majesty applied to the Old Testament Deity, particularly during the late postexilic period, as a substitute for the personal name Yahweh, which was considered too sacred to pronounce.

Adonijah   The son of David who tried unsuccessfully to succeed his father to Israel's throne and whom Solomon put to death (1 Kings 1:9–2:25).

Ahab   Son of Omri and king of Israel about 869–850 B.C.E. Although Ahab practiced the Yahwist religion, he allowed his wife Jezebel, daughter of a Phoenician ruler, to encourage the Baal cult, which brought the condemnation of the prophet Elijah (1 Kings 17–22). A contemporary of Judah's King Jehoshaphat, Ahab was killed while defending Israel against Assyria's Shalmaneser III.

Ahasuerus (Xerxes)   Son of Darius Hystaspes and Atossa, daughter of Cyrus the Great, the Ahasuerus of the Book of Esther is usually identified with Xerxes I (486–465 B.C.E.), who led the second Persian invasion of Greece and was defeated at the Battle of Salamis (480 B.C.E.). There is no record that he ever had a Jewish queen named Esther.

Ahaz   King of Judah (c. 735–716 B.C.E.) and father of Hezekiah, who succeeded him. Although Ahaz reigned during the ministries of Isaiah and Micah, he compromised the Yahwist religion to curry favor with Assyria, whose vassal Judah became (2 Kings 16).

'Ai   meaning "the ruin" in Hebrew, 'Ai was a city reputedly destroyed by Joshua's conquest of Canaan (Josh. 7: 2–5; 8:1–29) but which archaeology has demonstrated to have been already an abandoned site during the thirteenth century B.C.E. when the Israelites entered Palestine.

Akhenaton   (1364–1347 B.C.E.)   Egyptian pharaoh who radically altered the state religion, introducing a monotheistic cult of the solar deity Aton and outraging the conservative priests of the Theban state god Amun.

Abandoning his original name, Amenhotep IV, Akhenaton founded a new capital, Akhetaton (now known as Tell el-Amarna); archaeologists call his reign the Amarna Period.

Akkad (Accad)   The narrow plain of Babylonia lying north of Sumer, locale of the Akkad dynasty, founders of the first real empire in world history (c. 2360–2180 B.C.E.). In Akkad, named for its capital city, were many of the great cities of antiquity, some of which are mentioned in Genesis 10.

Akkadian (Accadian)   (1) The period during which the early Semitic dynasty established by Sargon I dominated Mesopotamia (twenty-fourth–twenty-second centuries B.C.E.). (2) The Akkadian language, written in cuneiform script but sharing many features with Hebrew, Arabic, and Aramaic, was a Semitic tongue used in Mesopotamia from about the twenty-eighth to the first centuries B.C.E.

Alexander of Macedonia   One of the most brilliant leaders and military conquerors of the classical world, son of King Philip of Macedonia, Alexander was born at Pella in Macedonia in 356 B.C.E. and died in Babylon in 323 B.C.E. During his relatively brief career, he conquered most of the known world, created an empire that extended from Greece to India, propagated Greek culture throughout the Near East, and instituted a period of cosmopolitanism termed Hellenistic. His influence on Palestine is recounted in 1 Maccabees 1.

Alexandria   A major port city and cultural center founded by Alexander the Great on the Egyptian coast. The home of a large Jewish colony during the Hellenistic period, Alexandria nourished a fusion of Hebraic and Hellenic (Greek) ideas, one result of which was the Greek Septuagint translation of the Hebrew Bible.

allegory   A literary narrative in which persons, places, and events are given a symbolic meaning. Some Hellenistic Jewish scholars of Alexandria tended to interpret the Hebrew Bible allegorically, as Paul does the story of Abraham, Sarah, and Hagar (Gal. 4:21–31).

alpha   The first letter of the Greek alphabet, presented as a symbol of creation (Genesis). *See* Omega.

Amalekites   According to Genesis 36:12, these nomadic tribes were descendants of Esau who occupied the desert south and southeast of Canaan. Persistent enemies of ancient Israel, the Amalekites attacked Moses' group (Deut. 25:17–19), were defeated by Joshua at Rephidim (Exod. 17), and conquered by Gideon (Judg. 6: 33; 7:12) but were still troublesome in Saul and David's time (1 Sam. 15; 30:18).

Amarna Age   A title assigned to the reign of Pharaoh Amenhotep IV (Akhenaton), whose new capital had been built at Amarna, Egypt.

Amen   A term derived from a Hebrew work whose root suggests "so be it." Typically used as a confirmation (1

Kings 1:36), it implies agreement, as at the conclusion of a prayer (Matt. 6:13; 1 Cor. 14:16). In Revelation 3:14, "the Amen" is a synonym for Jesus Christ, who affirms the divine purpose.

Ammonites A Semitic group supposedly descended from Abraham's nephew Lot (Gen. 19:38). Chronic enemies of Israel (1 Sam. 11; 1 Kings 11), they occupied the eastern margin of the Transjordan plateau to harass the Israelites.

Amorites A Semitic people (called "Westerners" or "highlanders") who moved into the ancient Near East about 2000 B.C.E. and founded the states of Mari and Babylon, of which Hammurabi is the best-known Amorite ruler. The term was also applied to a tribe living in Canaan before the Israelite conquest (Num. 13:29; 21:26; Judg. 1).

Amos A shepherd and "dresser of sycamore [fig] trees" from the Judean village of Tekoa who denounced the religious and social practices of the northern kingdom (Israel) during the reign of Jeroboam II (c. 786–746 B.C.E.), Amos was the first biblical prophet whose words were collected and preserved in a book.

Amphictyony A confederation of tribes or cities (typically of six or twelve members) organized around a particular deity's shrine. The term is commonly applied to the league of Israelite tribes during the period of the judges (c. 1200–1000 B.C.E.).

Ananias II The high priest who presided over the full council (Sanhedrin) before which Paul was brought by Claudius Lycias for creating a "riot" in the Jerusalem Temple (Acts 22:22–23:22).

Anath A Canaanite agricultural goddess, sister-consort of the fertility god Baal.

Andrew A disciple of John the Baptist (John 1:35–40) who, according to John's Gospel, became the first of Jesus' followers and brought his brother Peter to Jesus (John 1:41–42). Mark gives another version of this calling (Mark 1:16–18; see also John 6:5; 12:22).

angel From a Greek work meaning "messenger"; angels were commonly conceived in biblical times as emissaries from the deity who employed them to communicate his will to humanity. The oldest known rendition of angels in art occurs on the stele of Urnammu, a Sumerian king, but many scholars suggest that Israel's belief in angelology derives from Persian sources. Angels named in canonical Scripture include Michael and Gabriel, although apocryphal and pseudepigraphal literature lists others. Angels are particularly important in the birth stories of Jesus (Luke 1–2; Matt. 1).

Annas A former high priest before whom Jesus was brought for trial (John 18:13), Annas was father-in-law of Caiaphas, then the currently reigning high priest (see also Luke 3:2 and Acts 4:6).

Annunciation The name given to the angel Gabriel's declaration to Mary of Nazareth that she was to bear a son, Jesus, who would inherit David's throne (Luke 1:28–32).

anthropomorphism Attributing human characteristics to something not human; particularly, ascribing human emotions and motives to a deity.

anti-Christ The ultimate enemy of Jesus Christ who, according to Christian apocalyptic traditions, will manifest himself at the End of time to corrupt many of the faithful, only to be vanquished when Christ appears. The term is used only in 2 and 3 John but is clearly referred to in 2 Thessalonians (2:1–12) and Revelation 13.

Antinomianism Literally meaning "opponents of law," the name applies to specific early Christian groups who argued that faith in Christ absolves the believer from obeying the moral law, a libertarian attitude attacked by Paul (Gal. 5:13–6:10) and the author of 1 and 2 John. See heresy.

Antioch Two Hellenistic cities famous in Maccabean and New Testament times bore this name. (1) In Syria, Antioch was the capital of the Macedonian Seleucid kings and, under Roman rule, the capital of a province of the same name. According to Acts, the first Gentile Christian church was founded in Antioch (Acts 11:20, 21), where followers of "the way" were first called Christians (Acts 11:26). Paul began all three of his missionary journeys from here. (2) Pisidian Antioch, a major city in Galatia (in Asia Minor), was also the site of an important early church, this one founded by Paul and Barnabas (Acts 13:14–50).

Antiochus The name of several Syrian monarchs who inherited power from Seleucus I, a general and successor of Alexander the Great. The most famous were Antiochus III, who gained control of Palestine from Egypt in 198/197 B.C.E., and Antiochus IV (*Epiphanes,* or "God Manifest") (175–163 B.C.E.), whose persecution of the Jews led to the Maccabean revolt.

Antonius Felix The Roman procurator or governor of Judea before whom Paul was tried at Caesarea about 60 C.E. (Acts 23:23–24:27).

aphorism A brief, pithy saying that challenges or overturns conventional wisdom. Jesus was believed to have favored aphorisms in speech.

'Apiru Egyptian version of the term *Habiru. See* Habiru.

apocalypse From the Greek *apokalypsis,* meaning to "uncover" or "reveal," the term refers to a special kind of prophetic literature that purports to foretell the future in terms of symbols and mystical visions and deals primarily with eschatological events.

Apocalypse of Peter One of many significant extracanonical works. This work exists only in an Ethiopian translation and conveys the eschatological terror described in Mark 13 and Matthew 24.

apocalyptic literature A branch of prophetic writing that flourished in Judaism from about 200 B.C.E. to 140

C.E. and greatly influenced Christianity. Works such as Daniel, Enoch, 2 and 3 Baruch, 2 Esdras, and the Christian Book of Revelation are distinguished by cryptic language, symbolic imagery, and the expectation of an imminent cosmic catastrophe in which the forces of Good ultimately defeat the powers of Evil, resulting in the establishment of a messianic rule and consequent transformation of the universe. Jesus' prophecies of his return (Mark 13; Luke 21; Matt. 24) are a form of apocalyptic discourse.

Apocrypha   From the Greek, meaning "hidden" books, Apocrypha refers to noncanonical or deuterocanonical literature, especially the fourteen books included in the Greek Septuagint and Latin Vulgate Bibles but not in the Masoretic Text of the Hebrew Bible. It also applies to a body of Christian works that typically parallel or spuriously "supplement" the New Testament canon.

Apodictic law   Law cast in the form of unconditional demands, such as the "thou shalt nots" in the Decalogue (Exod. 20).

apokalypsis   English transliteration of a Greek term meaning "a revelation, an unveiling of what is hidden." Paul uses the term to describe the divine source of his unique teaching (Gal. 1:12).

Apollos   A Hellenistic Jew of Alexandria, Egypt, noted for his eloquence, who was first a follower of John the Baptist, then embraced Christianity (Acts 18:24–28), and inadvertently became a rival of Paul at Corinth (1 Cor. 1:12; 3:4–6, 22–23; 4:6).

apostasy   From a Greek term meaning "to revolt," apostasy is the act of abandoning or rejecting a previously held religious faith. An apostate is one who has defected from or ceased to practice his or her religion.

apostle   A person sent forth or commissioned as a messenger, such as (but not restricted to) the Twelve whom Jesus selected to follow him. According to Acts 1, in the early Jerusalem church, an apostle was defined as one who had accompanied Jesus during his earthly ministry and had seen the resurrected Lord. Lists of the original Twelve differ from account to account (Matt. 10:2–5; Mark 3:16–19; Luke 6:13–16; Acts 1:13–14).

apothegm   A term in biblical criticism referring to brief sayings or instructive proverbs found in the Gospels. *See also* pericope.

Aqabah, Gulf of   A northern arm of the Red Sea, part of the Jordan rift, which separates the Sinai peninsula from Midian and Arabia.

Aquila   A prominent early Christian expelled from Rome with his wife Priscilla by Claudius's edict (49 C.E.), Aquila is often associated with Paul (Acts 18; Rom. 16:3–5; 1 Cor. 16:19).

Aram   According to Genesis 10:22, Aram was the son of Shem (a son of Noah) and progenitor of the Arameans, whom the Old Testament identifies with the Syrians (Gen. 24).

Aramaic   The language of the Arameans (Syrians), Aramaic was a West-Semitic tongue used in parts of Mesopotamia from about 1000 B.C.E. The official language of the Persian Empire after about 500 B.C.E., it was spoken by the Jews after the Babylonian exile. Parts of the Old Testament were composed in Aramaic, and a Galilean dialect of Aramaic was probably the language spoken by Jesus.

Areopagus   The civic court in Athens and the location of an important legal council of the Athenian democracy where, according to Acts 17, Paul introduced Christianity to some Athenian intellectuals.

Ark   The rectangular houseboat that Noah built to contain his family and pairs of all animals during the Flood (Gen. 6:14–16).

Ark of the Covenant   The portable wooden chest, supposedly dating from Mosaic times (Exod. 25:10–22), that contained sacred artifacts of Israel's religion, such as Aaron's staff and the two stone tablets representing the Decalogue. Sometimes carried into Battle (Josh. 6: 4–11; 1 Sam. 4), the Ark of the Covenant was eventually brought to Jerusalem and kept in the innermost sanctuary of Solomon's Temple. Its fate after the Temple's destruction is unknown.

Armageddon   A Greek transliteration of the Hebrew *Har Megiddon,* or "Mountain of Megiddo," a famous battlefield in the Plain of Jezreel in ancient Israel (Judg. 5:19; 2 Kings 9:27; 23:29). In Revelation 16:16, it is the symbolic site of the ultimate war between Good and Evil.

Artaxerxes   King of Persia (465–423 B.C.E.), son of Xerxes I. According to Nehemiah 2, Artaxerxes commissioned Nehemiah, his Jewish cupbearer, to go to Jerusalem and rebuild the city's walls. Scholars are not agreed on whether Ezra returned to Jerusalem during the reign of Artaxerxes I or Artaxerxes II.

Asa   Third king of Judah (about 913–873 B.C.E.) whose long reign was marked by various religious reforms. The authors of Kings and Chronicles judge him a "good" ruler (1 Kings 15:8–24; 2 Chron. 14:1–16:14).

ascension   The resurrected Jesus' ascent to heaven (Acts 1:6–11).

Ashdod   One of the five major cities of the Philistines (Josh. 13:3), where the captured Ark of the Covenant was placed in Dagon's temple (1 Sam. 5:1–8).

Asher   Reputed founder of an Israelite tribe that occupied a strip of Palestinian coast between Carmel and Phoenicia (Josh. 17:10–11; 19:24–31; Judg. 1:31–32; 5:17).

Asherah   Hebrew name for the Canaanite goddess Asherat, "Lady of the Sea," a consort of El, Canaan's chief deity, whom the apostate Israelites worshipped at various times (see 1 Kings 11:5; 16:33; 18:19; etc.).

Ashkelon   One of the five leading Philistine cities (Josh. 13:3; 2 Sam. 1:20).

Ashurbanipal Assyrian emperor (c. 668–627 B.C.E.), grandson of Sennacherib, son and successor of Esarhaddon; called Asnapper in Ezra 4:10.

Assur (Asshur) (1) Chief deity of the Assyrians, king of their gods, and personification of war. (2) Assyria's first capital, located on the west bank of the Tigris River, site of an earlier Sumerian city. (3) The name of the country from which the Assyrians took their name.

Assyria (1) A large territory centered along the upper Tigris River in Mesopotamia, including the major cities of Assur, Calah, and Nineveh. (2) The empire that dominated the Near East from the eleventh to the seventh centuries B.C.E. and whose leaders destroyed Israel in 721 B.C.E. and besieged Jerusalem in 701 B.C.E. It was destroyed by a coalition of Babylonians and Medes in 612 B.C.E.

Athens Greece's leading city-state and cultural capital in the fifth century B.C.E. and its leading intellectual center during Hellenistic and Roman times. According to Acts 17, the Apostle Paul introduced Christianity in Athens.

Aton *See* Akhenaton.

Augustus The first emperor of Rome (30 B.C.E.–14 C.E.), Augustus Caesar brought peace to the Roman Empire after centuries of civil war. According to Luke 2:1, his decree ordering a census of "the whole world" brought Mary and Joseph to register in their ancestral hometown, Bethlehem, where Jesus was born.

Azazel The unidentified place or demon to which the scapegoat was sent on the Day of Atonement (Lev. 16: 8, 10, 26).

Baal A Canaanite-Phoenician term meaning "lord" or "master," the name applied to Canaan's most popular fertility god. Worshiped as the power that caused germination and growth of farm crops, Baal was a serious rival to Yahweh after the Israelites settled in Palestine and became dependent on agriculture (Judg. 2:11–14). He is pictured as a god of storm and rainfall in a contest with the Yahwist Elijah on Mount Carmel (1 Kings 18: 20–46).

Babel A term meaning "the gate of God," Babel became synonymous with the confusion of languages that typified cosmopolitan Babylon (Gen. 11:4–9). The tower of Babel ("House of the Terrace-platform of Heaven and Earth") was a ziggurat. *See* ziggurat.

Babylon An ancient city on the middle Euphrates that was capital of both the Old and Neo-Babylonian empires. Under Nebuchadnezzar II (605–562 B.C.E.), who joined forces with the Medes to defeat Egypt at the Battle of Carchemish (605 B.C.E.) and create the second Babylonian Empire, Babylon destroyed Jerusalem and its Temple (587 B.C.E.). Babylon fell to the Persians in 539 B.C.E. Alexander the Great's plans to rebuild the old sanctuaries ended with his death in 323 B.C.E., and the city never regained its former glory. As the archetypal enemy of God's people, Babylon became the symbol of Satan's worldly power (Rev. 14:8; 18:2).

Babylonian exile The period between 587 and 538 B.C.E. during which Judah's upper classes were held captive in Babylon. An earlier deportation of Jewish leaders in 597 B.C.E. included the prophet Ezekiel. After Cyrus of Persia conquered Babylon in 539, Jews who wished to do so were encouraged to return to their Palestinian homeland.

Balaam A Bedouin prophet or fortune-teller from Pethor on the Euphrates River whom Balak, king of Moab, hired to curse the Israelites when they attempted to cross Moab on their way to Canaan. Yahweh caused the hired soothsayer to turn his curse into a blessing on Israel (Num. 22–24), although another tradition blames Balaam for corrupting the Israelites (Num. 31: 8, 15–17).

baptism A religious ceremony first associated with John the Baptist (Mark 1:4; 11:30; Luke 7:29) and performed on converts in the infant Christian community (Acts 2:38–41; 19:3–5). Baptism may have derived from ritual cleansings with water practiced by the Essenes, from some Pharisees' use of it as a conversion alternative to circumcision, or from initiation rites into Hellenistic mystery religions. In Christianity, it is the ceremony of initiation into the Church, performed either by total immersion in water or by pouring water on the head.

Barabbas A condemned murderer and possibly a revolutionary whom the Roman procurator Pontius Pilate released instead of Jesus (Mark 15:6–15; Matt. 27: 15–18; Luke 23:16–25; John 18:39–49).

Barnabas A prominent leader of the early Church in Jerusalem, associate and traveling companion of the apostle Paul (Acts 9:26–30; 11:22–30; 13:1–3; 13: 44–52; 14:1–15:4; 15:22–40; Col. 4:10; 1 Cor. 9:6; Gal. 2:1–13).

Barsabbas The Christian leader of the Jerusalem church who was considered but not chosen to replace Judas among the Twelve (Acts 1:23–26).

Bartholomew One of the twelve apostles mentioned in all three Synoptics as well as in the list in Acts (Matt. 10:3; Mark 3:18; Luke 6:14; Acts 1:13), Bartholomew is sometimes identified with the Nathanael of John's Gospel (John 1:45–51 and 21:2).

Baruch Secretary and friend of Jeremiah, Baruch ("blessed") recorded the prophet's message, which probably became the nucleus of the Jeremiah scroll (Jer. 36; 32:9–14; 43:6). The apocryphal Book of Baruch was attributed to him, as were the apocalypses of 2 and 3 Baruch in the Pseudepigrapha.

Bathsheba Wife of Uriah, a Hittite soldier working in King David's service, Bathsheba's adultery with David and his murder of her husband evoked the denunciation of the prophet Nathan (2 Sam. 11:1–4; 12:1–23).

Mother of Solomon, she conspired to place her son on Israel's throne (1 Kings 1:15–17).

Beatitudes The list of blessings or happinesses with which Jesus begins the Sermon on the Mount (Matt. 5:3–12). Luke gives a variation of these pronouncements (Luke 6:20–23).

Beersheba An ancient well in southern Palestine identified with the Genesis patriarchs (Gen. 21: 22–34; 26: 23–25, 32–33; 46:1); later a traditional location of the extreme southern border of the Israelite kingdom (Judg. 20:1; 2 Sam. 24:2; 1 Kings 4:25; etc.).

Behemoth A mysterious beast probably derived from Mesopotamian mythology but sometimes identified with the hippopotamus (Job 40:15–24). *See also* Leviathan.

Bel The Babylonian-Assyrian version of Baal, a common name for Marduk, chief god of Babylon (Isa. 46:1–4), sometimes called Merodach by the Jews (Jer. 50:2).

Belial An adjective meaning "not profitable" or "wicked" but used in the Old Testament as a proper name to denote an evil character, as "son of" or "daughter of" (Deut. 13:13; Judg. 19:22; 1 Sam. 10: 27). In 2 Corinthians, 6:15, Paul uses the term as if it were synonymous with the devil.

beloved disciple The unnamed "disciple whom Jesus loved" (John 13:23) whom the author of John's Gospel depicts as enjoying a more intimate relationship with Jesus than Peter or any other follower (John 13:21–29; 19:26–27; 20:2–10; 21:20–24). Although tradition identifies this disciple with the apostle John, neither the Gospels nor scholars can verify the assumption.

Belshazzar In Daniel, the last king of Babylon, son of Nebuchadnezzar (Dan. 5:1–31), though archaeological discoveries indicate that he was neither but merely prince regent for his father, Nabonidus.

Beltshazzar A name meaning "protect the king's life," given to Daniel by his Babylonian masters (Dan. 1:7; 2: 26; 4:8, 9).

Benjamin The twelfth and last son of Jacob, second son of the patriarch's favorite wife, Rachel, and thus full brother of Joseph and half-brother of Jacob's other ten sons. Benjamin figures prominently in Joseph's saga (Gen. 42–44) and is regarded as the founder of the tribe of Benjamin, which, under the Israelite monarchy, occupied territory adjacent to that of Judah (Josh. 18:11–28; Judg. 1:8, 21). When the ten northern tribes seceded from the Davidic monarchy, Benjamin remained with the southern kingdom of Judah (1 Kings 12:21; Ezra 4:1).

Bethany An impoverished suburb of Jerusalem, home of Jesus' friends Mary, Martha, and Lazarus (John 11: 1–44).

Bethel An ancient site, meaning "house of God," associated with the patriarchs Abraham (Gen. 12:8)

and Jacob (Gen. 28:11–13, 22). Under the divided kingdom, Jeroboam I built a shrine at Bethel, near Judah's northern boundary (1 Kings 12:32). Amos denounced a prophet at the royal sanctuary there (Amos 7:10–17).

Bethlehem A village about five miles south of Jerusalem, birthplace of David (1 Sam. 17:12) and the place where Samuel secretly anointed him king of Israel (1 Sam. 16:1–2; 20:6). According to Micah 5:2, it was to be the Messiah's birthplace, an idea that influenced the Gospel writers' accounts of Jesus' nativity (Matt. 2: 5–6; Luke 2; John 7:42).

Beth-peor An unidentified site east of the Jordan River in Moab, near which the Israelites camped before crossing Jordan and where Moses was buried (Deut. 3: 29; 4:46; 34:6).

Bethsaida A village on the north shore of the Sea of Galilee, the home of Peter, Andrew, and Philip (John 1:44; 12:21). In New Testament times, it consisted of an older Jewish section and a newer town, the capital of Philip the Tetrarch (see also Luke 10:13; Matt. 11:21).

Bildad One of Job's three friends who dispute with him the meaning of his afflictions (Job 2:11; 8; 18; etc.).

Bithynia In New Testament times, a Roman province in northern Asia Minor (modern Turkey) along the Black Sea coast and the location of several early Christian communities (Acts 16:7; 1 Peter 1:1).

Blasphemy Speech defaming the Deity, a capital offense in Old Testament times (1 Kings 21:9–13) and the charge the Sanhedrin levels against Jesus (Matt. 9:3; 26:65; John 10:36).

Boanerges "Sons of thunder," an epithet Jesus applies to James and John (Mark 3:17; Luke 9:52–56).

Boaz A wealthy landowner of Bethlehem (Ruth 2:1) who married the Moabite Ruth and became an ancestor of David (Ruth 4:22).

Booths, Feast of In ancient Israel, an autumn agricultural festival of thanksgiving during which the celebrants erected booths or shelters reminiscent of the wilderness encampments used during Israel's journey from Egypt to Canaan (Exod. 34:22); also known as the Feast of Tabernacles or Sukkoth (Lev. 23:39–44; Neh. 8:13–18).

Caesar A hereditary name by which the Roman emperors commemorated Gaius Julius Caesar, great-uncle of Augustus (Octavian), the first emperor (Luke 2:1; 3:1; Mark 12:14; Acts 11:28; 25:11).

Caesarea An important Roman city that Herod the Great built on the Palestinian coast about sixty-four miles northwest of Jerusalem and named in honor of Caesar Augustus. Caesarea was Pontius Pilate's administrative capital and later a Christian center (Acts 8:40; 10:1, 24; 18:22; 21:8). Paul was imprisoned there for two years (Acts 23:23–35; 24–26).

Caesarea Philippi   An inland city north of the Sea of Galilee built by Philip, son of Herod the Great (4 B.C.E.–34 C.E.), and named for the emperor Tiberius; the site of Peter's "confession" that Jesus was the Messiah (Mark 8:27; Matt. 16:13).

Caiaphas   Joseph Caiaphas, high priest of Jerusalem during the reign of the emperor Tiberius (Matt. 26:3, 57–66; John 9:49; 18:13–28; Acts 4:6). Son-in-law to his immediate predecessor, Annas, he was appointed to the office by the procurator Valerius Gratus and presided over Jesus' trial before the Sanhedrin.

Cain   According to the J source of Genesis, the first son of Adam and Eve, who slew his brother Abel, thus becoming the archetypal murderer and fugitive (Gen. 4). The "mark of Cain" is not a curse but a sign that Yahweh protected him from his enemies.

Calah   An ancient city on the Tigris, one of the early capitals of Assyria (Gen. 10:11–12).

Caleb   Along with Joshua, one of the two spies sent to reconnoiter Canaan who brought back a favorable report of Israel's chances (Num. 13:14). For his trust in Yahweh, Caleb was allowed to enter Canaan, while all others of his generation died in the wilderness (Num. 13:30; 14:38).

Calvary   The site outside Jerusalem's walls, exact location unknown, where Jesus was crucified (Luke 23:33). Calvary derives from the Latin word *calvaria*, a translation of the Greek *kranion*, meaning "skull"; Golgotha comes from the Aramaic for "skull" (Matt. 27:33; John 19:17).

Cana   A town in Galilee where Jesus turned water into wine at a wedding feast (John 2:1–11) and healed a nobleman's son (John 4:46–54).

Canaan   The Old Testament name for the land of Palestine west of the Jordan River, from Egypt in the south to Syria in the north (Gen. 10:19). According to Hebrew tradition, Canaan was the territory promised to Abraham's descendants (Gen. 15:7–21; 17:1–8) and infiltrated by the Israelite tribes during the thirteenth and twelfth centuries B.C.E. (Num. 21; Josh. 1–24; Judg. 1–2).

canon   A term derived from the Greek *kanon*, which may be related to the Semitic *qaneh*, a "reed," perhaps used as a measuring rod. In modern usage, a canon is a standard of measure by which a religious community judges certain writings to be authoritative, usually of divine origin. The Hebrew Bible alone is the canon of Judaism, whereas Christianity accepts both it (sometimes including the Apocrypha) and the Greek New Testament. The canon is thus an official list of books considered genuine, worthy to be used in teaching and liturgy, and hence binding in doctrine and morals. The adjective *extracanonical* refers to books not included in the official canon or list.

Capernaum   The "village of Nahum," a small port on the northwest shore of the Sea of Galilee that Jesus used as headquarters for his Galilean ministry and where he performed many "mighty works" (Matt. 9:1, 9–11; Mark 1:21–29; 2:3–11; Luke 7; John 4:46–54).

Carchemish   An important Hittite site in northern Syria that overlooked the main crossing of the Euphrates on the trade route from Assyria to the Mediterranean. In 605 B.C.E., Nebuchadnezzar II defeated the Egyptian forces of Pharaoh Necho II here (2 Chron. 35:20; Jer. 46:2), thus ending Egypt's last significant attempt to reassert its hegemony in the Near East and establishing Babylon as the dominant power.

Carmel   The name (meaning "garden" or "orchard") of a hilly range along the western border of Asher (Josh. 19:26), extending from the hill country of Samaria to the Mediterranean where Mount Carmel projects into the sea. Sacred to Baal because of its lush vegetation, Carmel was the site of Elijah's contest with the Canaanite priests (1 Kings 18).

case law   Law expressed in conditional terms: If such an act is committed, then such must be the punishment. This legal form characterizes ancient Near Eastern legal forms, including those found in Mosaic laws.

Catholic Epistles   A term referring to seven short New Testament documents, most of which were addressed to no specific person or church and therefore were intended for catholic ("universal") use.

centurion   A low-ranking officer in the Roman army in charge of a "century," or division of 100 men. A centurion named Cornelius became the first Gentile convert to Christianity (Acts 10).

Cephas   A name meaning "stone" that Jesus bestowed upon Simon Peter (John 1:42).

Chaldea   A Mesopotamian territory occupied by Semitic Arameans who founded the Neo-Babylonian Empire under Nabopolassar and his son Nebuchadnezzar, first in a brief line of Chaldean rulers (2 Kings 24: 2; 25:4–13; Jer. 37:5–12). The Chaldeans were famous for their mastery of astronomy and astrology.

Chedorlaomer   King of Elam, a country east of Babylonia on the Persian Gulf (Gen. 14).

Chemosh   The national god of Moab to whom children were sacrificed as burnt offerings (Num. 21:29; Jer. 48: 7, 13, 46). King Solomon erected an altar to Chemosh (1 Kings 11:7) that was not dismantled until Josiah's reforms more than three centuries later (2 Kings 23: 13). Like the Israelites, the Moabites ("people of Chemosh") attributed their country's defeats and failures to their deity's anger.

cherub, cherubim (pl.)   Mythological creatures—part bird, part human, part other animal—that were placed in pairs at each side of the mercy seat of the tabernacle, and later in the innermost sanctuary of Solomon's Temple, to protect the sacred relics in the Ark of the Covenant (Exod. 25:18–22). Their images were also embroidered on the veil of the Temple (2 Chron. 3:14) and sculpted on a frieze around the Temple walls and on the bases of the "Molten sea" (1 Kings 6:23; 7:29; 1 Chron. 28:18; Heb. 9:5). Such winged creatures, with a lion's or ox's body, eagle's wings, and human face, were common in ancient Near Eastern art and have been found in Byblos, Nineveh, and elsewhere. Originally the guardians of divine beings, they were later identified with the angels of Yahweh's heavenly court.

Christ From the Greek *Christos,* a translation of the Hebrew *Messiah,* meaning "anointed one," the term derives from the ancient practice of anointing kings at their coronation. The Messiah or Christ was to be a kingly descendant of David.

Christology The theological discipline that deals with the nature of Jesus Christ, particularly his divinity, relation to the Divine Father, and role in human redemption.

Church A term translating the Greek *ekklesia,* meaning "assembly of ones called out"; in New Testament usage, the community of believers in Jesus Christ. Individual churches or congregations make up the international Church, which is conceived as the visible part of Christ's spiritual body (Matt. 16:18; 18:17; Eph. 5: 27; 1 Tim. 3:15; 1 Cor. 12:12–27; Col. 1:18).

circumcision An ancient Semitic operation in which the foreskin of eight-day-old males is removed as a ceremony of initiation into the religion and community of Israel. Circumcision is represented as beginning with Abraham (Gen. 17:10–14) or Moses (Exod. 4:24–46; see also Lev. 1:59; 2:21; 12:3). The question of whether to circumcise Gentile converts to the early Christian Church was an important source of dissension (Acts 15; Gal. 2).

Claudius Fourth Roman emperor (41–54 C.E.), who expelled the Jews from Rome (Acts 11:28; 18:2).

Code of Hammurabi The compilation of Sumero-Babylonian laws inscribed on the basaltic Stele of Hammurabi (1728–1686 B.C.E.), founder of the first Babylonian Empire. A number of Hammurabi's statutes anticipate those of the biblical Torah.

codex A manuscript book of an ancient biblical text, first used by Christians to replace the unwieldy scrolls on which the Scriptures were first recorded.

Codex Sinaiticus An ancient Greek edition of the New Testament, which contains several books that supplement the central canon.

Colossae An ancient Phrygian city situated on the south bank of the Lycus River in central Asia Minor, important for its position on the trade route between Ephesus and Mesopotamia (Col. 1:1–2; 4:13).

conquest of Canaan The gradual occupation of Palestine during the thirteenth and twelfth centuries B.C.E. by previously nomadic Israelites, an idealized account of which is given in Joshua 1–24.

Constantine Roman emperor from 306 to 337 C.E. who was converted to Christianity and whose rule began a period of state support for the early church. Constantine issued the Edict of Milan in 313 C.E., mandating general tolerance of Christianity. He also presided over the Council of Nicaea in 325 C.E., establishing a precedent for imperial leadership of the church.

Corinth A cosmopolitan center of trade and commerce in ancient Greece, destroyed by the Romans in 146 B.C.E. but later rebuilt. Home of a large population of Hellenistic Jews, Corinth was later a Christian center established by the apostle Paul and his associates (Acts 18:24; 19:1; 1 and 2 Cor.).

Cornelius A Roman centurion associated with the Jewish synagogue in Caesarea who became the first Gentile convert to Christianity (Acts 10–11).

covenant In Old Testament terms: (1) an agreement or compact between individuals, such as Abraham and Abimelech (Gen. 21:27) or David and Jonathan (1 Sam. 18:3); (2) a promise Yahweh makes to certain people, such as Noah (Gen. 9:13) and Abraham (Gen. 15:18–21; 17:4–14); (3) a legal bond Yahweh forms with a chosen group, such as Israel, and the demands he makes in return. The Mosaic or Sinatic covenant is that from which the Old "Testament" (a synonym for "covenant" or "contract") takes its name (Exod. 20–24; 34; Deut. 29; Josh. 24). In Christian terminology, Jesus introduced a "new covenant" at the Last Supper (Mark 14:22–25; Matt. 26:26–29, etc.) that Christians believe superseded the Mosaic Covenant and embraced believers of all nations (1 Cor. 11:25).

Covenant Code A name given to the collection of ancient Hebrew laws found in Exodus 20:23–23:33, often called the Book of the Covenant (Exod. 24:7).

cult The formalized religious practices of a people, particularly its system of veneration, public rites, and liturgies.

cuneiform A wedge-shaped writing that originated in ancient Sumer about 3000 B.C.E. and spread throughout Mesopotamia.

Cyrus the Great Founder of the Persian Empire and conqueror of Babylon (539 B.C.E.) who liberated the Jews from captivity and decreed their return to Jerusalem to rebuild the Temple (2 Chron. 36:22–23; Ezra 1: 1–8). Second Isaiah calls him Yahweh's "shepherd" (Isa. 44:28) and his "Anointed" or "Messiah" (Isa. 45:1).

D *See* Deuteronomist.

Dagon An ancient Canaanite agricultural deity worshiped by the Philistines at Ashdod and Gaza (1 Sam. 5:1–7) and whose Gaza temple was reputedly destroyed by Samson (Judg. 16:23–30).

Damascus   The capital of Syria and terminus of ancient caravan routes in the Fertile Crescent. Damascus was supposedly founded by Uz, grandson of Noah's son Shem (Gen. 5:32; 6:10; 10:23), and was visited by Abraham (Gen. 11:31; 12:4; 14:14). Paul's conversion to Christianity occurred near Damascus (Acts 9).

Dan   (1) Son of Jacob and Rachel's servant, Bilhah (Gen. 30:1–6). (2) One of the twelve tribes of Israel, which first occupied a small territory between Judah and Ephraim (Josh. 19:40–48) but later migrated north to an area close to the Jordan's source (Josh. 19:47; Judg. 1:34; 18). (3) A Danite city formerly known as Laish, where Jeroboam I later established a cult center (1 Kings 12:26–30). As the phrase "from Dan to Beer-sheba" (Judg. 20:1; 2 Sam. 24:2; 1 Kings 4:25; etc.) indicates, the city of Dan was regarded as the extreme northern boundary of Israel.

Danel   An ancient king whose name (Danel) appears in the *Ras Shamrah* epics and who was incorporated into the same tradition as Noah and Job (Ezek. 14:14; 28:3). He is not the same as the character in the Book of Daniel, who is referred to in no other canonical Old Testament work.

Darius   The name of several Persian rulers mentioned in the Old Testament. (1) Darius I (522–486 B.C.E.), son of Hystaspes, was the emperor whose forces invaded Greece and were defeated at Marathon (490 B.C.E.). He continued Cyrus the Great's favorable treatment of the Jews (Ezra 5–6). (2) Darius "the Mede" (Dan. 5:31; 9:1), alleged to have condemned Daniel to the lion's den (Dan. 6:7–26), is unknown to history.

Dathan   A Reubenite who rebelled with Korah against Moses and Aaron in the Sinai desert (Num. 16:1–35; 26:7–11).

David   Son of Jesse (Ruth 4:18–22), successor to Saul, and second king of the united twelve-tribe monarchy (1000–961 B.C.E.), David expanded Israel's boundaries to their greatest extent, founded a new administrative and religious capital at Jerusalem, and created a prosperous though short-lived Palestinian Empire. His story is told in 1 Samuel 16 through 1 Kings 2; the Chronicler gives an often unreliable, idealized version of his cultic activities (1 Chron. 2, 3, 10–29). So great was David's effectiveness and popularity, especially in retrospect, that he became the prototype of the Messiah figure, who was prophesied to be his descendant (Isa. 9:5–7; 11:1–16; Jer. 23:5; 30:9; Ezek. 34:23–31; etc.).

Day of Atonement   (Yom Kippur) A solemn, annual Jewish observance in which Israel's high priest offered blood sacrifices ("sin offerings") to effect a reconciliation between the Deity and his people (Lev. 16). The banishment of a "scapegoat" to which the priest had symbolically transferred the people's collective guilt climaxed the atonement rites (Lev. 16). The Day of Atonement marked the once-yearly entrance of the priest into the Temple's Holy of Holies. The author of Hebrews argues that these ceremonies foreshadowed the sacrificial death of Jesus and his ascension to the heavenly sanctuary (Heb. 9).

Deacon   Literally, a "servant," a term applied to one of the lower orders of the Christian ministry—in the early Church, probably to the bishop's assistant.

Dead Sea   Known in biblical times as "the salt sea" (Gen. 14:3; Num. 34:3; Josh. 3:16; 12:3), the "sea of the plain [Arabah]" (Josh. 3:16; 12:3), and "the east sea" (Ezek. 47:18; Joel 2:20), this lake, forty-six miles long, was given its present name by Greeks in the second century B.C.E. Occupying a basin into which the Jordan River empties, and located in a geological fault zone that extends from Syria to the Gulf of Aqabah and thence into East Africa, it lies 1290 feet below sea level and has a depth of approximately 1200 feet, making it the lowest body of water in the world. With a saline content five times that of the ocean, it supports no fish or other forms of life.

Dead Sea Scrolls   Biblical and other religious manuscripts dating from the second century B.C.E. to the first century C.E., found in caves near Qumran on the northwest shore of the Dead Sea.

Deborah   A judge and prophetess who, with Barak, helped bring about Israel's victories over the Canaanite forces of Sisera (Judg. 4–5).

Decalogue   *See* Ten Commandments.

Delilah   A woman from Sorek whom the Philistines bribed to discover and betray the secret of Samson's strength (Judg. 16). Her name means "coquette" or "flirtatious."

Deuterocanon   The fourteen books or parts of books found in the Greek Septuagint and later editions of the Latin Vulgate—such as Tobit, 1 and 2 Maccabees, and the Wisdom of Solomon—but not included in the Hebrew Bible or most Protestant Old Testaments that Roman Catholics and some others regard as forming a second or later canon. After the Council of Trent, the books of 1 and 2 Esdras and the Prayer of Manasseh were deleted from the deuterocanonical list. When Protestant editions of the Bible include these works, they are typically classed as Apocrypha.

Deutero-Isaiah   Also known as Second Isaiah, the name assigned to the anonymous prophet responsible for Chapters 40–55 of the Book of Isaiah and to the work itself.

Deuteronomic Reformation   The label that biblical scholars apply to King Josiah's reforms of the Jewish religion following 621 B.C.E. The name derives from the assumption that the law book found during Josiah's repairs of the Temple was a form of the Book of Deuteronomy (probably Deut. 12–26) and that the work's insistence on the centralization of Israel's cult at a single (undesignated) sanctuary inspired Josiah's sweeping destruction of all rival shrines (2 Kings 22–23).

Deuteronomist (1) The unknown writer who compiled and edited the present form of the Book of Deuteronomy. Some scholars believe that he added the introductory material (Deut. 1–11) and appendixes (Deut. 27–34) to the older deuteronomic code (Deut. 12–26). (2) The redactor or editorial school that produced the entire Deuteronomistic History in something resembling its present form.

Deuteronomistic History The books of the Former Prophets (Joshua, Judges, Samuel, Kings) as compiled and revised from older sources by an anonymous author or editorial school deeply influenced by the historical philosophy of the Book of Deuteronomy. The first edition was produced late in Josiah's reign (about 610 B.C.E.), and a second edition followed Jerusalem's destruction in 587 B.C.E. It was further edited during the Babylonian exile.

deutero-Pauline New Testament books attributed to Paul but probably not written by him—e.g., Ephesians and the Pastorals.

devil The English word commonly used to translate two Greek words with different meanings: (1) *diabolos,* "the accuser" (John 8:44); (2) *daimonion,* one of many evil spirits inhabiting the world, who were thought to cause disease, madness, and other afflictions (see Matt. 10:25; Mark 3:22; Luke 8; 11:14–16; etc.) In Revelation 12:9, the devil is identified with the Hebrew Satan and the serpent of Genesis.

Diana (of the Ephesians) The Near Eastern form of the Greek goddess Artemis (whom the Romans identified with Diana) worshiped in Ephesus, which in Paul's time was the capital of the Roman province of Asia (Acts 19).

Diaspora Literally, a "scattering," the term refers to the distribution of Jews outside their Palestinian homeland, such as the many Jewish communities established throughout the Greco-Roman world.

Didache A two-part extracanonical work, also called the Teaching of the Twelve Apostles, that contains a manual of primitive church discipline that may date to apostolic times.

Dionysus Ancient Greek god of wine, ecstasy, and emotional freedom, he was the son of Zeus and a mortal woman, Semele. Representing the natural cycle of life, death, and rebirth, he is killed, descends into the underworld (Hades), and is resurrected to immortal life among the Olympian gods.

disciple From the Greek word meaning "learner," the term is applied in the New Testament to followers of particular religious figures, such as Moses (John 9:28), John the Baptist (Luke 11:1; John 1:35), the Pharisees (Mark 2:18), or Jesus. Although it applies especially to the Twelve (Matt. 20:17), it also designates others who

associated with Jesus (Matt. 14:26). Paul made numerous disciples "for Christ" (Acts 20:1, 7; 21:16).

documentary hypothesis A scholarly theory associated with Julius Wellhausen that argues the Pentateuch is not the work of one author but the result of many generations of anonymous writers, revisers, and editors (redactors) who produced the four main literary strands or components found in these five books: J (the Yahwist, about 950 B.C.E.); E (the Elohist, about 850 B.C.E.); D (the Deuteronomist, about 650–621 B.C.E.); and P (the Priestly component, about 550–450 B.C.E.).

Domitian Roman emperor (81–96 C.E.), younger son of Vespasian, who ascended the throne following the death of his brother Titus. The Book of Revelation was written late in his reign.

doublet A literary term denoting two or more versions, from different sources, of the same material (cf. Gen. 12:10–20; 20:1–18; 26:6–11; Exod. 3:1–20; 6:2–13; 20; Deut. 5; etc.).

doxology In a religious writing or service, the formal concluding expression of praise or formula ritually ascribing glory to God.

dragon A symbolic reptile derived from ancient Near Eastern mythology, related to the serpent in Eden (Gen. 3) and identified with the devil and Satan (Rev. 12). *See* Leviathan.

dualism A philosophic or religious system that posits the existence of two parallel worlds, one of physical matter and the other of invisible spirit. Moral dualism views the universe as divided between powers of Good and Evil, Light and Dark, which contend for human allegiance.

E *See* Elohist.

Ebedmelech The Ethiopian (Cushite) eunuch who rescued Jeremiah from the cistern where the prophet's enemies had left him to die (Jer. 38:1–13; 39:15–18).

Ebla A large ancient Canaanite city (located in modern Syria), Ebla contained an extensive library of clay tablets inscribed in Mesopotamian cuneiform. Compiled during the late third millennium B.C.E., Ebla's archives predate the oldest biblical documents by 1000 years.

Eber The legendary ancestor of various Hebrew, Arab, and Aramean tribes (Gen. 10:24–30; 11:15; 1 Chron. 1:18); listed in the New Testament as an ancestor of Jesus (Luke 3:35).

Eden The gardenlike first home of humanity (Gen. 2:8); an earthly paradise from which the first couple was expelled (Gen. 3:24). See also Ezekiel 28:13, where the "king of Tyre" enjoyed an "Eden," possibly a lush forested region (Ezek. 31:18; 36:25; Isa. 51:3; Joel 2:3).

Edom In Old Testament times, a region or country extending southward from the Dead Sea to the Gulf of Aqabah, bordered on the north by Moab, on the northwest by Judah, on the east and southeast by the Sinai desert (Num. 20:14–21; 2 Kings 3:20; etc.). It was also called "Seir" (Gen. 32:3; Num. 24:18; Judg. 5:4), identified with Esau (Gen. 36:1), and thought to be Yahweh's original homeland (Deut. 33:2; Judg. 5: 4–5; Hab. 3:3). Famous for its wisdom tradition (Obad. 8; Jer. 49:7), Edom is the setting for the Job story and may have contributed the central ideas of that philosophical work.

Edomites   According to Genesis, descendants of Jacob's twin brother, Esau, "who is Edom" (Gen. 36:1); a Semitic people who occupied the territory southeast of Judah and were among Israel's bitterest enemies (Judg. 11; 2 Kings 8:20–22; Ps. 137:7; Amos 1–2; 9; Ezek. 25:12–14; 35:1–15). The Edomites later infiltrated southern Judea, which in Hellenistic times was called Idumea (Mark 3:8).

Egypt   Ancient nation centered along the Nile River southwest of Palestine, visited by Abraham (Gen. 12:10–20) and settled in by his Israelite descendants (Gen. 41–50) for a reputed 430 years (Exod. 12:40). Moses, raised at the Egyptian court, led the enslaved Israelites from Egypt about 1280–1250 B.C.E. (Exod. 1–15). Many of Israel's classical prophets advised against turning to Egypt for political or military help (Isa. 30:1–7; 31:1; 36; Jer. 46; Hos. 7:11), although King Solomon had once made an alliance with the pharaohs (1 Kings 9:16–18, 24). Egyptian attempts to restore its hegemony in Palestine were finally ended at the Battle of Carchemish (605 B.C.E.), when Nebuchadnezzar of Babylon defeated Pharaoh Necho's troops.

El, Elohim (pl.)   A Semitic term for a divine being. In Canaanite religion, El was the high god, father of lesser deities. In the Hebrew Bible, El, when used as a name for the Israelite Deity, typically occurs as part of a phrase, such as El Shaddai ("God of the mountain"), El Bethel ("God of the House of God"), or El Elyon ("God Most High"). In its plural form, the Hebrew generic term for deity applied to both their national God (Gen. 1:1; 2:5; etc.) and foreign deities (Exod. 15: 2, 11).

Elam   An ancient civilized center across the Persian Gulf from Sumer (now in Iran), supposedly founded by Elam, son of Shem (Gen. 10:22). Chedorlaomer, king of Elam, headed several Babylonian states (Gen. 14: 1–11). Elamites later helped Assyria invade Judah (Isa. 11:11; 22:6).

Eleazar   (1) The third son of Aaron, a chief of the Levites, who succeeded his father as high priest (Exod. 6: 23; Num. 3:2, 32; 20:25–29; Josh. 14:1). (2) In 2 Maccabees, the aged "teacher of the Law" who was bludgeoned to death for refusing to eat pig's flesh (2 Macc. 6:18–31).

Eli   In 1 Samuel 2:22–4:18, an ineffectual judge and priest at Shiloh under whose jurisdiction young Samuel served (1 Sam. 3:1).

Elihu   A young man who condemns Job's alleged self-righteousness (Job 32–37).

Elijah   Literally, "Yahweh is my God"; a fiercely Yahwist prophet from the northern kingdom whose anti-Baalism and attacks on Ahab's dynasty had a tremendous impact on Israel's political course during the ninth century B.C.E. and who shaped his nation's prophetic traditions for centuries thereafter (1 Kings 17–19; 21; 2 Kings 1–2). Reportedly carried to heaven in a fiery chariot (2 Kings 2:1–13), he was expected to reappear shortly before the Day of Yahweh arrived (Mal. 4: 5–6). Although some Christian writers identified John the Baptist with Elijah (Luke 1:17; Mark 9:12–13), some contemporaries viewed Jesus as Elijah returned (Mark 9:28; 16:14). Along with Moses, Elijah appears in Jesus' Transfiguration (Mark 9:4; Matt. 17:3; Luke 9:30).

Eliphaz   The most moderate and restrained of Job's critics (Job 4; 8; 15; 22–24; etc.).

Elisabeth   A Levite, wife of the priest Zechariah, and mother of John the Baptist (Luke 1).

Elisha   A ninth-century prophet in the northern kingdom, successor to Elijah (1 Kings 19:15–21; 2 Kings 2: 1–15). Like his predecessor, Elisha was a clairvoyant who worked numerous miracles, including the resuscitation of a dead child (2 Kings 4:18–37; 6:32–7:2; 8: 7–13; 13:14–19). So great was his prestige that he not only brought an end to the Omri-Ahab-Jezebel dynasty in Israel by having the upstart Jehu anointed king (2 Kings 9:1–13) but also made Hazael king of Syria (2 Kings 8:7–15).

Elohim   *See* El.

Elohist   The scholarly term designating the anonymous author or compiler responsible for the E document or tradition in the Pentateuch. The name arose from his characteristic use of *Elohim* to denote the Hebrew Deity.

El Shaddai   Although commonly translated "God Almighty," this term probably means "God of the Mountain," referring to the Mesopotamian cosmic "mountain" inhabited by divine beings. One of the patriarchal names for the Mesopotamian tribal god, it is identified with Yahweh in the Mosaic revelation (Exod. 6:3). Except for a few occurrences in Job (5:17, 8:5; etc.), Isaiah (13:6), and Ezekiel (10:5), it appears chiefly in the Pentateuch (Gen. 17:1; 28:3; 35:11; 43:14; 48:3; Exod. 6:3, etc.). *Shaddai* alone appears in Ruth 1:20–21 and Job 13:3; 20:15–20; 31:2; 40:2; etc.

Emmaus   A village (site unknown) near Jerusalem, along the road to which the resurrected Jesus appeared to several disciples (Luke 24:13–32).

Endor   Literally, "fountain of habitation"; a small town southeast of Nazareth, remembered for its witch whom King Saul solicited (1 Sam. 28:7–25).

Enoch   A son of Cain (Gen. 4:17, J's account) or of Jared (Gen. 5:18, P's version) and father of Methuselah (Gen. 5:21). P's statement that "God took him" (Gen. 5:24)—apparently to heaven and without death—strongly influenced later Hebrew notions of immortality and gave rise to a whole body of pseudepigraphal literature in which Enoch is a model of divine wisdom.

Enuma Elish   The Babylonian creation epic that takes its name from the opening phrase (in Akkadian), "when above."

Epaphras   An early Christian of Colossae who reported on the Colossian church to the imprisoned Paul (Col. 1:7; 4:12; Philem. 23).

Epaphroditus   A Macedonian Christian from Philippi who assisted Paul in prison (Phil. 2:25–27).

Ephesus   A wealthy Hellenistic city, later capital of the Roman province of Asia, site of the famous temple of Artemis (Diana) (Acts 19–20). Ephesus is frequently mentioned in various Pauline and deutero-Pauline letters (1 Cor. 16:19; 2 Cor. 12:14; 13:1; 1 Tim. 3:1; 2 Tim. 4:12; etc.). The author of Revelation (Rev. 2:1–7) judged the church there favorably. Later Christian traditions made it the site of the Virgin's assumption to heaven and the final ministry of the apostle John.

Ephod   An apronlike garment worn by the high priest Aaron and his successors (Exod. 28).

Ephraim   (1) Son of Joseph and Asenath (daughter of the priest Potipherah) and adopted by Jacob (Gen. 48:1–20). (2) The Israelite territory occupied by the tribe of Ephraim, bordered on the south by Dan and Benjamin, on the west by the Mediterranean, on the north by Manasseh, and on the east by the Jordan Rift Valley. Shechem (Josh. 21:20) was its most important city and served as an early capital of the northern kingdom (1 Kings 12:1). (3) The half-tribe of Ephraim, along with Manasseh, was one of the twelve tribes. After the ten northern tribes seceded (922 B.C.E.) from the Davidic union, Ephraim became dominant in Israel and was commonly used as a synonym for the whole ten-tribe nation.

epiphany   An appearance or manifestation, particularly of a divine being; typically sudden and accompanied by dramatic natural effects (Exod. 3; 6; 19; 24; Isa. 6; Job 38–42; etc.).

epistle   A formal letter intended for a wide public audience rather than for a specific group or individual.

eponym   The person from whom a people or group is reputed to have taken its name (Gen. 36:1).

Erech (Uruk)   An ancient Sumerian city, home of the legendary King Gilgamesh.

Esarhaddon   Son of the Assyrian Emperor Sennacherib, Esarhaddon ruled from about 680 to 669 B.C.E., despoiled Tyre and Sidon, colonized Samaria, and reputedly took Manasseh, king of Judah, captive to Babylon (2 Kings 19:37; Isa. 37:38; 2 Chron. 33:11; Ezra 4:2).

Esau   Firstborn son of Isaac and Rebekah, twin brother of Jacob (Gen. 25:25–34), Esau gave up his birthright to his cleverer sibling (Gen. 27–28), thus becoming the prototype of the person who is insensitive to his heritage (Heb. 12:16). He was thought of as the progenitor of the Edomites, traditional enemies of Jacob's descendants (Israel) (Gen. 36).

eschatology   From the Greek, meaning a "study of last things," eschatology is a doctrine or theological concept about the ultimate destiny of humanity and the universe. Having both a personal and a general application, it can refer to (1) beliefs about the individual soul following death, including divine judgment, heaven, hell, and resurrection; or (2) larger concerns about the fate of the cosmos, such as events leading to the Day of Yahweh, the final battle between supernatural Good and Evil, judgment of the nations, and the establishment of the Deity's universal sovereignty. In Christian terms, it involves the *Parousia* (return of Christ), the chaining of Satan, introduction of the millennium, etc. Apocalyptic works like Daniel, Revelation, 2 Esdras, and the books of Enoch typically stress eschatological matters.

Essenes   According to Josephus, one of the three major sects of first-century C.E. Judaism. Semi-ascetic in nature, the Essenes were spiritual descendants of the Hasidim ("pious") who had resisted Antiochus IV's attempts to destroy the Jewish religion. Their apocalyptic convictions and certain of their rituals akin to baptism have suggested to some scholars that they were an influence on such representative pre-Christian figures as John the Baptist. They are commonly identified with the Qumran community, which produced the Dead Sea Scrolls.

Esther   Heroine of the canonical book bearing her name, cousin and adopted daughter of Mordecai (Esther 2:15), queen of Persia under Xerxes (Esther 1:1–2:18), Esther became a national heroine by delivering her people from a mass slaughter planned by Haman (Esther 2:19–4:17). The Book of Esther commemorates the Feast of Purim (Esther 9:17–10:3).

Ethiopia   An area of northeast Africa (Abyssinia), which the Hebrews called Cush or Kush, supposedly settled by a son of Ham (Gen. 10:6–8). Classical writers mention a line of Ethiopian queens named Candace, one of whom is cited in Acts 8:27.

etiology   Literally, a statement of causes or origins; in literary terms, a narrative created to explain the origin or meaning of a social practice, topographical feature, ritual, or other factor that arouses the storyteller's interest.

Eucharist   From the Greek work for "gratitude" or "thanksgiving," Eucharist is a name for the Christian ceremony of consecrated bread and wine that Jesus initiated at the Last Supper (Mark 14:22–25; Matt. 26: 26–29; etc.).

Euphrates River   The longest river of southwest Asia; one of the four streams of Eden (Gen. 2:14), the Euphrates was the extreme northeastern border of Israel's kingdom at its height (2 Sam. 8:3; 10:16; 1 Kings 4:24).

evangelist   The New Testament name for a Christian who traveled from place to place proclaiming the Gospel (Acts 6:1–5; Eph. 4:11; 2 Tim. 4:5). The term is also used for the authors of the four Gospels and means "one who proclaims good news."

Eve   The first woman, wife of Adam, who derived her name from the Hebrew verb "to live" because she was "the mother of all those who live" (Gen. 3:30). Paul's interpretation of her role in the fall of humanity is given in 2 Corinthians 11:3. (See also 1 Timothy 2:11–15.)

Evil-merodach   Son and successor of Nebuchadnezzar who reputedly treated well Judah's captive monarch Jehoiachin (2 Kings 25:27–30; Jer. 52:31–34). The name means "man of Marduk."

exegesis   A literary term denoting close analysis and interpretation of a text to discover the original author's exact intent and meaning. Once this has been established, later interpretations may also be considered.

exile   Period during which the Jews were captive in Babylon (587–538 B.C.E.).

Exodus   A Greek term meaning "a going out" or "departure." In the Old Testament, it refers to the escape of Israelite slaves from Egypt under Moses' leadership (c. 1280–1250 B.C.E.), an event the Hebrews regarded as Yahweh's crucial saving act in their history (Exod. 15; 20:1–2; Deut. 5:6; Josh. 24:1–13; Ps. 105:26–39; Amos 2:10; etc.).

exorcism   The act or practice of expelling a demon or evil spirit from a person or place (Tob. 8:1–3; Mark 1: 23–27, 32–34; 5:1–20; Matt. 8:28–34; Acts 19: 13–19; etc.).

expiation   In religious terms, the act of making atonement for sin, usually by offering a sacrifice to appease divine wrath (Lev. 16).

Ezekiel   A major prophet of the sixth century B.C.E., exiled to Babylon, who was distinguished by his strange visions and priestly concerns. The name means "God strengthens."

Ezra (Esdras)   A postexilic Jewish priest who returned to Jerusalem from Babylon during the reign of the Persian Emperor Artaxerxes (Ezra 7:1) to promulgate the Mosaic Torah and supervise a reformation of the Jewish religion (Neh. 8–10; Ezra 7–10). His influence on later Judaism was so great that he was conceived as the re-creator of the Hebrew Bible and author of several pseudohistorical and apocalyptic works (1 Esd. 8–9; 2 Esd. 14).

faith   In biblical terms, the quality of trust, reliance on, and fidelity to God. Both the New Testament and the Greek translation of the Hebrew Bible use two terms (*pistis, pisteuein*) to express the concept, which reaches its fullest development in Paul's doctrine of salvation through trust in the saving power of Christ (Rom. 10: 17; Gal. 3:5–29, 5:6, etc.).

fall, the   In some Christian theologies, a term that denotes humanity's loss of innocence and divine favor through Adam's sin of disobedience (Gen. 3). According to some interpretations of Pauline thought (Rom. 5:12–21; 1 Cor. 15:45–49), the primal human sin resulted in the transmission of death and a proclivity toward depravity and evil to the entire human race. As a medieval rhyme expressed it, "In Adam's fall, we sinned all." Despite the emphasis given the fall by some theologians, such as Augustine, the Yahwist's account of Adam's behavior is never mentioned again in the Hebrew Bible.

Fast of the Ninth Ab   A solemn observance mourning the two destructions of the Jerusalem Temple, the first by the Babylonians (587 B.C.E.) and the second by the Romans (70 C.E.), both in the month of Ab (August). The dirges in the Book of Lamentations are read to commemorate the sanctuary's dual fall.

Feast of Dedication   An eight-day Jewish celebration (now known as Hanukkah) instituted in 165 B.C.E. by Judas Maccabeus and held annually on the twenty-fifth day of Kislev (November–December) to commemorate the cleansing and rededication of the Jerusalem Temple, which Antiochus IV had polluted. Referred to in John 10:22–38, it is also known as the Festival of Lights.

Fertile Crescent   The name by which James H. Breasted designated the arch or semicircle of fertile territory stretching from the Persian Gulf on the northeast to Egypt on the southwest and including Mesopotamia, Syria, and Palestine.

Festus, Porcius   The procurator of Judea whom Nero appointed to succeed Felix and through whom Paul appealed to be tried by Caesar's court in Rome (Acts 24:27–26:32).

firmament   The Old Testament term for the vault or arch of the sky that separated the earthly oceans from the heavenly ocean of rain-giving clouds and in which Elohim placed the sun, moon, and stars (Gen. 1:6–8, 16–20, 7:11; 2 Sam. 22:8; 2 Kings 7:2; Pss. 24:2; 78: 23; 104:2, 5; Job 26:11; 27:18).

Flood, the   The global deluge of Noah's day (Gen. 6: 5–8:22), based on ancient Mesopotamian flood stories akin to that found in the *Epic of Gilgamesh* and later used as a prototype of world judgment and destruction (Matt. 24:36–41; Luke 17:26–30; 2 Pet. 2:5; 3:5–7).

form criticism   An English rendition of the German *Formsgeschichte,* a method of biblical criticism that attempts to isolate, classify, and analyze individual units or characteristic forms contained in a literary text and to identify the probable preliterary form of these units before their incorporation into the written text. Form criticism also attempts to discover the setting in life (*Sitz-im-Leben*) of each unit—i.e., the historical, social, religious, and cultural environment from which it developed—and to trace or reconstruct the process by which various traditions evolved from their original oral state to their final literary form.

Gabriel   In the Hebrew angelic hierarchy, one of the seven archangels whose duty it was to convey the Deity's messages. Gabriel explained Daniel's visions to him (Dan. 8:15–26; 9:20–27) and, in the New Testament, announced the births of John the Baptist and Jesus (Luke 1:5–17; 26–38). The name may mean "person of God" or "God has shown himself mighty."

Gad   (1) Firstborn son of Jacob and Zilpah (Gen. 30: 1–11; 35:26), Gad was the eponymous ancestor of the Israelite tribe of Gad (Num. 2:14) whose territory was located northeast of the Dead Sea, east of the Jordan River (Num. 32; Deut. 3:16–20). Gad joined the revolt against Rehoboam and was part of the ten-tribe northern kingdom. (2) A prophet at David's court (1 Sam. 22:5; 2 Sam. 24; 1 Chron. 21; 2 Chron. 29: 25, 29).

Gadara   A Hellenistic city belonging to the Decapolis (ten-member league of Greek cities in Palestine), where Jesus exorcised a demoniac (Mark 5:1–20; Matt. 8:28–34; Luke 8:26–39).

Galatia   A region in the interior of Asia Minor (Turkey) settled by Gauls; in New Testament times, a Roman province visited by Paul and his associates (Acts 16:6; 18:23; 1 Cor. 16:1; Gal. 1:2; 1 Pet. 1:1).

Galilee   From the Hebrew term *Galil ha-goyim*, meaning "circle of Gentiles," the name given northern Palestine lying west of the Jordan, an area originally assigned to the tribes of Ashur, Zebulun, and Naphtali, who failed to evict the Canaanites living there (Josh. 19; Judg. 1; 4; 5). The region where Jesus grew up (Matt. 2:23; Luke 2), Galilee was then under Roman control but administered by the tetrarch Herod Antipas (4 B.C.E.–39 C.E.) (Luke 23:5–7).

Galilee, Sea of   The major body of fresh water in northern Palestine and source of livelihood to many Galilean fishermen, such as Peter, Andrew, and John (Matt. 4: 18–22). The towns and fields along its shores were the site of many of Jesus' public discourses and miracles (Mark 6:30–52; etc.) and of a resurrection appearance as well (John 21:1–14).

Gallio   A proconsul of Achaia (the Roman province of Greece) who dismissed charges brought against Paul by Corinthian Jews (Acts 18:12–17), Gallio was a brother of Seneca, the Stoic philosopher.

Gamaliel   A leading Pharisee, scholar, member of the Sanhedrin (Acts 5:34), reputed teacher of Paul (Acts 22:3), and exponent of the liberal wing of the Pharisaic party developed by his grandfather Hillel, Gamaliel persuasively argued for a policy of toleration toward the new religion preached by Peter and other apostles (Acts 5:38–40).

Gath   Of the Philistines' five major cities, the one nearest to Hebrew territory (Josh. 13:3; 1 Sam. 17; 27; etc.).

Gaza   The southernmost of the Philistines' five principal cities (Josh. 13:3) where Samson destroyed the temple of Dagon (Judg. 16). During the Israelite monarchy, Gaza marked the southernmost boundary of Judah (1 Kings 4:24).

Gehenna   New Testament name for the "Valley of the Son [or Children] of Hinnom" that bordered Jerusalem on the south and west and was the site of human sacrifices to Molech and other pagan gods (Jer. 7:32; Lev. 18:21; 1 Kings 11:7; 2 Chron. 28:3; 33:6). Later used as a dump in which to burn garbage, it became a symbol of punishment in the afterlife and is cited as such by Jesus (Matt. 5:22; 10:28–29; 18:8; 25:30, 46; etc.).

Gemara   The second part of the Talmud; an extensive commentary, in Aramaic, on the Hebrew Mishnah.

Gentile   Someone who is not a Jew, an uncircumcised person, one belonging to "the nations" (Ps. 9:17; Isa. 2:2; Zeph. 2:1; Hag. 2:7; Matt. 1:11; 12:21; Luke 21: 24; etc.).

Gethsemane   The site of a garden or orchard on the Mount of Olives where Jesus took his disciples after the Last Supper; the place where he was arrested (Matt. 26: 36–56; Mark 14:32–52; Luke 22:39–53; John 18: 1–14).

Gibeah   A small hill town in the territory of Benjamin, prominent in the eleventh century B.C.E. because it was the home of Saul (1 Sam. 10:26) and the first capital of the united monarchy (1 Sam. 13–14; 2 Sam. 21:6).

Gibeon   A city of the Hivites ("Horites") (Josh. 9:17; 11:19), whose people deceived Joshua into making a treaty of protection with them (Josh. 9–10), Gibeon became an Israelite cult center (2 Sam. 21:1–9; 1 Kings 3:4–5; 1 Chron. 16:39–40; 2 Chron. 1:3, 13; etc.).

Gideon   Also called Jerubbaal ("Contender against Baal"), a military judge who delivered Israel from the Midianites (Judg. 6–8). Although Gideon refused to accept a crown (Judg. 8:22–32), his son Abimelech reigned for three years at Shechem (Judg. 9).

Gilboah   A prominent hill on the west side of the Jordan Valley, site of the battle in which the Philistine armies defeated King Saul and killed three of his sons, including Jonathan, thus clearing the way for David to mount Israel's throne (1 Sam. 31; 2 Sam. 1).

Gilead   A rugged highland in central Transjordan located between the Yarmuk and Arnon rivers (Josh. 13; Jer. 8:22; 46:11).

Gilgal   The name of several Old Testament towns, including one located southeast of Jericho where Joshua erected twelve stones symbolic of Israel's twelve tribes (Josh. 4:1–9, 20); the site of the confirmation of Saul's kingship (1 Sam. 11:15; 13:4–15); and a cultic center in southwest Samaria associated with a school of prophets, particularly Elijah and Elisha (2 Kings 2:1–4; 4:38).

Gilgamesh Legendary king of Uruk, hero of the Sumero-Babylonian *Epic of Gilgamesh,* fragments of which date from shortly after 3000 B.C.E., describing his adventures battling Evil and searching for immortality. The Babylonian version incorporates a story of the Flood narrated by Gilgamesh's ancestor Utnapishtim.

glossolalia A religious phenomenon in which a person is inspired to speak in a language not his own. In Acts 2, this emotional "speaking in (foreign) tongues" symbolizes the multinational nature of the early Christian movement.

Gnosticism A movement in early Christianity which taught that salvation was gained through special knowledge (*gnosis*) revealed through a spiritual savior (presumably Jesus) and was the property of an elite few who had been initiated into its mysteries. Gnosticism became a major heresy in the primitive Church, though little is now known about its precise tenets.

Gog The term Ezekiel uses to depict a future leader of Israel's enemies (Ezek. 38) whose attack on the Jerusalem sanctuary will precipitate Yahweh's intervention and the ultimate destruction of the wicked (Rev. 20:8).

Golden Calf (1) An image that the apostate Israelites fashioned out of gold jewelry and other treasures taken from Egypt and which, under Aaron's direction, they worshiped as their deliverer from slavery (Exod. 32: 1–6; Deut. 9:16). (2) Two calf images that Jeroboam I set up at Bethel and Dan as rivals to the Jerusalem sanctuary were probably not revered as idols in themselves but as visible pedestals of the invisibly enthroned Yahweh (1 Kings 12:29).

Goliath The Philistine giant from Gath whom the young David defeated with a slingshot (1 Sam. 17; 2 Sam. 21:19).

Goshen An area in northeastern Egypt where Jacob and his clan settled to escape a Near Eastern famine (Gen. 46:28–34; 47:5–12).

Gospel (1) The Christian message—literally, "good news." (2) The name applied to the literary form of the religious biographies of Jesus, especially Matthew, Mark, Luke, and John.

Gospel of Peter An early noncanonical gospel ascribed incorrectly to Peter. This gospel, which may date from as early as the first century C.E., is the only Gospel that depicts Jesus' actual rising from the tomb during the Resurrection.

Gospel of Thomas A Gnostic collection of approximately 114 sayings attributed to Jesus and allegedly the work of his disciple Didymus Judas Thomas. Although

found in Egypt in 1945 as part of a thirteen-volume work containing forty-nine Coptic-language books dating from the fourth and fifth centuries C.E., it may have been written as early as the last part of the first century C.E.

Habakkuk A prophet of the late seventh or early sixth century B.C.E., perhaps a Levitical temple musician (Hab. 1:1; 3:1, 19), and presumed author of the book bearing his name.

Habiru An ancient Near Eastern term designating people or clans who were outside the urban social and legal structure. The Habiru appear to have been nomads who raided the settled populations during the Amarna Period (fourteenth century B.C.E.) in Palestine. The biblical Hebrews may have been related to this group.

Hades The Greek term for the Underworld, abode of the dead, named for Zeus's brother Hades, god of the nether regions. In the Septuagint Bible, it is used to translate *Sheol,* the Hebrew word for the gloomy subterranean place where all the dead, good and evil alike, were eternally housed (Gen. 42:38; 1 Sam. 2:6; Job 7: 9; Ps. 6:5; Prov. 27:20; Eccles. 9:10; Isa. 38:18; etc.). In the New Testament, *Hades* is also the usual term for the Underworld, although *Gehenna* (often translated "hell") is cited as the place of punishment (Matt. 5:22, 29, 30; 16:18; Mark 9:43, 45, 47; Luke 12:5; Acts 2: 31; Rev. 1:18, 20:14; etc.).

Hagar In Genesis 16, Sarah's Egyptian handmaiden, who bears Abraham's first son, Ishmael. In Genesis 21, the jealous Sarah persuades Abraham to drive Hagar and Ishmael into the wilderness, whence an angel rescues them.

Haggadah Jewish narrative writings dating from the early centuries C.E. illustrate and interpret the nonlegal portions of the Torah (law).

Haggai A postexilic prophet who, with his contemporary Zechariah, urged the restored community of Jerusalem to rebuild the Temple (520 B.C.E.).

Hagiographa A Greek term, meaning "sacred writings," that applies to the third major division of the Hebrew Bible (the Kethuvi'im), encompassing books of poetry, wisdom, late historical books (Chronicles-Ezra), and the apocalypse of Daniel.

Halakah A collection of Jewish interpretations and applications of the Mosaic law dating from the early centuries C.E.; a part of the legal sections of the Talmud.

Ham According to Genesis, a son of Noah (Gen. 5:32; 6:10; 7:13; 9:18, 22) and the father of Canaan (Gen. 9:22), Ham was considered the progenitor of various nations in Phoenicia, Africa, and West Arabia (1 Chron. 8). "The land of Ham" is usually taken to be Egypt (Pss. 78:51; 105:23; etc.).

Haman An official at Ahasuerus's (Xerxes') court who attempted to engineer the mass extermination of the Jews (Esther 3,7).

Hammurabi   Sixth king of Babylon's First Dynasty (1728–1686 B.C.E.) and founder of the first Amorite Empire in Mesopotamia. Hammurabi is best remembered for his law code, inscribed on an eight-foot stone monument in Akkadian cuneiform, whose legal forms resemble those of Hebraic covenant law. *See* Code of Hammurabi.

Hannah   Wife of Elkanah and mother of Samuel (1 Sam. 1). Hannah's lyric prayer (1 Sam. 2:1–10) anticipates the Magnificat of Mary (Luke 1:42–45).

Hanukkah   *See* Feast of Dedication.

Haran   An ancient trade center in northwestern Mesopotamia, about sixty miles above the confluence of the Belikh and Euphrates rivers, Haran was the site of an important moon cult and of Abraham's call to follow Yahweh (Gen. 11:28–12:5, 24). The last refuge of the Assyrians, it was destroyed by the Medes about 606 B.C.E. (Zeph. 2:13–15; Nah. 3:1–3).

hasidim   Devout Jews who refused to forsake their religion during the persecutions of the Syrian monarch Antiochus Epiphanes (second century B.C.E.).

Hasmoneans   The Jewish royal dynasty founded by the Maccabees and named for Hasmon, an ancestor of Mattathias. The Roman conquest of Palestine in 63 B.C.E. brought Hasmonean rulership and Jewish independence to an end.

Hazael   An Aramean official of Damascus who murdered his king, Ben-hadad II, at the prophet Elisha's instigation (2 Kings 8:7–15; see also 1 Kings 19: 15–18), usurped the Syrian kingship, and despoiled parts of Israel and Judah (Amos 1:3; 2 Kings 12; 2 Chron. 22). The name means "God sees."

Hebrew   (1) A member or descendant of one of a group of northwestern Semitic peoples, including the Israelites, Edomites, Moabites and Ammonites. According to Genesis 10:21–31 and 11:15, the Hebrews were descended from Eber, great-grandson of Shem (1 Chron. 1:18; Luke 3:35), and apparently belonged to an Aramean (ancient Syrian) branch of Semites who had originally migrated from Arabia. The Israelites' Aramean ancestry is referred to in the famous creed of Deuteronomy 26:5 (see also Gen. 25:20; 28:5). (2) The Semitic language spoken by the Israelites.

Hebron   An ancient city nineteen miles southwest of Jerusalem (Num. 13:22), located near the sacred oaks of Mamre associated with Abraham (Gen. 13:18; 18; 35: 27), and one of the oldest continuously inhabited sites in Palestine.

Heilsgeschichte   A term from German biblical scholarship, usually translated as "sacred history" or "salvation history," which refers to the fact that Old Testament writers told Israel's story not as an objective series of events but as a confession of faith that their God was operating through the history of his chosen people, directing events in order to save them, or at least those faithful to their covenant relationship.

Hellenism   The influence and adoption of Greek thought, language, values, and culture that began with Alexander the Great's conquest of the eastern Mediterranean world and intensified under his Hellenistic successors and various Roman emperors.

Hellenists   Jews living outside Palestine who adopted the Greek language and, to varying degrees, Greek customs and ideas (Acts 6:1; 9:29).

henotheism   The worship of a single god with a belief that other gods exist. Psalm 82 appears to represent a henotheistic stage of Israelite religion, as do such passages as the victory song in Exodus 15.

heresy   Holding or teaching a religious opinion contrary to Church dogma. Applied to Christianity by its detractors (Acts 24:14), the term was not generally used in its modern sense during New Testament times except in the pastoral Epistles (1 Tim. 1:3; 2; Titus 3:10).

hermeneutics   Study of the methodology of applying the principles and rules of interpreting a biblical text; especially, applying the results of such analysis to a contemporary situation, as one might apply the message of Hosea to modern problems of monogamy and religious faith.

Herod   The name of seven Palestinian rulers.

(1) Herod I (the Great), the Idumean Roman-appointed king of Judea (40–4 B.C.E.), was ruling when Jesus was born (Matt. 2:1). An able administrator who completely reconstructed the Jerusalem Temple, he was notorious for reputed cruelty and was almost universally hated by the Jews.

(2) Herod Antipas, son of Herod I, tetrarch of Galilee (Luke 3:1) and Perea (4 B.C.E.–39 C.E.), is frequently mentioned in the New Testament. Jesus, who called him "that fox" (Luke 13:31–32) and regarded him as a malign influence (Mark 8:15), was tried before him (Luke 9:7, 9; 23:7–15). Antipas was also responsible for executing John the Baptist (Matt. 14:1–12).

(3) Herod Archelaus, ethnarch of Judea, Samaria, so misruled his territory that he was recalled to Rome, an event to which Jesus apparently refers in Luke 19:12–27. Archelaus's evil reputation caused Joseph and Mary to avoid Judea and settle in Nazareth (Matt. 2:22–23).

(4) Herod, a son of Herod the Great and half-brother to Herod Antipas (Matt. 14:3; Mark 6:17).

(5) Herod Philip II, son of Herod the Great and half-brother of Herod Antipas, ruled portions of northeastern Palestine and rebuilt the city of Caesarea Philippi near Mount Hermon (Luke 3:1).

(6) Herod Agrippa I, son of Aristobulus and grandson of Herod the Great, ingratiated himself at the im-

perial court in Rome and, under Claudius, was made king over most of Palestine (41–44 C.E.). A persecutor of Christians, he reportedly died a horrible death immediately after accepting divine honors (Acts 12:1–23).

(7) Herod Agrippa II, son of Herod Agrippa I and great-grandson of Herod the Great, was the first king of Chalcis (50 C.E.) and then of the territory formerly ruled by Philip the Tetrarch, as well as of the adjoining area east of Galilee and the upper Jordan. This was the Herod, together with his sister Bernice, before whom Paul appeared at Caesarea (Acts 25:13–26:32).

Herodians   The name applied to members of an influential political movement in first-century C.E. Judaism who supported Herod's dynasty, particularly that of Herod Antipas. Opposing messianic hopes (Mark 3:6), they conspired with the Pharisees to implicate Jesus in disloyalty to Rome (Mark 12:13; Matt. 22:16).

Herodias   Granddaughter of Herod the Great, daughter of Aristobulus, and half-sister of Herod Agrippa I, Herodias was criticized by John the Baptist for having deserted her first husband for her second, Herod Antipas, who divorced his wife to marry her. In revenge, she demanded the head of John the Baptist (Mark 6:17–29; Matt. 14:1–12; Luke 2:19–20).

Hexateuch   A term meaning "six scrolls" that scholars use to denote the first six books of the Old Testament—the Torah plus the conquest narrative in Joshua—which some experts believe once formed a continuous account (J).

Hezekiah   Son of Ahaz and fourteenth king of Judah (c. 715–686 B.C.E.). Hezekiah ruled during the Assyrian crisis when Sargon II and then Sennacherib overran Palestine. His reign was notable for the prophetic careers of Isaiah and Micah and for sweeping religious reforms, which included purging the Jerusalem Temple of non-Yahwistic elements (2 Kings 18–20; Isa. 22:15–25; 36–39; 2 Chron. 29–32).

hierocracy   A form of government controlled and administered by religious authorities, the term characterizes Jerusalem and Judah followed the return from exile and the rebuilding of the Temple in the late sixth century B.C.E. and after.

hieroglyphic   The ancient Egyptian system of writing in pictorial script.

higher criticism   The branch of biblical scholarship that attempts to analyze biblical writings for the purpose of determining their origins, their literary history, and their authors' purpose and meaning. Unlike lower criticism, which confines itself to studying the written texts to discover (if possible) the authentic words of the original writers or their redactors, higher criticism endeavors to isolate and interpret the religious, political, and historical forces that produced a given book and caused it in many cases to be revised and reedited by later hands. *See* textual criticism.

Hinnom, Valley of   A topographical depression lying south and west of Jerusalem; also called "the Valley of the [Children] of Hinnom" (Jer. 7:32; 2 Chron. 28:3; 2 Kings 23:10, etc.). *See also* Gehenna (a corruption of *Ge-Hinnom*).

Hiram   (1) The name of a series of rulers of Tyre, an ancient Phoenician seaport, with whom David and Solomon engaged in trade and commerce (2 Sam. 5:11; 1 Kings 5:1; 9:11; 1 Chron. 14:1; 2 Chron. 3; Ezek. 26–28). (2) A half-Tyrian, half-Israelite architect and craftsman whom King Hiram sent from Tyre to cast the bronze or copper fixtures and decorations of Solomon's Temple (1 Kings 7:13–51; 2 Chron. 2:13–14; 4:16).

historical criticism   Analyzing a written work by taking into consideration its time and place of composition in order to comprehend the events, dates, personages, and other factual elements mentioned in or influencing the text.

Hittites   Mentioned forty-seven times in the Old Testament either by this name or as descendants of Heth (a grandson of Ham, son of Noah), the Hittites were among the most powerful people in the ancient Near East. A non-Semitic Indo-European group, they formed an older kingdom (c. 1700–1400 B.C.E.) contemporaneous with the Hebrew patriarchal period (Gen. 23), as well as a later "new kingdom" (c. 1400–1200 B.C.E.). Archaeologists have found remains of their cities in Asia Minor (central Anatolia), northern Mesopotamia, Syria, and Palestine, where the Pentateuch and Joshua list them among the nations occupying Canaan (Gen. 15:20; Exod. 3:8; Deut. 7:1; 20:17; Josh. 3:10, 11:3; 24:11).

The Hebrews from Abraham to Solomon had various commercial and political relations with the Hittites (Gen. 23:1–18; 26:34; Josh. 1:4; Judg. 3:5–6; 2 Sam. 11:2–27; 1 Kings 9:20–22; 11:1; 2 Kings 7:6; 2 Chron. 1:17; 8:7–9; Ezek. 16:3, 45). About 1200 B.C.E., however, the Hittite Kingdom in Asia Minor fell to an invading Aegean people, probably Thracians and Phrygians. The Hittites centered near Carchemish in northern Syria were defeated by Sargon II in 717 B.C.E. and absorbed into the Assyrian Empire.

Holiness Code   The name given to the body of laws and regulations set forth in Leviticus 17–26 derives from the code's emphasis on holiness (separateness, religious purity) of behavior, which was to distinguish Israel and set its people apart from the rest of the world.

Holy of Holies   In Hebrew, a superlative referring to the Most Holy Place, the innermost room of the tabernacle and Temple, where Yahweh was believed to be invisibly present.

Holy Spirit, the   The presence of God active in human life, a concept most explicitly set forth in John 14:16–26 and in the Pentecost miracle depicted in Acts 2. The Old Testament speaks of "the spirit of God" (based on the Hebrew word for "wind" or "breath") as the force that created the universe (Gen. 1:2; Job 26:13; Ps. 104:29–30) and that inspires humans to prophesy and otherwise carry out the divine will (Exod. 31:3; Judg. 3:10; 1 Sam. 16:13–14; Isa. 61:1–3; Joel 2:28–30). In post–New Testament times, the Holy Spirit was declared to be the Third Person in the Trinity (Matt. 28:19–20).

Horeb, Mount   The name that the E and D traditions use for the mountain in the Sinai desert at which Moses received Yahweh's law (Exod. 17:6; 33:6; Deut. 1:2, 6, 19; 4:10, 15; also Ps. 106:19). Called Sinai in the J and P sources, its exact location is unknown. According to 1 Kings 19:1–21, Elijah fled there to renew his prophetic inspiration.

Hosea   An eighth-century prophet active in the northern kingdom from before the death of Jeroboam II (d. about 746 B.C.E.) until shortly before its fall to Assyria in 721 B.C.E.; the source of the Book of Hosea, first in the printed list of Minor Prophets.

Hoshea (Hosea)   Last king of Israel (732–724 B.C.E.).

Huldah   A woman prophet associated with King Josiah's royal court in Jerusalem who pronounced on the authenticity of a "book of law" thought to be an early form of Deuteronomy. In the biblical record, she is the first person to decide on the authority of a scriptural document and thus stands at the head of the canonizing process (2 Kings 22; 2 Chronicles 34).

Hyksos   The Egyptian name (perhaps meaning "rulers of foreign lands") for a racially mixed but largely Semitic group that infiltrated and overran Egypt about 1720–1570 B.C.E., establishing the Fifteenth and Sixteenth Dynasties; themselves expelled by the Theban kings Kamose and Ahmose I, who founded the native Egyptian Eighteenth Dynasty. Some scholars believe that the Hebrews entered Egypt during the friendly rule of the Semitic Hyksos and were enslaved when the native Egyptians returned to power.

Hyrcanus   Name of John I, son of Simon Maccabeus, Hasmonean king and high priest of Judah (134–104 B.C.E.). John II (63–40 B.C.E.), a high priest and puppet ruler installed by Rome, was succeeded by Herod the Great.

Idumea   The name, meaning "pertaining to Edom," that the Greeks and Romans applied to the country of Edom, Judah's southern neighbor; the home of Herod the Great (Mark 3:8; 1 Macc. 4:29; 5:65).

Immanuel   The name ("God is with us") that Isaiah gave to a child whose birth he predicted as a sign to King Ahaz during the Syro-Ephraimite War (late eighth century B.C.E.). Although not presented as a messianic prophecy, it was nevertheless interpreted as such (Mic. 5:3; Matt. 1:22–23).

Incarnation   The Christian doctrine asserting that the prehuman Son of God became flesh, the man Jesus of Nazareth, to reveal the divine will to humanity—a doctrine based largely on the Logos hymn that opens the fourth Gospel (John 1:1–18, especially 1:14; see also Col. 1:15–20; 2:9–15; Phil. 2:5–11; Heb. 1:1–4; 2:14–18).

Infancy Gospel of Thomas   A noncanonical gospel that dates from the mid-second century C.E. and is ascribed to the apostle Thomas. This work provides a fictional account of Jesus' youth.

Isaac   Son of Abraham and Sarah (Gen. 21:1–7), child of the covenant promise by which Abraham's descendants would bring a blessing to all the earth's families (Gen. 17:15–22; 18:1–15) but whom Yahweh commanded to be sacrificed to him (Gen. 18:1–18). Reprieved by an angel, Isaac marries Rebekah (Gen. 24:1–67), who bears him twin sons, Esau and Jacob (Gen. 25:19–26), the latter of whom tricks his dying father into bestowing the firstborn's birthright on him (Gen. 27:1–45). Paul interprets the near-sacrifice of Isaac as an allegory of Christ (Gal. 4:21–31).

Isaiah   An eighth-century prophet and counselor of Judean kings, Isaiah of Jerusalem was active during the reigns of Uzziah, Jothan, Ahaz, and Hezekiah (collectively, 783–687 B.C.E.) (Isa. 1:1; 6:1; 7:1–12; 38:1–6). Oracles attributed to this historical figure are found in Isaiah 1–39, particularly in Chapters 1–11, 20, 22, and 28–31. (Chapters 24–27, 33–35, and 36–39 are thought to be by other hands.) Second Isaiah, who lived during the Babylonian exile (587–538 B.C.E.), contributed Chapters 40–55. Third Isaiah, whose work is found in Chapters 56–66, lived during the postexilic period. A complete text of Isaiah, possibly dating from the second century B.C.E., was found among the Dead Sea Scrolls.

Ishmael   The son of Abraham and Sarah's Egyptian handmaiden Hagar (Gen. 16), Ishmael and his mother were exiled to the desert, where an angel rescued them (Gen. 21). Cited as the eponymous ancestor of twelve princes (Gen. 25:12–16), he is also regarded as the progenitor of the Arabs and a forefather of Mohammed, founder of Islam. In Galatians 4:21–31, Ishmael son of a slave woman, is compared to the Jerusalem of Paul's day.

Ishmaelites   The name the J sources apply to caravan merchants trading with Egypt (Gen. 37:25–28; 39:1) but whom the E document calls Midianites (Gen. 37:28, 36). Although the twelve tribes of Ishmael were a populous nation (Gen. 17:20), the biblical record seldom refers to them.

Ishtar   Goddess of love and war in the Assyrian and Babylonian religions; prototype of later fertility and erotic deities such as Ashtoreth, Aphrodite, and Venus (Jer. 44).

Isis   Ancient Egyptian goddess, wife of Osiris and mother of Harus, who was worshiped from prehistoric to Roman times. As a beneficent mother who protected her devotees, Isis was pictured in Egyptian art as a madonna with child, an iconography that influenced later Christian portraits of Mary and the baby Jesus.

Israel   (1) The name given Jacob by an angel in Transjordan (Gen. 32:28, J source) and by Yahweh at Bethel (Gen. 35:10, P source). Although interpreted as "he has been strong against God" (Gen. 32:28), it probably means "may God show his strength" or "may God rule." (2) The Israelite nation descended from the twelve sons of Jacob (Israel); the covenant people chosen at Sinai. (3) The northern kingdom as opposed to the southern state of Judah during the period of the divided monarchies (922–721 B.C.E.).

Issachar   Son of Jacob and Leah (Gen. 30:14–18), the eponymous progenitor of the inland tribe bearing his name (Gen. 49:14–15; Josh. 19:17–23; Deut. 33:18–19; Num. 1:29; 26:25; 1 Chron. 7:2).

J   *See* Yahwist.

Jabal   According to Genesis 4:20, a son of Lamech and Adah whom the J source regards as the progenitor of itinerant tent dwellers and keepers of livestock.

Jabesh-gilead   An Old Testament city built in the rugged country east of the Jordan River, destroyed by Israelites who resented the town's failure to send representatives to a tribal assembly at Mizpah (Judg. 21:8–14). Men from this city rescued the decapitated body of Saul from the Philistines (1 Sam. 11; 31:12; 1 Chron. 10:11–12), for which courageous feat David rewarded them (2 Sam. 2:5–7).

Jachin and Boaz   Names that Hiram, a half-Phoenician craftsman, gave to the twin pillars of copper decorating the entrance to Solomon's Temple (1 Kings 7:13–22; 2 Chron. 3:17). Their exact appearance, religious function and significance, and the meaning of their names are conjectural.

Jacob   The younger of twin sons born to Isaac and Rebekah (Gen. 25:21–26), Jacob is famous for his shrewdness, opportunism, and craftiness. He stole his brother Esau's birthright and Isaac's blessing (Gen. 25:29–34; 27:1–29), acquired great wealth in stock breeding (Gen. 29–30), and absconded with his father-in-law's household gods (Gen. 31:1–21) but later concluded a covenant with him (Gen. 31:22–25). Jacob was also the recipient of several divine visitations: the dream vision of a ladder to heaven at Bethel (Gen. 28) and wrestling with a divine being at Jabbok, Transjordan, after which his name was changed to Israel (Gen.

32:24–32; 33:4), a revelation renewed at Bethel (Gen. 35:1–15).

Father of twelve sons, eponymous ancestors of Israel's twelve tribes (Gen. 46:1–27), Jacob suffered in old age largely because of the temporary loss of his favorite children, Joseph (Gen. 37:2–36) and Benjamin (Gen. 43:1–14), and other filial problems reflected in his deathbed blessings (Gen. 49:1–28). In accordance with his wishes, he was buried in a cave near Mamre, which his grandfather Abraham had purchased from a Hittite (Gen. 49:29–33; 50:7–13).

Jael   Wife of Heber the Kenite (member of a nomadic tribe of metal workers), who offered hospitality to Sisera, the Canaanite general, and then murdered him, thus becoming a national heroine in Israel (Judg. 4:11–22; 5:24–31).

Jairus   The head of a synagogue in Galilee who asked Jesus to heal his dying child, for which act of faith he was rewarded with the girl's miraculous cure (Luke 8:41–42, 49–56; Mark 5:35–43; Matt. 9:18–20, 23–26).

James

(1) Son of Zebedee, brother of John, and one of the twelve apostles (Mark 1:19–20; 3:17; Matt. 4:21–22; 10:2; Luke 5:10; 6:14). A Galilean fisherman, he left his trade to follow Jesus and, with John and Peter, became a member of his inner circle. He was among the three disciples present at the Transfiguration (Mark 9:2–10; Matt. 17:1–9; Luke 9:28–36) and was at Jesus' side during the last hours before his arrest (Mark 14:32–42; Matt. 26:36–45). James and John used their intimacy to request a favored place in the messianic kingdom, thus arousing the other apostles' indignation (Mark 10:35–45). James was beheaded when Herod Agrippa I persecuted the Jerusalem church (41–44 C.E.) (Acts 12:2).

(2) James, son of Alphaeus and Mary (Acts 1:13; Mark 16:1), one of the Twelve (Matt. 10:3–4), called "the less" or "the younger" (Mark 15:40).

(3) James, the eldest of Jesus' three "brothers" (or close male relatives) named in the Gospels (Mark 6:3; Matt. 13:55), first opposed Jesus' work (Matt. 12:46–50; Mark 3:31–35; Luke 8:19–21; John 7:3–5) but was apparently converted by one of Jesus' post-resurrection appearances (1 Cor. 15:7) and became a leader in the Jerusalem church (Acts 15:13–34; 21:18–26). According to legend, a Nazirite and upholder of the Mosaic law, he was known as James "the righteous." James apparently clashed with Paul over the latter's policy of absolving Gentile converts from circumcision and other legalistic requirements (Gal. 1:18–2:12). The reputed author of the New Testament Epistle of James, he was martyred at Jerusalem in the early 60s C.E.

Jamnia   Coastal village in Palestine. *See* Academy of Jamnia.

Jamnia, Academy of   An assembly of eminent Palestinian rabbis and Pharisees held about 90 C.E. in the coastal village of Jamnia (Yabneh) to define and guide Judaism following the Roman destruction of Jerusalem and its Temple. According to tradition, a leading Pharisee named Yohanan ben Zakkai had escaped from the besieged city by simulating death and being carried out in a coffin by his disciples. Yohanan, who had argued that saving human lives was more important than success in the national rebellion against Rome, was given Roman support to set up an academy to study Jewish law. Under his direction, the Pharisees not only preserved the Torah traditions but also apparently formulated what was to become the official biblical canon of Palestinian Judaism. Out of the deliberations at Jamnia came the authoritative list of books in the Writings, the third major division of the Hebrew Bible.

Japheth   According to Genesis 5:32; 6:10; 9:18, and 10:1, one of Noah's three sons, the eponymous ancestor of various Indo-European nations, especially Aegean Sea peoples, including the Greeks (Ionians) and Philistines (Gen. 10:1–5).

Jashar, Book of   Apparently a collection of Hebrew poetry (since lost), quoted in Joshua 10:12–13; 2 Samuel 1:18, and 1 Kings 8:53 (Septuagint version only).

Javan   According to Genesis 10:4–5, the fourth son of Japheth and progenitor of the Ionian Greeks and other coastal and island peoples of the northeastern Mediterranean (1 Chron. 1:5, 7).

JE   The designation scholars give the hypothetical document uniting J's (the Yahwist's) account of Israel's beginnings with E's (the Elohist's) parallel narrative. After the northern kingdom of Israel fell to Assyria in 721 B.C.E., refugees may have brought the E document south to Jerusalem, where it was combined with the older J to produce JE, thus preserving E's northern tribal stories about the national ancestors and Exodus.

Jebus   The city held by Jebusites, an ancient Canaanite tribe (Gen. 10:16; Josh. 11:3; 1 Chron. 1:14; Ezek. 16:3), which later became Jerusalem, it may have been the same town called Urusalim ("city of peace") in the Amarna letters and called Salem, city of Melchizedek, in Genesis 14:18–20 (see also Josh. 18:16, 28; Judg. 19:10; 1 Chron. 11:14). David captured the city and made it his capital (2 Sam. 5:7–9; 6–10; 1 Chron. 11:4–9), placed the Ark of the Covenant there (2 Sam. 6:4–5), and purchased from a Jebusite an ancient stone threshing floor (2 Sam. 24:16–24; 1 Chron. 21:15–28) that became the site of Solomon's Temple (1 Kings 6: 1–8:66).

Jeduthun   The representative leader or eponymous founder of a guild of Temple singers and musicians (1 Chron. 25:1, 3, 6; 16:40–42) who provided music for services at the Jerusalem sanctuary. This group offici-

ated during the reigns of Solomon (1 Chron. 5:12–13), Hezekiah (2 Chron. 29:14), and Josiah, whose magnificent revival of the Passover liturgies they helped celebrate (2 Chron. 35:15–16). Jeduthun's name appears in the superscriptions of Psalms 39, 62, and 77 and among the list of exiles returned to Jerusalem from Babylon (Neh. 11:17).

Jehoiachin   King of Judah (598/597 B.C.E.), son and successor of Jehoiakim. After inheriting the throne at age eight and reigning for only three months and ten days, he was taken captive to Babylon (2 Kings 24:10–12; 2 Chron. 36:9–10), where he remained the rest of his life. Babylonian records indicate that he was at first accorded favored status but later imprisoned until Nebuchadnezzar's successor, Evil-merodach (Amel-Marduk), released him (562 B.C.E.) and honored him above other captive kings (2 Kings 25:27–30; Jer. 52: 31–34).

Jehoiakim   Second son of Josiah, Jehoiakim was made king of Judah about 609 B.C.E., when Pharaoh Necho of Egypt placed him on the throne, deposing his brother Jehoahaz who had reigned only three months (2 Kings 23:34; 2 Chron. 36:4). Another brother, Zedekiah, replaced Jehoiakim's heir, Jehoiachin, to become Judah's last Davidic monarch. The Deuteronomistic historians, the Chronicler, and the prophet Jeremiah all denounced his religious apostasy and misguided attempts to combat Babylonian domination with Egyptian alliances (2 Kings 23:36–24:6; 2 Chron. 36:5–8; Jer. 25–26; 36). Ignoring Jeremiah's advice (Jer. 36: 1–26), Jehoiakim died or was assassinated before paying the consequences of his rebellion against Babylon (2 Kings 24:6). The Chronicler states that he was chained and carried off to Babylon (2 Chron. 36:6–7), but this was the fate of his son and heir, Jehoiachin (2 Kings 24: 12–16; 2 Chron. 36:10).

Jehonadab   Son of Rechab the Kenite (1 Chron. 2:55), he assisted Jehu in massacring King Ahab's family and slaughtering Baal worshipers in Israel (2 Kings 10: 14–27). According to Jeremiah 35:1–19, he was a nomadic ascetic who condemned drinking wine, planting vineyards, cultivating fields, or building cities. His support of Jehu's fanatical Yahwism may have been in part a revolt against Ahab's urban culture.

Jehoram   (1) A son of Ahab and king of Israel (849–842 B.C.E.) who enlisted King Jehoshaphat's help in quelling Moab's rebellion against paying Israel tribute (2 Kings 3:1–27). Jehu later murdered him (2 Kings 8: 25–29; 9:22–26). (2) Son of Jehoshaphat and king of Judah (839–842 B.C.E.), he married Ahab's daughter Athaliah and fostered the religion of Baal in Judah (2 Kings 8:16–24; 2 Chron. 21:1–20). His reign was marked by wars with the Arabs and Philistines and by the loss of Judah's control of Edom. The name means "Yahweh is exalted."

Jehoshaphat   Son of Asa and king of Judah (873–849 B.C.E.), his name means "Yahweh judges." Although the Deuteronomistic historians give him short shrift (1 Kings 15:24; 22:41–51), the Chronicler emphasizes the general success of his twenty-four-year reign (2 Chron. 17:1–21:1), which was marked by important religious reforms, effective wars against Edom, Moab, and Ammon (2 Chron. 20:1–30), and the achievement of relative political security and prosperity for his people.

Jehovah   An English rendering of the divine name created by adding the vowels of *Elohim* and *Adonai* to the four consonants (YHWH) of the Tetragrammaton, the term entered the language via a Roman-Catholic Latin translation about 1518 C.E., though the name *Yahweh* is considered a more accurate rendition of the Hebrew original.

Jehu   A son of Jehoshaphat (not the king of Judah) whom the prophet Elisha had anointed king of Israel in 842 B.C.E. (2 Kings 9:1–3), fulfilling an earlier command of Elijah (1 Kings 19:16–17). Thus commissioned by Israel's prophetic guild, Jehu proceeded to slaughter Ahab's family and all connected with it (2 Kings 9: 14–10:27), including King Jehoram, King Ahaziah of Judah and his forty-two sons, Queen Jezebel, Ahab's seventy sons, and numerous other Israelites who worshiped Baal. Jehu's long reign (842–815 B.C.E.) saw Israel's territory shrink to a fraction of what it had been under Omri and Ahab (2 Kings 10:32–33). Although he murdered in Yahweh's name, his actions were condemned by the prophet Hosea (Hos. 1:3–5). Nor was he a wholehearted Yahwist (2 Kings 10:31), though his name means "Yahweh is He."

Jephthah   The son of Gilead and a harlot, Jephthah was driven as a youth from the area of Gilead by his legitimate brothers (Judg. 11:1–3) but was recalled by Gilead's elders when the Ammonites attacked Israel. An effective military leader, he defeated the Ammonites and was judge (general) in Israel for six years (Judg. 12: 7). Best known for vowing to make a burnt offering of the first person he met after the battle if Yahweh would grant him victory, he presumably immolated his own daughter, who had come to congratulate him on his success (Judg. 11:29–40; see 2 Kings 3:27). The author of Hebrews praises him for his faith (Heb. 11:32).

Jeremiah   One of Israel's greatest prophets, Jeremiah warned Jerusalem and its kings of their misdeeds and of coming doom by the Babylonians for approximately forty years (c. 627–587 B.C.E.) (Jer. 1:1–3). Beginning in the thirteenth year of Josiah's reign (640–609 B.C.E.), he also prophesied during the reigns of Jehoiakim (609–598 B.C.E.), Jehoiachin (598/597 B.C.E.) and Zedekiah (597–587 B.C.E.), continuing after Jerusalem's fall (587 B.C.E.) and during a forced exile in Egypt (Jer. 40–44).

Although usually ignored by the royal family, persecuted by both government officials and his compatriots for his unpopular (and seemingly treasonous) message that Yahweh had forsaken Judah and determined its annihilation, Jeremiah persisted in attacking official policy and denouncing those who trusted in the Temple (Jer. 1:11; 15; 21–22; 25–28; 36–38). After Jerusalem's fall, he was treated well by the Babylonians (Jer. 39–40), but his fellow survivors forcibly transported him to Egypt (Jer. 42–44). His message is known for its promise of a new covenant and a restoration of Judah (Jer. 30–33).

Jericho   One of the world's oldest cities, Jericho's ruins lie near an oasis on the west side of the south Jordan River Valley. Partly excavated by archaeologists, its earliest occupation dates to about 7800 B.C.E. Although according to Joshua 2 and 5:13–6:26 its fortified walls crumbled when the Israelites marched around the city, radiocarbon dating indicates that the site was already abandoned at the time of the conquest (thirteenth century B.C.E.). Jericho was partly rebuilt by Hiel of Bethel during Ahab's reign (869–850 B.C.E.) (1 Kings 16:34), but no evidence of this occupation remains. It was extensively rebuilt during Herod's day (40–4 B.C.E.) and is mentioned several times in the New Testament (Matt. 20:29; Mark 10:46; Luke 10:30; 18:35; 19:1; Heb. 11:30).

Jeroboam I   An Ephraimite who led the ten northern tribes' secession from the Davidic monarchy and became the first ruler of the northern kingdom (1 Kings 11:26–12:33). Jeroboam I reigned from approximately 922–901 B.C.E. His first capital was Shechem, site of the old tribal confederacy (Josh. 24), but he later moved his administration to Tirzah, his former home and an ancient Canaanite royal sanctuary (1 Kings 12: 24–25). The Deuteronomistic historians condemned Jereboam I for establishing rival Yahwist shrines at Bethel and Dan to compete with the Yahwist Temple at Jerusalem, and they condemned him for tolerating the worship of such foreign deities as Chemosh, Ashtoreth, and the Ammonite Milcom (1 Kings 11:33; 12: 26–13:34).

Jeroboam II   A descendant of Jehu, son of King Jehonash, and ruler of Israel (786–746 B.C.E.) whose long reign brought relative peace and material prosperity to the northern kingdom, Jeroboam II won major victories over Ben-hadad, king of Syria, and extended Israel's territory so that it included almost all the territory over which David and Solomon had ruled, except Judah. The Deuteronomistic account of his reign (2 Kings 14:23–29) gives no indication of its importance. The prophets Amos and Hosea, who were active during the time of Jeroboam II, denounced the country's economic oppression of the poor as well as its widespread materialism.

Jerome   Eminent Christian scholar and teacher (347–419/420 C.E.) known for his translation of the Bible into Latin. *See* Vulgate.

Jerusalem   An ancient Palestinian holy city, sometimes identified with the Salem of Genesis 14:17–20 but more often with Jebus, a city of the Jebusite tribe (Josh. 18:28; Judg. 19:10), Jerusalem became King David's capital after he had captured it from the Jebusites (2 Sam. 5:6–10; 2 Chron. 4:5). Solomon centralized the worship of Yahweh on a hill called Zion there (1 Kings 5–7; 2 Chron. 2–4), and Jerusalem remained the capital of Judah after the secession of the northern tribes (922 B.C.E.). The city suffered three major destructions: in 587 B.C.E. when the Babylonians razed Solomon's Temple; in 70 C.E. when the Romans destroyed the city and its Herodian Temple; and in 135 C.E. when the Romans decimated the city for the last time.

Jerusalem church   According to Luke-Acts, the original center of Christianity from which the "new Way" spread outward to "the ends of the earth" (Acts 1–15). Inspired by the Spirit at Pentecost, the Jerusalem believers formed a commune led by three "pillars"—Peter (Cephas), John, and James, Jesus' kinsman (Acts 2–3; Gal. 1:18–2:10).

Jesse   The son of Obed and grandson of Ruth and Boaz (Ruth 4:17, 22), Jesse was a Judean shepherd and father of seven or eight sons, including David (1 Sam 16:10–11; 17:12; 1 Chron. 2:12–17) who became king of Israel. He is mentioned in the messianic prophecies of Isaiah 11:1, 10, and in Matthew's and Luke's genealogies of Jesus (Matt. 1:5–6; Luke 3:32; see also Rom. 15:12).

Jesus   The English form of a Latin name derived from the Greek *Iesous,* which translated the Hebrew *Jeshua,* a late version of *Jehoshua* or *Joshua,* meaning "Yahweh is salvation." The name was borne by several biblical figures, including Joshua, leader of the conquest of Canaan; an ancestor of Jesus Christ (Luke 3:29); and a Jewish Christian, also called Justus (Col. 4:11). It appears several times in the Apocrypha, notably as the name of the author of Ecclesiasticus, Jesus ben Sirach.

Jesus Christ   The name and title given the firstborn son of Mary and Joseph (the child's legal father), the one whom Christians regard as the Spirit-begotten Son of God and Savior of the world. According to Matthew 1:21 and Luke 1:31, he received the name Jesus because he was to "save his people from their sins." The term *Christ* is not a proper name but the English version of the Greek *Christos,* a translation of the Aramaic *Meshiha* and the Hebrew *Mashiah* ("Messiah," "the Anointed One"). Although we know almost nothing about the historical Jesus, the New Testament presents a thorough documentation of what the early Christian community believed about the historical Christ.

Jesus Seminar   A group of about 100 leading New Tes-tament scholars in North America who are attempting to reconstruct Jesus' actual teachings in Scripture. Among their contribution to biblical scholarship is their work, *The Five Gospels: The Search for the Authentic Words of Jesus* (1993).

Jethro   A shepherd and priest of the Kenites, a Midianite tribe of coppersmiths, with whom Moses took refuge during his flight from Egypt and whose daughter Zipporah he married (Exod. 2:15–22; 18:1–12). Moses apparently identified Jethro's god, El Shaddai, with Yahweh, god of the Israelites (Exod. 3; 6; 18).

Jew   Originally a member of the tribe or kingdom of Judah (2 Kings 16:6; 25:25), the term later included any Hebrew who returned from Babylonian captivity and finally encompassed Hebrews scattered throughout the world (Esther 2:5; Matt. 2:2). Some New Testament writers refer to "the Jews" as any Israelites opposing Christianity (John 1:19; 5:16, 18:20; Acts 14:19; 16:20; 1 Cor. 1:23; Rev. 2:9).

Jezebel   Daughter of King Ethbaal of Tyre and wife of King Ahab, Jezebel promulgated Baal worship in Israel and persecuted Yahweh's prophets (1 Kings 16:29–33; 18:4, 19; 19:1–3). After she perverted the Mosaic law to confiscate Naboth's vineyard (1 Kings 21:1–16), Elijah predicted her shameful death (1 Kings 21:24–26), a prophecy fulfilled when Jehu threw her body for dogs to eat during his bloody purge of Ahab's dynasty (2 Kings 9:30–37). In Revelation 2:20, she is a symbol of false religion.

Jezreel   (1) A fertile valley, known as the Plain of Esdraelon, extending southeast across Palestine from north of Mount Carmel to the Jordan River. (2) A fortified city and the site of Naboth's vineyard (1 Kings 21:1–24) and of Jehu's murders of King Joram, of the Queen-mother Jezebel (2 Kings 9:24, 30–37), and of all Ahab's heirs (2 Kings 10:1–11).

Joab   A son of Zeruiah, half-sister of David (2 Sam. 2:18), Joab was the cruelly efficient commander-in-chief of David's armies who managed the capture of Jerusalem (2 Sam. 5:8; 1 Chron. 11:6–8) and successful wars against the Syrians, Ammonites, and Edomites (2 Sam. 12:26–31; 1 Kings 11:15–17). He murdered Abner, general of the northern tribes under Saul's heir, Ishbaal (2 Sam. 2:18–23; 3:22–30); arranged Uriah's death so that David could marry Bathsheba (2 Sam. 11:6–21); reconciled David and Absalom (2 Sam. 14:28–33) but later murdered David's rebellious son (2 Sam. 18:9–17); and supported the wrong contender for David's throne (1 Kings 1:5–33), for which he was executed early in Solomon's reign (1 Kings 2:28–34), supposedly on David's deathbed advice (1 Kings 2:5–6).

Joanna   Wife of Chuza, an administrator in Herod Antipas's Jerusalem household, who became a follower of Jesus (Luke 8:3) and was among the women who discovered his empty tomb (Luke 23:55–24:11).

Joash (Jehoash)   The name of several Old Testament figures. (1) Judge Gideon's father (Judg. 6:11, 31–32). (2) A son of King Ahab (1 Kings 22:26–27; 2 Chron. 18:25–26). (3) The eighth king of Judah (c. 837–800 B.C.E.), a son of Ahaziah, who reduced Baal worship and repaired the Temple but later had to forfeit some of its treasures to pay Hazael, king of Aram, who besieged Jerusalem. Joash's reign, including the machinations of his grandmother, the Queen-regent Athaliah, is recorded in 2 Kings 11–12; 13:10–13; and 2 Chronicles 22:11–24:27. (4) The twelfth king of Israel, third of the Jehu dynasty, who recovered some of the Israelite territory that his predecessors had lost to Syria, defeated King Amaziah of Judah, and transported some of the Temple's treasures from Jerusalem to Samaria (2 Kings 13:1–25; 14:8–16; 2 Chron. 25:18–19).

Job   The name apparently dates from the second millennium B.C.E. and may mean "one who comes back to God," a penitent. It may derive from the Hebrew *ayab,* "to be hostile," denoting one whom God makes his enemy. The central character of the wisdom book bearing his name, Job is linked with Noah and Daniel as a person of exemplary righteousness (Ezek. 14:14, 20). All three of Ezekiel's heroes were non-Israelite; Job was probably an Edomite.

Joel   Although numerous biblical figures bore this name (meaning "Yahweh is God"), the best known is the son of Pethuel (Joel 1:1), a prophet of postexilic Judah (perhaps about 350 B.C.E.).

John the Apostle   A son of Zebedee and brother of the apostle James, John was a Galilean fisherman whom Jesus called to be among his twelve most intimate followers (Mark 1:19–20; Matt. 4:21–22). Jesus called James and John *Boanerges* ("sons of thunder"), possibly because of their impetuous temperaments (Mark 3:17; 9:38; Luke 9:52–56). Always among the first four in the Gospel lists of the Twelve (Mark 3:14–17; Matt. 10:2; Luke 6:3–14), John was present at the Transfiguration (Matt. 17:1; Mark 9:2; Luke 9:28) and at Gethsemane (Matt. 26:37; Mark 14:33). Tradition identifies him with the "beloved disciple" (John 13:23; 21:20) and as the author of the Gospel of John, a premise that most scholars believe is impossible to prove. Along with Peter and James, he was one of the triple "pillars" of the Jerusalem church (Acts 1:13; 3:1–4:22; 8:14–17; Gal. 2:9). He may have been martyred under Herod Agrippa, although a late second-century tradition states that he lived to old age in Ephesus.

John the Baptist   The son of Zechariah, a priest, and Elisabeth (Luke 1:5–24, 56–80), John was an ascetic who preached the imminence of judgment and baptized converts in the Jordan River as a symbol of their repentance from sin (Matt. 3:1–12; Mark 1:2–8; Luke 3:1–18). The Gospel writers viewed him as an Elijah figure and forerunner of the Messiah (Luke 1:17; Matt. 11:12–14; John 1:15, 9–34; 3:22–36) who baptized Jesus but also recognized his superiority (Matt. 3:13–17; Mark 1:9–11; Luke 3:21–22). When imprisoned by Herod Antipas, he inquired whether Jesus were the expected "one who is to come." Jesus' answer was equivocal but he praised John's work as fulfilling prophecy (Matt. 11:2–19; Luke 7:24–35). At his stepdaughter Salome's request, Herod had John beheaded (Matt. 14:6–12; Mark 6:17–29). Some of John's disciples later became Christians (John 1:37; Acts 18:25).

John of Patmos   The author of Revelation, exiled to the Aegean island of Patmos where he experienced visions of heaven and End time (Rev. 1:1, 4, 9; 22:8). He is not to be confused with the apostle John, son of Zebedee and brother of James.

Jonah   A son of Amittai, a Zebulunite from Gath-hepher whom Yahweh sent as prophet to warn Nineveh of its impending doom (Jon. 1:1–16). The "sign of Jonah," who was reputedly delivered from death inside a sea monster (Jon. 1:17–2:10), is cited in the Synoptics as prophetic of Jesus' death and resurrection (Matt. 12:40; 16:4; Luke 11:29–30).

Jonathan   Son and heir of King Saul (1 Sam. 13:16; 14:49; 1 Chron. 8:33) and famous for his unselfish devotion to young David (1 Sam. 18:1–5; 19:1–7; 20:1–21:1; 23:15–18). Along with his father, Jonathan was killed by the Philistines at the Battle of Gilboa (1 Sam. 31:1; 2 Sam. 1:16), a loss David lamented in one of his most moving psalms (2 Sam. 1:17–27).

Joppa   An important harbor of ancient Palestine, located on the Mediterranean coast about thirty-five miles northwest of Jerusalem and now a suburb of Tel Aviv (1 Macc. 10:76; 12:33–34; 13:11; 14:5, 34; 2 Macc. 12:3–4). It was in Joppa that Peter resurrected Tabitha (Acts 9:43) and experienced his vision welcoming Gentiles into the Church (Acts 10:1–48).

Jordan River   The main river of Palestine, which occupies a deep north-south rift valley connecting the Sea of Galilee with the Dead Sea (a distance of about sixty-five miles) and forms the boundary between east and west Palestine. The Jordan is mentioned in the narratives concerning Lot, Abraham, and Jacob (Gen. 13:10; 14:12–16; 32:10) but is best known as the last barrier Israel crossed before entering Canaan—an event marked by a miraculous stopping of the river's flow (Josh. 3:1–5:1)—and as the site of John the Baptist's activity (Matt. 3:5; Mark 1:5; Luke 3:3), including the baptism of Jesus (Matt. 3:13–17; Mark 1:9–11; Luke 3:21–22). Naaman was cured of leprosy by bathing in the Jordan (2 Kings 5:10–14).

Joseph

(1) The son of Jacob and Rachel, who aroused his ten brothers' jealousy, was sold into slavery and taken to Egypt where, aided by his ability to interpret dreams, he rose to power second only to that of

pharaoh himself. His story is told in Genesis 30: 22–24; and Genesis 37–50. The name *Joseph* is used to represent the combined tribes of Ephraim and Manasseh (Josh. 16:1–4) and the northern kingdom (Ps. 80).

(2) The husband of Mary and legal father of Jesus, a descendant of the Bethlehemite David (Matt. 1:20) but who lived in Nazareth (Luke 2:4) where he was a carpenter (Matt. 13:55). Little is known of him except for his piety (Luke 2:21–24, 41–42) and his wish to protect his betrothed wife from scandal (Luke 2:1–5). Because he does not appear among Jesus' family members during his (supposed) son's public ministry, it is assumed that he died before Jesus began his preaching career (Matt. 1:18–2:23; 13:55–56).

(3) Joseph of Arimathaea, a wealthy member of the Sanhedrin and, according to John 19:38, a secret follower of Jesus who claimed Jesus' crucified body from Pilate for burial in his private garden tomb (Matt. 27:57–60; Mark 15:42–46; Luke 23:50–53; John 19:38–42).

Josephus, Flavius   An important Jewish historian (c. 37–100 C.E.) whose two major works—*Antiquities of the Jews* and *The Jewish Wars* (covering the revolt against Rome, 66–73 C.E.)—provide valuable background material for first-century Judaism and the early Christian period.

Joshua   The son of Nun, an Ephraimite, Joshua ("Yahweh is salvation") was Moses' military assistant (Exod. 17:8–13), in charge of the tabernacle (Exod. 33:11), one of the two spies optimistic about Israel's prospects of conquering Canaan (Num. 13:1–16; 14:6–9), and chosen to succeed Moses (Num. 27:18–23; Deut. 3: 28; 31:23; 34:9). He led the Israelites across the Jordan (Josh. 3), captured Jericho (Josh. 6) and Ai (Josh. 7–8), warred against the Canaanite kings (Josh. 10–12), allotted the land to various tribes (Josh. 13:1–22:8), and made a covenant with Yahweh and the people (Josh. 24).

Josiah   Son of Amon (642–640 B.C.E.), Josiah ("Yahweh heals") became king of Judah after his father's murder. The outstanding event of his reign (640–609 B.C.E.) was the discovery of a Book of the Law (probably an early edition of Deuteronomy) and the subsequent religious reform it inspired (following 621 B.C.E.). Josiah purged Judah and part of Israel's old territory of their rural shrines and "high places," centering all worship at the Jerusalem Temple (2 Kings 23:27). He was killed at Megiddo attempting to intercept Pharaoh Necho's army on its way to support the collapsing Assyrian Empire (609 B.C.E.) (2 Kings 22:1–23:30; 2 Chron. 34: 1–35:27).

Jotham   (1) The youngest son of Jerubbaal (Gideon) (Judg. 9:5), who denounced his brother Abimelech to the people of Shechem for the latter's murder of Jerubbaal's seventy sons (Judg. 9:7–21). (2) Son of Uzziah, who was king of Judah as regent for his father (c. 750–742 B.C.E.) and later in his own right (742–735 B.C.E.) (2 Kings 15:32–38; 2 Chron. 27:1–9). The name means "Yahweh is perfect."

Jubilee   Derived from the Hebrew word for "ram's horn" or "trumpet," the term refers to the sabbatical year described in Leviticus 25:8–24 to be kept every half-century and proclaimed by a trumpet blast on the Day of Atonement. During a Jubilee year, all debts were to be canceled and private property returned to its rightful owners.

Judah   (1) The fourth son of Jacob and Leah (Gen. 29: 35) who, according to the J account, received his father's most powerful blessing (Gen. 49:8) and became the progenitor of the tribe of Judah, which along with that of Ephraim was the most important in Israel's history. David was of this populous tribe, which loyally supported his dynasty (2 Sam. 2:4; 1 Kings 12:20). (2) The kingdom of Judah, the southern kingdom of the divided monarchy, was composed chiefly of the tribes of Judah and Benjamin, which supported the Davidic dynasty when the northern ten tribes seceded from the union (922 B.C.E.). It was destroyed by the Babylonians in 587 B.C.E.

Judaism   The name applied to the religion of the people of Judah ("the Jews") after the northern kingdom of Israel fell (721 B.C.E.) and particularly after the Babylonian exile (587–538 B.C.E.).

Judas   A late form of the name Judah, popular after the time of Judas ("the Jew") Maccabeus and borne by several New Testament figures: (1) the brother (or son) of James, one of the twelve apostles (Luke 6:16), who is sometimes identified with the Thaddeus of Matthew 10:3 or the Judas of John 14:22; (2) the "brother" or kinsman of Jesus (Mark 6:3; Matt. 13:55); (3) Judas Iscariot ("Judas the man of Kerioth"), son of Simon Iscariot (John 6:71; 13:26), the apostle who betrayed Jesus to the priests and Romans for thirty pieces of silver (Mark 3:19; 14:10; Luke 6:16; Matt. 26:14–16, 47; John 18:3) but later returned the blood money and committed suicide (Matt. 27:3–5; Acts 1:18–20). The Gospel writers little understood Judas's motives, attributing them to simple greed or to the influence of Satan (Luke 22:3; John 6:71; 12:1–8; 13:11, 27–29).

Judas the Galilean   A Jewish revolutionary who led a revolt against Rome when Quirrnius was governing Syria (6 or 7 C.E.) (Acts 5:27).

Jude   An Anglicized form of the name Judah or Judas; one of Jesus' "brothers" (or a close male relative) (Mark 6:3; Matt. 13:55), perhaps a son born to Joseph before his marriage to Mary. Jude is less prominent in the early Christian community than his brother James (Jude 1: 1) and is considered, according to tradition, the author of the Epistle of Jude, though most scholars doubt this claim.

Judea   The Greco-Roman designation for territory comprising the old kingdom of Judah, the name first occurs in Ezra 5:8, a reference to the "province of Judaea." In the time of Jesus, Judea was the southernmost of the three divisions of the Roman province of western Palestine, the other two of which were Samaria and Galilee (Neh. 2:7; Luke 1:39; John 3:22, 11:7; Acts 1:1; Gal. 1:22).

judge   (1) In the Old Testament, a civil magistrate (Exod. 21:22; Deut. 16:18), administrator of a judiciary system traditionally organized by Moses (Exod. 18:13–26; Deut. 1:15–17; 16:18–20; 17:2–13; 19:15–20). Under the monarchy, the king became the supreme civil judge (2 Sam. 15:2; 1 Kings 3:9, 28; 7:7). (2) In the Book of Judges, the term refers primarily to people of God who led military revolts against Israel's foreign oppressors. There were twelve officially designated as such: Othniel of Judah, Ehud, Shamgar, Deborah, Gideon, Tola, Jair, Jephthah, Ibzan, Elon, Abdon, and Samson, though Eli and Samuel were also spoken of as judges (1 Sam. 4:18; 7:15).

Judgment, Day of   A theological concept deriving from the ancient Hebrew belief that the Day of Yahweh would see Israel's triumph and the destruction of its enemies, a confidence the prophet Amos shattered by proclaiming that it would mean calamity for Israel as for all who broke Yahweh's laws (Amos 5:18–20). This view prevails in Zephaniah 1:1–2; 3 and Malachi 3:1–6; 4:1–6. Isaiah also refers to "that day" of coming retribution (Isa. 11:10–16; 13:9, 13), while it is given an apocalyptic setting in Daniel 7:9–14, an idea developed in several apocryphal and pseudepigraphal books as well as in the New Testament (Matt. 25; Rev. 20).

Jupiter   Latin name of the chief Roman deity, counterpart of the Greek Zeus, king of the Olympian gods for whom some ignorant men of Lycaonia mistook Paul's companion Barnabas (Acts 14:12–18).

Kadesh   The central campsite of the Israelites during their wanderings through the Sinai wilderness (Num. 13:26–33; 20:1–11; 32:8; Deut. 1:19–25).

Kenite hypothesis   A theory arguing that Yahweh was originally the tribal god of the Kenite clan from which Moses and his Hebrew followers borrowed and adapted their religion (Exod. 18:1–12).

Kenites   A Midianite clan of nomadic coppersmiths and metalworkers to which Jethro, Moses' father-in-law, belonged (Exod. 18:1–12; Num. 10:29–32; Judg. 1:16; 4:11; 1 Sam. 15:6).

Kethuvim (Ketubim or Kethubim)   The Hebrew term designating the Writings, the third division of the Hebrew Bible: Psalms, Job, Proverbs, Song of Songs, Ecclesiastes, Esther, Ruth, Lamentations, Daniel, Ezra, Nehemiah, 1 and 2 Chronicles.

Kittim   Originally an Old Testament name for the Island of Cyprus and its inhabitants (Gen. 10:4), thought to be descendants of Noah's grandson Javan, it was later applied to Macedonian Greeks (1 Macc. 1:1) and others (Dan. 11:30).

KJV   Abbreviation for the King James Version of the Bible, published in 1611.

Koheleth (Qoheleth)   The title—meaning "the president" or "the preacher" of an assembly or church (*qahal*)—that the otherwise anonymous author of Ecclesiastes (the Greek equivalent of the term) gives himself (Eccles. 1:1; 12:9–10).

koine   The "common" or popular form of Greek spoken by Alexander's soldiers and transmitted as an international language throughout the Greco-Roman world. The Septuagint and New Testament are written in koine.

Korah   The son of Izhar, who rebelled against Moses' leadership during the Sinai wanderings (Num. 16–17).

Laban   A descendant of Nahor, brother of Rebekah (Gen. 24:29; 25:20), father of Leah and Rachel, and thus father-in-law of Jacob. An Aramean living in Haran, Laban was noted for his duplicity and greed (Gen. 24:29–31:55).

Lachish   A major fortified city in Judah about thirty miles southwest of Jerusalem and twenty miles from the Mediterranean coast (2 Kings 14:19; 2 Chron. 11:5–12; 14:6; 32:9; Jer. 34:7).

Lamech   According to J, the son of Methuselah and father of Tubal and Jubal (Gen. 4:1–24); according to P, the son of Methuselah and father of Noah (Gen. 5:25–31). His boastful song of vengeance is given in Genesis 4:23–24.

Laodicea   A commercial city on the Lycus River in Asia Minor and one of the seven churches of Asia (Col. 4:15–16; Rev. 3:14–22).

Latter Prophets   Also known as the "writing prophets," the term refers to the books of Isaiah, Jeremiah, Ezekiel, and the twelve Minor Prophets.

Law   The Torah ("teaching," "instruction") or Pentateuch, the first five books of the Bible containing the legal material traditionally ascribed to Moses.

Lazarus   (1) The brother of Mary and Martha, a resident of Bethany whom Jesus resurrected (John 11:1–12:10). (2) The beggar in Jesus' parable of rewards and punishments in the afterlife (Luke 16:20–25).

Leah   Laban's older daughter, whom he married to Jacob by trickery after the latter had worked seven years for her younger sister, Rachel (Gen. 29:16–30:21; 31:14). Although Jacob disliked Leah, she bore him six sons and a daughter: Reuben, Simeon, Levi, Judah, Issachar, Zebulun, and Dinah (Ruth 4:11).

legend   A term denoting unverifiable stories or narrative cycles about celebrated people or places of the past. Legends grow as the popular oral literature of a people.

Their purpose is not to provide historical accuracy but entertainment, to illustrate cherished beliefs, expectations, and moral principles. Scholars consider much of the material associated with the stories of the patriarchs, Moses, and prophets as legendary.

Levi   The third son of Jacob and Leah (Gen. 29:34; 35: 23), Levi earned his father's disapproval for his violence in slaughtering tribal neighbors (Gen. 34:30; 49:5–7). He was the eponymous ancestor of the tribe of Levi to which Moses, Aaron, and Miriam belonged (Exod. 6: 16; Num. 3:1–39).

Leviathan   A mythical sea monster, the ancient Near Eastern dragon of chaos and symbol of Evil which Yahweh defeated in creating the universe (Ps. 74:14; Dan. 7:2; Isa. 27:1; Job 41:1–34; see also Rev. 11:7; 12:3; 13:1–8).

Levites   The Israelite tribe descended from Levi, son of Jacob (Num. 3; 1 Chron. 5:27–6:81) that was given priestly duties in lieu of land holdings when Israel conquered Canaan (Deut. 18:1–8). According to P, only descendants of Aaron were to be priests (Exod. 28:1; Num. 18:7); the Levites were regarded as their assistants and servants (Num. 18:2–7; 20–32). They served as priests of secondary rank and as Temple functionaries during the postexilic period, which was dominated by a priestly hierarchy (1 Chron. 24–26). Other stories involving Levites appear in Judges 19–21 and Luke 10:32.

lex talionis   The law of strict retaliation, the principle of retributive justice expressed in the Torah command to exact "eye for eye, life for life" (Exod. 21:23–25; Lev. 24:19–20; Deut. 19:21) and rejected by Jesus (Matt. 5: 38–39).

literary criticism   A form of literary analysis that attempts to isolate and define literary types, the sources behind them, the stages of composition from oral to written form with their characteristic rhetorical features, and the stages and degree of redaction (editing) of a text.

Logos   A Greek term meaning both "word" and "reason," used by Greek philosophers to denote the rational principle that creates and informs the universe. Amplified by Philo Judaeus of Alexandria, Egypt, to represent the mediator between God and his material creation, as Wisdom had been in Proverbs 8:22–31, the term found its most famous expression in the prolog to the fourth Gospel to denote the prehuman Jesus—"the Word became flesh and dwelt among us" (John 1:14).

Lord's Supper   The ritual meal that Jesus held with his closest disciples the night before his death. Here he introduced the new covenant and shared the bread and wine that symbolized his body and blood about to be sacrificed on behalf of humanity (Mark 14:22–25; Matt. 26:26–29; Luke 22:14–20). Paul first calls the Christian "love feast" (*agape*) or Communion by this

name in 1 Corinthians 11:20, where he describes the ceremony of the Eucharist (1 Cor. 11:23–26). John's version of the event (John 13:1–35) differs strikingly from that in the Synoptics.

Lot   Nephew of Abraham, with whom he migrated from Ur to Haran and finally to Canaan (Gen. 11:31; 12:5). Lot separated from his uncle, who rescued him from kidnappers (Gen. 13:1–14:16). Lot later entertained angels come to destroy Sodom (Gen. 19:1–29), who directed his escape from the doomed city. He reputedly fathered the nations of Moab and Ammon by incest with his two daughters (Gen. 19:30–38). Jesus referred to Lot's experience in Sodom (Luke 17:28–30), as did the author of 2 Peter 2:6–8.

Lucifer   A term meaning "light bearer" and referring to the planet Venus when it is the morning star, the English name Lucifer translates the Hebrew word for "shining one" (Isaiah 14:12). An epithet applied to the king of Babylon, it was later mistakenly taken as a name for Satan before his expulsion from heaven.

Luke   A physician and traveling companion of Paul (Col. 4:14; Philem. 24; 2 Tim. 4:11) to whom a late second-century tradition ascribes the Gospel of Luke and Book of Acts.

LXX   A common abbreviation for the Septuagint, the Greek translation of the Hebrew Bible made in Alexandria, Egypt, during the last three centuries B.C.E.

Lycaonia   A district in Asia Minor added to the Roman Empire around 25 B.C.E., where Paul endured persecution (Acts 13:50; 14:6–19).

Lycia   A small province in southwestern Asia Minor, bordering the Mediterranean, which Paul visited on his missionary travels (Acts 21:1; 27:5–7).

Lydia   A once powerful kingdom of western Asia Minor with its capital at Sardis, Lydia (Lud) is mentioned in Jeremiah 46:9 and Ezekiel 30:5.

Lystra   A city in the Roman province of Galatia where Paul and Barnabas performed such successful healings that they were identified as Zeus and Hermes (Jupiter and Mercury) (Acts 14:6–19; 16:1; 18:23).

Maat   Ancient Egyptian goddess of truth and justice.

Maccabees   A name bestowed on the family that won religious and political independence for the Jews from their Greek-Syrian oppressors. Judas, called Maccabeus ("the hammerer"), son of the aged priest Mattathias, led his brothers and other faithful Jews against the armies of Antiochus IV (Epiphanes) (175–163 B.C.E.). The dynasty his brothers established was called Hasmonean (after an ancestor named Hashmon) and ruled Judea until 63 B.C.E., when the Romans occupied Palestine.

Macedonia   The large mountainous district in northern Greece ruled by Philip of Macedon (359–336 B.C.E.), whose son Alexander the Great (356–323 B.C.E.) extended the Macedonian Empire over the entire ancient

Near East as far as western India, incorporating all of the earlier Persian Empire. Conquered by Rome (168 B.C.E.) and annexed as a province (146 B.C.E.), Macedonia was the first part of Europe to be Christianized (Acts 16:10–17:9; 18:5; 19:29; 20:1–3).

Magdala   A town on the northwest shore of the Sea of Galilee and home of Mary Magdalene ("of Magdala") (Matt. 15:39).

Magnificat   Mary's beautiful hymn of praise, recorded in Luke 1:46–55.

Magog   *See* Gog.

Malachi   The title of the last book of the Minor Prophets, the word means "my messenger" (Mal. 3:1) and may have been affixed by an editor (Mal. 1:1) who mistook it for a proper name.

Mamre   A plain near what later became the city of Hebron in southern Palestine, where Abraham temporarily settled under its ancient oaks (Gen. 13:18) and where angels on the way to Sodom visited him (Gen. 18). From a Hittite, Abraham bought a cave near Mamre in which his wife Sarah (Gen. 23:17, 19) and then he himself (Gen. 50:13) were buried.

Manasseh

(1) The elder son of Joseph and the Egyptian Asenath, daughter of a high priest at On, who received a lesser blessing from the dying Jacob than his full brother Ephraim (Gen. 48:1–20), reflecting the tribe of Ephraim's greater importance in the later history of Israel.

(2) One of Israel's twelve tribes, divided into two sections and occupying land east and west of the Jordan River (Josh. 17:1–18).

(3) A son of Hezekiah and Hephzibah who was king of Judah longer than any other Davidic monarch (c. 687–642 B.C.E.). Despite the Deuteronomistic condemnation of him as the most evil ruler of Judah for his encouragement of Baalism, astrology, and human sacrifice, he proved an effective king, maintaining his country's relative independence during troubled times (2 Kings 21:1–18; 2 Chron. 33: 1–20). The historicity of his supposed deportation to and return from Babylon has been questioned. In 2 Kings 23:26–27, Judah's final destruction is attributed to Manasseh's wickedness.

manna   The food miraculously supplied the Israelites during their wanderings in the Sinai wilderness (Exod. 16:1–36). Described in Numbers 11:7–9 and commonly referred to as "bread" from heaven (Deut. 8:3; Nah. 9:20; Ps. 78:24; John 6:31–35; Heb. 9:4; Rev. 2: 17), its appearances ceased when Israel entered Canaan (Josh. 5:12).

Manoah   A pious member of the tribe of Dan and father of Samson, Israel's Herculean judge (Judg. 13:2–25; 14:2–10; 16:31).

Mari   An ancient Near Eastern city located on the Middle Euphrates River near the boundary of modern Syria and Iraq. Destroyed by Hammurabi of Babylon (c. 1738–1686 B.C.E.), Mari's royal palace has yielded thousands of clay tablets that preserve a rich array of information about the Mari period (c. 1750–1697 B.C.E.).

Mark (John Mark)   Son of Mary, a Jerusalem Jew who accompanied Barnabas (his cousin) and Paul on an early missionary journey (Acts 12:12–25; 13:5, 13; 15: 37). For reasons unstated, he left them at Perga (Acts 13:13), which so angered Paul that he refused to allow Mark to join a later preaching campaign (Acts 15:38), though he and the apostle were later reconciled (Col. 4:10; Philem. 24). Some identify Mark with the youth who ran away naked at the time of Jesus' arrest (Mark 14:51–52). An early tradition ascribes authorship of the Gospel of Mark to him, as Papias and Eusebius (*Ecclesiastical Histories* 3.39.15) testify.

Martha   The sister of Mary and Lazarus of Bethany (Luke 10:38–42; John 11:1–12:2), whose home Jesus frequently visited.

martyr   A "witness" for Christ who prefers to die rather than relinquish his faith. Stephen, at whose stoning Saul of Tarsus assisted, is known as the first Christian martyr (Acts 22:20; Rev. 2:13; 17:6).

Mary   From the Latin and Greek *Maria,* from the Hebrew *Miryam* (Miriam), a name borne by six women in the New Testament.

(1) Mary the virgin, wife of Joseph and mother of Jesus, who, the angel Gabriel informed her, was conceived by Holy Spirit (Matt. 1:18–25; Luke 1: 26–56; 2:21). From her home in Nazareth, Mary traveled to Bethlehem, where her first son was born (Luke 2:1–18), and thence into Egypt to escape Herod's persecution (Matt. 2:1–18), returning to Nazareth in Galilee after Herod's death (4 B.C.E.) (Matt. 2:19–23). She had one sister (John 18:25), probably Salome, wife of Zebedee, mother of James and John (Matt. 27:56), and was also related to Elisabeth, mother of John the Baptist (Luke 1:36). Gabriel's annunciation of the Messiah's birth occurs in Luke 1:26–36; the Magnificat, in Luke 1:46–55.

Mary visited Jerusalem annually for the Passover (Luke 2:41) and reprimanded the twelve-year-old Jesus for lingering behind at the Temple (Luke 2: 46–50). She may have been among family members convinced that Jesus' early preaching showed mental instability (Mark 3:21) and apparently humored his requests during the wedding celebration at Cana (John 2:1–12). Although Jesus showed his mother little deference during his ministry (Mark 3:31–35; Luke 11:27–28; John 2:4), on the cross he entrusted her care to his "beloved disciple" (John 19:25–27). Mary last appears in the upper room praying with the disciples just before Pentecost (Acts 1:13–14).

(2) Mary Magdalene, a woman from Magdala, from whom Jesus cast out seven demons (Luke 8:1–2) and who became his follower. A common tradition asserts that she had been a prostitute whom Jesus had rescued from her former life (Mark 16:9; Luke 7:37–50), but this is by no means certain. She was present at the crucifixion (Mark 15:40; Matt. 15:47), visited Jesus' tomb early Sunday morning (Matt. 28:1; Mark 16:1; Luke 24:10; John 20:1), and was one of the first to see the risen Jesus (Matt. 28:9; Mark 16:9; John 20:11–18), although the male disciples refused to believe her (Luke 24:9–11).

(3) Mary, sister of Lazarus and Martha, whose home at Bethany Jesus frequented (Luke 10:38–42; John 11:1–12:8).

(4) Mary, wife of Cleophas, mother of James the Less and Joseph (Joses), was a witness of Jesus' crucifixion, burial, and resurrection (Matt. 27:56–61; 28:1; Mark 15:40, 47; 16:1; Luke 24:10; John 19:25).

(5) Mary, sister of Barnabas and mother of John Mark, provided her Jerusalem home as a meeting place for the disciples (Acts 12:12; Col. 4:10).

(6) An otherwise anonymous Mary mentioned in Romans 16:6.

Masada   A stronghold built by Herod the Great on a fortified plateau 800 feet above the Dead Sea, Masada was captured by Zealots during the revolt against Rome (66 C.E.). When the attacking Romans finally entered Masada (73 C.E.), they found only seven women and children alive, 953 others having died in a suicide pact.

masoretes   From a Hebrew term meaning "tradition," the name given to medieval Jewish scholars who copied, annotated, and added vowels to the text of the Hebrew Bible.

Masoretic Text (MT)   The standard text of the Hebrew Bible as given final form by the Masoretes in the seventh through the ninth centuries C.E.

Mattathias   A Jewish priest who, with his sons John, Simon, Judas, Eleazar, and Jonathan, led a revolt against the oppressions of Antiochus IV (c. 168–167 B.C.E.) (1 Macc. 2:1–70).

Matthew   A Jewish tax collector working for Rome whom Jesus called to be one of the twelve apostles (Matt. 9:9; 10:3; Mark 2:13–17; 3:18; Luke 5:27–32; 6:15; Acts 1:13), Matthew (also called Levi) is the traditional author of the Gospel of Matthew, an attribution contested by most scholars.

Matthias   The early Christian elected to replace Judas among the Twelve (Acts 1:23–26). The name means "gift of Yahweh."

Medes   An ancient Ayrian (Iranian) Indo-European people occupying mountainous country south of the Caspian Sea who established a kingdom that by 600 B.C.E. extended from near the Persian Gulf to the Black Sea.

In 612 B.C.E., they joined the Neo-Babylonians and Scythians to destroy Nineveh and terminate the Assyrian Empire. They were subdued by Cyrus the Great (549 B.C.E.), whose dominion was commonly known as the Medo-Persian Empire (Nah. 2:3–3:19; Esther 1:19; Dan. 5:28). The "law of the Medes and Persians" was traditionally immutable (Esther 1:19; Dan. 6:8, 15) and once given could not be rescinded, a factor that plays an important part in the Book of Esther (Esther 8:7–12).

Megiddo   An old Palestinian city overlooking the Valley of Jezreel (Plain of Esdraelon), the site of numerous decisive battles in biblical history (Josh. 12:21; 2 Kings 9:27; 23:29–30; 2 Chron. 35:20–24; Zech. 12:11) and symbolic location of the climactic War of Armageddon (Rev. 16:16).

Megillot   A Hebrew word meaning "scrolls"; the five Old Testament books—Song of Songs, Ruth, Lamentations, Ecclesiastes, and Esther—each of which was read publicly at one of Israel's annual religious festivals.

Melchizedek   The king-priest of Canaanite Salem (probably the site of Jerusalem) to whom Abraham paid a tenth of his spoils of war (Gen. 14:17–20); cited by the author of Hebrews as foreshadowing Jesus Christ (Ps. 110:4; Heb. 5:6–10; 7:1–25).

Mercury   Roman name for Hermes, Greek god of persuasion, business, trade, and messenger of Zeus, for whom Paul was mistaken in Lystra (Acts 14:12).

Merneptah   Egyptian pharaoh, son and successor of Ramses II, who reigned about 1224–1211 B.C.E. His stele commemorating the defeat of several Canaanite nations include the earliest known reference to Israel, which Merneptah claimed that he had totally eradicated.

Merodach   A Hebrew form of the Akkadian Marduk (also called Bel), the chief Babylonian god, ridiculed by Second Isaiah (Isa. 46:1–4) and Jeremiah (Jer. 51:44–45).

Mesopotamia   The territory between the Euphrates and Tigris rivers at the head of the Persian Gulf (modern Iraq); cradle of the Sumerian, Akkadian, Assyrian, and Neo-Babylonian civilizations (Gen. 24:10; Judg. 3:8–10; 1 Chron. 19:6; Acts 2:9; 7:2).

messiah   A Hebrew term meaning "anointed one," designating a king or priest of ancient Israel who had been consecrated by having his head smeared with holy oil, marking him as set apart for a special role. King David is the model of Yahweh's anointed ruler; all his descendants who ruled over Judah were Yahweh's messiahs (2 Sam. 7:1–29; Ps. 89:3–45). After the end of the Davidic monarchy (587 B.C.E.), various Hebrew prophets applied the promises made to the Davidic dynasty to a future heir who would eventually restore the kingdom of David (Pss. 2; 110; Dan. 9:25–26). Christians believe that Jesus of Nazareth was the promised Messiah

(Christ) as expressed in Peter's "confession" (Matt. 16: 13–20; Mark 8:27–30; Luke 9:18–22; etc.).

Methuselah According to Genesis 5:21–27, an antediluvian patriarch descended from Seth and Enoch who attained an age of 969 years. He appears as Methushael in Genesis 4:18 and in Luke's genealogical list (Luke 3:37).

Micah A Judean prophet of the late eighth century B.C.E. and younger contemporary of Isaiah of Jerusalem (Isa. 2:2–4; Mic. 4:1–3). A rural figure who denounced the evils of urban life (Mic. 1:5) and predicted Jerusalem's fall (Mic. 3:12; cited in Jer. 26:18–19), his oracles form most of the present Book of Micah in the Minor Prophets. His name means "Who is like Yahweh?"

Micaiah An eighth-century B.C.E. prophet who predicted Ahab's defeat and death at the Battle of Ramoth-gilead (1 Kings 22:8–28; 2 Chron. 18:6–27).

Michael The angel whom the Book of Daniel represents as being the spirit prince, guardian, and protector of Israel (Dan. 10:13, 21; 12:1). Jude 9 depicts him as an archangel fighting with Satan for Moses' body. In Revelation 12:7, he leads the war against the dragon (Satan) and casts him from heaven. His name means "Who is like God?"

Michal A daughter of Saul (1 Sam. 14:49) who was offered to David as his wife for his exploits against the Philistines (1 Sam. 18:20–27). Michal helped David escape Saul's wrath (1 Sam. 19:11–17), only to be rejected when she criticized his dancing naked before the Ark (2 Sam. 6:14–23).

Midianites An ancient nomadic people inhabiting an area in the northwestern Arabian desert, east of the Gulf of Aqabah, opposite the Sinai peninsula, and south of Moab. According to Genesis 25:1–4, they were descended from Abraham and his wife Keturah. Judges 8: 24 identifies them in Gideon's time as Ishmaelites, the name given in Genesis 37:25 to the merchants to whom Joseph was sold. Moses took refuge with the Kenites, a Midianite group (Exod. 2:15–3:1; 18:1–15) into which he married. The judge Gideon defeated some Midianites who encroached on Israel's territory (Judg. 1:16; 4:1; 6–8).

Midrash From a Hebrew work meaning "to search out," Midrash refers to a commentary on or interpretation of Scripture. Collections of such haggadic or halakic expositions of the significance of the biblical text are called Midrashim.

millennium A 1000-year epoch, particularly the period of Christ's universal reign (Rev. 20:1–8) during which Satan will be chained and the dead resurrected.

Minor Prophets Twelve prophetic books short enough to be recorded together on a single scroll: Hosea, Joel, Amos, Obadiah, Jonah, Micah, Nahum, Habakkuk, Zephaniah, Haggai, Zechariah, and Malachi.

Miriam The daughter of Amram and Jochebed, older sister of Aaron and Moses, who brought her mother to nurse the infant Moses after he was found and adopted by pharaoh's daughter (Exod. 2:4–8; Num. 26:59; 1 Chron. 6:3). Miriam led the victory celebration after the crossing of the Sea of Reeds (Exod. 15:20–21). Although later stricken with leprosy for criticizing Moses, she was cured and readmitted to Yahweh's favor after her brother interceded for her (Num. 12:2–15).

Mishnah From the Hebrew verb "to repeat," a collection of Pharisaic oral interpretations (Halakah) of the Torah compiled and edited by Rabbi Judah ha-Nasi about 200 C.E.

Mizpah The name of several Old Testament sites, the most important of which was located in the territory of Benjamin (Josh. 18:26) near the border of Judah and Israel, perhaps a cult site (Judg. 20:1–11) on Samuel's prophetic circuit (1 Sam. 7:5–16; 10:17–24) and the temporary center of Jews remaining in Palestine after Nebuchadnezzar's deportations (2 Kings 25:23; Jer. 40–41).

Mizraim According to Genesis 10:6, a son of Noah's son Ham and the progenitor of the Hamitic nations of Lower Egypt, North Africa, and Canaan. It is also the Hebrew name of Egypt.

Moab An ancient neighbor-state of Israel located in the Jordan highlands east of the Dead Sea and north of Edom. Supposedly descended from Lot's incestuous union with his daughter (Gen. 19:30–38), the Moabites were Israel's traditional enemies (Num. 22:3; 24: 17; Judg. 3:12–20; 11:15; 2 Kings 1:1; 3:4–27) and frequently denounced by the prophets (Isa. 15:16; 25: 10; Jer. 9:26; 25:26; 48; Ezek. 28:8–11; Amos 2:12; Zech. 2:8–11; Ps. 60:8). Yet, both David and Jesus were descended from Ruth, a Moabite (Ruth 4:13–22; Luke 3:31–32). In extreme emergencies, the national god Chemosh was sometimes worshiped with human sacrifice (2 Kings 3:27; 13:20).

Molech (Moloch) The national god of Ammon whose worship characteristically involved human sacrifice, an act specifically forbidden the Hebrews (Lev. 18:21; 20: 2; Amos 5:26) but allegedly introduced by King Manasseh (2 Kings 21:6; 2 Chron. 33), rooted out by Josiah (2 Kings 23:10), and denounced by the prophets Jeremiah (Jer. 7:29–34; 19:1–13) and Ezekiel (Ezek. 16:20–21; 20:26, 31).

Money In early biblical times, before coins were first minted, value in business transactions was determined by weighing quantities of precious metals. In the early period, the term *shekel* refers not to a coin but to a certain weight of silver. The use of coinage was first introduced into Palestine during the Persian era when the daric or dram, named for Darius I (521–486 B.C.E.), appeared. After Alexander's conquest of Persia, Greek coinage became the standard. The silver drachma (Luke 15:8), a coin of small value, was equivalent to the Roman denarius. The lepton was a small copper coin (Luke 12:59; 21:2), the least valuable in circulation, and one of the denominations coined by the Jews for use in the Temple. This was the "widow's mite" (Mark 12:42). The talent (Matt. 18:24) was not a coin but money of account; it was divided into smaller units—60 minas or 6000 drachmas—and was worth at least $2000. The denarius (Matt. 18:28), the basic unit in the New Testament, was a silver coin, the day's wage of a rural laborer (Matt. 20:2).

monolatry   The worship of one god while conceding the existence of others.

monotheism   Belief in the existence of one god, a major theme of Second Isaiah (Isa. 40–46).

Mordecai   His name derived from Marduk or Merodach (the chief Babylonian deity), Mordecai was the cousin and foster father of Esther, who according to the book bearing her name, was the Jew married to Ahasuerus, emperor of Persia. Representing the typically devout but politically ambitious Jew living in the diaspora, Mordecai saved his sovereign's life (Esther 2:21–23) and outwitted Haman, who attempted to exterminate him and all Jews throughout the Persian domain (Esther 3:6–15), a plot he employed his beautiful cousin to foil so that, by his astuteness, he became second in power to the emperor (Esther 8–10).

Mosaic Covenant   An agreement between God and the nation of Israel that was mediated by Moses. According to the terms of this pact, Israel swore to keep all of the laws enumerated in the Torah. Failure to do so would result in suffering all the curses contained in Leviticus and Deuteronomy.

Moses   The great Hebrew lawgiver, religious reformer, founder of the Israelite nation, and central figure of the Pentateuch was the son of Amram (a Levite) and Jochebed and brother to Aaron and Miriam (Exod. 2:1–4). Adopted by pharaoh's daughter and raised at the Egyptian royal court (Exod. 2:5–10; Acts 7:22), he fled Egypt after killing an Egyptian bully and settled in Midian among the Kenites, where he married Jethro's daughter Zipporah (Exod. 2:11–22).

After an encounter with Yahweh at the burning bush (Exod. 3:1–4:17), he returned to Egypt (Exod. 4:18–31), interceded with pharaoh during the ten plagues (Exod. 5–11), led the Israelites across the Reed Sea (Exod. 14–15) to Sinai where he mediated the law covenant between Yahweh and Israel (Exod. 19–31), pled for his people (Exod. 33–34; Num. 14), directed their migration through the Sinai wilderness (Num. 11–14; 20–25), appointed Joshua as his successor (Num. 27:18–23), and died in Moab (Deut. 34:1–7; Acts 7:20–44). He is also credited with building the tabernacle (Exod. 35–40), organizing Israel (Exod. 18:

13–26), restating Israel's law code shortly before his death (Deut. 1–31), and composing several hymns (Deut. 32–33; Ps. 90).

Although Moses' name became synonymous with the covenant concept and Israel's traditions (Pss. 77:20; 103:7; 105:26; 106:23; Isa. 63:12; Mic. 6:4; Matt. 17:3; Luke 16:29; John 1:17; 3:14; 5:46; 7:19; 9:29; Acts 3:22; 21:21), modern scholars have concluded that much of the material in the Pentateuch dates from post–Mosaic times. (*See* documentary hypothesis.) Moses also figured prominently in Paul's theology (Rom. 5:14; 10:5; 1 Cor. 10:2; 2 Cor. 3:7; 3:15) and that of the author of Hebrews (Heb. 3:2; 7:14; 9:19; 11:23). Jude preserves an old tradition, probably derived from the pseudepigraphal Assumption of Moses, that the devil disputed the angel Michael for Moses' body (Jude 9; Rev. 15:3).

mystery   Derived from a Greek word meaning "to initiate" or "to shut the eyes or mouth," probably referring to the secrets of Hellenistic "mystery religions," the term is used variously in the New Testament. Jesus speaks at least once of the "mystery" of the kingdom (Matt. 13:11; Mark 4:11; Luke 8:10), but Paul employs the term frequently as if the profounder aspects of Christianity were a religious secret into which the Spirit-directed believer becomes initiated (Rom. 11:5; 16:25; 1 Cor. 2:7; 4:1; 13:2; 14:2; 15:51; Col. 1:26; 2:2; 4:3; 2 Thess. 2:7; 1 Tim. 3:9; 3:16; see also Rev. 1:20; 10:7; 17:5–7).

myth   From the Greek *mythos*, a "story," the term denotes a narrative expressing a profound psychological or religious truth that cannot be verified by historical inquiry or other scientific means. When scholars speak of the "myth of Eden," for example, it is not to denigrate the tale's significance but to emphasize the Eden story's archetypal expression of humanity's sense of alienation from its creator. Myths typically feature stories about divine beings and national heroes who represent natural or psychological forces that deeply influence humans but that they cannot control. The psychologist Carl Jung interpreted myth as humanity's inherited concept of primeval events that persists in the unconscious mind and finds expression through repeated reenactments in ritual worship and other cultic practices. Israel's covenant-renewal ceremonies and retellings of Yahweh's saving acts during the Exodus are examples of such cultic myths.

mythology   A system or cycle of myths, such as those featuring the deities of ancient Greece or Rome. Once the embodiment of living religious beliefs, Greco-Roman and other mythologies are now seen as archetypal symbols that give philosophic meaning to universal human experiences. Mythologies are thus "falsehoods" only in the narrowest literal sense. They are probably akin to dreams in revealing persistent images and attitudes derived from the human subconscious.

Naaman The Syrian commander-in-chief of Benhadad, king of Damascus and an enemy of Israel, whom the prophet Elisha bathes in the Jordan River to cure his leprosy (2 Kings 5:1–27).

Nabal An epithet meaning "fool," the name applied to the rich shepherd, husband of Abigail, who refused to feed David's band of outlaw guerrillas (1 Sam. 25:2–42).

Nabonidus Son of Nabu-balatsuikbi, father of Belshazzar, and last ruler of the Neo-Babylonian Empire (556–539 B.C.E.).

Nabopolassar The name means "son of a nobody." Nabopolassar founded the Neo-Babylonian Empire by revolting against Assyria, a move that enabled King Josiah of Israel to carry out his religious reforms without Assyrian interference and to regain much of the old territory of the northern kingdom. Allied with the Medes, Nabopolassar destroyed Nineveh (612 B.C.E.) and was succeeded by his son Nebuchadnezzar II (Nah. 3:1–3; Zeph. 2:12–14; Jer. 46). *See also* Josiah.

Naboth A landowner in the city of Jezreel whose vineyard King Ahab coveted, Naboth was illegally executed through Queen Jezebel's machinations (1 Kings 21:1–16). This crime, denounced by the prophet Elijah, became the focal point of resistance to Ahab's royal dynasty and culminated in its extermination by Jehu (1 Kings 21:17–29; 2 Kings 9:1–10:11).

Nahor According to Genesis 11:27–30, the son of Terah, brother of Abraham and Haran. By Milcah (and a concubine) Nahor fathered twelve sons, eponymous ancestors of the north-Semitic Aramean tribes (Gen. 21:33; 24:24; 29:5–6).

Nahum A prophet from Elkosh (Nah. 1:1) who delivered poems rejoicing in Nineveh's fall and the destruction of the Assyrian Empire (612 B.C.E.).

Naomi Wife of Elimelech of Bethlehem (Ruth 1:2) and mother-in-law to Ruth, whose marriage she arranged to her Jewish kinsman Boaz (Ruth 3–4). Her name means "my pleasantness."

Naphtali (1) According to Genesis 30:7–8, Naphtali was the son of Jacob and Rachel's handmaid Bilhah and compared to a wild hind in his father's blessing (Gen. 49:21); the eponymous ancestor of one of the northern tribes of Israel (1 Chron. 7:13; Exod. 1:4; Num. 1:15, 42; 26:50). (2) The tribe of Naphtali was assigned territory north of Megiddo along the upper Jordan and western shores of the Sea of Galilee (Josh. 19:32–39; Judg. 1:33). It supported King David (1 Chron. 12:34–40) but became part of the northern kingdom after 922 B.C.E. (1 Kings 15:20) and was dispersed by the Assyrians in 722–721 B.C.E. (2 Kings 15:29).

Nathan (1) A son of David (2 Sam. 5:14; Zech. 12:12; Luke 3:31). (2) A prophet and political counselor at David's court who enunciated the concept of an everlasting Davidic dynasty (2 Sam. 7), denounced the king for his adultery with Bathsheba (2 Sam. 12:1–23), revealed Adonijah's plan to seize power (1 Kings 1:5–8), helped Solomon succeed to David's throne (1 Kings 1:8–45), and is credited with writing a history of David and Solomon's reigns (1 Chron. 29:29; 2 Chron. 9:29).

***Navi* (*Nabi*)** The Hebrew word for "prophet," a spokesperson for Yahweh who delivered his God's judgments on contemporary society and expressed his intentions toward the world (Deut. 13:1–5; 18:9–22; Amos 3:7; etc.).

Nazarenes A name applied to early Christians (Acts 24:5).

Nazareth A town in Lower Galilee above the Plain of Esdraelon (Megiddo) where Jesus spent his youth and began his ministry (Matt. 2:23; Luke 1:26; 4:16; John 1:46).

Nazirites From the Hebrew *nazar* ("to dedicate"), referring to a group in ancient Israel that rigorously observed ascetic principles, including refusing to drink wine, cut their hair, come in contact with the dead, or eat religiously "unclean" food (Num. 6:1–21). Samson, despite his ill-fated love affairs, belonged to this sect (Judg. 13–16).

Nebuchadnezzar (1) A Fourth Dynasty king of the Old Babylonian Empire (twelfth century B.C.E.). (2) Son of Nabopolassar and the most powerful ruler of the Neo-Babylonian Empire (605–562 B.C.E.), Nebuchadnezzar II defeated Pharaoh Necho at the Battle of Carchemish (605 B.C.E.) (2 Kings 24:1–7; Jer. 46:2) and brought much of the Near East under his control. He attacked Judah and deported many of its upper classes in 598–597 B.C.E., besieged and destroyed Jerusalem in 587 B.C.E., and took much of its population captive to Babylon (2 Kings 24:10–25; 25:11–21; 2 Chron. 26:6–21; Jer. 39:1–10; 52:1–30). The portrait of him in Daniel is probably not historical (Dan. 2:1–13; 3:1–7; 4:4–37).

Nebuzaradan Commander of the Babylonian guard under Nebuchadnezzar who was sent to oversee the destruction of Jerusalem (587 B.C.E.) and the deportation to Babylon of Judah's population (2 Kings 25:8–20).

Necho Pharaoh Necho II, son of Psammetichus I (Psamtik), second king of the Twenty-Sixth Egyptian Dynasty (610–594 B.C.E.), defeated and killed King Josiah of Judah at Megiddo (609 B.C.E.), thus ending Josiah's religious reforms and Judah's political renaissance (2 Kings 23:29–35; 2 Chron. 35:20–24; 36:4). His plans to reassert Egyptian hegemony in the Near East were permanently thwarted when Nebuchadnezzar of Babylon defeated Egyptian forces at Carchemish (605 B.C.E.) (2 Kings 24:7; Jer. 46).

Negeb, The The largely desert territory south of Beersheba in Judah (Deut. 1:42–46; Josh. 10:40; 15:21–32; 19:1–9; Judg. 6:3; 1 Sam. 27:5–10; etc.)

Nehemiah   A Jewish court official (cupbearer) living at the Persian capital in Susa who persuaded Emperor Artaxerxes I (465–423 B.C.E.) to commission him to go to Judea and rebuild Jerusalem's walls (Neh. 1:1–2:20). Although he encountered resistance from Judah's jealous neighbors, Nehemiah finished the rebuilding in record time (Neh. 3:33–6:19) and, with the priest Ezra, effected numerous social and religious reforms among the returned exiles (Neh. 8:1–9:3; 11:1–3; 12:27–13:3).

Nergal-sharezer   A high Babylonian official present at the capture of Jerusalem who at King Nebuchadnezzar's orders helped protect the prophet Jeremiah (Jer. 39:1–14). He later became king of Babylon (560–556 B.C.E.) after murdering Amel-Marduk (the Evil-merodach of 2 Kings 25:27).

Nero   Nero Claudius Caesar Augustus Germanicus, emperor of Rome (54–68 C.E.), the Caesar by whom Paul wished to be tried in Acts 25:11 and under whose persecution Paul was probably beheaded (64–65 C.E.). A first-century superstition held that Nero, slain during a palace revolt, would return at the head of an army. Regarded by some Christians as the anti-Christ, Nero's reappearance is apparently suggested in Revelation 13:4–18.

Nethinim   A group of Temple servants who performed such menial tasks as carrying wood and water (Ezra 7:7, 24; 8:20; Neh. 3:26–31; 10:28–31).

Nevi'im (Prophets)   The Hebrew term designating the second major division of the tripartite Hebrew Bible (Tanak), the Prophets.

New Year Festival (*Rosh Hashanah*)   Also called the Feast of Trumpets (Lev. 23:23–25), this was a time when work ceased and the Israelites assembled together (Num. 29:1–6). Before the exile (587–538 B.C.E.), the Jews observed the festival in the autumn, but afterward they adopted the Babylonian celebration held in the spring, the first day of the month of Nisan (March–April). With a new emphasis on atonement, it became the first of Ten Days of Penitence, a solemn introduction to the Day of Atonement (*Yom Kippur*) (Lev. 16). Ezekiel urged the keeping of both New Years (Ezek. 40–48).

Nicanor   (1) A general of Antiochus IV whom the Maccabees defeated (1 Macc. 3:38; 7:26–32). (2) A deacon in the Jerusalem church (Acts 6:1, 5).

Nicodemus   A leading Pharisee and member of the Sanhedrin (John 3:1; 7:50; 19:39) who discussed spiritual rebirth with Jesus (John 3:1–21), visited him by night and defended him against other Pharisees (John 7:45–52), and with Joseph of Arimathaea, helped entomb his body (John 19: 38–42).

Nimrod   According to J, the great-grandson of Noah, grandson of Ham, son of Cush, and a legendary hunter and founder of cities in Mesopotamia (Gen. 9:19; 10:8–12). Several ruined sites in Iraq preserve his name.

Nineveh   The last capital of the Assyrian Empire, located on the east bank of the Tigris River, and supposedly founded by Nimrod (Gen. 10:11), Nineveh was one of the greatest cities in the ancient Near East (Jon. 1:2; 3:2–4; 4:11). Several Judean kings, including Hezekiah, sent tribute there (2 Kings 18:13–16). Its destruction was foretold by the prophets (2 Kings 19:5–37; Zeph. 2:13) and celebrated by Nahum (Nah. 1–3). Assyria's last major ruler, Ashurbanipal (668–627 B.C.E.), was an antiquarian who collected thousands of literary works on clay tablets—including the *Epic of Gilgamesh* and the *Enuma Elish*—for the royal library at Nineveh. After a three-month siege, the city was destroyed in 612 B.C.E. by a coalition of Medes, Babylonians, and Scythians. Jesus ironically refers to the "men of Nineveh" as more spiritually receptive than his contemporaries (Matt. 12:41).

Noah   The son of Lamech (Gen. 5:28–30), father of Ham, Shem, and Japheth (Gen. 4:32), whom Yahweh chose to build a wooden houseboat containing pairs of all living creatures to survive the Flood (Gen. 6:13–8:19) and with whom Yahweh made an "everlasting" covenant (Gen. 8:20–9:17). In another story (Gen. 5:29; 9:18–27), Noah is the first vinegrower and a victim of excessive drinking. Infrequently mentioned elsewhere in the Old Testament (Isa. 54:9; Ezek. 14:14), he and the Flood are often cited in the New Testament as examples of divine judgment (Matt. 24:37–39; Luke 17:26–28; Heb. 11:7; 1 Pet. 3:20; 2 Pet. 2:5; 3:5–6).

Obadiah   (1) One of Ahab's stewards who hid 100 Yahwist prophets in caves during Jezebel's persecutions and who arranged the meeting between Ahab and Elijah (1 Kings 18:3–16) that resulted in a contest between Yahweh and Baal on Mount Carmel (1 Kings 18:17–46). (2) Traditionally recognized as author of the Book of Obadiah, about whom nothing is known. His book is fourth and shortest among the Minor Prophets.

Obed   Son of Ruth and Boaz, and father of Jesse, father of David (Ruth 4:17–22; 1 Chron. 2:12; 11:47).

Obed-edom   (1) A citizen of Gath in whose house David placed the Ark of the Covenant before taking it to Jerusalem (2 Sam. 6:10–12; 1 Chron. 13:13–14). (2) The founder of a group of singers at the second Temple (1 Chron. 15:21; 16:5).

Olives, Mount of (Olivet)   A mile-long limestone ridge with several distinct summits paralleling the eastern section of Jerusalem, from which it is separated by the narrow Kidron Valley. Here David fled during Absalom's rebellion (2 Sam. 15:30–32), and according to Zechariah 14:3–5, here Yahweh will stand at the final eschatological battle, when the mountain will be torn asunder from east to west. From its summit, with its panoramic view of Jerusalem, Jesus delivered his apocalyptic judgment on the city that had rejected him (Matt. 24–25). He often retreated to its shady groves in the evening (John 7:53; 8:1), including the night before his death (Matt. 26:30–56; Mark 14:26; Luke 22:39; see also Matt. 21:1; Mark 11:1; Luke 19:29; Acts 1:12).

omega   The last letter in the Greek alphabet, used with alpha (the first letter) as a symbol of the eternity of God (Rev. 1:8; 21:6) and Jesus (Rev. 1:17, 22:13), probably echoing Isaiah's description of Yahweh as "the first and the last" (Isa. 44:6; 48:12).

Omri   Sixth ruler of the northern kingdom (876–869 B.C.E.) and founder of a dynasty that included his son Ahab (869–850 B.C.E.), his grandson Ahaziah (850–849 B.C.E.), and a younger son Jehoram (849–842 B.C.E.), whose important military, political, and economic successes are minimized by the Deuteronomistic historians (2 Kings 16:23–28). Omri's leadership raised Israel to a power and prestige considerably above that of Judah. Even a century after his death and the extinction of his dynasty, Assyrian records referred to Israel as the "land of the House of Omri."

Onesimus   The runaway slave of Philemon of Colossae whom Paul converted to Christianity and reconciled to his master (Philem. 8–21; Col. 4:7–9).

Ophel   The southern end of Jerusalem's eastern or Temple hill, the site of David's city (2 Chron. 27:3; 33:14; Neh. 3:26–27; 11:31).

oracle   (1) A divine message or utterance (Rom. 3:2; Heb. 5:12; 1 Pet. 4:11) or the person through whom it is conveyed (Acts 7:38). (2) An authoritative communication, such as that from a wise person (Prov. 31:1; 2 Sam. 16:23). (3) The inner sanctum of the Jerusalem Temple (1 Kings 6:5–6; 7:49; 8:6–8; Ps. 28:2). (4) The supposedly inspired words of a priest or priestess at such shrines as Delphi in ancient Greece and Cumae in Italy.

oral tradition   Material passed from generation to generation by word of mouth before finding written form. Scholars believe that much of Israel's early history, customs, and beliefs about its origins, such as the stories about the patriarchs and Moses in the Pentateuch, were so transmitted before J first committed them to writing about 950 B.C.E..

Osiris   Ancient Egyptian god of fertility and also of the underworld.

P   *See* Priestly document.

Palestine   A strip of land bordering the eastern Mediterranean Sea, lying south of Syria, north of the Sinai peninsula, and west of the Arabian desert. During the patriarchal period, it was known as Canaan (Gen. 12:6–7; 15:18–21). Named for the Philistines, it was first called Palestine by the Greek historian Herodotus about 450 B.C.E.

Pamphylia   A small area (after 74 C.E., a Roman province) along the southern coast of Asia Minor where Paul broke with Barnabas and John Mark (Acts 13:13; 14:24–25; 15:38; 27:5).

parable   From the Greek *parabole* ("a placing beside," "a comparison"), a short fictional narrative that compares something familiar to an unexpected spiritual value. Using a commonplace object or event to illustrate a religious principle was Jesus' typical method of teaching in the Synoptic Gospels (Matt. 13:3–53; 22:1; 24:32; Mark 4:2–3; 13:28; Luke 8:4–18; 13:18–21; 21:29). Yet, a recurrent tradition held that Jesus used parables to prevent most of his hearers from understanding his message (Mark 4:10–12; Matt. 13:10–15; Luke 8:9–10). Famous Old Testament parables or fables include Nathan's (2 Sam. 12:1–14), Isaiah's (Isa. 5:1–7), Jotham's (Judg. 9:7–21), Jehoash's (2 Kings 14:8–10), and Ezekiel's (Ezek. 17:22–24; 24:1–14), the last two of which are allegories.

Paraclete   A Greek term (meaning "an advocate" or "intercessor summoned to aid") that the Gospel of John uses to denote the Holy Spirit, Paraclete is variously translated "Comforter," "Helper," "Advocate," or "Spirit of Truth" (John 7:39; 14:12, 16–18; 15:26; 16:7; see also 1 John 2:1).

paradise   Literally, a "park" or walled garden, paradise is the name applied to Eden (Gen. 2:8–17) and in post–Old Testament times to the abode of the righteous dead, of which the lower part housed souls awaiting the resurrection and the higher was the permanent home of the just. It is possible that Jesus referred to the lower paradise in his words to the thief on the cross (Luke 23:43). Paul's reference to being "caught up" into paradise may refer to the third of the seven heavens postulated in later Jewish eschatology (as in the books of Enoch) (2 Cor. 12:2–5). John's vision of the tree of life in "the garden of God" (Rev. 2:7; 22:1–3) depicts an earthly paradise.

parallelism   A structural feature typical of Hebrew poetry, consisting of the repetition of similar or antithetical thoughts in similar phrasing: "The wicked will not stand firm when Judgment comes nor sinners when the virtuous assemble" (Ps. 1:5).

Parousia   A Greek term (meaning "being by" or "being near") used to denote the Second Coming or appearance of Christ, commonly regarded as his return to judge the world, punish the wicked, and redeem the saved. It is a major concept in apocalyptic Christianity (Mark 13; Matt. 24–25; Luke 21; 1 and 2 Thess.; 2 Pet. 2–3; Rev.); but see also John 14:25–29; which emphasizes Jesus' continued spiritual presence rather than an eschatological apparition.

Passion   The term commonly used to denote Jesus' suffering and death (Acts 1:3).

Passover   An annual Jewish observance commemorating Israel's last night of bondage in Egypt when the Angel of Death "passed over" Israelite homes marked with the blood of a sacrificial lamb to destroy the first-born of every Egyptian household (Exod. 12:1–51). Beginning the seven-day Feast of Unleavened Bread, it is a ritual meal eaten on Nisan 14 (March–April) that traditionally includes roast lamb, unleavened bread, and bitter herbs (Exod. 12:15–20; 13:3–10; Lev. 23:5; Num. 9:5; 28:16; Deut. 16:1). The Passover was scrupulously observed by Israel's great leaders, including Joshua (Josh. 5:10), Hezekiah (2 Chron. 30:1), Josiah (2 Kings 23:21–23, 2 Chron. 35:1–18), and the returned exiles (Ezra 6:19), as well as by Jesus and his disciples (Matt. 26:2, 17–29; Mark 14:1–16; Luke 22:1–13; John 13:1; 18:39). According to the Synoptics, Jesus' Last Supper with the Twelve was a Passover celebration (Matt. 26; Mark 14; Luke 22) and the model for Christian Communion (the Eucharist) (1 Cor. 11:17–27).

Pastoral Epistles   The name applied to the New Testament books of 1 and 2 Timothy and Titus, presumably written by the apostle Paul to two of his fellow ministers (pastors), but which modern scholars believe were composed by an anonymous disciple of Pauline thought living near the mid-second century C.E.

Patmos   A small Aegean island off the coast of western Asia Minor (Turkey) where John, author of Revelation, was exiled by the emperor Domitian about 95 C.E. (Rev. 1:9).

patriarch   The male head (father) of an ancient family line, a venerable tribal founder or leader; especially: (1) the early ancestors of humanity listed in Genesis 4–5, known as the "antediluvian patriarchs"; (2) prominent "fathers" living after the Flood to the time of Abraham (Gen. 11); (3) the immediate progenitors of the Israelites: Abraham, Isaac, and Jacob (Gen. 12–50; Exod. 3:6; 6:2–8). Acts 7:8–9 includes Jacob's twelve sons among the patriarchs.

Paul   The most influential apostle and missionary of the mid-first-century Church and author of seven to nine New Testament letters. Saul of Tarsus (Paul's original name) was born in the capital of the Asia Minor province of Cilicia (Acts 9:11; 21:39; 22:3) into a family of Pharisees (Acts 23:6) of the tribe of Benjamin (Phil. 3:5) and had both Roman and Taurean citizenship (Acts 22:28). Suddenly converted to Christianity after persecuting early Christians (Acts 7:55–8:3; 9:1–30; 22:1–21; 26:1–23; 1 Cor. 9:1; 15:8; Gal. 1:11–24; Eph. 3:3; Phil. 3:12), he undertook at least three international missionary tours, presenting defenses of the new faith before Jewish and Gentile authorities (Acts 13:1–28:31). His emphasis on the insufficiency of the Mosaic law for salvation (Gal. 3–5; Rom. 4–11) and the superiority of faith to law (Rom. 4–11) and his insistence that Gentiles be admitted to the Church without observing Jewish legal restrictions (Gal. 2; 5; Rom. 7–8) were decisive in determining the future development

of the new religion. He was probably martyred in Rome about 64–65 C.E.

Pella   A Gentile city in Palestine east of the Jordan River, to which tradition says that Jesus' family and other Jewish Christians fled during the Jewish revolt against Rome (66–70 C.E.). Before this time, Jerusalem had been the center of the Palestinian Jewish-Christian church. References in Acts and Paul's letters indicate that Palestinian Christian teachings differed significantly from those Paul stressed in the churches of Gentile Christianity. No writings from the Palestinian Christians survive, so the fate of the Pella community is not known.

Pentateuch   From a Greek word meaning "five scrolls," the term denotes the first five books of the Hebrew Bible, the Torah.

Pentecost   (1) Also known as the Feast of Weeks (Exod. 34:22; Deut. 16:10), the Feast of Harvest (Exod. 23:16), and the Day of the First Fruits (Num. 28:26), Pentecost was a one-day celebration held fifty days after Passover at the juncture of May and June. (2) The occasion of the outpouring of Holy Spirit on early Christians assembled in Jerusalem (Acts 2:1–41), regarded as the spiritual baptism of the Church.

Peniel   A site on the Jabbok River in Jordan where Jacob wrestled with El (God) and thereby won a blessing (Gen. 33:22–33).

Peor   A mountain in Moab on which King Balak commanded the prophet Balaam to build seven altars (Num. 23:28–30), Peor may also have been the place where Israel sinned by worshiping Baal (Num. 25:1–18; Josh. 22:17).

Peraea (Perea)   A name the historian Flavius Josephus gave the area that the Old Testament called the land "beyond" or "across" (east of) the Jordan River (Gen. 50:10; Num. 22:1; Matt. 4:14; 19:1; John 10:40). Both John the Baptist and Jesus retreated to this rugged territory (John 1:28; 10:40–42; 11:3).

Pergamum   A major Hellenistic city in western Asia Minor (modern Bergama in west Anatolian Turkey), site of a magnificent temple of Zeus, which some commentators believe is referred to as "Satan's Throne" in Revelation 2:13, Pergamum is one of the seven churches that the author Johnny Patinos addresses (Rev. 1:11; 2:12–17).

pericope   A term used in form criticism to describe a literary unit (a saying, anecdote, parable, or brief narrative) that forms a complete entity in itself and is attached to its context by later editorial commentary. Many of Jesus' pronouncements probably circulated independently as pericopes before they were incorporated into the written Gospel records.

Persepolis   A capital of the Persian Empire established by Darius I (522–486 B.C.E.) and burned by Alexander the Great (330 B.C.E.) (2 Macc. 9:2).

Persia   A large Asian territory southeast of Elam inhabited by Indo-European (Ayrian, hence "Iran") peoples, Persia became a world power under Cyrus the Great, who united Media and Persia (549 B.C.E.), conquered Lydia (546 B.C.E.) and Babylon (539 B.C.E.), including its former dominion, Palestine, then permitted the formerly captive Jews to return to their homeland (2 Chron. 36:20–22; Ezra 1). Under Emperor Darius I (522–486 B.C.E.), the Jerusalem Temple was rebuilt (Ezra 3–6). A son of Darius, Xerxes I (486–465 B.C.E.) was probably the Ahasuerus of the Book of Esther (Esther 1:2; 2:1; 3:1; 8:1). Artaxerxes I (465–423 B.C.E.) decreed the return of two other exile groups under Ezra and Nehemiah.

pesher   A Hebrew word denoting an analysis or interpretation of Scripture, it is applied to the commentaries (*persherim*) found among the Dead Sea Scrolls.

Peshitta   A version of the Old Testament translated for Christian churches in Syria during the fifth century C.E.

Peter   The most prominent of Jesus' twelve chief disciples, Peter was also known as Simon (probably his surname), Simeon (Symeon), and Cephas (the Aramaic equivalent of *petros,* meaning "the rock" or "stone") (John 1:40–42). The son of Jonas or John (Matt. 16: 17; John 1:42; 21:15–17), brother of the apostle Andrew, and a native of Bethsaida, a fishing village on the Sea of Galilee (John 1:44), he was called by Jesus to be "a fisher of men" (Matt. 4:18–20; Mark 1:16–18; Luke 5:1–11). The first to recognize Jesus as the Messiah (Matt. 16:13–20; Mark 8:27–30; Luke 9:18–22), Peter later denied him three times (Matt. 26:69–75; Mark 14:66–72; Luke 22:54–62; John 18:15–18).

   Commanded to "feed [the resurrected Jesus'] sheep" (John 21:15–19), Peter became a leader of the Jerusalem church (Acts 1:15–26; 2:14–42; 15:6–12) and miracle worker (Acts 3:1–10) and was instrumental in bringing the first Gentiles into the Church (Acts 10–11), although Paul regarded him as a conservative obstacle to this movement (Gal. 2:11–14). He appeared before the Sanhedrin (Acts 4:1–12) and was miraculously rescued from at least one imprisonment (Acts 5: 17–42; 12:1–19). A married man (Matt. 8:14; Mark 1: 30; Luke 4:8; 1 Cor. 9:5), Peter was to be the "rock" on which Jesus' Church was built (Matt. 16:16–20). Although some scholars regard him as the source of 1 Peter, virtually all experts deny Petrine authorship to the second epistle bearing his name. He was martyred under Nero about 64–65 C.E.

pharaoh   The title of Egypt's king, commonly used in place of a ruler's proper name in the Old Testament. Thus, the pharaohs who confiscated Abraham's wife (Gen. 12:14–20), rewarded Joseph (Gen. 41:37–57), enslaved the Israelites (Exod. 1:8–22), and opposed Moses (Exod. 5:1–6:1; 6:27–15:19) are all anonymous, although many scholars believe that the pharaoh of the

Exodus was Rameses II (c. 1290–1224 B.C.E.). Solomon later made Egyptian pharaohs his allies (1 Kings 3: 1; 7:8). Pharaoh Shishak (Sheshonk I) sacked the Jerusalem Temple during King Rehoboam's time (c. 922–915 B.C.E.) (1 Kings 14:25–28; 2 Chron. 12: 2–9). Pharaoh Necho killed King Josiah at Megiddo but was later defeated by Nebuchadnezzar at Carchemish (2 Kings 23:29–34; 24:7; 2 Chron. 35:20–36:4).

Pharisees   A leading religious movement or sect in Judaism during the last two centuries B.C.E. and the two first centuries C.E., the Pharisees were probably descendants of the Hasidim who opposed Antiochus IV's attempts to destroy the Mosaic faith. Their name may derive from the Hebrew *parush* ("separated") because their rigorous observance of the law bred a separatist view toward common life. Although the New Testament typically presents them as Jesus' opponents, their views on resurrection and the afterlife anticipated Christian teachings. The "seven woes" against the Pharisees appear in Matthew 23:13–32. Paul was a Pharisee (Acts 23:6; 26:5; Phil. 3:5).

Philadelphia   A city in Lydia (modern Turkey) about twenty-eight miles from Sardis, one of the seven churches in Revelation 3:7–13.

Philemon   A citizen of Colossae whose runaway slave, Onesimus, Paul converted to Christianity (Philem. 5, 10, 16, 19).

Philip   (1) King of Macedonia (359–336 B.C.E.), father of Alexander the Great (1 Macc. 1:1; 6:2). (2) One of the Twelve, a man of Bethsaida in Galilee (Matt. 10:3; Mark 3:18; Luke 6:14; John 1:43–49; 12:21–22; 14: 8–9; Acts 1:12–14). (3) An evangelist of the Jerusalem church who was an administrator (Acts 6:1–6) and preacher (Acts 8:4–8), the convertor of Simon the sorcerer (Acts 8:9–13) and of an Ethiopian eunuch (Acts 8:26–39). Paul visited Philip at Caesarea (Acts 21: 8–15). (4) A son of Herod the Great and Palestinian tetrarch (4 B.C.E.–34 C.E.) (Luke 3:1).

Philippi   A city of eastern Macedonia, the first European center to receive the Christian message (Acts 16: 10–40), Philippi became the apostle Paul's favorite church (Acts 20:6; Phil. 4:16; 2 Cor. 11:9) and the one to which his letter to the Philippians is addressed.

Philistines   A people from Aegean Sea islands (called Caphtor in Amos 9:7) who settled along the southern coast of Palestine during the twelfth century B.C.E. to become the Israelites' chief rivals during the period of the judges and early monarchy (c. 1200–1000 B.C.E.) (Josh. 13:2–4; Judg. 1:18–19; 13:1–16:31; 1 Sam. 4: 2–7:14; 13:1–14:46; 17:1–54; 2 Sam. 5:17–25; 8:1– 2; 21:15–18; see also Jer. 47:1–7; Zeph. 2:4–7).

Philo Judaeus   The most influential philosopher of Hellenistic Judaism, Philo was a Greek-educated Jew living in Alexandria, Egypt (c. 20 B.C.E.–50 C.E.), who promoted a method of interpreting the Hebrew Bible allegorically (which may have influenced Paul in such passages as 1 Cor. 10:4 and Gal. 4:24, as well as the authors of the fourth Gospel and Hebrews). His doctrine of the Logos (the divine creative Word) shaped the prolog to the Gospel of John.

Phinehas   Grandson of Aaron, son of Eleazar, Israel's third high priest (Num. 10:8–10; 25:6–13; Josh. 22: 13, 30–32; 24:33).

Phoebe   A servant or deaconess of the church at Cenchrae, a port of Corinth, whose good works Paul commends in Romans 16:1–2.

Phoenicia   A narrow coastal territory along the northeast Mediterranean, lying between the Lebanon range on the east and the sea on the west. It included the ports of Tyre and Sidon. Notable Old Testament Phoenicians are Ethbaal, king of Tyre (1 Kings 16:21); his daughter Jezebel, wife of Ahab (1 Kings 18:19); Hiram, king of Tyre (2 Sam. 5:11; 1 Kings 5:1–12; 2 Chron. 2:3–16); and Hiram, the architect-decorator of Solomon's Temple (1 Kings 7:13–47; 2 Chron. 2:13). Jesus visited the area, where he healed the daughter of a Syro-Phoenician woman (Matt. 15:21; Mark 7:24, 31; Acts 15:3; 21:2–7).

phylacteries   One of the two small leather pouches containing copies of four scriptural passages (Exod. 13:1–10, 11–16; Deut. 6:4–9; 11:13–21), worn on the left arm and forehead by Jewish men during weekday prayers (Exod. 13:9, 16; Deut. 6:8; 11:18; Matt. 23:5).

Plato   Greek philosopher (427–347 B.C.E.) who postulated the existence of a dualistic universe consisting of an invisible spiritual realm containing Ideal Forms of everything that exists and an inferior material realm composed of imperfect replicas of those forms. Plato's view of the immortal human soul and its posthumous destiny greatly influenced virtually all subsequent Western thought, including that of official Christianity.

Polycarp   A bishop of Smyrna who was reputed to have been a disciple of John and who was martyred in 155 C.E. Letters to and from Polycarp are considered important noncanonical works.

polytheism   Belief in more than one god, the most common form of religion in the ancient world.

Pontius Pilate   The Roman prefect (also called a procurator) of Judea (26–36 C.E.) who presided at Jesus' trial for sedition against Rome and sentenced him to be crucified (Luke 3:1; 13:1; 23:1–25; Matt. 27:1–26; Mark 15:1–15; John 18:28–19:22; Acts 3:13; 13:28; 1 Tim. 6:13).

Potiphar   The head of pharaoh's bodyguard who placed Joseph in charge of his household but later threw him in prison when the Hebrew slave was accused of seducing Potiphar's wife (Gen. 37:36; 39:1).

Priestly document   The Priestly composition, referred to as P. This is the final written addition to the Pentateuch, consisting largely of genealogical, statistical, and legal material compiled during and after the Babylonian exile (c. 550–450 B.C.E.). Major blocks of P occur in Exodus 25–31; 35–40; Leviticus 1–27; and Numbers 1–10. P incorporated the earlier J and E sources and provided an editorial framework for the entire Torah. Some recent scholars believe that P is responsible for most of the Pentateuch.

Priscilla   (Prisca)   The wife of Aquila and a leading member of the early Church (Acts 18:18; Rom. 16:3; 2 Tim. 4:19).

proconsul   A Roman governor or administrator of a province or territory, such as Gallio, proconsul of Achaia, before whom Paul appeared (Acts 18:12).

procurator   The Roman title of the governor of a region before it became an administrative province. During the reigns of Augustus and Tiberius, Judea was governed by a prefect, the most famous of whom was Pontius Pilate. The office was upgraded to the level of procurator under Claudius.

prophet   One who preaches or proclaims the word or will of his or her Deity (Amos 3:7–8; Deut. 18:9–22). A true prophet in Israel was regarded as divinely inspired. *See Navi.*

Prophets   (Nevi'im)   The second major division of the Hebrew Bible, including Joshua through 2 Kings, Isaiah, Jeremiah, Ezekiel, and the twelve Minor Prophets.

Protoevangelium of James   Also called the Book of James, a noncanonical gospel, supposedly written by James (pictured as Jesus' older step-brother), that provides an account of Jesus' parents and family. Although this work is not part of the New Testament canon, it has been influential in church history because of its portrait of Mary, Jesus' mother.

proverb   A brief saying that memorably expresses a familiar or useful bit of folk wisdom, usually of a practical or prudential nature.

Providence   A quasi-religious concept in which God is viewed as the force sustaining and guiding human destiny. It assumes that events occur as part of a divine plan or purpose working for the ultimate triumph of Good.

psalm   A sacred song or poem used in praise or worship of the Deity, particularly those in the Book of Psalms.

Pseudepigrapha   (1) Literally, books falsely ascribed to eminent biblical figures of the past, such as Enoch, Noah, Moses, or Isaiah. (2) A collection of religious books outside the Hebrew Bible canon or Apocrypha that were composed in Hebrew, Aramaic, and Greek from about 200 B.C.E.–200 C.E.

pseudonymity   A literary practice, common among Jewish writers of the last two centuries B.C.E. and the first two centuries C.E, of writing or publishing a book in the name of a famous religious figure of the past. Thus, an anonymous author of about 168 B.C.E. ascribed his work to Daniel, who supposedly lived during the 500s B.C.E. The Pastorals, 2 Peter, James, and

Jude are thought to be pseudonymous books written in the mid-second century C.E. but attributed to eminent disciples connected with the first-century Jerusalem church.

Ptolemy　(1) Ptolemy I (323–285 B.C.E.) was a Macedonian general who assumed rulership of Egypt after the death of Alexander the Great. The Ptolemaic dynasty controlled Egypt and its dominions until 31 B.C.E., when the Romans came to power. (2) Ptolemy II (285–246 B.C.E.) supposedly authorized the translation of the Hebrew Bible into Greek (the Septuagint).

publican　In the New Testament, petty tax collectors for Rome, despised by the Jews from whom they typically extorted money (Matt. 9:10–13; 18:17; 21:31). Jesus dined with these "sinners" (Matt. 9:9–13) and called one, Levi (Matthew), to apostleship (Matt. 9:9–13; Luke 5:27–31). He also painted a publican as more virtuous than a Pharisee (Luke 18:9–14).

Purim　A Jewish nationalistic festival held on the fourteenth and fifteenth days of Adar (February-March) and based on events in the Book of Esther.

Q　An abbreviation for *Quelle,* the German term for "source," a hypothetical document that many scholars believe contained a collection of Jesus' sayings (*logia*). The theory of its existence was formed to explain material common to both Matthew and Luke but absent from Mark's Gospel. It is assumed that Matthew and Luke drew on a single source (Q), assembled about 50 C.E., for this shared material.

Queen of Heaven　A Semitic goddess of love and fertility worshiped in various forms throughout the ancient Near East. Known as Ishtar to the Babylonians, she was denounced by Jeremiah but worshiped by Jewish refugees in Egypt after the fall of Jerusalem (Jer. 7:18; 44: 17–19, 25).

Qumran　Ruins of an Essene monastic community located near the northwest corner of the Dead Sea, near which the Essene library (Dead Sea Scrolls) were hidden in caves. The Romans destroyed it in 68 C.E.

rabbi　A Jewish title (meaning "master" or "teacher") given to scholars learned in the Torah. Jesus was frequently addressed by this title (Matt. 23:8; 26:25, 49; Mark 8:5; 10:51; 11:21; 14:45; John 1:38, 49; 3:2; 4: 31; 6:25; 9:2; 11:8; 20:16), as was John the Baptist (John 3:26), although Jesus supposedly forbade his followers to be so called (Matt. 23:7–8).

Rachel　Daughter of Laban, second and favorite wife of Jacob, mother of Joseph and Benjamin (Gen. 29:6–30; 30:1–24; 35:16–19). When Rachel fled her father's house with Jacob, she stole Laban's household gods (Gen. 31:32–35). Jeremiah prophesied that Rachel (Israel) would "weep for her children," which the author of Matthew's Gospel regarded as fulfilled when Herod slaughtered the children of Bethlehem (Jer. 31:15; Matt. 2:18; see also Ruth 4:11).

Rahab　(1) A prostitute of Jericho, possibly a priestess in a Canaanite fertility cult, who hid Israelite spies and was spared her city's destruction (Josh. 2:1–24; 6:25; Ps. 87:4; Heb. 11:31). (2) A mythological sea monster, the dragon of chaos, whom Yahweh subdued before his creation of the universe (Ps. 89:10); also a symbol of Egypt (Ps. 87:4; Isa. 30:7).

Rameses (Raamses)　One of the two "store cities" that the enslaved Israelites built for pharaoh (probably Rameses II) (Exod. 1:11; 12:37; Num. 33:3–5).

Rameses II　Ruler of Egypt (c. 1290–1224 B.C.E.) who many scholars think was the pharaoh of the Exodus.

Ramoth-Gilead　A town in Gilead, east of Jordan near the Syrian border, that was a city of refuge (Deut. 4:43; Josh. 20:8) and a Levitical center (Josh. 21:38; 1 Chron. 6:80) for the tribe of Gad. Ahab of Israel (869–850 B.C.E.) was killed trying to recapture it from Aram (Syria) (1 Kings 22:1–38; 2 Chron. 18:1–34), and the usurper Jehu was anointed there (2 Kings 9:1–21).

Ras Shamra　*See* Ugarit.

realized eschatology　A belief that events usually associated with the eschaton (world End) are even now realized or fulfilled by Jesus' spiritual presence among believers.

Rebekah (Rebecca)　The daughter of Milcah and Bethuel, son of Abraham's brother Nahor (Gen. 24:15, 47), and sister of Laban (Gen. 25:20), whom Abraham's representative found at Haran and brought back to Canaan as a bride for Isaac (Gen. 24). Of Esau and Jacob, the twin sons she bore Isaac, she preferred Jacob and helped him trick her dying husband into giving him the paternal blessing (Gen. 25:21–28; 27:5–30; see also Rom. 9:10).

Rechab　The father of Jehonadab (Jonadab), who assisted Jehu in exterminating Ahab's entire household and associates (2 Kings 10:1–28). The Rechabites were a group of ascetics who abstained from wine, settled dwellings, and other aspects of what they considered urban corruption.

redaction criticism　A method of analyzing written texts that tries to define the purpose and literary procedures of editors (redactors) who compile and edit older documents, transforming shorter works into longer ones, as did the redactor who collected and ordered the words of the prophets into their present biblical form.

redactor　Editor. *See* redaction criticism.

Rehoboam　A son of Solomon and Naamah (an Ammonite princess), the last ruler of the united kingdom (922–915 B.C.E.), whose harsh policies resulted in the ten northern tribes' deserting the Davidic monarchy in Judah and forming the independent northern kingdom of Israel (922 B.C.E.) (1 Kings 11:43; 12:1–24; 14: 21–31; 2 Chron. 9:31–12:16) and in Pharaoh Shishak's

(Sheshonk I) despoiling the Jerusalem Temple (1 Kings 14:25–28).

resurrection The returning of the dead to life, a late Old Testament belief (Isa. 26:19; Dan. 12:2–3, 13) that first became prevalent in Judaism during the time of the Maccabees (after 168 B.C.E.) and became a part of the Pharisees' doctrine. Like the prophets Elijah and Elisha (1 Kings 17:17–24; 2 Kings 4:18–37), Jesus performed several temporal resurrections: of the widow of Nain's son (Luke 7:11–17), the daughter of Jairus (Mark 5:21–43), and Lazarus (John 11:1–44). Unlike these personages, however, Jesus ascended to heaven after his own resurrection (Acts 1:7–8). Paul gives the fullest discussion of the resurrection in the New Testament (1 Thess. 4; 1 Cor. 15), although he leaves many questions unanswered (see also Matt. 25: 31–46 and Rev. 20:13).

Reuben (1) The son of Jacob and Leah, eldest of his father's twelve sons (Gen. 29:32; Num. 26:5), Reuben slept with his father's concubine (Gen. 35:22), which cost him a paternal blessing (Gen. 49:3–4), but he defended Joseph against his brothers (Gen. 37:21–30). (2) The northern Israelite tribe supposedly descended from Reuben (Num. 32:1–38) that along with Gad settled in the highlands east of the Jordan River.

rhetorical criticism A method of textual analysis that studies not only the form and structure of a given literary work but the distinctive style of the author.

Roman Empire The international, interracial government centered in Rome, Italy, that conquered and administered the entire Mediterranean region from Gaul (France and southern Germany) in the northwest to Egypt in the southeast and ruled the Jews of Palestine from 63 B.C.E. until Hadrian's destruction of Jerusalem during the second Jewish revolt (132–135 C.E.).

Rosetta Stone A granite block bearing the same message inscribed in both Greek and ancient Egyptian hieroglyphics, a bilingual inscription that enabled scholars to decipher the language of the pharaohs. Discovered in 1799 and translated by the French linguist Champollion, it records a proclamation by Ptolemy V (c. 203–181 B.C.E.).

Ruth A widow from Moab who married Boaz of Bethlehem and became an ancestor of King David (Ruth 4:17).

Saba (Sheba) A Semitic kingdom in western Arabia noted for its merchants and luxury trade but best known for the visit of one of its queens to Solomon's court (1 Kings 10:1–13; 2 Chron. 9:1–12; 2 Matt. 12: 42; Luke 11:31).

Sabbath The seventh day of the Jewish week, sacred to Yahweh and dedicated to rest and worship. Enjoined upon Israel as a sign of Yahweh's covenant (Exod. 20: 8–11; 23:12; 31:12–17; Lev. 23:3; 24:1–9; Deut. 5: 12–15) and a memorial of Yahweh's repose after six days of creation, the Sabbath was strictly observed by leaders of the returned exiles (Neh. 13:15–22; Isa. 56: 2–6; Ezek. 46:1–7). Jesus was frequently criticized for his liberal attitude toward the Sabbath, which he contended was made for humanity's benefit (Matt. 12: 1–12; Mark 2:23–28; Luke 6:1–9; John 5:18).

Sabbatical Year According to the Torah, every seventh ear was to be a Sabbath among years, a time when fields were left fallow, native-born slaves freed, and outstanding debts canceled (Exod. 21:2–6; 23:10–13; Lev. 25:1–19; Deut. 15:1–6).

sacrifice In ancient religion, something precious—usually an unblemished animal, fruit, or grain—offered to a god and thereby made sacred. The Mosaic law required the regular ritual slaughter of sacrificial animals and birds (Lev. 1:1–7:38; 16:1–17:14; Deut. 15: 19–23; etc.).

Sadducees An ultraconservative Jewish sect of the first century B.C.E. and first century C.E. composed largely of wealthy and politically influential landowners. Unlike the Pharisees, the Sadducees recognized only the Torah as binding and rejected the Prophets and Writings, denying both resurrection and a judgement in the afterlife. An aristocracy controlling the priesthood and Temple, they cooperated with Roman rule of Palestine, a collusion that made them unpopular with the common people (Matt. 3:7; 16:1; 22:23; Mark 12:18; Luke 20:27; Acts 4:1; 5:17; 23:6).

saints Holy ones, persons of exceptional virtue and sanctity, believers outstandingly faithful despite persecution (Dan. 7:18–21; 8:13; Matt. 27:52; Acts 9:13; 26:10; Rom. 8:27; 1 Cor. 6:2; 1 Thess. 3:13; 2 Thess. 1:10; Heb. 13:24; Rev. 5:8; 13:7–10; 17:6; 20:9).

Salome (1) Daughter of Herodias and Herod (son of Herod the Great) and niece of Herod Antipas, before whom she danced to secure the head of John the Baptist (Matt. 14:3–11; Mark 6:17–28). Anonymous in the New Testament, her name is given by Flavius Josephus (*Antiquities* 18.5.4). (2) A woman present at Jesus' crucifixion (Matt. 27:56; Mark 15:40) and at the empty tomb (Mark 16:1).

Samaria Capital of the northern kingdom (Israel), Samaria was founded by Omri (c. 876–869 B.C.E.) (1 Kings 16:24–25) and included a temple and altar of Baal (1 Kings 16:32). The Assyrians destroyed it in 721 B.C.E. (2 Kings 17), a fate the prophets warned awaited Jerusalem (Isa. 8:4; 10:9–11; Mic. 1:1–7).

Samaritans Inhabitants of the city or territory of Samaria, the central region of Palestine lying west of the Jordan River. According to a probably biased southern account in 2 Kings 17, the Samaritans were regarded by orthodox Jews as descendants of foreigners who had intermarried with survivors of the northern kingdom's fall to Assyria (721 B.C.E.). Separated from the rest of Judaism after about 400 B.C.E., they had a Bible consisting of their own edition of the Pentateuch (Torah) and a temple on Mount Gerizim, which was later destroyed by John Hyrcanus (128 B.C.E.) (Matt. 10:5; Luke 9:52; John 4:20–21). Jesus discussed correct worship with a woman at Jacob's well in Samaria (John 4:5–42) and made a "good Samaritan" the hero of a famous parable (Luke 10:29–37).

Samson   Son of Manoah of the tribe of Dan, Samson was a Nazirite judge of Israel famous for his supernatural strength, abortive love affair with Delilah, and spectacular destruction of the Philistine temple of Dagon (Judg. 13–16).

Samuel   The son of Hannah and Elkanah, an Ephraimite (1 Sam. 1:1–2), Samuel was Israel's last judge (1 Sam. 7:15; Acts 13:20), a prophet and seer (1 Sam. 9:9) who also performed priestly functions (1 Sam. 2:18, 27, 35; 7:9–12). Trained by the high priest Eli at Shiloh (1 Sam. 2:11–21; 3:1–10), he became the single greatest influence in Israel's transition from the tribal confederacy to monarchy under Saul, whom he anointed king (1 Sam. 8:1–10:27) but later rejected in favor of David (1 Sam. 13:8–15; 15:10–35).

sanctuary   A holy place dedicated to the worship of a god and believed to confer personal security to those who took refuge in it. Solomon's Temple on Mount Zion in Jerusalem was such a sacred edifice, although Jeremiah denounced those who trusted in its power to save a disobedient people from punishment (Jer. 7; 26).

Sanhedrin   The supreme judicial council of the Jews from about the third century B.C.E. until the Romans destroyed Jerusalem in 70 C.E., its deliberations were led by the high priest (2 Chron. 19:5–11). Jesus was tried before the Sanhedrin and condemned on charges of blasphemy (Matt. 26:59; Mark 14:55; 15:1; Luke 22:66; John 11:47). Stephen was stoned as a result of its verdict (Acts 6:12–15). Peter, John, and other disciples were hailed before its court (Acts 4:5–21; 5:17–41), and Paul was charged there with violating the Mosaic Torah (Acts 22).

Sarah   The wife and half-sister of Abraham (Gen. 11:29; 16:1; 20:12), Sarah traveled with him from Ur to Haran and ultimately to Canaan and after a long period of barrenness bore him a single son, Isaac (Gen. 18:9–15; 21:1–21). She died in Hebron (Gen. 23:2) and was buried at Machpelah in Canaan (Gen. 23:19; see also Rom. 4:9; Heb. 11:11; 1 Pet. 3:6).

Sardis   Capital of the kingdom of Lydia (modern Turkey), captured by Cyrus the Great (546 B.C.E.); later part of the Roman province of Asia and the site of a cult of Cybele, a pagan fertility goddess (Rev. 3:1–6).

Sargon I   The Semitic founder of a Mesopotamian Empire incorporating ancient Sumer and Akkad and stretching from Elam to the Mediterranean (about 2360 B.C.E.).

Sargon II   Successor of Shalmaneser V and king of Assyria (722–705 B.C.E.) who completed his predecessor's three-year siege of Samaria and captured the city, bringing the northern kingdom (Israel) to an end in 721 B.C.E. (Isa. 20:1; 2 Kings 17).

Satan   In the Old Testament, "the satan" appears as a prosecutor in the heavenly court among "the sons of God" (Job 1–2; Zech. 3:1–3) and only later as a tempter (1 Chron. 21:1; cf. 2 Sam. 24:1). Although the Hebrew Bible says virtually nothing about Satan's origin, the pseudepigraphal writings contain much legendary material about his fall from heaven and the establishment of a hierarchy of demons and devils. By the time the New Testament was written, he was believed to head a kingdom of Evil and to seek the corruption of all people, including the Messiah (Matt. 4:1–11; Luke 4:1–13). Satan (the "Opposer" or "Adversary") is also "the Evil One" (Matt. 6:13; 13:19; Eph. 6:16; 1 John 2:13; 5:18–19), "the Devil" (Matt. 4:1; 13:39; 25:41; John 8:44; Eph. 4:27), and the primordial serpent who tempted Eve (Rev. 12:9).

Saul   Son of Kish, a Benjaminite, and the first king of Israel (c. 1020–1000 B.C.E.), Saul was anointed by Samuel to meet the Philistine crisis, which demanded a strong centralized leadership (1 Sam. 9:1–10:27). He defeated the Ammonites (1 Sam. 11:1–11) and Philistines at Geba and Michmash but rapidly lost support after antagonizing Samuel (1 Sam. 13:8–15) and refusing to kill the Amalekite king (1 Sam. 15:7–35). He was also upstaged by David, of whom he became intensely jealous (1 Sam. 18:6–24:23). Saul and his son Jonathan were killed by the Philistines at the Battle of Gilboa (1 Sam. 31) and commemorated by one of David's most beautiful psalms (2 Sam. 1:17–27).

Saul of Tarsus   According to Acts, the name by which the apostle Paul was known before his conversion on the road to Damascus. *See* Paul.

Savior   One who saves from danger or destruction, a term applied to Yahweh in the Old Testament (Ps. 106:21; Isa. 43:1–13; 63:7–9; Hos. 13:4) and to Jesus in the New (Luke 2:11; John 4:42; Acts 5:31; 13:23; Phil. 3:20; 1 Tim. 4:10; 2 Tim. 1:10; 1 John 4:14).

scapegoat   According to Leviticus 16, a sacrificial goat on whose head Israel's high priest placed the people's collective sins on the Day of Atonement, after which the goat was sent out into the desert to Azazel (possibly a demon). The term has come to signify anyone who bears the blame for others (see Isa. 53).

scribes   Professional copyists who recorded commercial, royal, and religious texts and served as clerks, secretaries, and archivists at Israel's royal court and Temple (2 Kings 12:10; 19:2; Ezra 4:8; 2 Chron. 34:8; Jer. 36:18). After the Jews' return from exile, professional teachers or "wise men" preserved and interpreted the Mosaic Torah (Ezra 7:6; Neh. 7:73–8:18). In the New Testament, scribes are often linked with Pharisees as Jesus' opponents (Matt. 7:29; 23:2, 13; Luke 11:44) who conspired to kill him (Mark 14:43; 15:1; Luke 22:2; 23: 10), although some became his followers (Matt.8:19; see also Acts 6:12; 23:9; 1 Cor. 1:20).

scroll   A roll of papyrus, leather, or parchment such as those on which the Hebrew Bible and New Testament were written. The rolls were made of sheets about nine to eleven inches high and five or six inches wide, sewed together to make a strip up to twenty-five or thirty feet long, which was wound around a stick and unrolled when read (Isa. 34:4; Rev. 6:14; Jer. 36).

Scythians   A fierce nomadic people from north and east of the Black Sea who swept southward toward Egypt and Judah about 626 B.C.E. Jeremiah prophesied that Judah would be devastated (Jer. 4:5–31; 5:15–17; 6: 1–8, 22–26), and Zephaniah saw the invasion as a sign that the Day of Yahweh had arrived (Zeph. 1:7–8, 14–18); but the Scythians were bribed by Pharaoh Psammetichus I (664–610 B.C.E.) and returned north by the coastal route without attacking Palestine.

Sea of Reeds   A body of water or swampland bordering the Red Sea that the Israelites miraculously crossed during their flight from Egypt (Exod. 14:5–15:21). The origin of the name is uncertain because there are no reeds in the Red Sea, which is more than 7200 feet deep.

Second Isaiah   *See* Isaiah.

Secret Mark   One of several noncanonical gospels. This gospel may provide a link between the Synoptic Gospels and the fourth Gospel's account of Lazarus' resurrection.

seer   A clairvoyant or diviner who experiences ecstatic visions (1 Sam. 9:9–11); forerunner of the prophets.

Seir   A mountain range running through Edom almost to the Gulf of Aqabah through which the Israelites passed during their desert wanderings (Deut. 2:1; 33: 2). Seir was regarded as the home of the Esau tribes, rivals of Israel (Gen. 36:8, 20–21; Josh. 24:4) and was also an early name for Edom (Gen. 32:3; 35:20–21, 30; Num. 14:18).

Seleucids   The Macedonian Greek dynasty founded by Alexander's general Seleucus (ruled 312–280 B.C.E.), centered in Syria with Antioch as its capital. After defeating the Ptolemies of Egypt, it controlled Palestine from 198 to 165 B.C.E., after which the Maccabean revolt defeated the forces of Antiochus IV and eventually drove the Syrians from Judea (142 B.C.E.) (1 and 2 Macc.).

Seleucus   *See* Seleucids.

Semites   According to Genesis 10:21–31, peoples descended from Noah's son Shem, whose progeny included Elam, Asshur, Arpacshad (Hebrews and Arabs), Lud (Lydians), and Aram (Syrians) (Gen. 10:22). In modern usage, the term applies to linguistic rather than to racial groups, such as those who employ one of a common family of inflectional languages, including Akkadian, Aramaic, Hebrew, and Arabic.

Sennacherib   Son of Sargon II and king of Assyria (704–681 B.C.E.). In 701 B.C.E., Sennacherib devastated Tyre and besieged Jerusalem, after which he levied heavy tribute upon King Hezekiah of Judah (2 Kings 18). A clay prism recording Sennacherib's version of the Judean campaign tallies well with 2 Kings 18:14–16 but strikingly diverges from the story of 185,000 Assyrian soldiers slain by Yahweh's angel in a single night (2 Kings 19:10–35; Isa. 37:9–36).

Septuagint (LXX)   A Greek translation of the Old Testament traditionally attributed to seventy or seventy-two Palestinian scholars during the reign of Ptolemy II (285–246 B.C.E.), the Septuagint was actually the work of several generations of Alexandrine translators, begun about 250 B.C.E. and not complete until the first century C.E. The later additions to the Septuagint were deleted from the standard Hebrew Bible (Masoretic Text) but included in the Christian Scriptures as the Apocrypha.

seraphim   Heavenly beings, usually depicted with six wings (Isa. 6), who attended the throne of God; perhaps derived from Assyrian or Egyptian mythology.

serpent   A common symbol in Near Eastern fertility cults, a snake was the original tempter of humanity (Gen. 3–4) and a symbol of Assyria, Babylon (Isa. 27: 1), and the Israelite tribe of Dan (Gen. 49:17). A bronze image of a snake that was used to heal the Israelites during a plague of snakes in the wilderness (Num. 21:4–9) was later destroyed by King Hezekiah (2 Kings 18:4). Revelation 12:9 identifies the serpent with the devil and Satan (the primordial dragon).

Seth   The third son of Adam and Eve (Gen. 4:25–26; 5:2–8), cited as the first man to invoke Yahweh's sacred name.

Shadrach   The name the leading eunuch of Babylon gave the Hebrew boy Hananiah (Dan. 1:7; 2:49). Along with Abednego and Meshach, he survived incarceration in a fiery furnace (Dan. 3:1–30).

Shalmaneser   The name of five Assyrian kings, two of whom appear in the Old Testament. (1) Shalmaneser III (859–824 B.C.E.), one of Assyria's most effective rulers, defeated a coalition of Syrian and Palestinian states led by Ben-hadad (Hadadezer) of Damascus and King Ahab of Israel, a defense league that disintegrated largely because of Elijah's and Elisha's interference in Israelite and Syrian politics (2 Kings 8:7–15, 9–10). Shalmaneser's Black Obelisk shows either Jehu, who overthrew Ahab's dynasty, or one of his representatives groveling at the Assyrian king's feet and paying him tribute. (2) Shalmaneser V (726–722 B.C.E.), successor to Tiglath-Pileser, extorted tribute from Hoshea, last ruler of the northern kingdom (732–724 B.C.E.). When Hoshea later refused payment, Shalmaneser captured him and laid siege to Israel's capital, Samaria, for three years but died before taking the city (2 Kings 17: 3–5; 18:9).

Shamash Babylonian sun god associated with justice and prophecy, the Akkadian counterpart of the Sumerian Utu.

Shaphan Scribal secretary of state for King Josiah (640–609 B.C.E.), to whom Hilkiah the priest entrusted the "lost" Book of the Law (probably Deuteronomy) found during repairs on the Jerusalem Temple. After reading it to Josiah, Shaphan was sent to ask the prophetess Huldah what Yahweh wished done with the book. He may have been instrumental in the subsequent religious reforms (2 Kings 22:3–20).

Sharon, Plain of The most fertile part of the coastal plain of Palestine, stretching about fifty miles north to the headland of Mount Carmel, belonged to the northern kingdom after 922 B.C.E. Its desirable fields became an image of the messianic bounty (Isa. 35:2).

Sheba, Queen of *See* Saba.

Shechem (1) The son of Hamor the Hivite from whom Jacob bought land in Canaan and who later raped and wished to marry Jacob's daughter Dinah (Gen. 33: 18–20; 34:1–31). Despite Hamor's friendly wish to ally his clan with Jacob's, Simon and Levi led Jacob's sons in a murderous attack on Shechem's clan to avenge their sister's dishonor. (2) An ancient Canaanite city located about forty-one miles north of Jerusalem in the hill country later allocated to the tribe of Ephraim, Shechem was the first site in Canaan that Abraham visited (Gen. 12:6) and the first place where the Hebrews came in touch with Canaanite culture (Gen. 33:18–20; 34:1–31). Here Joshua held a covenant-renewal ceremony uniting the Israelite tribes under Yahweh and, according to some scholars, including native tribes friendly to the Israelites. Abimelech attempted to make himself king here (Judg. 9), and here Rehoboam came to be crowned (1 Kings 12), only to be divested of his northern territories by Jeroboam I, who made Shechem his capital. Although the Deuteronomists mention its religious importance (Deut. 11: 26–32; 17:1–26; Josh. 8:30–37), Shechem fell into obscurity until the mid-fourth century B.C.E. when the Samaritans built a temple on Mount Gerizim. The city was destroyed by John Hyrcanus in the late second century B.C.E. but rebuilt as Flavia Neapolis.

Shem Noah's oldest son, brother of Ham and Japheth, the eponymous ancestor of the Semites, including the Arameans, Hebrews, Akkadians, and Arabs (Gen. 5:32; 9:21–27; 10:1).

Shema Judaism's supreme declaration of monotheistic faith, expressed in the words of Deuteronomy 6:4–9 beginning "Listen (Hebrew *shema,* "hear"), Israel, Yahweh our God is the one Yahweh." It also includes Deuteronomy 11:13–21 and Numbers 14:37–41 (cf. Mark 12:29–34).

Sheol According to the Old Testament, the subterranean region to which the "shades" of all the dead descended, a place of intense gloom, hopelessness, and virtual unconsciousness for its inhabitants. The term was translated *Hades* in the Greek Septuagint and in later Hellenistic times was regarded as an abode of the dead awaiting resurrection (Gen. 42:38; 1 Sam. 2:6; Job 7:9; 14:13–14; 26:6; Pss. 6:5; 16:10; 55:15; 139:8; Prov. 27:20; Eccles. 9:10; Isa. 14:15; 28:15; 38:10, 18; Hos. 13:14; Jon. 2:2; cf. references to Hades in Matt. 16:18; Luke 10:15; Acts 2:31; Rev. 1:18; 20:15). It is *not* the same theological concept as hell or Gehenna (Matt. 10:28; 23:33; Mark 9:43; Luke 12:5).

Shepherd of Hermas One of several extracanonical works contained in the Codex Sinaiticus. This mystical, apocalyptic work incorporates documents that may date from the first century C.E.

Shewbread The term the King James Version uses for the twelve loaves of consecrated unleavened bread placed in the Holy Place of the tabernacle and Temple (Exod. 25:30; Lev. 24:5–9; 1 Sam. 21:2–6).

Shibboleth The password Jephthah used to determine whether fugitives from a battle between the Ephraimites and his own Gileadites were his people or the enemy's. The Ephraimites pronounced *sh* as *s* (Judg. 12:4–6). In contemporary usage, the term refers to the slogans or distinctive values of a party or class.

Shiloh A prominent town and religious center that the Israelites established in the highlands of Ephraim, where Joshua assigned the tribes of Israel their territorial allotments (Josh. 18). Apparently a headquarters for the tribal confederacy during the time of the judges (Josh. 21:2; 22:9; Judg. 21:15–24; 1 Sam. 2; 12–17; 3: 30), the Ark of the Covenant was kept there until the Philistine war, when it was taken to a camp at Ebenezer, where the Philistines captured it (1 Sam. 4). Returned, it was not again placed in Shiloh (1 Sam. 6: 21–7:2), possibly because the Philistines had devastated the site. Jeremiah predicted that Yahweh would deal with Jerusalem as he had with Shiloh (Jer. 7:12–15; 26: 6–9).

Shinar, Plain of An alluvial lowland between the Tigris and Euphrates rivers at the head of the Persian Gulf. Settled by Sumerians about 4000 B.C.E., it was later known as Babylonia after the principal city in the area (Gen. 11:2; 14:1, 9). This region is the traditional homeland of Abraham, ancestor of the Israelites (Gen. 11:31; see also Isa. 11:11; Zech. 5:11; Dan. 1:2).

Shishak An Egyptian pharaoh (Sheshonk or Sheshonq I) (935–914 B.C.E.), founder of the Twenty-Second Dynasty, who during Solomon's reign gave asylum to the rebellious Jeroboam (1 Kings 11:40) but later invaded Judah and stripped the Temple of many of its treasures (1 Kings 14:25–28; 2 Chron. 12:2–9).

Shittim Site of the Israelites' encampment in Moab, opposite Jericho, prior to their crossing the Jordan River into Canaan (Num. 24–36).

Shrine   A sacred place or altar at which a god is worshiped, usually with ritual sacrifices. The discovery of Deuteronomy (621 B.C.E.), which prohibited sacrifice at any but a designated central sanctuary (assumed to be the Jerusalem Temple), inspired Josiah's sweeping destruction of all rival shrines in Judah and Samaria (2 Kings 22–23; 2 Chron. 34–35).

Shunammite   The "Shulamite" bride who is praised in the Song of Solomon 6:13; the origin and meaning of the name are uncertain.

Sibylline Oracles   A collection of futuristic visions written in imitation of Greco-Roman prophecies attributed to Apollo's oracle, the Sibyl.

Sidon   A wealthy Phoenician port city (Gen. 10:15, 19; 1 Chron. 1:13) that suffered repeated destructions during the Assyrian, Babylonian, and Persian periods (Jer. 25:22; 27:3; Ezek. 27:8; 28:21–23) but was rebuilt and visited by Jesus and Paul during Roman times (Mark 7: 24–31; Acts 27:3). *Siddonians* is a common biblical term for Phoenicians.

Silas   The Semitic, perhaps Aramean, name of an early Christian prophet (Acts 15:32), otherwise called Silvanus, who accompanied Barnabas and Paul to Antioch with decrees from the Jerusalem council (Acts 15: 1–35) and who joined Paul on his second missionary journey (Acts 16–18; 1 Thess. 1:1; 2 Thess. 1:1). He may have been the author of 1 Peter (1 Pet. 5:12).

Simeon   (1) The second son of Jacob and Leah (Gen. 29:33) who helped avenge his sister's rape upon the people of Shechem (Gen. 34). The tribal group named after him, the Simeonites, was probably absorbed by Judah and is seldom mentioned in the Old Testament (Deut. 27:12). (2) Another name for Simon Peter (Acts 15:14; 2 Pet. 1:1). (3) The devout old man who recognized the infant Jesus as the promised Messiah (Luke 2:22–34).

simile   A comparison, usually to illustrate an unexpected resemblance between a familiar object and novel idea. Jesus' parables about the kingdom of God are typically cast as similes (Matt. 13:31–35, 44–50; Mark 4:26–32; Luke 13:18–19).

Simon   The name of several New Testament figures. (1) Simon Peter (Matt. 4:18; 10:2). (2) One of the twelve apostles, Simon the Canaanite (Matt. 10:4; Mark 3:18), a nationalist Zealot (Luke 6:15; Acts 1:13). (3) One of Jesus' "brothers" (Matt. 13:55; Mark 6:3). (4) A leper whom Jesus cured (Mark 14:3–9). (5) Simon of Cyrene, the man from North Africa who was forced to carry Jesus' cross (Mark 15:21). (6) A Pharisee who entertained Jesus in his home (Luke 7:36–50). (7) Simon Iscariot, father of Judas the traitor (John 6:71; 13:26). (8) A leather tanner of Joppa with whom Peter stayed (Acts 9:43; 10).

Simon Magus   A Samaritan sorcerer ("magus") who tried to buy the power of the Holy Spirit from Peter (Acts 8:9–24); thought by some to be the forerunner of the Faust figure. The sale of church office is known as *simony*.

Sin   An Akkadian deity known to the Sumerians as Nanna, the moon god.

Sin, Wilderness of   A desert plain on the Sinai peninsula through which the Israelites passed on their way to Mount Sinai (Exod. 16:1; 17:1; Num. 33:11–12).

Sinai   (1) A peninsula at whose southern apex the Gulf of Aqabah joins the Gulf of Suez at the head of the Red Sea. Its 150-mile inverted base borders the Mediterranean, forming the boundary between Egypt and Palestine. (2) According to the J and P accounts, Mount Sinai, the sacred mountain in the wilderness where Moses experienced Yahweh's call (Exod. 3; 6) and to which he led the Israelites from Egypt for Yahweh's revelation of the Torah (Exod. 19–24; 34:4). This site, which has never been positively identified, is called Horeb by E and D (Exod. 3:1; 17:6; Deut. 1:6; 4:10).

Sisera   The Canaanite leader whose forces Deborah and Barak defeated and whom Jael, wife of Heber the Kenite, murdered in her tent (Judg. 4–5).

Sitz-im-Leben   German term used in form criticism to denote the social and cultural environment out of which a particular biblical unit grew and developed.

Smyrna   An Aegean port city of western Asia Minor (Turkey), site of an early Christian church that the author of Revelation praises for its poverty and faithfulness (Rev. 1:11; 2:8–10).

Sodom   Along with Gomorrah, Admah, Zebolim, and Zoar (Gen. 13:10–12; 14:2; Deut. 29:23), one of the "five cities of the plain" (near the south shore of the Dead Sea) destroyed by a great cataclysm attributed to Yahweh (Gen. 19:1–29). Abraham, who had been royally welcomed by Sodom's king (Gen. 14:13–24), pleaded for it to be spared (Gen. 18:16–32). Contrary to legend, its sins were regarded as violence and inhospitality to strangers rather than homosexuality. Later Bible writers cite it as a symbol of divine judgment upon wickedness (Isa. 3:9; Lam. 4:6; Matt. 10:15; 2 Pet. 2:6; Jude 7; Rev. 11:8).

Solomon   Son of David and Bathsheba and Israel's third king (c. 961–922 B.C.E.) (2 Sam. 12:24–25), who inherited the throne through David's fondness and the intrigues of his mother and the prophet Nathan (1 Kings 1:9–2:25). He became famous for his wisdom (1 Kings 3:5–28); allied himself with Hiram of Tyre (1 Kings 5); built and dedicated Yahweh's Temple in Jerusalem (1 Kings 6, 8); built a huge palace for himself (1 Kings 7:1–12); received Yahweh's renewal of the Davidic covenant (1 Kings 9:1–9); was visited by the Queen of Sheba (1 Kings 10:1–13); worshiped other gods than Yahweh, presumably because of his foreign wives' influence (1 Kings 11:1–40); and died leaving his people financially exhausted and politically discontented (1 Kings 11:41–12:25). An idealized account of his reign is given in 2 Chronicles 1–9.

Solomon's Porch   A magnificent covered colonnade built along the east side of Herod's Temple in Jerusalem in which Jesus walked (John 10:23); the site of several apostolic miracles (Acts 3:11; 5:12).

Son of Man

(1) An Old Testament phrase used to denote a human being (Pss. 8:4; 80:17; 144:3; 146:3; Isa. 56:2; Jer. 51:43), including a plural usage (Pss. 31:19; 33:13; Prov. 8:4; Eccles. 3:18–19; 8:11; 9:12). The phrase is characteristic of the Book of Ezekiel, where it is commonly used to indicate the prophet himself (Ezek. 2:1).

(2) In Daniel 7:12–14 "one like a son of man" refers to Israel itself or to a divinely appointed future ruler of Israel, although this figure is not given specific messianic significance.

(3) In some pseudepigraphal writings, particularly the Similitudes of the Book of Enoch, he who serves as Yahweh's agent in the coming Day of Judgement is variously called "the Elect One," "the Anointed One," and "the Son of Man."

(4) In the Gospels, the phrase is always spoken by Jesus and in most cases applied to himself (Matt. 8:20; 9: 6; 11:19; 12:8; 16:27–28; 19:28; 24:30; 28:31; Mark 2:28; 8:38; 9:31; 10:45; 13:26; Luke 12: 8–10; 18:8; 21:27; 22:22; John 3:14). Outside the Gospels, it is used only once (Acts 7:56), although the author of Revelation echoes Daniel 7:13 (Rev. 14:14).

sons of thunder   An epithet (*Boanerges*) applied to the apostles James and John (Mark 3:17), possibly because of their impulsive temperaments (Luke 9:52–56).

Sopherim   The name applied to Jewish scribes, from the time of Ezra and after, who copied and transmitted the manuscripts of the Hebrew Bible.

soul   In Hebrew, *nephesh* ("breath"), applied to both humans and animals as living beings (Gen. 1:20; 2:7; 2: 19; 9:4; Exod. 1:5; 1 Chron. 5:21). It was translated *psyche* in the Greek Septuagint, the same term used (commonly for "life" rather than the immortal personality) in the New Testament (Matt. 10:28; 16:26; Acts 2:27; 3:23; Phil. 1:27; Rev. 20:4).

source criticism   Analysis of a biblical document to discover the sources, written or oral, that the author(s) incorporated into it. Close study of the Pentateuch has led scholars to conclude that at least four main literary units—J, E, D, and P—were blended in its composition.

speaking in tongues   An ecstatic phenomenon of the early Church (Acts 2:1–45), presented at first as a miraculous and intelligible speaking and understanding of foreign languages by those who did not know these tongues (Acts 2:5–12) but later criticized by Paul as an inferior spiritual gift (1 Cor. 12–14).

stele (stela)   An upright slab or pillar inscribed with a commemorative message, such as those bearing the law Code of Hammurabi (early seventeenth century B.C.E.) or that of King Mesha of Moab (about 835 B.C.E.) who commemorated his victory over Israel following Jehu's revolution.

Stephen   A Hellenistic Jew of Jerusalem who was stoned for his Christian heresy (Acts 6:8–60), thus becoming the first martyr of the early Church. The name means "royal" or "crown."

Stoicism   A Greek philosophy that became popular among the upper classes in Roman times; Stoicism emphasized duty, endurance, self-control, and service to the gods, the family, and the state. Its adherents believed in the soul's immortality, rewards, and punishments after death, and in a divine force (providence) that directs human destiny. Paul encountered Stoics when preaching in Athens (Acts 17:18–34), and Stoic ideas appear in Ecclesiastes, the Wisdom of Solomon, Proverbs, John 4:23 and 5:30, James 1:10, and 1 Peter 2:17.

Succoth   An Old Testament term meaning "booths." (1) A town east of the Jordan River in the area allotted to Gad (Josh. 13:27), where Jacob had erected booths (Gen. 33:17). (2) An Egyptian site in the Nile delta given as the first Israelite camp during the Exodus (Exod. 12:37; 13:20).

Sukkoth   *See* Feast of Booths.

Sumer   The land at the head of the Persian Gulf between the Tigris and Euphrates rivers, site of the oldest high civilization in the ancient Near East, and traditional homeland of Abraham and his ancestors. Its cities include Erech (Uruk), Ur (Gen. 10:10; 11:10–27; 15:7), and Calah (Nimrud). Whereas Sumer occupied southernmost Mesopotamia, Akkad lay to the north (Gen. 10:11–12); the two regions together were later known as Babylonia.

symbol   From the Greek *symbolon,* a "token" or "sign," and *symballein,* to "throw together" or "compare." In its broadest usage it means anything that stands for something else, as the star of David signifies Judaism and the cross represents Christianity. The use of symbols characterizes prophetic and apocalyptic writing. In Daniel, for example, wild beasts symbolize pagan nations; in Ezekiel, Yahweh's presence is symbolized by his radiant "glory."

synagogue   In Judaism, a gathering of no fewer than ten adult males assembled for worship, scriptural instruction, and administration of local Jewish affairs. Synagogues probably began forming during the Babylonian exile when the Jerusalem Temple no longer existed. Organization of such religious centers throughout the diaspora played an important role in the faith's transmission and survival. The synagogue liturgy included lessons from the Torah, the Prophets, the Shema, Psalms, and eighteen prayers.

syncretism   The blending of different religions, a term Bible scholars typically apply to the mingling of Canaanite rites and customs (Baalism) with the Israelites' Mosaic faith. Although a practice repeatedly denounced by the prophets (Judg. 2:13; 3:7; 6:31; 8:33; 1 Kings 16:31; 18:26; 2 Kings 10:18; Jer. 2:8; 7:9; 19:5; 23:13; Hos. 2:8), Judaism borrowed many of its characteristic forms, psalms, concepts, and religious rituals from earlier Canaanite models.

Synoptic Problem   The scholarly term for the problem of relationship—the nature of the literary interdependence—of the first three Gospels, Matthew, Mark, and Luke. Most scholars believe that Matthew and Luke are expanded editions of Mark.

Synoptics   The first three Gospels, so named because they share a large quantity of material in common, allowing their texts to be viewed together "with one eye."

Syria   (1) The territory extending from the upper Euphrates River to northern Palestine. (2) The kingdom of Aram, with its capital at Damascus (Isa. 7:8). As the creed in Deuteronomy 26:5 states, the Israelites regarded themselves as descended from Arameans (Syrians). Isaiah 7 refers to the Syro-Ephraimite coalition against Assyria.

Syro–Phoenician   The name applied to a woman living near the Phoenician cities of Tyre and Sidon whose daughter Jesus healed (Mark 7:24–30; Matt. 15:21–28).

Tabernacle   The portable tent-shrine, elaborately decorated, that housed the Ark of the Covenant (Exod. 25–31; 35–40; Num. 7–9) from the Exodus to the building of Solomon's Temple (1 Kings 6–8); used in both Old and New Testaments as a symbol of God's presence with humanity (Num. 9:5; Deut. 31:15; Pss. 15:1; 43:3; 61:4; 132:7; Isa. 4:6; 33:20; Hos. 12:9; Acts 7:46; Heb. 8:2; 9:11; 2 Pet. 1:14; Rev. 21:3).

Tables (Tablets) of the Law   The stone slabs on which the Ten Commandments were inscribed (Exod. 24:12; 32:15–20).

Tabor   A prominent limestone hill in Galilee (Deut. 33:19; Josh. 19–22; Judg. 4:6; 5:15–21; Ps. 89:12–13; Jer. 46:18).

Talmud   A huge collection of Jewish religious traditions consisting of two parts: (1) the Mishnah (written editions of ancient oral interpretations of the Torah), published in Palestine by Judah ha-Nasi (died about 220 C.E.) and his disciples; (2) the Gemara, extensive commentaries on the Mishnah. The Palestinian version of the Talmud, which is incomplete, was produced about 450 C.E.; the Babylonian Talmud, nearly four times as long, was finished about 500 C.E. Both Talmuds contain Mishnah and Gemara.

Tamar   (1) The wife of Er, son of Judah (Gen. 38:6), who when widowed posed as a prostitute to trick her father-in-law into begetting children (the twins Pharez and Zerah) by her (Gen. 38: 6–30). (2) Absalom's sister who was raped by her half-brother Amnon, whom Absalom later killed (2 Sam. 13:1–32; 1 Chron. 3:9).

Tammuz   An ancient Near Eastern fertility god, a counterpart to the Semitic-Greek Adonis, at whose mythic death women ritually wept (Jer. 22:18; Amos 8:10; Ezek. 8:14).

Tanak   A comparatively modern name for the Hebrew Bible, an acronym consisting of three consonants that represent the three major divisions of the Bible; the Torah (law), the Nevi'um (Prophets), and the Kethivium (Writings).

Targum   Interpretative translations of the Hebrew Bible into Aramaic, such as that made by Ezra after the Jews' return from the Babylonian exile (Neh. 8:1–18). The practice may have begun in the postexilic synagogues, where Hebrew passages were read aloud and then translated into Aramaic with interpretative comments added.

Tarshish   (1) A son of Javan (Greece, Aegean peoples) (Gen. 10:4; 1 Chron. 1:7). (2) An Old Testament term used to designate ships and ports, particularly the Phoenician variety (1 Kings 10:22; 22:48; Jon. 1:3; 2 Chron. 20:36).

Tarsus   Capital of the Roman province of Cilicia (southeastern Turkey) and birthplace of Paul (Saul) (Acts 9:11; 11:25; 21:39; 22:3); a thriving commercial center in New Testament times.

Tell   Flat-topped artificial mounds consisting of the ruins of ancient cities that dot the landscape of Mesopotamia, Syria, and Palestine.

Temple, the

(1) The imposing structure built by King Solomon (using Phoenician architects and craftsmen) on Mount Zion in Jerusalem to house the Ark of the Covenant in its innermost room (the Holy of Holies) (1 Kings 5:15–9:25). Later recognized as the only authorized center for sacrifice and worship of Yahweh, it was destroyed by Nebuchadnezzar's troops in 587 B.C.E. (2 Kings 25:8–17; 2 Chron. 36:18–19).

(2) The second Temple, rebuilt by Jews returned from the Babylonian exile under Governor Zerubbabel, was dedicated about 515 B.C.E. (Ezra 1:1–11; 3:1–13; 4:24–6:22; Hag. 1–2; Zech. 1:1–8:13).

(3) Herod's splendid Temple replaced the inferior edifice of Zerubbabel's time and took nearly a half-century to complete (John 2:20).

Jesus, who visited the Temple as a child (Luke 2:22–38; 41–50) and often taught there (Matt. 21:23–24:1; Luke 20:1; John 7:14–52; 10:22–39), cleansed it of its money changers (Matt. 21:12–17; Mark 11:15–19; Luke 19:45–46; John 2:13–22) and prophesied its destruction (Matt. 24:1–2; Mark 13:1–4; Luke 21:5–7), which was fulfilled when the Romans sacked Jerusalem in 70 C.E. Until that event, the apostles continued to preach and worship there (Acts 3:1–26; 5:42; 21:26–22:29).

Ten Commandments (Decalogue)   The set of ten religious and moral laws that Yahweh inscribed on stone tablets and gave Moses (Exod. 20:1–17; repeated in Deut. 5:6–21). Some scholars believe that a ritual Decalogue is contained in Exodus 34:1–16 and 22: 29b–30; 23:12, 15–19 (see also Exod. 31:18–32:16).

Tent of Meeting   *See* Tabernacle.

Terah   A son of Nahor, father of Abraham, a younger Nahor, and Haran (Gen. 11:26; 1 Chron. 1:26–27), Terah migrated from the Sumerian city of Ur to Haran in northwest Mesopotamia (Gen. 11:27–32).

teraphim   Household gods, probably in the form of human figurines, perhaps representing a family's guardian spirit or ancestors and thought to confer good luck on their possessor. When secretly absconding with her husband Jacob, Rachel stole and hid her father's teraphim (Gen. 31:30–35). Even as late as the monarchy, owning such domestic idols was not necessarily viewed as conflicting with Yahweh's worship (Judg. 17:4–13; Hos. 3:4), although Samuel likened their use to idolatry (1 Sam. 15:23) and King Josiah outlawed them (2 Kings 23:24). They may have been used in fortune-telling.

testament   From the Latin for "covenant," this is the term used for the two main divisions of the Bible—the Old Testament (canonical Hebrew Scriptures) and the New Testament (Christian Greek Scriptures).

Tetragrammaton   The four consonants (YHWH) comprising the sacred name Yahweh, the God of Israel. Although the name appears nearly 7000 times in the canonical Old Testament, some modern Bible translations continue the Jewish practice of inaccurately rendering it as "the Lord."

Tetrateuch   A critical term for the first four books of the Bible. Genesis through Numbers are composed primarily of J, E, and P material, with little or no discernible contribution from the Deuteronomist (D), who is responsible for Deuteronomy, the fifth book of the Torah.

textual criticism   Comparison and analysis of ancient manuscripts to discover copyists' errors and, if possible, to reconstruct the true or original form of the document; also known as *lower criticism.*

Thaddeus   One of the most obscure of Jesus' apostles, he is listed among the Twelve in Matthew 10:3 and Mark 3:18 but not in Luke 7:16 or Acts. 1:13.

theodicy   From a Greek term combining "god" and "justice," theodicy denotes a rational attempt to understand how an all-good all-powerful God can permit the existence of Evil and undeserved suffering. Job, Habakkuk, and 2 Esdras contain notable theodicies.

theophany   From the Greek, meaning an appearance of a god to a person, as when El wrestled with Jacob (Gen. 32:26–32), Yahweh appeared to Moses (Exod. 3:1–4: 17; 6:2–13) and the elders of Israel (Exod. 24:9–11), or the resurrected Jesus revealed himself to Thomas (John 20:24–29) and Paul (Acts 9:3–9).

Theophilus   The otherwise unknown man to whom the gospel of Luke and Book of Acts are addressed. He may have been a Roman official who became a Christian.

Thessalonica   A major Macedonian city (modern Salonika) where Paul and Silas converted "some" Jews, "many" Greeks and "God-fearers," as well as numerous "rich women," to Christianity (Acts 17:1–9). Paul later revisited the city (1 Cor. 16:5) and wrote two of his earliest surviving letters to its congregation (1 and 2 Thess.)

Third Isaiah   *See* Isaiah.

Thomas   One of the twelve apostles (Matt. 10:3; Mark 3:18; Luke 6:15; Acts 1:13), seldom mentioned in the Synoptics but relatively prominent in the fourth Gospel, where he is called Didymus ("twin") (John 11: 16; 20:24; 21:2). Unable to believe the other disciples' report of Jesus' resurrection, Thomas is suddenly confronted with the risen Jesus and pronounces the strongest confession of faith in the Gospel (John 20:24–29).

Thummim   See Urim and Thummim.

Thyatira   A city of ancient Lydia in Asia Minor (modern Turkey), original home of Lydia, Paul's first European convert (Acts 16:14) and one of the seven churches of Asia in Revelation 2:18–29.

Tiberias   A city on the western shore of the Sea of Galilee founded by Herod Antipas and named for Emperor Tiberius; a well-known spa in Jesus' day.

Tiberius (Tiberius Claudius Nero)   Stepson of Augustus and second emperor of Rome (14–37 C.E.). According to Luke 3:1, Jesus came to John for baptism in the fifteenth year of Tiberius' reign. Except for Luke 2: 1, he is the Caesar referred to in the Gospels (Matt. 22: 17; Mark 12:14; Luke 20:22; John 19:12).

Tiglath-Pileser III   Emperor of Assyria (745–727 B.C.E.), the biblical "Pul" (2 Kings 15:19) who captured Damascus in 732 B.C.E. and coerced tribute from kings Menaham of Israel and Ahaz of Judah (2 Kings 16:7–18; 2 Chron. 28:20–25). Ahaz's stripping of the Jerusalem Temple and sponsoring of pagan cults were probably done to placate Assyria's king.

Tigris River   According to Genesis 2:14 (where it is called the Hiddekel), the Tigris was the third of four rivers that watered Eden (see Dan. 10:4). Approximately 1146 miles long, it forms the eastern boundary of Mesopotamia (the land between the Tigris and Euphrates). On its banks rose the ancient cities of Nineveh, Asshur, and Calah (Gen. 10:11), centers of the Assyrian Empire.

Timothy   Younger friend and fellow missionary of Paul, who called him "beloved son" (1 Cor. 4:17; 1 Tim. 1: 2–28; 2 Tim. 1:2), Timothy was the son of a Greek father and devout Jewish mother (Acts 16:1; 2 Tim. 1: 5). To please the Jews, Paul circumcised Timothy before taking him on his second evangelical tour (Acts 16: 1–4; 20:1–4). Paul later sent him to Macedonia (1 Thess. 3:6) and thence to Corinth to quiet the dissension there (Acts 19:22; 1 Cor. 4:17; 16:11), which he failed to do (2 Cor. 7:6, 13–14; 8:6, 16, 23; 12:18). The picture of Timothy in the pastoral Epistles seems irreconcilable with what is known of him from Acts and Paul's genuine letters.

Tirzah   A Canaanite city that Joshua captured (Josh. 12: 24), later the home of King Jeroboam (1 Kings 14:17), and the northern kingdom's capital during the reigns of Baasha (c. 900–877 B.C.E.), Elah (877–876 B.C.E.), Zimri (seven days in about 876 B.C.E.), and Omri (c. 876–869 B.C.E.), who took it by siege and ruled there for six years until he transferred the capital to Samaria (1 Kings 15:33–16:28).

Tishbite   A term used to describe the prophet Elijah (1 Kings 17:1; 21:17; 2 Kings 1:3, 8; 9:36). Its origin and meaning are uncertain.

tithe   Paying a tenth of one's income in money, crops, or animals to support a government (1 Sam. 8:15–17) or religion (Lev. 27:30–33; Num. 18:24–28; Deut. 12: 17–19; 14:22–29; Neh. 10:36–38). In Israel, the high priest, Levites, and Temple upkeep were supported by required levies. Abraham is reported to have paid Melchizedek tithes (Gen. 14:20; see also Heb. 7:2–6). Jesus regarded tithing as an obligation of his people (Luke 11:42; 12:13–21; 18:12).

Titus   A Greek whom Paul converted and who became a companion on his missionary journeys (2 Cor. 8:23; Gal. 2:1–3; Titus 1:4), Titus effected a reconciliation between Paul and the Corinthians (2 Cor. 7:5–7; 8: 16–24; 12:18). A post-Pauline writer makes him the type of the Christian pastor (Titus 1–3).

Titus, Flavius Sabinius Vespasianus   Son and successor of Vespasian and emperor of Rome (79–81 C.E.), he directed the siege of Jerusalem, which culminated in the destruction of the city and Herodian Temple in 70 C.E. His carrying of the Temple treasures to Rome is commemorated in the triumphal Arch of Titus that still stands in the Roman Forum.

Tobiah   A partly Jewish Ammonite who occupied a storeroom in the rebuilt Temple area after the exile and whom Nehemiah threw out of his lodgings (Neh. 13: 6–9). Tobiah allied himself with Sanballat the Samaritan in opposing Nehemiah's reconstruction of Jerusalem's walls (Neh. 2:10; 4:3, 7; 6:1–19).

Torah   A Hebrew term usually translated "law," "instruction," or "teaching," it refers primarily to the Pentateuch, the first five books of the Hebrew Bible, and in a general sense to all the canonical writings, which are traditionally regarded as a direct oracle or revelation from Yahweh.

tradition   (1) Collections of stories and interpretations transmitted orally from generation to generation and embodying the religious history and beliefs of a people or community. Traditions of the patriarch were eventually included in the J and E sagas and finally incorporated into the first book of the Torah. (2) Oral explanations, interpretations, and applications of the written Torah (1 Chron. 4:22; Mark 7:5, 9; Matt. 15: 2; Gal. 1:15), many of which were eventually compiled in the Mishnah. (3) Recollections and interpretations concerning Jesus that circulated orally through various early Christian churches and some of which were included in the Gospel narratives (1 Cor. 15:1–8; 2 Thess. 2:15).

tradition criticism   Analysis of the origin and development of specific biblical themes—such as the Exodus motif in the Old Testament and the eschatology of the Kingdom of God in the New—as presented by different Bible writers. In some cases, tradition criticism emphasizes the early and oral stages of development.

Trajan (Marcus Ulpius Nerva Trajanus)   Emperor of Rome (98–117 C.E.) who was born in Spain about 53 C.E., became a successful military leader, and brought the Roman Empire to its greatest extent, annexing Dacia, Armenia, Mesopotamia, Assyria, and Arabia. Probably following the policies of Vespasian (69–79 C.E.), he conducted a persecution of Christians, although he wrote to Pliny the Younger, governor of Bithynia, that they were not to be sought out or denounced anonymously.

Transfiguration   A supernatural happening that Jesus' three closest disciples—Peter, James, and John—experienced when, alone with him on an isolated mountaintop, they saw Jesus transformed into a being of light accompanied by Elijah (symbolizing the Hebrew prophetic tradition) and Moses (symbolizing the Torah) (Matt. 17:1–13; Mark 9:2–13; Luke 9:28–36). A heavenly voice identified Jesus as his "beloved son," thus revealing Jesus as the culmination of and superior to the law and prophets.

Transjordan   The rugged plateau area east of the Jordan River, a region Joshua assigned to the tribes of Reuben, Gad, and half of Manasseh (Josh. 13) but which they failed to wrest from other Semites living there.

tree of life   An ancient Mesopotamian symbol of rejuvenation or immortality (as in the *Epic of Gilgamesh*), the J (Yahwist) author places in the Garden of Eden, humanity's original home, where its fruit would confer everlasting life on the eater (Gen. 2:9; 3:22–24). Yahweh's express motive for expelling the first human couple from Eden was to prevent their rivaling him further by eating from the tree of life (Gen. 3:22–24). It is often referred to in apocalyptic literature (En. 24:4; 25: 4–6; Asmp. M. [Life of Adam and Eve] 19:2; 22:3; 28: 2–4; XII P.: Levi 18:11), where it is usually reserved for the righteous to eat after the Day of Judgment (2 Esd. 8:52; cf. Rev. 2:7 and 22:2, 24).

Trinity   A post–New Testament doctrine that posits God existing as three divine Persons in One, although he manifests himself on different occasions as Father, Son, or Holy Spirit. After generations of ecclesiastical debate on the subject had seriously divided the Church, Constantine, the first Christian emperor of Rome but then unbaptized, called a council of church leaders in Nicea to settle the issue (325 C.E.). The council decreed the orthodoxy of the trinitarian formula, so that the mystery of trinity in unity henceforth became central to the Christian faith (Matt. 28:19–20; 2 Cor. 13:14; Gal. 1:1–5).

Trumpets, Feast of   The Hebrew month began with a new moon. On the first day of the seventh (sabbatical) month, a festival, assembly, and sacrifice were to be held (Lev. 13:23–25; Num. 29:1–7).

Tubal-cain   According to J, the son of Lamech and Zillah and the ancestor of all metalworkers in bronze and iron (Gen. 4:19–26). He may have been regarded as the eponymous progenitor of the Kenites.

Twelve, Book of the   The twelve books of the Minor Prophets—Hosea to Malachi—originally compiled on a single scroll.

Twelve, the   The twelve apostles whom Jesus specifically chose to follow him. Different names appear on different New Testament lists of the Twelve (Matt. 10:1–5; Mark 3:16–19; Luke 6:12–16; Acts 1:13–14).

Twelve Tribes of Israel   In ancient Israel, tribes were confederations of clans, which in turn were composed of families related by blood, adoption, or long association, all forming a corporate community with a distinct social, religious, or ethnic identity. Traditionally believed to have descended from the twelve sons of Jacob (Israel) (Gen. 49:2–28; a parallel list, Moses' Blessing, mentions only eleven, omitting Simeon; Deut. 33: 6–25), the tribes were Reuben, Simeon, Levi, Judah, Issachar, Zebulun (born of Jacob's wife Leah), Joseph (later divided into the tribes of Ephraim and Manasseh) and Benjamin (both born to Jacob's favorite wife, Rachel), Gad and Asher (by the slave girl Zilpah), Dan and Naphtali (by another concubine, Bilhah).

The apportionment of tribal territories in Palestine is described in Joshua 13–19. Ezekiel foresaw an idealized tribal state in Israel (Ezek. 48), and the author of Revelation multiplied the traditional twelve tribes by 12,000 to symbolize the number of Jews redeemed in Christ (Rev. 7:4–8). (See also Matt. 19:28; Luke 22:30; James 1:1, where the twelve tribes represent "spiritual Israel," the Christian community.) The so-called ten lost tribes were those of the northern kingdom assimilated into the Assyrian Empire after 721 B.C.E. (2 Kings 17).

Tychicus   A loyal helper and companion of Paul who accompanied him through the Roman province of Asia on his third missionary journey (Acts 20:4), Tychicus delivered Paul's letters to the Colossians (Col. 4:7–9) and Ephesians (Eph. 6:21).

Tyre   An ancient Phoenician seaport famous for its commerce and wealth, Tyre was originally built on a small offshore island about twenty-five miles south of Sidon. King Solomon made an alliance with its ruler, Hiram, the skills of whose architects and craftsmen he used in constructing the Jerusalem Temple (1 Kings 5:15–32; 7:13–51). Its power and luxury were later denounced by the prophets (Isa. 23; Ezek. 26–28; Amos 1:9–10; Zech. 9:3–4). Alexander the Great sacked the city in 332 B.C.E., although it had been rebuilt by Jesus' day (Mark 7:24–31; Luke 3:8).

Ugarit   Ancient Canaanite city (Arabic Ras Shamra) in modern Syria where cuneiform archives were found that preserve prebiblical religious texts and myths about El and Baal, some of which anticipate traditions later associated with Yahweh.

under the thigh   A euphemistic expression for the grasping of another's male organs during the conclusion of a vow, oath, or covenant (Gen. 24:2, 9; 47:29; see also Judg. 8:30).

Ur   One of the world's oldest cities, in Sumer, Ur was the ancestral homeland (Gen. 11:28–31) from which Abraham and his family migrated to Haran, although some scholars have suggested a northern location for the Abrahamic Ur. Archaeologically, the Sumerian Ur is notable for its well-preserved ziggurat and "royal Cemetery," whose tombs have yielded a number of beautifully crafted artwork, furniture, jewelry, and other sophisticated artifacts (mid-third millennium B.C.E.).

Uriah   (1) A Hittite practicer of Yahwism and soldier of David whose wife Bathsheba the Israelite king seduced and wished to marry. David ordered him exposed in the front lines of battle so that he was inevitably killed, a crime the prophet Nathan denounced to the king's face (2 Sam. 11–12). (2) A priest whom King Ahaz of Judah (c. 735–716 B.C.E.) commissioned to remodel the Temple area and construct an altar modeled on that which Ahaz had seen in Assyrian-dominated Damascus (2 Kings 16:10–16). (3) A Judean prophet who predicted the Babylonian destruction of Jerusalem, fled to Egypt to escape King Jehoiakim's wrath, but was murdered and his body returned to Judah where it was buried in a common grave (Jer. 26:20–23).

Urim and Thummim   Undescribed objects (whose names may mean "oracle" and "truth") that were used by Israel's priests in casting lots to determine Yahweh's will on a specific matter. They could apparently indicate only yes or no responses (Exod. 28:29–30; Num. 27:21; 1 Sam. 28:6; Ezra 2:63; Neh. 7:65).

Uz   Job's unidentified homeland, which various scholars have suggested to be Edom, Arabia, or a location east of the Jordan River.

Uzziah (Azariah)   Son of Amaziah, king of Judah (783–742 B.C.E.), and a contemporary of King Jeroboam II of Israel (786–746 B.C.E.) (2 Kings 14:22; 15: 1–7; 2 Chron. 26:1–23), Uzziah fortified Jerusalem; defeated the Philistines, Ammonites, and Arabs; and greatly extended Judah's political jurisdiction. Both the Deuteronomist and Chronicler rate him as "pleasing" Yahweh, although the latter attributes the king's leprosy to his usurping priestly functions in the Temple.

Vashti   The empress of Persia (unknown to history) who refused to exhibit herself to the male friends of her husband, Ahasuerus (Xerxes I), and whom Esther replaced as queen (Esther 1:9–2:18).

veil   The elaborately decorated curtain separating the Holy Place from the Most Holy Place in the tabernacle and Jerusalem Temple (Exod. 26:31–37), which was reputedly rent in two at Jesus' crucifixion (Matt. 27:51; Heb. 6:19; 9–10).

Vespasian   Emperor of Rome (69–79 C.E.) who led Roman legions into Judea during the Jewish revolt (66–70 C.E.), the siege of Jerusalem passing to his son Titus when Vespasian became emperor.

Vulgate   Jerome's Latin translation of the Bible (late fourth century C.E.), including the Apocrypha, which became the official version of Roman Catholicism.

Wisdom   A personification of the divine attribute of creative intelligence, pictured in the form of a gracious woman (Yahweh's daughter) who mediates between God and humanity (Prov. 1:20–33; 8:1–31; 9:1–6; Ecclus. 24; etc.). This Hebrew concept of Wisdom merges with the Greek philosophic doctrine of the heavenly Logos in John's Gospel (John 1:1–18) and Colossians (1–2).

wisdom literature   Biblical works dealing primarily with practical and ethical behavior and ultimate religious questions, such as the problem of Evil. The books include Proverbs, Job, Ecclesiastes, Ecclesiasticus, and the Wisdom of Solomon. Habakkuk, 2 Esdras, and the New Testament Book of James also have characteristics of wisdom writing.

woes, the seven messianic   The series of seven condemnations of scribes and Pharisees attributed to Jesus when he was rejected by official Judaism (Matt. 23: 13–32).

Word, the   (1) The "word" or "oracle" of Yahweh, a phrase characteristic of the Hebrew prophets, typically referring to a divine pronouncement, judgment, or statement of purpose that the prophet delivers in his God's name. (2) The preincarnate Jesus (John 1:1–3). *See* Logos.

Writings   *See* Kethuvim.

Xerxes I   (486–465 B.C.E.); thought to be the biblical Ahasuerus, emperor of Persia (Esther; Ezra 4:6).

Yahweh   A translation of the sacred name of Israel's god, represented almost 7000 times in the canonical Old Testament by the four consonants of the Tetragrammaton (YHWH). According to Exodus 6:2–4, it was revealed for the first time to Moses at the burning bush; according to J, it was used from the time of Enosh before the Flood (Gen. 4:26). Scholars have offered various interpretations of the origin and meaning of the divine name. According to one accepted theory, it is derived from the Hebrew verb "to be" and means "he is" or "he causes to be," implying that Yahweh is the Maker of events and Shaper of history.

Yahwist   The name scholars give the anonymous writer or compiler who produced that J document, the oldest stratum in the Pentateuch (about 950 B.C.E.).

Yom Kippur   *See* Day of Atonement.

Zadok   A priest officiating during the reigns of David and Solomon who supported the latter's claim to the throne and was rewarded by being made chief priest at the Temple (2 Sam. 15:24–29; 17:15; 19:11; 20:25; 1 Kings 1:7–8; 32–39; 45; 2:35; 1 Chron. 6:4–15, 50–52; 12:28). Ezekiel regarded Zadok's descendants as the only legitimate priests (Ezek. 40:46; 43:19; 44: 15; 48:11). After the exile, they apparently enjoyed a monopoly in the second Temple (1 Chron. 24:2–19; 27:17; 29:22).

Zaphenath-paneah   According to Genesis 41:45, the Egyptian name given Joseph, son of Jacob. It has been variously translated as "says the God: he will live," "revealer of secrets," and "minister of agriculture."

Zarephath   According to 1 Kings 17:8–24, a Phoenician town near Sidon where Elijah befriended a widow during a famine and resuscitated her son (Luke 4: 25–27).

Zealots   An extremely nationalistic party in first-century Judaism dedicated to freeing Judea from foreign domination by armed revolt if necessary. Their militarism and fanatical patriotism generated several uprisings, culminating in the great rebellion against Rome (66–73 C.E.). According to Flavius Josephus' possibly biased account, their intransigence led to the destruction of Jerusalem and the Temple. The Simon of Luke 6:15 and Acts 1:13 is called a "zealot."

Zebedee   A Galilean fisherman, husband of Salome, father of the apostles James and John (Matt. 27:56; Mark 1:19–20; 3:17; 14:33; 15:40).

Zebulun   (1) The sixth son of Jacob and Leah, full brother of Reuben, Simeon, Levi, Judah, and Issachar (Gen. 30:20; 35:23). (2) The tribe of Zebulun, represented in Jacob's blessing (Gen. 49:13) as a seagoing group located near the Phoenician port of Sidon, actually settled in a landlocked farming area of northern

Palestine (Josh. 19:10–16), although they were on a main trading route with coastal cities. Except for their failure to expel the Canaanites from their allotted territory and their joining Barak and Deborah against Sisera (Judg. 1:27–30; 4:10–16; 5:18), they are seldom mentioned in the Old Testament.

Zechariah

(1) The son of Jehoiada the priest, Zechariah was stoned to death for denouncing Judah's idolatry (late ninth century B.C.E.) (2 Chron. 25:20–22; he is usually identified with Zacharias in Matt. 23:35 and Luke 11:51).

(2) The son of Jeroboam II and the last king of Jehu's dynasty in Israel, who reigned only six months (about 746/745 B.C.E.) before he was murdered (2 Kings 10:30).

(3) The son of Berechiah or the priest Iddo (Zech. 1:1, 8; Ezra 5:1; Neh. 12:16), a Judean prophet whose message is contained in the book of the Minor Prophets bearing his name.

The latter, a contemporary of Haggai (c. 520–515 B.C.E.), urged the returned exiles to rebuild Yahweh's Temple in Jerusalem. Although Judah was then part of the Persian Empire ruled by Darius, he apparently regarded the Jewish governor, Zerubbabel, a descendant of David, as a potential messianic king (Zech. 4:6–15; 6:9–14). His work is characterized by strange imagery and apocalyptic visions. Chapters 9–14 of the Book of Zechariah are thought to have been appended by a later author.

(4) A Judean priest married to Elisabeth, a descendant of Aaron, whose long childless marriage was blessed in his old age by the birth of the future John the Baptist (Luke 1:5–25, 57–80; 3:2). A vision foretelling the birth rendered him temporarily paralyzed, but he recovered his speech in time to name the child and to utter a prayer of thanksgiving—the Benedictus (Luke 1:67–79).

(5) A Jewish martyr mentioned in Jesus' phrase "from Abel to Zecharias" (Matt. 23:35; Luke 11:51), usually identified with Zechariah, son of Jehoiada in 2 Chronicles 24:20–24.

Zedekiah A son of Josiah and the last king of Judah (c. 597–587 B.C.E.), Zedekiah reigned as a tribute-paying vassal of Nebuchadnezzar (2 Chron. 36:13; Jer. 29:3–7; Ezek. 17:15–18). A weak ruler, he consulted the prophet Jeremiah (Jer. 21:1–7) but acceded to his advisers' pressures to seek help from Egypt in overthrowing Babylon's yoke (Jer. 27:12–22; 37:6–21; 38:7–28). When he rebelled against Babylon, Nebuchadnezzar laid siege to and destroyed Jerusalem (587 B.C.E.). Zedekiah tried to escape but was captured, tried, and condemned to having his sons slain before his eyes and his own eyes put out, after which he was imprisoned in Babylon, where he died (2 Kings 24:17–25:7; 2 Chron. 36:10–21; Jer. 39:6–14; 52:1–27).

Zephaniah (1) Son of Maaseiah and second-ranking priest under King Zedekiah who acted as go-between for the king in his consultations with Jeremiah (2 Kings 25:18; Jer. 21:1; 29:25–32; 37:3–4; 52:24–27). After Jerusalem's fall, he was executed by the Babylonians. (2) A seventh-century Judean prophet whose pronouncements of judgment are collected in the book bearing his name (Zeph. 1:1). Virtually nothing is known of his life.

Zerubbabel A son of Shealtiel or Salathiel (Ezra 3:2, 8; Hag. 1:1; Matt. 1:12) or of Pedaiah (1 Chron. 3:19), Zerubbabel (meaning "begotten in Babylon") was a grandson of Jehoiachin, the king of Judah imprisoned in Babylon (1 Chron. 3:17), and therefore a legitimate heir to the Davidic throne. Appointed governor of the restored Jewish community in Jerusalem (Ezra 3; Hag. 1:1, 14) he returned from Babylon with the first group of exiles and, with Joshua, the high priest, set up an altar to Yahweh and made arrangements to rebuild the Temple. Between the time the work began and the Temple's dedication in 515 B.C.E. (Ezra 6), however, Zerubbabel disappeared from history. The prophets Haggai and Zechariah, who had urged the rebuilding, had both regarded him as a potential messianic king (Hag. 2:20–23; Zech. 4:6b–10a; 6:9–15—the latter passage reworked by later scribes). When these political expectations failed to materialize, hopes were focused on a priestly hierarchy represented by Joshua (Zech. 3:1–4; 6:11–12).

Zeus In Greek mythology, the son of Cronus and Rhea, king of the Olympian gods, and patron of civic order. A personification of storm and other heavenly powers, he ruled by wielding the lightning bolt. The Romans identified him with Jupiter (Jove). Some people of Lystra compared Barnabas to Zeus and Paul to Hermes (Acts 14:12). The erection of his statue in the Jerusalem Temple courts helped spark the Maccabean revolt (c. 168 B.C.E.).

ziggurat A characteristic architectural form of Sumerian and Babylonian temples, the ziggurat was a multi-leveled tower resembling a stepped or recessed pyramid consisting of succeedingly smaller platforms built one atop the other. At its apex was a chapel dedicated to a major civic god. Broad ceremonial staircases used for liturgical processions led to the ziggurat's summit, to which it was believed the gods invisibly descended. The story of the Tower of Babel in Genesis 11:1–9 is probably based on a misunderstanding of the ziggurat's function.

Zilpah The handmaid of Leah by whom Jacob begot Gad and Asher (Gen. 29:24; 30:9–13, 35:26).

Zimri A chariot captain who murdered King Elah and seized Israel's throne, which he held for only seven days (876 B.C.E.). When Omri, leader of the military, attacked him at Tirzah, Zimri set the palace on fire and perished in the ruins, after which Omri became king (1 Kings 16:8–20).

Zion   The name, probably meaning "citadel," for a rocky hill in old Jerusalem, it was originally a Jebusite acropolis that David captured and on which he built his palace and housed the Ark of the Covenant (Judg. 19: 11–12; 2 Sam. 5:6–12; 6:12–17; 1 Chron. 11:5–8). David purchased a threshing floor in Zion (2 Sam. 24: 18–25) on which Solomon later built the Temple. In time, the term referred either to the hill on which the Temple stood or to the surrounding city of Jerusalem (Pss. 2:6; 9:11; 76:2; 127:3; Isa. 1:26–27; 10:24; 30:19; 64:10; Jer. 31:6; Amos 1:2; Mic. 3:12).

Zipporah   A daughter of Jethro, a Midianite shepherd and priest, Zipporah became Moses' wife (Exod. 2: 11–22) and bore him at least two sons, Gershom (Exod. 2:22) and Eliezer (Exod. 18:3–4), saving the latter from Yahweh's wrath by circumcising him with a flint stone (Exod. 4:18–26).

Zoar   One of the five "cities of the plain" on the eastern shore of the Dead Sea (Gen. 13:10; 14:2, 8) that Lot reached as Sodom was being destroyed (Gen. 19:20–23). Because it is referred to by the prophets, it may have survived the catastrophe (Isa. 15:5; Jer. 48:34).

Zoroastrianism   The official religion of imperial Persia, it was founded in about the sixth century B.C.E. by the east Iranian prophet Zoroaster. According to his followers, the universe is dualistic, composed of parallel worlds of matter and spirit in which legions of good and evil spirits contend. In a final cosmic battle, Ahura Mazda, god of light and righteousness, will totally defeat Ahriman, embodiment of darkness and chaos. Historians believe that many biblical concepts of angelology and demonology, including the character of Satan, ultimately derive from Zoroastrian influence.

Zophar   A Naamathite, one of Job's three companions (Job 2:11; 11:1; 20:1; 42:9).

General Bibliography

This bibliography provides a representative list of important scholarly works on the Hebrew Bible and New Testament. Many additional references on specific topics and individual biblical books are included in the Recommended Readings appended to particular units throughout the text.

Bible Commentaries, Dictionaries, and Old Testament Introductions

Achtemeir, Paul J., ed. *Harper's Bible Dictionary*. San Francisco: Harper & Row, 1985. An excellent one-volume dictionary.

Ackroyd, P. R., et al., eds. *The Cambridge Bible Commentary*. Cambridge, Eng.: Cambridge University Press, 1972.

Anderson, Bernhard. *Understanding the Old Testament,* 4th ed. Englewood Cliffs, N.J.: Prentice-Hall, 1986.

Black, Matthew, and Rowley, H. H., eds. *Peake's Commentary on the Bible,* rev. ed. New York: Nelson, 1962.

Brown, Raymond E.; Fitzmyer, Joseph A.; and Murphy, Roland E. *The New Jerome Biblical Commentary,* 2nd ed. Englewood Cliffs, N.J.: Prentice-Hall, 1990.

Eissfeldt, Otto. *The Old Testament: An Introduction*. New York: Harper & Row, 1965.

Fohrer, Georg. *Introduction to the Old Testament*. Nashville, Tenn.: Abingdon Press, 1968.

Gottwald, Norman K. *The Hebrew Bible: A Socio-Literary Introduction*. Philadelphia: Fortress Press, 1985.

Humphreys, W. Lee. *Crisis and Story: Introduction to the Old Testament,* 2nd ed. Mountain View, Calif.: Mayfield, 1990.

Keck, Leander E., ed. *The New Interpreter's Bible*. Nashville: Abingdon Press, 1994. The complete biblical text in 12 volumes with scholarly commentary. (Vols. 1, 8, and 9 currently available.)

Metzger, B. M., and Coogan, M. D., eds. *The Oxford Companion to the Bible*. New York: Oxford University Press, 1993.

Pfeiffer, Robert H. *Introduction to the Old Testament,* rev. ed. New York: Harper & Row, 1949.

Soggin, J. Alberto. *Introduction to the Old Testament,* 3rd ed. Translated by J. Bowden. Louisville: John Knox Press, 1989.

Suggs, M. J., Sakenfeld, K. D., and Mueller, J. R., eds. *The Oxford Study Bible*. New York: Oxford University Press, 1992.

Ancient Texts Relating to the Old Testament

Beyerlin, Walter, ed. *Near Eastern Religious Texts Relating to the Old Testament*. Translated by J. Bowden. Philadelphia: Westminster Press, 1978.

Coogan, Michael David. *Stories from Ancient Canaan*. Philadelphia: Westminster Press, 1978. A paperback collection of Canaanite myths and their biblical parallels.

Cross, Frank M. *Canaanite Myth and Hebrew Epic, Essays in the History of the Religion of Israel*. Cambridge, Mass.: Harvard University Press, 1973.

Dalley, Stephanie. *Myths from Mesopotamia: Creation, The Flood. Gilgarmeds and Others*. New York: Oxford University Press, 1989.

Gardner, John, and Maier, John. *Gilgamesh*. New York: Knopf, 1984. A new translation with scholarly annotations.

Gaster, Theodor H. *Myth, Legend, and Custom in the Old Testament*. New York: Harper & Row, 1969.

Heidel, Alexander. *The Gilgamesh Epic and Old Testament Parallels*. Chicago: University of Chicago Press, 1949.

———. *The Babylonian Genesis,* 2nd ed. Chicago: University of Chicago Press, 1951. A paperback translation of the *Enuma Elish* with commentary.

Matthews, Victor H. and Benjamin, Don C. *Old Testament Parallels: Documents from the Ancient Near East*. Mahwah, N.J.: Paulist Press, 1991.

Pritchard, James B. *The Ancient Near East: An Anthology of Texts and Pictures*. Princeton, N.J.: Princeton University Press, 1965. A text that contains excerpts from the following two books:

———. *The Ancient Near East in Pictures Relating to the Old Testament*. Princeton, N.J.: Princeton University Press, 1965.

———, ed. *Ancient Near Eastern Texts Relating to the Old*

Testament. 3rd ed. supp. Princeton, N.J.: Princeton University Press, 1969. Translations of relevant Egyptian, Babylonian, Canaanite, and other ancient literatures—the standard work.

Sanders, N. K. *The Epic of Gilgamesh.* Baltimore: Penguin Books, 1972. A readable paraphrase of the *Epic of Gilgamesh* with a scholarly introduction.

———. *Poems of Heaven and Hell from Ancient Mesopotamia.* London and New York: Penguin Books, 1971.

Biblical Archaeology

Albright, William F. *Archaeology and the Religion of Israel.* Garden City, N.Y.: Doubleday/Anchor Books, 1960.

———. *Yahweh and the Gods of Canaan: A Historical Analysis of Two Contrasting Faiths.* Garden City, N.Y.: Doubleday/Anchor Books, 1969.

Báez-Camargo, Gonzalo. *Archaeological Commentary on the Bible.* Garden City, N.Y.: Doubleday, 1984. A book-by-book study of archaeology's contribution to understanding biblical literature.

Burrows, Millar. *What Mean These Stones?* New York: Meridian, 1957.

Finegan, Jack. *The Archaeology of the New Testament,* rev. editions. Princeton, N.J.: Princeton University Press, 1992.

Frank, Harry T. *Bible, Archaeology, and Faith.* Nashville, Tenn.: Abingdon Press, 1971.

———. *Discovering the Biblical World.* New York: Harper & Row, 1975.

Freedman, David N., and Greenfield, J. C., eds. *New Directions in Biblical Archaeology.* Garden City, N.Y.: Doubleday, 1969.

Harris, Roberta L. *The World of the Bible.* London: Thames and Hudson, 1995.

Kenyon, Kathleen. *Archaeology in the Holy Land,* 3rd ed. New York: Praeger, 1970.

Landay, Jerry M. *Silent Cities, Sacred Stones.* London: Weidenfeld and Nicolson, 1971.

Magnusson, Magnus. *Archaeology of the Bible.* New York: Simon & Schuster, 1977.

Mazar, Benjamin. *The Mountain of the Lord.* Garden City, N.Y.: Doubleday, 1975.

Moscati, Sabatino. *The Face of the Ancient Orient.* Garden City, N.Y.: Doubleday/Anchor Books, 1962.

Pritchard, James B. *Gibeon, Where the Sun Stood Still.* Princeton, N.J.: Princeton University Press, 1962.

———, ed. *The Harper Atlas of the Bible.* New York and San Francisco: Harper & Row, 1987. Includes beautifully illustrated discussions of archaeological sites.

Shanks, Hershel. *The City of David.* Washington, D.C.: The Biblical Archaeology Society, 1973.

Winton, Thomas D., ed. *Archaeology and Old Testament Study.* Oxford, Eng.: Clarendon Press, 1967.

Wright, George E. *Biblical Archaeology,* rev. ed. Philadelphia: Westminster Press, 1966.

———, ed. *The Bible and the Ancient Near East.* Garden City, N.Y.: Doubleday/Anchor Books, 1965.

Hebrew Bible History, Theology, and Interpretation

Ackroyd, Peter R. *Exile and Restoration: A Study of Hebrew Thought in the Sixth Century B.C.E.* Philadelphia: Westminster Press, 1968.

Ahlstrom, Gosta W. *Who Were the Israelites?* Winona Lake, Ind.: Eisenbrauns, 1986.

Albrektson, Bertil. *History and the Gods.* Lund, Sweden: Gleerup, 1967.

Albright, W. F. *From the Stone Age to Christianity.* Garden City, N.Y.: Doubleday, 1957.

———. *The Biblical Period from Abraham to Ezra.* New York: Harper & Row, 1963.

Alt, Albrecht. *Essays on Old Testament History and Religion.* Translated by R. A. Wilson. New York: Doubleday, 1967.

Alter, Robert, and Kermode, Frank, eds. *The Literary Guide to the Bible.* Cambridge, Mass.: Harvard University Press, 1987. Scholarly essays on the critical interpretation of biblical literature.

Anderson, Bernhard W., ed. *Creation in the Old Testament.* Philadelphia: Fortress Press, 1984.

Anderson, G. W., ed. *Tradition and Interpretation.* Oxford, Eng.: Clarendon Press, 1979.

Avi-Yonah, Michael, ed. *A History of the Holy Land.* New York: Macmillan, 1969.

Bright, John. *Early Israel in Recent History Writing.* London: SCM Press, 1956.

———. *A History of Israel.* Philadelphia: Westminster Press, 1972.

Bruce, F. F. *Israel and the Nations: From the Exodus to the Fall of the Second Temple.* Grand Rapids, Mich.: Eerdmans, 1963.

Childs, Brevard S. *Biblical Theology in Crisis.* Philadelphia: Westminster Press, 1970.

Clements, Ronald E. *A Century of Old Testament Study.* London: Lutterworth Press, 1976.

Coote, Robert B., and Coote, Mary P. *Power, Politics and the Making of the Bible.* Minneapolis: Ausburg Fortress Press, 1990.

Cross, Frank M. *The Ancient Library of Qumran and Modern Biblical Studies.* Garden City, N.Y.: Doubleday, 1961.

de Vaux, Roland. *Ancient Israel: Its Life and Institutions.* Translated by D. Smith. New York: McGraw-Hill, 1961.

———. *The Early History of Israel.* Translated by D. Smith. Philadelphia: Westminster Press, 1978.

Eichrodt, Walther. *Theology of the Old Testament,* Vol. 1. Translated by J. A. Baker. Philadelphia: Westminster Press, 1961.

————. *Theology of the Old Testament,* Vol. 2. Translated by J. A. Baker. Philadelphia: Westminster Press, 1967.

Eliade, Mircea. *Cosmos and History: The Myth of the Eternal Return.* New York: Harper Torchbooks, 1954.

————. *The Sacred and the Profane: The Nature of Religion.* New York: Harper Torchbooks, 1961.

Ellis, Peter. *The Yahwist: The Bible's First Theologian.* Notre Dame, Ind.: Fides, 1968.

Fohrer, Georg. *History of Israelite Religion.* Translated by D. Green. Nashville, Tenn.: Abingdon Press, 1972. Traces the development of Israel's characteristic religious concepts and traditions.

Freidman, Richard E. *Who Wrote the Bible?* San Francisco: Harper & Row, 1987. A superb analysis of theories about biblical authorship, including the suggestion that J (the Yahwist) was a woman.

Fromm, Erich. *You Shall Be as Gods.* Greenwich, Conn.: Fawcett, 1966.

Gabel, John B. *The Bible as Literature: An Introduction,* 3rd edition. New York: Oxford University Press, 1996.

Gaster, Theodor H. *Thespis: Ritual, Myth, and Drama in the Ancient Near East.* New York: Abelard-Schuman, 1950.

————. *Myth, Legend, and Custom in the Old Testament.* New York: Harper & Row, 1969.

————. *The Dead Sea Scriptures in English Translation.* Garden City, N.Y.: Doubleday, 1976.

Gottwald, Norman K. *The Tribes of Yahweh: A Sociology of the Religion of Liberated Israel, 1250–1050 B.C.E.* Maryknoll, N.Y.: Orbis Books, 1979.

Grant, Michael. *The History of Ancient Israel.* New York: Charles Scribner's Sons, 1984.

Gray, John. *Near Eastern Mythology.* New York: Peter Bedrick Books, 1982.

Halpern, Baruch. *The First Historians: The Hebrew Bible and History.* San Francisco: Harper & Row, 1988.

Hillers, Delbert R. *Covenant: The History of a Biblical Idea.* Baltimore: Johns Hopkins University Press, 1969.

Jagersma, Henk. *A History of Israel in the Old Testament Period.* Philadelphia: Fortress Press, 1983.

Kaufmann, Yehezkel. *The Religion of Israel.* Translated by M. Greenberg. Chicago: University of Chicago Press, 1960.

Klein, Ralph W. *Textual Criticism of the Old Testament: The Septuagint after Qumram.* Philadelphia: Fortress Press, 1974.

Koch, Klaus. *The Growth of the Biblical Tradition: The Form-Critical Method.* Translated by S. M. Cupitt. New York: Scribner, 1969.

————. *The Prophets.* Vol. I, *The Assyrian Age.* Translated by M. Kohl. Philadelphia: Fortress Press, 1982.

Kohler, Ludwig. *Old Testament Theology.* Translated by A. S. Todd. Philadelphia: Westminster Press, 1958.

Levenson, Jon D. *Creation and the Persistence of Evil.* San Francisco: Harper & Row, 1988.

Lindblom, Johannes. *Prophecy in Ancient Israel.* Philadelphia: Fortress Press, 1963.

Mays, James L., ed. *Harper's Bible Commentary.* San Francisco: Harper & Row, 1988. Provides clear, scholarly discussions of each book in the Old and New Testament Aprocrypha.

McCurley, Foster R. *Ancient Myths and Biblical Faith: Scriptural Transformations.* Philadelphia: Fortress Press, 1983.

McKenzie, John L. *A Theology of the Old Testament.* Garden City, N.Y.: Doubleday, 1974.

Mendenhall, George. *Law and Covenant in Israel and the Ancient Near East.* Pittsburgh: Biblical Colloquium, 1955.

————. "Biblical History in Transition." In G. E. Wright, ed., *The Bible and the Ancient Near East.* New York: Doubleday/Anchor Books, 1965.

————. *The Tenth Generation: The Origins of the Biblical Tradition.* Baltimore: Johns Hopkins University Press, 1973.

Miller, J. Maxwell. *The Old Testament and the Historian.* Guides to Biblical Scholarship. Philadelphia: Fortress Press, 1976.

Noth, Martin. *The History of Israel.* New York: Harper & Row, 1960.

————. *A History of Pentateuchal Traditions.* Englewood Cliffs, N.J.: Prentice-Hall, 1972.

Orlinsky, Harry M. *Ancient Israel.* Ithaca, N.Y.: Cornell University Press, 1960.

Raitt, Thomas M. *A Theology of Exile.* Philadelphia: Fortress Press, 1977.

Redford, Donald B. *Egypt, Canaan, and Israel in Ancient Times.* Princeton, N.J.: Princeton University Press, 1992.

Ringgren, Helmer. *The Faith of Qumran.* Philadelphia: Fortress Press, 1961.

————. *Israelite Religion.* Translated by D. E. Green. Philadelphia: Fortress Press, 1966.

————. *Religions of the Ancient Near East.* Translated by J. Sturdy. Philadelphia: Westminster Press, 1973.

Robertson, David. *The Old Testament and the Literary Critic.* Guides to Biblical Scholarship. Philadelphia: Fortress Press, 1977.

Robinson, H. Wheeler. *Worship in Ancient Israel: Its Forms and Meaning.* Philadelphia: Fortress Press, 1967.

Sanders, James A. *Torah and Canon.* Philadelphia: Fortress Press, 1972. A concise and helpful introduction to canon information.

Shanks, Hershel, ed. *Ancient Israel: A Short History from Abraham to the Roman Destruction of the Temple.* Englewood Cliffs, N.J.: Prentice-Hall, 1988.

————, ed. *Understanding the Dead Sea Scrolls.* New York: Random House, 1992.

Smith, Morton, and Hoffman, R. Joseph, eds. *What the Bible Really Says.* Buffalo: Prometheus Books, 1989. A collection of essays on key biblical topics, for the nonspecialist.

Soulen, Richard N. *Handbook of Biblical Criticism.* Atlanta: John Knox Press, 1976.

Tucker, Gene M. *Form Criticism of the Old Testament.* Guides to Biblical Scholarship. Philadelphia: Fortress Press, 1971.

von Rad, Gerhard. *Old Testament Theology.* Vol. 1, *The Theology of Israel's Historical Traditions.* Translated by M. G. Stalker. New York: Harper & Row, 1962.

————. *Old Testament Theology.* Vol. 2, *The Theology of Israel's Prophetic Traditions.* Translated by M. G. Stalker. New York: Harper & Row, 1965.

————. *God at Work in Israel.* Translated by J. Marks. Nashville, Tenn.: Abingdon Press, 1980.

Westermann, Claus, ed. *Essays on Old Testament Hermeneutics.* Translated and edited by J. L. Mays. Richmond, Va.: John Knox Press, 1963.

————. *The Promises to the Fathers: Studies on the Patriarchal Narratives.* Translated by D. E. Green. Philadelphia: Fortress Press, 1980.

Wolff, Hans W. *Anthropology of the Old Testament.* Translated by M. Kohl. Philadelphia: Fortress Press, 1981.

————. *Confrontations with Prophets.* Philadelphia: Fortress Press, 1983.

Wright, G. Ernest. *The Old Testament and Theology.* New York: Harper & Row, 1969.

Zimmerli, Walther. *Man and His Hope in the Old Testament: Studies in Biblical Theology,* 2nd series. Naperville, Ill.: Allenson, 1968.

————. *Old Testament Theology in Outline.* Translated by D. E. Green. Atlanta: John Knox Press, 1978.

Old Testament Apocrypha, Pseudepigrapha, and Apocalyptic Writings

Becker, Joachim. *Messianic Expectation in the Old Testament.* Translated by D. E. Green. Philadelphia: Fortress Press, 1980.

Charles, R. H., ed. *The Apocrypha and Pseudepigrapha of the Old Testament in English,* vols. 1 and 2. New York: Oxford University Press, 1913, 1963.

Charlesworth, J. H., ed. *The Old Testament Pseudepigrapha.* Vol. 1, *Apocalyptic Literature and Testaments.* Garden City, N.Y.: Doubleday/Anchor Books, 1983.

————, ed. *The Old Testament Pseudepigrapha.* Vol. 2, *Expansions of the "Old Testament" and Philosophical Literature, Prayers, Psalms, and Odes, Fragments of Lost Judeo-Hellenistic Works.* Garden City, N.Y.: Doubleday/Anchor Books, 1985.

Cohen, Shaye J. D. *From the Maccabees to the Mishnah.* Philadelphia: Westminster Press, 1987.

Hanson, Paul D. *The Dawn of Apocalyptic: The Historical and Sociological Roots of Jewish Eschatology.* Philadelphia: Fortress Press, 1979.

Mowinckel, Sigmund. *He That Cometh.* Translated by G. W. Anderson. Nashville, Tenn.: Abingdon Press, 1956.

Nickelsburg, George W. E. *Jewish Literature Between the Bible and the Mishnah: A Historical and Literary Introduction.* Philadelphia: Fortress Press, 1981.

Ringgren, Helmer. *The Messiah in the Old Testament: Studies in Biblical Theology,* no. 18. Chicago: Allenson, 1956.

Rost, Leonard. *Judaism Outside the Hebrew Canon: An Introduction to the Documents.* Nashville, Tenn.: Abingdon Press, 1976.

Russell, D. S. *The Method and Message of Jewish Apocalyptic: 200 B.C.–A.D. 100.* Philadelphia: Westminster Press, 1964. A useful review of apocalyptic literature of the Greco-Roman period.

————. *Apocalyptic: Ancient and Modern.* Philadelphia: Fortress Press, 1978.

New Testament Introductions, Theology, Criticism, and Interpretation

Boring, M. E., Berger, Klaus, and Culpe, Carsten, eds. *Hellenistic Commentary to the New Testament.* Nashville: Abingdon Press, 1995.

Duling, Dennis C., and Perrin, Norman. *The New Testament: Proclamation and Parenesis, Myth and History,* 3rd edition. New York: Harcourt Brace, 1994.

Ferguson, Everett. *Backgrounds of Early Christianity,* 2nd edition. Grand Rapids, Mich.: Eerdmans, 1993.

Funk, R. W. *New Gospel Parallels.* Vols. 1 and 2. *Foundations & Facets.* Philadelphia: Fortress Press, 1985. A major achievement in New Testament scholarship. Volume 1 provides parallels to the three Synoptic Gospels. Volume 2 assembles parallels to the Gospels of John, Thomas, and Peter, the Infancy Gospel of Thomas, the Protoevangelium of James, the Acts of Pilate, and various manuscript fragments.

Funk, Robert W., Hoover, Roy W., and the Jesus Seminar. *The Five Gospels: The Search for the Authentic Words of Jesus.* A new translation that color codes Jesus' sayings according to the translators' belief in their relative authenticity.

Goppelt, Leonhard. *Theology of the New Testament,* vols. 1 and 2. Translated by J. E. Alsup and edited by J. Roloff. Grand Rapids, Mich.: Eerdmans, 1981.

Guthrie, Donald. *New Testament Theology.* Downers Grove, Ill.: Inter-Varsity Press, 1981.

Hahn, Ferdinand. *Historical Imagination and New Testament Faith: Two Essays.* Philadelphia: Fortress Press, 1983.

Harris, Stephen L. *The New Testament: A Student's Introduction.* Mountain View, Calif.: Mayfield 1995, 2nd edit.

Kee, Howard C. *Understanding the New Testament,* 5th ed. Englewood Cliffs, N.J.: Prentice-Hall, 1993. A scholarly, analytical approach to New Testament study.

Koester, Helmut. *Ancient Christian Gospels: Their History and Development.* Philadelphia: Trinity Press International, 1990.

Koester, Helmut. *Introduction to the New Testament,* vol. 1.

History, Culture, and Religion of the Hellenistic Age, rev. edition. New York: Walter de Gruyter, 1995.

Kummel, W. G. *Introduction to the New Testament.* Translated by H. C. Kee. Nashville, Tenn.: Abingdon Press, 1975.

Ladd, George Eldon. *A Theology of the New Testament.* Grand Rapids, Mich.: Eerdmans, 1974.

McGrath, Alister E. *Christian Theology: An Introduction.* Oxford, England: Blackwell Publishers, 1994.

Miller, Robert J. *The Complete Gospels,* rev. edition. San Francisco: HarperSanFrancisco, 1994. Contains both canonical and all extant noncanonical gospels.

Pfeiffer, Robert. *History of New Testament Times: With an Introduction to the Apocrypha.* New York: Harper & Brothers, 1949. Covers Roman rule from Pompey's conquest (63 B.C.E.) to the outbreak of the Jewish revolt (66 C.E.).

Tyson, Joseph B. *The New Testament and Early Christianity.* New York: Macmillan, 1984. An introduction that places early Christian literature, including noncanonical gospels, in its historical Jewish-Hellenistic context.

Birth, Trial, and Resurrection Narratives

Brown, Raymond E. *The Birth of the Messiah: A Commentary on the Infancy Narratives in Matthew and Luke.* New York: Doubleday, 1977. A comprehensive analysis of the historicity and theological implications of the infancy narratives.

————. *The Death of the Messiah,* vols. 1 and 2. New York: Anchor Doubleday, 1994.

Brown, Raymond E., Donfried, K. P., Fitzmyer, S. J., and Reumann, John, eds. *Mary in the New Testament: A Collaborative Assessment by Protestant and Roman Catholic Scholars.* Philadelphia: Fortress Press, 1978.

Catchpole, David R. *The Trial of Jesus.* Leiden: Brill, 1971. Argues that Jesus was executed for religious offenses.

Crossan, John Dominic. *The Historical Jesus.* San Francisco: HarperSanFrancisco, 1991.

Denielou, Jean. *The Infancy Narratives.* Translated by R. Sheed. New York: Herder and Herder, 1968. Attempts to discern historical worth of the birth stories.

Fuller, Reginald H. *The Formation of the Resurrection Narratives.* Philadelphia: Fortress Press, 1980.

Funk, Robert W. and Hoover, Roy W. *Five Gospels, One Jesus.* Sonoma, Calif.: Polebridge Press, 1992. Includes Gospel of Thomas and the four canonical Gospels, with the probable words of the historical Jesus printed in red or pink.

Marxsen, Willi. *The Resurrection of Jesus of Nazareth.* Translated by M. Kohl. Philadelphia: Fortress Press, 1970.

Meier, John P. *A Marginal Jew: Rethinking the Historical Jesus.* 3 vols. New York: Doubleday, 1991.

Perrin, Norman. *The Resurrection According to Matthew, Mark, and Luke.* Philadelphia: Fortress Press, 1977.

Rivkin, Ellis. *What Crucified Jesus? The Political Execution of a Charismatic.* Nashville, Tenn.: Abingdon Press, 1984. Presents Jesus as a victim of "the system," a Roman-Jewish establishment devoted to preserving the political status quo.

Sanders, E. P. *The Historical Figure of Jesus.* New York: Viking, 1994.

Winter, Paul. *On the Trial of Jesus.* Berlin: Walter de Gruyter, 1977. Emphasizes the political charges against Jesus.

Women and the Bible

Daly, Mary. *Beyond God the Father: Toward a Philosophy of Women's Liberation.* New York: Harper & Row, 1980.

Frymer-Kensky, Tikva. *In the Wake of the Goddesses: Women, Culture, and the Biblical Transformation of Pagan Myth.* New York: The Free Press, 1992. A superb scholarly study of biblical religion's relation to older Near Eastern pantheons.

Gerstenberger, Erhard S., and Schrage, Wolfgang. *Woman and Man.* Translated by D. W. Scott. Nashville, Tenn.: Abingdon Press, 1982.

Jeunsonne, Sharon P. *The Women of Genesis, From Sarah to Potiphar's Wife.* Minneapolis: Augsburg Fortress Press, 1990.

LaCocque, André. *The Feminine Unconventional: Four Subversive Figures in Israel's Tradition.* Minneapolis: Augsburg Fortress Press, 1990.

Myers, Carol. *Discovering Eve: Ancient Israelite Women in Context.* Oxford, Eng.: Oxford University Press, 1988.

Otwell, John H. *And Sarah Laughed.* Philadelphia: Westminster Press, 1977.

Ruether, Rosemary R. *Sexism and God-Talk.* New York: Harper & Row, 1982.

Wolkstein, Diane, and Kramer, Samuel N. *Inanna, Queen of Heaven and Earth.* New York: Harper & Row, 1980.

Index